DATE DUE

MY 4 '98			
AP 3 '99			
AT 4 '05			
MY 2 2 '06			

DEMCO 38-296

A TWILIGHT STRUGGLE

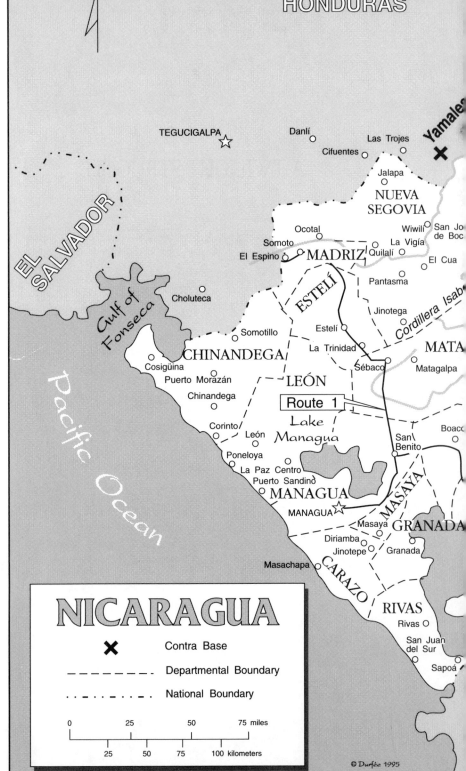

HONDURAS

Yamale

TEGUCIGALPA ☆

Danlí ○

Cifuentes ○

Las Trojes ○

✖

Jalapa ○

NUEVA
SEGOVIA

Ocotal ○

Wiwilí ○

San Jo
de Boc

Somoto ○

La Vigía ○

El Espino ○ ○ MADRIZ Quilalí ○

El Cua ○

EL
SALVADOR

Choluteca ○

Gulf of
Fonseca

Pantasma ○

ESTELÍ

Jinotega ○

Cordillera Isab

Somotillo ○

Estelí ○

MATA

CHINANDEGA

La Trinidad ○

Cosigüina ○

Sébaco ○

Matagalpa ○

Puerto Morazán ○

LEÓN

Chinandega ○

Route 1

Pacific Ocean

Corinto ○ León ○

Lake
Managua

Boaco ○

Poneloya ○
La Paz Centro ○
Puerto Sandino ○

San
Benito ○

MANAGUA

MASAYA

MANAGUA ☆

Masaya ○ GRANADA

Diriamba ○
Jinotepe ○ ○ Granada ○

Masachapa ○

CARAZO

RIVAS

Rivas ○

San Juan
del Sur ○

Sapoá ○

NICARAGUA

A TWILIGHT STRUGGLE

American Power and Nicaragua
1977–1990

ROBERT KAGAN

THE FREE PRESS

New York   London   Toronto   Sydney   Tokyo   Singapore

The Free Press
A Division of Simon & Schuster Inc.
1230 Avenue of the Americas
New York, N.Y. 10020

Printed in the United States of America

printing number

1 2 3 4 5 6 7 8 9 10

Text design by Carla Bolte

Map of Nicaragua is courtesy of Albert D. McJoynt.

Library of Congress Cataloging-in Publication Data

Kagan, Robert.
    A twilight struggle : American power and Nicaragua, 1977–1990 /
Robert Kagan.
        p.   cm.
    Includes bibliographical references and index.
    ISBN 0-02-874057-2
    1. United States—Foreign relations—Nicaragua.   2. Nicaragua—
Foreign relations—United States.   3. Nicaragua—Politics and
government—1979–1990.   4. Frente Sandinista de Liberación Nacional.
I. Title.
E183.8.N5K28   1996
327.7307285'09'047—dc20   95-47303
                                                              CIP

For my parents,
Donald and Myrna Kagan

CONTENTS

PART FIVE: THE IRAN-CONTRA SCANDAL AND ITS CONSEQUENCES

PART SIX: DOWNFALL OF THE SANDINISTAS

CONCLUSIONS

ACKNOWLEDGMENTS

This project could not have been completed without the generous and patient support of the Lynde and Harry Bradley Foundation and the Carthage Foundation. At the U.S. Naval War College Foundation, with which I was affiliated as a Senior Research Fellow, Robert B. Watts, the late Walter B. Woodson, Jr., and Marion Gomez all helped immeasurably. Alvin H. Bernstein, the first director of the Naval War College Foundation and now director of the George C. Marshall Center in Germany, has been a cherished friend and mentor for almost 30 years.

Glen Hartley and Lynn Chu have been the finest of literary agents, not only for me but for members of my family and my closest friends; we have all benefited from their shrewdness and their tenacity. At the Free Press, Adam Bellow and David Bernstein have been wise, thoughtful, and considerate editors. I am especially grateful to Sherwood Harris, who skillfully and almost painlessly turned an obese book into a merely fat one. Jacqueline Mahal, Aaron Bernstein, and Danyako Amahdu were outstanding research assistants, and Julienne Lindley a master coordinator and fairy godmother.

In the course of my research, I benefited from the generosity of several individuals. William Ratliff of the Hoover Institution made available an early draft of his book, written with Roger Miranda, about the inside workings of the Sandinista National Directorate. Former Secretary of State George P. Shultz generously shared with me an early draft of his memoirs. Dan Fisk provided important declassified documents made available to the Senate Foreign Relations Committee. I am particularly indebted to Peter Kornbluh of the National Security Archives for allowing me to look at mountains of declassified documents before they were published.

As this book evolved, several friends and colleagues were kind enough to look at drafts. Peter W. Rodman and M. Charles Hill, two of America's most accomplished foreign policy-makers and for whom I was privileged to work in the State Department, lent the wisdom of their years in diplomacy. Luigi Einaudi, a veritable State Department institution, made helpful comments on early chapters. Crescencio Arcos, a close friend and comrade-in-arms, read some of the later sections. Doyle McManus, one of the finest journalists in Washington, read a very large portion of the book and did his best to save me from errors. I am sure he failed. Eddie Lazarus read parts of an early draft and has been an indispensable friend and soulmate throughout the years. My brother, Fred Kagan, a professor of military history, helped with the portions of the book dealing with Soviet military policy and strategy and was a constant source of wisdom and warmth. Gary Schmitt, in a singular act of friendship, read the entire manuscript and offered many valuable suggestions for improvement.

Bruce Cameron, who has given himself over many times to the pursuit of noble, losing causes, adopted this project as one of them. I am ever grateful for his friendship. Arturo Cruz, Jr. led me through the labyrinths of Nicaragua's political culture, and I came to love both the journey and the guide. Elliott Abrams hired me to work as his deputy in the State Department a decade ago. In all the years since, he has been a mentor, a friend, and a rare example of courage and conviction to all who know him.

My parents, to whom this book is dedicated, were a never-ending source of strength and encouragement. My mother, Myrna Kagan, lent me some of her infinite fortitude at moments when mine flagged. My father, Donald Kagan, read and commented on every word of this book. My debt to him for this and for every other act of love and kindness in my lifetime can never be repaid.

Finally, my wife, Victoria Nuland, gave me confidence and happiness, her strength of character matched only by her loving heart. In ways I cannot begin to describe, this book was possible only because of her.

INTRODUCTION

From 1977 to 1990 the United States and Nicaragua were locked in a bloody and conflict-ridden embrace. The Nicaraguan people lurched from dictatorship to revolution and then from dictatorship to free elections, their course determined at every step by the interaction of their own political culture with powerful outside forces. In the United States, three presidents tried to influence Nicaragua's course with a minimum of effort and expense, but their policies were plagued by controversy and scandal. The American intervention raised fundamental issues of national interest and ideals, and in so doing it cast in sharp relief the jagged fault lines in America's own political and ideological landscape. It exposed the American people's profound ambivalence about their country's great power and about the morality of exercising it in world affairs.

For more than two centuries the United States has steadily expanded its power and influence in the world, and that expansion began in the Western Hemisphere. In the nineteenth century, the United States established itself as hegemon over the weaker, poorer, and smaller nations to its south. The great and growing disparity of power between the United States and its southern neighbors made some degree of hegemony inescapable, but Americans actively pursued a position as the region's dominant people. And like powerful peoples throughout history, they tried to shape the world around them to suit their material needs and their ideals. They sought to defend their national security against threats, real and imagined, expelling or, in the case of the British, amicably ushering out all foreign powers whose foothold in the hemisphere posed a challenge to American supremacy. Within the cordon created by the Monroe Doctrine, Americans also pursued goals that were only tangentially related to security. In the early part of the twentieth century, presidents as different as Theodore Roosevelt and Woodrow Wilson assumed for the United States a responsibility for political and moral leadership in the Western Hemisphere. They would lift the troubled peoples of the region "upward toward peace and order" and teach them "to elect good men." For the rest of this century, the United States sought to impose in the hemisphere, in a sporadic and distracted manner, its view of a decent international order.

In exercising their great influence over their weaker neighbors, however, Americans have often been plagued by bad conscience. A nation founded in rebellion against an imperial master, with a passionate commitment to national sovereignty and self-determination, could not ignore that, in pursuing its interests and imposing its view of a proper international order, it was also invading the sovereignty and limiting the self-determination of others. This conundrum has been at the heart of what one scholar has called "the tragedy of American diplomacy."[1] Tragic or not, the ambivalent soul of America has consistently sought the fruits of hegemony in this hemisphere but just as consistently balked at the moral costs of exercising it. The result has been a repeated cycle of intervention, withdrawal, and intervention again.

———

In the highly charged atmosphere of the Cold War, especially in the tumultuous years described in this history, this deep ambivalence about the use of power to impose an "American order" in the hemisphere became more pronounced. The experience of the Vietnam War aroused strong passions in the United States against further American interventions abroad. At the same time, the spread of left-wing revolutionary movements in Central America posed a comprehensive challenge to the "American order" in a part of the world where Americans had grown used to exercising the greatest influence. Marxist-Leninist revolution attacked America's liberal capitalist values. And the revolutionaries in Central America and the Caribbean put force behind their defiance by allying with America's great Cold War adversary, the Soviet Union, thus threatening what many Americans perceived as their fundamental security.

The political crisis in Nicaragua at the end of the 1970s thus proved the spark to ignite another passionate American debate. The fall of the Somoza dictatorship in 1979, and its replacement by a revolutionary Sandinista government allied to Cuba and the Soviet Union, raised the most profound issues for many Americans and renewed the century-old clash between competing visions of America's proper role in the world. Americans who wished to end a long history of intervention in Nicaragua and other nations in the hemisphere battled against those who continued to see both right and reason in maintaining an "American order" in the region, especially against the threat of communism.

The conflict over Nicaragua also put a great strain on the American system of government. The two political parties used it as a means of defining themselves and attacking each other, continuing an old American tradition of exploiting foreign policy controversies for domestic political purposes. The legislative and executive branches swept the Nicaraguan dispute into their 200-year struggle for supremacy in the conduct of foreign policy, as a resurgent post-Watergate Congress battled against the modern, "imperial" presidency. Much of the prolonged fight in the United States was not about Nicaragua at all. It was a battle to define America at home and abroad.

The stakes were high for all the politicians and policymakers who took part in the shaping of U.S. policy in Nicaragua in the last decade of the Cold War. Jimmy Carter suffered in the 1980 election from Republican accusations that he had "lost" Nicaragua to communism. Ronald Reagan entangled himself in the Iran-contra affair, a political scandal so severe that his top aides feared impeachment, and senior Reagan officials went to trial or pleaded guilty to a variety of crimes and misdemeanors. The Nicaraguan controversy also helped drive from office the powerful Democratic Speaker of the House, Jim Wright, whose free-lance diplomacy in Nicaragua aroused Republican resentment. Small wonder that when George Bush became President, he made escaping Nicaragua his first foreign policy goal.

The clash of interests, institutions, and ideologies forged an American policy toward Nicaragua that was chaotic, lurching, changeable, and often inherently contradictory. Although participants and observers spoke of a "Carter policy" or a "Reagan policy" toward Nicaragua, the more complex truth was that no administration pursued the course it would have preferred. Presidents Carter, Reagan, and Bush found their policies hampered, blunted, sometimes negated, and always shaped by the conflict between the executive and legislative branches of government, the rivalry between the political parties, and the conflicting aims of ambitious individuals.

In time, however, out of this roiling conflict emerged one common American goal: to seek free and fair democratic elections in Nicaragua. It is doubtful that anyone in the American debate began with that goal clearly in mind. Even after it became the declared purpose of American policy to bring democracy to Nicaragua, the disputes over how to do so all but obscured the aim. In the end, nevertheless, elections in Nicaragua became the grand compromise that alone could settle the American conflict. Free elections offered an apparent solution to the old conundrum. They were a way of restoring sovereignty in Nicaragua and ending American intervention in a manner consistent with the "American order." The imposition of democratic elections in Nicaragua, which most Nicaraguans welcomed, proved to be a type of hegemony acceptable to the broadest spectrum of Americans.

In hindsight, the outcome in Nicaragua might appear logical and even inevitable. To participants and observers at the time, however, it was neither. The path toward elections in Nicaragua was uneven and unpredictable. The Sandinistas had come to power in 1979 not as democrats but with plans to build a socialist state with themselves as the ruling vanguard. Their model was Fidel Castro's Cuba, and they knew that the only way to fulfill such aspirations in a region dominated by the United States was to forge a close, strategic alliance with the Soviet Union. They aimed to defy American hegemony, not to accommodate themselves to American power and American values.

For President Jimmy Carter and his advisers, the rise of the Sandinistas posed an especially difficult challenge. Strongly influenced by a post-Vietnam desire to end American intervention and hegemonic pretensions in the Western Hemisphere and elsewhere, they also feared the strategic and political consequences of "losing" Nicaragua to a pro-Soviet Marxist-Leninist revolution. Caught between these conflicting aims, the Carter administration pursued a policy of half-hearted intervention that not only failed to prevent a Sandinista victory but instead eased the Sandinistas' path to power.

Faced with a successful Marxist revolution in Nicaragua, and the danger of further Marxist victories in neighboring El Salvador and Guatemala, the Carter administration tried to persuade the Sandinistas to pursue a more democratic and pro-Western course by the gentle device of friendly relations and the provision of economic aid. Carter's goal was to stop the spread of communism in Central America and forestall political attack at home, but without the threat or use of force. The policy of friendly persuasion, however, was unsuccessful. In the absence of a direct threat to their survival in power, it was neither in the Sandinistas' interest, nor in keeping with their ideological convictions, to meet American standards of "bourgeois democracy." In the bipolar world of the Cold War, the Sandinistas had made the strategic choice to join the Soviet camp and to defy the United States.

When Ronald Reagan took office in 1981, the new president and his conservative Republican advisers took a very different view of the proper course for American policy. After a brief flirtation with negotiations, Reagan officials decided that only armed pressure could persuade the Sandinistas to moderate their policies at home and abroad. But the President and his advisers confronted a strong popular aversion to the direct use of American military power in Central America and a Congress still reluctant, after Vietnam, to approve even the dispatch of American military advisers to the region. The Reagan administration, therefore, chose what one official called the "lowball option": covert support for a small army of rebels—who became known to the world as the "contras"—fighting to overthrow the Sandinista government.

The controversy that erupted over this covert American intervention in Nicaragua dominated the Reagan years. The clash between the administration and Congress over funding for the contras led first to a scandal over the CIA's mining of Nicaragua's harbors in 1984 and then to the Iran-contra affair which all but crippled the Reagan presidency in 1987. Congress in 1988 refused to vote more military aid for the contras, and by the time Reagan left office even his Republican successors declared that his policy had "failed."

The contra war had taken a terrible toll on the Sandinistas, however. Their Soviet patron was in decline and their economy in collapse. By the time President Bush took office, the Sandinistas were desperate to end both the war and their long confrontation with the United States. Seizing on the diplomatic plan proposed by Costa Rican President Oscar Arias, the Sandinistas agreed to hold free and fair elections in exchange for an end to American support for the contras. For President Bush, free elections provided a welcome escape from the Nicaraguan political quagmire. For the Sandinistas, the elections proved a disastrous mistake. Certain of victory, they allowed thousands of international observers to monitor the campaign and the voting. But when the results were tallied on February 25, 1990, the Sandinistas had been buried in a landslide.

————

The election of Violeta Chamorro as President of Nicaragua was widely recognized as a success for American policy, but who deserves credit for it has been the subject of much debate. This book proposes no simple answers. It is not a story about inevitability, about the success of a single, consistent policy, but about the complex interaction between broad historical trends and unpredictable individual actors which makes every event in history unique and beyond the capacity of humans perfectly to plan or foresee.

————

For several years I was a direct participant in the events described in this history. As a member of the State Department's Policy Planning Staff and as principal speechwriter to Secretary of State George P. Shultz, I helped draft broad statements of Reagan administration foreign policy, including the fullest official explication of what has been called the "Reagan Doctrine." Then, as Deputy for Policy to Assistant Secretary of State Elliott Abrams, I helped carry out U.S. policy toward Nicaragua and, in particular, American support for the armed Nicaraguan Resistance.

This book, however, is neither a personal memoir nor a defense of the Reagan administration and its policies. My time in government helped me better understand how American policy was formulated and conducted, and my personal acquaintance with central figures both inside and outside the American and Nicaraguan governments gave me valuable insight into their actions and motives. But the narrative, the interpretation, and the analysis are based primarily on documentary evidence, from both Nicaraguan and American sources. A wealth of secret government documents from the Carter and Reagan administrations has been declassified in recent years as a result of congressional inquiries, and these, along with the public information available in newspapers, in the records of Congress, and in the public pronouncements of the White House and the State Department, make up the body of evidence upon which all significant conclusions in this book are based.

I also conducted extensive interviews with key actors in both the American and Nicaraguan governments—from George P. Shultz and Robert McFarlane in the United States to Sandinista Defense Minister

Humberto Ortega, contra leaders in Nicaragua and Miami, and former President Oscar Arias in Costa Rica. Many works on this subject have claimed to understand the goals and tactics behind American, contra, and Sandinista policies, but this book allows all sides in the U.S.-Nicaraguan conflict to speak for themselves.

Most of the interpretations of U.S. policy in Nicaragua were published during the contentious years of the last decade of the Cold War. Many were written to discredit the policies of the Reagan administration and did not look broadly at both Reagan and his opponents in Congress. Generally focused on the formulation of U.S. policy, they tended to ignore the Nicaraguan side, neither seriously analyzing the actions and motives of the Sandinistas and their opponents, nor describing with any care the ever-shifting patterns of Nicaraguan politics. Those few studies which focused on Nicaragua, in turn, neglected serious attention to the American side. And since most of the studies concentrated on the highly controversial "covert" war waged during the Reagan years, they did not provide the perspective on U.S. policy that can be gained by a longer view, one that stretches across the three presidencies of Carter, Reagan, and Bush.

With the passage of some years, and of the Cold War itself, the time has come for a more complete treatment. This book is an attempt, finally, to address that most contentious of American foreign policies not as an occasion for polemic but as a serious subject of historical investigation.

Part One

INTERVENTION AND WITHDRAWAL

1

Occupation and Its Consequences

This history recounts 13 years of conflict involving the United States and Nicaragua, but the events of these 13 years had roots in a longer history of relations between the world's great democratic power and its small, turbulent neighbor. In the mid-nineteenth century, Nicaragua was ruled briefly by the infamous American "filibuster," William Walker. Later in the century it became a favored location for a U.S.-built isthmian Canal. The United States intervened with troops in 1912 and occupied Nicaragua for most of the next 21 years, assisted in a war against the rebel Augusto César Sandino from 1927 to 1933, and was involved in the birth of the Somoza dynasty in 1936 and its perpetuation for another 43 years. Most informed Americans were not proud of that history, and vague memories of these events and the myths surrounding them influenced the course of American policy in the 1970s and 1980s.

Those myths resonated especially powerfully in an America racked by doubts about its role in the Vietnam War. The marines' campaign against Sandino was portrayed by critics in the post-Vietnam era as an exertion of imperial power in the service of American big business against the leader of an anti-imperialist, revolutionary class struggle—Sandino as a prototype of Ho Chi Minh. The Somoza dynasty was portrayed as the servant of successive American administrations looking for a reliable protector of corporate interests and a bulwark against the spread of communism in

Central America. These caricatures were not all invented in the 1970s: contemporary critics of the Coolidge and Hoover administrations had also assailed their "imperialist" policies and lionized Sandino as a revolutionary patriot.

Even a brief look at America's involvement in Nicaragua in the early decades of the twentieth century reveals a more complex story, however. For one thing, it is a story not only of constant American intervention, but also of constant withdrawal. As early as the 1920s, American presidents were eagerly searching for a way out of the entanglement that had begun in 1909. Even the Somoza dynasty was as much a product of hasty American withdrawal as it was of American intervention.

————

At the beginning of the twentieth century, in the wake of the Spanish-American War, President Theodore Roosevelt sought to place the United States in the first rank of the world's great powers as befitted its new economic and military might. The prerequisite to playing a great power's role in the world, Roosevelt believed, was to assume a great power's responsibilities in its own sphere. Because of America's preponderant power in the hemisphere, the United States had to "assume an attitude of protection and regulation in regard to all these little states." Because America was a democratic country, Roosevelt also declared as part of this responsibility the need to help Central Americans acquire the "capacity for self-government," to assist their progress "up out of the discord and turmoil of continual revolution into a general public sense of justice and determination to maintain order."

Just at the moment when the United States was beginning to assume "responsibility" for the "little states" of the Caribbean, however, the Nicaraguan dictator, José Santos Zelaya, was creating turmoil. A general who had seized power in 1893, President Zelaya "thought a higher manifest destiny—his own—commanded that he and Nicaragua control all of Central America."[1] In 1907 Zelaya invaded Honduras to install a provisional government under his control. In an effort to bring stability to the region, the United States joined Mexico in sponsoring a Central American peace conference, where all the parties agreed to denounce unconstitutional seizures of power. But within months of the conference Zelaya returned to supporting rebellions against his neighbors.[2]

By the time President William Howard Taft took office in 1909, American patience with Zelaya was exhausted. In 1909 rebels led by Juan

Estrada, a dissident from Zelaya's Liberal Party, and by Emiliano Chamorro, a Conservative Party leader, began an uprising on the Atlantic Coast of Nicaragua. Although Secretary of State Philander Knox professed neutrality, American officials were known to favor the rebels, American businessmen allegedly donated several hundred thousand dollars, and American citizens helped the rebels directly in their struggle. When two Americans were caught laying mines in the San Juan River, President Zelaya ordered them executed. This was the last straw for the Taft administration. In a public letter Knox called Zelaya "a blot on the history of his country" and threw America's moral support behind the Conservative rebels who represented "the ideals and the will of a majority of the Nicaraguan people more faithfully than does the Government of President Zelaya." Faced with this thundering pronouncement from the northern power, Zelaya resigned and fled the country. In 1910 the Conservative Party, led by Estrada and Chamorro, regained power for the first time in 17 years. The "Knox letter" would long be remembered by Nicaraguans as the first great intrusion of American power into Nicaragua's affairs in the twentieth century.

Zelaya's forced resignation and the Conservative victory left the United States with responsibilities in Nicaragua. The country was in a state of near-anarchy, the Conservatives found the treasury empty, and the Liberals waited for an opportunity to reverse their recent defeat. Through a policy that the Taft administration itself dubbed "dollar diplomacy," the United States in effect put Nicaragua in receivership. It placed an American in charge of the Nicaraguan customs house, with instructions to divide the receipts between the government and foreign creditors. The Taft administration then forced the new Nicaraguan government to begin paying off its debts to British and other foreign lenders and to borrow exclusively from American banks. The result was that the new Nicaraguan government was stripped of much of its control of the nation's economy. As security for the new loans, the American banks took controlling interests in Nicaragua's National Bank and railroads. Control of these assets did not return to Nicaraguan hands until the early 1920s. In the words of one historian, "a supposedly sovereign republic had become the virtual ward of New York bankers, acting informally for the American government."[3]

"Dollar diplomacy" soon proved inadequate to its purpose, however. In 1912 the Conservatives placed Adolfo Díaz in the presidency through an election which the Liberals had no chance of winning and in which they did not participate. Under the leadership of a dissident Conservative general, the Liberals revolted. Their slogan was, "Down with Yankee Imperialists," and the resulting disorders threatened to tear the country apart once more. Americans and other foreigners clamored for protection amid the violent anarchy.

The Taft administration promptly sent more than 2,500 marines to Nicaragua to put down the rebellion and keep Díaz in office. Claiming a "moral mandate to exert its influence for the preservation of the general peace of Central America, which is seriously menaced by the present uprising," the Taft administration crossed the threshold to armed intervention and occupation. The Liberal rebellion was quickly put down. A 100-man legation of marines remained, ostensibly to continue protecting American citizens. The marines also became the effective guardians of a Conservative Party dynasty that was to rule unchallenged until 1924.[4]

The years of Conservative rule and American occupation were relatively calm and prosperous for Nicaraguans. In the early 1920s the government was able to buy back control of both the National Bank and the railroad. Woodrow Wilson made few changes in the policies of his Republican predecessor, even though the Democrats had denounced "dollar diplomacy" during the 1912 campaign. The Wilson administration obtained a $4 million loan for Nicaragua from American banks and found no cause to withdraw the marine legation.

On the contrary, Wilson undertook similar interventions and occupations in Haiti and the Dominican Republic. The President expressed his intention to "teach [Latin] Americans to elect good men," and continued stewardship of Nicaragua seemed to him to be compatible with that goal. Secretary of State William Jennings Bryan completed negotiations for the purchase of rights to an alternate canal through Nicaragua for a sum of $3 million, and Foreign Minister Emiliano Chamorro signed the treaty for Nicaragua. Nicaraguan and American critics would cite the Bryan-Chamorro treaty as an example of the abject subservience of the Conservative governments to American imperialism,[5] but since no canal was ever built in Nicaragua, the Nicaraguans can hardly be said to have been mistreated. For State Department officials, the treaty had been "a convenient excuse for giving Nicaragua urgently needed financial help."[6]

The calm in Nicaragua during these years was not destined to last. Order and prosperity did not appease the Liberals who clamored for a return to power and the end of the Conservative dynasty. Since Conservative power depended heavily on American support, the Liberals began to see their chance when the United States became disenchanted with its policy toward the entire world after 1920.

By the 1920s Wilson's military occupations of Haiti, the Dominican Republic, and Nicaragua had become unpopular, and anti-imperialists, pacifists, and isolationists in both parties demanded withdrawal. When President Warren G. Harding took office in 1921, having promised a "return to normalcy," his Secretary of State, Charles Evans Hughes, was determined to end the occupations as soon as possible.

Stability in Nicaragua seemed to require a return of the Liberals to power, but that return had to be achieved peacefully. For American policymakers, the answer to this conundrum was a free election. "If we could bring about the election in 1924 of a government which had real popular support," one State Department official later recalled, "we could extricate ourselves from a situation which was increasingly embarrassing."[7]

This American goal collided with the ambitions of Emiliano Chamorro, the Conservative Party boss who commanded the loyalty of the Conservative Party's army. Chamorro sought the presidency a second time in 1924, knew that a fair election would bring the Liberals to power, and was prepared to use his army to prevent such an occurrence. Only the United States stood in his way, but Secretary Hughes was bent on withdrawal. Republican isolationists like Senator William Borah warned the State Department against involvement in Nicaragua's internal affairs. Chamorro, aware of the Americans' desire for withdrawal, waited for his moment.

The 1924 elections, partially supervised by the American marines, were the fairest in Nicaragua's history. As predicted, the incumbent Chamorro was defeated in a landslide by a Liberal-Conservative coalition. Secretary Hughes, believing America's work finally done in Nicaragua, ordered the immediate departure of the marines. Despite pleas from the new government for protection against Chamorro's army, the marines withdrew in August 1925. A few weeks later Chamorro and his loyalists in the army seized power. Chamorro purged his opponents from the Congress, drove the newly elected Liberal Vice President, Juan Sacasa, into exile, and had himself named President.

Chamorro's coup put the United States and the new administration of Calvin Coolidge in an impossible position. Unable to recognize the Chamorro government without violating its own prohibition against unlawful seizures of power, unwilling to intervene to force the restoration of the elected coalition government including Vice President Sacasa, but also unwilling to countenance the inevitable armed revolt by the Liberals, the United States was paralyzed. In 1926 U.S. officials forced Chamorro to resign, but recognized another Conservative, Adolfo Díaz, as the new President. Recognition of the Liberal Sacasa as President might well have precipitated another Conservative military coup. The Coolidge administration hoped to stabilize Nicaragua through support of the post-Chamorro Conservative government and without sending the marines back to Managua.[8] American recognition of Díaz, however, only fanned the crisis. The Liberals refused to accept the Conservative Party's Díaz as President and launched their rebellion, demanding the "constitutional" restoration of their own party's leader, Juan Sacasa.

The leader of the Constitutionalist army was General José Maria Moncada, and among the Liberals preparing for battle was a young man who returned from Mexico in June, Augusto César Sandino, and another young Liberal general, Anastasio Somoza García. As fighting erupted along the Atlantic Coast, the newly installed President Díaz asked for support against the Liberal rebels, but Coolidge's Secretary of State, Frank Kellogg, refused. On December 8 Kellogg expressed his "regret that there appears to be a tendency on the part of the Díaz administration to rely upon the Government of the United States to protect it against the activities of the revolutionists by physical means."[9] And although Díaz pleaded for military support from the United States, Kellogg refused to intervene in the conflict.[10]

The Coolidge administration did send warships to Nicaragua's Atlantic Coast and landed some marines to protect American citizens, but these measures were not meant to stem the Liberal rebellion. Arms coming from Mexico gave the rebel army the means to advance, and at the end of December General Moncada scored victories along the Atlantic Coast which forced the government forces to withdraw. On the Pacific Coast, wild rumors of approaching ships filled with armed men prompted President Díaz to threaten the United States with immediate surrender.

The impending collapse of the government in Managua and the eruption of panic and chaos throughout the country forced the Coolidge administration to take the decision it had long been avoiding. With the British, Belgian, and Italian governments insisting on American protection of their citizens, on January 6, 1927, President Coolidge ordered the marines back to Managua to shore up Díaz. Although the Coolidge administration did not claim any interest or goal beyond protecting the welfare of foreign and American citizens, the return to full-blown intervention in Nicaragua could not be hidden.

Senators William Borah and George Norris condemned Coolidge's actions as "shocking to every peace-loving citizen in civilization" and a "blot on the national honor."[11] Senator Burton K. Wheeler declared that Nicaragua, which had long been trampled "under the merciless heel of the State Department and the New York bankers," was at that moment "in the bitterest bondage in which any free people ever found themselves."[12] President Coolidge, in response, cited the arms coming from radical Mexico, warned of dangers to American businesses, of the strategic threat posed by a possible alternative canal in Nicaragua under foreign control, and even invented an illusory danger of Russian bolshevism.[13]

But Coolidge's main interest lay in returning Nicaragua to some semblance of stability so that American intervention could end without further embarrassment. On April 9, 1927, Coolidge sent the former and future American Secretary of War, Henry L. Stimson, on a mission to settle the problems in Nicaragua. Coolidge's instructions to Stimson before the latter's departure for Nicaragua were free of any injunctions about Mexican radicalism or about the alleged threat to American businesses. "I want you to go down there," President Coolidge said, "and if you can see a way to clean up that mess, I want you to do it."[14]

Stimson arrived in Nicaragua a few days later. The civil war that had been blazing in the country for almost a year had taken its toll. "[T]he fields were uncultivated and little farming was going on. A large portion of the city of Chinandega was in ashes. Almost every man or boy whom one met either in the country or cities was armed. It was a common sight to see a farmer driving his cattle or leading his pack horse with a military rifle strapped across his back, while the butt ends of revolvers and automatics produced telltale creases in the garments of such male Nicaraguans as one met or did business with in town."[15]

Stimson knew that the history of Nicaragua in the nineteenth and early twentieth centuries presented "a picture of successive periods during which one or the other of the two great parties was successful in holding the reins of government" while the other attempted revolutions that either succeeded or were violently suppressed. "The results of elections were habitually controlled by the man or men who held the machinery of government, including the army and the police." As a result, Nicaraguans had "come to realize that an election meant nothing" and that the only means of transferring power was by force. Armed rebellion had thus become "a regular part of their political system."[16] Stimson was also aware, of course, that U.S. intervention had also become "a regular part" of Nicaragua's political culture.

Stimson's main task was to persuade the Liberals to accept a plan that would allow Díaz to remain president until the 1928 elections, to permit the supervision of the elections by the American government, to support the creation of a neutral constabulary to keep order and safeguard free elections once the marines departed, and to give up their weapons. Stimson also knew that only the leader of the Liberal army, General Moncada, had the power to decide when the fighting would end and on what terms. In May Stimson met Moncada near the town of Tipitapa to gain a final settlement of the war.

As Moncada later recalled the conversation, Stimson's message was blunt and imperious. "My government has recognized President Díaz," Stimson declared, "and the United States cannot make an error." Moncada replied, "You have made one." Stimson said he had come to obtain peace, but he had instructions to win the acquiescence of the Liberal army by force if necessary. Moncada declared that for him the issue was a matter of honor.[17] According to Stimson's recollection of the meeting, Moncada said "he could not in honor ask his army to accept" the retention of Díaz, "as it had been fighting Díaz all winter." But if Stimson would assure Moncada that the United States "insisted on Díaz as a necessary condition to our supervision of the election, he would not fight the United States." If Stimson would give him a letter to that effect, "he would use it to persuade his army to lay down its arms."[18] The exchange was virtually an orchestrated performance: Stimson and Moncada both knew the Liberal army would submit before American military might. Moncada himself had much to gain in the agreement, which effectively made him the Liberals' leader and likely presidential candidate for 1928. On May 11 all but one of the Liberal generals agreed to the terms of the Peace of Tipitapa. The lone dissenter was Sandino, who slipped off into the mountains of Nueva Segovia with a few dozen demoralized followers.

Despite President Coolidge's alleged concerns about Central American "bolshevism", Stimson's intervention almost guaranteed the electoral victory of the Liberal "revolutionists" in the 1928 election. Liberals who opposed the Peace of Tipitapa at the time, and many did, objected to Stimson's apparent anointing of Moncada as the Liberals' leader more than to the agreement itself.[19] A few Liberals feared that the election in 1928 would not be fair and that General Moncada had surrendered for nothing. Sandino, who soon led dissident Liberals into battle in the hills of northern Nicaragua, claimed at the time to be worried principally that Moncada and the other Liberal leaders had been hoodwinked and that the result would be a continuation of the Conservative dynasty. Most Liberals with whom Stimson spoke, however, "were even more emphatic than the Conservatives in demanding that [American] supervision should be thorough and effective."[20] As it became clear that the elections would be fairly conducted, and that a Liberal victory in 1928 was likely, fewer and fewer Nicaraguans in either camp lamented the Peace of Tipitapa.

Stimson left Nicaragua proud of his work, and in later years he defended his actions against many critics.

> [I]t was legitimate to hope that if a generally admitted fair election could once be held, it might serve as a guide and pattern toward which the minds of the Nicaraguan people might turn in the future, and that having been shown by Americans that such an election was possible, they would be encouraged in the future to adopt permanently a system of free elections with their own efforts. The saving of a nation from anarchy; the termination of a century-old political vice which had destroyed its attempted democracy; the setting of that nation upon the road to a possible orderly self-government— all seemed to me to be a goal worthy of every possible effort.[21]

2

The Rise of Sandino

Like most Nicaraguans, Augusto Sandino had been born into a political party. His father, Gregorio Sandino, was a well-to-do provincial landowner and a devoted Liberal. Augusto Sandino was the product of an affair between his father and a family servant, but his father raised him as a member of the family. Sandino, who was 14 years old when José Santos Zelaya fled under American pressure, undoubtedly grew up sharing the common Liberal's sour view of the United States' intervention at that time. His family's fortunes were not affected during the Conservative Party's reign, however, and Sandino himself had left Nicaragua in 1920 for personal, not political reasons. He spent several years as a laborer in Tampico, Mexico, where he was allegedly influenced by the anti-Americanism of the Mexican revolution. He returned to Nicaragua in June 1926, however, not to make a revolution but to help the Liberal Party in its struggle against Emiliano Chamorro.

Sandino's career as a general began inauspiciously. He launched his first small attack on a government post in northern Nicaragua on November 2, but the attack failed and he made his way east to join Moncada and the nascent Constitutionalist army at Puerto Cabezas. By the time he reached the coastal town in December, the United States had recognized Díaz. Sandino went to Moncada to seek weapons and supplies and to offer his services as a general. Moncada, however, snubbed Sandino and at first declined his request for weapons. When Sandino caught up with Moncada a second time at Prinzapolka, the Liberal leader rebuffed him again. Sandino, described by one of his lieutenants as "very vain and sophisticated, fully believing that his wisdom was infallible," never forgave Moncada for these repeated slights.[1]

On May 5 Moncada summoned Sandino to tell him of the agreement reached with Stimson at Tipitapa. He offered Sandino the governorship of Jinotega, one of seven provinces to be returned to Liberal hands under the agreement, as well as $10 in back pay for all the days he had fought in the Constitutionalist cause. Moncada also told Sandino he could keep all the mules he had taken for his army. Sandino rejected the offer, considering Moncada's agreement with Stimson an abject betrayal of the Liberal cause.

The war that Sandino waged for the next six years, and which was celebrated by revolutionaries in Nicaragua and by their sympathizers in the United States 50 years later, was not the simple story of a Nicaraguan nationalist fighting imperialism. Sandino's motives were complex and ever-shifting. He began fighting in 1926 not to force out American marines and to return Nicaragua to Nicaraguans but to force out a Conservative government and return Nicaragua to the Liberals. He continued the fight, after the Peace of Tipitapa was concluded, not because he opposed American imposition of a settlement, but because he opposed the imposition of a settlement that placed either the Conservatives or his nemesis, General Moncada, in the presidency. And when the American marines finally withdrew in 1933, and the United States washed its hands completely of any further military role in Nicaragua, Sandino did not lay down his arms, content to see Nicaragua at last in the hands of Nicaraguans, but held onto his army and demanded a role for himself in the governance of Nicaragua.

Sandino's behavior does not square with modern efforts to portray him as a forerunner of the revolutionary, anti-imperialist movements of the 1960s and 1970s: At one time or another, Sandino claimed to adhere to a dozen different political and religious doctrines. Much depended upon who his audience was and on who was giving him money. To members of the "American Anti-Imperialist League" and other socialist groups, or to representatives of the Comintern, he often spoke of the "proletarian revolution" he wanted to lead across the globe. To American isolationists he spoke only of seeking independence from American dictates. To others he claimed religious motives or to speak for the Indo-Hispanic race.[2] To his peasant followers, he claimed mystical powers. Attempts to impose ideological coherence on these utterances have produced some amusing conclusions. One scholar, for instance, has claimed to discover that "the intellectual foundations of Sandino's philosophy" could be found in a blend of "Mexican anarchism, Spiritualism, Freemasonry, and theosophy, and in the Magnetic-Spiritual School of the Universal Commune's custom-made fusion of anarchism and Spiritism."[3]

Efforts to depict Sandino as an early Communist or socialist revolutionary are no more successful. Even Sandinista theoreticians in the 1970s, who insisted that Sandino was the forerunner of their own socialist revolution, despaired of finding "clear ordered statements about the means of production or class struggle." To see Sandino's "true position" as a revolutionary, they claimed, it was "necessary to see whose side he was on and whom he was against."[4] Others who insist upon the ideological motives behind Sandino's actions and statements have been forced to the last refuge: that Sandino had cleverly "learned to keep his political convictions to himself." Sandino's contemporary and sometime ally, the Salvadoran communist revolutionary, Augustín Farabundo Martí, offered a better interpretation. Sandino's banner, he said, "was only a banner of independence, a banner of emancipation." Sandino "did not want to embrace the communist program for which I was fighting."[5]

Even the conclusion that Sandino was a nationalist and a patriot seeking to free his country from the North American yoke cannot be accepted without qualifications. Some scholars argue that Sandino opposed Díaz and the Conservatives because of "their ties to the Americans," but it would be more accurate to say that he opposed the Americans because of their ties to the Conservatives.[6] Sandino held President Coolidge responsible for the war because Coolidge had "persisted in maintaining in power his lackey Adolfo Díaz, a person who enjoys the contempt of every good Nicaraguan."[7] Sandino's army was made up of "Liberal Nicaraguan volunteers" whose goal was "the defense of our sovereignty and maintenance of the rights of the Liberal party."[8] And Sandino proved himself no devotee of elections, no matter how free, that did not put his preferred party or candidate in power. One strong piece of evidence that Sandino was a Liberal first and an anti-imperialist chiefly when it was useful was a letter he wrote to the American marines in May 1927. His proposal for peace, for which he later suffered much embarrassment,[9] suggested that "a United States military governor take power" in Nicaragua until new presidential elections could be carried out. The elections were to be "supervised" by the American marines.[10] Sandino changed his mind only when the United States abandoned strict neutrality and put its forces at the service of the Díaz government against him.

In November 1928 Nicaraguans voted in what were perhaps the fairest elections in their history, thoroughly supervised and monitored by American military officials.[11] Sandino, who foresaw a victory by General Moncada, did all he could to disrupt the voting. His men assassinated local officials in the northern provinces, both Liberals and Conservatives. Over the years Sandino and his fighters used terror to punish "traitors," employing such means of execution as the "gourd cut," slicing off the top of the victim's skull, the "vest cut," chopping off the head and both arms, and the "bloomers cut," chopping off the legs and allowing the victim to bleed to death. "Liberty is not conquered with flowers," Sandino once declared. "For this reason we must resort to the cuts of vest, gourd, and bloomers."[12] But Sandino's efforts at intimidation failed. Ninety percent of the registered voters cast their ballots. Even in Nueva Segovia, one of the northern provinces where Sandino held the most sway, 82 percent of registered voters went to the polls.[13] This high turnout casts doubt on assertions that Sandino had gathered a large and devoted following among the northern peasant population.[14] Marines chasing the guerrilla leader found local peasants unhelpful to them and "strong for Sandino," but the vast majority of these peasants went to the polls in defiance of Sandino's orders.[15] Liberal voters, rich and poor alike, came out in force in 1928 to elect General Moncada president by 20,000 votes.

The election brought the Liberal Party to unfettered power for the first time in almost 20 years. It was also the first peaceful transfer of power between the two parties in Nicaragua's history. Leaders of both sides respected the results over the coming four years, and both parties requested American supervision again for the 1932 elections. The Conservatives did not try to upset the new government by force, and Moncada was restrained by the continuing presence of the American marines and guided by the advice of Henry Stimson.[16]

In spite of the elections and the peace wrought between the two factions, Sandino continued his struggle in the northern hills. Since 1927 Sandino had proven a brilliant guerrilla commander, capable of making use of all the advantages afforded guerrillas by the Nicaraguan geography and terrain. The American marines and the new trainees in the National Guard could not deal with him. At various times, the number of marines in Nicaragua was reduced to a minimum, in the hope that Sandino would fade away or that the newly trained Nicaraguan National Guard could handle him alone. When the marines slackened their attacks, however, Sandino increased his. He sought every opportunity to strike at marine outposts, to embarrass the Americans, and thus enhance his own reputation as Nicaragua's emancipator. Periods of ignoring Sandino, therefore, were followed by increased efforts to track him down and eliminate him.

But the Nicaraguan terrain confounded the marines, as it had confounded Managua-based Nicaraguan governments since independence and would confound future governments from the Somozas to the Sandinistas in their own fights against rebel forces. The sparsely populated and undeveloped mountain and jungle regions of northern, central, and eastern Nicaragua were always one step away from escaping the grip of any central government. The marines and the Guard could not cut off Sandino's supply or escape routes which weaved along the northern border with Honduras. To stop Sandino would seem to have required "a continuous occupation of the whole five-hundred-mile border."[17] The National Guard at its height had fewer than 3,000 men; the number of American marines fluctuated between 1,000 and 3,000.

The leaders of the marine contingent in Nicaragua repeatedly told officials in Washington that putting down Sandino's rebellion would require a far greater commitment of resources by the United States. But the U.S. government was unwilling either to withdraw or to intensify the intervention. Especially after the election of Herbert Hoover, the new administration's only goal was to end American involvement, to "Nicaraguanize" the war as quickly as possible, and to prepare for the final evacuation of American troops immediately after the 1932 elections.

By the first half of 1930, the marines were no longer leading National Guard troops in the fighting but spent most of their time guarding the cities. In February 1931 Secretary Stimson ordered the withdrawal of all marine units by June of that year. Only an "instruction battalion" would remain to continue training the National Guard in Managua. Even if Stimson had wanted to keep the marines in longer, pressures from Congress were becoming irresistible. In March 1929 isolationists almost succeeded in cutting off all funds for the marines in Nicaragua. In January 1931 the powerful Senator Borah renewed his demand for the removal of all American forces, and Stimson decided to begin the evacuation.

Sandino's response to the diminishing American presence was to strike even more aggressively at American positions. On December 31, 1930, his troops ambushed and killed eight marines, causing an outcry in the

United States against continuing the occupation. In March 1931, just one month after Stimson ordered the beginning of the withdrawal, Sandino ordered attacks on American citizens and their property in Nicaragua. In a historic departure from American policy in Nicaragua, Stimson declared that the United States government could "not undertake general protection of Americans throughout [Nicaragua] with American forces. To do so would lead to difficulties and commitments which this Government does not propose to undertake." He recommended that American citizens who did not feel secure in Nicaragua should leave the country.[18]

Sandino did not defeat the United States in Nicaragua. The American retreat was due to the much broader movement toward isolationism in the United States during the depression era. Sandino played a significant role, however, in undermining an already declining American will. By shedding American blood, he gave powerful arguments against the intervention to its opponents in the United States. Sandino himself, moreover, had become a potent symbol for anti-imperialist movements in America and throughout the world. In 1928 the American Anti-Imperialist League and the editors of the *Daily Worker* and the *Nation* joined to raise funds for "medical supplies" and circulated pamphlets calling on supporters to "Enlist with Sandino" and "Defeat the War against Nicaragua." The Sixth World Congress of the Comintern, meeting in Moscow, sent "fraternal greetings to the workers and peasants of Nicaragua, and the heroic army of national emancipation of General Sandino, which is carrying on a brave, determined struggle with the imperialism of the United States."[19] An American journalist named Carleton Beals spent weeks with Sandino and wrote articles for the *Nation* recounting the exploits of the brave Nicaraguan patriot. Congressional opponents of the marine intervention likened Sandino to George Washington. According to Senator J. Thomas Heflin of Alabama, "Sandino crying for liberty, begging for the deliverance of his country from the invader, sounds like the cries our fathers made in the days of the Revolution. . . . We are seeking this man out to kill him for fighting for principles that we fought for in 1776."[20] Efforts by Stimson and other administration officials to portray Sandino as nothing more than a "bandit" had little success. Sandino's struggle captured the imagination of many Americans, and his international popularity helped doom the marines' already difficult struggle.

By the early 1930s no clear economic or strategic interests were at stake in Nicaragua, and the high political costs of continuing the occupation outweighed any political benefits to President Hoover. Far from remaining in Nicaragua to protect American financiers, the marine legation by 1931 was, on Stimson's directive, not even attempting to protect American lives and property. Secretary Stimson and other American officials, however, still felt a sense of responsibility for what happened in Nicaragua after the marines' eventual departure. The leaders of both Nicaraguan parties pleaded with the United States government to keep the marines in the country. From January 1929 until the 1932 elections, both the Conservatives and the Liberals led by Sacasa saw the American presence as a check on the ambitions of Moncada, as well as a safeguard against the Sandinistas. Stimson and other American officials considered it irresponsible to withdraw without making some arrangements for Nicaragua's future stability.

The Nicaraguan National Guard was the product of this American sense of obligation. Designed to substitute for American power, to safeguard elections, and to maintain stability, the Guard under its American commanders had carried the brunt of the fighting against Sandino. In 1932 the rebel army increased the pace of its attacks, however, and the Guard took some shocking losses. Low on arms and ammunition, and lacking well-trained leaders to take over from the withdrawing Americans—who themselves had not fared well against Sandino—the Guard's morale reached a low ebb as the elections approached.

In November 1932 Nicaragua held its second consecutive fair election. The American government again supervised it, although earlier in the year the American Congress had cut funds for the delegation of election observers so that Americans were present at only 182 out of 429 polling places. Nevertheless, the resulting victory by the Liberals' Dr. Sacasa over the Conservative candidate, Adolfo Díaz, was widely accepted as fair and reflective of popular opinion. Sacasa's triumph completed the process of the Liberal Party's restoration begun in 1924. The vanquished Conservatives would remain out of power for the next 58 years.

The first problem faced by the new Liberal president was that Moncada, though no longer President, intended to wield influence in Nicaragua from behind the scenes as the leader of his faction. Moncada named the first chief of the newly independent Nicaraguan National Guard: Anastasio Somoza García, one of the generals in Moncada's Liberal Constitutionalist army. The American ambassador, who liked the affable and English-speaking Somoza, warmly approved the selection.

The significance of Somoza's appointment was obscured by the continuing war against Sandino. With the American withdrawal due to be completed within three months after the elections, leaders of both parties feared being left alone to face Sandino's increasingly threatening army. Sacasa, like his predecessors, pleaded in vain with the American government to keep the marines in Nicaragua a little longer. When the Hoover administration refused, Sacasa and the other political leaders resigned themselves to seeking a peace with Sandino.

President-elect Sacasa wasted no time in offering a peace conference when the rebel leader called for the creation of an enormous, new department in northern Nicaragua in which his army would remain and his followers would hold all government positions. Sacasa agreed to negotiate these demands rather than see a renewal of the war. Sandino's army was "as strong as, if not stronger than any time in the past."[21] At the end of January Sandino, "feeling romantic and tragic," as he put it, traveled to Managua to meet Sacasa. He embraced the President, and he embraced Somoza, and on February 2, 1933, he declared his crusade for Nicaragua's freedom ended. Sandino was granted a tract of land in the Coco river valley, where he planned to begin an agricultural commune. The government agreed to let Sandino keep an army of 100 men, supported by government funds, for a period of one year. The remainder of Sandino's troops were to turn in their arms. When Sandino agreed to these terms, some of his lieutenants objected, just as Sandino himself had objected to Moncada's acquiescence at Tipitapa. Unlike Moncada, Sandino had the dissidents shot.

Sandino's own acquiescence to the government's terms, however, was far from complete. When Sandino's army was disarmed on February 22, 1,800 fighters turned themselves in but only 361 weapons were collected. Sacasa and Somoza suspected that Sandino had kept a large cache of weapons for future use. Sandino confirmed these suspicions later in the year when he offered to send 600 armed fighters to defend President Sacasa against an alleged Conservative uprising.[22] By the spring of 1933, Sandino was already making known his defiance of Managua. In a "Manifesto to the Peoples of the Earth and in Particular to the People of Nicaragua," Sandino declared that he would "morally support Doctor Sacasa during his administration," but that he was "independent of the government." He announced plans to create a "Federal District of Central America" in his Coco valley preserve.[23] Sandino often discussed the more practical goals of forming his own political party and running for the presidency on his own ticket. No one doubted that Sandino's ambition was to take a part in ruling Nicaragua, one way or another.

3

The "Good Neighbor" and the Rise of Somoza

President Sacasa soon became even more concerned about the growing power of the National Guard chief, Anastasio Somoza. Chamorro and Moncada both offered their support to Somoza as a way of weakening Sacasa, but it soon became clear that there was, in fact, a five-way struggle for power under way in Nicaragua. When President Sacasa contracted malaria in November 1933, rumors spread of an impending takeover of the government by the Guard. While Chamorro and Moncada supported Somoza, Sandino repeatedly offered his army to protect President Sacasa. But Sacasa, fearing that reliance on Sandino would soon become subordination to Sandino, did not accept the offers.

Nicaraguans on all sides of the struggle looked north to see what role the United States would play. It took them some time to realize that the Americans, under their new President, Franklin D. Roosevelt, had no intention of playing any role at all. The policy of the "Good Neighbor," which Roosevelt announced in his inaugural address, was little more than a continuation of policies already begun by Hoover and Stimson. Unlike its predecessors, however, the Roosevelt administration intended to adhere rigidly to the principle of non-intervention, regardless of the consequences in Nicaragua. The United States, it soon became clear, was prepared to be a "Good Neighbor" to any Nicaraguan leader, regardless of how he came to power or how he wielded it.

Without American involvement after January 2, 1933, events in Nicaragua took what history had shown to be their natural course. The triangular relationship between Sacasa, Sandino, and the Guard was inherently unstable. Sandino declared the Guard unconstitutional and demanded its reorganization, and the Guard wanted to be let loose to destroy Sandino. Somoza suggested that Sandino be imprisoned and then exiled. While Sacasa temporized, the Guard took action. On February 21, 1934, Guard officers captured Sandino and shot him.[1] Somoza, who now had the only armed force in Nicaragua, expressed undying loyalty to President Sacasa, but everyone in Nicaragua knew he harbored ambitions for the presidency.

If Somoza sought to gain power by illegal means, which was the only way he could take power, it was widely believed in Nicaragua that only the United States government could prevent him. Since 1907 the United States had refused to recognize governments in Nicaragua that came to power by illegal or violent means. This "non-recognition" policy had been the downfall of Emiliano Chamorro, even though he was widely presumed to have been a friend of the United States. Since 1927 the United States had acted as a guardian of the Nicaraguan constitution and of agreements reached between the parties. It had blocked Moncada's efforts to prolong his stay in power; it had insisted on fair elections and constitutional transfers of power in 1928 and 1932.

The Roosevelt administration, however, was unwilling to take any action to block Somoza. When the American marines withdrew from Nicaragua on January 2, 1933, the State Department released a statement declaring an end to the "special relationship" between the United States and Nicaragua. Saying that the United States had considered it "a privilege to assist Nicaragua" and would "always look with friendly sympathy and satisfaction upon the progress which Nicaragua through her own efforts will inevitably achieve in the future," the State Department officially removed itself from any further role in Nicaraguan politics.[2]

President Sacasa, who had the most to lose from America's sudden lack of interest, repeatedly implored the American Ambassador, Arthur Bliss Lane, not to declare America's rigid commitment to non-intervention lest this "encourage some of his political adversaries to take steps to satisfy their political ambitions by forcible or other extra-constitutional action."[3] The State Department, however, would not permit Ambassador Lane to make any public statement, not even in support of constitutional government or free elections, since even the most anodyne statements might be interpreted as taking sides. As Secretary of State Cordell Hull explained, the United States "desire[d] not only to refrain . . . from any interference, but also from any measure which might seem to give the appearance of such interference."[4] Lane complained to Washington that he sometimes found it difficult to be a "good neighbor" to Nicaraguans while scrupulously observing such strict principles of non-intervention.[5]

In September 1935, officials approached Lane with a plan to demand Somoza's resignation from the National Guard and asked what the United States would do if Somoza should respond with force. The State Department instructed Lane to reply that the United States did not "intend to intervene in the internal affairs of Nicaragua."[6] The Nicaraguans responded angrily: "In other words we are to do nothing. We are to allow the present fine situation to continue. Somoza will be President and then the United States will be satisfied."[7] In Washington, American officials complained that the Nicaraguans behaved as if they were "incapable of self-government." One Nicaraguan official sadly admitted that "sometimes it occurred to him that such was the case."[8]

Somoza, freed from any restraint by the northern power, pressed ahead in his plans to seize the presidency. In May, fighting between Somoza's and Sacasa's forces began around León. As the danger grew, Nicaragua's neighbors approached the United States to discuss some form of mediation between the warring parties. The Roosevelt administration remained aloof.[9] When the Sacasa government appealed to the entire diplomatic corps in Managua to issue a statement calling upon Somoza to cease fighting "in the name of humanity," the governments of Great Britain, France, El Salvador, Honduras, and Mexico signed the appeal, hoping a halt in the fighting might lead to negotiations among all the Nicaraguan factions. The new American Ambassador, Boaz Long, was instructed not to sign.

At the beginning of June, President Sacasa resigned and Somoza became de facto ruler of Nicaragua. Although Somoza had not yet even worked out the arrangements for his formal assumption of the presidency, the State Department cabled Ambassador Long that "on the basis of information available here, there appears to be no reason why you should not treat with the present Government which seems to be in control of the country and all governmental machinery."[10]

Six months later Somoza had himself elected President in a vote which all his prospective opponents boycotted. In the days leading up to the vote, Somoza's opponents made a final, vain plea to the Roosevelt administration. The deposed President Sacasa, his longtime enemy Emiliano Chamorro, and the former Conservative President Adolfo Díaz joined in appealing for American intervention. "The principle of non-intervention," they wrote, although "dear to all the Latin-American peoples," must nevertheless "not exclude the friendly cooperation between the American countries. . . . [I]ndifference to the struggles and misfortunes of a friendly or sister nation can in no way denote goodwill towards her."[11] Despite their plea, the Somoza dynasty was born under the watchful but studiously indifferent eye of Nicaragua's good neighbor to the north.

———

Nicaragua was not the only country where dictatorship was born and prospered during the years of Roosevelt's "Good Neighbor" policies. With Fulgencio Batista in Cuba, Rafael Trujillo in the Dominican Republic, and Somoza in Nicaragua, a Mexico City newspaper could complain in 1939 that the hemisphere was "transforming itself into a league of 'mestizo' dictators, with the United States destined to guarantee the slavery of Latin American peoples."[12] Since most Mexican writers and politicians had always been among the most fervent advocates of non-intervention by North America, this complaint was ironic. Neither in the Dominican Republic nor in Cuba nor in Nicaragua could the United States be held responsible for dictatorship. In Nicaragua dictatorship had been the normal state of affairs since its independence; tyranny and one-party rule had been interrupted only by periods of revolution and near-anarchy. To be sure, the United States had helped create a new army, the National Guard, which had been used to put its leader into the presidency. But the use of national armies by individuals seeking power was common in Nicaragua. Had control of the Guard been given to Chamorro, to Moncada, to Sandino, or to any number of other would-be *caudillos*, the results would probably not have been very different. Somoza had the skills and wiles to keep himself in power for 20 years. He may, therefore, be considered one of Nicaragua's most successful dictators, but he cannot be considered the creation of the United States.

If the American intervention which ended in 1933 had had any special effect in Nicaragua, it had been to temper the tendency to dictatorship and violent revolution. Not all the elections held during the American occupation were fair, but three of them were fairer than any elections held in Nicaragua before or since—until the internationally supervised elections of 1990. Under American occupation, one Nicaraguan party transferred power peacefully to the other for the first time in their history. The price for Nicaraguans was their sovereignty. For Americans, the price was responsibility and guilt. There was little financial cost to the occupation and perhaps some gain for a few American bankers and businessmen. American losses in the war against Sandino were very small. But after more than a dozen years of occupation, the American people, through their Congress, grew weary of the responsibility and ashamed of the hegemonic behavior of their government.

The result of America's non-intervention in Nicaragua, however, was dictatorship. Over the next 40 years, successive American governments supported, disdained, or ignored the Somozas. For most of this period the United States did not keep the Somozas in power any more than it had put them in power. Indifference and non-interference had been all Somoza required in 1936; it was enough for the next 40 years. Since the beginning of the century, Nicaraguan dictators had fallen for one reason alone: because the United States withdrew its support and gave encouragement, intentionally or not, to the dictator's challengers. So long as the United States remained aloof, the Somoza dynasty was not likely to end.

Part Two

THE LAST SOMOZA AND THE TRIUMPH OF REVOLUTION

4

Human Rights and "Dissociation"

During the first year of the presidency of Jimmy Carter, Nicaragua was a subject of little interest to the American press, less to the American Congress, and still less to the young administration. All were struggling with what were thought to be larger issues in America's wide-ranging foreign policy, from peace in the Middle East and Africa to "Third World" poverty, the Panama Canal treaties, and the search for an arms agreement with the Soviet Union. In the four decades since Anastasio Somoza first seized the presidency in Nicaragua, the United States had evolved into the world's foremost military and economic power. After securing victory in World War II, the United States had gone on to expand its global interests and involvement beyond anything Theodore Roosevelt or Woodrow Wilson could have imagined. The United States had become a superpower, and its sphere of influence was no longer the Western Hemisphere but the world.

Just as the country's experiment in internationalism in the early part of the century had led to a period of disillusionment and withdrawal after World War I, however, many Americans suffered a similar disillusionment in the 1970s as the Vietnam War drew to a close. A campaign theme of George McGovern in the 1972 presidential elections was "Come Home, America," and although McGovern lost, this sentiment found full expression in the liberal wing of the Democratic Party throughout the 1970s.

The call for an end to the "immoral" policies of recent presidents echoed the earlier complaints against American "imperialism" by isolationists, pacifists, and other critics of American intervention in the first two decades of the century. Like the earlier anti-imperialists, many of the new generation of liberals sought a retraction of American involvement and influence overseas. There were no occupying troops to remove in Latin America, but there were unsavory dictators whose rule seemed to many to be every bit as much a manifestation of American imperialism. The Somoza dynasty in Nicaragua, which many believed had been installed by American marines and preserved by American power ever since the 1930s, provided an inviting target.

By the 1970s, the four-decades-old family dictatorship in Nicaragua was one of the few remaining Latin dynasties. Anastasio Somoza Debayle, the son of the Somoza dynasty's founder, had had himself elected president in 1967. Less politically adept than his father, less inclined to moderation and compromise than his brother, Luis, who had ruled Nicaragua from 1957 to 1967, the younger Somoza aroused opposition at home and abroad. He used his power both to expand his family's wealth and to suppress all potential challenges to the continuation of the dynasty. In 1972, when a large earthquake devastated Managua, Somoza and his political allies took most of the international relief aid for themselves. Their behavior attracted international attention, and in 1975 the American columnist Jack Anderson wrote a series of articles calling Somoza the "world's greediest dictator."

The bad international publicity spurred attacks on the regime at home. Opposition groups, sensing Somoza's weakness, looked for opportunities to strike. In 1974 an armed attack and kidnapping by a small leftist guerrilla movement, the Sandinista National Liberation Front, prompted Somoza to impose a state of siege and wipe out the guerrilla bands in the countryside. But the success of the counter-insurgency campaign carried an enormous price. Members of the National Guard imprisoned, brutalized, and killed not only Sandinista fighters, but also hundreds of peasants suspected of helping them. The private human rights monitoring organization, Amnesty International, charged that "Torture, arbitrary detention and disappearances" had become "increasingly characteristic of the human rights situation in Nicaragua." More damaging to the Somoza regime were accusations by Nicaragua's Roman Catholic bishops in February 1977 that the National Guard had carried out widespread torture, rape, and summary executions of civilians in their battle against the guerrillas.[1]

Somoza chose a particularly inopportune moment to crack down. In the late 1960s and early 1970s, American policy had been indifferent to Somoza's activities. In the early Nixon years, Somoza had even found a close ally in Ambassador Turner Shelton. But Nixon resigned amidst the Watergate scandal, and by 1974 the mood in the United States had shifted dramatically. A new American Ambassador, James Theberge, began distancing the Ford administration from the dictatorship. A State Department human rights report at the end of 1976 leveled harsh criticism at the Somoza regime, the first public attack by the U.S. government in many years. By the beginning of 1977, Somoza faced a determined assault from powerful American opponents.

In the spring of 1977, Edward I. Koch, the Democratic congressman and future mayor of New York City, began the first effort to cut off all U.S. military aid to Nicaragua. Congressman Koch was part of a new political movement in Congress that emerged in the mid-1970s after the end of the Vietnam War and the Watergate scandal. Made up of 80 to 90 young liberal Democrats, mostly elected in 1974 and 1976 as part of the anti-war, anti-Nixon vote across the country, this bloc sought a sweeping revision of American foreign policy in the post-Vietnam era. Under the banner of "human rights," the new generation of liberal Democrats focused their attack on American policies that appeared to coddle foreign dictators and military governments. They demanded withdrawal of American support for those right-wing governments which engaged in repression and brutality. They were less concerned with reforming these regimes than they were with cleansing America's dirty hands. Their goal was "dissociation."[2]

The new President who took office in January 1977 generally shared the goals of the "new foreign policy." In his campaign Jimmy Carter had promised to make human rights a central part of American foreign relations, not only with the Soviet Union and other communist countries but also with those governments long supported by the United States. "[I]f any nation, whatever its political system, deprives its own people of basic human rights," candidate Carter had declared, "that fact will help shape our own people's attitude toward that nation's repressive government. . . . [W]e should use our tremendous influence to increase freedom, particularly in those countries that depend upon us for their very survival."[3] Carter insisted he would not let concerns about communist revolutionaries determine America's policy toward right-wing tyrants. In May 1977 he urged Americans to rid themselves of their historical "inordinate fear of

Communism which once led us to embrace any dictator who joined us in that fear."[4]

Carter's strong language did not immediately translate into dramatic actions, however. Although one prominent journalist, the *New York Times'* Alan Riding, decided to make Nicaragua his own test of the new administration's commitment to human rights,[5] few observers expected Carter's deeds to match his words. For one thing, both Congress and the Democratic Party were divided. Koch and other liberal Democrats railed against Somoza and spared no hyperbole, calling Nicaragua "one of the most disgusting, cruel and corrupt governments in the world . . . beyond hope of redemption."[6] But from the other side, conservative Democrats like Charles Wilson from Texas railed against the "double standard" erected by the liberals. According to Wilson, "Nicaragua's main sin seems to be that it is friendly to the United States." While aid flowed freely to many other countries with worse records, Wilson argued, "We should not single out one country, and if we are going to single out one country, we should not single out one of our best friends in this hemisphere."[7]

The Carter administration was itself divided on the issue, between advocates of the new emphasis on human rights and those who favored more traditional and cooperative relations with allied governments. In the early months of 1977 the State Department became tangled trying to find an acceptable compromise. The Carter administration began by seeking $3.1 million in military aid for Somoza's army. One senior official, however, when asked why military aid should be given to Somoza's regime, could give no good reason and testified that Nicaragua was really of no strategic importance to the United States.[8] The Assistant Secretary of State for Inter-American Affairs, Terence Todman, on the other hand, insisted that the United States had significant security interests in Nicaragua, including "prevention of the introduction of hostile forces and bases into the region, limitation of hostile influences, protection of lines of communication, and maintenance of regional stability." Todman argued that "for political reasons Nicaragua should continue to receive the modest amount of security assistance from the U.S."[9] The result was a stalemate that at first seemed to favor Somoza. On June 23 the House approved the Carter administration's request for military aid for Nicaragua by a vote of 225–180; 107 Democrats joined 118 Republicans in approving the aid.[10]

Somoza, in turn, took steps to appease his American critics. In the spring he ordered the National Guard to curb its violent behavior, and in

September he lifted the three-year-old state of siege against the Sandinista guerrillas and ended press censorship. His purposes were obvious enough. For Somoza the actions were part of a deal: "The U.S. wants philosophy, we want international cooperation. So we trade: I give them philosophy and they give me international cooperation and that's the name of the game. You never get anything free."[11]

But Somoza's "trade" did not satisfy some senior Carter officials, who were determined to put pressure on the dictator for further reform. The State Department's human rights bureau argued that all aid be withheld from Nicaragua, despite the vote in Congress. Deputy Secretary Warren Christopher agreed. He decided that the United States would sign the 1977 military aid agreement but withhold the aid pending further progress in the human rights situation.[12] Christopher also decided to withhold approval for two development loans totaling $10 million which Congress had approved. This step went beyond what even Koch and the human rights lobby had sought.[13] It amounted to a complete suspension of all aid to Nicaragua.

With Christopher's decision to withhold aid, the Carter administration and the Congress turned their attention away from Nicaragua. In November of 1977, Ed Koch was elected mayor of New York City. For those who remained in Washington there were other, more important matters to consider. The stakes in Nicaragua seemed tiny, both to Somoza's friends and to his enemies. Not only was Nicaragua deemed strategically insignificant, but the possibility of dramatic change in this insignificant country was remote. Somoza's opponents were weak. The Sandinista guerrilla forces had been all but wiped out by the National Guard since 1974, which was why Somoza felt free to lift the state of siege. The CIA estimated the number of guerrilla fighters at 50.[14] The suspension of aid, therefore, was presumably without cost to the United States or even to Somoza. The argument over Nicaragua began and ended in 1977 as a dispute between competing views about American foreign policy in which Nicaragua was but a test case.[15]

5

Shaking the Foundations

These small and rather haphazard decisions in Washington, however, blew down across Nicaragua like a hurricane. Nicaraguans knew from historical experience that even small shifts in American policy could have a direct and powerful effect on the balance of political power in Nicaragua, and in 1977 many Nicaraguans believed that Carter's promises to distance the United States from right-wing dictators were aimed specifically at Somoza. Had Warren Christopher approved the release of military and economic aid, Nicaraguan expectations of a change in American policy might have subsided. But the suspension of aid in October stoked flames that had begun building earlier in the year.

The Carter administration was not Somoza's only problem in 1977. In July the tall and stout 51-year-old president suffered a serious heart attack, which kept him hospitalized in Miami for more than a month. The illness and long absence from the country created inevitable problems for the dictator. Nicaraguans contemplated Somoza's mortality and began thinking about the succession—three years before the scheduled elections. Somoza's recent elevation of his son to a senior position in the military appeared calculated to catapult the next generation of Somozas into the presidency, a prospect that caused unease among those opposition leaders who might otherwise have been inclined to wait patiently for the next electoral contest. Close friends and advisers were urging Somoza to resign in favor of a unity government—a ploy which might have allowed him to preserve his power behind the scenes, as his father and brother had once done.[1] But Somoza was determined to hold onto the presidency.

The heart attack, together with the new American hostility, brought to the surface long-simmering discontents in Nicaraguan society. Tolerance of Somoza's rule had already begun to deteriorate in the early 1970s when the Somozas expanded their control of the nation's economy. After the earthquake leveled Managua in 1972, the Somoza family exploited the devastation by buying up businesses. Nicaraguan businessmen were angry and worried about their pocketbooks, but personal wealth was not the only issue. By increasing his family's grasp on the economy, Somoza broke a tacit agreement that had kept Nicaragua's business elite quiescent. Nicaragua under Somoza, though bad for politics, was supposed to be good for business.

Indeed, for that very reason Nicaraguan businessmen were a rising force in Nicaraguan society. The development of cotton as a major industry in the 1950s and 1960s had brought new wealth to Nicaraguans outside the traditional landed families. One prominent entrepreneur, Alfonso Robelo, for instance, did not belong to any of the great clans from the major cities of León or Granada. An attractive, intelligent, and ambitious young man, Robelo had made millions by manufacturing cottonseed oil that could be used for cooking. He and others with new economic power increasingly aspired to a commensurate share of political power that would protect their rights and interests. The obstacle was Somoza. The perpetuation of the dynasty promised permanent exclusion from any share of real power in Nicaragua for young and eager men like Robelo.

Despite their growing antipathy to Somoza, however, and their desire to get involved with politics, the young businessmen did not have a ready vehicle to promote their interests. The established political parties lacked a large popular following and were much discredited because they had acquiesced to, and cooperated with, Somoza rule for so long. In the early 1970s the Conservative Party had made a political deal with Somoza and been granted a large but worthless minority proportion of seats in the Congress. This "pact" was widely considered a disgrace, and the party had subsequently splintered into factions.

Some Nicaraguan politicians, however, had not been discredited. One former Conservative politician who had refused to cooperate with Somoza was Pedro Joaquín Chamorro, descendant of the Conservative Party leader Emiliano Chamorro and leading heir of the prominent Nicaraguan family that had ruled Nicaragua for many years in the nineteenth century and during the years of the marine occupation. Chamorro was an aristocrat whom many found autocratic, but he had won widespread popularity, in Nicaragua and abroad, for his forceful opposition to the Somoza dictatorship. In 1959 Chamorro had led a small, ill-conceived invasion from Costa Rica against the government of Luis Somoza. The attack failed, Chamorro was arrested, and then later released. After that incident, he gave up armed efforts against the Somozas and became editor of the newspaper owned by his family, *La Prensa*, making it a platform for outspoken opposition to the Somoza regime. In the early 1970s, when the Conservative Party had made its "pact" with the Somoza government, Chamorro had broken away from the party and in 1974 founded UDEL, the Union for Democratic Liberation, a coalition of political and labor groups opposed to the government.

Chamorro and the other leaders of UDEL were inspired by progressive and socialist ideas sweeping through the hemisphere in the early 1970s. The electoral victory in 1970 of Salvador Allende and a coalition of social democratic and Marxist forces in Chile seemed to provide an exciting example of peaceful and progressive change. Chamorro had traveled to Chile to witness the "revolution" there, studied the methods of political organization, the social programs, and the electoral skills of the victorious parties. When Allende veered toward outright Marxism and was then toppled and killed in a military coup, the lesson Chamorro drew was that radical change was dangerous. He sided with the anti-Marxist Chilean democrats who silently supported the coup. The party he founded in Nicaragua in 1974 was to be an opposition movement for peaceful, progressive change, anti-Somoza but also anti-communist. By 1977 Chamorro had become a leader of the growing political opposition to the Somoza family and UDEL was his vehicle. His efforts attracted the sympathies of young men like Robelo, as well as of other Nicaraguan businessmen like Adolfo Calero, manager of the Coca-Cola bottling factory and a leader of another Conservative Party faction that had broken off from the "official" Conservatives in the government.

Chamorro's ascendancy represented something new in Nicaraguan political life. The rise of a moderate, non-violent opposition to Somoza that crossed family lines and encompassed several classes of society was a departure from the historical pattern of Nicaraguan politics, which had usually been a struggle among elite families fought by armed *campesinos*. The novel developments in Nicaragua coincided with the complex changes in Washington, and the blend was potentially explosive. The Carter administration's new policy of hostility to Somoza offered Chamorro and his followers the opportunity they had long sought to put an end to the dynasty and carry out a kind of political revolution in Nicaragua. Chamorro declared that Somoza's "lifting of the censorship and state of siege [were] concrete results of the change in U.S. policy toward Nicaragua," and he expected to ride peacefully into power on the new winds blowing down from Washington.[2]

———————

The Carter administration's decisions in 1977 also spurred another group of Nicaraguans into action against Somoza. For the leaders of the Sandinista National Liberation Front, however, the new American policy held as many risks as opportunities. The peaceful departure of Somoza sought by Chamorro and the Nicaraguan business and aristocratic elite was anathema to this small but energetic group of Nicaraguan revolutionaries. They had no interest in exchanging one U.S.-backed oligarchy named Somoza for another named Chamorro. The Sandinistas instead sought a thorough transformation of Nicaraguan society, a complete liberation from American influence. And they insisted that only the Sandinista party, as the Nicaraguan people's vanguard, could lead the country through this historic revolutionary transformation.

The Sandinista National Liberation Front (known by its Spanish acronym, FSLN, for *Frente Sandinista de Liberación Nacional*) had been founded by Carlos Fonseca, Tomás Borge, and Silvio Mayorga in 1961. The small movement was born out of frustration with the Moscow-line Nicaraguan Socialist Party which had shunned violent revolution as a means to power. Its founders chose Augusto César Sandino to evoke the memory of his defiant stand against the invading marines, but the movement's real inspiration was Fidel Castro, whose dramatic revolutionary triumph in Cuba in 1959 had sent shock waves through Latin America. "The victory of armed struggle in Cuba," Tomás Borge recalled, "was a spark which brought light to the midst of naive and boring dogmas of the time. . . . We left the country and we began to organize forces abroad."[3] According to the "FSLN Program of 1969" the Front was to be "a political-military organization whose objective is the seizure of political power through the destruction of the bureaucratic and military apparatus of the dictatorship." That destruction, Fonseca and Borge believed, would only "come about as a consequence of the development of a hard and prolonged people's war."[4]

Although differences often arose among the Sandinista leaders over how to achieve their goal, there was full agreement on the problems facing Nicaragua. The early Sandinistas, who read Marx, Engels, and Lenin, argued that the forces of imperial capitalism had seized control of the country, forcing its people to serve the interests of the monopolies based in the United States. The victims of this imperialist system—the poor, the workers, and Nicaragua itself, which had lost its independence—needed a champion, a vanguard—the FSLN. "Reformist" solutions demanded by Pedro Joaquín Chamorro and other opponents of the Somozas were worse than futile; they were dangerous. Liberalization, elections, even legal trade unions could only soften the "contradictions" of society and perpetuate the system of capitalist dominance. Change had to come through violent upheaval, not "electoral farces." Armed revolution, the creation of the new, just society that Marx envisioned, and of a "new Nicaraguan man," were the only answer. Fonseca had traveled to Moscow in 1957 and wrote admiringly of the post-Stalin order there. The 1969 program called for "the establishment of a Revolutionary Government based on a worker-peasant alliance and the support of all the anti-imperialist patriotic forces of the country."

While the "bourgeois" opponents of Somoza over the years swung between hostility and accommodation to the dynasty, the Sandinistas passed through several stages of revolutionary work, never wavering in their goals but adjusting their tactics frequently in response to repeated failure. In the early days of the movement, the Sandinista founders had planned to carry on their revolutionary struggle in accord with the "foco" strategy of guerrilla warfare, which they believed had made possible Castro's victory in Cuba. The idea of the "foco" was that an isolated band of guerrillas, fighting the government's troops in the hills and jungles—in Castro's case, the Sierra Maestra—could spark a popular rebellion and topple the dictatorship. By 1969, however, it was clear that the "foco" strategy was a failure in Nicaragua, having achieved nothing for the Sandinistas but devastation by the National Guard. With the FSLN program of 1969, Carlos Fonseca attempted a shift in revolutionary theory and strategy. His new doctrine called for a larger "people's army" and a long, drawn-out popular struggle, and it took for its model the successful struggles of Mao Tse-tung and the Vietnamese General Giap.

The difference between the old and the new strategies, however, was less than Fonseca and the others suggested. After 1969, bands of Sandinista fighters still operated mostly in the hills. The universities and high schools, swept up in the worldwide student movement and suffused by radical politics, became rich reservoirs for developing Sandinista cadres. But political activity in the main centers of population—Managua, León, Granada, and Estelí—was insignificant. It was still a "jungle war," and the prospects for mass insurrection seemed remote. By 1976 the Sandinistas, few in number and periodically mauled in clashes with the Guard, remained no more than an annoyance to the Somoza government.

In the mid-seventies some of the young Sandinista cadres at the universities, mostly from the upper and upper-middle classes, did not follow their elders into the jungle to fight the prolonged war, but went abroad for study. Like Pedro Joaquín Chamorro, they were inspired by progressive and leftist thought sweeping through Latin American universities. And like Chamorro, they were drawn after 1970 to Allende's Chile. Some worked with radical youth groups in Chile and learned about urban mass organizing and revolutionary party work. When Allende fell in 1973, the young Sandinistas drew a different lesson from Chamorro. They were more convinced than ever that socialist revolution was essential in Nicaragua, but it had to be carefully studied and prepared for if it was to succeed and avoid the fate of Allende.

When these younger Sandinistas returned to Nicaragua in 1975, they launched an attack on the strategy and tactics of the older leaders of the FSLN, Borge and Fonseca. Borge responded by purging them from the movement, and the Sandinistas split into two hostile factions that remained sharply at odds for the next three years of the revolution. Borge's faction, the old-line Sandinistas, became known as the Prolonged Popular War faction. The younger Sandinistas who splintered off were known as the Proletarian Tendency because they favored careful preparation of the Nicaraguan working class. The struggle between the two factions grew violent and threatened to do the Guard's work by destroying the entire movement. Carlos Fonseca had to return from exile in Cuba to resolve the dispute at enormous personal risk. The Guard found and killed him in 1976. In subsequent months the Sandinistas suffered heavy casualties and many arrests. Borge and others were jailed.

In 1976, therefore, the Sandinista movement was at its nadir; but within three years it would be challenging Somoza for control of the nation. While Jimmy Carter was campaigning for the presidency in the

United States, yet another new group of young leaders was emerging in the FSLN. This group, which became known as the Insurrectionary faction or *Terceristas*, tried to bridge the personal and doctrinal gap between the older leaders of the Prolonged War faction and the young turks of the Proletarian Tendency. More than bridge the gap, however, they filled the vacuum of leadership. Led by Humberto Ortega and his brother Daniel, the *Terceristas* began by mediating, but soon moved into the front ranks of the Sandinista leadership.

In 1977 the shift in American policy heralded by the election of Jimmy Carter and the resulting rise of a broader opposition to the dynasty convinced *Tercerista* theorists that a decisive opportunity was at hand. As *Tercerista* leader Humberto Ortega recalled, "In mid-1977, there was great political activity among the bourgeois opposition resulting from the shift given to U.S. foreign policy by the Carter Administration."[5] Humberto Ortega and Carlos Coronel laid out the *Terceristas'* new strategy in a "General Political-Military Platform." The *Tercerista* plan attacked the passivity of the other Sandinistas and their inability to see the opportunities before them. It quoted Lenin: "today the misfortune is in our routine, in our doctrinism, in intellectualism's immobility, in the senile fear of all initiative."[6] The *Tercerista* strategy called on the movement to adopt a new military doctrine of "uninterrupted offensive," which would constantly harass the forces of Somoza, spur the rest of the country to insurrection, and place the FSLN in the vanguard of that struggle.

The *Tercerista* "Platform" also broke from orthodox Sandinista doctrine by calling for "tactical and temporary" alliances with bourgeois "progressives" to form a "broad anti-Somoza Front" along with the peasants and workers. This "triple bloc made up of the proletariat, the peasantry, and the petite bourgeoisie" would comprise the "moving force of the revolution." In order to achieve this alliance, the plan stated, the Sandinistas would have to submerge the rhetoric of Marxism-Leninism and speak only of the anti-Somoza struggle and the goal of democracy in terms that would not frighten off the bourgeoisie. Inherent in this strategy, as well, was a recognition that the new American administration was amenable to a change of government and could be induced to undermine Somoza—but only so long as the alternative did not appear to be communism. The *Tercerista* platform made clear that the bourgeoisie would play a decidedly secondary part in the revolution; its role was to be as a shield and a mask for the real revolution. Within the broad opposition coalition, the platform made clear, the FSLN was to be "hegemonic."[7]

Both prongs of the *Tercerista* strategy clashed with the more orthodox Marxist strategies of the other Sandinista factions, who argued that "objective" conditions had to be ripe before the insurrection could begin, and that even "tactical" alliances with the bourgeoisie were a dangerous betrayal of the workers and peasants. Nevertheless, the *Terceristas* went ahead with their plans, and the other factions, weakened by the imprisonment of their leaders and their isolation in the Nicaraguan hills, were dragged into the fighting.

The occasion for the Sandinistas' first attacks came in September 1977 when Somoza bowed to U.S. demands to lift the state of siege. Somoza's retreat, which cheered Pedro Joaquín Chamorro's followers, caused nervousness among the Sandinistas. "[T]he enemy had taken a step forward by lifting the state of siege," Humberto Ortega recalls, "and was considering an amnesty." The Sandinistas "saw that if this happened, we would be in a difficult position. So we decided to speed up the offensive."[8] In October 1977 the *Terceristas* launched several small but well-publicized attacks on National Guard posts near Nicaragua's southern border with Costa Rica. The assaults took the Guard by surprise, and Sandinista fighters killed or wounded more than a dozen government soldiers. The Sandinistas, outmanned and outgunned, suffered proportionally much heavier casualties, but the political impact of the October attacks more than compensated for the military failure.

When the fighting subsided, the *Terceristas* unveiled their new political strategy. A group of twelve Nicaraguan businessmen, academics, and priests publicly announced their support for the Sandinista Front, shocking much of Nicaraguan elite society. As the respectable front for the Sandinista movement, the "Group of Twelve" was designed to persuade others that the Sandinistas sought a democratic, not a communist solution for Nicaragua and that it was safe to help them with money and political support. One of the Twelve was Sergio Ramírez, a clandestine member of the FSLN who had helped conceive and carry out the strategy with Coronel and the Ortega brothers. Ramírez had contacted Joaquín Cuadra Chamorro, a prominent and prosperous lawyer, whose son was a Sandinista fighter, but who, according to Ramírez, "was a man the bourgeoisie would find trustworthy beyond reproach." Another figure beyond reproach was Arturo Cruz, an official with the Inter-American Development Bank in Washington. In the wake of the Sandinista attacks, the Twelve called for a national dialogue to bring about democracy in Nicaragua. They praised the Sandinistas' political "maturity" and insisted that the Sandinistas had to be part of any national solution. This was the first time prominent Nicaraguans had said a kind word about the guerrilla movement.

The Sandinistas were fortunate that the *Times'* Alan Riding decided to make himself the tribune of their new approach. In articles on October 20 and 26, Riding wrote of a new "major drive" by the Sandinistas to "topple Somoza." And he reported that the FSLN's goals had become "ideologically more modest," that "committed Marxists" had been forced to break away from the movement, and that the "new objective" of the Sandinistas was "to overthrow General Somoza through a 'popular insurrection' and to call free elections."[9]

The *Terceristas'* political strategy appeared to be working. While purists in the other factions complained that the *Terceristas* had "grotesquely" sought the Carter administration's approval by presenting themselves "to the bourgeois press as the standard-bearers of a democracy," the *Terceristas* could take satisfaction from having raised their movement from moribund obscurity to the pages of the *New York Times*.[10]

———

Chamorro and the Sandinistas, meanwhile, eyed each other warily. The aristocrat had a disdain for the guerrillas which he did not try to conceal. Chamorro spoke warmly of "these young people [who] are looking for an end to Somoza," but in the next breath assigned them no role in the future of Nicaragua. "As soon as Somoza is finished," Chamorro said, "the *Frente Sandinista* will have no reason to exist . . . I don't believe they would be very successful if there were free elections . . . [t]hey are very courageous young people. . . . But as an army, they are not trained to govern."[11]

Chamorro may have hoped that the violence might help force Somoza out and bring in a democratic government in which he, the rightful heir to power in Nicaragua, would play the leading role. And in some ways the *Terceristas'* October attacks did play into Chamorro's hands. The Sandinistas were far too weak to take on the Guard; but their attacks caused alarm in Nicaragua and possibly in the United States, as well. Chamorro and other opposition leaders expected the United States to move even more swiftly against Somoza now that a communist threat had appeared. Chamorro told American reporters that "without Somoza there would never be a [Sandinista Front]. Just as without Batista there would never be a Fidel Castro in Cuba." He said the majority of Sandinistas were not Marxist, "just anti-Somoza," but he also warned that "the longer Somoza is in power, the longer there will be a Marxist tendency in the Sandinistas." Chamorro undoubtedly envisioned an American policy that aimed to remove Somoza and replace him with a moderate, democratic government—led by Pedro Joaquín Chamorro.[12]

President Somoza, in the meantime, was still trying to quell the storm at home and appease officials in Washington. He seized on the Group of Twelve's proposal for a dialogue and stalled for time. Nicaragua's Archbishop, Obando y Bravo, formed a committee, with Alfonso Robelo as the representative for private enterprise, to coordinate plans for holding the discussions. Somoza met with this committee once at the end of November and insisted that the dialogue be deferred until after municipal elections scheduled for February 1978. Publicly, he argued that the will of the people, as expressed in those elections, could guide the negotiators and give meaning to the dialogue. Privately, Somoza believed his party would win another landslide over the weak Conservatives, thus discrediting his opposition and undermining their strength in a dialogue. He also hoped to gain time, to let the Sandinista attacks fade into the past and allow the opposition's ardor to cool. As for the Carter administration, Somoza intended to "crawl into his shell like an armadillo and wait for the wind to pass."[13]

On New Year's Day 1978, Somoza announced that the National Dialogue, which he now scheduled for March 1, would lay the "foundations for national harmony." Five days later, Chamorro issued a list of "minimum" demands that had to be met before a dialogue could begin. One demand was that the dialogue begin in early January, before the municipal elections. Now it was Somoza and the Sandinistas who joined forces, to denounce the moderates' proposal. Somoza's newspaper called the opposition demands "absurd."[14] The Sandinistas declared that the whole idea of a dialogue was "a lie against the people," with obvious implications for any opposition leaders who engaged in it.[15] The *Terceristas* did not have to worry about angering Chamorro and the other moderates with such statements; the unarmed opposition was already consumed with anger at Somoza's haughty rejection of its demands.

———

Nicaraguan politics had undergone an important transformation during President Carter's first year in office. The officials in Washington who helped spark these changes, however, saw no special reason to change the course of American policy in response to them. The small size of the Sandinista forces, the insignificance of their attacks on a few barracks in October, and the dispatch with which Somoza's National Guard put down the offensive calmed any concerns that might have appeared at the State Department, the Pentagon, or the CIA.

To be sure, American officials in Nicaragua were concerned. The new Ambassador, Mauricio Solaun, had only arrived in Managua in August, but by December he was already traveling to Washington to argue for more pressure on Somoza to open up the political system and allow a transition to another government. But Assistant Secretary Todman, engaged in a battle with the human rights bureau for control of the policy, opposed doing anything further to upset his preferred approach of quiet and constructive diplomacy in Latin America.[16] Warren Christopher and the advocates of a tougher policy against Somoza had turned their attention elsewhere. In any case, their prescriptions for Nicaragua did not go beyond the suspension of aid, and they had already accomplished that goal.

6

The Death of Chamorro

On January 10, 1978, Pedro Joaquín Chamorro was shot to death in his car. No one ever found out who ordered the assassination, but Chamorro's murder set off an explosion of protests against Somoza.[1] Thousands took part in the funeral procession, which quickly became an anti-Somoza rally and then a riot in the streets of Managua, where "some carried the black and red colors" of the Sandinista Front.[2]

Like the assassination of Benigno Aquino in the Philippines a few years later, the murder of Chamorro revolutionized Nicaragua. Chamorro's assassination at once deprived the opposition of its most important leader and gave it a *cause célèbre* around which to rally national support. The murder, whether Somoza's responsibility or not, stirred fear as well as indignation throughout Nicaragua's privileged class. Like Somoza's encroachment into the private economy after the 1972 earthquake, the murder of the dictator's leading opponent was a dramatic abrogation of the silent compact between the ruler and the upper classes. Now the fears and frustrations of the Nicaraguan aristocracy combined with the rise of a politically active business class and the new radicalism and violence of the Sandinistas to create a powerful force that threatened to shake the foundations of the Somoza dynasty. A priest presiding at the memorial service predicted that "those who murdered Dr. Chamorro to extinguish a light have, in fact, lighted a flame."[3]

43

Chamorro's killing ended all discussion of a dialogue between the opposition and Somoza; now no opposition leader dared call for less than the immediate resignation of the dictator. "Reform" was out of the question. Chamorro's successor as president of UDEL declared that "one cannot ask the Devil to reform Hell. . . . The people of Nicaragua have no alternative but to end the Somoza regime and install a just, republican regime."[4] The *Terceristas* declared that "the people have no other alternative but to fight without quarter to overthrow the tyranny." They renewed their call for a "great anti-Somoza popular front that will include all the nation's democratic forces so that the revolutionary violence of the masses headed by our political-military organization will give the final blow to the dictatorship and create a popular democratic government."[5]

For the time being, however, the Sandinistas had no bullets in their chambers and no new offensive to unleash on the regime. The moderate opposition politicians and businessmen thus took center stage and for a time became the "vanguard" of popular anger against Somoza. They sought a peaceful means of pressuring the dictator to resign, and they used the one weapon at their disposal: money. On January 23 Nicaragua's leading businessmen, organized by Alfonso Robelo and other entrepreneurs at the Nicaraguan Development Institute, began a nationwide general strike. "In an effort to avoid greater sorrow and anxiety among the Nicaraguan people," the private sector leaders declared on January 24, "we demand justice and state that through peaceful means we shall continue to struggle for the establishment of an order that will guarantee freedom and respect for the citizens' rights."[6]

In the first few days the strike brought much of Nicaragua to a halt and galvanized the political opposition. Factions of the Conservative Party and other, smaller opposition parties joined with UDEL in support of the strike. The new coalition appeared to comprise "the whole civic society plus the church," one opposition leader recalls.[7] Not in many years, if ever, had such broad and spontaneous opposition arisen to challenge the Somoza regime.

Even as the disparate factions joined together in support of the strike, however, differences over goals and means—how peaceful the confrontation, how sweeping the change, and how "constitutional" the succession—led to disagreement and acrimony. The political breadth of the opposition gave it power in confronting the regime, but it also made agreement on these important issues difficult.

Leaders of UDEL were more radical in their demands for Somoza's immediate resignation, whether or not it could be achieved within the existing constitution. The business leaders who had formed the "National Strike Committee," on the other hand, were more cautious in urging Somoza to "give serious consideration to the constitutional means which could lead the country to permanent peace based on justice, freedom and democracy."[8] Some opposition leaders, especially from the Socialist and Communist parties and their affiliated labor unions, spoke of the need for a radical transformation of society. Some of the younger businessmen spoke out for a more equitable distribution of wealth.

Many of Somoza's opponents, however, were more conservative in their goals. They sought to preserve the existing political and economic system of Nicaragua, which had brought a measure of prosperity to the country. They believed Somoza had become the gravest threat to that system but only because they feared that the longer Somoza remained in power, the more radical and revolutionary his likely successors would be. A peaceful and constitutional change was essential to forestall anarchy, violence, and the rise of the Sandinistas. Riding reported at the end of January that "more and more opponents of the Somozas" were "recognizing [the Sandinista Front] as the vanguard of the present struggle," but this was *Tercerista* propaganda.[9] The great majority of opposition leaders were opposed to the Sandinistas, most feared them, and some even preferred to live with Somoza rather than to live through a Sandinista-led revolution in Nicaragua.[10]

This fear of anarchy and violent revolution was a serious weakness for the unarmed opposition in its competition with both Somoza and the Sandinistas, neither of whom had such fears. Somoza believed the Sandinista threat was an important asset. He expected the United States to back him against an armed, communist revolutionary movement. He liked to rebuke the businessmen and aristocrats, warning that "it was my government which gave my little capitalist colleagues the social tranquility to build their fortunes."[11] The Sandinistas, of course, counted on violence and anarchy as the key to victory, and the *Terceristas*, or "Insurrectionaries," were the most devoted to violent actions. Constitutional reform was the last thing the Sandinistas wanted.

On February 3 the general strike began to falter. The private sector was losing about $2 million a day, and the larger businesses gradually began to reopen. By February 5, the day of the municipal elections called by Somoza, the strike was virtually over. Business leaders declared they would continue to fight for freedom and justice in Nicaragua and called the strike "a temporary renewable struggle," but they went back to business.[12] The strike leaders put the best face on the situation, boasting that "never before have workers, businessmen and politicians been so united against the regime," but the failure of the strike after less than two weeks showed the limits of civic protest against Somoza.[13]

The Sandinistas reveled in the failure of the strike, which they had denounced as a "bourgeois maneuver." But they were still far too weak to take advantage of the situation. They vowed that "the FSLN's rifles of justice will continue to support the people," and they threatened to take harsh measures against those businessmen who had "play[ed] the game of the dictatorship by reopening their businesses or factories."[14] In February, however, they managed only a few small attacks on National Guard posts, and were easily repulsed by the army. The unarmed opposition's loss was not yet the Sandinistas' gain.

The real beneficiary of the strike's failure was Somoza, who by the end of February seemed back in control. The opposition leaders had hoped for dramatic defections from the government or the National Guard, but none occurred. Somoza instead went on the attack, belittling the strike leaders and playing on the growing antagonisms between the labor unions and the businessmen; he mocked the "capitalists' strike," the "strike of the millionaires."[15]

On February 5 the municipal elections went ahead as planned. A majority of Nicaraguans stayed away from the polls, the opposition decried the vote as illegitimate, and Somoza's Liberal Party won by a landslide— more than a ten-to-one margin. Somoza proclaimed that the opposition had no support among the people. From this position of strength, Somoza resumed efforts to appease Washington and demonstrate his own popularity among the Nicaraguan "masses." He renewed his call for a dialogue, introduced legal reforms to grant official status to a greater number of opposition parties, and promised to pass legislation that would favor the workers—a one-month's pay bonus at the end of the year and an expansion of the social security program. Somoza dismissed all talk of his resignation. "This has been a definite countdown," he announced publicly, "to see if the Somozas are in or out. Well, in my view, the answer is that we're very much in."[16]

With the failure of their strike, Nicaraguan opposition leaders turned for help to the United States and the Carter administration. Throughout the strike opposition politicians and businessmen had met frequently with officials at the American embassy and believed that Ambassador Solaun sympathized with their struggle. William Baez Sacasa spoke for many when he said, "People realize that the Carter administration is different. With Nixon in the White House and a pro-Somoza ambassador here, this strike simply would not have taken place. No one was prepared to take on both the Somozas and the United States. . . . Happily, the United States is no longer identified with the Somozas."[17] Even the strike had been designed more to spur the United States to action than to force Somoza to capitulate.[18]

Others shared these expectations of American intervention. Venezuela's President Carlos Andrés Pérez had been a close friend of Pedro Joaquín Chamorro and an ardent critic of Somoza. After Chamorro's murder, Pérez began publicly denouncing the Somoza regime, almost to the point of breaking relations and calling for Somoza's overthrow. On January 31, 1978, he sent President Carter a letter seeking joint efforts against the Nicaraguan government.[19] At the end of the strike, Venezuela sought President Carter's support for an investigation by the OAS (Organization of American States) of human rights violations by the Somoza regime, and Pérez raised the matter of Nicaragua again when President Carter traveled to Caracas in the spring of 1978.

The Cuban government also fully expected the United States to remove Somoza from power and replace him with an acceptable moderate government in order to forestall a revolutionary victory. According to one Cuban commentator, the United States had pinned its hopes on Chamorro and after his murder had lost the "main card" in its "pseudodemocratic maneuvers."[20] Another speculated that, nevertheless, the United States realized that "its protégé of so many years has entered a crisis and cannot survive much longer."[21]

Somoza himself shared these fears. He believed Ambassador Solaun and the Carter administration aimed to overthrow him, and at times the American ambassador gave him reason to be concerned. After the February elections, Somoza later recalled, Ambassador Solaun told him there were countries who wanted to see him overthrown. When Somoza asked what it would take to "get them off my back," the ambassador suggested he might "shorten" his term of office. Somoza asked, "Are you trying to say I should resign?" According to Somoza, Solaun said "yes." Somoza recalls,

> My ire was rather obvious at that point and I decided it was time for frankness. I looked at him squarely in the eye and said: "Mr. Ambassador, whose brainchild is that? Your government's? Because I want to know officially!"

[Solaun] denied that such was the official position of the United States and remarked that it was just a personal thought of his. Based upon the previous conversations which my friends had with the Ambassador, I was sure he was lying to me.[22]

Ambassador Solaun had not lied to Somoza, however. His suggestion that Somoza consider early retirement was entirely his own and not a reflection of attitudes in Washington. On the contrary, the Carter administration acted in the first months of 1978 as though it were unmoved by the violence and popular uprising against Somoza and unwilling to consider a more energetic American role in shaping political developments in Nicaragua.

Days after the end of the businessmen's strike, the Carter administration released its international human rights surveys for 1978. The report on Nicaragua exposed a large gap between American and Nicaraguan perceptions of the nature of the problem. It praised Somoza for lifting the state of siege in September 1977 and for his "elimination" of press censorship. Since these actions, politics in Nicaragua had been "characterized by vehement and lively press and public debate, attacks on National Guard installations, and steps toward a 'national dialogue' between the government and opposition groups."[23] Although the Somoza government remained "an authoritarian political regime," the State Department's report noted that "stability has been maintained, the economy has expanded, the legally recognized opposition Conservative Party has been allowed to contest elections and participate in governmental bodies, and other non-violent opposition groups have been allowed to function." The report made no mention of the broad, moderate opposition that had arisen in 1977 and been further inflamed by the murder of Chamorro. Indeed, the report barely mentioned Chamorro's assassination, the event that had catapulted the moderate opposition into open confrontation with Somoza. The State Department's account merely noted that "planning for the [national] dialogue" had been "interrupted by the assassination of opposition leader Pedro Joaquín Chamorro in early January 1978."

The human rights report reflected the State Department's considered judgment as well as its preferred policy.[24] Assistant Secretary Todman and his aides were pursuing a policy that could be called "constructive engagement" with the Somoza government. At a February 16 congressional hearing Todman's deputy, Sally Shelton, testified that "although problems remain, it is our opinion that marked progress [on human rights in Nicaragua] has been manifested since early 1977." "By all appropriate means," Shelton stated, "we will continue to impress on the Government of Nicaragua our concern regarding human rights violations and the effect such violations have on the totality of our relations, not just our bilateral assistance programs." State Department officials even expressed a measure of understanding for some of Somoza's harsher actions, noting that the Nicaraguan government had "a duty to protect the population from terrorism and acts of violence."[25] Todman envisioned a process of gradual reform in Nicaragua, leading to free elections in 1980 and a change of government. He told members of Congress that Somoza's conciliatory statements—his promise to step down as president in 1981, his offer to enact political reforms, and his renewed call for dialogue—were all signs "that we may be on the road back." Todman hoped that once Nicaragua's opposition leaders saw that Somoza had taken these actions, there might be a "return to faith in the word of the person [Somoza], which is obviously fundamental to any settlement."[26]

Further outbreaks of violence in Nicaragua did not shake the Carter administration from this course. At the end of February riots broke out spontaneously in Monimbó, a neighborhood of Masaya, where the large Indian population rose up in protest against poverty and government repression. The National Guard suppressed the uprising violently, firing machine guns at the crowd from armored cars and helicopters. As many as 100 were killed in the massacre, which was intended to discourage any further acts of rebellion. The Monimbó uprising, although neither led nor planned by the Sandinistas, became part of the lore of the Sandinista revolution, a symbol of the hatred the "common people" of Nicaragua had developed for Somoza.

The Guard's brutality outraged all Nicaraguans and increased the sense of crisis in Nicaragua. The Carter administration, however, responded in measured tones. Official spokesmen called for an end to *all* violence in Nicaragua and did not single out the Guard's actions for special condemnation. One American official testified at a congressional hearing that the National Guard had "acted with considerable constraint during the disorders."[27] On March 9, Terence Todman expressed hope that "the violence will stop and that there will be a peaceful solution to help Nicaragua toward its democratic development."[28]

The Carter administration, in other words, had gone as far as it intended to go. Pushed by Congressman Koch to show consistency in its human rights policy, the administration had cut off aid to the Somoza regime. At the beginning of 1978 Warren Christopher and the human rights bureau maintained the suspension of all aid and proposed, rather oddly, only an allocation of $150,000 for training the National Guard. Beyond this act of dissociation from the Somoza regime, however, the Carter administration had no further plans.

7

The Carter Doctrine

President Jimmy Carter was at heart an anti-interventionist, especially in Latin America where, in Carter's eyes, the many U.S. invasions and occupations over the past century were a stain on the nation's character. Carter's non-interventionism was also an outgrowth of the Vietnam War. In one of his earliest speeches on foreign policy, as a candidate for the Democratic nomination in May 1975, Carter had argued that "Our over-involvement in the internal affairs of Southeast Asian countries" required a "reassessment by the American people of our basic foreign policies." The lesson of Vietnam was that the United States should never again "become militarily involved in the internal affairs of another nation unless there is a direct and obvious threat to the security of the United States or its people." Even with the best of intentions, Carter believed, intervention was a serious mistake. He argued that "we cannot impose democracy on another country by force," and he expressed hope "that our days of unilateral intervention such as occurred in Vietnam, Cambodia, and the Dominican Republic are over."[1] Carter's opposition to intervention applied not only to armed invasions but to covert activities by the CIA, as well. Another main issue of the 1976 campaign had been Chile and the CIA's role in toppling the government of Salvador Allende. Candidate Carter had insisted that "We must not use the CIA or other covert means to effect violent change in any government or government policy."[2]

As events in Nicaragua were already demonstrating, however, the Carter administration's human rights policies were themselves a potent form of intervention. With a few words and a suspension of loans, the United States had helped alter the political balance in Nicaragua in potentially revolutionary ways. Carter officials showed some understanding of this point. At the beginning of 1978 they described the administration's policy as an attempt "to detach itself from a regime that has long enjoyed Washington support without provoking a blowup in Nicaragua that could impair stability throughout Central America."[3] The act of American dissociation from the Somoza regime, however, was not passive or neutral, nor could it be the last chapter in the story. It was only a first step toward some new configuration of power in Nicaragua, and the United States could not help but play a crucial role in determining what that new configuration would be.

The Carter administration had reasons other than non-interventionist principles to refrain from deeper involvement in Nicaragua. In February and March Congressman Charles Wilson renewed his attack on the administration for continuing to deny aid to the Somoza regime. Wilson ominously predicted that "Nicaragua will be in great focus in the Congress this year. I expect many confrontations."[4] He complained that the continued suspension of aid to Nicaragua was extremely unfair: "The current mayor of New York [Koch] chose Nicaragua for his demonstration of human rights effectiveness";[5] Nicaragua had been made a "test case" by the "Christopher committee" and "the Human Rights Bureau in the State Department";[6] and now the Carter administration had gone even further in denying aid to Nicaragua than Koch had originally demanded. Wilson insisted that the administration immediately release the two development loans approved by Congress for Nicaragua.[7]

Congressman Wilson accompanied his demands with some explicit threats. "I am a supporter of the Panama Canal Treaty," he warned, "but I do insist on consistency in our human rights policy. . . . If we are going to treat Nicaragua as the State Department wants to treat it, then I am going to insist on similar treatment for a neighboring country that has a much worse human rights record."[8] Wilson soon opened public hearings on human rights in Panama. He also threatened to block the entire foreign aid bill if the Carter administration did not release the two loans for Nicaragua.

The Carter administration did not want to provoke Wilson further, and in May Warren Christopher's committee approved the two loans. In announcing the decision, the Carter administration reiterated its policy of "strict non-intervention in the internal political affairs of Nicaragua and our continuing desire for a steady non-violent transition to genuine democratic rule."[9]

The Carter administration's apparent reversal shook the Nicaraguan political system once more. The approval of the loans angered Nicaraguan opposition leaders. Somoza declared victory and thumbed his nose at his dismayed opponents. Even before the loans had been approved, he had warned them to forget about turning the United States against him. "There are people who had hoped that with President Carter's arrival in office the U.S. Government was going to come here to overthrow the Nicaraguan Liberal government. . . . [T]hey now realize that things are not that way, that the United States cannot intervene in the domestic affairs of another country and that we are a responsible government."[10]

Moderate opponents of Somoza in Nicaragua were discouraged by American policy, but they continued to try to rally domestic and international support against Somoza. In the summer of 1978 the "Broad Opposition Front," known by its Spanish acronym FAO (*Frente Amplio Opositor*), was born. The FAO consisted of 15 opposition organizations. These included the MDN (Nicaraguan Democratic Movement) led by Alfonso Robelo and other young businessmen; UDEL led by Rafael Córdova Rivas; three factions of the splintered Conservative Party; and the Group of Twelve, represented by Sergio Ramírez, who was known to speak also for the *Terceristas*. Other opposition parties joined, including the Social Christians, Social Democrats, and the Liberal Independent Party, an anti-Somoza group formed in the 1940s. The Nicaraguan Communist Party, and the Nicaraguan Socialist Party were also represented, along with several business organizations and two trade unions, one Marxist and one non-Marxist.

The FAO represented almost every political strand in Nicaraguan society, but its strength was also a weakness. For such a broad alliance of disparate forces, unity of action and purpose was elusive. Opposition leaders jostled one another for political prominence, as if the competition to succeed Somoza had already begun. Ambassador Solaun reportedly complained that the Nicaraguan opposition was "hysterical, conceited and full of complexes."[11]

Efforts at unity were hampered even more by the growing radicalism of some important opposition leaders and by the presence within the opposition front of the *Tercerista* spokesman, Sergio Ramírez. The radicalization of the FAO was the *Terceristas*' main goal. And in the effort to capture the opposition front and drive it toward acceptance of violent solutions, Alfonso Robelo soon became their most important ally. The more conservative opposition leaders like Xavier Zavala and Adolfo Calero watched in dismay as Robelo moved ever closer to Ramírez and the *Tercerista* position.

Robelo, who at heart was no radical, probably hoped to exploit the Sandinistas to achieve power for himself and his moderate colleagues— just as the Sandinistas hoped to exploit him. According to one Sandinista official responsible for forging ties with the moderates, "Robelo and the other businessmen thought they would outmaneuver the Sandinistas because they were smarter. But, in fact, [the moderates] did not have the cohesiveness of the FSLN."[12] As Robelo increasingly hewed to the radical line of his new Sandinista allies, as he began publicly to support a "final massive offensive by the guerrillas," the more conservative opposition leaders saw the FAO slipping out of their grasp.[13]

As the opposition to Somoza grew more radical, the Carter administration continued to take no sides in Nicaragua. From the early spring to the late summer of 1978 the State Department was without an Assistant Secretary for Latin American, Terence Todman having resigned in frustration over his constant battles with the human rights bureau. President Carter's only noteworthy action in the summer of 1978 was to send a personal letter to Somoza praising him for the progress he had made in improving the human rights situation in Nicaragua and urging him to continue to keep his promises. When the letter became public in early August it caused an uproar both in Nicaragua and in the United States. State Department officials let it be known that they had opposed sending the letter but had been overruled by Zbigniew Brzezinski at the National Security Council. Actually, the letter was President Carter's own idea, part of his new effort to show that the human rights policy included constructive praise as well as criticism.[14] Carter was especially pleased that Somoza had agreed to allow political opponents, like the Group of Twelve, to return from exile and that he had invited the Inter-American Human Rights Commission to investigate allegations of human rights abuse in Nicaragua.

Somoza was delighted: "The letter from President Carter came at a time when I needed encouragement, and particularly from the United States." He thrust it in the face of Venezuelan President Pérez as proof that "at least some of the things I was doing in Nicaragua were pleasing to President Carter." Pérez said he didn't "care what Carter says. Our position is firm and you have to go."[15] But Somoza, with Carter's letter in his pocket, boasted confidently to reporters: "I don't think the United States would have the nerve to ask me to resign. No, I don't think so."[16]

8

"Viva el Frente Sandinista"

A t the beginning of August 1978, the *Washington Post* criticized the
Carter administration's policy toward Nicaragua in a remarkably pre-
scient editorial:

> American policy toward that small and dependent country has come to be
> taken as symbolic of whether the administration is "serious" about human
> rights.
>
> But what the United States is really dealing with, or so we increasingly
> suspect, is a revolution. It is comforting to think that the aging dictator So-
> moza will somehow fade away and be replaced in the scheduled 1981 elec-
> tions by moderate democrats friendly to the United States. Such is the po-
> larization and violence now building, however, that President Somoza may
> be forced out in an explosion well before 1981 and replaced not by centrist
> democrats but by elements politically and ideologically beholden to the
> guerrillas of the Sandinista National Liberation Front. A "second Cuba" in
> Central America? It is not out of the question.
>
> [President Carter] would do better to figure that the imminence of a
> major upheaval requires an urgent diplomatic initiative, one meant to bring
> representative popular government to Nicaragua before that possibility is
> preempted by escalating violence.[1]

On August 22 two dozen Sandinista commandos led by Edén Pastora of the *Tercerista* faction attacked and seized control of Nicaragua's National Palace, where the Congress was in full session. For two days the commandos held the entire Nicaraguan legislature hostage while Pastora negotiated terms with Somoza. Somoza, fearing great loss of life and the murder of several of his relatives, finally gave in to Pastora's demands. He promised the Sandinistas money, allowed the publication and radio broadcast of a long Sandinista communiqué in his own media, and released Tomás Borge and other Sandinista prisoners from jail. Somoza guaranteed Pastora, his fighters, and the released prisoners safe conduct out of the country. While most went quietly to Cuba, others took well-publicized refuge in Panama and Venezuela to demonstrate that the Sandinistas had the support of Latin leaders other than Fidel Castro. After his stunning success, Pastora declared from Panama that the Somoza regime would now certainly fall. "What I cannot tell you is whether that will happen tomorrow or next year. But he will fall. . . . This will hasten the process."[2]

The raid on the National Palace shook the Somoza regime. His capitulation to Sandinista demands made him appear impotent, both to the outside world and to his fellow Nicaraguans. His weak response angered some senior officers in the National Guard and led to rumblings about a coup. Even before the raid, a plot against Somoza had been brewing among some colonels who feared that their commander was leading the country to disaster. In one blow the Sandinistas shattered the image of invincibility that Somoza had carefully built up since the beginning of the year.

The *Terceristas'* bold and spectacular stroke was part of their strategy to spark a general insurrection through violent attacks on the government in full view of the urban population. The results must have exceeded their expectations. Crowds lined the streets to cheer for "Commander Zero," Pastora's *nom de guerre*, as he and the released prisoners were driven to the airport. For the first time, the Sandinistas had a hero for the people to admire and follow. The triumphant arrival of Sandinista fighters and released prisoners in Panama was front-page news in the United States and throughout the world. The image fit the stereotype of dashing Latin guerrillas, enthusiastically supported by the Nicaraguan people and Latin American presidents, fighting a cruel but powerful dictator. Pastora was a swashbuckling David outwitting and outdaring an inept Goliath. The Sandinistas rose to international prominence as never before in their history.

The sensation of the palace raid easily eclipsed the more ordinary efforts of the opposition that had coalesced in the Broad Opposition Front. The opposition called for a second nationwide strike, which it claimed would last until Somoza resigned. Riding reported that the leaders of the strike considered it a "last opportunity for a relatively nonviolent and nonextremist solution to the country's year-old political crisis."[3] The shutdown got off to a slow start, however, and the world paid little attention.

Moderates in the opposition were especially alarmed by the Sandinista communiqué read over radio and television and reprinted in *La Prensa* in the days after Pastora's attack on the palace. The communiqué, entitled "The Maneuvers of the New Somocismo," signed by Humberto and Daniel Ortega, assailed broad sectors of the moderate and conservative opposition as allies of "*Somocismo*" and called on the Nicaraguan people to "unmask and crush" them. The *Terceristas* attacked Archbishop Obando's peace proposals, denounced the "financial bourgeoisie" for plotting with Somoza, and accused the "industrial bourgeoisie, the business people, the small and medium bourgeoisie, the factory workers, the farm workers," in other words, most of the FAO, of being opportunistic latecomers to the anti-Somoza struggle. The *Terceristas* proclaimed that their revolution would be waged only for the workers and peasants, "those who have supported the entire weight of economic exploitation and political-military repression of the Somoza tyranny." Any alliance with the bourgeoisie was a temporary and distasteful necessity. The *Terceristas* made clear that they opposed the peaceful resignation of Somoza.[4]

The *Terceristas'* August communiqué was a tactical error, an outburst of honest triumphalism after the smashing military victory. Allies of Somoza believed the communiqué had done the government a favor by clearly delineating the *Terceristas'* differences "with the Church, capital, and the medium and small bourgeoisie." They urged the opposition to unite with the government and "defend themselves against the intent of the Sandinista front, whose objective is to eliminate the present Nicaraguan system of pro-Western democracy."[5] President Somoza seized on the occasion to chastise the foreign press, and particularly Riding, for its previous characterizations of the Sandinistas. It was now "evident that the orientation which Mr. Alan Riding wanted to ascribe to the Sandinista front, that is that they accepted any ideology and were trying to recruit democratic supporters to strengthen their movement, has been discredited. . . . [T]hey have totally disavowed Alan Riding as their spokesman."[6]

The communiqué and the palace raid gave energy to conservative groups that had fretfully but silently watched the leftward slide of the opposition front. One business group openly denounced the communiqué's appeal to "violence and destruction" and called on Nicaraguans who were "neither with Somoza nor with the Sandinistas [to] form a large civil force and . . . support the political parties who seek constitutional change." Business leaders called for the overthrow of Somoza, but "without participation of the Sandinists." They wanted a new government that was "neither Somozist nor Sandinist."[7] In September 1978, ten months before the Sandinista revolution triumphed, signs of the "counterrevolution" had begun to appear.

The *Terceristas* in their overzealousness had sparked this backlash from the more conservative groups, but they moved swiftly to hold onto their more important ally in the opposition. They invited Alfonso Robelo to serve in the new government junta they intended to form after Somoza fell.[8] With Robelo officially on their side, the *Terceristas* effectively captured the leadership of the FAO. On September 15 the FAO elected to a three-man Political Committee Robelo, Rafael Córdova Rivas and Sergio Ramírez. A week later the *Terceristas* publicly named the same three men to lead a revolutionary "provisional government" after Somoza's fall.

The *Terceristas* were also saved from their error by Somoza, who in the days after the palace raid began arresting leaders of the opposition, including such well-known moderates as Adolfo Calero. Somoza also arrested 85 members of the National Guard for plotting against him. So long as the only alternative to him was violent revolution, Somoza believed he stood a better chance of gaining the support of most Nicaraguans and of the United States. After the palace raid, Somoza's message was "*après moi le déluge*": "To resign would be to open this country to chaos and anarchy. . . . [The guerrillas] will not stop [their] campaign of terror if I step down. They have pledged to continue the bloodletting until they establish in this country a Marxist state or die trying."[9]

In the first days of September the most intense violence in years broke out across the country. The rioting erupted spontaneously, and the Sandinistas were initially caught off guard without the strength to mount an offensive. At the end of August fighting broke out in Matagalpa between the National Guard and the young boys in the poor barrios, spurred to violence by the heroic feats of Pastora. The bloody street battles lasted several days and spread to four other cities. Most of the Sandinista leaders were either out of the country or hiding in the safety of the hills outside Managua and had to scramble to make the uprising their own. As Humberto Ortega later recalled, "The people were the ones in the vanguard of that struggle. There was no alternative but to put ourselves at the head of that upsurge and try to obtain the most positive outcome. . . . It was the first national uprising led by the FSLN but that was chiefly due to pressure by the masses."[10] On September 9, the *Terceristas* announced the start of a "final offensive" against the Somoza regime and launched simultaneous attacks on police stations and National Guard posts in Managua, León, Estelí, Masaya, and Chinandega. The attacks were weak and unsustainable, however, and within days the small *Tercerista* forces had to withdraw to avoid being wiped out by the Guard. The local youths kept up the fighting after they left and suffered high losses.

The fighting in the streets was nevertheless a great political victory for the Sandinistas. The youths told journalists that they were "fighting for the '*Frente*' here." And the street battles radicalized the general population. As one Nicaraguan demonstrator explained, "Nobody here says '*Viva* the Broad Front' or '*Viva* the Conservative Party.' What we say is '*Viva el Frente Sandinista.*'" Peasants interviewed around Matagalpa said the Sandinistas alone had won victories against the government.[11]

The September uprising did Somoza inestimable damage at home and abroad. After his weak response to the palace raid, Somoza unleashed the full fury of the National Guard against the barrios. Under the command of Somoza's son, elite troops of the National Guard used tanks and trucks to shell and overrun the poorly armed youths in the streets. The small Nicaragua Air Force bombed and strafed barricaded blocks in Matagalpa, killing civilians and damaging homes in poor neighborhoods. As the Guard retook control of the five embattled cities, troops executed young men they found in the streets, firing submachine guns at point-blank range. "For the National Guard," one American journalist reported, "which ostensibly believes it is saving the country from an imminent guerrilla-led communist threat, every Nicaraguan youth has become a potential terrorist, and every closed door a potential hideout."[12] The dead youths became martyrs of the Sandinista revolution. The Guard's brutal behavior won the Sandinistas hundreds if not thousands of new, young recruits, spoiling for revenge.

International attention was riveted on the carnage. The National Guard's furious assault was the most visible act of bloodletting in recent Nicaraguan history. A sensational front-page headline in the *Washington Post* read: "He Was Crying, 'Don't Kill Me, Don't Kill Me!'"[13] Venezuela's President Pérez called on the Organization of American States to intervene in Nicaragua to "seek a process of democratization . . . and avert further bloodshed." He declared "No one has the right, no matter how powerful he is or how many weapons he has, to sacrifice the life of his nation. . . . [This is] a situation that should awaken the conscience of America."[14] Within a month after the uprising, Pérez and the Panamanian President, General Omar Torrijos, began shipping weapons to the Sandinistas in Costa Rica, with the assistance of Costa Rica's President Rodrigo Carazo. In the fall of 1978 the political struggle in Nicaragua had become an international affair.

———

The Sandinistas' palace raid and the ensuing bloody confrontation between the Nicaraguan government and the urban youths startled the Carter administration into a hurried reassessment of its policy. Despite its declared intention to stay aloof from what it had called a purely Nicaraguan problem, the Carter administration was soon drawn into the more traditional American role as arbiter of a brewing Central American crisis. Horror at the bloodshed was one motive; fear of a Sandinista revolutionary victory was another. After the Sandinistas' "final offensive" in early September, Carter officials said they had gained "a greater appreciation" of the guerrillas' strength. The Sandinistas were a more serious contender for power than they had thought.[15]

The new Assistant Secretary of State for Latin American Affairs, Viron Vaky, came to Washington from his post as ambassador to Venezuela. There he had watched events unfold in Nicaragua along with President Pérez and had come to similar conclusions. Somoza could not last, Vaky believed, and the only serious question was whether he would be replaced by pro-American moderates or pro-Cuban revolutionaries. Vaky believed the United States had to step in and ensure the victory of the moderates through a peaceful transfer of power.

In meetings with other senior officials at the end of August, Vaky argued that the administration had only three options: "to disassociate, to stay neutral and let nature take its course," as the administration had been doing so far; "to support Somoza . . . to shore him up"; or "to try to promote some constructive alternative to . . . a continuation of the Somoza regime." Vaky argued vigorously for the third course. The Carter administration's "neutral," "hands off" policy in recent months had allowed the moderate, "responsible" opposition "to get chewed up." Somoza's actions were "destroying this opposition and making [Somoza's] depiction of the situation [as a choice between him and the communists] a self-fulfill-ing prophecy." The moderate opposition leaders feared opening a dia-logue with Somoza because they expected it to be futile and dangerous. As a result, "a rather classical case of polarization [was] beginning to set in." Vaky believed the United States had to move into the breach, to act as an "outside catalyst," a "marriage counselor" to forge "an agreed upon solution to the end of the dynasty," one that would offer "some moderate third choice between these two poles that are emerging." Vaky believed, further, that only the United States, "given its weight down there and its acceptability on all sides," could play this role.[16]

Vaky considered it essential that the Carter administration move quickly and resolutely, before the embattled moderate opposition forces disintegrated. At a meeting on August 29, Vaky sought agreement within the administration on a plan to force Somoza to resign. American officials would explicitly tell Somoza that the time had come for him to leave of-fice, for the good of his country. Officials in Managua would begin talks with the National Guard and the ruling Liberal Nationalist Party to un-dermine him, spreading word that the general had lost American support. Vaky expected that Somoza's allies would abandon the dictator to protect themselves and their institutions. If Somoza or his supporters resisted, the United States would use economic and trade sanctions or whatever might be necessary, short of assassination, to bring Somoza down.[17]

Vaky's plan, which entailed a dramatic about-face in the administra-tion's policy toward Nicaragua, met overwhelming opposition within the administration. No one disputed Vaky's analysis of the situation in Nica-ragua. But for a variety of reasons senior officials rejected Vaky's proposal for direct action by the United States, either as mediator or as arbiter in Nicaragua.

Anthony Lake, the State Department's Director of Policy Planning, and Robert Pastor, Zbigniew Brzezinski's assistant on the National Secu-rity Council staff, opposed Vaky on philosophical grounds. To abandon the policy of non-intervention required President Carter to undermine what was to be his own unique contribution to a new, more respectful American policy in Latin America. Pastor argued that "our current prob-lems in [Latin America] stemmed in part from the history of U.S. inter-ventionism, which, although almost always undertaken with good inten-tions, frequently had adverse effects on U.S. interests that outweighed any shorter-term benefits."[18] Lake, who had resigned from the Nixon ad-ministration over the bombing of Cambodia in 1970, recalled "the experience of the American-approved coups in Saigon in late 1963 and early 1964, which had ushered in a period of severe instability while convincing many Vietnamese (inaccurately) that the American embassy was calling all the shots in Vietnamese politics." The United States had been "blamed for the ensuing political chaos" and Vietnamese hostility to the American-backed government had proved "a fatal disability in a war for 'hearts and minds.'" Lake and Pastor believed the United States "should not assume the responsibility for removing" Somoza; they opposed "going to a chief of state to ask him to step down."[19]

Zbigniew Brzezinski had no particular objection to American intervention, but he doubted the wisdom of removing Somoza when guerrillas were waging a revolutionary struggle which he feared would lead to the establishment of a pro-Cuban, pro-Soviet communist government in Nicaragua. He publicly expressed hope that "any further changes in the nature of the Nicaraguan political system will not create a repetition of the Castro situation." He might favor Somoza's resignation, "but only . . . in a way that ensured the result was not a victory by the extreme left."[20] Brzezinski and Warren Christopher both feared that, even if successful, Vaky's plan would bring to power a moderate government too weak to hold off the Sandinistas. Christopher later complained that Vaky and his aides "wanted us to oust Somoza, but they never really showed us how, or what would follow." Brzezinski and Christopher had the Joint Chiefs of Staff on their side. The Chiefs' representative reduced the issue to a simple question: who was worse, Somoza or the Sandinistas?[21]

Over these discussions hung an unspoken but pervasive fear of the political repercussions of any action against Somoza. On September 22 more than 70 congressman, led by powerful Democrats Charles Wilson, Jack Murphy, and the House Majority Leader, James Wright, wrote Carter to demand that he "do your utmost to demonstrate the support of the United States Government for the Government of Nicaragua and President Anastasio Somoza, a long and consistent ally of the United States."[22] In the face of such pressures, Carter's top advisers were not about to recommend that the President force Somoza to resign. Among all the many difficult and politically risky policies Carter was pursuing around the world, Nicaragua was too small for such a high price.

If the option of forcing Somoza from power was unacceptable, however, so too was the option of supporting him. On the same day that Carter received the letter from Wilson, Murphy, and Wright, the Senate voted to cut off most of the remaining aid for Nicaragua.[23] Liberal Senator

Frank Church, chairman of the Foreign Relations Committee, declared that Somoza faced "a national mutiny in which almost every sector of the country has united against [him.] The question is not whether Somoza falls, but when."[24] Were President Carter to seek to shore up Somoza against the Sandinistas, he would face an outcry from liberal Democrats no less deafening than the conservatives' outcry if he acted to overthrow Somoza. Of the three options open to the administration, therefore, Carter officials found none acceptable.

Their frustrating and futile deliberations soon became well known in Washington, and in Managua. The *Washington Post* described the administration as "immobilized by its internal contradictions" and warned that Somoza, who could see this for himself, "quite possibly believes he can hang on."[25] But the Carter administration was desperate for a solution to the Nicaraguan crisis that required none but the most minimal American action.[26]

When Costa Rica's President Carazo proposed a mediation in Nicaragua by Central American governments, therefore, the Carter administration seized on the proposal. As Robert Pastor recalls, "the United States did not decide to mediate, but rather decided to support an initiative that had been proposed by Costa Rica." Vaky was skeptical that any mediation without the United States could succeed, but Christopher strongly favored the idea of a Central American mediation in which the United States played only a distant, supporting role.[27] On September 12, the State Department spokesman called on "all sides in Nicaragua to engage in discussions toward creating a national consensus for a peaceful, democratic solution," and he urged that all sides make "appropriate concessions and sacrifices" to avoid further bloodshed. The spokesman insisted that the statement was not meant as an American call for Somoza's resignation.[28] Anonymous Carter officials nevertheless told reporters that they hoped Somoza would resign voluntarily. That same day the administration dispatched an emissary, Ambassador William Jorden, on a tour of Latin American nations to build support for the Costa Rican-led mediation. Vaky hoped Jorden might also visit Somoza and make American views of his situation plain, but Christopher rejected the idea as entailing too direct an American role.[29]

President Carazo's mediation, however, collapsed before it began. Somoza had little difficulty persuading the other three Central American governments, all under some form of military rule, that the mediation was a bad idea. As for Costa Rica, Somoza on September 12 drew attention to the fact that the *Terceristas* had their base of operations there by sending the Nicaraguan air force on a raid across the border. Some Costa Rican students were injured in the attack. President Carazo professed that he could no longer be neutral in the mediation and called for an OAS investigation of the attack. President Pérez promptly dispatched planes from the Venezuelan air force to defend Costa Rica, and President Torrijos threatened to bomb Somoza's bunker in Managua. The Carter administration's hopes for a peaceful Latin American mediation in Nicaragua had in two weeks turned into fears of a regional war.[30]

President Pérez was furious at the Carter administration's inaction. A Sandinista victory, he told Jorden, would "open the door to Castro. . . . This will end in Cuban hands. The shame is this could be avoided, but the United States has not been decisive enough." Pérez declared he did not trust the United States anymore.[31] President Torrijos agreed: His idle threat to bomb Managua had been aimed at rousing the United States to action.

Despite the growing crisis, the Carter administration stepped forward with the utmost reluctance. On September 22 the President stated at a press conference that he was "trying through peaceful means to . . . put an end to the suffering. . . . We don't want to intervene in the affairs of a sovereign country. . . . [But] we are trying to work with our friends and well-meaning neighbors of Nicaragua to perhaps mediate the disputes . . . using . . . the OAS as a vehicle whenever possible." Brzezinski added that the administration's policy was neither a "hands-off policy" nor "engaging in interventionism." Some mediation was necessary to end a polarization in Nicaragua that could only lead to "extremism."[32] All Carter officials now agreed, however, that the mediation would have to be led by the United States, and on September 23 Jorden was dispatched to Nicaragua to gain Somoza's agreement.

Jorden's meeting with Somoza was predictably unpleasant. The Nicaraguan President knew that the real purpose of the pending mediation was to force his early resignation, and he regarded Jorden's offer of America's "friendly, good offices" cynically. The Carter administration, after all, had treated him "like an enemy" and was the "main party responsible" for all his problems; his opponents in Nicaragua had since 1977 believed that "with the attitude of the Carter Administration, they would have 'Carte Blanche' to do as they pleased."[33]

Jorden rather timidly told Somoza that "the possibility of your departure from office before 1981 is one of the possibilities that has to be considered," but he immediately added that whether, in fact, this was "necessary, or how it might be arranged, is quite a different matter. That's a matter for you and your people to decide." Jorden promised that the United States would not impose any solution, but only wanted to "make some suggestions and perhaps serve as a kind of bridge at the outset so that Nicaraguan elements can gradually pull together." Jorden's statements may have indicated to Somoza that, although the Carter administration wanted him to resign, it was not quite comfortable saying so, in public or in private.

To protect his political stocks in the United States, Somoza would not reject the mediation outright. He hoped that with the Carter administration's evident timidity, and the proven support of influential members of Congress, he could survive the mediation no matter what its hidden purpose. Somoza accepted, therefore, telling Jorden, "I want you to know that I am doing my utmost to accommodate the United States without losing my pants." Somoza also wasted no time in testing the Carter administration's resolve. He summarily rejected President Carter's first choice as American mediator, a demand to which Carter officials acquiesced, as Robert Pastor recalls, a little too quickly.[34]

With Somoza's formal agreement in hand, the Carter administration won adoption of an OAS resolution providing the "umbrella" for American mediation. The resolution approved on September 30 asked Nicaragua to agree "in principle, to accept the friendly cooperation and conciliatory efforts that several member states of the Organization may offer toward establishing the conditions necessary for a peaceful settlement . . . without prejudice to full observance of the principle of nonintervention." The OAS designated a three-member team comprised of the United States, Guatemala, and the Dominican Republic as the International Commission of Friendly Cooperation and Conciliation. At the beginning of October the American mediator, William Bowdler, a trained diplomat with long service at the State Department, traveled to Managua to begin the negotiations.

9

The Return of Stimson

Bowdler's instructions reflected the Carter administration's ambivalence as it entered the Nicaraguan fray. A half-century earlier, President Coolidge had instructed Henry Stimson simply to "clean up the mess." The Carter administration's directive in October 1978 was a bit more complicated. The instructions written by Vaky but rewritten by Christopher and Pastor directed Bowdler to "facilitate the achievement of a national consensus on Nicaragua's future political evolution."[1]

The desired solution was the resignation of Somoza and a transition to democratic elections, but precisely how Bowdler was to achieve this was left ambiguous. On the one hand, Bowdler was authorized to "persuade Somoza and his close relatives to step down in advance of 1981 and not run for office," if this was "necessary" to assure a peaceful and democratic solution. Bowdler was encouraged, however, "to the greatest extent possible," to "allow the solution to emerge from the play of the positions taken by the two sides." Bowdler was to try to "work out between the government and the opposition groups" the nature and the timing of the transition.[2] The Carter administration's instructions to Bowdler attempted to strike a compromise between Vaky's insistence that the United States directly pressure Somoza to resign and the preference of all other Carter officials that Somoza's resignation be obtained without direct American pressure and, as it were, voluntarily. In public statements, administration spokesmen insisted on the "neutrality" of the mediation and described the American role as providing "friendly assistance," as stipulated by the OAS resolution. Privately, American officials let it be known in Washington and Managua that they expected the result of the mediation to be Somoza's departure.

On one point Bowdler's instructions were not ambiguous. Whatever the outcome, Bowdler was to "seek to preserve the National Guard as an institution capable of maintaining law and order while insuring acceptable new leadership [i.e., not Somoza family members] and the establishment of discipline and restraint."[3]

Over the next three weeks Bowdler succeeded in pulling the FAO back from its more radical demands and closer to the positions long advocated by the more moderate members of the opposition. The exercise of American influence undid months of hard work by the Sandinistas. The proposal for transition to a new government presented by the FAO to Bowdler and the mediation team on October 25 was so moderate that Sergio Ramírez and the *Terceristas* had to resign from the coalition in angry denunciation. Vaky was glad to see the Sandinistas depart. "At the end of 1978," he later recalled, "the Sandinistas were not a force whose agreement you needed" to forge a peaceful and democratic settlement in Nicaragua. "When you had the businessmen, why go for these people?" Over the course of the mediation effort, Vaky and Bowdler had become convinced they could bring about a change of government in Nicaragua that could remove Somoza, exclude the radical revolutionaries, and keep the Guard intact.[4] Bowdler's efforts seemed about to accomplish that goal.

The Sandinistas agreed. Ramírez later recalled that during Bowdler's mediation the "State Department decided to bring down Somoza but conserve the fundamental structures of *Somocismo*, in alliance with some of the traditional forces that were at that moment in the 'civic' opposition." Ramírez believed that if the Carter administration had managed to remove Somoza, "it provided the opportunity—the last one for imperialism—to bring down Somoza and try to preserve *Somocismo*."[5] The fact that Alfonso Robelo remained with the FAO when the *Terceristas* broke away was perhaps the clearest sign that Bowdler's mediation was succeeding for the United States.

The main demand of the Nicaraguan opposition had not changed since the Chamorro assassination, however: Somoza had to resign from the presidency and from his role as supreme commander of the National

Guard; he and his family then had to leave Nicaragua. The FAO no longer insisted that he leave immediately, but it was understood that a "peaceful and democratic solution" required his departure, and the sooner the better.

Much to the displeasure of the Sandinistas, the opposition had accepted American dictation on the subject of the National Guard. The FAO's October 25 proposal gave the new junta responsibility for "professionally reorganizing" the Guard to make it the armed force of the whole republic, charged with guaranteeing the sovereignty, independence, and territorial integrity of the nation. "Reorganization" was a codeword for removing the most brutal and corrupt officers, and it would be carried out with the "advice" of a "technical council" made up of National Guard officers.[6]

Bowdler's labors had produced an opposition plan that required Somoza's resignation. Now the opposition leaders waited for the United States to fulfill its part of the bargain. But Somoza was not behaving like a man who intended to give up power. At a press conference on October 19, Somoza declared that he could not, even if he wanted to, "negotiate or compromise with the mandate that the people gave me in the 1974 elections when they elected me for this term." The opposition, he declared, did not "have the strength to make me resign. I would never allow that to happen, because it is my duty to defend the country's constitution. . . . I cannot be thrown out by mere words; it must be done through a vote." Asked what he would do if the United States tried to overthrow him, Somoza was defiant: "Well, let them come here and throw me out."[7]

Vaky believed Somoza needed a stern message from the United States, and he proposed that the Carter administration immediately impose an array of economic sanctions against Nicaragua to convince Somoza to accept the FAO's plan and resign. "Somoza knew we were divided," Vaky recalled, "and he believed President Carter was some kind of mystic who was out of touch with reality."[8] If the administration hesitated, Vaky feared, Somoza would interpret it as a sign of weakness. As Pastor wrote to Brzezinski, Vaky also worried "that unless we move now, there will be further polarization [in Nicaragua], and . . . the mediation effort may collapse."[9]

Pastor led the opposition to Vaky's plan for quick action against Somoza. In a memorandum to Brzezinski he argued that the timing was bad for an ultimatum to Somoza. "By far the most important" of Pastor's concerns was that the U.S. congressional elections were less than a week away, and there was "a strong conservative current . . . flowing through" the American electorate. If the Carter administration delivered an ultimatum before the elections, Somoza would "unquestionably convey our message to the right in the U.S., and we cannot exclude the possibility that the Nicaragua issue will be injected into the campaign in a way which will hurt the President." Carter could be "criticized for destabilizing Somoza . . . and for making it easier for the communists to come to power in Nicaragua."[10] Brzezinski followed Pastor's advice, and on October 31 he rejected Vaky's proposal for immediate sanctions.[11]

Carter officials instead compromised among themselves again. At the end of October the United States asked the International Monetary Fund to delay its decision on a $20 million loan for Nicaragua, and on November 1 the IMF announced a postponement of "two or three weeks," which in fact lasted until May. Somoza recalled in his memoirs that the IMF's decision was a "strong signal" from the United States with serious financial repercussions. "Our much-needed financing was dead."[12] Somoza was shaken by the decision, not only because of its immediate financial impact but as stark evidence of the extraordinary power of the United States to make matters impossible for a small country.

By itself, however, the IMF's decision was not enough to scare Somoza into capitulation. Somoza aimed to drag out the negotiations and test the Carter administration's resolve. Bowdler reported to Washington that Somoza appeared "committed to resisting outside pressure and hanging on to power at all costs." Bowdler shared Vaky's concern that delay would be dangerous for the moderates in the opposition front.[13] With the mediation faltering, Robelo was back to praising the Sandinistas.[14] One FAO leader told the *New York Times,* "We can't play along with Somoza's delaying tactics indefinitely if we are to retain any credibility among the people."[15] Another opposition leader laid the problem on the doorstep of the Americans: "The issue is whether the United States has enough power in the short term to force Somoza to resign. This is the only way that a bloodbath can be avoided."[16]

To shore up the moderate opposition Bowdler on November 7 went a bit beyond his instructions and presented Somoza with a thinly veiled ultimatum. The mediators asked Somoza, in writing, if he was "disposed to consider [his] constitutional separation from the presidency" before 1981. "[T]he departure of Your Excellency from the Presidency of the Republic," the mediators stated, "reflects a broad sentiment of the Nicaraguan people. . . . [T]he situation in Nicaragua is truly grave and alarming and

. . . a new bloodbath can only be avoided by conducting negotiations on a realistic basis."[17] This was the bluntest request yet from the United States government, and Vaky believed Somoza was shaken by its directness. With the IMF's recent announcement, Somoza later recalled, Bowdler's demand had "maneuvered the situation to the extent that I was almost in that proverbial corner."[18]

Most observers in Washington and Managua believed the Carter administration was on the verge of forcing Somoza from power. President Carter himself declared on November 9 that "we are negotiating actively now to reach an agreement in Nicaragua to control bloodshed, to minimize disputes, and to set up a government there that will have the full support of the Nicaraguan people."[19] The next day *La Prensa* reported in banner headlines: "Carter: I Support a New Government."[20] The *Washington Post* praised this apparent shift in the President's approach to Nicaragua. After coming to office "eager to put intervention, even of a political sort, behind and to let Latins sort out their own affairs," the Carter administration had "found it necessary to fudge its commitment to non-intervention in order to pursue its other political goals. . . . Under the guise of a 'mediation' mission . . . the United States is conducting in Nicaragua a bold and unprecedented political intervention pointed at securing President Anastasio Somoza's resignation."[21]

On November 11 Somoza, trying to keep the Carter administration at bay, publicly announced his counterproposal: He would hold a national plebiscite to measure the strength of the political parties arrayed against him. This "democratic" formula, he insisted, was only fair and ought to be embraced by the Carter administration. Vaky and Bowdler, however, thought it was a trap. Bowdler warned the State Department that Somoza's proposal had to "be assessed within the unique context of Nicaragua, a country which has had no formal political life or free competition among political forces for almost half a century."[22] More importantly, Bowdler saw Somoza's counterproposal as just "a stalling tactic"; Vaky believed Somoza was just "throwing sand in our faces."[23]

But Pastor and other Carter officials in Washington were reluctant to reject Somoza's proposal out of hand, since to do so meant committing the United States to Somoza's overthrow. As Lake recalls, "To be accused on Capitol Hill and before the American public of overthrowing an anti-Communist friend of America would be bad enough. . . . But to overthrow a government that was proclaiming its desire for elections would be still worse." Pastor proposed a modification of Somoza's plan: Instead of holding a plebiscite on the strength of the opposition parties, Somoza would have to allow a vote on his own continuation in power. Vaky and Bowdler objected again, but Brzezinski, Secretary of State Cyrus Vance, and Warren Christopher liked Pastor's plan. They instructed Bowdler to seek the FAO's support for a national plebiscite on Somoza's rule.[24]

Somoza and his opponents recognized immediately that the Carter administration had reached a moment of decision and had decided against forcing Somoza from power. The idea of a plebiscite on Somoza's rule was quickly dubbed the "Washington Plan" because no Nicaraguan opposition leader wanted to be associated with it. The FAO announced its intention to quit the mediation on November 21 if Somoza did not immediately agree to resign. Even the moderate Adolfo Calero publicly asked "How can a popular consultation be conceived in a country where the people are the victims of military repression, where there is martial law and a curfew has been imposed, where the citizens are persecuted, where many have sought refuge and gone into exile and where the people live in a state of terror? Who is going to guarantee free and democratic voting under these conditions with a government that has made a constant mockery of elections and disregards the aspirations of the Nicaraguan people?" Bowdler reported to Vaky that many in the opposition front had "lost faith in the mediation effort: [The] only alternative, they say, is war against Somoza and the National Guard."[25] Even Archbishop Obando y Bravo, usually a cheerleader for the mediating commission, expressed pessimism. "I note," he said "that the international mediators have not obtained what we wanted, although we must admit they have worked hard."[26]

On November 21 the FAO broke off negotiations as promised but left open the possibility of resuming the talks. Bowdler and the mediators formally presented the "Washington Plan" for a "popular consultation" on whether Somoza should stay in power or resign. If the vote favored Somoza, then the government would be restructured. If Somoza lost, a new Government of National Unity would be established according to the FAO's October 25 proposal. On November 24, both the FAO and Somoza formally rejected the "Washington Plan." Somoza's negotiators declared the plan unconstitutional because it called for Somoza to resign if he lost the plebiscite. The FAO dismissed the plan on the grounds that "the presence of Somoza and his family . . . makes a national democratic process impossible."[27]

On November 27, however, the international mediation commission resubmitted its plan to both sides, threatening to leave Nicaragua in 24 hours if it did not receive a favorable response. The mediators criticized both sides, declaring Somoza intransigent and accusing the FAO of demanding a U.S.-assisted coup d'état.[28] Bowdler hoped that both sides, seeking to avoid blame for the collapse of the talks, would find some way to agree to the plan. On November 29, after much urging by the mediators, the FAO did finally agree to the American plebiscite proposal, in principle. The next day, November 30, Somoza's negotiators also agreed, in principle.

Neither side was sincere, and both were only trying to appease Washington. Nevertheless, on December 2 Bowdler called on the two sides to begin direct negotiations on the terms of the plebiscite. Somoza eagerly agreed, and as a sign of good faith he lifted martial law, restored press freedoms, declared a general amnesty for all political prisoners, and allowed the return of all exiles, including "the members of the Sandinista National Liberation Front." Bowdler told Somoza that he hoped these actions would "lead to quick acceptance by the FAO of direct talks."[29] The FAO vacillated, however, fearing that negotiations with Somoza would unravel the opposition alliance. Bowdler became angry and impatient. In his meeting with the opposition front, "we listened to the now familiar cant over Somoza's untrustworthiness and the necessity for full compliance with the general amnesty before the FAO could sit down at the same table" with Somoza. "We were dumbfound[ed] by the short-sightedness and the pettiness of the argumentation. As a result all three of us spoke forcefully about the need for the FAO to seize this opportunity or lose this opportunity with unforeseen consequences."[30]

The FAO agreed to sit down with Somoza's Liberal Party negotiators on December 8, but the negotiations accomplished nothing. On December 16 Bowdler cabled to Vaky that "none of the parties . . . are enthusiastic about joining into these talks."[31] Indeed, only the United States was making any effort to keep the negotiations alive. Alfonso Robelo expressed concern that the FAO was "losing its prestige and credibility by yielding to too many American demands and concessions to Somoza."[32] Just entering direct talks with Somoza had cost the FAO the defection of several more opposition parties and the strengthening of the Sandinistas' hand.

On December 20 the mediators presented a modified "final" proposal to both sides. Bowdler agreed to allow Somoza to remain in Nicaragua during the plebiscite, but in order to give the opposition confidence in the vote, he proposed that the plebiscite be conducted under the "supervision and control" of an International Authority. Not only would foreign supervisors oversee the voting areas, but the International Authority would also establish new electoral districts, decide the number and location of voting places in each district, and collect votes from Nicaraguans abroad. If Somoza lost, he would have to leave the country for at least two years.

On December 21, the FAO accepted the mediators' "final" proposal, fully expecting that Somoza would not. Somoza was silent. With the "final" offer on the table, the Carter administration decided to give Somoza an unmistakable warning. When Bowdler next visited Somoza, he was accompanied by General Dennis McAuliffe, the commander of all U.S. forces in Latin America. The general sought to assure Somoza "that every member of the Joint Chiefs of Staff is concerned about the instability, the potential for violence which exists here in Nicaragua. It is of military significance that we maintain peace and stability in Central America." "Speaking very frankly," McAuliffe declared, "it is our view that peace will not come to Nicaragua until you have removed yourself from the presidency and the scene."[33]

Although shaken by the general's warning, Somoza still hoped to survive the Carter administration's pressures. He neither accepted nor rejected the mediators' "final" proposal but responded with another counterproposal. Arguing that an "International Authority" to supervise the plebiscite constituted an unacceptable intrusion into Nicaraguan sovereignty, Somoza proposed that a "National Authority" conduct the vote "under the supervision of the Organization of American States."

Senior Carter officials were not prepared to accept Somoza's new plan. On December 26, Secretary of State Vance called a meeting of top officials to decide how best to force Somoza to accept Bowdler's "final" proposal. According to Pastor, "the only debate was between those who wanted to apply the pressure in a phased approach . . . or all at once." Vaky argued for immediate sanctions, but was overruled again. President Carter, meanwhile, had read Somoza's counterproposal and, much to the surprise of his advisers, found many of its arguments persuasive. According to Pastor, Carter believed Somoza's objection to an "International Authority" was reasonable. Indeed, Carter thought the proposal his own advisers had devised and presented in Managua was "interventionistic" and "an excessive demand."[34] On January 5 President Carter approved a new proposal which accepted Somoza's demand that a "National Authority" conduct the plebiscite monitored by an "International Authority."

Bowdler was sent back to Managua to convince the FAO to accept the Carter administration's new version of its "final" proposal, modified to include Somoza's suggestions.

But Somoza himself demanded further changes to the modified plan. He opposed allowing the International Authority to arbitrate disputes. This time, Somoza's refusal to accept the final, "final" proposal brought an end to the mediation. Bowdler left Nicaragua, telling Somoza he would not return until Somoza agreed to the plan. On January 19, the FAO publicly denounced "the brutal intransigence of the dictator" and declared the mediation ended. Carter officials prepared to enact the first "phase" of sanctions.

President Carter came under immediate pressure from Congressmen Murphy and Wilson, however. Throughout the mediation these two congressmen had worked openly to thwart any attempt by the administration to undermine Somoza. On November 17 they had stood at Somoza's side at a press conference in Managua, urging the opposition to accept Somoza's original plebiscite proposal. In the first week of December, Wilson renewed his threat to "torpedo" legislation on the Panama Canal treaties if the administration did not disburse the $12 million in economic assistance loans, as he claimed he had been promised. He charged that the State Department was being run by a "bunch of adolescent anarchists" and was "encouraging communism in the Caribbean."[35] On January 19 Congressman Murphy met with President Carter to discuss the Panama Canal Treaty legislation, and he took the opportunity to raise the matter of Nicaragua. Carter told Murphy that Somoza "could not go on as he was," and he rejected any suggestion that the Nicaragua issue should be linked to the Canal legislation.[36] Murphy reported back to Somoza that he had made no progress with the President.

A week later, however, the administration did not respond so firmly when Congressman Wilson threatened to retaliate if economic aid to Somoza were cut further. Wilson called Vice President Mondale and another influential member of the administration, Henry Owen. Owen reported Wilson's threat, which he deemed genuine, to other senior officials: "He can single-handedly eliminate Latin America from the aid program this year." When senior Carter officials met on January 26 to discuss the imposition of sanctions against Somoza, Brzezinski decided that "cutting off all economic aid at this time was not necessary or appropriate; some room should be left for the next stage."[37] Brzezinski and other senior officials recommended that the United States take actions against Somoza that were "symbolic," such as termination of the $150,000 for military training for the National Guard. On January 31 President Carter approved the more limited, symbolic sanctions.

That still did not end the matter, however. Congressman Murphy, after his meeting with Carter, had sent a letter to the President in which he argued the case for each of Somoza's objections to the final plebiscite proposal. The letter was passed to the President on January 31, along with his advisers' recommendations on sanctions. Once again, the President expressed sympathy for Somoza's complaints. As Pastor recalls, "Carter read through Murphy's point-by-point rebuttal of the mediation team proposal and jotted in his neat script those points, for example, on prior registration of voters, that struck Carter as sensible. Indeed, on many of the differences, Carter's notes suggest he found the Somoza/Murphy position better than the mediators' proposal."[38] Carter's famous attention to such details led him, once again, to reopen matters his administration had already settled and to modify the proposal his envoy had already presented in Managua. When Pastor called to tell Vaky of the President's sympathetic response to Murphy's letter, he heard "silence and then a thud, the sound of a forehead hitting a desk." Pastor deftly solved the problem by ignoring the President's notes. He sent a memorandum to Carter informing him that the mediation had ended and the United States was going ahead with the limited sanctions he had approved. "If the President wanted to change course, he would stop us. As it turned out, it was the same day that the Ayatollah flew to Teheran on a chartered 747, signaling the collapse of the Administration's Iran policy. The memorandum was returned the next day without comments."[39]

More than six weeks after Bowdler had presented the Carter administration's first "final" proposal to Somoza, the United States imposed its first phase of sanctions against Somoza. On February 8 the State Department spokesman, Hodding Carter III, announced the withdrawal of 47 officials from the American embassy in Managua, including the four-man military assistance group and 21 Peace Corps volunteers. The administration formally ended the military assistance program that had been suspended the previous year and prohibited all new economic aid projects. Assistance programs already under way were to continue. The spokesman declared these gestures "an expression of hope that a settlement is still possible." When a journalist asked whether the Carter administration's actions did not "call into question" the legitimacy of the Somoza government, Hodding Carter responded, "I hope you read my statement very carefully before you run out of here and write a lead that in any way reflects what you just said." According to Anthony Lake, the State Department's spokesman had his "eye on his pro-Somoza audience in Congress and the criticism that would follow a headline saying the administration was calling for Somoza's resignation."[40] Conservative criticism was mild, however. Congressman Wilson kept up his threats to sabotage various bills, but mostly to prevent any further moves against Somoza. The Carter administration had no further actions in mind. After imposing the sanctions on February 8, the administration turned away from Nicaragua. As Pastor recalls, "With the passing of the atmosphere of crisis, and no new ideas or options, the Administration turned its attention to other areas that had been neglected."[41]

Somoza was unruffled by the administration's sanctions. More than three weeks earlier he had told reporters that "if they remove the military people and lower representation, materially I would not lose anything else but a few nice American gentlemen who are living in Nicaragua."[42] Although he accused President Carter, Secretary Vance, and the "liberal wing of the Democratic Party" of "finagling" to bring him down, Somoza said he would keep his "foot in the door" in Washington and continue "playing politics with Jimmy Carter." "If you analyze what is going on here," he told reporters at the end of February, "you'd have to say I'm pretty patient . . . [I'm] angry, but I keep my cool."[43]

———

The moderate opposition in Nicaragua was devastated and embittered by the failure of the mediation. So was Viron Vaky. Several months later Vaky described in a letter to Congress what he believed had been the opportunities and the failures of the administration's attempt to settle the Nicaraguan conflict.[44] "[T]he decision to attempt a mediation effort aimed at persuading Somoza to step down and facilitate an orderly transition to an interim government made up largely of moderates was, in my view, a sound one." The United States "tackled the succession crisis at a time when it was still possible to achieve a moderate outcome and hold the radical elements of the Sandinista movement in check." Bowdler's mediation brought a period of peace and "forced the Sandinista guerrilla activity into the background and into virtual suspension." The opposition coalition had been fragile, but Bowdler and his colleagues had been able to "bring them along to direct talks and still preserve the essential unity of the group." The American mediation in October had "catalyzed the moderate opposition elements into a relatively cohesive group capable of functioning."

"What was not foreseen," Vaky argued, "was the obduracy of Somoza in negotiating his resignation and departure. . . . Somoza used the mediation to gain time in the belief that he could strengthen the National Guard and simply hold on. Somoza's fundamental rigidity shattered any possibility for compromise and a peaceful end to the Somoza dynasty." "The tragedy in the Nicaraguan situation," Vaky concluded, "may in historical perspective lie in the perhaps unknowable answer to the question of whether we should have—or could have—exerted greater pressure and leverage to secure agreement to a peaceful transition when that was relatively easy to accomplish." Vaky regretted the consequences of that failure by the United States. "One of the agonizing things that the mediation process did," he later testified, "was to bring people out whom you would not have thought would oppose the regime. People of the establishment, businessmen, and the like came out and declared their opposition. And they did it on our word that we were trying to resolve the problem."[45] "The failure of the mediation," Vaky told Congress in the summer, "came close to destroying the moderate opposition, leaving it with no alternative but withdrawal or radicalization."[46]

10

"It Was More Important for Somoza to Fall Than to Keep Out the Cubans"

The collapse of the American mediation gave an enormous boost to the Sandinistas' fortunes. In the first months of 1979 the long-squabbling Sandinista factions united behind a combined political-military strategy that soon proved remarkably successful.[1] To ease their rapprochement, Fidel Castro stepped in and made unity a condition of his support in the battles to come.

The biggest disputes had been over military strategy. Some Sandinistas clung to the idea of prolonged "guerrilla war" in the hills and opposed the *Terceristas'* "insurrectionary" strategy of large offensives and spectacular urban attacks. In the view of the other factions, the Sandinistas' weakness in the September uprising had been an embarrassment and an example of the high cost paid for the *Terceristas'* "reckless adventurism."[2] Castro agreed. Although he believed Central America was ripe for revolution, he thought the struggle in Nicaragua would take time.[3] He told Humberto Ortega to refrain from frontal attacks on the National Guard and to concentrate on more common guerrilla tactics of harassment and deception. In December Castro told *Tercerista* leaders to abandon plans for a large military offensive because he did not believe the FSLN had the logistical capability or the organization to sustain conventional operations against the Guard. Castro believed the war against Somoza could be won, but only after several years of struggle.[4]

At first, Humberto Ortega seemed to acquiesce to Castro's demands. In the weeks that followed, however, the *Terceristas* carried the main burden of the fighting and kept up the "insurrectionary" approach. Edén Pastora led the Southern Front from Costa Rica and fought almost conventional battles against the National Guard across the Nicaraguan border. Pastora's fighters took a pounding from the superior Guard troops and suffered the worst losses, but the threat Pastora posed to Managua and the Pacific Coast tied down many of the National Guard's best troops and diverted attention from the Northern Front. They also provided a diplomatic benefit: Each time Somoza's troops chased Pastora back into Costa Rican territory, these incursions into Costa Rica brought a storm of international criticism.

In the most populated cities along the Pacific Coast, Joaquín Cuadra Lacayo led the *Terceristas'* Internal Front, arming and organizing the youths in the barrios to harass the Guard and prepare for a general insurrection. German Pomares led a *Tercerista* Northern Front, which carried out raids on National Guard posts, ambushed convoys, and sporadically stole into the isolated towns and villages near the Honduran border. In the mountains were small bands of guerrillas led by Henry Ruiz of the Prolonged Popular War faction. In the cities, leaders of Jaime Wheelock's Proletarian Tendency worked to organize and raise the "proletarian consciousness" of the workers and peasants in preparation for the eventual uprising, to infiltrate and agitate in the unions, and to work with the leftist organizations in Moises Hassan's United People's Movement.

On March 7, 1979, the Sandinistas announced the formation of a nine-man directorate with three members from each of the three factions.[5] They pledged themselves to collegial deliberations and equality. There was no denying, however, that the *Terceristas* were in the ascendancy if only because of their larger numbers of fighting forces. And despite Humberto Ortega's concessions to Castro, his "insurrectionary" strategy soon became the accepted military doctrine of the revolution.[6] Premature frontal attacks in the cities would be avoided, but the cities remained the target, and the plan was to move against them as soon as weapons and manpower afforded. All Sandinista factions agreed that the main threat to the revolution was the United States government, which was "still trying to advance their plan to scare Somoza, to leave us the famous Somozism without Somoza, trying to create in the Broad Opposition Front a political alternative to guarantee imperialist interests."[7]

Humberto Ortega's strategy needed a steady supply of weapons to have any hope of success. As late as March the rebel army had less than 2,000 regular fighters. Somoza's National Guard had close to 10,000 troops, a small air force, a tank battalion in Managua, and an elite force led by Somoza's son. Carter officials withdrew from the mediation fairly confident that this imbalance would continue to favor Somoza and ensure his grip on power until at least 1981. When the State Department announced the sanctions on February 8, it called on all nations to refrain from sending arms to either side in the Nicaraguan war. By then, however, several Latin leaders had already stepped in to help the Sandinistas in their struggle.

Venezuela's President Pérez had been the first to send arms to the Sandinistas. Using a special group of officers and a National Security Council that reported only to him, Pérez had secretly shipped rifles and ammunition to Pastora and the *Terceristas* in Costa Rica beginning in early 1978. He delivered one final shipment of arms in February 1979, the last month of his presidency. According to Humberto Ortega, as Pérez neared the end of his term, he turned to Castro and asked him to take over the supply of arms to the Sandinistas.[8]

Panama's General Torrijos had also begun arming the Sandinistas in late 1978. He sent his top intelligence officer, Colonel Manuel Noriega, to Havana to talk to Fidel Castro about setting up an arms supply system for the Sandinistas through Panama and Costa Rica.[9] In September the Cuban government shipped eight crates of arms, including .50 caliber machine guns to be used as anti-aircraft weapons, to Panama for later delivery to Sandinista troops in Costa Rica.[10] In November three Panamanian air force planes carried crates of AK-47 rifles, .50 caliber machine guns, and hand-held mortars from Cuba to Panama. Beginning in December, as the American mediation faltered, the triangular route from Havana to Panama to Costa Rica carried an increasingly heavy flow of arms. Cuban officials established a command center in Costa Rica to oversee the distribution of weapons and advise the Sandinistas on military operations. One of these Cubans, Julian López, later became his country's ambassador to Sandinista Nicaragua. Although President Pérez's successor, Luis Herrera Campíns, ended Venezuela's participation in the arms supply in March, the combined efforts of Cuba, Panama, and Costa Rica by that time more than made up for the loss. Between February and July 1979, millions of pounds of arms and ammunition reached Sandinista forces in Costa Rica.

The intervention of Panama, Venezuela, Costa Rica, Cuba, and other nations on the side of the Sandinistas had significance beyond the purely military, however. It established a new Latin solidarity with the anti-Somoza forces, Sandinista and non-Sandinista alike, that eventually played a decisive part in bringing down the dictatorship. Each of the principal Latin leaders—Pérez, Carazo, Torrijos, Castro, and the Mexican government of José López Portillo—had their own reasons for wanting to force Somoza from power. Costa Ricans remembered that the Somoza dictatorship in 1955 had supported, and Nicaragua had served as a launching point for, an armed insurrection against the government of the hero of Costa Rican democracy, José "Pepe" Figueres. Nicaraguan opponents of the Somozas had, over the years, found refuge in Costa Rica, where they became friends and business partners of the Costa Rican elite. The Chamorro clan, in particular, had always found a second home in Costa Rica, and Pedro Joaquín Chamorro was popular there as he was in many strongholds of the Latin Democratic Left. The National Guard's attacks on Costa Rican territory, as well as Somoza's repeated threats of retaliation against Costa Rica for supporting the Sandinistas had the effect of further angering and scaring President Carazo and the Costa Rican people.[11] The gun-running business, moreover, was extremely rewarding, and Costa Rican officials made a great deal of money helping the Sandinistas.[12]

Carlos Andrés Pérez's opposition to the Somoza dynasty was long-standing, but he took an active role in internal Nicaraguan affairs only after the murder of his good friend, Pedro Joaquín Chamorro. Pérez became offended and annoyed when Somoza did not simply take his advice and resign in 1978, and this, combined with his frustrations with the Carter administration, led him to redouble his efforts, while still president, to help the Sandinistas overthrow Somoza. Pérez had developed an affection for the flamboyant Edén Pastora who, though a Sandinista, proclaimed himself a 'social democrat' and no Marxist.

General Torrijos also personally disliked Somoza and in a memorable statement once declared that "the crisis in Nicaragua can be described as a simple problem: a mentally deranged man with an army of criminals is attacking a defenseless population. . . . This is not a problem for the OAS; what we need is a psychiatrist."[13] Torrijos and his top deputy, Manuel Noriega, liked to keep a foot in both camps in the hemisphere, playing along with Castro and the Americans simultaneously. Gun-running was also a good business in Panama.

The Latin-wide assault on Somoza, moreover, followed a long tradition of inter-American intervention. Nicaragua was only the latest battleground in a decades-long war between the Latin American democratic Left and the authoritarian Right. The heroes of the democratic Left's struggle were President Rómulo Bétancourt, the democrat who came to power in Venezuela in 1958 after the fall of the dictator Marcos Pérez Jiménez; "Pepe" Figueres of Costa Rica, who disbanded the Costa Rican army in 1948 and played a large role in securing democracy in Costa Rica for the next four decades; and Fidel Castro, who led a successful armed struggle against the Batista dictatorship in Cuba in 1959 and brought communist government to Latin America.

The historic villains were the powerful *caudillos* in the hemisphere who had reigned together in the 1940s and 1950s: Rafael Trujillo in the Dominican Republic, Pérez Jiménez in Venezuela, Batista in Cuba, and Somoza in Nicaragua. When Rafael Calderón Guardia led his invasion from Nicaragua against the Figueres government in Costa Rica in 1955, he had the support of Somoza, Batista, Trujillo, and Pérez Jiménez. When Castro fought to overthrow Batista in the late 1950s, he had the support of Figueres and Bétancourt (who employed Carlos Andrés Pérez as a principal emissary to Castro.)

For the political descendants of Rómulo Bétancourt and Pepe Figueres, a quick look around the hemisphere revealed only one surviving remnant of the 1950s clique of dictators: the Somoza dynasty. When the possibility began to emerge that Somoza could be toppled—in no small part because the United States seemed willing to help remove him—the Latin democratic Left jumped into the fray.

There was a difference between Castro and the others: the Cuban communist leader wanted a revolutionary victory and the establishment of a socialist ally in Nicaragua; the others expressed hope for something more like a social democracy, a new ally of the democratic, not the communist, Left. Pérez, Carazo, and Torrijos all insisted, then and later, that their support for the Sandinistas was meant to prevent the revolution from becoming too radical. President Pérez, according to Vaky, did "not want the FSLN to be left entirely to Castro's influence."[14] General Torrijos had decided, for similar reasons, to "buy a share" of Sandinista stock and believed the Americans would have been wise to do the same.[15] The actions of these Latin presidents were not always consistent with their stated intentions, however. In the end, all three Presidents helped Castro deliver weapons to the Sandinistas and made it possible for the Cubans to play a critical role in the Nicaraguan revolution. As President Carazo later admitted, "It was more important for Somoza to fall than to keep out the Cubans."[16]

After the failure of the American mediation, the Sandinistas reaped the full military and diplomatic benefits of Latin solidarity. The arms that flowed into Nicaragua in increasing amounts enabled the Sandinistas to expand their attacks on the National Guard. The increasing international isolation of Somoza, and the growing legitimacy of the armed struggle against him, strengthened the Sandinistas' position in Nicaragua and in the world.

The growth in the Sandinistas' military capabilities was dramatic. In February and March Sandinista military actions were light and sporadic.[17] By the end of March, however, the quality and quantity of arms supplied to the Sandinistas began to have an effect in the war. At the beginning of April, the Sandinistas launched a new offensive, attacking cities, small towns, and National Guard patrols in the north and northwest regions of the country. The largest attack in the offensive began on April 7 when several hundred Sandinistas led by the *Terceristas'* Northern Front commander, German Pomares, attacked the city of Estelí. The Sandinista forces occupied much of the town, while about 100 National Guardsmen remained near their command headquarters, waiting for reinforcements. There was some heavy fighting inside the city, but the National Guard did not attempt to uproot the Sandinistas from their positions, even after the reinforcements arrived. Somoza, who was at the time on vacation in the United States, did not want a repetition of the September bloodshed. The National Guard commanders were under orders not to bombard the town from the air or to launch a large ground attack.[18] At the end of one week, the Sandinistas escaped in the night through a gap in the Guard's positions. After the Sandinistas escaped, the Guardsmen reportedly dragged about 40 young men out of their hospital beds, some of them unconscious, and executed them in the street along with one of the hospital's physicians.[19]

Somoza belittled the guerrilla attacks across the country as a "mimicry of an offensive,"[20] but the fighting resumed at the end of April with a Sandinista attack on the city of León. This time Somoza's air force did bomb the city. Once again the Sandinistas withdrew. At the beginning of May, the guerrillas announced the beginning of another "final offensive" against the regime. On May 29 about 300 guerrillas of the Southern Front launched an attack from Costa Rica against the Nicaraguan town of Rivas. The Sandinistas announced that the "hour for the overthrow" of Somoza had arrived. In Mexico City, a Sandinista spokesman told reporters, "This is what we've been preparing for. We're throwing everything we have into the final offensive. Somoza's days are numbered."[21] Rivas, however, did not fall.

By the beginning of June the Sandinistas had changed the nature of the war. Although still too weak to defeat the National Guard anywhere, the Sandinistas had picked up the pace of the conflict. They had developed the capacity to attack significant targets in the north and south simultaneously. They could not capture and hold towns, but they were beginning to spread the National Guard thin and to force its commanders to make decisions about what to defend. The increase in arms had allowed the Sandinistas to increase the numbers of fighters in the field and to regroup quickly after each offensive. By May the Sandinistas had reportedly increased their strength to over 2,000—the *New York Times* estimated 5,000—from less than 1,000 in 1978.

The Sandinistas' new capabilities began to attract attention in Washington. Analysts at the CIA and the Pentagon, however, discounted the Sandinistas' offensives because they failed to take and hold their objectives. At the beginning of June, the CIA "undertook a rapid assessment" of the conflict "and concluded that the fighting could conceivably develop into a second insurrection on the level of the September crisis, but it would not be adequate to displace Somoza."[22] Although the Sandinistas took control of León on June 6, General McAuliffe told the Panama Canal Subcommittee that "the FSLN very recently mounted a series of hit-and-run type attacks. . . . The Nicaraguan forces of President Somoza are, in my judgment, entirely capable of dealing with this threat. . . . [They] are reacting, in my judgment, adequately to the situation and are able to regain control in the contested areas fairly quickly."[23] The American embassy reported that while the Sandinistas appeared "to have larger numbers with substantially better equipment and better training than during the fighting in September 1978," the National Guard remained "better armed, better trained and larger in numbers." The Guard had "soundly defeated" Pastora's troops near Rivas and, "despite current difficulties in maintaining control of cities such as León, Matagalpa and Masaya, we have no evidence of any loss of morale, above-normal desertions, or serious doubt in their eventual ability to regain control of those cities." In the White House, Robert Pastor believed that both Somoza and the National Guard would "emerge battered, hopefully shaken, and intact in a few weeks."[24]

Other observers in Nicaragua told a more alarming story. The *Times*'s

Alan Riding reported on June 8 that the guerrillas had "seized all or most of Matagalpa, Ocotal and Chichigalpa in the north, Masaya near the capital and Diriamba and Granada in the south." Riding quoted one observer saying: "It looks like the whole country is slowly catching fire. The firemen are running around desperately, but new blazes keep erupting."[25] The real battlefield situation lay somewhere between Riding's excited reports and the low-keyed judgments of Carter officials. The Sandinistas were creating havoc around the country in part because Somoza had adopted a patient, defensive strategy. The key to Nicaragua was Managua and the central Pacific Coast, and Somoza kept most of his forces in and around the capital. Except in the south, where a successful guerrilla offensive could directly threaten the Pacific Coast region, National Guard troops concentrated on holding their barracks and command posts. "The Sandinista strategy," one Guard officer told a reporter, "is to draw our troops to the provinces, but we're not falling for that."

The Carter administration's analysts may have accurately portrayed the military balance as it stood on June 8, but they underestimated the potential strength of the Sandinistas. The momentum in the war had shifted: the Sandinistas were on an upward course and the Guard on a downward course. The main reason was the disparity in the flows of weapons to the two sides. Although the only clearly articulated goal of American policy since January had been to stop the flow of arms to both sides in Nicaragua, the Carter administration had succeeded only in cutting off supplies to the Somoza regime. A decision on June 11 to issue "clear, forceful private and public warnings to cease the arms flow to both sides" resulted in a "tough statement" to Israel to stop delivering arms to Somoza,[26] and on June 14 an Israeli ship with arms approaching the Atlantic coast of Nicaragua turned around and went home.[27] Throughout the spring and early summer, however, arms flowed in steadily increasing amounts to the Sandinistas.

According to Robert Pastor, the Carter administration "received some information about arms smuggling [to the Sandinistas], but until *late June* it never suspected that the arms flow was very large or that both the Cuban and Costa Rican governments were directly involved."[28] This understates the level of the Carter administration's suspicions, however. Torrijos, Carazo, and Pérez tried to conceal their arms shipments from American eyes, and they repeatedly lied about their role when asked by Carter officials, but it was impossible to keep such a large flow of weapons secret. As early as May 2 the CIA produced a report on "Cuban Support for Central American Guerrilla Groups" that described in some detail the direct roles played by both the Cuban and Panamanian governments in shipping arms to the Sandinistas, as well as the role of Costa Rica as the main staging area for this network of support for the Sandinistas. The report specifically stated that the Cuban government had "limited its own direct involvement by relying on the Panamanian government to transport the arms," and it described the "recent reactivation of the Panama-Costa Rica resupply route to the FSLN." The CIA report also described the use on two occasions of the Panamanian air force to ship weapons from Cuba, as well as an agreement reached at the beginning of January between Castro and Torrijos to transport FSLN fighters to Cuba for training and to use Panama as a "bridge" between Nicaragua and Cuba.[29] The CIA's report was based, in part, on a very reliable source. Colonel Noriega, who was on the CIA's payroll, had handed American intelligence officers documents describing the arms supply effort, including the names of pilots, airplane tail numbers, and Cuban companies involved.[30]

The Carter administration had been suspicious about Panama and Costa Rica even before the CIA's May 2 report. In March the National Guard had seized weapons coming by truck from Costa Rica and showed American journalists 49 Belgian-made FAL automatic rifles, 99 U.S.-made M-1 rifles, and 6 Soviet-made RPG-2 rockets.[31] The American Ambassadors in Costa Rica and Panama repeatedly asked government officials if reports of their countries' involvement in gun-running were true.[32] Ambassador Moss, in Panama, recalls that he was given instructions "at least a dozen times to go in and make demarches to Torrijos in the sense that Washington certainly hopes that nobody in this area is fueling this war and we wouldn't want to see guns going through Panama and there are rumors that guns are going through Panama." Torrijos "with an absolutely straight face" denied that any guns were passing through Panama. He even wrote in a note for President Carter that "if anybody is caught running guns, I'll have him put in jail."[33]

The Carter administration reached a point where it simply did not want to know precisely what Torrijos was up to. According to one official, intelligence agents in Panama were asked by their CIA superiors to stop paying so much attention to documenting all the arms shipments the Panamanian government was involved in.[34] When a State Department intelligence analyst did try to present "incomplete but suggestive evidence of the growing flow of supplies to the Sandinistas, he found considerable resistance to his proposal of a Cuban connection."[35] One Defense

Department official testified in June 1979 that the Carter administration had "long had extensive information indicating Cuban, Panamanian, Costa Rican, and, at times, Venezuelan support for the Sandinistas. Yet the administration has been strangely quiet regarding this aspect of the problem."[36]

The reason for the Carter administration's silence about Panamanian gun-running was the Panama Canal treaties. With legislation on the treaties coming up for a vote in May or June, and conservative hostility to the treaties high in both parties, the administration could not afford charges that Torrijos, the man who would be entrusted with the Canal, was supporting a communist revolution in Nicaragua. Allegations of Torrijos's support for the Sandinistas were so widespread, however, that opponents of the treaties called hearings in June to "examine" them. On June 4, two days before the hearings were to begin, Robert Pastor flew to Panama on a "secret mission" to "try to persuade Torrijos to *stop* sending arms to the Sandinistas."[37] At a meeting on Contadora Island off the coast of Panama, Pastor sternly informed Torrijos that his continued "playing with the Sandinistas" could make passage of the Canal treaties "impossible." Pastor requested a letter from Torrijos to President Carter giving "assurances of Panamanian non-intervention in Nicaragua's internal affairs."[38] The letter was of dubious validity, since the Carter administration had its own evidence that Panama was involved in arms smuggling to the Sandinistas,[39] and according to Pastor, "none of us was quite sure what [Torrijos' assurances] meant."[40] But Pastor brought the letter back to Washington. At the hearings two days later General McAuliffe insisted there was "no evidence" that the "Panamanian Government" had any role in arming the Sandinistas.[41]

The Carter administration was not eager to acknowledge Cuba's growing role in the arms supply effort, either. For many months, Carter officials had avoided mentioning Cuba in connection with the Sandinistas. When the CIA's May 2 report leaked to the press, conservative columnists Rowland Evans and Robert Novak went so far as to accuse the Carter administration of "sub rosa encouragement of leftist efforts to overthrow Nicaragua's dictatorship."[42] The danger that Nicaragua could become a "second Cuba" was a Republican and conservative charge that the administration always refuted.

One result of the Carter administration's efforts to shield the Congress from news about the Panamanian and Cuban roles was that Carter officials themselves discounted the importance of the arms supply network.

Torrijos reduced Panama's involvement in the first weeks of June, but at the same time Castro began to pour weapons into Nicaragua, flying them directly from Havana to Costa Rica without stopping in Panama. According to some reports, over one million pounds of arms, ammunition, and supplies were delivered from the beginning of June to the end of the war in mid-July. The shipments included not only rifles and ammunition, but larger weaponry, including rocket-launchers, bazookas, and anti-aircraft guns. "Needless to say," Humberto Ortega recalls, "the armament that was received played quite a decisive role in hastening the victory and, in some cases, in deciding a few battles which otherwise would have been lost."[43] The Carter administration had averted its eyes at a particularly important moment and, therefore, overlooked the significance of the Sandinista arms buildup in June.

Carter officials also missed the significance of the international forces lining up against the Somoza regime. In the middle of May Fidel Castro traveled to Mexico to meet with President José López Portillo. There he predicted that "Somoza will soon be in the garbage can of history" and denounced the Carter administration.[44] In their private conversations, Castro urged the Mexican President to take public action against Somoza. Two days later Costa Rica's President Carazo, who had already broken relations with Nicaragua, urged the same.[45] On May 20, at a luncheon in honor of President Carazo, López Portillo announced that Mexico was severing ties with the Nicaraguan government because of the "horrendous genocide" Somoza was committing. The next day, Mexico's foreign minister, Jorge Castañeda, expressed hope that international isolation of the Somoza regime would lead to the "downfall of sanguinary government," and he called upon the United States to cut all ties to Somoza.[46] The Carter administration, on the contrary, quickly tried to stave off any further actions by Latin governments.

11

Damage Limitation and the "Second Pillar"

The escalating violence and growing international support for the Sandinistas had a predictable effect on the FAO and moderate opposition forces in Nicaragua. Since April important leaders in the FAO had become more willing to consider an alliance with the Sandinistas to overthrow Somoza. In part, they feared that the Sandinistas would soon win the widest popular following, and they did not want to be left behind. Since the failure of the mediation at the beginning of the year, Sandinista cadres had successfully put together an alternative coalition of political groups, the National Patriotic Front (FPN). Their goal had been to lure away disaffected FAO members into this more radical alliance. On April 23 FPN leaders announced the beginning of dialogue with the FAO to unite "all the country's forces in order to overthrow President Anastasio Somoza's dictatorship." Julio López reassured the FAO that "we are anti-imperialists, but that does not mean we are anti-capitalists."[1]

The FAO's leaders demanded first that the Sandinistas stop their verbal attacks on the bourgeoisie. This was quickly agreed to, but the negotiations were periodically suspended because, as the American embassy reported, "FPN firebrands have found it very difficult to avoid belittling the moderates."[2] The FPN wanted in return an agreed plan for unified action against the regime, including another nationwide strike. The negotiations dragged on without result for some time, but at the end of April Somoza all but threw the moderates into the FPN's arms. He had Robelo and Córdova Rivas arrested on charges of involvement with gun-running. After forceful protests by the American government—Warren Christopher summoned the Nicaraguan ambassador to his office and demanded the release of the opposition leaders—Somoza let Robelo and Córdova Rivas go.[3] But when Robelo emerged from prison on May 14, he traveled to Costa Rica to seal his alliance with the *Tercerista* leaders.[4]

For the remaining moderates and conservatives in the FAO, Robelo's defection was a severe blow. Another blow fell at the beginning of June when the Nicaraguan Episcopal Conference released a statement apparently endorsing armed struggle against the dictatorship. Perhaps the result of a temporary victory by the more left-wing Nicaraguan clergy over the more conservative hierarchy led by Archbishop Obando, the statement declared that "the extremist actions of the revolutionary insurrection affect us all, but it is not possible to deny their moral legitimacy in the face of a blatant and prolonged tyranny which violates the basic rights of individuals."[5]

As the FAO's center dissolved, moderate and conservative leaders reached out in desperation to the United States. On June 1 the American embassy reported receiving two separate appeals for help from moderates who were "looking for an international intervention approved by the OAS or a restarting of the mediation" as well as for money to compete with the better financed political forces of the Left and the regime. "Both appeals were for rapid action in light of the possibility the FSLN still could force a national strike and a major insurgency in Managua."[6] The Sandinistas sought to capitalize quickly on their victories and issued the call for a nationwide strike on June 4. Fully aware that the unions and business groups in the FAO opposed another strike, the Sandinistas explicitly threatened those who refused to honor their call.[7] When the strike began on June 4, there were mixed reports as to whether the private sector and FAO unions were complying. The strike was successful enough, however, and combined with a new wave of Sandinista attacks on several Nicaraguan cities, it moved Somoza to declare a 90-day state of siege on June 6.[8]

Since the announcement of the sanctions back in February, the Carter administration had let events take their course in Nicaragua. Many other international problems had occupied the attention of senior Carter officials in the first six months of 1979. The Shah had fallen from power in

Iran, and the world was watching the first stages of the Ayatollah Khomeini's Islamic revolution. Carter's conservative critics charged that his human rights policy was responsible for this setback and that America's strategic position in the Persian Gulf had been gravely damaged. The SALT II treaty negotiations with the Soviet Union were coming to an end—Carter and Brezhnev signed the agreement in Vienna in the middle of June—but a conservative Democrat, Senator Henry Jackson, was leading the charge to defeat the treaty in the Senate. The Panama Canal legislation was due for a final vote at the beginning of June, and conservative opposition remained fierce.

Other events around the world added to a growing perception that President Carter's foreign policies were failing, and this was not just the perception of conservatives. Democratic Congressman Lee Hamilton, a reliable supporter of the administration, had noted earlier in the year that many Americans had come to "a very pessimistic view of . . . our position in the world and our ability to maintain our national interests." Hamilton cited several troubling developments, from the "pro-Soviet coups in Afghanistan, South Yemen, and Ethiopia" to the difficulties in Iran and Turkey, "the stalemate in the Middle East talks, the tensions in the Persian Gulf, Rhodesia." President Carter faced political problems at home, as well. In the spring of 1979 growing gas lines helped damage Carter's popularity, as measured in opinion polls. On May 25 a frustrated President worried that the American people were "disturbed . . . doubtful . . . uncertain about the future."[9]

It was understandable that in such difficult times, the Carter administration did not seek out additional difficult and controversial policies to pursue. The veiled intervention in Nicaragua of the last months of 1978 had not fared well, and an attitude of deliberate non-intervention in Nicaraguan affairs had seemed appropriate once again, this time more out of a sense of futility than ideological commitment. Vaky described the months between February and June 1979 as a time when "we didn't know where we were going. There was no point in talking anymore about getting Somoza out because there was no center [i.e., moderate opposition] to replace him, and there was no point shoring him up because he was a losing wicket."[10]

The crescendo of violence and instability in Nicaragua in June, however, once more made inaction impossible for the Carter administration. Very reluctantly, Carter officials returned to the fray. As one official told reporters in early June, "The United States has to do something. We'd prefer not to be out in front. But, given the intense emotion the situation is generating throughout Latin America, we can't be the last to act."[11]

All Carter officials agreed in June that Somoza had to resign quickly. This once contentious issue ceased to be a matter for debate when the intelligence reports were predicting Somoza's imminent demise. In June Carter officials had to debate a new question: Should the United States try to prevent a Sandinista victory or accept it as inevitable?

Vaky had six months earlier been the mastermind behind American efforts to prevent the Sandinistas from coming to power. In June, however, he argued that the United States should accept a Sandinista victory and try to make the best of it. "I didn't change," Vaky later recalled. "Everything else changed. . . . Half [of the moderates] were already gone, the other half didn't trust us anymore." The Sandinistas, who had been too weak to worry about in October 1978, were too strong to ignore in June 1979. Vaky hoped it would be possible at least to steer the Sandinista revolution in a moderate direction and to establish some influence over the next government in Managua. In Vaky's view, the Ortega brothers and some of the other Sandinista commanders were not committed Marxists but "classic *caudillo* types, searching for an ideology to sustain their search for power." They would need American economic assistance and diplomatic recognition; these needs would in turn make them more responsible and less radical. Vaky recognized his policy was not ideal; it was a policy of "damage limitation." In Vaky's view the United States had already missed its chance to prevent the Sandinistas from taking power; now it would have to devise a policy to live with them.[12]

On the other side of the debate in June 1979 was Zbigniew Brzezinski, who now took a more direct role in the brewing Nicaraguan crisis. Brzezinski shared neither Vaky's hopes for moderating the Sandinista revolution nor his pessimism about the possibility of preventing a Sandinista victory. Brzezinski's eagerness to block a guerrilla victory in Nicaragua was based on both political and strategic concerns.[13] He worried that the "loss" of Nicaragua, coming so soon after the fall of the Shah, would hurt the President. He also feared its effect on the upcoming Senate debate over the ratification of the SALT II treaty. Brzezinski was eager to dispel criticisms of an America "in retreat." He also worried about the strategic consequences of a Sandinista victory, fearing that U.S. passivity in Nicaragua would embolden an already aggressive Soviet Union. Since the beginning of Carter's presidency, Brzezinski had argued that "Soviet military activities by proxy in the Third World" required a strong American response.[14] The "proxy" that concerned Brzezinski most was Cuba. America's bargaining position with the Soviets, in Brzezinski's view, was eroding with each failure by the Carter administration to resist Soviet meddling in regional conflicts, and Nicaragua was fast shaping up as another failure. Brzezinski aimed to prevent a Sandinista triumph.

The policies proposed by Vaky and Brzezinski were mutually exclusive. The United States could not acquiesce in a Sandinista victory in the hopes of gaining influence with the new government and, at the same time, try to prevent the Sandinistas from coming to power. Yet despite the contradictions the administration did try to pursue both policies.

The Carter administration began by trying to muster international support for renewing the mediation in Nicaragua. As in September 1978, Carter officials placed their hopes first in a Latin-led mediation to remove Somoza. On May 29 the foreign ministers from the Andean Pact nations—Venezuela, Bolivia, Ecuador, Colombia, and Peru—had met and offered their "good offices" to Nicaragua. They hoped to establish a cease-fire, persuade Somoza to resign and then hand over power to a new junta.[15] The State Department endorsed the Andean Pact mission, and on June 11 Bowdler met with the foreign ministers of Ecuador and Venezuela to offer the quiet cooperation of the United States.[16] On June 13 Secretary Vance asked the OAS to authorize the new mediation in Nicaragua.

But the Andean Pact mission collapsed immediately. Somoza bluntly rejected the foreign ministers' offer of "good offices," and the ministers left Managua furious at the rebuff. Then on June 16, much to the Carter administration's surprise and dismay, the Andean Pact formally recognized the Sandinistas as a "legitimate" army eligible for "treatment and prerogatives" as a belligerent under international law. The Carter administration had tried to prevent the announcement, but the Latin governments, according to Pastor, "still thought that the United States was looking to save its longtime client, Anastasio Somoza."[17]

As Carter administration officials hurriedly debated the proper response to events in Nicaragua in the middle of June, the ground was shifting under them. Deliberations had barely started in Washington when events began to preclude any policy except acquiescence to a Sandinista victory. As the Carter administration set off to promote diplomatic efforts by Latin American nations, to look for a moderate alternative among the opposition forces in Nicaragua, to choke off the flow of arms to the Sandinistas, to preserve the National Guard, it found each path all but blocked. On all three fronts—diplomatic, political, and military—the Carter administration had arrived late and discovered that the Sandinistas had already taken the high ground and prepared fortifications.

The Andean Pact's announcement on June 16 was accompanied by other dramatic news that day. The Sandinistas announced from Costa Rica the establishment of a provisional government with a five-member junta of Alfonso Robelo, Violeta Chamorro, Moises Hassan, Sergio Ramírez, and Daniel Ortega.[18] The surprising presence of Robelo and Chamorro on the junta was a stunning victory for the Sandinistas. Since Robelo was still officially the representative of the FAO and Chamorro was the publisher of *La Prensa*, the "moderate" credentials of the new Sandinista junta were impressive. The Sandinista Front suddenly appeared to many in Nicaragua and abroad as the undisputed leader of all anti-Somoza forces.[19]

Although events were rushing toward the outcome Vaky had already predicted, Brzezinski remained determined to prevent it. His strength within the administration insured that his strategy would be tried, for a time. On June 18, the State Department proposed reconvening the OAS foreign ministers in the hope of renewing the international mediation, obtaining Somoza's resignation, and getting agreement to a cease-fire in Nicaragua. Vaky and his colleagues were primarily concerned with stopping the bloodshed in Nicaragua and sought the OAS' involvement for that purpose.[20] Brzezinski, however, had more ambitious goals in mind.

Brzezinski aimed to establish an alternative to the Sandinista junta, a "second pillar of power" in Nicaragua with the strength to prevent an outright Sandinista victory. This American-backed "Government of National Reconciliation" would replace Somoza, with the support of the National Guard, and then negotiate the terms of a final political settlement with the Sandinista junta. To ensure the peaceful transfer of power from Somoza to this "National Reconciliation Government," Brzezinski also proposed the creation of an "inter-American peacekeeping force" that would enter Nicaragua when Somoza agreed to resign and would guarantee the U.S.-brokered settlement against Sandinista attacks.[21]

Vaky and other State Department officials opposed both aspects of Brzezinski's plan. Vaky, Bowdler, and the new American Ambassador to Nicaragua, Lawrence Pezzullo, believed it was too late to pull together a moderate alternative to the Sandinista junta. In Vaky's view, "a second nucleus of opposition leadership" was simply not available. Ambassador

Pezzullo reported on June 27, his first day in Managua, that it was already "apparent that we have little if any chance of putting together" a new moderate coalition.[22] State Department officials also objected that any effort to establish a "second pillar" would only anger the Sandinista junta and undermine any hopes for good relations with the next government of Nicaragua. If the "FSLN-supported Provisional Government should win, our relationship will have begun on a hostile note. . . . [W]e would have structured the situation so that the government would view us as hostile . . . and would therefore be most receptive to Cuban support."[23] Vaky and Christopher also opposed Brzezinski's proposal for a "peacekeeping force," believing the OAS would never approve such a plan, especially if it appeared to be an American attempt to impose its own junta in Nicaragua.[24]

Brzezinski had President Carter's support, however, and for a time the National Security Advisor's geostrategic and political arguments were more persuasive to the President than the State Department's case for a policy of relative passivity. In the middle of June, the President was more concerned than usual about Soviet and Cuban behavior in Central America, and the effect of their actions on the arms control process and domestic politics. He had just returned from the Vienna summit, where he and Soviet Secretary General Brezhnev had signed the SALT II agreement. Passage of that agreement in the Senate, already a difficult battle, could be made more difficult by a Sandinista victory in Nicaragua.[25]

The President's concerns were not just political. The more aggressive behavior of the Soviets in the Third World, even as they negotiated an arms agreement with the United States, supported arguments by Brzezinski that the Soviets sought only what they needed from the United States without moderating their behavior on issues the United States cared about. Carter wanted Brezhnev to understand that the United States took Soviet actions in these regional conflicts seriously and that the Soviets' geopolitical behavior was as important as arms control treaties. At the summit meeting in Vienna in the middle of June, he told Brezhnev "we should avoid further confrontation by refraining from intrusions into troubled areas, either directly or indirectly through proxies." Carter said he considered Cuba "a proxy or surrogate of yours, supported and financed by you." Brezhnev was unmoved. The Soviet Union was "dedicated to support the struggle for emancipation and solidarity," he declared, although these "revolutions, which the Soviets do support, emerge only within other nations. The instigation for them never originates with us." Carter, dissatisfied with Brezhnev's response, afterwards told reporters that he had warned Brezhnev that "growing Cuban involvement in the problems of Central America and the Caribbean can only have a negative impact on U.S.-Soviet relations."[26]

With these geostrategic and political considerations in the background, Brzezinski could insist that Vance do more than ask for Somoza's resignation at the OAS meeting on June 21. He wanted the Secretary of State to call for the establishment of the inter-American peacekeeping force and to make explicit reference to Cuban involvement in Nicaragua. With President Carter's backing, the State Department's objections were overruled.

The Carter administration now paid a price for pursuing two different policies at once. The OAS was no place to look for help in blocking the Sandinistas. The most influential Latin leaders were pursuing only one goal in June: the removal of Somoza. Some governments, like Mexico, were actively providing a political shield for the Sandinistas to prevent any U.S. attempts to keep them from power. Pastor blamed State Department officials for seeking support in the OAS: "The decision to use the OAS was a sign that the [State] department had not fully grasped the implications of the Andean Pact statement" of June 16.[27] But Vaky and other State Department officials had not planned to ask the OAS for anything beyond a resolution calling for a cease-fire and Somoza's resignation. It was Brzezinski who demanded that Vance also seek the OAS' approval for an American attempt to keep the Sandinistas from power.[28] Vaky and other State Department officials continued futilely to resist Brzezinski's plan. Their draft of Vance's speech made no mention of a peacekeeping force or Cuban involvement. President Carter, however, after consulting with Brzezinski, personally wrote in both statements.

The only matter on which all Carter administration officials agreed was that Somoza should be asked to resign. By June 21 two events had loosened most of the political constraints that had earlier caused the administration to pause. On June 20 the House of Representatives defeated all amendments aimed at crippling the Panama Canal legislation. The administration could now call for Somoza's ouster without fear of retaliation by Murphy and Wilson. (In response to this victory, General Torrijos immediately broke relations with Nicaragua.) On June 20, as well, the National Guard executed an American journalist in Nicaragua. Bill Stewart, an ABC news correspondent, was ordered to his knees and killed with a gunshot to the back of his head, in full view of the television cameras. The horrible and irrefutable evidence of the Guard's brutality was shown on the evening news in the United States and became a national and international scandal. As Pastor recalls, "The response by the public was unlike anything I had seen since I had been in the White House. . . . One consequence of the tragedy was that it quieted the thunder from the right in the United States."[29]

Secretary Vance's call for Somoza's resignation on June 21, therefore, came as no surprise. The other parts of Vance's request, however, aroused indignation and suspicion among the assembled Latin delegations at the OAS meeting that day. As Carter and Brzezinski requested, Vance called upon the OAS to seek "the replacement of the present government with a transitional government of national reconciliation, which would be a clear break with the past." He asked the OAS to send a special delegation to Nicaragua to "facilitate" the formation of this transitional government and the holding of free elections. He called for an end to all arms shipments to Nicaragua, and, in words written by President Carter, warned of the "mounting evidence of involvement by Cuba and others in the internal problems of Nicaragua." Secretary Vance asked all member states to "consider on an urgent basis the need for a peacekeeping force, to help restore order and to permit the will of the Nicaraguan citizens to be implemented in the establishment of a democratic and representative government."[30]

A request that might have been greeted with cheers in Latin America had the United States made it in January was greeted with hostility on June 21. With Somoza's departure a foregone conclusion, many Latin leaders worried only that the United States would intervene to prevent a Sandinista victory. Pérez, Figueres, and Torrijos agreed with Vaky that the Sandinistas were going to win and that the time had come to begin influencing them, not to try to stand in their way. At the beginning of June Torrijos had told Robert Pastor, "It's too bad the United States is always so slow to recognize new realities, and that you didn't have the foresight to buy a share of Sandinista stock when I was first offering it." To which Pastor had replied "General, we have not come to buy Sandinista stock, but to try to get you to sell yours."[31]

The OAS meeting was a disaster for the Carter administration. As Pastor recalls, "Mexico, Panama, and the Andean nations not only did not share U.S. anxiety and reservations about a Sandinista military victory but had decided to run interference for the Sandinistas."[32] The Panamanian representative formally recognized the Sandinistas' five-day-old junta as the "government of national reconstruction;" he then offered Sandinista leader Miguel D'Escoto a seat on the Panamanian delegation. Mexico's foreign minister, Jorge Castañeda, insisted it was "not up to the O.A.S. or anyone else to tell them how they should constitute their government once they knock down the dictator." Even before Vance spoke, the Cuban Foreign Ministry circulated a statement accusing the United States of seeking a military presence in Nicaragua, using the OAS "as a cover."[33]

The American proposal for a peacekeeping force was crushed in a vote by the OAS members. The resolution passed by the OAS on June 23, after hours of negotiations by Warren Christopher, called for the "immediate and definitive replacement" of Somoza, but without suggesting how this might be accomplished other than to urge member nations to "take steps that are within their reach to facilitate an enduring and peaceful solution of the Nicaraguan problem"—words insisted upon by the United States. The OAS called for the installation of a democratic government in Nicaragua and "the holding of free elections as soon as possible." It also called on all nations to respect "scrupulously the principle of nonintervention." Christopher told reporters afterwards that there was "no precedent for the broadly based and far-reaching resolution adopted today." The OAS resolution, however, was designed to open a clear path for the Sandinistas. It opened only a small crack through which the United States could try, once again, to shape the next government of Nicaragua.

Brzezinski was unhappy with the course of events. At a meeting with the President and other senior officials on June 22 he argued for direct American intervention in Nicaragua, reminding the President that there were "major domestic and international implications [in] a Castroite take-over in Nicaragua. [The United States] would be considered as being incapable of dealing with problems in our own backyard and impotent in the face of Cuban intervention. This will have devastating domestic implications, including for SALT."[34] President Carter, however, rejected any consideration of unilateral American intervention. He placed his hope in further mediation.

Brzezinski continued to look for a solution in the "second pillar." On June 25 he again proposed creating an alternative governing structure, an "Executive Committee" with the support of the National Guard, that could negotiate with the Sandinista junta.[35] Vaky proposed working instead with the Sandinista junta, seeking perhaps to strengthen Robelo and Chamorro by broadening the junta to include other moderates. The Carter administration decided, again, to pursue both plans, in the hope that one might succeed and that in any case pursuing both tracks could only enhance American influence over the final outcome. The plan for a "second pillar" was presented to Somoza on June 25, and two days later Bowdler traveled to Panama to present the plan for broadening the junta to the Sandinista junta members.

Events in Nicaragua, however, had just about foreclosed both options. The Carter administration's plans to broaden the junta or set up a "second pillar" aroused heated opposition from the two moderates on the Sandinista junta. On June 18 Violeta Chamorro had insisted that the junta was the "true government of national unity" which already represented "all ideological, social, political, insurgent and intellectual sectors."[36] On June 20 Chamorro, Robelo, and the rest of the junta publicly rejected any American plan to establish an alternative government of national reconciliation.[37]

Even moderates outside the junta were finding it prudent to seize their last remaining opportunity to play some role in the next government and to protect their political and economic interests. The Sandinistas worked quickly to convince moderates that the moment to get on board was passing by. In the third week of June the Sandinista junta announced its program of government. The fruit of Robelo's bargaining with the Sandinistas over several weeks, the program of government was a compromise between the *Terceristas'* "minimum program"—the basic points that could be agreed upon with the bourgeoisie without blocking the socialist aims of the revolution—and Robelo's effort to ensure that his own position in the new government would be as strong as possible. The plan called for the creation of a Council of State, which would be made up of 30 members representing the FSLN, FPN, FAO, and even COSEP (Superior Council of Private Enterprise), a powerful, and rather conservative, alliance of Nicaraguan business leaders. Many moderates took the plan seriously. The American embassy in Costa Rica reported that "major jockeying for position" was already under way for participation in the Council of State.[38]

After Robelo struck his deal, the FAO leaders decided they could not afford to be left out of the grand plan the Sandinistas were orchestrating. They announced that "the junta, on which the FAO is represented and which the FAO has supported and continues to support, constitutes the beginning of that democratic and pluralist regime which must accede to power upon the fall of the Somocista government."[39] When on June 28 the *New York Times* revealed the details of the Carter administration's plan to establish a "second pillar," even conservative business leaders joined the Sandinistas in rejecting the "U.S. Plan."[40]

Faced with these developments, Vaky argued that "the time had come to choose which side of the street we wanted to work." Warren Christopher also worried that the United States would lose its chance to moderate the Sandinistas if it didn't try to work with them before Somoza was overthrown. The important goal, Vaky insisted, was to stop the fighting as soon as possible so that a peaceful transition to the Sandinista junta could occur.[41]

Pastor was appalled by these suggestions. It was "the first time in a year of NSC meetings that anyone had suggested the central U.S. objective was something other than preventing a Sandinista victory." Pastor questioned "whether one could realistically expect to win over the military leaders of the Sandinistas in the last days of their revolution after they had been fighting U.S. imperialism for two decades." He argued that "as long as there was any possibility of placing a buffer between them and exclusive power," the United States should try.[42]

On June 30, however, Ambassador Pezzullo reported from Managua that no opposition leader would join an alternative government "without greater assurances . . . that a reconstituted National Guard would stand firm and support them." Potential leaders of the opposition saw "the Junta in San José supported by an FSLN force and such countries as Panama and Costa Rica, while they would have nothing but helpful words from the US Government as of the moment."[43]

The preservation of the National Guard was essential to Brzezinski's plan, but by the beginning of July, as the Sandinistas, the moderates, and the Americans all knew, the National Guard's prospects had become bleak. This was not because they were fighting poorly or suffered from bad morale, yet. In the south, National Guard troops led by Commander "Bravo" were tearing into the Southern Front forces led by Edén Pastora. All of the major northern cities had been lost to the Sandinistas, but Managua was still in the hands of the government. In all likelihood, the Guard could hold out, even after the departure of Somoza, if it was well led, well supplied, and confident of support from the United States.

All Carter officials agreed that the National Guard should be kept intact during and after the transition from Somoza to a new, provisional government. Vaky believed it necessary "to preserve the integrity of the National Guard as an important element of moderation in future arrangements" because "a full military victory by the FSLN could reduce the future strength of moderate forces substantially."[44] Pastor and Brzezinski believed the political balance in Nicaragua would depend entirely on "who had the guns." "If the Sandinistas were left with a monopoly of military power," Pastor argued, "the moderates in the Junta would be at the mercy of the [Sandinista] Directorate."[45] But Carter officials also knew that the National Guard was running out of ammunition and supplies to conduct the war. By July 7 Pezzullo was reporting from Managua that "the [National Guard's] supply lines have been severely restricted whereas the FSLN has an open supply line." He guessed that the Guard would run out of ammunition in "less than two weeks."[46]

But apparently none of the senior policymakers in the Carter administration ever suggested that the United States should resume, or even promise to resume, arms shipments to the Guard.[47] Vaky opposed the idea because he was resigned to dealing with a Sandinista government. But Pastor and Brzezinski, who were not so resigned, also made no effort to arm the Guard. Pastor acknowledged that as the war in Nicaragua "became more ferocious, the idea of permitting the survival of any part of the Guard became increasingly problematic."[48] After the murder of Bill Stewart, the idea of renewing military assistance to the Guard was politically difficult and maybe even morally repugnant to President Carter.

While refusing to provide arms, senior American officials nevertheless devoted great efforts to finding the right person to take charge of the Guard and hold it together during the transition. They tried to have a former National Guard officer, Bernadino Larios, named to an expanded Sandinista junta to "assure the [National Guard] officers who will survive after Somoza that the [National Guard] is not being forgotten or abandoned."[49] Vaky instructed the American ambassador in Guatemala to tell another prospective Guard chief that "he may wish to keep in mind the importance of providing [Guard officers] with hope for the future."[50] The Carter administration, however, would not provide what the Guard really needed to have hope for the future. At their meeting on June 27, Pezzullo asked Somoza directly, "How do we preserve the Guard?" Somoza answered, "By giving them the logistics they need to make themselves felt in the country—that's all." Pezzullo responded that the Carter administration was "willing to do what we can to preserve the Guard," but it was "not going to come in here with the wherewithal to do it now. . . . I don't think we could get that through our Congress. . . . We are talking about the impossible. . . . We do want to preserve the Guard, we would like to see a force emerge here that can stabilize the country, we might never see that happen."[51] By July 10 Vaky was telling Pastor that "the Guard would not hold together, and that we should discard the illusion that it would."[52]

12

"Those Plans Have a Way of Not Working Out"

At the beginning of July the Carter administration finally abandoned Brzezinski's plan to establish a moderate alternative government to act as a second pillar of power alongside the Sandinistas. At a meeting with the President on July 2, Brzezinski made one final attempt, proposing to replace the Sandinista junta with a new one that would include the National Guard commander and only one leftist, Sergio Ramírez. President Carter took the State Department's side and rejected Brzezinski's suggestion as impractical. He accepted Vaky's plan to add moderates to the junta. According to Pastor, "Carter understood the importance of having a moderate on the Junta, which would have effective control of the army. 'We don't want Ortega to be Minister of Defense,'" the President said.[1]

The administration spent the next two weeks trying to broaden the junta with the addition of more moderates and to select a new commander for the National Guard who could hold the force together after Somoza's departure and negotiate a cease-fire with the Sandinistas. On July 3 Vaky flew to Venezuela to discuss with the Andean Pact foreign ministers ways of expanding the junta and moderating the next government. That same day, President Carter met with Torrijos in Washington and presented him with a seven-step plan for replacing Somoza with a broadened junta and a new Guard commander. On July 4, Bowdler met with Carazo in Costa Rica and suggested adding moderates like Adolfo Calero to the junta. Carazo presumably conveyed the message to the Sandinistas.

The idea of expanding the junta to include more moderates certainly had the support of Latin leaders. Carazo, Torrijos, Pérez, and Figueres had all grown nervous at the last minute about the possibility that a Sandinista government might be thoroughly Marxist and beholden to Castro, a concern that was amply shared by President Luis Herrera Campíns in Venezuela. In the second week of July, Figueres said publicly that he feared Somoza would be replaced by a Marxist government, which would lead eventually to a U.S. intervention. Figueres told reporters he was trying to find out from the Marxist members of the FSLN how far they wanted to go in carrying out reforms in Nicaragua. He singled out Edén Pastora as a "moderate and democratic element" within the Sandinista Front.[2] At the beginning of July, then, at the prompting of the United States, Panama, Costa Rica, and the Andean Pact began separate discussions with the Sandinista junta to broaden its membership and to seek understandings that could form the basis for a cease-fire and the formation of a transition government.[3]

Senior Carter officials now believed that one of their last remaining weapons for influencing the transition in Nicaragua was the ability, which the United States alone possessed, to choose the moment of Somoza's departure. "The main card the U.S. had to play," Pastor writes, "was Somoza's resignation."[4] The irony of the American mediation in July of 1979 was that, while it could no longer accomplish what Bowdler had a half-year earlier—the strengthening and consolidation of a moderate alternative to both Somoza and the Sandinistas—it could with little difficulty achieve the goal that had eluded Bowdler and Vaky in 1978: obtaining Somoza's departure from power.

By July Somoza was quite ready to quit both the presidency and the country. He had erred disastrously. In January he had confidently and stubbornly rejected American demands for a plebiscite which he might have won, but which at worst would have transferred power peacefully to the FAO. Six months later Somoza was preparing to flee Nicaragua with only his family and his money and to bequeath his country to the Sandinistas. When Ambassador Pezzullo came to Managua on June 27 to tell Somoza to resign, the last defender of the dynasty put up no argument. "I don't pretend to negotiate," Somoza told Pezzullo at their first meeting. "I am willing to sacrifice myself—whatever pride I might have. . . . I am not interested in influencing events in Nicaragua; I have been President twice and certainly I don't want this to be a bloodshed."[5]

The June OAS resolution calling for his resignation was the final act which had convinced Somoza his position was untenable—since the day of the vote Somoza had carried a letter of resignation in his pocket. His supporters in the American Congress were no longer of any use. When Pezzullo arrived to meet with Somoza for the first time, he found Congressman Murphy at Somoza's side, but Murphy was only there as a witness to ensure that the Carter administration kept whatever deal it struck with Somoza.[6]

Ambassador Pezzullo asked not only that Somoza resign, but that he do so in a way least likely to cause the Carter administration political difficulties. "If you left with a certain amount of dignity and you left with class, I think that's the touch," Pezzullo suggested. If, on the other hand, "you walk out of here and went after . . . the Carter administration, talk[ed] to Reagan and coo[ed] up to the Reagan campaign, it might make you feel better but it wouldn't help you."[7] Pezzullo knew how badly Somoza wanted asylum in the United States, which Somoza called "my other country," and Pezzullo's threat to deny him asylum if he did not behave was implicit but clear.[8]

Pezzullo also made clear that the Carter administration depended on Somoza's cooperation to ensure a moderate outcome in Nicaragua. If Somoza would not resign at the appropriate moment, Pezzullo explained, the Carter administration would not "have the capacity to make any of the other moves." The United States had to "deliver up something" if it was going to demand a peaceful and moderate transition. If the Carter administration failed to deliver, the Sandinistas "would come and sweet-talk to us that they are nice people, and so on. But give them five years and they would nationalize banks, and so on. We see all that."[9] In his conversations with other Nicaraguans, Pezzullo tried to make clear that the Carter administration held the "Somoza card" in its hands and would only play it when confident of an acceptable outcome. On July 2 Riding reported that the ambassador had told opposition leaders that "the existence of a democratic regime in the future must be guaranteed in Nicaragua before General Somoza's departure."[10]

As it turned out, however, the Carter administration placed more value on the "Somoza card" than it was worth. The Sandinistas did not want the United States to force Somoza's early resignation and preserve the National Guard. Indeed, the longer Somoza stayed, the better chance there was of defeating the National Guard—so long as the Carter administration continued to deny the Guard weapons and supplies. The Sandinistas knew, moreover, that the administration could not keep Somoza in power for long. It was the American Secretary of State, after all, who had led the OAS to call for Somoza's resignation. The United States could not easily bargain with something it had already promised to give away.

By the beginning of July, the "Somoza card" had actually become not only useless but a growing embarrassment and burden to the administration. On July 7 Somoza himself told the *Washington Post* that he was ready to resign, which ended any pretense that only the United States could persuade Somoza to quit. The *Washington Post's* headline read: "Somoza Agrees to Quit, Leaves Timing to U.S."[11] The Sandinista junta charged that instead of ending the war, the United States was extending it and was using the Somoza resignation as a "blackmail tool to guarantee its interests in Nicaragua."[12] Alan Riding wrote on July 10 that "while the main purpose of the war—General Somoza's ouster—has apparently been achieved, the bloody conflict goes on." The United States government "assuming its traditional role as final arbiter of Nicaragua's political destiny . . . has indicated that General Somoza's resignation will become effective only when the United States is satisfied with the composition and political program of the successor regime."[13]

Sandinista successes on the battlefield also had the effect of devaluing the "Somoza card." By the beginning of July, it was clear that while the Guard might hold out in Managua for a month or more, it had little hope of regaining control in the northern cities. As the guerrillas advanced, one observer speculated that the Sandinistas would "not need Washington [to get rid of Somoza] because they are making faster inroads than anyone expected."[14] On July 7, Sergio Ramírez candidly told one reporter, "If the Sandinistas continue advancing, we won't have to broaden the junta."[15]

The Sandinistas only fear was of American military intervention. That fear, and not the "Somoza card," was what caused the Sandinistas to make some compromises in the days before their victory. On July 10 Carter officials decided to present the junta with an "ultimatum." The junta would have to accept additional moderate members, call for a ceasefire, and organize elections, or the U.S. would seek "alternative approaches." Pastor recalls that "the administration had no idea what alternatives were available, but threats made in desperation are not generally inhibited by the absence of rational alternatives."[16] The Sandinistas, however, could well imagine what the "alternative approaches" might be. As late as July 18 Tomás Borge stood at a rally in León warning his countrymen against an imminent intervention by the United States "with the marines or through the forces of the Central American Defense Council."[17]

To prevent an American intervention, the Sandinistas needed to maintain the support of important Latin leaders. Those leaders, however, were growing more and more nervous about the Marxists in the Sandinista Front and about the possibility that the Nicaraguan revolution would become Castro's triumph. On July 8 the Sandinista junta's "foreign minister," Miguel D'Escoto, complained that Latin governments were threatening to cut off their support for the Sandinistas unless the junta was expanded and the structure of the National Guard preserved.[18] The *Terceristas* believed they had no choice but to try to appease Carazo, Pérez, Torrijos, Figueres, and even Bowdler, as best they could without compromising on strategically vital points.

Torrijos, Pérez, and even Castro advised the Sandinistas to accept an expansion of the junta. Castro, at least, considered it a minor concession since he, like Pastor and Brzezinski, did not expect the junta to have any real power in the next government.[19] Much to the surprise and chagrin of the Carter administration, however, it was Violeta Chamorro and Alfonso Robelo, not the Sandinistas, who rejected any plan to put more moderates like themselves on the junta. They may have feared the dilution of their own power. Pérez, a close friend and protector of Violeta and her late husband for many years, tried to persuade her, but she broke down in tears and said she preferred to resign rather than accept the expansion.[20] Robelo rejected the plan publicly. He saw "no reason why the United States should lay down conditions on how we should run Nicaragua."[21]

While Robelo and Chamorro took a hard line, however, the Sandinistas tried to accommodate the concerns of Latin leaders and the Carter administration. On July 14 the Sandinista junta announced their government's "cabinet," and the selections were notable for their "moderate" coloration. The twelve figures named included Joaquín Cuadra Chamorro, Arturo Cruz, and Roberto Mayorga, all members of the Group of Twelve, but also members of the Nicaraguan bourgeois elite. To meet another American demand, the Sandinistas offered the post of Defense Minister to the former National Guard colonel, Bernadino Larios. This answered President Carter's stated concern that an Ortega not have that post. The only troubling appointment was Tomás Borge as Interior Minister, but Borge was the only Sandinista named, and both the *Times* and the *Post* reported that his appointment was, in fact, good news for the United States.[22]

In keeping with their political-military strategy, the *Terceristas* were willing to compromise extensively in stating the political goals of the revolution. On July 12 Ramírez, Ortega, Borge, Pastora, Robelo, and Chamorro met in Costa Rica on President Carazo's ranch at Puntarenas with Carazo, Figueres, Pérez and Torrijos. Determined to win the unequivocal support of these Latin notables, and with it the international legitimacy necessary to forestall any last-minute American intervention, the Sandinistas agreed to modify the junta's political program. The new program they announced on July 12 was strikingly moderate. The junta pledged itself to install a government of "democracy, justice, and social progress," with full guarantees for *all* Nicaraguans to participate in the political system, not just those who had proven themselves in the struggle against Somoza. The junta promised not to persecute members of the National Guard who had not committed crimes against the people and to permit those who so wished to join the new national army.

The junta also specifically pledged for the first time that it would preserve a mixed economy in Nicaragua and that, although there would be an agrarian reform and a "transformation" of key sectors of the economy, including the financial system and the trade sector, nevertheless there would also be guarantees and full respect for the "properties and activities of the private sector" not otherwise affected by the government program. Although it was the junta's commitment to elections and human rights that received the most international attention both at the time and later, the junta's promise to respect private property and economic activities may have been the most important and decisive for Nicaraguan moderates and businessmen. At the most basic level, it gave them some assurance that they might at least survive economically in Sandinista Nicaragua, and perhaps economic survival would also mean political survival.

Even the announcement of this revised political program did not satisfy the Latin leaders assembled at Puntarenas. Pérez and the others also asked the Sandinista junta to send a letter to the OAS officially committing the junta to hold free elections. The junta did so, declaring to the OAS General Secretary that after it took power it would hold the "first free elections . . . in a century" in Nicaragua, for local offices, a constituent assembly, and later the "supreme authorities" of the country.[23]

The concessions the Sandinistas made in the last days before their defeat of Somoza were "dictated by the need to neutralize Yankee interventionist policies in light of the imminent Sandinista victory."[24] Although unnecessary to prevent an American intervention, which the Carter administration never seriously contemplated, the concessions won the Sandinistas enormous goodwill in the United States and throughout Latin America. Vaky considered the Sandinistas' letter to the OAS a first and important step toward the kind of moderation he hoped to foster in the new government. Carlos Andrés Pérez announced on July 13 that he was "deeply satisfied with the sense of responsibility shown by the members of the Government of National Reconstruction and the clear and categoric democratic program they have submitted to America and the world. . . . In my contacts with the [junta] and the Sandinist Front commanders, I have been surprised by the equanimity, the deep sense of responsibility and the democratic feeling which determines all their actions."[25] With Pérez's statements, the question of the legitimacy of the Sandinista junta was settled. The timing of Somoza's resignation, however, still rested with the United States.

The Carter administration was no longer able to resist the tide of events in Nicaragua. Although an exasperated Brzezinski warned his colleagues on July 13 that in Central America "the baton [was] being passed from the United States to Cuba," it was Vaky's strategy of accommodation that the Carter administration now adopted, more by force of circumstances than by conviction.

The Carter administration's new policy was shaped by a hope that what appeared to many to be a communist victory in Nicaragua need not be one at all. In appearances before Congress, Assistant Secretary Vaky portrayed the situation in Nicaragua with as much optimism as he could. Although he acknowledged Cuba's significant role in supplying arms to the Sandinistas, he pointed out that Cuba was "not the only or even the most important of the supporters of the anti-Somoza rebellion. Nicaraguans and our democratic friends in Latin America have no intention of seeing Nicaragua turned into a second Cuba, and are determined to prevent the subversion of their anti-Somoza cause by Castro." In response to concerns that the Sandinistas would control the direction of the next government, Vaky argued that the Nicaraguan people themselves would not permit a radical revolution. There were "large elements, including some now associated with what is called the Sandinistas, who are not Castroist or Marxist. There are elements ranging from the Conservative Party which has been the long-time opposition party to business groups, bankers, political parties like the Christian Democrats [Social Christians], all of them engaged in relating to this particular fight."[26] Vaky said that even most Sandinista fighters were not "ideological" and argued that the *Terceristas* were not "Marxist ideologues."[27]

Since Vaky wanted the United States to provide economic aid quickly to the new regime, he may have understated the prospects for a radicalization of the revolution. Vaky sincerely believed, however, that a pluralist, democratic government with a mixed economy and a neutral foreign policy could emerge from the Nicaraguan revolution, if the United States conducted itself wisely and prudently, and if it greeted the new Nicaraguan leaders with friendship and assistance rather than suspicion and hostility. "You would hope," as he later put it, "that they [the Sandinistas] would behave realistically."[28]

Vaky was by no means alone in his hope that circumstances would constrain whatever radical desires some Sandinistas might harbor. The *Washington Post*, which had earlier expressed concerns about a Sandinista victory, in July recommended embracing the Sandinista junta and "to use the embrace to hold them to the democratic standards they profess." Nicaragua's "need for vast economic repair ensures a respect for its neighbors' anti-Communist political sensitivities." The *Post* considered it "inconceivable, moreover, that Moscow will take on another billion-dollar baby."[29] Alan Riding of the *Times* also argued that "the political moderation of any successor regime seems guaranteed by the need for enormous assistance from the United States during reconstruction."[30]

The great ideological and political debate that was to dominate American policy toward Nicaragua over the coming decade thus took full shape in the last days before the Sandinista triumph. Opposed to Vaky's hopeful, accommodationist approach was Brzezinski's conviction that the Sandinistas' impending victory was a defeat for the United States and a victory for the Soviet Union and Castro. Warren Christopher, who shared Vaky's view, skeptically asked Brzezinski what he meant by a "Castro-ite" government in Nicaragua. Brzezinski responded that a Castro-ite government would be one that "supported Cuban and Soviet foreign policy and insurgencies abroad—for example, in El Salvador."[31]

Conservative critics of the Carter administration soon began arguing that the President was "losing" Nicaragua to the Communists and was doing so deliberately.[32] Such perceptions were encouraged by "off-the-record" statements that emanated from the American embassy in Managua, possibly from Ambassador Pezzullo himself. Alan Riding reported that "One United States official said Washington wanted to help Nicaragua 'but can't be seen helping a bunch of radicals.' He said the junta had 'to look moderate for us to be able to sell the package back home.'"[33] Conservative Democrats were just as troubled by the course of events as Republicans. At the last minute, Congressman Murphy even persuaded Majority Leader Jim Wright to intercede on Somoza's behalf. Wright asked Secretary Vance to allow Somoza to speak directly with President Carter by phone. The House Majority Leader believed it was "extreme" to ask a head of state to step down.[34]

Despite these pressures, the Carter administration now sought as rapid a conclusion to the conflict as possible, in part so that the Guard might not be completely destroyed. In the end, the American plan was not very different from what the Sandinista junta had already proposed. Somoza would resign and turn power over to an elected member of the Nicaraguan Congress, who, in turn, would call for a cease-fire, begin negotiations between the new Guard commander and the leaders of the Sandinista forces, and then transfer power to the junta. It would be an unconditional and immediate transfer of power.

According to the American plan, Somoza would resign at one in the morning on July 17 and hand over power to Francisco Urcuyo, a physician in his sixties chosen by the Nicaraguan Congress at the Americans' behest. The Guard would be put under the control of Lieutenant Colonel Federico Mejía, who had been chosen by American officials and approved by the junta. The final two days, however, were tragicomic, as almost nothing worked out as planned. Somoza did resign and flew to Miami on July 17. Before leaving, he retired 100 senior officers in the Guard and Mejía was named as the new commander. Urcuyo became interim president, and then the plan broke down.

Urcuyo announced to the nation that a time for healing had come and made clear that he had no intention of immediately passing power to the junta. He told Ambassador Pezzullo that he would not transfer power to a "communist junta," but only to a democratic one. He told reporters he might have to stay in power "one, two, or three months," and he denied landing rights to the plane that was supposed to bring the junta from Costa Rica to Managua.

The Carter administration was furious and publicly denounced Urcuyo's violation of the terms worked out for Somoza's departure. The State Department threatened Somoza with expulsion from Miami if he did not convince Urcuyo to relinquish the presidency, and the ex-president pleaded with Urcuyo by telephone. "You are ruining me," Somoza told Urcuyo. "They will deny me political asylum here if you don't do this." Urcuyo responded, "I'll never give it [the presidency] to the Communists."[35]

In the meantime, before Urcuyo had made his surprise announcement, rumors spread in Managua that Sandinista forces were advancing from all directions to take the city. After Urcuyo's statements, the Sandinistas announced that the United States had reneged on its deal and, therefore, they refused to negotiate a cease-fire with the Guard. Now they demanded the Guard's unconditional surrender. With Somoza gone, the National Guard was without a leader; it was also without ammunition as the Sandinistas advanced on Managua. The Guard's new leader asked Pezzullo if the United States was going to resupply his troops. Pezzullo said it would not. In the early morning hours of July 18, the National Guard disintegrated. As Bowdler prepared to leave Nicaragua he, quite uncharacteristically, spoke to an American journalist. "I think it would have been better if things had gone according [to the original plan]," he said. "But those plans have a way of not working out."[36]

That day the new Nicaraguan government junta made its first pronouncement, albeit from Costa Rica. Read by a Sandinista spokesman, it instructed the people of Nicaragua to remain calm and wait for instructions from their new leaders. The statement, though issued by the junta, left no doubt about who had achieved the great victory. "The Sandinist National Liberation Front has proclaimed that it is implacable in combat and generous in victory. . . . Long live the Sandinista National Liberation Front!"[37] On July 19 the Sandinista junta entered Managua and took control of the government. It was not a transition or a succession; it was the triumph of the revolution.

13

New Terms for the Alliance

On July 18 interim president Francisco Urcuyo fled Nicaragua on a plane to Guatemala, and the National Guard had disintegrated after futile attempts to arrange a cease-fire-in-place with the Sandinista forces. Hundreds of officers of the Guard commandeered planes and flew to Honduras. Thousands of other soldiers made for the Honduran border on foot, while still others took to boats and went across the Gulf of Fonseca to El Salvador. Several thousand more were trapped inside Nicaragua and either surrendered or were captured. The 40-year-old edifice of the Somoza dynasty collapsed in a day. On July 17, two armed factions struggled for power in Nicaragua; by July 19, only one remained.

———

The collapse of the National Guard had immediate and profound consequences for the arrangements of power in the new government. The Sandinistas had not expected to find themselves without an armed opponent.[1] The dissolution of the Guard removed the most important rationale for the *Terceristas'* bourgeois alliance. Assistant Secretary of State Viron Vaky had worried that a "full military victory by the FSLN could reduce the strength of moderate forces substantially," and in the first week after Somoza's fall the leaders of the Sandinista Front made clear that they considered their earlier arrangements with Robelo obsolete.[2]

In theory, at least, the government that took power on July 19 gave the moderates a significant if minority role. The new junta included Robelo and Chamorro and three Sandinistas: Daniel Ortega, Sergio Ramírez, and Moises Hassan.[3] Moderate groups were represented in all the provisional governing institutions except the army and the police. In the proposed 33-member Council of State, the business groups of COSEP, the six political parties and trade unions formerly of the FAO, and the Nicaraguan clergy were promised 14 seats, while the Sandinistas and affiliated groups were to have 19 seats. The government cabinet announced on July 19 also contained many businessmen and financial technocrats. As the Sandinistas had promised, former National Guard Colonel Bernadino Larios, who had been arrested by Somoza for allegedly plotting a coup, was named Defense Minister.

The formal arrangements in the new government, however, did not reflect the real distribution of power. Adjustments were inevitable, and the first three months saw a contest for power and preeminence between the Sandinistas and their erstwhile allies. Within a week it became clear that the government junta was at best a rubber stamp for decisions taken by the Sandinista Front's nine-man National Directorate. Robelo and Chamorro approved some of the early decrees: the imposition of an immediate state of emergency; the expropriation of land and businesses owned by the Somoza family and close associates; the nationalization of the banks, mines, and transportation system; and the abolition of the constitution, the court system, and the Congress. With their approval the government decreed the establishment of new "special public order courts," charged with handing down three- to ten-year sentences for a variety of crimes, including stiff sentences for those found to have aided "*Somocismo.*"

Many other important actions, however, were taken by the Sandinistas without approval by or even consultation with the junta's two moderates. The most dramatic sign of the government junta's near-irrelevance came on July 28, when the Sandinista Directorate held its own press conference to announce the reorganization of the Sandinista army. Neither the government's Defense Minister, Bernadino Larios, nor the two moderate junta members were present when Humberto Ortega named the new General Command of Tomás Borge, Luis Carrion Cruz, and himself. Joaquín Cuadra, leader of the *Terceristas'* Internal Front during the war, was named chief of staff. When asked by reporters why Defense Minister Larios was not present to announce the new leaders of Nicaragua's armed forces, a Sandinista leader replied "We came here to speak primarily about things that concern *us*."⁴ Three days later, Daniel Ortega declared that the Sandinistas had "borne most of the burden of the struggle against Somoza" and would continue to be "the spearhead of the revolution."⁵

Before the fall of Somoza, Vaky had speculated that most of the Sandinista leaders were more interested in power than in revolutionary ideology. But the Sandinistas quickly demonstrated that power and ideology were closely connected. Whether or not they were genuinely committed Marxist-Leninists, they found the ideological precepts of Marxism-Leninism helpful in their effort to consolidate power. If nothing else, the Sandinistas' claim to be the revolutionary "vanguard" of the people justified the accumulation and centralization of power in their hands, and the denial of power to others. The alliance between the Sandinistas and the moderates before the victory had proclaimed a single, "democratic revolution." But the Sandinistas now argued, in effect, that there had really been two revolutionary victories on July 19, 1979. One was the "bourgeois revolution" of moderates like Robelo, Chamorro, and the FAO, which aimed at replacing the Somoza dictatorship with a version of free-market capitalist democracy; the other was the Sandinista revolution, which aimed at a far more radical transformation of Nicaraguan society. With the new balance of power after July 19, the Sandinistas acted to insure the victory of their revolution over Robelo's. In their struggle with the moderates, ideology was a potent and necessary weapon. What justified the Sandinista leaders' demand for the greatest share of power in post-Somoza Nicaragua, after all, if not their unique commitment to a complete transformation of Nicaraguan society? After their triumph, therefore, they returned to the language of class war, in which the erstwhile bourgeois allies became enemies, no less odious or dangerous than the Somoza dictatorship itself. The bourgeoisie believed it had won a share of power in the revolution, but in fact "the war had been won by Sandinismo, and the people recognized above all the total victory of Sandinismo."⁶

It followed, according to this logic, that the bourgeoisie would soon try to recapture what they had lost. A "counterrevolution" was inevitable, for in Marxist it terms it was the "class interest" of the bourgeoisie to try to reverse its unexpected defeat, to seek the return of its power and wealth, and to do so with the support of its patron, the United States. The bourgeoisie's control of national financial institutions and most Nicaraguan businesses gave it the ability to pursue its "class interest" to the detriment of the people's revolution and their Sandinista vanguard. As Tomás Borge said in the first days after the Sandinistas' triumph: "where in the world did a revolution not have its counterpart, a counter-revolution?"[7]

Most foreign observers, including most American officials, assumed that by "counterrevolution" the Sandinistas meant efforts by Somoza's family, his followers, and the National Guard to regain power. The Sandinistas, however, were not yet worried about the exiled guardsmen.[8] It was, rather, the "traitorous bourgeoisie" that was now "the principal instrument of the counterrevolution."[9] Everything the Sandinistas did to enhance their own power in the first weeks and months was justified by the need to respond to this danger.

According to the doctrines propounded by the Sandinistas in the first weeks of the revolution, the way to combat this threat was to attack the bourgeoisie, isolate it from the rest of the population, take away more of its economic powers, and force it to accept the supremacy of the revolution. Sandinista leaders determined to attack the bourgeoisie's "most representative elements as soon as they give us the first opportunity. By striking political and economic blows, we will greatly reduce its power and its capacity for counterrevolutionary maneuvering."[10] At the same time, the Sandinistas would organize the people and build up the strength of the workers and peasants in whose name the Sandinista Party would rule. What was required were "economic and social transformations" which would irrevocably change "the relations of power between workers and capital." This meant not only the transfer of political and military power to the revolutionary vanguard, but also a transfer of economic power to "the people." "[O]nly a change in the relations of production . . . will really tilt, this time in depth, the balance of power between classes in favor of the oppressed." To accomplish this transformation required an all-out assault on the "traitorous bourgeoisie," on the "vestiges of *Somocismo*," and on the inchoate "counterrevolution."

One of the principal tools of the revolutionary transformation was to be the "mass organizations," associations of workers, peasants, writers, women's and student groups. The Sandinistas established the Association of Rural Workers for peasants in the countryside and began to organize the Sandinista Labor Central to unite all labor organizations in the country under one, party-directed federation. Funds and facilities for all the mass organizations were appropriated on behalf of the government by Sandinista officials, although the junta members never officially authorized them. As Robelo recalls, these decisions "were never discussed.

They just happened."[11] Among their other roles, the mass organizations were the means by which opponents of the revolution could be identified and then purged. All who joined the organizations were local defenders of the revolution; all those who did not were branded as counterrevolutionaries. In the first two weeks after the defeat of Somoza, the Sandinista Party also organized Civil Defense Committees throughout the country into one centralized bureaucracy with headquarters in Managua.[12] The committees were to be the "eyes, ears, and hands" of the revolution. A leaflet distributed by the Sandinista-created United People's Movement urged all Nicaraguans to work in the Civil Defense Committees, warning that anyone who refrained would be regarded as "opposed to the revolution" and suggesting that "Somozists" undergo a process of reeducation.[13]

The revolutionary transformations aimed also at redirecting Nicaragua away from the idea of "bourgeois democracy" toward a "popular democracy" based on what the Sandinistas called the "daily popular consultation." In practice, this meant that all important decisions would be made by the National Directorate. There was no need for formal elections. Addressing the crowds assembled at the Plaza de la Revolución in Managua on July 20, Daniel Ortega declared that the "people of Nicaragua" were already "voting at this time for the Sandinista National Liberation Front" by their very presence in the square.[14] In the middle of August, a typical "election" of local leaders was held in the town of Estelí. Ortega, speaking at a rally before the assembled townspeople, proposed five names to serve in the local junta. As one journalist reported, "All proposed members were elected by a show of hands."[15]

One of the best-publicized endeavors of the Sandinista revolution was the National Literacy Crusade, a huge, year-long effort to teach poorer Nicaraguans in the barrios and in the countryside to read and write. Modeled after a similar effort in Cuba early in Castro's revolution, the Literacy Crusade won applause and admiration from around the world. The national campaign aimed at more than just literacy, of course; it was a massive attempt at political indoctrination. As one sympathetic scholar has noted, "The crusade was always considered a political project first and an educational one second."[16] For decades the Nicaraguan people had received the kind of education that favored the Somoza dynasty. Now they needed an education that would aid in the socialist transformation of Nicaragua.

The Sandinistas' struggle for revolutionary transformation and predominance did not go unanswered by the moderates. From the first day,

Robelo worried about the course of the revolution and his own decline in power, although in public he showed his differences with his Sandinista allies in subtle ways. At rallies he shouted "Long live the Sandinista Front!" and he wore a revolutionary bandanna around his neck. But unlike the other leaders he also shouted "Long live Pedro Joaquín Chamorro!"[17] He told reporters there was "no need to be afraid. No second Cuba will take place in our country."[18]

Other moderate leaders were not so sure. At the end of July the Nicaraguan Catholic church and the business organizations represented by COSEP spoke out against the trend they were witnessing. On July 31 Archbishop Obando and six bishops issued a pastoral letter in which they urged the government to restore freedom of expression.[19] The Church leaders regretted that "after so much blood has been shed and so many sacrifices made," the Nicaraguan people were being "compelled to forget their primary respect for life and human values." The Nicaraguan people had "fears and anguish during this transition period." The pastoral letter specifically complained about the work of the Civil Defense Committees and criticized the "indoctrination process being carried out now in Nicaragua."[20]

At the beginning of September, moderate political parties began to emerge or, more accurately, to reemerge in opposition to Sandinista policies. Some factions of the Conservative Party and other moderate opposition groups of pre-revolutionary days joined together and renamed themselves the Sandinista Social Democratic Party, hoping to claim the mantle of revolution for themselves. The new party claimed the support of such international social democratic luminaries as Carlos Andrés Pérez, and it included among its members some from Robelo's organization, the Nicaraguan Democratic Movement, as well as Jaime Chamorro, brother of Pedro Joaquín. The party leaders set as their principal goal "to struggle so that Nicaragua can have a true democracy with free, just and honest elections so that the people, after this transition government, can determine at the polls the system they prefer."[21] They declared themselves a barrier against those who sought to "detour the revolution onto a totalitarian path not wanted by the majority of Nicaraguans."[22] A party spokesman was applauded at a political rally when she compared the Sandinistas to the Somozas: "There is fear among our people. And, gentlemen, it is not fear of Somozism—it is fear of Sandinism. . . . The enemies of the revolution are inside the revolution. . . . Friends, Somoza at least took two years to show his claws in 1939. But [those] who are now in possession of the weapons have not waited even 2 years."[23]

The stirrings of opposition forces only further convinced the Sandinistas of the need to consolidate economic and political power more quickly. Sandinista leaders called the new opposition parties "counterrevolutionary" and insisted that the FSLN was "not prepared to yield to anyone or to retreat a single inch."[24] Humberto Ortega warned on September 3 that the "revolution could wipe out the Nicaraguan bourgeoisie right now because it has the power and the people's support." At the end of September, the Sandinista newspapers and radio stations announced that one of the revolutionary slogans, "Implacable in combat, generous in victory," had been changed to "implacable in combat, implacable in victory." Radio Sandino announced a new nationwide effort called "Death to Somozismo" to be carried out by the Sandinista Defense Committees "for the purpose of discovering all persons who have infiltrated organizations, ministries" and other parts of the government, including the army, and "eradicating all harassment and expelling all Somozist henchmen from Sandinist organizations."[25]

The official encouragement to inform against suspected "counterrevolutionaries" had an immediate effect. At the beginning of October, the Sandinista police and army launched "Operation Sandinista Fist," arresting hundreds and perhaps thousands throughout the country. The ostensible purpose of the operation was to seize arms scattered around the country. Many Nicaraguans were arrested, and many had their houses searched after neighbors informed on them for "counterrevolutionary activities."[26] Humberto Ortega declared that

> strong measures should be adopted against the Somozist lackeys still at large, against the treacherous bourgeois reaction, against the mercenaries who obey the orders of American imperialism, and against the so-called Social Democrats, who are nothing but servants of the treacherous bourgeois reaction and the foreign bourgeois reaction of imperialism. We are also prepared to use a strong hand against the ultra-left-wing sectors who claim to be more revolutionary than the Sandinistas but who are really nothing but treacherous servants of imperialism.[27]

The "ultra Left" was a minor but vexing problem for the Sandinistas. A labor group known as the Worker's Front was resisting inclusion into the Sandinista Labor Central; an "ultra Left" newspaper, *El Pueblo*, was criticizing the Sandinistas for not moving more quickly toward socialism; and a faction of the Nicaraguan Socialist Party was challenging the Sandinistas "from below" by criticizing the alliance with the bourgeoisie, and by organizing workers and inciting them to demand higher wages. By themselves, these were minor irritants, but the danger was that the "ultra Left" challenged the Sandinistas' revolutionary legitimacy.[28] Tomás Borge's State Security officials arrested the Socialist Party leader and several leaders of the Worker's Front, raided the offices of *El Pueblo*, and threw several of its staff in jail. "Journalism has a right to be free," declared Joaquín Cuadra, the new Chief of Staff of the Sandinista army, "but it does not have the right to attack this process, even indirectly."[29]

In the crackdown against the "ultra Left" and the "treacherous bourgeoisie," the Sandinista mass organizations played a central part. In the countryside, the peasantry was exhorted to pursue its "class interest" against landowners. Members of the new Sandinista Rural Workers Association (ATC) were encouraged to report on landowners who left their fields fallow, on excessive slaughtering of livestock, and on reductions in the amount of land under cultivation. According to government decrees, failure to cultivate fields and produce at certain levels constituted "economic sabotage" and could justify state expropriation of "unused" lands. Many times, the ATC's members did not wait for the government to act against the landowner, but occupied the land themselves and then demanded that the government "intervene" and confiscate the property. A communiqué from the Conservative Democratic Party on October 19 charged the Agrarian Reform Ministry with having "tolerated, permitted and promoted the occupation of land owned by Nicaraguans which is not provided for by decrees . . . carried out on the basis of unsubstantiated denunciations, which is a violation of the rights of the legitimate owners."[30] In the Sandinistas' eyes, however, these complaints only confirmed the dangers posed by the bourgeois counterrevolution.[31]

The same pattern was repeated in the cities, where store-owners and factory-owners suffered constant work stoppages and strikes by Sandinista labor union members and also by the "ultra Left." Workers accused owners of "economic sabotage" and demanded state intervention. They demanded 100 percent wage increases. Sometimes, the Sandinista authorities brokered a deal acceptable to both sides. Sometimes, as in the case of strikes by "ultra Left" unions, they cracked down on the union. Other times, they allowed the workers to seize a factory and then expropriated it on some legal pretext. Labor troubles and state interventions happened frequently enough to owners who had in some way resisted Sandinista demands to convince many in the private sector that the Sandinistas used them as a political weapon. Sandinista leaders responded that only "Somozists" should "feel anxiety or uneasiness."[32]

In the middle of October the government declared that the State of Emergency instituted in July would continue for an indefinite period and announced that the long-delayed inauguration of the Council of State would not occur until May 4, 1980. The Sandinistas also declared that the composition of the Council would have to be changed to conform to the new realities of the revolution. The reorganization had to be "based on the reality of the nation's true political forces." "Counterrevolutionary" parties were out. The 19th of July Sandinista Youth, the Sandinista Labor Central, the Association of Rural Workers, and the Sandinista Civil Defense Committees, on the other hand, would all have significant representation in the Council because they represented "the people."[33] These announcements put an end to the opposition's hope of wielding influence in at least one branch of the government.

That blow was compounded on October 28 when Alfonso Robelo, responding to demands by businessmen and politicians for some reassurances regarding the real intentions of the government, declared that "the Sandinist government is headed toward a Nicaraguan socialism within the scheme of Sandinist ideology. . . . [A]ll production assets in Nicaragua will gradually pass from private property to collective social property." Robelo told his private sector colleagues that he could not give them, as they had requested, an absolute guarantee that Nicaragua was not heading toward communism. He could only guarantee, he said, "that I shall strive within the Sandinist Government for a socialization process in which justice, freedom, and order are respected."[34] Robelo had reached the conclusion, he said, that the old Nicaraguan structure, "where only the capitalists obtained benefits in a disproportionate manner," was immoral. Just three months earlier, Robelo had assured the private sector that the nationalizations and expropriations would end after the initial decrees. Robelo's statements at the end of October were taken by many moderates as a sign that he had completely abandoned his old allies in the private sector and thrown in his lot with the Sandinistas. Perhaps, however, Robelo was simply reporting what had become obvious to him after three months in the junta. The day after Robelo's comments, two of Nicaragua's most prominent businessmen were arrested after accusations by labor leaders that they were engaged in "dubious" business practices. The government transferred management of their firm to the Sandinista labor union.

In less than three months since the revolutionary victory, the Sandinistas had given their bourgeois opponents a lesson in what Tomás Borge liked to call "the new rules of the game." The Sandinistas did not intend to wipe the bourgeoisie out as a class. They recognized that the well-being of the Nicaraguan economy depended to some extent on production by the businessmen and landowners. But precisely because of this economic reality, the Sandinistas were determined to wrest all power from the "bourgeoisie" and to make Nicaragua's private sector as much as possible a willing servant of the new revolution. The Sandinistas' somewhat contradictory attitude toward the bourgeoisie was neatly expressed by the slogan introduced in October: "Let us increase production, let us crush counterrevolution."[35] But while depending on the bourgeoisie to produce for the revolution for the time being, the Sandinistas made clear that their ultimate goal was to do away with the bourgeoisie altogether. "We are getting ready for the people to control the nation's wealth," Jaime Wheelock declared. The goal was to "improve our work capacity so the workers can start replacing the bourgeoisie and little by little can take actual control of production."[36]

If *Tercerista* leaders Humberto and Daniel Ortega dissented from the prevailing tendencies of the young revolution, they gave no outward sign. While Borge, Wheelock, and other Sandinista leaders sundered the tactical alliances with the bourgeoisie, Humberto Ortega concerned himself chiefly with building the new Sandinista army into a powerful and disciplined force, and Daniel worked to consolidate his own position within the leadership. In the competition for position and power within the Sandinista hierarchy there was, for the moment, no virtue in moderation. Once again the Sandinistas' ideological posture, whether real of feigned, favored radicalism. Individual Sandinista leaders, even the *Terceristas*, were not about to make common cause with what Humberto Ortega called the "treacherous bourgeoisie." Humberto himself rather conspicuously cast off close allies and advisers, like Carlos Coronel, who had helped him devise and carry out the *Tercerista* strategy of bourgeois alliance.[37] As he later recalled, during the revolutionary struggle there had been "unity around the thesis of *Tercerismo*," but "after we took over, *Tercerismo* weakened. In fact, the *Terceristas* themselves became more radical." The trend toward radicalism was part of the jostling for power among the competing individuals and tendencies in the Directorate. Fidel Castro lay at the center of this power struggle. "The one who wanted to gain hegemony within the FSLN," Humberto Ortega later explained, "had to get closer to Fidel."[38]

One of the first victims of the post-revolutionary competition for power was Edén Pastora. The only man with his own army on July 19, Pastora had immediately, in an act of faith or foolishness, turned command of his fighters over to Humberto Ortega. The Ortegas had acted quickly to ensure that he did not take it back. The best-known hero of the revolution received no post in the army in the reorganization announced on July 28, but was instead appointed Deputy Interior Minister, under Borge. The Sandinistas slighted Pastora again at the beginning of August, when they awarded honorary ranks to the heroes of the revolution. All nine members of the Sandinista National Directorate received the highest rank of "Revolutionary Commander," though a number of them had done little fighting and were not even in the country in the final months. Pastora, who had led troops in the ferocious battles against Commander "Bravo" in the south, received the secondary rank of "Guerrilla Commander."[39] The break with Pastora was a clear sign of the shifts in the Sandinista movement.

It was not all cynical calculation. The revolutionaries were flushed with enthusiasm and even a measure of arrogance after their surprising victory. Humberto Ortega, no less than his colleagues, was swept away by what he later called a "youthful romanticism" about the new Nicaragua they were going to build. They felt no further need for the kinds of compromises that had been necessary to defeat Somoza. After their victory, Ortega recalls, "we radicalized our model to look more like Cuba. Whether *Terceristas* or not, we wanted to copy in a mechanical way the model that we knew—which was Cuba—and we identified ourselves with it. . . . We didn't want to follow the other models."[40]

14

The "Mask of Democracy"

Events in Nicaragua in the first months of the revolution ran counter to the hopes and expectations of senior Carter officials. Viron Vaky had hoped that by offering American friendship and economic assistance at the very beginning of the revolution, the United States could steer the Sandinistas along a moderate course. In the last days of July, therefore, the administration sent several million dollars worth of food and supplies for the Red Cross to distribute as emergency relief in Nicaragua. The administration requested that Congress reallocate an additional $8–10 million in emergency economic assistance. On July 28, eight days after the revolutionary junta took power, Ambassador Pezzullo flew into Managua on a plane loaded with medical supplies and other emergency relief from the United States.

The Carter administration's strategy toward Sandinista Nicaragua was based on its perception of the errors of past American responses to revolution in Latin America, especially in Cuba. Carter officials "tended to believe that hostile policies by the United States had been counterproductive, giving revolutionary regimes the excuse or the reason for radicalization." After failing to prevent the Sandinistas from coming to power, therefore, "the Administration wanted to avoid repeating the rest of the Cuban experience in Nicaragua."[1] The administration would seek to embrace the revolution, not isolate it; it would try to assist Sandinista

123

leaders in the task of reconstruction, not challenge them. As Cyrus Vance put it in a memorandum to President Carter, the Nicaraguan government's "future policies" were "likely to be influenced by whether the Sandinistas perceive the United States as sympathetic or hostile. . . . [O]ur ability to exert influence during this formative period is contingent on their believing that our polices are not aimed against them."[2] By denying the Sandinistas an enemy, Vance, Vaky, and other Carter officials hoped to avoid pushing them into the arms of Castro and the Soviet Union.

The central assumptions underlying Vaky's policy were that the Nicaraguan revolution had not yet embarked on an irrevocably radical course and that the United States could still influence it along a more moderate path. "The course of the Nicaraguan revolution," Vaky argued before Congress in mid-September, could be "affected in no small way by how the U.S. perceives it and relates to it." The United States might "write off" Nicaragua as "already radicalized and beyond redemption," but that would "not only be untrue at this moment, it would also surely drive the revolution into radicalization."[3] To perceive Nicaragua as radical would help make it radical; to perceive it as moderate would help make it moderate.

In any case, Carter officials argued, some Sandinistas were likely to be more radical than others:

> There were likely to be some important differences, say, between a Tomás Borge, who had been a member of the Communist Party, and the rest of the leadership, which was young, much less educated, and unlikely to have his deep doctrinal convictions. Some Sandinistas might be social democrats; others might only be superficial leftists or Marxists without being Leninists. The question was who would prevail, and whether ideology could be moderated by a tolerant U.S. policy.[4]

The notion that there were important differences between members of the Sandinista Directorate was an elusive hope of officials in the State Department, whose desire to find these moderates led them through an endlessly shifting maze. As one official at the American embassy in Managua later recalled, "Ambassador Larry Pezzullo and I were hoping that there was a moderate element that we could identify, and at various times we identified different people. Occasionally even Tomás Borge sounded like a moderate." The Sandinistas were well aware of the Americans' hopeful search, and they seemed to take turns throughout the 1980s adopting the role of "Sandinista moderate" as circumstances dictated.

Carter officials later admitted that they "were never really able to identify the moderate, or to use a better term, the pragmatic factions. . . . Frankly, we never really understood the dynamics of the leadership."[5]

Even if the Sandinistas were Communists, Carter officials argued, "perhaps it would be better to treat them like democrats, and maybe even the Sandinistas—or rather some of the key leaders—might even begin to behave like democrats." Carter officials believed that instead of trying to lift the "'mask of democracy' from the faces of the Sandinistas to show they were really Communists," it would be better to "take the mask seriously . . . and by doing so, try to graft the masks to their faces."[6] Thus Deputy Secretary of State Warren Christopher testified before Congress in September that the Nicaraguan government's "orientation" was "generally moderate and pluralistic," even though events of the previous two months suggested otherwise.[7]

Denying that the Sandinistas were Communists put off the day when President Carter could be accused of having "lost" Nicaragua. Under criticism from conservatives who accused him of actually having supported a communist takeover in Nicaragua, Carter took pains to insist that the revolution was not a victory for Castro and did not presage a Cuban-style government in Nicaragua. It was a mistake, he argued, "to assume or to claim that every time an evolutionary change takes place in the hemisphere that somehow it's a result of secret, massive Cuban intervention." Vaky's insistence that the course of the Nicaraguan revolution had yet to be determined, despite the apparently radical direction of the first days and weeks, was helpful to Carter. "I think the people of Nicaragua have got enough judgment to make their own decisions," the President declared hopefully, "and we will use our efforts in a proper fashion without interventionism to let the Nicaraguans let their voice be heard in shaping their own affairs."[8]

In fact, although Christopher publicly declared the Nicaraguan government "not Marxist or Cuban" in its orientation, most Carter officials had no "illusions about the Sandinista Directorate's preferences for Cuba and Marxism, and its visceral hatred of the United States."[9] Nor were Carter officials unaware that the Sandinistas had already embarked on a radical course immediately upon Somoza's overthrow. Within six days of the July 19 revolutionary victory, senior intelligence officials predicted that "the hard-core Marxists in the regime quickly will begin trying to neutralize the influence of the junta's more moderate members and seize control." One anonymous official told reporters that Borge's appointment as Interior Minister could be the first step in "a 'textbook example' of gaining power 'a slice at a time' by progressively maneuvering into control of key posts."[10] The elimination of Edén Pastora's power was another early blow to the Carter administration's hopes: On July 21 the American embassy had reported optimistically that Pastora's nationwide popularity and "charisma" gave him "potential to become a key actor on the new Nicaraguan stage;"[11] a week later Pastora had been effectively removed from that stage.

Equally troubling to Carter officials were the large numbers of Cuban officials who flew to Managua immediately after July 19 and began advising the Sandinistas on all aspects of their foreign and domestic policies. Vaky admitted in September that the Cuban government "certainly has the gratitude of the Sandinista leadership for the assistance provided, and considerable ties with key figures in the revolution." He insisted, however, that it was "not automatic that—whatever Havana's intentions—the interests of the Sandinistas as the Government of Nicaragua will become identical with those of Cuba."[12] Ambassador Pezzullo told congressmen that the new rulers of Nicaragua were "relatively intelligent people. They are not deluded. Castro and what he developed in Cuba is not a perfect model of anything." To which Congressman Dante Fascell, a Democrat from southern Florida, replied, "Yes, it is Mr. Ambassador. It is an excellent dictatorship."[13]

Despite their optimistic public statements, Carter officials knew that a slight modification of American policy was going to be necessary. As the weeks passed and the Sandinistas acted in ever more radical fashion, Carter officials began placing their hopes less on the "rationality" of the revolution's leaders and more on the anti-revolutionary moderates in the government and society. If the "Marxist elements" were indeed "well-positioned to exert power," Vaky now argued, at least they did not "yet dominate the situation."[14] The presence in the junta of Robelo and Chamorro, and in the economic ministries of technocrats like Arturo Cruz, gave the United States an important lever to use in shaping the future of Nicaragua. Vaky argued that "the whole economic planning sector of the Cabinet is in the hands of moderate, democratic, responsible bankers and professionals who are well known in international circles." These individuals, along with the influential private sector and the independent newspaper, *La Prensa*, all stood in the way of revolutionary radicalism. "Nicaragua's future internal policies and relationships with the outside world," Vaky argued, would be determined "by those Nicaraguans who best define and meet the country's needs during the reconstruction period."[15] The best policy for the United States, then, was to insure that the moderates in the government and in Nicaraguan society had the resources to help the nation rebuild, which in turn would help them gain influence and even a measure of control of the government. Vaky hoped that the Sandinistas would "find themselves so hemmed in that their game plan does not quite work."[16]

After initially pursuing a policy of denying the Sandinistas an enemy, therefore, the Carter administration shifted to a policy of open support for the Sandinistas' adversaries in Nicaragua. Instead of using economic assistance as a way of displaying American goodwill to the Sandinistas, the Carter administration would use it to strengthen their opponents. From a policy of accommodation, the Carter administration had moved subtly to a policy of indirect confrontation with the Sandinistas.

The increasingly anti-communist tenor of the administration's policy became even more pronounced in late September and early October. Even as Carter officials argued publicly that Nicaragua had not been "lost" to communism, they debated among themselves about how best to prevent "another Nicaragua" from occurring in neighboring El Salvador and elsewhere in Central America. Senior officials from the Defense Department and the intelligence agencies, according to reports, feared that Cuba would use the momentum of the Sandinista victory in Nicaragua "to try and breathe new vigor into the guerrilla movements stirring in El Salvador, Guatemala and Honduras."[17] In the midst of these concerns, the news exploded in Washington that a Soviet military brigade had been stationed in Cuba.

By October 1 the anxiety about communist advances in the Caribbean was enough to force the administration to address the matter publicly and to portray their policy in Nicaragua as fundamentally anti-communist. Even Secretary Vance, usually the most reluctant to sound alarms about Soviet and Cuban penetration in Central America, sought to justify aid to Nicaragua as necessary to stem the communist advance. On September 27 he declared that by "extending our friendship and economic assistance, we enhance the prospects for democracy in Nicaragua. ... We cannot guarantee that democracy will take hold there. But if we turn our backs on Nicaragua, we can almost guarantee that democracy will fail." Vance expressed concern "over Cuba's efforts to exploit for its own advantage social and political change within its neighbors," and he explicitly pointed out that Cuba's actions were "reinforced by its close military ties with the Soviet Union. The recent confirmation of the presence of a Soviet combat unit in Cuba has further heightened this concern."[18]

President Carter was even more direct in his October 1 address. He promised to respond to the Soviet presence in Cuba with increased military maneuvers in the Caribbean, increased surveillance of Cuba, and an increase in economic assistance to some countries "to alleviate the unmet economic and human needs in the Caribbean region and further to ensure the ability of troubled peoples to resist social turmoil and possible Communist domination." The President announced a series of steps designed to reassure countries in Central America and the Caribbean which, the President said, were becoming fearful "that they may come under Soviet or Cuban pressure."[19] The administration's heightened concern about communism in the Caribbean, and the political consequences of these apparent Soviet and Cuban advances, inevitably came to envelop its policy toward Nicaragua. The increase in economic assistance to the region turned out to be mostly the $75 million for Nicaragua. Of the $75 million in proposed loans and grants, 40 percent was to be provided to the Nicaraguan government, chiefly through the moderate-controlled Central Bank; 60 percent would be provided directly to the private sector for economic reconstruction.

————

The Sandinistas could not be expected to welcome the Carter administration's new, openly declared goal of "hemming in" their revolution. The Carter administration's plans to provide aid only fulfilled their expectations of American policy. As Humberto Ortega put it, "We truly believed the United States would not accept the revolution as we had designed it."[20] The aid bill, according to Sandinista theorists, was "financial pressure organized by imperialism to destabilize the social and economic foundation of the Sandinista revolution." The support the United States planned to give to "free enterprise" and the "traitorous bourgeoisie" were meant to strengthen the bourgeoisie at the expense of the revolution. In a more general sense, the Sandinistas viewed the Carter administration's goal, correctly, as one of trying to "lock our country to the international capitalist system . . . shackling our economy to all the extortionist policies of imperialism in matters of control of investments, employment, wages, exchange rate, taxation, etc., which, of course, are at odds with revolutionary policy."[21]

The Sandinistas were not oblivious to what Vaky called "practical realities." The Nicaraguan economy did need assistance from the United States and the capitalist world. At the very least they needed to renegotiate the nation's debt with international lenders. They also needed the Nicaraguan bourgeoisie, at least for the time being, to attract this outside support and to produce for the revolution. Sandinista leaders acknowledged that a period of cautious pragmatism might be necessary in the "expectation of financial aid from the Western bloc" and that, for the moment, a slower pace of revolutionary transformation might be desirable in order "to eliminate any legitimacy from imperialism's tactics of undermining our position."[22] Fidel Castro himself advised Sandinista leaders to go slowly in the revolutionary process in order not to close off the possibility of Western assistance.[23] The Sandinistas understood that Nicaragua's "private sector" was the "bait for getting foreign capital" and would have to be mollified for a time. "As for the country's political future," Tomás Borge said, "we will see."[24]

At several moments in the first year of the revolution, therefore, the Sandinista leaders made concessions toward the private sector and moderate opposition parties. These moments of tactical flexibility frequently coincided with the rhythm of the American congressional calendar. When President Carter sent the aid legislation to Congress on November 9, the two-month crackdown by the Sandinistas was replaced by a temporary effort at compromise. On November 9, Robelo announced the creation of an economic planning commission, with private-sector representatives, to devise the reconstruction plan for 1980 and to define the role of private enterprise in the revolution.[25] On November 10, the government released the "ultra Left" prisoners, the El Pueblo newsmen and the members of the Workers Front, who had been arrested a month earlier in "Operation Sandinista Fist". That same day, the government, led by Borge, met with the leaders of the Catholic church—the first meeting between the government and the Church since late July. The revolution, Borge declared, "belongs to all of us."[26] On November 14, Borge rebuked Nicaraguans who had made false accusations of "counterrevolutionary" behavior during the mass arrests in October.[27] On November 15, Borge called on all bourgeois "experts" to join the revolution.[28] On November 21, the government temporarily suspended the decree which since July had given the government legal grounds for seizures of private property.

Through deft compromise, therefore, the Sandinistas prevented in November what might have become an open rift with the moderate groups in the country, just at the time when the United States was beginning to debate the aid package. The promise of American economic assistance was enough to achieve a rescheduling of Nicaragua's foreign debt. It was the key that unlocked the banks of the world. By December 18 the Reconstruction Minister, Alfredo César, was able to announce that the major American and European banks had agreed to a two-year moratorium on debt repayment.

The period of conciliation did not last long, however. There were limits to the Sandinistas' flexibility. As much as they needed Western economic assistance, they also feared its corrosive effect on their power in Nicaragua. Ultimately, the national economy had to be made independent of the "system of extortion and subordination imposed by imperialism worldwide." This meant rejecting "the notion of reconstruction based on massive infusions of foreign capital," controlling the banking and financial systems "both by government decrees and through politically trustworthy cadres," and forbidding "foreign banks from making loans to the private sector." As Directorate member, Luis Carrion Cruz, explained, the compromise between the revolution and the bourgeoisie would "only last for a certain time; the revolutionary process will continue to press forward and deeper, and the two will eventually become incompatible."[29]

The Sandinistas had another important reason to resist Vaky's strategy. They were convinced that their future lay in a strategic partnership with the Soviet Union and Cuba. Defiance of the United States might indeed have been be foolhardy if the Nicaraguan government planned to face the superpower alone. But the Sandinistas were confident of the protection and support of the Soviet bloc. "The leadership in the Soviet Union at that moment was very supportive," Humberto Ortega recalls. "Cuba looked strong, with its forces in Africa. We thought we would have substantial support."[30] Far from being pushed into the arms of the Soviets and Cubans by American policy, as many critics of American policy later claimed, the Sandinistas actively sought to align themselves with Soviet foreign policy. They took every opportunity to show the Soviet Union where their loyalties were. They even voted to abstain on a January 1980 United Nations resolution condemning the Soviet Union's invasion of Afghanistan, even though many of the other "non-aligned" nations voted for the resolution. By March of 1980, the Sandinistas had already signed a party-to-party agreement with the Soviet Communist Party, as well as secret military protocols to begin receiving arms from the Soviet bloc. Deliveries of Soviet weapons from Cuba began almost immediately thereafter.

By the end of December 1979 the Sandinistas were back to a more radical course in their domestic policies, as well. On December 4, all the cabinet ministers were asked to submit their resignations, and the Sandinistas reshuffled the government. When the new cabinet was named on December 27, the Sandinistas had strengthened their control of the key economic positions.[31] The Defense Ministry was formally given to Humberto Ortega. Only a few of the less important ministries were retained by the moderates.[32]

Throughout January and February workers, with obvious government encouragement, continued seizing factories. On February 19, for instance, a large food-processing firm, El Caracol, was occupied by workers who charged management with "economic sabotage." The next day, the government confiscated the firm citing "proof," supplied by the workers, that the owners had ties to Somoza. Another large company, Sovipe, was taken over by workers on February 23 amid more allegations of "sabotage." According to reports by the American embassy, Sandinista officials had wanted to buy a 51 percent controlling interest in the company. They began harassing the firm by calling in all outstanding loans and taking away all government contracts. When the workers occupied the company, Sandinista officials told the managers that their financial and labor problems would not be resolved until they sold the majority share. "[I]n at least some of the cases [of company seizures]," the embassy reported, "the government appears to be using labor disputes to extend its control over selected private businesses."[33]

In mid-February, junta member Alfonso Robelo broke his silence and made the beginning of an open political challenge to the Sandinistas. In a speech to 5,000 supporters in northern Nicaragua, he urged his audience to join his party, the MDN (Nicaraguan Democratic Movement), and to struggle for a "pluralist revolution." "If you have any complaint, make it known and if you want to belong to a political organization you have the right to do so because we live in a free Nicaragua." Robelo said his party stood for "socialism with freedom," and he declared that "the Sandinist revolution has only one owner and that is the Nicaraguan people."[34]

―――――――

Faced with the Sandinistas' determined refusal to conform to American expectations, the Carter administration chose to continue putting the best face on the situation. When Sandinista leaders denounced American policy, Carter officials turned the other cheek. When the Sandinistas sent Tomás Borge to greet Ambassador Pezzullo at the Managua airport on July 28, Pezzullo commented hopefully that this was "a significant gesture by this new government. They selected the individual they knew would be the most suspect to us and had him carry the olive branch."[35] Nine days earlier Borge had stood in the Plaza de la Revolución in Managua warning of intervention by that "traditional enemy of Latin America, the United States" and declaring that "the FSLN will take up their rifles against the enemies of our people."[36] After less than three weeks in Managua, Ambassador Pezzullo told reporters that "our relations [with Nicaragua] are as cordial and as easy as I've ever witnessed with any government. There is no great policy agony on our part as far as I know, and I'm Ambassador here."[37]

Most Carter officials did not try as hard as Pezzullo to hide the direction the Sandinista revolution was taking. In February, administration officials in Washington acknowledged that "the revolution in Nicaragua could move toward an authoritarian, Cuban-style system, seeking to cope with scarcity and hardship by imposing sacrifices on the Nicaraguan people in the name of economic autarchy. This would probably mean alignment with the Cubans and Soviets, and would be likely to lead to support for radical revolutionary movements elsewhere in Central America."[38] The Sandinistas, who were the "dominant influence" in Nicaragua, clearly wanted to lead the country "toward a Marxist model, drawing heavily on the Cuban example, and on Cuban advice and support." Carter officials attributed this inclination to fear, of the private sector and of "Somoza plots for a counterrevolution," and to lingering "uncertainties" about the "'true' intentions of the United States." Under the circumstances the Sandinistas could well decide that "an authoritarian, Marxist state offers a simplistic but attractive solution."[39]

Vaky and other Carter officials insisted, nevertheless, that Nicaragua's future was not yet decided. "Many outcomes or scenarios" were "still possible within the framework of the Sandinista revolution."[40] The revolution could yet "move towards an open, pluralistic society with a mixed economy. This would imply a pragmatic international policy of normal relations with the West, to gain assistance and release the energies of the Nicaraguan people to rebuild their economy." Vaky insisted that the Nicaraguan moderates still had a "strong influence, even among the Sandinistas." Despite some "contrary trends," Nicaragua remained "surprisingly open to moderation and pragmatic considerations." Vaky admitted it was "conceivable, if you did everything right, it might still go sour,"[41] but he insisted that if the United States was "not in the ball game, if we do not try, we will almost surely see adverse developments."[42] Vaky's mild optimism was somewhat contradicted by his own actions, however, for in December 1979 Vaky resigned as Assistant Secretary of State.

15

Passing the Aid and Averting Crisis

As the Congress proceeded to debate the Carter administration's Nicaraguan aid bill at the beginning of 1980, the most compelling argument in its favor was that there was nothing to lose by trying. Opponents of the aid offered no promising alternative. Even some conservative critics agreed that if American financial assistance could "save the private sector, that is certainly worth doing."[1] The Sandinistas' January vote against condemning the Soviet invasion of Afghanistan convinced a majority of Republicans, and many Democrats, that Nicaragua was a lost cause, but enough supported the aid to pass it by five votes on February 27. Among the conservatives who supported the aid was Congressman Henry Hyde of Illinois. Hyde declared he had "no way of knowing whether or not Nicaragua is gone," but he did not want to "slam the door. . . . I want to try to put my foot in the door. . . . I want to nurture . . . [the Church, the private sector, and the press] . . . not extinguish them."[2]

The bill passed this first hurdle only after several conditions were attached, however, mostly concerning Nicaragua's foreign policy. One required the President to certify, before disbursing the aid, that Nicaragua was not supporting terrorists or terrorist acts in other countries. This amendment, sponsored by Republican Congressman C. W. Bill Young of the House Intelligence Committee, passed by an overwhelming vote of 392–3 and soon became a great problem for Carter officials. Another pro-

vision called for the termination of aid if Nicaragua allowed foreign combat troops on its soil. In the end the Carter administration also agreed to
language in the final legislation encouraging the Sandinistas to hold early
elections and to respect the political rights of their opponents, but the
President did not have to certify that such steps had been taken before releasing the aid.

The approval of aid did little to stem the Sandinistas' radical course.
After the aid bill passed at the end of February, the Sandinistas denounced all the conditions, correctly, as "a new form of intervention."[3]
Five days after the House vote, the Sandinistas took further steps to
weaken their bourgeois opponents. On March 2 and 3 the government issued two decrees aimed directly at private-sector businessmen and
landowners. One decree outlawed "decapitalization," a vague concept
that covered any expenditure of funds for purposes other than those the
Sandinistas deemed "productive."[4] The decree encouraged more worker
takeovers and government confiscations. The second decree gave legal
title to peasants who had taken over lands since the beginning of the revolution—including those lands occupied without official government
sanction.

The Sandinistas' opponents responded angrily to the new decrees. On
March 16 Alfonso Robelo finally came out in open opposition to Sandinista policies. On the second anniversary of the founding of Robelo's
Nicaraguan Democratic Movement, he told a "wildly enthusiastic" crowd
in Managua that his party stood for "ideological pluralism, effective
democracy . . . electoral freedoms, the free interchange and publication of
ideas and freedom to organize."[5] Two days after Robelo's speech, workers
took over a company owned by Robelo's uncle, charging that the ownership had ties to Somoza. The Sandinista-controlled media heavily publicized the takeover and the charges in what the American embassy reported was an effort to "smear" Robelo.[6] At the end of March, during a
visit by Venezuelan President Herrera Campíns, a truckload of Sandinista
Labor Federation members tried to break up a political rally, burning the
party's flags and tearing up its signs. Later, when President Herrera
Campíns called for "political pluralism" in Nicaragua, the Sandinistas responded with billboards proclaiming that "the people have already
voted. . . . People's power is Sandinista power." The *Washington Post* reported that, as a result of events in March, "[a] growing political polarization has come into the open" between the Sandinistas and their moderate
opposition.[7]

That confrontation erupted into crisis in the month of April. On April 11, Luis Carrion Montoya, one of the last remaining private-sector representatives with an important title in the government, resigned as Executive Director of the National Financial System. Ten days later he was replaced by a Sandinista, Alfredo César. On April 12 Manuel José Torres, one of the most prominent private-sector figures and the Minister of Agriculture between July and December 1979, had his cattle farm seized by peasants at the apparent instigation of government officials. The American embassy reported that "the invasion of the land of such an important and respected person has sent shock waves" through the town of Rivas where Torres lived. "Torres' anti-Somocista credentials," the embassy noted, "were impeccable."[8] On April 17 Radio Sandino announced that the State of Emergency would be extended for another full year. Ambassador Pezzullo interpreted the government's action as a sign that it was "clearly unwilling to expose itself to the test of a wholly free political system and prefers the advantages offered by maintaining a state of siege."[9] The public confrontation in Nicaragua, meanwhile, threatened the aid bill in Washington, where it had to clear several more hurdles before becoming law. On April 17 the House Democratic leadership withdrew the bill at the last minute from a scheduled vote, fearing that a majority was lacking.[10]

The conflict between the Sandinistas and the moderates finally exploded over the composition of the Council of State. The original plan for the Council, agreed upon before the ouster of Somoza, was to give all participants in the anti-Somoza revolution a relatively equal share of seats. Since December, however, the Sandinistas had insisted that the Council reflect the strength of their mass organizations. On April 11, in a meeting of the government junta at Violeta Chamorro's house, the Sandinista representatives presented a draft plan in which they proposed that the number of Council seats be raised from 33 to 47, of which the Sandinistas would hold a guaranteed majority.[11] Sergio Ramírez candidly explained the Sandinistas' purpose to foreign journalists: "Originally, before the revolutionary victory, the Sandinist Front, which was trying to create a broad spectrum of alliances, proposed that it hold one-third of the seats on this council. But now that it is in power it has been trying to guarantee itself a parliamentary majority." Ramírez assured his listeners that "the increase in the number of seats held by Sandinist organizations is not totalitarianism but purely a matter of parliamentary practice. It needs a majority to carry out its political plan. This is why the Sandinist Front will now hold 53 percent of the seats."[12]

On April 16 the government junta met again and voted on the Sandinista plan. With Daniel Ortega out of the country, and Robelo and Chamorro voting against the plan, the vote was a tie. However, several Sandinista *commandantes* present at the meeting cast Daniel Ortega's vote to break the tie.[13] Three days later Violeta Chamorro resigned from the junta, claiming poor health.[14] The next day *La Prensa* was shut down and occupied by its employees at the order of the Sandinista Directorate.[15] On April 21 Robelo asked Sergio Ramírez to reverse the vote to expand the Council of State, but Ramírez insisted the Directorate's decision was final. The decree giving the Sandinistas a guaranteed majority in the expanded Council was published that day. Robelo promptly resigned. He told reporters "it was becoming a situation where I was not doing anything. To continue there would just have been to lend my presence to the appearance of a pluralism that was not listening to our point of view."[16]

Robelo hoped his resignation would provoke a crisis that would "make the FSLN reflect on what it is doing. We hope they will reconsider."[17] His resignation did spur others. Arturo Cruz, who had been head of the Central Bank, also resigned, though he claimed his resignation had nothing to do with Robelo's. Seventeen members of Robelo's political party quit their positions in the government.[18] The leaders of the opposition business alliance, COSEP, also joined the attack on the government, publicly expressing indignation at "the alarming and constant deviations [from] the nation's fundamental statute and the program of the Government of National Reconstruction."[19] The American embassy reported that opposition leaders had become convinced that the Sandinistas would "change the rules of the game here as it suits their purposes" and that "cooperation with the [Sandinistas] puts [the opposition] in a no-win situation."[20]

Robelo and other opposition leaders hoped the Sandinistas would be forced to make concessions or risk losing international support. The success or failure of Robelo's strategy, therefore, depended heavily on the American reaction to the crisis. With the next vote on aid approaching, the Sandinistas were eager to satisfy the concerns of the Carter administration and the Congress. Ambassador Pezzullo warned the Sandinistas that the aid bill would be defeated unless they replaced Robelo and Chamorro with two other reputable moderates.[21] At the end of April the Sandinistas announced that they would lift the recently renewed State of

Emergency, and they promised to enact a law of rights and guarantees to protect businessmen against further seizures. Sandinista leaders freely admitted that they were pressed by the need "to renegotiate the foreign debt and wanted to avoid economic reprisals by the Carter administration or international agencies."[22] They asked COSEP leaders to present their complaints and to discuss a compromise that would allow the businessmen to take their seats in the new Council on May 4.

The COSEP leaders responded with a written set of demands that aimed at returning to the original plan of government to which the Sandinistas had agreed before the victory over Somoza: the Sandinistas would have to lift the State of Emergency, set a date for presidential elections, decree a formal separation of the Sandinista Party from the army and the government, pass laws against arbitrary confiscations of property, guarantee freedom of the press, return control of *La Prensa* to Violeta Chamorro and her Board of Directors, and provide access to television and radio for all opposition groups.[23]

The Sandinistas declared these demands unacceptable: Directorate-member Bayardo Arce vowed the Sandinistas would never give up their power, even if it meant that Nicaraguans had to eat grass.[24] The most the Sandinistas would offer was to suggest that COSEP's demands be taken up in the Council of State, after it was convened. COSEP responded that if some of their demands were not met immediately, including the restoration of the original Council of State, they would boycott the Council's inauguration.

The Carter administration's priority was passing the aid bill in Washington. In Managua, therefore, Ambassador Pezzullo's priority was ensuring that the opposition did not boycott the Council of State's first meeting on May 4. Since COSEP's hard line was an obstacle to compromise, Pezzullo urged the business leaders to soften their demands. Pezzullo also sought other ways around the obstacle. He advised the Sandinistas to open negotiations on "more than one front," with other opposition groups and private-sector leaders who were not closely associated with COSEP.[25] As talks with COSEP proceeded, the Sandinistas contacted Arturo Cruz, whom Pezzullo favored to replace Robelo or Chamorro on the junta.

Pezzullo's mediation turned the tide. When Sandinista and COSEP leaders met on May 2, the Sandinistas demanded prior assurances that the businessmen would take their seats in the Council on May 4. At first, the three COSEP representatives—Enrique Dreyfus, Reinaldo Hernandez, and Jorge Salazar—were defiant. They insisted that the Council had to be restored to its original form and that a date for elections had to be set before they would agree to participate. At one point Jorge Salazar, a powerful and popular landowner, jumped to his feet shouting, "We're tired of threats. If you're going to confiscate, do it. We're not afraid."[26] But the COSEP leaders were isolated. Before the meeting Pezzullo had urged them to abandon their plans to boycott, and in the end COSEP leaders bent to the combined pressures of the Sandinistas and the American ambassador. They agreed to take part in the Council of State's inauguration on May 4 and dropped most of their demands. In return, they won only the Sandinistas' promise to announce a date for elections sometime before July 19, the first anniversary of the revolution. As part of the deal, *La Prensa* was returned to Violeta Chamorro.[27]

The deal with the Sandinistas opened a wide rift within COSEP's ranks. José Francisco Cardenal, the president of the Chamber of Construction, was furious at what he considered the COSEP representatives' betrayal. He denounced COSEP's accommodation to the "evident, irreversible tendency of the current Nicaraguan regime toward a rigid and abusive Marxist-Leninist system."[28] His anger grew when the Sandinistas named him Vice President of the new Council of State without consulting him. On May 11 Cardenal left Nicaragua for Costa Rica; two days later he flew with his family to Miami, where he became one of the first leaders of an incipient armed counterrevolution. Pezzullo commented that "Cardenal's action represents the first major split in the organization. Cardenal is widely respected among the business members of the country for his moral uprightness, although he has a reputation for volatility."[29]

The agreement between COSEP and the Sandinistas, nevertheless, all but ended the crisis. At the May 4 inauguration of the Council of State only Robelo's MDN, the Conservative Democratic Party, and the Social Christian Party refused to take their seats. The rest of the opposition parties followed COSEP into the new assembly. Pezzullo reported to Washington that the Council was "off to a more auspicious and dignified start than seemed possible a few days ago." It remained only for the Sandinistas to name two moderates to the junta to replace Robelo and Chamorro. On May 13 the Speaker of the House, Tip O'Neill, told reporters that the House Democratic leadership would delay further action on the Nicaraguan aid bill until the two vacancies on the junta were filled by non-Sandinista moderates.[30] Six days later the Sandinistas named the two new junta members. Once again following Pezzullo's recommendation, they selected Arturo Cruz, who accepted despite his earlier resignation from the Central Bank. The Sandinistas also named Rafael Córdova Rivas, who had taken over UDEL after Pedro Joaquín Chamorro's assassination in 1978.

The American embassy reported that the "FSLN's naming of Cruz and Córdova pulled the rug out from under COSEP's feet."[31] The business leaders "sensed that Larry Pezzullo's candidates, not theirs, had been selected" for the junta.[32] And if COSEP felt like "a jilted lover," as the American embassy put it, Alfonso Robelo became an outcast. He denounced the "totalitarian" drift of the Sandinista government and the growing Cuban influence in Nicaragua, but with the naming of Cruz and Córdova Rivas, and with COSEP's participation in the Council of State, Robelo and his party grew irrelevant. He was a nuisance to the government but no longer a threat.[33] The Sandinistas emerged from their worst crisis without any diminution of their political, economic, and military control of the country.

The settlement of the May crisis eased the way for passage of the Carter administration's aid proposals in Washington. Although conservatives like Senator Jesse Helms complained that the Sandinistas had "dropped this little mask they were wearing,"[34] Senate Democrats, led by Nebraska's Edward Zorinsky, argued that the aid would put the United States government in "a strong position to compete in Nicaragua . . . against the Cubans, the Soviets, the Somoza types and anybody else who would attempt to influence the new government and direct its national character."[35] The Senate passed the bill easily, and on May 31 President Carter signed it into law. "This legislation," the President declared, "will signal to the Cubans and others who might wish to interfere in Central America that the United States intends to resist their efforts throughout the region in order to support the forces of democracy."[36]

In the House the battle to approve more aid to Nicaragua was led by Democratic Majority Leader Jim Wright.[37] In a rare, personal plea Wright implored his colleagues "to lock horns with socialism and communism in Latin America" by passing the administration's request. Wright acknowledged that he had had "more friendship for President Somoza than most of the people in our State Department," but that was now in the past. "What we have to do now is look to the present and to the future. There is a chance, maybe an outside chance, but a chance that we can win in Nicaragua."[38]

Wright and other Democrats based their optimism largely on the presence of Arturo Cruz in the new junta. The soft-spoken, gentlemanly banker traveled to Washington on June 4, at Pezzullo's suggestion, and lobbied hard and successfully with congressmen across the political spectrum. Wright was buoyed by Cruz's assurances that an "overwhelming majority of the people of Nicaragua" wanted to live in freedom and did not want to be "dominated" by Cuba and the Soviet Union. With Cruz in the junta, Democrats argued, "no one faction controls the government, nor does the FSLN directorate, nor the FSLN military forces, nor the junta, nor the Cabinet." Speaker O'Neill, in an unprecedented intervention in the debate, declared that by passing the aid the House would be "supporting Dr. Cruz and those like him who are working to promote democracy in Nicaragua."[39] On June 6, the aid passed by a large margin, 243–144.

Majority Leader Wright hoped that as the leading supporter of aid, he would be able to exercise some influence with the Sandinistas. On June 7 he flew to Nicaragua with three other southern Democrats to secure pledges from the government.[40] At the airport he jokingly asked Nicaraguans not to say, "Yankee, go home." "We came as friends and as equals, with a belief in the principle of self-determination. On behalf of President Carter and our Congress, we say sincerely that we wish to be friends and we understand that the best way to do this is by being friends."[41] Wright said he had come to Nicaragua with the hope that restoring the Nicaraguan people's dignity would not mean simultaneously depriving them of their individual rights. He called upon the Nicaraguan government to hold elections.[42]

On the surface, tensions in Nicaragua appeared to have eased. Cruz returned to Nicaragua a hero and gave interviews describing how he had helped convince the U.S. Congress to approve the aid.[43] The two political parties that had boycotted the Council of State were deliberating whether to rejoin and end their political isolation. COSEP and Jorge Salazar's organization of coffee growers, UPANIC, believed they had reached an agreement with the government at the end of May on the return of some expropriated lands.[44]

But the facade of national harmony was cracking even as Wright and his delegation arrived in Managua. On June 7, the day after the House passed its aid bill, the Sandinista leaders renewed their attacks on the bourgeois opposition. Robelo and his party had scheduled a rally in the neighborhood of Nandaime for June 8, but the Sandinistas held their own rally in the same town to preempt them. Humberto Ortega denounced the "oligarchs ... who believe they are kings just because they have money." "We will get on our knees," Ortega vowed, "only to sow the earth or to take up rifles against the reaction and in defense of the revolution." The crowd roared in unison: "People's power, people's power; we do not want Robelo on this soil; National Directorate, give us your orders!"[45] On June 10, about 80 Sandinista youths threw stones at Robelo and his supporters when they tried to open an MDN party office in Chinandega. *La Prensa* denounced what it called the "neo-Somozist mobs," or *turbas*.[46]

Wright and his fellow delegates were fully aware of the continuing confrontation between the government and its opponents whom American aid was meant to help. "[A]mid surface professions of unity and fairness," one member wrote, ". . . undercurrents of antagonism run deep, strong and dirty." Archbishop Obando told Wright that Nicaragua was "moving toward Marxism." The Church was still strong but Obando didn't know "for how long." A member of the Chamber of Commerce told the congressmen that he was "opposed to Marxism, but the Sandinistas have the guns." Congressman Bill Alexander, a southern moderate Democrat, described the Sandinistas as "highly politicized and radical," in need of an enemy, with a "tendency to suspect counter-revolution everywhere." "Their tolerance for moderate elements," he reported, was "diminishing daily." Alexander also noted reports that there were 2,000 Cubans and 200 "Russians" working in Nicaragua, many of whom were "'internal security advisors,' training the Sandinista military in the rudiments of counter-intelligence and the development of population control methods."[47]

Wright and his delegation returned to Washington for one final vote on aid to Nicaragua, the House–Senate conference report, which passed narrowly on July 2.[48] What the congressmen saw in Managua did not lessen their enthusiasm for the assistance.[49] The moderate political leaders and businessmen, besieged as they were, had implored Wright and his colleagues to speed up the delivery of aid. They continued to view the American help as their last hope, though not principally for financial reasons. One businessman told the congressmen, "If the loan is granted, it will be clear to the communists that the United States has not abandoned us."[50]

Whatever concessions Wright may have won on behalf of the opposition, however, did not prove lasting. In preparation for the first anniversary of the revolution, the Sandinistas launched "Operation July 19," a nationwide raid on suspected counterrevolutionaries "to guarantee tranquillity" during the festivities.[51] Hundreds were arrested in Managua alone.[52] On

July 19, the featured speaker at the revolutionary celebration was Fidel Castro. Because Castro had been invited, Presidents Carazo of Costa Rica and Torrijos of Panama did not come—a bad sign for Carter officials who hoped the two presidents would continue to play a moderating role in Nicaragua. The United States sent UN Ambassador Donald McHenry to lead its delegation, but McHenry and his companions walked out during the playing of the Sandinista anthem, which contained the phrase "Yankee, enemy of mankind."

Contrary to their promises to COSEP in the agreement mediated by Pezzullo, the Sandinistas failed on July 19 to name a date for elections. They assured Ambassador McHenry privately that they would eventually hold elections, but in public Sandinista leaders declared that the July 19 celebration was itself "a sort of plebiscite," in which the Nicaraguan people were already expressing their "support for the Sandinist people's revolution, support for the Sandinist Front, support for the National Reconstruction Government." Sandinista leaders said they had no interest in holding a "lottery or a raffle."[53]

Daniel Ortega complained that COSEP and the other opposition parties were "just talking about elections, elections, elections."[54] But on August 23 Sandinista leaders put an end to speculation about elections. Humberto Ortega declared that the Sandinistas intended to remain in power until at least 1985. "Democracy," Ortega announced, "does not consist merely of elections; it is something more—much more. To a revolutionary, to a Sandinist, it means the people's participation in political, economic, social and cultural affairs." The Sandinistas argued that Nicaragua's "underdevelopment and the economic, social and moral destruction in the country is so great and extended that we cannot expect the country to be rebuilt before 1985." When Humberto Ortega finished reading the proclamation, he asked, "Do we agree that they should stay until 1985?" The crowd shouted back: "Yes!" "This is democracy," Ortega declared. "This is elections. This is the popular vote. Let us raise our hands, those of us who are in agreement."[55]

Present at Ortega's speech, which was originally planned as a commemoration of the recently completed Literacy Crusade, were Costa Rica's President Carazo, Ambassador Pezzullo, and a senior AID (Agency for International Development) official, Lawrence Harrison. When President Carazo told the crowd that governments obtained legitimacy only through "open and free elections," he was greeted with chants of "We don't want elections."[56] When Ortega launched into a particularly vituperative attack on Republican presidential nominee Ronald Reagan—the "so-called Reagan, who promotes imperialism, armaments and fascism"—and on the American aid bill—"the famous $75 million that the Yankees have used to pressure us"—the U.S. officials walked out. "Harrison," writes Shirley Christian, "watching the young people in uniforms as they responded to Ortega's words, was reminded of films he had seen of Nuremberg during the 1930s."[57]

Four days after announcing the postponement of elections until 1985, the Sandinistas issued three new decrees. One prohibited all political campaigning and organizing before 1984, thus making all opposition political activities punishable under the Law on Public Order and Security. A second decree, announced by Arturo Cruz, restricted media reporting on economic shortages of "strategic" goods. All reports had to be submitted to the government for review prior to publication. The third decree placed similar restrictions on all reporting on "national security" matters. On August 28, all three laws were approved by the Council of State. Ambassador Pezzullo commented hopefully that the new laws would "be applied elastically." Pezzullo wanted to "wait to see if the atmosphere of intimidation softens, or if the FSLN leadership will use the mechanisms set in place to muzzle *La Prensa* and other critics."[58]

A strong reaction from the United States might have forced the Sandinistas to soften their intimidation, but the announcements and decrees at the end of August provoked no response from either the Carter administration or from Congressman Wright. American press coverage of the Sandinistas' new decrees was scant. Although the prohibition on political activities until 1984 and the limiting of press freedoms contradicted assurances Wright had received in Managua in June, Deputy Secretary Warren Christopher recommended disbursing the aid to Nicaragua on schedule. Although the law that passed Congress included hortatory language concerning free elections, a free press, and other guarantees of individual rights, the words expressed only the concerns of Congress and did not bind the President. The flow of aid, therefore, did not depend on the Sandinistas holding an election sooner than 1985 or on their eliminating censorship. On September 12 President Carter officially certified that the Nicaraguan government was abiding by the terms of the legislation and released the remaining aid. In the first week of September, with the Carter administration's quiet support, the Nicaraguan government completed negotiations with international banks to reschedule the national debt on "extremely favorable" terms.

With the aid issue settled in Washington, the Sandinistas did not feel the same urgency to compromise as they had in April and May. Instead, the Sandinistas became more defiant and implacable in the face of opposition complaints. On September 16 the government junta dropped all pretense and officially declared its subordination to the Sandinista National Directorate. In a communiqué signed by all five junta members, including Arturo Cruz, the government formally recognized the Sandinista Party as the vanguard of the revolution.[59]

The Sandinistas thereafter announced that all discussion of political matters was to cease. Victor Tirado, one of three *Tercerista* members on the Directorate, declared that "the top priority in this country is economic reactivation." The Sandinistas were not "willing to waste time on sterile talk about elections." At a meeting of party leaders and cadres the Sandinistas declared that the recently completed debt renegotiation had "smashed a plan by the most reactionary imperialist sectors to dominate the revolution through financial strangulation." Now the task was to continue the reconstruction of the economy, to channel investment toward productive areas, to create "labor discipline" in state-controlled sectors of the economy—that is, to discourage workers' demands for higher wages—and to institute a program of austerity, restricting the import of "luxury items," decreasing the numbers of government employees, and freezing the 1981 budget at the 1980 level. Tirado also declared that the area of "people's property" was to expand in the coming year, which meant more confiscations. The Sandinistas would "stimulate the private sector," but only for the "patriotic businessmen who are not seeking large profits."[60]

Alfonso Robelo complained that while the Sandinista government was heading "toward a completely totalitarian position," the world was paying no attention. This "second stage" of the revolution was not being watched as carefully as the struggle against Somoza.[61] Indeed on October 17, despite the acrimony in Nicaragua, American officials held a public signing ceremony with the Sandinista government to make the aid agreement official. The senior American official, Lawrence Harrison, noted that the United States had provided post-Somoza Nicaragua with $63 million in addition to the $55 million agreement signed that day.

In an attempt to spark another crisis and draw international attention, Robelo again called for a large protest rally in Nandaime, just outside Managua, to be held on November 9. As the day approached, the Sandinistas tried to dissuade Robelo, claiming that his rally violated the new prohibition on political campaigning and citing reasons of "national security." Tomás Borge would not authorize the rally because "armed activities ... planned against our revolution and our country" had been timed to coincide with the rally. According to Borge, "I told Robelo: You would have a hard time explaining why you were carrying out this activity in Nandaime while our country was being attacked. We even did them the favor of telling them this. We not only banned [the rally] but gave them an explanation."[62] When Robelo refused to yield, the Sandinistas abandoned explanations. On November 8 and 9 members of the Sandinista youth movement gathered outside MDN headquarters. The Sandinista group chanted "People's power" and "Down with the bourgeoisie;" the MDN's members shouted back insults of their own. The confrontation ended with the sacking of the MDN's offices by the Sandinista youths "under the tolerant eyes of the [Sandinista] police."[63] Throughout the confrontation the Nicaraguan press, under strict instructions from the government, kept silent about the rally and the political events surrounding its cancellation. On November 10 Robelo declared that Nicaragua had "emerged from one dictatorship and entered another."[64]

This time Robelo won the support of most of the opposition. COSEP issued a statement on November 11 declaring that "the Government of National Reconstruction is no longer pluralist or a government of national unity." While the Sandinistas had "tried to sell abroad the image of a Social Democratic Nicaragua with a mixed economy," in reality the government sector was "destined to become a state capitalism, thriving on a mechanism of confiscation and expropriation which, with apparently unlimited voraciousness, often functions on the margin of revolutionary legality."[65] The Sandinistas had become both "the executive and legislative branch" and had subordinated the judicial branch as well. Nicaragua existed in "a state of political uncertainty in which the specter of Marxist-Leninist socialism looms in the panorama of national life."[66] Radicals in the government were "laying the groundwork to establish a communist political and economic system with totalitarian state capitalism and the attendant restrictions on the citizens' freedom in Nicaragua."[67] On November 12, the four opposition parties, along with COSEP and two non-Sandinista unions, walked out of the Council of State. The boycott by 11 out of the 47 Representatives forced the Council to adjourn for lack of a quorum. *La Prensa* described the situation as a "definitive break" in the historic alliance forged between the Sandinistas and the moderates in the struggle against Somoza.

The Sandinistas responded by calling for national unity against the traitors. "What we have in Nicaragua is a people's democracy," Ramírez declared, "where power is obviously not in the hands of millionaires but where the millionaires and the rich have the right to participate in political affairs and production."[68] Moises Hassan accused opposition leaders of harboring "dangerous visions." The election of Ronald Reagan on November 4, he said, had created hopes among the opposition that the "U.S. Government will put an end to the Sandino-Communists and . . . support the Nicaraguan Democratic Movement millionaires, the slaves of Yankee imperialism." Hassan warned that "if circumstances in this country forced the hand of the Nicaraguan people and the Sandinist Front, it would be no trouble . . . to crush these enemies of the people. We can crush them in 24 hours."[69]

16

The Origins of the Counterrevolution

The Sandinistas' actions in the summer and fall of 1980 had indeed set off the first stirrings of armed counterrevolutionary activity in Nicaragua. Since July violence had been increasing in the Nicaraguan countryside, although the incidents were sporadic and could not have been perceived as an organized counterrevolution. Most of the clashes the Sandinistas blamed on armed "counterrevolutionaries" were isolated instances of banditry and cattle-rustling in the northern part of the country. Ex-National Guardsmen encamped in Honduras were making forays across the border to pilfer from unprotected farms and villages, and renegade ex-Sandinista fighters fended for themselves with weapons they had refused to give up after the revolution.

At the same time, there were scattered efforts to organize an armed counterrevolution. One group known as the Democratic Armed Force was made up chiefly of former National Guardsmen and, although very small, was causing enough trouble that the Sandinistas sent Edén Pastora with a special battalion to put it down. Another small armed group, led by Fernando "El Negro" Chamorro, operated in the south near the border with Costa Rica. Chamorro had attracted some of Pastora's followers, disillusioned by the Sandinistas' disdainful treatment of them and their leader.

A more serious anti-Sandinista movement was forming in northern

Nicaragua. In the last days of the war against Somoza, groups of pro-Sandinista fighters had formed the Anti-Somoza Popular Militias, or MIL-PAS. When the Sandinistas triumphed in 1979, however, the MILPAS held onto their weapons and kept themselves apart from the new revolutionary government. The leader of the MILPAS, Pedro Joaquín Gonzalez, known as "Dimas," was a farmer from Matagalpa who had joined the FSLN in 1972 and become a commander during seven years of combat.[1] In 1979 "Dimas" had liberated Quilali for the Sandinistas in the northern province of Nueva Segovia. The new government had named him commander of Quilali after the revolutionary victory. Like Sandino 50 years earlier, however, this conqueror of the Segovias soon grew disenchanted with his erstwhile leaders. He complained that too many positions in the new Sandinista government had been given to members of the old aristocracy, while men like himself had been consigned to the hinterlands. In early 1980, after Sandinista land policies and the government's intrusiveness had angered many landowners and peasants in the northern countryside, "Dimas" resigned his post and transformed the MILPAS into the Anti-Sandinista Popular Militias. Like Sandino, "Dimas" led a few dozen men into the mountains of Segovia and began a new rebellion. Among his followers were other former Sandinista fighters, many from Quilali and other towns in the northern provinces of Nueva Segovia, Matagalpa, and Jinotega, who defected from the army to join the new fight.[2] On July 23 "Dimas" and his men attacked the Sandinista police headquarters in Quilali, killing three Sandinistas and wounding five. Later that day they ambushed a government car on a road outside Quilali.[3]

Another group of armed peasant rebels was stirring near El Cua in Jinotega province. Encarnacion Baldivia, an illiterate shopkeeper known as "Tigrillo," had also fought with the Sandinistas against Somoza. After the revolution's triumph he had trained with the Sandinista army for a year. Then he, too, had deserted with rifles into the hills with three dozen followers.[4]

While these small groups of peasants, farmers, and former soldiers began an almost invisible rebellion in the summer of 1980, the more prosperous Nicaraguans from the Pacific Coast cities—the political elite—did not begin organizing until the fall. The northern peasants and farmers were historically jealous of their independence, as Moncada and the American marines had learned a half-century before. They were also among the first to feel the effects of the Sandinistas' new agrarian policies. For opposition political leaders and businessmen in the cities, however, the catalyst was the Sandinistas' announcement about elections and the new decrees. The failure of the Carter administration and the Congress to denounce the Sandinistas' actions helped convince many of the Sandinistas' opponents that peaceful measures of protest were no longer adequate. Any hope that the private sector could become an "equal partner" in the revolution was fanciful. Any hope that the political parties would be allowed to challenge Sandinista supremacy or shape the direction of the revolution, or that *La Prensa* and the Church would become the rallying points of a growing opposition movement, began to fade. Some in the opposition, the private sector, and the Church were now coming to believe that direct confrontation with the Sandinistas was futile, and they sought just to survive and preserve the limited political space the regime allowed. Others still planned to resist through peaceful, political means. Overall, however, the organized political parties began to decline in importance, and the struggle against the Sandinistas passed to Nicaraguans outside the political parties. Delegates to the Federation of Cattlemen's Associations, for instance, announced that they would resist the invasions of their properties and the new dictatorship "even at the cost of our own lives, if necessary."[5]

Already by the summer of 1980, a few of these Nicaraguans, both inside and outside the opposition parties, had begun to set their hopes on the nebulous forces of armed men who were gathering in exile. At the end of August, Francisco Urcuyo, the man who had succeeded Somoza as interim president for two days, announced the formation of a "government-in-exile" in Guatemala and promised to raise support for a struggle against the Sandinistas. Other plots were known to be afoot. On September 9 Lenin Cerna, the chief of the State Security Office, announced the arrest of the former Defense Minister, Bernadino Larios. Two days later the Sandinistas declared that they had uncovered a plot by Larios and others to assassinate all nine Directorate members. The plot allegedly involved a network of former Guardsmen, some based in Miami, including Colonel Enrique Bermúdez.[6] According to Borge's aides, Larios had been making contact with Bermúdez's group, the Fifteenth of September Legion, in Miami and Honduras. The Sandinistas even intimated that Larios had been meeting with officials in the American embassy, and according to Lenin Cerna, "we do have serious suspicions that CIA elements are behind this plot by Bernadino Larios and the national guardsmen who are in this country."[7]

And in fact the CIA was involved in supporting some opposition leaders and parties. At the beginning of 1980 President Carter had signed an intelligence "finding" that authorized the CIA to support "democratic elements" in Nicaragua. In practice, this support took the form of money for opposition leaders and parties to pay for organization and propaganda. The Carter administration did not approve money for armed actions, but one of the recipients of CIA funds was José Francisco Cardenal, who had begun to organize political and military groups in Miami after he resigned from the Council of State in May 1980.[8]

Whether or not there had been a plot by Larios, the links between some members of the "civic" opposition in Nicaragua and the remnants of the National Guard in Honduras, Guatemala, El Salvador, and Miami had been growing since the summer.[9] José Francisco Cardenal, who had left Nicaragua in May, had since joined a group of exiles in Miami, most of whom, according to Edgar Chamorro, were from the Conservative Party factions. In the fall of 1980 these exiles formed themselves into a political organization, the Nicaraguan Democratic Union, and concentrated their efforts on "writing letters to Congress urging them to cut off aid to the Sandinistas."[10] As the year wore on, however, and "the Sandinistas grew more repressive . . . many of us became convinced that they had to be replaced, and that only armed opposition could do it." Cardenal met with the former National Guard colonel, Enrique Bermúdez, who had begun organizing the Fifteenth of September Legion in May 1980. Cardenal and Bermúdez formed a new group called the Nicaraguan Democratic Revolutionary Alliance. This political-military alliance would later become the Nicaraguan Democratic Force, the main army of "contras" supported by the Reagan administration. In 1980, however, the nascent "contras" did little but travel around the Western Hemisphere looking for support, mostly in vain.

Others in the bourgeoisie also flirted with the idea of an armed attack against the Sandinistas. In the summer of 1980 Jorge Salazar, the president of the private coffee growers' association and a former Sandinista supporter, apparently became involved in a conspiracy to support a coup by Sandinista officers who disapproved of the direction of the revolution. Whether there ever was such a conspiracy within the Sandinista military remains unclear. Friends of Salazar had been approached by members of the Sandinista army who claimed that there was a dissident group of officers willing to overthrow the government and looking for a respected civilian leader to organize the effort and form a new government.[11] According to his cousin, Salazar first rejected the idea, but as the Sandinistas reneged on their agreements with COSEP, he began to believe that the only way to change the direction of the revolution and get the Sandinistas out was "to shoot them out." Salazar first approached Robelo, who declined to join this particular conspiracy. Salazar then sought out Leonardo Somarriba, the vice president of the Nicaraguan Chamber of Commerce, who agreed to help. Although the plan was allegedly for Sandinista officers to stage a coup, Salazar also tried to gather weapons to distribute among some of the coffee growers he represented. "The general idea was that the army people would begin the uprising, arrest as many members of the Sandinista Directorate and other FSLN leaders as possible, then seize a radio station and announce that a change of power was underway."[12]

Salazar contacted José Francisco Cardenal, Enrique Bermúdez and "anyone who wanted to fight for the liberation of Nicaragua"—but he opposed open collaboration with the ex-National Guardsmen for fear of the "political consequences."[13] Salazar instead made contact with a number of Sandinista army officers, including a man named Alvaro Baltodano, who was from one of the more respected Nicaraguan families and whom Salazar had known most of his life. Salazar became more confident of the veracity of the conspiracy.

Salazar and his colleagues apparently expected at least tacit support from the American government. According to Robert Pastor, the U.S. embassy was told in October that "a group of moderate civilians, led by Salazar, and non-Marxist Sandinistas in the Nicaraguan military were conspiring to overthrow the directorate. The Ambassador was informed; he was not asked for help."[14] In the midst of the heated contest against Ronald Reagan, Carter officials were reluctant to get involved in a plot that was unlikely to succeed, but they also worried that if the United States remained passive and a coup attempt against the Sandinistas failed, "not only would that extinguish any remaining hope for moderation, but the United States would appear once again several steps behind events, or worse, irrelevant (at a moment when the President needed desperately to look assertive)." On the other hand, if the administration supported the coup and it failed, the President would be charged with ineptness and the "strategy of trying to moderate the Sandinistas would be finished." Carter officials were divided about what to do. "Some of the suspicions that the Carter Administration had about the Directorate had been confirmed in the past year. Those who were most pessimistic and suspicious of the Sandinistas tended to be in favor of supporting a coup, and those who were less pessimistic both about what had happened in Nicaragua and what could be expected in the future were more inclined to resist the temptation."[15] Ambassador Pezzullo opposed aiding the coup in part because he believed it was a trap set by the Sandinistas. Pezzullo warned Salazar to stay away from it, and the United States took no action.

Pezzullo was right: The conspiracy was a trap, orchestrated by Borge's State Security office, probably with advice from the Cubans. Castro in the early years of the revolution had created mock conspiracies against himself to lure oppositionists, as well as disloyal aides and officers, into revealing their hostility and unreliability. On November 17, Leonardo Somarriba, Mario Hanon, the president of the National Association of Ricegrowers, and several others involved in the conspiracy were suddenly arrested by State Security officers. Borge had decided on a different fate for Salazar, however. While getting out of his car at a gas station, Salazar was ambushed by State Security agents and shot to death. The agents then planted several M-16 rifles in the trunk of Salazar's car, to prove he had been assembling an arsenal. In fact, Salazar had not yet gotten that far in his conspiracy.[16]

Salazar's assassination stunned the moderate opposition, much as Pedro Joaquín Chamorro's murder had stunned the country almost three years before. As Shirley Christian recounts the concerns of the opposition, the killing "seemed to change the rules of the game. Did it mean that in a country without the death penalty opposition was to be dealt with by assassination? Why, it was asked, had he not been arrested and tried?"[17] There could be little doubt that Salazar, who was arguably the most popular of Nicaragua's business leaders, had been chosen for assassination as a message to others like him. It was a calculated killing for calculated political purposes. As Edgar Chamorro, put it, "the assassination of Jorge Salazar . . . made it clear that the Sandinistas would not tolerate any serious political opposition."[18] One associate of Salazar's told *Washington Post* reporter Christopher Dickey that "whether Jorge was involved in a plot or not, you don't kill a guy who was unarmed. And if Jorge Salazar was involved it shows the desperation of people like him."[19] At Salazar's funeral, the crowds chanted, "Who killed Jorge? Tomás Borge."[20]

While the murder of Pedro Joaquín Chamorro had shaken the Somoza regime and begun the unraveling of the dictator's power, however, the killing of Salazar had quite the opposite effect. It helped the Sandinistas consolidate their power. The killing of Salazar not only frightened other opposition leaders, but in proving the Sandinistas' claims about the connection between the "civic" and armed opposition, it tarred the bourgeois groups with the stain of Somocista revanchism and the exiled menace of the National Guard. The opposition and business groups pressed Arturo Cruz, whom they still considered a loyal representative of their interests, to resign in protest. But Cruz resisted the pressure, saying "I have the obligation to continue to offer my contribution as member of the government of the junta, because my conscience is totally clear."[21]

The killing of Salazar also did the Sandinistas little obvious damage abroad. The *Washington Post* did not even run a story on the Salazar assassination until a week after the killing, when the Sandinistas held a press conference at which Somarriba and two others made a public confession of their conspiracy.[22] The *New York Times* noted that "Nicaragua's politics have become rougher and nastier." The *Times* did not know whether Salazar had "strayed from the path of legitimate dissent," but suggested that "Mr. Salazar's alleged conduct would certainly be understandable."[23]

The Carter administration did not publicly denounce the Sandinista government for the killing of Salazar. On November 18, the State Department spokesman said only that the United States "deeply regrets" the killing of Salazar, who had "played an active and courageous role against the Somoza regime, and [who] was working, as a prominent leader of the private business community, for a democratic political future in Nicaragua."[24] The next day, in his fifth and final speech before the OAS, President Carter mentioned Nicaragua only briefly, saying, "In Nicaragua many of us have been working together to help that country heal its wounds. It's in the interest of all who care about freedom to help the Nicaraguan people chart a pluralistic course that ends bloodshed, respects human rights, and furthers democracy."[25]

17

"It Is the Duty of Every Revolutionary to Make the Revolution"

I n Washington, the assassination of Salazar was not the only, or even the most important event shaping U.S.-Nicaraguan relations in the last three months of the Carter administration. In the United States the issue had become less the threat of communism within Nicaragua, or the well-being of the bourgeoisie, than the export of revolution from Nicaragua to El Salvador.

The legislation passed earlier in the year did not require the Carter administration to suspend aid to Nicaragua over an event like Salazar's assassination. What was binding on the President was the Young amendment, which prohibited aid for Nicaragua unless the President certified that the Nicaraguan government was not supplying arms or otherwise offering support to "terrorists" in other countries. This was the only weapon available to conservatives who wanted to stop aid, and so the battle had shifted in August from a debate over Nicaragua's internal politics to an examination of its external policies. To disburse the aid, the Carter administration had to respond to charges that the Sandinistas were indeed aiding and abetting "terrorists" in El Salvador.

The congressional battle concerned more than aid to Nicaragua, of course. With the presidential election fast approaching, Republicans were seeking ways to weaken Carter and boost Reagan. As the Iran hostage crisis dragged on, foreign policy became a bigger issue than usual in the campaign. The Republican litany of Carter's failures and "losses" included the hostages, the Iranian revolution, the Soviet invasion of Afghanistan, the shelving of SALT II, and the Panama Canal treaties. Nicaragua was a smaller political issue, but linked with El Salvador it allowed Republicans to portray President Carter as soft on communism and in retreat to the Soviet Union all around the world. For conservative Republicans, the matter of Sandinista aid to El Salvador was both a genuine concern and a useful campaign issue. If Carter admitted the Sandinistas were supplying arms to the Salvadoran guerrillas, he would be forced to abandon his entire policy toward the Sandinistas and admit the "loss" of Nicaragua. On the other hand, if he ignored the reports of Sandinista arms shipments to El Salvador and signed the certification, the Republicans would have another weapon. *Time* magazine predicted that Carter would "put off signing the bill until after the November elections. To sign it now might give the Republicans a campaign issue that the President scarcely needs."[1] But Carter did not put off the certification. According to Pastor, the "politics of the issue did not deter Carter."

In the summer of 1980 reports of Sandinista support for guerrillas in El Salvador had become widespread. A Panamanian airplane carrying weapons had crashed in El Salvador in June. The weapons were Venezuelan, but they were identified by their serial numbers as part of the arms shipment that President Pérez had provided the Sandinistas in 1978. The pilot's flight plan listed Nicaragua as one of his stops. The Sandinistas vigorously denied any involvement, but on June 22 *La Prensa* had printed a story from El Salvador of a guerrilla who declared that the Sandinistas were, indeed, supplying arms to the Salvadoran revolution.[2] The Sandinista leaders denounced *La Prensa*, called it "counterrevolutionary," accused it of "sowing distrust," and gave orders to the People's Militia to burn copies of the newspaper throughout the country.[3]

Nevertheless, the reports of the Sandinistas' support for the guerrillas were accurate.[4] At the beginning of June, the FSLN National Directorate told the Salvadorans they were willing to take on the guerrillas' cause as their own and "to contribute in material terms." They offered the guerrillas a headquarters in Managua, and the visit of the Salvadoran guerrilla delegation had ended with dinner at the home of Humberto Ortega.[5] The Sandinistas were concerned lest their role be discovered by the Carter administration. The Salvadorans sometimes complained that the Sandinista "Front was very conservative and . . . had a tendency to look down on the situation in [El Salvador] and to protect the Nicaraguan revolution." But in the summer of 1980 and throughout the next ten years, arms flowed freely from Nicaragua to El Salvador.

Carter officials may not have been aware of the first meetings and the agreement reached between the Sandinistas and their Salvadoran "cousins" in June and early July. By the end of July, however, intelligence officials in Washington had become convinced that the Nicaraguan government was directly involved in arms shipments to the guerrillas. After reviewing several months' worth of intelligence reports, CIA analysts reported to the White House that the Sandinista Directorate had officially "adopted a policy of providing assistance to Salvadoran insurgents in the form of training, transit, material, and arms." Even State Department officials, who were more reluctant to reach such conclusions about Sandinista activities, conceded that there was "a persuasive case of involvement by individual Sandinistas, including some members of the government."[6] The intelligence community's conclusions quickly leaked to the public. On August 1 the columnists Evans and Novak reported that according to U.S. officials "two convoys of ships carrying Soviet arms from Cuba" had been unloaded in Nicaragua. The weapons were part of "a growing arms cache" to be used "in the coming battle for El Salvador." Conservatives in Congress charged that for the administration to provide aid after such revelations constituted a willful violation of the law.[7]

Carter officials faced a difficult decision. Robert Pastor argued that the administration "must deliver on the $75 million if we are going to get in the game in Nicaragua and provide businessmen and 'pluralists' with the wherewithal to counter the Cubans." It was necessary, therefore, "for the President to make a certification to Congress."[8] If the CIA would not change its evaluation,[9] the Carter administration would have to interpret the demands of the legislation to meet its needs. The State Department thus took the position that although there was "a persuasive case of involvement by individual Sandinistas, including some members of the Government" in supporting violence or terrorism abroad, nevertheless there was "no *conclusive* evidence" of direct involvement by the Sandinista Directorate or the Nicaraguan government.[10] Brzezinski recommended to President Carter that he accept this interpretation and go ahead with the certification, although the National Security Adviser warned that this was "a controversial decision, which the Republicans may attack." Brzezinski argued, however, that "we are already committed to the $75 million and to the policy."[11]

On September 12 President Carter certified that "on the basis of an evaluation of the available evidence, the Government of Nicaragua 'has not cooperated with or harbors any international terrorist organization or is aiding, abetting, or supporting acts of violence or terrorism in other countries.'"[12] The certification made no mention of the fact that the CIA had come to a contrary conclusion and that only by insisting on "conclusive" evidence did the State Department justify the certification.

Conservatives were outraged and declared the President might "well be purposefully and willfully violating the law." Congressman Bill Young, sponsor of the restrictive legislation, declared that he had personally examined the "information made available to the President by our intelligence agencies, and no reasonable man, after examining that evidence, could reach the same conclusion contained in the president's certification. . . . I can tell you that the intelligence reports confirm in overwhelming detail that the Sandinista clique that rules Nicaragua is engaged in the export of violence and terrorism."[13] The administration's case was not helped when Anastasio Somoza was assassinated in Paraguay on September 17. At the beginning of October even the State Department's own counterterrorism expert believed the certification had been a mistake. While he understood "the political importance of assisting Nicaragua," he had "no doubt that the Nicaraguan Government is deeply and directly involved" in supporting violence and terrorism.[14]

Senior Carter officials were intensely worried that between the time of the certification and election day the Sandinistas would present a "smoking gun" which would leave the President in "an untenable position."[15] On September 27, therefore, the State Department sent Deputy Assistant Secretary James Cheek to Managua to warn the Sandinistas against providing arms to the Salvadoran guerrillas. In Managua, Cheek and Ambassador Pezzullo implicitly reminded the Sandinistas that President Carter had exposed himself to acute embarrassment by certifying the Sandinistas' non-involvement even though "the evidence . . . raised serious questions about Nicaragua's role in El Salvador."[16]

The Sandinistas got the message and promptly suspended the arms deliveries. On September 30 a Salvadoran guerrilla commander wrote his colleagues that, "regarding the next shipments, there are problems."[17] The Sandinista Front had decided to "suspend shipments during a period of approximately one month," from the beginning of October to the beginning of November. The Sandinistas explained that the suspension was due to the visit from Cheek on September 27. "They say that [Cheek] manifested knowledge about shipments via land through Nicaragua; in small vehicles and that we carried out attempts by sea." The Sandinistas, annoyed at the discovery of their arms supply routes, blamed the Salvadorans for "bad management" and began an investigation into the matter. The Salvadorans, for their part, were puzzled by the Sandinistas' report of their meeting with Cheek. "[I]t seems very strange to us that a gringo official would come to them to practically warn about a case such as this. If it were true that [the Americans] have detected something concrete, it is logical that they would hit us and they would arm the great propaganda machine and not that they would warn us (we are not friends.)" The Salvadoran guerrillas interpreted the Carter administration's "warning" to the Sandinistas as related to the American presidential elections. They speculated that the administration and the Sandinistas had come to "a possible understanding in order not to cause problems to Carter before November." Perhaps "a breather in the fighting must be considered in order to see how the Carter-Reagan problem is resolved."

The Sandinistas certainly hoped Carter would be reelected. In a July 19 speech, Daniel Ortega referred to Reagan as "Somoza's brother," much to the chagrin of Carter officials who believed such attacks by Ortega and Castro could only help Reagan in the election. After more than a year of criticizing the Carter administration's "imperialist" policies, Sandinista officials had begun praising Carter's efforts to "change the traditional policy toward our people."[18] Even hard-liner Bayardo Arce said, "We believe that one must learn to recognize the differences among imperialism. We cannot deny that following the revolutionary triumph there has been an official policy of the United States and especially from Carter to try to prevent [imperialist aggression against Nicaragua]. . . . [I]f Carter intends to follow a policy involving certain changes in our relations, we believe that we can consider the differences although this does not mean that we are abandoning our anti-imperialist attitude." In their effort to ease Carter's political difficulties, the Sandinistas not only suspended the arms shipments in October, but they also canceled a meeting of Central American communist groups that they had planned to host.[19]

The Sandinistas often had mixed feelings about aiding the Salvadoran guerrillas, in part because they did not want to risk American retaliation, but also because they did not believe before the middle of 1980 that the guerrillas had much chance of success. The guerrillas reported that "the Front did not have confidence in the maturity of the Salvadoran left and in the degree of true unity" among the guerrilla factions. As Castro had pressured the Sandinistas to unite and develop a coherent strategy before he would provide them with a large supply of arms, the Sandinistas presumed to make the same argument to the Salvadoran guerrillas. And just as Castro had doubted, as late as January 1979, that the Sandinistas could defeat Somoza without a protracted struggle of at least two years, so the Sandinistas often doubted that the Salvadoran guerrillas had much chance of victory in their struggle any time soon. The Sandinistas were willing to be helpful, but they asked themselves how much they should risk, at a perilous time in their own revolution, to support a rebel force in El Salvador. They could reasonably argue that as long as the revolution was strong in Nicaragua, there was always hope for El Salvador. But if the Nicaraguan revolution failed, the chances for success in El Salvador would greatly diminish.

Nevertheless, the Sandinistas did not waver in their fundamental commitment to the Salvadoran guerrillas in the last half of 1980. There were three important reasons why the Sandinistas decided the risk was worth taking. First, they honored their commitment because Cuba, the Soviet Union, and much of the socialist world, from Bulgaria to Vietnam, had by the fall of 1980 pledged some form of support to the Salvadoran guerrillas. Hundreds of tons of arms were arriving in Cuba, from where they were to be shipped to Nicaragua and then on to El Salvador. Any hesitation by the Sandinistas in shipping the arms in the last three months of 1980 for the Salvadoran guerrillas' "final offensive" would have blocked the entire arms supply effort. With the whole socialist world watching, the Sandinistas, who had twice traveled through that world looking for economic and military assistance for their own revolution, must have felt constrained to carry out their assigned role in El Salvador. "It is the duty of every revolutionary to make the revolution," Castro had proclaimed in 1962. "In America and in the world, it is known that the revolution will be victorious, but it is improper revolutionary behavior to sit at one's doorstep waiting for the corpse of imperialism to pass by."[20] The Sandinistas were probably under some pressure to carry out a more massive assistance effort than they might have liked, and at moments not always of their own choosing.

Changed circumstances in El Salvador in the second half of 1980 also shaped the Sandinistas' decision however. A "final offensive" planned by the guerrillas for the end of 1980 looked promising, and, as Humberto Ortega later recalled, "from an objective point of view . . . the region was most ripe for revolution." The Sandinistas were very enthusiastic. "We thought the FMLN [Farabundo Martí National Liberation Front] would win very quickly. They were pursuing our same insurrectional strategy, and we were confident it would work."[21] The Sandinistas hoped, as the Salvadoran guerrillas did, that the "final offensive" would succeed and that the next President of the United States, whoever he was, would be confronted by a *fait accompli* in El Salvador. Such an important strategic victory was, they believed, worth the risk.

Finally, and most importantly, the Sandinistas considered a successful revolution in El Salvador to be in their strategic interests.[22] As Arturo Cruz, Jr., who worked in the Foreign Ministry during the early years of the revolution, has argued, "According to the National Directorate, a region as small as Central America allowed for only one of two options: a revolutionary solution for the entire region . . . or the eventual defeat of Nicaragua."[23] The reactionary states on Nicaragua's borders posed a threat to the revolution by their very existence. Honduras was inevitably a haven for Nicaraguan counterrevolutionaries; right-wing forces in the governments and militaries of El Salvador and Guatemala could provide arms to rebels; and even Costa Rica posed a threat, with its reactionary newspapers and radio stations. It was a simple calculus: To the extent that Nicaragua's reactionary neighbors were strong and unthreatened by internal problems, they posed a greater threat to the Sandinista revolution. If they were preoccupied by civil conflict, or in the best case, were overthrown by Sandinista-supported leftist movements, the revolution was safer. As early as March 1979 the Sandinistas had agreed that their posture of "nonalignment" in foreign policy would be a necessary tactic "to neutralize . . . the chance of a military intervention by Yankee imperialism. . . . [However,] strategically we will strengthen an alliance with the revolutionary forces of the region and the governments of the socialist camp."[24]

As Daniel Ortega later explained, the Sandinistas considered El Salvador a northern front against the Americans. He called it "our shield." The Sandinistas hoped that if the United States was preoccupied with preventing a communist victory in El Salvador, it would devote less time and energy to undoing the communist victory in Nicaragua.

On October 25, after a one-month hiatus, the Sandinistas notified the Salvadoran guerrillas that they would resume arms shipments on a large scale beginning November 4, Election Day in the United States. Weapons were piling up in storehouses in Cuba awaiting transshipment through Nicaragua to El Salvador by air, land, and sea, and the Sandinistas were eager to carry out the deliveries as quickly as possible. As the Salvadoran guerrillas stationed in Managua noted, the Sandinistas were "in a hurry and determined.... [T]hey have been packing the bundles day and night. In fact, these people from Lago [Nicaragua] have stepped things up. It is such a hot potato for them."[25]

Some analysts of this period have argued that the Sandinistas finally decided to ship the arms to the guerr. .as only when they saw that Ronald Reagan had been elected President of the United States.[26] The Sandinistas, however, had established their plans for resuming arms shipments at least two weeks before the American election, at a time when the contest was judged too close to call, by pollsters and by Carter officials themselves. Leading American pollsters on Election Eve had declared the contest a "dead heat," and weapons from Nicaragua began pouring into El Salvador before any returns had been announced on November 4.[27] The Sandinistas certainly preferred to see Carter elected and that was why they had held up the shipments for one month. Nevertheless, their decision to resume shipping the weapons was unrelated to the American election results. As the Salvadoran guerrillas noted at the beginning of November, the "U.S. elections no longer pose any problems (the results do not matter). The comrades in the [Sandinista] Front are ready to take a firm step in an irreversible manner. Also, they are pressured by the next stronger wave already in sight, and that is the shipment that is being delayed in Esmeralda [Cuba]."[28]

The Sandinistas paid no immediate price for their resumption of arms shipments to the guerrillas in November. The Carter administration, now a lame duck, was not eager to draw attention to the Sandinistas' violation of their pledges. According to Pastor, the administration did not find "conclusive" evidence of official Sandinista involvement until January 2, 1981, when CIA aerial photography showed a large cargo plane on a small airstrip north of Managua, "just a short hop across the Gulf of Fonseca to El Salvador." Between July and December, the airfield had been converted from a small dirt strip to "a 1,200-meter graded strip with turnarounds, hard dispersal areas, and storage buildings." The CIA sent a report to the White House on January 6, combining information about the airstrip with a "vast quantity of new intelligence" collected during the previous month. Pastor recalls that it was only this January 6 report which "for the first time . . . provided conclusive proof that the Nicaraguan government was providing significant amounts of aid to the insurgency in El Salvador. Such an airstrip could not have been built or operated without a decision by the Nicaraguan Directorate or its Military Commission. The law on Nicaraguan aid did not leave the Executive Branch with any option but to terminate aid."[29]

The Carter administration sent Ambassador Pezzullo to deliver one final demarche to the Sandinistas. Pezzullo was instructed to tell them that the United States had "substantial evidence" that the Sandinistas were "cooperating in supplying weapons and providing other facilities to the guerrillas in El Salvador"; that Nicaraguan territory was "being used to channel arms clandestinely to El Salvador and that Cubans are involved; we have very precise information in this regard"; and finally that the United States regarded these actions "as the most flagrant intervention in the internal affairs of El Salvador."[30] The demarche was delivered as preparation for a cutoff of U.S. aid to Nicaragua.

The consequences of Sandinista support for the "final offensive" in El Salvador for the future of U.S.-Nicaraguan relations were enormous, perhaps greater than the Sandinistas imagined. Even as a lame-duck administration, the Carter administration could not tolerate this Sandinista behavior. In November and December El Salvador fell into acute crisis. As the guerrillas began their offensive, right-wing death squads and army officials kidnapped and killed several leading opposition politicians. On December 2, four American nuns working in El Salvador were kidnapped and killed by the same right-wing political-military forces. The Carter administration was determined both to help the government defeat the guerrilla offensive and to end the killings by right-wing forces connected to the military. Under the circumstances, evidence of Sandinista complicity in arms shipments to the guerrillas was not only unwelcome but intolerable, politically and strategically.

The Carter administration, therefore, dramatically shifted course in the last days of the term. After months of trying to understate reports of the Sandinista role in supplying arms to El Salvador, senior officials now discussed "how to use the evidence [of Sandinista support] at international forums to both condemn the Nicaraguan intervention and forge an international response." The State Department was instructed to compile all the evidence on outside support to the Salvadoran guerrillas.[31] Publicizing Nicaraguan involvement was a way for the Carter administration to strengthen its case for resuming military assistance to the Salvadoran government, which it had suspended after the murders of the nuns. The Salvadoran guerrillas launched their "final offensive" on January 10. Carter resumed the military assistance to El Salvador on January 14 and increased it three days later, citing the need to "support the Salvadoran Government in its struggle against left-wing terrorism supported covertly ... by Cuba and other Communist nations." The statement cited two reasons for releasing the funds for El Salvador: agreement by the Salvadoran government to a series of reforms requested by the Carter administration and "evidence of outside support for the guerrillas."[32]

The policy reversal by the Carter administration in its last weeks left a significant legacy for the incoming Reagan administration. On the weekend before the inauguration of President Ronald Reagan, Ambassador Pezzullo was instructed to tell the Sandinista government that American aid had been suspended, although in the United States the administration made no official announcement of its decision. The night before Reagan's inauguration, Pastor writes, "As I was cleaning out my desk, I received a draft memo from the State Department for Carter to give to Reagan the next day on whether to terminate aid to Nicaragua."[33]

The incoming administration's anti-communist zeal was well-established, its likely attitude toward Sandinista Nicaragua easy enough to predict. Nevertheless, as would become clear in the first months of the new administration, its policy toward Nicaragua was not set. One can only wonder what that policy might have been had the Sandinistas been willing or able to refrain from supporting the Salvadoran guerrillas in November and December. That they did not refrain was an act of enormous importance. If the Carter administration could not countenance the Sandinistas' involvement in El Salvador, there was little hope that the Reagan administration would be any more tolerant. Years later, Humberto Ortega recalled that the decision to arm the Salvadoran guerrillas at the end of 1980 was a critical error: "We paid a heavy price for our internationalist romanticism."[34]

Part Three

THE REAGAN REVOLUTION

18

"Ideologues" vs. "Pragmatists"

The transition from Carter to Reagan was the most dramatic changing of the guard of the Cold War era. The contrast between the man who had warned against an "inordinate fear of communism" and the old Republican anti-communist who warned against insufficient vigilance against the Soviet threat had been sharply etched in the 1980 campaign. Not since the middle years of the Truman administration had a group of men and women come to power in the United States so suspicious of Soviet intentions, so alarmed at the possibility of a shift in the world's strategic balance, and so unsure of the will of the American people to meet the challenge. If Carter officials were guided by the lessons of Vietnam and Cuba, the new Republican administration, like Truman's decades before, believed the most important lessons were learned at Munich in 1938. Reagan and his advisers saw themselves as Churchill to the Carter administration's Chamberlain.

For the new administration, the struggle against the Soviet Union and world communism required more than an arms buildup and a more assertive foreign policy, although these were essential. There was also an important battle to be fought at home. Conservatives were convinced that the corruption of America's political and intellectual elite was a deadly weakness in the global struggle. Jeane Kirkpatrick, a leading conservative commentator and President Reagan's choice for ambassador to

the United Nations, wrote in January 1981 that nothing was "as important as understanding the relationship between the recent failures of
American policy—in Latin America and elsewhere—and the philosophy
of foreign affairs that inspired and informed that policy." The philosophy
of liberal Democrats was to blame for the conviction of many Americans
that the United States was "on the wrong side of history." Its counsel of
defeat declared that, in Kirkpatrick's words, "we must try to make amends
for our deeply flawed national character by modesty and restraint in the
arenas of power and the councils of the world."[1]

The Reagan administration and its supporters drew strength and confidence, however, from the 1980 elections. For conservatives, Reagan's
overwhelming victory represented an emphatic popular rejection of the
liberal wing of the Democratic Party. This conviction was supported by
leading pollsters who wrote in 1980 that the American people felt "bullied" and "humiliated" by the Iranian ayatollah and "out-gunned by the
Russians." "Fearing that America was losing control over its foreign affairs," the pollsters argued, "voters were more than ready to exorcise the
ghost of Vietnam and replace it with a new posture of American assertiveness."[2] On January 27, at a White House ceremony for the 52 hostages released by Iran minutes after Carter left office, President Reagan appealed
to this new mood in simple terms: "We hear it said that we live in an era
of limits to our power. Well, let it also be understood, there are limits to
our patience."[3]

Yet the confidence the new administration derived from the President's
popularity was tempered by a sense of being surrounded by hostile forces,
at home as well as abroad. In the conservatives' view, against the tide of
popular support for President Reagan and the philosophy he represented
stood the liberal "elite" which, despite the shift in national mood, held
bastions of power in the Congress and in the national media. Conservatives who came to Washington to put their own philosophy in place thus
felt at once supremely confident and desperately embattled. This mixture
was to play a significant part in shaping both the Reagan administration's
policies and its rhetorical style.

The 1980 elections affected the Democratic Party in equally paradoxi-
cal and contradictory ways. The party was badly shaken by the 1980 election results, and its center was moving swiftly rightward. The party's liberal wing fared poorly in the elections. Prominent spokesmen for the "new
foreign policy" lost their seats in the Senate, and the Republicans won
control of the Senate for the first time in 25 years. Among the defeated

Democratic senators was George McGovern, the symbol of post-Vietnam liberalism and, for conservatives, of the party's descent into appeasement.[4] The liberal senator from Massachusetts, Paul Tsongas, lamented after a few weeks of the new administration that "the last election changed things. Not only did we lose Democrats and liberals, but those who are left are so weary. Everyone is running for cover from Reagan and the conservative trend."[5]

The vast majority of the young Democrats elected in 1974 survived the Reagan landslide, however. They expected to play an important role, especially on the issue of Central America, and in the early weeks of the year, liberal Democrats managed to capture control of the Foreign Affairs Subcommittee on Latin America.[6] With a conservative Republican in the White House, liberals found greater freedom to attack administration policies than they had under a president from their own party. A clash of philosophies was inevitable, and especially in those areas where the Reagan administration was most determined to reverse course and the American public least inclined to support him. Opponents of the new conservative philosophy would not take their stand against tax cuts, but they would stake out a position against a more aggressive, anti-communist policy in Central America.

Central America was an especially divisive issue in the Reagan years because it brought together two issues on which liberals and conservatives strongly differed. One issue of dispute was the size of the threat posed by the Soviet Union and communism around the world and the amount of force the United States needed to exert to meet that threat. While some Democrats believed the Reagan administration exaggerated the Soviet threat, especially in Central America, Secretary of State Alexander Haig placed the Central American conflict squarely in the context of the worldwide confrontation between the United States and the Soviet Union. It was one of the places where Western resolve would be tested in the 1980s, a "strategic chokepoint" where the Soviet Union hoped to "exploit the gap" in America's "unmanned" or "thinly held" line of defense.[7]

This disagreement over the real threat posed by the Soviet Union was related to the second major issue of dispute: The origins of the revolutionary movements in Central America. Liberal critics of the Reagan administration denied that the Soviet Union was behind the spread of communism in Central America; indeed they denied that either the Sandinistas or the Salvadoran guerrillas were Communists. The revolutions in Central America were indigenous uprisings of the people against injustice and imperialism—American imperialism. The problem in Central America, therefore, was not the Soviet Union but the United States, which was pursuing the same old, immoral policies of domination and exploitation. By supporting local governments against the revolutionaries the United States was standing in the way of popular aspirations for freedom, economic equality, and human rights.

These two views of the Central American conflict were irreconcilable, or so it seemed at first. An administration seeking deeper involvement in order to stem the Soviet advance was met by an opposition seeking less American involvement in order to end a sorry history of imperialism. Over the course of President Reagan's two terms, this fundamental clash of views continually produced political compromises that satisfied no one and an American policy that pulled in two directions at once.

Partly because of this ideological and partisan confrontation, the Central American crisis was an unwelcome distraction from the Reagan administration's broader plans in the first year. The "Reagan revolution" was to be primarily a domestic revolution of reduced taxes, reduced domestic spending, and increased defense budgets. President Reagan's manner of handling the Central American crisis in his first year in office was marked by a keen desire to submerge the issue while the major battles of the Reagan revolution were waged.

———

Indeed, American policy toward Nicaragua in the 1980s might have been very different if the Reagan administration had not been greeted in its first days with a crisis in El Salvador. Reagan officials believed the Carter administration had bungled badly in Nicaragua, but Nicaragua had been Carter's "loss." If the Salvadoran government fell, on the other hand, it would be Reagan's loss. American intelligence officials predicted that the government of El Salvador might fall by the end of the year and that the government of Guatemala could fall soon thereafter.[8] Senior officials in the new administration feared that their first year in office could be plagued by communist triumphs in Central America. From the very first days, they were preoccupied with putting out the fire in El Salvador as best they could. But they moved cautiously. In February Reagan officials acted quickly to send emergency military assistance to the Salvadoran army, but increasing only marginally the amounts already sent by the Carter administration. They also added about two dozen additional American military advisers. These steps were hardly dramatic. Less than

$100 million more in aid and another two dozen military advisers represented something less than a national mobilization for war. Yet even these minor steps immediately revealed the extent to which Central America was to become the main battleground of the political and ideological war of the 1980s.

The strong statements by Secretary of State Alexander Haig, along with the administration's actions, met with varied responses that exposed the divisions in Congress and within the Democratic Party. The House majority leader, James Wright, declared that Central America was "probably more vitally important to us than any other part of the world" and said he fully expected the President to receive bipartisan support for his policies.[9] Within days, however, House Appropriations Subcommittee chairman, Clarence Long, asked whether the Reagan administration's policies were not "creating a situation in which we may be doing what we did in Vietnam, saying, 'Move over boys. We're going to fight this war'?" Walter Cronkite began his first interview with the President by asking, "Do you see any parallel in our committing advisers and military assistance to El Salvador and the early stages of our involvement in Vietnam?" At his first news conference, the first question Reagan had to answer was "how do you intend to avoid having El Salvador turn into a Vietnam for this country?"

Reagan, who had eluded Democratic efforts to paint him as a war candidate in the campaign, now had to do so again in the very first weeks of his presidency. He denied any parallel between El Salvador and Vietnam and disavowed any intention of sending American troops to fight anywhere, but he was exasperated by the questioning. After all, he complained to reporters, "I didn't start the El Salvador thing. I inherited it. And the previous administration, which probably was as vociferous as anyone in talking about my threat to peace, they were doing what we're doing, sending aid to El Salvador." As for charges that he was leading the nation to war in Central America, Reagan joked, "I've been here more than 6 weeks now and haven't fired a shot."

White House polls showed, however, that the discussion of El Salvador was making many Americans nervous about the prospects for war. Reagan's closest political advisers, eager to make the most of the President's honeymoon to enact the important legislation concerning the economy, urged the President and his foreign policy advisers to avoid these heated exchanges with their ideological adversaries. The early clash over El Salvador thus quickly revealed a schism in the Reagan administration to match that in the Democratic Party.

What later became known as the battle between the "ideologues" and the "pragmatists" in the administration, did not, as in the Democratic Party, derive from fundamental differences over the goals of foreign policy. The two factions consisted, on the one hand, of senior White House officials James Baker and Michael Deaver, and the President's wife, Nancy Reagan, and on the other hand, the President's senior foreign policy advisers, CIA Director William Casey, Secretary of Defense Caspar Weinberger, Deputy Secretary of State and then National Security Adviser, William Clark, United Nations Ambassador Jeane Kirkpatrick, and, on issues like Central America, Secretary Haig. The principal difference between the factions was over the question of how, when, and on what issues to use President Reagan's political power. The latter group favored ideological confrontation with the liberal Democrats, in which the personal appeal of the President could be summoned to winning the domestic battle for the American soul as well as the strategic battle against the Soviet Union. They tended to oppose compromise with the Democrats in Congress and sought mainly to exploit the acute Democratic vulnerability on the issue of communism.

Baker, Deaver, and other White House political advisers, on the contrary, feared the erosion of the President's political strength that could result from this constant confrontation. They did not disagree with the general conservative view of the Soviet Union and communism. As a matter of political tactics, however, they favored compromise and bargaining with House Democrats, limiting the areas of confrontation to those few important, and chiefly domestic, issues that usually made the difference between successful and unsuccessful presidencies.

The President himself acted from the beginning of his term as the embodiment of compromise between these two often incompatible views. At times confronting his political adversaries in the most aggressive manner, at times submerging the differences between himself and his ideological opponents, Reagan was both pragmatic politician and hidebound ideologue. Nowhere did this compromise seem more impossible to achieve than in Central America. While Reagan's political advisers did not want to engage in a debilitating public controversy, Haig and most conservatives believed it was precisely the place to draw the line, against the Soviet Union and its proxy, against the post-Vietnam liberalism that sapped the nation's strength, and against the Democrats in Congress. Reagan went back and forth between the two.

Although the immediate crisis the administration had to confront in

Central America was in El Salvador, officials in the State Department and other agencies believed the origins of this crisis lay in Nicaragua and Cuba. While both politics and practical necessity forced the administration to address El Salvador first, privately the administration debated what to do next about Castro and the Sandinistas. Here, too, the inner discussions of the Reagan administration were heavily influenced by the larger ideological conflict some wanted to wage and others wished to avoid.

Previous administrations, from Eisenhower and Kennedy to Johnson and Nixon, facing less troublesome situations and less defiant governments in Latin America, had consistently responded by using American power in a variety of forms. Rather than allow victories by radical forces, each of these presidents supported coups (Guatemala, 1954), insurgencies (Cuba, 1961), invasions (the Dominican Republic, 1965) and covert political programs (Chile, 1973). The first decision the Reagan administration faced was trivial by comparison: whether or not to resume economic aid to Nicaragua that had been suspended by the Carter administration. On January 23 the *New York Times* reported the suspension of economic aid, which the Carter administration had never made public. The State Department declared that the new administration would conduct its own review of the evidence of Sandinista misbehavior before making any decision and claimed to have reached "no conclusion yet about the evidence that we have."[10]

The idea of a "review" by the new administration was ludicrous. On January 29 the outgoing Secretary of State of the Carter administration, Edmund Muskie, told the *Washington Post* that there was "no question" that Nicaragua had shipped arms from Cuba to El Salvador and that this had happened with the knowledge "and to some extent the help" of officials in the Nicaraguan government.[11] In Managua, Ambassador Pezzullo told Sandinista leaders, "you people are just irresponsible. We've got you red-handed."[12] The State Department's review was only a means of gaining time while Secretary Haig and other officials decided what to do in Central America. At the beginning of February, Ambassador Pezzullo returned to Washington to consult with the new Secretary of State.

Pezzullo was one of the few senior officials to survive the transition from Carter to Reagan, but he had not changed his views of the correct policy in Nicaragua. He advised Haig to delay any decision on aid to Nicaragua and to give the Sandinistas another chance to end their support for the Salvadoran guerrillas. Cutting off American economic assistance,

Pezzullo argued, could only hurt the chances of reaching some agreement with the Sandinistas. Haig surprised everyone by agreeing. When Ambassador Pezzullo repeated his recommendation to Reagan, the President also agreed. Reagan even recalled what he said a Mexican friend had told him: "Don't make the mistake of Americanizing the Central American problem."[13]

Haig's agreement to let Pezzullo talk to the Sandinistas again did not reflect any optimism about the results of such discussions, however, much less any intention to renew economic aid to Nicaragua. The Secretary of State considered Nicaragua a distraction from the real problem in the Western Hemisphere. Haig wanted to "go to the source" of the problem, which was Castro's Cuba. Cuba, not Nicaragua, "was at once the source of supply and the catechist of the Salvadoran insurgency." Nicaragua was just a transshipment point, a cog in the machine run by Havana and Moscow. The way to prevent further aid to guerrillas in Central America was not to harass Nicaragua, but to "carry the consequences of this relationship directly to Moscow and Havana, and through the application of a full range of economic, political, and security measures, convince them to put an end to Havana's bloody activities in the hemisphere." What Haig feared most was a policy of "incrementalism." Trying to approach the problems of El Salvador and Nicaragua without addressing the role of Cuba was folly. Haig had learned lessons of his own in Vietnam. "To start small, to show hesitation, was to Vietnamize the situation. To localize our response was to Vietnamize the situation. Such a policy, in my view, could only lead us into the old trap of committing ever larger resources to a small objective."[14]

Immediately upon taking over as Secretary of State at the end of January, Haig had instructed Robert McFarlane, then State Department Counselor, to develop a plan for isolating and then rolling back Marxist control of Cuba.[15] Haig's view, according to McFarlane, was that during the President's political honeymoon, he should use his great popularity to push forward a tough policy in the Western Hemisphere, where the most immediate problems required the most difficult and most politically unpopular actions. McFarlane had assembled a group of officials from the Pentagon, the CIA, and the State Department to make a set of recommendations that Haig could bring to the President for approval.

After several meetings, however, the group decided, without dissent, that Haig's plans were unwise. Isolating, rolling back, or overthrowing Castro, the group decided, would require substantial military efforts that the American people would not support. In addition, military officials feared the use of so many ships and troops to accomplish this mission in the Caribbean would detract from American forces elsewhere, opening up areas of weakness that the Soviet Union could exploit. What if Brezhnev takes Berlin, McFarlane recalls one official asking.[16] Instead of focusing on Castro and Cuba, McFarlane's group recommended the United States build its strategy on two pillars: isolating Nicaragua and stimulating the economic development of the surrounding countries in Central America.

Haig was unhappy with McFarlane's recommendations. He wanted to propose to the President a plan for "noticeably higher levels of U.S. aid, the introduction of reasonable numbers of military advisers, and most important, an augmented U.S. military presence in the region . . . a carrier group, or two, maneuvering between Cuba and the Central American mainland" that would serve as "a useful reminder of the revival of keen U.S. interest in these waters and coasts and of our ability to blockade Cuba if that became necessary." "Direct military action was neither required nor justified," Haig writes in his memoirs, "and . . . I never contemplated it." He believed that stationing American warships in the Caribbean would alone cow Castro into ending his support for revolutions in Central America, since it was "obvious that Cuba . . . simply could not stand up to the geostrategic assets available to the larger country."[17] McFarlane drew up the plans as Haig requested, and they called, among other things, for the stationing of American vessels in a position to cut off Cuban supplies of oil and block both the import and export of weapons.[18]

When Haig brought these plans to the White House in March, however, he met a wall of disapproval. Haig recalls that "very nearly the first words spoken on this subject in the councils of the Reagan Administration made reference to the danger of 'another Vietnam.'" For the White House political advisers, "another Vietnam" meant engaging in an unpopular military action that would soon make for an unpopular and ineffective president.[19]

The Secretary of Defense also raised objections. Haig recalls that Weinberger "genuinely feared the creation of another unmanageable tropical war into which American troops and American money would be poured with no result different from Vietnam. . . . In the [National Security Council] and in private meetings with me over breakfast, Cap Weinberger insistently raised the spectre of Vietnam and worried over the possibility that the President would be drawn into 'involuntary escalation.'"[20] The Joint Chiefs of Staff expressed their concern that the Soviet Union might respond to any blockade of Cuba by attacking an American ally somewhere else in the world. The United States would not be able to respond adequately, they argued, if its forces were engaged in the Caribbean.[21]

Secretary Haig's influence on the subject of Central America waned rapidly after March. The attempted assassination of the President on April 1 not only delayed any further consideration of Central America and other matters, but it provided the occasion for one of Secretary Haig's more notable political calamities (when he told reporters at the White House that he was "in charge.")[22] After April Haig turned his attentions elsewhere.[23] Later in the year, Haig again set forth his plan to "go to the source," and once again it languished without support from the President or the rest of the cabinet.

With the rejection of Haig's policy, however, the administration found itself with no policy at all. McFarlane later lamented that in its first two years, the administration never collected itself to form a comprehensive strategy for Nicaragua and the region, but simply approached it crisis by crisis. The Reagan administration's failure to settle on a policy, however, was understandable. The extended debates over Haig's proposals revealed just how limited the administration's capacities were in confronting the problems in Central America. All the choices were politically and, in the view of some, even strategically unattractive.

Meanwhile, Ambassador Pezzullo was trying to convince the Sandinistas to stop arming the Salvadoran guerrillas. When Pezzullo returned to Managua in the second week of February, he told the Sandinista leaders the United States had evidence that they were continuing to supply the Salvadoran guerrillas, despite their past promises to stop. He revealed that the United States knew about the airstrip in the north of Nicaragua that was being used for arms shipments to El Salvador. Pezzullo explained that promises were no longer enough. The Sandinistas had to prove their good intentions by taking visible steps, like ending the use of the airstrip and Sandino airport for shipments to El Salvador and by closing down the Salvadoran guerrilla headquarters in Managua. In return, he said, the United States would offer Nicaragua "a way out" of the impending confrontation and would consider establishing normal ties, including eventually the resumption of aid.[24] The Sandinistas received the same advice from Democrats in Congress. On March 13 Congressman David Bonior traveled to Nicaragua and "implor[ed]" Sergio Ramírez to "do what he could to stop the arms flow to El Salvador through the Honduras borders and through Nicaragua."[25]

Without quite admitting to their past involvement, the Sandinistas told Pezzullo they did not want to "risk our revolution for an uncertain victory in El Salvador," and Daniel Ortega said he understood that the credibility of the Nicaraguan government was at stake.[26] Sandinista leaders admitted they had been "very permissive" in allowing the FMLN to use Nicaragua as a base of operations, but insisted they had now made a firm decision to prevent the transfer of arms to El Salvador through Nicaraguan territory. They told reporters that "Washington's message has been received loud and clear," and they understood "the very high cost to Nicaragua of involvement in El Salvador."[27]

Despite their assurances to Pezzullo, however, the Sandinistas did not end all aid to the guerrillas. In the spring of 1981 the Cubans and Sandinistas shared the view of American intelligence officials that a guerrilla victory in El Salvador might be close at hand. The Sandinistas stopped using the airport at Papalonal but diverted the arms shipments overland by truck and across the Gulf of Fonseca by boat.[28] American intelligence officials were also aware that large stocks of weapons were still in Cuba awaiting shipment to Nicaragua and then El Salvador. The military headquarters of the Salvadoran guerrillas remained on Nicaraguan soil.

On April 1 the Reagan administration finally announced it was suspending aid to Nicaragua indefinitely. The decision was made by Thomas Enders, just then taking over as the new Assistant Secretary of State for Latin America, and it represented less a careful judgment of the costs and benefits of providing aid to Sandinista Nicaragua than the first effort by the new Assistant Secretary to take control of a policy that had had no direction for three months. Assistant Secretary Enders asserted that intelligence reports showed unmistakably that the Sandinistas had resumed arms shipments after a brief halt in February. Ambassador Pezzullo believed, on the contrary, that his diplomatic efforts had succeeded in reducing the arms flow to a trickle, and he was furious at the decision.[29] But Enders's assessment proved more accurate. The decline in arms shipments to the guerrillas was temporary and reflected no shift in policy by the Sandinistas. The reduced flow of weapons lasted only until July, when the next large shipment of arms from overseas replenished the Sandinistas' stocks. Pezzullo's arguments were, in any case, irrelevant to the Reagan administration's calculations. As Haig declared in his memoirs, from the very beginning he had little intention of renewing aid to a "government that was working so assiduously against American interests."[30]

19

"Alien Cadres, Alien Models, and Alien Ideas"

The Sandinistas roundly denounced the April 1 decision, calling it an act of aggression and a human rights violation, and in the years that followed, critics of the Reagan administration would argue that the suspension of aid ended hopes of a diplomatic rapprochement and drove the Sandinistas to take more radical actions at home and abroad. The Sandinistas, however, had chosen their course before President Reagan was even inaugurated. Starting weeks before Ronald Reagan took the oath of office, the Sandinistas had begun warning of an imminent American invasion, a counterrevolutionary uprising, or an economic blockade—or all three at once. The suspension of aid by the Reagan administration in April was not a turning point but a way-station on a journey already underway.

The Sandinistas' alarmist warnings in 1981 had their roots in domestic rather than foreign concerns. As Ambassador Pezzullo reported at the end of January in a cable entitled "FSLN Stirs War Psychosis," the Sandinistas had launched a "major propaganda barrage" which had "hit new, shrill tones" long before Reagan officials had made any decisions about aiding Nicaragua. Pezzullo attributed the campaign primarily to fears of domestic unrest and opposition, to concern about the "difficult economic conditions ahead and the FSLN's urgent need to lay blame for failures to some non-Sandinista force."[1]

With the excuse of preparing for imminent invasion, the Sandinistas hoped to consolidate their power and weaken their increasingly numerous enemies. The central part of the propaganda barrage was a call to all Nicaraguans to join the Sandinista Popular Militias. The main purpose of the militias was to incorporate more and more Nicaraguans into a Sandinista-controlled organization, to give them a stake and a means of participation in the revolution, and to isolate the revolution's opponents. "If we had gained power having won elections," Sergio Ramírez explained, "perhaps we would not have had to concern ourselves so much with defense. But we are experiencing a revolutionary process which stemmed from armed struggle and we are altering the face of the country. There are enemies of this process both at home and abroad. In order to advance the revolution it is necessary to defend it. Well, the foundation of our defense is the people's militia."[2]

In their search for justifications for this massive recruitment of citizens into the militia, the Sandinistas could not yet claim that armed counter-revolutionary activities on the Honduran border posed a threat. As late as February 1981, Alan Riding wrote that there had been "surprisingly little" armed activity anywhere in Nicaragua.[3] The Sandinista Army Chief of Staff Joaquín Cuadra called the small bands of fighters in the north "mosquitoes." Ambassador Pezzullo speculated that "as popular discontent" continued to grow, the Sandinistas would have a "difficult time whipping up genuine war hysteria in the absence of concrete threats to the country."[4] The Sandinistas had to justify the mass recruitment into the militias by the threat of an American invasion, even though the militias would be ineffective in preventing or repelling such an attack if it ever came.

The militias were but one response to the growing political difficulties the Sandinistas faced in 1981. After the Sandinistas' postponement of elections until 1985 and then the assassination of Jorge Salazar, the Sandinistas and their increasingly outspoken opposition stood in angry confrontation. The opposition political parties, business groups, and labor unions had been boycotting the Council of State since the fall of 1980. The Sandinistas permitted some open dissent, and protests rang on the pages of *La Prensa* and on opposition radio stations. Political and business leaders did their best to discredit Sandinista rule in the eyes of both their fellow Nicaraguans and the world, hoping to force the government to come to terms or face international isolation and economic ruin. Businessmen insisted that without help from the private sector, the economy could not produce enough for genuine recovery. But they insisted that the private sector would not and could not invest and produce so long as the Sandinista government promoted "class hatred," repression, and violence by the workers against managers and owners. As Sandinista leaders conceived it, the opposition leaders were engaged in simple blackmail, threatening economic disaster if their political demands were not met.[5]

To confront this political challenge, the Sandinistas linked the complaints of the bourgeoisie with the alleged foreign aggression, thus asserting the government's right to suppress opponents in the name of national defense. "We will simply put an end to this project," Bayardo Arce warned on January 23 when news of the Carter administration's aid suspension appeared in the *New York Times*. He was referring to the "project" of a mixed economy and political pluralism. "Just imagine our situation if we were short of foreign currency. . . . Can we allow reactionary groups to continue saying and doing what they and the businessmen want, robbing and exploiting at will?"[6] The Sandinistas hoped to silence the complaints of the bourgeoisie by drowning them in appeals for national unity in the face of the foreign danger. "Imperialism," Tomás Borge asserted on January 1, 1981, "is the godfather of all the reactionary and counterrevolutionary attempts that might take place in this country." "Our people," he declared, "must prepare for combat."[7] But combat against whom? It was not so much in the northern countryside that the Sandinistas began cracking down in early 1981, but in Managua. In February, for instance, the head of an independent human rights group was arrested after accusing the government of engaging in the systematic torture of political prisoners, as well as other repressive actions.[8] The government also arrested one COSEP official, harassed opposition political parties with verbal and physical threats, and warned *La Prensa*, whose barrage of criticism was unceasing, that "the cup of our patience runneth over."

Clashes with opponents took violent form only on the Atlantic Coast, where traditionally independent Indian, black, and Creole populations resented and resisted encroachment by the Managua government. On February 19 the Sandinistas arrested the Miskito delegate to the Council of State, Steadman Fagoth, on charges of having collaborated with Somoza's security forces before the revolution.[9] An American embassy officer who toured the Atlantic Coast at the end of February reported a "very high level of tension and animosity among the black and Indian population against the [government] and the Sandinistas."[10] On February 24, a shooting incident in the village of Prinzapolka left several local residents dead, and rumors circulated that the much-resented Cuban advisers had given Sandinista troops the orders to fire. The American embassy reported that the Sandinistas appeared "to be moving down a path toward arousing the lasting antipathy of the Indian as well as black communities of the region."[11]

Within the government itself, changes in the political leadership showed the accelerating trend toward radicalism. On March 4, still a month before the Reagan administration's decision to suspend aid, the Sandinistas announced another reorganization of the government junta. Arturo Cruz and Moises Hassan were dropped, leaving Sergio Ramírez, Rafael Córdova Rivas and Daniel Ortega, whose new title became coordinator of the junta. Cruz was named ambassador to Washington and Hassan was given a post in the newly created Government Council, but the reorganization only barely disguised the fact that Cruz, at least, had resigned in protest.[12] Cruz's opposition to the direction of the Sandinista government had been an open secret for months. While Cruz had tried to defend the Sandinistas throughout much of 1980, after the murder of Salazar he had begun to challenge them. On January 26 Cruz had warned that "those who commit undemocratic abuses do not realize the damage they do to the revolution by trying to revive the medieval inquisition." At a rally of his own political party, Cruz gave approval to "civic actions guaranteed by the fundamental statute of rights and guarantees" of the original government program, knowing full well that these same activities were denounced as "counterrevolutionary" by the Sandinistas.[13] Opposition party and business leaders had come to consider Cruz their only friend in the junta, but Cruz was already looking for a way out of the government.[14] Upon accepting his new assignment in Washington, Cruz pledged his "absolute faith" in the revolution, but everyone knew that the "revolution" to which he pledged himself was not the revolution under way in Nicaragua.[15]

The reorganization of the junta in March was followed by more violent confrontations with the opposition. During the week of March 11, Alfonso Robelo challenged the government by scheduling yet another rally at Nandaime. This time Borge granted a permit, but days before the rally the MDN's headquarters were attacked, and crowds of pro-government demonstrators assembled in Nandaime to oppose the rally. Leticia Herrera, the national coordinator of the Sandinista Defense Committees and thus a subordinate of Borge, denounced Robelo and called on the Sandinista faithful to "repudiate" the rally. The next day, March 15, violent demonstrations erupted against opposition institutions throughout Nicaragua. According to Robelo, "mobs led by Sandinista Front members blocked all the roads in Nicaragua, set fire to houses in Nandaime, overturned cars and in Managua completely destroyed two radio stations . . . and partially destroyed [another.]"[16]

Other reports described the burning of MDN headquarters in Chinandega, the burning of cars in front of an opposition union headquarters, and the kidnapping by armed civilians of an MDN official.[17] The American embassy reported that Sandinista "militiamen out of uniform led and filled out the crowds." Observers of the demonstrations, according to the embassy, could not believe that "the violence and blocking of Nandaime [were] spontaneous." Sandinista leaders were openly "euphoric at the 'popular' repudiation of the MDN which they interpret[ed] in their media as a Sandinista 'victory.'"[18] Robelo called March 15 a "night of terror."[19] Fearing for the safety of his party members, he canceled the Nandaime rally. He warned that "we Nicaraguans are increasingly losing hope of a civic struggle." *La Prensa* did not circulate that day or the next because Borge warned the publishers that he could not guarantee the newspaper's safety against the mobs.[20]

At the end of March, the Reagan administration announced its decision to suspend economic assistance to Nicaragua. Oddly enough, the Reagan administration gave little sign that its decision had anything to do with events in Nicaragua.[21] The State Department spokesman did not remark on the violence of March 15, nor on the "reorganization" of the junta which dropped Arturo Cruz, the last remaining moderate representative. Asked by reporters on March 19 whether any developments in previous weeks indicated that the Marxists might be extending their control further in Nicaragua, the State Department spokesman said nothing had occurred to change the situation, so far as he knew.[22] If Nicaraguans understood anything about what the United States was up to, therefore, they had reason to believe the Reagan administration cared more about Sandinista support for the guerrilla war in El Salvador than about the well-being of political opponents in Nicaragua.

The suspension of American aid had no noticeable impact on the trend of events in Nicaragua. Private-sector leaders took a "generally relaxed view" of the aid decision, according to the American embassy, and did not regard it "as threatening to them directly."[23] The Sandinistas continued along their previous path. On May 2 they decreed another reorganization of the Council of State, expanding its membership to 51 and giving Sandinista-affiliated parties and organizations an even larger majority of more than 40.[24] On May 22, the main opposition radio station, Radio Corporación, was shut down for 48 hours by the government for reporting on new confrontations between the Sandinistas and Miskito Indians on the Atlantic Coast.[25] When Archbishop Obando, after a meeting with the Pope in Rome, publicly accused the regime of moving toward Marxism, Nicaraguan state television promptly pulled the archbishop's Sunday mass off the air for the first time in eight years and replaced it with a mass led by a priest sympathetic to the revolution.[26] On July 10 the government shut down *La Prensa* for two days "for failing to tell the truth" about Sandinista relations with the Catholic church.

On July 19 Daniel Ortega announced a new set of decrees aimed at further weakening the private sector's remaining economic power and punishing capital flight. The most dramatic of these was the confiscation of 14 large businesses as "revolutionary punishment" for the crimes of capital depletion and economic sabotage. In at least two of the cases, the decision to confiscate shocked the private sector because the companies had been showing large profits. Another decree called for the confiscation of all financial assets of Nicaraguans who had been out of the country for more than six months. Another confiscated additional "unused" farmlands, some of which were to be given to peasants as part of the agrarian reform. In announcing the measures, Daniel Ortega sought the approval of the "popular assembly": "Do you agree with this decree?" he asked the crowd in the Plaza de la Revolución, and the crowd responded with its approval. The decrees were not submitted to the Council of State, nor were they discussed with political parties. "We are not going to continue discussing the rules of the game," Ortega declared. "The people know the rules of the game and if anyone wants to play, he must abide by the rules of the game or leave, because otherwise the people will crush him. . . . I do not want to hear tomorrow that all this is unjust and abusive, that we do one thing today and another thing tomorrow, because this is not the case. These measures are just."[27]

Ambassador Pezzullo lamented the continuing radicalization of the Sandinista revolution. In May Pezzullo had informed Washington that the main reason for Nicaragua's precarious economic situation was the government's assault on the private sector. "Rather than provide incentives to production," the Sandinistas had "opted for centralized state control of a major public sector and have condoned assaults on the remaining private sector, thus inhibiting private investment." As a result, Pezzullo explained, all the foreign assistance received by the Sandinistas since July 1979 had not been enough to reactivate the economy "in the face of poor management and anti-private sector policies." Rather than cooperating with the private sector, the Sandinistas had chosen to create "an exclusivist system in which non-Sandinista forces were effectively barred from a share of power. Skeptical of ideological purity or domestic talent, the FSLN turned elsewhere and came to rely heavily on Cuban and leftist technical support in all major areas." In Pezzullo's view, the importation of "alien cadres, alien models, and alien ideas" had cost the FSLN heavily in "domestic acceptability."[28]

It was once again Humberto Ortega who made clear that the link between power and ideology was indissoluble and that the Sandinistas had no intention of pursuing the course preferred by the bourgeoisie. "The democracy that Robelo wants" was the democracy in which the bourgeoisie "have the army, the power, and that we Sandinistas be what the Left is in Costa Rica, a sector, an organization that is free to move about, that publishes its newspaper, but that they, the bourgeoisie, be the ones to control power." What existed in Sandinista Nicaragua was "the reverse. Here in Nicaragua power is held by Sandinismo. The people have it. And [the bourgeoisie] must be, insofar as we want them to be, a political force that moves within the limits that the revolution has imposed. That's the way it has to be." The bourgeoisie had "spoken of elections from the beginning, but we have not compromised ourselves with the elections that they think we are going to promote. And we are never . . . going to discuss power, because the people took this power with arms. The power of the people will never be in play here."[29]

Talk of armed counterrevolution now pervaded Managua. Arturo Cruz's defection had been followed in July by another that was even more dramatic. On July 9 the Sandinistas announced that Edén Pastora had resigned his post in the government and left the country. In a letter to Humberto Ortega, Pastora claimed he was off to fight with revolutionary forces in other countries, in the manner of Che Guevara, but many Nicaraguans suspected that Pastora's departure marked the denouement of a power struggle that the popular hero of known anti-communist views had long ago lost. Pastora, more than any other rebel leader, resembled the legendary Sandino, certainly in temperament. Inclined to mysticism, and philosophical incoherence, Pastora was convinced of his own historical role, not only on the Nicaraguan but on the world stage. He sometimes claimed to have been Sandino in a previous life. When he re-emerged in 1982 to lead the fight for a "true, democratic revolution," he would accuse the Sandinistas of bringing "foreign soldiers", that is, Cubans, to "the fatherland's soil." But it was well known that Pastora's chief complaint was in having been snubbed and relegated to secondary status in the revolution by the Ortegas and by Borge.

Pastora's defection had created "shock waves throughout Nicaraguan society." According to Ambassador Pezzullo, no event since the victory of the Sandinista revolution had "been more dramatic than the Pastora departure, or has greater potential to influence the course of events here."[30] If Pastora emerged in open opposition to his erstwhile Sandinista colleagues, as many expected, divisions might appear in the Sandinista army, where Pastora had allies and followers. Other Sandinistas of a social democratic inclination might be inclined to join Pastora in opposition. Pastora's defection thus raised both hopes and fears of anti-Sandinista political and business leaders. Pezzullo reported that many Nicaraguans were "reaching the conclusion that the on-going political crisis here will degenerate into violence."[31]

Since the election of Reagan, many Nicaraguans had believed the United States would eventually lend support to an armed counterrevolution against the Sandinistas, much as it had once supported rebels against President Zelaya more than 70 years before. José Francisco Cardenal's group had even sent a letter to Richard Allen during the transition asking for help from the incoming President.

In the first half of 1981, however, the Reagan administration had approached the idea of aiding a counterrevolution cautiously and skeptically. For conservatives inside and outside the government there was an attractive quality to the prospect of aiding an insurgency against the Sandinistas in response to the insurgency the Sandinistas were aiding in El Salvador. Since the time of the Republican convention in 1980, a handful of Americans with some political influence in Washington, including an aide to Senator Jesse Helms, had taken up the cause of the Nicaraguan armed resistance groups and lobbied on their behalf in Washington, in Honduras, and in Argentina.[32] Policy analysts at conservative think tanks like the Heritage Foundation had recommended support for armed anti-Sandinista groups before Reagan's election, and some of these analysts had become senior officials in the Reagan administration.

A more aggressive policy against the Sandinistas was becoming easier to contemplate as their already tarnished reputation in the United States declined even among former defenders. Senator Zorinsky rose in the Senate on July 30 to express "very grave concerns about the increasingly troubled path and direction of the Nicaraguan revolution." Citing the closing of La Prensa and Radio Corporacion, the "unprincipled attack on freedom of religion," reports that the Sandinista government was not "really serious" about elections, the announcement of new economic laws and confiscations on July 19, and the large buildup of Soviet-supplied weapons, Zorinsky said he had concluded that the Sandinistas were "backing off" from their original commitments to political pluralism and a mixed economy. "Unless and until the Nicaraguan Government rededicates itself to the principles for which the revolution was fought," the Democratic Senator warned, "neither the majority of the Nicaraguan people, nor their friends in the United States will continue to lend their support."[33]

While Senator Zorinsky worried about the closing of La Prensa, Reagan officials worried almost exclusively about the Sandinistas' continuing support for the Salvadoran guerrillas. El Salvador remained the main problem in Central America, and for Assistant Secretary Enders it still held a much higher priority than Nicaragua. As his first major act in his new post, Enders in July set forth a comprehensive strategy toward El Salvador that aimed to prevent a guerrilla victory while quieting, as much as possible, the clamor in the Congress and among the American public. Enders's policy, worked out with Ambassador Deane Hinton in El Salvador and army officers in Panama, set the general course of the Reagan administration's policies toward El Salvador for the next eight years. Thanks to efforts by the Carter administration in 1980, Enders could attempt to pursue in El Salvador a policy similar to what Vaky had hoped to pursue in Nicaragua before the mediation collapsed. A shaky coalition of the center, represented by José Napoleon Duarte's Christian Democratic Party, was allied with the nation's military against the guerrillas on the left and political and economic enemies on the right.[34] This alliance provided the United States an opportunity to fend off a communist victory without supporting a dictatorship.[35] Enders's strategy called for American military aid to the Salvadoran army in its fight against the guerrillas, economic aid to shore up the civilian government, and pressure for an open electoral process and social reforms, including a controversial land reform.

Enders's strategy for El Salvador faced formidable obstacles. As El Salvador moved toward elections and toward moderate and reformist leadership in the early 1980s, the Salvadoran guerrillas, although weakened politically, did not give up the military struggle. Since their defeat in the January 1981 "final offensive" the guerrillas had shifted back to a longer-term strategy, requiring lower levels of fighting and fewer weapons. In the view of Enders, Ambassador Hinton, former Carter officials, and senior foreign service officers at the State Department, the war in El Salvador could drag on for years if the guerrillas received a steady supply of arms. The government's inability to defeat the guerrillas could, in the meantime, destroy the process of democratization and reform by splitting the fragile alliance between the military and the civilian government. Failure to foster democratic and civilian rule in El Salvador could in turn undermine support in the American Congress for military and economic aid. A key element of Enders's strategy was winning the war against the guerrillas quickly, and that required closing off the guerrillas' outside sources of supply.

Since suspending aid on April 1, however, administration officials had been at a loss to find a way to achieve even this limited goal in Nicaragua. On June 3 Enders declared that "efforts to supply from Nicaragua arms, headquarters and training to guerrillas in neighboring countries" was continuing, although at a lower rate than before the January "final offensive." In the middle of July he told Congress that "an ominous upswing" in arms shipments had risen "to levels that enable the guerrillas to sustain military operations despite their inability to generate fresh support."[36] Although critics would later claim the administration exaggerated the levels of arms shipments from Nicaragua, news reporters at the time declared it was "fairly common knowledge that the flow of arms to El Salvador [was] once again increasing fairly precipitously."[37] Indeed, in July a large shipment of weapons for the FMLN arrived at the port of Corinto from Vietnam. The Vietnamese donation, which had been arranged at the beginning of the year but was delayed, included 1,500 American-made M-16 rifles with more than a million cartridges.[38]

In light of these developments, it was predictable that the Reagan administration would seriously entertain the idea of supporting armed rebels as a way of forcing the Sandinistas to "turn inward," protect their own revolution, and leave El Salvador alone. With Haig's proposal to "go to the source" in Cuba ruled out by President Reagan and his advisers, the next logical target for American pressure was Nicaragua. With American economic aid suspended, and the Sandinistas' unarmed opponents practically eviscerated by government actions, one means of increasing pressure on the Sandinistas was to arm those who wanted to fight.

Some of the foundations for such a policy had already been laid. CIA officials had already begun to make preliminary contacts with Nicaraguans to discuss the possibility of an armed effort against the Sandinistas. Some of these Nicaraguans had already received money from the CIA in 1980 under the intelligence finding signed by President Carter, and on March 9 President Reagan had signed a new finding authorizing covert activities in Central America to help interdict the flow of arms to El Salvador.[39] This gave the CIA the presidential authority to meet not only with Nicaraguan but also with Honduran military officials who had been giving occasional support to some of the bands attacking parts of northern Nicaragua. Neither Carter's finding nor Reagan's March 9 finding gave the CIA authority to begin arming groups directly or indirectly, however.[40]

For all its attractions, the idea of arming anti-Sandinista fighters sparked little enthusiasm among senior administration officials. Ambassador Pezzullo argued that it would only strengthen the Sandinistas.[41] In Secretary Haig's view, arming guerrilla bands to fight communism in Central America was entirely inadequate, the worst kind of "incrementalism." Since Nicaragua was not even Haig's main target, Enders recalls, the Secretary of State "did not want to be involved in an effort that centered on the Sandinistas." He also did not want to "create and arm something only to abandon it in the jungles."[42] Secretary of Defense Weinberger also doubted the effectiveness of such a policy and worried that the United States would be dragged into war in Central America. At first, even the new CIA Director, William Casey, whose agents in Central America were making contact and discussing future arrangements with the armed Nicaraguans, was reluctant to involve his agency in a paramilitary effort against Nicaragua. Casey's first priority was to rebuild the agency's reputation and its professionalism after what he believed were years of neglect and unfair criticism.[43]

While the CIA explored the idea of supporting armed groups against the Sandinistas, therefore, Enders searched for a tidier solution. In the middle of the summer, he persuaded a skeptical Secretary Haig that the Reagan administration should make a serious diplomatic approach to the Sandinistas to persuade them to end their support for the Salvadoran guerrillas. If the plan failed, the administration would be free to try whatever other options remained. Haig, although dubious about the prospects for success, agreed, and no one else in the Reagan administration opposed Enders's plan. To protect himself against attacks from conservatives in

Congress, Enders met with Senator Helms and asked him to support negotiations with the Sandinistas over the next six months. If the talks
failed, he told Helms, then the United States could seek ways to force the
Sandinistas to agree to American demands. Helms told Enders to take a
year if he needed it and if the Sandinistas appeared to be negotiating in
good faith.[44]

20

The Enders Mission

The Reagan administration turned to diplomacy in the summer of 1981, not because it preferred negotiations to confrontation but because it lacked the means of effective confrontation. Assistant Secretary Enders wanted to see if he could "use the threat of confrontation rather than confrontation itself" to make the Sandinistas stop what they were doing in Central America.[1] Although few perceived it, and Enders did his best to conceal a rather weak hand, the United States approached the Sandinistas in the summer of 1981 not to dictate terms but to get help with a problem it could not easily solve in any other way.

Enders traveled to Managua on August 11 and, in two days of meetings with Daniel Ortega and other Sandinista officials, proposed a full discussion of possible solutions to the problems between the two countries. The talks were often blunt, and Enders rather imperiously pointed out to the Sandinistas their obvious weaknesses against the northern superpower. Amid the threats, Enders proposed a deal. "You see your revolution as irreversible and so do we," he told Ortega. "We do not share many political and social ideas but acknowledge that the defeat of Somoza is an accomplished fact and we consider it as such and, moreover, a necessary fact."[2] Enders said the United States preferred to see Nicaragua more free and democratic, but what most concerned American officials was "the continued flow of arms, munitions and other forms of military aid to El Salvador [and] the rapid expansion of military power in Nicaragua."[3]

Enders speculated that the Sandinistas most feared efforts by the Reagan administration to "destabilize and attack the revolution." He suggested that these mutual concerns could provide the foundation for an agreement. If the Sandinistas would commit themselves to ending support for guerrillas in neighboring countries, the United States would commit itself not to threaten or use force "either bilaterally or by other means." Enders proposed to look more closely at "the problem of Nicaraguan political exiles in the United States," and he suggested that economic assistance to Nicaragua could be resumed if Nicaragua halted the arms flow to El Salvador. The United States was prepared to consider the question of food and development aid, as well as assistance from the Peace Corps, almost immediately.

Enders declared that the United States and Nicaragua had reached a "fork in the road." Their future relationship could either be one of accommodation or one of confrontation. To avoid confrontation, the Sandinistas "could take the necessary steps to ensure that the flow of arms to El Salvador is again halted as in March of this year." The United States would "monitor the results," but it would not make up imaginary shipments. The Reagan administration, Enders insisted, was "not setting impossible conditions or playing some diabolical game which you cannot win."[4]

Enders proposed that over the next weeks both sides should take steps to reduce polemical attacks. During that time he hoped that steps would be taken "to halt the arms flow to El Salvador." Enders proposed to make another trip to Nicaragua at the end of September "to review the programme which has been drawn up and see if conditions are ripe to go on to the next stage." He concluded by emphasizing that failure to reach agreement in the present negotiations would bode ill for the future of U.S.-Nicaraguan relations. Enders did not want to "go into the alternatives before us in any detail," but he warned that there were "only two things which could oblige us to involve ourselves militarily in this region." One was if "this idea of doing the utmost to halt the arms flow to El Salvador is rejected"; the other was "if the arms race in Central America is built up to such a point that some of your neighbors in Central America seek protection from us under the Inter-American Treaty." "We have nothing to gain in such a situation," Enders told Ortega. "[T]he cost would be excessive—but if it is forced upon us, the present American administration would be prepared to take a decision in that situation." Enders declared that relations between the Reagan administration and the Sandinistas were "now at a crossroads, and if we do not take these steps we will not achieve any detente."

Enders had posed for the Sandinistas a critical choice, and only later did the Sandinista leaders realize just how significant their decision would be for the future of their revolution. At the time, still flushed with the confidence of victory and infused with anti-imperialist zeal, the Sandinistas simply found Enders's tone arrogant and his offer unacceptable.[5] Daniel Ortega responded that the Sandinistas had also "seen the crossroads" and had already "considered the two alternatives." They had "decided to defend our revolution by force of arms, even if we are crushed, and to take the war to the whole of Central America if that is the consequence." When Enders ridiculed the idea of the Sandinistas defending themselves against an American invasion, Bayardo Arce yelled "All right, come on in! We'll meet you man to man. You will kill us, but you will pay for it. You will have to kill us all to do it."

Ortega rejected any deal which included a commitment to stop aiding the Salvadoran guerrillas. He declared frankly that the Sandinistas were "interested in seeing the guerrillas in El Salvador and Guatemala triumph." For reasons of ideology and affinity there was "a great desire here to collaborate with the Salvadoran people [including] among members of our armed forces." Ortega told Enders that the guerrilla war in El Salvador was "our shield—it makes our revolution safer."[6]

Enders, who evidently did not want to close the door on further negotiations, said he understood "that a revolution which has recently triumphed will find it necessary to take arms to defend itself and protect other revolutionary movements with which it has affinity." He also understood that it was "more advantageous" to the Sandinistas "if the struggle takes place in other countries rather than your own." But Enders asserted that such behavior by the Sandinistas could "become a challenge to the United States to which the latter has to respond." It was a "vicious circle which we must escape from." Enders concluded by emphasizing once again "the importance of stopping the flow of arms to El Salvador, for if this is not done, I could not suggest to my government that we pursue the line we have discussed."

When Enders returned to Washington, he was harshly criticized by other officials for demanding too little of the Sandinistas and especially for offering to accept the Sandinista revolution without demanding political or economic reforms.[7] In Haig's opinion, the problem was not that Enders had asked for too little, but that the Sandinistas had not even agreed to what little he had asked. In response to a memorandum from Enders, in which the Assistant Secretary suggested there might be some hope for an agreement with the Sandinistas, Haig wrote back, "I'll believe it when I see it, and meanwhile let's not hold up on the other plans."[8]

Enders went ahead with the diplomatic efforts nevertheless. He and his staff drew up a series of proposals for consideration by the Sandinistas, and on August 31 he sent a message to Ortega proposing that "illustrative drafts" of these proposals as well some prospective joint statements by the two nations be sent through diplomatic channels. Enders repeated his earlier warning that "the continued use of Nicaraguan territory to support and funnel arms to insurgent movements in the area would pose an insurmountable barrier to the development of normal relations."[9] And he went a step further, telling Ortega that "unless this support is terminated right now, I don't think there can be the proposed dialogue, so I will say this has to be a *sine qua non* for any dialogue."[10] A week later, although he had received no response from the Sandinistas, Enders sent Ortega another diplomatic note containing the draft of a statement that the United States would release publicly if an agreement were reached.[11] Again, there was no response from the Nicaraguan government. On September 16 Enders sent another diplomatic note, proposing that a joint statement be issued by both countries promising adherence to the principles of non-intervention and non-interference in the internal affairs of other nations.[12] In this second proposal, Enders also invited Ortega to Washington to make the joint statement.

On September 19 the Sandinista government broke its silence to protest a U.S. military exercise in Central America planned for October 7–9. The maneuvers were to be held off the Caribbean coast of Honduras and involved 400 troops. Enders, in a letter on September 28, offered to let Nicaragua send observers and then sent an American general to Managua to explain the purpose of the maneuvers.[13] Enders also took the opportunity to ask the Nicaraguan government for some reaction to the two draft proposals he had sent.[14]

Enders believed the Sandinistas spent the month of September debating how to respond to his proposals. But on October 7 Daniel Ortega attacked the United States harshly in a speech at the United Nations, and to Enders, Ortega's speech signaled the end of whatever debate the Sandinistas had waged among themselves.[15] At the end of the month, the Sandinistas formally rejected Enders's proposals as "sterile."

The Sandinistas' decision to reject Enders's offer in the fall of 1981 was not just an emotional response to a seemingly imperious American envoy, nor was it the result of a misunderstanding. Arturo Cruz, the Sandinistas' envoy to Washington, met with Enders many times during these months and recalls that the American's "message was clear: in exchange for nonexportation of insurrection and a reduction in Nicaragua's armed forces, the United States pledged to support Nicaragua through mutual security arrangements as well as continuing economic aid. His government did not intend to interfere in our internal affairs."[16] Ambassador Pezzullo believed the Sandinistas understood perfectly well what was being proposed.[17]

Sandinista leaders also understood the political motives that lay behind the Reagan administration's proposals. During a visit to Havana, Edén Pastora later recalled, Daniel Ortega told Castro that "Enders had come to Nicaragua as President Reagan's representative to say that Nicaragua had been given up as lost—that it was the problem of the Democratic Party in the U.S., and that the Republicans' problem was not Nicaragua, but El Salvador, which they had no intention of losing. Furthermore, Enders had told Daniel that the Nicaraguans could do whatever they wished—that they could impose communism, they could take over *La Prensa*, they could expropriate private property, they could suit themselves—but they must not continue meddling in El Salvador, dragging Nicaragua into an East-West confrontation, and if they continued along these lines, Enders said, they would be smashed."[18]

The revolutionary leaders of Nicaragua based their decision on what they believed were rational strategic and political calculations: about the global and regional balance of power, about domestic forces at work in the United States and in Europe, and about the requirements of their own power in Nicaragua, all of which pointed to defiance of what would later prove to be the most limited of American demands.[19]

By far the most decisive issue in the Sandinistas' calculations was their conviction that the power of the Soviet Union and the socialist bloc would allow them to challenge American hegemony even in the Western hemisphere. American observers who later believed the United States forced the Sandinistas into the arms of the Soviets by its aggressive policies failed to understand the Sandinistas' strategic assessment at the time.[20] The Sandinistas earnestly sought alliance with the Soviet Union, and by the time Enders arrived in Managua the Sandinistas had already made a strategic decision to align themselves with the socialist bloc precisely so that they might resist such pressures from the United States to change either their foreign or their domestic policies.

Many contemporary observers believed the Sandinistas would pursue a course of nonalignment between the superpowers, but the Sandinistas simply did not believe nonalignment was possible in a region dominated by the United States. Humberto Ortega saw the world as divided into two camps, "one side the camp of imperialism, the camp of capitalism headed by the United States and the rest of the capitalist countries of Europe and of the world, and on the other side the socialist camp, composed of distinct countries of Europe, Asia, and Latin America, with the Soviet Union as their vanguard."[21] Nicaragua could be in one camp or the other, but not in both.

The Sandinistas, therefore, were eager suitors of Soviet patronage—more eager, in fact, than the Soviets were to act as patrons. For, contrary to Secretary Haig's assertions, Soviet leaders had not embarked in the late 1970s on a "four-phase plan" or any other kind of plan for the conquest of Central America. After the Sandinista victory in Nicaragua, the head of the Soviet Communist Party's International Department, Boris Ponomarev, had expressed new enthusiasm for the "liberation movements" in Central America, and Leonid Brezhnev at the 26th Party Congress in 1981 spoke at length about the newly "liberated countries" in Central America and elsewhere.[22] For the Soviets, however, the region was at most a target of opportunity, worth exploring but only if success seemed likely. If the Sandinistas hoped to benefit from Soviet largesse and protection, they believed they had to demonstrate to Soviet leaders the value of making an unprecedented investment in Central America, in the shadow of American power. And that meant aiding the revolution in El Salvador.

While most Americans and Nicaraguans might consider a decision to join the socialist bloc impractical if not suicidal in the face of America's economic and military dominance of the hemisphere, the Sandinistas did not share such a fatalistic view. To them the Soviet Union appeared to be a superpower equal in strength to the United States, economically as well as militarily, one that could eventually provide a shield against American aggression in Central America as it had once provided a shield for Castro. Indeed, at the time of the Sandinista revolution the Soviets appeared to be in the ascendant and the United States in retreat—even politicians and political analysts in the United States suggested as much. Neither Nicaraguans nor Americans, from the most conservative to the most liberal, saw the signs of Soviet economic stagnation or global overextension in the early 1980s that would lead to such revolutionary changes by the late 1980s. "Remember," Humberto Ortega would later explain, "this was the strong Soviet Union. . . . We thought it would last."[23]

The Sandinistas also believed the Soviet Union and its allies could and would help keep the Nicaraguan economy afloat. Nicaragua might not prosper as it had when integrated into the American market, but it could survive with Soviet support. Humberto Ortega recalls that at the time of Enders's diplomatic mission, "we thought the Soviet Union was as rich as the United States. . . . We truly believed that the utopia existed."[24] The Soviet bloc, moreover, would provide arms free of charge and without accompanying demands for concessions to the Sandinistas' domestic enemies.

The Sandinistas were well aware that their choice of foreign policy would affect their own power in Nicaragua. To seek integration with the West required giving greater political space to the opposition, enhancing the role of the private sector, accepting limitations on the pace and direction of the revolution, and sharing power with the bourgeoisie. The Sandinistas understood that these were the only terms under which good relations with the United States could be maintained. Even if the United States left the Sandinistas alone, as Enders promised, it would never offer the kind of support the Sandinistas needed to hold power in Nicaragua unchallenged. For Humberto Ortega, in particular, a close relationship with the Soviet Union and Cuba offered far better prospects for his army and his continued rule than even the warmest of ties with the United States. Ortega had no reason to believe the United States would ever fund and equip his force, provide the tanks and aircraft he sought, as the Soviet Union was already doing.

While Enders hoped to draw a clear line between the Sandinistas' domestic and foreign policies, the Sandinistas themselves recognized no such clear distinction. Their ideology, their claim to be the heirs of Sandino, and the requirements of power all required that domestic and foreign policies be intimately related. As Sergio Ramirez put it in April 1981, the Sandinista revolution "cannot stop being anti-imperialist if it is going to be a true popular and democratic revolution." To ally with the United States was to "risk . . . the loss of our nationality."[25] Humberto Ortega told a group of Sandinista military officers in August 1981 that "our revolution has a profoundly anti-imperialist character, profoundly revolutionary, profoundly classist; we are anti-Yankee, we are against the bourgeoisie . . . we are guided by the scientific doctrine of the revolution, by Marxism-Leninism."[26] As for supporting the Salvadoran revolution, Tomás Borge explained that "our solidarity with that country and that people are part of the consolidation of our revolutionary process."[27] He declared, not as a provocation but as a statement of logical fact, that "this revolution goes beyond our borders. . . . Our revolution was always internationalist from the moment Sandino fought in La Segovia. With Sandino were internationalists from all over the world. . . . With Sandino was that great leader of the Salvadoran people, Farabundo Martí."[28]

The link between foreign and domestic policies was never clearer than during the three months after Enders's last visit to Managua. As the Sandinistas chose the course of confrontation with the United States, they also took further steps against their bourgeois opponents. One week after Enders left Managua, the Sandinistas closed *La Prensa* for three days. At the beginning of September the government announced a state of "economic and social emergency" that was to last for one year. The new state of emergency made all strikes illegal, tightened existing laws against capital depletion, and added to the list of statements and actions punishable by law those that might cause harm to the economy or endanger foreign aid.[29] The Sandinista Media Directorate warned that attempts to discredit the Nicaraguan government "fall within the framework of attempts by forces opposed to the people's interests to destabilize the process at times of economic and social emergency."[30]

The rallying cry was anti-imperialism. In response to the American military maneuvers in Honduras, the Sandinista government called for an "anti-intervention mobilization" of the masses and militia, and Humberto Ortega gave a speech that would long be remembered by the bourgeoisie. He called upon the Sandinista militias to draw up lists of the revolution's opponents and warned that anyone supporting "the plans of North American imperialism" would "be the first to appear hanging by the lamp posts along the roads and highways of the country."[31]

The Sandinistas' actions in the fall of 1981 showed their enormous confidence in the future. It was not fear of the United States that prompted the Sandinistas to take a hard line in their foreign and domestic policies, but rather their lack of fear. The Sandinistas, of course, wanted to preserve their revolutionary victory. If faced with a clear choice between aiding the Salvadoran guerrillas and surviving, they would undoubtedly have chosen to survive. But the Reagan administration did not present the Sandinistas with such a clear choice. Despite its power, and despite the new administration's threatening rhetoric, the United States posed no direct threat to the Sandinistas, and by the fall of 1981 the Sandinistas understood this perfectly well. They were aware that a Secretary of State who came to office promising to "go to the source" had been able to do nothing of the kind, and that the administration had considerable difficulties just sending 30 military advisers to El Salvador. The Sandinistas watched the congressional debate over El Salvador and believed there were powerful forces in the U.S. Congress and in the American public that served to check the Reagan administration's more aggressive inclinations.[32]

The Sandinistas knew, as well, that the Reagan administration faced international obstacles to an aggressive policy in Central America. The French Foreign Minister had already stated his opposition to American policy during a visit to Managua. Germany's Willy Brandt and Spain's Felipe González, both important leaders of the Socialist International, gave political and financial support to the Sandinistas. González declared in Managua that the Socialist International would act as an "umbrella" to shield the revolution against the United States. In Latin America, Mexico and Venezuela, both powerful, oil-rich countries, loudly opposed any American aggression against Nicaragua. The Sandinistas understood that while American military power might be preponderant in the hemisphere, the power of international and American domestic opinion to prevent the use of that power could be even greater. Enders's trip to Managua had itself been a sign of the administration's weakness, an attempt to solve through negotiations what the United States could not easily solve through the exercise of its power.

The Sandinistas' confidence was such that even when their actions at home threatened to alienate their supporters in the United States, they made only half-hearted efforts to repair the damage. On October 20 the Senate passed an amendment, sponsored by Senator Zorinsky, which required that any aid sent to Nicaragua in the future had to go only to the private sector. Even the liberal Democratic Senator Edward Kennedy supported the amendment, calling the Nicaraguan government "an authoritarian regime of the left."[33] Another Democratic Senator, Thomas Eagleton, criticized the Nicaraguan government for "exporting its revolution," silencing *La Prensa*, and "most troubling" of all, developing "one of the largest military forces in Central America with the help of several hundred Cuban military advisers and military equipment supplied by Fidel Castro and his Soviet bloc colleagues."[34] The Sandinistas dispatched a Foreign Ministry official, Julio López, to meet with members of Congress. But at a lunch with several congressmen on October 27, López was unapologetic. When Majority Leader Jim Wright asked pointed questions about the agreement that had been reached between the Sandinistas and the private sector back in 1980, López evaded the question and instead launched into a lengthy attack on U.S. policy in El Salvador, which one American observer called the "most insulting performance I have ever seen."[35] Wright, who "had viewed the outcome of those [1980] negotiations almost as a personal commitment to him," walked out of the dining room. Congressman Michael Barnes, a liberal Democrat and chairman of the House Subcommittee on Latin America, told reporters that the support for the Sandinistas on Capitol Hill was dropping away. On November 9 the *Washington Post* expressed concern that Nicaragua "seem[ed] to be becoming a Communist-controlled police state."[36]

For Reagan officials, even those who wanted to make a distinction between the Sandinistas' foreign policy and their domestic actions, the events of October strengthened the case for supporting an armed anti-Sandinista movement.[37] On October 31 Nicaragua's Vice Foreign Minister, Victor Tinoco, finally made formal reply to Enders's proposals. Tinoco declared the proposals "sterile," and he concluded his message by stating that further consideration of U.S. proposals would depend on American actions, "above all the relaxation of tensions that your government generates with concrete acts in the area of Central America and the Caribbean." Tinoco declared that Nicaragua hoped for realistic proposals from the United States and wanted to continue the dialogue.[38]

The Sandinistas could not have expected, however, that the Reagan administration would feel obliged to continue after the rejection of its first diplomatic approach. Enders had already been criticized for his efforts, and after Ortega's October 7 speech to the United Nations Enders had decided that the Sandinistas were not interested in pursuing his proposals. Had the Sandinistas responded with greater interest, Enders claims, "we would have seen the diplomatic effort to its completion, and as an alternative to the course we took."[39] Instead, the administration determined on a more aggressive strategy to confront the Sandinistas.

21

The "Lowball Option"

"In the end," Alexander Haig recalls, "the decision to go covert was a decision almost by default." It was, he believed, a failure of the "policy-making apparatus."[1] Robert McFarlane also believed that the decision to arm the contras was taken in a haphazard manner, divorced from any larger strategy. Throughout the summer and into the fall, while Enders pursued his negotiations with the Sandinistas, the CIA was preparing an alternative policy of arming anti-Sandinista fighters if and when the negotiations failed. Despite the general lack of enthusiasm, support for anti-Sandinista fighters was ultimately seen by many officials as one arrow in a rather empty American quiver. After Tinoco's response to his diplomatic overtures, Enders himself had come to the conclusion that the Sandinistas required more forceful persuasion. As Enders's deputy, Craig Johnstone, recalls, he wanted a "bargaining chip" that the United States could trade in return for an end to the Sandinistas' support for the Salvadoran guerrillas. The bargaining chip was to be the anti-Sandinista military groups forming in Honduras. CIA Director Casey required little further persuasion. As one CIA official later told a reporter, "[Casey] was aware that this was going to be a problem, but it was decided there was no other way to do it."[2]

The government of Argentina had begun aiding Enrique Bermúdez and his Fifteenth of September Legion earlier in 1981, providing money, training, and, by the summer, advisers in Honduras. Sixty Nicaraguans had been flown to Argentina for training.[3] In August the new CIA official in charge of Latin American operations, Duane Clarridge, traveled to Honduras, and met with the Argentine advisers, representatives from the Honduran military and the leadership of the newly formed Nicaraguan Democratic Force (FDN). The FDN was the product of an alliance between Enrique Bermúdez's Fifteenth of September Legion and José Francisco Cardenal's Nicaraguan Democratic Union. The Argentines and Nicaraguans present at the meeting believed the United States had tacitly agreed to support their efforts, although in fact the decision had not yet been made in Washington.[4]

There things had stood while Enders conducted his negotiations with the Sandinistas through the beginning of October. With Ortega's speech on October 7 and Tinoco's note three weeks later, Enders believed the United States could make no further progress in the negotiations unless the Sandinistas were put under some pressure. "We thought we would see whether the insurrection would produce conditions for negotiations," he recalls.[5] On November 1, CIA Director William Casey met with the Argentine military's Chief of Staff, General Leopoldo Galtieri, and the two agreed that the Argentines would manage operations in Nicaragua and that the United States would provide the money and the weapons.[6]

Secretary Haig, however, had still not given up hope of more vigorous action against Cuba. Although he was losing the debate in private, in public he tried to keep the option of military action open, if only so that "regimes that are moving toward totalitarian government" would know that their actions in Central America entailed risks that "exceed whatever advantages they seek for themselves." But Congressman Michael Barnes pounced on Haig's statements, declaring "if I were a Nicaraguan, I'd be building my bomb shelter." Haig's statements soon had anonymous administration officials telling reporters that "a resort to military contingencies is unlikely, largely because Defense Secretary Caspar W. Weinberger and the Joint Chiefs of Staff are understood to have strong reservations."[7] President Reagan had to deny once again that he had any "plans for putting Americans in combat any place in the world."

While Haig rattled sabers in public, the administration's real options were discussed at a meeting of the National Security Council on November 16. Assistant Secretary Enders described for President Reagan the broad strategy for Central America that he and other officials had agreed on. At the heart of the program was Enders's plan to support democratic reforms in El Salvador while fighting the guerrillas, and all the other parts of the strategy were directly or indirectly aimed at achieving the central goal of saving El Salvador from communism. The ten-point strategy, which the President approved a week later as National Security Decision Directive 17 (NSDD 17), included calls for: an additional $250–$300 million in economic assistance for Central American and Caribbean countries to strengthen local economies;[8] more military assistance for El Salvador and Honduras and additional training for Salvadoran military forces; increased American intelligence and surveillance efforts in the region; and, to combat the charges of liberal Democrats and the "elite media," a public information program in the United States to build domestic support for the administration's policies in Central America.[9] In deference to Haig's continuing insistence that the administration "go to the source," NSDD 17 also called for a strengthened American military presence in the Caribbean and a tightening of the economic sanctions against Cuba.[10]

Within this overall strategy there was also a new plan for covert actions against the Sandinistas. Enders presented President Reagan with a rather stark choice: "We must find a way to return to negotiations with Nicaragua or we will have to send troops." The plan Enders proposed had already been set in motion by Casey's meeting with General Galtieri. President Reagan was informed that the Argentines were already training 1,000 Nicaraguans and the United States would simply be supporting them with money, arms, and equipment.[11] The Nicaraguan forces would attack Cuban and Sandinista targets "in the [Nicaraguan] highlands and on the East Coast."[12] The proposal for covert action "was presented to [Reagan] as pressure rather than conquest," Enders recalls, "a lowball option, a small operation not intended to overthrow." The purpose of the operation, Enders explained, would be to "harass the government, waste it."[13]

Enders recalls that President Reagan was "skeptical" of the covert military activities presented in the plan. The President doubted that a paramilitary effort would succeed in pressuring the Sandinistas, and according to Enders he was "profoundly averse to violence." Officials therefore discussed the idea of destroying only economic targets in Nicaragua as a way to bleed the Sandinistas while endangering as few civilians as possible. As one official explained to reporters, reflecting the President's opposition to violence, "If you blow up a dam, you cause a lot of trouble, but you're not killing people." Another official confided that "Ronald Reagan has the reputation of being a gunslinger, but he [was] the most cautious, conservative guy in those meetings."[14] As a result of Reagan's objections, the idea of an American-directed commando unit to carry out attacks against targets in Nicaragua was apparently dropped.[15] Even after discussing ways to modify the plan to make it less deadly, Reagan "did not immediately grasp for it," according to Enders.[16] The President made no final decision at the November 16 meeting. A week later, he approved Enders's overall strategy and signed NSDD 17. But it was not until the beginning of December that Reagan signed the intelligence finding authorizing the covert actions against Nicaragua.

During those two weeks, the Reagan administration made another diplomatic approach to try to settle the problem of arms shipments to El Salvador, this time by discussing the matter directly with the Cuban government. As Haig recalls, President Reagan believed that "some sort of direct contact with Castro, or even with the Soviet leaders, might produce a desirable result" in Central America. Haig had opposed the idea from the beginning, wanting Castro to feel the pressure and the isolation produced by American diplomacy and military maneuvers, "but Reagan persisted." When Haig continued to balk, an aide to Reagan's national security adviser, Richard Allen, took matters into his own hands and tried to arrange a meeting with Castro through the columnist, Jack Anderson. Haig put a stop to the effort but felt under increasing pressure to follow his President's wishes. Reagan's enthusiasm for a diplomatic initiative was strengthened when Mexico's President and Foreign Minister joined in pressing for a "reconciliation" between the United States and Castro. Unable to convince his colleagues and the President to keep the threat of military pressure on Castro, Haig decided that "nothing could be lost by testing the waters."[17] Haig himself traveled to Mexico City for a secret meeting with Cuban Vice President, Carlos Rafael Rodríguez.

The meeting between Haig and Rodríguez, however, accomplished little, in part because Haig had little to say. He was in a weak position and later recalled that "there were formidable difficulties in convincing [the Cubans] of our seriousness of purpose."[18] Haig told Rodríguez that "time [was] running out." But the Cubans had good reason to wonder about the new administration's commitment to an aggressive policy. Almost a year of threatening rhetoric had passed and President Reagan could still put off his critics by pointing out that he hadn't fired a shot yet. Public statements by Reagan officials and anonymous leaks to reporters consistently undercut Haig's threats of military action. Secretary of Defense Weinberger told interviewers on November 22 that the administration was "well away" from "drawing a line in the sand." Military officials were reported to be "very nervous about the potentially disastrous impact" that any use of force might have on public support for the defense budget.[19] The Cubans and Sandinistas could not have failed to see what was apparent even to a casual reader of the American press. On November 25 the *Washington Post* noted that "the Reagan administration has shown a good deal more restraint than many of its press notices and its own pronouncements have indicated." With respect to Nicaragua, in particular, the *Post* found the Reagan administration was "much less the tiger than the tabby." If the Sandinistas wanted a "decent settlement," the *Post* suggested, "they can have one."[20]

The Reagan administration, however, had for the moment given up hope for a "decent settlement." On December 1, with all other options exhausted or rejected, including the option of doing nothing, Reagan signed the finding prepared for him by the CIA. For the President and his advisers, the "lowball option" appeared the *least* controversial means of applying pressure on the Sandinistas to change its policy toward El Salvador. The covert program kept the United States government at a distance from the violence it was intended to support. The only involvement of the United States would be through Argentina, although the wording of the finding did not rule out the occasional direct involvement of the United States in supporting individual operations against specific targets inside Nicaragua.

National Security Decision Directive 17 and the accompanying plan for covert options, therefore, were a compromise between President Reagan's desire to avoid the appearance of aggressive intervention in Central America, on the one hand, and his strategic and political concerns about losing El Salvador, on the other. Reagan officials still feared the fall of the Salvadoran government either before or after the elections that had been scheduled for March of 1982. Reagan intended to stop the advance of communism in Central America, but he wanted to do so in the least violent and least controversial manner possible. This unusual combination of anti-communist belligerence and post-Vietnam reluctance to use American power drove Secretary Haig to distraction. It was, however, a policy shaped by the politics of ideological confrontation in Washington.

For Reagan officials, one of the main virtues of the new covert program was that it required no public explanation, no public defense, and no public vote by Congress. The administration had only to inform the intelligence committees in both houses of the new finding and gain their quiet acquiescence. Days after President Reagan approved the covert program, CIA Director Casey met with the two intelligence committees to explain the new covert plan. Casey's explanations, however, sowed seeds of confusion and contention that later blossomed into full-blown controversy.

The new procedures for consultation with Congress, instituted after the controversies over CIA activities in the mid-1970s, were largely untested. Before the reforms in the intelligence oversight process, a President had not been compelled to tell Congress anything about planned covert operations. Most administration officials and most members of Congress involved in the new process expected that covert programs approved by the President would generally be approved by the two committees. In the charged political climate of the 1980s, however, when not just partisan politics but strong philosophical disagreements were turning many debates over policy into heated confrontations between competing views of America's proper course, the smooth and informal process of consultation was bound to be severely tested. William Casey, whose disapproval of and disdain for the new congressional oversight mechanism was apparent from the first, may not have been aware of the difficult course ahead when he first went before the intelligence committees to explain the new covert program in Nicaragua.

Casey described the program's principal aim of pressuring the Sandinistas to end their support for the Salvadoran guerrillas, but he may have stumbled in explaining the means by which this was to be accomplished. Instead of presenting the contras as a "bargaining chip," intended to pressure the Sandinistas into agreeing to end support for the Salvadoran guerrillas, Casey gave some members of the committee the impression that the contras would themselves be interdicting the arms flow. According to one account of Casey's meeting with the House intelligence committee, the CIA director spoke of a planned "500-man force as a carefully limited group whose target was the Cuban support structure in Nicaragua."[21] Members of the committee later told reporters that they understood Casey to mean "crack teams of commandos hitting arms caches, ammunition dumps, Cuban military patrols and a couple of key bridges along the arms supply route in the dead of night and withdrawing unseen from Nicaragua to their Honduran bases."[22] In other words, they believed the program was meant, literally, to interrupt the flow of arms to El Salvador.

Whether Casey himself was confused or intentionally vague, or whether members of the committee were confused or were just not paying close attention, is difficult to determine. One of Enders's principal aides, Craig Johnstone, recalls that he was "absolutely stupefied" when he heard how the program had been described to the committees. "No one thought that we're going to send a group out and capture some guy running across with weapons."[23]

Some members of the committee later claimed that Casey "did nothing to suggest an anti-Sandinista political dimension" to the covert program.[24] Others recall that he did. Casey certainly should have mentioned a "political dimension," since according to the December 1 finding, the goal of supporting the armed groups in Nicaragua was "to build popular support ... that will be nationalistic, anti-Cuban and anti-Somoza" and to "support and protect the opposition" in Nicaragua by "developing and training action teams that will ... engage in paramilitary ... operations."[25] Congressman Lee Hamilton wrote years later that Casey told the committee "there would be a military arm and a separate political arm which would attempt to secure support from other nations." Other members recalled that the administration had hoped to force the Sandinistas to "turn inward."[26]

Casey's briefing of the committees was clearly inadequate, and one result was that the majority of members found the plan shoddy and in many respects objectionable. They asked Casey questions about the methods, the goals, and the risks of the program. Would the Sandinistas not respond to cross-border attacks from Honduras by attacking that country? How would the administration respond if the Sandinistas requested Cuban troops to help them against the attacks? Casey's answers did not satisfy them, and even a conservative Republican complained that the Reagan administration had not thought through all the repercussions of its new policy.[27] Ironically, amidst all the tough questioning, the members apparently never asked Casey exactly how he expected the program to interdict weapons going to El Salvador, later the matter of greatest controversy.

The intelligence committees did not attempt to block the new program, however, since most of the members did not consider that the purpose of the intelligence oversight process. After the meeting the chairman of the House Intelligence Committee, Congressman Edward Boland, sent a letter to Casey which repeated the concerns expressed by the members of the committee and requested regular briefings from Casey and other officials to keep them informed of the development of the new covert operation.[28]

———

The first year of Reagan's presidency closed with what later proved to have been a momentous decision. At the time, it was perceived by most Reagan officials as far from momentous. The year had been spent arguing over the proper responses to the communist threat to Central America, from blockades and embargoes of Cuba to the deployment of troops in Central America. The product of these lengthy and heated discussions was the decision to support the bands of anti-Sandinistas struggling for survival on the Honduran-Nicaraguan border. McFarlane and Haig bemoaned the lack of a coherent strategy or a plan for the long-term. The President was unenthusiastic about the plans set before him. Those congressmen who knew about the new covert program were bothered but kept their concerns to themselves.

Nicaragua's leaders, meanwhile, remained defiant as the first year of the Reagan administration closed. On December 4 Secretary Haig met with Nicaraguan Foreign Minister Miguel D'Escoto at the OAS meeting in St. Lucia. In his speech to the OAS Haig declared that "we do not close the door to the search for proper relations," but that the United States intended to protect its allies under attack. "When the townsmen come to drive the wolf away from the sheep's throat," Haig said, "the wolf should not then cry that his liberty is being violated."[29] Daniel Ortega responded the next day that "we do not accept the door that the Americans are opening for us because [it] is too small . . . so small that in order to pass through it, we would have to do it on our knees and we are not going to do that."

22

The Birth of the Reagan Doctrine

In 1981 President Reagan and his advisers had concentrated on domestic affairs to the exclusion of most foreign policy matters. In 1982 President Reagan turned his attention to foreign affairs and to making his own mark on American foreign policy. New philosophies were promulgated, new rhetoric employed, and the "war of ideas" was fought on matters of foreign policy with a new vigor. Just as President Carter's reformulation of America's foreign policies and goals in 1977 had direct consequences for Nicaragua, so Reagan's announcement of his own broad doctrines in 1982 substantially reshaped the policy he had approved at the end of 1981 in ways that would have similarly dramatic effect in Nicaragua.

For the second year in a row, American policy toward Nicaragua derived from its policy toward El Salvador. The year 1982 began as 1981 had, with a spectacular offensive by the Salvadoran guerrillas. On January 27 the guerrillas overran the main military airport in El Salvador, destroying over half of the air force's fleet of planes and helicopters. Within days, the Reagan administration sent an additional $55 million in emergency military assistance to El Salvador, once again arousing the ire of liberal Democrats in Congress. This year, however, the administration was better prepared to confront the political challenge at home. Thanks in large part to Enders, and to José Napoleon Duarte, the Reagan administration had begun to discover the power of "democracy" as a weapon in the American political and ideological battle.

In 1981 the divisive debate over aid to El Salvador had led to an uneasy political compromise. The Reagan administration had won approval for aid to El Salvador because many conservative and moderate Democrats feared the "loss" of another Central American country to communism.[1] But liberal Democrats, who opposed Reagan's anti-communist policies, had attached a requirement that the President certify every six months that the Salvadoran government and military were improving their record in the area of human rights. Despite this measured victory, the Reagan administration faced the probability of ever-dwindling support among moderate Democrats and Republicans, disgusted or embarrassed by American support of a regime whose only claim to virtue was its bloody struggle against the communist guerrillas. In the summer of 1981, therefore, the Reagan administration had begun to make democracy its goal in El Salvador, not just defeat of the guerrillas. Although liberal Democrats doubted the Reagan administration's sincerity, this strategy succeeded in gaining the support of important moderate Democrats, like House Majority Leader Jim Wright, and insured a steady supply of aid to El Salvador throughout the 1980s.

After March 28, when El Salvador held its first free elections in many years, the political strategy invented for El Salvador grew into a broader doctrine that extended beyond El Salvador and beyond Central America. Although the sweeping victory of the right-wing parties in El Salvador nearly undermined American efforts to support Duarte's centrist faction,[2] the spectacle of masses of Salvadoran voters ignoring guerrilla threats and going to the polls won the administration broader and deeper support in Congress. It also bolstered the President's confidence. Indeed, what came to be known years later as the "Reagan Doctrine" may have been born in El Salvador in 1982.

The Reagan Doctrine has been widely understood to mean only support for anti-communist guerrillas fighting pro-Soviet regimes, but from the first the doctrine had a broader meaning. Support for anti-communist guerrillas was the logical outgrowth, not the origin, of a policy of supporting democratic reform or revolution everywhere, in countries ruled by right-wing dictators as well as by communist parties. The intellectual author of this more even-handed approach was Elliott Abrams, then Assistant Secretary of State for human rights and later Assistant Secretary for

Latin American affairs. In a memorandum to Secretary Haig in late 1981, Abrams had argued that, for reasons of both morality and political necessity, the United States had to prove itself just as committed to democracy in countries ruled by allied dictatorships as in those ruled by communist adversaries.[3]

The first and fullest public exposition of the new doctrine came in June 1982, less than three months after the elections in El Salvador and as a direct consequence of those elections. In his speech to the British Parliament at Westminster, Reagan for the first time in his presidency proclaimed America's support for democratic change everywhere in the world. Reagan cited the struggle of Solidarity in Poland and the "decay of the Soviet experiment." He proclaimed it the right of all human beings to struggle for freedom and democracy and the obligation of the United States to support that struggle. "If the rest of this century is to witness the gradual growth of freedom and democratic ideals," he declared, "we must take actions to assist the campaign for democracy."

The shift in rhetoric from the previous year was dramatic. Throughout most of 1981 administration officials had eschewed the word "democracy" when speaking of the developing world.[4] Reagan's rhetoric in June 1982 bordered on the extravagant. "Since the exodus from Egypt," Reagan told the Parliament, "historians have written of those who sacrificed and struggled for freedom—the stand at Thermopylae, the revolt of Spartacus, the storming of the Bastille, the Warsaw uprising in World War II. More recently, we've seen evidence of this same human impulse in one of the developing nations of Central America." Reagan obviously enjoyed pointing out how the elections in El Salvador had disproved his critics in Congress and in the press. "Day after day we were treated to stories and film slanted toward the brave freedom-fighters battling oppressive government forces on behalf of the silent suffering people of that tortured country. And then one day those silent, suffering people were offered a chance to vote. . . . Suddenly the freedom-fighters in the hills were exposed for what they really are—Cuban-backed guerrillas who want power for themselves, and their backers, not democracy for the people." Reagan's new crusade for democracy was designed to lend a powerful aura of legitimacy to his old crusade against communism. It shifted the ground under his opponents. Liberal Democrats might argue that El Salvador was not nearly democratic enough, but few elected American officials would deny, publicly, that an imperfect democracy in El Salvador was preferable to a guerrilla victory.

The new doctrine gave President Reagan a new basis for demanding support for a more aggressive anti-communist strategy. In his speech at Westminster, Reagan called it a "preposterous notion . . . that we should encourage democratic change in right-wing dictatorships, but not in Communist regimes." Even the Soviet Union was "not immune from the reality of what is going on in the world," and in what proved to be one of the most far-sighted declarations of his presidency, Reagan offered an optimistic vision of the Soviet Union's future:

> It has happened in the past—a small ruling elite either mistakenly attempts to ease domestic unrest through greater repression and foreign adventure, or it chooses a wiser course. It begins to allow its people a voice in their own destiny. Even if this latter process is not realized soon, I believe the renewed strength of the democratic movement, complemented by a global campaign for freedom, will strengthen the prospects for arms control and a world at peace.[5]

If Reagan envisioned the peaceful transformation of Soviet society from within, however, he had in mind a more violent struggle for freedom in some other communist countries. "Any system is inherently unstable that has no peaceful means to legitimize its leaders," Reagan declared. "In such cases, the very repressiveness of the state ultimately drives people to resist it, if necessary, by force." This was the argument liberals had used to justify the attacks of leftist guerrillas on right-wing dictatorships. Reagan turned it into the philosophical basis for what became the best-known element of the Reagan Doctrine: the support of anti-communist guerrillas fighting Soviet-backed governments in Afghanistan, Cambodia, Angola, and Nicaragua.

While the less idealistic of Reagan's advisers might have seen in this strategy only an effective means of bleeding the Soviet Union's resources and punishing it for expanding its reach in the late 1970s, that was not the way Reagan, the politician, explained his policies to the American people. The purpose he proclaimed was democracy, not aggressive containment waged to the last Afghan or Nicaraguan. Indeed, with his new doctrine Reagan ventured onto new ideological terrain, leaving traditional Republican foreign policy behind. Dominated by "realists" for whom such democratic "messianism" was a recipe for endless disillusionment and failure, and by more traditional anti-communists, highly skeptical that democracy among allied countries in the developing world could be pursued without undermining American interests, the Republican party and the conservative movement were not the natural home for the Reagan Doctrine in its double-edged form. Supporting anti-communist guerrillas was welcome, but insisting on democratic reform among allies and adversaries alike was almost anathema.

Reagan's own views were probably those of his party: He rarely showed personal distaste for allied dictators, especially those under siege from the left. As the standard-bearer for the conservative wing of the Republican party throughout the mid-to-late 1970s, he had defended American allies such as the Shah of Iran and Somoza against the Carter administration's attacks. As President he stunned American liberal sensibilities by declaring that Guatemala's military dictatorship had gotten a "bad rap." His cabinet officials in the first year-and-a-half behaved similarly: Vice President Bush toasted Philippine President Ferdinand Marcos's "commitment to democracy"; Ambassador Kirkpatrick raised eyebrows with her apparently warm relations with the military junta in Argentina before the Falklands war; and Alexander Haig frequently objected to imposing "Western standards" on allied countries in the developing world.

The Reagan Doctrine began as an act of political salesmanship. It wrapped a conservative Republican president's aggressive anti-communist strategy in a broader cloak that appealed to moderate Democrats while it confounded liberals. It recognized the political circumstances of post-Vietnam America, in which unabashed support for right-wing dictatorships, even those fighting communist guerrillas, could not withstand popular scrutiny and distaste, and in which the support of anti-communist guerrilla groups had to be justified on more than "realist" or anti-communist grounds. For President Reagan, the new doctrine suited his preferred political style. It completely reversed the grim pronouncements of Haig and the other more traditional conservative Republicans. It was a message of optimism, rather than of despair; it pointed to opportunities rather than dangers. Reagan did not have to tell Americans that support for brutal dictatorships was a necessary evil, nor that the struggle with communism was endless. The new doctrine offered the possibility of an end to the Cold War that was both peaceful and democratic.

The promulgation of this new doctrine soon affected American policy toward Nicaragua in important and ultimately decisive ways. It changed the style of the administration's rhetorical attack on the Sandinistas. It changed the terms of the diplomatic settlement the administration was willing to entertain, and by the end of the year it began to affect the nature and the goals of the new covert operation. These were not entirely unintentional consequences of the new doctrine. A few administration officials, especially in the CIA, had already begun to harbor greater ambitions in Nicaragua than the strategy of containment Enders had proposed in Managua in August 1981. Nevertheless, it is important to recognize that the President's broad doctrine shaped the specific policy toward Nicaragua far more than that policy shaped the doctrine.

In 1981 questions of democracy and human rights in Nicaragua had received little attention in the public statements of Reagan officials, who concentrated almost exclusively on the issue of arms shipments to the Salvadoran guerrillas. In 1982 Reagan officials picked up that rhetorical weapon as part of their broad assault on the Sandinistas. On March 1 Ambassador Kirkpatrick denounced the Sandinistas' forced relocation of Miskito Indians on the Atlantic Coast as a "massive" human rights violation.[6] Days later Secretary Haig described the Sandinistas' attacks on the Indians as "genocide." At the end of February President Reagan made the broader case against the Sandinistas' domestic policies. In a speech to the OAS he noted that the Sandinistas had broken their promises to respect human rights and hold free elections in Nicaragua. "Two years later these commitments can be measured by the postponement of elections until 1985, by repression against free trade unions, against the media [and] minorities."

Once again, Reagan's assault on the Sandinistas' shortcomings as democrats was connected to events in El Salvador where, "in contrast," the government had agreed to hold elections and had called on their opponents to "join the democratic process."[7] The Reagan administration's new tactic struck a chord with those moderate and conservative Democrats who remembered their support for Nicaragua's "private sector," the hard-won battle for aid in 1980, and who were disillusioned and embittered by the Sandinistas' subsequent behavior. Even liberal critics of the administration's policies would not defend Nicaragua against the administration's charges,[8] though they noted with irony the Republicans' new-found concern for Indian rights in Latin America.[9]

––––––

The Reagan administration's new enthusiasm for the "democratic revolution" immediately raised questions about the purposes of the recently approved covert operation in Nicaragua. A plan designed in 1981 to force the Sandinistas to end their support for revolutions in neighboring countries did not conform to President Reagan's new promise to support "democratic change" in communist as well as non-communist countries. Enders's original conception of the anti-Sandinista forces as a "bargaining chip" was especially out of step with the administration's overall change of direction in 1982. As Enders's deputy, Craig Johnstone, recalls, there was a growing conviction inside and outside the administration that "people were not bargaining chips." Even in meetings with members of Congress, Johnstone was "brutalized" when he tried to explain the purpose of arming Nicaraguans.[10] The anti-Sandinista guerrillas began to take their place as part of the doctrine of democratic aspirations that would bear the President's name.

Enders and Johnstone resisted these new pressures to redefine the purposes of their original "lowball option." They objected not to the desirability or appropriateness of seeking democratic change in Nicaragua, according to Johnstone, but because they believed the Nicaraguan forces just then assembling along the Honduran border were an inadequate means for achieving such an ambitious end. The small guerrilla force might be sufficient to "waste" the Sandinistas and force them to "turn inward," but it was not capable of waging a democratic revolution in Nicaragua. To set such a goal was to embark on a policy with no foreseeable end and no prospect of success.[11]

Enders and Johnstone, however, were a small minority in an administration increasingly animated by the President's call for a global offensive against communism and for support of the "democratic revolution." Secretary Haig, who had consistently opposed treating Nicaragua rather than Cuba as the main problem, was rapidly losing influence and resigned in June. CIA Director Casey, who had begun to recognize the enormous role his agency might play in implementing the President's new doctrine in Afghanistan, Nicaragua, and elsewhere, was in the ascendant. CIA officials charged with managing the covert operation in Nicaragua were becoming more ambitious as new opportunities arose for supporting a full-scale assault on the Sandinistas' rule. The most dramatic development came in April, when Edén Pastora announced that he was taking up arms in the name of a "true, democratic revolution." When Robelo and his followers in the MDN joined Pastora's struggle, CIA officials even drafted a new intelligence finding to authorize support for these "efforts by democratic Nicaraguan leaders to restore the original principles of political pluralism, non-alignment, a mixed economy and free elections to the

Nicaraguan revolution."[12] Although the finding was never signed, it indicated the evolving views of administration officials.

The Reagan administration's march toward support of "the campaign for democracy" in Nicaragua was slowed only by resistance in Congress to such a policy. The Congress was itself divided, however, and its efforts to constrain the Reagan administration were both half-hearted and inconsistent.

For members of Congress, and particularly for Democrats, the idea of supporting a democratic revolution in Nicaragua struck at the heart of the ideological debate that had rent American politics and the Democratic Party since the mid-1970s. The silent uproar and confusion Casey had created when he briefed the intelligence committee members in December 1981 were not just the product of a misunderstanding between the cagey, often incomprehensible CIA director[13] and the occasionally inattentive committee members who differed even among themselves as to what had been said. Even with the clearest of explanations and the most limited of goals, the Reagan administration's decision to begin an armed covert attack on the Sandinista government could hardly have been better designed to ignite conflict in the Congress. That the administration was conducting a covert intervention against a left-wing government was controversial enough; whether or not that intervention aimed at overthrow or merely harassment was a question of vital political and ideological importance. The most liberal wing of the Democratic Party had no representatives on the House intelligence committee, but the committee's chairman, Edward Boland, was well aware of the political difficulties posed by the administration's covert program—difficulties not only for the country, but for him personally.

The administration's shift in rhetoric came at a time when its quiet policy of covert operations against the Nicaraguan government was being stripped of both its secrecy and its silence. Less than three months after Reagan signed the finding, and before the effects of that decision had even begun to be felt in Nicaragua, Reagan administration officials were already being called to account for their actions—and so were the members of the intelligence committees. In February and March news of the covert program in Nicaragua was revealed to the *Washington Post* and *New York Times*. The revelations of a covert action against Nicaragua, of which the committee had been informed, put the committee's members and its chairman, Edward Boland, in a difficult spot. Liberal Democrats not on the committee, like David Bonior and Michael Barnes, immediately attacked the Reagan administration for "trying to overthrow the legitimate government of Nicaragua," and on March 15 Barnes declared he would introduce legislation to prohibit the United States from "engaging in or supporting military or paramilitary operations against Nicaragua."[14] On March 11 the *Washington Post* expressed the common view of most moderate Democrats in and out of Congress that matters were "getting out of hand in respect to Nicaragua." In approving a covert program against Nicaragua, President Reagan was "moving rapidly toward the outer limit of the support he can reasonably expect from the American people and from this country's friends in the hemisphere."[15]

The consensus of the Democratic Party was that American intervention for the purpose of overthrowing a foreign government was unacceptable. In fact, no more than in the Carter years could most American politicians, Republican or Democrat, openly proclaim the goal of American policy to be the overthrow of another regime. Insofar as the administration suggested that the covert paramilitary effort might have the political goal of ending Sandinista rule, Chairman Boland and other Democratic committee members had to oppose such a plan.

A substantial number of moderate Democrats could support the Reagan administration's efforts to block arms shipments to the Salvadoran guerrillas, however. And they supported the more limited, strategic goals that Enders had pursued in 1981.[16] Some liberals in Congress and some journalists tried to cast doubt on the administration's assertions that Nicaragua "was being transformed into an ever more efficient platform for supporting insurgency in El Salvador."[17] The *New York Times* editorial page insisted there was "no proof."[18] Congressman Barnes simply denied that arms shipments were occurring. Charging that the Reagan administration lacked "credibility," Barnes said he waited "with bated breath" for some "concrete and verifiable evidence . . . that the Nicaraguan Government has been directly involved in the El Salvadoran war."[19] But moderate and conservative Democrats generally accepted the administration's claims. They had good reason. Members of both intelligence committees who were given classified briefings by the administration expressed no doubts about the continuing flow of arms from Nicaragua to the guerrillas in El Salvador. One week *before* Congressman Barnes professed to be waiting "with bated breath" for the administration's evidence of Sandinista complicity, Congressman Boland had released a public statement supporting the administration's claims.[20] The House intelligence committee reported that available intelligence showed convincingly that the Nicaraguan government was "helping train insurgents and [was] transferring arms and financial support from and through Nicaragua to the insurgents." The Sandinistas had provided "the insurgents bases of operation in Nicaragua," and Cuban involvement "especially in providing arms" was "also evident." The intelligence committee's report emphasized that "contrary to the repeated denials of Nicaraguan officials, that country is thoroughly involved in supporting the Salvadoran insurgency." The support was "such as to greatly aid the insurgents in their struggle with government forces in El Salvador."[21]

The Sandinistas were actually making less effort to hide their support than they had in 1980 and 1981. In the first three months of 1982 the amounts of weapons flowing to the Salvadoran guerrillas through Nicaragua reached their highest levels since the "final offensive" of 1981. The Salvadoran guerrillas were stockpiling weapons for an offensive to disrupt the elections scheduled for March,[22] and Tomás Borge declared in February that the Sandinistas had a duty to help their revolutionary brothers in El Salvador. "How can we keep our arms folded in the face of the crimes that are being committed in El Salvador and Guatemala? . . . If we are accused of expressing solidarity, if we are forced to sit in the dock because of this, we say: We have shown our solidarity with all Latin American peoples in the past, we are doing so at present and will continue to do so in the future."[23] In February a large shipment of arms arrived by sea from Nicaragua to the coast of El Salvador; early in March, a guerrilla unit in El Salvador received several thousand sticks of TNT and detonators.[24] Guerrilla commandante "Montenegro" later told reporters that throughout 1982 "urban commandos and 200 guerrillas under his command in Guazapa received monthly arms shipments from Nicaragua that were trucked across Honduras, hidden in false panels and floors. . . . Each truck, he said, carried roughly 25 to 30 rifles and about 7,000 cartridges of ammunition."[25] The arms shipments were too large and too frequent to evade American scrutiny, but the method of their transport made their capture difficult if not impossible. Nevertheless, even a liberal senator like Paul Tsongas declared after being briefed by intelligence officials that "those of us who are opposed to the policy accept the fact that there is indeed Nicaraguan involvement in El Salvador."[26]

Many critics of the administration also had to accept the fact that the Sandinistas were engaged in a large buildup of the size and capability of their own armed forces. At the beginning of March CIA officials released aerial reconnaissance photographs showing the location of the Sandinistas' new battalion of 25 Soviet-made T-55 tanks, two Soviet-made Mi-17 helicopters, and four airfields being lengthened and fitted to accommodate advanced fighter aircraft. The *New York Times* declared that the "debate will continue about exactly why Nicaragua is building airfields, multiplying training camps and buying Soviet-made tanks. But that the buildup is going on need no longer be a matter of argument."[27]

The consensus among Democrats in Congress supported efforts to halt the Nicaraguan military buildup, and intelligence committee members from both parties "shared the administration's stated policy goal—stopping a flow of arms from Nicaragua to the Salvadoran rebels."[28] It was on this broad consensus that Boland attempted to build a case for supporting the Reagan administration's covert operation in Nicaragua, even as the administration's own goals were shifting and expanding.

Boland's first problem was the legislation that Congressman Barnes had threatened to introduce banning all covert actions against Nicaragua. Barnes's proposal ran roughshod over the intelligence committee's prerogatives and violated the compromise between the branches on how Congress was to play its role in overseeing the executive branch's covert policies. For this and other reasons, Boland's friend, Speaker O'Neill, asked Barnes not to introduce the legislation banning funds for the covert program, but rather to let Boland handle the problem in the proper manner within the intelligence committee.[29]

In the first week of April Boland's committee met to consider the 1983 intelligence authorization bill. Some committee members proposed denying funds for the covert operation in Nicaragua altogether, but as Boland later reported, "the Committee considered, but rejected, motions to strike all funds for the program. Instead, the Committee adopted language in the classified annex to the report accompanying the bill that limited the uses to which funds authorized for the program could be applied." With the Reagan administration's concurrence, Boland added a phrase to the secret annex to the intelligence authorization bill declaring it the will of Congress that none of the funds appropriated could be spent "for the purpose of overthrowing the government of Nicaragua or provoking an exchange between Nicaragua and Honduras."[30]

The compromise served the immediate interests of both the committee and the administration. Reagan officials quietly took note of the fact that Boland's restriction did not constrain their support of the contras in any way, since Boland had addressed only the administration's intent rather than its actions. So long as the covert support for the anti-Sandinista forces was not "for the purpose" of overthrowing the government in Managua, it did not matter if the contras themselves were fighting to remove the Sandinistas from power. For Boland, the compromise meant that no one could accuse the committee and the Democratic Party of cutting off a program to stop the spread of communism in Central America, but neither could they be accused of supporting intervention against a sovereign government. In this respect the compromise resembled the one reached earlier over military aid to El Salvador. Both compromises were designed to cover over splits in the Democratic Party and disagreements between the executive and legislative branches.

The compromise over covert operations in Nicaragua, however, brought the executive and legislative branches into uncharted, and possibly unchartable, territory. When the intelligence committees were established and the 1980 Intelligence Oversight Act passed, members of both the executive and legislative branches anticipated that in the unlikely event that the congressional committees strongly opposed a covert program, but the President went ahead with it nevertheless, then the committees might vote to deny funds for the program altogether in the annual intelligence authorization legislation. Boland, however, had overruled efforts to block all funding for the covert program in Nicaragua. Instead he used restrictive language in the legislation to shape a policy that could fit within political constraints imposed by a divided Congress.

Both branches thus joined in averting their eyes from the contradiction at the heart of the covert program. The administration's stated intentions and the Congress's expressed aims, after all, did not affect the goals of the Nicaraguans they were supporting with American dollars. No one could seriously believe the anti-Sandinista fighters were risking their lives merely to "interdict" the flow of arms from Nicaragua to El Salvador. Boland certainly knew better. The Reagan administration was more disingenuous than the Congress, however, because despite Enders's minority view, the administration as a whole could not honestly deny that its goals were evolving and becoming more ambitious. With the defection of Pastora and President Reagan's growing attraction to the idea of a fight for democracy in Nicaragua, the distinction between the contras' goals and those of the Reagan administration was becoming smaller. As the contras' apparent capabilities grew beyond anything originally planned by the Reagan officials, so too did the administration's ambitions. The CIA's new finding, which proposed aiding "the democratic Nicaraguans in their efforts . . . to restore freedom and democracy to Nicaragua," fell by the wayside after the compromise with Boland and never reached President Reagan's desk.[31] The goals it set forth, however, were a closer approximation of the administration's evolving policy than the new language in the secret annex of the intelligence authorization bill.

23

Nicaraguan Explosions

While Congressman Boland and the Reagan administration were reaching their uneasy truce, anti-Sandinista fighters in Honduras and Nicaragua were only beginning to receive American resources and to carry out their own ambitious struggle. For all the attention the covert program had already received in the United States, the program itself was slow in getting started, and it was not until the late spring and early summer of 1982 that the anti-Sandinista fighters began making their presence felt in Nicaragua.

Even in theory, covert assistance to anti-Sandinista fighters was an uncertain instrument for achieving the precise and limited goal Enders had in mind. In practice, it depended heavily on groups of men of unproven abilities and sometimes unclear motives. The Nicaraguans who began receiving American assistance at the beginning of 1982 were a disparate lot. Most Reagan officials knew little or nothing about them. At the beginning, American contact with the forces was limited. Argentines trained and commanded the contras from camps in Honduras. A lone CIA official visited the camps on occasion or met with Bermúdez and other leaders in Tegucigalpa.[1]

The Argentines had chosen the contra general staff and leadership according to their own tastes, not all of which the Americans shared. Nor could the Reagan administration have any confidence in the military capabilities of the inchoate guerrilla forces, even as their goals for them expanded. When President Reagan signed the intelligence finding in December 1981, the Argentines had barely begun to assemble a force of Nicaraguans willing and able to fight. The National Guard colonels, majors, and lieutenants of the Fifteenth of September Legion led by Enrique Bermúdez had become the general staff of the new FDN, and these were the men the Argentines established as the generals of the new war, the recipients of the impending American aid, and the putative leaders of the troops in the field. Those troops, however, neither fully respected nor always took orders from their general staff. The forces that had become the centerpiece of U.S. policy toward Nicaragua were still mostly bands of marauders, fighting their own private wars in the northern countryside of Nicaragua where most of them were born.

Like the general staff, some of the fighters were also former National Guardsmen, but they had been sergeants and enlisted men, platoon leaders and foot soldiers. Poorly educated, the sons of farmers in the northern mountains and countryside of Nicaragua, many of them had more in common with the peasants of the north, and even with the Sandinista militiamen, than they did with the officers who led them. They had been surviving on the border of Honduras and Nicaragua for more than two years since they escaped after the revolution, foraging and cattle rustling, fighting only to stay alive and, on occasion, for revenge. The Argentines had given them some money and training to carry out isolated assassinations of Sandinista party leaders or Cubans, more in the style of the Argentine "dirty war" than of an insurrection. Of these former National Guardsmen, Pedro Pablo Ortiz Centeno became the most famous, and infamous, as "Suicida."[2] In 1979 Sergeant Ortiz had belonged to a tough little force in the National Guard called the Rattlesnakes, and in June and July of that year he and his comrades fought Edén Pastora's troops to a standstill in the south of Nicaragua while the other Sandinista forces in the north moved into Managua. After the collapse of the National Guard leadership on July 19, they made their way by boat to El Salvador and then traveled to Honduras where they lived as refugees. Throughout 1980 and 1981, "Suicida" and others like him had moved back and forth across the border between Honduras and the northern Nicaraguan province of Nueva Segovia. They found some support among the independent mountain people scattered sparsely throughout the region. When the Argentines and the FDN general staff began looking for men willing and able to fight in Nicaragua, "Suicida" and other National

Guardsmen of the lower ranks were already there. Even among these National Guardsmen there were important differences. Some had fought in units like the Rattlesnakes, others belonged to Somoza's elite guard led by Somoza's son, and still others had joined the National Guard only in the last few months of the war.[3] Some had reputations in Nicaragua as killers, others as good men, and others had been too young to develop any reputation at all.

In addition, there were the MILPAS, the anti-Somoza militias who had turned against the Sandinistas. Many had left after the death of their leader, "Dimas," in August 1981, but some had kept fighting along the northern border. There were "Tigrillo" and his men, and there were others who had defected from the ranks of the Sandinista army or militias. In the summer of 1981 "Tigrillo" and another former Sandinista named "Jhonson" had attacked El Cua unsuccessfully before deciding to go north to Honduras where Bermúdez's new organization was recruiting.[4] There were also followers of Edén Pastora from the old Benjamin Zeledon/Southern Front, who after Pastora's defection had left or been chased out of the Sandinista ranks.[5] Among the contras was a group of Protestant evangelicals, including an assistant pastor and a seminarian.[6]

The fourth and by far the largest group of anti-Sandinista fighters was the force of Miskito, Sumo, and Rama Indians and black "Creoles" on the Atlantic Coast. With little outside encouragement, the Indians and Creoles had been clashing sporadically with the Sandinistas since the beginning of the revolution. After the Sandinistas' arrest of the Miskito leader, Steadman Fagoth, and the shootings at Prinzapolka in February 1981, relations between the government and the Indian and Creole communities had steadily deteriorated. When Fagoth was arrested, Miskito Indians occupied a town on the Atlantic Coast to demand his release. The Sandinistas freed Fagoth and he fled to Honduras where, with 3,000 Miskitos, he sought support from the Honduran army and the FDN for armed actions against the Sandinistas on the Atlantic Coast.[7] The Sandinistas grew alarmed at the possibility of losing control of the Atlantic Coast altogether, which they feared could be followed by a declaration of independence by Miskito and Creole leaders and then a formal secession. In the last days of 1981, after Christmas, the Sandinistas launched attacks on several Miskito villages, including, according to the Honduran government, some on the Honduran side of the border which contained thousands of refugees. The Hondurans alleged that the Sandinista forces killed hundreds of Indians in a "massacre," but the Sandinistas denied the charges. A week later the Sandinista army relocated by force about 20 villages in northeastern Nicaragua with about 10,000 inhabitants, while thousands more fled into Honduras. It was the largest military operation yet conducted by the new government, and Sandinista officials declared it had been necessary to prevent the region from becoming a "theater of operations for counterrevolutionary actions."[8]

Altogether the number of potential anti-Sandinista troops at the beginning of the American covert program stood at something less than 2,000, more than half of whom were Atlantic Coast Indians and Creoles. The number of fighters in the main force of the FDN commanded by Bermúdez, however, was no more than a few hundred. They faced a Sandinista army of close to 25,000, not including the hastily trained militia which the government claimed had reached 50,000, as well as the armed collective farmers and coffee pickers. Humberto Ortega's strategy was to let the militia fight the counterrevolutionaries in the hills and jungles of northern and eastern Nicaragua, while the Sandinista regular army stayed behind to guard the more heavily populated sections of the Pacific Coast. When necessary, regular army units would be flown to forward positions in the Soviet-supplied Mi-17 helicopters. At the beginning of 1982, the Sandinistas did not fear the forces that the Americans and the Argentines were slowly pulling together.

The Nicaraguans, Americans, and Argentines who assembled in Honduras were more optimistic. They believed that with U.S. financial assistance and a permanent, secure base of operations in Honduras, the anti-Sandinista forces could survive indefinitely. The provisions of arms, equipment, and money would attract more fighters. The diverse groups of fighters, if unified and coordinated, could cause the Sandinistas problems on three fronts: from the north with the FDN, on the Atlantic Coast with the Miskitos, and from the south with fighters from Pastora's old Southern Front.

What the contra forces lacked was a political identity attractive to the outside world and to the Nicaraguan political class. In meetings through the fall and winter of 1981, Enders and CIA officials and the Argentines had agreed that the political coloration of the anti-Sandinista fighters was important. The Reagan administration had come to support the former National Guard officers out of necessity, for these were the men whom the Argentines had chosen and because they believed there was no one else to lead the fighting. But they considered this a serious weakness in the program because the contras were vulnerable to the charge of representing a return to Somocism in Nicaragua. The presence of the Argentines further tarnished the contras' image, since the Argentine military had earned a reputation as among the most brutal in Latin America.

A more significant weakness was that the small fighting force had no political face at all, at least not in traditional Nicaraguan terms. The anti-Sandinista fighters, whether they had been footsoldiers in the National Guard or guerrillas in the struggle against Somoza, were mostly campesinos, small farmers, and petty landowners from a rural and less civilized Nicaragua. Their backgrounds and families were unknown to the aristocratic families of Granada and León. They had nothing to do with the political world of Managua. They had not been leaders in the governments and the legislatures of the Somozas, nor in the parties that had opposed them. Although the Guardsmen may have fought for Somoza, unlike many leading opposition politicians they did not actually know him or do business with him. And if they had fought for the Sandinistas, they were less well connected to the new government than many of the opposition leaders who were related to leading Sandinista officials by blood or by marriage. The Sandinistas and their political opponents in Granada, Managua, and León had more in common with each other than either of them had with the Nicaraguans assembling on the Honduran border.

In no sense were these farmers and campesinos politicians. Their complaints against the Sandinistas were narrow and specific, not philosophical. If they were farmers, it was fixed government prices for their produce or the creation of cooperatives, or confiscations, or failed expectations of the revolution. If they were devout Catholics or evangelical Protestants, it was Sandinista hostility to their church. If they were former Guardsmen, it was revenge. If they were MILPAS, it was betrayal. These complaints were not the stuff of political platforms. The anti-Sandinista fighters, therefore, were left to do their explaining and their campaigning with their guns and their knives. While the politicians in Managua debated, they killed, and they did so without the benefit of a political plan save the removal of the Sandinistas from power.

In the first six months of 1982, the newly organized rebel forces did very little other than train and receive new supplies. Their existence had been so precarious before that they were delighted to be receiving the grand sum of $9,000 each month for the entire force.[9] While the fighters trained, their Argentine and American supporters, eager to show something for the money being spent on the new forces, decided to strike a mostly symbolic blow. On March 14 anti-Sandinista fighters trained by the Argentines set off explosives at two bridges in northern Nicaragua, badly damaging one and completely destroying the other. One of the bridges, at Somotillo, was on the main route along which arms were being shipped to the Salvadoran guerrillas in trucks. Thus the first blow fit precisely the description of the covert program Casey had given the intelligence committees in December. The dramatic explosions, like the Sandinistas' own small attacks in October 1977, were also an announcement to Nicaraguans that the struggle had begun. They were intended as "an inspiration to other Nicaraguans and a provocation to the Sandinistas."[10]

The hope of CIA officials was that the explosions would force the Sandinistas to take harsh, unpopular measures against political opponents, and the strategy worked. The Sandinistas immediately imposed a new state of emergency throughout the country, began another crackdown on political opposition in Managua, and tightened press restrictions. On March 18 Humberto Ortega announced a new "patriotic tax" on businesses to pay for the nation's defense against the "imminent invasion."[11] A week later the government suspended *La Prensa* for carrying reports supporting "the anti-patriotic game of the Nicaraguan right." On April 14 the government extended the State of Emergency for another month, and at the beginning of May, the *Washington Post*'s Christopher Dickey reported from Managua that "many Sandinista officials are beginning to portray the move toward socialism as their only chance for survival in a hostile world." Tomás Borge, speaking to a crowd of supporters in Managua, said playfully that the Americans and the Western world did not seem to realize where the revolution was going. The crowd chanted back: "Socialism! Socialism! Socialism!" To which Borge replied: "Our hardworking people know where we are headed."[12]

The latest radical turn by the Sandinistas, and the signs of a new America willingness to intervene, proved to be the decisive moment for many leading Nicaraguan moderates, both in the opposition and in the government. In April and May first Robelo and then Alfredo César left Nicaragua for Costa Rica, with no intention of returning. Haroldo Montealegre, another moderate technocrat in the Sandinista government, also left. Most dramatic of all was the surprising reemergence on April 15 of Edén Pastora. After months of silence, including a period of "house arrest" in Havana followed by several meetings with the CIA's Clarridge, Pastora announced from Costa Rica his decision to take up the struggle against the Sandinistas. Claiming to represent the true revolution and the real spirit of Sandino, Pastora condemned the "bourgeois" lifestyles of the nine commandantes. "I will drag them with bullets from their mansions and Mercedes Benzes," he declared. Adopting the rallying cry of Sandino, he called on "all Nicaraguans to put themselves on a war footing as long as there is a single foreign soldier on the fatherland's soil." At the end of May small numbers of Sandinista soldiers began defecting to Costa Rica to join Pastora in the fight. Alfonso Robelo, who had once denounced the armed path, declared his allegiance to Pastora's struggle.[13]

Pastora's defection further damaged the Sandinistas' reputation throughout the hemisphere. The dashing revolutionary warrior traveled to Venezuela, Mexico, and elsewhere courting the support of disillusioned liberals and "trying to rebuild something of the regional alliance that helped the Sandinists topple the Somoza regime." In Washington Pastora won "the backing of liberals on Capitol Hill" disappointed by the Sandinistas' radicalism. His defection, according to one observer, "dramatically changed the panorama of exiled opposition, which until then had been dominated by extremely conservative groups formerly associated with the late General [Somoza] and his National Guard."[14]

The American and international press focused most attention on the Sandinista crackdown in Managua and the decision by leading members of the Nicaraguan political elite to begin an armed struggle against the government. Less visible but equally significant was the government's crackdown in the northern and eastern provinces, where opposition to the government among peasants and small landowners had been building for two years and where support for the anti-Sandinista fighters based along the Honduran border was starting to grow rapidly. Over the course of the summer, the government sent greater and greater numbers of militia forces to police the areas near the Honduran border. Local Sandinista defense committees increased their vigilance and denounced those in the villages who did not prove their devotion to the revolution. Campesinos were recruited into the militias or thrown in jail for refusing. Many campesinos fled north to Honduras to avoid the recruiters. Some joined the anti-Sandinista forces assembling across the border. The Sandinistas reported to the press that the campesinos were kidnapped by the contras, and some probably were. The majority, however, left willingly.

Campesinos who joined the anti-Sandinista forces during the coming year all told journalists similar stories. To one reporter they "complained about having to sell whatever crops or livestock they raised to state stores at prices set by the government. They detest rationing, which sometimes requires them to walk miles to get necessities." The peasants also resented "Sandinista propaganda and pressures against the evangelical churches many of them attend." They believed the government in Managua was "communist and atheist."[15] Another journalist reported that "the rebels and their noncombatant collaborators" complained about "enforced food rationing, expropriation of the farmer's markets, enforced organization of peasant co-ops, the Sandinistas' anti-religious policies and harassment of the Catholic Church." Another reporter found that "the opposition to the Sandinistas seems to spring mainly from resentment over acute shortages of daily necessities and the imposition of Marxist ideology over religion."[16]

A prominent Sandinista leader and theorist, Luis Carrion Cruz, later acknowledged that widespread peasant support for the armed rebels was early "evidence that, at some point, the alliance of the revolution with an important sector of campesinos was broken." The problem, as Carrion explained, was that the Sandinista revolution had been "eminently urban— in its bases and in the vast majority of its leaders—and it triumphed with an insurrection that was decided in the cities." As a result, Sandinista leaders had given "privileges to urban interests to the detriment of the campesinos." The government had angered peasants by establishing "checkpoints on the highways to guarantee, coercively, that the campesinos would deliver their production to the state at the official price. The objective was to sell it cheaply to the population in the cities."

Even policies publicized as beneficial to the Nicaraguan peasant left many nervous and angry. The agrarian reform, which took properties away from well-to-do landowners—the peasants' "class enemies"—created more tension than satisfaction. The hope of many campesinos, the Sandinistas soon discovered, was "to become like the landowners," and the reforms were seen "as a denial of their own chance one day to become large landowners themselves." Finally, Carrion recognized the damage done by the confrontation between the government and the Catholic and Protestant churches in Nicaragua. The churches had done "a great deal of work in the countryside where religion has much greater weight than in urban areas."[17]

The clash with the Catholic church hurt the Sandinistas in cities, as well. After a visit by Archbishop Obando at the end of June, Pope John Paul II sent the archbishop back to Nicaragua with a letter assailing the Sandinistas' attempts to undermine the authority of the Catholic bishops by supporting a pro-Sandinista "People's Church." The Pope called on

Nicaraguan priests and nuns to unite behind the bishops, who enjoyed, he said, the support of "the overwhelming portion of the people."[18] A few weeks later, in one of the more bizarre episodes in the confrontation, a close aide to Archbishop Obando was photographed naked on the street outside a woman's home, after being accosted by officials of the Interior Ministry, ordered to disrobe, and forced out the door. Tomás Borge had looked on from a van parked on the street. When Sandinista newspapers published the picture, protesting students from a Catholic school clashed with Sandinista militants, resulting in deaths on both sides.[19]

Less well-publicized was the government's crackdown on several evangelical Protestant sects: Jehovah's Witnesses, Mormons, and Seventh-Day Adventists.[20] Most of these Nicaraguan Protestants lived in the isolated northern and eastern parts of the country, where English and German missionaries had settled and proselytized a century or more earlier. Many were Indians and Creoles; almost all were campesinos. Local Sandinista defense committees accused these groups of having links with the CIA. The evangelicals were singled out to be drafted into the militias, or were arrested, or were killed. In the spring of 1982, in a small village near the Honduran border, more than a dozen were rounded up by a Sandinista battalion and taken away as their families watched. Eight years later, their skeletons were found in a mass grave.[21] In the spring and summer of 1982, the ranks of the contras filled with evangelical Protestants.

As the Sandinistas approached the celebration of the third anniversary of the revolution, they faced a population "openly disillusioned with the revolution" due to the growing economic crisis that brought increases in both inflation and unemployment. According to Alan Riding, many Nicaraguans believed that "unless the regime dramatically moderates its policies and finds ways of reviving the economy, a new violent struggle for power will sooner or later erupt."[22] The *Washington Post's* Christopher Dickey found the revolutionary celebrations "desultory." "The revolution, once marked by a contagious enthusiasm that united this country's people and inspired sympathy throughout the world, has begun to appear drab and embattled, its ranks divided."[23]

The Sandinistas' international support was also fast diminishing. The new president of Costa Rica accused the Sandinistas of "totalitarian Marxism-Leninism." Venezuela's president publicly called on them to "confront their conscience" and honor their promises to respect pluralism.[24] A meeting of the Socialist International scheduled to be held in

Caracas in the middle of February had to be canceled when Venezuela's Acción Democrática Party, the party of Carlos Andrés Pérez, demanded that the Sandinistas not be granted their usual observer status.[25] In the United States, liberal Democrats who opposed the Reagan administration's policies began to preface their attacks with a caveat: "I hold no brief for the Sandinistas."

24

Diplomacy—Round Two

The growing confrontation between the Reagan administration and the Sandinistas troubled politicians and diplomats up and down the hemisphere. In both Latin America and the United States, many feared that the growing isolation of Nicaragua and the growing confidence of the Reagan administration's rhetorical attacks could eventually lead to American intervention. Short of that, the Reagan administration and the Sandinistas were already forcing everyone in the hemisphere to take sides between the distasteful regime in Managua and an administration in Washington bent on intervening in a sovereign Latin nation.

For Latin and American liberals alike, one way out of this tangled and difficult problem was a quick negotiated settlement. By pressing the Reagan administration to pursue a diplomatic rather than a belligerent course, they could oppose American intervention without having to defend the Sandinistas' record. The first diplomatic initiative came from the Mexican government in February. As the relatively poor and weak neighbor of the world's richest and most powerful country, Mexico had for decades struck a careful balance between confrontation and accommodation with its northern neighbor. "The resulting policy of loud words and cautious action" had always allowed Mexico "to challenge Washington in diplomatic forums without threatening fundamental U.S. interests in Mexico."[1] Throughout the 1960s and 1970s, Mexico had served as Cuba's strongest and sometimes only defender in the hemisphere and, although Mexicans liked to allude to their own revolutionary heritage, the relationship did not rest on ideological affinity. In part, this stance kept Castro from stirring up trouble in a country many thought perpetually ripe for revolt. Mexico's relations with Cuba also "served as a vital symbol of Mexico's independence: It was a policy designed for Washington, not Havana."[2]

The noisy confrontation building between the Reagan administration and the Sandinistas put the Mexicans in an awkward position. Since the Sandinistas' reputation had already become tarnished, even in Latin America, Mexico could not simply take their side and join Cuba in unabashed defiance of the United States. Silence and neutrality, on the other hand, implied acquiescence and impotence in the face of an aggressive American administration. With ambitions of playing an important role in international diplomacy, Mexico thrust itself forward as the arbiter between the aggressive, hegemonic, northern superpower and the defiant, if immature, Sandinistas.

On February 21, 1982, Mexican President José López Portillo traveled to Managua to receive the Order of Sandino in appreciation for his government's support of the Sandinistas before and after the 1979 revolution. He had demanded beforehand that the Sandinistas release the three COSEP leaders imprisoned since the previous October, and Daniel Ortega had personally commuted their sentences a week before the visit. In Managua López Portillo proclaimed his solidarity with the revolution and warned the United States of "historic condemnation if there is a violent curtailment of the rights that the U.S. people undoubtedly demand for themselves; self-determination with independence, dignity and the exercise of sovereignty."[3]

The Mexican president proposed three points to begin a process of negotiations between the United States and Nicaragua. "Invoking the close relationship between Mexico and its neighbor to the north," he called on the United States to rule out the threat or use of force against Nicaragua, and he called on Nicaragua to agree to a balanced reduction of military forces in the area.[4] Finally, Portillo proposed a system of nonaggression pacts between Nicaragua and the United States and between Nicaragua and its neighbors. "[I]f this system of pacts became a reality," he proclaimed, "the main points of dispute in relations between Nicaragua and the United States could be resolved by negotiations immediately afterward."[5]

In the United States liberal congressmen seized on the Mexican initiative and in a letter to President Reagan called it "an important opportunity to resolve the conflict in the region."[6] Both the Reagan administration and the Sandinista leaders, however, were suspicious. Sandinista leaders, and especially Humberto Ortega, were not pleased with López Portillo's call for a reduction in their armed forces and an end to the supply of Soviet military equipment. From the administration's point of view, the Mexican proposal lacked the main point: an explicit promise by the Sandinistas to end covert support for the Salvadoran guerrillas.[7] It was a step backward from Enders's proposal in August 1981. Under pressure from liberal Democrats and Republicans in Congress, the administration publicly welcomed the Mexican government's intervention but tried to reshape it. Enders appreciated "the sincerity with which the President of Mexico has put forward his most recent proposal," but noted that "so far, a vital element is missing. And that is the continued very substantial support of Nicaragua for insurgency (in El Salvador.)"[8] Or as Haig put it three days later, in his inimitable fashion, the Mexican proposal "unfortunately lacked the definitive in the *sine qua non* area." It simply "did not touch upon in specific terms the guarantee to keep the hell out of the affairs of neighboring states. Without that, it only becomes a delaying negotiating tactic to permit the activity to continue . . . and we cannot permit that."[9]

Although Congressman Barnes called Haig's comments "a virtual declaration of war," the administration persisted in trying to change the Mexican plan.[10] On March 14 Haig presented the Mexican foreign minister a five-point American proposal and said he would send Enders to Managua in April to renew his earlier talks with the Sandinistas. The new proposal was almost identical to what Enders had offered the Sandinistas in August 1981: a commitment by the United States to nonaggression and enforcement of the Neutrality Act against Nicaraguan exiles; a commitment by all Central American nations to reduce foreign advisers to "a reasonably low level" and to refrain from importing "heavy offensive weapons"; the renewal of American economic assistance to Nicaragua; and, finally, a call "for the Nicaraguans to get out of El Salvador—to wind up the command and control, the logistics, including weapons, ammunition, and training camps." Haig repeated once again that this last point was the "*sine qua non*."[11] Mexican Foreign Minister Castañeda agreed a solution could be found in such a "tradeoff." "[T]his supply of arms [to the Salvadoran guerrillas] must stop," Castañeda declared, "but also in exchange for something" which would allow the Sandinistas "to feel secure from foreign dangers." Castañeda delivered the American proposal to the Sandinistas in Managua, expressing hope that direct negotiations might begin after the March 28 elections in El Salvador.[12]

The Sandinistas now had a second opportunity to reach agreement with the United States on Enders's terms. Publicly, Daniel Ortega said the new proposal "could be considered an encouraging element."[13] Privately, however, Sandinista officials believed no useful end could come from a negotiated agreement with the United States. As one official in the Sandinista Party's International Directorate later recalled, the Sandinistas were "supremely confident" of their position in March of 1982.[14] Relations with the powerful Soviet Union were improving dramatically. At the beginning of May Daniel Ortega visited Moscow and was honored with a state dinner attended by the entire Soviet leadership. Even the ailing Yuri Andropov emerged from his sickbed for the first time in weeks to greet Ortega and to declare Nicaragua a "fraternal country," greatly increasing the Sandinistas' standing among Third World allies of the Soviet Union. The Soviet government pledged $166.8 million in technical assistance and credits for Soviet-built projects, not an enormous amount but welcome.[15] More important to the Sandinistas was the unpublicized Soviet military assistance, which increased sharply in 1982.

Sandinista leaders saw the "correlation of forces" shifting in their favor in Central America, as well. They remained optimistic about the revolution in El Salvador, especially in the weeks leading up to the March 28 elections. According to one close adviser to Humberto Ortega, the Sandinistas had drawn up a "balance sheet on the activities of the FMLN" at the beginning of 1982, "weighing the levels of success in El Salvador with the international political cost of continuing support." The guerrillas, in their view, had started 1982 "stronger than ever" and stood a good chance of victory that year. The Sandinistas even considered secretly sending some of their own troops to help in the fighting.[16] The Sandinistas hoped, and the Reagan administration feared, that the guerrillas could disrupt the March 28 vote sufficiently to throw El Salvador, and Enders's policy, into chaos.

Sandinista leaders were also optimistic about the economy. Although the Nicaraguan business class was not investing and producing at high levels, the nation's economy had grown substantially since the disastrous year of the revolutionary victory. Much of this growth was based on the large amounts of American and other foreign aid the government had received in 1980 and 1981 and was, therefore, not the best measure of the true state of the economy. Nevertheless, the healthy economic growth of the preceding two years made Sandinista leaders confident about their future.[17]

Finally, the government's foreign policy analysts continued to view the Reagan administration as unwilling or unable to make good on its threats. As one former official explained, "the Reagan administration had barked many times but never bitten."[18] Sandinista leaders saw perfectly well the political constraints on the American President and his most belligerent cabinet officials.[19] As the Mexican government pushed the negotiations forward, Sandinista spokesmen began to stir up another "war scare" as they had in the spring of 1981. When the two bridges were sabotaged in northern Nicaragua on March 14, the Nicaraguan government called for a meeting of the UN Security Council to block an "imminent invasion," not by the small rebel forces in Honduras but by the United States. Foreign Minister D'Escoto told reporters that an American invasion was not just "possible, nor even probable, but rather we're convinced that the decision has been taken and they're just awaiting a propitious moment."[20]

Liberal Democrats in the U.S. Congress also spread the fear of impending war among the American public, even before the bridge explosions. Congressman Barnes declared the situation "frightening. . . . It is almost as if the administration wants a war in Central America."[21] Polls taken by the White House showed growing public anxiety and "overwhelming opposition to intervention by U.S. troops."[22] But even Barnes knew that the threat of American intervention was non-existent; indeed, he called Sergio Ramírez to assure him and other Sandinista leaders that the United States would not invade Nicaragua.[23] The Reagan administration, meanwhile, did all it could to dampen the fear of war.[24] When President Reagan was asked if there were "any circumstances under which we would be sending U.S. combat troops to El Salvador?" Reagan responded by joking, "Well, maybe if they dropped a bomb on the White House I might get mad."[25]

The Sandinistas had thus "taken an inventory of power" and found themselves in a good position. In Nicaragua "we controlled the army, the police, the ideological apparatus, the popular organizations and the commanding heights of the economy." The international "correlation of forces," in both material and political terms, was in their favor. Under these circumstances, there was simply no need to seek agreement with the Reagan administration.[26]

Reagan officials were aware of both the Sandinistas' confidence and their hopes to delay reaching a settlement. They saw no sign of any change in the Nicaraguan government's attitude since Enders's visit to Managua in August 1981. Enders believed the Sandinistas only "wanted to appear to negotiate without actually doing so."[27] In any case, Argentina's invasion of the Falkland Islands at the beginning of April, and Great Britain's decision to defend the islands, quickly engulfed both Secretary Haig and Assistant Secretary Enders, leaving them little time for negotiations with Nicaragua.

Once again events in El Salvador influenced the direction of U.S.-Nicaraguan relations. The March 28 elections, although they resulted in a sweeping victory for right-wing parties, brought 80 percent of eligible voters to the polls. The guerrillas' threatened assault on the elections proved inconsequential. The success in El Salvador gave new confidence to Reagan officials. Enders and Johnstone were optimistic that, after inheriting a "chaotic situation" from the Carter administration, "the trend of events is now in our favor." The elections in El Salvador were "a psychological and military disaster" for the guerrillas, and a blow as well to the Sandinistas. American allies in Central America were rallying to the anti-communist cause. The new civilian government in Honduras was "willing to cooperate in the struggle against guerrillas in El Salvador and against anti-democratic forces in Nicaragua," and Costa Rica's new government shared the conviction "that Nicaragua must be dealt with firmly." Even "Mexico's unhelpful role [was] diminishing as that country focuse[d] more on domestic economic concerns."[28]

The elections in El Salvador also led to a small but potentially significant change in the Reagan administration's negotiating position. On April 7 the new American ambassador in Managua, Anthony Quainton, delivered a new eight-point proposal to the Sandinista government. The points repeated Enders's original proposal, added a demand for international verification of the Nicaraguan government's compliance with any agreements[29] and in a final, eighth point, noted that the Sandinistas' adherence to earlier democratic commitments would be an essential element in determining the future course of relations between the two countries. Enders had resisted including a call for democracy in Nicaragua, but other officials argued that after elections had been held in El Salvador, the Sandinistas should be held to the same standards.[30] Critics of the Reagan administration's policies have argued that the inclusion of the eighth point on democracy alone destroyed the chances of a negotiated settlement in 1982, but that was not the case. On April 11 the Sandinistas rejected the entire proposal without expressing any preference for one point over another.[31]

The Salvadoran election dismayed the Sandinistas almost as much as it buoyed the Reagan administration. It represented a decided shift in the "correlation of forces" because it appeared to end prospects for a quick guerrilla victory. The Sandinistas responded to the new circumstances by softening their own negotiating position slightly. In the middle of April the Nicaraguan government repeated its desire to begin negotiations, as soon as possible, at the highest level and with the Mexicans as mediators. The Sandinistas put forward a thirteen-point proposal of their own, repeating past demands for an end to CIA support for counterrevolutionaries, an end to patrols by U.S. warships near Nicaragua, to overflights by U.S. spy planes, and to the use of Honduras as a "base for armed aggressions and terrorist operations," as well as a new demand that the United States renounce the imposition of any "economic, financial, or commercial blockade" against Nicaragua. In a diplomatic note delivered to the State Department on May 7, the Nicaraguan government also declared its willingness to discuss its alleged ties to the Salvadoran guerrillas, although without conceding that such ties existed.[32]

Within the Reagan administration, however, the little enthusiasm for negotiations that existed before the Salvadoran election had about disappeared once that crucial event passed. Enders and his colleagues were not interested in prominent high-level negotiations in Mexico. "We don't think it's a serious offer," one official told reporters, "and we don't intend to give [the negotiations] any priority . . . given our evaluation of their intentions."[33] Ambassador Quainton offered to begin discussions at a low level with the Sandinistas, but any high-level talks would be held only when aid to the guerrillas had stopped. Daniel Ortega responded in pique that the Sandinistas could not "dedicate our intelligence effort and security forces to pursuing those who are trafficking in arms when we have to defend ourselves against those who are attacking us from Honduras and the North American aggression."[34] The two sides traded proposals and insults throughout the summer, but negotiations had ended for the moment. When President Reagan next discussed negotiations in the fall, he made it clear that the United States was no longer interested in bilateral talks with Nicaragua, but would discuss issues only in a multilateral forum with all the Central American governments.

25

The Boland Amendment

By April 1982, the Reagan administration had come to rely primarily on one tool for shifting the balance of forces in Nicaragua: the anti-Sandinista movement in its various armed and unarmed forms. Despite the optimism of administration officials, little had been accomplished so far. American money and arms had barely begun to reach the hands of anti-Sandinista fighters, and the Falklands crisis caused a further temporary disruption. Officials believed "the greater effectiveness of anti-Sandinista groups operating along the country's borders has increased the pressure on the Nicaraguans," but this remained more a hope than a statement of fact.[1] The FDN had built five small base camps spread out along the Nicaraguan-Honduran border, but the fighters in these camps made only brief forays into Nicaragua. "Units loaded up with ammunition, hiked inside [Nicaragua] for two or three days until they found something to shoot at, and them came right back out."[2]

More promising developments came in late spring and early summer, however. The campesino leader, "Tigrillo," had great success recruiting new fighters in the areas where he had lived all his life. Bermúdez trained and equipped the new recruits and sent "Tigrillo" back in, accompanied by a 23-year-old former National Guard second lieutenant, now calling himself "Mike Lima."[3] In July the two commanders led 59 fighters into Jinotega, ambushed a Sandinista patrol, and then struck deeper into Ze-

238

laya province. The FDN's leaders were shocked to find many campesinos ready to join the new rebel army. When "Tigrillo" arrived at a farm, "soon there were peasants converging from several directions, bearing reports on the Sandinistas' movements." "Mike Lima's" unit swelled to 240 men, many more than he could equip.[4]

In July, as attacks along the Honduran border increased, the Sandinistas and Hondurans charged each other with violating the border in pursuit of, or in aid of, the contras. Both sets of charges were probably correct, but the Honduran actions were the more egregious, since on repeated occasions, Honduran forces provided cover fire with mortars and heavier weapons for contra forces moving back and forth across the border. The Sandinistas occasionally ventured into Honduras in pursuit of the contras and to test the Honduran army's mettle. They had to show great care, however, lest they provoke a violent response by the Hondurans' superpower patron. An illustration of the Sandinistas' predicament came on July 24, when 100 contras launched an attack five miles across the border against the small town of San Francisco. That same day, the United States conducted joint military exercises with the Honduran army simulating the rapid delivery of U.S. weapons to Honduran forces operating close to the Nicaraguan border.

Since the Sandinistas could not end this difficult military situation by military means, they sought to relieve the pressure by appeals to world opinion. Borge and D'Escoto warned at the end of July that "a real state of war" existed between the two countries, and the Latin leaders responded. On September 7 the presidents of Mexico and Venezuela offered their services to mediate between Honduras and Nicaragua.[5] The Reagan administration had no interest in a bilateral settlement between Nicaragua and Honduras which resulted in a *cordon sanitaire* to prevent contra infiltrations, while Nicaragua's support for the Salvadoran guerrillas proceeded unchallenged. President Reagan responded that any solution would have to include:

Democratic pluralism within each nation that includes free and fair elections in which all those who wish to do so may participate freely;

An end to support for terrorist and insurgent groups in other countries of the region;

A fully verifiable regional agreement banning the importation of heavy weapons; and

A fully verifiable regional agreement limiting foreign security and military advisors.[6]

The emphasis on democracy had become a major theme of all the administration's policies in Latin America. After helping to organize the Central American Democratic Community earlier in the year, a group which consisted of every country in Central America except Nicaragua, the administration helped arrange a "Forum for Peace and Democracy" in San José on October 4. Representatives from Colombia, El Salvador, Honduras, Jamaica, Belize, and Costa Rica signed the "Declaration of San José," which stated, more than a dozen times, that democracy and elections were the key to peace in Central America.[7] In his letter to the presidents of Mexico and Venezuela, Reagan suggested that the meeting at San José offered a promising opportunity for Latin Americans to decide how best to proceed toward peace. Venezuela and Mexico, however, did not stoop to participate in so obvious an American diplomatic ploy. The hemisphere was becoming divided. The Mexicans pressed for bilateral talks between Nicaragua and Honduras, but the Honduran government refused. President Suazo Córdova told the Mexican foreign minister that he was "too busy" to go to Caracas for a meeting with the Sandinistas. In addition to their hostility to the communist government across the border, the Honduran government and military saw in the Reagan administration a seemingly unlimited reservoir of economic and military assistance. Since 1980 American military aid had tripled to over $10 million; the Reagan administration planned further increases; and in July Honduras's President Suazo Córdova and General Gustavo Alvarez had visited Washington to ask for even more. Senior Mexican officials let it be known they suspected the hand of the Reagan administration behind the Hondurans' refusal to negotiate, but there was little they could do.[8]

The flurry of diplomatic activity in September and October did have a number of important consequences. As a result of the heightened international attention to the presence of thousands of contras on Honduran soil, the Honduran government put pressure on contra leaders to move as many of their forces into Nicaragua as possible. Contra leaders like Suicida needed little encouragement, and in November he and more than 2,000 others marched into Nicaragua to take up permanent positions in the northern and central provinces. "Mike Lima" and "Tigrillo" led more than 100 fighters across the Bocay River and attacked a Sandinista post in northern Jinotega. The Sandinistas chased them around the countryside with 2,000 men, but the rebels slipped away—just as Sandino's fighters had once eluded American marines.[9]

Some of the rebel leaders were re-enacting Sandino's style of warfare in other ways, as well. Tigrillo's brother, "Dimas Tigrillo," set himself up as a peasant warlord, defiant of the FDN leaders based in Honduras. Establishing his base at Wina, he "began thinking about where to plant crops, and even began to plot out a primitive taxation scheme." He also went on a killing spree, murdering local peasants and his own troops, before the Sandinistas overran his ill-conceived base in November, using long-range artillery, attack helicopters, aerial bombers, and hundreds of troops in a coordinated assault.[10] Another commander whose reputation as a rebel leader grew notorious at the end of 1982 was the former National Guard sergeant, Suicida. In November Suicida led several hundred men in an assault on the Segovian town of Jalapa. After ten days and a million rounds of ammunition, the attack failed.

Despite their erratic and sometimes murderous behavior, the rebel leaders attracted almost 1,000 new recruits in the last six months of 1982.[11] The infiltration of armed fighters into Nicaragua had an electrifying effect in the northern countryside, where campesinos angry at government interference in their daily lives turned in increasing numbers to the rebel army. While the Reagan administration, Congress, the Sandinistas, and Latin American presidents vied for control of the diplomatic process, the contra forces grew in the rugged and isolated northern provinces, assuming a size and aggressive temperament beyond the expectations of everyone, including the Sandinistas and the Reagan administration. The Sandinistas took sterner measures to control the peasant populations of north, central, and eastern Nicaragua, declaring martial law in the five northern provinces. The ranks of the contras, in turn, doubled and then tripled as whole villages in northern Nicaragua emptied and families made their way north to Honduras.

––––––

The contras' winter offensives had dramatic effect in Washington, too, igniting an explosion of protests against the increasingly visible "secret war" the Reagan administration was waging against the Sandinistas. At the beginning of November, *Newsweek* magazine ran a long story describing American support for the contras as much larger than ever anticipated and quoting anonymous American officials in Central America who warned that the covert program was almost out of control.[12] The article quoted one U.S. official saying "this is the biggest fiasco of this administration. . . . This is our Bay of Pigs." The *Newsweek* article also asked whether the covert operation violated "the spirit if not the letter of congressional restrictions on dirty tricks?" This was a matter that soon became the subject of debate in the Congress and in the Reagan administration.

The *Newsweek* article prompted a series of news reports and editorials in other publications throughout the month of November. Reagan administration officials rebutted some of *Newsweek*'s allegations and criticisms: "We are not waging a secret war, or anything approaching that," one senior intelligence official said. "What we are doing is trying to keep Managua off balance and apply pressure to stop providing military aid to the insurgents in El Salvador."[13] Back in April, Congressman Michael Barnes had been dissuaded by the House Democratic leadership from openly opposing the covert operation planned by the administration. By November, the press made clear that the covert attacks against Nicaragua had gone well beyond those plans and had become an assault into Nicaraguan territory by thousands of contras. The leadership of the Democratic Party, including Congressman Boland, remained quiet, but the liberal wing of the party determined to raise a public objection to the Reagan administration's growing secret war.

On December 8 Congressman Tom Harkin rose in the House to offer an amendment prohibiting all support for paramilitary activities in or against Nicaragua. His concern was not with fine legal distinctions but with the morality of American foreign policy. Referring to the *Newsweek* article, Congressman Harkin told his colleagues that "news reports of late . . . clearly indicate that we are becoming ever more mired in the jungles and swamps of Latin America." "[T]he real mistake we are making," he said, "is not only in doing something that is clearly illegal, but in siding with perhaps the most hated group of Nicaraguans that could exist outside of the borders of Nicaragua, and I talk about the Somocistas." Such support for "vicious, cutthroat murderers" was "antithetical to our own beliefs and what we want in Central America." "[R]egardless how one may feel about the Sandinistas . . . in the name of all that is right and just and decent, we should end our involvement with this group."[14]

Other liberal Democrats joined Harkin. Congressman George Miller called on Congress to "go on record in getting control of those agencies who have convinced the White House to substitute covert action for policy, to substitute covert action for diplomacy, and take an action that without the express consent of this Congress is in fact illegal, unethical and against the best interests of this country." Miller called on his colleagues to take a stand against the Reagan administration as Democrats had once challenged the Nixon and Ford administrations. "You are now on notice. This is not speculation about another Vietnam. This is a first step of our Vietnam. Some of us came here to stop Vietnam. And here is a chance to stop the new one."

Miller and his colleagues spoke for a generation of younger Democrats in the House.[15] They did not command a majority of votes or the support of the House leadership, and they did not expect Harkin's amendment to win. What they did hope, however, was to embarrass their party leaders into joining their assault on the administration's policy in Nicaragua.

The clear implication of their charges was that Boland and the intelligence committee were either willing participants in an illegal and immoral war, or dupes of the Reagan administration. Chairman Boland took the floor to defend himself, saying that "those who are supporting the Harkin amendment had a field day here and I do not blame them. I can say to my friend [Harkin] and all of those who have made these magnificent appeals that I share their concern for the news stories. . . . these concerns are shared by the Permanent Select Committee on Intelligence, make no mistake about it."[16] Boland insisted, however, that he had already addressed the problem. Both intelligence committees in the House and Senate and even the Reagan administration had agreed to prohibit the use of funds "to overthrow the Government of Nicaragua or to provoke a military exchange between Nicaragua and Honduras," and so Harkin's amendment was unnecessary.

Boland went further, asserting the exclusive competence of his committee to oversee covert operations run by the executive branch. Congressman Harkin's amendment, he said, "sets a bad precedent. We ought not to legislate in an area such as this without the benefit of all the facts. That is why the Intelligence Committee was established, and its effectiveness depends on its ability to keep the Nation's secrets and exercise sensible and prudent oversight." Aware that it was his own ability to serve as the watchdog for Congress that was being questioned, Boland gave assurances "that the committee certainly does understand its obligations to rein in activities which can get out of control or which could threaten to involve this Nation or its allies in a war." He requested that Harkin withdraw his amendment on the grounds that the "Intelligence Committee's oversight is such that the assurances I have given can be relied upon."[17]

Congressman Harkin did not let his elder colleague escape so easily.[18] Boland was forced to offer his own amendment, which repeated publicly the restrictions he had set forth in the secret annex in April. Boland's amendment prohibiting the use of funds "for the purpose of" overthrowing the government of Nicaragua or provoking a war between Nicaragua and Honduras passed by a vote of 411–0.

Passage of the Boland amendment perpetuated the unusual compromise that had been reached between the intelligence committee and the Reagan administration back in April. Even more than before, however, the two sides now became equal partners in evasion. The Boland amendment preserved the "loophole" of the earlier agreement: the Reagan administration could aid the contras, who sought to overthrow the Sandinista government, so long as it was not the Reagan administration's intent to overthrow the Sandinistas. Thus, even after the spate of news stories suggesting that the contras, by virtue of the size of their forces and their own statements, seemed to be seeking the overthrow of the Sandinista government, Boland and 410 members of Congress voted to allow the administration to continue supporting the war under precisely the same terms as before. In speeches, testimony before Congress, and public diplomatic proposals, the Reagan administration had already made clear that one of its principal goals was democratic reform in Nicaragua, and the contras had become the administration's main tool for carrying out its policy. Still, no congressman rose to suggest the administration was in violation of the restrictions now passed into law. Boland, in fact, stated that he believed his agreement with the administration to be intact.

Congressman Boland and the House of Representatives, moreover, had a chance to close the loophole and chose not to. Just before the final vote on the Boland amendment Congressman Harkin offered a modification that resembled Boland's legislation in all respects except one: Harkin's amendment specifically addressed the question of the contras' intent, saying that no funds could be provided to an individual or group "which is already known by [the CIA or Defense Department] to have the intent of overthrowing the government of Nicaragua."[19] Harkin's amendment would still have been subject to interpretation by an executive branch looking for loopholes, but it would have gone a long way toward undoing the ambiguity that Boland's language deliberately perpetuated. The modified amendment was rejected without even a recorded vote.[20]

Harkin and his colleagues nevertheless achieved their more limited objectives. Were it not for Harkin's efforts there might have been no public vote on covert aid to the contras in 1982. The passage of the Boland amendment now made it a matter of public record that the United States was supporting a covert war in Nicaragua. Congress, meanwhile, put itself on record as simultaneously supporting aid to the contras, supporting restrictions on that aid, and consciously providing the loophole through which those restrictions could be made irrelevant.

The unanimous vote resulted from lobbying by the Reagan administration in concert with Boland and the House leadership in a deal that had been made beforehand. Within the Reagan administration, some officials argued that the Boland amendment should be opposed, in part because they feared it was impossible for the administration to avoid falling afoul of the new law. They were overruled.[21] William Casey went to Capitol Hill during the debates in the House and Senate to assure members that the program would remain within the prescribed limits and that, even though the contras' intent might be to overthrow the Sandinistas, this would not be the goal of the Reagan administration. Minutes before the vote, Congressman Barnes rose to urge fellow liberal Democrats to accept Boland's language "so that we can go on record" and because if Boland's substitute amendment did not pass, then "we will not pass anything, I fear."[22] Harkin and his colleagues laid aside their objections and voted with Boland, secure in the knowledge that they had made their point and put both the Reagan administration and their own leaders on notice.

In the Senate, Senator Christopher Dodd of Connecticut forced consideration of a measure to prohibit American support for any "irregular or paramilitary groups operating in the Central American region." His amendment, which eschewed even Harkin's efforts to win support by narrowly addressing aid to the contras, failed decisively by a vote of 56–38. Like Harkin's amendment, however, Dodd's was a symbolic effort to expose not only the Reagan administration's secret war, but the Congress's willful acquiescence. The Boland amendment was passed into law on December 21.

The day before the House passed the Boland amendment, the CIA hurriedly organized a news conference in Fort Lauderdale to unveil a new "political directorate" for the Nicaraguan Democratic Force (FDN), the main group of rebels fighting out of Honduras and in the north of Nicaragua. In response to criticism as old as the FDN itself that the fighting force represented a return to Somocismo and rule by the National Guard, the Reagan administration brought five members of the Nicaraguan bourgeois political class to the fore. One was Edgar Chamorro, the descendant of two prominent families of the Nicaraguan aristocracy. José Francisco Cardenal, the political leader of the political-military alliance, had quit, or been expelled, in a dispute with Bermúdez over control of the movement but the FDN leadership acquired a more significant political figure when, at the beginning of 1983, Adolfo Calero finally left Nicaragua and joined the FDN directorate. Calero had played a prominent and outspoken role in the struggle against Somoza throughout 1978 and 1979. He had been jailed briefly by Somoza in the crackdown against moderates in the fall of 1978. He led a Conservative Party faction and had continued his struggles for democratic government in Nicaragua well into the second and third year of the Sandinista revolution. Not surprisingly, when he joined the FDN at the beginning of 1983 he quickly became the directorate's leader, both by the force of his personality and thanks to the effective support of the CIA. He also soon forged a strong and potent alliance with the former National Guard colonel, Enrique Bermúdez, the senior military officer in the contra movement.

Some opposition politicians in exile argued against joining with the former Guardsmen, but Chamorro and others responded that Bermúdez and his group "were professional soldiers and not necessarily bad guys. Besides, I pointed out, we didn't have the capacity to train a fighting force, and we had to work with people who did."[23] Just as most moderate leaders in the days of the FAO, including Robelo, had been willing to form a new government with the support of a reformed National Guard, so these FDN political leaders were willing to join a political-military alliance in which Guardsmen like Enrique Bermúdez, whose reputation for decency was not even questioned by the Sandinistas,[24] led the fighting. Nicaraguan moderates, as always, lacked the guns which they considered essential to force political change. In 1979 many moderates had hoped the Sandinistas' guns would force Somoza from power while the guns of the National Guard would prevent a Sandinista victory. Now some Nicaraguan moderates turned again to the National Guard to do the fighting they could not do.

At the December 7 press conference, the new political directorate declared it was opening its arms "to all those who wish to join us" and expressed the "patriotic intention of cooperating with any group which shares our objectives." The directorate appealed to the nations of the hemisphere for help, using the rhetoric and the symbols of the democratic revolution. "[J]ust as they supported our first effort to free ourselves from dictatorship, they might now, convinced that our struggle is also their struggle, offer us their decided support in our effort to complete the patriotic task." Invoking the words of Pedro Joaquín Chamorro, they looked forward to the day when "Nicaragua can again be a Republic."[25]

The new rhetoric and composition of the contra leadership fit well with the foreign policy President Reagan had outlined that year. While Congress and the administration shook hands behind closed doors over the Boland amendment's restrictions, the new contra political leaders proclaimed a democratic revolution in Nicaragua.

26

"With a Gun at Our Heads"

While the rebel leadership was being reshaped in Florida and Honduras, rebel fighters moved into Nicaragua in unprecedented numbers. In Nueva Segovia, the Sandinistas estimated that almost 1,000 had entered and taken up positions by the end of December.[1] In northern Zelaya, according to a Honduran military officer, five columns of 125 fighters each crossed over from Miskito Indian camps in Honduras.[2] The fighters moved in during the coffee-picking season, hoping also to disrupt the harvest. They ambushed trucks carrying coffee-pickers to the fields, sometimes forcing the trucks to turn back after lecturing the campesinos, other times firing on them, especially when the trucks were escorted by armed Sandinista militia. The Miskito fighters headed for their homelands in the northeastern portion of the country and began by attacking near the border villages of Waspan and Bilwaskarma. The FDN troops in Nueva Segovia prepared to make another attack on Jalapa. According to a local Sandinista commander, "their plan was to take Jalapa from different sides, then cut off the highway south and declare this a liberated territory."[3] In the first weeks of 1983 Suicida occupied a 200-square-mile area around Jalapa in the center of Nueva Segovia, striking out periodically against civilian and military targets to undermine the government's control of the region. In March the Sandinistas reported heavy fighting around Quilali, 20 miles south of Jalapa. They estimated the number of rebel fighters in the area at about 2,000.[4]

A group of fighters led by a former National Guard lieutenant, "Toño," organized for more ambitious ventures. At the end of December Toño trained and organized 240 fighters into a unit called the Jorge Salazar Task Force. His plan was to travel deep into the central Nicaraguan province of Matagalpa and establish a permanent base. The Jorge Salazar Task Force crossed into Nicaragua in February 1983, and although some of the men deserted for their homes, the rest of the force found an open path to the central regions of the country. Toño discovered that once rebel forces made their way past the Sandinista forces blocking infiltration at the border, there were many fewer Sandinista units to impede their southward progress. Toño's men set up camp in the mountains at El Rosario and on March 8 cut off the road from Waslala to Rio Blanco, overrunning three Sandinista military garrisons.[5]

The rebel fighters found themselves in friendly territory in both the Segovias and further south in Matagalpa. At the end of March, two journalists, Christopher Dickey from the *Washington Post* and James LeMoyne from *Newsweek*, joined a group of contras in Honduras and marched with them into Nueva Segovia to meet up with Suicida and get a close look at the war from the contras' perspective. The fighters they traveled with were mostly "small landowners and local country people." The commanders were "tough professional soldiers from the old National Guard." The guerilla units "appeared to be as well trained and well armed as virtually any regular infantry in Central America," fully equipped with American weapons and supplies, seasoned by months of combat, and their morale was high. The contra forces led by Suicida "appeared to count on considerable and invaluable support among the few peasants left in the increasingly deserted war zone."[6]

When peasants were asked why they were offering the rebel fighters food, "sometimes bringing it unbidden to mountaintops for them," or why they offered the rebels shelter and gave them information about the whereabouts of Sandinista troops, or why they joined the rebel army, the peasants "said nothing about fear. Instead they talked in terms of what they view as Sandinista threats to their economic, social and cultural survival."[7] The peasants complained about Sandinista rationing and low government prices for their crops and livestock. They said they were infuriated by Sandinista troops who took their food and supplies, leaving behind a slip of paper. The contras, on the other hand, paid in cash: The patrol Dickey traveled with "carried the equivalent of several thousand dollars in Nicaraguan currency."

In addition, the local farmers and country folk were strongly religious Catholics and evangelical Protestants, who resented the government's pressures on them and believed the Sandinistas to be atheists. "They find it easier to sympathize with the contras," Dickey wrote, "some of whom carry weathered Bibles to leaf through during breaks in their long marches and wear large crucifixes around their necks and religious medals on their fatigue hats."[8]

One civilian told reporters that in December the contras had escorted 600 residents from the village of Los Encinos across the border into Honduras. "The Sandinistas try to keep people from leaving," the man said, "so we had to flee at night. We walked for three days." Another group of refugees said that 30 families had been displaced near Jalapa after Sandinista troops burned their homes. Another journalist traveling with the contras reported that "conversations with the combatants over the five days left the impression that even if covert American aid ends, deep-rooted unhappiness with the Government among the people in northern Nicaragua will keep the insurgency boiling for a long time."[9]

To maintain their position in the countryside, contra leaders used brutal intimidation as well. Although there were no reports of Sandino's infamous "gourd cut," reports of campesinos murdered by contras who suspected them to be informers, of women raped and men beaten, circulated the countryside. In some towns and villages hostility toward the contras was as great as support for them was elsewhere. After an attack on the small village of Rancho Grande, a few miles south of the Honduran border, the contras were driven off by a combination of militia and local people. One 70-year-old man holding an old Soviet-made rifle said he had shot at the contras and would do so again if they returned.[10]

The contras routinely executed Sandinista soldiers and militia captured in ambushes or Sandinista officials sent from the cities to teach in the schools or work in the fields. They frequently killed lay preachers and religious workers who came to the countryside to pick crops in support of the revolution and in service to the "People's Church." The contras treated these civilians as enemies, and on this basis justified their rape, torture, and murder. Some of the contras simply enjoyed killing the "*piricuacos*," or rabid dogs, as they called the Sandinistas and their official supporters; others executed captured soldiers and militia because it was too difficult to bring them along as prisoners while the unit moved quickly through the hills and jungles. Still others killed whenever and whomever they chose.

"We walk here as lords of this land," Suicida told Dickey. The tradition of local warlords in the rugged hills of Nicaragua was an old one. Sandino had made Nueva Segovia his own fiefdom in the 1920s and 1930s, and many contras, including Suicida, looked to Sandino as a model.[11] As Adolfo Calero told Dickey, "This is not the second civil war that Nicaragua has had. We've had dozens of them." None of these Nicaraguan wars had been fought without brutality.

Sandinista army commanders expressed concern, nevertheless, that the contras enjoyed "at least tolerance, if not support, from some farmers and villagers in the region."[12] Over the course of several months, the Sandinista commanders had witnessed a rapid improvement in the contras' military abilities. "On their own, the contras would have taken 10 to 15 years to achieve this level of arms and organization," one commander in the northern provinces told reporters, "but now they have small combat units equipped with M-60 mortars, M-79 rocket launchers, automatic rifles, communications and so on, which gives them tactical independence." A Sandinista commander said, "we'd like to see the contras invade in a conventional way because we would whip them, but they're not going to do us that favor. They're going to keep chipping away and we have to learn to live with the problem. This could go on for a long time."[13]

Toño's drive into Matagalpa made the Sandinistas especially nervous. The Jorge Salazar Task Force was hardly in a position to conquer the Sandinista army from Matagalpa, but the location of the new offensive was troubling to Sandinista commanders who had hoped to keep the rebels bottled up along the Honduran border. Instead, the fighting had "moved to what was always seen to be—indeed what is—the central province."[14] On March 22 Sandinista officials reported that between 200 and 500 contras had entered the city of Matagalpa, and Humberto Ortega told reporters that Sandinista soldiers and militiamen were fighting against at least 1,200 guerrillas around Matagalpa. Ortega dispatched regular army forces, including a specially trained army battalion, to push back the rebels. Hundreds of militia were also rushed to Matagalpa to man defenses.

Although the loss of Matagalpa would be disastrous, the Sandinistas were reluctant to send more reinforcements. Worrying as the deep penetration was, the Sandinistas considered it a ruse to draw their forces away from the border area around Jalapa—a tactic they used themselves in the fight against Somoza. Borge explained to reporters on March 24 that Matagalpa was "merely diversionary to make us lower our guard in the north."[15] Despite Sandinista efforts to dislodge them, the contras remained in Matagalpa province into April.

In the end, the Sandinistas counted on the contras' impossibly long supply lines to thwart any sustained attack so deep into the country. Ortega insisted the rebels had "no chance of taking a single town" because it was "impossible for them to be supplied from Honduras."[16] He was right. By the second week of April, large numbers of contra troops began their trek back toward the Honduran border for rest and resupply. Those who had penetrated as far as Matagalpa found the trip back particularly rough going. "It took us 20 days to walk out of there," one contra spokesman told a reporter afterwards.[17] On their way out they were attacked repeatedly by Sandinista forces and, as the contras weaved their way quickly through the difficult terrain, they sustained heavy losses. According to the Nicaraguan Defense Ministry, 196 guerrillas were killed between March 30 and April 11. Most of the casualties were suffered by columns of contras making their way back into Honduras. During the entire March offensive, the Sandinistas reported killing 402 contra fighters while losing 91 men of their own.[18]

After their successes early in the year, rebel leaders complained bitterly that the CIA and their own military leaders were not providing them with the long land and air supply lines necessary to sustain the offensive. By April 1983 the FDN had acquired two C-47 cargo planes, but their range was too short to reach the forces that most needed resupply. Contra political leaders outside Nicaragua told reporters that "the United States is helping us in ways we don't want. They are saying no, no, no to everything. Our men want to do spectacular things. You have the momentum and they stop you. It's like an invisible hand holding the strings." Others expressed their concern and puzzlement at the restrictions imposed by the Boland amendment, and they questioned the extent of America's commitment to their fight. "I would like to know where they stand," one rebel leader told Christopher Dickey. "Why must this be a covert thing if they are for us?"[19]

American officials in Washington and Central America, however, had not been prepared for the enormous growth of the rebel forces that began at the end of 1982 and continued throughout 1983. When Mike Lima told Bermúdez in August 1982 that he was bringing back 180 new recruits, Bermúdez had asked him not to "bring such a mountain of men. The Americans don't want us to grow so much."[20] The Reagan administration had simply underestimated the potential strength of its "lowball option."

The retreat from Matagalpa did not end the contras' months-long offensive, however. In May Suicida and his men launched another assault on Jalapa. It failed like the last, but only after the Sandinistas rushed several battalions of regular army and reserve troops to the isolated northern town.[21] On June 7 the contras took a small hamlet on the Honduran border known as El Porvenir. They held it for eight days, with the Honduran army providing covering fire with rifles and mortars from the other side of the border. Although the Sandinistas finally retook El Porvenir on June 15, a Sandinista military spokesman, Roberto Sanchez, declared that the war had entered a "totally different" phase.[22] As one journalist reported at the beginning of July, "Although [the Sandinistas] managed to repel efforts to take any of the major towns in Nueva Segovia . . . they lost at least temporary control of a number of small villages and strategic sites and still do not exercise complete control over a significant part of the border region."[23]

None of the contras' successes in 1983 made any great impression on officials in Washington. American observers inside and outside the Reagan administration labored under the misapprehension that the contras could pose no threat to the Sandinistas until they struck at the populated Pacific Coast. Twice in 1983 the CIA sent rebel commando teams on a difficult and dangerous mission to destroy a heavily guarded tank battalion in Chinandega; both times the mission failed.[24] In Washington, the rebels' activities in the eastern portions of the country were considered peripheral. The Sandinistas understood, however, that the fall of any major town in northern and eastern Nicaragua would mean serious trouble. No more than Somoza or any other Managua-based government in Nicaraguan history could the Sandinistas afford to see "liberated territory" carved out of the Nicaraguan countryside. Such a setback could mean, if not the end, at least the beginning of the end for the regime.

The unexpected strength of the rebellion forced the Sandinistas to reconsider their tactics. Before the 1983 offensives, the Sandinista army's strategy had been to throw the militia at the contras, perhaps employing some regular army troops in blocking positions near the Honduran border, but holding the bulk of the regular forces in reserve to protect strategic positions near the major military bases and large cities near the Pacific

Coast. The theory was to defend against the possibility of an American invasion, although Humberto Ortega recognized that any attempt to repel such an invasion would be futile. The strategy had obviously not worked. The government was alarmed to learn how close the contras had come to dealing it a significant blow in the north, and, just like Somoza, the Sandinistas were forced to send regular battalions to the front to prevent the loss of a single town. Transportation for Sandinista forces in the north was difficult, however. There were few roads—only one between Jalapa and Ocotal—and these were subject to constant ambush by contra forces.[25] With an estimated 2,500 fighters operating in columns of 500–600 moreover, the rebels could pose a threat in several locations at once, and the Sandinistas could not afford to be caught short.

A complete change of strategy was called for. No sooner had the heaviest fighting come to an end in the middle of June than reports circulated in Managua that a high-ranking Cuban general, Arnoldo Ochoa, had arrived to take charge of the war against the contras.[26] General Ochoa had commanded the Cuban expeditionary forces in Angola, and his dispatch by Castro to take control of the situation in Nicaragua suggested that the contras' bold actions in the spring worried the Cuban military high command, as well as the Sandinistas.[27] Whether on the advice of Ochoa or on their own, the Sandinistas immediately set about revising their military strategy, tactics, and capabilities. Rather than using the militias and reserves as the sole buffer against contra attacks in the north, the Sandinistas reoriented their army toward more aggressive counterinsurgency warfare. They began to train special counterguerrilla battalions that could move quickly and over extended periods of time in search of contra forces. The changes came slowly, however. For the next several months the Sandinistas could do no more than repeat their earlier tactics more effectively. When most of the contras withdrew back into Honduras from northern Nicaragua, Sandinista troops immediately set about digging trenches and foxholes in rice fields, and reinforcements were brought in to block the next offensive. On June 19 reporters counted at least 1,000 Sandinista troops deployed around Jalapa.[28] More arrived in the weeks that followed. The Sandinistas learned that blocking infiltration of rebel forces was almost impossible along the 500-mile long border.

The Sandinistas desperately needed greater mobility for their army if the new strategy was to succeed. Here the Soviet Union stepped in with a vital contribution of weapons and equipment. After Ochoa's arrival, the weaponry flowed at unprecedented levels. Soviet deliveries reportedly included up to ten Mi-8 helicopter transports, over 300 new trucks—increasing the number of trucks by one-third—20 to 25 armored fighting vehicles and personnel carriers, a number of multiple rocket launchers—the so-called "Stalin organs"—and additional tanks that increased the total number of tanks in the Sandinistas' inventory to 60. These additional weapons, vehicles, and helicopters increased the mobility of Sandinista forces responding to contra attacks far from the strategic center of the country. They also permitted larger numbers of Sandinista forces to be supplied for longer stretches in forward positions near the borders.

The cost of conducting this different type of war against the contras went beyond weapons and supplies, which the Soviets provided for little or nothing. The military's demand for oil to operate all the new vehicles and aircraft also grew, as did the Sandinistas' vulnerability to sabotage of its oil supplies. More significantly, the new counterinsurgency strategy required an increase in the already large numbers of men under arms. On July 15 Humberto Ortega announced plans to begin universal military conscription in order to make possible the "massive defense" necessary to protect the revolution.[29] The political price of universal conscription promised to be high. In the cities, where most citizens had so far been able to ignore the war in the northern provinces, opposition to the new draft law would be stiff. The Sandinistas could expect to anger many middle- and lower-class Nicaraguans who had been at worst indifferent to the revolution, but who now saw their sons taken into the army. The draft issue immediately strengthened the hands of opposition parties representing the interests of the urban bourgeoisie.

———

The expanded rebellion forced the Sandinistas to change their political and diplomatic strategies, as well as their plan for fighting the war. One of the first shifts could be seen in the Sandinistas' agrarian reform program. As reporters traveling with the contras in May reported again and again that the rebels, for all their violent misdeeds, enjoyed significant support among the peasants, the Sandinistas looked for ways to repair their own relations with the campesinos. Along with their opposition to the Sandinistas' alleged atheism and to their military conscription policies, the campesinos complained most bitterly about the government's land policies. Beginning in May and June of 1983, the Nicaraguan government reversed its course of the previous two years and began distributing parcels of land to peasants along the northern and southern borders of the country. The new program did not exactly give ownership of the land to those who farmed it; the peasants were given title to lands which they were to work as cooperatives. The titles had symbolic and political importance, however. Rebel leaders in the north frequently proclaimed their desire to return lands confiscated by the Sandinistas to their original owners, which in the case of many contra fighters meant to themselves and their families. The new titles presented by the Sandinistas in the summer of 1983 presumably gave those who received them an incentive to defend their claim to the land against rebel attacks. Along with their new titles, the peasants were also handed guns.

The government handed out titles to more land in two months than in all the previous four years of the revolution. At the same time, to win greater support among farmers, cattle-growers, and small landowners, the government announced it was considering pardoning some outstanding debts owed the Central Bank. These new policies completely reversed the original conception of the Sandinista agrarian reform. At the beginning of the revolution, the Sandinistas had been committed to keeping intact the large estates confiscated from Somoza's family and friends, in part to produce more efficiently for the agricultural export market, and in part to avoid "the enlargement of a peasant class of small property owners with 'bourgeois' interests."[30] Four years later, concern about the "bourgeoisization" of the peasantry gave way to concerns about blocking political and strategic inroads by the contras.

Under the pressure of the rebel war, and the international scrutiny it was attracting, the Sandinistas began to make some concessions to their unarmed political opponents. Not much had been heard from these groups since the Sandinistas had imposed a State of Emergency throughout the country in March 1982. The opposition's newspaper, *La Prensa*, had been heavily censored, its radio stations shut down. Its political rallies were prohibited, the opposition's properties periodically confiscated, and its leaders periodically arrested. Now the Sandinistas loosened the restraints, spoke of a new flexibility and even hinted of the possibility of elections. At the beginning of 1983 the leaders of a coalition of political parties, unions, and business groups known as the Democratic Coordinating Board, or Coordinadora, traveled throughout Latin America to gain international support for their efforts in Nicaragua. In particular, the Coordinadora's leaders sought to bring pressure on the Sandinistas to hold free elections sooner than 1985.[31] In pursuit of this goal, the leaders of the opposition parties demanded that the Sandinista-controlled Council of

State finally pass a law on political parties making clear the terms by which the opposition would be allowed to compete in any election.[32] The Sandinistas were uncharacteristically tolerant of the opposition's public complaints.

The Sandinistas did not hide the fact that their more moderate stance was the result of new economic and military pressures. When the second wave of the contras' northern offensive was in full swing, Carlos Nuñez, the president of the Council of State, addressed the legislature's opening session and made clear the growing conviction among Sandinista leaders that the pressure exerted by the United States demanded in response a greater degree of political flexibility. "The imperialist enemy wants us to make mistakes now, when it would be most advantageous to that enemy for impatience to prevail over prudence and revolutionary ire over good sense. The enemy wants us to respond irrationally and to push aside our mixed economy and our political pluralism. . . . [But w]e won't make any mistakes. We can't afford to."[33] Over the course of several months, the passage of the new political laws and the holding of elections had ceased to be the annoying refrain of the opposition parties and had become, in Nuñez's words, "tasks made necessary by the defense" of the revolution.[34]

The pressure brought by the rebel forces also forced the Sandinistas to reconsider their diplomatic position. In January 1983 the foreign ministers of Mexico, Venezuela, Colombia, and Panama met on the island of Contadora to inaugurate a new effort to find diplomatic solutions to the growing crisis in Central America. Unfortunately for the Sandinistas, the new "Contadora Group" seemed more interested in negotiating an end to the violence in Nicaragua than about furthering the Sandinistas' interest in bilateral negotiations with Honduras. Indeed, the Contadora Group soon began to bend to American insistence on multilateral talks involving all Central American nations, where Nicaragua would likely be outvoted 4–1.[35]

At the beginning of May, therefore, the Sandinistas took their case to the United Nations Security Council, where Nicaragua had won a two-year membership the previous year. Nicaraguan Foreign Minister Miguel D'Escoto demanded that the Security Council take up the issue of U.S. support for the rebels, pass a resolution denouncing American aggression against Nicaragua, and designate the UN Secretary General to intervene directly in the crisis.[36] But again the Sandinistas were rebuffed. On May 19 the Security Council voted unanimously to support the "efforts of the Contadora Group to achieve solutions to the problems that affect Central

American countries and to secure a stable and lasting peace in the region." The final resolution did not condemn American aggression: It reaffirmed "the right of Nicaragua and of all the other countries of the area to live in peace and security, free from outside interference"—a phrase that could be said to refer not only to American support for the contras but also to Nicaraguan, Cuban, and Soviet interference in El Salvador.[37] Except for the fact that the United Nations officially put the issue of Nicaragua on its agenda for the first time,[38] the resulting resolution was a defeat for the Sandinistas and a victory for the United States.[39]

Having openly attempted to displace Contadora as the mediator and failed, the Sandinistas now risked diplomatic isolation if they refused to bend. When the foreign ministers of the four Contadora countries called a meeting in Panama on May 28 with the five foreign ministers from Central America, the Sandinistas had no choice but to attend. This time, Foreign Minister D'Escoto sat at the same table with the other Central American foreign ministers and held "bilateral" discussions with his Honduran counterpart while the others looked on.

As the international talks proceeded, the Sandinistas found themselves increasingly outnumbered. The Nicaraguan government had hoped that the Contadora Group, led by a sympathetic Mexico, would protect its interests against the United States and its allies. The other Central American governments, however, had demanded a greater say in settling the region's conflicts, and the Contadora Group had not resisted. This opened the door to a number of strong demands by the Sandinistas' adversaries. The other Central American governments insisted, for instance, that the question of democratization be part of any peace proposal devised by the Contadora Group. The Nicaraguan political opposition leaders also lobbied to make their demands for free elections and broad political reforms part of the Contadora Group's deliberations.[40]

The Sandinistas saw that the negotiations were turning against them. In the middle of June, D'Escoto was still declaring that "the real test" for the Contadora Group would be to bring Honduras back into bilateral talks with Nicaragua. But on July 17 the presidents of the Contadora Group met at Cancun and issued a statement supporting continued dialogue "with the participation of all the governments in Central America." The Contadora Group went even further and endorsed the Reagan administration's new political goals in Nicaragua. In their declaration from Cancun on July 17, the four presidents called not only for commitments to cease delivery of weapons to insurgencies, to freeze arms levels, to prohibit installation of foreign military bases in the region, and to reach agreement on other security matters; they also called for "a great effort to strengthen democratic institutions and guarantee the observance of human rights." "To this end," the communiqué continued, "we must perfect the methods of popular consultation, guarantee free access of the different currents of opinion to the electoral process, and promote the full participation of citizens in their country's political life."[41]

The Sandinistas had little choice but to bend further or suffer international isolation. On July 19, at ceremonies celebrating the fourth anniversary of the revolution, Daniel Ortega announced that his government, despite its "absolute conviction that the real threat to peace in the region demands bilateral solutions," nevertheless agreed to accept the Contadora Group's multilateral format "so there will be an end to the excuses." D'Escoto complained that Nicaragua was being forced to negotiate "with a gun at our heads."[42]

Meetings among the Central American foreign ministers at the end of July yielded no progress, so the Contadora ministers pressed ahead on their own. On September 8 and 9, they drafted and then presented to the Central American foreign ministers a "Document of Objectives," which became know as the "21 points," a concatenation of different proposals.[43] Although intended as a compromise among all the involved parties, the 21 points fell hardest on the Sandinistas. The first points of substance had to do with internal political reforms, and point four called for the adoption of "measures conducive to the establishment and, where appropriate, improvement of democratic, representative, and pluralistic systems that will guarantee effective popular participation in the decision-making process and ensure that the various currents of opinion have free access to fair and regular elections based on the full observance of citizens' rights." Point five called for the promotion of "national reconciliation efforts wherever deep divisions have taken place within society, with a view to fostering participation in democratic political processes in accordance with the law."[44]

The points concerning security in the region also addressed few of the Sandinistas' demands. Except for calling on all governments to prevent the use of their territory for the destabilization or subversion of other governments in the region (points 10–13)—a demand aimed at both Nicaragua and Honduras—the rest of the security provisions rejected Sandinista demands and were more favorable to the requirements of the United States and its allies. While the Sandinistas had insisted that all deliveries of weapons to both sides in the Salvadoran conflict be stopped—which would have prevented the United States from sending arms to the Salvadoran government—Contadora's 21 points opposed weapons deliveries only to groups seeking to destabilize other governments. While the Sandinistas had demanded an immediate signing of a nonaggression pact between Nicaragua and Honduras, the Contadora document was silent on this point. While the Sandinistas called for commitments that no foreign military bases be established and that no military exercises be conducted in the region by foreign armies, the Contadora proposal—drawn up in the very midst of large American exercises—called only for a ban on foreign military bases "or any other type of foreign military interference."

Moreover, the Contadora Group added points that the Sandinistas had consistently rejected when presented by the Americans and that clearly worked against their strategic interests. One was a call for reductions in stocks of weapons and in the numbers of armed troops which, given the size of the Sandinista army in relation to those of its neighbors, could only result in a sharp reduction of the Sandinista army at a time when Humberto Ortega was seeking its rapid expansion. The other was a call for reductions in the number of foreign military advisers "and other foreign elements involved in military and security activities, with a view to their elimination"—a measure that would also fall heavily on the large numbers of Cuban and Eastern bloc advisers in Nicaragua, numbers that had been growing since the spring in order to help the Sandinistas handle the contra war.

The Central Americans, including Nicaragua, had little choice but to agree to the 21 Points or face international opprobrium. In the days following the Contadora meeting, D'Escoto grumbled that although the United States was not "physically represented in the Contadora Group, its militaristic attitude is present in every discussion."[45] Nevertheless, at the end of September Daniel Ortega wrote to express his agreement with the Contadora Group's "Document of Objectives."

While maneuvering to avoid isolation abroad, the Sandinistas also continued to loosen restraints on their opposition within Nicaragua. They sped up the process of approving an electoral law, and on August 20 the Council of State announced that it had completed work on the laws to govern political parties in the next election. Opposition leaders told reporters they had won some concessions from the Sandinistas in the law, including guarantees that parties could hold meetings and public rallies, maintain offices, and distribute literature, so long as their proposals and platforms were "constructive" and respected "the basic principles of the Sandinista revolution." The law also gave parties the right to "aspire to power." What remained unclear was whether the Sandinistas intended to put their control of the government at risk.[46]

Whatever the Sandinistas' ultimate intentions, however, their small opening permitted opponents a forum denied them for over two years. At the end of August, 90 members of the Conservative Democratic Party met in a movie theater to hold the first convention by an opposition party since the victory of the revolution. There the opposition party delegates pledged publicly to do whatever they could to prevent the consolidation of "totalitarian Marxist-Leninist regimes which are in the Soviet orbit and are rejected by the immense majority of our people." Neither Sandinista police nor Sandinista-controlled mobs disrupted the remarkable gathering. Earlier in the week, the Social Christian Party held a meeting of 200 activists in Chinandega. The party's leader, Adan Fletes, spoke cautiously about the new opening provided by the government. "The meetings that are going on these days would never have been permitted three months ago. But we remember the years of dictatorship, when there were periods of looseness interspersed with repression. Perhaps that same cycle still exists. We shall see."[47]

27

A "Violation of the Law"

While the Sandinistas bent under the new international and domestic pressures created by the Reagan administration's covert program, that program itself came under severe pressures in Washington. The very visibility of the larger war proved disruptive of the thin consensus that had been reached in Congress at the end of 1982. By April 1983 the covert war in Nicaragua was anything but covert. Television reporters flown to the scenes of battle by the Sandinistas filmed the dead and wounded campesinos. American viewers, who had not followed the obscure debates over the Boland amendment, understood only that a "secret war" allegedly supported by the United States was being waged against Nicaragua, and the dead and wounded campesinos they saw on the television were the casualties of this secret war.

Many observers believed that if the administration was involved at all in support of the fighting in Nicaragua, then it was somehow in violation of laws passed by Congress. The Boland amendment's subtle distinctions and loopholes were either misunderstood, or ignored, or forgotten.[1] Even Congressman Michael Barnes told reporters that "Congress intended to prohibit the administration from trying to take paramilitary action against Nicaragua. But they have ignored it. I think they're in pretty obvious violation of the law." Senator Patrick Leahy of Vermont, a liberal member of the Senate intelligence committee, told reporters on April 4 that the press accounts alone suggested wrongdoing by the Reagan administration.[2] The *New York Times* reported that the "recent increase in fighting between the military and anti-Government forces in Nicaragua . . . according to members of both the Senate and House intelligence committees, has raised questions about whether the CIA has aided the anti-government forces, violating the amendment passed by Congress."[3] The vice chairman of the Senate Select Committee on Intelligence, Daniel P. Moynihan, said there was "a crisis of confidence building between the committee and the intelligence community over this issue. . . . They say it complies with the law. Committee members are saying we're not so sure." Moynihan insisted that there was "evidence every night on television" that the law was being violated.[4]

Members of the intelligence committees, like Moynihan and Leahy, knew better. Even the administration's harshest critics knew that the Boland amendment's loophole allowed the administration to support the rebels. Congressman Barnes obviously knew the Boland legislation did not bar "paramilitary action against Nicaragua," because in March he introduced new legislation to close the loophole Boland had left open: Barnes's proposal barred funds "which would have the effect of supporting, directly or indirectly, military or paramilitary operations in or against Nicaragua by any nation, group, organization, movement or individual."[5] Senator Moynihan had been among the few to point out in December 1982 that the Boland amendment was fraught with ambiguity. He had warned it would be "difficult to draw the line between harassment activities and a deliberate attempt to destabilize or overthrow a government." Even when he declared the Reagan administration was violating the law in April, Moynihan said that Congress might "have to rewrite the law to make more explicit what our intentions are."[6] The new legal interpretations in Congress were the result of the new publicity given the war, publicity which was as unwelcome to members of the intelligence committees as it was to the Reagan administration. The *New York Times* reported on April 10 that "as recently as three weeks ago, before the activities in Nicaragua moved into the headlines, half a dozen members of the Senate Intelligence Committee said they had no anxiety about the legality of the operations. Some of the same members now express serious doubts."[7]

The Reagan administration was confounded by the new controversy. Officials would scarcely talk about the covert program, much less defend it. President Reagan would not comment. Secretary of State George Shultz had replaced Al Haig in the summer of 1982, after Haig had resigned in anger over what he believed was mistreatment at the hands of White House officials. Shultz knew little about the covert program and referred all questions to the intelligence committees.[8] The Senate majority leader, Howard Baker, denied any knowledge of what was going on in Nicaragua.[9]

Boland's loophole, which Reagan officials had quietly accepted rather than face a public battle in the House, had become a trap. As a legal matter, the administration could cling to the Boland amendment's fine distinction between the U.S. government's intentions and those of the contras.[10] But the technical legality of the administration's actions did not provide a satisfactory political argument now that the covert war had become a public controversy. President Reagan was his own worst enemy, telling reporters on one occasion that his policy aimed only at "trying to interdict the supply lines, which are supplying the guerrillas in El Salvador." On another occasion he argued that since it was impossible for the contras to defeat the large, well-equipped Sandinista army, then his policy could not be in violation of the Boland amendment.[11] Reagan's weak and inaccurate responses did not stem the tide growing against his policies. Although some Republicans and conservative intellectuals pleaded with the administration to defend itself openly and vigorously, the President and his advisers simply denied they were violating the law and asked Congress to continue supporting the administration's foreign policies.[12]

Eventually the Senate intelligence committee acknowledged that the CIA was not violating "the letter or the spirit" of the legislation.[13] The House intelligence committee, however, was under too much pressure from liberal colleagues to admit that the Reagan administration was only doing what Boland's amendment had allowed. Boland himself was traveling in China when the controversy broke out, but he quickly became a target for liberals opposed to the covert war. *Washington Post* columnist Mary McGrory claimed Boland did "not like to upset the CIA," which was why he had "put over the loophole version" and overrode Harkin's objections in December. McGrory reminded Boland that he had then "assured the House that he would personally see to it that the situation 'did not get out of control.'" But now that it had, she wrote, "he is in China on tour."[14] With Boland out of the country, other members of the committee took matters into their own hands. On April 7 Congressman Wyche Fowler, a moderate Democrat from Georgia, declared that the administration's support for the Nicaraguan rebels did not fully comply with the law. To one observer, Fowler's announcement "suggested that Democrats, breaching what has generally been a bipartisan approach to intelligence matters in Congress, might seek to gain political advantage from the Reagan Administration's intelligence activities in Central America."[15]

Fowler's charge, which in effect put the House intelligence committee on record declaring the Reagan administration's activities illegal, opened the floodgates. On April 10 Senator Christopher Dodd of Connecticut declared that the administration was "clearly breaking the law" and called for new legislation barring "any funding by the Central Intelligence Agency and the Defense Department for any paramilitary group operating in Central America." Dodd proposed a closed session of the Senate "so that we can find out exactly what our government is doing, who we are supporting and how far we intend to go."[16] The next day, the House Foreign Affairs subcommittee on Western Hemisphere Affairs, of which Congressman Barnes was chairman, voted in favor of Barnes's legislation prohibiting aid to the Nicaraguan rebels unless such aid was approved openly by both houses of Congress.

Congressman Boland, still traveling in China, was incensed when he heard about Congressman Fowler's unprecedented news conference. But when he returned to Washington on April 12, he took the measure of the furor that had arisen against him within his own party. A generational confrontation was brewing between young liberals of the post-Watergate era and their older colleagues. Members of the intelligence committee told reporters that "the driving force" behind the opposition to the covert policy in Nicaragua was a "group of 40 to 50 members, mostly young and Democratic, who have worked behind the scenes during the last 18 months to persuade their colleagues that current policies are dangerously misguided."[17] The younger members believed that old liberals like Boland had allowed the country to go to war in Vietnam, had allowed the CIA to become a "rogue elephant" in Latin America, and would allow the Reagan administration to carry out its covert war against the Sandinistas. "Eddie Boland tends to be of the old school," one liberal Democrat told reporters. "He sees his role as being supportive of the Administration, and he gives a strong benefit of the doubt to the Administration. He's less skeptical than some others, and that's why he was chosen to be chairman. . . . Eddie reflects how things used to be, before the turmoil surrounding the Central Intelligence Agency about abuses in the past."

Boland angrily denied he was "of the old school," but he acknowledged differences with the young liberals. "I think there's more of a willingness and a desire to cooperate on my part and get along with different Administrations. I think there's a responsibility on the part of the chairman to cooperate with any Administration that's in." Boland declared himself in "complete sympathy" with President Reagan's efforts to deter communist expansion in Central America and agreed that "the United States has a vital interest in the area."[18]

Boland would not resist the party's liberals on this increasingly embarrassing issue, however. On April 13 Boland declared that the administration was in apparent violation of the law. The chairman of the intelligence committee based his contention solely on the news stories coming out of Nicaragua. "The question," he argued, was whether the contras "have gone beyond merely stopping the infiltration of arms and equipment into El Salvador. It is my judgment that there has been an apparent violation of the law. If you look at the stories that have come out of there, from reporters and members who have gone down there, the evidence is very strong."[19] According to one reporter who interviewed Boland at the end of April, "junior members of the committee were the first ones to insist that the Boland Amendment was being violated. The chairman agreed with their judgment only reluctantly, and even now says that he is able to see the argument on 'both sides.'"[20]

Having declared the Reagan administration in violation of the law, Boland promptly invited administration officials to meet with the committee and discuss how best to proceed. Boland refused to give any further endorsement to the covert war, but he wanted to block the legislation proposed by Congressman Barnes which would be an embarrassing infringement on the intelligence committee's domain. To protect his prerogatives, and to defend himself and his party from charges of "softness" in Central America, Boland proposed his own legislation to cut off aid to the anti-Sandinista rebels. Boland's bill would provide $80 million in overt assistance to El Salvador, Honduras, and Guatemala for the purpose of preventing the flow of arms from Nicaragua across their borders.[21] His legislation was soon endorsed by the chairman of the House Foreign Affairs Committee, Clement Zablocki, another member of the "old school" of liberal Democrats. By the end of April, the "Boland-Zablocki" legislation supplanted the Barnes legislation as the main Democratic challenge to the Reagan administration's policies. In this way the more venerable

Democratic leaders wrested control of events back from their younger and more radical colleagues.

––––––

The uproar in the middle of April dealt a blow to the Reagan administration, which was already reeling from other setbacks to its policies in Central America. The controversy over the covert program in Nicaragua was almost subsumed in a larger crisis over the administration's policies in El Salvador. Since the beginning of the year, senior administration officials had been very concerned about the erosion of public and congressional support for aiding both the Salvadoran army and the contras. Much of the concern was based on extremely pessimistic reports about the situation in Central America, especially in El Salvador. When the year began Enders reported to Shultz that the crisis seemed almost without solution. "Cuban-type communism" was being consolidated in Nicaragua. Nicaragua, in turn, was "promoting a revolution against El Salvador," and Cuba was planning to "step up support for a similar insurgency in Guatemala." So far, Enders said, "we don't see the endgame." Enders's assessment was more sanguine than that of other officials. Shultz's military adviser told him it was the view of the Joint Chiefs of Staff that "we are losing. It could be finished by the end of the year."[22]

Such dire reports seemed to demand drastic measures, but the Reagan administration was already having a hard time maintaining support in Congress for limited amounts of aid to the Salvadoran army and the stationing of a few dozen military advisers. At the end of 1982 William Casey had complained to Secretary of State Shultz in exasperation that the American people were "not behind our policy in Central America," support in Congress was fading, and, as a consequence, the administration was "in danger of losing on what is by far the most important foreign policy problem confronting the nation." Casey even told Shultz he should not be spending his time "traveling around Europe" but should be "going around the United States sounding the alarm and generating support for tough policies on the most important problem on our agenda." Force, Casey reminded Shultz, was the "only language the Communists understand."[23]

The alarm within the administration exacerbated divisions that had opened among senior officials. For several months a bureaucratic battle had been brewing between Reagan's second secretary of state, George

Shultz, and his second national security adviser, William Clark. Differences over policies in Central America provided the highly inflammable substance of this dispute and drew others into the fight on both sides. The foreign policy-making apparatus of the Reagan administration came unhinged in 1983, and largely over the issue of Central America.

As Casey's attack on Shultz showed, mistrust of the new secretary of state was rampant among President Reagan's more conservative advisers. The principal issue between them was negotiations. Casey had once warned Shultz not to be a "pilgrim," which he explained meant "an early settler," in Central America.[24] From the point of view of Casey, Weinberger, Clark, and Kirkpatrick, however, Shultz *was* an early settler. The moment he had turned his attention to Central America as secretary of state, Shultz had begun to search out opportunities to begin or to encourage negotiations. He wanted "a vigorous negotiating track to reach an agreement if we could." He wanted to work closely with Latin American governments, and not only with American allies in Central America but also with the "three major regional nations: Mexico, Colombia, and Venezuela."[25]

In seeking a negotiated settlement, Shultz adhered to certain general principles, but he was sometimes less concerned with the details of a possible agreement than his colleagues might have wished. In April, for instance, he met with Mexican Foreign Minister Sepulveda in Mexico City, where the two men agreed on an informal list of principles that could serve as the basis for talks in Central America. Most American officials knew that, when it came to Nicaragua, Mexico was likely to be the least helpful of all the Latin governments and Sepulveda the least helpful of all Mexican officials.[26] The two foreign ministers were, indeed, able to agree on only broad, general points. The principles Shultz brought back to Washington, therefore, were less specific in their demands on the Nicaraguan government than all previous American proposals and scarcely represented an advance.[27] While Shultz rather naively suggested that cooperation between the United States and Mexico might create a "potentially new and positive force for change," Clark objected both to Shultz's principles and to the whole idea of a common proposal with the Mexicans. Clark bluntly told Shultz that "we do not want the Mexicans to deal bilaterally with Central America." Shultz believed Clark was "entirely missing the point," but he had "no time to fight this issue."[28] Clark, however, was right to find Shultz's and Sepulveda's principles inadequate. A few months later the Contadora Group, of which Mexico was a member, produced its Document of Objectives, which contained points far more specific, far more demanding of the Sandinistas, and far more favorable to the United States.

Clark mistrusted Shultz, and as the crisis in Central America grew more alarming, he tried to seize control of policy in Central America with the support of Casey and Weinberger. Shultz returned from a trip to China in February to find that "the political atmosphere was bitter."[29] Assistant Secretary Enders was under fire for a memorandum outlining what became known as the "two-track" strategy in Central America. In El Salvador, the two-track policy meant arming the Salvadoran army against the guerrillas while simultaneously supporting negotiations with the guerrillas for a political solution. In Nicaragua it meant arming the contras while seeking an eventual negotiated settlement with the Sandinistas. Clark and other critics of Enders inside the administration suggested that the two-track policy really meant letting the guerrillas negotiate their way into a share of power in El Salvador and letting the Sandinistas win their security through talk rather than actions. Secretary Shultz, who always favored combining what he called "power and diplomacy," supported Enders's approach, and he recognized that the assault on Enders was really an indirect attack on him and his policies.

Shultz and his colleagues differed, as well, on the best approach to take toward the Democrats in Congress who opposed the President's policies. Casey favored "doing what we can and not being afraid of Congress." He was sure the Democratic Party would "never take the risk of losing Central America." Shultz had an entirely different view. He did not believe the Democrats could be bullied into supporting the administration's policies. He wanted to "get a workable policy in place, and workable meant a policy with congressional support." There was a strong connection between Shultz's more accommodating approach to Congress and his vigorous support for negotiations. He believed it was necessary to convince Congress that the administration intended to be forceful in defending American interests and yet also willing to pursue diplomatic solutions in Central America. Shultz wanted to "demonstrate that we were working to achieve a peaceful solution."[30]

Shultz did not disagree with his colleagues' assessment of the strategic stakes in Central America. He said he found the growing Cuban and Soviet influence "alarming." If the "Soviets consolidated a Communist regime on the mainland of the Americas," he argued, "they could tie us down and preoccupy us right on our southern border in the hope that we would not attend adequately to the Soviet challenges in the farther reaches of the world." Implicit in Shultz's assessment, however, was a conviction that the Reagan administration should not do the Soviet's work by preoccupying itself with Central America and engaging in endless, divisive battles with the Democrats in Congress. The Soviets understood "full well," Shultz argued, "that Central America and the Caribbean was the region where the American press and American public opinion were the most sensitive to the possibility of 'another Vietnam.'"[31] The question in Shultz's mind was whether his colleagues at the National Security Council and the CIA understood this as well as the Soviets did. A Gallup poll taken in the middle of March showed that of 87 percent who claimed to have heard or read about "the situation in El Salvador," a large majority opposed the President's request for military aid, and a majority opposed raising the number of American military advisers in El Salvador. A majority believed that "U.S. involvement in El Salvador could turn into a situation like Vietnam." Shultz believed these fears were in part the product of the administration's own threats. Told that Clark and the other "hard-liners" feared the Reagan administration was losing its battle, Shultz responded that "we are losing because of them."[32]

Shultz's concern about maintaining the support of Democrats in Congress led him to oppose many of the actions that his colleagues believed necessary to confront the crisis in Central America. Clark wanted more drastic steps taken to prevent the fall of El Salvador, including the dispatch of many more military trainers and advisers. Shultz considered the plan to send more advisers a "wholesale 'Americanization' of the effort," and in a meeting with Reagan in March he argued that seeking congressional approval for this idea was "a self-inflicted wound that would soon amount to suicidal behavior on our part."[33] President Reagan and his political advisers agreed, and the request was not made. At the end of May, senior officials at the Pentagon, the NSC, and the CIA proposed a plan to place mines in Nicaragua's ports, while high-speed patrol boats fired at oil tanks and port facilities. Shultz thought the plan was "outrageous" and persuaded President Reagan to reject it. On this and other matters, Shultz found Reagan to be "a cautious though decisive man, sensitive about being viewed as too pugnacious."[34]

While Shultz believed the problem was the administration's threatening style, Clark, Casey, Weinberger, and Kirkpatrick all believed the problem was that the President and the administration had not effectively made their case to the American people. President Reagan himself believed the public was confused and didn't understand what was going on in Central America. They were misled by a liberal media and liberal members of Congress, who warned of war every time he lifted a finger. His more conservative advisers complained repeatedly that the "Great Communicator" had not lent his personal efforts to this task of persuasion. They proposed he deliver a televised address on Central America to a joint session of Congress in the hopes of intimidating the Democrats by appealing directly to the American people. The President's political advisers opposed the idea of a speech on the grounds that it could only stir greater fears. To the White House chief of staff, James Baker, to Michael Deaver and to Nancy Reagan, the whole topic of Central America was to be avoided as much as possible. Shultz also believed a speech to Congress was ill-advised. But Clark and others believed in Reagan's power to persuade, and the President agreed to do what they considered necessary to save his policies.

On April 27 Reagan addressed the Congress, trying to balance alarm with optimism. Given the enormous strategic stakes involved, Reagan declared, he could not believe there was "a majority in this Congress or the country that counsels passivity, resignation, defeatism, in the face of this challenge to freedom and security in our own hemisphere." Senator Dodd, speaking for the Democrats, evoked the memory of the Vietnam War: "The American people know that we have been down this road before—and that it only leads to a dark tunnel of endless intervention."

Reagan's speech had little immediate effect. The polls showed no change. On May 3, just a week after the speech, the House intelligence committee voted to cut off funding for the covert program in Nicaragua and approved the Boland-Zablocki proposal. President Reagan denounced the intelligence committee's action as "irresponsible" and defiantly told reporters, "We'll keep right on fighting." In a long interview with journalists at the White House, an angry Reagan revealed the true contours of his thinking about Nicaragua, denying altogether the legitimacy of the Sandinista government—"it was a Government out of the barrel of a gun"—and referring to the contras as "freedom fighters."[35] Reagan's first use of this term caused another scandal in the press and in Congress. Senator Moynihan declared there existed "an unmistakable sense" that he and other senators were still "not fully apprised of the purposes" of the covert program.

When Secretary Shultz returned from the Middle East in the middle of May he found that once again "people at Defense and the CIA and Jeane

Kirkpatrick [had] all surged into a heightened state of alarm over Central America." Their immediate target was Assistant Secretary Enders, but Shultz saw Clark's attack on Enders as a grab for power. He decided to sacrifice Enders in the hope of thwarting Clark's broader ambitions.[36] He demanded assurances from the President that he would be in charge of policy in Central America, and he asked the President to reconfirm that a negotiated settlement was the goal of American policy. "Though we must continue to strengthen the shield against the Salvadoran rebels and keep the pressure on Nicaragua," Shultz wrote in a May 25 memorandum, "we cannot expect a military solution, at least in the next several years." The only way to establish peace in Central America, "free from foreign incursions into democratic countries," was by "regional negotiations leading to a reciprocal and verifiable agreement in which the Nicaraguans come to terms with the need for them to mind their own business." In a bow to the President's oft-stated views, Shultz also insisted that democracy in Nicaragua ought to be a goal of the negotiations. "[I]n forcing Nicaragua to the negotiating table," Shultz wrote, "we must not sell out the Nicaraguan patriots who wish their government to live up to the promises of free elections and a pluralistic society made when the Sandinistas came to power."[37] Reagan responded that Shultz's "judgments regarding our policy toward the region are correct," thus approving both the negotiating "track" and Shultz's statement that the contras should not be "sold out." Reagan also agreed that the secretary of state was to have full charge of the government's policy in Central America.

Shultz had to wait before reaping the fruits of this bureaucratic victory, however. As Clark and Casey grew still more alarmed about the situation in Central America over the summer, they in turn alarmed the President, and Reagan looked to them, not to Shultz, for answers. Officials worried that the Salvadoran government's position was deteriorating and that the guerrillas were increasingly dangerous. In the meantime, Soviet arms shipments to Nicaragua had increased dramatically in the first six months of 1983 in response to the growing effectiveness of the contras.[38] In July, American intelligence officials estimated that the rate of Soviet weapons and supply deliveries had doubled in 1983 compared with previous years, from about 10,000 tons of equipment per year to 20,000 tons.[39] By August American officials were estimating that the Soviets had already delivered twice as much military equipment in the first seven months of 1983 as in all of 1982. Ten Soviet arms shipments had arrived in Nicaraguan ports compared with only five in the previous year, and ten other ships from the

Soviet bloc were due to arrive within the coming weeks. The Soviets also increased the number of advisers from 70 to 100, and the Cubans had increased their numbers of advisers from 7,500 to 9,000, of which more than 2,000 were military and internal security advisers.[40] The chief of naval operations warned that "integral Cuban units" had begun arriving in Nicaragua in the wake of Cuban General Ochoa's visit. The contras were on the verge of being cut off by Congress and were not, in any case, the answer to the new influx of Soviet weaponry and Cuban military expertise. Administration officials believed more was needed to show American resolve in the region, to intimidate the Cubans and Sandinistas, to signal the Soviet Union that the administration was serious about preserving its hegemony in the region, to bolster allied governments in Central America, and to undo the damage being done by the Democratic opposition in Congress.

Ironically, Clark and Weinberger now looked to "the source," as Haig once had, hoping to intimidate both Castro and the Sandinistas with a demonstration of American military might. At an NSC meeting on July 8 the President was presented with a list of military responses to the crisis in Central America and had asked "How do we stop Castro with exercises?" Within days Clark and Weinberger had won Reagan's approval for large naval maneuvers in the Caribbean and off Nicaragua's Pacific Coast to last for six months. In Honduras, up to 3,000 American troops were to conduct joint maneuvers with the Honduran army. Scheduled to begin at the end of July, after the House vote on the Boland legislation, the military maneuvers aimed at President Reagan's twin frustrations, at the Communists who challenged America in its own backyard, and at the Congress which stood in the way of meeting that challenge. The President approved the plans without discussing the matter with Shultz, who later complained that he had been "totally blindsided."[41] The decision to hold the exercises became public almost immediately, causing another stir in Congress about a week before the critical vote on aid to the contras.

28

"An Amendment to the Amendment, As Amended"

While Reagan administration officials fought amongst themselves, the Democrats in Congress confronted their own difficulties. CIA Director Casey was not wrong to believe that the Democrats were politically vulnerable and fearful of standing in the way of President Reagan's anti-communist policies. Although the polls showed little effect from the April 27 speech, a substantial minority of Democrats in Congress sought some means of supporting the President. Even Democrats who disagreed with the President said they did "not want to be labeled the party that lost El Salvador, or the group that walked away." In the South, where the population was more conservative, and especially in Florida, where large numbers of Cuban immigrants were politically powerful and virulently anti-communist, this concern was acute. Florida Democrat Dante Fascell, a high-ranking member of the House Foreign Affairs Committee, was already working on a compromise on aid to El Salvador that would be more to the administration's liking.[1] The House majority leader, Jim Wright, quickly pronounced himself in favor of the President's efforts to support the government in El Salvador—in a clear break with the northern, liberal wing of his party represented by the Speaker, Tip O'Neill.[2]

For many of the more conservative Democrats, the easiest answer to the problem was to support Reagan in El Salvador but oppose him in Nicaragua. Wright thus declared himself, on the one hand, "absolutely, firmly and enthusiastically" behind the President's support for El Salvador's battle against the insurgents, but on the other hand "totally opposed" to covert operations against Nicaragua. It was one thing to provide arms to a government, and quite another to be "financing the invasion of another country."[3] The legislation proposed by Boland and Zablocki offered the perfect balance: a cutoff of aid to the contras and an $80 million increase in aid to El Salvador and the other three American allies. Democratic members of the House intelligence committee could thus insist that "they shared the Administration's objectives in Central America, but disagreed with administration policy" toward Nicaragua.[4]

Southern Democrats remained nervous, however, lest their cutoff of aid to the contras appear to their constituents as an endorsement of the Sandinistas. When a Republican charged that the committee's decision gave a "great morale boost" to the Sandinistas, Congressman Fowler responded heatedly that the Democrats on the committee had "serious troubles, all of us . . . with the repressive nature of the Sandinista regime in Nicaragua. What the committee did today was by no way, in any manner, to be construed as any sort of favor to the Sandinista government."[5] On June 2, Congressmen Wright, Hamilton, Zablocki, and Fascell joined liberals Barnes, Solarz, Mikulski, and Torricelli in sending a strongly worded letter to Daniel Ortega, criticizing the "conspicuous Cuban presence, serious human rights violations, and absence of democratic rights" in Nicaragua. They called on the Nicaraguan government to negotiate with its political opponents to "arrest the trend toward civil war, repression, and Cuban domination." As one congressional observer has noted, these Democrats were "reluctant to let the Sandinistas' increasingly restrictive domestic behavior become a political liability."[6]

Even though it was almost impossible for most of these Democrats to support continuation of covert aid to the contras in any form, they eagerly sought negotiations with the Reagan administration to demonstrate their desire to work with Reagan. Congressman Lee Hamilton met with Enders in May "to find a middle ground that would show congressional unhappiness with the covert action while preserving some flexibility of action for the president." Hamilton even complained that the more liberal members of his party wanted "to make a political issue of this and do not want a compromise at any point."[7] In June and July, moderate and conservative Democrats such as Fascell, Mica, Congressman Dave McCurdy of Oklahoma, and Majority Leader Jim Wright all took part in negotiations with the Reagan administration to find a compromise.

The much larger, liberal wing of the Democratic Party was just as determined to prevent a compromise. After the meeting between Enders and Hamilton, Speaker O'Neill said he hoped there would be no agreement to allow the Reagan administration "to continue to break the law for the rest of the year."[8] O'Neill's opposition to the contras was, by his own account, virulent and emotional, and this visceral feeling was shared by other liberal Democrats.[9] For reasons of moral conviction O'Neill was not interested in compromise, and neither were the other liberals in the House. Congressman Robert Torricelli from New Jersey told reporters he was "disappointed" that some Democrats were negotiating with the administration, "because American laws are being violated and a sovereign nation is being invaded and those are two actions that defy compromise."[10]

O'Neill and the liberal bloc favored confrontation for political reasons, as well. The frustration of Democratic leaders after two years of Reagan administration legislative victories was acute.[11] Buoyed by polls that showed the American people very much on their side on Central America, O'Neill and other leaders relished the prospect of dealing the President a resounding, partisan defeat in an open vote on the House floor. Congressman Peter Kostmayer spoke for many when he suggested that "as Central America becomes an issue in the national presidential campaign, it is important for the Democratic party to take a position"; the longer the issue was "dragged out the less decisive impression there is in the country that the Democrats have taken a clear-cut stand." It was not long before Congressman Hamilton was declaring that he and the administration were actually "a long way away from any agreement."[12]

Under pressure from the liberal wing of the party, moderate Democrats had to ask more from the Reagan administration than it was prepared to give. Congressman McCurdy complained that he could not get a clear answer from administration officials when he asked whether Nicaragua had to agree to stop sending weapons to guerrillas in the region in order to trigger the cutoff of aid to the contras, or whether in addition the Sandinistas had to agree to adopt democratic political reforms. "The problem I had all along," McCurdy insisted, was that "there appears to be a shifting of conditions and escalation of the conditions."[13] Administration officials, locked in battle on so many issues, did not agree among themselves on exactly what they wanted. According to Robert McFarlane, who conducted much of the negotiations with Congress, Reagan officials would "not agree to a straight trade," exchanging American support for the contras for Nicaraguan support for the Salvadoran guerrillas. The administration wanted commitments from the Sandinistas to allow a "free press, freedom of religion, to conduct negotiations with the opposition, and to hold free elections." Moreover, McFarlane insisted that the administration "would not give away our authority to support the contras," by which he meant that the administration did not want to leave to Congress the decision of when and how to end assistance to the rebels. This just about precluded any hope of an agreement with moderate Democrats like McCurdy, who demanded much greater congressional control of the covert program. According to McFarlane, he and other administration officials were aware that by insisting on such terms they could lose the vote in the House in July. In their view, however, the alternative was worse. Tying aid to the contras to some promise by the Sandinistas to end support for the Salvadoran guerrillas was, in their view, dangerous and fanciful. They preferred to lose, blame the Democrats for "losing Central America," and come back to fight another day.[14]

The Reagan administration did not stop negotiating, however. In the first two weeks of July the White House chief of staff, James Baker, held talks with Congressmen Fascell, Mica, McCurdy and, most significantly, Jim Wright. More than anyone else, it was Wright whose decision would determine the outcome of the vote on contra aid in 1983, and many believed Wright might be amenable to a compromise that would preserve aid to the contras in some form. Wright was known to feel personally betrayed by the Sandinistas, whose broken promises to allow greater freedom in Nicaragua had left him angry and embarrassed after his visit in the summer of 1980.[15] Republicans involved in the negotiations considered Wright "a key figure" who was "trying to bridge the gap" between the two sides. Liberal Democrats, worried that Wright might indeed strike a deal with the administration, warned their leader against any concessions. Speaker O'Neill publicly declared that he expected Wright to support the Boland-Zablocki bill, and younger liberals let it be known that they expected party members "to take a stand" against contra aid.[16] According to one observer, Wright was "under instruction from freshman members who think there is a difference between Republicans and Democrats." The liberals in the caucus had "delivered the unspoken message that if Wright wants to be speaker, he must be more liberal."[17]

The race for Tip O'Neill's job was already on, and everyone knew that Wright badly wanted it.[18] He needed a majority of Democratic votes in the House, and most Democrats were northern liberals and moderates, not southern conservatives. Wright, whose appreciation and understanding of his party's ideological composition was as keen as anyone's, did not need to be told where his political vulnerability lay. His relationship with the liberal wing of his party had never been friendly.[19] He had barely won the post of majority leader. Wright had overcome the liberals' opposition only when O'Neill's close friend in the Massachusetts delegation, Edward Boland, announced his support.[20] Wright had since tried to conform himself as best he could to soften the opposition against him in the party's liberal wing. The *Congressional Quarterly* reported he had "moved somewhat to the left since he became majority leader."[21] In the middle of July, he reversed himself on the issue of the MX missile and joined the liberals in their losing effort to defeat funding for the weapon.[22] Conservative Democrats complained that Wright was abandoning them, but they understood his reasons. Congressman Charles W. Stenholm, a fellow Texan who became a leader of the Conservative Democratic Forum in the House, lamented in early 1984 that "the Jim Wright I know is a moderate, not a liberal. But he has come to be known as a liberal." Stenholm conceded, however, that Wright's shift "has been a matter of necessity to be a leader in our Democratic Party. I don't hold that against Jim."[23] Wright had angered liberals by supporting President Reagan on El Salvador; he could never hope to win their support if he crossed them again on Nicaragua.

Wright appeared to be looking for compromise, however, almost until the day of the vote. Other moderate southern Democrats, like McCurdy, also appeared to be unsure. The Oklahoma congressman with three military bases in his district was sufficiently worried about appearing "soft on communism" that he commissioned a poll in his district to help him decide if it was safe to vote against aid to the contras.[24] The problem was that the Boland-Zablocki legislation was clearly inadequate for the more conservative segment of the party. Even after the House Foreign Affairs Committee passed the legislation on June 6, Congressman Hamilton predicted it was "not going to become law" in its current form.[25] Congressman Dante Fascell argued that the bill did not "come to grips with the complex problem we face of Soviet penetration" in Central America, and another Florida Democrat, Dan Mica, declared he would try to modify the bill "in a way that would be acceptable to all."[26] "The question," Mica told a reporter, "is how you extricate yourself from this covert operation without abandoning your opposition to the Sandinistas. Our cause in opposing the Nicaraguan export of revolution is just. Our methods are illegal. We're trying to find a reasonable way to resolve that problem."[27]

As Congressman Barnes explained, moderate and conservative Democrats were desperately looking for "a way to be on both sides of the issue."[28] The inadequacy of Boland-Zablocki meant that some other alternative would have to be proposed, and there was no telling how close such an alternative might come to providing for a renewal of the covert aid in some form. Congressman Mica proposed continuing aid to the contras until the Sandinistas ended their aid to the Salvadoran guerrillas, and this proposal seemed to gain support as the day of the vote approached. By July 14, less than two weeks before debate was scheduled to begin on the Boland-Zablocki bill, House Democratic leaders pronounced themselves worried about the outcome of the vote. O'Neill predicted it would be "very close," and Congressman Zablocki admitted to reporters that he did not have the votes to pass his bill "as of today."[29]

The Reagan administration had made some effort to win wavering Democrats, not by making concessions, but by appealing to the spirit of bipartisanship. A week before the scheduled vote Reagan announced the appointment of a bipartisan commission on Central America. Recommended by the conservative Democrat, Senator Henry Jackson, the commission was modeled after another panel led by General Brent Scowcroft, which had eased passage of funding for the MX missile by uniting moderates and conservatives around a compromise plan. Reagan's announcement of the commission and its chairman, Henry Kissinger, was hailed by moderate Democrats.[30]

The helpful effect of this announcement was immediately destroyed the very next day, however, when the *New York Times* revealed the Reagan administration's plans to conduct large naval and land exercises around Nicaragua beginning at the end of July. The *Times* reported that senior administration officials had not ruled out the possibility of a quarantine around Nicaragua and suggested that other actions were also under consideration, including increased military assistance to countries in the region and the prepositioning of American weapons in Honduras to enable U.S. troops to deploy quickly in a crisis.[31] In addition to the leaks about the exercises, there were reports that the Defense Department proposed raising the number of U.S. military advisers in El Salvador from 55 to 125. Other reports claimed that the CIA had formulated ambitious new plans for expanding the covert program in Nicaragua and intended to support between 12,000 and 15,000 fighters over the course of the coming fiscal year.

Liberal Democrats seized on the reports as further proof that the administration wanted war. Democratic presidential candidate Walter Mondale told reporters it was clear that "[Reagan] is on a course that will lead us into war." Speaker O'Neill called the exercises "an unneeded show of strength," intended for domestic political purposes. The administration got support from some conservative Democrats, like Georgia Senator Sam Nunn, who called it "a strong message . . . to Cuba and Nicaragua . . . that needs sending."[32] Overall, however, news of the exercises damaged the administration severely. Even Republican leaders were angry that the White House had not consulted with them before going ahead with the maneuvers, just at the moment when they were trying to woo Democrats to support the controversial aid for the contras.[33] Democrats and some moderate Republicans worried that their vote on the covert program would later turn out to have been a vote to approve a panoply of as-yet undisclosed military actions by the Reagan administration. The covert aid program, objectionable by itself to liberals and moderates, had to carry the additional burden of being only a first step down Senator Dodd's "dark tunnel of endless intervention." A vote for continuing aid to the contras, the liberals claimed, amounted to another "Gulf of Tonkin" resolution.

Secretary Shultz found both the administration's actions, and the Congress's response "bizarre." He was angry at Caspar Weinberger's Pentagon, which "seemed to take any means to avoid the actual use of American military power but every opportunity to display it." He lamented that the Reagan administration was "engaged in a continuous, divisive debate about the use of strength versus diplomacy at a time when we needed both and had neither in Central America." Meanwhile, "we had a Congress whose most active members saw the specter of another Vietnam and seemed determined to prevent such an outcome by denying the United States the ability to use any aspect of national power to deal with Communist advances in Central America."[34] As the day of the vote approached, the Reagan administration and its supporters in Congress found the prospects for victory slipping away.

The first true vote on the administration's covert program in Nicaragua was a legislative tangle. Since neither the Boland-Zablocki legislation nor the administration's request for unfettered covert aid was capable of gaining a majority of House members, complicated compromise proposals abounded. Congressman Mica's amendment, for instance, delayed any cutoff of aid to the contras until October 1, 1983. It required the President to submit a new plan for interdicting arms to El Salvador that would conform to the Boland amendment, and then cut off the covert program only if Nicaragua agreed "by formal action" to end its support for guerrilla groups in the region, and even then only after the President or the OAS verified that the Sandinistas were abiding by their commitment. Mica's bill did not have the Reagan administration's enthusiastic support, but it was the only proposal for a continuance of covert aid that stood any chance of passage.[35] At the other extreme, Congressman Barnes offered an amendment which would cut off aid to the contras, while expressing the "sense of the Congress" that Nicaragua and its neighbors should reach an agreement not to support subversion against one another.

In a choice between the amendments offered by Mica and Barnes, Democratic Party leaders feared most southern moderates and conservatives would support Mica. The House leaders, therefore, used clever parliamentary procedures to avoid a direct vote on the Mica amendment. Before any vote was taken, an amendment to Mica's amendment was hastily drawn up by a New York Democrat, Stephen Solarz, and presented in the name of Congressman Boland. The trickiest proposal yet offered, the Boland-Solarz amendment to the Mica substitute amendment for the Young amendment to the Boland-Zablocki amendment turned Mica's proposal on its head. Aid to the contras would end immediately, but if after 30 days the President reported to Congress that Nicaragua was still aiding the Salvadoran guerrillas, Congress could renew support for the contras. Solarz called his amendment a "compromise to the compromise." "We would take the first step," he argued, by cutting off contra aid. If the Sandinistas did not reciprocate, the United States would be "in a position to resume paramilitary operations against Nicaragua." As both conservatives and some liberals were quick to point out, the Solarz-Boland amendment undermined Boland's original, stated goal of ending an immoral and illegal covert war.[36] The only purpose of the Solarz-Boland amendment, however, was to drive a wedge between Mica and some of his more moderate supporters.

As the debate on the amendment drew to a close, Congressman Wright rose to throw his considerable influence on the side of Solarz-Boland. Proclaiming his support for a bipartisan compromise, Wright said that "while we agree on certain things, we come to one unbridgeable gulf. . . . We want to put a stop to that U.S.-financed military intervention, and we want to put a stop to what the Sandinistas are doing." Wright insisted the only question was "Who goes first?" In the kind of rhetorical flourish for which he was famous, Wright suggested this question addressed "the fundamental flaw in human character that has always led to war. . . . [M]en go on dying, and infants crying at mothers' breasts, and blood comes instead of milk because the statesmen of the world are insisting that 'no, you go first, and then we will follow suit.'" Wright suggested that the United States must "wash our hands clean, come into the court with clean hands, expunged of our own sin, and then say to the court, 'require the same compliance from Nicaragua.'"[37]

The House voted first on the Barnes amendment, which lost by only one vote, 213–214, a bad sign for Mica and the Reagan administration. Wright supported the straight cutoff, as did McCurdy and most of the more moderate southern Democrats. The Solarz-Boland amendment came up next, and it passed by a vote of 221–205. Other votes followed on amendments proposed by Republicans, but the battle was over. Mica angrily insisted that a vote be taken on his own amendment, but Wright and the House leaders had already maneuvered successfully to divide his southern colleagues. Mica's amendment was defeated, 203–223.

Just before the final vote on the Mica amendment, Wright rose to offer yet another modification to the pending legislation, or as the brilliant Texas parliamentarian put it, "I offer an amendment to the amendment, as amended, offered as a substitute for the amendment, as amended." Wright's amendment was simply a strong denunciation of the Sandinistas. The Nicaraguan government, it stated, had "failed to keep solemn promises, made to the Organization of American States in July 1979, to establish full respect for human rights and political liberties, hold early elections, preserve a private sector, permit political pluralism, and pursue a foreign policy of non-aggression and non-intervention." The amendment further declared that the Sandinistas, "by providing military support (including arms, training, and logistical, command and control, and communications facilities) to groups seeking to overthrow the Government of El Salvador and other Central American governments," had "violated article 18 of the Charter of the Organization of American States." Wright declared that the Nicaraguan Government ought to be "held accountable" before the OAS, and he called upon the President to seek a reconvening of the Seventeenth Meeting of Consultation of Ministers of Foreign Affairs—which had presided over the transfer of power from Somoza to the Sandinistas in 1979—for the purpose of finding "effective measures" to bring about compliance by the Nicaraguan government.

President Reagan himself could not have more fervently laid out the accusations against Nicaragua nor been more extreme in his demands of the Sandinistas, including the demand for full and rapid democratization. Wright professed himself more angered by the Sandinistas' internal policies than by their support for the Salvadoran guerrillas, and he made clear that he took their broken promises as a personal betrayal.

> We asked them [back in 1980], can we tell our colleagues in the Congress that you will assiduously observe the political rights, free speech, free press, free assembly? Yes, they said, you may.
>
> They have not done that.
>
> We said can we tell our colleagues in the Congress that you will observe a pluralistic political system in which you honor the rights of other political parties to participate. They said, yes you may.
>
> They have not done that.
>
> And we asked if they would observe the rights of private property, refusing to confiscate such property except by due process of law, and they said, yes, you may indeed.
>
> We asked if we might report that they would have early, free elections to ratify by the vote of the people the government by which they would be governed. They said yes, we intend to do that very soon.
>
> They have not really obeyed the spirit or, I am convinced, the letter of those commitments.[38]

Wright's amendment thus cast the pending legislation as a measure against the Sandinistas. Although Wright was sincere in his strong denunciations of Nicaragua, he also created a shield against charges by Republicans and conservatives that the Democratic party was "soft" on Nicaragua. He reassured the few uneasy moderates that a vote against the Mica amendment was not a vote for appeasement.

Wright had not yet finished for the day. With a majority of votes firmly in hand and all dangerous amendments including Mica's defeated, Wright now delivered the *coup de grace* to the administration. He reintroduced the original Boland-Zablocki legislation, which put a final end to aid for the contras, amended only by his own proposal concerning Nicaragua and the OAS. His maneuver stripped away the Solarz-Boland amendment, revealing it for what it was, merely a device for splitting moderate votes away from Mica. The Boland-Zablocki legislation that probably could not have passed earlier in the day was now ushered through the House by Wright with the largest margin yet, 228–195.

The defeat, which Shultz called "the worst legislative defeat of the Reagan administration to that date," had many causes. Shultz and others blamed the announcement of the Big Pine II military exercises, and that was certainly a large contributor. Congressman Mica ruefully told reporters afterwards that he "wish[ed] the president hadn't sent his boats down there just two days before the vote." Congresswoman Olympia Snowe, one of a handful of moderate Republicans who voted for the Boland-Zablocki amendment, said her vote was "a message to the administration that I have concerns about its Central America policy." If the Reagan administration was willing to undertake such extensive military maneuvers, she said, "I can only wonder what we can expect in the future."[39] Congressman Solarz rightly surmised that "in the process of scaring the Sandinistas, the President scared Congress."[40]

It is impossible to know how many votes the administration lost as a result of the exercises. It is also hard to know how the voting might have turned out had not Wright and the House leadership used clever parliamentary tactics to split southern moderates. The House was closely divided, even more closely than the final vote suggested. As the coming years proved, at any given time the House of Representatives could vote one way or another on aid to the contras.

Nicaragua was such a contentious issue because it involved political needs and ideological principles that contradicted one another. The Sandinistas were unpopular, and Democrats did not want to appear indifferent to the spread of communism in Central America. But there was also broad agreement within the Democratic Party that the United States ought not to confront the Sandinistas with force, directly or indirectly. Congressman Barnes insisted the only question at issue was "Will we or will we not authorize the Government of the United States of America to seek by military means to overthrow the duly constituted government of another nation."[41] Many liberals and moderates in both parties found such an idea objectionable. The post-Vietnam Democratic Party, in particular, had become devoted to undoing a history of American intervention, in Latin America and in Southeast Asia, and the July 28 debate was replete with the phrases of the 1970s. Boland compared the contra program to "a rogue elephant, doing what it wanted to," a pointed allusion to Democratic assaults on the CIA in the 1970s.[42] As part of his personal peacemaking with the younger liberals in the party, Boland apologized for his generation's errors in Vietnam. Comparing the current vote on contra aid to the vote on the Gulf of Tonkin resolution in 1964, he explained that then "we did not have all the facts. We could not—many of us could not—see where it would take us. Today the House does not suffer from that disadvantage." Boland, in fact, renounced any further role in the distasteful program. It was "no longer a matter for the fourteen members of the Intelligence Committee. It is an action that must be justified in the full light of American values, American responsibilities, and future American involvement."[43] The covert program was dirty, like the Bay of Pigs and the covert undermining of Allende. Wright spoke of it as a "sin" and asked that Americans come to "court" with "clean hands."

Nicaragua evoked such feelings because it had already been the site of American intervention in the past and because an overtly anti-American revolution had finally succeeded in challenging America's hegemony in Central America. "I'm not crazy about the Sandinistas," Tip O'Neill explained, "but their country was ravaged by the Somozas and their cronies for forty-five years, when we virtually forced their people into servitude through our corporations." This sinful behavior by the United States had been undone by the Sandinista revolution. Now the Reagan administration was trying to reverse the defeat and return American policy to its past ways. The liberals' insistence that the contras were all "Somocistas," instead of mostly illiterate peasants, was crucial to their effort to cast present American policy in the light of past sins. After the Somozas had been "thrown out of office," O'Neill argued, the Reagan administration was "trying to put them back in."[44] There was a strong sentiment among liberals and moderates in Congress that, in Nicaragua, no matter how distasteful the Sandinistas might be, it was wrong for the United States to try to reverse its defeat and return to the dominant style of its unsavory past.

———

The covert program had been rejected in the House, but not in the Republican-controlled Senate, where it continued to have some support in both parties. A few days after the House vote on July 28, CIA Director William Casey went before the Senate intelligence committee to present a new intelligence finding, as part of an agreement reached with the committee earlier in the year. In May, both Goldwater and Moynihan had proposed continuing covert aid until September 30, the end of the fiscal year, and had allocated $19 million to the CIA's reserve fund for the next fiscal year. In order to receive these funds, President Reagan had to submit a new intelligence finding which restated his goals. Goldwater had said the President needed to explain "just a little more clearly just what it is he wants to do," and Senator Moynihan insisted the new finding would have to be approved by a majority vote in the committee.[45]

Casey's ambitions had not been lessened by the defeat in the House. On August 3, he told the Senate intelligence committee he wanted to increase support to the contras significantly and frankly suggested that the administration did indeed seek a change of government in Nicaragua.[46] Casey's proposals got a poor reception from the committee. According to Moynihan, committee members believed the administration's new proposal was "much too broad and ambitious," and they had "no hesitation" in telling Casey "precisely that."[47] Administration officials went back to the drawing board and, after close consultation with the intelligence committee, put together a new proposal which the President signed on September 19 and which Casey brought to the committee on September 20. This time Casey was accompanied by Secretary Shultz—Senator Moynihan had insisted that Shultz attend to demonstrate that aid to the contras was not "a substitute for, but rather an aid to American diplomatic efforts."[48]

With one exception, the new finding did little more than go back to the administration's own interpretation of the earlier Boland amendment. It stated that the purpose of the covert program was to "provide support, equipment and training assistance to Nicaraguan paramilitary resistance groups as a means to induce the Sandinistas and Cubans and their allies to cease their support for insurgencies in the region; to hamper Cuban-Nicaraguan arms trafficking; to divert Nicaragua's resources and energies from support for Central American guerrilla movements; and to bring the Sandinistas into meaningful negotiations and constructive, verifiable agreement with their neighbors on peace in the region."[49] After the committee hearing on September 20, an administration official explained to the *New York Times*, "We were always being questioned on whether we were going beyond our program of interdicting arms. Now we say, 'Yes, we are supporting the rebels until the Nicaraguans stop their subversion in neighboring countries.'"[50] Senator Moynihan declared that this description of the administration's intentions, even as expressed anonymously, was "a welcomed statement."[51] The committee's members pronounced themselves satisfied by the "limited nature" of the program and declared that the new plan was "much more sensible than in the past" and "looked as if it had some coherence and practicality," a quality they attributed to the intercession of Secretary Shultz.[52]

On September 22, the Senate intelligence committee voted 13–2 to approve the President's "new" program and agreed to release $19 million for the Fiscal Year 1984.[53] The CIA could also spend $10 million in unused funds left over from the Fiscal Year 1983 budget, making the total amount approved by the committee $29 million. Given that in Fiscal Year

1983 the contra program cost almost $50 million, the committee planned to force the administration to come back for more money at some point in 1984. Sources on the committee made clear that their intention was to keep the Reagan administration on a tight leash.[54]

The debate in the Senate on November 3 was perfunctory.[55] Senator Moynihan delivered the only interesting and important speech, and as vice chairman of the intelligence committee and a northern Democrat, he wielded the kind of influence in the Senate that Boland wielded in the House. Moynihan chided the administration for the "vagueness with which the goals of the program" had been stated from the beginning. "[A]t times," Moynihan declared, "the covert program appeared to be preceding policy and not following it."[56] Having dismissed the administration's arguments, Senator Moynihan chose to justify his own support of covert aid to the contras firmly on the basis of international law. "[T]he Government of Nicaragua has violated international law" by providing military support to the Salvadoran guerrillas, Moynihan argued. "From that view," he declared, "it follows that we have obligations as well as rights to respond to the violations of law by these other nations."[57]

"Our goal," Senator Moynihan said, "should be nothing more, nor nothing less, than bringing the Government of Nicaragua into conformity with the accepted norms of international behavior." The solution Moynihan sought was a negotiated settlement in which the Sandinistas agreed to abide by those norms. He asked the administration to take recent diplomatic proposals by the Sandinistas seriously. Even though "a measure of caution was warranted," since the timing of Sandinistas' proposals—right after the House vote and right before the Senate's deliberations—was suspicious, still "the *bona fides* of the probe should be tested to determine whether it might indeed constitute a first step by Nicaragua in reaching a *modus vivendi* with its American neighbors or merely another propaganda ploy." Moynihan said he and the intelligence committee intended to "watch with some care the seriousness with which the administration takes the Nicaraguan proposals."[58]

Led by Moynihan and Senator Goldwater, the Senate saved the covert program for the administration. On November 2 the House had approved the Boland-Zablocki legislation again as part of the Fiscal Year 1984 Defense Appropriations bill, where the appropriations for the intelligence agencies were "hidden." On November 17 and 18, House and Senate conferees met to resolve differences in both the intelligence authorization and defense appropriations bills. The outcome provided a small victory for Reagan. Boland fought a lonely battle in the conference against Republicans from both chambers and with little help from Senate Democrats. The conferees approved money for the covert program and dropped the Boland amendment restrictions as "unnecessary" in light of the President's new intelligence finding.[59] Boland succeeded only in winning an absolute "cap" of $24 million on the amount of money the administration could spend on the covert program in Nicaragua in fiscal year 1984. To spend more out of the CIA's contingency fund, which would become necessary within six to eight months, the administration would have to seek approval of Congress. Boland was not happy with the compromise, but he tried to convince the rest of the House to accept it as the best that could be obtained. The compromise, he said, would "force either a significant phase-down of the covert action or a situation where the administration will have to come back and request additional funds if the covert action is to continue."[60]

The limited victory in Congress at the end of 1983 did not make administration officials sanguine about the future. Opposition in the House to aiding the Nicaraguan rebels seemed almost insurmountable, and it would be easier for House Democrats to block passage of a new aid authorization in 1984 than it had been to cut it off in 1983. Even in the Senate support for the rebels was less sure than the outcome in November suggested. Moderate Republicans on the intelligence committee, like Senators Cohen of Maine and Durenberger of Minnesota, were uneasy with the program, and other moderate Republicans in the Senate, like Senator Nancy Kassebaum of Kansas, consistently expressed their discomfort with the President's policies in Central America. It was hardly a sign of strength that a liberal senator from New York, Daniel P. Moynihan, held this fragile coalition together. If Moynihan dropped his support, the battle in the Senate could become as brutal as that in the House.

With congressional approval hanging by a thread, administration officials grew impatient with what seemed to them the slow progress of the rebel army. If funding for the rebels could be cut off within six or twelve months, some Reagan officials wanted the rebels to make extraordinary and even decisive gains during that period. William Casey told Duane Clarridge, the covert program's chief, that he wanted the rebels to come out of the hills and do "the urban bit," a shift in strategy for which the rebel army was ill-prepared. Casey also asked other analysts for ways to increase the pressure on the Sandinistas more quickly, to make them "sweat."[61] Congressman Hyde told McFarlane "our guys have to win one occasionally. People don't like to back losers."[62]

Intelligence analysts assessing the war wrote disparaging reports about the rebels' abilities, leading McFarlane and others to the conclusion that the rebels "were not fighting that well."[63] Failed rebel attacks on Ocotal and on five other towns in Nueva Segovia during September and October confirmed the impression that the guerrillas were failing. So, too, did the controversy that erupted over the behavior of Suicida in the second half of the year. After his second failed attack on Jalapa, Suicida and some of his lieutenants went on a rampage of murder and torture, mostly of their own followers. Frustrated by what they considered the lack of support from the FDN leadership, they became virtual renegades within the movement until they were captured and executed. The reports of abuses badly damaged the rebels' already poor reputation and caused Reagan officials further anxiety. The "lack of a credible political leadership," McFarlane feared, was a "significant vulnerability" that could undermine the rebels' already tenuous support in Congress.[64]

The notable failures of the rebels at the end of 1983, combined with the precarious political situation in Washington, distracted attention away from the rebel army's successes that year and from its potential successes in coming years. When not measured against the demands in Washington for immediate, crushing blows against the Sandinistas, the rebels' progress was impressive. The growth of the forces had been extraordinary: from less than 1,000 fighters at the end of 1981, to more than 2,000 at the end of 1982, to as many as 6,000 by the end of 1983.[65] In its first full year of receiving consistent foreign support, the rebel army had managed to conduct major offensives in the spring, summer, fall, and winter, and in the northern, central, and eastern parts of the country. In September some 450 rebel fighters had penetrated as far south as Boaco and Chontales.[66]

If Reagan officials and members of Congress were not impressed, Sandinista army leaders were. Humberto Ortega admitted publicly for the first time that the military situation in the north was "difficult."[67] At the end of August Sandinista officials reported rebel attacks in eight different locations in northern Nicaragua. The officials confirmed that the rebel forces seemed better disciplined, better trained, and better armed than in the past. They also reported that contra forces were now obviously being resupplied by air. The CIA had, indeed, established a crude system to resupply contra forces using two or three small planes to drop weapons, ammunition, medicines, food, and clothing at pre-determined locations. Adolfo Calero confirmed that whereas before "we didn't have the capacity to supply our people. . . . Now we are better prepared logistically."[68]

If the rebels failed to "do the urban bit" or seize "liberated territory," they accomplished other goals more appropriate to a guerrilla army in its infancy. They were already forcing the government to spend scarce resources to prevent the fall of any major towns in the north, to impose an unpopular draft on an unwilling urban population, and to crack down on, and thereby alienate, much of the rural population of the north. The rebels penetrated deep into the central provinces of Matagalpa, Boaco, and Chontales; they grew in size and fighting ability; and they posed enough of a threat to the regime to give encouragement to its opponents. Although some attacks failed, others succeeded. In October forces led by Mike Lima attacked and occupied Pantasma, just 80 miles north of Managua. The setbacks at the end of 1983 which so troubled Reagan officials, moreover, soon proved only temporary. In the first six months of 1984, the rebels would mount the most spectacular offensives of the war and drive the Sandinistas to the point of desperation.

The Reagan administration, however, preoccupied with the brutal political battle at home, took little notice of these trends. In the last months of 1983, therefore, it was the American government that reached the point of desperation. Officials searched for ways to turn the tide in Nicaragua quickly, before congressional support evaporated. As they searched, the foreign-policy-making bureaucracy was torn apart by internecine feuds. In the wake of the congressional outcry concerning the naval maneuvers in July, Secretary Shultz had threatened to resign. He told Reagan that "the process of managing foreign policy has gone completely off the track."[69] After several weeks of bitter infighting, Reagan's second national security adviser, William Clark, was forced to resign his post. The battle to succeed him pitted Shultz and his allies at the White House, Baker and Deaver, against Weinberger, Casey, and Kirkpatrick. Shultz and the White House advisers wanted Baker; Casey and Weinberger proposed Kirkpatrick.[70] Either of these individuals might have proved a strong force in the National Security Council, strong enough to tilt the battles over policy decisively one way or the other. For that very reason, the two sides compromised on a weaker candidate, Robert McFarlane, under whose leadership these battles would continue.

In the midst of this frenetic transition, the Reagan administration continued to thrash about for quick answers to its problems in Central America. Even State Department officials, who had been a voice for restraint for much of the year, began searching for a rapid way out of the increasingly controversial Nicaraguan imbroglio. With the State Department's constraints lifted, Casey and Clarridge gave freer rein to their imaginations. And if the rebels themselves were incapable of carrying out some of the more spectacular projects Casey and Clarridge had in mind, the CIA had other men on its payroll who could.

The first of the new spectaculars was carried out by a hitherto unknown rebel "air force." On September 8 two airplanes flown by contra pilots bombed Sandino airport outside of Managua—the first air attack of the war. One of the planes was shot down and crashed into the control tower. Unfortunately for the Reagan administration, Senators Cohen and Hart were flying into Managua that day. They arrived at Sandino airport seven hours after the attack, incensed at the CIA.[71] Edén Pastora immediately claimed responsibility for the attack, declaring that "our objectives were to bomb military installations of the Sandinista Air Force as well as the Soviet electronic telecommunications station known as Santa Maria." Neither goal was accomplished.

According to the Sandinistas, flight documents on the downed plane showed that it had taken off from an airfield in Costa Rica.[72] The Costa Rican government promptly arrested more than 80 of Pastora's followers,[73] but two weeks later Pastora's new "air force" carried out two more raids, hitting a military installation near the port of Puerto Sandino and a distillery near Montelimar, once the summer retreat of Somoza, now the retreat of the Sandinistas. Pastora's air attacks were more sensational than effective; or as Robelo put it, they had a "purely political value," and Pastora traveled to the United States soon afterward to try to win some financial support.[74]

On October 2, fuel tanks at a Nicaraguan port on the Atlantic Coast were destroyed by shots fired from motorboats. On October 11, armed men in motorboats attacked dock installations at Corinto on the Pacific Coast, blowing up five fuel storage tanks which contained more than three million gallons of gas. The fires raged out of control for most of that day and 25,000 residents had to be evacuated from the port city.[75] According to one report, the attacks on the ports left the Nicaraguan government with less than a month's worth of oil reserves.[76]

The *New York Times'* Philip Taubman reported from Washington on October 16 that the CIA had recommended and helped plan the attacks.

According to administration officials he interviewed, the CIA had decided over the summer that direct attacks on industrial and transportation targets inside Nicaragua would be a quicker and more effective way of hurting the Sandinistas. Officials also told Taubman they hoped the attacks would show members of Congress that the rebels could be more effective in harassing the Nicaraguan government.[77] What the officials did not tell Taubman, however, was that the men carrying out the attacks from the motorboats were not Nicaraguan fighters. They were contract employees of the CIA, so-called "unilaterally-controlled Latino assets," men of Hispanic origin hired by the CIA to carry out these special covert actions. These actions were the closest the United States had come to a direct role in the attacks on Nicaragua.

Other actions by the CIA followed at the end of the year. For several months Clarridge, encouraged by Casey, had advocated mining the harbors of Nicaragua to discourage oil shipments and strangle both the Nicaraguan economy and the Sandinista military effort. The mines would be designed not to destroy ships, but to frighten their captains. Mere rumors that harbors and ports were mined could be enough to reduce shipping significantly. For months, State Department officials, led by Craig Johnstone, had rejected the idea as both reckless and futile. Mining harbors recalled the Vietnam War, Johnstone argued, and would be poorly received in the United States; and the benefits were unlikely to justify the risks.[78] Shultz had fought the idea in meetings with Reagan. In the winter of 1983, however, State Department officials changed their minds. Frustrated at their inability to force concessions from the Sandinistas, and at what Johnstone called their "empty quiver," they wanted some way to turn up the pressure.[79]

The decision to mine the harbors of Nicaragua, which would have such a devastating impact on the Reagan administration's policy in 1984, was made without debate or rancor. At the end of 1983 American policy in Nicaragua had been overshadowed by two far more dramatic events: the bombing of the marine barracks in Beirut on October 23 and the American invasion of Grenada that same week.

———

The second half of 1983 ended in considerable frustration for Reagan officials concerned with Central America. Congress had slashed aid for a covert program that was not, in any case, living up to the expectations of many Reagan officials. To others it had become more and more apparent that the contra program was inadequate as the sole tool of policy. No immediate victories and no end to the conflict lay in sight, either in Nicaragua or in Washington. Without consciously choosing it, the Reagan administration was pursuing a policy Johnstone called "playing for the breaks."[80] This approach fell well short of a strategy. On the other hand, in a confrontation between a superpower and a much weaker nation in its sphere of influence, the larger power could afford many more errors and failures than the smaller.

29

The Correlation of Forces

In 1983 the Reagan administration's bumbling efforts to confront the Sandinistas, as well as the Democrats in Congress, did not appear to hold much promise of success. In 1984 even more damaging errors and internal divisions would bedevil the American government, while the Sandinistas would improve both their military and their political response to the North American aggression. The year 1984 was, nevertheless, a turning point in the confrontation between the two countries. The Sandinistas were forced along a different path from the one they had originally intended. The Reagan administration, though suffering its worst legislative defeat in four years, took the first step toward future legislative victories. More generally, the enormous disparity of power between the two countries began to manifest itself, lessening the effect of many American errors and making any Sandinista victories limited and temporary.

The United States brought to the struggle the raw economic, political, and military power of the world's most potent nation. American influence in the international economy reinforced its political influence with the major Western powers and with many other nations in the developing and newly industrialized world. In the Western Hemisphere the predominance of American power was overwhelming. Virtually every country in the hemisphere depended for its economic and political well-being on American trade or aid, and thus, in a general sense, on American goodwill. The one country that stood in open defiance against the northern superpower, Cuba, was admired by many Latins for its brave stance, but few wished to emulate its poverty and isolation. Viron Vaky had once argued that the Sandinistas would never be so foolish as to follow Castro into challenging American economic, political, and military hegemony in the hemisphere, that the realities of life in the shadow of the superpower would convince the Sandinistas that they had to "behave realistically."

But the Sandinistas *had* challenged American hegemony, in pursuit of power and independence at home and security abroad. In so doing they depended heavily on three sources of strength: the Soviet Union and the Eastern bloc for the military means to resist American direct and indirect intervention; the international community for the diplomatic means to isolate the Reagan administration and block its aggression; and the American domestic opposition to Reagan for the political means to undermine the American administration's strategy from within.

In 1984 at least two of these sources of strength suffered erosion. The Soviet Union's economic and political strength, its ability to compete on an equal footing with the other superpower, came under question during an unprecedented crisis of succession when Yuri Andropov died and Konstantin Chernenko was chosen as Soviet leader. In this difficult phase of Soviet history, the Sandinistas were among the first to sense a shift in the global "correlation of forces." Meanwhile, the international diplomatic community, though clearly in disagreement with the Reagan administration's policies in Central America, proved at best unable and at worst uninterested in stopping American intervention in its own sphere of influence. This was just one of the troubling lessons of the American intervention in Grenada. Reagan's dispatch of troops to that tiny Caribbean island in October 1983 had aroused little international condemnation.

Ultimately, the key to ending U.S. aggression seemed to lie in the American domestic political arena. From the days of their revolutionary struggle the Sandinistas had understood that by actively exploiting the political, ideological, and institutional schisms in the American system they might be able to constrain even an aggressive administration such as Reagan's. With the Soviets and the Europeans unable to stop the Reagan administration, the Sandinistas' best strategy for ending American aggression was to persuade America to constrain itself. But, once again, Reagan's decision to intervene in Grenada, and the overwhelming support he received from the American people, including even erstwhile Democratic critics, forced the Sandinistas to reassess their vulnerability to an American invasion and to change their political and military strategies in response to all the other forms of American aggression.[1]

————

The immediate problem facing the Sandinistas in the first months of 1984 was the growing rebellion in Nicaragua. Militarily, and even politically, the contras reached a level of strength and effectiveness in the first six months of the year previously unimagined by their supporters in the United States or by their adversaries in Nicaragua. In the United States, the contras' successes actually received less attention than their more modest gains in the spring of 1983. In Nicaragua, however, the contras were unmistakably shifting the political and military balance of power.

The sheer number of rebel fighters infiltrating from Honduras and Costa Rica and taking up positions deep inside Nicaragua in 1984 was frightening to Sandinista military leaders. In the first months of the year as many as 6,000 fighters pushed into the northern, eastern, central, and southern portions of the country. Communiqués from the Sandinista Ministry of Defense charted the rebels' southward drive beginning in January. On January 15 the Defense Ministry announced the start of a new offensive by contra forces in the northern provinces of Nueva Segovia and Jinotega, with some clashes occurring deeper, into northern Matagalpa province, some 30 kilometers north of the town of Rio Blanco.[2] Two days later, Humberto Ortega announced that FDN forces were engaged in a coordinated assault employing 3,000–4,000 fighters in Nueva Segovia with the aim of occupying Jalapa.[3] By February the FDN claimed to hold territory in northern and central Nicaragua, allegations which the Sandinistas soon confirmed.[4] By the middle of March, according to Sandinista military reports, Tigrillo's Rafael Herrera forces had taken control of San José de Bocay in the Bocay river valley in Jinotega. According to the Sandinistas, Tigrillo held this territory in his native province for almost two months.[5] The rebel forces also claimed control of another river valley in Madriz near the town of Talpaneca. From January to June, contra forces numbering in the thousands fought continuously against Sandinista regular army and militia units in Jinotega, Madriz, Nueva Segovia, and northern Matagalpa.

While the FDN penetrated from the north, Edén Pastora's forces drove across the southern border from Costa Rica. On April 11, they laid siege to and eventually overran a Sandinista military garrison at San Juan del Norte on the Atlantic Coast at the mouth of the San Juan River—one of the most spectacular raids of the war. Pastora's men held the garrison for five days. Before Pastora could establish his "provisional government," Sandinista forces counterattacked and drove Pastora's force of about 300 men back across the Rio San Juan into Costa Rica. Pastora's raid never-theless forced the Sandinistas to send more than 2,000 troops to the southern border in April and May to prevent any renewed offensive.[6]

By the beginning of April, Sandinista leaders were calling on civilians to prepare for what Daniel Ortega called "the largest military offensive that the United States has launched." The government put 20 towns on alert in the northern provinces of Madriz, Nueva Segovia, and Estelí, and Ortega warned that 8,000 rebels were attacking in both the north and the south of the country.[7] On April 13, Tomás Borge spoke in even more dire tones. "In this offensive," he declared, "the largest mounted to date, there are more than 8,000 mercenaries of the CIA participating inside the country. And many have even entered central regions of Nicaragua. Fighting is under way in the Departments of Matagalpa, Jinotega, Nueva Segovia, northern Zelaya, southern Zelaya." Borge also noted that "for this operation the CIA is employing an enormous apparatus of logistical support and is maintaining a steady supply of arms, ammunition, food-stuffs, information, and communication for its mercenary army."[8] The next day, Daniel Ortega reported that "fighting is constant, in the north-ern area of our country, the Departments of Nueva Segovia, Jinotega, and Northern Zelaya, even on the border area of Chinandega Department. These are areas where we are being attacked continuously."[9]

Although Humberto Ortega and the Cuban general Ochoa had begun to devise new tactics to respond to the rebels, by the beginning of 1984 few of these new tactics had yet reached the field. In March the Sandin-ista army brought tanks and heavy artillery up to the border in northern Nueva Segovia and Jinotega to meet the FDN's attacks.[10] The Sandin-istas also made increasing use of their new irregular combat battalions, the BLIs (*Batallóns de Lucha Irregular*). The more mobile BLIs, now better trained in counterinsurgency operations and directed in many cases by Cuban military advisers, began chasing rebel units around the country-side, making it more difficult for the rebels to rest and receive supplies. The Sandinistas still did not have the manpower they needed to meet rebel offensives in so many parts of the country at once, however. They were "unable to protect [government installations] and lacked the manpower or mobility to pursue the guerrillas."[11] Although the Sandinistas had announced the beginning of universal conscription in 1983, Humberto Ortega recalls, "we didn't start recruiting until 1984."[12] Their efforts to block the rebels' infiltration failed, and while they concentrated their efforts on blocking in the north, the forces of the Jorge Salazar Regional Command drove deeper into the central provinces. In the middle of May, Adolfo Calero, a member of the FDN Directorate, declared that the FDN task forces had "penetrated the center of the Nicaraguan territory in our southbound march" and had reached into the provinces of Boaco and Chontales.[13]

The rebels' 1984 offensive was marked by a return to more classic guerrilla tactics. There were fewer pitched battles like Suicida's mad attacks on Jalapa, more hit-and-run raids and ambushes designed to undermine government authority in the hinterlands. The offensive also heralded a shift in the organizational structure of the rebel army. Rebel task forces like the Jorge Salazar grew so quickly that they were redesignated as "regional commands" containing several task forces. In some of the regional commands, even the task forces grew so large that they became virtually autonomous armies, and the task force subcommanders grew in stature equal to that of the regional commanders. This development began a transformation in the rebel leadership that would soon become an important asset both inside and outside Nicaragua. Within the Jorge Salazar Regional Command, which penetrated deepest into the provinces of Matagalpa, Boaco, and Chontales, the new task force chiefs symbolized the evolution in the social composition of the rebel army's leadership. Unlike Toño and Quiche, the two ex-National Guardsmen who founded the Jorge Salazar Command, young leaders like "Rigoberto," "Franklyn," "Emiliano," "Fernando," and "Dumas" were representative of the farmers, petty landowners, and campesinos who had always made up the bulk of the contra forces but had hitherto been kept out of the leadership ranks.

The Jorge Salazar Regional Command was unique among the task forces in displaying this degree of social mobility, but it was also the largest and most wide-ranging rebel force in Nicaragua. The success of the Jorge Salazar task forces as they drove down through Matagalpa into Boaco and Chontales was unforeseen by American or Sandinista strategic planners. While there were at times reports of murders and kidnappings by contra forces, the rebels nevertheless appeared to enjoy a good deal of support from the local populations in these provinces. In Matagalpa, small farmers had many political and economic grievances against the government. In Boaco and Chontales, the cattle-growers who dominated the sparsely populated regions were famous for their independence and resistance to control from any regime in Managua. Wherever people had held land or depended on good market prices for their produce, discontent with the Sandinistas was high, and so was the level of support for the contras.

Defense Minister Humberto Ortega best summed up the problems the government was having. On June 5 he explained that the Reagan administration's "open war strategy" consisted of "permanently weakening our country through counterrevolutionary activity in the large territories of Segovia, Matagalpa, Jinotega, the Atlantic Coast, part of Chontales, and Rio San Juan in order to dismember the country's economy." The widespread rebel offensive was "aimed at dispersing the [Sandinista Army], weakening it, and affecting the basic military structure throughout the country," to make possible an American invasion of the Pacific Coast left unguarded by the dispersed government forces. The rebel army had been "reorganized to better respond . . . to act as real military units in a modern army. From more than 20 military bases in Honduras and Costa Rica on the border with Nicaragua, the supplies are brought in by air and land . . . [and] more than 10,000 genocidal individuals are constantly launching criminal attacks." The CIA, meanwhile, was "unleashing campaigns to confuse the people, with the objective of blaming the revolutionary government for the grave economic problems we are experiencing."[14]

On May 24, FDN officials declared their goal was "to deepen our penetration from the north and the south, to tie the two fronts together in the central Department of Matagalpa and thus to divide the country in two . . . in this way it would be very hard for the Sandinist Army to break our resistance and our supply lines, while we would be isolating the Pacific coast from the Atlantic."[15] This goal, unimaginable at the beginning of 1983, no longer seemed implausible, even to the Sandinistas. "We faced a grave situation in the summer of 1984," Humberto Ortega later recalled. "The war was very, very hard."[16]

On June 15, the same day the Sandinista army sent 2,000 troops to the southern border to liquidate what remained of Pastora's forces near San Juan del Norte, the government suddenly announced that senior officials led by Daniel Ortega were heading off on an unscheduled trip to Moscow. Ortega told reporters only that the delegation would discuss with the Soviet leaders "matters pertaining to the situation of aggression experienced by Nicaragua and the economic problems we face because of this aggression."[17] The Sandinistas were off to Moscow to ask for more military assistance and to win a greater degree of Soviet commitment to their survival.

———

The Soviet patrons the Sandinistas turned to in 1984 were not the same as those whom they had found when they arrived in power five years earlier. By the middle of 1984, the Soviet Union had chosen Chernenko as its third leader in as many years, and the Brezhnev era in Soviet politics and foreign policy was closing quickly. The most committed Brezhnevites and devotees of active Soviet support for radical states in the Third World were growing old, changing their tune, or otherwise waning in strength in the upper reaches of the foreign policy apparatus.[18] The changing faces reflected subtle shifts in Soviet foreign policy doctrine, and while these shifts did not suggest immediate problems for the Sandinistas, they did portend a future different from the one Humberto Ortega and others had envisioned.

The weakness of the Soviet economy had become an inescapable fact. As far back as June of 1983, then-General Secretary Andropov had made the Soviet Union's poor economic performance the main theme of his speech to the Central Committee Plenum. In addition to forcing the Sandinistas to recalculate their earlier perception of Soviet-American equality—especially since the American economy now appeared as strong as the Soviet Union's was weak—the Nicaraguan leaders also had to confront the implicit suggestion in Andropov's speech that the Soviet Union could not continue to sustain its Third World allies economically.[19] To be sure, Soviet economic support, while important, had never been enough to float the Nicaraguan economy. Symbolically, however, the Soviet Union's increasingly open acknowledgment of its economic crisis threatened to weaken the main pillar of the Sandinistas' entire strategy toward the United States and the West.

Even more dramatic than the Soviets' admission of their own economic weaknesses were the signs that proliferated in 1983 and 1984 that the "correlation of forces" had shifted against the Soviet Union along the entire range of U.S.-Soviet competition. Most notable was the successful deployment of Pershing and cruise missiles by the NATO alliance in December 1983. Soviet leaders had lobbied hard to prevent this deployment by both threatening and cajoling Western European nations for over three years, hoping in the process to separate the United States from its allies, particularly West Germany. The deployment thus had not only strategic but broad political ramifications. Far from opening cracks in the alliance, the Soviet challenge succeeded only in reestablishing American leadership in the Atlantic alliance. Andropov had retaliated by withdrawing from all talks on strategic nuclear weapons with the United States, but rather than creating panic in the West, this tactic only allowed Reagan to appear the willing peacemaker without having to make any concessions. When, after the death of Andropov in February 1984, the Soviet leadership saw the futility of its position, it took steps to repair relations with the same American President who had in both word and deed assaulted the Soviet Union for nearly four years. Although the crisis in U.S.-Soviet relations was the central theme of Walter Mondale's campaign against Reagan, the Soviet leadership did Reagan the favor at the end of September of permitting a highly publicized meeting between the President and Foreign Minister Gromyko at the United Nations—thus helping to put a final nail in the coffin of the Democrat's campaign.[20] Soon after Reagan's re-election, the Soviets agreed to begin new negotiations over nuclear and space-based weapons, thus abandoning their earlier refusal after less than a year.

Those who relied on Soviet power to check that of the United States could not fail to take note of these developments, and Sandinista leaders had many occasions to view the Soviets firsthand during this period. They met with senior Soviet officials three times in the first six months of 1984: Daniel Ortega attended Andropov's funeral in February, where he met Chernenko and Gromyko. Humberto Ortega met with Soviet military chiefs Ustinov and Ogarkov, and Admiral Gorshkov, in April. Daniel Ortega returned to Moscow in June for another emergency meeting with Chernenko to obtain further Soviet military support. Humberto Ortega recalls he could "see within the party a serious crisis of succession." Worse still, although the meetings were friendly and Soviet military aid continued to flow to Nicaragua at record levels, the Sandinistas detected a growing reticence by their Soviet patrons to challenge American hegemony in Central America.[21]

For the Sandinistas a key test of Soviet will came on the question of advanced fighter aircraft. Soviet officials had promised to deliver MiG fighters to Nicaragua; Sandinista fighter pilots had been training for a year in Bulgaria; airstrips in Nicaragua had been lengthened and configured by Eastern bloc engineers to handle advanced fighter aircraft; and MiG

fighters earmarked for Nicaragua were said to be in Cuba awaiting shipment. Nevertheless, Soviet leaders and Castro rebuffed repeated Sandinista pleas in 1984 to deliver the planes. At the beginning of 1984, the
American administration had delivered a stiff warning that the introduction of advanced fighter aircraft into Nicaragua would not be tolerated,
and now it appeared that the Soviets would not challenge Reagan's ultimatum. "On the military level," Humberto Ortega recalls, "the Soviets
were being very careful with us. Their unwillingness to provide the MiGs
was either prudence or shyness." In either case, from the Sandinistas'
point of view, the Soviet Union had made a decision to let the United
States dictate what was and was not permissible for Nicaragua's defense.
The military value of the Migs would have been small, except as a coun-
terweight to American-made fighters in the hands of the Honduran and
Salvadoran air forces. In the Sandinistas' battle against the contras they
would have been nearly useless. But they were important as a symbol of
the Soviet commitment to the Sandinista revolution. Cuba, after all, had
entire squadrons of Migs. The fact that the Soviets had considered sending the planes to Nicaragua, but apparently changed their mind in the
face of American warnings, greatly disturbed Sandinista leaders. Viewed
in the context of the overall decline in Soviet power and will relative to
those of the United States, the Soviets' failure to deliver on this implied
promise boded ill for the future. Humberto Ortega warned his colleagues
in the Directorate that "the correlation of forces in the world" had become "very difficult for the socialist camp."[22]

As in the past when faced by threats to their survival, the Sandinistas
moderated their course. The simple strategy of revolutionary consolidation that had guided them for the past two years gave way to the far more
complicated political and diplomatic strategies necessary to blunt American aggression, forestall international isolation, and defeat internal counterrevolutionary forces of both the armed and unarmed variety. As early
as the summer of 1983, after the first big waves of contra offensives, after
failed efforts to enlist the support of the United Nations against the
United States, and after the Sandinistas were forced to agree to Contadora's Document of Objectives, the Sandinistas had begun to discuss publicly the possibility of holding elections. In November of 1983 the Directorate had voted by a narrow margin to hold elections in 1984 as a way
out of the increasingly dangerous confrontation with the United States.

On December 4, 1983, Daniel Ortega announced that the electoral process would begin on January 31, 1984, and on February 21 the government declared that the elections would be held on November 4, two days before the American election.[23]

Bayardo Arce, next to Tomás Borge the most radical member of the Sandinista directorate, elaborated the new strategy candidly in a speech to the Nicaraguan Socialist Party in May.[24] The Sandinistas, Arce suggested, now had to pay the price for the promises made to Carlos Andrés Pérez, José Figueres, and others in the summer of 1979. The Sandinistas had promised "revolutionary change based on three principles which made us presentable in the international context . . . [:] non-alignment abroad, a mixed economy, and political pluralism. With those three elements we kept the international community from going along with American policy in Nicaragua"[25] Five years later, prudence once again required a measure of flexibility to prevent the defeat of the revolution.

Elections were, of course, "a nuisance." "What a revolution really needs," Arce insisted, "is the power to act. The power to act is precisely what constitutes the essence of the dictatorship of the proletariat—the ability of the [working] class to impose its will by using the means at hand [without] bourgeois formalities." And "of course," Arce explained, "if we did not have the war situation imposed on us by the United States, the electoral problem would be totally out of place in terms of its usefulness. . . . But from a realistic standpoint, being in a war with the United States, those things [i.e., elections] become weapons of the revolution to move forward with the construction of socialism. . . . [I]t is well to be able to call elections and take away from American policy one of its justifications for aggression against Nicaragua."

"Imperialism asks three things of us," Arce explained: "to abandon interventionism, to abandon our strategic ties with the Soviet Union and the socialist community, and to be democratic." The first two could not be conceded. "We cannot cease being internationalists unless we cease being revolutionaries," Arce declared, referring to Sandinista support of the Salvadoran and other local guerrillas. "We cannot discontinue strategic relationships [i.e., with the Soviet Union and Cuba] unless we cease being revolutionaries. It is impossible even to consider this." But democracy, "bourgeois democracy," had "an element which we can manage and even derive advantages from for the construction of socialism in Nicaragua." The Sandinistas would use elections, Arce explained, "to legitimize the revolution."

Arce was putting the best face on the Sandinistas' adjustment to their increasingly dire circumstances. As Humberto Ortega later recalled, the Sandinistas agreed to hold elections in 1984 "because we began detecting that the Soviet Union was not strong . . . [and because] we had the counterrevolution. The elections were a tactical tool, a weapon. They were a bitter pill that had to be swallowed."[26]

That the Sandinistas did not intend to give their opponents a fair chance to win the elections was an article of faith among opposition leaders. The Democratic Coordinator (in Spanish, *Coordinadora*),[27] the main opposition alliance, from the first saw the elections as an opportunity to expose the Sandinistas to the world as tyrants. For the first time since the imposition of the State of Emergency in 1982, opposition leaders were near the center of international attention. They were invited to Caracas to meet with Contadora leaders; they had played a part in devising the 21-point Document of Objectives; they had the public backing of leading American politicians like Jim Wright. They knew, however, that the attention they received was due to the war. Indeed, they went out of their way to associate themselves with the contras. On December 24, 1983, the Coordinadora had set forth a set of nine demands to ensure that the elections would be "authentic."[28] The demands included complete separation of the Sandinista Party from the state, the transformation of the Sandinista People's Army into a national army "removed from political or ideological sectarianism," the repeal of the law establishing universal military conscription, the law allowing censorship of the media, and the law under which private land and businesses had been confiscated. The opposition demanded an end to the state of emergency that had been in place since March 1982; the promulgation of an amnesty law pertaining to political crimes; full respect for freedom of worship; freedom for opposition labor unions; full autonomy for the judicial branch of government; and the restoration of habeas corpus. The Coordinadora called for a national dialogue on the elections "among all the political parties and movements, including those in arms." And finally, the opposition leaders demanded that any elections had to be supervised by an international body.

The Sandinistas paid no attention to these demands, and from the first opposition leaders believed the Sandinistas' motives were entirely cynical. A prominent young businessman, Antonio Lacayo, declared that expecting free elections from the Sandinistas was like "saying you're going skiing without snow." The Sandinistas were playing "a very cool game," another opposition leader told American journalists. It was "a chess game with your American leaders and with our people, with the opposition."[29] On January 27 Arturo Cruz wrote in the *New York Times* that the Sandinistas were "not interested in a genuine electoral contest but in a farcical vote that will give a veneer of legitimacy to their de facto Government." Nicaragua's "erstwhile liberators," Cruz wrote, had become "addicted to power."[30] Under the circumstances, the opposition would also play a game. The Sandinistas had given the opposition "an '*apertura*,' a little opening, and we are fighting to widen that hole," Enrique Bolaños explained. "We're telling the world: stop and think. Don't be fooled. Please keep the pressure on and let us inside Nicaragua make our demands for democratization of Nicaragua, hoping no blood will be shed."[31] Opposition leaders hoped, however, that the war and the attendant international pressure would mount and, eventually, bring the Sandinistas to their knees.

30

Divided Counsel

While the Sandinistas reeled in the first months of 1984, the Reagan administration seemed to recover from its earlier missteps. President Reagan and his advisers began the year in a mood of greater optimism. The invasion of Grenada had brought a surge of popular support for the President, and the booming economy helped push Reagan's popularity ratings to their highest level since early 1982. Reagan's advisers looked ahead confidently to the coming re-election campaign: Over the first six months of 1984 Reagan's lead in the polls over his Democratic challenger, Walter Mondale, grew steadily to ten and fifteen points.

Even on the troublesome issue of Central America, there were favorable developments. The release of the report of the Kissinger commission in January gave Reagan officials more confidence to press their case in Congress. The report fully endorsed the administration's strategy in Central America, calling for vastly increased economic and military aid to the four U.S. allies and even for aid to the "democratic forces" in Nicaragua.[1] These findings came as little surprise, since all but one of the Democrats on the commission were moderate, conservative, or even hawkish members of their party.[2] Still, the report gave the administration's policy an elaborate explanation and justification that had been lacking.

A second boon for the administration came in March, when the first round of presidential elections was held in El Salvador. Salvadoran voters turned out in great numbers despite threats from the guerrillas. Both the fact of the elections and their result—the election of José Napoleon Duarte in the second round in May[3]—served the administration's political needs. Duarte's election proved a decisive turning point in the long congressional fight over aid to El Salvador. Jim Wright, who personally witnessed the voting, told reporters he would press fellow Democrats "to defend the freely chosen government" in El Salvador.[4] On May 10 Wright led 55 Democrats in approving most of President Reagan's request for military and economic aid, in defiance of the Democratic leader, Tip O'Neill. El Salvador thereafter faded as a controversial subject in American politics—and was more than adequately replaced by Nicaragua.

A memorandum from Secretary Shultz to the new national security adviser, Robert McFarlane, expressed the State Department's measured optimism as 1984 began. There had been "substantial gains" in Central America: "destabilization" supported by Cuba and the Soviet Union had been "blunted," and the United States had shown that "with our help, the rest of Central America need not go the way of Nicaragua." With democracy strong in Costa Rica and taking root in El Salvador, the Sandinistas were "increasingly isolated." American military aid to the region had "strengthened the resolve of Honduras," improved the performance of the Salvadoran military, and "increasingly placed the Sandinista government on the defensive."[5]

————

Shultz and his advisers at the State Department began pressing for a renewed diplomatic effort early in the year. With the Sandinistas' acceptance of the Contadora Group's 21 points and their agreement to hold elections in 1984, Shultz argued, the Nicaraguan government was "attempting to appear more reasonable" and might even be "signal[ling] a desire to reach some form of accommodation."[6] Eager as he was for a negotiated settlement, Shultz was even more hopeful of ending what he considered the administration's increasingly futile struggle to win new aid for the contras from Congress. Shultz did not favor the repeated clashes with Congress and the immobilizing controversies they stirred.[7] He claims to have been convinced the rebels could somehow continue fighting, "with or without congressional aid," but he was willing to accept the demise of the contras. American strength, he argued, could be demonstrated in other ways, "in naval exercises, in intelligence overflights, in the assistance Congress votes for El Salvador, in our determination to stand by our friends."[8]

Shultz was not especially optimistic that a negotiated settlement could be reached with the Sandinistas. Deputy Assistant Secretary of State Craig Johnstone had developed an elaborate four-stage proposal, by which both the United States and the Sandinistas would take simultaneous steps toward solving their differences and achieving normal relations. If carried out faithfully by both sides, the four-step plan was designed to achieve, after 90 days: the withdrawal of all Cuban and Soviet military and security personnel from Nicaragua; the full termination of all Sandinista support for the Salvadoran guerrillas; a negotiated agreement on the size of all armed forces in the region and the beginning of steps to reduce the Nicaraguan army to meet the agreed limits; the holding of "free and fair democratic elections" in Nicaragua allowing full participation by the opposition parties, to be verified by international observers. In exchange for these concessions by the Sandinistas, the United States would: end all support for the contras; significantly reduce the size of its military presence in Central America; reduce arms shipments to the region; and begin to provide economic assistance to Nicaragua. Shultz was not at all sure the plan would work, but he was "willing to give it a serious try." "Even if we failed," he later wrote, "the demonstration that I was seriously pursuing a diplomatic track was essential if we were to have any hope at all for support from Congress for our Central America policy."[9]

Anticipating opposition from the rest of the administration, State Department officials moved with stealth in formulating their plans. No one outside the State Department saw the four-step plan until the early summer. Then, only McFarlane was let in on the idea so that he might transmit it to Reagan. McFarlane believed the proposal had "teeth" and provided for a "much more demanding standard of performance by the Sandinistas."[10] McFarlane's support proved crucial as the State Department moved to the next phase of its plan, the beginning of direct talks with Sandinista leaders. Shultz also had important support from Reagan's top political advisers, James Baker and Michael Deaver, as well as from Nancy Reagan.[11] All wanted to end the politically damaging debate over contra aid and approved the idea of a diplomatic effort during the campaign season.

As in 1983, however, Reagan received divided counsel. While Shultz and his advisers looked forward to a possible negotiated settlement, other officials were preoccupied with finding more aid for the contras. Robert McFarlane advised the President on February 21 that "unless an additional $14M is made available, the program will have to be drastically curtailed by May or June of this year." McFarlane argued that not just Central America but the credibility of the United States in the world was at stake. While Shultz believed other forms of American power could be used to persuade the Nicaraguans, McFarlane argued that the rebel forces were the "*only* significant pressure being applied against the regime in Managua." If the covert program had to be ended, the United States would lose its "principal instrument for restraining the Sandinistas from exporting their revolution and, in fact, for facilitating a negotiated end to the regional conflict." The "international repercussions of this failure" would "affect friends and adversaries alike." McFarlane insisted that "the only practical alternative" was to approach Congress "with a concerted effort to obtain additional funding for this program, despite the anticipated strong resistance we expect."[12] The President accordingly directed Shultz, Weinberger, Casey, and the chairman of the Joint Chiefs of Staff, General Vessey, to make aid to the contras "a matter of highest priority" in order to "prevent a major foreign policy reversal." President Reagan was "determined that this program should continue."[13]

Given the near certainty that the House would not vote new aid for the contras, administration officials knew they would have to win the Senate's approval for new money first, and then try to force the House to compromise again in a conference. In March the Senate intelligence committee voted 14–0 to approve $21 million in new aid for the rebels, to supplement the $29 million that had been approved at the end of 1983.[14]

The unanimous vote masked the fact, however, that support for the covert program was quietly eroding in the intelligence committee. Senator Moynihan, running for re-election in New York, was under pressure from fellow liberals in his party to withdraw his support for the aid.[15] Moynihan's discomfort was shared by others on the committee, including two moderate Republicans. Senator Cohen warned that the Reagan administration was "ignoring the Contadora process" and not "paying enough attention" to the "very strict restrictions" the committee had placed on the conduct of the covert war. Senator Durenberger complained there was "no real evidence that the covert action effort" had brought about "changes in Sandinista policy."[16]

No sooner had the $21 million aid bill passed the Senate than disaster struck. The mines planted in Nicaragua's harbors earlier in the year, though they did little damage to the Sandinistas, exploded into scandal in Washington. Minutes before the final vote to pass contra aid, Senator Goldwater was handed a report from a member of the intelligence committee staff who had learned that the President had approved the mining of Nicaragua's harbors and that the action had been carried out directly by the CIA. For senators on the intelligence committee, the mining itself was no surprise, but the extent of the CIA's participation was. Goldwater rose in fury and, much to the surprise of assembled senators and intelligence committee staff members, began reading the note aloud to his colleagues while the Senate stenographer transcribed his words into the public record of the Senate proceedings. Senator Cohen had to rush over and tell Goldwater that the information he was reading into the public record was highly classified. Goldwater's words were deleted from the Senate record, but a *Wall Street Journal* reporter heard what he had said and rushed it into print the next day under the headline: "U.S. Role in Mining Nicaraguan Harbors Reportedly Is Larger Than First Thought."[17]

In the weeks that followed, the CIA's direct role in the mining was the subject of angry, private exchanges between the Reagan administration and the Senate intelligence committee and above all its chairman and vice chairman, Senators Goldwater and Moynihan. In the public debate, however, it was the mining itself that came under attack. Critics denounced it as an act of war, and on April 10 the Senate voted 84–12 to condemn the mining. The uproar put Senate intelligence committee members in a doubly embarrassing position. Accused of having known about the mining but done nothing to prevent it, the committee members could not explain to the public that their real complaint with Casey was that he had never told them about the extent of the CIA's direct involvement.[18] Indeed, they could hardly say anything without revealing highly classified information.

Members of the committee were thus vulnerable to attack from all sides. One member of the intelligence committee, Senator Leahy, charged his colleagues with hypocrisy: "There were senators who voted one way the week before," in support of aid to the contras, and "a different way the following week," to condemn the mining, "who knew about the mining in both instances. And I think they were influenced solely by public opinion. And I think that's wrong and that's a lousy job of legislative action."[19] After all, Leahy argued, the mining "was a logical extension of an undeclared, secret war." What did members of Congress "think organizing and supplying the contra army of thousands was? Peace?"[20]

Leahy, of course, could afford to make such statements, since he had consistently opposed the covert program. For senators like Moynihan, however, who had supported aid to the contras and had raised no objection to the mining, but only to the CIA's role, the political embarrassment was acute. Even Senator Goldwater said he had been humiliated "because I did not know the facts on this." Moynihan's vote for contra aid in March of 1984 was the last he would cast to support the Nicaraguan rebels.

The embarrassment felt by senators was nothing as compared to the damage done to the Reagan administration's covert program. And that was nothing compared to the disaster the entire episode brought down on the heads of the guerrillas fighting in Nicaragua. Enders and Johnstone had been right to resist the mining idea early in 1983, before giving in in desperation. As Johnstone had feared, the scandal put an end to already dim hopes of obtaining new funding for the contras in fiscal year 1984. The Senate could, and eventually did, pass the $21 million, but after the mining scandal it was unlikely to overrule the House in a conference as in 1983. On May 24, the House voted against aid to the contras by an overwhelming margin of 241–177. In the absence of any effort by the White House to hold its troops together, sixty Republicans from the north and midwest joined the Democratic majority, no doubt eager to distance themselves from the embarrassing affair with elections just six months off.

———

A week after the devastating defeat in the House, Secretary Shultz paid a surprise visit to Managua to open a new round of direct negotiations with the Sandinistas. On June 1 Shultz spent two-and-a-half hours with the Sandinista leader in a meeting he publicly characterized as "constructive."[21] The two sides scheduled another round of talks. The Sandinistas designated Vice Foreign Minister Victor Tinoco to represent them, and the United States named as presidential envoy, Harry Shlaudeman. They set the first meeting for late June in the Mexican town of Manzanillo.

Shultz had succeeded in winning Reagan's approval for his plan without any formal meeting of the President's national security advisers, however, and before Shlaudeman and Tinoco could exchange a word, the inevitable battle erupted within the Reagan administration.[22] Weinberger, Casey, and Kirkpatrick demanded a chance to express their objections. With congressional support for aid to the contras collapsing, and Ambassador Shlaudeman about to begin the first round of negotiations in Manzanillo, the President met with his advisers on June 25 to reconsider the administration's strategy.[23]

The President was offered sharply divergent advice by his senior policymakers. Weinberger and Kirkpatrick implored Reagan to put a stop to Shultz's negotiations immediately and to devote his efforts instead to finding new aid for the contras. Even as they were meeting, Senate Republican leaders were acting to strip contra aid from an "emergency" supplemental appropriations bill, thus dooming the prospects for any assistance to the rebels in Fiscal Year 1984. Kirkpatrick insisted that the time had come to "require the Democrats to stand up and be counted" and to make their responsibility "clear to the U.S. public." She warned that "the coincidence of our undertaking this bilateral negotiating effort at the same time as the Congress fails to support funding for the Contras" was enough "to totally unravel our entire position in the region."

Some discussion on June 25 was devoted to finding alternative sources of funding for the contras if and when the Congress cut them off. Kirkpatrick and Weinberger favored seeking aid from third countries.[24] Robert McFarlane limited himself to expressing the hope that "none of this discussion will be made public in any way," and Reagan agreed that if "such a story gets out, we'll all be hanging by our thumbs in front of the White House until we find out who did it." Unknown to Shultz, Weinberger, and Kirkpatrick was the fact that Reagan and McFarlane had already been promised funds for the contras by the Saudi Arabian government.

Shultz argued that seeking money from third countries was "very likely illegal." He insisted that while he agreed on the need to save the contras, his negotiating strategy offered the only way to regain congressional support. Posing an analogy with recent events in Europe, Shultz argued that "we would not have gotten the deployment of Pershing missiles in Europe if people had not seen that we had a credible, vigorous negotiation going on." Similarly, he told Reagan, "you have moved to get yourself in a position with the USSR where we have made credible proposals and they have walked out." That had been "useful because it shows who is at fault for the lack of progress." In Central America, too, Shultz argued, an "essential ingredient in [our] strategy is that we can say, if Nicaragua is halfway reasonable, there could be a regional negotiated solution." He did not claim that a satisfactory settlement with the Sandinistas was likely. "I give the chances of a positive negotiation outcome with Nicaragua as two-in-ten," he told Reagan, "but if it doesn't succeed, it needs to be clear where the responsibility is, and that we have tried to help our Contadora friends obtain a positive outcome."[25]

While it was often President Reagan's custom to sit silently while his advisers argued, keeping his own counsel and making his decision known only afterwards, this time he openly agreed with his secretary of state that the direct talks with the Sandinistas should go forward. His goal, he made quite clear, was not a negotiated settlement, but more aid for the contras. The question, he insisted, was "How can we get that support in Congress?" Participation in negotiations was "important from that standpoint, to get support from Congress." Reagan said he could not "imagine that Nicaragua would offer anything reasonable in a bilateral treaty." But he insisted that "to back away from talks" would "look like a defeat."[26]

Having lost in their attempt to cancel the negotiations,[27] Weinberger, Kirkpatrick and NSC staff official, Constantine Menges, fought to prevent Shlaudeman from presenting the State Department's four-stage proposal, which Menges regarded as "a false agreement" because it "would not assure implementation of genuine democracy in Nicaragua."[28] The details of the plan were less at issue, however, than the fact that Shultz was conducting negotiations at all. At bottom, Weinberger, Kirkpatrick, and Menges believed Shultz could not be trusted to avoid a bad deal that would leave the United States and its allies helpless to resist communism in Central America.[29] "Everybody was worried," Kirkpatrick recalls, that Shultz was "about to definitively compromise something, but we weren't quite sure what. . . . And since he didn't keep anybody informed, Casey or Cap or anybody, everybody felt free to develop their own fantasies."[30]

The President, however, proved to have a keener sense of the likely outcome of negotiations than his nervous advisers. The lengthy battles over the State Department's proposal, which Menges and other officials did manage to dilute and delay, proved superfluous. The Sandinistas approached the negotiations in 1984 guided by the same principals that Foreign Ministry officials had set forth in 1982: "that the negotiation process was a tool to buy time"; that the negotiators themselves "had to be weak, so they could not make any decisions"; and that the negotiating strategy had to "take advantage of American dissension over Central America."[31]

Shlaudeman held four rounds of talks with the Sandinistas at Manzanillo between June 25 and August 15. At first he was instructed to read only summaries of the State Department's proposal; then he was permitted to read the entire plan orally, although at the insistence of Menges, Defense Department officials and, ultimately President Reagan, some of the proposed American concessions were left vague.[32] The Sandinistas did not respond favorably to any aspect of the State Department's proposal. Tinoco and the other negotiators, Shlaudeman reported to Shultz, "were clearly operating under a tight rein, without authorization to discuss substance."[33]

The State Department's demand for elections was the least of the Sandinistas' concerns, since they planned to hold elections that year. But they were not about to forgo their strategic relationships with Cuba and the Soviet Union, nor their support for the Salvadoran guerrillas, no matter what the Americans offered in return. While Menges and other critics of the State Department's plan worried about the inadequate guarantees for "genuine democracy," and liberal critics of the Reagan administration believed the call for any democratization killed any chance of agreement, it was on the security provisions that the Sandinistas found the State Department's proposal far too demanding.[34] Shlaudeman himself ultimately decided that the entire State Department proposal was "not worth a damn" and took it upon himself to seek a more limited agreement with the Sandinistas. "I had in mind to get something concrete in the security field that we could then go forward on."[35] This independent attempt to find grounds for a settlement would have justified the worst suspicions of Menges and others if they had known about it. But Shlaudeman's independent efforts achieved nothing. Shlaudeman later recalled his conviction that "the chances of a really stable agreement with the Sandinistas were nil, regardless of the Reagan administration's position."[36]

Although there was never any progress at Manzanillo, Shultz regarded his initiative as "a ten-strike" and told Reagan so on several occasions. The Sandinistas, he argued, were "defensive" and isolated. When Robert McFarlane asked what the point of continuing the talks was, Shultz argued that the "ill repute of Nicaragua" could be used "to build support for our efforts in El Salvador."[37] Shultz obviously could not claim, as he once had, that the talks with the Sandinistas were bolstering support for contra aid in the Congress. Indeed, the Manzanillo talks were proving anything but a deft combination of "power and diplomacy," as Shultz liked to put it. Peter Rodman, director of the State Department's Policy Planning office, had warned Shultz that negotiations undertaken without the "leverage" of contra aid could lead to an outcome favorable to the Sandinistas.[38] With the danger of "another Grenada" clearly passed, aid to the contras was all that remained to frighten the Sandinistas sufficiently to consider the large concessions demanded in the State Department's proposal.[39] Whatever signs of accommodation State Department officials detected at the beginning of the year diminished as the pressures on the Sandinistas diminished. By the end of the summer, contra forces began retreating from Nicaragua back into Honduras in a state of disarray. Honduras's support for the contras was wavering. The Reagan administration openly admitted the futility of pursuing more contra aid for the remainder of the year. Under the circumstances, the Sandinistas felt no pressure to accept the State Department's four-step plan. In time, moreover, they would find a better alternative.

While Shultz and his advisers at the State Department pursued the bilateral talks at Manzanillo, the negotiations sponsored by the Contadora Group seemed fatally stalled. On June 8, the Contadora ministers produced a preliminary draft treaty for discussion and comment by the five Central American governments. At a meeting of the Contadora Group's vice ministers in Panama at the end of August, Nicaraguan Vice Minister Tinoco rejected major provisions in the draft, telling reporters that Nicaragua would "not tolerate arms limitation nor the suspension of its electoral process and reserves the right to decide on foreign advisers."[40] The next day Costa Rican President Alberto Monge told reporters that Contadora had "made an extraordinary effort and carried out sincere labor" but had reached a point where it could go no further. Monge recommended turning the matter over to the OAS, where it was sure to be buried.

The governments of Mexico and Colombia, however, were not willing to see their negotiations fail. With the American elections approaching in November, they wanted to reach a quick agreement on the assumption that Reagan in a second term would have far less political interest in seeking peace. As the U.S.-Nicaraguan talks went ahead fruitlessly at Manzanillo, the two governments determined to push the Contadora negotiations forward to a resolution. Rather than allowing the Central American governments to control the pace and substance of the talks, as they had over the past year, Mexico and Colombia decided to break the logjam by taking matters into their own hands and drafting their own treaty.

The United States and its allies had long demanded that any treaty had to be "comprehensive," that is, covering all issues from arms levels to support for insurgencies to domestic political reforms; "verifiable," that is, subject to strict, meaningful international monitoring; and "simultaneous," meaning that all provisions, from arms reductions to political reforms, must occur at the same time. But the Mexicans and Colombians decided that, in the words of Colombia's President Betancur, "to conclude a binding, comprehensive, verifiable agreement in treaty form was impossible." It was better to gain agreement on general points first, and then later "press for results."[41] The Mexicans called an emergency meeting of Contadora on September 6 and wrote a new draft of the agreement with provisions more palatable to the Sandinistas. On September 7 the Contadora Group submitted the new draft for approval by the Central American governments.

The new draft agreement abandoned the points of greatest importance to the Reagan administration: simultaneity and verifiability. Immediately upon signature, for instance, the United States would have to suspend all military maneuvers in Central America and end aid to the contras. While these main demands of the Sandinistas were to be satisfied immediately, however, matters of interest to the United States and its allies—the size of the Sandinista armed forces, the number and type of weapons in the Sandinistas arsenal, and the limits on the numbers of foreign advisers—would be the subjects of future negotiations. The methods for verifying compliance with the agreement, moreover, were weak. Each nation was to take the main responsibility for ensuring that its own territory was not used to harbor or support irregular forces. The highly visible presence of the contras on Honduran territory, therefore, would be a bigger problem for the Hondurans than the highly secretive support for the FMLN would be for the Sandinistas. Overall verification of security matters was to be left to a commission of delegates "representing states of recognized impartiality," and these independent commission members, not the parties to the treaty, would decide if violations of the provisions of the treaty had occurred. Secretary Shultz considered the draft "most unsatisfactory," just the sort of "trap" the State Department had hoped to avoid by presenting its own proposal at Manzanillo.[42]

Under the weight of the Contadora Group's pressure, most of the Central American governments were inclined to agree to the new draft. But despite the Contadora Group's concessions to their interests, the Sandinistas remained ambivalent. On September 8 Nicaraguan Foreign Minister D'Escoto rejected any provision on disarmament, even a speculative one.[43]

The Sandinistas still objected to the security provisions of any treaty more than to the calls for democratization—and with good reason. The strategic relationships with Cuba and the Soviet Union, all Sandinista leaders agreed, were critical and non-negotiable. On the other hand, the Sandinistas had every intention of holding elections in 1984 and putting to rest this element of international criticism. The only question for the Sandinistas was the amount of risk they would have to take in holding elections deemed acceptably free and open to the West.

31

The Nicaraguan Elections of 1984

For the first six months of 1984, the Sandinistas had not worried much about their upcoming elections. The opposition was weak, lacking organization and the means of campaigning, while the government enjoyed a near monopoly of the public media and a seemingly unlimited reserve of funds and material for conducting an electoral campaign. The opposition was also divided by the usual personal jealousies, seemingly unable to agree on a single candidate out of all its ambitious party and factional leaders. For most of the year, it never occurred to Sandinista leaders that they would not overwhelm any opposition slate and achieve their goal of legitimizing the revolution. The Ortega brothers, moreover, looked forward to the popular endorsement of "President" Daniel Ortega, making the Ortega family the unquestionable leaders within the Directorate.

What complicated this happy scenario was the selection of Arturo Cruz as the Coordinadora's candidate in July. Cruz's name had often been mentioned by the more progressive factions of the opposition. The former president of the Central Bank, member of the government junta, and ambassador to the United States was fairly well known in Nicaragua and very popular among American politicians. Indeed, his selection owed much to the intercession of the State Department's Craig Johnstone, who persuaded Cruz to accept the nomination and persuaded the other opposition leaders, including Calero and the contra leaders, to accept Cruz.

The announcement of Cruz's candidacy on July 20 attracted considerable attention in the United States, both to the candidacy itself and to the question of whether the Sandinistas would actually allow him to run under reasonably fair conditions.

In the eyes of many American observers, particularly those of a moderate and liberal cast, the elections had become the true test of the Sandinistas. As a way out of the increasingly unpleasant confrontation between the Reagan administration and the Nicaraguan government, elections began to take the place of the stalled diplomatic efforts. In the middle of July the *Washington Post* editorialized that "those with misgivings about American support of the Nicaraguan insurgents ought to have none about American support of a Nicaraguan democratic process."[1] In Congress, Democrats opposed to the covert war against Nicaragua supported the goal of fair elections if only because they would end the divisive debate over President Reagan's policy. At the end of March, Jim Wright and several other liberal and moderate Democrats had sent a letter to Daniel Ortega, commending him for "taking steps to open up the political process in your country." "We write with hope," the letter continued, "that the initial steps you have taken will be followed by others designed to guarantee a fully open and democratic electoral process." If the Sandinistas followed this course, Wright and his colleagues would protect the Sandinistas from the Reagan administration. "We have been, and remain, opposed to U.S. support for military action directed against the people or government of Nicaragua." If the Sandinistas did what was necessary, "[t]hose responsible for supporting violence against your government . . . would have far greater difficulty winning support for their policies than they do today."[2]

With this broad support in the American Congress, Arturo Cruz arrived in Nicaragua at the end of July. He immediately spelled out tough demands of the Sandinistas. Cruz stood by the nine-point Coordinadora document of December 1983 which called, in effect, for the dismantlement of Sandinista controls of all the levers of power in the country. The Sandinistas, as one observer has written, "had overwhelming advantages, beginning with their control of the press, the police, and the three-member Supreme Electoral Council charged with overseeing the campaign. They had set the voting age at sixteen to take advantage of their support among young people, and had insisted that soldiers, who were required to attend Sandinista 'political education' classes and were cut off from contact with the opposition, be allowed to vote at special polling places adjacent to military bases. Mayors and provincial governors used their control over ration cards and business permits to discourage people from supporting the opposition."[3] As long as such controls remained in place, Cruz and his opposition colleagues argued, the electoral campaign would be an unequal test between one party with all the powers of government at its disposal and an opposition with none.[4] Cruz refused to register his candidacy formally with the electoral council until his demands were met. In addition, Cruz and the Coordinadora insisted that the date of elections had to be postponed so that if and when agreement was reached, the opposition parties would have sufficient time to campaign under more favorable conditions.

Cruz made these demands because he believed that "the Sandinistas had decided on a Somoza-style election ... a propaganda extravaganza aimed at an international audience."[5] But he also believed the Sandinistas needed the opposition's participation in the elections and that this gave him a strong bargaining position. He told supporters in Nicaragua "that the Sandinistas were using the proposed elections to buy an international certificate of legitimacy and that they hoped that the opposition would cosign the purchase check. I insisted that for this to happen, legitimate elections were required; otherwise the check would be fraudulent."[6]

From the first Cruz understood that he might be forced to drop out of the race if the Sandinistas would not provide fair electoral conditions. His plan was to remain in the contest as long as possible, demanding concessions from the Sandinistas to the limit of their tolerance. When the Sandinistas finally refused to offer a fair contest, he would expose them to the world as totalitarians. Alfonso Robelo, who advised Cruz, employed a stark metaphor to describe this strategy: "Sandinista duplicity in the elections was like an abyss"; Cruz had to have "the courage of advancing to the very cliff's edge in order to demonstrate that one more step would have been fatal."[7] Advancing to the edge, however, required clever and flexible negotiating by Cruz and the Coordinadora. The appearance of inflexibility by Cruz and his allies could give the Sandinistas the chance to declare to the world that the opposition did not really want to participate in the elections and, repeating Somoza's standard charge, that the opposition in fact feared the elections because it had no popular support.

Cruz's flexibility was constrained, however, by the opposition factions he represented in the Coordinadora. The opposition was divided "between those who wished to participate in the elections and those who wished to abstain," but the decisions of the Coordinadora had to be unanimous. Cruz's personal advisers favored taking risks in bargaining with the Sandinistas, but "what developed was a process that bestowed virtual veto power on the hard-liners." The business leaders of COSEP wielded great influence within the group, and COSEP's leader, Enrique Bolaños, adhered to the position, in Cruz's words, "that no gratuitous legitimacy be given to the Sandinista Front." "Instinctively," Cruz recalls, "I agreed with the viewpoints of the pragmatists. Nevertheless, I opted to remain neutral because I was afraid to polarize the differences, which would then be exploited by the Sandinistas."[8] Cruz worried that the more conservative members of the coalition would turn on him if he compromised too much. As in the days of Somoza, the charge of being a collaborator, a "pactist," was always a dangerous possibility.[9]

The Reagan administration also had mixed feelings about the elections. Although united behind Cruz's candidacy, officials differed over the goals of his campaign, just as the Nicaraguans in opposition did. Most American officials, in the CIA and at the White House, expected that the Sandinistas would refuse to hold fair elections and that this would strengthen the case in Congress for a renewal of contra aid. President Reagan himself was convinced the Sandinistas would not hold a fair election, but a "rubber stamp" election of the kind "that we see in any totalitarian government."[10] A handful of officials in the State Department, led by Craig Johnstone, genuinely hoped that elections would begin to moderate the regime and make the continuing contra war unnecessary.[11] For most of the campaign these divergent strategies were not at odds, since both required making extensive demands of the Sandinistas that both believed were unlikely to be met.

Most Reagan officials, however, remained more concerned about the fate of contra aid than about the fate of Cruz. They had given up hope of obtaining money for the contras before the end of the 1984 fiscal year, but hoped to renew aid after October 1. Above all, they wanted to avoid any effort by House Democrats to ban future aid to the contras.[12] That, however, was exactly what was coming. The Senate version of the authorization bill contained $28 million for the contras, but in the House the Democrats led by Congressman Boland sought to impose a comprehensive ban on all aid to the contras for the coming fiscal year. The language proposed by Boland and the House Intelligence committee stated that, "During fiscal year 1985, no funds available to the Central Intelligence Agency, the Department of Defense, or any other agency or entity of the United States involved in intelligence activities may be obligated or expended for the purpose or which would have the effect of supporting directly or indirectly, military or paramilitary operations in Nicaragua by any nation, group, organization, movement or individual."

What later became known as the second Boland amendment was for all intents and purposes the amendment originally proposed by Harkin but rejected by the House at the end of 1982. Secretary Shultz and other officials argued in vain that the talks at Manzanillo and in Contadora required that the contras be supported to keep pressure on the Sandinistas. Boland argued that, to the contrary, "the secret war hasn't brought Central America closer to peace or Nicaragua closer to democracy. What it does is to provide the Sandinistas with the perfect excuse to foist unfair elections, a huge army, censorship and the draft on the Nicaraguan people."[13] On August 1, the House passed the intelligence authorization bill in which Boland's language was embedded by an overwhelming margin of 294–118. The prospects for a compromise between the Senate and the House after such a lopsided vote were slight.

The effect of the House vote was felt immediately in Nicaragua. The very next day negotiations between Cruz and the Sandinistas over the terms of the Nicaraguan elections broke down. The Sandinistas had extended the deadline for opposition parties to register their candidates until August 5, but they made no concessions to Cruz's substantive demands. Their attitude hardened as Cruz campaigned and denounced the government at opposition party rallies, first in Cruz's hometown of Jinotepe at the beginning of August. After a week of tolerance the Sandinistas began to show their displeasure with the opposition's political activities. The rally in Jinotepe drew a large number of anti-Sandinista protesters. But when Cruz traveled to the next planned meeting, in Matagalpa, the Sandinistas took steps to disrupt the gathering. Directorate-member Bayardo Arce had warned in May that at some point the "divine mobs" would intervene in the political contest with the bourgeoisie.[14] In Matagalpa on August 4 these *"turbas divinas,"* as the Sandinistas called them, appeared in front of the theater where Cruz and his supporters were meeting and verbally and physically assaulted those who attended the opposition meeting as they left the event.

The response by local residents, however, surprised both the opposition and the Sandinistas. Young boys threw rocks at the Sandinista group and chanted anti-Sandinista slogans. Cruz was amazed by the local reaction: "These were the younger brothers of the boys who six years previously had fought alongside the Sandinista Front against the forces of Somoza.

The Sandinistas had sunk to the same level of popular repudiation that Somoza's forces had previously occupied—a categorical moral defeat."[15]

That same day, Daniel Ortega traveled to a city near Chinandega, the site of the next opposition meeting, and personally rallied supporters to prevent a repetition of the events in Matagalpa. On the morning of August 5, according to one American observer, "fifty *turbas* burst into the soccer field [in Chinandega], tearing down the banners and dispersing the organizers [of the opposition rally.]" As a consequence of these and other actions by the *turbas*, "many who wished to go to the Cruz rally stayed home. On the day of the rally, local authorities also impeded traffic from outlying areas into Chinandega. As Cruz marched through the city, many people opened their doors, gave the 'V' for victory sign, and then ducked back into their homes to avoid the ever-present eyes of the [Sandinista Defense Committees.]"[16]

Observers estimated that, despite the harassment, at least 7,000 Nicaraguans assembled in Chinandega to hear Cruz speak on August 5. The crowd chanted, "What do the people want? That the Sandinistas go away!" ("Que quiere la gente? Que se vaya el Frente!"); and "The Sandinistas and Somoza are the same thing. ("El frente y Somoza son la misma cosa.") As one observer recounted, "When Cruz began to speak, dozens of *turbas* armed with sticks, stones, and machetes surrounded the field. They came on what appeared to be army trucks chanting, 'Power to the people.' They proceeded to break the windows and puncture the tires of demonstrators' cars. The police seemed to make no serious effort to restrain them. When the *turbas* attacked the demonstrators themselves, opposition youths dispersed, only to return wielding their own sticks and stones. Outnumbered, the *turbas* were routed."[17] As William Baez recalls, "Our mob was bigger than their mob."[18]

News of these events did not reach Washington until September, for on the same day that Daniel Ortega announced the lifting of press censorship, the Sandinistas censored all reporting on the Chinandega rally in *La Prensa*. The American press did not report at all on the events of August 5.[19] Nevertheless, the episode at Chinandega had an enormous emotional impact on Cruz, on the Sandinistas, and eventually, on opinion in the United States.

Cruz, who had until then been pursuing the campaign with every expectation that his efforts would be both futile and brief, became infused with a new enthusiasm for the race. Surprised both by his own favorable reception and by the evident hostility of many Nicaraguans toward their government, Cruz leaned toward mounting a serious challenge to the Sandinistas and seeing the campaign through to the end. In Chinandega, he recalls, "a peasant girl handed me a simple note. . . . It said: 'Don Arturo, the Sandinistas are fooling the people outside Nicaragua. Go and tell the world the truth. It isn't true that the people like them; what we want is for them to leave us alone so we can live in peace.'" Cruz had "suspected that anti-Sandinista feelings were strong, but that morning I reached the conclusion that the Sandinista vanguard that formerly had the backing of the Nicaraguan people and the sympathy of the world was now, due to its own excesses, reduced to an armed minority that held the country captive."[20] Cruz began to believe that if the Sandinistas held a fair election, they could lose.

The Sandinistas were taken aback by the degree of popular antipathy revealed in the rallies at the beginning of August. They had thought hostility to their rule was confined to the bourgeoisie, while the "people" who presumably benefited from the revolution were supportive. No more than other Managua governments did the Sandinistas maintain close contact with the "masses," however. They "receive[d] favorable reports from lower-level cadres whose jobs depend[ed] on the perception of success."[21] Roger Miranda, a senior aide to Humberto Ortega who defected to the United States in 1987, confirmed that Ortega and the other commanders were not aware of their political weakness, especially outside Managua. Miranda reported that he himself understood the seriousness of the problem only after touring the Northern Front and seeing the extent to which the campesinos were disaffected by the revolution.[22]

As the summer wore on, the Sandinistas had come to discover that the risks of elections were greater than they had thought. The risk was not that they would lose—that seemed inconceivable—but that they might not win by a large enough margin. It was one thing to prove to the world that pluralism existed in Nicaragua; it was another thing to show that the "traitorous bourgeoisie" and the "Somocistas" were almost as popular as the revolution. A very narrow victory over Cruz could be dangerous. For Daniel Ortega, the Sandinistas' presidential candidate, it could be humiliating.

While the dangers of holding fair elections appeared to grow, moreover, the risks of not holding them had diminished with passage of the Boland amendment. The combination was enough to determine the Sandinistas' course. After Chinandega, Cruz believed, "the Sandinistas had reevaluated the [Coordinadora's] participation in the elections and had decided that it constituted an unacceptable political challenge to Sandinista control. . . . That first weekend in August furnished enough evidence for them to imagine what could happen throughout Nicaragua."[23] On August 6 the Supreme Electoral Council declared that the Coordinadora would be barred from participating in the elections as a result of Cruz's failure to register as a candidate by the August 5 deadline.

To increase international pressure on the Sandinistas after Chinandega, Cruz set off on a tour of Latin and European capitols. Some questioned Cruz's decision to leave Nicaragua just as the momentum of his campaign was beginning to build,[24] but Cruz and his advisers believed their challenge to the Sandinistas would depend on foreign as much as on Nicaraguan opinion. The lack of international coverage of the events at Chinandega was a problem they wanted to overcome by directly addressing foreign leaders. "[The Sandinistas'] policy consisted of deceit and force," Cruz recalls, "and it was designed to give absolute advantage to the ruling party. In order to counter these tactics, we decided to go on a tour outside Nicaragua, seeking international support for our efforts."[25] As a former member of the Group of Twelve, Cruz well understood the importance of inviting foreign intervention in any battle with the regime in Managua.

Cruz returned to Managua on September 13 with enhanced authority to challenge the Sandinistas. His successful tour of Latin American, in which he met with the presidents of Venezuela, Costa Rica, El Salvador, Ecuador, and Colombia, increased his stature both inside and outside Nicaragua and showed just how vulnerable the Sandinistas had become to foreign meddling. Colombia's President Betancur, in particular, made common cause with Cruz in his campaign to pressure the Nicaraguan government to make concessions in the nature and timing of the electoral campaign. Betancur believed "Contadora's fate might well hinge on the Nicaraguan elections. Peace not only in Nicaragua but in the whole region was at stake." Betancur began to mediate between the two sides in Nicaragua, urging Cruz to show more flexibility and telling the Sandinistas that the elections were the "best defense against any possible U.S. intervention."[26]

Cruz thus returned to Nicaragua with a new set of more limited demands. At the urging of the Colombian government, and of Craig Johnstone at the State Department,[27] Cruz dropped the Coordinadora's insistence that the Sandinistas engage in a dialogue with the contras. He also dropped all demands having to do with the basic structures of the Sandinista state. Instead, Cruz recalls, "We were careful to propose only those electoral guarantees that were directly related to the electoral process, specifically the essential freedoms previously outlined by us and the length of time required for a fair campaign."[28] The most important issue quickly became the date of the elections. If the elections took place on November 4 as planned, Cruz would have only a few weekends to campaign. He wanted to be able to spend at least one Sunday in every capital of Nicaragua's sixteen departments.[29] Betancur agreed that Cruz's demands constituted the "*mimimas minimorum*."[30]

Faced with the new challenge posed by Cruz's more reasonable demands and his potent international patrons, the Sandinistas had a difficult choice to make. In addition to Betancur, a number of leading Latin politicians, including members of the Socialist International like Carlos Andrés Pérez, called the Sandinistas repeatedly in the first two weeks of September to urge them to negotiate an agreement with Cruz. Prominent liberal and moderate Democrats in the United States, including Jim Wright, Edward Kennedy, and Michael Barnes, also made appeals.[31] The Sandinistas were willing to continue talking with Cruz, but they insisted that postponement of the elections was "not negotiable."[32] On September 18 Humberto Ortega stated that "for practical and technical reasons" the Sandinistas had ruled out the possibility of postponing elections. Cruz declared that if the Sandinistas would not "consider the first demand, which was postponing the elections, there was no sense even talking about the other demands."[33]

The Sandinistas, in turn, toughened their measures against Cruz's campaign. After the turbulent rallies in Matagalpa and Chinandega at the beginning of August, the government decided to prohibit the opposition from holding any more outdoor meetings. The Coordinadora had thus begun organizing indoor meetings in a variety of cities. In León on September 18, a meeting of 100 opposition supporters was surrounded by what Cruz described as a "shouting and threatening mob that in my estimate consisted of about 600 individuals"[34]—Sandinista radio boasted the number was more like 2,000. On his way out of the building Cruz was hit by a stone thrown by one of the demonstrators, had his hair pulled, and was spat upon. The police, after watching the attacks for a while, finally escorted Cruz and his supporters from León. (The *Washington Post* thus carried a brief account of the incident under the headline, "Nicaraguan Police Aid Opposition Leader."[35]) In Boaco and Masaya over the next few days, the violent mobs came again: Cruz's car was pelted with rocks; demonstrators brandished machetes. The Sandinistas, as in the past, called these riots a "spontaneous popular repudiation" of Cruz. Daniel Ortega declared "We are not ashamed to be *turbas*, because to be part of the *turba* is to be part of the people."[36]

International pressures on the Sandinistas increased. Leading Democrats in the United States took a harsh line. Presidential nominee Walter Mondale expressed his intention, if elected, to "quarantine" Nicaragua if the Sandinistas did not stop supporting insurgencies in Central America. The *Washington Post*'s Stephen Rosenfeld noted that some opponents of contra aid were beginning to believe that, "with the terms of the Nicaraguan elections still unsettled, this may not be the right moment to take the heat off Managua." The issue of democratization was beginning to unite Americans where "supporting an armed intervention in another country" had divided them. Democracy was "an issue tailor-made for a bipartisan approach," and it was "playing right into the hands of Ronald Reagan." Rosenfeld predicted the Reagan administration would "be able to argue, if Cruz continues to be denied a fair crack, that the Sandinistas have left no alternative but further support of the Nicaraguan insurgency."[37] Rosenfeld was ahead of most Democrats, who were not prepared to agree that the pressure of the contras, as Reagan argued, was necessary to force the Sandinistas to hold fair elections. What was striking, however, was how many moderate and liberal Democrats had begun publicly holding the Sandinistas to a standard of behavior in their internal affairs that hitherto only conservative "ideologues" had demanded. Past concerns about intervention and sovereignty were temporarily submerged as many American politicians of all political stripes now felt justified in demanding that the Sandinistas hold free, "Western-style" elections. That some did so mainly in order to deny Reagan the chance to seek more aid for the contras did not make matters any easier for the Sandinistas.

Under great pressure from all sides to show some flexibility in both the elections and in the Contadora talks, the Sandinistas made a daring effort to finesse the problem. On September 21 they made two surprising announcements. First, they announced once and for all that the date of elections would not be postponed. But second, the Sandinistas announced they would sign the current draft of the Contadora agreement, provided there were no further changes made in the draft and provided the United States would agree in a separate, bilateral treaty to cease its aggression against Nicaragua.

As the Sandinistas had hoped, their announced willingness to sign the Contadora draft at first drew far more international attention than their decision not to postpone the elections. In his letter to the Contadora Group, Daniel Ortega met the insistence of Betancur, Sepulveda, and others "to reach as quickly as possible a peace accord for the whole region." Further amendments to the agreement, he declared, would only "obstruct the peace." And he deftly shifted the burden of achieving a peaceful settlement onto the Reagan administration, insisting that "the accord among the five Central American nations ... will only be sufficient if it can count on a formal and obligatory commitment by the United States."[38]

With this one stroke, the Sandinistas threw the Reagan administration into embarrassing disarray. Reagan officials had been so preoccupied with their struggle over the terms of the State Department's four-step proposal that they had lost track of the Contadora talks and missed the decisive shift engineered by Mexico and Colombia at the beginning of September. It was several days before the State Department could publicly explain its opposition to the Sandinistas' maneuver. Spokesman Alan Romberg declared that Nicaragua was "clearly seeking to close off debate on those provisions of the latest draft concerning the size of military forces and procedures for verification and control. They talk about open elections but their actions belie their promises."[39] But the Sandinistas did what the Contadora Group had hoped all the Central American countries would do. While the United States complained that the Sandinistas were engaged in chicanery, the Contadora foreign ministers worked to convince the other Central American governments to join Nicaragua in agreeing to the document.

Within days the Reagan administration was in retreat. Now it was the United States that faced international isolation, and there was the added danger that the other Central American governments might agree to the draft treaty.[40] Secretary Shultz and his advisers scrambled to avoid what could be at the very least a public relations disaster. State Department officials were confident the Sandinistas had only agreed to the draft because they knew it was unacceptable to the United States. If the United States and its allies could force the Contadora Group to accept some important changes, Shultz considered it "unlikely that Nicaragua would sign on."[41]

Insisting that "the drafting process is not over," the State Department declared there was still a "need for all the provisions, including those on troop levels, armaments and foreign advisers, to go into effect at the same time."[42] From the end of September through the first three weeks of October, the Reagan administration worked with its four allies on an alternative draft. Shlaudeman, at his sixth meeting with Vice Foreign Minister Tinoco on September 25, dropped the State Department's four-step proposal altogether and suggested using the Contadora Group's September 7 draft treaty as the basis for further negotiations. Tinoco refused. Shlaudeman returned to Washington convinced the Sandinistas were "just stringing us along" at Manzanillo.[43] In Shultz's view, the Sandinistas were "reading the U.S. congressional votes."[44]

The Sandinistas were certainly enjoying the Reagan administration's discomfort.[45] They had supported the Contadora draft not because they liked it, but because they knew the Reagan administration did not like it.[46] The Sandinistas also knew that the United States would come back to seek changes—as Shlaudeman was now trying to do—but they saw no need for further concessions. They had played their best card in the diplomatic game and were content to watch the Americans scramble. At the end of October, Tinoco suggested to Shlaudeman that perhaps the United States and Nicaragua could sign a secret bilateral treaty, "on the side," as Shlaudeman recalls, "about maneuvers, support for contras, no organized Soviet presence, no FMLN support, verification." Shlaudeman considered the proposal a disingenuous ploy. He explained to Tinoco that the United States would enter into no secret agreements, and certainly none with the Sandinistas.[47]

By the middle of October, the State Department's alternative draft had been completed in consultation with the four other Central American governments. The draft restored the simultaneity of all parties' actions, proposed a detailed timetable for the withdrawal of all foreign troops and advisers, tightened the requirements for democratic elections, and strengthened provisions for verification. Without such changes, Shultz told reporters, Washington would regard any treaty as "just a piece of paper." Daniel Ortega complained that the Americans were raising questions just "to slow the process. . . . The important thing is to sign the act; in the implementation these details will be taken care of." The Mexicans agreed with Ortega, but they could not budge the Reagan administration. After a testy meeting with Mexico's foreign minister, Bernardo Sepulveda, Shultz told reporters, "There's a real difference between agreeing on the idea that verification is necessary and important, and agreeing in advance that it will be done and here's how." Sepulveda reluctantly gave in, abandoning hopes for a settlement before Reagan's anticipated re-election.[48]

The struggle within the Reagan administration continued to be as brutal as ever. While Shultz and his aides set about trying to strengthen the Contadora treaty without appearing to obstruct an agreement, Constantine Menges and others in the administration charged that Shultz was looking for an "October surprise"—a "false agreement" to ensure the President's re-election in November.[49] On his way to the inauguration of a new Panamanian president on October 10, Shultz was contacted by McFarlane, who reported "great consternation" in Washington that Shultz was about to sign a pact with Daniel Ortega and "give it all away."[50] Menges was convinced Ortega would agree to the State Department's new draft in Panama. This was only one of several misreadings of the Sandinistas by the more hawkish wing of the Reagan administration. Daniel Ortega did not even attend the Panamanian inauguration on October 10, knowing he would be pressed by other Latin leaders to make concessions on both the Contadora treaty and on the elections. While many Reagan officials were convinced, then and later, that the Sandinistas would sign almost any agreement, with the full intention of evading its provisions, the Sandinistas proved to take the agreements far more seriously. Despite many false alarms rung in Washington, the Sandinistas never actually signed any Contadora draft.

This did not mean that the more hawkish Reagan officials were wrong about Shultz, however. The secretary of state would have been pleased if Daniel Ortega had agreed to the State Department's revised draft. Even after October 10 Shultz claims to have hoped to use the coming months "to develop a negotiated settlement in Contadora if at all possible."[51] It was not possible. On October 19 the four other Central Americans, meeting in Tegucigalpa, formally agreed to present an alternative draft to Contadora. By November, the Contadora Group reluctantly agreed to consider the new Tegucigalpa draft, thus ensuring that the negotiations would continue fruitlessly well into 1985.[52]

––––––––

Despite the great success of their diplomatic maneuver on September 21, the Sandinistas still faced the problem of Cruz and the elections. The international pressure to reach agreement with Cruz did not diminish as much as they might have hoped. The Reagan administration continued to emphasize the point, of course, and on October 1, the State Department spokesman told journalists that "Nicaragua's rush to pre-empt the process involving the Contadora act was designed to take the spotlight off" elections while they "shut out Arturo Cruz and the major opposition parties."[53]

The Sandinistas were also aware that, in the last week of September, the issue of the elections had become enmeshed in the continuing wrangle in Congress over aid to the contras. The Senate was due to vote on aid once again, in the Defense Appropriations section of the giant continuing resolution being assembled for the President's signature. According to reports in the *Washington Post*, "pressure on Nicaragua has been intense from its friends in Congress to concede the [election] date this week, in time for the Senate vote." One congressional aide told reporters, "[The Sandinistas] really have nothing to lose, and talk about a propaganda victory . . . !"[54] Many moderate and liberal Democrats sincerely wanted the Sandinistas to allow Cruz to run, but Democrats in Congress also had another motive. To kill Reagan's covert program in Nicaragua, liberal Democrats needed the Sandinistas to make a good showing in the elections.

In Latin America, Carlos Andrés Pérez, the broker of Nicaraguan political deals in the past, invited Cruz to a meeting of the Socialist International in Rio de Janeiro on September 30. Bayardo Arce was there representing the Sandinistas, and Pérez aimed to forge an agreement between Cruz and the Sandinistas before midnight of October 1, the Sandinistas' latest deadline for registration of candidates in the Nicaraguan elections. Cruz arrived in Rio very suspicious of the Sandinistas' intentions. "The Sandinista leaders wanted to appear to agree to the wishes of foreign democratic leaders," he believed, and would make "only cosmetic concessions while demanding fundamental concessions that the [Coordinadora] would find unacceptable."[55] With the U.S. Congress about to vote on contra aid, Cruz knew the Sandinistas were telling members of Congress that they would not be to blame if the talks in Rio failed.[56]

Cruz also wanted to appear as flexible as possible in the talks. "[W]e had to exhaust our efforts to seek a real solution and, if that were not possible, to leave no doubt about our sincerity so that responsibility for the failure would fall on the Sandinistas." But Cruz was hampered by opposition in his own ranks and in the Reagan administration to any deal with the Sandinistas. As a shield against the pressure that would come from both the Sandinistas and his own allies, Cruz sought the assistance of Pérez and Betancur.

Before the talks began, Cruz made two points clear to Pérez and Arce: First, that he had not come with authority to speak for the Coordinadora, whose members in Managua were scarcely aware that a negotiation was even taking place. Second, however, Cruz declared that he was the presidential candidate of the Coordinadora. While any agreement reached in Rio could not technically be considered final, Cruz would negotiate on his own and then stake his reputation on carrying the Coordinadora with him.

On October 1 Cruz, Arce, Pérez, and an assortment of mediators from the Socialist International met as the midnight deadline for registration in Managua approached. Cruz repeated his offer to participate in the elections if the Sandinistas provided guarantees to the opposition concerning campaign rights and agreed to postpone the elections until February 24, 1985. After some discussion, Arce agreed to postpone the elections until January 13, 1985, if the Coordinadora registered by midnight and provided that the contras agreed to a cease-fire by October 10 and pulled their forces out of Nicaragua by October 25.

Arce's counteroffer was a clever stroke, well-suited to exploit the schisms in the Coordinadora and the divided counsels of the Reagan administration. It was a proposal designed for rejection. It required Cruz to deliver the contras' surrender, almost three months before Election Day, in return for assurances by the Sandinistas that the campaign would be fair. The Sandinistas fully expected that the Coordinadora, the contras, and the Reagan administration would all insist that Cruz reject such a deal, and they believed Cruz lacked the authority to act on his own in Rio. As Sergio Ramírez put it, "Cruz never had authority over Bermúdez and Calero ... and the Coordinadora didn't have that authority." According to one observer, "Arce had made the offer in the knowledge that it wasn't acceptable."[57]

As the Sandinistas predicted, Arce's offer raised a storm among the opposition. Cruz called Coordinadora leaders in Managua to relay the proposal and urged them to register before the midnight deadline to put more pressure on the Sandinistas. "Do it, register, because we have all the necessary safeguards not to be trapped," Cruz told them. "Do something really meaningful and we will really grow in stature." But the Coordinadora leaders demanded that Cruz return to Managua and discuss the offer with them before agreeing.[58] The Reagan administration, meanwhile, sent mixed signals to Cruz. In Washington, Craig Johnstone and CIA officials supported efforts to reach an agreement with the Sandinistas in Rio.[59] But in Central America, other CIA officials told Cruz to reject Arce's offer.[60]

The Sandinistas knew that Cruz was being urged to reject the offer because they had tapped his phone lines. Daniel Ortega, then traveling in New York, was kept informed of the conversations.[61] As a result, even before Cruz had decided how to respond to Arce's proposal, the Sandinistas declared that the talks had collapsed. Daniel Ortega announced in New York that the date of the elections would not be changed. "We were flexible on the date until a few days ago," he told reporters. "The elections are going to take place on November 4. At this point we cannot continue to play with the date." According to Ortega, Cruz himself was "acting in good faith but he is a victim and an instrument of the policy of aggression against Nicaragua. He said he was powerless and couldn't do much against the Coordinator."[62]

The Sandinistas had misjudged Cruz's independence, however. When Cruz returned to the negotiations after consulting with his allies in Managua, he stunned everyone by accepting Arce's offer. With Carlos Andrés Pérez and several West German party officials as witnesses, Cruz declared that while he could not personally order a cease-fire and withdrawal by the contras, he promised to work to persuade both contra leaders and American officials to accept the terms demanded by the Sandinistas. And he enlisted the support of Pérez and Socialist International President Willy Brandt as "guarantors" of the agreement. "I agreed to a proposal that a Socialist International delegation should intercede in Washington, San José and Tegucigalpa to assure the suspension of aid to the rebel groups." If the contras refused to accept the terms for a cease-fire and withdrawal by October 25, Cruz promised to resign as the Coordinadora's presidential candidate.[63] In the meantime, Cruz declared, he would register his candidacy as soon as he returned to Managua for a "vote of confidence" from the Coordinadora. If the Coordinadora voted against him, he would resign and the Sandinistas could proceed with elections on November 4. With Pérez as his witness, Cruz pledged his "full personal guarantee of the agreement. . . . If the [Coordinadora] did not approve my petition, I would be obliged to separate myself, and the Sandinistas would be able to throw the blame on the [Coordinadora] for its intransigence."[64] Cruz asked for a two-day extension of the deadline to register his candidacy and persuade his colleagues in the Coordinadora to accept the agreement.

Now it was Bayardo Arce's turn to make a decision. But Arce no longer had the authority to agree to his own proposal. In New York Daniel Ortega had already declared the negotiations ended and had reaffirmed that the election date would be November 4. Under strong pressure from Pérez, Arce for a moment appeared willing to sign the agreement. Indeed, one witness to the talks recalled that "for twenty minutes we had an agreement."[65] Just as the terms of the agreement were being put in writing, however, Arce abruptly stood up from the table, shook hands with the officials from the Socialist International, and left. He went immediately to a press conference and announced that the Coordinadora had "lost their last chance to register. There is no longer any question. The elections will be held in Nicaragua on November 4."[66]

Despite the Sandinistas' obvious unwillingness to let Cruz campaign on fair terms,[67] some critics of the Reagan administration have placed the blame for the failure of the 1984 elections on the Reagan administration, others on Cruz. One critic argues that "[o]f the many missed opportunities to achieve at least some of the stated U.S. goals in Nicaragua, perhaps none compared to" Cruz's failure to run for president in 1984. "The division in Washington all but assured an inconclusive contest."[68] Carlos Andrés Pérez later tried to claim that negotiations failed because "the CIA had given instructions, had put pressures [on representatives of the Coordinadora] against Cruz's candidacy and therefore it wasn't accepted. They just didn't want someone with the prestige of Cruz to enter the elections, because it would validate them. They wanted to demonstrate there was no freedom of elections in Nicaragua."[69] The *New York Times'* Stephen Kinzer, while arguing that "Sandinista leaders bore ultimate responsibility for breaking off the talks in Rio de Janeiro, and, by extension, for the failure of the election," nevertheless blamed Cruz for a failure of nerve. Cruz "could have saved the day if he had been willing to take the bold stand many of his friends expected of him. He had known all along that he had no chance of defeating Ortega for the presidency, and that the election would be less than pristine." Kinzer argued that if Cruz had agreed to run in the elections, "despite all the obstacles placed in his way, he would have run a strong campaign and attracted much sympathy for the abuses to which the Sandinistas would probably have subjected him. He would have finished with a third of the vote or more, and become Nicaragua's undisputed opposition leader. . . . But he flinched at the crucial moment, refusing to re-enter the campaign and thus retreating from the historic challenge before him. Never again would Nicaraguans turn to him for political leadership."[70]

Cruz himself shared these misgivings and regretted his lack of flexibility at Rio. "When the [Coordinadora] was unable to enter the race on 1 October," he recalled later ". . . it may have lost a salient opportunity to show the Sandinistas for what they really are. . . . [E]ven though our decision not to participate was justified . . . it would have been better if our side had allowed us the authority to make an agreement in Rio."[71] "In hindsight," as he later told a journalist, "we should have gone, with or without conditions. In hindsight, I feel you must go to elections to prove there has been a fraud. From a purely political standpoint, against a totalitarian system, you might as well go and bloody your nose."[72]

How different would the course of events have been in Nicaragua if Cruz had participated in the 1984 elections? Kinzer and Cruz agree that the election would have been marred by violent attacks on opposition rallies, press censorship, and other forms of manipulation—as indeed proved to be the case with those few, small opposition parties that did take part. Cruz believes that "if the [Coordinadora] had been in the race there would have been more incidents of mob terror, like those in Chinandega and Masaya, and that Sandinista hypocrisy could have been irrefutably demonstrated."[73] As for the fairness of the balloting, when the vote was actually held on November 4 the Sandinistas, even though they faced no serious opposition, felt compelled to censor all news reports that suggested electoral irregularities and decreed a ban on all references to the election "in terms that directly or indirectly express or suggest citizens' abstentions, fraud, manipulation of figures or lack of confidence in electoral authorities."[74] The Sandinistas allowed informal international observers to attend the elections; but like Somoza they refused international "supervision" of the elections, and in 1984 the level of international scrutiny was nothing like what it would be in 1990. The debate over whether or not the Sandinistas rigged the elections of 1984 has raged for years, but Kinzer's statement on this subject seems to be the truest: There was simply "no way for outsiders to determine if vote counts were genuine."[75]

Whether or not an election held under such circumstances would have resulted in a political opening in Nicaragua in 1984 would have depended heavily on the intentions and the behavior of the Sandinistas after the elections. Pérez and others believed the Sandinista regime might have evolved toward the kind of one-party rule that exists in Mexico, which Gutman describes as "left-of-center, semidemocratic, broadly based one-party rule." Pérez argued that the election was thus "not a solution to the problem, but it certainly was an opening."[76]

Such judgments represent wishful thinking more than understanding of the Sandinistas' goals in 1984. The Sandinistas themselves later recalled that they were not prepared to make a real change in their political strategy in 1984. "The great majority of the FSLN," according to Humberto Ortega, "didn't see the election as strategically significant. They only saw it as a game. . . . The fact that we had elections in 1984 didn't mean anything."[77] At Rio the Sandinistas had the opportunity of bringing Cruz and the bourgeois elites he represented into the political process, but they declined. Nor did this decision represent a victory of the "hard-liners" over the "moderates" in the Directorate. It was the Ortegas who finally rejected the deal proposed by the "hard-liner" Arce at Rio de Janeiro.[78] It was Daniel Ortega, not Tomás Borge, who incited local Sandinista officials and "divine mobs" to break up Cruz's rallies in August. According to Rafael Solís, a well-known Sandinista "moderate," and Augusto Montealegre, an assistant to Humberto Ortega, all the Sandinistas "were crippled by fear of democracy." The moderate Sergio Ramírez was "vehement against the deal" in Rio in September. The Ortegas "wanted to win quickly" and decisively, and the margin of victory, they feared, "would not have been large enough"[79] if they had postponed the date of elections. An election that demonstrated widespread popular opposition—in the streets or at the ballot box—was more than the Sandinistas were prepared to concede in 1984.

Nor did the Sandinistas believe they had to pay such a high price in the fall of 1984. Although the contras had proven dangerous, they were in retreat after the cutoff of American assistance. By the end of the year, at least half of the contra forces inside Nicaragua had returned to their bases in Honduras. The Sandinistas shared the view of most Americans that Congress would never again vote aid to the contras. The Soviet Union had not agreed to deliver the MiGs, but Soviet arms shipments in 1984 surpassed all previous years, and by the fall the Sandinistas had begun receiving the Hind helicopters which proved to be such a formidable weapon in anti-guerrilla warfare. On the heels of their political coup over the Contadora agreement, the Sandinistas may have believed they did not need to make further concessions to international opinion. Their prospects for the future were not favorable, but they were also not as glum as they had been in June. Rather than take the significant risk posed by a Cruz candidacy, the Sandinistas chose—as governments often do—to secure immediate gains and worry about future problems later.

32

The Boland Amendment and Beyond

The immediate price the Sandinistas paid for ending the talks with Cruz was small. On October 10 the Reagan administration gave up trying to win renewed funding for the contras in the Fiscal Year 1985 supplemental appropriations bill that Congress was trying to pass before the elections. Negotiators from the House and Senate had been wrangling for weeks over this huge continuing appropriations resolution, in which contra aid was only one of many controversial provisions. At the last minute, Senate negotiators dropped their insistence on this and several other measures included in the Defense Appropriations legislation, in return for the House dropping its insistence on a variety of water projects. Boland's legislative restrictions banning direct and indirect support for the contras by intelligence agencies thus became part of the law governing the next fiscal year as well.

President Reagan would later be criticized by conservatives for not vetoing the appropriations bill containing the Boland restriction—the violation of which was later to erupt into the Reagan administration's greatest scandal. The Republican minority report of the Congressional Committees investigating the Iran-contra affair, though sympathetic to Reagan, concluded that "the President should simply have vetoed the strict Boland Amendment in mid-October 1984, even though the Amendment was only a few paragraphs in an approximately 1,200-page-long continuing appropriations resolution and a veto therefore would have brought the Government to a standstill within 3 weeks of a national election."[1] The very wording of this criticism showed how unreasonable it was to blame Reagan for this failure, however. A veto of the entire appropriations bill because of the Boland amendment would have been an act of political folly; and only subsequent events could make it appear the lesser of many bad choices. As it happened, this appropriations bill was already on the President's desk for a second time; a week before, Reagan had vetoed a first version of the bill because it contained "budget-busting" expenditures. Thus he had already put government employees on furlough and infuriated members of Congress. Now senators and congressmen were desperate to return to their districts for the last days of campaigning. Reagan and his advisers did not relish explaining to the American people, three weeks before the election, that it had been necessary to shut down the government again so that the secret war against Nicaragua could be supported out of the CIA contingency fund.[2]

Another reason the Reagan administration accepted the new legislation was a provision added by Senate negotiators at the last minute that insured another vote on aid to the contras on or after February 28, 1985. The measure, which reserved $14 million in military assistance for the contras to be released by a joint resolution of the two houses, showed how the Cruz candidacy had already begun to affect the deliberations in Congress. Although introduced by Republican senators, the idea was the brainchild of moderate Democrats troubled by the Sandinistas' refusal to accede to Cruz's demands. The *Washington Post* expressed the view of moderate Democrats when it acknowledged "the possibility that the insurgency [had been] one factor inclining the Sandinistas to consider broadening the elections."[3] Robert Leiken, an increasingly influential adviser of moderate Democrats, argued that "our best hope to avoid regional war and a national bloodbath [in Nicaragua] would be to suspend a decision on aid to the contras until after the Nicaraguan elections." Leiken suggested that while "aid to the contras was the outcome of a misguided approach," nevertheless the Congress "should consider carefully when and how to terminate funding for them. Not only domestic sobriety but also the fate of Central America demand deliberation, not haste."[4]

The Republican Senator Tad Stevens, who introduced the measure delaying a decision on contra aid until February 1985, expressed the view of many that the contras could support themselves in the meantime "with assistance they are getting from elsewhere in the world." Stevens hoped that the possibility of renewed aid in 1985 would "encourage that assistance from other sources to the Contras during this period."[5] As the tempestuous year came to a close, in fact, some members of Congress and officials in the Reagan administration comforted themselves with the expectation that the contras would somehow find a way to survive even without direct support from the United States.

Secretary Shultz had made this argument both publicly and privately. On June 29 he told the *New York Times* that the Nicaraguan insurgents would "continue one way or another" and that the Reagan administration would give "moral support" to their efforts to obtain funds elsewhere.[6] In his memoirs Shultz recalls he had confidence that the contras could "survive and fight" without congressional aid. His advisers "felt that the Contras could scrape up enough money themselves to hold together."[7] Such faith in the contras' fund-raising abilities would become the cornerstone of not only the administration's but also the Congress's strategy in 1985.

Yet Shultz and members of Congress had reason to assume that, in fact, it would be the Reagan administration's fund-raising abilities that would be tested. Even before the cutoff of funds in May, Reagan officials had begun searching for ways to provide temporary funding for the contras until Congress could be brought around. The idea of turning to another source for temporary assistance to the contras seems to have been discussed at least as early as the fall of 1983. Secretary Shultz himself wrote about finding "alternative benefactors" for the contras in a September 6, 1983, memorandum to President Reagan.[8]

Indeed, McFarlane had taken it upon himself to seek "alternative benefactors," not always keeping his colleagues informed of all his efforts. Even before the mining scandal, McFarlane had asked an Israeli government official if Israel might be willing to assume for a time the instruction, guidance, and support of the contras. The Israeli government declined, no doubt fearing the repercussions in Congress if its role in such a controversial program became public. On March 27, however, William Casey urged McFarlane on, "in view of the possible difficulties in obtaining supplemental appropriations to carry out the Nicaraguan covert action project through the remainder of this year."[9] Late in April, McFarlane made a second, weaker attempt to obtain assistance from Israel, which the Israeli government again rejected.[10]

At meetings in the early spring of 1984, all senior foreign policy advisers discussed in greater detail the prospect of asking for help from third countries. Secretary Shultz expressed reservations about all of the recommendations. He flatly opposed asking Israel for help, on the grounds that it would be unwise for the United States to incur such an important, secret, and potentially explosive debt to that country. In addition, there was a legal question about whether a recipient of American aid could be asked to perform a function for which Congress had denied funds to the administration. Shultz wondered more generally about the legality of the United States acting as a conduit for funds from a third country to the contras.[11]

Nonetheless, in early summer Robert McFarlane had continued to seek a benefactor for the contras. Worried that the contras would become demoralized by the cutoff of funding, President Reagan told McFarlane to reassure the contras of his continuing support, and McFarlane had dispatched one of his aides, Lieutenant Colonel Oliver North, to Honduras. McFarlane understood his charge from President Reagan to keep the contras together "body and soul."

The controversy that later erupted in the Iran-contra scandal in 1987 had to do with elaborate efforts by North and colleagues outside the government to raise private funds for the contras and, finally, to "divert" money from the proceeds of arms sales to Iran. These were not, however, what kept the contras alive during the cutoff of congressional aid. The crucial contribution, without which the rebel army might have disintegrated in 1985, came from Saudi Arabia. In a meeting with the Saudi Arabian ambassador to the United States, Prince Bandar, McFarlane let it be known that "it looked as though we were heading for a defeat regarding congressional support for the Contras, that it was almost inevitable that the administration would fail in getting any support for the contras and, because of that, it would represent a substantial loss for the President."[12] The Saudi ambassador understood the point and returned to McFarlane days later with the news that his government had decided to provide the contras with $1 million each month through the end of the year. The Saudi donations would eventually amount to some $32 million.

McFarlane did not consider this veiled solicitation illegal but says he did not tell Secretary Shultz about it.[13] In early July, after the Saudi government had deposited the first million dollars in the contras' bank account, McFarlane met privately with Shultz and Secretary of Defense Weinberger. With the situation in Congress hopeless, Weinberger asked, according to McFarlane, what the administration was going to do. McFarlane recalls that he responded, "It is taken care of. If you want to know how I will tell you, but you two are the ones who have to testify" before the intelligence committees.[14] According to McFarlane, "neither gentleman pressed the matter further."[15] Shultz recalls hearing "about efforts within the NSC staff to drum up private donations to support the contras."[16] McFarlane, in fact, told Shultz the contras were "getting a million each month," and although McFarlane said he didn't know where the money was coming from, he did say he was "confident they can get it for the next six months."[17] Only by assuming that *someone* in the administration was looking out for the contras could anyone share Shultz's conviction that the contras would have enough money to continue "one way or another" without the aid they had been receiving from Congress.

———

As 1984 drew to a close, the Sandinistas and the Reagan administration stood about as they had at the beginning, bloodied but ready for the next round of confrontations. Both ended the year with damaged images in international and American domestic opinion. The general perception in Congress and in Latin America was that the United States had blocked the signing of a peace treaty in Central America, although Shultz's efforts in October and November left a muddle sufficient to confuse the issue. The World Court condemned the Reagan administration's mining of Nicaragua's harbors, and the administration was doubly criticized for refusing to participate in the adjudication. The Reagan administration and the contras suffered another blow in the last weeks of the American presidential campaign when it was revealed that the CIA had produced a manual for the contras suggesting, among other things, that local Sandinista officials should be "neutralized" as part of the contras' political-military strategy. In addition to the immediate scandal this caused, the manual raised the issue of the contras' human rights record to a new prominence. Walter Mondale made much of the CIA manual in his second presidential debate with Reagan, and Reagan had no answer to the charge other than to disavow the manual and blame it on low-level CIA officials. The second-to-last thing American voters heard about Nicaragua before they went to the polls on November 6, therefore, was the CIA's "assassination manual."

The last thing Americans heard about Nicaragua was the victory of Daniel Ortega on November 4. Ortega won over 60 percent of the vote, and many international observers attested to the fairness of the voting, but the elections did not confer the legitimacy the Sandinistas had sought. Cruz's withdrawal from the campaign hurt them, particularly in the American Congress. Some time after the elections were held, Carlos Andrés Pérez wrote to decline an invitation to attend the inaugural ceremonies scheduled for January. In his letter, which was made public, Pérez explained to Daniel Ortega that "those of us who believe we have done so much for the Sandinista revolution feel cheated, because sufficient guarantees were not provided to assure the participation of all political forces. Sadly, the limiting in this way of true political pluralism weakened the credibility of elections."[18]

There was a difference between the political damage suffered by the Sandinistas and that suffered by the Reagan administration. While the harm done to the Sandinistas in 1984 pertained to their legitimacy as rulers of Nicaragua, the harm done to Reagan concerned only his policy of support for the contras. President Reagan, himself, ended 1984 far more powerful than he had begun it. On November 6 Reagan crushed Walter Mondale with 59 percent of the vote and swept 49 out of 50 states. In Congress, the Republican Party fared less well, gaining only 11 seats in the House and none in the Senate, but Reagan's personal triumph matched that of his 1980 election and promised to give him a similarly strong hand in dealing with the next Congress.

Part Four

THE REAGAN DOCTRINE

33

The "Non-Lethal" War

The landslide re-election of Ronald Reagan guaranteed another battle with Congress over aid to the contras in 1985. The first second-term President since Nixon, and the most popular second-term President since Eisenhower, Reagan stood ready to turn his enormous popularity into legislative successes across a broad range of foreign and domestic issues. Critics both inside and outside the Reagan camp complained that Reagan's "issueless" 1984 campaign left him no mandate to demand actions from Congress. Over the course of 1985, however, it became clear that Reagan's second landslide victory carried a message to the Democratic Party that a majority of voters understood in general what Reagan stood for and preferred it to what the Democrats had been offering.

The nation's overwhelming support for Reagan did not translate directly into support for the contra war in Nicaragua. Polls still showed the American people opposed to the covert war, insofar as they knew about and understood it. But the 1984 elections demonstrated in a more general way, as the 1980 elections had, that the constellation of political and ideological forces in the American system favored a more aggressive, anti-communist foreign policy than that advocated by Reagan's Democratic opponents. While 1984 ended with the contra program all but dead, at a broader level the entire 1984 campaign, from the Democratic primaries to Election Day, had once again revealed Democratic vulnerabilities and Republican strengths that were likely to affect the debate over contra aid in 1985.

For Democrats, the invasion of Grenada in October 1983 had cast a shadow over the entire 1984 campaign. In the Democratic primaries at the beginning of the year, ideological differences among the party's candidates were delineated in part by their stated view of whether the invasion was justified or not. And the party's eventual nominee, Walter Mondale, intentionally staked out a position on this question clearly to the right of his most significant challenger, Gary Hart. Hart never expressed even qualified approval of the invasion, but by September Mondale was saying that he, too, would have ordered the troops into Grenada "to go in there and protect American lives." On the subject of Central America, Hart clearly spoke for the party's liberal wing, and Mondale just as clearly for the more moderate and conservative wings. While Hart introduced legislation in February 1984 to remove all U.S. forces from the region, Mondale promised he would not "pull the plug" in Central America. While Hart reminded Democrats that Mondale had supported the war in Vietnam, suggesting he might support "another Vietnam" in Central America, Mondale sought to portray Hart as an irresponsible isolationist who did not understand the importance of defending American interests.[1] On the stump, Senator Hart accused the Reagan administration of providing the "bodyguards for Central American dictators."[2] But Mondale attacked Hart repeatedly for once having suggested that Fidel Castro was not a dictator.

When Mondale turned his attention to the general election after defeating Hart in the primaries, he moved even further to the center, trying to win back the "Reagan Democrats" who had defected in 1980. On one occasion he deliberately chose Nicaragua to burnish his centrist credentials, promising to "quarantine" Nicaragua if the Sandinistas continued to "export" their revolution. This evocation of President Kennedy's naval blockade of Cuba during the missile crisis of 1962 aimed, as *New York Times* reporter Leslie Gelb suggested, at "sharpening and toughening [Mondale's] positions on what [his] aides call 'strength issues' to broaden his appeal to moderates and conservatives."[3]

So while it was true, as has often been noted, that Reagan did not run a campaign designed to highlight specific issues—least of all Nicaragua—the campaigns of both parties and Reagan's monumental victory portended a more conservative political atmosphere for the coming year, one that could not help but shape the debate over issues such as Nicaragua. Reagan was not a suicidal politician; thus he had not made contra aid the centerpiece of his 1984 election bid. Instead, Reagan began his campaign for contra aid after his landslide victory, taking advantage of his own popularity and Democratic unease. In each phase of the battle, he pushed the congressional consensus as far as he believed it could go and then settled, always a bit short of his goals, but always further along than before. One result was that the compromises he made along the way sometimes became traps, both for his policy and for him. The other result was that in the Sisyphian task of winning congressional support for the contras, he did finally push the stone to the top of the hill.

———

To some of President Reagan's leading advisers, the effort seemed a waste of energy and political resources. Under the legislation passed in October 1984, Reagan could ask Congress to release the $14 million in covert military assistance any time after February 28. Before the new year had even begun, however, Reagan officials believed there was little chance of Congress passing such aid. Some in the State Department suggested forgoing the battle for aid altogether. Secretary Shultz recalls that he "did not favor continued futile efforts . . . [which] only underlined and contributed to our problem." Assistant Secretary Motley and Craig Johnstone tried to start a discussion about "the possibility of life in Central America policy after the contras."[4] As late as January 17, Robert McFarlane told Adolfo Calero that if the contras could not prove themselves a more potent force politically and militarily, then "I thought we owed it to them and to ourselves [to] cut both our losses and theirs." McFarlane's comment reflected his conviction that without much greater congressional support the contras were a hopelessly weak reed on which to rest American policy.[5]

Officials at the NSC, the State Department, and the CIA discussed a variety of options for responding to congressional objections—from providing aid to the contras "overtly" to seeking financial support from third countries—but the consensus was that these alternatives were not satisfactory.[6] The idea of "overt" assistance had come from Congress. The new chairman of the Senate intelligence committee, Senator David Durenberger, said he favored "any open policy to support the democratic revolution" in Nicaragua, but "under covert action, I'll vote against it."[7] Durenberger didn't want to give the money "to Bill Casey and have it end up as a manual floating down into the jungle in a balloon or a mine going off in the harbor."[8]

Supporting the contras overtly, however, posed political and legal problems. The administration considered declaring the contras a "government" eligible for foreign assistance, but since the contras did not hold any territory and could not qualify for recognition under international law, this was quickly rejected.[9] A more palatable, but far from desirable, "overt" option was for the United States to provide only "non-lethal" or "humanitarian" assistance to the contras, while relying on other countries to provide military assistance, intelligence, tactical advice, logistical support, and training. McFarlane's aides believed this option had a number of political advantages: It excluded "the most controversial aspects of the original program," covert military assistance provided by the CIA; and it would "not requir[e] opponents of the old program to reverse their previous votes" against covert aid.[10] To make up for the lack of direct U.S. military assistance, McFarlane's staff recommended increasing the amount of assistance from the $14 million in the current legislation to as much as $100 million.[11]

But this plan for overt, "non-lethal" assistance also had significant drawbacks. Under existing legislation it turned out to be almost impossible to ask Congress for more than $14 million, even in "humanitarian" aid.[12] Another problem was the complex legal issue of requesting support from third countries, much discussed by senior officials the previous year. Shultz and James Baker had argued that the administration could not do indirectly what Congress had forbidden it to do directly, and the CIA's general counsel declared the agency could not seek aid from third countries "without running afoul" of the Boland amendment's restrictions.[13] In January 1985, one of McFarlane's aides, Oliver North, recommended that the administration seek explicit approval from Congress for soliciting aid from third countries, on the assumption that Congress favored doing something against the Sandinistas so long as Congress did not have to take responsibility for it.[14] Secretary Shultz seems to have broached the idea with Senator Richard Lugar, who told reporters in January "if you cannot get $14 million" out of Congress, "then you find a different route" through third countries. But another McFarlane aide, Donald Fortier, was not as optimistic that the House would agree.[15] At the end of January, Congressman Fascell told Fortier he opposed the administration trying to raise money on its own.[16] McFarlane was unenthusiastic in any case. Although he had secretly solicited help from the Saudi government, he was reluctant to continue relying on such help in the future. Donations from third countries were unreliable; the administration lost control over contra forces when they provided only indirect support. McFarlane told President Reagan he preferred to seek congressional approval for new aid rather than further help from other countries. According to McFarlane, Reagan agreed: "He wanted this program to be one that was American-funded and supported without any other involvement."[17] This did not stop either McFarlane or Reagan from gratefully accepting one final, and very large, donation to the contras from Saudi Arabia in February.

One of the Reagan administration's biggest concerns about any "overt" program, however funded, was that Honduras might refuse to cooperate. Were the United States to declare its support for the contras openly, Honduras would lose even the thin veneer of official deniability with which it had deflected international criticism for harboring the contras. American relations with the Honduran government were severely strained at the beginning of 1985, in part because a coup within the Honduran military in March of 1984 had brought a less pliant group of officers to power. The massive return of contra fighters to their Honduran bases at the beginning of 1985 particularly troubled the Hondurans. The presence of so many armed Nicaraguans caused the government political problems. The army feared a Sandinista military strike at the contras' sanctuary. In the third week of January, McFarlane went to Honduras to reassure the government and army, who in turn demanded that the contras move back into Nicaragua, armed and supplied or not. They also demanded more economic and military assistance, as well as a written promise of American military support in the event of a Nicaraguan attack on Honduras. The meeting broke up in disagreement, and McFarlane reportedly stalked out.[18] On March 16, Vice President Bush had to travel to Honduras and publicly declare the administration's "deep commitment to Honduran security," adding that the United States would "strive to go the extra mile for economic aid to Honduras."[19] Given the continuing problems, administration officials feared that the passage of an overt assistance program in Congress might be more than the U.S.-Honduran relationship could bear.

On January 23, the President himself publicly rejected the idea of an overt program on the grounds that it would be tantamount to a declaration of war against Nicaragua, and Senator Lugar agreed that there was "no consensus in the public for that."[20] On January 24, the President's spokesman reiterated the administration's concern that overt financing of the rebels would raise questions under international law as to whether the United States was not itself at war with Nicaragua. At the beginning of February, an NSC staff memorandum listed the administration's options and recommended that non-lethal aid might be acceptable, but only as a "bottom line" in any negotiations with Congress.[21]

While the situation seemed hopeless to Reagan's top advisers, however, the President himself remained determined to win support for the contras or to find some way to back their cause. He put an end to further discussion of cutting the contras loose. Administration officials thus turned back to their original plan to seek new covert aid from Congress. Some had a lingering hope that Congress might yet be persuaded to approve the original program; others were merely following the President's clearly stated desire.

In Congress, hostility to the Sandinistas had grown since the Nicaraguan elections in November. The Sandinistas had withheld exit visas from more than a dozen political leaders in the Coordinadora, arrested a local opposition leader in León, severely tightened censorship of *La Prensa* and the few remaining opposition media outlets, and declared that the "rightist sector" was now "without rights."[22] Having survived the political challenge of Cruz and the military challenge of the contras in 1984, the Sandinistas were determined to prevent any recurrence of such a dangerous combination in 1985.

The crackdown spawned the second exodus of opposition leaders since 1982. On December 14, Pedro Joaquín Chamorro, Jr., co-editor of *La Prensa*, chose exile in Costa Rica. Other less prominent figures also left the country, while those who did not began calling themselves the "captive dissidents." Most damaging to the Sandinistas, however, was Arturo Cruz's decision to lend his support to the armed opposition. It was not a choice he made easily. In the first weeks after the November elections, Cruz had called upon the United States to eschew "military solutions" and allow Daniel Ortega "a period of grace." He predicted that the Ortegas would "make an effort to reach national reconciliation."[23] By January 3, however, Cruz had changed his mind. At a press conference with Chamorro he called on the United States to resume aid to the contras and declared his intention to lobby for the aid in Congress.[24]

Cruz's announcement was a boon to the contras' flagging reputation in Congress. He had attracted a loyal following among moderate Democratic congressmen during and after his aborted campaign for the presidency, and his change of heart had a strong effect on the attitudes of some of these "swing" votes.[25] Even liberals like Congressman David Obey told reporters there was "something to be said for keeping the Sandinistas under pressure or in doubt as to our intentions." Congressman Bill Richardson, a strong opponent of aid to the contras in 1983, called Daniel Ortega "a little Castro,"[26] and even Congressman Michael Barnes professed to be "struggl[ing] ... to find a compromise that could achieve the ends the administration wants to achieve, while getting us out of this [contra] program."[27] Reagan officials believed they saw an opening in such statements.

In February the administration shifted tactics to try to win support for a covert military aid bill. Private negotiations with Congress turned into public confrontation, as the President sought to bludgeon the Congress into doing what it would not be cajoled to do. Within the administration there was no shortage of enthusiasm for this new battle. A reshuffling of the President's staff after the election had already made for a more confrontational disposition in the White House. The President's chief of staff, James Baker, had traded jobs with the secretary of the Treasury at the beginning of the year, and the new chief of staff, Donald Regan, was as contemptuous of Congress as Baker was solicitous. Regan hired Patrick Buchanan, a conservative columnist, to serve as director of the White House Office of Communications, and Buchanan became a strong advocate of confrontation with the Democrats. The loss of Jeane Kirkpatrick, who left her post as UN ambassador after the election, and the almost complete isolation of Constantine Menges on the NSC staff,[28] reduced the ranks of the confrontational camp in the administration, but this was more than made up for by the apparent enlistment of a new recruit: George P. Shultz.

After months of seeking diplomatic settlements with both the Sandinistas and the Democrats, Shultz by 1985 was reserving his moderate advice for the more promising field of U.S.-Soviet relations. On the subject of Nicaragua, he became a devoted and outspoken hawk, following the lead of his President. Shultz's shift to a harder line was attributed by some observers to his desire to mollify conservative critics, to "give" Nicaragua to the Republican right wing so that he might have a freer hand in dealing with the Soviet Union. With the failure of negotiations in the fall of 1984, the constant attacks from the President's more conservative advisers, and then the embarrassment caused by the Sandinistas' clever ploy in the Contadora talks, Shultz, as Shlaudeman put it, had been "burned." The results of all his risky undertakings had been neither a diplomatic settlement nor increased support in Congress for the contras. In February, at a confrontational meeting with the House Foreign Affairs Committee, Shultz declared sharply that Nicaragua had fallen "behind the Iron Curtain" and that the United States could not "put up with a Brezhnev Doctrine"—by which he meant the permanent control of Nicaragua by the Sandinistas. And while Shultz did not completely close the door on the diplomatic "track,"[29] he told the committee members that he had "put on ice" the talks at Manzanillo.[30] In a break with his past statements, Shultz on February 22 declared it "immaterial to us" how a change in Nicaragua was achieved, whether through negotiations or "through the collapse of the Sandinista regime."[31] Liberal commentator Tom Wicker was shocked to find George Shultz—"supposedly the steady man of the Reagan Administration"—engaging in the kind of "inflammatory discourse" he had come to expect only from the President.[32]

President Reagan himself was eager to do battle on the issue of Nicaragua. He intended to wield his restored political power to make the members of Congress "feel the heat" if they refused to "see the light."[33] Less constrained after his landslide re-election, Reagan gave fuller voice to his moral convictions about communism and America's role in fighting it. As a means of selling his unpopular covert war in Nicaragua, President Reagan elaborated more fully on themes he had adumbrated at Westminster in 1982.[34] Linking together the popular Afghan and unpopular Nicaraguan rebellions and putting both in a broader historical and ideological context that stretched from the American Revolution to the French Resistance, Reagan elaborated an international strategy that was revolutionary abroad and politically potent at home.

The "Reagan Doctrine," as it was dubbed by columnist Charles Krauthammer in 1985, was a sweeping application of American political philosophy and morality to the conduct of international affairs. It denied the fundamental legitimacy of all communist governments, and by implication all non-democratic governments, declared them to be essentially transient, affirmed the right of democratic movements to challenge them, and proclaimed the right, even the responsibility, of the United States to provide assistance to those movements. "There are those who say America's attempt to encourage freedom in Nicaragua interferes with the right of self-determination," Reagan said in April. ". . . [But] when a small clique seizes a country there is no self-determination, and no chance of it."[35] Reagan was thinking primarily about communist governments, but Secretary Shultz took the doctrine to its logical conclusion and declared that "as a matter of fundamental principle, the United States supports human rights and peaceful democratic change throughout the world, including in non-Communist, pro-Western countries."[36] Pushed by the difficult task of selling its policy in Nicaragua, and emboldened by the continued success of democratic reform in El Salvador, Reagan and Shultz thus called for an unprecedented ideological consistency in American foreign policy.

The departure from traditional Republican policies was striking. For most of the twentieth century, Republicans had been isolationists, anti-Communists, or practitioners of realpolitik. Even Democratic presidents, from Kennedy to Carter, had hesitated to question the legitimacy of noncommunist dictatorships. The Reagan Doctrine was the unique product of a unique combination of circumstances in the United States. At the height of the cold war, with the most fervently anti-communist President in American history, a Congress half-controlled by Democrats, and an American public moved by conflicting desires for national assertiveness and withdrawal, by belligerent anti-communism and post-Vietnam moralism, the Reagan doctrine came as close as any other international political strategy to answering the contradictory demands of the country.

And as intended, the Reagan Doctrine proved both attractive and frightening to a Democratic Party divided between anti-Communists and liberal idealists and seeking a marriage between the two. More than even Reagan officials might have imagined, the idea of supporting armed rebellions against communist regimes, at least in some parts of the Third World, found increasing support among moderate and even liberal Democrats over the course of the year.[37] The tearing down of the old "double standard"—by which conservatives and liberals accused one another of coddling dictators of the left or right—came as welcome relief to many Democrats, who could better justify their anti-communism when it was explicitly tied to support of democracy. For moderate and conservative Democrats the attraction of the Reagan Doctrine was that its anti-communism was subsumed in a higher idealism with Democratic roots; it removed some of the stigma that Democrats had long attached to Republican anti-communism.

The fuller elaboration of the Reagan Doctrine in the first months of 1985 helped force an important shift in the terms of the Nicaragua debate, although that shift had begun before the Nicaraguan elections. More and more Democrats now expressed the view that the Sandinistas should be urged and even pressured to reform their regime and institute democracy. Few disputed the administration's claim that the 1984 elections in Nicaragua had been illegitimate—in contrast to the popular perception of El Salvador's elections. If anything, the Sandinistas' election only increased Congress's scrutiny of their internal politics; and it whetted the appetites of American politicians in an increasingly idealistic and intrusive mood. Many were not prepared to take the next step with the Reagan administration by supporting the contras, but the enunciation of the Reagan Doctrine inevitably drew attention to the supposed "forces of freedom" in Nicaragua whom Reagan even referred to as "the moral equal of our Founding Fathers."[38]

34

The "Freedom Fighters"

While the Reagan Doctrine provided the rationale for long-term support of the contras, however, it also placed a heavy burden on the rebel movement, a burden which the contras could not easily sustain. As the terms of the American debate shifted to democracy, both critics and would-be supporters of the Reagan administration's policy asked the obvious question: Were the contras capable of bringing democracy to Nicaragua? That question broke down into two parts: Were the contras democrats, and could they win?

The scandal of the CIA's "assassination" manual in the fall of 1984 had raised again the question of the contras' conduct of the war, and their opponents focused new attention on the issue in the months leading up to the vote on contra aid in April 1985. New allegations of widespread human rights abuses by contra forces struck at President Reagan's arguments on his own ground. A New York lawyer, Reed Brody, compiled a list of 200 abuses committed by the contras over the previous three years, including "assassination, torture, rape, kidnapping and mutilation of civilians." The Sandinistas, recognizing the importance of Brody's investigation, did their best to help him, arranging interviews with victims of contra attacks,[1] providing transportation and escort to the interviews, paying Brody's three-month hotel bill, and even providing office space.[2] If Brody's report was thus somewhat tainted, however, more independent human rights monitors also found evidence of violations by the contras. In March Americas Watch cited abuses by both the contras and the Nicaraguan government, but singled out the contras for what it called "the deliberate use of terror."[3] Other reports attacked the composition of the contras' top leadership, which was still dominated by former National Guardsmen.[4] These reports bolstered charges by Democrats that the contras were, in the words of New York Democrat, Thomas Downey, "thieves, brigands, and butchers." Enrique Bermúdez, returning from a trip to the United States at the beginning of March, reported to his troops that "we have a terrible image [in Washington]."[5]

In response to these charges, the President's speech-writers pulled out all the stops, resulting in the President's ill-advised comparison of the contras with the Founding Fathers.[6] But while the allegations of contra abuses were sometimes exaggerated by human rights monitors hostile to Reagan's policies, it was indisputable that contra troops in their attacks and ambushes often made no distinction between civilians and armed Sandinista soldiers. It was the contras' policy, *de facto* if not always *de jure*, to treat civilians who helped the Sandinistas as combatants. In years past, there had been many incidents of campesinos murdered as "informers" without evidence or investigation. Contra officials complained that the Sandinistas often placed those whom they considered civilians in harm's way—for instance, in the lead truck of a convoy—and that they were not to blame for civilian deaths under such circumstances. But rebels also admitted to journalists that they "often killed Sandinista prisoners and Government officials and that they believed the Sandinistas would kill them."[7] In the United States, the violent behavior of the contras became the rallying point for the nationwide movement of church organizations that in 1985 turned their attention from stopping aid to El Salvador—efforts which were having less and less effect in Congress—toward the more promising goal of stopping further aid to the contras.

The critics' case against the contras on moral grounds was complemented by arguments that the contras were also too weak militarily to achieve the goals that Reagan had set for them. The timing of this second argument was apt, because in the first four months of 1985, the contras had reached a nadir in their three-year struggle against the Sandinistas. Nineteen-eighty-four had ended in disaster as contra forces, cut off entirely from American supplies and logistical support, began pulling out of Nicaragua. In the last three months of 1984, more than three-fourths of the FDN's forces retreated back across the border into their camps in Honduras. Those that remained in Nicaragua were low on supplies and chiefly tried to avoid engagements with the Sandinista army. In the view of State Department officials, the contras had been largely ineffective since the U.S. funding had run out.[8]

Money raised by McFarlane from the Saudi government did help a little. From July through the end of 1984, the Saudis had deposited $6 million into an account controlled by Calero, and the FDN leader had begun making purchases of arms. In the fall Calero bought $2 million worth of rifles, ammunition, and hand grenades from a retired American colonel— the former military attaché in Nicaragua during the fall of Somoza.[9] He also placed an order for weapons through Richard Secord, whom Oliver North had asked to serve as a liaison between the contras and international arms dealers. Secord's shipment of weapons, however, which included surface-to-air missiles, did not arrive until the spring of 1985.[10] By December of 1984, the contras' stocks of weapons and materiel had fallen dangerously low, and Calero asked Secord for a shipment of "emergency supplies" to relieve what had become in his words "a very, very difficult situation."[11] The emergency supplies Calero requested still did not reach contra base camps until February.[12] As 1985 began, the contras' ability to move supplies into Nicaragua had also been severely weakened by the loss of CIA logistical support. Contra forces returned to primitive methods they had used in the early years of the war, marching equipment in by mule or on the backs of young boys. The mobility of contra forces was consequently dramatically reduced.

The weakness of the contras at the end of 1984 and beginning of 1985 gave the Sandinista army a much-needed pause to repair weaknesses revealed during the previous year's battles. In 1984, according to Humberto Ortega, "We did not have a young and properly trained force . . . the EPS [Sandinista Army] had no specialized forces and virtually no helicopters . . . its logistics system was weak and lacked a number of resources, for which it had already signed contracts but had not yet received. . . . Our situation was very difficult." By the beginning of 1985, however, Sandinista forces were well on their way to a peak in their performance in the ten-year war. The addition of new Soviet attack helicopters, the Mi-24s, or "flying tanks," was about to shift the equation dramatically against the contras.

The strategic goal of the Sandinistas in 1985 was to drive the contras back into Honduras and Costa Rica, keep them from reinfiltrating back into Nicaragua, and then, with luck, destroy them in their sanctuaries. The Sandinista army took the opportunity of the contras' retreat to move large forces into the former contra strongholds up near the Honduran border and to begin an operation to wipe out Pastora's smaller force on the Costa Rican border. They abandoned their previous, exclusive reliance on fixed, defensive positions around northern towns and villages, manned by ill-trained and poorly equipped local militias. Instead, the Sandinistas made increasingly good use of the Irregular Warfare Battalions, or BLIs, which though still not manned by the Sandinista regular army[13] were well-trained, highly mobile units, independent of fixed bases and able to operate for weeks at a time in the hills and jungles, searching for the enemy.[14] In the northern provinces, the BLIs chased small units of contras around the mountains and countryside while other Sandinista forces set up blocking positions along the contras' customary routes of infiltration from Honduras, deploying troops in fixed positions and planting thousands of mines along roads and paths.[15] According to some estimates, 6,000 Sandinista army troops moved to the immediate border area in the first four months of 1985.[16]

The Sandinistas also brought heavy artillery and tanks up to the front, along roads which they gradually built or improved to allow more rapid reinforcement and resupply of new forward bases.[17] The tanks served as "mobile gun platforms, self-propelled howitzers," according to one military analyst, in terrain where artillery could not move.[18] The Sandinistas also made increasing use of the Mi-8 helicopters to transport troops quickly to the sites of contra attacks, forcing the contras to scatter quickly after any attack and making it difficult to sustain their assaults for more than a couple of hours.

To accomplish these simultaneous missions of chasing contras and holding fixed positions on the borders, the Sandinistas had to increase the number of men under arms. "We must achieve numerical superiority over the enemy," Bayardo Arce declared on February 3, and throughout 1985 the Sandinistas placed their highest priority on recruitment.[19] Until the middle of 1984, the universal conscription announced by Humberto Ortega in October 1983 had not been strictly enforced. In the last months of 1984, however, the government began a more active draft of young men from the urban middle class, and these began manning the BLIs and the forward units in 1985. With superior numbers, increased firepower, and new forward positions, Humberto Ortega and his top commanders hoped to deal the contras a fatal blow in the first few months of 1985 while aid from the United States remained cut off, thus rendering moot any future vote by the U.S. Congress to provide new aid to the rebels.[20]

The contras were not entirely passive during these months. Some forces had begun to move back into the northern provinces of Jinotega and Nueva Segovia in early December, replenished with the arms Calero had purchased. In the first three weeks of January, these contra forces swept through the northern town of Pantasma in Jinotega province, blew up four electric towers south of the town, interrupting power throughout much of the province, and partially destroyed two bridges on the Coco River. Journalists reported at the end of January that the rebels had "begun descending from the mist-shrouded mountains often enough so that unarmed Sandinistas now rarely travel here."[21]

Despite their low levels of supplies and uncertain future, moreover, the contras' ranks were still swelling, thanks in part to the very same Sandinista draft that was manning the BLIs.[22] While the Sandinista army conscripted thousands of young men into its ranks, thousands of others fled the country to avoid the draft.[23] Sons of the middle and upper classes fled to Costa Rica and elsewhere; but thousands of young campesinos from the northern provinces fled to Honduras, where a small but significant percentage joined the contras.[24] Explaining their decision to dodge the Sandinista draft and then risk their lives with the contras, these youths told reporters that "fighting with the rebels was different because it was 'voluntary.'"[25] That the contras, even at their weakest moment, could continue to attract such strong support in the northern provinces exasperated Sandinista political and military leaders, who finally lost patience.[26] Near the end of February, Sandinista forces reportedly used mortars and long-range cannons to shell 15 small communities in Jinotega where contra forces had been operating.[27]

This heavy-handed tactic was soon followed by a more coordinated, and less bloody, effort to empty northern villages. On March 17, Daniel Ortega announced the resettlement of 7,000 families or more than 20,000 people in Jinotega and their relocation to government-controlled farm cooperatives.[28] Families ordered from their homes, with little notice and little time to pack, watched as soldiers set fire to their shacks and slaughtered or hauled away their livestock. Sandinista political officials declared it "an opportunity to reorder the population, which has been very dispersed."[29] Tomás Borge put the matter differently: The removal of civilians made it "easier to use our artillery. It clearly becomes a war zone." One Sandinista soldier told a reporter: "There will be nobody left but them and us."[30]

By March, the Sandinista army's actions in the north, combined with the contras' uncertain and sporadic supply of weapons and materiel, had stymied the rebels. Enrique Bermúdez reported that only a quarter of his troops were in the field, with the rest sitting in Honduras. Contra commanders told reporters their men needed "guns, boots, everything." Although some supplies were coming in, it was not enough to outfit the entire force; some had been waiting five months for supplies.[31] In February, the "emergency" airlift of weapons bought through Secord had arrived in Honduras carrying 90,000 pounds of ammunition and grenades. Another airlift came in March with more ammunition, rocket-propelled grenades and launchers, mortars, rifles and explosives.[32]

Between the end of February and the end of March the Saudis deposited $24 million in Calero's account, bringing their total contribution to $32 million. With this assistance, Calero was soon able to purchase all the weapons and ammunition the contras needed for the remainder of 1985 and well into 1986. The future looked better than the present, however. The shortage of weapons was relieved, but it remained extremely difficult to transport the weapons into Nicaragua to replenish forces deep inside the country. Oliver North advised Calero in the middle of February to set aside "$9–10 million for nothing but logistics." But the contras faced the threat of annihilation before any supply system could be set up. North told Calero of American intelligence reports that between 45,000 and 60,000 Sandinista troops were involved in operations in the northern provinces, nearly a third of which were up near the Honduran border. He recommended that contra forces go into hiding in an effort to survive the Sandinistas' attempt to destroy them, even providing Calero and Bermúdez with a map from the CIA showing concentrations of Sandinista forces and places where contra forces could safely wait out the current offensive.[33] "While I know it hurts to hide," North wrote Calero, "now is the time to do it. . . . Most important is saving the force from what I believe will be a serious effort to destroy it in the next few weeks."[34]

If Nicaragua was dangerous for the contras, however, Honduras was an unreliable haven. The presence of so many contras posed problems for the Honduran government. With presidential elections approaching, every candidate promised to rid the country of the Nicaraguan rebels.[35] At the beginning of February, the Honduran army told the contra leaders to move their entire force of 5,000 troops back into Nicaragua within one week. "The Hondurans," Motley wrote in a memorandum to Shultz, "are evidently anxious to avoid a Nicaraguan cross border attack against such a large FDN concentration on Honduran territory."[36] Such an incursion threatened a double embarrassment for the Hondurans—first, because it would reveal the extent of Honduran support of the contras, and second, because it could reveal the Honduran army's unwillingness or inability to defend Honduran territory. The Hondurans wanted the contras out, whether they had the supplies to fight the Sandinistas or not, and the contras were badly squeezed.

————

The contras' military setbacks in the winter of 1984–85 wiped out what little memory there was of their successes in the spring and summer of 1984, when they had the Sandinistas in a very difficult spot. The contras became victims of a vicious circle: weakness in the American political system in 1984 had translated into weakness on the battlefield in 1985, which undermined support for contra aid as the next vote approached. When the retiring commander of American forces in Latin America, General Paul Gorman, told members of Congress in February that "overthrow is [not] feasible in the near future," his statements were seized upon by critics of the administration's policy as conclusive evidence that the contras could never "win" in Nicaragua.[37]

General Gorman's testimony had two sides, however. The general said he didn't see "any immediate prospect that these guys in blue suits in the hills are going to march into Managua," and he argued that "the whole resistance movement has got another year or more of slogging to go before" that would ever be possible.[38] But while a "year or more" seemed a long time to officials in Washington, Nicaraguans had seen their guerrilla wars stretch across decades.

For Humberto Ortega, the most important issue was what Americans would call "momentum." Ortega defined a Sandinista victory as the moment when "the mercenary forces cannot develop strategically as a military threat to the revolution." Short of that, there was always the possibility that the contras could win growing support in the country. As Gorman put it, "The nature of the beast is that you join what you think is a winning cause."[39] The Sandinistas did not fear an outright contra military victory, moreover. They feared their own defeat under the combined pressures of domestic dissatisfaction, economic failure, military confrontation, and diplomatic isolation. President Reagan's "master plan" in 1984, in Ortega's view, had been to "make the balance of forces tilt in favor of the mercenaries by November 1984 . . . to isolate us from the foreign community, and particularly from Latin America." "[H]e wants to enclose us financially," Ortega explained. "He wants to create huge economic problems for us so that the people will become dissatisfied with the revolution. A dissatisfied and disgusted people will turn against the revolution and that will be the end of the revolution."[40] Ortega and his colleagues recognized this multi-pronged strategy as the one they themselves had employed to defeat Somoza. General Gorman argued that combined military, diplomatic, economic, and political pressures could eventually "bring the Sandinistas to a reckoning," even though it might take several years.

President Reagan said much the same in a televised news conference on February 21, when he declared his desire to see the Sandinista government "removed in the sense of its present structure in which it is a communist, totalitarian state." Asked whether he was not, in that case, advocating the overthrow of the present government, Reagan responded, "Not if the present government would turn around and say, all right, if they'd say, 'Uncle. All right, come on back into the revolutionary government, and let's straighten this out and institute the goals.'"[41] Although the President was probably unaware of this, the hope he claimed to harbor was precisely the hope of many members of the Nicaraguan political and economic elite. They, too, entertained the possibility that the Ortega brothers, at least, could be forced to restore the *Tercerista* alliance to what the Nicaraguan moderates thought it would be back in 1979, before the revolutionary triumph. Nicaraguans like Arturo Cruz held out such hopes and believed that military pressure by the contras was required to achieve it. In the United States, however, Reagan's hopeful scenario was roundly attacked by critics who considered it so far-fetched as to be indistinguishable from a call for overthrow. "Say, 'Uncle,'" became another embarrassing presidential gaffe.

The contras' military and political weaknesses forced the Reagan administration to seek remedies. Democrats wary of the Sandinistas needed something more to support than Adolfo Calero, Enrique Bermúdez, and 10,000 contra fighters sitting in Honduras. Reagan officials believed the main weakness of the contras was their lack of "legitimate" leadership, which in American terms meant moderately progressive, anti-Somoza, bourgeois politicians or business leaders. McFarlane believed that in order to pass aid to the contras, "Congress had to find the Contra movement a more appealing, legitimate movement oriented toward political goals, pluralism, and so forth."[42] He had told Don Fortier and Oliver North that "to help win the vote" they should try "to expand the base of the Contra leadership to include acknowledged, credible, political figures in Nicaragua."[43] After the 1984 elections there were few more credible political figures than Arturo Cruz.

Cruz and his advisers had the same idea. Near the end of 1984, Cruz's son, Arturo Cruz, Jr., argued that liberal and moderate Democrats in Congress "needed their own pretext" to approve contra aid. He compared the situation to that of El Salvador. The rebels needed to "find our own Duarte to lay the basis for a bipartisan consensus. Then the liberals can say that they do not necessarily approve of the policies of the Reagan administration, but rather are approving aid in order to strengthen the center, and Nicaraguan Democrats."[44] Cruz's analogy with the congressional politics of aid to El Salvador was apt, and there was another pertinent analogy: the Carter administration's attempt to block the Sandinistas in 1978 and 1979. Then, too, Vaky and Bowdler had searched for moderate Nicaraguans like Robelo and Calero to forge an anti-Sandinista, anti-Somoza, centrist alliance with a "reformed" and purged National Guard.

Grafting Cruz onto the contra leadership was no simple matter, however. Cruz did not want to become just another rebel. His strength lay in his political appeal inside Nicaragua, in his connections with the internal opposition groups that had chosen him as their candidate, in his role as a leader of the Democratic Coordinadora. These connections made him popular abroad, in no small part because it made Cruz a part of the peaceful, not the armed, struggle against the Sandinistas. The prize Cruz represented to the Americans, and the danger he posed to the Sandinistas, was as the solitary link between the bourgeois political opposition in the cities of the Pacific Coast and the armed campesinos in the northern hills of Jinotega. He could do for the contras what he and the Group of Twelve had done for the Sandinistas. Cruz refused, however, to play the role of facade a second time. As Cruz and his allies contemplated a merger with Calero and the forces of the FDN, they wanted to make sure Cruz had some control of the guns, too.

Cruz's international prestige was as much a threat to Calero and Bermúdez as to the Sandinistas. Bermúdez had not led his troops for five years in order to turn them over to Arturo Cruz and Alfonso Robelo. As the negotiations between the two sides proceeded in February, Bermúdez insisted that he owed it to his fighters to remain in a position of power and to ensure that "all we have told our fighters about our principles would not be deviated from or distorted."[45] The contras' top commanders, in turn, pledged the loyalty and solidarity of the "15,000 fighters of the FDN" to Calero and Bermúdez and attacked "certain propagandist, anti-patriotic, and sectarian campaigns carried out by persons incapable of any struggle for liberty."[46] According to North, Calero was "uncomfortable with both Cruz and Robelo in that they were in the Sandinista government which expropriated his property and jailed him," but Calero's real fear was that Cruz would now try to expropriate the FDN.[47]

The confrontation between Cruz and FDN leaders was not only over personal power, but also over fundamental political goals. Their differences emerged as the two sides set about drafting a declaration of common principles that would serve as the first step toward formal alliance. Cruz genuinely hoped for a peaceful solution, though he agreed with the FDN and the Americans that military pressure was necessary, for the moment. And the elements of a peaceful solution, in Cruz's mind, could well include a reconciliation with the Sandinistas, at least with the Ortega brothers. As a member of the junta in the early years of the revolution, Cruz had never fully abandoned the hope that the Ortegas would come to their senses.[48]

Calero viewed the possibility of conciliation with the Ortega brothers as a dangerous illusion.[49] Cruz's flirtation with the idea of a negotiated settlement struck Calero and Bermúdez and the contra fighters as vaguely treasonous. The "loyalty proclamation" signed by the FDN's regional and task force commanders in February left no room for conciliation: It ended with the words "until the final victory." Calero had reason to suspect that Cruz in the end was more likely to find common cause with the Sandinistas than to help him and Bermúdez into power.

But Calero was under enormous pressure from the Reagan administration to accept Cruz and Robelo into the contra leadership. McFarlane warned him in January that if the contras could not "produce a political leadership" that was more appealing, then perhaps it was best to forget about further aid from the United States. North had cajoled Calero, saying "You and I both know [Cruz's] value and limitations,"[50] but North left no doubt where the Reagan administration stood. At the end of February Calero, Robelo, and Cruz agreed to work together.

The symbol of the new alliance was a document released in San José, Costa Rica, in the first week of March. Signed by Cruz, Calero, Robelo, Pedro Joaquín Chamorro, Jr., Carlos Coronel, and other opposition leaders, the San José document served Cruz's interests as well as the Reagan administration's. It called for a church-mediated dialogue between the Sandinistas and their political opponents. The subject of the dialogue would be the return to the "original plan of government." The San José declaration emphasized "reconciliation of the Nicaraguan family" and sought no victory over the FSLN. On the contrary, it implicitly held out the hope of a return to the original *Tercerista* alliance between the moderate Sandinistas and the progressive bourgeoisie, suggesting that the "totalitarian tendency" in Nicaragua had only *"for the moment . . .* accepted the Sandinista Front as its vanguard," implying that the Sandinistas themselves might choose a different course.[51] The signers even declared that if national dialogue with the Sandinistas proceeded, "we pledge to accept that Mr. Daniel Ortega continue as acting head of the Executive Branch until such time as the people pronounce themselves in a plebiscite." For Reagan officials, the declaration was designed only to forge a union of the armed and unarmed opposition to the Sandinistas—with Cruz as the vital link between the two. For Cruz, however, the San José document expressed the hope that "maybe, just maybe one of the Sandinista leaders will stop to meditate for a moment, to ponder the situation and say: Well, we should be more Nicaraguan than communist."[52]

The opposition leaders gave the Sandinistas a short deadline to meet their demands, however. If the national dialogue was not making progress by April 20, the war would continue. This deadline coincided with the expected vote in Congress on contra aid, and was put in at the request of Reagan officials.[53] It was also the *sine qua non* for Calero. As he told reporters, "If the Sandinistas don't agree [to the negotiating proposal], I take it to mean that Mr. Cruz agrees with those of us re-enforcing our quest with military efforts."[54]

On March 3 Archbishop Obando endorsed the opposition's plan informally in a Sunday homily, and Cruz planned to meet with Archbishop Obando and the opposition leaders in Managua to show the unity of opposition forces.[55] On March 7 the Sandinistas denied Cruz entry into Nicaragua. Borge's Interior Ministry released a communiqué denouncing a "CIA plan" which aimed to "give the Nicaraguan Democratic Force the status of an internal political force."[56] On March 9 the ten top opposition leaders in Nicaragua, including the editor of *La Prensa*, were summoned to State Security headquarters, where the director, Lenin Cerna, warned them against participating in the "plot."[57] On March 11 Daniel Ortega insisted that Cruz's efforts to establish "unity between the mercenary forces abroad and the political forces inside the country" were impermissible.[58]

In Washington, Cruz's efforts had more success. According to North, the San José document was intended "to convince the U.S. Congress that the opposition was led by reasonable men,"[59] and it went a long way to accomplishing that goal. Cruz's devoted following, which included Robert Leiken, an influential liberal writer, and Bruce Cameron, a liberal human rights lobbyist, worked to build Cruz's image on Capitol Hill. Moderate Democrats like Ike Skelton began arguing that "we have to change the perceptions of the American public and international opinion toward the contras. This means we have to support Arturo Cruz in the Nicaraguan situation in much the same way we supported Napoleon Duarte in El Salvador."[60] As his son had foreseen, Arturo Cruz now came to represent both a centrist alternative and the hope for a negotiated solution, a national reconciliation in Nicaragua. "These people were not talking overthrow," Congressman McCurdy recalled. "They were talking some opening of the political process." With Cruz and Robelo in the contras' leadership, South Carolina Democrat John Spratt said, there was a "genuine opportunity for social democracy in Nicaragua."[61] And the *Washington Post* called the opposition's proposal "entirely fair and reasonable" since it required only that the Sandinistas return to the "original goals of *their own revolution.*"[62]

35

The "Humanitarian" War

The enlistment of Cruz did not solve the Reagan administration's problem in Congress, however. Most moderate Democrats were still not ready to vote for military aid to the contras, even though Cruz's plan for a national reconciliation required it. At the beginning of March, the President remained at least 20 to 30 votes shy of a majority for his proposal in the House.[1] On April 3 House Minority Leader Robert Michel told Reagan his contra aid plan was "dead in the water," and the White House legislative director agreed the administration was short of the necessary votes.[2] Even in the Republican-controlled Senate, Majority Leader Dole considered the contra aid vote a quixotic distraction from more important issues.[3]

Some of Reagan's advisers recommended extraordinary measures. Oliver North recommended that the President go around Congress and appeal directly to the American people to "contribute funds ('. . . send your check or money order to the Nicaraguan Freedom Fighters, Box 1776, Gettysburg, PA . . .') to support liberty and democracy in the Americas."[4] Pat Buchanan and Constantine Menges wanted the President to make a nationally televised speech to put more pressure on the Democrats to approve his proposal. Conservatives inside and outside the administration wanted to fight and lose, if necessary, so that the American people "would know who was responsible and which policy failed."[5]

McFarlane, other White House officials, and ultimately Reagan himself rejected this strategy. White House officials adamantly opposed a televised speech by Reagan on Nicaragua, fearing it would put the President's prestige on the line in a losing cause.[6] McFarlane was intent on finding an agreement with House Democrats, not in proving them irresponsible.[7] With the latest Saudi contribution to the contras in the bank, McFarlane sought to win broad support for a policy "which the administration could sustain through the Congress and the American people."[8] Conservatives like Henry Hyde recommended to McFarlane that the administration should just "expand private sector and third country assistance . . . in the effort to support the resistance."[9] Instead, McFarlane and North put together a compromise designed to win the votes of some moderate Democrats.

On April 4 Reagan announced that if Congress approved his request for $14 million in covert military aid, he promised to withhold weapons and ammunition from the contras and provide them only with "humanitarian" assistance until June 1. If the Sandinistas agreed to a cease-fire on the terms presented in the contras' March 1 proposal in San José, Reagan would continue withholding military aid for an additional 60 days, while negotiations toward a final settlement on national reconciliation were completed. If the Sandinistas did not agree to a cease-fire by June 1, Reagan would resume military aid to the contras.[10] Reagan officials assumed, correctly, that the Sandinistas would never agree to a proposal they had already rejected in March.[11] McFarlane hoped, however, that moderates in Congress would be attracted to the President's effort to find a compromise.

The proposal, sponsored in the House by Minority Leader Robert Michel, forced the House leadership to respond with a compromise of its own. Speaker O'Neill lashed out in a fury at the President, calling the proposal a "dirty trick" and accusing Reagan of "hoodwinking the American public" with his talk of "humanitarian aid" to "butchers" who were "killing people out there, ravishing the villages."[12] But observers noted that the plan "put Reagan's Capitol Hill critics on the defensive."[13] Congressmen Hamilton and Barnes quickly prepared a letter to their colleagues urging them not to decide yet how to vote on the aid request.[14] With Reagan's surprise "peace proposal" on the table, Congress adjourned for a two-week Easter recess.

The coming days were consumed by a public relations battle mounted across the country. The President opened the week on April 15 by declaring that a vote against his proposal was more than "a rejection of the freedom fighters . . . [it was] literally a vote against peace."[15] A private conservative group, "Citizens for America," working in consultation with North, organized a public relations campaign "to take the President's case right to the people, to hop right over the national media."[16] The campaign cost about $300,000 and included visits by 22 Central American business officials to cities across the United States and then to the offices of selected congressmen. Another group, the "Nicaraguan Refugee Fund," to whom Reagan delivered his April 15 speech, brought six Nicaraguan refugees to Washington to tell their stories. "Resistance International," a group of European politicians and writers, visited the White House on April 18 to endorse Reagan's proposal.[17] New York millionaire Lewis Lehrman, then director of "Citizens for America," made speeches in several cities. The State Department's Office of Public Diplomacy released documents like Bayardo Arce's "secret speech" of May 1984 and studies alleging a variety of Sandinista misdeeds, including involvement in the international drug trade. Former UN Ambassador Jeane Kirkpatrick gave a speech in Pennsylvania. Cruz, Calero, and Robelo were brought up to lobby members of Congress.

While opponents of contra aid, then and later, complained about this "barrage" of public diplomacy,[18] the campaign was more than matched by what the *Congressional Quarterly* called a "well-organized drumbeat of opposition to [President Reagan's] policies in Central America." A broad coalition of church groups, peace groups, human rights groups, environmental groups, labor and professional organizations, and "solidarity" networks across the country had mobilized at the beginning of the year, loosely coordinated by the "Coalition for a New Foreign and Military Policy."[19] With their historical roots in the small human rights movement of the late 1970s, these groups had been transformed by the Salvadoran "death-squad" murders of American nuns and Archbishop Oscar Romero into a nationwide movement of activists opposed to the Reagan administration's policies in Latin America.

After four fruitless years trying to block American aid to the Salvadoran government, these groups shifted their attention to Nicaragua, drawn by reports of atrocities by the contras, by the desire to prevent President Reagan's intervention against another poor Latin American country, by a "concern as U.S. citizens" about what such policies "say about our national character," and by a conviction that "the difference between Vietnam and Central America is that the Catholic Church stands between us and Central America."[20] The U.S. Catholic Conference, the United Church of Christ, the Presbyterian Church U.S.A., and the American

Baptists all worked to "activat[e] their congregations," while the Protestant Inter-Religious Task Force on Central America and the Catholic-based Religious Task Force on Central America coordinated from Washington the grassroots lobbying efforts in the home districts of congressmen. During the Easter recess and in the week before the vote, congressional offices reported receiving hundreds of phone calls from church members opposed to contra aid.[21] In addition, dozens of national celebrities, former government officials, and other notable figures took part in the lobbying campaign against contra aid.[22] "By the time the votes occurred on April 23rd and 24th," one coordinator of the lobbying effort recalled, "opponents to contra aid had involved more than 150 national organizations and their constituencies in the efforts to terminate the aid—it would be the largest organizing effort to that date (and many believe, ever) on a Central America-related policy issue, and would set the standard for all future campaigns."[23]

Both supporters and opponents of contra aid concentrated on the "swing" votes of moderate southern Democrats. The President's combination of political pressures and his apparent compromise had exposed the strained seam of a Democratic Party that was pulling itself in two opposite directions at once. Concern among leading Democrats about the disastrous results of the 1984 presidential elections had been growing since the beginning of the year. House Democrats went off on retreats and formed new policy groups to discuss how to respond to what seemed to them the "far more conservative" mood of the country; southern Democrats in particular believed the party's leaders needed to "develop the perception that they favor a strong defense."[24] Liberal Democrats, on the other hand, took an opposite view of their party's predicament, arguing for a more forceful assertion of liberal principles in foreign and domestic policies.

For both factions, Nicaragua had become a defining issue. Southern Democrats feared opposing Reagan too stridently, out of concern that he could successfully "blame them later if all of Central America erupts into conflict."[25] Although they opposed covert military aid, they did not want the Democratic Party to appear to be "abandoning" the contras altogether.[26] During the Easter recess, one prominent southern moderate, Congressman Dave McCurdy, traveled to Nicaragua and was "disturbed . . . by evidence of growing Sandinista repression, censorship and duplicity, and by the escalation of their military forces." While he had always voted against aid to the contras, McCurdy told reporters, he believed "more strongly than ever that there is a compelling case for continued

American involvement in Central America . . . [and that] to relieve the outside pressure on the Sandinistas would be a mistake."[27] Liberal Democrats felt just as strongly that Reagan's policies were immoral, however, and the liberals held a majority within the caucus, as well as the support of Speaker O'Neill.[28] O'Neill turned control of the issue over to the liberal wing by appointing David Bonior as head of a new Task Force on Nicaragua. Bonior was a young, articulate, and virulent opponent of Reagan's policies, sure to carry out the liberals' desire to confront and defeat Reagan on the question of aid to the contras, even as more conservative party leaders hoped to avoid precisely such a confrontation.

The man who stood in the middle of the Democratic Party's ferment was the majority leader from Texas. A southerner who nevertheless depended on the liberal majority to elevate him to Speaker after O'Neill's retirement in 1986, Wright embodied his divided party; and its strains pulled at him from both directions. Liberals suspected him of being too conservative.[29] Conservatives suspected him of selling out to liberals to win the Speakership, and indeed, Wright could no longer command the allegiance of conservative colleagues even in his own state.[30] Wright searched for safe ground on the divisive issue of Nicaragua. Even though a poll conducted by Democrats in the House showed that Reagan's request would probably be defeated by 10–20 votes, Wright convinced a reluctant O'Neill to let Congressmen Hamilton and Barnes put together an alternative to the President's proposal that could give moderates the protection they needed without betraying the liberals' goal of defeating contra aid. Wright told reporters "It often is best if, in addition to saying what you're not for, you're able to say what you're for."[31]

Finding a proposal that appealed to both northern liberals and southern moderates, however, was no easy task. With a few days left before the vote, Barnes and Hamilton proposed that $10 million in humanitarian assistance be provided to Nicaraguan "refugees" through the Red Cross or other international relief agencies; the rest of the money would be given to the Contadora countries to support negotiations. This was not the same "humanitarian" aid the administration had in mind; indeed, the purpose of the Barnes-Hamilton proposal was to end the war. Barnes and Hamilton made one concession to win the support of moderates like McCurdy: their bill provided an opportunity for the President to return to Congress for more aid to the contras on October 1, the beginning of the next fiscal year. This was less than McCurdy and other moderates asked for,[32] but more than House liberals had wanted to give. The minor concession attracted moderates from both parties in search of a comfortable "middle course" between supporting the President's plan for covert military aid or doing nothing.

In the Senate, Georgia Democrat Sam Nunn offered a similar "humanitarian" aid proposal, but without the provision limiting aid to "refugees." Nunn's intent, unlike Hamilton's, was not to end the war but to keep the contras alive while the Sandinistas were tested. If the Sandinistas did not change their behavior, Senator Nunn declared, "the President could come back to Congress and request resumption of military aid. At that point, a request for military aid would be on a very different foundation. I would support and am certain that many others would support an expedited procedure in both the House and Senate for such a Presidential request."[33] Nunn's proposal did have the effect of scuttling military aid for the time being. The day after Nunn's speech, President Reagan agreed to compromise once more and to forgo military aid for the rest of the fiscal year.[34] Henceforth the debate in Washington would be about "humanitarian" aid only.

Moderate Democrats in the House and Senate hoped their proposals could attract broad support from both parties. The larger the consensus, they believed, the safer the vote in favor of compromise. But efforts to achieve a consensus across the political and ideological divides failed in both Houses. Liberal Senators would not accept Nunn's proposal, and neither conservatives in the House nor the Reagan administration would accept the Barnes-Hamilton proposal. On April 23, the Senate passed Nunn's "humanitarian" aid plan by a narrow margin, 53–46. In the House that day, the contest was even closer. Speaker O'Neill wanted a clear victory over President Reagan, after losing to the President on MX missile legislation the previous month, and he used all his power as Speaker to muster the necessary votes. An aide to O'Neill later said he hadn't seen the Speaker work so hard on a vote in ten years. "You could hear the sound of elbows crunching," the aide recalled, as swing voters and freshman members were called into O'Neill's office for one-on-one encounters.[35]

As moderates took to the floor to support the Barnes-Hamilton proposal, however, their arguments revealed their discomfort with the plan to end support for the contras. Congressman Richardson, a former contra aid opponent who had begun to shift his position after the 1984 elections in both Nicaragua and the United States, argued that pressure on the Sandinistas "should be increased so that the Sandinistas negotiate with the Contras."[36] Passing the Barnes-Hamilton bill, Richardson insisted, would send "a message to Managua." "It says to the Sandinistas very forcefully: You have to reduce your Soviet and Cuban ties. . . . You have got to negotiate with the Contras besides cleaning up your act or else . . . there will be Members of Congress like myself who agonized over this vote who will not continue to support the Sandinista efforts as we have indirectly."[37]

The crucial assumption that underlay such statements was that the contras were going to find their own sources of military aid, no matter what kind of "humanitarian" aid the Congress passed. Congressman Richardson could argue that "the conflict [in Nicaragua] won't end with this vote" because "we all know that there is a lot of private aid that is going to flow to the Contras." Senator Cohen similarly satisfied himself that the contras didn't need American military aid: "They can raise $14 million with a couple of fund-raisers in Florida, Texas, or California."[38] Few knew what McFarlane and North knew about efforts to raise funds for the contras, but members of Congress, like Secretary Shultz a year earlier, simply assumed the funds could be found. This was the centerpiece, albeit largely unmentioned, of the moderates' new policy. The expectation of private or third-country military aid to the contras was what made it possible for a moderate Democrat like McCurdy to declare the Barnes-Hamilton proposal, which officially cut off congressional support for the contra war, as a "symbol of bipartisan determination to stand firm for democracy in Central America."[39]

Even so, the voting on the amendments was close. The administration-backed Michel amendment lost by two votes, 213–215. The Barnes-Hamilton proposal passed, 219–206, due as much to the defection of 14 liberal Republicans as to lack of support among moderate Democrats.[40] The Democrats had no time to rejoice, however. Throughout the debate, a number of liberal Democrats had expressed objections to all contra aid proposals, including the Barnes-Hamilton amendment.[41] And so, in the vote on final passage of the amended bill, more than 100 liberal Democrats and three moderate Republicans joined almost 200 conservative Republicans and Democrats in voting "no." The Barnes-Hamilton proposal fell under an avalanche, 123–303. At the end of the day, no aid of any kind had been provided to the contras, and the moderate Democrats were left stranded.

———

On April 23, after the House voted down the President's original request, but before it voted on a final contra aid bill, the Nicaraguan government announced that President Ortega would travel to Moscow to meet with

General Secretary Gorbachev at the beginning of May. Some House members heard the news during the voting on April 24, but it wasn't until the next day's morning papers that word spread throughout Washington, and the recriminations began.[42] Senator Sasser of Tennessee, who had voted against the administration's aid bill on April 23, told reporters he would have voted in favor had he known of Ortega's planned trip. The "ill-timed and ill-advised" visit to Moscow showed that Ortega was "either naive, incompetent or not as committed to negotiations as recent statements would indicate."[43] Even Sasser's strong comments gave only a hint of the anger and embarrassment felt by those moderates who had voted against Reagan.

During his visit to Moscow at the beginning of May, the Sandinistas claimed, Ortega won Soviet agreement to supply 80–90 percent of Nicaragua's oil needs.[44] The Sandinistas later insisted that Ortega's trip had been forced by economic emergency,[45] that the government was facing an oil shortage after Mexico cancelled oil shipments on April 16 and badly needed a Soviet commitment to fill the gap.[46] But the trip also revealed an uncharacteristic tactical inflexibility by the Sandinistas. Oil crisis or not, the Sandinistas did not have to conduct their visit to Moscow in such a clumsy manner. Sandinista leaders knew their decision to go to Moscow at that moment could cause them difficulties in Congress.[47] Once the votes in Congress had been scheduled for April 23, Ortega could have put his trip off for a month to allow a decent interval to pass. Or, if he feared the Soviets would not reschedule the meeting, he could have made Moscow and the East bloc capitals the last stops of a longer world tour, perhaps landing first in Madrid or Stockholm.[48] Nor did the Sandinistas have to send President Ortega. A trip by the planning minister, Henry Ruiz, would have attracted far less notice.[49]

No special oil emergency was required to explain Ortega's eagerness to travel to Moscow, however, regardless of the cost in the United States. The visit was part of a consistent pattern, the eighth by a senior Sandinista leader in five years. Three of these visits had been to attend the funerals of Soviet leaders, and after each funeral, there had always been a second visit soon afterwards to meet with the new leader. Thus Daniel Ortega went to Brezhnev's funeral at the end of 1982 and then traveled again to Moscow in March 1983 for a meeting with Andropov; Ortega met Chernenko at Andropov's funeral in February 1984 and then met with Chernenko again in June 1984; and he met with Gorbachev at Chernenko's funeral in March 1985 and managed to schedule this second visit with Gorbachev two months later, perhaps, as one scholar humorously suggests, "to make sure that Mikhail Gorbachev did not leave the scene before [Ortega] could make contact."[50] The specific agendas for the eight meetings with Soviet leaders varied, but the Sandinistas' main purpose was always the same: to establish good personal relations with the new leadership as quickly as possible.

In 1985, the Sandinistas' relationship with the new Soviet leadership was more important than ever. Not only were the Sandinistas more dependent on Soviet support—not just for oil, but for an increasing supply of fairly high-quality weapons—but they also had more reason to worry about the depth and longevity of that support. To be sure, the weapons flowed in greater abundance than ever in 1985, the Soviets were willing to solve the Sandinistas' oil problems, and Gorbachev's public rhetoric in 1985 gave little hint of any softening. But the Sandinistas in their strategic planning had once counted on thirty years of Soviet support, not just five or ten,[51] and they rightly perceived that Gorbachev and his associates were even less enthusiastic about Third World revolutionary movements than Andropov had been. In Moscow, Ortega held meetings and was honored at the highest levels, but he was probably aware that Foreign Minister Andrei Gromyko was lately more interested in repairing U.S.-Soviet relations;[52] nor could it have escaped Ortega's notice that one of the earliest supporters of the Nicaraguan revolution, the Communist Party's International Department chief, Boris Ponomarev, was now 80 years old.[53] If U.S.-Soviet relations improved, which by 1985 seemed increasingly likely, the Sandinistas wanted to ensure that their revolution would not become a casualty.

The vital importance of close relations with the Soviet Union had been one of the few constants in Sandinista theory and policy since their earliest pre-revolutionary days. Since taking power they had been eager suitors in an effort to prove themselves Moscow's most reliable allies, much as Somoza had once sought to prove himself Washington's best friend in Central America. The Sandinista government had decreed three days of national mourning after the death of "Comrade Chernenko," though surely the Soviets would not have taken amiss some smaller gesture.[54] The Sandinistas clung to their geopolitical ally, however, even though that alliance, when openly flaunted, earned them the hostility of the U.S. Congress.

In the United States the trip was a disaster for the Sandinistas. Senator Dodd could well express wonder "that some Democrats were surprised that Daniel Ortega went to Moscow. Where do my colleagues think he was going to go? Disney World?"[55] But what so offended moderate Democrats about the timing of Ortega's trip to Moscow—aside from the immense political embarrassment it caused them—was that it cast in stark relief the strategic choice the Sandinistas had made and apparently always would make. Rather than put their fate in the hands of the American Congress, the Sandinistas ran off to seek the succor of the Soviets. Butler Derrick, a Democrat from South Carolina, told reporters he "took it as an international slap at the Congress and a slap at those of us who had gone out on a limb to come up with something." Congressman Charles Schumer, a Democrat from New York, said members of Congress considered the trip to Moscow "a personal rebuke to Congress."[56] Members of Congress knew how to respond to such treatment.

The defeat of the Barnes-Hamilton proposal had already begun a migration of moderate southern Democrats away from the House leadership;[57] Ortega's trip turned it into a stampede. Two days after O'Neill had twisted the arms of wavering moderates, the Speaker and other House leaders now bore the brunt of the moderates' fury at Ortega. One angry southern Democrat, Congressman Tommy Robinson from Arkansas, was still fuming more than a month later and publicly chastised himself for letting "my leadership and the liberals in this Congress convince me that Daniel Ortega was going to do right. He did not do right. They have a Neville Chamberlain mentality." O'Neill's aides confirmed that Ortega's trip "undercut enormously the position of the leadership."[58] O'Neill's helplessness to undo the damage became apparent when the Speaker hastily called a meeting of the top Democratic leaders on May 4 and told Lee Hamilton to "see what you can work out" in the way of a compromise to pass some form of aid to the contras. But this then raised a "firestorm" among party liberals, and O'Neill was forced to deny the next day that he had considered "reversing our position on financing the contras."[59] The House leadership was paralyzed and unable to bridge the now yawning gap between the two wings of the party.[60] This allowed the moderates, led by McCurdy, to chart their own course and to draw up compromise legislation that more faithfully reflected their true aims.[61]

The Reagan administration, after a week of hesitation, responded to one of the moderates' demands and imposed a trade and economic embargo against Nicaragua. The embargo was another idea that came from Congress, especially from Democratic Senators Lloyd Bentsen and Sam Nunn.[62] Reagan officials were unenthusiastic. Secretary Shultz believed an embargo would be ineffective: the United States supplied only 20 percent of Nicaragua's imports and bought 18 percent of its exports. Other officials considered it a weak measure designed only to make congressmen feel better about their votes against contra aid. But Senator Bentsen privately pushed the administration to respond to his suggestion, and on April 27 Senator Dole publicly called on the administration to impose an embargo. "I think it's time to get tough . . . and stay tough," the majority leader declared.[63] On April 29, Shultz gave in and President Reagan approved sanctions against Nicaragua. "It's not going to be an overpowering event," Shultz told reporters, "but there's a certain sense of feeling that regardless of the effect, certain kinds of relationships with countries we think are doing a lot of damage are undesirable."[64] Reagan announced the sanctions on May 1, the same day he arrived in Bonn, West Germany, for the beginning of an economic summit, and the timing could hardly have been worse. American allies had not been notified in advance, and they unanimously denounced the decision.[65]

On May 7 McCurdy and his moderate colleagues introduced their new legislation.[66] Like the Michel amendment the moderates had just voted down two weeks before, McCurdy's bill provided the $14 million in "humanitarian" aid directly to the "Nicaraguan resistance forces." And while the Barnes-Hamilton legislation had stated that aid "may not be provided . . . with the intent of provisioning combat forces," McCurdy's bill included no such restriction, stipulating only that the United States could not provide weapons or equipment of a lethal nature. Both the intent and the certain effect of McCurdy's legislation was to provide "food, clothing, medicine and other humanitarian assistance" to a fighting force in the field.

McCurdy's bill also included the provisions favored by moderates in both House and Senate during the previous debate and promised by President Reagan in his letters to both Houses: an economic embargo against Nicaragua, the removal of human rights violators from the contras' ranks, and the resumption of bilateral talks between the United States and Nicaragua "with a view of encouraging" a church-mediated dialogue between the contras and Sandinistas, national reconciliation in Nicaragua, and a Contadora agreement.[67] McCurdy's bill also stipulated that if the President determined that diplomatic and economic pressures had failed to produce a negotiated agreement, Reagan could ask Congress for more aid for the contras "in such amount and of such a nature as the President deems appropriate"—which amounted to an invitation for the President to seek military aid if the Sandinistas did not agree to negotiations with the contras. McCurdy had skillfully placed himself at the head of the moderate bloc that held the balance in the House. He no longer had to bend to the dictates of his own leaders in the House, but neither was he subservient to the Reagan administration.

At the beginning of June, Senator Nunn introduced his own bill co-sponsored by four southern Democrats—Bentsen of Texas, Boren of Oklahoma, Chiles of Florida, Johnston of Louisiana[68]—that provided $14 million in humanitarian assistance in Fiscal Year 1985, and another $24 million in Fiscal Year 1986. Nunn's bill lifted the Boland restrictions altogether and did not specifically preclude the CIA from delivering the aid, but it prohibited the President from providing any other material assistance to the contras. On June 6 the Senate passed Nunn's amendment 55–42.

In the debates in both Houses during the second week of June, the forces led by McCurdy and Nunn had a better chance than ever to lay out their goals, their political concerns, and the logic behind the policy toward Nicaragua they were shaping for the United States. McCurdy and his colleagues took pride in offering a "moderate" synthesis of the two "extreme" positions that had been tearing the Congress and the country apart, not just over Nicaragua but on many foreign policy issues since the end of the Vietnam War. Between the morally pure isolationism of the liberal Democrats and the morally tainted anti-communist interventionism of the Reagan administration, they argued, lay a third path: a modern, liberal anti-communism that blended elements of both the pre-Vietnam and post-Vietnam Democratic foreign policy, the cold warrior tradition of Truman, Kennedy, and Johnson with the idealism of the human rights lobby and anti-war movement. McCurdy and his colleagues would support a fight against communism, on moral and strategic grounds, but they would support it only on behalf of a democratic, not authoritarian alternative. They would support the use of force, but only in pursuit of an eventual negotiated settlement, not outright victory.

As Democrats, McCurdy, Nunn, and other moderates necessarily defined their policy by the ways in which it was not like President Reagan's, and, as Arturo Cruz, Jr., had predicted, they used El Salvador as the model. The Reagan administration had been "firmly allied with the extreme right" in El Salvador, Bernard Aronson[69] wrote in the *New Republic*, until forced by "strong Democratic criticism of human rights abuses and a deteriorating military situation" to take action against death squads and support President Duarte. In Nicaragua, the Reagan administration was "allying with the Somocista right," but Democrats could once again force the administration to reform its ally by conducting a "purge" of ex-Guardia from the military high command and of human rights abusers from the entire force.[70] Thus would the United States be giving its full support to the "genuine democrats"[71]—Cruz, Robelo, and Calero—"men of sterling credentials resembling that of El Salvador's Duarte."[72]

In both El Salvador and Nicaragua, the moderates asserted, President Reagan preferred a military victory to a peaceful settlement, and their role was to force the administration to support negotiations for a "political solution." Moderate Democrats had to "bring[] the President a long way from the warmongering statements of the past," Congressman Jones declared.[73] Robert Leiken summed up the views of McCurdy and other moderates in an editorial later in the year. "Consider what happened in El Salvador. The Administration had little success until, under pressure from Congress it began to speak out against the death squads, urge military reform and support President José Napoleon Duarte in his efforts to open a dialogue with the rebels."[74] The moderates proposed the same strategy for Nicaragua, and the same roles for themselves. They would steer an indifferent President toward support for human rights, a war-loving President toward support of diplomacy and peace.

Finally, the moderates claimed their policy was superior to Reagan's because it created consensus in the United States instead of confrontation. It aimed as much at binding the political wounds of post-Vietnam America—and patching the rifts in the Democratic Party—as at solving problems in Nicaragua. The United States had so far avoided both "another Vietnam" and a communist victory in El Salvador, wrote Bernard Aronson, "largely because we have achieved something approaching a consensus uniting moderates in both parties."[75] That consensus was built around the unique mixture of anti-communism, liberal interventionism, human rights, and peace. A principal virtue of McCurdy's proposal for Nicaragua, Congressman Jim Jones argued, was that it represented "an El Salvador-style coming together of both sides."[76] That coming together provided protection to those who would otherwise be caught in the crossfire of the ideological war, and the broader the consensus, the more the protection.

While the moderates' doctrine was thus defined by the ways in which it differed from, and corrected, Reagan's policies, it also shared important elements of those policies. McCurdy, Nunn, and their colleagues shared the conviction that the United States had a strategic interest in resisting the expansion of communism in the Western Hemisphere. More significant still was their belief that the United States had a moral interest in seeking what McCurdy called "genuine democracy" in Nicaragua. While Jim Wright continued to insist that whether one liked the Sandinista government or not, it was "the established government of that country,"[77] Democrats like McCurdy, Nunn, and their supporters rejected this non-interventionist principle in favor of a more intrusive concept of American policy. Aronson argued that the Sandinistas had forfeited "any legitimate claim to invoke the principle of 'sovereignty'" since they themselves had received foreign help in overthrowing Somoza; and he asked fellow Democrats: "Why was it 'legitimate' to help the Nicaraguan people wage their revolution in 1979 but 'illegitimate' to help the Nicaraguan people save their revolution today?"[78]

This had been President Reagan's argument for the past three years. It was, moreover, the novel principle that underlay the newly enunciated Reagan doctrine, which questioned the legitimacy of all non-democratic governments everywhere and asserted the right of the United States to interfere on behalf of democratic forces fighting those governments. When McCurdy insisted that American foreign policy be guided by "standards that are the same for El Salvador, Nicaragua, South Africa, Chile, and other nations throughout the world," he was only echoing what Secretary Shultz had said in February.[79]

Nor did McCurdy, Nunn, and others disagree with the Reagan administration's assertion that military pressure, as well as economic and diplomatic pressure, was necessary to force changes in Nicaragua. McCurdy's proposal gave "humanitarian" aid to a fighting force in the field because McCurdy and other moderates believed the Sandinistas had to be convinced to negotiate and make reforms. "The Sandinistas can hardly be expected to hold a political dialogue about the future of their country with a group of exiled refugees," Aronson wrote.[80] Even the moderates' support for reform of the contras aimed not only at reducing human rights abuses, but at enhancing the contras' political appeal in Nicaragua, particularly in the cities where they were weakest, and thereby improving their capacity to challenge the Sandinistas. On many occasions, McCurdy and other moderates declared the contras could never "win" unless they made the necessary reforms.

The moderate Democrats who supported McCurdy's proposal were fond of arguing that Reagan's goals were unclear and his means of attaining them uncertain or inadequate. Their own policy was not immune to such charges, however. The centerpiece of their strategy for achieving a "political solution" in Nicaragua was a dialogue between the Sandinistas and the contras, which the Sandinistas had adamantly and repeatedly rejected. The purpose of this unlikely dialogue was to discuss the conditions for national reconciliation and the creation of genuine democracy, meaning among other things new elections for President. In the absence of any Sandinista willingness to hold a dialogue and then make concessions, McCurdy's policy appeared to be indistinguishable from Reagan's: more military pressure.

The main distinction between McCurdy's and Reagan's strategy, in the end, was one of emphasis. Both sides agreed on the need to pressure the Sandinistas by supporting the contras, but the Reagan administration preferred victory to negotiations and the moderates preferred negotiations to victory. McCurdy and his colleagues wished to support the war as briefly and as parsimoniously as possible, while probing constantly for any signs of Sandinista accommodation. Their great hope was that the Sandinistas would eventually see reason. The Reagan administration's great hope was that the Sandinistas would eventually collapse.

The distinction was lost on many of McCurdy's more liberal colleagues in the Democratic Party. When debate began on McCurdy's bill on June 12 there was fundamental disagreement on the most fundamental question: whether the aid in McCurdy's bill did or did not support a resumption of congressional aid for the contras' war against the Sandinistas. McCurdy's coalition of moderates included members from both parties who simply were not prepared to say that they were supporting war or even military pressure against the Nicaraguan government. Both McCurdy and Nunn had insisted that their respective amendments in the House and Senate moved "any military options to the back burner,"[81] which wasn't quite true. But Congressman Jones of Oklahoma went much further. Jones was in the awkward spot of having co-sponsored the Barnes-Hamilton amendment in April and was now a co-sponsor of McCurdy's bill in June. Naturally, he tried to argue that "the policy goals of Barnes-Hamilton and that of McCurdy-McDade are virtually the same."[82] He even persisted in referring to the intended recipients of McCurdy's aid as "refugees" and to the aid itself as "relief."

Pursuit of an acceptable compromise had required deliberate avoidance of unpleasant facts. McCurdy could only gain the support of more liberal Democrats because he was not asking them to vote for military aid to the contras. But his goal of increasing the pressure on the Sandinistas depended very much on the contras receiving that aid from other sources. McCurdy's liberal opponents were at pains to point this out. Congressman Boland insisted that McCurdy's concept of "humanitarian" aid was "a fig leaf. . . . [A]s we all know, the private groups will continue to provide money for arms and ammunition. The effect of [McCurdy's] amendment, and that private aid, is going to be more money for the Contras than they have ever received in the past."[83] Boland argued that the "humanitarian aid" in McCurdy's amendment actually constituted more than "logistical support to an army in the field." In reality, he asserted, it was "difficult to distinguish between logistical support to an armed force in the field that is receiving arms from other sources . . . and direct arming of that force," since the contras could simply use the money they had been spending on logistical support to buy more arms—which is precisely what they did.[84] As Congressman Spratt, a close ally of McCurdy, later admitted, the real purpose of McCurdy's bill was, indeed, "to maintain the contras as a fighting force."[85]

McCurdy's compromise straddled incompatible positions on another point, as well. Many members of his coalition wanted the Reagan administration to begin direct negotiations with the Sandinistas. Reagan officials, however, had little interest in bilateral talks. In a letter to McCurdy on June 11, written at the congressman's request, Reagan stated his reservations: It was possible, he wrote, "that in the proper circumstances, such discussions could help promote the internal reconciliation called for by Contadora and endorsed by many Latin American leaders. . . . However, such talks cannot be a substitute for a church-mediated dialogue between the contending factions. . . . Therefore, I will have our representative meet again with representatives of Nicaragua *only* when I determine that such a meeting would be helpful in promoting these ends."[86] McCurdy gave up trying to get stronger assurances,[87] and his legislation simply "urged" that the President resume the talks, and then only "with a view to encouraging" negotiations between the contras and Sandinistas and a "comprehensive, verifiable" Contadora agreement.

While McCurdy himself did not claim to have exacted any promise from Reagan concerning bilateral negotiations, others in his coalition did.[88] In rising to cast "one of the most agonizing votes" of his career, Congressman Bill Richardson declared he would vote for the McCurdy amendment, in part, "because I think the President of the United States for the first time is saying that he is for negotiations and meaning it. . . . I am willing to give the President of the United States a chance and the benefit of the doubt. I hope and pray he does not let us down."[89]

On June 12 the House approved McCurdy's amendment by a margin of 248–184, with 73 Democrats (59 from the South) joining 175 out of the 182 Republicans. Coming less than two months after the defeat of contra aid in April, the vote was a remarkable turnabout, and the large margin of victory owed much to McCurdy's efforts to bring as many moderates into the deal as possible. Both Democrats and Republicans found safety in numbers.

Just as the unanimous 410–0 vote on the first Boland amendment in December 1982 had proven completely deceptive, however, so the large majority that passed aid to the contras on June 12, 1985, was a deeply divided group, and the "coming together" engineered by McCurdy on this one vote masked a world of different intentions and expectations. Of the 248 members who voted in favor of the winning amendment, about 180 did so with the intention of resuming American support for the contras' war against the Sandinistas and would have voted for military aid if given the chance.[90] But few of the remaining 70–80 members who voted for the McCurdy amendment shared those intentions. Of the 73 Democrats who voted for the McCurdy amendment, no more than 25 were hard-core conservatives.[91] The rest were split between moderate conservatives in the mold of McCurdy and Democrats substantially more liberal than McCurdy. They voted more out of anger and fear than out of conviction, anger at Ortega and fear of the political consequences of voting against aid to the contras.

Political fear played a critical role in pushing moderates further than many might otherwise have gone. During the debate, conservative Virginia Democrat Dan Daniel sternly reminded his more moderate colleagues that their party had been "trampled at the polls" in the presidential election and that "postelection polls indicated that one of the reasons for that political loss was the perception that the Democrats were soft on defense." "If we now fail to oppose the spread of communism in this hemisphere," Daniel warned, "and we are once more perceived to be soft on defense, and communism, then we could be shut out completely in the next election." Senator Nunn called Central America "a great testing ground for our nation and also for the Democratic Party." And even a young moderate like Congressman Richardson believed "it was critical for the Party not to be the typical no response, don't intervene in my country [party.] There was a division in the country. We had just taken a terrific beating with Mondale defeated."[92]

Southern Democrats were particularly susceptible to these arguments, since Reagan had compiled some of his biggest margins in their districts. In Texas, Florida, Oklahoma, North and South Carolina, for instance, all states where Reagan won more than 60 percent of the vote and Mondale less than 40 percent, the effect on House members' votes was most dramatic.[93] In July 1983, the 50 House Democrats in these states had voted 34–16 to cut off all aid to the contras; in June 1985, the 43 Democrats who survived the elections in these states voted 30–12 to restore "humanitarian" aid to the contras.[94] At a time when the Republican Party was making disturbing gains in the "solid South," both at the presidential and congressional levels, southern Democrats were paying especially close attention to their constituents, whom Congressman Spratt of South Carolina described as "pro-military, pro-intervention, and pro-anti-communist."[95] "One of the lessons of 1984," one keen observer of Congress writes, "was that foreign policy issues had domestic consequences; for some members the contra votes posed a critical test before the U.S. electorate of Democrats' willingness to employ military force in fulfilling U.S. global objectives."[96]

Contra aid was only one issue where moderate Democrats sought to redirect their party's foreign policy and change its image in 1985. What McCurdy did for aid to the contras, Les Aspin, a northern moderate, did for the MX missile funding, and Stephen Solarz, a northern liberal, did for aid to anti-communist rebels in Cambodia. In May the Senate voted to provide $5 million in military aid for the non-communist guerrillas in Cambodia, and on July 9 the House passed a similar amendment sponsored by Solarz, 288–122.[97] On June 11, a day before the House passed contra aid, the Senate voted 63–34 to repeal a ten-year-old ban on CIA support for guerrillas in Angola. A month later the House also voted to repeal the ban, 236–185, with 60 Democrats (46 from the South including McCurdy) joining the majority. Aid to the Afghan guerrillas continued with broad support in both parties. Summing up the legislative events of the year, observers noted a "new mood" in Congress, the most visible manifestation of which was "the House's willingness to intervene around the world" on behalf of anti-communist forces. Congressman Hyde traced the beginnings of the new attitude to the October 1983 invasion of Grenada. Congressman Solarz told reporters, "only half-jokingly," that Congress's message was: "we are ready to march on Moscow."[98]

McCurdy's "humanitarian" aid to the contras was only a half-step, however, intentionally designed to give only equivocal support to the anti-communist forces in Nicaragua. Congressman Stewart McKinney, a liberal Republican from Connecticut, characterized the House as divided into three groups: those who "hoped the current conflict in Nicaragua would just go away"; those who "felt we should intervene"; and those who "were terribly afraid of being misinterpreted for either action."[99] It was this third group of moderate southern Democrats and northern Republicans who provided the margin of victory for the legislation to resume American support for the contras' war. It was this third group, moreover, afraid of misinterpretation, that tried to interpret their action to suit their complex political needs. Thus did a Republican liberal like McKinney speak for all the moderates in both parties when he explained the meaning of the legislation just passed: "We do support the Contadora process; we do support humanitarian aid; we do support negotiation; and we want peace talks."[100]

36

"The Administration Would Be Well Advised Not to Push the Law *Too Far*"

If the moderates' purpose in passing "humanitarian" aid to the contras was to foster dialogue, national reconciliation, and peace in Nicaragua and Central America, however, events after the June 12 vote moved in quite the opposite direction. Throughout the summer of 1985 Sandinista and contra forces continued as before trying to inflict as much damage on one another as possible, and they moved no closer to dialogue. Tensions along Nicaragua's borders with Honduras and Costa Rica reached new heights. Within Nicaragua, the Sandinistas cracked down further on their unarmed, political opponents. The Contadora talks all but collapsed when the Sandinistas walked out of the negotiations.

Ironically, the passage of "humanitarian" aid neither benefited the contras' war effort nor brought a respite in the fighting. The new legislation did not reach the President's desk for signature until August, and shipments of U.S. "humanitarian" aid did not begin arriving in Honduras until October. In the summer and early fall of 1985, the contras relied almost exclusively on the money provided by the Saudi king and on the arms and ammunition bought with that money in the first months of the year.[1] Reliance on this kind of support was what members of Congress expected. The most common assumption was that the contras were raising money themselves and buying arms on the international arms market. A less common but still prevalent assumption was that the Reagan administration was facilitating these transactions somehow, as indeed was the case. Earlier in the year reports surfaced in the newspapers of alleged diversions of American aid to El Salvador and Honduras into the hands of the contras. Those reports proved unfounded. The most important source of funds for the contras, the Saudi government, somehow remained secret.

Oliver North's role did not, however. In August, reports in the *Miami Herald* and then in the *New York Times* described in some detail North's increasing efforts to assist the contras since the cutoff of American aid in 1984. On August 8 the *Times* reported that the contras had been "receiving direct military advice" from an official on the National Security Council staff since the summer of 1984. The official met "frequently with rebel leaders in Washington and on trips to Central America," gave "frequent speeches and lectures on the subject of Nicaragua and, when asked, advise[d] people on how they might donate money to the rebel cause." The anonymous officials providing the information were prolific with their comments and judgments. "[Y]ou know our policy is to support them," one official explained, "and that's his job. . . . [W]hen the right people can't manage the operation, you have to look for other alternatives." Another "senior Administration official" told reporters that the contras were this NSC official's "account" and complained that there was "a lot of frustration within the White House, because they do not believe the N.S.C. is the logical place to manage the program. The staff is too small." Oliver North was soon revealed as the man whose "account" was the contras.[2]

Members of Congress reacted slowly and uncertainly to these rather detailed, if anonymous, comments from administration officials. The first congressman to express an opinion on these reports was Congressman George E. Brown, Jr., of California, a liberal Democrat and member of the House intelligence committee. Brown told reporters, "If the President wants to use the N.S.C. to operate a war in Nicaragua, I don't think there's any way we can control it." Brown said he and other intelligence committee members had discussed the operation but hadn't taken "any formal action."[3] The chairman of the Senate Foreign Relations Committee, Senator Lugar, said the National Security Council staff was "carrying out the president's policy." Lugar even said he "knew essentially what the administration was doing, and I approved [of] it."[4] Congressman Brown thought better of his passive stand a day later, when he told reporters "It appears on the surface that the NSC is attempting to circumvent the law. The intent of Congress was clear that all direct involvement with the contras was to be cut off . . . all intelligence-related matters go through the NSC; the question is whether it's considered an intelligence activity. I'm going to ask for very close scrutiny by the intelligence committee and, if there is any evidence, I will ask for hearings."[5]

The House intelligence committee did not rush into action, however. "As a source of opposition," Mary McGrory complained on August 13, "the Democratic House has flopped."[6] On August 14, a private "watchdog" organization, Common Cause, wrote to the two intelligence committee chairmen calling for investigations. Still the committees were slow to respond. Congressman Barnes of the House Foreign Affairs Committee then took it upon himself to write McFarlane seeking "all information, including memoranda and any other documents, pertaining to any contact between Lt. Col. North and Nicaraguan rebels as of enactment of the Boland amendment in October, 1984."[7] McFarlane waited almost a month before responding to Barnes that all actions by the NSC staff had complied "with both the spirit and the letter of the law." There had been no "expenditures of NSC funds which would have the effect of supporting directly or indirectly military or paramilitary operations in Nicaragua by any nation, group, organization, movement or individual." McFarlane further denied any "parallel efforts to provide, directly or indirectly, support for military or paramilitary activities in Nicaragua." On September 30, Barnes wrote back asking McFarlane again to provide the "pertinent documents."[8] McFarlane again delayed.

The House intelligence committee took a very different tack from Barnes. On August 20 Chairman Lee Hamilton wrote McFarlane on August 20 asking for a "full report on the kinds of activities regarding the contras that the NSC carried out and what the legal justification is for such actions given the legislative prohibitions that existed last year and earlier this year."[9] On September 5 Hamilton announced his intention to hold hearings. "It seems to me," he told reporters, "that the N.S.C. is involved in intelligence activities and I don't see how they can escape the Boland amendment." Since North's activities were no longer secret, Hamilton stated his opinion that "[North] had to travel, he had to do some things that involved spending money. If Colonel North was spending money to meet them that is an expenditure of funds. I do not prejudge the question of legality. But I do have questions about whether what they did was in compliance with the Boland Amendment." The administration, Hamilton believed, would have a "tough case to make" to show that it did not violate the law. Unlike Barnes, however, Hamilton made no request for documents. McFarlane responded immediately with a letter to

Hamilton similar to the one he sent Barnes. Seeing that the matter would not die on its own, McFarlane took steps to put out the fire.

On September 5, McFarlane met alone with Senators Durenberger and Leahy of the Senate intelligence committee. After the meeting, Durenberger told reporters "we came away from the meeting feeling that from Bud McFarlane we're getting what he believes to be the situation with regard to his staff. Are we satisfied that this sort of concludes the matter and that no one was in any way involved in directing the effort? No, you can't be satisfied. You can be satisfied with Bud McFarlane telling you the truth as he perceives it. But you can't be satisfied that you know all the factors." Leahy agreed that "Mr. McFarlane told us what he had been told." "I am also satisfied," Leahy told reporters, "that if the law has been broken either in spirit or in fact, it will come out."[10] With this feeble vote of confidence from the Senate committee, McFarlane met on September 10 with Hamilton and the House intelligence committee and repeated his denials. After the meeting, Hamilton said, "I, for one, am willing to take you at your word."[11] The next day, Hamilton canceled his investigation and his plan to hold hearings. He told reporters "It was the testimony of the adviser to the President versus some stories in the press based on undisclosed sources. It was a court with only one witness."[12]

The investigations by the two intelligence committees did not exactly exhaust the investigatory powers at their disposal. On September 12, 31 congressmen wrote Hamilton and Senator Durenberger urging them to pursue their investigation more actively. Hamilton responded on September 18 that "at this time the committee does not have any information to contradict Mr. McFarlane except several unsubstantiated news stories."[13] Hamilton and presumably other members were aware of Congressman Barnes's request for documents and McFarlane's demurral. In response to Barnes's September 30 letter, McFarlane finally invited Barnes to his office to see the documents pulled together by his aides. McFarlane and his staff had discovered six potentially damaging memoranda, mostly written by North, which showed the extent of North's activities and McFarlane's personal awareness of them. McFarlane considered invoking executive privilege, but instead he brought Barnes to his office, without staff, placed a tall stack of documents in front of the congressman, and invited him to look through them. Barnes angrily rejected the offer, telling McFarlane: "You'll hear from us." Barnes was convinced McFarlane was withholding evidence of a possible crime,[14] but he and his small subcommittee lacked the political clout to force the administration to divulge the documents.

Hamilton and the intelligence committee, now aware that Barnes had actually seen a stack of relevant documents, still did not ask McFarlane to make them available to Congress. On October 7 McFarlane responded to a list of further questions from Hamilton, but wrote testily that "this process of constantly responding to unsubstantiated allegations by unnamed individuals" was hampering the effort to bring democracy to Nicaragua. McFarlane expressed the "sincere hope" that his response would "suffice to put this matter to rest."[15] It did, as far as Hamilton was concerned. On October 29, Congressman Barnes made one more attempt to obtain the documents he had seen in McFarlane's office. In his final letter to McFarlane, Barnes requested again that the documents be provided, but this time to the House intelligence committee. Barnes wrote that he had "consulted" with the House leadership, and also with Chairman Hamilton, but McFarlane heard nothing further from Hamilton or from Speaker O'Neill. He simply rebuffed Barnes once again, and there the matter ended.

As in 1982 and 1983, the intelligence committees' passivity in pursuing charges of alleged law-breaking by administration officials had a political context. Divisions in Congress, and within the Democratic Party, restrained Hamilton and other Democrats. In the event of a showdown between the administration and the House intelligence committee, Congressman Brown complained in October, "the vote will be 8 to 8 or even 9 to 7 for the White House." Hamilton agreed that Nicaragua was "a very exceptional case" because Congress was divided along "partisan lines" on how much to constrain the actions of the White House. Hamilton, like Barnes, Leahy, Durenberger, and most other members following the issue, spoke as if they had little doubt they had not been told the whole story by McFarlane. But they did not wish to press the contentious issue that had so recently been settled.[16] Hamilton suggested only that "the Administration would be well advised not to push the law *too far*."[17]

Indeed, far from hounding the administration about North's activities, the House and Senate intelligence committees took steps before, during, and after their investigations to give the administration even greater legal latitude in dealing with the contras. From the end of June to December, the Boland amendment's restrictions on the role of the CIA were loosened in the 1986 intelligence authorization bill to allow the agency to provide training and intelligence information to the contras, so long as such assistance did not "amount to participation in the planning or execution of military or paramilitary operations" or participation in "logistics activities integral to such operations." The language was necessarily imprecise, and even the two intelligence committee chairmen disagreed about what they were permitting.[18] A report by the *Congressional Quarterly* noted that the new language allowed the purchase of radios "that would allow contra leaders at their base camps . . . to receive intelligence information from the United States and to pass that information along to units stationed deep in Nicaragua." Whether or not the passing of such information followed the "intent" of Congress, the CIA was left to "make its own determination of what kinds of information it could provide." The intelligence authorization bill approved in November also allowed the Reagan administration to provide trucks, helicopters, and communications gear to the contras as part of the "humanitarian" assistance, so long as the vehicles were not modified to "be used to inflict serious bodily harm or death." Finally, the House and Senate conferees acquiesced to demands from Reagan officials that the administration be allowed to solicit aid from third countries for the contras. The foreign aid bill approved on July 26 had contained language inserted by Senator Claiborne Pell prohibiting any "understanding, either formal or informal, under which a recipient of U.S. economic or military assistance . . . shall provide assistance of any kind to the contras." Reagan administration officials threatened to veto the whole bill if that language was not changed. Pell agreed to new language which prohibited the administration from conditioning its assistance to another country, "expressly or impliedly," on support for the contras.[19] In the ever-shifting legal terrain shaped by Congress, donations like those of Saudi Arabia, not explicitly prohibited by Congress when first solicited by McFarlane in 1984, possibly illegal when next proffered in 1985, were now, perhaps, possible under the new legislation.[20]

The desire of members of Congress to move away from the divisive contra aid issue was powerful. Laws governing the administration's behavior since October 1984 had been significantly altered. Congress had passed "humanitarian" aid to the contras with the understanding that military aid would come from other sources, and the desire to examine carefully the administration's role in those acquisitions was lacking, except among a handful of liberal Democrats. It was the intent of Congress that the contras continue to apply military pressure on the Sandinistas; it had to be the intent of Congress, as well, that the contras find the weapons with which to carry out their military campaign. With help from the Reagan administration, this is what they did.

37

"I Think We're Surrounded"

Armed with weapons purchased by Richard Secord at the request of Oliver North with Saudi money sent at the request of Robert Mc-Farlane, contra forces throughout the summer launched potent offensives in northern and central Nicaragua. The rhythms of the war in Nicaragua followed a different pattern from the rhythms of the legislative process in Washington. Congress passed aid bills in the spring and early summer, which the President signed in late summer or early fall. The contras began their offensives in the spring when the rainy season started, and ended them in the fall when the rains let up and the roads used by Sandinista troops hardened. By the time the contras received the first penny of "humanitarian" aid voted by Congress, therefore, they had already struck their blows deep inside Nicaragua and were on their way back to the safety of Honduras.

The Sandinistas tried hard to prevent the contra offensives of 1985. The CIA had been predicting a Sandinista attack on contra bases in Honduras since the start of the year, but the Sandinista army waited until the beginning of May to launch what they hoped would be a crushing and demoralizing blow. With several thousand troops up near the border, new roads built northward to support them, artillery in place at the front, tens of thousands of peasants evacuated from both northern and southern border areas, the Sandinistas' preparations had been extensive.[1] Thousands of new draftees had been trained and sent into battle, and even some soldiers from the regular army, hitherto held in reserve, were now sent to the front.[2]

Sandinista forces hit contra units at the end of April as they tried to move from the Las Vegas salient into Nueva Segovia and Jinotega. The contras sustained heavy losses and retreated back into Honduras.[3] In the first week of May, several hundred Sandinista troops entered Honduras in and around the Las Vegas salient, cutting through the contras' customary infiltration routes, and striking at the FDN's main base camp.[4] Preceding the advancing forces was a barrage of artillery rounds fired from Nicaragua into Honduras, striking the contras' camp and its environs and scattering the contra forces. Then elements of several Sandinista light infantry battalions drove to the perimeter of the contras' main camp, forcing the rebels to pull back even deeper into Honduras.[5] As the Sandinista troops withdrew across the border into Nicaragua, they laid mines along the contras' infiltration routes.[6]

The Sandinistas' cross-border raid did not destroy the contras, but with only several hundred Sandinista troops involved in the operation that could not have been its purpose. The Sandinistas' goal was to eliminate the contra threat in 1985, but their strategy was a combination of military, political, and diplomatic tactics. The Sandinistas envisioned nothing so crude as an invasion of Honduran territory, which would have required thousands of troops to destroy the contras in one blow. That option was denied them by American military power and by the Sandinistas' strong belief that President Reagan would not hesitate to use it if given adequate justification. Rather, the Sandinistas' plan was to keep the contras bottled up in Honduras and Costa Rica while pressing on the increasingly vulnerable link of the U.S. policy chain: the contras' unhappy hosts.

The incursion of May 1985 severely embarrassed the Honduran military and government, further shaking already fragile Honduran support for the contras and U.S. policy. The attack not only drew international attention to the presence of several thousand Nicaraguans on Honduran soil, but it drew domestic attention to the Honduran army's apparent inability either to control or protect Honduran territory. The Sandinistas' artillery bombardments had forced about 1,000 Honduran civilians to flee their villages in the area,[7] but the Honduran army had not responded. A few days after the first incursion, Sandinista forces attacked again, this time striking at a Honduran border patrol, killing one Honduran soldier and wounding four others, the first publicly acknowledged Honduran casualties of the Nicaraguan war.[8] Still there was no response. The Honduran army was hampered by lack of adequate transport helicopters to move large numbers of troops to the isolated border area, by lack of maps and communications gear, and by the fact that the Sandinistas held the high ground around the salient.[9] They were hampered still more by their keen desire to keep secret their support for the thousands of contras on their territory, even though this secret had long since become impossible to keep.

The American ambassador in Honduras, John Negroponte, reported after the incursions in May that the contras' presence in Honduras had become "a truly neuralgic point" in U.S.-Honduran relations since the cutoff of U.S. aid to the contras in 1984. The defeat of contra aid in the U.S. Congress at the end of April 1985, followed by the Sandinista incursions in May, left the Honduran government "exposed and carrying what it believes to be an undue share of the burden of confrontation with Nicaragua."[10] The Hondurans were in "dismay" over the damage done to their "international image" by the contras' presence. They "squirm over anything which contributes to a reputation of contributing to regional tensions or serving as a cat's paw for the United States."[11] Their first response was to try to sweep the contras under a rug. After the Sandinistas' incursion, the Honduran military ordered the contras to disperse their forces out of the Las Vegas base camps immediately, both to prevent further Sandinista attacks and to reassert Honduran sovereignty over its own territory. The high command sent 1,000 Honduran troops to the border, not to defend against Sandinista attack, but to supervise the dismantling of contra base camps and their relocation to new "secret" camps further north and east along the border.[12] The new camps were in even more isolated jungle terrain, thus worsening the contras' already difficult supply problems.[13]

After the incursion, the Sandinistas went out of their way to exploit the Hondurans' concerns. Far from denying that their forces crossed the border, Sandinista officials declared that Honduras had brought the attack on themselves. "Sometimes rockets cross the border," Sandinista military intelligence chief Julio Ramos told reporters several days after the raid; Nicaragua had warned Honduras "that any camp that is so close to the border, it is impossible to avoid that once in a while a bullet goes across."[14] Before and after striking into Honduras, the Sandinistas offered to meet with senior Honduran officials to discuss the border problem, and on several occasions meetings between the two sides were held, quietly—

General **Augusto César Sandino** (second from right) in 1931 with his "internationalist" colleagues, including the Salvadoran Communist leader, **Augustín Farabundo Martí** (last on right). (AP/Wide World)

General **Anastasio Somoza García**, President of Nicaragua, riding with President **Franklin Delano Roosevelt** during a 1939 visit to Mount Vernon. President Roosevelt is alleged to have said of Somoza: "He's a son-of-a-bitch, but he's our son-of-a-bitch." (AP/Wide World)

Pedro Joaquín Chamorro, editor of *La Prensa*, outspoken opponent of the Somoza dynasty. His assassination in January 1978 shook the Somoza regime to its foundations. (AP/Wide World)

Four of the five members of the original government junta that replaced the Somoza dictatorship in July 1979. From left to right: **Sergio Ramírez, Violeta Chamorro, Alfonso Robelo,** and **Daniel Ortega.** This picture was taken in San Jose, Costa Rica on July 14 — four days before the junta was to take power in Managua. (The missing junta member was Moisés Hassán.) (AP/Wide World)

Deposed Nicaraguan President **Anastasio Somoza Debayle**, speaking to reporters in Miami on July 17. He had fled Nicaragua early that morning. (AP/Wide World)

President **Jimmy Carter** greets **Daniel Ortega** (in uniform), **Alfonso Robelo** (far left) and **Sergio Ramírez** (far right) at the White House. At the September 24 meeting, Carter said: "If you don't hold me responsible for everything that occurred under my predecessors, I will not hold you responsible for everything that occurred under your predecessors." (AP/Wide World)

(Left) **Edén Pastora**, the Sandinista guerrilla leader who led the assault on the National Palace in August 1978. Shortly after the Sandinistas took power, the disillusioned Pastora became an anti-Sandinista guerrilla leader but had no similar successes. (AP/Wide World)

(Below) **Arturo Cruz**, campaigning in Boaco for the presidency of Nicaragua in 1984. The day this picture was taken, September 22, Cruz was attacked by about 300 Sandinista militants, who threw rocks at his car in breaking up his political rally. Cruz eventually dropped out of the campaign and in 1985 became a leader of the contra rebels. (AP/Wide World)

Contra task force commander, "Kaliman." Under Edén Pastora, he commanded 100 men in the fight against Somoza on the Sandinistas' southern front from 1978 to 1979. After the revolutionary victory he became a lieutenant in the Sandinista army, but in September 1980 he deserted the army and left for Costa Rica. He later emerged as one of the top commanders in the contras' Southern Front. (AP/Wide World)

Two Faces of the Contras

A 14-year-old Nicaraguan named Miguel from the province of Leon poses on a jungle trail along the Rio Bocay, six kilometers from the Honduran border. "I am fighting," he told the photographer, "because I love my country." May 4, 1987. (AP/Wide World)

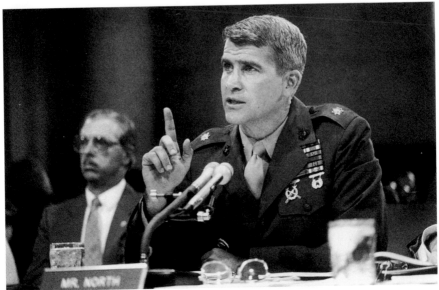

Lt. Col. **Oliver North**, testifying before congressional committees investigating the Iran-Contra affair, July 7, 1987. As two senators on the committee later recalled, the contest between "one Marine against twenty-six lawyer-politicians . . . wasn't even close. North held a Gatling gun while we sat like ducks in a shooting gallery. The American people loved it." (AP/Wide World)

An unusual summit meeting between Speaker of the House **Jim Wright** (left) and Secretary of State **George Shultz** (right) to settle disputes over Wright's intervention in U.S.-Nicaraguan relations. Democratic power-broker **Robert Strauss** (center) had to be called in to bring the two men together. (AP/Wide World)

Costa Rican President **Oscar Arias** meets with President **George Bush**, April 4, 1989. (AP/ Wide World)

Violeta Chamorro campaigning for the presidency on February 11, 1990. Her unexpected victory over Daniel Ortega was two weeks away. (AP/Wide World)

Sandinista Defense Minister **Humberto Ortega,** posing with the author under a portrait of Sandino after interview in May 1990.

a source of concern to the Americans. While Ambassador Negroponte was "reasonably confident" that the Hondurans' "basically helpful position" toward the contras remained firm, he warned Washington that the Honduran government had delivered the "not-so-subtle message . . . that a negotiating option" was available to them "if sufficient help for the FDN and assurances of various kinds to the [Government of Honduras]" were not forthcoming from the United States.[15]

The Sandinistas pursued the same strategy in the south, along the border with Costa Rica, though with greater military force and more ambitious aims. At the end of May, the Sandinista army and air force launched a large offensive against troops led by Edén Pastora along the San Juan River on the Costa Rican border with the aim of wiping out those much smaller forces altogether. Heavy shelling and aerial bombardment of Pastora's positions on both sides of the border and of the small landing strip at La Penca scattered the several hundred contra forces operating in the region, and several thousand Sandinista infantry troops closed in to mop up.[16] Sandinista forces chased the contras into Costa Rica, prompting Costa Rican President Monge to denounce the new Nicaraguan "aggression."[17] In Costa Rica as in Honduras, however, anger at the Sandinistas mingled with discontent and embarrassment at playing host to the contras, and this discomfort was precisely what Humberto Ortega hoped to exploit. "We cannot go into Honduras or Costa Rica," he told a reporter, ". . . [but] the presence of the contras in Costa Rica and Honduras creates problems for Honduras and Costa Rica because the contras are not going to defeat us."[18]

It was a subtle strategy that required careful weighing of the risks of American retaliation, and over the course of 1985 and 1986 Ortega gambled several times, probing the limits of American tolerance. In May 1985 the Reagan administration did little to publicize the attacks on Honduras, fearing that government's response to international publicity. After the attack against contra positions in Costa Rica, the White House spokesman warned the Sandinistas "to halt immediately any further military operations against its neighbors" and expressed concern "at signs of increased aggressive behavior by the Government of Nicaragua."[19]

The Sandinistas' cross-border raids caused barely a stir in the United States. The Reagan administration's warning came on June 4, a week before the moderates voted to support renewed aid to the contras, but the Sandinistas' military actions were not even mentioned in the congressional debate. Reagan was a long way from building a case for direct

American retaliation, and the Sandinistas knew it. Although the Sandinistas dramatically moved their Soviet-made T-55 tanks into positions around Managua, León and, Chinandega, and although Daniel Ortega declared that "if the U.S. troops intervene, we will be ready to resist and win,"[20] the Sandinista army continued its operations against the contras along the borders.

For the contras and the Americans, there were two answers to Humberto Ortega's political-military strategy: win congressional support for the contras to reassure the Hondurans and, more importantly, move as many contra troops as possible out of Honduras and Costa Rica and back into Nicaragua to fight. At the end of April, no more than 2,000–3,000 contras held positions in Nicaragua, one cluster of about 1,000 in the area of eastern Jinotega, northeastern Matagalpa, and central Zelaya,[21] another cluster of several hundred in the central provinces of Boaco and Chontales,[22] a few hundred more scattered in the northwestern provinces of Nueva Segovia and Madriz, and a few hundred in southern Zelaya.

The Sandinistas had launched their attacks at the very end of the dry season, a time of advantage for an army still heavily dependent on dirt roads for ferrying supplies to forward troops. When the roads turned to mud, it was the time for guerrillas to move. Even as moderates in the U.S. Congress prepared to vote in the spring for "humanitarian" aid to bring peace to Nicaragua, therefore, the contras had begun infiltrating large numbers of fighters back into Nicaragua in preparation for a new rebel offensive. That offensive began shortly after McCurdy passed his bill.

In regrouping and preparing for their June 1985 offensive, the contras faced a two-fold problem. The Sandinistas had mined or blocked with troops many of the old infiltration routes into the northwestern provinces, especially in Nueva Segovia, Madriz, and western Jinotega, where in 1984 the contras had raised such havoc and even exerted significant control with support from the local population. The Sandinistas had run roads up to the border along the Bocay valley, north from Wiwili and northeast from Murra. Even if the Honduran army hadn't forced a large number of contras to move north and east along the border, placing them across from northeastern Jinotega and Zelaya, the contras would have had to find some new routes into Nicaragua. The result was that in May and June of 1985 most of the contras' task forces had to enter Nicaragua some 200 kilometers further east than in previous years, down through northeastern Jinotega and Zelaya into sparsely populated country along the eastern slope of the hills and mountains that cut through the middle of the country. Even this was no easy task. One contra task force tried to infiltrate at the beginning of June along the banks of the Bocay river, 200 kilometers east of the Las Vegas salient, and was reportedly met and turned back by Sandinista troops.[23] Others had similar difficulties. Once inside the country, there was still no safe refuge, as the more mobile Sandinista forces, complete with air support, struck at any large concentrations of rebels they could find.

The contras' plan of attack, which Sandinista military officials referred to as "Rebellion 85," was to move several thousand troops into the country, link up with the forces that had hunkered down in remote areas along the eastern slope of the hills and mountains that divided northern Nicaragua, and then swing northwest over the mountains toward Matagalpa and Estelí and southeast toward the central provinces of Boaco and Chontales, where other forces were awaiting resupply. By far the largest part in this plan was to be played by the Jorge Salazar Operational Command. Under the overall leadership of "Quiche," the Jorge Salazar force had grown so large from absorbing recruits and other task forces that it had been divided into two large Regional Commands led by "Rigoberto," the former MILPAS fighter, and "Franklyn," the former small farmer from Matagalpa.[24] The Jorge Salazar Command had become not only the largest force within the FDN, but with its two non-Guardia leaders— "Rigoberto" and "Franklyn"—it had emerged as a potent political force in rural Nicaragua.

The June offensive began badly for the contras. The forces of the Jorge Salazar Command had been inside Nicaragua for weeks awaiting resupply, but in April and May, Sandinista forces hit their camp at Cerro Verde in Central Zelaya and forced them to disperse and regroup further north before they could be reached by the reinforcements sent down from Honduras. Those reinforcements, the Andres Castro Regional Command led by "Dimas," were hit by the Sandinistas on their way to the scene of fighting. According to Sandinista reports, the situation for the contra forces in the interior "turned desperate." "Every day they asked for reinforcements from Honduras. . . . Besides reinforcements, they requested food, ammunition and boots." Contra forces bringing fresh supplies, however, were trapped by Sandinista Light Infantry Battalions and had to split up. By the time they arrived to join the forces they had been sent to help, "they were tired and had very little material." The contra forces continued to receive strict orders not to take on Sandinista forces, but to lie low and disperse. Some forces began heading northward again. On June 6, *Barricada* reported that the area once occupied by the Jorge Salazar Operational Command had been cleared. The Sandinista party newspaper noted triumphantly that this "'Jorge Salazar' operational command had become the counterrevolution's strategic force within Nicaragua and as such would have played the main role in the so-called 'final offensive' to be unleashed in mid-June."[25]

Barricada's optimism proved premature. The contras' plans were disrupted, but fierce fighting continued in the area of San José de Bocay and El Cua into late June, with both sides taking heavy casualties. The struggle for control of the Bocay valley was of vital importance, since for the contras it was both an infiltration route and a potential staging ground for attacks in the northwest. The Sandinistas fought hard—one of Humberto Ortega's aides was killed in the fighting—but the rainy season took its toll. At the end of June the Sandinistas' regional subcommander told *Barricada* that "operational conditions" were "hazardous." Sandinista troops "depended on airborne and land operations under conditions which have been extremely adverse, due to the intense rainfall in that zone at this time of year." Moreover, Sandinista commanders found that "there are still some civilians supporting the mercenaries, either out of ignorance or fear."[26]

By the beginning of July it was clear that the Sandinistas had failed to block the reinfiltration of at least 3,000 contra forces from Honduras, and several hundred from Costa Rica, and would soon begin paying the price.[27] At the end of June, rebel forces of the Segovia Regional Command returned to make trouble in their old strongholds in Nueva Segovia and Jinotega and, according to Sandinista reports, were attempting to cut the lines of communication to northern towns and villages in the area with the support of other contra forces operating south of Quilali in Jinotega.[28] In the third week of July, the Sandinista army reported more than 90 clashes over the previous month with contra forces in Military Regions I and VI, comprising the provinces of Neuva Segovia, Madriz, Estelí, Jinotega, and Matagalpa.[29] Another contra force of over 1,000, the Diriangen Regional Command, which had at various times been led by former National Guard officers "Mike Lima" and "Benny," had entered Jinotega in the middle of July and made its way westward toward the province of Estelí and its capital of the same name, according to the Sandinista regional commander.[30] By the end of the month, the Diriangen Regional Command was ambushing Sandinista army trucks and blowing up bridges on the outskirts of Estelí.[31] On August 1, FDN forces destroyed a bridge on the road between

Sébaco and San Isidro southeast of Estelí in western Matagalpa, temporarily cutting off the Pan American highway and isolating a number of towns in Madriz and Nueva Segovia Departments.[32]

That same day, the Sandinista Defense Ministry reported heavy fighting at La Trinidad, a town of 8,000 people 13 kilometers southeast of Estelí. Some 200 contras had entered the town in the morning and surprised the local militia.[33] Residents told reporters that the contra troops had swarmed over the hills around the town at dawn and then engaged in a three-hour fire-fight with Sandinista militia and later Sandinista army reinforcements before taking control of the center of the town. "The contras had this town for several hours this morning," a woman told reporters, and a Sandinista official in Estelí called the fighting in the region "the most serious we have seen around here" since the start of the war in 1982.[34] From the air base at Estelí the Sandinistas sent light planes and Mi-24 helicopters to bomb the contras' positions and drive them out of La Trinidad.[35] By August 5, the Sandinista regional commander reported that the army and air force had broken up the contras' assault on Estelí and charged that the contras were "carrying out offensive actions deep into Nicaragua in an attempt to portray before the world that they are strong."[36]

On the same day that the Diriangen forces attacked La Trinidad and the roads around Estelí, the Jorge Salazar Regional Command struck at a small village called Cuapa, some 200 kilometers to the south in Chontales province. The August 1 attack on Cuapa became both famous and notorious. It was famous for the blow it struck so deep inside Nicaragua and the proof this provided of the contras' presence in the geographical heart of the country, and notorious for the manner in which the blow was struck. The rebels swept into Cuapa in the early morning, overrunning the small Sandinista militia garrison. The Sandinistas sent a truckload of reinforcements, but the contras ambushed the truck, killing most of the 40 soldiers, who turned out to be local boys just recently drafted into the army.[37] The contras took charge of the town and called residents into the main square. "They said they were going to march to Managua," one resident told reporters. "They said they represented Christianity and democracy." The contras asked the townspeople about the town mayor, who had been appointed by the Sandinistas. The mayor, a native of Cuapa, was well liked: "We told them he had done some good things for the town," one man told reporters.[38] The contras rounded up eight other Sandinista officials, not natives of Cuapa, including local Sandinista Defense Committee officials, marched them along with the mayor out into the woods, set the mayor free and executed the rest.[39]

The execution of the eight local officials became one of the most frequently cited examples of the contras' murderous treatment of civilians, all the more so since at least one of the contras involved called himself "Atila" and was a former National Guardsman.[40] Such executions were hardly rare, but this event was special because of the numbers involved and the publicity it received in the United States. Attacks like that on Cuapa were common in Chontales, according to local residents. Squads of contras often descended into villages, killed or kidnapped local Sandinista officials and military recruiters, and held political meetings for the villagers. Perhaps more remarkable than the killings themselves was that the contras had asked the townspeople their opinion of the Sandinista-appointed mayor and abided by it.[41] For the contras, it remained not only standard practice but publicly declared policy to execute local Sandinista officials.

Despite such abuses, the forces of Jorge Salazar operating in Boaco and Chontales were in friendly territory, so much so that by August they had established a base from which they could not be dislodged by Sandinista army or air force. American journalists visited the region in August and wrote that the people who lived in these provinces "considered themselves frontier people, cowboys and hillbillies who loved open spaces and bridled at government regulation. Many sympathized with the contras, which meant that contra units operating there had sources of food and shelter that they did not have in other areas."[42] Local ranchers and farm workers told reporters "that on at least two occasions in recent weeks brigades of contras numbering several hundreds had arrived peacefully at ranches in Chontales and had been given permission to rest overnight."[43]

The Sandinista commander in charge of the Boaco and Chontales region, Roberto Calderón, tried to explain that while some peasants supported the contras and even took up arms with them, "we would not say the peasant is a political or ideological enemy of the revolution, or that he is convinced because he is carrying a weapon."[44] But the Sandinistas knew they had problems with the rural population, and not just in the ranchlands of Boaco and Chontales. Tomás Borge noted that many of the contras who attacked La Trinidad and the roads around Estelí were young boys who had evaded the draft, been sent to Honduras by their parents, and then joined the contras. But he insisted that the number of youths joining the army was still higher than the number of draft evaders joining the contras.[45] In Chontales the roads were not safe.[46] One resident in the town of La Libertad, a Sandinista military base 30 kilometers east of Cuapa, told reporters: "The roads are too dangerous to use, so people don't leave town. Nobody knows where the contras are, but . . ." "But what?" a reporter asked. "But I think we're surrounded."[47]

Although Sandinista officials after every battle claimed to have "eliminated," "annihilated," or "neutralized" contra forces in Estelí, Chontales, and Boaco, the clashes continued. In the first week of August senior Sandinista officials called the contra attacks publicity stunts, designed to create the "image of active belligerency in areas that have important roads and where they had not previously acted."[48] But a week later the Defense Ministry reported that the army was preparing for yet another rebel offensive against Estelí, and Comandante Luis Carrión Cruz was dispatched to organize the defense of the province.[49] During the first three weeks of August, the FDN reported 99 clashes with Sandinista forces: 31 in Jinotega, where the battle for the Bocay valley and contra infiltration routes continued; 23 in Chontales, where the Jorge Salazar Regional Commands were moving in and out of villages and setting ambushes on the roads; 18 in Matagalpa, connected to the fighting in both Jinotega and Estelí; 12 in Estelí itself; the rest in central Zelaya, Boaco, Madriz, and even León.[50] On August 24, the Sandinista army announced it was beginning "a second phase of massive attacks against approximately 4,400 anti-Sandinistas mobilized mainly in the country's north-central region." This second phase meant increasing Sandinista forces along the Honduran border to prevent the continuing reinfiltration of contras as well as increasing the number of forces assigned to fight the contras "deep inside Nicaraguan territory."[51] The large Sandinista army and militias were being stretched thin.

The second phase of the Sandinista army's counteroffensive led to another confrontation with Honduras. On September 13, according to a communiqué released by the Sandinistas, approximately 800 contras were attempting to infiltrate into Nueva Segovia through the Las Vegas salient with "Honduran army troops and the Honduran Air Force" providing cover fire. Sandinista ground and airborne forces fought all day to repel the infiltration. In the afternoon the Honduran air force launched strikes against the Sandinista forces inside Nicaraguan territory.[52] The Honduran government's story was only a little different. President Suazo announced that the Honduran air force had struck positions in Nicaragua and shot down a Sandinista helicopter, but only after a Sandinista mortar attack against positions inside Honduras killed at least one Honduran soldier and seriously wounded eight others.[53] On September 14 the Honduran government declared a state of alert for land, sea, and air forces, President Suazo called an emergency session of the National Congress, and in an evening address on television and radio told the nation that the Honduran air force, in a limited defensive action, had repelled a Nicaraguan invasion.[54]

Whether the Sandinistas "invaded" or only fired mortar shells across the border was of less importance than the aggressive posture assumed by the Honduran military, in stark contrast to its behavior in May. Clearly, the Honduran military had decided to provoke an exchange by letting the contras pass through the salient and by providing cover fire for them. Whether or not the Hondurans' new-found confidence was due to the presence of large numbers of American soldiers in Honduran territory, the bombing of Nicaraguan positions was a shot across the Sandinistas' bow and a sign that the United States had, at least for the moment, improved its difficult relationship with the Honduran government.

Meanwhile the fighting around Estelí and Chontales continued. On September 20, the Sandinistas reported resettling 200 peasant families to cooperatives from their homes in Estelí, a sign of the contras' strength in the area.[55] General Joaquín Cuadra reported that 4,500 contras were in action in the northern and central regions of the country, with 2,500 more prepared to move in from Honduras against Estelí. The contras' aim, according to Cuadra, was to divide the Sandinista army between the fighting in Chontales and the conflict in Estelí, 200 kilometers to the north, and then try to occupy the northern city and take control of the Pan-American highway.[56] The Honduran army continued to play a supporting role in this latest offensive. According to Cuadra, the Hondurans had placed four infantry battalions, three artillery battalions, and several armored units up near the border, thus protecting contra forces from further Sandinista attempts to disrupt their infiltration.[57]

Such was the military state of affairs in Nicaragua near the end of October when "humanitarian" aid from the United States was only just beginning to trickle in to contra camps in Honduras. October was the last month of the rainy season, and the Sandinistas welcomed the reprieve. "The dry season will come soon," Humberto Ortega said, "and it will be much easier to act against the enemy because we will be able to use our means of transportation, and deployment will be much easier."[58] Indeed, the onset of the dry season, and continuing supply problems on the contras' side, forced the guerrillas to pull back from their offensive in the last two months of 1985, regardless of the new flow of American aid. A significant portion of the troops began withdrawing back into Honduras, much to the chagrin of the Reagan administration and the Honduran government.

———

The contras' summer offensive was another rude shock to the Sandinistas, but the future looked better to Humberto Ortega for the first time in over a year. Ortega was particularly pleased with the advances made in the air with the new Soviet helicopters, perhaps the most significant military development in the war. During the fighting at La Trinidad and Estelí, he noted, the helicopters had played a critical role, and he cited as the army's principal advance over 1984 the introduction of "the different types of helicopters that we needed to support counterinsurgency operations, combat helicopters and support helicopters."[59] The contras agreed: the Soviet helicopter gunships were terrifying weapons for rebel forces in Nicaragua as in Afghanistan.

Another advance over the previous year was the enormous growth of the Sandinista armed forces, now believed to number over 60,000 men, a growth Ortega considered of "strategic" significance. Still more were needed. "In the next few weeks and months," Ortega declared in the middle of August, "we are going to mobilize thousands of additional men because only through massive mobilization of the people will we be able to quickly end the war." At the end of August *Barricada* printed the names of 4,000 youths who had to report for their physicals, and on September 2 Ortega officially announced resumption of the draft which had been suspended for four months.[60]

A third improvement over the previous year was the Sandinistas' successful relocation of the rural population in the north, which had been so helpful to the contras in 1984. Thousands of peasants who the Sandinistas believed supported the contras were now in "relocation camps." Other thousands were benefiting from changes in the agrarian reform program which were beginning to give them a stake in the revolution. Finally, almost all northern peasants, who in 1984 had seen contras much more frequently than government troops in their remote hills, now saw mostly Sandinista army uniforms. "Peasants that were confused because the revolution had not reached them," Humberto Ortega explained, "or because we had committed errors, or because they feared the armed presence of the counterrevolutionaries coming from abroad, [those peasants] willingly or by force joined the counterrevolution. . . . [But] just a couple of thousand were affected, and now they are affected less severely because the peasant sees the revolution and how we are hitting the counterrevolution."[61]

The contras, with their support structure thus severely weakened in traditional strongholds, had been forced to move into new areas like Estelí and Chontales, and so their successes in these areas were signs of both strength and weakness. In the new regions, the contras had to begin from nothing to establish their presence, instead of building on networks and relationships already in place. In effect, the contras had lost an entire year of development, and Humberto Ortega, at least, was confident that they could not replicate their earlier successes. Most of the contras were natives of Nueva Segovia, Jinotega, and Matagalpa; many fewer were from Estelí and Chontales. From the Sandinistas' point of view, the only serious problem arising from the battles of 1985 was the establishment by the Jorge Salazar forces of a near-permanent base in the center of the country.

Humberto Ortega declared optimistically in October that "we have brought [the contras] to a defensive situation, a situation in which they do not have any prospects for strategic, military, and political development because they do not have their own social base for that. . . . From the military point of view, even though we have not exterminated them— and we think that will take time—they cannot, on their own, become an army capable of defeating us. That is impossible."[62]

———

Humberto Ortega knew better than anyone, however, that wars were not won by military means alone. Earlier in the year, the Sandinistas had invited two Salvadoran guerrilla leaders to study the war against the contras and recommend improvements in the Sandinistas' counterinsurgency efforts. The Salvadorans did not paint an optimistic picture. One told his "Nicaraguan comrades" that they were "in a situation like Mozambique with South Africa." The war would drag on, and with American economic pressure the Sandinistas could be "slowly strangled."[63] Even Humberto Ortega acknowledged that the Sandinistas would probably never obliterate the rebels entirely but would have "to coexist" with them so long as the United States continued to provide aid.[64]

The Sandinistas understood from their own experience that all that was required for guerrillas to win was for the government to lose. In 1985

Sandinista leaders sometimes talked about losing. Ortega's rival, Tomás Borge, had said in April that "the only revolutions which have been defeated . . . are those which have been destroyed by the revolutionaries themselves. Revolutions are immortal provided the revolutionaries act in accordance with the laws of historical development."[65] To Borge, this meant hewing more closely to Marxist-Leninist principles and not succumbing to the threats and entreaties of the bourgeois imperialists. It also meant not giving in to bourgeois notions of "popular support."

Humberto Ortega was more worried about losing the support of important sectors of the population. "Why does the United States want to aid the contras at this time when they know that they are strategically defeated?" Ortega asked. Because "they want them to continue to pressure us, to economically weaken us, to distract us militarily so that we will not consolidate our Army." The contras were going to "continue wearing us down" while Reagan tried to "completely drown our economy" until a "dissatisfied and disgusted people will turn against the revolution and that will be the end of the revolution."[66]

The deterioration of the Nicaraguan economy, which so concerned Ortega, had begun accelerating in 1984. By 1985 Sandinista leaders were flatly acknowledging that the economy was in crisis. During the early eighties, when the high price of oil and low price of export commodities depressed the economies of all Latin America, Nicaragua's economic problems did not stand out. Large amounts of foreign aid in the first two or three years masked weaknesses in the economy's productive capacity. But by 1984 the foreign aid had fallen dramatically, and when the other Central American countries began to pull out of their recessions, Nicaragua did not. Latin American countries averaged a 2.6 percent growth rate in 1984; Nicaragua's rate was 0.5. The low growth rate, combined with the high rate in the growth of the Nicaraguan population, resulted in a plummeting level of per capita gross national product. By the end of 1984, Nicaragua's per capita GNP hovered around 500 dollars; in the Western Hemisphere, only Haiti's, Bolivia's, and Honduras's were lower.[67]

Nicaragua's debt of $4.5 billion, half of it owed to American banks, was requiring yearly interest and amortization payments of nearly $300 million dollars. The Sandinistas did not want to default, but by 1985 Nicaragua had nevertheless become the first country ever to fall six months in arrears to the World Bank. In June of 1985, Nicaragua signed an agreement with the private banks to pay $15 million over the next year, while delaying the rest of the payments for one year. The agreement avoided default, but Nicaragua became one of a handful of countries declared "value impaired" by American bank regulators.[68] In addition, the Sandinistas still had not paid for past oil shipments from Mexico, a debt amounting to some $300 million. Without oil the Sandinista army, increasingly dependent on trucks and helicopters, would grind to a halt; only the intercession of the Soviet Union had filled the gap left by Mexico.

Even without the debt burden, Nicaragua's estimated $460 million in annual exports fell well short of the more than $700 million it needed to import raw materials and keep the economy afloat. "The low prices of our export products," Daniel Ortega told his fellow Nicaraguans in February 1985, "the financial obligations imposed by our creditors, and the economic damage caused by U.S. attacks have resulted in a shortage of foreign exchange. This has resulted in limitations in obtaining raw materials, spare parts, machinery, medicines, food, and basic products, all of which are vital resources for production and our people's survival."[69]

The Sandinistas' answer to these problems from the beginning of 1985 had been to impose a traditional, "capitalist" austerity program. They tried to boost exports and cut government spending; they tried to remove price supports to cut spending and stimulate production, but without raising wages so much as to spark hyper-inflation and increase the price of exported goods. Nothing much worked, however. Exports fell, in part because shortages of foreign exchange prevented the purchase of enough fertilizer and machinery for the growing and harvesting of crops, and so crop yields fell. Industrial production also declined sharply in 1985.

The cuts in government spending, meanwhile, caused pain and anger at home, especially among those in Nicaragua who had been loyal to the revolution because they were the beneficiaries of the very programs now being cut. Over the course of 1985 the government reduced subsidies of foods, which earlier in the revolution had aided the cities at the expense of the countryside. And from February to May of 1985, prices were allowed to rise some 333 percent for major consumer goods. Wages were raised also, but not enough to keep up with this inflation. "The worker will not enter paradise," Sandinista Directorate-member Carlos Nuñez stated after one large wage hike in February 1985. "[W]e must at least offer our people our basic products and tell them that this is all. . . . We must also abandon social programs that are not related to defense and face new sacrifices." Nuñez hoped the government would thereby "maintain the authority, respect, and leadership of a government before its people by telling them the truth."[70] The truth, however, was not welcome.

The wage hikes were criticized by Nicaraguan businessmen as inflationary, and by "leftists" and union leaders as insufficient. On the day the increases were considered in the National Assembly, opposition parties from the far left to the far right walked out and left the Sandinista deputies to pass the measure themselves.[71]

While the wage increases satisfied no one, the huge price increases still did not put more food and consumer goods in the stores. A flourishing black market provided some rare items, although at prices even higher than those set by the government. The government tried again and again to crack down on the "parasites," "gouging merchants," and "speculators" who continued to benefit from the shortages and the price increases.[72] These "gouging merchants," however, included tough old ladies in Managua's Eastern Market, and the Sandinistas' efforts to crack down on these "speculators" aroused popular protests and were repeatedly rebuffed by the market women themselves, sometimes by force.

The state of the Nicaraguan economy had reached crisis proportions before the United States imposed its trade embargo in May, but the embargo made an already dreadful economic situation worse. The Sandinistas had to lower the prices of their diminishing exports—bananas, coffee, cotton, seafood, and meat—in order to open new markets, but this in turn reduced foreign exchange earnings needed to buy more raw materials for the next plantings. Contrary to Shultz's expectations, the embargo really did hurt the Sandinistas, economically and politically. Some observers saw virtue in Nicaragua's economic straits. The *Times'* Stephen Kinzer wrote at the beginning of June that perhaps the American embargo would "provide the Sandinistas with an opportunity to do what they have always wanted to do: pull Nicaragua out of the American orbit completely. . . . There may well come a time when Nicaragua will need almost nothing from the United States. That is a measure of independence to which many Latin American countries have aspired."[73] The price of independence, however, was poverty.

The Sandinistas' allies in the socialist countries could not offer much help to compensate for the lack of American aid and trade. Even under Andropov, the Soviet Union had made clear that subsidization of the economies of friendly governments, never very large, would vanish. Soviet officials were tending more and more to offer only friendly advice to allies—and their advice more often than not was to move toward free markets and to integrate themselves into the Western economy. The socialist bloc had little hard currency to spare to buy Nicaraguan goods, and except for meeting Nicaragua's oil needs, the Soviet Union and Eastern bloc had little to offer Daniel Ortega during his trip in May. Ortega had to return to Managua with the sobering report that "the socialist countries will not solve Nicaragua's problems."[74] During his travels through Western Europe, Ortega's pleas for help attracted little new aid. He won agreement from the Italian government to build a power plant in Nicaragua; Finland promised $10 million in aid over three years; Yugoslavia agreed to provide "cultural, educational and scientific-technical cooperation." But West Germany could not be persuaded to resume the aid it had cut off after the 1984 elections; and worse still, even socialist Spain cut its small aid program.[75]

Humberto Ortega told an American reporter in October that "when a real revolution has been made, the people understand that they must sacrifice much in order not to surrender."[76] In his own mind, however, Ortega had to know that the Nicaraguan people's commitment to sacrifice on behalf of the revolution was in doubt. Tomás Borge knew it and attributed this lack of commitment to the requirements of *Tercerismo*, to the need to bend and distort the revolution to appease imperialism. The pressure from the United States under Reagan had forced the Sandinistas, "independently from our will, to develop political pluralism and a mixed economy." Once only a "tactic," the mixed economy had by necessity become a "strategy." This, in turn, had made "much more difficult the role of the revolutionary leadership within the masses. Political pluralism, mixed economy, and the more general traits of the revolution tend to confuse the masses." It would have been better to pursue "an ideological project which is as clearly defined as the one that existed in Cuba," but this had proven impossible.[77]

Borge spoke as if he believed that the revolution, at least the revolution he fought for, had already failed. "Originally, the Sandinista Front had conceived of a different kind of revolution," Borge said a few months later. "In ideal terms, it would be a deeply radical revolution, even at some point reaching the abolition of private property, a revolution within the classically socialist framework. But reality taught us that in the special conditions of Nicaragua, this was not possible."[78] No doubt Borge's bitterness at losing power to the Ortega brothers contributed to his pessimism, but the accuracy of his analysis was hard to refute. The reality was that great numbers of Nicaraguans did *not* understand the need for more sacrifice, and the majority would sacrifice only if given no choice by the government.

The continuing war with the contras thus posed a serious problem even if the contras remained far from any conceivable military victory. The enemies of the revolution—economic, political, religious, and military—were multiplying and increasingly acting in concert, or so it seemed to the Sandinistas. On May 1 the two independent unions had celebrated May Day with a demonstration and a mass, led by Archbishop Obando, at El Calvario church near the market—the so-called "church of the market vendors." Here were three potent political and economic forces united in their common opposition to the Sandinistas. The Sandinistas found the demonstration so intolerable that they sent the Sandinista police, not even the *turbas*, to break it up.[79]

The Sandinistas' most powerful unarmed opponent was also the one least vulnerable to government pressure. Nicaraguans angry at the government needed a symbol to rally around, a means of venting their anger, and as Ortega rightly noted, that symbol was neither Calero, nor Robelo, nor Bolaños, nor even Arturo Cruz. It was the Catholic church and the church's leader, Obando y Bravo. Obando's popularity alone posed a serious problem for the Sandinistas; what was unacceptable, however, was Obando's use of his great influence on behalf of the contras and against the revolution. Obando had already supported the contras by praising the March 1 San José proposal and by offering the Church's services as mediator to a negotiation the Sandinistas firmly rejected—the same role he had once played on behalf of the Sandinistas in their struggle against Somoza.

On May 25, another enemy of the Sandinistas, Pope John Paul II, struck a blow by elevating Archbishop Obando to cardinal, an unprecedented event for Central America. When Cardinal Obando y Bravo returned triumphantly to Managua, he was greeted at Sandino airport by the largest spontaneous demonstration of popular support since the Pope's own arrival in 1983. The demonstration's political character was unmistakable: The cardinal was cheered not just as head of the Nicaraguan Catholic church but as a symbol of anti-Sandinism. The crowd of over 100,000 jeered at one truckload of Sandinista police, while another group of police was pelted with rocks when it used fire hoses to disperse an unruly crowd near the airport. The blue and white flag of pre-Sandinista Nicaragua flew everywhere. As the cardinal made his way through the crowd that lined the road into Managua, for nine hours on the back of a pick-up truck, a young man with a megaphone walked in front shouting "Do you want communism?" "No!" the crowd shouted back. "Do you want Christianity?" "Yes!" A Nicaraguan in the crowd told reporters that "the Cardinal has his people too, people who are against the government."[80] The following Sunday, the Sandinista government banned the regular weekly broadcast of Cardinal Obando's mass and homily over Radio Catolica.[81]

Some bishops in the rural areas of Nicaragua did not hesitate to show their hostility to the government and their sympathy for the contras. During the heavy fighting in Jinotega at the end of August, the bishop of Jinotega attacked the government in a homily, saying "We want no more indiscriminate aerial bombardments, killing campesinos in our mountains."[82] Humberto Ortega was forced to respond at a press conference, "I really don't know what the bishop was talking about . . . perhaps he was talking about Somoza times, because the sights of our shrapnels and helicopters are well directed toward CIA mercenaries."[83] After the contras attacked Cuapa and ambushed the truckload of young Sandinista draftees, Pablo Antonio Vega, the bishop of the provincial capital and also president of the Nicaraguan Episcopal Conference, criticized only the Sandinista army. Ignoring both the executions of eight Sandinista officials by contra forces and the ambush which killed 40 Sandinista troops, Bishop Vega told reporters that "what caused outrage in many families was that these kids [the Sandinista reinforcements] were sent into a situation without any real training. We know of two cases where the mothers destroyed Sandinista coffins and bought their own so their sons would not be buried as soldiers."[84]

One of the Church's greatest offenses was its stand, along with the opposition parties, against the military draft and in favor of those who evaded it—this at a time when Humberto Ortega considered it essential to expand the size of his army to fight the contras on two fronts. The Church leaders would not be silenced, however. Efforts to divide the Church by supporting a "popular church" based on liberation theology had failed. Obando traveled throughout the country and overseas. Nicaraguans, and the international press, followed his every word.

Another potent and almost unassailable critic was *La Prensa*. In March the editor of *La Prensa* felt confident enough to tell a visiting group of Americans that aid to the contras was "fundamental to preventing the entrenchment of a communist regime" in Nicaragua. "War is an unfortunate thing," Jaime Chamorro said. "We don't want it, but it is necessary to counter the Sandinistas. . . . [The] Contras fight with weapons and we, with political parties and the private sector, are putting up a different kind of battle. We are both working to prevent the entrenchment of a communist regime in Nicaragua."[85] *La Prensa*, too, was a symbol, and almost as untouchable as the Church, even though it had begun to receive money from the Americans' National Endowment for Democracy.[86] The link between such increasingly vocal domestic political opposition and the contra war, even if only implicit, was intolerably dangerous for the government.

This at least was the rationale for the Sandinistas' decision on October 15 to declare a new state of emergency with more sweeping restrictions on political and press rights.[87] The new restrictions seemed aimed principally at two sectors of the opposition: the Church and *La Prensa*. Earlier in the month, officials from Borge's Interior Ministry had forcibly entered the offices of Church spokesman Bismarck Carballo to prevent publication of a new magazine.[88] Following the October 15 announcement, *La Prensa* came under heavier censorship than ever before. Journalists estimated that, before the decrees, about one-third of *La Prensa*'s articles had been censored; afterwards, the proportion rose to two-thirds.[89] With their international reputations and access to Western reporters and politicians, however, both *La Prensa* and the Catholic church could still make their protests heard in Washington and around the world.

Less fortunate were the other targets of the October crackdown. On October 19 the Sandinista government announced the arrests of 134 people accused of collaborating with the contras, passing information, distributing propaganda, and planning acts of sabotage.[90] This was in Matagalpa alone; no doubt other "collaborators" were arrested in the other departments where fighting had been heavy. Although the Western press and the political debaters in Washington tended to focus on the effects of the new decrees on the Church and *La Prensa*, the Sandinistas made no secret of their additional purpose in the countryside. In announcing the new decrees, President Daniel Ortega declared they were necessary to prevent the contras from forming an "internal front" and provoking "discontent and confusion among the masses."[91]

––––––––

The Sandinistas knew that their new decrees would bring a storm of criticism from the United States, and it was Daniel Ortega's unfortunate task to travel to New York for the United Nations General Assembly meeting at the end of October and defend the action as best he could. Much to his displeasure, he found another Nicaraguan in New York at the same time: Cardinal Obando was denouncing the Sandinistas' harassment of the Church in the most strident terms, and with great success.

The most fervent American opponents of the Reagan administration's policy were befuddled and dismayed, even angry with the Sandinistas. President Ortega and his wife appeared on the "Phil Donahue Show" on October 22 to explain the government's actions to what was surely the largest American audience ever addressed by a Nicaraguan leader. Donahue was dejected. While he and "millions of Americans" were embarrassed by the Reagan administration's policies, Donahue told Ortega, the Sandinistas had nevertheless "apparently scored, without meaning to, a tremendous public relations victory for the Reagan administration." The Sandinistas' October crackdown "looks like the work—I'm not saying it is Mr. President—it looks like the work of a fascist government. . . . How could you impose such radical measures on your own people at a time when you claim to be on the edge of victory?" Ortega patiently tried to explain that "when you're at the point of reaching a victory, but you have an opponent who has many resources, then you have to make a maximum effort to assure your victory, and thus bring nearer the possibilities for peace." But Donahue responded, "You've snatched defeat from the jaws of victory! You've got the whole Catholic Church angry with you. . . . Let them speak. Your revolution is popular."[92] Liberal columnist Mary McGrory, in a column entitled "Ortega Has No Use for Friends," declared that Ortega knew he was "a terrible trial for people in the United States who have gone bail for him," but he was nevertheless "washing his hands of his congressional sympathizers—as they doubtless will of him—leaving Reagan free to continue the inconclusive war and all the misery it entails for Nicaragua."[93]

As for the American moderates' hopes that their "humanitarian" aid bill might prod the Sandinistas to be more forthcoming in the Contadora negotiations, once again it had the opposite effect. The day the House had approved McCurdy's bill, the Sandinistas announced in a communiqué that the entire agenda of the Contadora talks would have to be reviewed and "adjusted to the actual political conditions in the Central American region." On June 17 Tinoco said the Sandinistas were no longer interested in discussing "theoretical formulas for future peace while the war goes marching on." Further talk about security issues and verification had to be set aside in favor of "an in-depth discussion of the fundamental problems affecting the Central American region," above all, continuing U.S. aid to the contras. For the next four months, the Sandinistas refused to discuss further any of the pending issues in the draft treaty until U.S. aggression ended. The Contadora Group, led by Mexico, tried to meet Sandinista demands by calling for the resumption of bilateral talks between the United States and Nicaragua. But Secretary Shultz reiterated in Mexico City on July 26 that the United States would only resume those talks if the Sandinistas agreed to begin a dialogue with the contras.[94] The Contadora Group's call for bilateral talks, however, encouraged the Sandinistas to hold firm in their refusal to proceed with negotiations.

The price the Sandinistas paid was gradual isolation. The Contadora Group did not hold another meeting with the five Central American governments until September 12. At that meeting the group tabled a third draft of the treaty, in hopes of resuming discussions. The draft was not to the Sandinistas' liking. It struck a compromise between the September 1984 draft the Sandinistas had agreed to sign and the "Tegucigalpa draft" drawn up by the other four Central American governments with U.S. support in October 1984. As a compromise, it had necessarily moved closer to the position of the four and further from what the Sandinistas had been willing to accept the previous year. On two points in particular—international military maneuvers and the timing of negotiations on arms and troop limits—the draft was closer to American demands for "simultaneous" and "verifiable" actions by all sides. The Sandinistas objected to the changes.[95] At the next set of meetings on October 7 in Panama, Costa Rica announced it would sign the draft, El Salvador and Honduras expressed general support with reservations, Guatemala as usual said nothing, and Nicaragua declared it was not ready to give its views.[96]

On November 11, the Nicaraguan government released a letter from Daniel Ortega to the Contadora Group presidents outlining Nicaragua's objections to the latest draft, and the Sandinistas withdrew once more from any further consideration of the draft. They declared that Contadora had been "crushed" and that the Latin American countries were a "disgrace."[97] On December 3 the Nicaraguan government submitted a formal request that the Contadora talks be suspended until at least May of 1986.[98] On December 9, the OAS General Assembly voted 25–1 to urge that the Contadora talks continue. Nicaragua alone voted against the resolution. The Sandinistas stood firmly by their new position: All American aggression against Nicaragua had to stop before discussions about a Contadora treaty could resume.[99]

38

The $100 Million Aid Vote—Round One

Nothing that had occurred in the months since passage of McCurdy's bill surprised Reagan administration officials. On the contrary, the Sandinistas fulfilled all the administration's worst predictions, increased its determination to press ahead for a full program of military aid to the contras, and appeared to provide the necessary justification to seek the support of Congress. The Reagan administration's attitude toward the Sandinistas could have been described by Lenin's dictum: the worse the better.

Other events at the end of the year helped strengthen the administration's case for new aid to the contras. At the end of November a Nicaraguan helicopter shot down by contra forces near the Honduran border was found to have Cuban soldiers aboard. On December 5 the new assistant secretary of state, Elliott Abrams, told a congressional committee that intelligence analysts had been receiving "more and more reports" of Cuban involvement as part of what Abrams called "a massive Soviet and Cuban intervention" in Central America. General Ochoa had just recently ended his tour in Nicaragua. He had publicly received a decoration from Humberto Ortega and was promptly replaced by another high-ranking Cuban general. American officials believed Cuban advisers were now also involved at all levels of the Nicaraguan counterinsurgency effort, down to "very small units of the Nicaraguan army." Abrams warned that "we may be seeing Cubans move into a combat role on the mainland of North America." He argued that Congress ought to renew military aid to the contras "or we are going to be seeing a Soviet base in Nicaragua."[1] Later in the month a small car crashed in Honduras and was discovered to contain weapons, money, and communications equipment from Nicaragua destined for the Salvadoran guerrillas. The Sandinistas virtually acknowledged their continuing support for the guerrillas when Daniel Ortega strongly implied that, in response to the contras' acquisition of anti-aircraft weapons (one of which had been used to shoot down the Sandinista helicopter near the Honduran border), the Sandinistas might provide the Salvadoran guerrillas with similar weapons.[2] On December 14 President Reagan appealed to the American people in a radio address: "If Nicaragua can get material support from Communist states and terrorist regimes . . . should not the forces fighting for liberty, now numbering over 20,000, be entitled to more effective help?"[3]

In the second half of December Abrams and other officials began discussing with conservative and moderate congressmen the prospects for passing military aid for the contras in 1986. Senator Lugar, a pragmatic and respected Republican on the Senate Foreign Relations Committee, believed military aid to the contras could pass, if the proposal was "done right."[4] Abrams and his colleagues needed little encouragement. On January 10 President Reagan decided to ask Congress for $100 million in new aid to the contras, $70 million of which was to be explicitly for military assistance, with all restrictions against the CIA and Department of Defense lifted.

The $100 million request was by far the Reagan administration's most audacious. After years of uncertainty and pretense, the new request represented a straightforward statement of the administration's goals in Nicaragua. One hundred million dollars was not harassment but full-fledged war. Openly aimed at increasing the contras' capacity to fight a full-scale war against the Sandinista army, the request challenged Congress to end its own equivocations of the previous year and to choose war over peace. The request was the product of a new consensus within the Reagan administration that had been lacking in years past when the means and ends of Nicaragua policy had been constantly debated amidst accusations of disloyalty or incompetence. From December 1985 through the first votes in March 1986, Secretaries Shultz and Weinberger, CIA director William Casey, the new national security adviser John Poindexter, the chief of staff Don Regan, and the President himself all favored military aid and from the start ruled out the possibility of settling for less.[5] Despite the usual efforts by the press to find disagreements between administration hawks and doves, between "ideologues" and "pragmatists," there were only hawks and ideologues to be found.

This new consensus had several causes. Chief among these were the dismal results of efforts since August to provide "humanitarian" aid to the contras. The State Department had most reluctantly accepted responsibility for managing the disbursement of aid, and the new Nicaraguan Humanitarian Assistance Office (NHAO) established at the State Department was plagued by problems from the first day. The program approved by Congress was necessarily an anomaly: "overt" in the United States but "covert" in Honduras. Much as Reagan officials feared when they first rejected the overt option in early 1985, the Hondurans refused to let State Department officials work in Honduras and manage the purchase, receipt, and delivery of goods, because to do so would be to acknowledge that the contras were based in Honduras. The NHAO officials, therefore, could not monitor most of the purchase and delivery of goods but had to accept the word of the contras and, later, CIA intelligence reports that the goods were indeed arriving. The problem arose when funds were sent to the region to pay the contras' suppliers. The State Department did not have any means of fully monitoring how all monies were spent nor any way of proving that items purchased eventually reached their destination. This in turn led to a scandal in the United States. When the General Accounting Office (GAO), the investigative arm of Congress, audited the NHAO accounts it found, among other things, that the State Department did not have "procedures and controls which would allow it to provide . . . assurances . . . that the funds are being used for the purposes intended by law and are not being diverted to other uses." Already by the end of 1985 reports that monies appropriated by Congress had been diverted or misspent or embezzled by contra leaders were raising trouble in Congress. While the GAO found no evidence of malfeasance,[6] the State Department could not prove that none had occurred, and over the course of 1986 the administration had a most difficult time meeting the charges. Congressman Barnes declared the administration once again in violation of the law.[7]

A more serious problem was that goods intended for the contras did not in fact reach them for months, not because of malfeasance but because of the Honduran government. The first airplane full of NHAO supplies did not leave the United States for Honduras until October 8—four months after the House passed McCurdy's bill. The second flight left New Orleans on October 10, with an NBC camera crew aboard courtesy of Adolfo Calero's brother who was managing the shipments in New Orleans. When the plane arrived in Honduras, on the military side of Toncontin airport, the Honduran army officials who greeted it were mortified to find American television reporters. The Honduran government summarily canceled all further NHAO flights into Honduras and could not be persuaded to allow flights to resume until February 1986, one month before the expiration of the "humanitarian" aid legislation.[8] Throughout those five months, the NHAO officials had to rely even more on purchases made in Central America, thus exposing themselves to even more criticism from Congress due to the lack of an "audit trail" for such expenses.[9] As a further consequence of the Honduran "blockade" and other problems, by the beginning of March only $11 million out of the $27 million voted by Congress had "actually been delivered into the hands of the democratic resistance in the region," according to the director of NHAO.[10] In response to complaints from Congress in December about the way the State Department was handling the delivery of "humanitarian" aid, Elliott Abrams spoke for the entire administration when he said, "If this program is unpleasing to you, it's not exactly the greatest program in the world from our point of view either."[11] Secretary Shultz was particularly eager to get the resupply operation out of his State Department.

The "humanitarian" aid program had been a military disaster for the contras as well as a logistical problem for Washington officials. Since November 1985 contra forces had retreated from Nicaragua in droves, and the ragged rebel forces were an alarming sight to CIA officials who watched them straggle into Honduras. Many of the troops entered Honduras barefoot.[12] By the beginning of 1986, more than two-thirds of all contra forces were sitting in their camps across the border, awaiting supplies that did not arrive, causing anxiety to the Honduran government and inviting a repetition of the May 1985 Sandinista incursion. For the first time in years, the contras made no effort to disrupt the coffee harvest in the northern countryside.[13] When it finally did arrive, the "humanitarian" aid voted by Congress was spent feeding the rebels in Honduras rather than in Nicaragua. By the time the next rainy season came in May, therefore, much of the "humanitarian" aid voted by Congress almost a year earlier had been used up without contributing to any contra offensive. The Sandinistas, meanwhile, took advantage of the contras' retreat to push new roads further up the Bocay valley, to set up strong positions along the

Coco River, and to make preparations to block the next wave of rebel infiltration. At the end of February, American officials were telling reporters they feared the contra war against the Sandinistas could collapse in 1986. The *New York Times'* James LeMoyne wrote that the contras were in the "worst military condition since [their] formation in 1982."[14]

Reagan officials believed the new $100 million aid request was essential not only to provide the contras with weapons, but to perfect a resupply system that would enable the contra fighters to get back into Nicaragua and stay there. The contras still lacked all but the most primitive means of supplying their troops deep inside Nicaragua, or even just across the border. They had a difficult enough time transporting supplies of weapons and materiel from storage depots in one part of Honduras to staging areas in another. Reagan officials believed a new resupply operation run by either the CIA or the Defense Department was desperately needed.

Those few officials who knew of Oliver North's nascent efforts to set up an air resupply system for the contras could not have placed much faith in that answer to the problem. The operation run by Richard Secord, later to become famous in the Iran-contra scandal, had gotten off to a very slow start and was not doing any better than NHAO at delivering supplies to the contras. North had first asked Secord to set up a logistics operation in July 1985, but the first supply flight did not take off until February 1986. The plane lost an engine flying toward contra camps in Honduras and crash-landed after the crew jettisoned all the supplies they were carrying.[15] The first flight carrying weapons arrived later in the month, but this was actually a NHAO flight, used surreptitiously by Secord's crew to deliver weapons.[16] Secord's operation did not begin flying regular missions until March, and even these were mostly flights from storage areas to staging areas in Honduras carrying weapons already purchased by the contras with the Saudi money. Few of the flights made air-drops to troops inside Nicaragua.[17] Neither North, nor presumably those officials who knew of his efforts, could believe that these private operations were any substitute for a well-funded program run by the CIA and the Defense Department.[18]

The traumatic experience of supplying the contras under McCurdy's 1985 compromise legislation greatly contributed to the wide consensus within the administration not to make any similar compromises in 1986. Most officials agreed it would be better to lose in Congress than to accept another year, or even another month, of "humanitarian" aid.

Nor did Reagan officials believe they would have to compromise with Congress in 1986. In the five years since Enders formulated his "low-ball option" for pressuring the Sandinistas, the political and ideological landscape of the United States had been transformed. The debate over the administration's policies in Central America had calmed. Five years after Enders set forth his strategy for El Salvador, Congress was regularly voting enormous amounts of military and economic aid to the popular Duarte government and was close to approving military aid to Guatemala for the first time in years. Contra aid remained controversial, but by 1986 the contras' struggle was now only one of four "covert" wars the Congress was openly supporting around the world. Aid to the Afghan Mujaheddin, to the Cambodian anti-communist rebels, and to the forces of Jonas Savimbi in Angola was gathering support among moderate and conservative Democrats concerned about their party's image.[19]

The decline of political opposition to the Reagan administration's policies helped bring unity within the administration. To an extent not sufficiently understood by many observers, the divisions in the Reagan administration had been the consequence of external political pressures more than of disagreements over policy. For Reagan administration officials from Enders to Motley to Shultz, pursuing the "diplomatic track" had been principally a response to congressional pressure; so too, of course, was the idea for "humanitarian" aid, which no administration official favored. In 1986 the "pragmatists" no longer had to counsel restraint in dealing with a Congress in which many Democrats were looking to "toughen" their party's image. Secretary Shultz, for one, had less reason to worry that a constant clash with Congress over contra aid would detract from the administration's ability to carry out other policies around the world. Fresh from the successful first summit between Reagan and Gorbachev in November 1985, Shultz threw himself into the battle with Congress over contra aid. Contrary to the assertion by some observers that Shultz "effectively withdrew from the highly politicized low-gain Nicaragua dispute," Shultz brought more energy than ever to the fight, yelling at reluctant congressmen and pounding the table for emphasis at committee hearings.[20] Calling Sandinista Nicaragua "a cancer, right here on our land mass . . . [that] has tried to spread itself around in a fundamentally evil way," Shultz demanded that Congress help those Nicaraguans who were "trying to attain freedom and independence in their country!"[21]

Another reason for the new unity in the administration was Elliott Abrams, who had replaced Langhorne Motley as assistant secretary of state for Latin American affairs in the summer of 1985. The shift from Motley to Abrams marked the final step in the gradual transition from the limited objectives and half-way measures of Enders's original "low-ball" strategy to the all-out military effort represented by the $100 million request. While Motley had inherited and kept alive an active "diplomatic track" that was favored by Secretary Shultz, Abrams had inherited a negotiating process that was moribund and a secretary of state who was disinclined to renew it. Abrams made clear from the beginning that he opposed negotiations with the Sandinistas as a general matter, and he certainly opposed talks without the "leverage" provided by a well-armed contra army. Replacing Motley's and Enders's quiet advocacy of diplomatic solutions, Abrams became the administration's most forceful and articulate spokesman for aid to the contras. As a young, neo-conservative intellectual and former "Scoop" Jackson Democrat, Abrams more than Motley or Enders saw himself not only as a policymaker but as a combatant in the "war of ideas." Described by one of his colleagues as "a combative, unapologetic defender of U.S. policy who found it congenitally difficult to show respect for those, particularly McGovernite liberals, for whom he had no respect," Abrams enraged staunch opponents of contra aid.[22] But he began with a good reputation among moderate and conservative Democrats, who recalled his work as an advocate for human rights and democratic reform in Chile, El Salvador, and other countries with right-wing dictatorships.[23] Until the explosion of the Iran-contra scandal at the end of 1986, many moderate Democrats considered Abrams one of the most reasonable, effective, and cooperative members of the administration.[24]

———

The Reagan administration's new-found determination to seek military aid for the contras, however, was unwelcome to the moderates who were still digesting the consequences of their vote for "humanitarian" aid. McCurdy's bill in 1985 had been a hesitant, half-way measure by Congress, designed to buy time and "give peace a chance." The new request, and the manner in which it was presented by administration officials, stripped the matter bare of soothing bromides. The Reagan administration now challenged Congress both to approve this commitment to see matters through to the end and to take responsibility for future events and future decisions yet unforeseen. This was not what most of the 70–80 moderates who voted for McCurdy's bill in June believed they had signed up for.

Even before the Reagan administration began talking about military aid, some moderates had begun to renounce their earlier vote for "humanitarian" aid.[25] At the beginning of February about 30 Democrats sent a letter to President Reagan asking him "to announce that you are postponing any decision on what kind of contra funding to request" until March.[26] In the meantime, the congressmen asked Reagan to launch a "major diplomatic initiative," to "put the power, prestige and good offices of the U.S. clearly and unequivocally behind the upcoming efforts of the Contadora Group to seek a negotiated end to the bloodshed in Central America." Of the 29 signers of the letter, 16 were moderate Democrats who had supported McCurdy's bill in June after voting against contra aid in April. The letter went unanswered for months. On February 5, McCurdy suggested in an op-ed article in the *New York Times* that he would vote against military aid if the President did not accede to their demand.[27]

Neither the letter nor McCurdy's article contained any specific proposals concerning the kind of negotiated settlement the United States ought to support. Approval of more aid, McCurdy declared, depended "on the President's ability to persuade moderate members of the House that he stands by his pledge, made in an open letter to me in June, that his Administration 'is determined to pursue political, not military solutions in Central America.'" The Democrats' letter made only two specific demands: first, that the President appoint a bipartisan delegation of "leading supporters and opponents" of contra aid to accompany administration officials to a meeting with Latin leaders "to explore how the U.S. can best support Contadora;" and second, to meet with the Presidents of the Contadora Group "to explore any actions the U.S. might take to facilitate a diplomatic solution."

The moderates did not hazard a guess as to how "determined" the Sandinistas were "to pursue political, not military solutions." Some simply declared the Sandinistas were ready to reach a settlement. Congressman Richardson, for instance, had speculated in November 1985 that the Sandinistas were "now ready to deal"—two weeks *after* the Nicaraguan government had formally withdrawn from the Contadora negotiations.[28] Some of the moderates were more interested in avoiding a vote on new military aid than in determining the willingness of the Sandinistas to reach an agreement.

At the time McCurdy was making his demands, in fact, the Sandinistas were trying to put an end to the Contadora negotiations. On January 8 President Ortega had sent a letter to the Contadora Group proposing an altogether new diplomatic process which would abandon the search for the comprehensive treaty sought by Contadora in favor of bilateral nonaggression pacts between Nicaragua and her neighbors. The proposal, as intended, drove the Contadora governments to take steps to keep the Sandinistas from departing the negotiations.

On January 11–12, the eight foreign ministers of the Contadora and Support Group[29] met in Caraballeda, Venezuela, and released a declaration that appeared to shift the negotiations significantly in the Sandinistas' favor. Fearing the "the possible risk of cessation of diplomatic action," the ministers called for renewal of the Contadora negotiations but also encouraged "the re-establishment of conversations between the Governments of the United States and Nicaragua, in order to settle their differences and to identify possible forms of agreement."[30] In addition, the Contadora ministers called for an immediate end to all support for guerrilla forces in Central America, thus taking one provision out of the comprehensive treaty and making it a prior action "necessary to create a climate of mutual trust" for the negotiation of the treaty. Similarly, the "message of Caraballeda" called for immediate suspension of international military maneuvers *prior* to the signing of a treaty. The new proposal eliminated the "simultaneity" that the United States and its allies had successfully reinserted into the Contadora draft treaty. Instead, the United States would have to end aid to the contras and suspend military maneuvers as an incentive for the Sandinistas to return to the talks.[31] The Contadora Group also dismissed the administration's position, hitherto shared by McCurdy and other moderates, that the Sandinistas should hold a dialogue with the contras. When the Sandinistas insisted that the United States "must not only be willing to resume the dialogue, but also to . . . abandon the idea of turning it into an instrument to force Nicaragua to hold an immoral dialogue with terrorist forces," the Contadora Group agreed.[32] The Contadora Group's ambassadors in Washington delivered the "message of Caraballeda" to Secretary Shultz, who accepted it without comment.

When McCurdy and his colleagues demanded that the Reagan administration "explore how the U.S. can best support Contadora," therefore, they already knew Contadora's answer: stop aid to the contras immediately, end all military maneuvers, conduct bilateral talks with the Sandinistas, and drop the demand that the Sandinistas meet with the contras. McCurdy and his colleagues stopped short of making these demands their own, since most had already endorsed Arturo Cruz's earlier proposal for negotiations between the Sandinistas and contras. McCurdy simply called on the Reagan administration to "propose and sign a peace agreement" that would be "so reasonable, in Latin American terms, that the Sandinistas cannot reject it without destroying whatever legitimacy they have in the eyes of the world."[33]

In congressional hearings at the end of February Secretary Shultz explained in detail why the administration opposed any delay in requesting contra aid, much less the unconditional resumption of bilateral talks with Nicaragua. The Sandinistas' "game plan," Shultz argued, was "to somehow or other persuade people not to help the Contras for long enough so that, with this big Soviet buildup of advanced weapons, they will wipe them out before we wake up. So I am a little dubious about proposals to hold off while negotiations take place." Senator Claiborne Pell told Shultz the United States should "let the Contadora countries and the support group take the lead," but Shultz responded that such a course meant leaving defense of American security interests "up to the Soviets, the Cubans, and the Nicaraguan Communists." Shultz insisted that before any negotiations could succeed, Congress had to approve contra aid first. "[I]f you do not have any cards to play," he argued, "you cannot get into the card game." The Sandinistas might eventually be willing to negotiate on American terms, but only when "the present government sees that it cannot win militarily, that it is losing its base of support, and that its best hope for retaining some part in the government of the country is to sit down and negotiate. . . . [U]nder those circumstances, it will do it." Shultz stood firm against the kinds of compromises moderate Democrats were requesting. "[T]here is a program there and the Congress either supports it or does not support it, it is not to be fussed around with."[34] On February 25 President Reagan formally delivered his $100 million request to Congress.

Without the support of some moderate Democrats and Republicans, however, the administration's request had little chance of passing. House Democratic leaders counting votes in both parties were confident of victory.[35] Reagan officials, who had mistaken their own enthusiasm and unanimity for that of Congress, were surprised to find themselves apparently "dead in the water." The opposition in Congress, Buchanan admitted, "was broader and deeper than we thought." Having announced the new proposal, however, administration officials were reluctant to compromise. Instead, the President and his advisers first tried to bludgeon Congress into acquiescing. They set Buchanan free to make the case "clearly, boldly and starkly," as he and other conservatives had wanted to do in 1985. To Buchanan this meant turning the debate into a sharply partisan confrontation.[36] On March 5 Buchanan published an op-ed article in the *Washington Post* asserting that the Democratic Party had "become, with Moscow, co-guarantor of the Brezhnev doctrine in Central America." The Democratic Party's vote on the President's $100 million request would "reveal whether it stands with Ronald Reagan and the resistance—or Daniel Ortega and the communists."[37] Speeches written for President Reagan at the beginning of March contained the same kind of attacks in only slightly less partisan form. "If the members of Congress hide their heads in the sand and pretend the strategic threat in Nicaragua will go away," Reagan warned, "they are courting disaster and history will hold them accountable." The map of Central America would be "covered in a sea of red, eventually lapping at our own borders."[38]

Buchanan's aggressive tactics certainly made southern Democrats nervous. While Tip O'Neill declared bravely on March 12 that there would be "no deals," other congressional leaders said they were "scared to death that [Reagan would] pull another rabbit out of the hat, turn another loser into a winner, and leave us totally vulnerable."[39] At the same time, however, the raw partisanship of Buchanan's attacks sent some Democrats rallying around their party leaders. Democrats charged that Buchanan's statements amounted to "red-baiting" and "McCarthyism."[40] Even moderate Republicans, themselves unenthusiastic about military aid for the contras, complained about the administration's "highly offensive . . . distortions."[41] Conservative lobbying groups across the country, employing the same strong rhetoric as Buchanan, did more harm than good for the administration's cause. In the Florida district of Buddy MacKay, "Citizens for Reagan" ran newspaper ads with the headline "Whose Buddy Is He? . . . Your Congressman and Communist Nicaragua." MacKay took a defiant stand and said the conservatives could "take their out-of-state campaign and shove it."[42] The National Conservative Political Action Committee sent letters to Democratic members warning them not to drive a "nail into the coffin of liberty and democracy in Nicaragua" and enclosed a nail in the envelope. One southern Democratic congressman sent a letter back enclosing a screw.[43]

Buchanan, to be sure, was at least as interested in attacking the Democratic Party as in winning approval for aid to the contras. His conviction that it was more important to frame the issues clearly and place blame where it belonged than to win any given vote was a legacy of the Vietnam

War. In the eyes of many conservatives, Democratic congressmen and liberal activists had forced an American surrender and then escaped blame for the consequences of their actions. When the Democrats "lost" Nicaragua, Buchanan was determined that the American people should know who was responsible. "Having voted to abandon Southeast Asia to Hanoi and Moscow," Buchanan wrote, "the Democratic Party would not likely survive the ceding of Central America to the Warsaw Pact." Many leading Republican members of Congress felt the same way. Congressman Lott declared that if the Reagan administration lost the vote for contra aid, "My recommendation will be that we walk away from it and say that Tip O'Neill and the Democrats lost Nicaragua."[44]

President Reagan, however, was more interested in winning the vote than in setting the historical record straight. Within days of Buchanan's editorial, Reagan took a more conciliatory tack, suggesting that members of Congress act "not as Republicans, nor as Democrats, but as Americans."[45] By the end of the first week of March, the Reagan administration, still short by as many as 20–25 votes in the House, began talking about a compromise. Abrams held talks with moderates in both houses, and McCurdy predicted the administration would "be dragged kicking and screaming to another position."[46]

From the beginning of the year McCurdy had insisted no military aid could be passed unless the Reagan administration made a greater effort to pursue a diplomatic settlement. In March McCurdy proposed, as a compromise, that Congress approve the President's request but bar the expenditure of the military aid for several months while the administration resumed bilateral negotiations with the Sandinistas. If the Sandinistas refused to talk, or negotiated in "bad faith," then Congress could vote again to release the military aid.[47] A similar plan was proposed in the Senate by Tennessee Democrat Jim Sasser, although Sasser's plan called for a full six-month delay. Reagan officials were unhappy with both proposals—the President insisted a six-month delay was too long—but Sasser correctly surmised that administration officials were "smelling defeat on the question of direct aid to the contras" and were "starting to feel around for a compromise position that might be acceptable to all sides."[48]

By the middle of March Reagan declared he would be "willing to talk" about a 60- or 75-day delay in releasing aid to the contras.[49] In the meantime the Reagan administration tried to appease the Democrats' desire for more negotiations by appointing a new special envoy to replace a tired Shlaudeman, who after more than 50 meetings with Central American leaders over two years had lost his value as a symbol of hope for a negoti-ated settlement. At the suggestion of Shultz and Abrams, the President appointed Philip Habib, one-time negotiator in the Middle East who, at the beginning of March, was fresh from a successful mission to help ease out Philippine President Marcos. President Reagan sent Habib immedi-ately to Central America for talks with officials in El Salvador, Honduras, and Guatemala. Reagan even suggested that Habib might go on to Nica-ragua, if there could be "any benefit" in such a visit.[50] Habib's first desti-nation, however, was Capitol Hill, where he told members that if they sent him to Central America "without something in my tool box, the Sandinistas will laugh at me."[51]

With both McCurdy and the administration agreeing that disburse-ment of military aid could be delayed while diplomatic efforts proceeded, the only outstanding issue was who would decide whether or not to re-lease the aid when the time came. Moderate Democrats led by McCurdy in the House and by Sasser in the Senate insisted that the military aid could only be released by another vote in Congress. Republicans and Rea-gan officials insisted the decision had to be left to the President. On this point the negotiations between McCurdy and the administration broke down. McCurdy and other moderate Democrats suspected the Reagan administration opposed any negotiated settlement with the Sandinistas and that the President's decision to disburse the military assistance was a foregone conclusion. That meant a vote for the President's proposal amounted to a vote for military aid, regardless of the delay. Reagan offi-cials, on the other hand, suspected that McCurdy and his colleagues did not want to vote for military aid at any time, that they were looking for a way to avoid such a vote altogether, and that their demand for a negoti-ated settlement was really a demand for an American capitulation. Agreeing to give Congress another vote, therefore, meant continuing the disastrous "humanitarian" aid program indefinitely.

Reagan officials still hoped that the President could overawe his oppo-nents by appealing directly to the American public. On March 16 Reagan addressed the nation on television, and both sides paused in their negoti-ations to see what impact the "Great Communicator" might have on American public opinion. Reagan gave the speech Buchanan and other conservatives had long been clamoring for. He warned of the "mounting danger" that threatened "the security of the United States." The unfold-ing strategic nightmare the President described began with the Soviet Union and Cuba using Nicaragua as a base to "become the dominant power in the crucial corridor between North and South America." From there they would "be in a position to threaten the Panama Canal, interdict our vital Caribbean sea lanes, and, ultimately, move against Mexico." Presumably saving the worst for last, the President warned that, should the Soviets move against Mexico, "desperate Latin peoples by the millions would begin fleeing north into the cities of the southern United States."

The President's speech was aimed directly at the constituents of southern Democrats, whom White House speechwriters cynically but probably correctly suspected of having greater fear of Latin immigration than of Soviet interdiction of American sea lanes and the fall of Mexico to communism. Reagan's speech gave no hint of compromise, nor paid much attention to the question of negotiations. Reagan did not utter the word "Contadora," nor mention Philip Habib, nor hint at any new effort to pursue talks. Reagan more than hinted at the pressure he wanted to put on members of Congress, however. Echoing Buchanan's March 5 article, the President insisted "the Congress must decide where it stands." It would be "remembered as that body of men and women that either stopped the communists before it was too late—or did not."[52] The President asked the American people to contact their congressmen directly and urge them "to help the freedom fighters—help us prevent a communist takeover of Central America."[53]

Reagan's lack of subtlety was an effective tactic for the South. The Democrats' response, read by Tennessee's Senator Sasser, emphasized the degree to which the Democratic Party agreed with Reagan about "what our goals should be in Central America," about the behavior of the Sandinistas, and about the principle that "Nicaragua must never become a base for Soviet military adventurism in this hemisphere. Never." The Democrats' only concern, Sasser suggested, was that President Reagan was "seizing military options before he has exhausted the hope of a peaceful solution." With subtlety equal to Reagan's, Sasser concluded that "as the father of a 17-year-old son, I say, Mr. President, let's not rush blindly into that quagmire. We've done that before."[54]

The President's speech brought an increase in public support for contra aid—as much as a twelve-point jump in one poll.[55] Its effect in the south was sufficient to make House Democratic leaders even more nervous. Congressman Jim Chapman had been in office less than a year after winning a special election in his staunchly conservative Texas district by a margin of 50.9 to 49.1. After Reagan's speech on March 16, Chapman's aides said his Texas constituents saw the communist presence in Central

America as an "immediate threat" and that consequently the congressman was "wide open" on the question of contra aid.[56] Chapman received special briefings from the CIA and a personal meeting with Reagan. A handful of other southern Democrats, like Marilyn Lloyd of Tennessee and Alberto Bustamante of Texas, were also wavering as late as March 18, the day before debate was to begin. Between Reagan's speech and his appointment of Habib, the President had moved closer to securing a majority in what was certain to be a very close vote.[57] At the same time, compromise proposals were proliferating. Speaker O'Neill and the Democratic leadership recognized that one of these compromises might just give Reagan enough southern votes to win.

O'Neill had originally established the voting procedure to permit no amendments to the President's proposal, which would either pass or fail on a single vote. Designed to prevent McCurdy from repeating his victory of the previous year—which liberal Democrats had rued even more than the Reagan administration—O'Neill's tactic was a reassertion of his prerogatives as Speaker and an attempt to deal Reagan a clear defeat on this most contentious of issues. By the day before the vote, however, O'Neill recognized that he once again lacked the strength to defeat Reagan's proposal on a straight vote. And once again, McCurdy held the balance. The moderates wanted to vote for some form of contra aid, even if they were reluctant to support the President's plan. McCurdy, who was still negotiating with Reagan officials, warned O'Neill that some of his colleagues would have to vote with the President if given no other choice. O'Neill finally gave in and made McCurdy an offer he could not refuse: If McCurdy and his group would vote with the party leadership against the President on March 19, O'Neill promised to give McCurdy a chance to offer his own alternative contra aid proposal on April 15. O'Neill's concession was an admission that there was no longer any stopping aid to the contras.[58] Perhaps Reagan was short of a majority for his own proposal, but O'Neill and the liberal Democrats were also short of majority to oppose further aid to the Nicaraguan rebels.

O'Neill's concession turned the tide in the March 19 vote. Moderate Democrats announced they would vote against the President's proposal in anticipation of voting for an alternative contra aid proposal a month hence. McCurdy continued negotiating with Reagan officials until the last minute, but the two sides could find no compromise on the question of releasing the military aid. "I need something more than a letter of a promise from the President," McCurdy told reporters. "He needs pressure from Congress." The talks broke down in mutual accusations of bad faith.[59] On March 20, with McCurdy's group of Democrats standing firm with the House leadership, the House defeated the President's proposal 222–210.

The vote against contra aid in March 1986 was deceptive, for the Speaker's control of legislative procedures had turned a probable majority in favor of aid into a temporary majority against it.[60] The moderate Democrats led by McCurdy remained an insurmountable obstacle to O'Neill's efforts to kill contra aid. Whether out of political fear exacerbated by Reagan's speech, or out of a conviction that pressure on the Sandinistas was necessary to achieve a variety of moral and strategic goals, McCurdy and other southern Democrats were determined that contra aid in some form must pass. As it was, 46 Democrats voted for the President's proposal, 39 of these from the South.

The President's defeat, in fact, owed as much to Republican defections as to the loss of McCurdy's Democrats. Sixteen Republicans, all from the North, voted against their President. These defections were the natural if unintended consequence of Buchanan's political strategy, which had been designed to frighten southern voters without appeasing the more liberal sensibilities of the north. Republicans from northern blue-collar districts found their pro-contra stance costly. Even Minority Leader Michel reported that people in his district were more "worried about jobs and losing their farms" than about a red map of Central America.[61] In the Pennsylvania offices of Republican Senator Arlen Specter, telephone calls after the President's March 16 speech were evenly divided between opponents and supporters of aid. Pennsylvania Congressman Tom Ridge, who had won his seat in 1982 by a margin of 50.2–49.8 while other Republicans in the state lost during the recession, voted against the President. The administration, he complained, had "ignored" moderates like him and this problem had been "exacerbated by the rhetoric."[62] Chalmers Wylie had held his Republican seat in Ohio since 1966 and had supported the President five times on contra aid votes in previous years. He had second thoughts, however, when phone calls from his district ran heavily against the President after the speech. Wylie voted against the proposal, hoping the Sandinistas would "take it as a sign of peace and friendship."[63] Congressman John Rowland of Connecticut was a freshman Republican trying to hold on to his seat in a district where registered Democrats outnumbered Republicans. He voted against Reagan despite an imploring phone call from the President.[64]

The loss of these Republicans was vexing to Republican leaders and White House officials. On the other hand, they knew they had only to win back seven of the sixteen to pass their aid bill the next time. They were likely to gain at least as many southern Democrats. Despite their defeat on March 19, therefore, Republicans and White House officials did not believe they would have to accept even McCurdy's terms for a compromise. "I'll frame this as the day they voted for communism in Nicaragua," Congressman Lott declared after the vote. And, looking to the future, Lott told reporters: "I'm not going to vote for a pile of pabulum with Dave McCurdy's name on it."[65]

39

"It's Not Easy Selling McCurdy"

The defeat of contra aid in the House, though presumably temporary, provided an opening for those in the hemisphere eager for a negotiated solution. Between the end of March and April 15, when O'Neill had promised another vote, the Contadora Group hoped to resolve the outstanding disputes in the negotiations among the five Central American governments and obtain final agreement on a treaty. An agreement would doom any hope of passing contra aid in the American Congress, and whether the Reagan administration supported the agreement or not, the signing of a final document by all five Central American governments would force the contras out of their bases in Honduras and Costa Rica.

The Sandinistas, whom American and Latin observers expected to welcome the reprieve from Congress, responded by launching an attack on the main contra base camp in Honduras. The Sandinistas, engaged in a brutal war, were not interested in Congress's "sign of peace and friendship"; Humberto Ortega had begun the operation before the March 20 vote and had obviously planned to proceed regardless of Congress's decision. The strategic purpose of the mission, he explained later, was to strike at "mercenary bases, against their training centers, against their camps, their redoubts, their central bases of operations."[1] One observer called it "a high-stakes gamble by the Sandinistas that the political risk of crossing into Honduras was outweighed by the chance to destroy the main guerrilla camps."[2] On March 22 some 1,500 Sandinista army troops attacked the main contra base camp 10 miles inside Honduras near Los Trojes and other contra staging areas further east at Bocay on the Coco River. The heaviest fighting took place on March 23 when Sandinista forces engaged several thousand rebel fighters in an all-day battle that left heavy casualties on both sides. The contras were surprised by the attack and fell back from the main camp, allowing the Sandinistas to penetrate the perimeter before regrouping to mount a counterattack. Then it was the Sandinistas' turn to be surprised by the numbers of well-armed, veteran contra troops who put up a stout defense.[3] As the contra forces began encircling the smaller Sandinista units, the attackers fought their way out supported by Sandinista artillery barrages from BM-21 multiple rocket launchers across the border in Nicaragua.[4] At the same time, additional Sandinista forces in Nicaragua moved up to provide support and, possibly, to renew the offensive.[5] To the east, another Sandinista force attacked and destroyed the rebel airstrip at Bocay.[6]

The Sandinistas' cross-border attack did not come as a complete surprise, either to the Honduran government or to the Reagan administration. On March 18, while McCurdy was negotiating with Reagan and O'Neill, a column of Sandinista armored personnel carriers and trucks had moved out of Estelí along the Pan American highway northward to the Honduran border. On March 19, while the House was debating contra aid, the Honduran army general staff had placed its forces on alert and dispatched 5,000 troops to the border area in response to what an army spokesman called "an unusual movement of Nicaraguan troops" armed with anti-aircraft guns and tanks.[7] Honduran officials passed intelligence reports to the American embassy warning of Sandinista preparations for an attack on March 20 on Honduran border positions.[8] On March 21, the day after the House defeated aid to the contras, Elliott Abrams and General John Galvin had flown to Tegucigalpa to reassure the Hondurans of the American commitment to their security. American officials had discussed the provision of new weapons and, if necessary, American airlift capacity to Honduran troops near the border area in the event of a Sandinista cross-border attack.[9] On March 22 a Honduran helicopter was shot down near the rebel camps by Sandinista forces, and on March 23 Honduran army units near the border had again been put on alert.[10]

On the morning of March 24, the day after the heaviest fighting began near Los Trojes, President Azcona called the State Department directly to ask American officials to provide Honduras with the emergency military assistance they had talked about, including help in transporting Honduran troops closer to the border.[11] Elliott Abrams and other officials in Washington were eager to respond favorably for several reasons: to fulfill their earlier promises, to help protect the contras from the Sandinista attack, to show the Sandinistas the United States was prepared to use its military forces in the region if necessary, and to dramatize for members of Congress the danger the Sandinistas posed to their Central American neighbors. The President's spokesman made a special point of stating that the incursion had occurred "within 48 hours" of the vote in the House.[12]

In the United States, however, critics of the administration greeted reports of the incursion skeptically. The Nicaraguan government categorically denied that its troops had entered Honduran territory and accused the Reagan administration of fabricating the entire story in an effort to win congressional support for the contra aid bill. The American press, which had no confirmation of the administration's claims, was skeptical that an incursion had occurred at all, let alone in the proportions suggested by administration officials.[13] The Honduran government added fuel to the charges by the way it handled publicity of the incident. President Azcona asked for American emergency assistance privately; publicly, his government began by denying the attack had even occurred,[14] and then denied that the attack threatened Honduras' security.[15] Indeed, after some initial fears, the Honduran government had decided that only the contras' security was threatened. Honduran military leaders asked for American help "mainly to test the United States' commitment to a new security arrangement under which the [Reagan administration had] agreed to aid Honduras if Nicaraguan troops cross the border."[16] They wanted reassurance, but they wanted to avoid the glare of international publicity which drew attention to the presence of contra base camps on Honduran territory. As one Honduran official later explained, "The United States interest was that this situation have the connotation of an international incident. We had no interest in this."[17]

The Reagan administration needed public declarations from the Hondurans, however, not only to help its case for more aid to the contras, but, of more immediate significance, to justify the provision of the emergency assistance the Honduran government had requested. After the Hondurans' public professions of ignorance, State Department officials called the Honduran government again to ask whether Azcona really wanted American assistance.[18] Assured that he did, the officials demanded not only that the Honduran president put his request in writing, as required by law, but that the Honduran government publicly state that an incursion had indeed taken place, that Honduran security was threatened, and that American assistance was required.[19] While awaiting these assurances, Reagan officials went ahead with their plans. On March 25 President Azcona sent a letter to President Reagan "formally and urgently" requesting military assistance "to repel the Sandinista forces and to prevent these attacks from occurring in the future."[20] Having made this official request for emergency aid, the Honduran president went off to the beach.

American helicopters did not begin carrying Honduran troops to their "rear staging area" until late in the afternoon of March 26.[21] Even so, the show of force may have been decisive in cutting short the Sandinista army's offensive. As late as March 25 Humberto Ortega was still sending reinforcements up to the border area. It was not until the American military forces in Honduras were officially instructed to begin operations that the Sandinista forces in Honduras broke down into small units and began making their way back to Nicaragua as quickly as they could. When Honduran troops finally began arriving to sweep through the area of the incursion, most of the Sandinista forces had returned back across the border. The *New York Times'* James LeMoyne believed the Sandinistas had counted on another passive response by the Hondurans, and "had it not been for the strong reaction from Reagan Administration officials the Sandinista calculation may have proved correct."[22]

By March 27 the Sandinista troops had completely withdrawn, and Sandinista leaders were freely acknowledging that their troops had attacked and destroyed several contra base camps in Honduras.[23] Daniel Ortega told reporters that Honduras had "lost sovereignty over [the] part of its territory" occupied by the contras.[24] Since Nicaragua was "interested in fighting the mercenary forces and occupying those camps," it was impossible to avoid "military operations by our Army in the entire border area where, logically, our fighters look for the contras camps." That area of Honduras, Ortega declared, had become "a war zone."[25]

Democrats who had just voted against President Reagan's aid proposal were once again embarrassed by the Sandinistas' actions. Some still claimed that the Reagan administration had fabricated the incident or at least greatly exaggerated the risk in order to pass contra aid.[26] Since the Sandinistas themselves had admitted crossing the border, however, some critics shifted their argument and alleged that the Sandinista army had only pursued contras fleeing back into Honduras. This charge, too, was contradicted by Humberto Ortega himself.[27] Liberal accusations succeeded in muddying the waters, however, long enough for the Senate to vote on the President's bill on March 27. The Senate passed the bill, as expected, but only by a margin of 53–47, the weakest showing yet for the administration.

In the end, however, the Sandinistas suffered in Congress more than the Reagan administration. Opponents of contra aid could not hide their embarrassment at the Sandinistas' warlike response to their peaceful overtures. Speaker O'Neill called Ortega "a bumbling, incompetent Marxist-Leninist Communist"; Democratic whip Thomas Foley called the incursion "unjustified and stupid"; and Majority Leader Wright declared the Sandinistas' action "a clear violation of the Rio Treaty" under which the United States had "a clear and unequivocal responsibility" to respond.[28]

The Sandinistas' actions boded ill for the ongoing Contadora negotiations. At the next meeting of the thirteen foreign ministers on April 5–7, Nicaragua's D'Escoto insisted that negotiations simply could not proceed until the United States ended aid to the contras. D'Escoto also made clear the Sandinistas' unbending opposition to any discussion of arms limits.[29] The Contadora Group, displeased at the lack of progress, gave Nicaragua and the other Central American countries eight days to respond to the latest draft of the treaty and pressed for a final agreement by June 6.

Both the Contadora ministers and Democratic opponents of contra aid were eager for an agreement before the next vote scheduled for April 15. Tip O'Neill expressed hope that Nicaragua would sign the treaty and put an end to the political struggle in the United States. The Sandinistas did not welcome this concerted effort to force an agreement. "We reject the 1985 proposal, we reject it," Ortega insisted on April 10. But to escape their worsening international isolation, the Sandinistas responded with a half-gesture. On April 12 Ortega accepted the Contadora Group's invitation to return to negotiations, but only on the understanding that this "should not and cannot be linked with a Nicaraguan literal acceptance of the proposal of the modified Contadora Document." The latest draft, the Sandinistas insisted, had been shaped by the United States and contained "points that are unacceptable as they seriously harm the country's sovereignty and security." One point in particular was troubling: that the Sandinistas would be asked to make a commitment regarding limits on the size of their army on the date of signature. "[I]f the U.S. aggression does not end," the Sandinistas insisted," they would "under no circumstances . . . agree to disarm." They agreed to sign the document on June 6, there-

fore, only "so long as the U.S. aggression against Nicaragua has completely ended by that date and so long as an agreement is reached on the
points pending in the modified document."[30]

The Sandinistas shared the common assumption in Washington that
McCurdy's bill would pass on April 15, providing "humanitarian" aid to
the contras in some form and thus continuing the American aggression.[31]
Nicaragua's ambassador in Washington emphasized that "*any form* of aid
approved by the U.S. Congress for the contras would be an obstacle for
the Contadora Group's process."[32] Opponents of contra aid may have
hoped that such statements indicated the Sandinistas' desire to sign a
Contadora treaty if only aid to the contras were ended. But frustrated Democrats reported from the Contadora meeting in Panama that
Nicaraguan officials were "being intransigent" and that the Sandinistas'
"commitment to peace [was] suspect."[33] Instead of using progress in the
Contadora talks as a means of killing contra aid, as these Democrats had
hoped, the Sandinistas seemed to be using contra aid as a means of killing
Contadora.

On April 15 with no diplomatic progress to report, the House of Representatives met to consider McCurdy's alternative proposal for contra
aid. Speaker O'Neill had thus fulfilled his promise to give the moderates
a vote on their bill, but he had done so in such a way as to make passage
of McCurdy's legislation difficult if not impossible. First, the legislation
to which he attached McCurdy's bill, a $1.7 billion supplemental appro-
priation, was almost certain to be vetoed by President Reagan.[34] Second,
the rule O'Neill and his deputies had devised to consider the bill built a
complex labyrinth which made it very difficult for McCurdy to assemble
the necessary coalition of moderate Democrats and conservative Republicans.

According to O'Neill's rule, House members could vote on three different versions of the contra aid bill. Liberals favored an amendment by
Congressmen Hamilton and Richardson to provide $27 million in refugee
assistance only to contra fighters who turned in their arms. That amendment would be voted on first. If, as expected, it was defeated by a coalition of McCurdy's moderates and conservative Republicans, the next
vote would be on McCurdy's amendment. Most observers expected the
Republicans to vote against McCurdy's proposal so that they might then
vote for their own amendment, the proposal supported by the Reagan administration. The problem for Republicans was that, according to
O'Neill's rule, if either Hamilton's or McCurdy's amendment passed, the

administration-backed bill would not even come up for a vote. To win approval of his amendment, therefore, McCurdy could not count on the Republicans. Instead, he would have to gain the support of almost all the Democratic Party's most liberal members. These anti-contra liberals, according to the common wisdom, would vote for McCurdy's amendment if only to block passage of the Reagan administration's bill. If all went as planned, and McCurdy's amendment was approved by this coalition of moderate and liberal Democrats, then there would be one last vote on final passage of the legislation. But for McCurdy to win on final passage, he would have to change partners yet again. The liberals would be expected to vote "no" on final passage, thus achieving their goal of killing all forms of contra aid. McCurdy, therefore, would need to get the support of conservative Republicans once more. The Republicans, presumably, would approve McCurdy's bill on final passage rather than see aid to the contras defeated altogether.

The biggest problem with this tortuous scheme was that both the liberal Democrats and the conservative Republicans had grown to mistrust and even to dislike McCurdy and his compromise proposals. Congressman David Bonior, who had the unpleasant task of convincing his liberal colleagues to go along with the plan, told Mary McGrory that it was "not easy selling McCurdy."[35] As the day of the vote approached, some 70 liberal Democrats remained unsure of what to do. Conservative Republicans, meanwhile, were loathe to follow the course laid out for them by the Democratic leadership. O'Neill's procedure forced them to pass "a pile of pabulum with Dave McCurdy's name on it," as Congressman Lott put it, or risk sharing the blame for the demise of the contras.

The Republicans mutinied. When the Hamilton amendment came to a vote on April 16, Republicans held their ballots until, on a signal from Michel, they cast their votes en masse—*for* the amendment. As a result, an absurd combination of liberal, anti-contra Democrats and conservative pro-contra Republicans approved Hamilton's proposal overwhelmingly, 361–66. McCurdy's moderates were left standing by themselves, surprised and outraged. Approval of Hamilton's amendment ended action on the contra aid bill and prevented consideration of McCurdy's amendment. The Republican leader, Bob Michel, in a fiery speech after the vote, said Republicans had simply "refuse[d] to play the role assigned to us by the directors of this farce."[36] Congressman Foley asserted the Republicans had committed "parliamentary suicide," but the Democratic leadership was forced to scuttle further action on the contra aid bill. They stripped the Hamilton amendment from the supplemental appropriations bill and had to promise McCurdy another chance later in the year.

Republicans had taken advantage of the fact that the Democratic Party was really not prepared to live with the Hamilton amendment, despite its endorsement by O'Neill, Wright, and other party leaders. To bridge the gap in the party, something more than refugee assistance was required. The Republicans delighted in their victory over O'Neill and, perhaps even more, over McCurdy, who had been denied his chance to assert control over policy in Nicaragua. "Rather than play that game," Congressman Cheney said after the vote, "we said, 'Screw it.'" McCurdy insisted his day was not over. The moderates, he declared, were "not going to be beaten into submission by either side."[37]

40

The "Phony Treaty"

In ways the Republican House leaders could not have anticipated, their surprising maneuver on April 16 also confounded the diplomatic strategy of the Sandinistas. The expected passage of McCurdy's bill—an official renewal of U.S. aggression—would have provided the Sandinistas a convenient excuse to avoid the increasingly problematic negotiations in Contadora. Instead, McCurdy's bill had failed, the Contadora Group had declared June 6 as the deadline for signature of a treaty, and Speaker O'Neill obligingly scheduled another vote on contra aid for June 9. Both opponents and supporters of contra aid knew for certain that if the Sandinistas signed a Contadora treaty on June 6, the House would not approve aid to the rebels three days later. The Sandinistas, however, did not welcome the new opportunity.

On April 20 Daniel Ortega told a gathering of party faithful that the Sandinistas could not sign a peace agreement until peace actually existed in Central America. If there was "no peace in Central America," he declared, "the [Contadora] document cannot be implemented and therefore the document cannot even be signed."[1] This insistence on peace as a precondition for signing a peace agreement was tantamount to rejection of further negotiations.

The Reagan administration was in a good position to take advantage of the Sandinistas' obvious reluctance to sign a treaty, but pressure from

439

conservatives inside and outside the administration forced Reagan officials instead to reveal their own discomfort with negotiations. Constantine Menges, who had left the National Security Council and was watching events from outside the administration, was again convinced that Secretary Shultz and the State Department were falling, or diving, headlong into a Sandinista trap. He successfully stirred like-minded administration officials and members of Congress to action against the impending "phony treaty."

On April 11 Philip Habib had inadvertently set off a conservative explosion with a letter to Congressmen Richardson, Barnes, and Slattery stating the administration's position on the Contadora talks. The letter, drafted by officials in the Latin America bureau and approved by Abrams, said the Reagan administration interpreted the provisions of the Contadora draft treaty "as requiring a cessation of support to irregular forces and/or insurrectional movements from the date of signature." Habib's letter further stated that while the United States was not a signatory to or legally bound by the treaty, it would "support and abide by a comprehensive, verifiable and simultaneous implementation of the Contadora Document of Objectives of September 1983, as long as such an agreement [was] being fully respected by all the parties."[2]

Habib's letter appeared to be a step back from the "simultaneity" previously sought by the Reagan administration. In Craig Johnstone's four-step plan of 1984, for instance, the cessation of aid to the contras was to be tied to the Sandinistas' implementation of other requirements in the agreement. What troubled conservatives was that Habib's letter suggested that the Reagan administration would end aid to the contras on the day a Contadora treaty was signed. Since many conservatives also believed the Sandinistas would sign the Contadora draft on June 6, Habib's assurance meant that a cutoff of aid to the contras was imminent. Congressman Jack Kemp, alarmed by Menges's warnings, called for Habib's resignation.[3] Jeane Kirkpatrick compared the Contadora treaty to the Yalta agreements of 1945.[4] Conservatives demanded that the Reagan administration state its objections to the treaty candidly or stand accused of complicity in another "sell-out" to Communists.

So far, the Reagan administration had refrained from publicly criticizing the draft treaty. Elliott Abrams and other Reagan officials had not wanted to repeat the mistake of 1984, when the administration's obvious opposition to Contadora's draft gave the Sandinistas an opportunity to score an easy propaganda victory. This time, with the Sandinistas openly shying away from the treaty draft, Reagan officials were content to let the Sandinistas do the complaining. The wording of Habib's letter had been an oversight rather than a shift in policy. And since most State Department officials assumed that no treaty would be signed on June 6, they considered Habib's letter irrelevant.

But the Reagan officials bent to conservative pressure. On May 22 the President's spokesman, declaring that Reagan remained "solidly behind" Habib, nevertheless bluntly declared that the United States "would not consider itself bound to support an agreement which failed to achieve in a verifiable manner all the agreed objectives of the Contadora Document of Objectives."[5] A few days later, Abrams told reporters that the wording of the Habib letter had been mistaken.[6] "Obviously, we're not going to drop the contras until the treaty has been not only signed but enacted and the provisions of the treaty carried out, and that would take quite a while."[7]

Constantine Menges, in the meantime, saw a "steamroller that was building toward a false treaty on June 6."[8] The Pentagon's analysts predicted that the Sandinistas would "conclude that a Contadora-like peace accord would provide them the shield from behind which they could continue their use of subversive aggression to impose Communist regimes throughout Central America."[9] The logic seemed inescapable: If the Sandinistas were sure to violate any treaty they signed, then why would they not sign any treaty? "The Soviet-supported Communists would be crazy not to sign," William Safire wrote. "The cutoff of aid to the pesky resistance is real, while honest elections with press freedom and an end to subverting neighbors are promises that fall trippingly from the tongue."[10] This was not only the conservatives' logic, moreover. It was the logic of the Contadora Group and many Democrats in Congress, who also assumed the Sandinistas would understand that the Reagan administration's policy of aggression could be crippled if the Sandinistas signed the Contadora draft in June.

The Sandinistas, however, continued to view matters differently. The best evidence of this was their reaction to the Habib letter and the ensuing controversy in Washington. At one point in April, before the Habib letter was released, Sergio Ramírez had suggested that if the Reagan administration promised to cease aiding the contras on the date of signature, Nicaragua might sign the treaty. No sooner had Habib's letter hinted at doing just that, however, than Sandinista leaders began adding new conditions. On April 25 Daniel Ortega declared it was not enough for the United States to promise to end support for the contras, it would also have to "accept a dialogue with Nicaragua in order to reach an agreement allowing the normalization of relations."[11] Two days later, Ortega insisted that the United States also had to sign the Contadora document. "[I]f they make no direct commitment to sign the document, then we cannot be carried away by what Mr. Habib or other U.S. officials have said."[12] The Sandinistas ran away from the Habib letter as fast as the Reagan administration did, and for the same reason. They did not want the Contadora treaty to be signed.

The May 8 inauguration of Costa Rican President Arias provided the next occasion for discussing the treaty, and Contadora ministers hoped that with the presence of so many Latin heads of state, there was the chance of a more serious dialogue.[13] On May 6, however, the Nicaraguan government announced that Daniel Ortega would not attend the inauguration, allegedly because the Costa Rican government would not provide adequate security. In Ortega's place, the Sandinistas sent not their foreign minister nor even their deputy foreign minister, but only their ambassador to Costa Rica, whose low status insured that she could not take part in negotiations with the other four Central American presidents or their foreign ministers.[14] The Sandinistas consequently suffered a number of rebukes. Peru's President Alan García publicly asked that they sign the Contadora agreement without demanding prior commitments from the United States. President Arias declared June 6 "a sacred date," and President Cerezo of Guatemala said it would be a "very sad day for the whole region" if the treaty were not signed.[15] Ortega responded from Managua two days later by saying it was "very risky" to establish a firm date for the signing of the treaty and a mistake to "create expectations."[16]

For the Sandinistas, the problem remained the draft treaty's proposed limits on armaments. Daniel Ortega declared on May 10 that he would not make "*any* commitment to Contadora that puts the people's weapons on the negotiating table."[17] Defense Minister Humberto Ortega made clear that it didn't matter what the United States did or promised to do: The size of the Sandinista army and the number of weapons it required were not negotiable. Even if the United States stopped supporting the contras immediately, Ortega insisted, Nicaragua still had to defend itself. "Who is going to guarantee that later on the United States will not attack us?" he asked. The Sandinistas had to have "an army capable of confronting the worst variation of interventionism." Ortega declared that if it was necessary to arm "400, 500, or 600,000 men we will do it. If all of them do not have rifles, grenade launchers, or modern weapons, we will make efforts to acquire them." Ortega further declared that the Sandinistas could not break their strategic ties with the socialist countries that supplied the Sandinista Army's weapons.[18]

If Nicaragua's defense requirements were to be defined as what was necessary to block an invasion from the world's most powerful nation, then it was difficult to imagine any agreement on arms limitations among the five Central American governments. Both friends and foes throughout the hemisphere had underestimated the Sandinistas' determination to preserve their armed forces, even if it meant a renewal of American military assistance to the contras. Democratic politicians in the United States and Latin American diplomats shared the goal of defeating President Reagan's request for contra aid, and they had asked the Sandinistas to put the revolution's fate in their hands. The Sandinistas, however, calculated their interests differently. Humberto Ortega told an American journalist in October 1985 that he favored a negotiated settlement, but one that did not mean "the self-destruction of the revolution."[19] Preservation of the revolution could not be placed in the hands of the Contadora Group, Presidents Arias and Cerezo, or the American Democratic Party. The only reliable guarantor was the Sandinista People's Army. Most other matters were negotiable: the amount of political space that could eventually be accorded the bourgeoisie, the businessmen, and the opposition parties; the extent of state control of the economy; perhaps even a degree of political reform and decentralization that would place some limits on the total power of the Sandinista Directorate. What could not be negotiated was the power of the Sandinista Directorate to determine the direction of the revolution, to oversee any process of reform, to impose changes, if any were necessary, from above, without losing control altogether.

The Sandinistas had reason to believe that the revolution as they had made it could not survive if they gave in to American and Latin pressures. And if the revolution did not survive, most if not all of the Sandinista leaders would not long survive in power either. It had been dismissed as rhetoric when Sandinista leaders argued that the only question being debated in the U.S. Congress was the means of destroying the Sandinista revolution. But the Sandinistas were right to be suspicious of their liberal friends in the United States. It was no comfort to hear leading opponents of contra aid like Congressman Hamilton suggest that arms reduction and changes in Nicaragua's "external behavior" were only first steps, that "over the long term" Nicaragua would be "unable to resist the tide of democracy in Latin America."[20] Perhaps for the moment the consensus in Congress opposed Reagan's war against Nicaragua; it was equally clear that a great majority of American congressmen in both parties was fundamentally opposed to the Sandinista revolution. The presence of four democratically elected Central American presidents at the inauguration ceremonies in Costa Rica cast in even starker relief the Sandinistas' form of rule. Both Democrats and Republicans in the United States hailed the "tide of democracy" in Latin America; both Democrats and Republicans declared that the Sandinistas were "out of step" with the democratic trend in the region.

The American Congress's dramatic switch in 1985 between April and June had been a rude lesson for the Sandinistas. If something as mundane as a trip to Moscow, the eighth in five years, was enough to turn a majority of congressmen in favor of contra aid, what faith could the Sandinistas have in Congress's reliability in the future? It was inevitable that the Sandinistas would have to take other actions in the future to defend the revolution against enemies both internal and external, actions the nervous Democrats in the United States might find even more objectionable than a simple trip to Moscow. Would American aggression be resumed by Congress every time the Sandinistas did what they deemed necessary for self-preservation?

As for the Sandinistas' putative allies in Latin America, their help could only be expected to go so far. Their immediate goal of ending Reagan's contra war stemmed from a vague commitment to an even vaguer concept of "Latin nationalism" against North American hegemony. But pitted against the Latin American governments' commitment to Latin solidarity was their grave economic plight, their debts to American bankers, and their dependence on American markets and financial assistance. Presidents Arias and Cerezo had publicly opposed aid to the contras, but the political climates in their countries, where the Sandinistas were widely disliked, and their almost complete dependence on American economic largesse, inevitably required some public hostility to the Sandinistas as a counterbalance. Even the Mexican government, presumably the Sandinistas' best ally in the hemisphere after Cuba, was divided between a new president eager for better economic ties to the United States and a foreign ministry that was allowed to play to the Mexican and Latin American Left by standing up to Reagan.[21] Such allies in a region where American economic hegemony was a fact were inherently unreliable. The

Sandinistas could look only to themselves, to the Cubans, and to the So-viets for their security.

The Sandinistas' dependence on these "strategic" alliances was one of the main reasons for their opposition to the Contadora treaty. In the era of blossoming détente between the superpowers, the Sandinistas did not dare risk giving the Soviets an excuse to reduce or cease their levels of arms shipments. Despite the fact that the Soviets were pouring weapons into Nicaragua at unprecedented levels, the Sandinistas were less and less impressed with the Soviet commitment to challenging American power, not only in Central America but around the world. Even back in October 1985, Humberto Ortega's exchange with the *Washington Post*'s Joanne Omang revealed concerns about the Soviet Union's staying power. Omang had said "The United States sees the Soviet Union everywhere; that is what it is afraid of." "Is that what they are afraid of," Ortega asked rhetorically, "the Soviet Union? . . . The Soviets have other problems, star wars, etc.; they do not need us for their problems with the United States."[22] The Soviets seemed committed to helping the Sandinistas with the arms necessary to resist American power, so long as the confrontation with the United States continued. But if the Sandinistas themselves agreed in a treaty to limit their supply of arms, they could be fairly sure the Soviet Union would comply.

Contadora, therefore, was a trap. The United States, Daniel Ortega warned, would "turn Contadora into an instrument of negotiation that will lead to the disarmament of the Nicaraguan people."[23] The Sandin-istas believed in 1986 that they were better off fighting the contras than locking themselves into a Contadora treaty that cut at the heart of their power.

Foreign Minister D'Escoto arrived at the May 16 round of talks, there-fore, with new proposals designed to complicate the negotiations on arms limits. The Sandinistas proposed dividing all weapons into two cate-gories—"offensive" and "defensive"—and then placing limits only on the "offensive" weapons. D'Escoto also declared that he did not "believe in the signing of papers while the United States refuses to honor the com-mitment it made not to attack Nicaragua."[24] But on both counts the San-dinistas ran into a solid wall of opposition.

Constantine Menges predicted that at this meeting of the Contadora Group and then at a meeting of the five Central American presidents a week later, Mexico would push the four Central American democracies to "sign the phony treaty ... [and] the likelihood was that Nicaragua, Guatemala, and now Costa Rica would try to pressure El Salvador and Honduras into signing."[25] It was the Sandinistas, however, who found themselves isolated by their four neighbors acting in concert. The Hondurans and Salvadorans responded with their own proposal on armaments, which called for counting practically all weapons as "offensive" and therefore subject to limitation. The Contadora Group, in the end, rejected the whole discussion of offensive and defensive weapons and called for counting all weapons to find a "reasonable balance" of forces among the five countries.

The Sandinistas were isolated, therefore, and not just on the subject of arms limitations. At a meeting of the five presidents in Esquipulas, Guatemala, at the end of May, the newly inaugurated President Arias decided to emphasize "democratization" in Nicaragua as a central requirement of any agreement. The Costa Rican president challenged Ortega at Esquipulas and even demanded removal of a phrase in the final communiqué which described the five presidents as "freely elected." Ortega had to acknowledge afterwards that the five presidents had been unable to agree on the "issue of democracy and pluralism in Central America."[26]

Arias's renewed emphasis on the issue of democratization was an open challenge not only to the Sandinistas but to the Contadora Group, which had all but declared that aspect of the negotiations closed. His reopening of the political section of the draft treaty owed much to the assiduous diplomacy of Habib, who tirelessly emphasized this issue in his trips throughout Central America, to the point where Daniel Ortega complained publicly that the United States was "encouraging certain Central American governments to propose, as a decisive issue, the definition and acceptance or nonacceptance of a given type of democracy." Ortega accused Arias of "sabotaging Contadora's negotiation efforts by discussing this topic of democracy now, by engaging in this somewhat philosophical and irrelevant discussion."[27] But on June 5, the day before Contadora's deadline, Guatemala's President Cerezo joined in insisting that "the Nicaraguan democratization process" had to be discussed before any treaty could be signed.[28] By the beginning of June it was clear that the Central Americans were no closer to agreement on the security issues and had moved further apart on the political issues in the treaty. The much-awaited June 6 deadline was destined to pass without consequence. At the Esquipulas summit, the Sandinistas balked at even mentioning the June 6 deadline in the final communiqué. They were not alone: The will to conclude a treaty by that date, or by any date, was lacking on all sides. The Contadora Group, never one to insist on its own deadlines, presented a new draft of the treaty on June 7 and proposed another deadline for responses from the Central American governments. The summer ended without further progress, however.

The Reagan administration breathed an audible sigh of relief, expressing contentment that the Central American governments had not been "forced into action."[29] The accusations from conservatives of an impending "sellout" subsided; Habib was given credit by Democrats for having made an effort to support negotiations. The Reagan administration, having weathered the storms from both right and left, turned its attention to the next battle for contra aid.

41

Contra "Reform"

The adverse developments in the Contadora negotiations did much to weaken earlier arguments by moderates that new contra aid should wait until diplomacy had been tried. Congressman McCurdy and twelve other moderate Democrats and Republicans had flown to Central America in the first week of June for meetings with all five presidents. They found the four democratically elected presidents pessimistic about the prospects for further negotiations led by the Contadora Group. The Sandinistas were "just drag[ging] this out," Guatemalan President Cerezo insisted, and Arias declared he was not "going to allow Contadora to go on and on and on." As usual, the delegation members added their own nuance to these statements when they returned to Washington, so that while Congressman Bustamante came back from Central America convinced that "the Sandinistas intend[ed] to delay and to stall for time, playing on public opinion in this hemisphere and in Europe,"[1] Congressman Spratt insisted that "all five" presidents believed a Contadora treaty "could be achieved in 90 days, provided the parties genuinely want a treaty."[2] Nevertheless, members of Congress had ample reason to understand that Contadora was on its last legs. The four presidents were, in fact, in the first stages of rebellion against the Contadora Group, and moderates in Congress applauded them for taking "destiny into their own hands."[3]

In addition to learning that the negotiations were stalled, perhaps permanently, the visiting members came away impressed with the four democratically elected leaders and appalled by Daniel Ortega—the only "national leader in military uniform," as one member remarked.[4] The evident unity of the four democratically elected presidents against the Sandinistas greatly influenced the approaching debate on contra aid. The rebels, President Arias said, had no chance of winning. He opposed supporting an endless war in Nicaragua which could only mean "no economic growth in Costa Rica." On the other hand, Arias argued, there would be "contras forever unless Nicaraguans feel they have free elections."[5] In general, he insisted, there would be "no peace in Central America if there is no democracy." The other presidents agreed that pressure on the Sandinistas to carry out fair elections was essential.[6]

McCurdy and his colleagues found a new dynamic at work in Central American politics. The four elected leaders had united around democratization as a matter of self-preservation. All four understood that their survival as national leaders rested heavily, if not solely, on the fact that they had been elected. Elections were their base of legitimacy, their chief source of power, and, in relation to the United States, the key to their economic and political survival. To ask the world to defend democracy in Central America was the same as asking the world to defend them, the elected presidents. With the exception of Arias, they all faced the same threats: powerful militaries accustomed to ruling; weak if not failing economies; and in El Salvador and Guatamela, leftist guerrillas. By displaying and emphasizing their democratic credentials, they could enlist broad American support from Reagan administration officials and members of Congress, from Republicans and Democrats, from liberals and conservatives.

McCurdy and his colleagues carried Arias's theme back to Washington. "These are impressive men with proven democratic credentials," McCurdy told reporters. "We should look to them on how to establish peace and democracy in Central America."[7] McCurdy and his colleagues left Central America believing "more than ever," according to Bruce Cameron, "that the Sandinistas were a threat to their democratic neighbors and that the solution to the Sandinista challenge was to force accountability upon them through the ballot. They believed that the contras were not the solution, but were indispensable to achieving one."[8]

The Reagan administration reaped the benefit, for the message of the four presidents that so appealed to McCurdy and his colleagues was nothing more than the central point on which President Reagan had long insisted. Two moderates who had voted against aid in March returned from the trip to Central America publicly espousing a policy toward Nicaragua fundamentally consistent with the President's. Congressman Bustamante from Texas, a consistent follower of McCurdy, told his House colleagues he "came away with the strong feeling that we need to continue to pressure the Sandinistas. . . . [T]here will be no peace in Central America until internal reform is forced upon the Sandinistas."[9] Indeed, of the thirteen members who traveled to Central America with McCurdy, four turned from opposition to support of the $100 million for the contras, and others in Congress were influenced by their conversion.[10]

McCurdy returned to Washington ready to negotiate again with the Reagan administration.[11] Most of McCurdy's suggestions were acceptable to Reagan officials. With their new-found admiration for the four democratically elected presidents, for instance, McCurdy and other moderates wanted to provide more than $300 million in economic assistance to Costa Rica, El Salvador, Honduras, and Guatemala, above and beyond the aid already provided them in the foreign assistance bill. The Reagan administration had no trouble embracing increased aid to its allies and welcomed the new congressional enthusiasm for what were now widely referred to as the "emerging democracies in Central America."[12]

The Sandinistas were not the only Nicaraguans to feel the pressure to reform. The growing consensus in favor of democratization also affected the contras and the continuing struggles among their political leaders. In the weeks leading to the next vote on aid to the contras, a long-simmering crisis in the contra leadership threatened to undermine the new support in Congress for the administration's policies. In the end, this crisis created even broader support for the contras.

Since June 1985 when Arturo Cruz, Alfonso Robelo, and Adolfo Calero had allied as the United Nicaraguan Opposition (UNO), a power struggle between Calero and the other two had threatened the contra leadership. Cruz and Robelo demanded at least equal control of the rebel army, and Calero resisted. While the two technically held a majority within UNO, Calero was president of the FDN, upon which UNO had been grafted. Any authority over the FDN's troops by the UNO Directorate depended on Calero.

Cruz and Robelo looked to the Reagan administration to force Calero to concede his exclusive powers. They argued that the Americans had made Calero the leader of the contras and could just as easily make them the leaders. The fight against Calero recalled the fight against Somoza in this and other ways. It again displayed the strength of Nicaraguan opposition politicians when courting sympathies in the American political culture and their weakness when facing the *caudillo* in the political culture of Nicaragua. It also revealed, again, the difficulties an American administration had in "intervening" in Nicaraguan political struggles on any side.

The first recourse of Cruz's supporters had been to the American press. Before this campaign, Adolfo Calero had led the FDN for three years without ever himself becoming the specific target of criticism in the United States.[13] His record as a staunch opponent of Somoza was undisputed, and in the Carter years William Bowdler had singled Calero out as an opposition leader officials in Washington should meet. As late as March 1985, James LeMoyne of the *New York Times* described Calero favorably as "an outspoken opponent" of the dictatorship who was "jailed for organizing a strike of businessmen against Somoza in 1978."[14] During the struggle with Cruz and Robelo, however, Calero's public image underwent a transformation. By May 1986 LeMoyne was describing Calero as an "extreme political conservative," and other journalists were calling him "an ultra-conservative"—the same term used to described supporters of the "death squads" in El Salvador.[15]

It was easier for supporters of Cruz and Robelo to tell Americans that Calero was an "ultraconservative" and thus a "Somocista" than to explain their real objection to Calero, which was that, regardless of politics or ideology, he had become a classic Nicaraguan *caudillo*.[16] It was not that Calero was himself a Somocista, Robert Leiken explained, but that he practiced politics in the "style of Somoza—relying on cliques rather than institutions."[17] Even this explanation fell a bit short, however, for in a rebel army there were no genuine "institutions" to rely on.

The view of Calero as *caudillo* was by no means limited to Cruz and his supporters, however. Oliver North had become sufficiently troubled by rumors of corruption surrounding Calero and his allies in the FDN that he had taken control of privately raised funds out of Calero's hands and given it to Richard Secord. Indeed, North's fateful decision to have Secord establish and manage resupply operations for the contras probably owed much to North's perception of Calero's failings as a leader and organizer. North's unofficial lieutenant in Central America, Rob Owen, grew sharply critical of Calero at the beginning of 1986. Calero had "used his strength and will and the FDN to further consolidate his hold on the resistance and to gain control of UNO." Owen described Calero as the "strong man. . . . What he says is law." Those who followed him were "liars" motivated by "greed and power." Owen also suspected that monies were being "pocketed" by FDN leaders, although he had no proof.[18] Owen doubted whether the United States retained any influence over Calero, suggesting that it was Calero who could and did "manipulate" the United States government. According to Owen, Calero and the FDN leaders no longer trusted even North, because they resented his and Owen's support for UNO, because they were angry that North had reduced their control over the finances and the army, and, in short, because even North, their closest American ally, was taking away Calero's exclusive control of the contras.[19]

Sympathy for Cruz's complaints about Calero was greatest at the State Department. Elliott Abrams had become the administration's leading spokesman for aid to the contras and was one of its most effective advocates on Capitol Hill. It was clear that the moderate Democrats and Republicans upon whom the administration depended were fond of Cruz and hostile to Calero. From purely political calculations, therefore, Abrams and other State Department officials wanted Cruz and Robelo to be content. Calero stood in the way. Cruz also appealed to Abrams's ideological proclivities. Calero, although no "ultra-conservative," did seem to stand only for anti-communism. The more progressive rhetoric of the Cruzistas was in keeping with Abrams's conception of the "Reagan Doctrine" as not just anti-communist but pro-democratic. It was an echo of the policies Abrams was conducting in El Salvador, in Haiti, and in Chile. Moreover, Abrams agreed with Cruz and his supporters that the broadest possible cross-section of the Nicaraguan opposition should be brought within the contra alliance.[20] Since Cruz had been the opposition's candidate for president in 1984, he seemed capable of uniting rather than dividing the armed and unarmed opposition to the Sandinistas. Calero's style, on the other hand, was exclusive, and the more Cruz and his American backers pushed, the more Calero resisted. This was a tactical error, ironically reminiscent of Somoza's. Flexibility would have served Calero better. Abrams had no special affection for Calero in any case, and Calero, who had developed close ties with CIA officials and North, had failed to notice Abrams's increasing influence within the Reagan administration.

Even State Department officials were not prepared to go as far and as fast as Cruz wanted, however. Cruz and his supporters insisted the "Somozists" had to be "purged" from the contras' leadership. Senior Reagan officials, including Abrams, did not agree. It did not seem conceivable to Reagan officials that Cruz and Robelo, who had visited the contras' camps less than a half-dozen times, could take over Calero's role. Indeed, it did not seem conceivable to Cruz's followers either. Cruz had never wanted to be a military chieftain. In public statements, Cruz disavowed military goals and spoke only of negotiations. Even when asked if he would support a military victory if the Sandinistas refused all peaceful settlements, Cruz responded, "No. No, no, no, no." He had cultivated over the years an image as senior statesman and man of peace. He was unwilling to see it tarnished, which was one reason he was always on the verge of resigning. His position as contra leader was an inherent contradiction. No Reagan officials, even those most partial to Cruz, saw him as the man to whom sole control of the military could be given.

Nor, however, could the Reagan administration afford to let Cruz resign. Congressman McCurdy had been quick to declare that if the rebels did not undertake necessary "reforms," which meant giving Cruz and Robelo the powers they demanded, then Congress would "walk away from them."[21] When the simmering mutual suspicions and resentments among the three leaders of UNO blossomed into full-blown confrontation in the spring of 1986, Reagan officials were forced to intercede to prevent the collapse of the alliance and the loss of crucial support in Congress.

In February Cruz's American and Nicaraguan supporters had presented Abrams with a list of demands designed to put UNO, and by implication Cruz, in charge of all aspects of the struggle.[22] Cruz and Robelo warned they would not lobby Congress for more aid to the contras if their demands were not met. "If I am to go the Hill and talk to Congress," Cruz told Abrams, "I must be honest and tell the truth. I will not tell them that we control the military." Calero angrily retorted, "You have control of the military through me. And you are forgetting your first responsibility. You promised the commanders in your first visit to Honduras that you would get aid for them." But Robelo responded that if the contra troops didn't recognize him and Cruz as their leaders, "why should we help them?"[23] Abrams agreed to pursue Cruz's requests, but he urged Cruz and Robelo to go to Congress in the meantime and lobby for the aid. He assured them the reforms would come after the vote was won.[24] "We just got rid of 'Baby Doc,'" Abrams told one Cruz supporter, referring to the recent ousting of the Haitian dictator, "we're about to get rid of Marcos, and in two years we'll be rid of Pinochet. Certainly, we can have Contra reform."[25]

Settling the disputes within the contra alliance required more than

Abrams's assent, however. Calero was a patient and stubborn man. Cruz was notoriously mercurial and given to bouts of frustration, a weakness Calero exploited. When Cruz and Robelo visited the contras' camps in Honduras, they were made to feel unwanted, and they returned from their infrequent visits sputtering with indignation. "Colonel Bermúdez didn't once mention Arturo or me," Robelo complained to Abrams about the contra commander's speech to graduating officers. "They don't recognize our leadership."[26] Bermúdez did not hide his contempt for the whole idea of UNO.[27]

Cruz's defeats among the contras were matched by successes in Washington. In the Senate, moderate Republicans and conservative Democrats made progress in contra "reform" their condition for passing the administration's proposal. The legislation required the administration to support both the broadening and the unification of the contra leadership. Its purpose was to encourage the inclusion of Nicaraguans perceived as more liberal than Calero and to subordinate the military force to civilian leadership, which really meant the subordination of Calero's FDN to Cruz's UNO. Buoyed by this victory in the Senate, Cruz demanded immediate action by the administration to redress the balance in the resistance movement. The CIA's Alan Fiers met with Cruz to reassure him that the reforms would take place. He told Cruz, "Arturo, I know you are concerned about the slow pace of reform, but I promise you it will come. But you have to be careful, you can't push them too hard. Without the FDN, there is no resistance to the Sandinistas. They are the core, the crucial, indispensable element. Give us time. They'll change." Cruz, incensed by what appeared to him to be Fiers's unshakable commitment to Calero and the FDN, stalked out of the room and promptly resigned.[28]

Cruz's supporters convinced him to suspend his resignation while Reagan officials took steps to answer his complaints. By April even the CIA's patience with Calero's obstructionism had worn thin and, with another vote approaching, administration officials agreed it was time to force Calero to make some sacrifices. Abrams gave Calero an ultimatum: Either he agreed immediately to negotiate with Cruz in good faith, or he would face a cutoff of the remaining American "humanitarian" assistance to the FDN.[29] Now Calero was furious. He told American officials that Cruz and Robelo had no following inside or outside Nicaragua. "Who has more people?" Calero fumed. "Ask yourself that question. Who has more followers? ... Cruz and Robelo are only two. How many do they represent?"[30] Calero agreed to Abrams's blunt ultimatum, however, and

meetings between Cruz, Robelo, and Calero were scheduled for the beginning of May.

As so often in the history of U.S.-Nicaraguan relations, the American
administration, having intervened partially to demand a change, could
not bring itself to intervene fully and impose a settlement of the conflict
among Nicaraguans. Instead, it preferred to force the two sides to work
out their differences, but with the clear understanding that it was the
caudillo who had to make concessions. And as usual, when the
Nicaraguans struggling against the *caudillo* were finally handed this opportunity to establish themselves, they faltered and showed their weakness. Given the chance to make demands of Calero at his moment of
weakness, Cruz and Robelo suddenly grew timid. In the second half of
April, Cruz's supporters, assigned to work with FDN officials to draft position papers for the May meetings, found their leader withdrawn, unwilling
to assert his views or even to involve himself in the preparatory deliberations.[31] Before the May meetings had even begun, therefore, Cruz's supporters conceded on their most important demand. Instead of eradicating
the FDN as an independent political-military organization and subsuming
it under UNO, they allowed the FDN to survive. Instead of fighting the
issue, one Cruz supporter recalls, "Cruz sulked."[32] The alliance between
Cruz and Robelo also cracked at this crucial moment. Perhaps Robelo's
instincts for survival led him to keep his distance from the erratic Cruz,
who so often seemed bent on resignation.[33] When Cruz and his supporters
demanded that all decisions of the UNO directorate be made by majority
vote, giving Cruz and Robelo dominance over Calero, Robelo undermined him, recommending that the minority in a losing vote would have
the right to appeal. Cruz again threatened to resign, and his American
supporters talked Robelo into backing down. The final compromise, however, gave Calero a veto over decisions affecting military strategy, appointments, and dismissals of military officials, and major political decisions—
thus preserving his hold over the FDN. These concessions would later
help erode the gains Cruz and Robelo had won.

For the time being, however, despite the weakness of the reformers, the
May meetings resulted in a significant diminution of Calero's authority
within the movement. With Reagan officials threatening a cutoff of aid,
Calero "voluntarily ceded some of his influence to ward off a move by administration officials to force him to do so."[34] Under pressure from U.S.
officials, particularly from the CIA, Calero made a tactical retreat. According to Cruz's supporters, Alan Fiers "delivered Adolfo."[35] The final

agreement did strengthen the authority of UNO over the FDN and other member organizations, specifically directing that all "political, financial, and military resources" were to be placed "at the service of UNO." While the FDN continued to exist as a political entity, the communiqué declared that "none of the groups in the alliance will have an army." The FDN army was now supposed to be UNO's army. Cruz's allies won control of foreign relations, and the document stated that a combined military and diplomatic strategy offered "the most effective means to force the Sandinist regime to adopt a real solution."[36] It also declared that UNO was to be governed by "the principle of civilian authority over the military, respecting the line of command in each structure."[37] To symbolize the new subservience of the military, Bermúdez was directed to submit his agreement to the new arrangements in writing to the UNO directorate and to pledge his subservience to the new civilian authority. Robelo declared that UNO was "in its most solid, firm position ever."[38]

The May 29 agreement turned a crisis into a political victory for the Reagan administration, and especially for Elliott Abrams. The press reported a measured triumph for Cruz and Robelo, a defeat for Calero's "conservative" forces, and, although doubts were raised about the real meaning of the changes made in Miami, members of Congress who followed the issue closely declared themselves satisfied with the results. Senators Kassebaum and Cohen, and Congressmen Aspin, Skelton, and Bustamante stood more firmly on the side of contra aid than earlier in the year.[39] Kassebaum expressed hope that the contras would become "a group we can be proud to support," Senator Lugar praised Abrams for "spurring Contra leadership reform,"[40] and supporters of aid put a provision in their bill placing the secretary of state, or his "designee," in charge of the overall program, making Abrams first among equals within the administration.

The benefit to the administration was nothing compared to the loss it would have suffered in Congress had Cruz resigned. On the eve of the Miami meetings, McCurdy had told reporters: "If Cruz walks, they might as well kiss support to the rebels good-bye. It would clearly be seen as a sign that the rebels refuse to become more democratic and provide a reasonable alternative to the Sandinistas."[41] Now that Cruz had not resigned, and even appeared to have won in his dispute with Calero, the contras more than ever appeared to many moderates in Congress as a movement with political promise. With the issue of "contra reform" temporarily settled, disagreements between the Reagan administration and McCurdy's moderates further narrowed.

42

The $100 Million Aid Vote—Round Two

McCurdy and the Republicans collided again, however, over the issue of a second vote. McCurdy still insisted that while "humanitarian" aid could begin immediately, military aid could not be released for 90 days, now October 1, to give time for a negotiated settlement under Contadora. Aid could then be released only by a joint resolution of the House and Senate. But administration officials still would not compromise on this point, nor did they feel they had to. As the negotiations proceeded, it became clear that a potentially decisive segment of moderates, including a portion of the McCurdy group, was prepared to support a bill acceptable to the administration. The Reagan administration and House Republicans believed they could win without McCurdy. They went forward with their own bill, adopting those aspects of McCurdy's plan they liked, and rejecting the rest.

While talks with administration supporters continued, McCurdy also met with the House Democratic leadership. With the possibility of a big defeat on contra aid looming, O'Neill made yet another concession to McCurdy. He offered to make McCurdy's amendment part of the underlying military construction bill so that when the overall bill passed, McCurdy's legislation would be approved automatically, without any direct vote. Liberals would be given an opportunity to defeat all contra aid by offering another amendment sponsored by Hamilton, but otherwise they were required to lend their support to McCurdy from the beginning, merely by agreeing to O'Neill's rule.[1] The only virtue of the rule, for liberals, was that they would not have to cast a vote for McCurdy's proposal. It was another painful concession for liberal members convinced that McCurdy supported the contra war almost as much as the Reagan administration.

The debate on the House floor on June 25 lacked the passion of previous encounters. Liberals knew the battle was lost. Moderate supporters and opponents of McCurdy's proposal had almost nothing to argue about. President Reagan had helped lower the heat of debate by giving a most conciliatory speech the day before. Designed to appeal to moderates of both parties, the speech was written by Bernard Aronson and gave favorable mention to a slew of moderate Democrats, including Les Aspin, who had traveled to Nicaragua with Aronson and Robert Leiken in April and come back supporting military aid to the contras. President Reagan, cutting short his usual litany of the Sandinistas' sins, said he knew "that even the administration's harshest critics hold no brief for Sandinista repression." Reagan credited his Democratic opponents with "honest questions" and "honest fears" about his policy. While he called McCurdy's bill a "tragic mistake," it was "offered I know in good faith." For the first time, Reagan acknowledged that the behavior of the contras was not above reproach, that human rights abuses had occurred "in the past" and were "intolerable." He promised he would "not permit this democratic revolution to be betrayed nor allow a return to the hated repression of the Somoza dictatorship." Paraphrasing Arias, Reagan declared that "the only way to bring true peace and security to Central America is to bring democracy to Nicaragua. And the only way to get the Sandinistas to negotiate seriously about democracy is to give them no other alternative."

Reagan, of course, had been saying much the same thing for more than three years. In a succession of widely celebrated "gaffes," the President had called for democracy in Nicaragua, stated this as his goal in supporting the contras, declared his intention to make the Sandinistas say "uncle" and give up their Marxist-Leninist project, and been forced to retreat in the face of those who claimed that insisting on democratization in Nicaragua was tantamount to calling for the Sandinistas' overthrow. By June 1986, however, such statements were on the lips of moderate Democrats and Republicans and elected presidents in Central America. Reagan's speech, widely praised for its "responsible" and bipartisan tone, was a rhetorical concession to the moderates in Congress; but it was a substantive concession by them to the President. Reagan could afford the conciliatory, even apologetic tone because the core of the argument had been conceded by a majority of Congress.

The floor debate on June 25 revealed the extent to which McCurdy had divided and weakened Reagan's opponents, even as he himself led the fight against Reagan's preferred amendment. Liberals did not bother to make the broader, ideological case against American intervention in Nicaragua. Instead they concentrated their attack on allegations of corruption in the distribution of NHAO funds.[2] Congressman Barnes proposed an amendment to withhold further aid until all past aid had been accounted for. It was defeated, 225–198.

The House leadership took little part in the debate. The Democratic whip, Thomas Foley, seemed positively grateful to the President for abandoning his earlier anti-Democratic rhetoric. "Yesterday I think the President approached the issue of good will of people on both sides of this question in the proper tone and sense. This body has no unpatriotic members."[3] For the first time in three years, neither Jim Wright nor Tip O'Neill spoke. For Wright, still balancing his party's divergent sectional interests just months before a general election and his own expected rise to the Speakership, there was nothing to be gained from speaking out.

As in the past, McCurdy's legislative tactic was to portray his policy as all things to all members. "For those opposed to military aid," Congressman Spratt argued, "we withhold aid for 90 days, and make it subject to a second vote. For those who demand aid now, we provide aid now, $30 million . . . enough . . . to sustain the contras as a force."[4] Jim Chapman, the besieged freshman from conservative eastern Texas, insisted McCurdy's was "a policy that exerts absolutely the maximum amount of pressure on Nicaragua" because "in the event of the failure of those negotiations, it is the McCurdy plan that delivers the heavy metal to the contras earlier."[5]

McCurdy's insistence on a second vote less than a month before the 1986 congressional elections lost the support of those who did not want to revisit the question in the middle of their re-election campaigns.[6] Many members were simply tired of the issue.[7] Others had become convinced that the Sandinistas were not ready to negotiate. Congresswoman Olympia Snowe declared that they had already "been provided ample time by this Congress to show a spirit of true conciliation and compromise." It was "time for the Congress to take decisive action on behalf of democracy in Central America."[8]

In the end, McCurdy's grounds for opposing the administration had become too narrow to sustain enough of his moderate followers. Of the two dozen members who clustered loosely around Congressman McCurdy, at least half, including McCurdy himself, favored contra aid in some form. They were more in agreement with the conservative authors of the administration-backed proposal, Democrat Ike Skelton and Republican Mickey Edwards, than with the majority of their fellow Democrats. Members who rose on June 25 to support McCurdy's bill spoke of "the emergence of a consensus position on Central America in the House." The similarity between the Skelton-Edwards and McCurdy proposals signified the establishment of "a near bipartisan consensus."[9] After the vote, even McCurdy privately expressed his satisfaction with the bill that had passed, which was not surprising, since he had done more than anyone to shape its terms.[10]

The administration-backed Skelton-Edwards amendment passed on June 25 by a margin of 221–209, a reversal of the 11-vote margin against military aid in March. As one of several close votes on contra aid over the years, the passage of the $100 million package in June 1986 has been viewed by some as transient, simply another swing by an ever-vacillating Congress.[11] This was not the common view at the time. Despite the slender margin, Reagan's victory was seen by supporters and opponents alike as both inevitable and decisive. The *Congressional Quarterly* noted that the House of Representatives, "[l]ong the center of opposition to military intervention against Nicaragua . . . for more than a year has been moving toward Reagan's position." The vote fulfilled the predictions of Senator Sasser months earlier that "some sort of military aid" would pass and that it was just a question of "what, if any, preconditions" were attached.[12] At the beginning of April the *New York Times'* Steven V. Roberts, surveying the legislative agenda, had predicted correctly that the President's biggest problem with Congress would be the budget "[w]hile Mr. Reagan seems to have the upper hand on contra aid."[13]

Indeed, as Congressman Barnes later pointed out, since the beginning of 1985 opponents of contra aid had been fighting an uphill battle against the majority in the House who supported aid to the contras. By controlling the rules by which contra aid measures were considered, Speaker O'Neill had reduced the margin of President Reagan's victories and on occasion had defeated him, but legislative tactics had only delayed the final result. "Our whole strategy," Barnes recalls, "was to postpone an up-

or-down vote for two years. We just didn't have the votes if Reagan ever presented it that way."[14]

Clearly, aid to the contras was no longer the political "poison" it had once been. In the spring a majority of Americans polled approved of President Reagan's handling of affairs in Central America, a sharp reversal from the very negative polls that had so troubled Reagan's political advisers three years earlier. By June the President's overall approval rating reached its highest point in six years: 68 percent.[15] Even some Democrats, seeking to define themselves as "centrists" for the coming presidential campaign, used the issue of contra aid to shape their image. The former governor of Virginia, Charles Robb, openly supported contra aid. The American public, he argued, would not "stand behind a party that won't stand up for American values and interests abroad."[16] Senator Bill Bradley of New Jersey also drew attention to himself by supporting contra aid. As one of only two Democratic senators above the Mason-Dixon line to vote for military aid in March, Bradley's choice was even more daring and looked to some like "an important signal of Mr. Bradley's growing interest in foreign policy, a broadening of the field of vision for the Senator."[17]

Keen observers of Congress recognized the broad implications of the June 1986 vote. The *Congressional Quarterly's* John Felton wrote that it "could signal a new consensus of congressional support for—or at least willingness to accept—Reagan's fundamental policy of using the contras to remove the leftist government in Nicaragua. If so, the vote would be comparable to House action in May 1984 that neutralized opposition to Reagan's support for the pro-United States government in El Salvador."[18] The vote on Salvadoran aid in 1984 had brought a consensus on that controversial issue that was never again seriously challenged. The vote on contra aid in the summer of 1986 seemed to have the same decisive quality.

———

In the week of July 4, the cover of *Time* magazine showed a picture of Reagan in front of the Statue of Liberty and called him a magician, the "Prospero of American memories." The consensus Reagan had muscled into place on contra aid, however, was not the product of magic. No policy of the Reagan administration had been more poorly stage-managed, more discordant, more fraught with controversy or more unpopular. Despite haphazard attempts at "public diplomacy," it was not White House theatrics that passed contra aid in June 1986, but two years of often brutal political confrontation and frequent compromise with an ideologically divided Democratic Party. In America's historic vacillation between intervention and withdrawal in Latin America, Reagan and congressional majorities in both houses had pulled the United States in the direction of idealistic intervention. As one Democratic supporter of contra aid put it on June 25, "For four decades we have been trying to induce the Central American republics to move toward democracy. Certainly, it is a form of interventionism, but it is not one we should shy away from. And now, for the first time in history, four of the five republics are democracies.... There can be no long-term peace and stability in Central America unless and until all five countries are democracies."[19]

––––––––––

The bill passed by the House did not become law until October, the consequence of delays in the legislative process both unavoidable and deliberate. The Senate did not vote to pass contra aid until August 13; Congress adjourned for its three-week summer recess; the fiscal year ended with no action; and the $300 million intended for the four Central American democracies had to be returned to the treasury. The omnibus resolution containing contra aid did not finally reach the President's desk for signature until October 18, a week short of four months after the House passed the $100 million aid legislation. Not until the end of November, therefore, did the first fruits of the June 25 vote begin to reach the rebel forces in Honduras.

Throughout those five months, Reagan administration officials feared the Sandinistas would try to deal a final blow to the contra forces before the new aid could take effect. Yet it was in Washington, not in Nicaragua, that the contras suffered their most staggering defeat. What in June had appeared to all observers as Reagan's inevitable triumph on this contentious issue gave way by December to another apparent inevitability, just as widely agreed upon, that the entire contra policy had been doomed from the start.

Part Five

THE IRAN-CONTRA SCANDAL
AND ITS CONSEQUENCES

43

The "Enterprise": A "Tainted Operation"

On October 5, a plane flying supplies to a contra task force in southern Nicaragua was shot down by Sandinista forces, and the one surviving crew member, Eugene Hasenfus, was captured. From Hasenfus's statements, and from documents recovered from the airplane, it was apparent that U.S. government officials could in some way be implicated in the flight, although Reagan officials denied any government involvement. Members of Congress were highly skeptical of the denials, but the relevant committees seemed no more eager to investigate the administration's activities in October 1986 than they had been in August 1985. As the initial furor over the shootdown subsided, moreover, another seemingly unrelated revelation pushed it aside entirely.

On November 2 the American hostage David Jacobsen was released by his captors in Lebanon. By November 6 Washington was abuzz with talk of a secret arms-for-hostages trade with Iran. President Reagan's insistence that he "did not—repeat, did not—trade weapons or anything else for hostages" did not convince many. The administration fell into a serious crisis. Secretaries Shultz and Weinberger made public their opposition to the deal with Iran, while Casey, Poindexter, and North began putting together inaccurate accounts of what had happened and when for the President's use. In his eagerness to deny any arms-for-hostages deal with Iran, Reagan himself made a number of incorrect statements that were quickly contradicted. A press conference on November 19 went terribly and showed the nation, for the first time, a confused and even frightened President Reagan. Attorney General Edwin Meese began an internal investigation to try to piece together an accurate account of what had occurred in the transactions with Iran.

Then on November 25, in an almost unbelievable linking of the explosive Iran arms sale controversy with the quietly simmering matter of the Hasenfus shootdown, Meese announced to the nation that in the course of their investigations officials had uncovered information suggesting that between $12 and $30 million dollars produced in the sale of arms to Iran had been "diverted" to the Nicaraguan contras. From that moment forward, the political controversies swirling around the two separate issues became joined into one "Iran-contra" affair. By the time the contras received the first dollar of new military aid in November, the Reagan administration had pulled itself down into the worst political scandal since Watergate, and the issue of U.S. policy in Nicaragua had become enshrouded in a thick haze of criminality.

The Iran-contra affair has been extensively examined in its legal and constitutional aspects. The effect of the operation on U.S. policy goals in Central America, however, and the actual benefit to the contras of the secret efforts to arm and supply them have received less attention. The scandal that ultimately did such damage to the contras was, of course, not of their own making. Nor, as it turned out, did they derive any more than marginal benefit from the exertions of Reagan officials and private individuals on their behalf. While the Saudi donations in 1984 and 1985 and the "humanitarian" aid voted by Congress in the summer of 1985 were probably essential to keeping the contra force in existence until full aid was restored in 1986, no similar claim can be made about the actions undertaken by North, Richard Secord, and other officials and private citizens from the end of 1985 through the fall of 1986. Indeed, those actions proved as unnecessary, and as futile, as they were ultimately destructive of the people and the policy they were meant to support.

————

Oliver North had approached Richard Secord in July 1985 and asked him to build and oversee an air resupply operation for the contras. By the beginning of 1986 the task still remained months from completion. If aid had passed both houses in March, Secord's entire operation, which by then had absorbed more than $2 million in funds donated for the contras by the Saudi king, by the Taiwanese government, and by private American citizens, would have ended without flying a single resupply mission. Using the money left over from the last Saudi donation in March 1985 and $1 million solicited from Taiwan by North in the fall of 1985, Secord had by January hired a few men on contract to run the resupply operation, gained agreement from the Salvadoran air force chief to use the military airfield at Ilopango as a main base of operations, purchased one Caribou C-7 aircraft, and begun construction of an emergency airstrip on land purchased in northern Costa Rica. In February, the government of Taiwan contributed another $1 million, and another several hundred thousand dollars were passed to accounts controlled by Secord from private fundraisers working with North. By April Secord had purchased another C-7 and a C-123 and the airstrip in Costa Rica was well on its way to completion. The first resupply mission, however, was not flown until April 1, 1986.[1]

Secord's operation began badly. Between April 1 and April 11, the C-7 flew a dozen missions, but these were "just short missions along the border," as Secord later recalled, delivering arms previously purchased by Calero from FDN warehouses to the FDN's staging areas in Honduras. These kinds of deliveries did not address the fundamental problem of supplying contra forces deployed in Nicaragua. The principal aim of Secord's operation—to deliver supplies to the small but needy forces in the south of Nicaragua—was not being accomplished at all.[2] After April 11, the operation abruptly stopped without having made a single delivery to any forces in the north or south of Nicaragua. Secord, acknowledging that his operation was "still not functioning correctly," hired a retired air force colonel, Robert Dutton, to look into the problem.[3] The new manager found that "the aircraft were in very poor condition. There was a lack of spare parts. We weren't able to keep them flying. Because the aircraft weren't flying, we weren't making any deliveries. . . . It just wasn't working."[4] Flights resumed in May, but by the end of May southern forces had still not received a delivery from Secord's operation, and the resupply of the FDN in the north still consisted almost exclusively of ferrying previously purchased weapons back and forth within Honduras.

From the start, the leaders of the FDN took a dim view of the new resupply effort. It was, after all, born of North's open suspicions of FDN corruption in the handling of the Saudi donations and other funds he had directed into Calero's accounts. Now North had given control of money and deliveries to people who rarely told FDN leaders what they were doing or why. The new resupply operation, such as it was, significantly reduced Calero's and Bermúdez's stature as leaders of the troops at precisely the same time that their political hegemony was being challenged by Cruz and Robelo in the battle for influence within UNO. The main purpose of the new resupply operation, moreover—to send weapons to the Southern Front—was anathema to FDN leaders. While from the perspective of military strategy, the establishment of a Southern Front was important to stretch the Sandinista army and take pressure off the forces in the north, FDN leaders hoped their own forces would eventually create a front in the south emanating from the strongholds of the Jorge Salazar task forces in the south-central province of Boaco. Bermúdez didn't believe there should be a Southern Front separate from the FDN.[5]

The Americans had other, non-military goals, however. A Southern Front independent of Calero and Bermúdez strengthened the more "progressive" Costa Rica-based politicians, like Cruz and Robelo, and thus had become an issue in the overall contra "reform."[6] Part of wooing Cruz and Robelo to the contras meant giving them a force they could call their own. The CIA, moreover, was trying to win the allegiance of Pastora's former commanders to the new UNO/South organization led by "El Negro" Chamorro, whose political allies were Robelo and Cruz. In the meantime Alfredo César was trying to bring Pastora's men under his own leadership.[7] In the midst of the contras' May meetings in Miami, Cruz and Robelo scored a victory, with the CIA's assistance, by persuading almost all the commanders once loyal to Pastora to unite with them in UNO as part of "El Negro's" southern forces.[8]

Bermúdez was furious.[9] From the point of view of Calero and Bermúdez, any strengthening of the southern forces further tipped the balance against them in the political struggle with these self-proclaimed "progressive" politicians. It was particularly galling to the FDN leaders that weapons in their stockpiles would be used to supply a competing force in the south, and that monies which they believed had been donated for the FDN were being used to supply other forces, while so many of their own men languished in Honduran base camps.[10] Such was the FDN's unwillingness to release weapons from their stockpiles that Secord finally had to purchase weapons specially for the southern front and stockpile them at Ilopango air force base in El Salvador, out of the FDN's reach.[11]

By the end of April, despite the fact that Secord's operation had absorbed over $2 million worth of contributions intended for the contras, leaving them with nothing in their coffers, the FDN had nothing to show for the effort and did not even control the planes that had been bought with donations given to support them. In late April, North visited the contras' camps and wrote despairingly to officials in Washington that "the lack of a viable source of resupply has not only affected combat operations but is now beginning to affect the political viability of the UNO leadership." Calero told North the whole operation was "lousy."[12] Bermúdez, North reported, questioned the need for a Southern Front and, for that matter, the need for the UNO alliance, right in front of the Southern Front commander "El Negro" Chamorro.[13] The FDN leaders' hostility to the new resupply effort undoubtedly played a part in its ultimate revelation in the press during the late spring and summer of 1986.[14]

By the end of April, Reagan officials were becoming deeply concerned at the prospect of the contras running out of supplies before the Congress approved new aid legislation. The concern was uniform both among those who knew what the so-called "private benefactors" were doing and among those who did not. North's reports were the most dire, but it is unclear whether his accounts of the contras' situation were genuine or designed to push the administration to take action. Although North reported at the end of April that the contras were down to one meal a day, that medical services were on the brink of shutting down, and that Bermúdez was warning of a lack of ammunition, Calero later recalled that the FDN still had enough arms and ammunition in the spring.[15] The CIA's analysts and NHAO officials estimated that the "humanitarian" aid would not run out until the end of June.[16] Even though Secord's resupply operation had so far failed to deliver much, the contras could survive until the next vote. The contras' military actions had dwindled considerably, to be sure, and were confined to scattered attacks by the Jorge Salazar forces in central Nicaragua and occasional raids in the northern provinces, but so long as they found safe haven in Honduras, they were not on the verge of elimination before June.

There was some doubt, however, that Congress would pass aid by the end of June. After the defeat of McCurdy's alternative on April 15, the prospects of quick action by O'Neill had turned bleak. Administration officials were aware that even if aid was passed at the end of June, it might be September before the legislation reached the President and the aid began flowing to the contras. How to bridge this gap became a consuming interest of administration officials at the beginning of May.

On May 1 President Reagan told Poindexter, "If we can't move the Contra package before June 9, I want to figure out a way to take action

unilaterally to provide assistance." Recalling his recent decision to provide emergency assistance to Honduras without congressional authorization, the President wanted some way of helping the contras equally immune from congressional meddling. According to Poindexter, Reagan was
"ready to confront the Congress on the Constitutional question of who
controls foreign policy."[17] A meeting of the National Security Planning
Group (NSPG) was scheduled two weeks later, at which Shultz declared
bluntly that "the real problem is that if we don't get money to the freedom
fighters, they are going to be out of business."[18]

At the meeting on May 16, both North and Alan Fiers, the chief of the
CIA task force running the contra war, urged their superiors to support a
plan to ask Congress to "reprogram" $15 million in "humanitarian" aid for
delivery by the CIA, which would keep the contras alive until legislation
passed and new aid could be disbursed. Fiers insisted this was the most
straightforward way to get the needed funds, and it had the added advantage of bringing the CIA fully into the program for the first time in two
years.[19] North was also increasingly eager to have the CIA take over the
resupply operation. His own efforts were showing little progress and were
exposing him to increasing danger of public exposure. To obtain a repro-
gramming of funds for this purpose, however, the administration needed
the agreement of both House and Senate intelligence committees and
both appropriations committees. Since the House had not yet voted to
provide aid at all, let alone to allow the CIA to deliver it, and since the
Senate Appropriations Committee chairman, Senator Mark Hatfield, was
a fervent opponent of contra aid, Secretary Shultz objected at the May 16
meeting that the idea was "breathtaking in improbability." Casey gave
in.[20] At one point, President Reagan asked, intriguingly, "What about the
private groups who pay for ads for the contras? Have they been contacted? Could they do more than ads?"[21] But the President's question apparently elicited no response from his advisers.[22] Instead, Secretary Shultz
recommended seeking funds for the contras from other countries, as allowed under the 1985 legislation. This plan was adopted, and Poindexter
instructed Shultz to draw up a list of potential donors.[23] Shultz and
Abrams settled on the idea of approaching the Sultan of Brunei, one of
the richest men in the world, for $10 million in "humanitarian" aid for the
contras. Shultz was due to visit Brunei later in June, and he considered
the possibility of making the request then.

North had other ideas, which he did not share at the May 16 NSPG
meeting. Since late 1985, North had been engaged in efforts to improve

relations with Iran and win the release of American hostages, by selling arms the Iranians needed in their war with Iraq. At some point in early 1986, North came upon the idea of overcharging the Iranians for the weapons and using the surplus to fund the contra resupply operation and other covert activities. Once again, he had turned to Richard Secord to serve as middleman, to handle the transfer of funds, and to manage the surplus in Swiss bank accounts controlled by Secord's partner, Albert Hakim. The first large sale of arms involving Secord occurred in February and generated a surplus of over $4 million. The second sale was to occur in May, and in a memorandum to President Reagan in the first of week of April, later to become famous as the "diversion memo," North advised that $12 million from the surplus "will be used to purchase critically needed supplies" for the contras. It was on the basis of this memorandum that Meese later made his dramatic announcement on November 25.[24]

On May 16, after the NSPG meeting where Shultz was assigned to seek aid from other countries, North reported privately to Poindexter that "the resistance support organization now has more than $6 [million] available for immediate disbursement." North wanted to call off the State Department's search for other funds, but he continued to press for the "reprogramming" due to "the urgent need to get [the] CIA back into the management of this program."[25] Poindexter neither reopened that question nor advised Secretary Shultz that he no longer needed to seek support elsewhere. In June North again expressed concern that the U.S. government was "bifurcating" its efforts to help the contras, with the State Department going in one direction while he went in another. "Money truly is not the thing which is most needed at this point. What we most need is to get the CIA re-engaged in this effort so that it can be better managed than it now is by one slightly confused Marine Lt. Col." Poindexter again declined North's advice. Far from discouraging Shultz and Abrams from seeking support abroad, Poindexter discussed with them the means for transferring the money to the contras while at the same time, as he told North, "not at all letting on that we had access to accounts." Poindexter told North that he, too, wanted to "get out of the business."[26]

North believed the pressure to find new money for the contras had abated. But so far the contras had received little if any money from the arms sales to Iran. The contras survived the months of June through September largely on resources they had already acquired before any "diversion." As it happened, the people whom North had called upon to assist the contras did not share his view of how the money in their accounts should be spent. As a result, nothing like $6 million, let alone $12 million, ever reached the rebel forces.

In his effort to get around the restrictions of the Boland amendment, North had encouraged the formation of an organization which he by no means fully controlled. What Richard Secord called the "enterprise" in his testimony before Congress was a hybrid organization. It carried out covert activities with the cooperation and encouragement of U.S. government officials, served as broker and financial manager in arms sales between the United States government and foreign officials, and was answerable, much of the time, to North. Yet it was also independent of the government and, on occasion, defiant. The "enterprise" had the attributes of a private company, seeking to enhance revenue, stay in business, and make money for its owners. Secord's partner, Hakim, who handled all the finances, described it as a "strange animal . . . with so many different identities."[27] Hakim was a businessman and believed he was "supposed to run things as a businessman does."[28]

When it came to providing money to supply the contras from the accounts they controlled, Secord and Hakim did not always consider North's instructions more important than their own judgments. Secord and Hakim were intent on building up what Hakim called "the financial backbone of the company." On occasion, Hakim explained, North wanted "too much money" for the contras, "and sometimes he gets it, sometimes [Secord] says, well, we cannot afford it. We got to keep the enterprise going."[29] From the first sale of American arms to Iran in February, Secord and Hakim had received the "surplus" of $4.6 million into their accounts. Hakim put $2 million in "reserve" in a certificate of deposit.[30] When North reported to McFarlane on April 21 that the contras' "pot is almost empty,"[31] and Secord reported to North that "current obligations" over the coming weeks would "nearly wipe us out,"[32] the balance in Hakim's account was a little over $2.3 million, with another $2 million in the certificate of deposit.

North himself had other uses in mind for this money besides aiding the contras. He had Secord purchase $100,000 worth of radios for donation to a country in the Caribbean; he also had him purchase a ship for use in future covert operations, at a cost of about $300,000; and he expected Secord to continue his role as middleman in upcoming sales of arms to Iran. What North may not have known was that after the first infusion of funds from the February arms sale to Iran, Secord and Hakim had also directed over $600,000 to various "capital accounts" for their own purposes, in addition to the $4.3 million in their main account and certificate of deposit.[33] In May, Hakim transferred $500,000 into another account for "investment purposes."[34]

The pattern of expenditures from Hakim's accounts suggests that Secord and his partner spent little of the "surplus" from the Iran deal on the contras, and that, insofar as the resupply operation could be sustained solely by other monies contributed specifically for the contras, Secord hoped to use the money from the Iran deals to shore up his company's "financial backbone." Through April, Secord had used only contributions for the contras to pay for the airplanes and the airstrip and the salaries of the pilots and crew. He had not anticipated spending any money on new weapons and only reluctantly purchased a little over $200,000 worth of weapons for the Southern Front in April. Then, when the resupply operation ground to a halt after a brief life in early April, Secord made other "unanticipated" expenditures for spare parts and maintenance to keep his few aircraft flying.[35]

When the second sale of American arms to Iran in May yielded an additional "surplus" of over $8 million, Secord and Hakim put another $2 million in the "reserves," leaving them with the $6 million that North told Poindexter was available for "immediate disbursement" to the contras. At the Iran-contra hearing in the summer of 1987, however, Secord denied that he had ever told North that the $6 million would be used for the contras. "I think he had an expectation that we would support the contras to the extent that we could," Secord told the congressional investigators. "We spent the money that we thought that we could spare from the Iranian initiative. . . . The enterprise needed money."[36]

Through May, June, and July, Secord's air supply operation continued to be plagued with problems. Deliveries in the north remained confined almost exclusively to ferrying the FDN's weapons and supplies from depots to forward positions in Honduras. Contra forces in the south had even more problems. No supply missions were attempted until June, when the airstrip in northern Costa Rica was completed. The first supply mission attempted on June 9, however, failed when the pilot could not find the troops. And when the plane landed at the brand new airfield in Costa Rica it got stuck in mud caused by inadequate drainage, and remained stuck for a day. The airstrip, paid for by funds donated to the contras, was never used again.[37] President Arias had declared Costa Rica's "strict neutrality" in the Nicaraguan conflict, and when he heard about the airstrip he asked that it be shut down.[38] The next two missions to the south also failed to locate forces to drop to, and on the second of these flights the plane struck a tree and lost one engine. Without a spare available, the aircraft was out of commission for almost a month.[39] There was a successful drop in June and one in July. Then the whole operation came to a standstill again in both the north and the south.

In May and June the "enterprise's" account balances ranged from $5 to $11 million, with "reserves" rising to $4 million. Hakim distributed still another $1 million to the partners' "capital" accounts. In the same months, Hakim's records show that a little more than $800,000 was spent on the resupply effort, with another $400,000 spent on arms and munitions. In July Secord spent another $600,000, improving his small, inadequate fleet with new spare parts and a new airplane.

Not only did Secord and Hakim spend little on the contra resupply effort. They planned to recoup all the money they did spend on the contras, and more, for the "enterprise." After the House passed aid to the contras at the end of June, Secord hoped to sell the "assets" of his air resupply operation to the CIA as soon as it was able to take control, presumably sometime in September. This was North's plan, as well, and from the end of June on he urged Poindexter and CIA officials to buy out Secord's operation. A report drawn up by one of Secord's colleagues "for presentation to the CIA" valued the operation's "assets" at over $4 million.[40] Almost all of the "assets" had been purchased not with money from the Iran deal, but with the other money raised for the contras. If Secord sold the planes and the airstrip for even $3 million, this would have more than compensated for any of the money he had so far spent from the Iran "surplus." North urged Poindexter in a July 15 message to convince the CIA to buy Secord's operation for $2.25 million, arguing among other things that Secord needed to borrow $2 million to provide food for the contras and could only do so if there were assurances that lenders could be repaid.[41] At the time of North's message, Hakim's accounts still contained almost $4 million, with another $4 million in "reserve."[42]

Officials at the CIA did not want to buy Secord's "assets," however, and by the beginning of July this had already been made clear to Secord and his associates. The main problem, in the view of Alan Fiers and other senior CIA officials, was that the whole Secord operation was "tainted," presumably by its dubious legality and the potential for scandal. Fiers said he would not "contaminate the new program with anything that's got any clutter from the past."[43] Another, less decisive problem was that Secord's operation had so far been most unimpressive. As his chief assistant in the resupply operation, Robert Dutton, recalls, "The feeling at that point was that it was a tainted operation, unsuccessful, the aircraft looked terrible. It wasn't something that was very attractive."[44] Secord could not do anything about the "taint" of the operation—he left it to North to argue this point with senior administration officials—but he was determined to improve the resupply operation to make it more attractive to the CIA. According to one of his employees, "General Secord continually stressed the fact that the aircraft were not operating at their maximum efficiency and that we should strive . . . harder to fly more and provide more air support in order to improve the image of that capability." Secord and North "would try to reverse that opinion by the Central Intelligence Agency while at the same time improving air operations support."[45] July and August passed, however, without any noticeable improvement.

The State Department's efforts to help the contras, meanwhile, had also made little progress by the end of August. Shultz had decided not to ask the Sultan of Brunei directly for the $10 million during his visit in June.[46] Instead, it was decided that Abrams would make the request. But it was not until August 8 that Abrams, armed with an account number given him by North, met with a Bruneian official in London and asked for the donation to the contras. The official said his government would consider the request, but as late as September no funds had been deposited in Secord's Swiss account.

Meanwhile, the secrecy surrounding North and Secord's operation began to be punctured from a variety of directions. Even in May, North himself had warned Poindexter that "the more money there is . . . the more visible the program becomes . . . and the more inquisitive will become people like Kerry, Barnes, Harkins [*sic*], et al. While I care not a whit what they say about me, it could become an embarrassment for the President and you." This was one reason North wanted the CIA back in the operation to cover his private resupply effort under an officially authorized program.[47] In late April and again in June, as North's informal representative in Central America, Robert Owen, had predicted, news stories suggesting North's involvement in resupply activities, and Owen's, began appearing in American newspapers. On June 24, the day before the House passed the $100 million aid legislation for the contras, Texas Democrat Ron Coleman introduced a Resolution of Inquiry, "directing the President to provide to the House of Representatives certain information concerning activities of Lieutenant Colonel Oliver North." Inspired by Congressman Barnes, it was another effort to get around the complacency of the intelligence committees and force a confrontation with the administration. The resolution specifically requested the President to hand over all documents concerning North's contacts with the contras, presumably including those McFarlane had showed Barnes in his office in the fall of 1985.

Once again, the effort to trap the Reagan administration received little support from the House leadership or from Democratic committee chairmen. Coleman's resolution was referred to the House Armed Services Committee, the House Foreign Affairs Committee, and the House Intelligence Committee for consideration. Chairmen Fascell and Hamilton sent letters to the White House seeking the administration's opinion of the resolution, to which Poindexter responded on July 21. Citing Robert McFarlane's denials of the previous year, Poindexter denied all allegations of non-compliance with the Boland amendment and declared the matter settled.[48] On July 30 the House Armed Services Committee, under Congressman Aspin, reported unfavorably on the resolution, which effectively killed it and made it unnecessary for the other two committees to report.[49] Hamilton nevertheless asked Poindexter to make North available to the intelligence committee for questioning, although Hamilton said he personally was not going to push the issue.[50] On August 6 North met with eleven members of the committee at the White House and denied the allegations against him. The committee members professed their satisfaction with North's answers, and Congressman McCurdy, in particular, expressed his view that the intelligence committee should report unfavorably on the resolution of inquiry, even though no report was necessary. Hamilton agreed and at the end of the meeting expressed his appreciation for North's testimony and his satisfaction with the answers given.[51] Administration officials left with the impression that Hamilton would "turn aside future offers of similar resolutions."[52]

Critics of the intelligence committee's second "investigation" of activities by the NSC staff later complained of its inadequacy. "It was as if law enforcement officers were to do nothing but interrogate a suspect, politely listen to his denials of wrongdoing, and straightaway let him go," Theodore Draper writes. "First, the committee did not know any more than they read in the newspapers, and then they did not want to know any more than North chose to tell them."[53] But Congress had finished with the divisive issue, and even staunch opponents of contra aid like Hamilton did not wish to reopen it. Even if he had, McCurdy's comments during the meeting indicated that a majority of intelligence committee members opposed further inquiry.

North's escape from the resolution of inquiry did not put an end to the gradual exposure of Secord's resupply operation, however. By the summer of 1986, North and his private associates were scrambling from one crisis to another. Since April a former CIA official working as an adviser to the Salvadoran air force had also been assisting the contra resupply effort at Ilopango. From the beginning, however, the ex-CIA agent, Felix Rodriguez (also known as Max Gomez), had expressed dissatisfaction with the way the operation was run. He sympathized with the FDN's growing complaints about shoddy aircraft and inadequate and sporadic supplies.[54] More significantly, he shared the FDN's conviction that the airplanes and equipment in Secord's operation rightly belonged to the contras, since they were paid for out of money donated for them. The commander of the Salvadoran air force, General Bustillo, agreed. Together, Rodriguez, Bustillo, and Enrique Bermúdez challenged Secord's and North's assertion that the resupply operation's "assets" belonged to Secord's company and could be sold.[55]

As the spring turned into summer, Rodriguez's complaints grew louder and the network of those he complained to grew wider. Secord and others suspected him of being the source of press stories about the operation. Matters came to a head at the end of June, when a confrontational meeting between Rodriguez, North, and one of Secord's colleagues settled nothing.[56] In July Rodriguez staged a minor revolt at Ilopango, taking control of the aircraft, winning the allegiance of the pilots and crews, and placing armed guards from the FDN on the planes to prevent them being taken away by Secord. No sooner was that dispute settled than Rodriguez traveled to Washington to rebut claims by North that he had tried to stop the resupply operation. On August 8, just two days after North's meeting with the House intelligence committee, Rodriguez met with Don Gregg, Vice President Bush's national security adviser and a longtime associate from the CIA. Disturbed by Rodriguez's charges that Secord's resupply operation was "essentially a money-making scheme," that Secord hoped to sell the aircraft to the CIA even though they rightly belonged to the contras, and that the operation was "corrupt, shoddy, unsafe,"[57] Gregg called an interagency meeting on August 12 to pass on the troubling news. He told Fiers and the CIA to have nothing to do with Secord's operation.[58]

Gregg's interagency meeting, so soon after the intelligence committee hearing, combined with the growing tensions in El Salvador between Bustillo's and Secord's people,[59] finally convinced North that the time had come to shut the whole operation down. On August 13 North sent instructions to Secord: "Conduct emergency recall immediately. Bring the maintenance and aircrews out of there quietly but quickly. Leave all the equipment, including airplanes. . . . Perhaps this thing can be patched back together for the transition. But for the moment the people must be gotten out of there."[60] August 13 was also the day the Senate passed a contra aid bill identical to the House version, avoiding the need for a conference on the issue and presumably opening the way for the legislation to become law some time in September. North may well have believed the contras could survive until the CIA took over and that the risks of continuing the private resupply operation had grown too great.

But Secord defied North's instructions. "There is more than 1 million dollars worth of equipment, spares, located at the airfield," he wrote back. "I must remind you that these assets are owned by Udall Research [one of Secord's shell companies] and there is no intention of abandoning them."[61] In another message that same day he insisted that his companies were "perfectly legal," and he threatened to "make this a major issue" if his operation shut down. "I will not permit [Rodriguez] to tear us up," he wrote, but he wanted North to know that the problem of the assets was "no small matter."[62] Secord later testified that his refusal to shut down the operation "had nothing to do with the money. What it has to do with is abandoning a project that we had sweated over for a long, long time and was finally functioning, and to abandon it simply because there are some personalities clashing was not acceptable to me, and I rejected that suggestion."[63] North backed down, and the supply operation continued.

Secord was already trying to divest himself of other "assets" he had acquired in the contra resupply operation. In the middle of July, Secord and Hakim had completed purchase of an additional $2.2 million worth of arms, purportedly for the contras, but they had never delivered the weapons. Instead, Secord sold the weapons to the CIA in September for $1.2 million. And because they knew this was to be their "last transaction in connection with the contras," Hakim recalls, Secord decided "we should maximize our profit." So although the weapons were never provided to the contras, Hakim in August paid Secord and himself a commission of $861,327 on the purchase, in addition to the $1.2 million from the sale, which was deposited back into the "enterprise" account.[64]

The next crisis came in early September, and again it involved the emergency airstrip in Costa Rica that Secord had purchased and built but had never successfully used. On September 5 North got word that a

Costa Rican official planned to hold a press conference to denounce the airstrip as a violation of Costa Rican law. The American Ambassador Lewis Tambs persuaded President Arias to cancel the press conference, and the crisis was averted, but only for the moment.[65] On September 10 Costa Rican security forces raided the airstrip and impounded 77 drums of gasoline that had been stored there,[66] and two weeks later the official went ahead with his press conference, revealing the existence of the airstrip and mentioning the name of Secord's company—which Hakim immediately shut down, transferring its assets to another shell company.[67]

After this near-disaster, the time might once again have seemed right to shut the entire resupply operation down. With October and the new fiscal year approaching, it was a short time before the contra aid legislation would become law and American aid would begin flowing. Between Rodriguez, the Costa Ricans, Bustillo, the FDN, and the press, the risks of complete exposure grew with each passing day. The Sandinistas, meanwhile, were doing their best to find and shoot down the resupply aircraft. At the end of August, the Sandinistas reported detecting "spy flights" over the southern region of Nicaragua.[68] On September 9 the Sandinistas accidentally shot down one of their own planes in a region where the resupply flights were occurring.[69] On September 11 Secord's pilots reported that the Sandinistas had set up extra guns along their flight paths.[70] Far from shutting his operation down, however, Secord in the second half of September began pushing it into high gear.

By early September the resupply operation had still not begun to work effectively, especially in the south. As Robert Dutton later recalled, "we were still not . . . accomplishing what we set out to accomplish. . . . [W]e were flying missions but nothing was being delivered because we couldn't find the troops to deliver them or they couldn't identify their own position where we could get to them."[71] As far as he was concerned, the entire resupply operation "didn't even become viable until mid-September."[72] At that point, however, the pilots began to solve their problems. They abandoned trying to locate troops all the time and instead began to drop to designated zones and let the troops find the supplies on their own.[73] They also took more risks. They flew during the day in order to see the drop zones better. They flew two planes at a time on some missions.[74] The risks paid off. For the first time ever, Secord's operation began to make regular drops in the south.

Secord urged his men on. He told Dutton to continue using two planes until the "surge" was well under way. He also told Dutton to start making drops even if there was no contact with troops on the ground. It was a "force feed" operation, he wrote. "Dry runs [are] not getting us out of [the] business." On September 13 Dutton reported proudly that all five planes were flying regular missions and had delivered 55,000 pounds of supplies in just two days.[75] By the end of September, Secord's resupply operation was flying missions almost every day and Dutton estimated that they had "put somewhere in the neighborhood of 180,000 pounds of munitions and supplies on the ground." Indeed, they were now delivering more than the southern forces needed.[76]

The "surge" that Secord referred to, in addition to supplying the Southern Front forces, was designed to prove that his operation was finally working. As Dutton later recalled, "since we had the aircraft now working and we had a means to make the deliveries . . . we were building up a case for the fact that the operation was now in fact a successful operating air resupply operation and that would be looked at by the CIA as something that was now a viable operation for them taking it over, purchasing it . . . [when] they came into the operation."[77] Dutton put together a photo album of the successful operation for North to show his colleagues, and on September 12, Poindexter told North that he had talked to Casey that morning "about Secord." He told North to "keep the pressure on Bill [Casey] to make things right for Secord."[78]

The recklessness of the late September "surge" finally came to disaster on October 5, less than two weeks before the President signed the $100 million aid package into law. A mission to supply forces in the south, this time FDN troops, went off during the day despite the greater risks involved. The pilot flew down the Pacific Coast of Nicaragua, but turned east over land sooner than usual. A special Sandinista unit, trained and equipped to shoot down the resupply aircraft, fired a missile and brought the plane down. Only Eugene Hasenfus parachuted to safety.

The resupply operation that exploded into the press that day had been in operation for six months, during most of which time few planes were flying and even fewer supplies were delivered. The question of whether the contras could have survived without North's and Secord's efforts to supply them, and without the State Department's efforts to solicit money for them, was answered by the fact that the contras *did* survive with almost no help from either of these sources. The $10 million from the Sultan of Brunei never reached the contras, as it turned out, because North's secretary had inadvertently transposed two numbers and the money was transferred to the wrong account.[79] There is reason to question how much of that $10 million the contras would have seen in any case, even if it had gone to the right account. According to Hakim, he understood that $3 million was going to be set aside for arms purchases for the contras, but he had no instructions for the other $7 million and, as he recalled, almost incredibly, "I believe we were short of money at the time."[80] There were, at the time, millions of dollars in the accounts of the "enterprise."

As for Secord's resupply operation and the famous "diversion," some members of the congressional committee that later investigated the matter suggested that the total amount of money "diverted" to the contras was no more than $600,000.[81] The logic behind that calculation was that only the arms bought by Secord and actually delivered to the Southern Front represented a real transfer of value to the contras. The more commonly accepted figure for the diversion is between $3 and $4 million, but even if one accepts the contention that $4 million was "diverted" on behalf of the contras, it is unlikely that the contras ever received anything like $4 million worth of benefits. Attorney General Meese's assertion on November 25 that the contras had received between $12 and $30 million worth of diverted profits from the sale of arms to Iran was wildly off the mark. For all the controversy raised about the diversion, the contras were fortunate if they received $2 million worth of tangible benefits during the entire nine-month stretch from January 1986 to the shootdown of the supply plane on October 5—an amount that paled in comparison to the far less controversial $32 million they had ultimately received from Saudi Arabia.

The mechanism that North helped set up for aiding the contras in 1986 had proven less dedicated to that task than North himself believed. And the politically disastrous downing of the Hasenfus plane in October, less than two weeks before the President signed contra aid into law, was also the product of motives that went beyond supporting the contras. When the Iran-contra scandal broke, Secord's and Hakim's "enterprise" accounts were frozen with a balance of more than $8 million. When North was asked during the Iran-contra hearings in 1987 if he was surprised that so much money remained in those accounts, he responded, "I was surprised. And I want to note I still don't understand that, and I am not willing at this point to accuse anybody, but I was surprised."[82]

44

The National Unity Government

Only hours after Attorney General Meese revealed the diversion at his November 25 press conference, Senator Durenberger declared it would be a "cold day in Washington" before Congress voted any more money for the contras.[1] Support for the contras in Congress actually proved more resilient in 1987 than most imagined, however. The scandal alone did not undermine support for that policy. Rather it was the scandal's effect on the Reagan administration that took the greatest toll. Since the consensus in Congress in favor of aiding the contras had been shaped not only by events in Central America, but also by the unremitting pressure of a very popular President on a wary and divided Democratic Party, it was vulnerable to any shift in the balance of political power in Washington. Little had changed in Central America between June 25 and November 25, or in American perceptions of the situation there, but the weakening of the Reagan presidency opened the way for others, in Washington and in Central America, to wrestle for control of American policy and change its course.

President Reagan's popular approval rating was 67 percent at the beginning of November; by the end of November it dropped to 46 percent. The 21-point decline was the sharpest ever recorded.[2] For Reagan, whose

482

greatest political weapon had been a popularity that overawed his opponents, the plummeting approval rating threatened his ability to lead effectively. Nor did the drop in popular approval measure the full depth of the crisis into which the Reagan administration fell at the end of 1986. For a time, in the view of the President's advisers, there seemed no limit to how far Reagan might fall. In the White House there were frightened whispers about possible impeachment. Worse still, President Reagan seemed incapable of finding his own way out of the morass. A President who had always depended heavily on his advisers to provide him with the facts and the details to carry out his broad visions and justify them to the public and Congress now found no one in the White House or the cabinet to help steer him through this most dangerous of political crises. The two men who knew most about what had happened, Poindexter and North, had been fired. When Meese's assertion of possible criminal wrongdoing was followed by the appointment of a special prosecutor, these two understandably refused to talk.

Another who might have provided Reagan some guidance, William Casey, was either confused about the nature and the timing of events or he was dissembling.[3] On December 15 Casey suffered a seizure and was found to have a serious brain tumor; he died a few months later. Secretary Shultz publicly distanced himself from the Iran operation, provoking charges of disloyalty from the President's advisers. Secretary of Defense Weinberger could offer the President no help. The chief of staff, Don Regan, tried to take control of the situation, but lacking all the facts he also stumbled and was widely blamed for the confusion and paralysis in the White House. When the President tried to explain what had happened, on the basis of briefings and chronologies prepared for him by Meese and others, he found that he had been given inaccurate or misleading information, which was quickly exposed by the press. When he departed from these prepared statements, he made his own mistakes, for his recollection of what he had approved was imperfect, at best. Reagan preferred to state what he wished to be true rather than what documents and testimony seemed to indicate.

In the early days of the crisis, some advised President Reagan to forget about trying to piece together all the facts, to declare executive privilege and put an end to further investigation of the matter. Senator Fritz Hollings, a South Carolina Democrat, suggested there was "nothing wrong with the President coming forward at this particular point and saying, 'I acted out of the national security interests, compassion for the hostages.'"[4]

Most leading Republicans, however, opposed a strategy of "stonewalling" the press and Congress. Howard Baker, the former Senate majority leader who had achieved national fame in the Watergate hearings, argued that "this thing is festering and going to get out of control . . . unless we get all these circumstances out and published as soon as possible. I think [the President's] in grave danger, not because of the substance necessarily, but because of the technique and the timing."[5] Senator Robert Dole called for thorough, and multiple, investigations. A candidate for the Republican presidential nomination in 1988, Dole told reporters, "There is a party interest here. This does reflect on the Republican Party and Republicans not just on the White House staff." Dole wanted to "cut our losses, and do it as quickly as possible."[6]

Reagan was deeply troubled by polls that showed a majority believed he was lying.[7] In an attempt to restore his reputation for honesty, Reagan submitted himself and his administration to three separate investigations: He appointed a commission led by former Senator John Tower to investigate and prepare a report on what had occurred; he promised full cooperation with the congressional investigating committees that had begun forming; and he approved the appointment of a special prosecutor to investigate and prosecute any criminal wrongdoing. None of these investigations solved Reagan's political problem, however. The worst of the political crisis did not pass until Reagan admitted, in a televised speech on March 4, that his administration had traded arms for hostages.

Although Attorney General Meese had decided that the "diversion" of money to the contras from the Iran arms sales was the most explosive discovery, polls throughout the crisis showed that very few Americans cared about the "diversion." When asked in December which was the worst aspect of the whole Iran-contra affair, 51 percent of those polled said it was the way the administration had handled the facts, 26 percent believed it was the sale of arms to Iran, and 7 percent said it was the use of the money to help the contras.[8] The President never acknowledged knowing about the diversion, and he never apologized for any aspect of covert efforts to support the contras, authorized or unauthorized. The day after Reagan admitted error in trading arms for hostages, his approval rating jumped nine points. The President was "not altogether out of the woods," Congressman Michel declared, "but he's certainly gotten to the firebreak."

Despite the congressional investigations of the Iran-contra affair that dominated the spring and summer of 1987, and despite predictions by Senator Dole that the government would be "in a holding pattern" until the next President took office,[9] the President had a fairly successful final two years. He signed a popular arms limitation treaty with the Soviet Union and held three summit meetings with Mikhail Gorbachev, the symbols of a blossoming détente. The economic recovery continued. In 1988 Reagan's popularity helped lift Vice President Bush into the presidency.[10]

The four months of crisis from the end of November to the beginning of March, however, profoundly transformed the character of the Reagan administration. The President restored his popularity with the American people, but the style of his presidency, his method of governing, had changed as a result of the scandal. "[T]he dominant Reagan presidency of the first six years," one Democratic senator noted, had ended.[11] Reagan's political survival had required setting aside partisan confrontation and accepting help from wherever it was offered. Since the Democrats in Congress had it in their power to do the greatest damage, the President and his advisers offered peace to the opposition party.[12]

To heal the breach of trust between the President and the Democrat-controlled Congress, Reagan and his political advisers filled the jobs of purged officials with appointments deemed acceptable to members of Congress from both parties. Although no Democrats were brought into the administration, the new team had the appearance of a national unity government. Popularity among Democratic as well as Republican congressmen became, for the first time, a prerequisite for a senior position in the Reagan administration. The new national security adviser, Frank Carlucci, named on December 2 to replace Poindexter, had been a career foreign service officer who held high posts in the Nixon, Ford, Carter, and Reagan administrations. To replace William Casey, Reagan settled on William Webster, who had been named director of the FBI during the Carter administration.[13] Most important was Reagan's selection of Howard Baker to replace Don Regan as chief of staff at the end of February. Baker had made his reputation first as a virtually non-partisan member of the Watergate committee. Later, as a moderate Republican Senate majority leader, Baker proved a natural conciliator whom Democrats liked and respected.[14]

Throughout the four months of political crisis, Democratic leaders had, of course, hoped to take advantage of the President's travails. The party's smashing victory in the 1986 elections for Senate, where the Democrats picked up nine seats and regained control of the chamber, was the first good news for the party since 1980. As the race for the presidency in 1988 began, Democrats hoped the scandal would place them in the White House, as well. Members clamored for seats on the House and Senate investigating committees in the hope of reaping some of the favorable publicity that had gone to members of the Watergate committee.[15] And as much as Republicans like Dole and Howard Baker wanted the investigations to begin and end as quickly as possible, Democratic leaders pleaded the difficulties of creating new investigative bodies and stretched the deadline for a final report out into the fall.[16]

The administration's offer of peace and conciliation in the depths of its crisis was accepted, nevertheless, by a Democratic Party that hesitated to make too much of their good fortune. Some Democrats feared that dragging the government through another Watergate-type affair would damage the nation at home and abroad.[17] Others feared that even if this was an acceptable price to pay for bringing Reagan down, the American people would lash out at the Democratic Party for taking partisan advantage of the President's crisis.[18] As Senators George Mitchell and William Cohen of Maine later wrote, while some Democrats were "eager to break out the long knives and deliver incapacitating, if not fatal, thrusts to the Republican Party's wounded Caesar," party leaders like the new Senate majority leader, Robert Byrd, "knew that the line between political opportunity and calamity is a thin one. . . . Ronald Reagan, whatever his personal or political weaknesses, remained a popular leader. The American people wanted the truth told, not exploited by opponents seeking political advantage."[19]

The price Democrats exacted in return was what Howard Baker and other members of the new team were offering, a greater share of power for Congress and for the Democratic leaders in Congress. The new Speaker of the House, Jim Wright, already had an ambitious conception of Congress's role, and his own, in the formulation of national policy. Even before his election as Speaker and before the Iran-contra scandal, Wright had asserted that the Speaker of the House had a constitutional role comparable to that of the President. He disagreed with the idea that "the President proposes and Congress disposes," arguing instead that there was a "creative role for the Legislative Branch and a leadership role for the Speaker."[20] Elected Speaker in the midst of the scandal, Wright sought a "new balance" that would "allow a Speaker to confront a strong President as a near equal and to dominate a weak President," in foreign as well as domestic policy.[21]

The shift in the political balance of power that resulted from the scandal was greater than the shift that had occurred on the issue of contra aid.

The Democrats' approach to the contra aid issue in 1987 was once again as divided as it had been in 1985. Opponents of contra aid had reason to expect that the scandal would inevitably undermine the consensus that had formed the previous year, just as the mining scandal of 1984 had. If the President was not to be the chosen victim of the Iran-contra affair, it seemed only natural that his cherished policy would be quickly defeated. The House Democratic Caucus briefly deposed Les Aspin as chairman of the armed services committee, in part to warn him and other moderate Democrats against further support for contra aid.[22] House Democrats, according to one observer, "intended to bring the White House to heel on foreign policy, and particularly in Central America."[23]

Wright acted quickly to dispel concerns among liberals that he would be any less forceful in opposing contra aid than his predecessor, Tip O'Neill. He appointed David Bonior, a leading opponent of contra aid, as chief deputy whip because Bonior's "constituency was precisely where Wright was weakest, among younger members and liberals opposed to Reagan's Central America policy. Those activists still resented Wright's having helped to pass Reagan's package of aid to El Salvador in 1982."[24] Wright wanted to make sure he did not stray from his party's liberal bloc on what was "perhaps the one issue over which a speakership could be lost."[25]

Despite all that had occurred, however, Wright still led a party divided over contra aid. While liberals demanded an all-out effort to kill the program when it was most vulnerable, moderates and conservatives in the part of the country Wright represented still had lingering fears of opposing Reagan's effort to "stop communism" in Central America. The Democrats' regaining of control in the Senate had not changed the equation on contra aid by more than one or two votes. The newly elected southern Democrats did not want to act hastily.[26] Senator Dodd of Connecticut found that even at the height of the President's travails in early February, the votes to disapprove release of the final $40 million of the $100 million aid bill were lacking.[27] The party's deep division was reflected even in the naming of members to the Iran-contra investigating committees in January. Of the six senators chosen by Majority Leader Byrd, three were supporters of contra aid—Nunn, Boren, and Howell Heflin of Alabama. House Democrats faced the same problem. Congressman Bonior soon found that he lacked the votes to disapprove the $40 million on a straight vote. Some conservatives and moderates suggested that perhaps later in the year they might vote against a request for new aid, but for now they were unwilling to cut off the aid they had so recently approved.[28]

The Iran-contra scandal probably caused a greater shift in the Reagan administration and in the Republican Party leadership than among the Democrats. A renewed ideological and political war over contra aid was not how the post-scandal Reagan administration hoped to begin its new "partnership" with Congress. The new national security adviser, Frank Carlucci, wanted a "serious review" of the policy and expressed his doubt that the contras could succeed.[29] Secretary Shultz recalls he wanted "to get the Nicaragua problem resolved if only because it had become too painfully divisive for the country."[30] Stalwart contra supporters like Casey, North, and Poindexter were gone, leaving only Secretary of Defense Weinberger and Assistant Secretary of State Elliott Abrams. But Abrams was badly damaged by charges that he had misled Congress about the administration's role in private supply operations and about his solicitation of Brunei.[31]

In the Congress, Minority Leader Michel advised the administration to shift its policy and to put off confrontation with Congress. In February 1987 he urged the White House to delay any request for a new $100 million in aid until September or later to give time for peace negotiations in Central America. A new request for aid, Michel believed, could not pass the House. Even conservative Republicans shared Michel's pessimism. Henry Hyde said the situation was "grim but not hopeless" and agreed that the administration had to support peace negotiations, so long as they didn't "sell out the contras."[32]

If President Reagan had not himself remained stubborn in support of the contras in early 1987, his new advisers would certainly have abandoned the controversial policy. But in his State of the Union Address at the end of January the President overruled the advice of White House officials to "play down the issue" and instead vowed to "fight any effort to shut off [the contras'] lifeblood and consign them to death, defeat or a life without freedom." Throughout the scandal Reagan never expressed any doubts about the contras or about America's right and obligation to support them. He apologized for selling arms to Iran, and he claimed ignorance of the diversion, but he never apologized or regretted the efforts that had been undertaken in his name to support the contras.[33] The President's stubbornness buoyed conservatives inside and outside the administration who opposed any conciliation with Democrats. With the election season approaching, conservatives made support for contra aid a requirement for their endorsement, considered essential for any Republican who hoped to win the party's nomination. As Congressman Jack

Kemp, the third leading candidate for the nomination and the one most closely associated with the conservative wing of the party, put it, "If we are to lose the $105 million, let the Democrats be the ones who vote it down."[34]

On this and other issues, a split in House Republican ranks opened wide between "main-stream" Republicans like Michel and the group of younger conservatives led by Kemp and Newt Gingrich.[35] Within the administration, as well, there were two factions contending for political control of the contra aid policy: Those who wished to put the issue aside and turn to more popular issues, and those who wanted to continue pressing the issue on Congress regardless of cost. Like the Democrats, the Republican Party began a search for some way to satisfy both its warring factions.

Amidst these shifting political forces, the issue of contra aid arose again at the end of February when a "second vote" on release of the final $40 million provided the occasion for another battle in the House and Senate in March 1987. There was no prospect of blocking release of the $40 million because the President could veto any resolution of disapproval, but opponents of contra aid saw an opportunity to strike a symbolic blow at the program in preparation for a *coup de grace* later in the year, when the President had to request new funds.

45

"I Am Not a Politician"

Following the pattern of previous years, the approach of a new vote on aid to the contras was accompanied by yet another crisis within the top ranks of the rebel leadership. The reforms instituted the previous May had inevitably not proceeded to the satisfaction of Cruz and Robelo. Calero had remained obdurate in protecting his position as both political and military leader. Bermúdez and his allies in the FDN command had resisted all efforts to subsume that organization under the UNO structure dominated by Cruz and Robelo, and even within the UNO organization Cruz and Robelo lacked the kind of control they sought. While all these failings of the "reform" effort dismayed Cruz and brought him once again to the verge of resignation at the beginning of the year, it may have been an entirely different issue that pushed him over the edge. Cruz was among the many public figures ensnared by the Iran-contra scandal.

On January 10, 1987, the *New York Times* revealed that a "senior Nicaraguan rebel leader" had been provided a "monthly stipend" for the better part of 1986 by a private fund-raiser associated with Oliver North.[1] In the middle of January Cruz quietly cleaned out his offices at the UNO headquarters in Miami, and on January 23 he told Abrams he intended to resign. Cruz was consumed with shame at having taken money from the CIA and then from North. He told his advisers he was looking for work so

490

he could "feel clean again." He felt his reputation had been terribly damaged: "I look at myself in the mirror, and I don't like what I see."[2]

Few of Cruz's closest associates were aware of just how strongly he had been affected by the scandal. Most believed his frustrations stemmed exclusively from the lack of progress in contra "reform." And Robelo and others used Cruz's threat to resign as leverage to force the Reagan administration to take stronger actions against Calero and Bermúdez. They knew that Elliott Abrams and other Reagan officials were desperate to keep Cruz in the leadership at least until the March contra aid votes. Congressman McCurdy was almost gleeful at the prospect of Cruz's resignation, calling Cruz "the essential ingredient in the glue that held the whole thing together." If Cruz left, McCurdy said, the administration "might as well kiss goodbye to the aid."[3]

Robelo reduced matters to the naked struggle for power.[4] Calero had to go, and the contra movement had to be restructured to give "clear command" to the "moderates."[5] If Calero and his "clique" were not forced out, Robelo insisted, he and Cruz would resign.[6] Calero's supporters denounced this "blackmail."[7] But Cruz and Robelo were in the ascendant in Washington, and Calero was at his most vulnerable and expendable. In the middle of February, Abrams asked Calero to resign for the good of the struggle, and Calero obliged.[8] Although Calero remained president of the FDN, he had been struck a fatal blow. His presidency of the FDN would quickly become meaningless as the FDN was soon to become integrated into one rebel army.[9] Even within the FDN, Calero's leading role would be challenged and undermined by both Bermúdez and Aristides Sanchez. The solitary leadership over the rebel forces that Calero had enjoyed since his appointment in 1983 had definitively ended. Conservatives led by Senator Jesse Helms lamented that Calero had been forced to resign in order to "appease certain legislators who don't support aid to the freedom fighters anyway." The conservatives strongly denounced the State Department's "intervention" into the contras' affairs.[10]

Despite the forced resignation of Calero, Cruz remained poised on the brink of resignation himself. But now Cruz felt "trapped," according to a close adviser, because "there was no way he could leave" after Abrams had secured Calero's dismissal. His demands for a purge of the FDN "clique," therefore, escalated. At times he demanded the removal of Bermúdez and his replacement by a Cruz ally with little experience as a military leader and virtually no experience with the FDN fighters. Although both Cruz and Robelo announced they would remain in the leadership until at least June "to make sure the reforms are implemented," Cruz at times insisted he would not stay long.[11] During meetings with Abrams, with his own advisers, and with moderates in Congress, Cruz practically sought permission to resign and seized on every excuse to justify it. Even as he agreed to stay, he told reporters of his shame and embarrassment.[12]

Reagan officials had decided the time had come to expand the contra directorate from three to seven, in part to avoid being held hostage by Cruz's constant threats of resignation. Elections would be held by the contras' newly formed "Assembly." Cruz insisted that the assembly was dominated by Calero's "clique," but he also had other problems with that body of Nicaraguan exiles. When American newspapers finally revealed at the end of February that it was Cruz who had received the "monthly stipend" from North, Cruz's enemies in the assembly demanded a public explanation. Cruz obliged, but on March 9, to the surprise and chagrin of Reagan officials and Cruz's own supporters, the rebel leader publicly resigned in a letter to the *Miami Herald*. He had told no one of his plan and gave no special reason for his latest change of heart. After having earlier declared his intention to stay at least until June while reforms were implemented, Cruz declared simply that "the time is up. I have given all that I can give."[13] Cruz told reporters he had "been wanting to do this for a long time."[14]

The timing of Cruz's announcement—just two days before the next vote on contra aid—seemed almost designed to pull down the temple walls. Moderates in Congress warned that Cruz's departure spelled the end of contra aid. His resignation, one supporter of contra aid suggested, would "give a lot of members the out they've been looking for without appearing to be Sandinista apologists." Senator Dodd declared that Cruz, who was a "real democrat" had "just discovered what many of us discovered a long time ago, that the contra movement is not a democratic movement."[15]

The resignation of Cruz did not put an end to the reform of the contras as a political movement. In May the contras' Assembly elected seven members of a new Directorate—one for each political tendency in Nicaragua. Robelo and Calero both won positions. The new Directorate announced the abolition of the FDN as a separate army and the integration of all rebel forces into the "Nicaraguan Resistance." In the new Directorate, no single individual had anything resembling the powers Calero once held over the rebel army. The opening up of the leadership allowed new forces to emerge, both among the politicians and among the rebel fighters, that had been suppressed for years. New members, like Alfredo César, proved to be adept diplomats, and relations between the contra leadership and many Latin governments improved. Others, like Azucena Ferrey, maintained good ties with political party leaders inside Nicaragua. Pedro Joaquín Chamorro, Jr., added his father's famous name and the luster of *La Prensa*.

Alfredo César was the biggest beneficiary of the reorganization and Cruz's departure. A former Sandinista, head of the Central Bank, and then leader of his own small "progressive" rebel organization, for two years César had carefully cultivated the moderate democrats of the Mc-Curdy group, at one point even winning a special portion of the contra aid legislation for his own small band of fighters. The big prize, however, was leadership of UNO, and to attain this César had played a careful game of shifting alliances. As a "progressive" contra, he had for years joined in the condemnation of Calero and the "Somocista" FDN. Through much of 1986, however, César had worked behind the scenes to forge an alliance with Calero, whose wife was a cousin of César's wife. During the crisis in February 1987 he had joined Calero and the FDN in denouncing the State Department's "intervention" on Cruz's behalf, and it was not surprising to see the two closely allied when the new directorate was named in May.[16]

César was a shrewd politician and a shrewd analyst of the international situation. In the search for some kind of accommodation with the Sandinistas, he was quick to pick up where Cruz had left off. He announced that the new directorate wanted "to use military action for political solutions, not as an end in itself."[17] Indeed, César would eventually go much further than Cruz ever dreamed toward a negotiated settlement with the Sandinistas.

What may have disappointed Cruz's supporters most, though few realized it, was how paradigmatic the entire struggle had been of the Nicaragua political culture. As Arturo Cruz, Jr., wrote despairingly in the midst of these struggles, "an entire generation of our beloved elites was excluded from the exercise of political power, and this explains the abundance of aspirants to the post of next supreme chief, both among the 'gentleman of the Revolution' and among our 'counterrevolutionary family.'" Cruz, Jr., saw it "as a hidden desire in some and an open desire in others, but in the final analysis it is the desire of all of us to be the next Somoza."[18]

If the goal in Nicaragua's political culture was to be the next Somoza, the two main tactics for achieving that goal were flexibility and single-minded attention to self-preservation and self-advancement. In a political culture without established institutions, political parties, or organized social movements, where all ties were personal and all deals temporary, the most important attribute for survival was flexibility. There could be no permanent friends and no permanent enemies, no fixed principles, no unshakable commitments. Hence the Nicaraguan tradition of "pacts," always vehemently denounced and always entered into with alacrity when the favorable moment came.

Stripped of its ideological content, the Ortegas' strategy of "tercerismo" had been the classic pact between temporary allies in pursuit of their own separate ambitions. Humberto Ortega was thus the consummate Nicaraguan politician, and his close adviser in the late 1970s, Carlos Coronel, the consummate Nicaraguan political theorist. It was not that either Ortega or Coronel lacked ideological convictions or aspirations for their country that went beyond personal ambition. Perhaps in their cases, and with other prominent Nicaraguan politicians and revolutionaries, there was a grand strategy, a distant, idealistic vision. Their self-justifying recipe for success was strategic rigidity and tactical flexibility. If so, however, the tactics often tended to overwhelm the strategy. The compromises necessary to survive in the political melee required putting off, again and again, any progress toward whatever ultimate goal was sought. Indeed, the tactical compromises more often than not undermined idealistic goals for the future by perpetuating the political culture of the past.

The most skillful Nicaraguan politicians did not let this get in the way of playing the required game successfully. In this respect, César was also the quintessential Nicaraguan politician. Arturo Cruz was not. A combination of integrity and vanity prevented him from striking the kinds of deals that made for a successful political career in Nicaragua. His unusual qualities appealed to Americans, but it made him incompetent to wage the political struggle in the Nicaraguan context. Cruz understood his own failings: "Part of my tragedy," he said, though with a touch of pride, "is that I am not a politician."[19]

———

The impact of Cruz's resignation on the March contra aid votes was less than many suspected it would be. Congressional support for aid to the rebels was sufficient to force Congressman Bonior and his liberal colleagues to devise a tricky parliamentary maneuver to avoid a straight vote on disapproval, which they feared they would lose. Bonior proposed voting on a different issue: a "moratorium" on releasing the remaining aid until all funds previously spent on the contras could be traced and accounted for.[20] By focusing on the question of "accountability," Bonior hoped to sidestep the divisions in his party and to take advantage of those aspects of the scandal that had nothing to do with the policy of supporting the contras. He assured Wright that only in this way could he "maximize our vote and give our opponents the most difficulty." By getting members to cast a negative vote, even if it wasn't directly against aiding the contras, Bonior argued, the moratorium could "build a nice bridge to moderates voting 'no' later," on the contra aid program itself.[21]

More moderate Democrats like Majority Leader Foley opposed Bonior's maneuver because it required the Speaker to ignore the existing legislation and impose his own rule.[22] Foley feared Republican outrage at such an arbitrary act by the new Democratic leadership.[23] But Wright supported Bonior's plan, in part to show party liberals he could be trusted to fight contra aid and in part to assert his own power as Speaker.[24] Republicans were indeed outraged, calling Wright's maneuver the act of a "one-party dictatorship," and the previously conciliatory Michel was humiliated. But Bonior's strategy worked.[25] On March 11 the moratorium resolution passed the House by a margin of 230–196.

As Bonior and Wright well knew, the 34-vote margin was not an accurate measure of support or opposition to contra aid in the House. Some of the more conservative members who voted for the "moratorium" were likely to vote for contra aid again in the future,[26] and a number of moderates who voted for the "moratorium" remained undecided.[27] At the same time, some members who voted against the "moratorium" might not vote for contra aid again in the future.

The vote in the Senate a week later did not clarify matters. The Senate defeated a straightforward resolution of disapproval of the $40 million, 52–48,[28] proving that the 1986 elections had scarcely changed the balance on contra aid.[29] But a number of senators from both parties warned the administration not to assume that its narrow majority was a stable one. Several echoed the warning of Senator David Boren, the new chairman of the Senate intelligence committee, that the administration "should not interpret my vote . . . as a blank check to continue with the present policy without broadening the approach." Boren insisted Reagan had to "work with leaders of both parties to develop a bipartisan, workable approach to Central America."[30] Senator Dole declared the Senate's vote provided "a new opportunity to convince the American people [that] what we're doing is right" and advised the Reagan administration to begin "rethinking" its strategy.[31]

The man who came forward with a possible solution to the latest political puzzle was not an American at all, but a Central American: the new president of Costa Rica, Oscar Arias. The peace proposal President Arias set forth in February 1987 transformed American policy in Nicaragua, and it did so in large measure by appearing to answer the demands of both sides in the American political stalemate.

46

The Arias Plan

When the Costa Rican people elected Oscar Arias their new president in February 1986, few knew exactly where he stood on many important issues, including the question of American aid to the contras. Indeed, few had given him any chance of winning the election. Arias ran as the more liberal of the two candidates. The largest Costa Rican newspapers were more conservative and favored his opponent, Rafael Calderón. Even the elder statesmen of Arias's own party, including two former presidents, did not fully support him.[1] Until the very last day before his election, the popular wisdom—which was dispensed widely, Arias recalls, by the American embassy in Costa Rica—gave Arias no chance to win.[2] Although the United States had adopted a strictly neutral stance, it was widely rumored that the Reagan administration would have preferred Calderón as the president most likely to continue President Monge's pro-American and pro-contra policies.

In his campaign, Arias had done little overtly to distinguish himself from Monge or Calderón. As one observer recalls, Arias "campaigned on familiar platitudes . . . [and] used much the same rhetoric" as Calderón.[3] Perhaps Calderón had been "more militantly anti-Nicaraguan" in his campaign and had openly "courted the backing of the Republican Party in the United States,"[4] but Arias also attacked the Sandinistas, an essential step for any candidate to win an election in Costa Rica.[5] "The great majority of Costa Ricans feels deceived by the Sandinistas," Arias often repeated. "They promised a new Nicaragua, not a second Cuba." On the question of the Reagan administration's $100 million contra aid bill, Arias, like Calderón, left many observers with the impression that he endorsed the Reagan administration's policies.[6] Only in the last weeks of his campaign did Arias seek to portray himself as a "peace candidate" and to declare that the presidential contest offered Costa Ricans a choice between "rifles and bread."[7] Even so, he recalls that the theme of "peace" stirred little interest among the voters, for whom it was an "abstract issue," while the conservative press declared that anyone who disagreed with President Reagan's policy "was a fool."[8]

As is often the case with elected officials, the nature of Arias's victory shaped the nature of his presidency. Winning the election without the support of the party hierarchy and the most powerful institutions of the press, and contrary to the proclaimed expectations of the United States government, made Arias's victory something of a political miracle. Not only did it give the new president an unusual measure of independence from the normally powerful arbiters of the Costa Rican political process, it also strengthened his resolve to pursue his own goals in the face of all the common wisdom.

The day Arias was elected, he declared that his victory meant "the overwhelming majority of Costa Ricans want peace. . . . We cannot develop our economy and at the same time spend our scarce savings on armaments." Arias said he had a mandate from the people to seek the peaceful settlement in Central America that alone could save the Costa Rican economy. The day after his election Arias proclaimed that Costa Rica would immediately adopt a position of strict neutrality with regard to the Nicaraguan conflict, by which he meant that Costa Rican territory would no longer provide a sanctuary for Nicaraguans fighting their government, as had been the case for years, first with the Sandinistas and then with the contras. Costa Rica, Arias insisted, would respect the principles of self-determination and non-intervention in the internal affairs of other nations. His government would support the Contadora negotiations, but not to the exclusion of other efforts to seek peace.[9] More importantly, Arias declared that Costa Rica itself would become "an active agent for peace" with hands that "will not tremble."[10]

The Sandinistas were delighted. Radio Sandino in Managua quickly declared that Arias's election was a setback for the United States.[11] Ten days later, the Nicaraguan government offered Costa Rica an apology of sorts for the killings of two Costa Rican border guards in May 1985. Daniel Ortega's note placed more blame for the incident on Costa Rica than on his own government, and Arias had to agree with critics that the diplomatic language was a bit "vague." The Costa Rican president-elect, however, immediately expressed his support for a resumption of diplomatic relations that had been suspended by President Monge.[12]

The most dramatic sign of Arias's new policy came on February 21, when he gave an interview on American television. To the surprise of many Costa Ricans, not to mention the Reagan administration, the president-elect declared his opposition to the $100 million contra aid bill then pending before Congress. "I don't think President Reagan can have what he wants with that money. On the contrary, the result of the aid to the anti-Sandinista rebels until now has been a more dictatorial and totalitarian government in Nicaragua." Democracy would not be achieved in Nicaragua by military pressure, Arias argued, but "through pressure exerted by all of Latin America." It would be better, Arias said, if President Reagan gave the $100 million as economic aid to Guatemala, Honduras, El Salvador, and Costa Rica.[13]

Arias's comments caused a sensation not only in the United States, where the House was about to vote on Reagan's request, but also in Costa Rica. Arias was still almost three months away from his inauguration, and the current president, Luis Alberto Monge, bridled at the president-elect's boldness.[14] Critics argued that Arias had contradicted a campaign promise. Worse still, he had criticized Reagan and thus risked damaging Costa Rica's relations with the United States. Arias's comments had come at "a crucial moment for President Reagan's internal policy," one Costa Rican opposition newspaper declared.[15] Some commentators went so far as to argue that Arias should resign or be prevented from assuming the presidency. Costa Rica was "a very pro-American country," Arias later recalled, "and so everyone asked how could I dare to disagree with Washington."[16]

Stung by the criticism, Arias in the weeks leading up to his inauguration embarked on a campaign against the Nicaraguan government, both rhetorical and diplomatic. At the beginning of March he declared that he would not visit Managua during his first trip through Central America.[17] In El Salvador he repeated a campaign charge that Nicaragua had become a "second Cuba,"[18] and he enthusiastically endorsed President Duarte's March offer to meet with the Salvadoran guerrillas if Daniel Ortega would meet with the contras, a proposal the Sandinistas had already angrily rejected. The day before the House vote in March, Arias publicly condemned the Sandinistas for turning down Duarte's offer, and the day after aid was defeated, he said the vote had opened "an opportunity for the Nicaraguan Government" to talk with its opponents.[19] On March 20 he declared "the Managua regime should change. . . . No country helped Sandinism more than Costa Rica. . . . [we] feel disillusioned, disappointed . . . betrayed."[20]

While vigorously denouncing the Sandinistas, Arias worked to ease Costa Rican concerns that his opposition to contra aid had damaged relations with the Reagan administration. He said he was sure that the United States would never "retaliate" against Costa Rica economically over a mere foreign policy dispute because he believed there was "a genuine and sincere U.S. desire to assist Costa Rica, especially because we are an exemplary democracy." On March 19 he declared that the United States would be the very first country he would visit after his inauguration.[21]

By April Arias had calmed the controversy in Costa Rica. It was clear that U.S.-Costa Rican relations had not suffered as a result of his opposition to contra aid, as even Reagan officials had found it useful to quote Arias's anti-Sandinista comments in the days leading up to the House vote in March.[22] At the same time, Arias's critics admitted that not only had no great damage been done, but Arias's "openly anti-U.S. attitude" had actually brought some benefits. "[T]he anti-U.S. position, which may bother us in a Costa Rican president," one opposition newspaper admitted, was nevertheless proving to be "a valuable asset internationally," one that could allow Arias "to assume a position of leadership among the Latin American presidents."[23] Arias may have made the same calculation. In April, May, and June he began to challenge the regional diplomatic heavyweights in the Contadora Group, above all Mexico, for control of the negotiating process.

In the spring of 1986 international attention turned to the Contadora talks, then reaching their most critical and, as it turned out, final stage. Far from relenting in his attacks on the Sandinistas, Arias pressed ahead. Abandoning his earlier commitment to non-intervention in the "internal affairs" of other countries, Arias mounted a political and diplomatic campaign to force the Sandinistas to make profound democratic reforms. He thus placed himself squarely in opposition to the Contadora Group, which considered all discussion of the political section of the treaty draft closed. Arias nevertheless insisted that the "totalitarian" nature of the Sandinista government was the source of the Central American crisis and that there would be no peace in the region until democracy flourished in Nicaragua. At the pivotal summit meeting of Central American presidents in Esquipulas, Guatemala, two weeks before the June 6 deadline imposed by Contadora, Arias stood firm in demanding that the Sandinistas make concessions and allow democratic reforms. Honduran President Azcona gave Arias credit for uniting the four democratically elected presidents against Daniel Ortega.[24] When the June 6 deadline passed without a signed treaty, Arias expressed no regrets. On the contrary, he had already declared that obtaining a signature of the Contadora agreement was not the most important goal. The "truly important goal," he said, was "achieving pluralism as soon as possible."[25]

The Reagan administration was pleased with Arias's performance. In the first week of June, Philip Habib came to Costa Rica and, according to Arias, thanked him for his stance against Nicaragua.[26] The next day Arias met with General John Galvin, commander of American forces in Panama, and declared his opposition to signing a Contadora agreement without a prior "guarantee" that democratic processes in each country could be verified. Contadora was, "for the time being," the only forum for negotiations, Arias said, but Costa Rica was not going to sign the treaty just to satisfy international opinion.[27]

The Sandinistas and their supporters were dismayed at the apparent reversal of Arias's position since his election. Radio Havana promptly dubbed Arias the "spokesman for Reagan" in Central America.[28] Daniel Ortega accused the United States of "sabotaging" the Contadora negotiations by "encouraging certain Central American governments to propose ... [the] acceptance or nonacceptance of a given type of democracy."[29] Costa Rica and other Central American countries, the Sandinistas declared, had succumbed to economic "blackmail" and become "instruments" of the United States.[30] Indeed, while Arias continued to repeat his opposition to contra aid, he helped erode any slim chance for a Contadora agreement which alone could have blocked passage of contra aid on June 26. Especially galling to the Sandinistas was the fact that when aid to the contras passed the House on June 26, the Congress also rewarded the four Central American democracies with "a prize" of $300 million in economic assistance.[31] In July Daniel Ortega warned that "some Central American leaders are playing with fire by becoming instruments of the U.S. Government's policy, by collaborating with the U.S. Government's warmongering plans.... The U.S. Government offers money, and the U.S. Government also exerts pressure, and some Central American presidents who call themselves democrats lack dignity. They lack dignity and pride."[32]

The Sandinistas sought revenge. Encouraged by the International Court of Justice's favorable decision on the Sandinistas' claim against the United States on June 25, 1986, the Nicaraguan government filed new claims against both Costa Rica and Honduras on July 18. The Sandinistas charged that despite President Arias's professions of neutrality, "the truth is that the complicity of the Costa Rican Government with the illegal policy of the U.S. Government has not ended, and the armed actions, the acts of intervention, and other illegal actions to the detriment of Nicaragua have continued."[33] On July 19, Daniel Ortega challenged Costa Rica and Honduras to "define" themselves "in view of the blackmail" of the United States: "either they decide on peace, or they will become instruments of U.S. policy"[34]

In the face of the Sandinistas' diplomatic and rhetorical attacks, Arias shifted course again. Throughout the summer and fall of 1986 Arias continued to denounce the Sandinista "dictatorship," at one point referring to them as "Somoza's heirs."[35] But he also spoke out increasingly against the dire consequences for Costa Rica of the new contra aid passed by the U.S. Congress. Continued war in Nicaragua, he argued, would increase the number of Nicaraguan refugees on Costa Rican soil. "These Nicaraguans, many of them contras, are probably the main obstacle we have in achieving the reactivation of our economy."[36] He appealed to Costa Rican nationalism, warning that the presence of so many foreigners would deprive Costa Rica of "its own identity."[37]

The Sandinistas responded quickly to Arias's latest shift in rhetoric and began portraying him more as the victim of American pressure.[38] They offered Arias a way to escape the charge of vassalage, and perhaps the International Court of Justice suit, as well. "The situation demands an honest and courageous attitude from the Costa Rican and Honduran presidents," Ortega declared on November 27, "They must tell the U.S. President: Look, mister, we can be your friends and allies, but you cannot ask us to commit suicide."[39]

———

In the months before the Iran-contra scandal broke in Washington, therefore, Arias held a unique position in the hemisphere. A frequent and vociferous critic of the Sandinistas, and of the Contadora Group, Arias had won praise from the Reagan administration and its supporters. Without changing his opposition to contra aid, Arias had helped pass aid in June by the timing of his diplomatic and rhetorical attacks on the Sandinistas. Shultz believed Arias had indeed become a "spokesman for democracy inside Nicaragua. . . . [H]is sincerity of purpose was never in doubt."[40] When Arias paid his first official state visit to the United States in early December, President Reagan extolled him for "your courageous defense of the right of the Nicaraguan people to liberty. Despite threats, insults, and provocation, Mr. President, you have not shrunk from your firm stand against totalitarianism next door. As the leader of the region's oldest and strongest democracy, your words have special significance and carry moral weight. As you've said: Democratization is the key to peace in Central America."[41]

Yet Reagan's critics were equally effusive in their praise of Arias. Although he had helped undermine the Contadora talks which they had doggedly supported for four years, and although he had done so by insisting on democracy in Nicaragua—a demand liberal Democrats and journalists associated with Reagan administration "zealots" and "ideologues"[42]—Arias nevertheless won praise for his forthright and consistent opposition to contra aid. The greatest symbol of the remarkably bipartisan support Arias had managed to achieve was the $300 million in economic assistance that had been enthusiastically endorsed, in an otherwise stingy Congress, by proponents as well as opponents of aid to the contras in the summer of 1986.[43]

Arias had won the approval of all sides by proclaiming two goals commonly thought to be incompatible: an immediate end to the contra war, and democracy in Nicaragua. For both sides in the American debate, Arias's two principles were contradictory: Supporters of the administration's contra policy believed the Sandinistas would not accept true democratic reform unless they faced defeat on the battlefield, if then. Opponents of contra aid argued that demanding democratic reform in Nicaragua meant demanding the Sandinistas' overthrow, because the Sandinistas would never voluntarily choose to remove themselves from power through a fair election. The Contadora Group had long ago rejected demanding democratization in Nicaragua, not only because it violated the principle of nonintervention but because the Sandinistas would never accept such dictates. The very inconsistency of Arias's proposals, however, made them attractive to members of Congress who, in the aftermath of the Iran-contra scandal, were looking for a way out of their own political impasse. Arias promised to give Reagan what he demanded, democracy in Nicaragua, and also what his opponents demanded, an end to the contra war.

The mammoth scandal that broke in the United States in November opened a wide path for Arias to pursue his ambition as peacemaker that otherwise would have been impossibly narrow. In the summer of 1986 Congress had settled the matter of contra aid, after painful and seemingly endless debate, and the new pact between the Reagan administration and majorities in both houses would have been largely immune to importunings by Latin leaders, at least until the fall of 1987. By December 1986, however, a weakened Reagan administration and a newly divided Congress practically invited foreign efforts to influence the tumultuous American debate. That month Senator Dodd traveled to Central America and paid a visit to President Arias. Dodd told Arias that, after the scandal and the Democratic victories in the Senate, Congress would never approve new aid for the contras. Arias had been casting around for some way to lead a new peace process, and before Dodd's trip he had begun discussing a Latin and European "peace alliance" to increase pressure on the Sandinistas. Listening to Dodd, however, Arias realized the extent of the shift in the American political balance, and he adjusted his plans accordingly. After Dodd's visit, the first outlines of the Arias peace plan began to emerge.[44]

At the end of January and beginning of February, 1987, Arias worked with his advisers to devise a new formula for peace in Central America. To begin the new negotiations, Arias called for a meeting of Central American presidents on February 15 in San José where he would present his peace plan. He did not invite Nicaragua to the meeting, however, and the common assumption in Washington and Latin American capitals was that his new plan would be difficult for the Sandinistas to accept and that Arias intended to isolate them once more. The Sandinistas immediately denounced Arias and the other presidents as "traitors and neo-colonies" of the United States.[45] The governments of Honduras and El Salvador anticipated a repetition of the Esquipulas summit the previous May, in which the four presidents would agree on a plan and present the Sandinistas with a united front. The Sandinistas would reject the plan and be held responsible for yet another failed effort at peace.[46] This was not the result Arias had in mind, however, and the plan he presented to his colleagues in San José surprised everyone, including the Sandinistas.

In the first place, the draft peace plan Arias drew up in February addressed not only Nicaragua, but all five countries in Central America. It ambitiously proposed to settle the Salvadoran and Guatemalan as well as the Nicaraguan civil wars, and it called for the same measures of national reconciliation and democratic reform in all the countries, even, theoretically, in Costa Rica. The Arias plan called for immediate cease-fires in Nicaragua, El Salvador, and Guatemala, the immediate suspension of all outside support for insurgencies in the region, and a prohibition on the use of territory in neighboring governments by insurgent forces. Within 60 days after signature of the agreement, governments in the region were to offer amnesty to guerrillas who had laid down their weapons, begin a "comprehensive dialogue" with opposition groups to establish terms for "national reconciliation," guarantee freedom of the press, show "clear evidence of unrestricted political party pluralism," initiate "an authentic, democratic, pluralistic and participative process" to promote social justice and human rights, and establish a timetable for the holding of free elections. The plan did not, however, demand that governments hold presidential elections sooner than planned, but rather made clear that elections should be held on schedules provided for in the existing constitutions in all five countries.

Beyond calling for an end to insurgencies in the region, the plan did not further address the regional security issues that had made up the bulk of the Contadora agreement. The Arias plan called for the start of negotiations on reduction of military forces in the region within 60 days after signature. It did not call for an end to outside military assistance to the governments in the region, nor did it address the questions of foreign military advisers or international military maneuvers. Arias believed the security provisions in the Contadora draft had been a principal obstacle to agreement and, in any case, avoided what he still believed were the essential truths: there could be "no peace without democracy in Central America," and "no democracy without peace." Ending insurgencies and promoting democracy were his chief concerns.

Arias did not share his draft plan with other governments until two days before the February 15 meeting in San José.[47] Reagan officials expected to be pleased with his plan. While the Contadora Group had promoted only "fake negotiations" that failed to address the threat of a Soviet-backed Nicaragua, Elliott Abrams said in January, the Central American democracies would never propose a treaty that did not "put enormous amounts of pressure on Nicaragua" because "their necks are on the line." In a meeting between Abrams, Habib, and Costa Rican Foreign Minister Madrigal in the first week of January, the two governments seemed to be in cordial agreement on most points.[48] Reagan officials welcomed declarations by Arias in January and early February that the Nicaraguan elections in 1984 had not been valid, that the Sandinista government could not claim legitimacy until it had been "chosen by the Nicaraguans in truly free elections," and that "if the Nicaraguan people were free to choose their leaders, they would not choose the FSLN, because after 7 or 8 years, the FSLN has only proven that it is good at impoverishing the people."[49]

What Reagan officials did not notice at first, or did not pay sufficient attention to, was that Arias's strategy for achieving democratic elections in Nicaragua was different from theirs and, above all, did not include any role for the contras. As one Costa Rican official noted, for Reagan officials "it was very hard later, once they learned the plan's contents, that they had drunk so deeply at that well, for the plan attacked their policy in Central America."[50]

When Arias finally revealed his plan, it was a most unwelcome surprise to the Reagan administration. While not objecting to Arias's proclaimed goals, which were after all their own, Reagan officials did object to his plan's call for the unconditional disbanding of the contras before the Sandinistas had to begin complying with the other provisions. Reagan officials insisted, as they had in the past, on "simultaneity": The contras should be disbanded only when the Sandinistas had taken significant steps to comply with all the terms of any treaty. Secretary Shultz was "baffled" by what he called Arias's "blind spot on the importance of pressure from the Contras to diplomatic movement by Nicaragua."[51] Reagan officials were dismayed to learn that in Arias's plan the Sandinistas would not even have to negotiate a cease-fire with the contras. The plan simply called on the governments in the region to declare cease-fires and expected insurgent forces and their outside supporters to abide by the terms of the agreement and lay down their arms. Habib found this aspect of the Arias plan simply "mad."[52] As one who had negotiated many cease-fires over the years, Habib believed that "the simple declaration of a cease-fire without some prior negotiations of the terms . . . [was] a guaranteed formula for failure of a cease-fire."[53] The American position, which Habib explained to Arias and the other three democratically elected presidents throughout the spring, was that the contras should take part in cease-fire talks; that they should also participate in the political dialogue on national reconciliation; that U.S. aid to the contras should be suspended only when an agreed cease-fire was in place; and that non-military assistance should continue to be provided after a cease-fire while the political dialogue continued and democratic reforms were carried out. The goal of the peace agreement, Habib explained, ought to be the "reintegration of Nicaraguans . . . into the political life of Nicaragua."[54]

Even on the matter of democratic reform, where the Arias plan went further than any of the Contadora drafts, Reagan officials believed it did not go far enough. Most Reagan officials had hoped for an agreement that would force the Sandinistas to hold free elections for president well in advance of November 1990, the date specified in the Sandinista constitution. Arias's decision to respect existing constitutions meant that the contras might be disbanded more than three years before the Sandinistas had to meet what Reagan officials believed was the only true test of their democratic intentions. Lifting press restrictions, declaring an amnesty, and holding a dialogue with opposition parties were inadequate measures of the Sandinistas' commitment to democracy. While Reagan officials welcomed the Arias plan's emphasis on political issues, they noted that the plan did not begin to address regional security concerns of the United States and its allies in Central America, especially the role of Cuba and the Soviet Union in supplying the Sandinista army, providing advisers, and possibly turning Nicaragua into a second base for Soviet power in the Western Hemisphere.

In 1984, 1985, and 1986 the Reagan administration had been reluctant to voice its specific objections to the Contadora treaty drafts, lest it be accused of undermining peace talks. In the first months of 1987 Reagan officials were even more reluctant to complain publicly about the Arias draft. With the Iran-contra scandal still at its height, with votes on contra aid pending in both houses in the first three weeks of March, and with many members of Congress from both parties warmly embracing the new Arias peace initiative as a possible escape from the next contra aid battle, the administration made its views known *sotto voce*.

On February 24 Secretary Shultz told the Senate foreign relations committee that the Arias initiative was "a healthy, welcome development," but said "we want to work with that process and not be too quick to pass judgment." Even so, important members of Congress like Republican Senator Nancy Kassebaum warned the administration not to insist on "trying to dot every 'i' and cross every 't'" before agreeing to support the Arias peace proposal.[55]

The governments of El Salvador and Honduras also withheld comment. At the February 15 meeting in San José they neither agreed to the draft plan nor stood in the way of further discussion. Elliott Abrams told a Senate committee on March 6 that both the administration and the Central American governments had "some ideas about how to improve the proposals and will make them known through appropriate channels at the appropriate time."[56] Privately, Habib began meeting with Arias and the other three presidents in an effort to modify the plan to meet the Reagan administration's concerns, or as Shultz put it, "to tighten up the Arias proposals and to close loopholes which we knew the Ortega regime would exploit."[57] Meanwhile, on March 13 the Senate passed a resolution supporting the "thrust" of the Arias plan by an overwhelming vote of 97–1.

Arias was under no illusion that the terms of his plan satisfied the Reagan administration. Nor was he inclined to bend to the administration's demands, no matter how quietly or cordially expressed by Habib. The Reagan administration was wedded to supporting the contras; Arias was equally intent on ending aid to the contras. Moreover, Arias assumed that contra aid was politically moribund in the United States as a result of the scandal, and the Reagan administration was quixotic to believe the contras would be sustained through the end of 1987. President Reagan's refusal to give up on this lost cause had succeeded only in isolating him, Arias believed, both in the United States and in the world.[58] Arias hoped the Reagan administration would eventually see merit in his strategy, but he had not devised his plan in order to win the support of the severely weakened American government. He was far more concerned with winning the support of his Central American colleagues, and especially of Presidents Duarte and Ortega. The terms of the plan that Reagan officials found objectionable were precisely those he considered necessary to accomplish that difficult task.

The Sandinistas, Arias assumed, would be the hardest to convince, since the burdens of his plan fell most heavily on them. Arias believed he had to keep the terms sufficiently flexible to entice the Sandinistas to go along. He declared, for instance, that he was "not going to be disrespectful" by proposing the Sandinistas talk with the contras, which he was sure they would reject.[59] Arias accepted the Sandinistas' claim that they could not undertake political reforms while the contra war continued."[60] Arias would not ask the Nicaraguan government "to move up its elections."[61] His plan recognized existing constitutions and electoral schedules because he knew the Sandinistas "would oppose the plan if we questioned their legitimacy."[62]

Arias thus retreated from positions he had held the year before, when he had suggested the Sandinistas should hold elections sooner than November 1990, and when he had called on the Sandinistas to negotiate directly with the contras.[63] But Arias responded that "things have changed since May 1986. . . . Central American geopolitics are always changing."[64] What had changed, however, were North American politics. What the Sandinistas wanted most out of any agreement, Arias believed, was an end to the contra war. If congressional support for contra aid had already been destroyed by the scandal, he reasoned, there was a limit to the concessions one could demand of the Sandinistas in return for what they might be able to get without making any concessions at all. The Reagan administration wanted Arias to make the plan tougher on the Sandinistas, but Arias was not even sure he could win their support on the terms he had already set forth.

The Sandinistas were ambivalent about the Arias plan from the start. When they recovered from their initial outrage at not being invited to the February 15 meeting in San José and finally looked at the plan, they saw much that was to their liking. The Arias plan did not require the Sandinistas to make any specific commitments to reduce the size of their armed forces, to limit the number and type of weapons in their arsenals, or to renounce further shipments of arms from the Soviet Union and Eastern bloc nations. While the Sandinistas still wanted limits on American military maneuvers in Honduras and off Nicaragua's two coasts, which the Arias plan also did not address, Humberto Ortega could rest comfortably knowing that his army would continue to be equipped at the levels he believed necessary. This was a big improvement over the Contadora negotiations of the previous year.

The most attractive part of the Arias plan was its demand for an end to the contra war on the date of signature, prior to all other actions. As the months passed in 1987, the well-financed contras were beginning once again to pose problems for the Sandinista army. As many as 10,000 contra fighters had slipped back into Nicaragua by April and were beginning to raise havoc in the north, south, and east-central parts of the country. The renewal of widespread fighting for the first time in more than a year promised to depress further the Sandinistas' already bankrupt economy, fan discontent in the countryside, and bolster opposition political movements in the cities. Sandinista leaders, as always, welcomed any plan that promised an end to the war without demanding a reduction in the arms and men needed to fight it.

The Sandinistas were wary of the provisions in the plan which called for democratic reforms, however. They had long avoided any explicit and detailed demands for reforms in the Contadora treaty, and to accept the Arias plan would be a significant concession, one that could prove dangerous if not carried out carefully. At the end of March Daniel Ortega repeated the Sandinistas' usual argument that "democracy" was in the eye of the beholder. In Nicaragua, Ortega explained, "We view democracy as the participation of the peoples and the creative effort of society in terms of actual independence and sovereignty of the country." Other countries should not insist on a uniformity of all democratic governments. "We have our idiosyncrasies and our own complexities," Ortega stated. "Based on these factors all of us are building democracy." The new Sandinista constitution guaranteed civil liberties and democratic government. "We have had a permanent dialogue with all the political parties that have accepted the constitutional order," Ortega pointed out. "There were political parties in the Constituent Assembly. . . . We have always been willing to talk with the domestic opposition."[65]

The Sandinistas did not view Arias as an enemy, and they were gratified to see the Reagan administration obviously discomfited by his plan, but they were nevertheless wary of Arias's ultimate intentions. In April Tomás Borge well expressed the Sandinistas' ambivalent attitude toward Arias and his plan. "One must objectively admit," he told reporters, "that the greater pressure of these parties is directed toward defending the Nicaraguan revolution, Nicaragua's existence as a nation, and its sovereignty, rather than applying pressure on us to change our structure." At the same time, Borge recognized that through the Arias plan "certain parties" were applying pressure on Nicaragua "'to find its place' within the framework of the traditional Latin American democracy. While they defend our existence, they simultaneously try to bring us closer to the Nicaraguan counterrevolutionaries and push us into the sheep pen of Latin American democracy."[66]

The Sandinistas thus moved cautiously. They did not reject the Arias proposal or complain about its contents, nor did they accept it. They welcomed "inclusion of the plan in the Contadora negotiating process," which was a way of hedging their bets and assuring the continued role of a friendly Mexico in the negotiations. And Daniel Ortega did agree to attend the next summit of all five Central American presidents which Arias scheduled for the end of June in Guatemala.[67]

Over the first five months of his peace initiative Arias had established the foundation on which to carry out his grand strategy. He had won broad support for his plan in the U.S. Congress and forced reluctant and tepid endorsements out of the Reagan administration, the Sandinistas, and the other Central American governments. The more endorsements he won, the more pressure he put on those who might want to stand in the way. Even the Contadora Group grudgingly gave its support to the plan, declaring it to be "within the framework" of their peace process, but only after Arias promised to call for a resumption of Contadora talks after his plan was signed.[68] Radio Havana commented cynically that Arias consistently tried "to please both friend and foe. . . . [H]is contradictory positions show what he is like. . . . [Arias] is always trying to seek respectability for his plans."[69]

By May, however, the momentum that Arias had built behind his peace process began to slow. The Reagan administration, with the worst of its political crisis behind it, managed to regain some influence over diplomatic developments in the region. Habib visited Presidents Duarte, Azcona, Cerezo, and Arias several times between March and June to explain more forcefully some of the administration's reservations about the plan. On May 3 President Reagan declared his general support for the Arias plan but insisted there remained "concerns which need to be resolved, particularly on the sequence of implementation. It's essential that any cease-fire be negotiated with the full range of the opposition." Reagan also stated that "For as long as I am President, I have no intention of withdrawing our support for these efforts by the Nicaraguan people to gain their freedom and the right to choose their own national future."[70] On June 17 Arias, who was traveling in the United States on a private visit, was invited to the White House and got an earful from the President and his top advisers. In what Costa Rican officials described as a "sharp, tense and blunt" discussion, Reagan told Arias, "the greatest concern is the need for the Sandinistas to act on genuine democratization before pressure on the regime is removed in any way." The next day, in a meeting with Vice President Bush, Arias expressed "sadness" that the administration focused only on the negative aspects of his plan and was disappointed that he had been unable to convince President Reagan that military pressure did not work and that his peace plan should be given a chance.[71]

The Honduran and Salvadoran governments also began to speak out against aspects of the Arias plan. After a visit from Habib at the end of March, the Honduran foreign minister declared that while Arias's plan was a "valid document," it lacked "some technical aspects that need to be corrected for it to be not only a valid document . . . but also a feasible document that can be implemented."[72] A couple of weeks later, the Salvadoran foreign minister weighed in with a list of proposed "modifications" that stressed "simultaneity and multilaterality, verification, control, and timing." The Salvadorans also wanted a "strict security plan" to accompany the Arias proposals. Both the Honduran and Salvadoran foreign ministers declared that the Arias plan was, after all, only a draft and ought therefore to be the subject of further negotiations.[73] Habib agreed that while the plan had shortcomings, it was only a "preliminary draft" and could be changed.[74]

Even the Nicaraguan opposition parties complained that the Arias plan would not guarantee "true elections" in Nicaragua since it did not call for amendments to the Sandinista constitution and electoral laws which they deemed essential. The Coordinadora stuck to its three-year-old demand for the election of a new constituent assembly to draft a different constitution "that would truly guarantee the democratic rights of the Nicaraguan people." And the Coordinadora joined in the call for negotiations that included the contras, fearing that unarmed opposition parties would have no strength alone at the negotiating table with the Sandinistas.[75]

Arias resisted all these appeals for changes in his draft.[76] Indeed, the common presumption that the peace plan was a "draft" subject to modification was not shared by its author.[77] Arias feared that if he accepted any modifications to his plan, the negotiations would immediately lead to stalemate and mutual recriminations. One summit meeting would lead to others as the opposing sides picked away at the provisions of the plan, and Arias feared his peace process would then "fall into the trap" of Contadora. After a meeting with Habib in April, he told reporters he could "accept many revisions," but if there were "deep changes, and the spirit of the proposal is distorted, then that can be viewed as a means to reject the proposal."[78] The key to Arias's strategy was actually to avoid negotiations. He hoped that if he could bring all the Central American presidents together at one summit and challenge them to say "yes" or "no" to his plan as it stood, then with the full attention of a hopeful world upon them, the Central American presidents would be cowed into agreement. The agenda at the next summit should have only one point, Costa Rican officials insisted: "to discuss Costa Rican President Oscar Arias's peace plan."[79]

Even Habib, who supported Arias's efforts more than most Reagan officials, grew frustrated at Arias's stubbornness. At one point Habib asked Shultz, "How firm should I be with Arias? He doesn't want to change a thing in his plan. The Democrats in Congress tell him it's perfect. It isn't." Shultz advised Habib to keep going over with Arias "what needs to be changed, and describe it as amplification."[80] Arias, however, remained unmoved. Shultz recalls with annoyance that "Arias seemed to alternate from one end of the spectrum to the other." He could be "statesmanlike" one moment, "but then the statesmanlike would slide off toward the saintly, and his eyes would grow sad and visionary. He seemed to believe that the world could be set right simply by saying it should be so. . . . I knew he simply could not understand how critical the growing contra pressure was to his negotiating efforts."[81] Arias, on the other hand, was annoyed at the Reagan administration for publicly supporting his plan but privately counseling El Salvador and Honduras to seek changes. "No one has said openly that they are against it," he complained in May. "But there are many ways in which to kill. Each man kills the thing he loves. The coward does it with a kiss."[82]

While Arias wrestled with the Reagan administration and its Central American allies, he also worried about the Sandinistas, who had adopted a strategy of silence in the hope that the Salvadorans, Hondurans, and Americans would derail the plan and relieve them of the burden of making a difficult decision. Arias, suspecting that the Sandinistas would not "show their cards until the Esquipulas meeting," did his best to reassure them that his plan made no unreasonable demands.[83] "We are not recommending a dialogue either with the contras in Nicaragua or with the guerrillas in El Salvador," Arias repeated. "At the same time we are calling for a cease-fire, an amnesty for the rebels in both countries, and the suspension of economic aid both to the Salvadoran guerrillas and to the Nicaraguan contras." We do not "question the legitimacy of existing governments or . . . call for elections to be brought forward—Each government must reach the normal conclusion of its constitutional term."[84] The Sandinistas' quiet aloofness nevertheless added to the growing perception that the Arias plan was going nowhere.

By May, Arias's hopes for a successful summit at the end of June were fading. He told reporters he no longer believed "that in a meeting of six to eight hours we will be able to accomplish what eight Latin American countries have not been able to achieve in four years." Faced with domestic criticism that he had spent too much time on his peace plan to the neglect of more pressing economic problems at home, Arias argued that "advancement in the direction of this peace so much longed for by all the Central American peoples will by itself constitute success."[85] In his May Day address he told the Costa Rican people that he was determined to surmount all obstacles. "Those who within and outside the country are hoping that the failure of a new peace initiative will turn us into allies of war actions should realize right now that it will never happen; they should know that we again will renew our faith in dialogue and our conviction in political solutions."[86] To win more support for his peace initiative and put pressure on his opponents, Arias went off on a long tour of European capitals.

By the time Arias returned, however, his June summit was collapsing. President Duarte insisted on a meeting of foreign ministers prior to the presidential summit at the end of June in order to prepare an agreed document for discussion. Duarte had no desire to go along with Arias's strategy for a single, highly publicized all-or-nothing summit in which he would be pressured either to agree to a plan he deemed faulty or be declared a saboteur of peace.[87] Arias, who was eager to satisfy Duarte and woo him away from the Reagan administration, agreed, and a preliminary foreign ministers meeting was scheduled for June 11. The Sandinistas, however, declared they would not attend and asked for a postponement until June 22, just three days before the summit. When the meeting was rescheduled for June 22 in Honduras, the Sandinistas then asked that it be held on June 23 in Guatemala.[88] The Sandinistas clearly hoped that their opponents would object, and they did.

On June 12 President Duarte demanded that the entire summit be postponed until August. The plan proposed by Arias, Duarte declared, would not yield the results "that we expect; therefore, we would rather not sign a document that is not good." He insisted that there should be at least four foreign ministers meetings prior to any summit to prepare an agreed text of the plan. The Salvadoran foreign minister declared that "only the postponement of the Central American presidents summit meeting" could save the Arias plan from failure. Arias grudgingly acquiesced. "What this demonstrates," he told reporters, "is that at this moment there is not a very favorable climate, which is absolutely necessary to hold this summit meeting." Arias agreed to reschedule the summit for the first week of August and to hold three foreign ministers meetings beforehand. "It is better we take our time."[89]

With the summit safely postponed, the Sandinistas could now demand that it be held as originally scheduled. The scheduling of foreign ministers meetings, Daniel Ortega declared, was an effort "to impede dialogue and a negotiated solution and to spread the war in the region."[90] Failure to hold the summit on June 25, Ortega insisted, would strike a "fatal blow" to the peace efforts of Arias.[91] The Sandinistas also showed signs of being afraid of the Arias plan. They demanded that negotiations revert back to Contadora, "the only serious and capable instrument" for peace in the region. At the end of June, Costa Rican officials declared that the Arias plan was on the "verge of collapse."[92]

47

The Iran-Contra Scandal: In Washington and Central America

News of the apparent collapse the Arias plan might have spurred some members of Congress to action had they not been distracted by a far more interesting spectacle: the opening of the Iran-contra hearings by the congressional investigating committees on May 5. The hearings, as expected, entirely consumed the American government for the better part of three months. What was not expected, however, was that the hearings would end up increasing support for aid to the contras. Yet from the very beginning of the public investigations, that is precisely what happened, and the result was a series of events that no one could have anticipated when the news of the scandal first broke.

If the Democratic members of the Iran-contra investigating committees "lost the Iran-contra hearings," as Mary McGrory later lamented,[1] it was probably for the very same reasons that Congress had ultimately been unable to resist President Reagan's appeal for contra aid—an evenly divided Congress and a nervous Democratic Party fearful of President Reagan and of any allegations of "softness" on communism. These political vulnerabilities made it hard for the Iran-contra committee to expose and condemn even possibly unlawful support for the contras. Indeed, the ambiguous results of the Iran-contra hearings perhaps justified in retrospect Congressman Hamilton's reluctance to pursue the allegations of wrongdoing by Oliver North in 1985 and 1986. Even with exciting revelations

516

about an Iran-contra diversion, the Congress was politically ill-suited to call the Reagan administration to account before the American people on the divisive issue of contra aid.

The Democrats and the moderate Republican senators, Warren Rudman and William Cohen,[2] intended to use the public hearings to reveal what they believed to be wrongful and even unconstitutional actions by Reagan administration officials. "The story that will be told is a sad one," Rudman declared when the hearings began. "There will be evidence of illegal behavior and contempt of our democratic form of government."[3] Evidence there may well have been, but by the end of the hearings the man most implicated in such behavior had also become one of the most popular men in America; and the House and Senate committee members who had tried to impugn his actions had become targets of hate mail.

Critics of the administration showed their vulnerability from the very beginning. Democrats who had feared taking on President Reagan at the height of the scandal in December were even more fearful of doing so on national television five months later. While the six House Republicans and Senators Hatch and McClure openly defended both President Reagan and his contra policy, the Democrats followed the advice of Majority Leader Foley: "Political instinct here happens to be that Democrats, I think, realize that if they were to appear to be using this national problem and controversy for narrow partisan gains, the public could be expected to react negatively."[4] Three weeks into the hearings, however, the public reaction even to implied criticism of the President had forced critics to retreat. As one House Democrat on the committee told reporters, "People like the President, even if they don't believe him, and they don't take kindly to what they see as political attacks on him."[5]

The committee proved reluctant not only to take on the President, but also to attack his policy of support for the contras. Of the 26 committee members, 17 had voted for military aid to the contras in 1986 and were not interested in publicly repudiating their own decision.[6] The issue was "a trap to be avoided," Senators Cohen and Mitchell later recalled. Rather than "argue the merits or morality of the Contra cause," the administration's critics wished to examine only "the means used by North and others to support it." As a result, House Republicans and a succession of witnesses advanced arguments for contra aid that went unanswered by Democratic critics. Weeks before Oliver North gave his now-famous testimony, Republicans on the committee reported that the hearings were giving contra aid "a tremendous boost."[7]

The task administration critics had left themselves—to explain the subtle and complex ways by which North and other officials had improperly aided the contras—proved immensely difficult. The questions they raised were important enough and worthy of serious discussion, but the difficult judgments and legal distinctions proved of little interest to the general public. It was especially hard in light of the Congress's own vacillating role over the years, and Republicans like Cheney asked from the beginning whether the "lack of a clear-cut policy by the Congress" had not contributed "to the events we will be exploring in the weeks ahead."[8] As Senators Cohen and Mitchell recall, "the public was not rushing to condemn the President over an issue in which the Congress was so divided and inconsistent."[9]

The committee members' eagerness for publicity also hindered their efforts. The fact that Reagan's presidency was not at stake had "removed the element of high drama from the proceedings." The committee thus acceded to Richard Secord's demand to testify first, allowing him to state his case before the public heard from anyone else, because "if we didn't capture the attention of the press and public at the outset we never would."[10] The committee's decision to allow Oliver North and his lawyer to dictate many of the terms under which North would testify was also based on an understanding that without North's dramatic testimony, the hearings would lose all interest to the viewing public.

The committee members were themselves especially susceptible to any hint of bad publicity. Long before North took the stand, committee members had begun a disorderly retreat before an angry public. Even Secord, arguably the least photogenic and sympathetic of all the witnesses, fared much better on television than the committee members expected.[11] The public reaction to the first week of hearings stunned the members. "The Committee as a whole had been perceived as hostile, belligerent, pompous, patronizing, or unpatriotic," its members recall.[12] By the time Oliver North appeared to testify on July 7, the off-balance committee and its unpopular lawyers had become a wide target for an extremely well-spoken, attractive, passionate, medal-clad marine.

As Senators Cohen and Mitchell later recalled, the contest between "one Marine against twenty-six lawyer-politicians . . . wasn't even close. North held a Gatling gun while we sat like ducks in a shooting gallery. The American people loved it."[13] After only one day of testimony, North instantly became one of the most popular men in America, and his erstwhile detractors on the committee hid in panic. "Soon the telegrams started to come," Senators Mitchell and Cohen recalled, "first in the hundreds, then in the thousands, then the tens of thousands."[14] Polls showed viewers supporting North by a margin of 43–14 percent, 50–9 in the South.[15] For weeks afterward, North maintained higher approval ratings than President Reagan. The Senate committee chairman, Senator Inouye of Hawaii, declared after North's testimony that "in the past week, I believe we have participated in creating and developing a new American hero."[16]

"The effect on the members was immediate and, in some cases, overwhelming," Senator Mitchell recalls. "All America was watching. And all America liked Ollie, or so it seemed. Careers hung in the balance. Committee members began to worry about how many constituents would remember their feelings of antagonism toward their representative on the next election day." When Senator Mitchell's turn came to question North, he made only a plaintive appeal to the colonel to "please remember" that others shared North's devotion to country and that it was "possible for an American to disagree with you on aid to the contras and still love God and still love this country just as much as you do."[17]

What troubled Mitchell and other liberal Democrats as much as North's personal triumph was the blow he struck on behalf of contra aid. "Hang whatever you want around the neck of Ollie North," North had stated to committee members before his enthralled television audience. "But for the love of God and the love of this nation, don't hang around Ollie North's neck the cut-off of funds to the Nicaraguan resistance again." Popular approval for contra aid surged.[18] A *Wall Street Journal*/NBC News poll taken after North's testimony showed that 40 percent of those asked favored contra aid, while 43 percent opposed it—compared to a margin of 32–54 two months earlier; a *Los Angeles Times* poll from July 10–13 found an even split, 42–42, compared to 31–54 in February.[19] Liberal Democrats were angry at their colleagues on the committee. "Someone should have brought [North] up short, and no one did," Senator Harkin complained. "What is now portrayed to the American people of the contras is 180 degrees out of whack."[20] The result of the Iran-contra hearings and North's testimony was that contra aid was, for a moment, more popular in the United States than before the scandal. Senator Dodd declared after the testimony that "if the contra aid vote were held today," President Reagan would win.[21] House Democrats said publicly that the hearings had made little difference, but privately, Bonior told Wright they were losing votes.[22]

————

The increase in support for contra aid complicated the plans of Howard Baker and President Reagan's new team of advisers. Since March, Baker and his staff had hoped to work out some deal with the Democrats to avert a confrontation over contra aid, but North's testimony now made compromise with the Democrats dangerous. Conservative Republicans, stirred to a frenzy by North, clamored for the Reagan administration to seize the moment and press Congress hard. "The time to launch the campaign for contra aid is now," Patrick Buchanan insisted, "when the iron is hot."[23] Congressman Kemp called on Reagan to double his $105 million request for the contras. After North's testimony White House officials did indeed shift with the prevailing winds, in part to avoid criticism from the right, but also in response to President Reagan's own renewed enthusiasm. White House officials leaked word that the President was considering putting forward a new, larger contra aid request before the August congressional recess.[24]

Privately, however, Baker and his deputies remained eager to avoid a clash with Congress. They wanted to turn the country's attention away from the scandal quickly and to begin rebuilding Reagan's political strength on a foundation of popular actions—like a new arms treaty with the Soviet Union. Even if support for the contras remained high, and they doubted it would, Baker and his colleagues did not want to fight the political battles that would be required to pass aid in the House of Representatives. The possible gain—another year's worth of contra aid—did not in their eyes justify the breakdown of the uneasy truce between the President and leading Democrats that even the Iran-contra hearings had not destroyed.

White House officials thus faced the difficult task of bargaining with the Democrats without falling prey to charges of appeasement from conservatives. At any previous time in the Reagan administration, the task would have been impossible. Since March, however, with Casey, North, and Poindexter gone, the National Security Council staff in the hands of Carlucci, and President Reagan licking his wounds, the proponents of conciliation with Congress dominated the administration for the first time.

On July 7, the day North began his testimony, the White House appointed former Texas congressman Thomas Loeffler to work as its congressional lobbyist on the Nicaragua issue. Elliott Abrams, who had led the administration's efforts on Capitol Hill for over a year, had been badly weakened in the Iran-contra hearings. Over a hundred liberal opponents of contra aid had written to Shultz demanding that Abrams be fired for misleading congressional committees about the solicitation of Brunei and administration involvement with the Hasenfus plane. Even conservative contra aid supporters like Senator Boren questioned Abrams's ability to work effectively with Congress.[25] The White House might well have let Abrams go, but Shultz refused, declaring that Abrams had done "an extraordinarily difficult job with great energy, with great skill and with great dedication" and should not be abandoned just because he had become a "lightning rod" for critics of contra aid.[26] Instead of firing Abrams, the White House hired Loeffler and brought full control of legislative strategy into Howard Baker's hands.

Loeffler's task was to find terms for compromise with the Democrats, and for this he naturally turned to his former Texas colleague, Jim Wright. The belief that Wright might be amenable to a deal on contra aid was widespread, even among some conservative House Republicans.[27] Loeffler first met with Wright on July 22, a little more than a week after North ended his testimony, and he warned the Speaker that the administration, buoyed by the recent rise in the polls, planned to seek as much as $200 million in new aid to the contras in September. Loeffler offered Wright a way to avoid another debilitating battle, however. Claiming that President Reagan was "really serious now about a diplomatic solution" to the conflict in Nicaragua, Loeffler asked whether Wright would be willing "to make a joint statement with the President in pursuit of a diplomatic settlement." Such an act would be "precedent-setting," Loeffler argued. "It would involve the Speaker of the House in foreign policy in a new way."[28]

Loeffler knew what Wright wanted to hear, of course, since Wright's ambitions as Speaker were no secret. Reagan's alleged interest in a "diplomatic settlement," moreover, offered Wright a chance to patch up the divisions in his party. "I remember executions in Cuba, in China," he told one colleague. "Where are we as a party if we beat contra aid and those terrible things happen?"[29] A combination of idealism, political interest, and personal ambition drove Wright to explore the deal Loeffler was suggesting.[30]

Wright's colleagues in the Democratic leadership, however, unanimously opposed any collaboration with the Reagan White House. "If the Sandinistas turn the plan down," Congressman Coelho warned, "then

Reagan's on TV pushing contra aid and we're trapped." Congressman Bonior suspected that Wright was being "set up."[31] Wright was undeterred. He warned Loeffler that "if the President is just going to go through the motions, with the idea of being rejected and using that as a justification to ask for more money to continue the war, count me out."[32] But Wright, who was not naive, believed that even if the administration did hope for such an outcome, he could turn their trap into an instrument for his own use, regardless of the administration's plans. Wright hoped and expected that a peace proposal offered jointly with Reagan could break the stalemate in the Central American negotiations, bring peace to Nicaragua, and make it impossible for the President to seek new aid for the contras.

The diplomatic situation in Central America at the beginning of August was confused, but not promising. While officials in Washington had been transfixed by the Iran-contra hearings, events in Central America had moved slowly. The temporary paralysis of the American government had had a generally paralyzing effect in Central America, where governments waited to see the outcome of the American conflict before deciding on their own course. But perceptions of the American political scene, and predictions of future American behavior, differed in each Central American capital. The political struggle in Washington in May, June, and July of 1987 had influenced Central American leaders in subtle and contradictory ways.

To Honduras and El Salvador, the two governments most dependent on Washington for aid and political support, the Iran-contra scandal had been a long-running nightmare. The prospect of Reagan's downfall at the hands of angry Democrats seemed more real to Central American than to Washington politicians. The consequences of a Democratic coup in Washington could be severe for the two governments that had conspired with the now-scandalous Oliver North and his colleagues.[33] Honduran officials and military leaders in late June were "jittery about what's going to happen on January 20, 1989, or maybe even before." They didn't want to be "left holding the bag" if and when the Democratic Party took control.[34]

To begin to undo the damage to their own reputations, Presidents Duarte and Azcona distanced themselves from the contra war. For the Hondurans, who harbored the contras, this was no easy task, but in June President Azcona refused to let contra leaders hold a public meeting in Tegucigalpa and suggested he would allow no such meetings in the future. A few days later, when a contra plane was shot down by the Sandinistas over Nicaragua and crashed in Honduras, the Honduran military deported the injured pilot and crew to Miami, and the government released a remarkable statement declaring the contras had "violated the government's policy of neutrality and nonintervention in the internal conflicts of other states."[35]

President Duarte did not face the same embarrassing problem as Azcona, but he had more to lose if the American Congress turned against him. With an ongoing guerrilla war, a weak economy, an angry right wing, and a restive military, Duarte depended on both the Reagan administration and Democrats like Jim Wright for continued economic and military aid. Knowing that Wright and most Democrats opposed contra aid and favored the Arias plan, Duarte took a risk by demanding postponement of the summit.

There were hints that the Salvadoran president had begun to ponder how he might salvage his own position amidst the possible wreckage of the Reagan administration. One of the few who saw these hints was President Arias. Duarte "knew the plan by heart," Arias recalls, and "was the one who took the peace initiative most seriously."[36] As the only president besides Ortega who faced a dangerous force of guerrillas,[37] Duarte took acute interest in those parts of the plan that favored incumbent governments over their armed challengers.[38] Arias's proposal had opened a gap between Duarte's interests and the Reagan administration's, and it had narrowed the gap between Duarte and the Sandinistas. Arias tried to make Duarte more independent of American influence. "I kept telling President Duarte that I wanted him to be more flexible, that he didn't have to accept all of Ambassador Habib's suggestions."[39] Between June and August Duarte grew more flexible than most American observers knew.

While the Honduran and Salvadoran governments worried about Reagan's weakness, the Nicaraguan government worried more about its own. The Sandinistas had learned from painful experience that contra aid was never as dead as Democratic politicians claimed, and Speaker Wright himself told the Sandinistas that, despite the scandal, new aid might yet pass.[40] Whatever the vagaries of American politics, the Sandinistas knew that their own predicament had grown even more dire since the spring—economically, politically, and militarily—and that they needed a reprieve from American pressure.

As commander of the Sandinista army, Humberto Ortega knew best how the war with the contras was eroding the government's strength. For the Sandinistas, perhaps the most troubling aspect of the war in 1987 was how it contrasted with the previous year of combat. In the last half of 1986 the contras had virtually ceased fighting, and by the time President Reagan signed legislation providing $100 million in aid most of the rebel forces had begun retreating back to Honduras to wait for the new supplies. Less than 2,000 contras remained in Nicaragua when the CIA returned to take charge of the war for the first time since the summer of 1984.

What the CIA managed to accomplish between November 1986 and July 1987 was a matter of great concern to the Sandinistas. CIA officials resisted political pressures to rush contra forces back into the country to make spectacular and probably futile raids against Sandinista military posts or towns—a strategy the Sandinista army would have welcomed. The director of the CIA's contra task force, Alan Fiers, had planned a more gradual crescendo of fighting, beginning in the first few months with small but well-coordinated attacks on lightly defended targets, electrical towers and transformers, telegraph, water works, small bridges, and other parts of the Nicaraguan infrastructure, and escalating in the second half of the year to more ambitious raids using larger concentrations of forces against Sandinista military posts in the hinterlands. A central aim of Fiers's strategy was to force the Sandinista army to respond to contra activities in several parts of the country at once, in the northern and southern border regions, in the central provinces of Matagalpa, Boaco, and Chontales, and in the northeastern part of Zelaya province: what Fiers called the "four-corner offense." In this way he hoped to "stretch the Sandinista army, deny them victory, erode their counterinsurgency capability and inflict maximum damage on their infrastructure."[41]

Thousands of well-trained and well-equipped contra forces had begun crossing back into Nicaragua in November. In the first week of December the Sandinistas launched an attack to block or slow the infiltration, employing several thousand troops up near the northern border and, at one point, launching another attack across the border into Honduras with about 1,000 troops.[42] But the attack succeeded only in frightening the Hondurans, and the contra forces "came right down through the heart" of the Sandinistas' defenses.[43] By the end of January, 2,500 contras had made their way past Sandinista blocking positions, and a month later Daniel Ortega reported that 6,000 contras had entered the country from Honduras.[44] By early spring Sandinista troops had no choice but to pull back from their positions along the northern border and begin chasing the contras around the countryside.[45]

At first the Sandinistas branded the contras' small unit attacks as mere propaganda,[46] but by the early summer the contras were successfully carrying out the "four-corner offense," attacking in larger units against better-defended targets.[47] New U.S.-supplied anti-aircraft missiles added to the contras' boldness and reduced the Sandinistas' most important technological edge in the war. As contra commander Mike Lima told reporters at the end of June, "Back in 1985 the Mi-24 [helicopter] was a terrifying weapon to our forces. We ran like rabbits when a hawk is overhead. Now our men can defend themselves better, When a helicopter comes, no one moves."[48] Defense analysts in Washington reported at the end of the July that the contras had shot down five Sandinista helicopters in the first seven months of the year and had gained the "tactical initiative" in the war.[49]

Over the course of the summer, the Sandinista army spread itself thin trying to respond to simultaneous attacks throughout the country. Despite the great numbers of troops in the Sandinista army and reserves, critical oil shortages and logistical problems limited the number of forces that could be sustained in combat at one time to between 30,000 and 40,000—only three times the 10–12,000 contras.[50] Observers criticized the Sandinista army for trying to respond to contra operations everywhere—like "firemen chasing fires"—which seemed a repetition of Somoza's futile efforts in 1979. But the Sandinistas, like Somoza, were reluctant to let the contras claim large pockets of "liberated territory" in Nicaragua unchallenged. As it was, wide swatches of the Nicaraguan countryside had come under the contras' control. By the end of the summer, the contras had established bases of operation in three regions inside Nicaragua: in the Bocay area of northern Jinotega, in southern Matagalpa and northern Chontales, and in the Nueva Guinea region near the Costa Rican border.[51] Sandinista authorities "evacuated" hundreds of peasant families from these areas, but could not eradicate the contras' growing network of supporters.[52] Enough young campesinos joined the contras' ranks in 1987, Humberto Ortega noted, to replace what he claimed were almost 3,000 killed in the fighting.[53]

Humberto Ortega's senior military aide, Roger Miranda, made a tour of Sandinista military posts in the countryside and returned with disturbing reports about widespread support for the contras and hatred of the government. In Boaco province, Miranda and his escort "felt such hostility they hardly dared stop to eat lunch. The possibility of being ambushed was very real." Miranda's escort, a brigade commander from Boaco, told him:

"Look, chief, all these peasants you have seen, all these little villages we have passed through, all these sons of bitches are Contras. All of them." Miranda returned to Managua "with the terrible feeling that he was regarded as the chief of an occupying military force in his own country."[54]

While the Sandinista army struggled for control in the countryside, the government faced continuing erosion of support in the cities. The Sandinistas had been laboring since the 1984 election to build a legal and respectable foundation for the revolution through the promulgation of a new constitution promising respect for fundamental rights and regular elections. But no sooner was the constitution put into effect at the beginning of 1987 than the Sandinistas reimposed the State of Emergency: *La Prensa* remained closed; business and opposition leaders were detained by the Interior Ministry; and the government stood in a pitched battle with Cardinal Obando and the Catholic church. Earlier the Sandinistas had expelled Bishop Vega of Juigalpa, the capital of Chontales province where support for the contras ran high, and the bishop's expulsion had drawn another sharp rebuke from the Vatican. Although the Sandinistas argued that the continuing war made such actions necessary, the arrests and abrogation of rights did not improve their reputation in the U.S. Congress or in Europe or in the cities of Nicaragua.

The biggest cause of domestic discontent in Nicaragua was the disastrous economy—a problem that compounded all the others. The contra war took an increasing toll on an economy that was plummeting anyway because of low world commodity prices, a lack of foreign assistance, the U.S. trade embargo, and the mismanagement and inefficiency of the Sandinistas' quasi-command economy. By the second half of 1987 inflation was out of control, goods of all kinds were scarce, and production had fallen to an all-time low. Daniel Ortega frankly told his countrymen on July 19 that Nicaragua's exports had declined steadily from $499 million in 1981 to a disastrous $230 million in 1986, and the outlook in the first six months of 1987 was no better. At the same time, while about 19 percent of the national budget had been devoted to defense in 1982, in 1986 the amount was closer to 40 percent, and in the first six months of 1987 it was 46 percent, one-third of the entire gross national product.[55] "We have no choice" but to make such expenditures for defense, Ortega declared. "Not doing this would allow the counterrevolution to advance and the revolution to be defeated."[56] Yet the plummeting economy raised the specter of slow strangulation if the Sandinistas could not turn it around.

To make up for the lack of foreign earnings, and the devotion of so many resources to defense, the Sandinistas relied on foreign assistance. Yet here, too, the story in the summer of 1987 was dismal. Ortega admitted to a budget deficit of $225 million—it was probably larger. "Who covers that deficit?" he asked rhetorically. "No one does." All the aid from the European countries, Latin America, China, India, Canada, Libya, and Iran, Ortega explained, was not enough to "cover the basic needs of the 1987 economic plans." West Germany, France, and even the Netherlands had halted or drastically cut aid programs for economic or political reasons. The Sandinistas were unable to make interest payments, and their crackdown on opposition politicians and Church officials hurt them in the West, where the Reagan administration constantly urged allies to cut the Sandinistas off.[57]

Soviet assistance, Ortega pointed out, although generous, was "not enough to cover Nicaragua's needs," and Henry Ruiz had returned from a meeting with Soviet Foreign Minister Shevardnadze at the beginning of the year obviously dissatisfied with what Gorbachev's government had to offer. In May Moscow announced it could not increase oil shipments beyond what had already been promised, and Ortega noted that the Soviet Union provided only enough oil "to cover 50 percent of our requirements."[58] The oil crisis not only harmed Nicaraguan industry and hampered civilian transportation, it forced a reduction in the use of military equipment like helicopters and trucks and diminished the army's mobility at a time when mobility was most needed.[59]

Signs of an ominous shift in the global balance of power were all around the Sandinistas. Humberto Ortega noted with dismay how the United States, which he insisted still threatened to invade Nicaragua, had over the past eight years built up an extraordinary military capability in Latin America. "[D]espite the international rejection" of American hegemony in the region, Ortega declared, "it has been impossible to halt it. . . . The United States has practically legitimized—as if it were a routine manner, as if it were not an alarming situation—the threatening presence, the actual deployment of its forces . . . the entire military, technological, electronic, political, and psychological setup."[60] While Reagan wielded this enormous American power against the Sandinista revolution, the Soviet Union under Gorbachev eagerly sought rapprochement with the United States.[61] From the Sandinistas' perspective, Soviet-American friendship only freed Reagan's hands in the American sphere of influence.[62] It was not that the Soviets were abandoning the Sandinistas. Military assistance from the Soviet Union had reached an all-time high in 1986 and continued to flow freely in 1987. The problem was that in the eight years since the Sandinistas swept into Managua, the correlation of forces had shifted dramatically against the superpower they had sought to make their patron and protector as they defied American hegemony.

With such unfavorable trends at home and abroad, the Ortega brothers "felt power slipping from their hands" in the summer of 1987.[63] They faced an old dilemma, however. They could win a reprieve from American pressure if they tacked back in the direction of "tercerismo," gave the bourgeoisie a share of economic and political power, ceased their aid to the Salvadoran guerrillas, reduced their Soviet and Cuban ties and sought integration in the West. Yet the danger of succumbing to American and bourgeois pressures was that having once retreated in the face of opposition, there might be no way to resist the forces thus unleashed.

The Arias plan offered a way out of the crisis that was at once tantalizing and worrying. Tomás Borge might be right to warn of the dangers of being herded into the "sheep pen" of Latin American democracy. For the Ortegas, on the other hand, flexibility and adaptability had always been essential ingredients of continued survival. And Humberto Ortega, with control of the army and ties, still, to the old bourgeois elite he had allied with in the 1970s,[64] could expect to survive a turn back toward tercerismo more easily than Borge. In the dire circumstances of 1987, the Ortegas did not so much develop an alternative strategy for the revolution as determine to keep their options open. Humberto and his brother Daniel sent subtle signals to the Reagan administration that they desired better relations, less in the hope of actually renewing talks than out of a desire not to burn all bridges with the Americans.[65] As for the Arias plan, they steered the government along a moderate course in the weeks leading to the summit. After Arias declared on June 21 that he would go to the summit meeting in August "with or without Ortega," the Sandinistas began to drop most of their objections to a meeting and by the end of July had agreed to attend both the foreign ministers meetings and the summit.[66]

————

Whatever the subtle shifts that had occurred in the attitudes of the Central American governments over the course of the summer, however, prospects for an agreement among the five presidents remained slim on the eve of the Guatemala City summit in the first week of August. Arias traveled through the Central American capitals on July 26–27 hoping to bridge differences but found objections to his plan on all sides. He accused the Honduran government of trying to "torpedo" the peace plan, but took a kinder attitude toward Duarte's "frank objections," which he believed could be "overcome."[67] Arias saved his strongest criticism for the Sandinistas, who on the one hand expressed support for his plan, but on the other hand seemed unwilling to commit themselves to the democratic reforms the plan called for. "They weren't prepared to accept anything," Arias recalls, "I was shocked. . . . I told them: 'You haven't read it. You have to understand that you are committing yourselves to adopt democracy.' |"[68] Daniel Ortega told reporters after meeting Arias that the Central American countries were all "accomplishing democracy through different ways and paths."[69]

The meeting of foreign ministers that began on July 31 revealed that the core of the Central American conflict was the confrontation between El Salvador and Nicaragua, and the Salvadoran foreign minister made clear that one issue mattered to his government above all others. He demanded that the Nicaraguan government "issue a statement at national and international levels stating that it no longer supports the FMLN-FDR," and he insisted that any treaty had to verify the expulsion of the Salvadoran guerrillas from Nicaraguan territory. "If Nicaragua does this," Foreign Minister Acevedo declared, "it will prove that it has the political willingness to attain peace and democracy in Central America."[70] Nicaraguan Foreign Minister D'Escoto refused to make such a declaration, however. The Honduran government, meanwhile, introduced a proposal to delay any cutoff of aid to insurgent forces until 180 days after signature, while steps toward democratization were to begin immediately. This proposal, which completely reversed the intent of the Arias plan— which was to end the contra war first—and which almost assured the renewal of contra aid by the United States Congress, was supported by the Salvadoran foreign minister.

The second foreign ministers meeting in Guatemala on August 4 thus opened "amid a climate of tension and recriminations."[71] The Sandinistas' apparent reluctance to accept the democratization provisions of the plan, the Salvadoran government's demand for an open acknowledgment of Sandinista support for the FMLN, the Honduran proposal to delay the cutoff of aid to insurgent forces, and the Reagan administration's known opposition to the Arias plan all pointed toward stalemate. The Sandinistas expected the summit to produce only a communiqué and an agreement to hold more talks.[72] President Azcona told military leaders before departing that he had no intention of signing any peace plan.[73] Arias himself lowered expectations by stating it was "not easy to attain peace in only one meeting"; he hoped the presidents would at least agree to meet again.[74]

48

The Wright-Reagan Agreement
and "Esquipulas II"

Such was the diplomatic impasse in Central America at the end of July
as Speaker Wright and Reagan officials began negotiating the terms of
their own political settlement. From the beginning the two sides proceeded on the basis of very different assumptions. The White House expected the diplomatic stalemate in Central America to continue during
and after the summit at Guatemala City. Few officials expected that any
agreement they reached with Wright was likely to be acceptable to the
Sandinistas. The White House aim in negotiating with Wright, therefore,
was only to forge a joint proposal that they could live with, in the unlikely
event the Sandinistas accepted it, but which they could use to seek more
contra aid in the almost certain event that the Sandinistas rejected it.

Baker and Loeffler, it appears, were not even thinking very much about
the Central American summit. They were simply looking for a bipartisan
agreement in Washington that could rid them of the tiresome and explosive contra aid issue. For them, agreement with Wright was an end in itself; whether the Sandinistas accepted an American proposal or rejected
it, the administration and Congress would be in accord, and a bruising
confrontation could be avoided. The actual terms of the proposal were,
therefore, of less concern. Those matters could be worked out by Secretary Shultz, whom they trusted to be reasonable. The primacy of the domestic political question in their minds was demonstrated by the fact that

the White House did not even invite Shultz into the discussions until a week after Loeffler's first meeting with Wright.

Wright was also primarily interested in the domestic political impact of his actions, but unlike Baker and Loeffler, he could not seek an agreement with the administration for agreement's sake. For Wright, a deal with the White House could be successful only if it ended contra aid; if it resulted in the renewal of aid, Wright would face a mutiny in his own party. Wright's future as Speaker thus depended on an outbreak of peace in Central America, and his whole aim in pursuing negotiations with the administration was to ensure this outcome.

Before Wright began negotiations with the administration over the actual terms of a peace plan, therefore, he took the measure of the different Central American governments. He learned from Arias that the summit meeting was likely to be "inconclusive" and that the Central American governments were "waiting to see what the United States would do" about contra aid. Wright invited the Nicaraguan ambassador, Carlos Tunnermann, to his office to inquire whether the Sandinistas were amenable to any kind of deal with the United States. Wright told Tunnermann he had lived through the "Who lost China?" debates of the 1950s and had no desire to open his party to such attacks again. He warned that Oliver North's testimony had changed the political equation in Washington and that "perhaps military aid to the contras will be extended." Wright told Tunnermann that there was "a small window of opportunity" for the Sandinistas: acceptance of a peace plan Wright intended to propose jointly with President Reagan. Wright wanted to know if the Sandinistas were interested in exploring such an agreement—at least in principle, since no plan yet existed. Ambassador Tunnermann instantly replied, "Yes."[1]

Baker and Loeffler brought Shultz into the discussions with Wright for the first time on July 30, just a week before the Guatemala summit. While White House officials were most concerned with striking a deal with the Speaker, Shultz also wanted to make sure that any peace proposal put forth by the President closed the "loopholes" in the Arias plan that he and Habib had labored over for the past four months. Shultz told Wright that any cease-fire talks had to include the contras.[2] More importantly, Shultz wanted to ensure that the threat of renewed war hung over the Sandinistas until they undertook serious democratic reforms and complied with other aspects of any agreement, and that if the Sandinistas rejected the Wright-Reagan plan, it "would result in resumption of military aid to the contras."[3]

Wright and his Democratic colleagues, who up until this point had been jollied along by Loeffler and Baker, were taken aback by Shultz's demands. Indeed, it was at this point that the negotiations should by all rights have collapsed because Shultz had exposed the inherent incompatibility of the two sides' positions. Shultz's insistence on continuing aid to the contras as pressure on the Sandinistas was unacceptable to Wright and other Democrats. Majority Leader Foley insisted there could be "absolutely no linkage" between the peace plan and contra aid, "no implication that if this fails, the Speaker is expected to support contra aid." Wright said the peace proposal had to stand "on its own, without a club in the closet"; there could be no "two track policy of subsidizing war while talking peace."[4] Wright insisted, moreover, that President Reagan delay requesting any aid for the contras until after September 30. Otherwise, Wright told Reagan officials, "I'd be screwed." The Sandinistas would suspect a trap, and Wright's own party would accuse him of treachery. "If we go forward together," Wright told Reagan, "then we just talk peace—peace—until then."[5]

A debate ensued over what conservatives called Wright's "gag rule" against any discussion of contra aid before September 30, but this debate evaded the more fundamental problem. It actually did not matter whether Wright committed himself to supporting aid for the contras if the peace plan failed. As Congressman Bonior warned Wright, "I think the initiative will fail and they'll be able to say, 'Look, we tried the Speaker's plan, it went nowhere, now give us the aid,' and they'll have the votes. I think the initiative will mean war, Mr. Speaker—three hundred million dollars worth of war."[6]

Baker and Shultz acceded to Wright's "gag rule" and exacted no explicit commitment from Wright except a promise to allow a vote on new contra aid if the peace plan failed. In negotiating the actual terms of the peace plan, Shultz also made other concessions. Although he wanted the Sandinistas to negotiate a cease-fire directly with the contras, Wright knew the Sandinistas still refused to meet with the contras. He suggested that perhaps "they could use a go-between." Shultz agreed to compromise. The final draft of the plan did not specify precisely who would have to negotiate with whom, but it did state that the terms of any cease-fire had to be "acceptable to the parties involved." Some "ambiguities" in the peace plan, Shultz argued, were "not necessarily bad."[7]

A second disagreement concerned elections. Congressman Cheney and other Republicans wanted to specify in the plan that the Sandinistas had to hold free elections for president in advance of those scheduled for 1990 under the new Sandinista constitution. "The heart of the whole issue," Cheney insisted to Wright, "is whether the Sandinistas will yield power peacefully." Wright, however, had already been told by Costa Rica's ambassador, Guido Fernandez, that the Sandinistas would never accept an explicit demand for "national elections," and he had agreed to drop that demand from an early draft. Wright now told Cheney, "You want to tell them to amend their constitution. I want them to live up to it." Again the negotiators compromised, calling for "an electoral commission [to] be established to assure regular elections open to free participation by all," but saying nothing about the timing of presidential elections.[8]

Reagan officials compromised on these points, in part, because on the matter of greatest concern to them, Wright put up no struggle. The final draft of the Wright-Reagan plan called for an immediate cease-fire "in place," which meant that the contras could remain intact as a fighting force in areas they controlled without turning in their arms. Once the cease-fire took effect, the United States would halt military aid to the contras, but not "humanitarian" aid. The Nicaraguan government would also have to cease receiving arms from Cuba and the Soviet Union. The United States could continue supplying "humanitarian" aid to the contras in their positions until an agreed plan of demobilization, by both the contra and Sandinista armies, was implemented and the safety of contra forces returning to political life in Nicaragua was "guarantee[d]." Shultz interpreted the overall agreement to mean that the contras had to be "satisfied that a cease-fire is going to be accompanied by such things as amnesty, release of political prisoners, the freedom of religion, freedom of the press and a process definitely under way that is going to lead to the kind of electoral system that we are advocating."[9]

One aspect of the proposal administration officials especially liked was the very short period the Sandinistas would be given both to agree to and then to implement the proposed reforms. Under the Wright-Reagan plan, negotiations toward a cease-fire would begin immediately and end by September 30, when current funding for the contras was to expire. If the Sandinistas did not agree to the conditions set forth, or refused to negotiate a cease-fire, the plan stated that other parties would be "free to pursue such actions as they deem necessary to protect their national interest." It was this phrase that caused Democratic leaders concern. When Shultz declared his satisfaction that the phrase kept the threat of renewed contra aid hanging over the Sandinistas' head, he provoked another outburst from Foley who warned that the negotiators were "on the verge of a very dangerous misunderstanding. If the assumption is, in the absence of Nicaragua's agreement, then Democrats will support aid, that's a mistake. We must reiterate as we have from the start: this is a peace plan. It has nothing to do with whether contra aid passes or not. The separation is absolute and antiseptic." The Democrats at the August 3 meeting were "nervous, nervous as hell."[10]

Because the Democrats were more nervous about the impact of the plan on Washington politics than about its effect on Central American diplomacy, they may have missed the most crucial elements of the Wright-Reagan plan. The final draft still embodied the Reagan administration's definition of "simultaneity" and thus differed sharply from the Arias plan, which proposed to end all aid to insurgent forces immediately from the date of signature. The terms of the Wright-Reagan plan inherently, if not explicitly, embodied Shultz's "two-track" approach of combining negotiations with the threat of renewed war, of keeping the contra option alive while the Sandinistas undertook reforms, of using force or the threat of force as a means of pressuring the Sandinistas to live up to their commitments. Moreover, the Wright-Reagan plan called for an end to the delivery of Soviet weapons and supplies to the Sandinistas in exchange for an end to contra aid. The Sandinistas could never agree to such a proposal and had resisted it through years of Contadora negotiations.

Wright's failure to perceive the importance of these points was due to several factors. First, he was under the impression that he had already received a kind of endorsement from both the Nicaraguan and Costa Rican governments. Wright had shown a preliminary draft of his plan to the ambassadors of both countries even before he began negotiating with Shultz. Costa Rican Ambassador Guido Fernandez had suggested some changes, which Wright agreed to, but Fernandez told Wright that if he and Reagan put forth such a proposal, it could spur the Central American presidents to reach an agreement in Guatemala. Wright gave a copy of his draft to Ambassador Tunnermann for the Nicaraguan government, who had also encouraged Wright in his peacemaking efforts. When Wright began negotiations with the administration on August 3 on the terms of a draft plan, therefore, he believed he had general support from the two most important Central American governments. While the heated objections of Wright's Democratic colleagues made him hesitate, this encouragement from Central American officials convinced him to go forward.[11] He actually feared only the opposition of El Salvador and Honduras who in his view were excessively under the sway of hostile Reagan officials.

Wright also believed his plan contained important incentives for the Sandinistas. Under the Wright-Reagan proposal, the United States would "suspend" military maneuvers in Honduras as a gesture of good faith. If and when the Sandinistas put the "national reconciliation" plan into effect, the United States would lift the trade embargo and begin to make Managua eligible for international aid programs. In addition, once the Sandinistas had implemented the required reforms, the United States would join in negotiations with all five Central American governments on matters of regional security—that is, arms levels, maneuvers, foreign advisers, and foreign military assistance. Wright thus hoped to offer the Sandinistas what they had long demanded—direct talks with the United States government.[12] Wright was also pleased to have included in the plan the statement that "the United States has no right to interfere or determine the identity of the political leaders of Nicaragua nor the social and economic system of the country."

The terms of the Wright-Reagan plan reflected the new political mood in Washington. Despite the Iran-contra scandal, the political will to cut off the contras completely and immediately, as Arias wanted to do, was lacking in both parties. North's testimony had made it impossible for the Reagan administration and the Republican Party to accept any such proposal, but it also made it difficult for Wright to insist on it, even if he was of a mind to do so. To straddle the gap in the Democratic Party Wright had to do more than demand an end to the contra war; he had to propose and support a plan that did not appear to "lose" Central America to communism. He hoped and expected that his plan would be accepted by the Sandinistas, but it could not be so weak as to make it too easy for the Sandinistas to accept. With all that had occurred since Congress passed aid to the contras in 1986, a consensus nevertheless remained in favor of "pressure" on the Nicaraguan government. Wright, who had spent years trying to find the middle path between the conservative and liberal wings of the party, and who shared the Southerner's concern that his party not be labeled forever "soft" on communism, devised a plan that, once again, expressed the desires of the center.

Conservatives inside and outside the administration immediately began attacking the Wright-Reagan plan as too soft on the Sandinistas, and White House officials, as usual, bent under the onslaught. On August

4 presidential spokesman Marlin Fitzwater made the mistake of publicly describing the deal as Reagan officials really understood it. The peace plan, he told reporters, "is tied to the request. Peace and funding are all tied together." Even Shultz annoyed Wright by telling an interviewer that while peace negotiations proceeded, "the contras will give a good account of themselves." Anonymous officials told reporters that the administration believed the Sandinistas would reject the plan, leaving the Democrats no choice but to support contra aid. Annoyed that administration officials weren't "playing straight," Wright complained to Baker, who reassured him that such statements were errors that would be corrected.[13] This was small consolation to Wright, who was already under attack from anti-contra liberals in his own party.[14]

More trouble was yet to come, however. While conservative Republican leaders in the House, like Cheney and Hyde, had participated in the negotiations with Wright and had given at least tacit support to the plan, Congressman Jack Kemp and conservatives in the Senate had been excluded. Kemp called Baker and accused him of "selling out" the contras.[15] Six conservative Republican senators met with Reagan on August 5 and warned him that, under Wright's "gag rule," he was "giving up 60 days of momentum and 60 days of holding the Democrats accountable . . . for nothing in return." Reagan assured the senators he was not giving up on the contras and would "beat the bushes" for aid in the fall if the peace plan failed. But the conservatives were sure that someone had "sold the President a bill of goods."[16] Abrams and NSC staff member José Sorzano also opposed the "gag rule," and found the plan in other respects only "barely acceptable," although Abrams defended it to Kemp and other House Republicans.[17] Another administration official who had been left out of the discussions with Wright, and who learned of the plan only from the newspapers, was Defense Secretary Weinberger. Weinberger heatedly opposed the entire plan and gave energy to other dissenters in the administration.

The conservatives set about trying to retract all the concessions that Shultz and Baker had made to Wright. As so often in the past they were convinced the Nicaraguan government would certainly accept a peace plan the conservatives considered so obviously flawed. At Weinberger's request, therefore, Sorzano and Abrams drew up a list of 21 points as the Reagan administration's "interpretation" of what the various ambiguous clauses in the peace plan really meant. At Weinberger's insistence President Reagan informally passed on the 21 points to Wright on August 5, but Wright rejected them, insisting the plan didn't need interpretation.[18]

Most State Department officials, however, did not really fear that the Sandinistas would accept the Wright-Reagan proposal with or without the administration's special "interpretation." They expected their close allies, El Salvador and Honduras, to endorse the American agreement but expected the final result of the summit to be continued stalemate. Wright, of course, had entirely different expectations. He still believed that his plan would spur the Central Americans. The Central American presidents, not President Reagan, would decide whether Congress would have to confront another request for contra aid.

President Reagan announced the joint peace proposal at a late afternoon press conference on August 5—on the very eve of the Central American presidents meeting in Guatemala. The State Department cabled the text of the Wright-Reagan plan, without comment or explanation, to Central America where it was delivered to the presidents as they prepared to depart for Guatemala. The lack of any accompanying explanation from the State Department was not so much an oversight as a reflection of the profound ambivalence of State Department and National Security Council officials about the plan's contents. After the flap over the administration's 21-point "clarification" of the Wright-Reagan plan—which Wright had rejected—Abrams and his colleagues could neither endorse nor condemn the plan as it was written. Publicly, Secretary Shultz would say only that the plan was "intended, and I hope it has this effect, of helping the Central American presidents to find a road to regional peace."[19] And indeed, the plan may have done just that, but not in the way Shultz, or Wright, expected.

No sooner was the Wright-Reagan plan announced than the Sandinistas denounced and rejected it. On the morning of August 6 Daniel Ortega declared that the American peace plan amounted to a "declaration of war against Nicaragua."[20] It kept the contras as a force-in-being while the Sandinistas carried out reforms; it required the Sandinistas to engage in some form of negotiations with the contras for a cease-fire; it gave the Sandinistas only a few weeks to comply, with an implicit threat of renewed contra aid if they did not; and it required a cut-off of military aid from Nicaragua's Soviet ally. Compared with the more lenient provisions of the Arias plan, the Wright-Reagan proposal held no attraction at all for the Sandinistas.

President Arias agreed that the Wright-Reagan agreement "had more teeth than mine" and was, therefore, "a plan against Nicaragua." Arias objected to the American proposal so vehemently that he called the other four presidents on the evening of August 5 and demanded that it not even be discussed at the meeting the next day. He threatened to walk out of the talks himself "if there is another plan on the table."[21] Somewhat more diplomatically, Arias asked Wright if the speaker insisted that all the terms of his plan had to be met. Wright, obviously sensing disaster if he stuck by terms so clearly objectionable to the Sandinistas and to Arias, quickly sent word to Arias and other Central American officials that he would "abide by any outcome they reach."[22] With this assurance, Arias dismissed the American proposal entirely and set about winning approval for his own. The Wright-Reagan agreement died at birth. The Reagan administration was not even aware that Wright had thus unilaterally abandoned the terms of the agreement they had so painstakingly negotiated.

To the surprise of most Reagan officials, Presidents Duarte and Azcona were scarcely more enthusiastic about the Wright-Reagan plan than Ortega and Arias. Conservative critics of the administration later charged that the Wright-Reagan agreement convinced the Salvadorans and Hondurans that Reagan had decided to "give up" on contra aid and would "abandon them in turn."[23] There is no question that the Reagan administration's political weakness after the Iran-contra scandal affected the judgment of the administration's closest allies in Central America, but conservatives overstated the importance of the Wright-Reagan plan in Duarte's and Azcona's calculations. While Republicans in Washington dubbed the Wright-Reagan agreement a "sellout," this was not the view in Central America. Duarte and Azcona were not less aware than Arias that the Wright-Reagan plan was a tougher proposal that could strengthen the administration's hand in the battle for contra aid, and that, for these very reasons, the Sandinistas had denounced and rejected it as a "declaration of war." This was not the first time Reagan had offered to end support for the contras in exchange for concessions the Sandinistas deemed unacceptable, and the Salvadoran government recognized President Reagan's political motives.[24]

President Duarte, moreover, had his own reasons for disliking the Wright-Reagan plan, which neither Wright nor Reagan administration officials had foreseen. Unlike Arias's proposals on the table in Guatemala, which promised to end foreign support for the FMLN guerrillas and which affirmed both the fundamental legitimacy of Duarte's government and the fundamental illegitimacy of the armed struggle against him, the Wright-Reagan peace plan did not even address these issues.[25] Indeed, ac-

cording to one Salvadoran official, Duarte feared the Wright-Reagan plan
not because it was a sign of surrender but because he worried it would
give the Sandinistas a pretext to withdraw from the talks without signing
any plan.[26] In the weeks before the summit meeting Duarte had begun to
have a change of heart about the Arias plan. "I decided if we were going
to have peace we had to have the political will to do it. We Central Americans had to start speaking the same language and we needed a coherent
plan *for all of us*."[27] Duarte's transformation was aided by his knowledge at
the end of July that the FMLN had rejected the Arias plan entirely.[28]
Duarte had come to see the Arias plan as a way of trapping his enemies
and securing a political victory for himself. The Wright-Reagan proposal,
therefore, was an obstacle to his plans.

When the five presidents met in Guatemala City on August 6, they
began by unanimously rejecting the Wright-Reagan plan out of hand. At
Daniel Ortega's suggestion, they agreed to discuss only the proposals
drawn up by their foreign ministers in preparation for the summit.[29]

The Wright-Reagan proposal had one important effect on the summit
meeting, however: It frightened Ortega into seeking an agreement on the
Arias proposal. Before the announcement of the American plan on August 5, the Sandinistas had been preparing for a diplomatic stalemate at
the summit. The draft proposals prepared by the foreign ministers were
stacked against Nicaragua. On every major point the vote of the foreign
ministers had been 4–1, with Nicaragua's D'Escoto the lone dissenter. On
one of the most important points—the timing of the cutoff of aid to insurgent groups—the sequence proposed by Honduras had been inserted into
the draft proposals, which meant the Sandinistas had to begin implementing democratic reforms 90 days before aid to the contras ceased.
Daniel Ortega had from the first resisted this reversal of the sequence
originally envisioned by Arias. He would not agree to lift the state of
emergency and allow a dangerous political opening while the war continued and American aid flowed to the contras. Before he had left for
Guatemala, Ortega won the Sandinista Directorate's permission to act
freely at the summit, but this was because Sandinista leaders expected
nothing would come from the meeting of the five presidents.[30]

But the Wright-Reagan plan changed Ortega's calculations. Obviously,
the Sandinistas had to reject the American plan. But if Ortega did so, and
then the five presidents reached a stalemate at the summit, there was a
good chance that the U.S. Congress might vote new aid to the contras.
This was precisely the scenario Reagan officials had hoped for, and which

Wright and his Democratic colleagues had dreaded. Ortega knew, therefore, that he had to reach agreement with the other presidents. The Wright-Reagan plan had left him no choice.

The astute Arias quickly perceived the pressure Ortega was under and the opportunity it created for an agreement. "On one side," Arias recalls, "Ortega had the threat of more aid to the contras. On the other side, he had a much tougher plan."[31] When the five presidents began their discussions, Arias turned to Ortega and bluntly asked if he was willing to make concessions, for if he was not it would be best if the five presidents just had a drink and went home. Both men understood the threat implied in Arias's question. President Ortega insisted he had come to talk.[32]

Over the next several hours, presidents Duarte and Ortega harangued each other over the support they had each given to the other's armed opponents.[33] During a break in the discussions, however, Ortega pulled Duarte aside. As Ortega later recounted to his brother, Humberto, he told Duarte "frankly that we acknowledge that we are still arming the FMLN but we think we have come to the moment to negotiate this point within the context of a regional accord." According to Ortega, this candid confession "did something to change Napoleon Duarte."[34]

Duarte responded to Ortega's frank admission by offering a compromise on the terms of the peace agreement. Instead of the sequence proposed by the Hondurans, Duarte proposed that all actions called for in the treaty go into effect at the same time 90 days after signature: on the same day the Sandinistas implemented democratic reforms there would be a cessation of aid to the contras, and to the FMLN. Duarte's proposal, he later recalled, "broke the deadlock." Ortega agreed to accept the terms, but Duarte wanted a solemn, personal commitment. As Duarte recalls the event:

> I asked him once and he said, "Yes." I asked him again. Then I asked him to shake my hand, and as we stood there with our hands locked I asked him a third time: "Do you commit your personal honor to comply with the agreement?" He said, "Yes."[35]

By the early morning hours of August 7, the presidents had still not left the hotel room, at Arias's insistence, and President Azcona alone stood in the way of an agreement. It was one thing for Duarte to compromise and change the sequence, after all, but Honduras was the country that hosted the contras, that was constantly urged by the United States to continue hosting them, and that would be exposed to international opprobrium if the contras refused to leave Honduran territory when the treaty called for their expulsion. Without the support of Duarte, however, Azcona's position was difficult. Arias made it impossible. At 4:30 a.m., Arias had Guido Fernandez, Costa Rica's ambassador in Washington, contact Wright and tell him that an outline of a peace agreement had been reached. Wright, in turn, told reporters the good news and by early morning Washington and Guatemala were abuzz with the word that peace had broken out in Central America. President Azcona gave in and signed.[36]

The Reagan administration was stunned; officials had never expected Duarte to sacrifice the contras for a personal commitment from Ortega to stop aiding the FMLN. But Duarte wasted no time in declaring that the five presidents had "rejected violence" as a means of taking power and that the guerrillas were thus an "illegitimate" force.[37] Congressman Wright was elated. He immediately endorsed the so-called "Esquipulas II" accords, declared that as a result of the peace agreement there would be no need for further contra aid, and expressed his hope that President Reagan would not seek any. It was Wright's greatest triumph as the new Speaker of the House, and he repeated to reporters what Guido Fernandez had told him early that morning: "President Arias wanted you to know that had it not been for the stimulus provided by your initiative there, he is not sure there would have been sufficient prodding and impetus to get all five to agree."[38] Wright probably did not understand that the "stimulus" he had provided with his proposal had been entirely negative.

The Central American presidents had adopted few of the changes to Arias's plan that Habib and Reagan officials had been pressing for since March and that had been contained in the Wright-Reagan proposal. The agreement signed in Guatemala gave no role to the contras, either as partners in discussions over the political future of Nicaragua or even as a party to cease-fire negotiations. Only "domestic opposition groups that have laid down their arms" would be part of the national dialogue.[39] The agreement called for a total cessation of aid to the contras, rather than the partial cutoff stipulated in the Wright-Reagan plan and long urged by Habib.[40] It called for the dismantling of guerrilla forces 90 days after signature, unlike the Wright-Reagan agreement which kept the contras as a force-in-being until they could be safely reintegrated into a democratic Nicaragua. And unlike the Wright-Reagan proposal, the Guatemala accords put no restriction on arms shipments from the Soviet bloc nor exacted any commitments from the Sandinistas regarding the use of Nicaraguan territory by the Soviet Union.

On the important, and increasingly confusing, issue of "simultaneity," the Guatemala accords were a slight improvement over the original Arias proposal, from the administration's point of view, but they fell short of the Wright-Reagan plan. According to the August 7 agreement, 90 days after the date of signature "the commitments with regard to amnesty, cease-fire, democratization, cessation of aid to irregular forces or insurgent movements, and the non-use of territory to attack other states . . . shall simultaneously begin to govern publicly." The ambiguity lay in the phrase "begin to govern." Did it mean the Sandinistas would complete implementation within 90 days, at which time the democratic reforms would "govern publicly" and aid to the contras would "simultaneously" cease? Or did it mean the Sandinistas only had to "begin" to implement democratic reforms "simultaneously" with the cessation of aid to the contras? The ambiguity of the treaty made it possible for all sides to assume that their idea of "simultaneity" had been adopted, but unfortunately for the Reagan administration, its preferred interpretation of the agreement's "simultaneity" was the least supportable. Arias's original plan had ended aid to the contras before demanding any steps toward implementation by the Sandinistas. If the five presidents had wanted to impose obligations on the Sandinistas from the date of signature they would have done so explicitly.[41] The compromise that Duarte had proposed at the summit was acceptable to Ortega precisely because it did not require the Sandinistas to loosen political controls before aid to the contras ceased.

49

"We Will Win This War in Washington"

Despite these shortcomings in the accords, when Secretary Shultz and Philip Habib read the terms in Shultz's office the evening of August 7 they declared it a "great agreement" and toasted each other on their success.[1] Shultz was evidently delighted at the prospect of putting an end to the contra aid battle with Congress—"a probable loser after the Iran-Contra revelations." He seemed to see in the agreement, moreover, more than was actually there. "To our relief and astonishment," he told President Reagan, "it has simultaneity—so it's a victory."[2] The President's first public reaction, therefore, was to welcome the new agreement, albeit with the warning that its true test would come with implementation. The State Department spokesman joined Wright in declaring that the "Esquipulas II" agreement superseded the Wright-Reagan plan. Habib asked Shultz to send him to Central America immediately to begin discussions with the Sandinistas. He wanted to "end the war on terms acceptable to us" and intended to concentrate his efforts on "strengthening the security aspects which were non-existent."[3] Shultz agreed to seek President Reagan's approval.

Shultz and Habib were alone in their happiness with the outcome of the Central American summit, however. Elliott Abrams, who read the text of the agreement along with them, found nothing to celebrate. Indeed, he found Shultz's reaction puzzling and Habib's enthusiasm alarming. Abrams believed that the agreement as written would lead to a cutoff of aid to the contras before any decisive steps toward democratization by the Sandinistas. He urged a more cautious reaction to the agreement and predicted that conservatives outside the administration, who shared his skepticism, would take the administration to task for embracing a treaty that put an end to the contras.

Far from quieting the furor over contra aid and putting the issue to rest, the signing of the peace plan in Guatemala inspired in conservative Republicans a new passion that the White House, and Republican candidates for the 1988 nomination, could not ignore. Conservatives rushed to declare that the "Esquipulas II" accords were a surrender to communism, and that the cause of this surrender had been the Wright-Reagan plan. Many administration officials, including the President himself, were rattled by the accusations and horrified to be apparently, and unexpectedly, on the verge of "selling out" the contras. As it was the presidential primary season, Republican candidates responded instantly to the party's right wing, and even moderate Republicans quickly became stalwart defenders of contra aid. On August 8, one day after the agreement was signed, Vice President Bush promised radio listeners in Miami that the Reagan administration was not "going to leave the contras twisting in the wind, wondering whether they are going to be done in by a peace plan."[4]

His two competitors for the 1988 nomination did not lag behind. Senator Dole declared that any peace plan must contain a "pledge" not to abandon the contras, and he called on the administration to seek a new package of military aid for the contras to be used if the peace plan failed.[5] Congressman Kemp called on Reagan to reject the Guatemala agreement altogether and immediately request $210 million in new aid from Congress.[6] Shultz recalls bitterly that "the right-wing ideologues did not want a negotiated settlement that would end Contra aid." Within the administration, the politically sensitive Howard Baker and his deputies quickly dropped their earlier efforts to set the contra issue aside.[7] President Reagan, counseled by Weinberger, Carlucci, and Abrams, opposed sending Habib to Central America to meet with the Sandinistas. "Communists win these kind of negotiations," Abrams told Shultz. Reagan told Shultz he feared he would be "skinned" by the right-wingers. Shultz suggested in a fury that if Habib was not to be allowed to do his job as negotiator, he ought to resign. On August 14 the administration announced Habib's resignation.[8]

Shultz himself stayed on, and in the view of many Republican observers, turned his energies to other matters, particularly the burgeoning rapprochement with the Soviet Union. The secretary of state, Senator John McCain later gently complained, was "a man who enjoys talking to Shevardnadze."[9] This was only partly true. Shultz's reaction to the agreement signed in Guatemala, when considered along with his earlier efforts in opening bilateral talks with the Sandinistas at Manzanillo, suggests indeed that he had none of the passionate commitment to the contra policy of most other senior officials in the administration, that he was less concerned about the prospects of permanent Sandinista rule in Nicaragua, and that at times he welcomed any opportunity to put the whole Nicaragua issue behind the administration.

Yet even after losing the dispute over Habib, Shultz, although bitter, continued to work hard to convince Congress to pass aid to the contras in 1987 and 1988, which was also consistent with his past behavior. It has often been suggested that Shultz's outspoken support of the contras was intended to keep American conservatives at bay. Perhaps it could also be said that Shultz's repeated abortive forays into Central American diplomacy were undertaken with an eye to appeasing liberals and moderates—certainly a no less significant force in Washington politics. There is, however, no hard evidence to support either charge. It is likely that Shultz had no irreversibly strong feelings one way or the other about Nicaragua and was prepared to live with more than one policy and more than one result. It was certainly not an issue on which he ever staked his career as secretary of state. At times Shultz acted out of loyalty to his President, at times out of genuine conviction, at times out of political or bureaucratic calculation, and at times out of a combination of all these. Throughout, however, Shultz remained wedded to his broad strategy of combining "power and diplomacy." It was not necessarily his fault that the vagaries of the American political system denied him the luxury of pursuing both elements of that strategy at the same time.

With the dispute over negotiations temporarily out of the way, Reagan officials, including Shultz, had no difficulty reaching agreement on the subject of contra aid. The aid would continue through September 30, the end of the fiscal year, and since the Guatemala agreement did not demand a cessation of aid to insurgent forces until 90 days after signature (November 5), the Reagan administration had every expectation of providing aid at least until then. Continuing aid beyond that date, however, required interpreting the Guatemala agreement differently from those who had signed it. And that is precisely what the administration proceeded to do.

Ignoring the unhelpful ambiguity concerning the plan's "simultaneity," Reagan officials simply interpreted the plan to conform with their own notion of simultaneity, as embodied in the Wright-Reagan proposal and in Habib's frequent conversations with Central American leaders. On August 15 President Reagan declared that American support for the contras would "continue until a satisfactory peace plan is in place, a cease-fire has occurred and a verifiable process of democratization is under way" in Nicaragua.[10] The State Department spokesman declared that the United States would preserve the contras as a military force until the Sandinistas had moved "irreversibly" toward democratic government in Nicaragua.[11] The administration also reinterpreted the "Esquipulas II" accord's proposal concerning a cease-fire. Although the agreement said nothing about negotiations between the contras and the Sandinistas, and in fact quite specifically did not call for such negotiations, Reagan officials nevertheless insisted that the Sandinistas negotiate a cease-fire with the contras, perhaps through a mediator, but preferably directly.[12]

The Reagan administration's interpretations of the treaty solved its most troubling problem. If these interpretations were accepted, then continued aid to the contras would be permissible under the treaty until the contras and Sandinistas successfully negotiated an agreement for a cease-fire. The contras would not have to agree to any final settlement until they were satisfied the Sandinistas had moved "irreversibly" toward democracy.[13] Since the prospects of an agreement between the contras and Sandinistas were slight, the administration's formula kept alive the hope of funding the contras well into the future. Under this interpretation of the treaty, the administration could not sell out the contras; only the contras could sell out the contras.

The Reagan administration could proceed to reinterpret the Central American treaty in this fashion only because its opponents in Washington still lacked the political strength or will to demand an unconditional end to contra aid. When Congress returned from its month-long summer recess on September 10, Secretary Shultz unveiled the administration's plans to seek $270 million in new aid for the contras sometime before Thanksgiving. Officials knew the amount was far higher than Congress was likely to approve, and it was only a matter of days before Shultz's promise to seek new aid before Thanksgiving was retracted in the face of massive opposition.[14] The administration's adamant refusal to "abandon" the contras nevertheless caused problems for leading Democrats. On August 7 Wright had appealed to the Reagan administration not to "renew the fangs of war when we have the dove of peace,"[15] but when his plea had been ignored Wright himself was unwilling to cut the contras off. Despite all that had occurred, from the Iran-contra scandal to the peace accord in Guatemala, Wright and the Democrats remained reluctant to end aid to the contras without President Reagan's blessing or tacit acquiescence.

On September 17 Wright agreed to extend support for the war past the end of the fiscal year and through November 10.[16] He promised angry liberals that this would be the last money approved for the contras, but his extension of aid set a precedent and implicitly acknowledged the validity of the administration's arguments. Once having failed to end further aid to the contras on the grounds that such aid violated the spirit if not the letter of the Guatemala agreement, the question of whether or not to continue funding was henceforth to be linked directly to whether or not the Sandinistas were complying with the terms of the treaty as the administration defined it. Howard Baker declared that the question of continued contra aid would be "answered in Managua by Daniel Ortega, rather than by Ronald Reagan in the White House," and leading Democrats apparently agreed. "If Ortega blows it," an aide to Wright said, "there will be problems for those who oppose contra aid."[17]

Daniel Ortega had signed the Guatemala agreement solely to put an end to the contras, but by the time he returned to Managua it was already clear that he had set the Sandinistas off on a difficult and dangerous journey. Rumbles of dissension led by Tomás Borge threatened the unity of the Directorate, and the Ortega brothers' dominance within it. No sooner had Daniel Ortega returned from Guatemala than he set off for Cuba to obtain Fidel Castro's approval and support for the treaty in order to quell any rebellion within the Directorate. When he returned from Havana with Castro's blessings, the Sandinista Directorate held a meeting with senior party cadres to explain what Ortega had done in Guatemala.

If the Reagan administration was engaged in reinterpreting the treaty to suit its own needs, the Sandinistas were embarked on a still more cynical project. In the secret meeting over the weekend of August 15–16, a defensive Daniel Ortega insisted that signing the Guatemala agreement did not mean a change in the strategic direction of the revolution. It was simply "one more arm that enables us to eliminate the Contras." On some issues, there would be no change in Sandinista policy, not even tactically. Ortega declared, for instance, that despite his thrice-repeated vow to President Duarte, "under no circumstances" would the Sandinistas "let the Esquipulas II accords cause a decline in the Salvadoran revolutionary organizations, whose level of military confrontations must be maintained and even increased"[18] Several weeks later Humberto Ortega met privately with a Salvadoran guerrilla leader and for the first time promised to send the FMLN new ground-to-air missiles.[19] Regarding the commitments to internal political reforms, however, Ortega argued for tactical flexibility. While adhering to the treaty would "in some degree benefit the internal reactionaries," Ortega insisted it was "better for us to take on the imperialists now on political terrain than to continue the war that is wearing us down in terms of human and material resources." "As in the case of Vietnam," Ortega declared, "we will win this war in Washington."[20]

The prospect of victory in Washington had been enhanced, Ortega argued, by the emergence of Speaker Wright as a "parallel power" in the U.S. government fully capable of "paralyz[ing] and def[ying] the authority of the President."[21] So long as the Sandinistas did not do "anything that will upset the majority vote in Congress," the mere "promise to comply with Esquipulas" would by itself be sufficient to defeat the contras on the American political battlefield.[22] The Sandinista Directorate and Assembly endorsed the Guatemala agreement on August 17—they had little choice—but Ortega's arguments could not conceal the risky nature of their new course.

The goal of the Sandinistas' strategy was to end aid to the contras; the price was greater freedom for the unarmed political opposition. That opposition, however, was a bomb waiting to explode, as the Sandinistas well knew. For eight years opposition leaders had been harassed and jailed, their newspapers and radio stations closed, and their organizations infiltrated and deprived of resources. These events had attracted little attention in the West, where debate had focused on the continuing contra war. When Ortega signed the Guatemala accords, however, he gave the Sandinistas' opponents unprecedented strength. With the world watching, and the question of war or peace in the balance, the opposition leaders could be expected to push the Sandinistas to the limits of their tolerance. In the difficult political environment created by the peace treaty, the government would have to find a way to keep the opposition from running rampant, but without being so heavy-handed as to offend the American Congress.

The Sandinistas at first hoped to abide strictly by the letter of the treaty. The only step required before November 5 was to appoint a national reconciliation commission to monitor political reforms and compliance with the agreement. This the Sandinistas did, approaching Cardinal Obando days after the summit meeting to seek his cooperation.

The opposition politicians, however, did not intend to wait until November 5. They planned to test the Sandinistas immediately and, if possible, to expose them before the world as insincere tyrants. On the evening of August 15, about 1,000 Coordinadora activists prepared to march through the streets of Managua. Five hundred relatives of political prisoners held a meeting at the headquarters of the Social Christian Party. As both groups prepared to move into the streets, Sandinista police wielding riot sticks, electrical cattle prods, and attack dogs descended upon them and violently dispersed the crowds. The police arrested two of the top leaders, and the Interior Ministry sentenced them to 30 days for disturbing the peace.[23] After the disturbances in Managua, the government announced it had no intention of lifting the emergency decrees until the contra war had ceased.[24]

The incidents on August 15 hurt the Sandinistas in Washington, where even sympathetic congressmen did not understand the reason for breaking up demonstrations by the unarmed opposition. The Reagan administration seized on the August 15 crackdown to justify continuing aid to the contras as "insurance" against Sandinista non-compliance. While some liberals told Ortega he could probably defeat contra aid with "relatively few steps" toward reform, House Democratic leaders feared the moderates in the party would turn toward support of contra aid if the repression continued.[25] Ambassador Tunnermann promised Wright it would not happen again, but Congressman Coelho warned that delays in implementing reforms could well lead to more contra aid.[26] For the first time since the revolution, the Sandinistas found themselves in the uncomfortable position Somoza once occupied—dependent on the favor of an American Congress, a majority of whose members had more sympathy for their political enemies.

The sharp response in Washington forced the Sandinistas to reconsider their position. If there was a dispute within the Directorate at this point, then the threat of renewed contra aid clearly strengthened the hand of those who argued for still greater flexibility. On August 25 Daniel Ortega named Cardinal Obando to the national reconciliation commission and offered to allow Bishop Vega and Father Bismarck Carballo to return from exile.[27] In the last week of August and first week of September, Sandinista leaders began warning the party faithful to prepare for the coming political assault of the Nicaraguan "right wing."[28] On September 6, 1,000 opposition party activists held a rally in Chinandega and were allowed to meet and disperse peacefully.[29] Two days later, the Sandinistas released to a visiting Senator Harkin the two opposition leaders imprisoned on August 15. On September 20 the government lifted restrictions on *La Prensa*, although not before trying to persuade Violeta Chamorro to accept limited, prior censorship, which she refused to do.[30] On October 1 *La Prensa* appeared on the streets of Managua for the first time in over a year, with a banner headline that declared, "The People Triumph!" and a front-page editorial that began "In the name of the people of Nicaragua, *La Prensa* today tells the Sandinista Front that Nicaraguans have never wanted and do not want a Communist-style totalitarian dictatorship."[31]

This was as far as the Sandinistas intended to go, however, without seeing evidence that the contra war would soon be brought to an end. When several thousand supporters of the Social Christian Party marched through the streets of Managua on September 27, in what reporters described as the largest protest since 1979, the Sandinista police arrested 18 party members.[32] Evidently Sandinista tolerance had reached its limits. In the last week of September Tomás Borge warned the opposition against harboring any "illusions that we are going to betray the principles of the revolution."[33] At the beginning of October, the Sandinistas found themselves in precisely the position they had hoped to avoid. They had permitted enough of an opening to allow an emboldened opposition to be heard by the world. Whatever freedoms they granted the opposition, however, were only used to demand more. What the world heard from opposition leaders was that the Sandinistas were not really complying with the "democratization" provisions of the treaty at all; they were merely making token gestures in a cynical "publicity show."[34] The opening of *La Prensa*, for instance, only sparked demands for the opening of all other press outlets to the opposition, including television. Cardinal Obando and his bishops became the champions of a direct dialogue between the government and the contras. They demanded an end to the draft and insisted that the amnesty called for in the treaty should include all political prisoners in Sandinista jails, including contras and their supporters. Leaders of the Coordinadora endorsed these positions, as did the editorial writers at *La Prensa* and the marchers in the streets of Managua.[35]

For those in Washington and Central America who wanted to end aid to the contras, the Sandinistas' refusal to take further steps before the November 5 deadline—justified though it might be under the treaty—posed serious political problems. On the one hand, Wright tried to argue that the November 5 deadline ought not to be considered a deadline at all. It was "an arbitrary time limit," Wright insisted, and should not be adhered to too rigidly. "It's not like a football game."[36] President Arias, who addressed Congress at Wright's invitation on September 22, also argued that some governments might "require a longer period" to fulfill their commitments. He warned against falling into a "trap set by someone who shows us a calendar every day, anxious to bury the last hope."

Both Wright and Arias recognized, however, that the Sandinistas would have to make more concessions to satisfy the American Congress. On October 8, therefore, Wright declared the Sandinistas' actions "far short of what I'd like to see" and warned that the peace accord "could be torpedoed if the Sandinistas were to renege on their commitments."[37] Arias told conservative Republican congressmen that he would seek "drastic action" through the OAS if the Sandinistas failed to comply with the agreement, which some took to mean an OAS-sanctioned American invasion.[38] Before leaving for Washington to address the Congress, Arias sent letters to Daniel Ortega and Cardinal Obando recommending that the Sandinistas also begin indirect negotiations with the contras using the cardinal as a mediator.[39] The Sandinistas tersely rejected Arias's suggestion.

The Nicaraguan government had its own plan for complying with what it insisted was the letter of the treaty. In an effort to prove that no negotiations were necessary to achieve a cease-fire, the Sandinistas announced a one-month unilateral truce beginning on October 7. In the first week of October the Sandinista army declared it had withdrawn its forces from four designated cease-fire zones of less than 800 square miles.[40] The government called on contra fighters to move into the zones, accept the amnesty and turn themselves and their weapons over to "peace commissions" established as part of the national reconciliation effort. In short, the Sandinistas' interpretation of the treaty was that the contras had simply to surrender by November 5, and then the Sandinistas' commitments concerning political reform would, as the treaty stated, "simultaneously begin to govern."

It was not an implausible interpretation, but it came nowhere near meeting the demands of the American political consensus. President Arias called it a "propaganda move."[41] The contras simply could not be done away with in this manner. The problem the Sandinistas faced was that since the summer the contras had earned a measure of respectability, both as a military and as a political force. The new contra Directorate was more diverse; its members, particularly César, were more adept at international diplomacy. Thanks to the efforts of the Reagan administration, moreover, the view had taken hold in Washington that the contras had to have some say in determining their own fate, and the Sandinistas could not simply demand an unconditional surrender. On October 13 Secretary Shultz reiterated that if the Sandinistas failed to negotiate a cease-fire with the contras, the United States would not consider itself bound to cut the contras off, and the Reagan administration would seek more aid from Congress.[42] President Reagan made a "solemn vow . . . as long as there is breath in this body" not to "walk away" from the contras.

Even the awarding of the Nobel Peace Prize to Arias on October 13 did not ease the pressures on the Sandinistas, although stopping Reagan's contra policy was the intent of the Nobel committee.[43] Arias did use his newfound influence to force an abandonment of the November 5 deadline for Sandinista compliance. The deadlines in his peace plan, he later recalled, had become "real traps, because every time the Sandinistas didn't fulfill their commitments on the timetable, there was a lot of criticism from the United States."[44] On October 28 the five Central American foreign ministers agreed to declare that November 5 was not a deadline, but only the beginning of a process that would end on January 5.[45] The Reagan administration had no choice but to delay its request for contra aid until after the new year.[46]

At the same time, Arias also used his new prestige to increase pressure on the Sandinistas. Only hours after winning the prize, Arias declared "Now more than ever I am going to insist that a negotiated cease-fire in Nicaragua is indispensable if we are to achieve lasting peace in Central America." And Arias went further, repeating many of the demands that Nicaraguan opposition leaders and Reagan officials had been making: that the amnesty had to be broad enough to cover "the largest number of political prisoners"; that the opening of La Prensa and Radio Catolica was "not enough" and that other press outlets, including television, should be made available to the opposition; and finally that Honduras would not have to expel the rebels from its territory until the Sandinistas had negotiated a cease-fire with the contras.[47] The logical implication of the last point was that the United States would also not have to end its aid to the contras until a cease-fire was negotiated.

The Sandinistas continued to resist strenuously. Daniel Ortega declared on October 18 that, regardless of what President Arias said, the Sandinistas would "never agree" to a dialogue with the contras because it was a "trap." The contras would make "totally unacceptable demands," the Reagan administration would blame the Sandinistas, and Congress would approve contra aid.[48] Yet as October came to an end and the erstwhile deadline of November 5 approached, the Sandinistas faced growing pressure to take some dramatic action to satisfy the growing demands for concessions. Even their few aid donors from Scandinavian and Asian countries told the Sandinistas their future depended on opening talks with the contras.[49] On October 28 President Arias declared his peace process "at an impasse" due to the Sandinistas' "intransigence and dogmatism." While Arias opposed further aid to the contras, he insisted that "the entire world should isolate" the Sandinistas if they refused to bend.[50]

On the weekend of October 28–29 the Sandinistas finally gave in. At a meeting of the Directorate with party cadres, they released a communiqué spelling out their plans. Declaring their intention to abide "by the letter" of the Esquipulas agreement, the Sandinistas noted that "without being obligated to do so we have made important decisions ahead of the deadlines established by the Guatemala agreements." The Sandinistas insisted they would not "continue acting unilaterally," however, and declared there could be no peace "as long as the counterrevolution is not ordered to end its illegitimate war against Nicaragua." Regarding calls for negotiations with the contras, the Sandinista Party declared that "under no circumstances and nowhere, with any intermediary whatsoever, will there ever be a political dialogue with the counterrevolutionary leaders."[51] The communiqué was widely seen by observers as a victory for the "hard-liners" in the party, but amidst the defiant rhetoric was concealed the crucial concession. By opposing a "political" dialogue, the Sandinista leaders had deliberately left open the possibility of a dialogue that was not "political." On November 5 Daniel Ortega announced that the Sandinistas would negotiate with the contras, through an intermediary, on the technical details of a cease-fire. Surrounded by banners proclaiming "Total Amnesty Never, Never, Never" and "No to Dialogue with the Contras," Ortega also announced the pardon and release of almost 1,000 political prisoners as partial compliance with the amnesty provision of the treaty. Further steps, such as lifting the State of Emergency and broadening the amnesty, Ortega declared, would not come until aid to the contras had been ended and the contras' facilities in Honduras had been dismantled.

The Sandinistas' dramatic concessions had a predictable effect on the debate in Washington. The Reagan administration and its supporters grudgingly welcomed the announcement but noted that as of November 5 the Sandinistas were still "far from being in compliance."[52] Opponents of contra aid hailed the Sandinistas' move as an important step toward peace, making it "more than likely," in Senator Dodd's words, that Nicaragua could fulfill its promises under the peace accord.[53] The fact that Ortega had made his announcement upon returning from a brief trip to Moscow even led some observers to believe, mistakenly, that the Sandinistas had acted under pressure from Gorbachev.[54]

50

"I Represent the American People, Too"

The real pressure on the Sandinistas had come from Arias, from the Reagan administration, and from the contras, whose gains since the beginning of 1987 had been extraordinary. Western journalists traveling with contra forces on several trips in September and October found that as much as 60 percent of Nicaragua was "contested" territory and that the contras moved freely up and down the mountainous spine in the center of the country from Honduras to Costa Rica.[1] In the Bocay river area near the border with Honduras, the contras had re-established a command and supply base in August after months of struggle. The remote region had proved too hard for the Sandinista army to resupply once the helicopters became vulnerable to contra anti-aircraft missiles.[2] In the southwestern part of Jinotega, in the area around the provincial capital, reporters found "solid support for the contras" and a "network of informers, couriers, lookouts, food suppliers and medical-support personnel" which one journalist described as "an underground civilian wing of the armed movement."[3] The contras' most important strategic base was in the central portion of the country, in the provinces of Matagalpa, Boaco, Chontales, and central Zelaya. An American peace activist captured by contra troops on October 17 near the town of Santo Domingo in southern Chontales was taken on a 14-day journey through what he described as "contraland." The rebels, he reported, "own Central Zelaya ... the

556

ranchers were absolutely fraternizing with the commandos. They all knew each other. The [contras] didn't seem to sense any more danger."[4] Further west, in Matagalpa and northern Boaco, the contras and Sandinistas contested daily for control. "There are armed groups all over the place, from both sides," according to one resident. Another resident described the evolution of the contra forces in the Matagalpa region: "At first, the contras were just a few guys with hunting rifles and civilian clothes. Then they came back with uniforms and better weapons. Now they are a regular army." In the six years of the war, the *Times*'s Stephen Kinzer wrote on September 11, the contras "have sought a territory inside Nicaragua where they can be based semipermanently and through which they can move freely. In the eastern sections of Matagalpa, Boaco, and Chontales provinces, they appear close to achieving that objective."[5]

The contras also began achieving more ambitious objectives in the fall of 1987. On October 15, contra forces launched a coordinated pre-dawn attack on five towns along the Rama Road and for two days closed down that most important strategic artery in Nicaragua.[6] They destroyed two bridges and seriously damaged another, ambushed a truck carrying Sandinista reinforcements, and occupied two of the towns for the better part of a day. Sandinista militia defending the towns withdrew after brief resistance, and the regular army, after losing two helicopters to contra missiles in less than a week, traveled by road and was slow in arriving.[7] James LeMoyne of the *Times* called the contras' assaults along the Rama Road "the most politically impressive and military damaging series of attacks in recent years."[8]

The October truce offered by the Sandinistas had aimed at slowing down these successes, and in the best case, drawing the body of contra fighters into small zones where they would either surrender or be more easily destroyed by Sandinista troops waiting outside the perimeters of the cease-fire zones. As a military maneuver, however, the truce had accomplished little. Although the cease-fire zones were meant to be traps, the contras had used them as safe places to receive air drops of supplies and weapons to last them through the end of the year. The Sandinistas estimated that several hundred contras accepted the amnesty, but even this probably inflated figure did not compensate for the number of volunteers who were daily joining the contras' increasingly successful struggle. Nor did the unilateral truce diminish the support contra forces were increasingly getting from local populations, reports of which in the Western press were also enhancing the contras' image. Reporters traveling with contra units through "contraland" wrote sympathetic portraits depicting contra fighters as genuinely popular among the local campesinos. The old image of the contras as revanchist ex-National Guardsmen was almost entirely replaced by a new picture of them as an army of "young peasants . . . too young to have served on anything but their farms a decade ago."[9] An inveterate critic like Senator Dodd had begun referring to the contras as mostly "young kids," rather than as Somocista thugs.[10] And even the Sandinistas had changed their rhetoric, albeit in an effort to sow divisions in the rebels' ranks, and begun to distinguish between the "corrupt political leaders" who lived in Miami, and the "peasants" who were doing most of the fighting and dying in the hills of Nicaragua.[11]

The Sandinistas' critical concessions at the end of October were aimed squarely at ending the mounting wave of contra successes. The price was high. Agreeing to negotiate with the contras, even through an intermediary, was a dangerous concession. It was a first step toward granting the contras the political legitimacy they had long struggled for and at a time when the contras' strength on the battlefield was growing. Once the negotiations began, contra leaders would insist on discussing political as well as military issues, thus uniting their cause with that of the internal opposition leaders in the cities. These opposition leaders, in turn, having acquired an armed wing as well as the support and sympathy of the Western democracies, would become bolder and more stubborn in their demands of the Sandinistas. When the Sandinistas rejected their demands, the Reagan administration would declare them intransigent, and the likelihood of renewed aid for the contras would grow. If not handled carefully the Sandinistas' dramatic concession, whose sole purpose was to defeat contra aid in Washington, could end up insuring its success. This danger must also have been apparent to Wright, who now had a pressing interest in seeing the negotiations proceed smoothly and quickly to a settlement before the next vote on aid to the contras.

For the Sandinistas, the choice of an intermediary was critical to the success or failure of their gamble. Cardinal Obando, the candidate pressed upon them by Arias and Wright, posed a most dangerous threat. The cardinal had long since proven that he was more interested in dismantling Sandinism in Nicaragua than in defeating contra aid in the United States. He could be expected to use his position as intermediary to press the demands of both the armed and unarmed opposition. This implacable enemy of the Sandinistas had a huge following in Nicaragua, the support of the Pope, and an unassailable international reputation. If the

Sandinistas rejected Obando's demands, they would in one stroke create a solid arch of opposition stretching from the contras in the hills to the political parties in the cities with the Catholic church as the keystone. The strength of the opposition in Nicaragua would be matched only by the diplomatic isolation of the Sandinista government overseas.

To avoid these dangers, the Sandinistas sought the assistance of someone they trusted more than the Cardinal, someone who they knew shared their interest in preventing a renewal of aid to the contras. On November 5 Vice Foreign Minister Tinoco formally invited Speaker Wright to serve as the mediator instead of the cardinal. Wright demurred, pleading a busy schedule and the criticism he would likely receive from the State Department. He suggested Cardinal Obando, but Tinoco declared the cardinal was "unacceptable." Later in the day Foreign Minister D'Escoto proposed that Wright accept the title of mediator and designate someone else to do the work. Again Wright resisted.[12] The Sandinistas' astonishing idea that the leader of the Democratic Party in Congress could serve as mediator between an American-backed guerrilla group and the government they were fighting so exceeded the bounds of American political decorum that it was either an act of cynicism or desperation. The Sandinistas had not entirely misjudged their man, however. If their original idea violated Washington's political etiquette, there were other ways to enlist Wright's assistance as a "parallel power" in the Congress.

On November 6 Ortega gave in and offered Cardinal Obando the job as mediator. Ortega's offer came with conditions, however. While Obando wanted the negotiations held in Nicaragua, Ortega insisted that the cardinal travel to Washington to receive the Sandinistas' cease-fire proposal in the presence of Wright. Wright, who suspected that the Sandinistas were somehow trying to limit Obando's independence, nevertheless accepted the invitation for a three-way meeting.[13] He also agreed to bring a team of American "technical advisers" to assist the Cardinal in his mediation.[14] Two days later Ortega showed Wright the Sandinistas' cease-fire proposal, virtually the same as their October unilateral truce, and asked for suggestions. Wright said he was in no position to negotiate cease-fire terms, but he recommended a few changes to make the plan more palatable to American ears.[15]

Nicaraguan officials made no secret of their plan to use Wright's involvement in the negotiations as a means of pressuring first the cardinal and then the contras to accept their terms. Wright's presence at the meeting with the cardinal, they explained, implied his approval of their cease-fire proposal even if he gave no public endorsement. By involving Wright directly in the negotiations, Nicaragua officials told reporters, they hoped to "leave the [Reagan] administration totally isolated."[16] The contras, in turn, would have no choice but to agree to their terms. As Ortega explained, those congressmen "interested in peace" would "really apply pressure to make the cease-fire a reality."[17]

Wright certainly fulfilled the Sandinistas' expectations when he met with the contra leaders later that same day. After saying he was encouraged by Ortega's evident intention to comply with the peace plan, Wright leveled a sharp warning. He told the contras that Congress would never again support military aid for them, no matter how "unpalatable" the Sandinistas became. Wright's message, according to one witness, was "Negotiate the best deal you can . . . because that is all you will get."[18]

Wright knew he was moving along a tricky path by involving himself in the negotiations in this way. When Secretary Shultz visited Wright's office two hours after Ortega left it, he was appalled to learn from the Speaker that the Sandinistas wanted him to name people "to assist them in the negotiations, probably oversee them." Shultz advised Wright to decline the invitation. If the cardinal wanted help, Shultz suggested, he should get it from Central Americans not from the U.S. Congress. Wright protested that the Sandinistas had "asked to talk. My instinct is I'm doing the right thing. I believe Ortega is ready to deal." Shultz scoffed that the Sandinistas hadn't "even come close to complying."[19] Wright dropped the issue, but proceeded as he had planned.

It was Cardinal Obando himself who undermined the Sandinistas' strategy. When the cardinal arrived at the offices of the papal nuncio in Washington on November 13, he found Daniel Ortega, Foreign Minister D'Escoto, Ambassador Tunnermann, Speaker Wright, David Bonior, and members of Wright's team of "technical advisers." The cardinal was polite but stubborn. He dismissed Wright's advisers and said he "would like to name my own team." He asked Ortega whether he was to be a "message carrier" or a mediator who could push both sides to agreement. And he insisted that future negotiations take place in Nicaragua, not in Washington.[20] Ortega held firm, insisting that the talks be held in Washington and that the cardinal's role was to deliver proposals not make them. He suggested to Wright how useful it would be if the Speaker would involve himself directly and maintain "liaison" with the cardinal, but Wright now beat a hasty retreat. He promised Cardinal Obando he would "not attempt to impose any help on you."[21]

Although Wright quickly backed away from his plans in the face of the cardinal's obstinacy, it was too late to avoid the political consequences of the actions he had already taken. When the meeting broke up, Wright came under attack from all directions. The Reagan administration publicly denounced him for engaging in "personal negotiations" with the Sandinistas, contrary to the stated policy of the U.S. government. Republicans in the House and Senate declared Wright's actions unconstitutional, and even normally cool heads like Congressmen Michel and Cheney were outraged. In Wright's own party only the liberals came unhesitatingly to his defense.[22] But a *Washington Post* editorial on November 16 charged that Wright had "overreache[d] recklessly" and asked if he was not "lending himself to a charade at which Daniel Ortega may be more clever than he is?"[23]

Wright responded that as Speaker of the House he did not need the "permission" of the administration. "I represent the American people, too," Wright declared, insisting the Executive and Legislative branches were "coequal" in matters of foreign as well as domestic policy. "The people who wrote the Constitution never intended the Congress to be subservient."[24] Behind this brave public front, however, Wright was politically wounded, isolated, and in retreat. On November 16 Wright met with an angry President Reagan and Secretary Shultz. "Ortega's a liar," the President insisted. "You can't believe anything he says. We started out with the Wright-Reagan plan. Now we've got the Wright-Ortega plan." This last charge Wright denied vehemently, but such a pithy comment, if uttered publicly by the President, would be damaging. Sensing Wright's defensiveness, Reagan's advisers now pressed him to help them pass a request for $30 million for the contras in the long-term continuing resolution before Christmas. Wright replied only that he doubted he could muster the votes. The next day the public feud ended when Shultz called on former Democratic Party chairman Robert Strauss to broker a reconciliation with Wright, and the three men held a press conference to announce a new pact which, despite its extremely vague wording, clearly drew Wright back from further involvement in the cease-fire negotiations.

The larger effect of the whole episode was to strengthen the administration's hand a little in the battle for more aid. While Wright and the Reagan administration were making peace, the new national security adviser, Colin Powell, was meeting with conservative and moderate House Democrats to seek their views on a new package of aid. Congressmen Skelton, McCurdy, English, and Spratt seemed receptive to his appeals.[25]

The Sandinistas were slow to realize that their plans had gone awry and that their hoped-for ally had withdrawn under fire. Daniel Ortega told reporters on his return to Managua that the Nicaraguan government had accepted Wright's four recommended advisers and that the cardinal was presenting the idea to the contras.[26] Obando, however, was doing no such thing. He was on a relentless campaign to force concessions from the Sandinistas. He publicly demanded official acknowledgment of his right to make substantive proposals in the talks, and on November 19 Ortega delivered a letter personally to the cardinal inviting his "suggestions and recommendations" as intermediary.[27] When the Sandinistas released 985 political prisoners as Ortega had promised on November 5, Obando declared they had not gone far enough to meet the terms of the Esquipulas agreement.[28] On points of dispute between the Sandinistas and contras, from the location of the talks to their content, Obando sided with the rebels. He insisted the next round of talks be held somewhere in Latin America, and he pressed for direct meetings between the two sides.

When the Sandinistas and contras began negotiations in Santo Domingo, the distance between their two proposals was predictably enormous. In discussing possible cease-fire zones, the contras asserted that their area of control stretched across 30,000 out of Nicaragua's 57,000 square miles. The Sandinistas were prepared to offer only 4,000 square miles. A more accurate figure fell somewhere between the two, but neither side was ready to compromise. While the Sandinistas' proposal envisioned the cease-fire zones as a place for the contras to turn in their weapons and accept amnesty, the contras had an entirely different conception. They demanded the establishment of air, land, and sea corridors to resupply their forces in the field with non-military supplies during their stay in the cease-fire zones, and they demanded that the Sandinistas' troops also be limited to non-military supplies. The contras' proposal was for a force-in-being, not a surrendering army. And while the Sandinistas' plan called for the contras to lay down their weapons during the cease-fire, which would be followed by the Sandinistas lifting the State of Emergency and restoring full political freedoms, the contras' plan called upon the government to take such steps simultaneously with the start of the cease-fire period and to complete them by its end.

The cardinal tried to bridge the gap between the two proposals, but his own proposal accepted the contras' main point. During the truce, the Sandinistas would have to decree a general amnesty, lift the state of emergency, and restore full press freedoms. The contras could continue to receive supplies and would remain in place until such steps were taken. The contras immediately accepted the cardinal's proposal, and the Sandinistas rejected it. Daniel Ortega defiantly declared there could "be no truce with the contras. . . . We are going to continue hitting them hard during this whole month of December."[29] The cardinal, in turn, publicly blamed the Sandinistas for the collapse of the talks.[30] What was more, as he told reporters, "I am going to talk directly to President Ortega and try to make him see that, to accelerate these negotiations, there has to be direct dialogue between the parties in conflict." The Sandinistas rejected this suggestion, as well, and proposed a second round of indirect talks in Santo Domingo for the middle of December. Oscar Arias, worried about the impasse, criticized the cardinal. Obando, he said, was "not an expert on cease-fires" and had proven to be not "very helpful."[31]

As the cardinal and the contras were pressing their political demands on the Sandinistas in Santo Domingo, the opposition groups inside Nicaragua were making their own parallel set of proposals. United as they had not been in years, the fourteen political, business, and labor groups demanded seventeen amendments to the 1987 Sandinista constitution. The demands were the same ones the opposition had been making for eight years, but the timing of their announcement to coincide with the cease-fire negotiations in Santo Domingo, the close similarity between their demands and those of the contras, and their insistence that "peace" could not be achieved unless their demands were met showed an unprecedented degree of explicit coordination between the internal opposition and the contras.

The Sandinistas, facing the very united front of armed contras, unarmed political opponents, and church that they had always sought to prevent, began to show signs of nervousness. It was clear that the opposition was preparing the way for passage in Congress of new aid to the contras by casting the government as intransigent, and over the weekend of December 12–13 the two Ortega brothers delivered stern warnings to the Managua politicians. "The distance is quickly closing between those contras who are armed and those who do not have guns in their hands," Daniel Ortega declared. He warned that the "new society" had no need of "rightists" and that the "mass of workers" might easily decide to deprive them of their political rights and property. If contra aid passed, "the right should not think that the workers will not force them to pay historically," Humberto Ortega warned. "Let the right tremble before the justice dealt by our people." Nor should the opposition maintain illusions of someday regaining power in Nicaragua. "In the hypothetical case that the Sandinista Front lost an election," Daniel declared, "the Sandinista Front would hand over government, not power."[32] The Sandinistas tried to get help from Wright, inviting his team of advisers to the next round of talks on December 13. But Wright's advisers, aware that the cardinal did not want them, declined. The Sandinistas postponed the talks with the contras and also put off any discussion of constitutional changes with the internal opposition. On December 15 the opposition coalition in Managua broke off its dialogue with the government.[33]

For all the risks the Sandinistas were taking, the goal which alone made the dangers worthwhile was no closer at hand. At the beginning of November Congress had quietly passed another resolution containing $3.2 million in aid for the contras to last through December 16. This came over the vehement objection of liberal House Democrats led by Bonior and Coelho, but House Democrats were once again "being torn apart" by the issue, and Jim Wright was in the middle.[34] "The pressures on him," Wright's biographer reports, "were the most intense he had ever experienced."[35] Wright had preferred to let the second short-term resolution slip by in the hope of taking a stand against further contra aid in the next continuing resolution due to come up on December 16.[36] Since November, however, the mood in the American Congress had shifted steadily in favor of continuing aid to the contras in some form. The contras, it was argued, could not be cut off while they were negotiating with the Sandinistas. The Reagan administration found even moderate Democrats sympathetic to its much-reduced request for $30 million. The proposed package extended the provision of non-military supplies and allowed delivery of military stockpiles left over from the $100 million, as well as improved air delivery capacity. Congressman Spratt of South Carolina, one of McCurdy's allies, said he would support an extension of non-military aid and "might even go for small arms and ammunition," although he had never voted for military aid before.[37] In the Senate, meanwhile, a majority in favor of some form of aid to the contras remained in place, despite the Iran-contra scandal and Democratic gains in 1986. On December 12 the Senate passed a contra aid package in the continuing resolution which included $9 million in non-military aid, another $7 million for airlifting both military and non-military supplies, and the provision of several million dollars worth of new electronic countermeasures equipment by the

Defense Department. Amendments to kill the proposal were defeated by wide margins. While a spokesman for Wright declared that the Senate package would never pass the House, Congressman McCurdy predicted it would. "Most people," he explained, "don't want the pressure on the Sandinistas released."[38] In the House, where Wright was trying to "lie low and heal" from recent political wounds, moderates like McCurdy and Spratt once again held the balance.[39]

The balance tipped decisively in favor of contra aid on the morning of December 13, when the *Washington Post* reported the surprising news that the Sandinistas secretly planned to increase their army to a staggering 600,000 in regular forces, reserves, and militia. The report also revealed that the Sandinistas had reached an agreement with the Soviet Union in October to supply this massive force over the coming five years. The new information came from a prominent Sandinista defector, Roger Miranda, an army officer who had served as Humberto Ortega's executive assistant. Miranda's report might normally have been greeted with incredulity by Reagan's critics in Washington, but his testimony was immediately confirmed by Humberto Ortega himself.[40] The revelations raised an outcry among Democrats and Republicans alike, who saw the planned military buildup as a violation of the spirit if not the letter of the Guatemala accords. For Democrats opposed to contra aid, the news was an embarrassment on a par with Daniel Ortega's trip to Moscow in 1985. Speaker Wright called the Sandinistas' planned buildup "preposterous" and noted ruefully that "the Sandinistas have had a history of snatching defeat from the jaws of victory."[41]

Days after Miranda's revelations, the Congress passed a new package of aid for the contras in the long-term continuing resolution. Wright was forced to pull back from a fight against both the White House and the Senate, and he agreed to extend aid to the contras through February 29, 1988. Liberals in the House Democratic Caucus resisted bitterly, complaining the contras kept "getting money without a floor vote." Majority Leader Foley pointed out, however, that House Republicans saw "a different conspiracy. They see the Sandinistas delaying things while aid is cut off and the contras wither and die." In the conference negotiations with the Senate, the House Democrats found themselves isolated, with the White House, Senate and House Republicans, and even Senate Democrats aligned against them. House leaders had hoped to cut off the delivery of military aid to the contras on January 1, while "humanitarian" aid continued until the end of February, but the Reagan administration insisted that previously purchased military supplies continue to be delivered until January 17, two days after the Central American presidents were due to meet and assess progress in the peace accords. The compromise passed by both houses as part of the continuing resolution on December 22 provided $3.6 million in additional non-military aid through the end of February, as well as $4.5 million for expanded and improved airlift of both military and non-military supplies. Military aid would be provided through February 3, when the House would vote on the President's new contra aid proposal.[42] House Democratic leaders, still seething after the Miranda disclosures, put the Sandinistas on notice. The new legislation, House Appropriations Committee Chairman David Obey told reporters, gave the Sandinistas "a window to be responsible, if they want to. If they don't, they damn well better duck."[43]

51

Soviet Policy in Nicaragua

While the revelations about the Sandinistas' military plans had great impact on the debate over Nicaragua policy, surprisingly little discussion was given to the implications for U.S.-Soviet relations. The five-year military protocol negotiated between July and October by Soviet, Cuban, and Nicaraguan military leaders constituted an enormous commitment of Soviet resources at a time when most American analysts assumed the Soviet Union was reducing its role in Central America. The weapons to be delivered between 1990 and 1995, in addition to rifles, ammunition, trucks, and spare parts, also included more advanced artillery and surface-to-air missiles, two dozen more helicopters, as well as a squadron of the long-promised MiG fighter aircraft. The five-year plan seemed to many Americans so inconsistent with Gorbachev's desire for rapprochement as to be explainable only by error, confusion, or sabotage within the Soviet government.

Since the first year after the Sandinista victory, the assumption shared by Viron Vaky and many other observers had been that the Soviet Union would not adopt another economic burden like Cuba. In the Andropov years the Soviets became more outspoken about their economic problems and declared that their ability to aid their friends and allies economically would indeed be limited. Even before the accession to power of Mikhail Gorbachev in 1985, American analysts had begun to detect a shift in offi-

567

cial Soviet attitudes towards its Third World clients and anticipated a shift in policy to match what by the late 1980s came to be called this "new thinking."[1]

A series of unrelated events in 1987 seemed to some observers to confirm the accuracy of that prediction. In the early summer, in response to the Sandinistas' cry for more oil, the Soviets had announced that they would provide no more than previously promised for the year, which was about 80 percent of the entire Nicaraguan supply. Soviet officials let it be known that they considered the Sandinistas inefficient in their use of Soviet economic aid—a charge the Sandinistas themselves did not deny[2]— and implicitly encouraged the Nicaraguans to close the remaining gap either by improving efficiency or by making greater efforts to convince non-communist suppliers to pick up a share of the burden. "The Kremlin," wrote Tad Szulc in the *New York Times* at the beginning of September, had "concluded that the Sandinistas have become an overall political liability" and had "resolved to begin cutting them off." Nicaragua was no longer "an inviting strategic investment for the Russians, who these days are much more careful about using their resources."[3] Vaky, who three years earlier had warned of a dangerous U.S.-Soviet confrontation over Nicaragua, argued in the same month that "the Soviet Union may well have no desire to challenge the U.S. on its own turf." Vaky also cited the oil dispute as a sign that "Moscow may wish to distance itself from the Sandinistas." Both Vaky and Szulc and a number of congressmen called on the Reagan administration to open negotiations with the Soviet Union in order to "make it easier for Moscow to disengage, not harder."[4]

The assumption that Moscow was looking to disengage and cut its aid to Nicaragua led to a second assumption: that the Soviets were pressuring the Sandinistas to make political and diplomatic concessions, both before and after the Esquipulas meeting. According to Szulc, Soviet military aid was supposed to "drop sharply if a Central American political settlement were achieved." Thus it was assumed Ortega had signed the Esquipulas agreement under Soviet pressure on August 7 and had agreed to negotiate with the contras under Soviet pressure on November 5. The tangible evidence of this pressure was the refusal to supply more oil and the expected reduction of military aid.

The evidence which Szulc and others cited, however, did not exist. And the evidence that did exist supported the opposite assumptions. Szulc's op-ed article appeared on September 6. On September 7 Soviet emissaries arrived in Managua bearing good news: The Soviet government would provide Nicaragua an additional 100,000 tons of oil to fill most of its needs for the rest of the year.[5] Then, in October, the tripartite protocols on military assistance between the Soviet Union, Cuba, and Nicaragua were secretly negotiated and agreed to. Preliminary discussions for these protocols had begun in July. Obviously, the timing and magnitude of the five-year military assistance plan were unrelated to diplomatic developments. If the Soviets were counseling the Sandinistas to make concessions, they were certainly not using the leverage of economic and military aid. In 1987 overall Soviet and Cuban economic and military aid for Nicaragua reached almost $1 billion. But there was little evidence that the Sandinistas were acting under Soviet instructions. Any careful review of diplomatic events shows that Daniel Ortega himself did not know he would sign the Guatemala accord before he met with the five presidents, much less could he have been under instructions from the Soviets to do so. And the decision to begin talks with the contras was taken before, not after, Daniel Ortega's trip to Moscow at the beginning of November.[6]

Coincidences of circumstances and events had been fitted together by American observers like Szulc to create a pattern that was misleading and inaccurate. What lay at the heart of the whole theory about this new Soviet policy toward Nicaragua, however, were more general and fundamental judgments: that the economic burden of aiding countries like Nicaragua was too great to be sustained at a time of Soviet economic failure; that Gorbachev intended to change Soviet foreign policy as dramatically as he was presumably trying to change its internal policy; and that Gorbachev considered support for Soviet clients in the Third World an obstacle to reaching arms agreements and an overall rapprochement with the United States. These were perfectly logical but nevertheless unwarranted assumptions.

To be sure, the Nicaraguan economy was in collapse, and the Soviets made clear that there were constraints on their largesse. They encouraged the Sandinistas, as they encouraged all their clients in these years, to seek greater efficiency through a more market-oriented system, as Gorbachev was attempting to do at home. Soviet dissatisfaction with the Sandinistas' misuse of their aid, however, no more indicated a desire to cut the Sandinistas off than American dissatisfaction with El Salvador's corruption and misuse of its aid signaled a desire to cut off President Duarte. The cost of supporting Nicaragua was, in any case, dwarfed by the $5 billion per year the Soviet Union spent supporting Cuba throughout the 1980s. Yet even after the collapse of the Soviet Union's East European empire, Gorbachev did not cut back significantly on that huge expenditure.

If anything, it is more likely that the Soviet government compensated for the lack of economic aid it could provide Nicaragua by offering ever larger amounts of military aid—a time-honored Soviet practice. The provision of weapons to clients, it seems, was never really considered by Soviet leaders to be a cost to their economy. For decades the Soviet Union had commonly provided large amounts of equipment to clients over long periods without any noticeable deviation in the timing or quantity of deliveries. A national economy run according to five-year production plans did not allow for the same flexibility, or unpredictability, as one run by yearly congressional authorizations. Decisions about the supply of military equipment to foreign countries, moreover, were not made by the Soviet Foreign Ministry alone, where Foreign Minister Shevardnadze's "new thinkers" had made tentative inroads,[7] but also by a Soviet military bureaucracy under the heavy influence of industrial baronies always eager for large state orders. The five-year military assistance plans, therefore, were not influenced by month-to-month diplomatic developments, but by long-term strategic considerations. Nicaragua was an anti-American client under attack from the United States, it was likely to remain so, and it was therefore equally likely to continue needing Soviet military assistance for the foreseeable future.

If Gorbachev put his personal imprint on Soviet policy toward Nicaragua, which seems unlikely given the many more important battles he had to fight, it was not reflected in the Soviet-Nicaraguan arms relationship. Soviet support for Nicaragua grew most dramatically *after* Gorbachev came to power. Soviet military aid to the Sandinistas reached its highest level in 1986. It dipped slightly in 1987, but the protocols the Soviet Union agreed to in the second half of 1987 promised ever higher amounts of military aid over the coming years. The five-year plans the Sandinistas worked out with their Soviet and Cuban counterparts, moreover, called for the largest build-up of forces *after* the contra war was to have ended. While the policy of expanding support to Nicaragua need not be attributed to Gorbachev personally, since it began with the delivery of the Hind helicopters several months before he came to power, the least that can be said is that Gorbachev did nothing to change the policy he inherited. The arms agreement in 1987 can be seen as a logical next step in a steady increase of Soviet support that had begun in the early 1980s and had proceeded almost without deviation through the regimes of Brezhnev, Andropov, Chernenko, and Gorbachev.

The assumption by Szulc and others that Nicaragua was not "an inviting strategic investment" was also mistaken. The Sandinistas, who were themselves taken aback by the size of the Soviet offer, speculated that the Soviets were "thinking in strategic terms" and wanted to make the Sandinistas "into the Israelis of Central America by developing our offensive and defensive capacities far beyond that of all our neighbors."[8] Even if Soviet plans were not that ambitious, the existence of the Sandinista regime exacted significant costs from the United States, which in the eyes of Soviet officials may have outweighed the cost to themselves.[9] Some American observers mistakenly compared the small cost to the United States of supporting the contras with the large cost to the Soviet Union of supporting the Nicaraguan government. The Soviets, however, quite reasonably looked at all of Central America as one strategic theater. What the United States spent in El Salvador, Honduras, and Costa Rica was more than six times what the Soviets spent in Nicaragua. Indeed, the Soviets may have noted that this unfavorable ratio for the United States in Central America was akin to their own unfavorable ratio in Afghanistan, where the Soviets had had to outspend the United States by quite a bit, and in a losing cause. By 1987 the Soviet Union was preparing to withdraw from that costly investment; no doubt Soviet officials believed the United States might also be forced similarly to cut its losses in Nicaragua.

The cost to the United States, moreover, was more than financial. In international forums the conflict was an embarrassment for the United States, the cause of an adverse ruling at the International Court of Justice and of repeated denunciations in the United Nations. It was an issue on which the United States could muster no support from its Western European allies, not even from the loyal Margaret Thatcher. The Soviet Union, on the other hand, stood squarely with the vast majority of the world's nations when it opposed American policy. The benefits to Soviet policy in Latin American were clear. One of the shifts in Soviet policy that had begun before Gorbachev, but which Shevardnadze assiduously pursued, was the courting of the large non-communist states of the region, like Argentina, Brazil, and Mexico. It was a policy driven as much by economic and trade interests as by any thought of relaxing the confrontation in the region with the United States, and it did not preclude continuing close relations with traditional Soviet clients like Cuba and Nicaragua. The Nicaraguan controversy, far from hindering Soviet efforts to expand its ties in Latin America, gave the Soviets an opportunity to join Mexico, Argentina, and Venezuela in a united front of Latin solidarity against the American aggressor.[10] Thus the Soviet Union had given its full support to the Contadora Group, taking its cue from Nicaragua and Cuba, and when the Esquipulas agreement was signed Soviet officials had no difficulty supporting it as well. On the contrary, Foreign Minister Shevardnadze and the rest of the Soviet government took every opportunity to declare their support for a peace agreement that called on the United States to end aid to the contras and required nothing of the Soviet Union. Soviet official statements interpreting the vague and often confusing terms of the agreement repeated verbatim those of the Sandinistas and gave no sign that the approach of the two governments on this matter differed by as much as a hair's breadth.[11]

In domestic American politics, the contra aid issue kept Reagan under constant attack from a virulent opposition. The Iran-contra scandal had shaken the administration to its very foundation and made Reagan a potentially ideal negotiating partner for Gorbachev's purposes: a conservative president who was yet desirous of resuscitating his presidency through arms agreements and rapprochement with the erstwhile "evil empire."[12] Yet, on the other hand, continued Soviet involvement in Central America seemed in no way to threaten the U.S.-Soviet relationship. This is perhaps where American analysts like Szulc made their greatest error, for while Szulc and others guessed that Gorbachev's interest in a rapprochement with Washington would make him want to smooth over a contentious point like Nicaragua, rather than exacerbate it, President Reagan himself showed Gorbachev that Soviet policy in Nicaragua did not stand in the way of improved relations.

Indeed, the circumstances surrounding Roger Miranda's revelations in December proved beyond any doubt that Reagan did not want disagreements over Nicaragua to stand in the way of rapprochement with Gorbachev's Soviet Union. The timing of Miranda's defection and subsequent debriefing by the CIA coincided with the summit between Reagan and Gorbachev that began in Washington on December 8. The administration could easily have made Miranda available to the press before Gorbachev arrived in the United States, but instead White House officials chose to wait until Gorbachev departed.[13] For the Reagan administration, the news of the Sandinistas' military plans and the Soviet role in supporting them was a matter distinct from and even antithetical to the purpose of the Reagan-Gorbachev summit. With the former, the administration hoped to persuade Congress to vote more aid to the contras; the purpose of the latter was to show the President and his Soviet counterpart in an amicable embrace.

While President Reagan may have been told about Miranda and the planned Sandinista buildup, he did not once raise it in his meetings with Gorbachev. Discussion of Nicaragua between the two leaders was brief and took a familiar course. Reagan told Gorbachev that if the Soviet Union stopped supplying weapons to Nicaragua, this would "go a long way toward improving U.S.-Soviet relations." Reagan afterwards could scarcely even recall what Gorbachev had said to him in response—a sign of how important the matter was to the President—but he told reporters that it was his impression that Gorbachev had simply agreed unilaterally to "withhold aid from the Sandinistas" as a way of supporting the Central American peace agreement.[14] Gorbachev could have said no such thing, of course. Colin Powell told reporters Gorbachev had made "a few cryptic references to an arrangement where they would reduce their level of arms support to something in the neighborhood of small arms, or he even said police weapons at one time. And he made a reference to our doing likewise."[15] Soviet officials, however, denied even Powell's version. They claimed Gorbachev had only offered to cut military aid to Nicaragua if the United States cut aid to its allies in Central America.[16] Gorbachev himself later responded to a query from President Arias by repeating that standard Soviet position.

Even if Gorbachev had offered to cut arms to the Sandinistas in exchange for an end to U.S. support for the contras, however, the Reagan administration would not have embraced such a deal. At a time when the administration was struggling mightily to pass a new contra aid bill, and with some hope of success, the President was not about to put an end to the contras with a handshake. To return to the *status quo ante*, in which the Sandinistas were left in power unchallenged by any military threat, was both unacceptable and unnecessary. The Reagan administration did not much care any longer how much aid was flowing from the Soviet Union. By late 1987 the geostrategic aspect of the administration's Nicaraguan policy remained a potent element of its rhetoric, but the genuine fear of Soviet expansion in Central America that had initially inspired Reagan officials in the early 1980s had passed. Reagan officials did not really believe the Soviets under Gorbachev would attempt to establish bases in Nicaragua. They did not really believe the Soviets would deliver Migs to the Sandinistas, no matter what the Soviets promised in the military protocols. And whatever other strategic advantages the Soviet Union had gained from Nicaragua, whether access to ports or landing fields, the administration had already grown accustomed to them after seven years. The important fact was that the Soviet Union by late 1987 was already clearly in a process of retrenchment, and possibly even retreat. It bore little resemblance to the Soviet Union that had so stirred the conservatives' fears during the Carter administration. By 1987 even President Reagan believed that, under Gorbachev, the days of Soviet acquisitiveness in the Third World had passed.

The struggle against the Sandinistas, meanwhile, had taken on a life of its own, independent of the Soviet threat. The Reagan administration no longer saw itself as battling the Soviet Union in Central America. It was now more concerned about an alliance of communists indigenous to the hemisphere—the Cubans, the Sandinistas, and the FMLN guerrillas—which the administration now saw as more violent and more radical than the Soviet Union, and just as threatening to American interests in a part of the world where the United States was most accustomed to enjoying unchallenged hegemony. Of course, this alliance of Latin adversaries depended on the Soviet Union for its weapons, but the high level of Soviet aid was far from the administration's biggest concern.

Despite all the aid the Soviets had provided in 1986 and 1987, the contras had still made significant military gains against the Sandinista army. Nor had unchecked Soviet aid prevented Nicaragua's slide into economic crisis or alleviated the diplomatic pressures under which the Ortegas now found themselves. To the Reagan administration, the ingredient to further success in Nicaragua was more aid to the contras, and on this point the American Congress had proved a far more serious threat than the Soviet Union. The Reagan administration used the Miranda revelations, therefore, strictly for its battle with Congress, not for its negotiations with Gorbachev. The Soviet leader, when he returned to Moscow, could not fail to recognize that by 1987 Reagan's talk of the Soviet menace in Central America was designed for American ears only. Gorbachev need have no fears that Soviet aid to Nicaragua stood in the way of what he wanted from the United States.

———

As 1987 ended, the Sandinistas were worse off than they had any reason to expect when the year began. In Washington, contra aid had survived both the Iran-contra scandal and, so far, the Esquipulas peace agreement. President Reagan's political well-being had been largely restored, thanks in some measure to the increasingly warm relations between the United States and the Sandinistas' strategic ally, the Soviet Union. The American Congress, because of the Miranda revelations, was more hostile than ever.

In economic terms the year 1987 had been calamitous for the Sandinistas. "By traditional standards," James LeMoyne wrote in December, "1987 is the year the Nicaraguan economy essentially collapsed."[17] The inflation rate had risen to 1,800 percent according to the government's own figures, but according to private economists it had accelerated sharply in November to an annual rate closer to 13,000 percent. Nicaraguan córdobas worth 8,000 to the dollar in the late spring of 1987 were by the end of the year trading on the black market at more than 43,000 to one. The government raised wages by 900 percent in 1987, but a worker's salary was worth only 6 percent of what it had been worth in 1979. The government added three zeros to 20- and 50-córdoba notes, and still Nicaraguans were carrying their money in paper bags. Nicaragua was heading toward a barter economy in 1988.[18]

Although the Sandinistas did not allow private polls, most observers believed their popularity was plummeting along with the economy. The political opposition parties were more outspoken and more unified than ever, brazenly challenging the Sandinistas to crack down and risk a renewal of contra aid. Opposition leaders, moreover, were associating themselves ever more closely with the contras, making demands in common with contra leaders and, in the eyes of the Sandinistas, generally turning the political opposition into an "internal front" of the rebel forces. The cardinal, in his role as mediator, was serving as the broker of this unacceptable marriage, but the Sandinistas had been unable to displace him with the more desirable figure of Speaker Wright and his team of advisers. The cardinal grew bolder with each passing day, chastising the Sandinistas for failing to take more steps toward compliance with the Esquipulas agreement and laying the blame for the failure of negotiations with the contras on "the egoism of those who place the interests of the party above the interests of the people and the common good."[19]

At the same time, the military strength of the contras increased with every passing month, and at the end of November Humberto Ortega admitted that the war with the contras was "the fiercest it's ever been." The number of clashes between contra and Sandinista forces had risen from about 25 a month at the beginning of the year to about 90 a month. Peasants and farmers throughout the central regions of the country from north to south provided the contras food, refuge, and intelligence on the whereabouts of Sandinista army units. The contras' anti-aircraft missiles had all but neutralized the Sandinistas' air superiority, as at least ten and perhaps as many as twenty helicopter transports and gunships were shot down over the course of the year. In the view of the *New York Times*'s military analyst, the war had reached the point of stalemate, in which the contras could not yet defeat the Sandinistas but the Sandinista army was "incapable of destroying the contras."[20]

In the last week of December the contras offered a preview of the next phase in the war, as planned by Fiers and his team at the CIA. On the morning of December 20, contra forces numbering around 3,000 men launched the largest coordinated attack of the war against three small towns in the central mining region of Zelaya province. In Siuna 1,000 contra troops struck from five directions, overwhelmed a government defense force of less than 400, killing as many as 40, destroyed the radar station and an arms warehouse, and occupied the town for more than a day. Obviously unconcerned by the threat of helicopter gunships, contra forces set ambushes along the few roads leading into the towns. The Sandinista army, unable to bring enough forces quickly into the area to contest the contras, resorted to aerial bombing of Siuna, but the air force had scarcely improved since Somoza's time and many of the bombs were apparently defective. Contra forces also occupied the town of Rosita for a day, and the town of Bonanza for two days. In addition to the arms warehouse and the radar station, the rebels destroyed an electrical plant, a police station, and a militia barracks in the attacks.[21] The *Times*'s James LeMoyne, who was the only American reporter to piece together an account of the attack from extensive interviews with villagers and Sandinista soldiers, called it "the contras' largest and most successful military operation of the war."[22]

In the United States, where lay the Sandinistas' only prospect of defeating the contras, the combined effect of the contras' military and political successes brought the rebels ever more support. So stalwart a spokesman for American centrist opinion as the *Washington Post* could declare that the contras were "entitled to a political role" and were "currently in an improved strategic position to claim such a role."[23]

52

"I Did Not Come to Washington to Preside over the Communization of Central America"

By the beginning of 1988 the Sandinistas had decided that their very survival depended on ending the contra war. It was imperative that they accomplish this to heal their failing economy, to call on the resources of the Western democracies, to resist the meddling encroachment of foreign powers into their internal affairs, and to establish a stable relationship with their political opponents now stirred into a frenzy of revolt. With each passing day the dangers grew. On January 10 a march by thousands of Nicaraguans in honor of the martyred Pedro Joaquín Chamorro turned into one of the largest anti-government rallies since 1979. Two days later, eleven of the most prominent opposition leaders met quietly in Guatemala with Alfredo César, Adolfo Calero, and other contra leaders to discuss plans for merging their two sets of talks with the Sandinistas into one overall political-military dialogue. The Sandinistas arrested the opposition leaders upon their return to Managua, despite the risk to Nicaragua's international image on the eve of the Central American summit. The "terrorist conspiracy" to form "an internal front with the contras" could not be tolerated.[1]

Stemming this dangerous tide required reaching an agreement with the other Central American governments on January 15, which in turn would lead Congress to vote against contra aid on February 3. By the beginning of 1988, however, the peace process inaugurated by Arias had broken down. Guerrilla wars continued in El Salvador and Guatemala, as well as in Nicaragua, and cease-fire negotiations in all three countries had stalled or collapsed. The Salvadoran government accused Nicaragua of continuing to support the FMLN, and the Sandinistas, in turn, accused El Salvador, Honduras, and Costa Rica of continuing to support the contras.[2] Pressures from the Reagan administration and from anti-contra Democrats, including threats of reduced American aid, encouraged the Central American governments to avoid any definitive declarations at the January 15 summit.[3]

An inconclusive summit posed the greatest danger for the Sandinistas, since it gave the Reagan administration an argument for renewing aid to the contras. Democratic opponents of contra aid bluntly warned Daniel Ortega to make further concessions or face renewed war. From the mouths of Congressman Bonior and Senator Dodd came the Reagan administration's insistence on immediate, "substantive, irreversible" steps by the Sandinistas, regardless of the actions of other governments.[4] Even President Arias, desperate to save his peace plan, placed the burden for compliance on Nicaragua alone. "If Nicaragua had complied [already]," Arias told reporters the day before the summit, ". . . no one would be thinking of more aid to the contras."[5] Any pretense that the Sandinistas were to carry out political reforms free from the threat of war was abandoned. Arias admitted what everyone else knew: The only meaningful judges of the Sandinistas were the members of the American Congress.

At the summit meeting on January 15, Daniel Ortega found himself isolated once again. Under pressure from the other presidents, he abandoned his demand for a 30-day extension of the deadline for compliance with the provisions of the Guatemala accords. Without pointing fingers at any one country for non-compliance, all five presidents sought safety in indecisiveness. "Because the commitments of Esquipulas II were not completely complied with," the final communiqué stated, the five presidents committed themselves "to unconditional and unilateral obligations that require of the governments a total compliance without excuses." Those commitments which had not been met "must be fulfilled immediately and in a public and evident way."[6] Faced with almost certain renewal of contra aid if the summit ended in this way, the Sandinistas gave ground. On January 16 Ortega dramatically announced two new concessions by the Sandinista government: the immediate lifting of the State of Emergency and the opening of direct negotiations with the contras.

The Sandinistas' concessions on January 16 transformed the debate in

Washington. Democrats applauded their actions and immediately demanded that the Reagan administration refrain from requesting new contra aid. The Sandinistas had gone "further than we expected would be the case," Bonior told reporters, and had "exhibited a great deal of good will toward complying." Ortega warned that "each dollar" approved by Congress "would be a dollar to kill the Central American accords," and Congressman Hamilton agreed that passage of new aid for the contras, just as the prospects for peace had improved, would be a tragic mistake.[7]

The Sandinistas knew that the battle in Congress would still be close. "The Congress," one official noted, was "very, very conservative, and no one is figuring that the ball game is over." President Reagan kept the pressure on Congress, declaring that it was "the freedom fighters and only the freedom fighters" who had forced the Sandinistas to make concessions and "wrung from them the limited reforms they've made." Moderate Democrats were torn. They wanted "to keep the pressure on" the Sandinistas, but not to give them an excuse to walk away from negotiations.[8] In McCurdy's view, a "delicate balance" of diplomatic and military pressures had forced the Sandinistas "for the first time in nine years . . . to recognize and pay more observance to the democratic principles." "Rather than offer Daniel Ortega a convenient escape clause," McCurdy argued, "let's strengthen the U.S. favorable position by challenging the Sandinistas to further concessions."[9] Moderates preferred to delay any consideration of further aid, but the February 3 vote could not be put off without agreement by both Speaker Wright and the Reagan administration. On January 22, therefore, McCurdy and 19 moderate colleagues once again asked President Reagan to request only "non-lethal" aid, which would be held in escrow pending the outcome of the cease-fire negotiations between the contras and Sandinistas.

Reagan officials remained as opposed to the idea of "non-lethal" aid as they had since the beginning of 1986. Three years before, the contras had been cut off at a time when the Sandinista army was reeling; it had taken the rebels three years to regain the lost ground. Now, with the war once again turning in the contras' favor and the Sandinistas again on their heels, Reagan officials were loathe to cut the rebel fighters off. Nor did CIA officials agree with the moderate Democrats' optimistic suppositions. They doubted that the contras could remain "militarily operational and adequately supplied till mid-July"; that the contras would "survive" and "be a presence" in Nicaragua for "3, 4, or 6 months"; and that if not, it would always be possible later "to rebuild the contra presence."[10] While the rebels might have enough weapons to last into the spring, CIA advisers feared that without assurances of a continued supply of weapons they would begin the long retreat back into their Honduran sanctuaries within a month or two. Few fighters would be so imprudent as to stay in the field until their last bullet was fired, and even retreat required weapons, ammunition, and supplies. The Sandinistas would not cease their attacks while peace talks proceeded; on the contrary, they had every incentive to increase the fighting, both to soften the contras at the negotiating table and to force rebel fighters to use up ammunition more quickly.

Elliott Abrams and other Reagan officials doubted, moreover, that McCurdy and his moderate colleagues would ever vote for new military aid, even if peace talks failed. McCurdy had never voted for military aid in the past, and some of the Democrats demanding concessions from the administration had not even voted with McCurdy for "humanitarian" aid in 1985.[11] If McCurdy considered the present situation too murky to support military aid in February, the situation in April, May, or June was not likely to be clearer.[12] The Reagan presidency was coming to a close; from July through November the country would be consumed by the presidential election campaign, and votes on contra aid would be unwelcome to both parties. To Reagan officials, the vote on February 3 seemed like the last chance to win Congress's support for the war.

Reagan officials believed that the Democrats could not be trusted to behave responsibly on the subject of Nicaragua. Democrats from Wright to Bonior to Dodd had acted as informal advisers to the Sandinista Directorate, telling them what they needed to do, and what they did not need to do, to prevent passage of contra aid. In the administration's view, Wright had tried to manipulate Cardinal Obando and had endorsed Sandinista cease-fire proposals calling for the surrender of the contras. Agreeing to McCurdy's demand for "non-lethal" aid amounted to moral, political, and ideological surrender. President Reagan declared that he had not "come to Washington to preside over the communization of Central America." He thus acknowledged that his aid request might be defeated but defiantly refused to lend himself to the Democrats' plan.

What finally convinced President Reagan and his advisers to insist on military aid on February 3, however, was the conviction that the vote might yet be won. In the last days of January the administration pared down its request to $50 million in an effort to meet the demands of some moderates. President Reagan promised that the "majority" of new aid would be "non-lethal," as McCurdy demanded, and Reagan officials agreed that the purpose of the aid would only be to "keep the contras in the field, in existence" over the next several months while the Sandinistas proved whether they really intended to comply or not. White House officials let it be known the President was even considering holding the military aid in escrow, pending the outcome of the cease-fire negotiations. The final request the President submitted on January 27 called for $36.25 million in assistance, of which less than $3.6 million was to be used for ammunition and surface-to-air missiles, with several million more to be used for transportation and logistical equipment, which the administration described as "non-lethal" aid, leaving the remainder for clothes, food, and medicine. Another $20 million was to be set aside as indemnification for replacement of lost aircraft. The new military assistance would not be delivered until March 31, supposedly to encourage the cease-fire negotiations. After March 31, if the President determined that there was no cease-fire in Nicaragua, that the failure of talks was due to Sandinista intransigence, and that in general the Sandinistas were not complying with the terms of the Esquipulas accords, he could order the release of military aid which would flow until the next vote in July.

Further than this the Reagan administration would not go. The small amount of military aid had become a symbol. The $3.6 million was not enough to make a big difference to the contras, but it was a challenge to Congress either to declare its support for the contra war or to abandon the contras and take responsibility for the consequences.

If the choice before Congress had been as simple as that, the Reagan administration might have won. But once again, Reagan's opponents avoided a definitive vote on contra aid. McCurdy met with Speaker Wright and, just as he had done three times in the past, demanded another vote on his own alternative package later in the month in return for defeating President Reagan's proposal on February 3. McCurdy warned that without such a commitment for another vote, he and his followers would support Reagan's request, guaranteeing its passage. The moderates in both parties, McCurdy explained, could not cut off the contras entirely. They needed to approve some form of aid. Wright granted McCurdy's request.

Wright's agreement to let McCurdy offer an alternative contra aid package after February 3 just about ensured the defeat of Reagan's proposal. The 1986 congressional elections had given the Democrats an additional five seats in the House, an inconsequential gain by the opposition party in an off-year election, but an important shift on contra aid: If all the freshman members followed their party leaders, the 221–209 margin in favor of military aid in June 1986 would be reduced to 216–214. The Reagan administration's problem was compounded by the unreliability of Republican moderates and liberals. Some of the freshman Republicans, like Congresswoman Constance Morella of Maryland, who replaced Michael Barnes, had already proven frequent defectors from party ranks.

On such a close vote, however, sheer happenstance played an inordinately large role. Virginia Congressman Dan Daniels, a staunch supporter of the contras, died eleven days before the February 3 vote.[13] New York Congressman Mario Biaggi, who had voted for military aid in June 1986, was not present for the vote in 1988.[14] Congressman Dan Mica of Florida, a consistent supporter of military aid to the contras, was running for the Democratic nomination for Senate in 1988 and apparently believed winning the support of Democrats across the entire state, as opposed to those in his own conservative district, required a more moderate stance. Maryland Congressman Roy Dyson, a conservative Democrat who had always voted for contra aid in the past, told President Reagan that he would support the administration again only if the Defense Department canceled plans to eliminate a squadron of aircraft at the Patuxent Naval Air Station in Dyson's district. The administration refused, and Dyson voted against the President's request.[15] Congressman Les Aspin, who had been punished by party liberals in 1987 for voting with the President on contra aid and the MX missile, would not vote for military aid to the contras again in 1988.

On the eve of the vote Republican leaders told Reagan he faced certain rejection without further concessions. Some advised dropping the military aid entirely. A "non-lethal" aid proposal was certain to pass, and if the President's proposal passed he was guaranteed another vote under "expedited procedures" in July. At least the administration would continue to control the legislative agenda.[16] The administration, however, would not drop the military aid. McCurdy and his colleagues, including a handful of moderate Republicans, voted against the administration's aid proposal, therefore, and their votes tipped the balance. On February 3 the House narrowly rejected Reagan's request, 219–211.

It is clear in retrospect that the Reagan administration made a monumental tactical error, for which it and the contras would pay dearly. Convinced of the duplicity of the Democrats, fearful of handing the Sandinistas an apparent victory, and refusing on principle to return to the old "humanitarian" aid compromise, the Reagan administration failed to see the advantages of a temporary, tactical retreat. In a confrontation that required as much flexibility as stolidity, the Sandinistas had proven both more adept and more daring.

The Reagan administration, consumed with its own problems, also failed to see how badly off the Sandinistas would have been even without passage of new military aid to the contras. The Sandinistas had already taken desperate measures to escape the vise that had been closing on them since August 1987: more and more pressure from the opposition, more and more scrutiny from the international community, and yet no end to the continuing contra war. Passage of "non-lethal" aid on February 3 would have prolonged this difficult situation, and it might have pushed the Sandinistas' tolerance and flexibility to the breaking point. The Sandinistas had never found the distinction between "lethal" and "nonlethal" aid very significant. Ortega argued that Reagan was "trying to frighten the U.S. Congress" into passing a "humanitarian aid" that was nothing more than "logistical aid . . . for those groups making war" against Nicaragua.[17] Ortega warned, as he had in April 1986, that renewal of *any* kind of aid to the contras would free the Sandinistas "to take all measures necessary to defend the sovereignty, self-determination and independence of our country."[18] It is possible that passage of the "nonlethal" aid proposal supported by Reagan would have prompted an angry and, for the Reagan administration, useful response by the Sandinistas.

The Sandinistas' opposition was as unruly as ever in the first months of 1988, and the Sandinistas had had to show more restraint than usual in responding. On January 21 the government sent *turbas* brandishing pistols to attack a demonstration by the Social Christian Party, and a Sandinista official said the attack was a "message that is meant to be heard."[19] On January 22, an indoor meeting of the Coordinadora was disrupted by another group of *turbas* who threw rocks through the windows.[20] On February 7 several thousand members of four non-Sandinista labor unions marched in Managua. "When the people move," they chanted, "the nine tremble!"[21]

On February 8 in Masaya, a spontaneous protest by mothers against the draft and forced recruitment of their sons erupted into a three-day melee between anti-government protesters and local Sandinista organizations. The anti-draft protesters burned cars, lit bonfires in the streets, threw rocks at a local Sandinista Youth headquarters and shattered windows of the town police station. The government sent 200 club-swinging riot police to disperse the demonstrators, arrested between 20 and 50 local opposition leaders, placed Masaya in a state of virtual martial law, and accused the opposition parties and *La Prensa* of inciting violence and trying to provoke an insurrection "in accordance with U.S. orders."[22] Had the Reagan administration passed a "non-lethal" aid bill on February 3, such actions would have been part of its case for a renewal of military aid to the contras.

Even with the defeat of the President's proposal, support for the contras did not disappear in Congress. On February 4 the Senate voted to approve the contra aid proposal 51–49. Congress was still closely divided and thus susceptible to further subtle shifts of mood.[23] The ambivalent policy of the moderates held sway: "Limited" support for the contras was "justified"; Congress had a "moral obligation to ensure that they are fed and clothed and remain a viable fighting force if the Sandinistas do not act in good faith"; the vote would "turn around next time" if the Sandinistas continued to "play games";[24] it was "very important that we not simply walk away from the situation or be perceived as walking away."[25] The position of the moderates—that the contras could not be "abandoned"— had become such an inviolable principle of American policy that it was mouthed even by liberal House leaders. House Whip Tony Coelho stated that the Democratic leadership did not "intend to turn our backs and run away."[26]

The advantages of compromising on February 3 may be no more than the speculations of hindsight. The costs of not compromising, however, were real and disastrous. Whatever the contras might have suffered from not receiving the $3.6 million in military aid paled beside the damage they suffered when the entire CIA supply program had to be shut down on February 29 as result of the February 3 defeat in Congress. The network of CIA support and advice, which had been so effective throughout 1987, was withdrawn entirely. The contras felt abandoned, bitter, and vulnerable as they entered negotiations with the Sandinistas. Because Reagan had lost and given up control of the legislative agenda, the contras now depended on Speaker Wright to hurry ahead with another vote on some form of "humanitarian" aid, as he had promised McCurdy and the moderates. The Sandinistas, meanwhile, were determined to exploit these circumstances to strike an immediate, crushing blow against the contras before the American Congress could act. On February 4 Daniel Ortega exhorted the Nicaraguan people to "complete the total defeat" of the rebels.[27]

When contra leaders postponed the next scheduled round of talks from February 10 to February 18, Wright publicly warned that if they delayed the talks he might delay the second vote on an alternative contra aid proposal.[28] Wright wanted the contras to go "back to the negotiating table" quickly, and Congressman Coelho warned that if they delayed the negotiations again, they might harm the prospects for passing an aid bill altogether.[29] Contra leaders promised Wright that they were committed to reaching an agreement with the Sandinistas when the talks resumed on February 18.[30]

The Sandinistas, however, delayed. By the middle of February Sandinista army troops were in an advanced state of preparation for an offensive planned for early March. The Sandinistas had a new and inviting target just across the border in Honduras. Toward the end of February, the CIA had begun moving large stockpiles of arms, ammunition, and supplies from Swan Island, where the CIA air resupply base had been located, to the contra base camps across the Honduran border. By the end of February, when as a result of the February 3 vote the CIA lost its legal authority to deliver supplies to the contras, 3,000 metric tons of arms, ammunition, and supplies had been stored at contra bases in Honduras along the Nicaraguan border. "Operation Danto," Humberto Ortega later explained, was to be the "culmination of a series of [Sandinista army] military offensives" in the first three months of 1988 "to eliminate completely the majority of the mercenary forces."[31] Sandinista negotiators were, therefore, instructed to stall for time, neither accepting nor explicitly rejecting Cardinal Obando's latest proposal for a new round of direct talks to be held in Nacaragua.[32]

While the talks stalled in Central America, Wright's half-hearted efforts to pass a watered-down contra aid bill foundered. A Democratic proposal to provide the contras $16 million through June 30 for food, clothing, medicine, and transportation was narrowly defeated on March 3.[33] A handful of liberals voted against the measure on final passage, prompting Wright to quote Will Rogers: "I don't belong to any organized political party. I'm a Democrat."[34] House Republicans had voted against the Democratic bill, hoping its defeat would lead to passage of a better alternative, but the Democratic leadership felt under no further obligations. Congressman Coelho insisted the Republicans had only themselves to blame for the lack of aid for the contras, and even moderate Democrats like McCurdy were content to blame the Republicans.[35] Wright noted "a weariness with the contra issue," and Congressman Bonior argued the

House was in a stalemate. He told reporters, "I think people have to step back a second and watch what happens in Nicaragua over the next couple of weeks."[36]

The second consecutive defeat of aid to the contras on March 3 dramatically altered the military and political balance that had already begun to shift against the rebels after the first defeat. Alfredo César, who believed he had been given some assurances of support by the Democrats, privately complained that they had let the contras down. Publicly, he castigated the Republicans and the Reagan administration, who in his view "felt it was better to leave our forces up in the air than vote with the Democrats." As a result of "some political battle in Washington," César noted despairingly, the contra forces had been "hurt in the field." As for the pending negotiations with the Sandinistas, now scheduled to begin in the small Nicaraguan town of Sapoa, César warned, "We feel weak."[37] After the February 3 vote some contra forces had already begun making their way back to sanctuary in Honduras; the March 3 vote threatened to turn that slow retreating trickle into a flood.

53

Sapoa

The Sandinistas, believing they had reached the endgame in the long and debilitating war with the contras, moved into the final stage of their months-long military offensive. From the beginning of March Sandinista diplomatic maneuvers were carefully coordinated with military actions to convince contra leaders that, in Daniel Ortega's words, their only choices were to "run the risk of total defeat and . . . end[] up with nothing, or . . . seek a negotiated solution and achieve something."[1] By the first week of March the Sandinista army was in the final phase of preparations for its offensive against the contra base camps that straddled the Nicaraguan-Honduran border near the conjunction of the Bocay and Coco rivers. It had set in place artillery batteries, called up reserve units, and moved large supplies of gasoline to staging positions in the northern regions to provide logistical support for a prolonged offensive in the remote region. Altogether 6–8,000 Sandinista army troops took up positions in and around northern Jinotega, along with a dozen or more transport and attack helicopters.

By March two company-sized units of Sandinista troops began infiltrating across the border into Honduras to test contra defenses and determine the exact location of their weapons stockpiles, while the Sandinista air force diverted the contras' attention with sporadic air strikes. On March 2 the Sandinistas abruptly dismissed Cardinal Obando as mediator, believing he was an obstacle to achieving the contras' surrender. On March 6 Daniel Ortega publicly announced the beginning of a major Sandinista offensive at the northern border. On March 7 the Sandinista air force began a steady bombardment of the upper Bocay river region, and on March 9 American intelligence officers began detecting the movement of large numbers of Sandinista troops northward to the border area.[2] Ortega said that the contras were in a "a position of weakness" after the March 3 vote. Their troops were retreating and "conserving their bullets." Contra leaders, Ortega suggested, would have to "accommodate themselves to a new situation. . . . The Reagan Presidency is coming to a close. If the contras don't reach a negotiated solution, they face the prospect of total military and political defeat."[3]

Wright, who was in frequent contact with both the Sandinista government and Alfredo César, sensed that the two sides were coming to a resolution of the conflict. While House Republicans and White House officials tried to persuade the Speaker to allow another vote on contra aid quickly, and Senate Democrats led by David Boren put together a proposal of their own, Wright said he did not want to schedule another vote until after the next round of cease-fire talks.[4]

On the morning of March 16 the Sandinistas launched their attack. Almost 5,000 troops pushed up across the Honduran border toward the contra camps from the south. Having learned the lesson of their failed incursion of 1986, the Sandinistas had also sent 1,500 troops deeper into Honduras to set up a blocking position behind the contra base at San Andres de Bocay to cut off any retreat. The contras tried to defend their positions with about 1,500 troops, but their bases on the Nicaraguan side of the border were quickly overrun and as they retreated they found themselves encircled. Their large weapons stockpiles were in danger. As the fighting continued through the morning of March 17, Sandinista troops penetrated as far as five miles inside Honduras.[5]

In the afternoon of March 16, President Reagan, along with Shultz, Powell, and Howard Baker called an emergency meeting with Wright, Michel, and other House leaders to inform them about the Sandinista incursion and to seek agreement from Wright for rapid consideration of a new aid bill. Shultz argued that with Nicaraguan troops in Honduras, the situation called for emergency measures. Wright and other Democratic leaders were skeptical of the administration's claims, however. On March 15 Coelho had charged that the administration was trying "to create an atmosphere of crisis" and that its "credibility on this issue is a little bankrupt."[6] Wright said he had been assured by Foreign Minister D'Escoto that there were no Sandinista troops in Honduras, and if there were they would be withdrawn immediately. A frustrated Shultz ended the meeting, saying if they could not even agree there was an emergency, there was not much chance of their agreeing on a new contra aid request.[7]

As word of the contras' increasingly dire military situation circulated through the administration on March 16, Reagan officials determined to do something to try to halt the Sandinistas' advance. In a repetition of previous comedic episodes concerning Sandinista cross-border attacks, the American ambassador in Honduras tried to coax the Honduran government into launching air strikes and moving ground forces forward, but the Hondurans were not eager to fight the Sandinistas in order to protect the contras. Instead, President Azcona called Ortega and demanded the immediate withdrawal of Sandinista troops from Honduran territory. Azcona finally did seek American assistance, and President Reagan ordered two battalions of the 82nd airborne to Honduras as a "measured response designed to show our staunch support for the democratic government of Honduras at a time when its territorial integrity is being violated."[8] On March 17 the Honduran air force ran a couple of half-hearted bombing raids—in one case dropping bombs near a group of American reporters being escorted by Sandinista army public affairs officers.[9]

President Reagan's action had a greater effect on the Sandinistas than on the Hondurans. The Sandinistas had always believed their most dangerous moment would come when President Reagan decided that his cherished contras were on the brink of annihilation. When they heard that Reagan had ordered the 82nd airborne to Honduras, Sandinista leaders feared it could be the first step toward a direct American attack on their forces. At midday on March 17 Humberto Ortega ordered a halt in the offensive. Some Sandinista forces continued to operate on Honduran territory for the next two days, prompting a second bombing raid by the Honduran air force, but the level of fighting decreased sharply after March 17. The contras, meanwhile, had put up a surprisingly stout defense, although suffering many casualties.[10] The Sandinistas fell short of their objective of capturing the weapons stockpiles. "[H]ad it not been for the virtual intervention of U.S. troops to save them," Ortega claimed later, the contra forces "in their bases in the border territory . . . [would have been] totally wiped out."[11]

As the fighting raged along the Nicaraguan-Honduran border, the battle in Washington was almost as fierce. Liberal Democrats charged that the Reagan administration had "discovered" an invasion of Honduras because, in the words of Congressman Coelho, it was "desperate to create a situation in Central American to justify military aid."[12] Coelho also suggested that the Reagan administration's actions were designed to undermine the cease-fire talks, or perhaps to divert attention from the indictments handed down against North and Poindexter by the Iran-contra prosecutor on March 16.[13]

As the administration briefed the two intelligence committees over the course of the day, however, the fact of the Sandinistas' incursion into Honduras came to be widely accepted. The chairman of the Senate intelligence committee, David Boren, denounced the attack; Senator Nunn, the chairman of the Senate armed services committee, and Congressman Aspin, the chairman of the House armed services committee, both declared their support for the administration's dispatch of troops. By the afternoon of March 17 Senator Byrd declared that "while the Sandinistas are to be condemned for their actions, and so far as I know they may be out of Honduran territory by now . . . I hope that the reaction that our country has had does not . . . derail the peace process."[14] Many journalists continued to write and speak of the Sandinistas' "alleged incursion" for more than a week—until a United Nations investigating commission, requested by Ortega, confirmed that Sandinista troops had indeed entered Honduras.[15] The debate in Washington quickly shifted from whether the incursion had occurred to whether the Sandinistas' offensive required a renewal of contra aid.

Moderate and conservative Democrats called for another vote on contra aid. According to one observer, "key House moderates whose votes had helped defeat the president's military aid request on Feb. 3 were clamoring for a new package that would resume limited munitions shipments to the contras and give Reagan the opportunity to demand a congressional vote for more."[16] Congressman Buddy MacKay of Florida, an opponent of aid in the past, warned that if Daniel Ortega was "reading the swing votes as being satisfied with the shutoff of aid, he's reading it wrong." MacKay introduced a bill to provide $48 million in non-lethal aid to the contras for a year, to let the CIA resume delivery of some $2.5 million worth of weapons, ammunition, and supplies left over from earlier purchases, and to give the President "expedited procedures" for a future military aid request. Senator Dodd believed moderate Democrats were now "more inclined to vote for military aid," and a bill in the Senate sponsored by moderates and similar to MacKay's appeared to gain new life. According to the *Congressional Quarterly*, the Sandinistas had "once again proven their ability to build political support in Washington for the contra guerrillas."[17]

Speaker Wright alone managed to hold back the tide. To discredit the Reagan administration's version of events, Wright distributed copies of the Iran-contra committee's report which alleged the Reagan administration had engaged in "intelligence misrepresentation" during the Sandinistas' March 1986 incursion. "[T]he campaign to cast doubt on the administration's version of events in Honduras," the *Washington Post* reported, "was part of a calculated Democratic strategy to ride out the storm that followed the incursion." Wright's strategy worked. Doubts and confusion reigned for days while Wright and Senate Majority Leader Byrd successfully blocked all action on contra aid measures, insisting that any consideration of additional aid should await the outcome of the next round of cease-fire talks.[18]

Meanwhile, contra leaders feared imminent destruction. Rebel forces in Honduras and Nicaragua were cut off from American assistance and had no hope of launching a counteroffensive. Adolfo Calero later recalled that "there were 5,000 men trapped in the Bocay, with only two or three days of food." Camps in the Bocay area which the contras had held for months were now in the hands of the Sandinistas, and thousands of well-equipped Sandinista troops remained poised to continue the offensive. The contra negotiators shared none of the administration's new optimism about restoring aid. Congressman Wright and Senator Byrd had made it clear to them that no aid bill would be considered until after a cease-fire had been reached with the Sandinistas, and by this point the words of Wright and Byrd carried far greater weight than those of State Department officials. Calero, César, and the other contra negotiators, including two field commanders representing the interests of the troops, all agreed that, in Calero's words, "Sapoa was our only hope."[19]

The negotiations at Sapoa provided the occasion for a convergence of common interests. Wright and other Democratic leaders needed a negotiated cease-fire to end the clamor for contra aid in the House and heal their divided party. The Sandinistas needed a voluntary agreement by the contra leaders to forgo further American assistance. The key part in this triangle was now the contras themselves. Ortega believed that "favorable conditions for an agreement with the mercenaries existed because the Yankee empire had shot its bolt."[20]

The rebel fighters, and most of their leadership, needed a respite from the fighting and a means of receiving supplies. They recognized that it was Wright, not Reagan, who held the key to their survival. They did not want a final cease-fire, however. To all the fighters, and most of the leaders, agreeing to a final cease-fire meant surrender, and surrender to Sandinista rule meant persecution, exile, or death.

The contra leadership did not speak with one voice, however. While Calero and other contra leaders went to the talks at Sapoa reluctantly, expecting and hoping for a failure which might then lead to more aid, Alfredo César saw an opportunity in the negotiations. Seeing that the balance of power in the United States had shifted, from the Reagan administration to Jim Wright, and understanding that Wright and the Sandinistas were in agreement on the need for a cease-fire, César presented himself as the man who could bring the contras to the table. Clearly, César hoped to be granted a significant role in Nicaraguan politics in return. If César's political "flexibility" was cynical, it was no more so than that of many Nicaraguan politicians in similar positions throughout the history of his country. Unlike Bermúdez, whose only hope of future power lay with a military victory by the forces at his command, or Calero, whose political future in Nicaragua was limited by a snobbish aristocracy, César was an agile politician of patrician manner who could achieve success in any number of possible Nicaraguan futures. As a former Sandinista, he could hope to act as a bridge between the elite business class and the revolutionaries—the keystone of a new "tercerismo." Oscar Arias, Carlos Andrés Pérez, and moderate Democrats supported César because they believed he was willing to work with the Sandinistas rather than insist on fighting against them. César offered himself as the key to a peaceful solution to Nicaragua's crisis. After the February 3 vote, César had begun to meet privately with the Sandinistas' lawyer and chief American representative, Paul Reichler. The meeting was arranged by House Democratic leaders, who told César, "'Look, the aid is defeated. . . . Reichler wants to talk with you, and we think he could help in the negotiations.'" Reichler wanted to "open up an informal channel" between César and the Sandinistas, and César, without telling his colleagues, agreed.[21]

César was not even included in the contras' delegation until a week before the meeting. Calero only decided to bring him because, as César recalls, Calero did not want to be blamed for the inevitable breakdown of the talks: "I was included to give legitimacy to the failure." While most contras, and most American officials, believed the Sandinistas' military offensive meant they were not interested in a negotiated settlement, César already knew otherwise. He recognized the incursion as a tactic to soften up the contra negotiators.[22]

Fortunately for César and the contras, the failure of the Sandinista army to accomplish its primary military objective, the surprisingly strong reaction of the Reagan administration, and the threat of renewed congressional support for aid to the contras put the two sides at Sapoa on more equal ground than the Sandinistas had anticipated. The contras were clearly at a disadvantage, but they did not come to the talks as mere supplicants. On the first day of negotiations, the Sandinistas insisted on signing a definitive cease-fire agreement to end the war then and there. They would stay at Sapoa as long as needed to reach a final agreement, but they wanted an overall political and military settlement before the fighting ended. The contras refused. "We weren't ready for that," César recalled.[23] The contras now knew that the American Congress would not completely abandon them, and this gave the rebels strength to resist outright surrender. Instead, they insisted on a temporary cease-fire, during which extended negotiations on a wide range of political and military issues would take place.

Much to the surprise of the contra negotiators, the Sandinistas retreated. At the end of the first day of talks, the two Ortega brothers and Joaquín Cuadra went back to their bungalow to consider their options. President Arias called both Ortegas and urged them to free political prisoners and allow the contras to join the political dialogue in Nicaragua. By morning the Sandinista leaders had decided to make some important concessions in order to reach an immediate agreement. In César's view, the Sandinistas "were worried about the situation in Congress. They knew that they would never have a better military situation than they had at that moment."[24] The Sandinistas decided to take what they could at Sapoa.

The Sandinista negotiators made two critical concessions to the contras' demands. Instead of demanding that the contras lay down their arms at the end of the 60-day cease-fire, the Sandinistas agreed to let the rebels keep their arms while negotiations for an overall settlement proceeded. The contras thus got what they most needed: a truce without surrender. Second, in connection with this prolongation of the talks, the Sandinistas conceded to the contras' long-held demand that political issues and military issues be linked. The Sandinistas undoubtedly understood that this point was critical for César. He would not negotiate the contras' disarmament without knowing what political role would be promised him in the future.

The Sandinistas' concessions exposed the subtle difference between César and the other contra negotiators. With the first round of talks about to end, some of the contra negotiators proposed delaying a final agreement until the next round. César strenuously objected. "I argued that if we had an agreement, we should close it that day. No extensions, no agreements in principle." Privately, César worried that if the talks were broken off, pressures from Washington and from the Nicaraguan exile community in Miami would make his colleagues back away from the agreement. The CIA, César believed, favored an agreement. Now that William Casey had been replaced by William Webster, CIA officials seemed intent on withdrawing from the controversial covert program. The White House also favored a settlement—César believed National Security Adviser Colin Powell was "very much involved" in pushing for an end to the war.[25]

But the State Department, led by Elliott Abrams, was bestirring itself against the emerging agreement. After the incursion into Honduras, and with moderate Democrats proposing new contra aid legislation, Abrams and his advisers believed the prospects for new aid were brighter, and they opposed what they considered a bad deal for the contras. When Calero called the State Department on the afternoon of the last day at Sapoa, he was told the Reagan administration opposed signing the agreement at that moment and recommended waiting. But César "wanted to resist these pressures." The Sandinista negotiators, meanwhile, worked hard to persuade other contra leaders of their sincerity. Humberto Ortega spent an hour alone with Calero; others talked with Aristides Sanchez; Sandinista military representatives met with the two contra commanders. There was, César declared, "a special nationalism" in the talks. "These were real Nicaraguan negotiations." César encouraged his colleagues to "try and get away from the superpowers."[26] In the end, the contra team agreed with César to make the deal final.

In the agreement announced on March 23, the Sandinistas and contras committed themselves to two phases of negotiations. The first phase was a temporary cease-fire during which the contra troops would move into designated cease-fire zones and be supplied with food, clothing, and medical equipment. Once the first phase was completed, negotiations for a "definitive" cease-fire and an overall political settlement would begin. The Sapoa agreement stated that the enforcement of a definitive cease-fire would "occur jointly with the Esquipulas II commitments to end the war." During the first phase, the Sandinistas committed themselves to guarantee freedom of speech and to declare a general political amnesty, releasing 50 percent of the political prisoners in Sandinista jails when the contras moved into cease-fire zones and another 50 percent when the "definitive" cease-fire agreement was signed. In addition, once the contra forces were in their enclaves, the contras could send representatives to the national dialogue between the opposition parties and government.

In return, the contras made the crucial concession the Sandinistas badly wanted. César and his colleagues agreed to forgo further American assistance. They would get no military assistance during the negotiating period, and they would receive food, medicine, and clothing only through a "neutral organization"—that is, not from an American government agency. What the Sandinistas won at Sapoa was a partial severing of the American umbilical cord that had for so long sustained the contras. Their agreement with the contras precluded any vote in the American Congress, for at least 60 days, on either military or "non-lethal" assistance, and ruled out the delivery of humanitarian aid by the CIA, Defense Department, or any other U.S. government organization. This aspect of the agreement was most welcome to Wright and other Democratic leaders. César was "100 percent sure" that Congress would approve new aid now that the deal was signed, and both he and Daniel Ortega publicly expressed their thanks to Speaker Wright for helping make the Sapoa agreement possible.[27]

The agreement at Sapoa permitted rapid passage of a humanitarian aid bill similar to the one defeated on March 3. Less than $18 million in food, clothing, and medical assistance were to be provided to the contras through September 30 by the Agency for International Development through "neutral" carriers agreeable to both the contras and Sandinistas. Republicans were dismayed at what they considered the forced surrender of the contras, for which they blamed Wright. But as one leading Republican declared, "You can't be more contra than the contras."[28] The Republicans demanded "expedited procedures" for the President to request new aid should the Sandinistas renege on their commitments, but Wright promised only that any request from the President would receive "prompt" consideration under a "fair and orderly procedure." The House passed the bill on March 30 by a 345–70 margin, with only liberal opponents of aid in opposition, and the Senate passed the identical bill the next day, 87–7. Wright declared that with the approval of this aid to the contras, Congress intended to encourage "both sides in Central America to reconcile their differences and bring about peace and democracy."[29]

The passage of aid, however, only encouraged both sides to hold fast to their positions. What they had conceded at Sapoa under pressure they sought to take back once the pressure was lifted. The Sandinistas immediately declared Wright's aid bill "illegal" and "interventionist," and while Americans ignored this seemingly *pro forma* protest, it was actually the opening salvo in a new effort to weaken the contras.[30] The Sandinistas planned to delay the delivery of food and supplies to the contra forces in Honduras and in Nicaragua for as long as possible and, in so doing, achieve what they had failed to gain at Sapoa: the contras' agreement to surrender their arms. By the time of the next high-level meeting, the Sandinistas were demanding that the contras agree to lay down their arms as the prerequisite to reaching an agreement on the cease-fire enclaves—contrary to the understanding reached at Sapoa.

The contras, on the other hand, encouraged by their lingering support in Congress, held out for terms that far exceeded what the Sandinistas were prepared to grant. Once the immediate danger of military defeat had passed and renewed humanitarian assistance was approved by the Congress, the contra leaders demanded broad political reforms in return for laying down their arms in a "definitive cease-fire." Contra negotiators also felt emboldened to insist that their troops be allowed to replenish their supplies of weapons during the cease-fire. Both of these demands exceeded the terms of the Sapoa agreement and the Sandinistas pronounced them "completely absurd."

Underlying the strategies of both sides were the simplest of motives: Peace agreement or no peace agreement, the contras were doing all they could to survive as a political and military entity, and the Sandinistas were doing all they could to destroy them. Given the Sandinistas' behavior after Sapoa, it is difficult to know whether they really hoped for an agreement with César, whether they had opened the "private channel" with him only to divide and demoralize the contras, or whether divisions in the Sandinistas' own ranks led to an inconsistent policy. Whatever the reason, the Sandinistas' tough policies in the spring and summer of 1988 made it very difficult for César to lead the contras to further agreements.

54

"Are You Selling Us Out?"

The Sapoa agreement had already opened a wide split within the contras' senior leadership. Enrique Bermúdez and some of the top military commanders in Honduras, as well as a large segment of the Nicaraguan exile community in Miami, declared it a shameful surrender. A contra radio station broadcasting to the troops in Honduras spoke of the "false signatures" at Sapoa.[1] Adolfo Calero found himself excoriated by conservative Nicaraguans, who accused him of having been "bamboozled" by Alfredo César and seduced by Humberto Ortega. Bermúdez denounced Calero and "Toño" and "Fernando," the two contra field commanders who had signed the accord. Aristides Sanchez disavowed his own signature on the agreement and made common cause with Bermúdez. These roiling dissensions put pressure on the contra negotiators to win back what had been given away at Sapoa. Commander Fernando's declaration on the first day of technical talks that the contras would "never lay down their arms until Nicaragua is democratic," was as much a promise to critics in the movement as a challenge to the Sandinistas.[2] Although the storm subsided a bit after the first two weeks, these underlying tensions in the movement did not fade.

The Sandinistas, intentionally or not, exacerbated the tensions in the contra movement. By April 14 the contra negotiators and the Sandinista negotiating team, led by General Joaquín Cuadra, had reached agreement

597

on all but a handful of the technical points. They delineated seven zones covering about 20,000 square miles of Nicaragua and settled matters of the verification and monitoring of supply deliveries and the protection of the combatants in the zones. When Calero, César, and the other contra negotiators arrived in Managua to discuss the means of delivery and other issues, however, they found Humberto Ortega and the other Sandinistas in an unyielding mood. In public Sandinista officials argued that the Sapoa agreement had just been a way "to help the contras save face, to give them an elegant political way out," or as President Ortega put it, "to end in negotiations a war the contras already lost militarily." In private, the Sandinistas refused to resolve the remaining issues concerning the enclaves until the contra leaders signed an agreement to turn in their weapons by June 28. This was a step back from the agreement at Sapoa, a virtual demand for the contras' surrender. If the contras could not move into enclaves because the Sandinistas would not agree on the enclaves, then the contras could also not begin to receive the shipments of American aid in Nicaragua. Alfredo César suggested that "if many members of the U.S. Congress recognize that the Sandinistas are holding the hunger of our troops hostage to a surrender, it could kick the mechanism very quickly in the law that provides for President Reagan to ask for more military aid."[3]

The Sandinistas were clearly trying to continue what "Operation Danto" had only begun. By mid-April contra fighters in Honduras and Nicaragua had not received a single shipment of American aid in six weeks and were beginning to suffer. Some managed to survive in Nicaragua among their peasant supporters, from whom, at first, they were able to buy food. Others hunted for deer and lived off the land. Many others began the long trek back to Honduras and, finding little or nothing to eat along the way, arrived in the camps nearly starving—only to find that there was not much food in the camps either. The problems in Honduras were exacerbated by the numbers of peasants who retreated with them, fearing violent reprisals by the Sandinista army. The camps in Honduras filled with thousands of armed men and women increasingly distraught and despairing. And with each passing week, as contra troops were transformed from fighters to refugees, the military balance shifted ever more in the Sandinista army's favor. On April 20 the Reagan administration, refusing to wait any longer for the negotiations to be completed, delivered 70,000 pounds of food by truck to the camps in Honduras. The Sandinistas protested that the deliveries were a "grave violation" of the Sapoa agreement, and Democrats in Congress charged again that the administration was violating the law.

The longer contra forces went without supplies, the more the military commanders and their troops came to view the Sapoa accord as a disaster and those who negotiated it as dupes or traitors. In a movement not known for its disciplined unity in the best of circumstances, the dissatisfaction caused by suffering increased the tensions and rivalries that always existed among the contra leaders, providing both motive and justification to those who wished to reorder the balance of power. The Sandinistas knew this and used the negotiations, in part, as a way of dividing their adversaries. As the Sandinistas were presenting their new demands, rewriting the agreement at Sapoa, and further delaying the delivery of supplies, a factional war exploded inside the contra movement.

The pressures on the contras in the spring of 1988 brought into the open a number of long-simmering conflicts at all levels of the rebel movement. In the top ranks of the leadership there was unfinished business left over from the last reorganization of the Directorate in the spring of 1987. Alfredo César had been catapulted into the fore by the resignation of Cruz, and Adolfo Calero had seen his earlier pre-eminence in the movement fatally undermined by his collision with Cruz. The alliance César had initially forged with Calero to consolidate his own position was tactical and temporary, and a fight between them for predominance in the movement was inevitable. Meanwhile, after years of chafing under Calero's leadership of the FDN, Aristides Sanchez and Enrique Bermúdez had won new independence and prominence in the 1987 reorganization, which in turn engendered new ambitions.

Tensions among the rebel field commanders were the product of deeper trends that had been developing over several years. The generation of former National Guardsmen that first led the campesinos into battle had given way to a new generation of veteran campesinos, former Sandinista army regulars and ex-MILPAS. The change was most noticeable in the enormous Jorge Salazar Regional Commands, whose leaders, the former Sandinista "Rigoberto," the farmer "Franklyn," and the evangelical pastor "Fernando," had become chieftains of near-legendary stature in the central regions of the country. Yet in the senior military command that surrounded Bermúdez, the ex-MILPAS and the ex-campesinos were scarcely represented. Bermúdez had kept all his old allies from the Guard in his general staff. Dissatisfaction with this imbalance had led to several confrontations over the previous two years, some of them bloody. While the war was going well, and the field commanders led their troops in ever-widening circles of influence in Nicaragua, the question of who was ostensibly running the war back in Honduras was of relatively little importance. As one contra field commander told reporters, "When we have everything, we do not care who is in charge of us."[4] While the Americans were directing the war, planning most of the military strategy, and operating a fairly reliable resupply operation, the general staff in Honduras were almost irrelevant figure-heads anyway. When the American program came to an end in March, however, and the supplies began to run out, leaders like "Rigoberto" came into the Honduran camps only to find Bermúdez's old guard still in charge. Long-suppressed discontents erupted.

Some field commanders demanded a reorganization of the General Staff to bring new blood into the command, but Bermúdez refused to satisfy many of the most discontented. Rigoberto, who fancied himself a reincarnated Sandino, was given an entirely non-military assignment by the senior command and felt dishonored. Fernando, who with Rigoberto had led Jorge Salazar troops in their assault on the three mining towns in December, was also annoyed at the way Bermúdez and his deputies were running things. Tigrillo, the oldest and most respected campesino leader, found no one in the camps who could provide food to his thousands of followers and summoned Bermúdez to a confrontational meeting toward the end of February. Nor were the ex-campesinos and ex-Sandinistas the only unhappy ones. Toño, a former Guardsman and adviser to Bermúdez, had also become dissatisfied with the military leadership and, like the other disgruntled commanders, thought he could do better.

This combustible mixture of leadership rivalry in the contra Directorate and generational conflict among the troops required only the proper spark to be ignited, and both the Sapoa agreement and then the Sandinistas' effort to prevent the delivery of supplies provided it. While the Sandinistas were laying down their new ultimatum in Managua on April 17, Toño and Fernando were back in Honduras denouncing Bermúdez and calling for his resignation. Joined by Rigoberto, the commanders engineered a dissident rebellion and found a ready ally in Adolfo Calero. With Calero financing their efforts, Tigrillo, Toño, Fernando, and Rigoberto worked to collect signatures on a petition calling for Bermúdez's replacement by a junta of field commanders. They gave interviews to the press denouncing Bermúdez as another Somoza, charges seconded by Calero, and by the third week of April had mustered the support of a third of the regional commanders and other important fighters.[5]

Bermúdez retaliated by expelling Toño and Fernando from the negotiating team, accusing them of defecting to the Sandinistas at Sapoa. He then stripped them and all the other dissidents of their ranks. These actions only further infuriated the dissidents and strengthened their support among troops in the camps. By the end of April, the effort to oust Bermúdez from the movement appeared to be succeeding. While the dissident commanders stirred up trouble in the ranks of the fighters, Calero sought the "legal" expulsion of Bermúdez by the contra Directorate. With Chamorro and Ferrey as likely allies of Calero, and Aristides Sanchez as the lone defender of Bermúdez, only César's approval was required to turn the tables decisively against the contra military commander.

The ouster of Bermúdez at the hands of Calero and his allies, however, was not a development to be welcomed by César. If Bermúdez were expelled from the movement, Calero's allies in the camps would rise to the fore and Calero would once again become the sole member of the directorate with close ties to the field commanders. In one stroke Calero could resume the preeminent position he had held years before. César, therefore, in yet another nimble shift of allegiance, came to the aid of the National Guard colonel he had once denounced as Somocista. His switch effectively blocked any chance that the contra Directorate could vote Bermúdez out as military commander. The CIA, meanwhile, with the aid of Honduran military officers, moved to quell the dissident rebellion against Bermúdez because they feared a civil war in the Honduran camps.

The Sandinistas fanned the flames of this internecine conflict by further tightening their demands at the next meeting at the end of April. On April 28 in Managua the Sandinista negotiators still would not agree to complete negotiations on an enclave agreement and proposed instead that the Red Cross should begin delivering aid to the contras in Nicaragua. The contra negotiators objected to this proposal on several grounds. Until the contra fighters could move into enclaves with appropriate guarantees, they could not safely go to the sites, which the Sandinistas had chosen, to pick up deliveries made by the Red Cross. Nor did the contras believe they could depend on the reliability of the Red Cross, which like any organization based in Nicaragua depended on the government's cooperation to function. Finally, the Sandinistas had already declared that the contras could propose their own preferred "neutral" agency to make the deliveries. They appeared now to be retreating from that earlier agreement, as well.[6]

By the beginning of May, therefore, the 60-day temporary cease-fire was more than half over, and the contras had yet to receive a shipment of supplies in Nicaragua. As many as 5,000 contra fighters had retreated to Honduras and more were arriving there each day in a state of near-starvation. For those contras remaining in Nicaragua, conditions were deteriorating as the troops ran out of money to pay local supporters for food and supplies. As the supply problems grew more acute, so did the political crisis within the movement. Reporters meeting with contra fighters in the camps found them "confused and demoralized" by the infighting and the shortages.[7]

On May 3 the dissident commanders came forward with their petition demanding the ouster of Bermúdez. The next day, three leaders of the rebellion—Rigoberto, Toño, and Tigrillo—were arrested by the Honduran military and swiftly deported to the United States, along with three civilian allies of Calero. Fernando, however, eluded capture and fled to the camps to rally support. By May 9 some 1,500 contra fighters led by Fernando had blockaded themselves in their camp at Yamales, disavowed Bermúdez as their leader, and declared their allegiance to the dissident commanders.[8] At one point troops loyal to Bermúdez fired on a group of dissidents traveling in Fernando's jeep. Fernando was finally arrested by the Honduran military and deported. With all their leaders removed, the dissidents gave in and on May 18 most declared their support for Bermúdez. The rebellion was thus quelled and Bermúdez retained control, although he could not have done so without the help of the CIA and the Hondurans.[9] The CIA's loyalty to Bermúdez proved more durable than its loyalty to Calero or indeed to the most distinguished of the contras' field commanders. The price of restoring unity was the loss from the contra ranks of some of their most famous and effective leaders.

With the contras in this weakened and divided condition, the Sandinistas tried to press their advantage. On May 1 Daniel Ortega warned that if the contras did not accept the government's offer before the cease-fire expired on May 31, the Sandinistas would "launch a major military offensive against the mercenary forces . . . that will make the Danto operation look small." The Sandinistas, he said, were offering the contras a chance to lay down their arms, and the contras "should be grateful that we are not offering them the guillotine or the firing squad, which is what they deserve."[10] American intelligence officials once again detected Sandinista troop movements up near the Honduran border in the Bocay region.

———

César, Calero, and other contra leaders hurried to Washington at the beginning of May to try to get Congress to put pressure on the Sandinistas. Either the Sandinistas had to settle the question of the enclaves, they insisted, or the United States had to begin delivering supplies directly. Wright publicly warned the Sandinistas against attacking contra forces and called for both sides in the negotiations to show "good faith." But he said that the contras' request for help in settling the resupply question put him in "a very awkward position: . . . I don't want to be a negotiator." Wright opposed the idea of direct deliveries by the United States because it would only give the contras the "impression that we want to rev up the war."[11] Wright and other Democratic leaders objected that AID was already violating the terms of the Sapoa accords by providing aid to the contras in Honduras without the Sandinistas' approval. Secretary Shultz protested to one congressional committee that it surely could not have been the intent of Congress to allow the Sandinistas to control the supply of aid to the contras, but House Democratic leaders nevertheless asked AID officials not to try to deliver food until the next round of negotiations between the contras and Sandinistas at the end of the month.[12]

César's efforts to muster some support in Washington were not entirely in vain. While Wright showed his annoyance with the contras, moderate and conservative Democrats were becoming impatient with the Sandinistas. On May 12 two dozen Democrats wrote to Ortega complaining of the Sandinistas' "apparent unwillingness . . . to facilitate delivery to the Resistance forces of food, clothing, and medical supplies" and about Ortega's "threats to launch a military offensive against the Resistance."[13] César boasted that these Democrats alone "represent[ed] the votes needed to change the U.S. Congress' decision on the approval of military aid."[14]

The Sandinistas had been taking a firm hand with unarmed opponents, as well as with the contras. At the end of April a two-month-old wildcat strike of construction workers erupted, provoked by the plummeting economy and the government's futile efforts to control wages and prices. Dozens of workers had begun hunger strikes, and their plight united the entire spectrum of opposition parties and unions, from far left to far right.

On April 26 the 14 opposition parties suspended their dialogue with the Sandinistas in sympathy with the strikers. Three days later Sandinista riot police wielding rubber truncheons broke up a crowd of several hundred workers and arrested dozens in a raid on one left-wing labor federation.[15] A few days later leaders of the 14 opposition parties were arrested and held for several hours after marching to the headquarters of the besieged union.[16] Over the next week the Interior Ministry banned the news broadcasts of three opposition radio stations, including Radio Catolica, because of their reporting on the strike. On May 14 the government instituted new rules to restrict news reports on the economy and the draft. "The Sandinistas see the contras falling apart, and they see the United States not disposed to help them," one opposition leader told reporters. "They feel that they now control the situation which means there's no reason to compromise on anything."[17]

In Washington, however, the Sandinistas' actions brought threats of renewed aid to the contras. Another letter from Democrats warned Ortega "that actions taken by your government will not only effect events in Nicaragua, but in Washington as well."[18] Speaker Wright himself came under fire. Wright was loath to declare that the Sandinistas were violating the terms of the Sapoa agreement, since to do so would have provided President Reagan the pretext to demand a quick vote on new aid.[19] The *Washington Post*, however, assailed Wright for not putting more pressure on the Sandinistas. Noting the Sandinistas' "hard line in cease-fire talks with the contras," the *Post* expected from Wright "the kind of words to the Sandinistas that would tend to balance the odds. . . . Instead there is earnest counsel to both sides to bargain in good faith and get the negotiations back on track. It is a pathetic performance."[20] A group of Senators and House members from both parties were preparing a bill for new aid that they threatened to introduce on June 1 if the Sandinistas were not more forthcoming. On May 26, Congressman Hyde surprised the Democratic leadership by proposing from the floor an amendment to the Intelligence Authorization bill allowing covert aid in the next fiscal year, and although the amendment failed by a margin of 214–190, it served as a warning to the Sandinistas that another attempt might succeed later if they were not careful.

The Sandinistas hurried to quell the building storm. Vice President Sergio Ramírez rushed to Washington to meet with Wright and "to clear up any misunderstandings about our intentions that Mr. Wright might have." Ramírez assured the Speaker the Sandinistas were not doing anything to stand in the way of deliveries to the contras, that they were not insisting on the Red Cross, and that any number of organizations could begin delivering supplies "tomorrow if possible."[21] Wright declared himself satisfied with Ramírez's explanations. Daniel Ortega announced the Sandinistas' intention to renew the cease-fire for another 30 days at the end of May, and he disavowed any plan to launch a new offensive against contra forces. Vice Foreign Minister Tinoco made a surprise visit to Miami and proposed a new round of talks with the contras at the end of the month, just two days before the Sapoa truce was due to expire.

The warnings from Congress buoyed the contras' hopes as they began the next round of talks. Reassured that the United States would not leave them to starve or be destroyed by the Sandinista army, contra negotiators had no reason to make only minimal demands of the Sandinistas. At the end of May they called for the establishment of a "new institutional order" in Nicaragua, which included the separation and independence of the army, the government, and the judicial system from the Sandinista Party, the elimination of compulsory membership in Sandinista mass organizations, the elimination of obligatory military service, guarantees for "unrestricted freedom of expression, including the opening and maintaining of private television channels," and a guarantee of the right to strike.[22] Wary of the Sandinistas' past record of proclaiming such principles without abiding by them, the contras also insisted that the Sandinistas agree to a timetable of specific steps to carry out the proposed reforms. They demanded agreement on a schedule for national and local elections, and specifically for the holding of elections by January 31, 1989, for a constituent assembly that would draft a new constitution. Only when these actions had been carried out, and were then verified by Cardinal Obando and the secretary general of the OAS, would the contras lay down their arms and reintegrate themselves into Nicaraguan political life.

To many observers, the contras' demands at the end of May seemed ridiculously extreme, especially in light of their military predicament. The contras clearly did not design their proposal with a view to winning the Sandinistas' acceptance. When asked what would be required to bring a more democratic government to Nicaragua, however, opposition leaders, both armed and unarmed, had always given the same answers. The contras' proposal was no more extreme than the others presented by Nicaraguan opposition leaders throughout the 1980s. It repeated demands made by Cruz and other opposition leaders in the San José document of March 1985.[23] It was almost identical to the nine-point platform the Democratic Coordinadora put forward in December 1983.[24] It contained many, but not all, of the seventeen proposed changes in the Sandinista constitution that opposition political and business leaders had been calling for since 1987. Citing the Sandinistas' commitments at Esquipulas, the contras now insisted that if a cease-fire were to be accompanied by democratization, these were the measures the Sandinistas would have to adopt. If such demands were declared "unreasonable," Alfredo César asserted, "then the resistance is not negotiating democracy in Nicaragua, but surrender."[25]

The contras, under the protection of the American Congress, had no reason to ask for less, and they could hope that if the Sandinistas rejected their proposal, the Congress might even vote them new aid. In this hope all the contra leaders were united: César hoped a new aid bill would strengthen his hand in the next round of talks, and Bermúdez hoped that he could resume the war and continue it into the next administration.

If the contras had no reason to ask for less than the maximum at the end of May, however, the Sandinistas had no reason to concede more than the minimum. Indeed, because of the ambivalent posture of the American Congress, neither side had any incentive to make the kinds of important political and military concessions that might make agreement possible. The Sandinistas' military situation was more favorable than it had been in two years. Since Congress cut off military aid to the contras, the dire circumstances the Sandinistas faced at the end of 1987 had improved considerably. So long as the Sandinistas did nothing to provoke a renewal of that aid, they like the contras did not have to fear defeat. Why, then, should they make the kinds of political concessions that could cost them control of the situation in Nicaragua and possibly lead to the very defeat they had avoided? The Sandinistas' mortal enemy, Ronald Reagan, was a few months from retirement, and Democratic presidential nominee Michael Dukakis, who had declared the contra war "immoral and illegal," was leading Vice President Bush by as many as ten points in the polls. As Sergio Ramírez put it, President Reagan's policy was in "complete ruins." The administration was "no longer able to reconstruct a policy against Nicaragua." Under the circumstances, Ramírez argued, the contras simply lacked the "military or political strength to impose their viewpoints at the bargaining table. . . . Two months from now they won't even be able to get what they can get now. . . . What we are working out here is a negotiated end to a war that is already over."[26] The Sandinistas had no reason to make dangerous concessions in May; if they could hold on until November and avoid a renewal of the war, then they might even be rid of the contras altogether by January 1989. They believed, moreover, that they had a hidden card still to play.

That card was Alfredo César. By the end of May César had emerged from the contras' internal struggles stronger than ever. He had been elected chief negotiator by his fellow directors in place of Calero. His private conversations with the Sandinistas' American lawyer, Paul Reichler, had continued and become more important. On May 23 César and Reichler met for several hours in Miami and for the first time discussed the broad outlines of a possible agreement. Over the next two weeks César held several private meetings with Sandinista leaders and representatives, unbeknownst to his fellow negotiators. The talks, therefore, proceeded on two levels: one, a public exchange between Sandinista and contra negotiators in a formal manner, the other, an informal discussion among César, Reichler, and the Ortegas. What transpired in the second remains almost entirely shrouded in secrecy.

In the formal discussions the Sandinistas and contras had little difficulty agreeing on many general points. "Unrestricted freedom of expression," "legal guarantees," "fair trial," "free and fair elections"—such phrases or their equal could be found in the Esquipulas accords, the Contadora draft treaties, and indeed in the Sandinista constitution. As the negotiations proceeded, therefore, the Sandinistas repeatedly declared that there was agreement on "80 percent" of the subjects under discussion.[27] It was the other 20 percent, however, where César and the other contra negotiators believed major concessions had to be made.

The most important difference between the two sides concerned the timing of the contras' disarmament. Under the Sandinistas' proposal, the contras would lay down their arms after the agreements were reached in the national dialogue. But the contras feared that by the time the government-controlled National Assembly got around to turning political agreements into law, under the Sandinistas' plan the contras would already be disarmed.[28] The contras, therefore, proposed that they not lay down their weapons until after Cardinal Obando and OAS Secretary General Baena Soares certified that the reforms agreed upon in the national dialogue had actually been enacted.

When the Sandinistas presented their counterproposal the next day, it incorporated verbatim six of the most general points from the contras' proposal but gave no specific dates for elections. On issues such as the separation of the army and the party, the Sandinistas' wording was vague and ambiguous. Humberto Ortega told reporters he didn't expect to have to make any changes in the Sandinista military in any case. "We are not afraid to discuss these points in the dialogue because our Army has already been moving for several years in that direction." César declared the counterproposal "incomplete." The Sandinistas, he claimed, refused to be pinned down; they would discuss broad issues of democratic reform, but "when we try to turn it into black and white, they avoid putting commitments into writing."[29]

The private discussions between César and the Sandinista negotiators also ranged over these issues. Reichler later claimed that he and César agreed that the national dialogue would take up six broad issues of democratic reform, such as "free expression" and "free elections," with the understanding that specific legal measures would then be enacted to carry out those reforms. In return for these assurances, the contras would agree to lay down their weapons. According to Reichler's account, César said he could sign such an agreement but doubted that Bermúdez would unless he were able to persuade Secretary Shultz to put pressure on Bermúdez. César denied that he ever made this offer. According to César's account, he and Reichler had identified several issues on which Reichler thought the Sandinistas could be flexible. César said he never committed the contras to any deal, however, and Reichler didn't commit the Sandinistas.[30]

What other questions were discussed in these conversations has been a matter of controversy. César, according to Humberto Ortega, said he wanted to run for president in 1990 and was prepared to make concessions in exchange for a guarantee from the Sandinistas that he would be allowed to run in a fair contest, perhaps even with the Sandinistas' support. The Sandinistas later recounted one evening when Humberto Ortega met for several hours with César and probed him for points of compromise in the contras' proposal. According to Reichler, César said the demand for a new constitution was negotiable, but when Ortega continued to press him, César broke off the discussions and abruptly left. The next day César publicly warned that if no agreement were reached with the Sandinistas, the contras would suspend the talks, allow the cease-fire to lapse, and go back to Congress for more assistance.

The contras did not end the talks, however, but called for another round to begin on June 7. César departed for Washington, and during the first week of June he met with Speaker Wright, moderate Democrats, and conservative Republicans and administration officials, including Elliott Abrams. He told Wright that a deal with the Sandinistas was practically completed; he could guarantee a majority of the contra directorate would vote for it, although he was unsure about Bermúdez.[31] César told reporters the Sandinistas had agreed to six of the contras' nine points and if they agreed to the other three a permanent cease-fire could be signed during the next round of talks. César even won the support of Elliott Abrams. He told Wright that for the first time Abrams had advised the contras to make the best deal they could. César publicly proclaimed that "If we decide we've got a good agreement, it will have the considered support of all the important sectors in Washington."[32]

César's statements were clearly meant to inform the Sandinistas that if they accepted his terms for agreement, he could deliver the contras and the Americans. No contra leader had ever been in a stronger position to make a deal. If Bermúdez refused to accept an agreement based on the nine points described by César to Abrams and others, he would be isolated. On the other hand, César could not accept any deal that fell far short of agreement on these nine points.

The fact that César was thus committed to a position seems to have convinced the Sandinistas that the first part of their strategy had failed. The "positive sign from Abrams," Nicaraguan officials later claimed, "immediately provoked the Sandinistas' suspicions."[33] It must have suggested to them that César was not going to play the role they had hoped for. Whether this was because he had not gotten what he wanted in his private talks, or because he could not bring the rest of the contras to agree to what the Sandinistas were officially offering, or both, can only be guessed.

The other contra leaders were certainly nervous about César's activities. He still had told them nothing about his talks with Reichler, but they had found out. The night before resuming talks with the Sandinistas, Bermúdez and Sanchez visited César in his hotel room. According to César, Bermúdez said, "I know you're talking to Reichler." César claims Bermúdez understood that he was acting "in good faith" and that the contra general didn't mind the private talks. But Bermúdez nevertheless confronted César directly: "What I want to know is whether I can trust your position—are you selling us out?" César promised Bermúdez he would "never agree to positions that are not those of the Nicaraguan Resistance."[34]

During the negotiations in Managua on June 8, the Sandinistas were troubled to find César deferring to Bermúdez rather than steering the contra delegation toward compromise. After the first day of talks, Vice

Foreign Minister Tinoco told reporters "a series of factors is coming together that reveals a conspiracy to break off the talks and blame the government." Bermúdez, speaking for the contras, declared that "the climate of the talks has deteriorated a lot. It's reinforcing our sense that we must proceed with caution." César complained again that whenever the contras tried to put issues "into black and white, they [the Sandinistas] avoid putting commitments into writing," especially on the question of elections. Vice Foreign Minister Tinoco admitted that this was the case: "If we begin to discuss democracy here, we get tangled up, because Sandinist revolutionary democracy could mean one thing, and we do not even know what democracy means to the contras." But Reichler said he was "getting a building feeling [the contras] don't really want an accord. They want to go back to Washington and ask for more military aid."[35]

The Sandinistas, therefore, went ahead with the second part of their plan. On the morning of June 9 they presented a new proposal during the morning session, and César and the other contra leaders rejected it. When the negotiators broke at midday, Reichler held a press conference to reveal his secret meetings with César. Reichler claimed César had "failed to fulfill his word of honor" and that Bermúdez was "holding Alfredo César hostage." When César and the other contra negotiators heard about Reichler's press conference, they hurriedly prepared a final proposal—lest they be held accountable for flatly rejecting the Sandinistas' plan. The contras' final proposal not only maintained all previous demands but added some new ones. The Sandinistas cried foul, and claimed that the contras were delivering an ultimatum at the eleventh hour. The meeting broke up in violent acrimony. Humberto Ortega accused César of going back on his word and warned that the next time the two sides met, they would be shooting and the contras would be among the dead. Ortega insisted the contra negotiators could not leave Nicaragua until he said so. The contras departed nevertheless, and the talks finally and officially collapsed.

The truth about what César and the Sandinistas really discussed may never be known. What seems clear is that the two sides had engaged in an elaborate, multi-dimensional game. César may well have tried to strike a deal with the Sandinistas that abandoned some of the contras' key demands, in the hope that the resulting deal would eventually clear the way for a political opening. If César privately offered a deal different from the one he discussed with Abrams and the other contras leaders, however, one wonders how he expected to get his own side to agree. Bermúdez and the fighters he represented had no interest in compromising their basic position.

In the end, César's intrigues could not bridge the gap between the contras and the Sandinistas. As Stephen Kinzer put it, "Contra leaders refused to order their troops to disarm until they had iron-clad guarantees of sweeping political reform. The Sandinistas were not prepared to offer any such concessions before a complete contra surrender."[36] The ambivalence of American policy practically insured this stalemate. The intransigence on both sides was the product of a divided American Congress which could not choose between abandoning the contras and letting them fight the Sandinistas.

55

Crackdown at Nandaime

The opposing sides in the contra aid debate in Washington predictably disagreed about who was to blame for the breakdown of the talks. Congressman Bonior accepted entirely the Sandinistas' account of events in Managua and blamed the contras alone for the breakdown of talks, insisting they had "walked away from a proposal that met virtually all their previous demands for democratization." The contras, he charged, were "not sincerely interested in peace."[1] Wright claimed he did not know who was to blame for the breakdown of the talks, but in any case he insisted he would not be bound by his March 30 commitment to give Reagan a quick vote on aid.[2] While conservatives in Congress were eager to provide the contras what they needed to "reconstitute themselves so they could fight," César and other contra leaders found the House Democratic leadership hostile to their request for more aid.[3] Wright warned the Reagan administration against seeking new military aid, insisting that "the armistice of the past several weeks is surely preferable to the bloodshed of the past several years."[4] Wright and Bonior told the contras they might eventually win an extension of humanitarian aid, but military aid was out of the question. Moderate Democrats were only slightly more encouraging. Congressman McCurdy said there was "little appetite" among his colleagues for another vote on aid at the moment. But he warned that the Sandinistas should not be "sanguine about delaying and expecting this to go away. It is a long time between now and October."⁵

The problem for the contras was that the United States was moving quickly into the election season, and the remainder of the congressional session was truncated. If Congress did not vote on aid by the end of June, the Democratic convention in the middle of July, followed by the Republican convention and a three-week congressional recess in August, virtually precluded any vote on aid before September.⁶

The Reagan administration itself was in no mood to rush ahead with a vote on contra aid, however. In the week after the contras left Managua, administration officials and even the President himself appeared reluctant to discuss another vote. On June 15 Reagan declared that the need for new aid to the contras was "so apparent" that it couldn't possibly be opposed, but when asked when he planned to propose new aid, Reagan gave no answer. Even when conservative congressmen pressed him privately and urged him to take the lead in the battle for aid, the President refused to make any commitments.⁷ The strong opposition by Wright and other House Democratic leaders was reason enough for the President's hesitation.

The onset of the presidential campaign helped shape the Reagan administration's approach. Vice President Bush had said little about the contras since securing the nomination, and his advisers let it be known they had little enthusiasm for a new battle over such a controversial issue in the closing months of the campaign.⁸ With the investigations of the Iran-contra special prosecutor continuing, and with frequently recurring allegations of Bush's or his staff's possible involvement in or knowledge of North's operations, the Vice President had an interest in keeping contras off the voter's mind. Governor Michael Dukakis's constant reference to the Reagan administration's "illegal" war was an attempt to exploit this vulnerability.

By the end of June, in fact, the Reagan administration was already beginning to set the contras aside as the principal tool of its Nicaragua policy. Under the direction of Secretary Shultz, now uncontested in his control of that policy, the administration began to abandon military pressure on Nicaragua and to seek other means. Shultz, hoping to make the most of a weak hand, scheduled a trip to Central America for the end of June, his first since 1984. His goal was to rally the four democratic governments in a "forward strategy" to demand enforcement of the democratization provisions of the Esquipulas agreement. Shultz hoped Arias might even become a mediator in the talks between the Nicaraguans, a role Arias himself was considering. The secretary of state had no illusions that the new strategy would necessarily bear fruit. "We are where we are," he told reporters after his trip. "That's my attitude. We work with the things we have to work with."[9]

The Reagan administration also gave greater attention to the opposition political parties, the labor unions, and the anti-Sandinista media in Nicaragua. The new American ambassador, Richard Melton, who had presented his credentials in Managua in April, took a more vigorous part than past ambassadors in encouraging the opposition to unify and to challenge the government to make good on its promises of reform. The administration was not alone in this effort to assist the opposition; in the American Congress it remained the one issue that united liberals and conservatives. In May the conservative Republican Mickey Edwards and the liberal Democrat Peter Kostmayer had proposed legislation to provide opposition parties, unions, and independent media $1 million through the National Endowment for Democracy (NED). In the Senate a bill providing $2 million through the NED passed the appropriations committee on June 22.

President Arias enthusiastically endorsed the administration's change of course. The theory of the Arias plan, widely praised by Democrats in Congress, was that the battleground in Nicaragua should be shifted from the military to the political front. After meeting with Shultz in San José on July 1, Arias declared that pressure on the Sandinistas "should not be imposed by once again firing rifles that have already been silenced . . . but by making them keep the promises they made at Esquipulas."[10]

The new strategy was a boon to the opposition in Nicaragua. The Guatemala accords were supposed to have given the unarmed opposition the leading role in demanding political reforms and to have placed them in the international spotlight. Ever since the Sandinistas had agreed to talk with the contras, in August 1987 however, the opposition in Managua had been shunted to the side. To be sure, the government had been forced to give the opposition greater freedom, so as to avoid a renewal of military aid to the contras, but while the opposition was freer to speak its mind, the world had not been paying much attention. Now the unarmed opposition could hope to have the best of both worlds: a Sandinista government still reluctant to clamp down for fear of angering the American Congress, and the full attention of the international community no longer distracted by the contras. The new ambassador, Richard Melton, and his staff did little more than play the role of cheerleader for the opposition, but this was enough to instill a new and almost giddy self-confidence.[11] The money voted for the opposition by Congress promised to support their activities long into the future and also served to underline the concern of the American government for their well-being.

The opposition leaders, and discontented Nicaraguans generally, were increasingly losing their fear of the Sandinista government. Nicaragua's economic troubles, which were surpassing even the most pessimistic predictions of a year earlier, had given opposition forces a steady supply of issues on which to attack the government and to enlist the support of the discontented. In this bolder mood, opposition leaders had begun talking openly about the need for a "government of national salvation," in which opposition politicians, businessmen, and technocrats would be brought in to share power and save Nicaraguan society. Coordinadora President Carlos Huembes publicly raised this challenge during a meeting on July 3 at which Ambassador Melton was present. The opposition leaders planned to meet with President Arias in the second week of July and invite him to mediate between the government and its opponents.[12] The opposition consciously set out to replicate the events of 1978, to make the comparison between Somoza then and the Sandinistas ten years later and, most importantly, to declare that once again an unhappy, oppressed people called out to the world for help against a tottering but still defiant dictatorship.

The Sandinistas understood perfectly well what their opponents were up to and how the activities of the opposition fit in with the shift in American policy and with the reawakening activism of President Arias. On July 10 the Sandinistas responded to the opposition's challenge. The occasion was an opposition rally at Nandaime. The historical significance of Nandaime was understood on both sides. In March of 1981 an opposition rally organized by Robelo's Nicaraguan Democratic Movement (MDN) had been disrupted by Sandinista mobs ordered into the streets by the government, and the *turbas* had burned down the MDN's headquarters in Nandaime. That event had marked a symbolic end of the Sandinista-bourgeois governing alliance and had been followed a few months later by the arrest of the most prominent opposition leaders. Now, in the days leading up to the Nandaime rally seven years later, Sandinista officials made clear their aim to see history repeated. "Remember there was a time when we burned down a house to prevent reactionaries from taking over the streets of Nandaime," one Sandinista told reporters in the first week of July. "This time we're ready to burn ten houses."[13]

The Sandinistas would later claim that the government police were "provoked" and physically attacked by the opposition at Nandaime. Accounts of the violence at Nandaime, however, especially that of the *New York Times*'s Stephen Kinzer, left no doubt that the clash was a premeditated show of force by the government. Days before the rally, a Sandinista official called an opposition leader with some friendly advice: "Some new repression is coming. We've decided to crack down. Don't send your people to Nandaime. We're going to kick ass down there." On the day of the rally, Kinzer recalls, "it took only a moment to see that the police were preparing for something extraordinary." The hundreds of officers lining the streets "seemed prepared for all-out war. Each carried an AK-47 assault rifle and extra ammunition clips. Some wore gas masks and bullet-proof vests." Several thousand opposition activists in the square were chanting anti-Sandinista slogans. The police shouted back and waved their clubs threateningly, but the chanting continued. Emilio Alvarez, the aging veteran of opposition against both Somoza and the Sandinistas, called out to Kinzer: "People aren't afraid any more. It means the Sandinistas' days are numbered." When Conservative party leader Miriam Arguello finally rose to speak, however, scuffling broke out at the back of the crowd. Perhaps some of the unarmed demonstrators attacked the heavily equipped army of police, as the Sandinistas later alleged, but in Kinzer's opinion the police "apparently had orders to escalate the provocations until there was a violent response." The police waded into the crowd and began firing tear-gas grenades. The first explosions dispersed the crowd immediately, but the "police were not satisfied with that." They fired more grenades and began chasing those fleeing, clubbing them as they ran, and kicking them when they fell. Kinzer himself was attacked by a policeman, who knocked him to the ground with his rifle butt.[14]

That day and the next Sandinista police arrested more than 40 protesters, including prominent opposition leaders. The president of the Coordinadora, Carlos Huembes, the leader of the Social Christian Party, Augustín Jarquín, and Conservative Party faction leader Miriam Arguello, were thrown in jail and summarily sentenced to six-month prison terms for "inciting" attacks on the police. State-run television showed Arguello in prison garb in her cell, looking worn and battered. Within the next 24 hours, the government ordered Radio Catolica and a handful of other private radio stations off the air for reporting "inaccurately" about the protest. *La Prensa* was ordered closed for 15 days. The government's account of the violence at Nandaime was that "the right-wing parties, *La*

Prensa, and unarmed contras, known as the civic opposition, incited incidents and attacked police in Nandaime." This "provocation," moreover, had been planned and orchestrated by the American embassy.[15] On July 11 Foreign Minister D'Escoto called Ambassador Melton to the Foreign Ministry and informed him that he and seven embassy employees were being expelled from the country. Melton was given 72 hours to leave Nicaragua.

The violent crackdown at Nandaime inaugurated five months of domestic repression and diplomatic intransigence by the Sandinistas. The arrested opposition leaders remained in jail awaiting trial until December, despite the pleas of Arias and other world leaders for their release. Relations between the United States and Nicaragua were severed, *de facto* if not *de jure*, when the Reagan administration expelled Ambassador Tunnermann in retaliation, leaving both countries without ambassadors for the remainder of the year. Secretary Shultz's new diplomatic initiative perished at birth, as the Sandinistas denounced his efforts to isolate them and called on their neighbors not to lend themselves to American aggression. A deeply dismayed President Arias tried briefly to persuade the Sandinistas to lift their repression and return to the reformist path, but he ran into an obdurate and defiant Daniel Ortega and had to retreat and wait for a better opportunity.

The Sandinistas' behavior in the summer and fall of 1988 was a great disappointment and embarrassment to those in Washington and Latin America who had hoped for moderation after the Sapoa agreement had virtually ended the war. Speaker Wright criticized the Sandinistas' "gravely serious and lamentable act of bad judgment and bad faith"; David Bonior complained that the crackdown at Nandaime could "only serve to heighten tensions at a time when diplomatic solutions should be pursued";[16] Senator Dodd called the Sandinistas' actions a "colossal blunder." President Arias openly lamented that while he had "always thought that the Sandinistas' steps toward a more pluralistic society and their compliance with the democratization stipulated by the peace plan [were] irreversible," he now found that this was not so. The Sandinistas had "unmasked themselves, proving to the world that there is no political will in Managua, that they were not honest when they committed themselves to democratize to comply with the accords."[17]

Some of the most outspoken critics of the Reagan administration traced the cause of the Sandinistas' tough behavior to the Reagan administration's own hard-line policies. One journalist charged that the contras' intransigence in Managua at the beginning of June had "handed Sandinista hard-liners the excuse for a domestic crackdown."[18] Speaker Wright created a scandal in September when he charged that the CIA had intentionally incited violent demonstrations to provoke the Sandinistas. Opponents of the contra war did their best to suggest that the Sandinistas' turn to a hard line was further evidence that the Reagan administration's aggressive policies were an abject failure. President Arias suggested that the Sandinistas' repressive actions in the last half of 1988 proved that they feared a political struggle with their unarmed opponents in Managua more than they feared continued war with the contras. Arias even implied, and some Nicaraguan opposition leaders declared openly, that the Sandinistas' actions in July were designed to provoke Congress to renew the war because the Sandinistas needed the "pretext" of the contras to justify their repression.[19]

But Arias knew perfectly well that the absence of any threat of renewed contra aid had made the Sandinistas more defiant, not less. The Sandinistas had been most flexible and moderate when the Reagan administration and the contras had been most warlike and intransigent: at the end of 1987 and the beginning of 1988. In January, with Congress poised to approve new aid for the contras unless the Sandinistas made concessions, they had clearly chosen the political struggle over war. It was only after Congress and the Reagan administration had abandoned a military role for the contras and had sought to pursue diplomatic avenues that the Sandinistas had cracked down in Nicaragua. The choice between the political struggle and war no longer existed, for by July 1988 the Sandinistas did not have to fear that their domestic crackdown would lead to a renewal of military aid to the contras.

After Nandaime the Senate passed a resolution condemning the "blatant" violations of human rights but warned only that continued failure to observe the peace accords and make democratic reforms "*could* cause Congress to reconsider the provision of additional humanitarian and other appropriate assistance, including military aid, if conditions so warrant."[20] A House resolution passed the next day did not even contain that warning.[21] President Reagan, asked by reporters on July 15 if he was in favor of more military aid for the contras, responded "You bet I am," but anonymous senior administration officials quickly explained that there was no desire in the White House or in the Bush campaign to fight for more military aid.[22]

On August 10 a bill extending "humanitarian" aid through March of

1989 passed the Senate narrowly, and the next day the House and Senate left Washington for a month-long recess.[23] The Sandinistas always knew that if they wanted to force a renewal of military aid to the contras, they had only to launch an offensive against the contras in Nicaragua or in Honduras. The temptation to strike another deadly blow at the demoralized rebel forces must have been great, but the Sandinistas assiduously avoided any hint of offensive action and, quite the contrary, repeatedly renewed the cease-fire.

56

"The Revolution Stays and Reagan Leaves"

In the last months of 1988 the Sandinistas knew that the Reagan administration, in Daniel Ortega's words, had "shot its bolt." Congress would take no further action for the remainder of the year, and the matter of contra aid would not be addressed in Washington until 1989 under a new American president. The most important development for the Sandinistas was the end of the Reagan presidency, and they had begun celebrating early.

"The revolution stays and Reagan leaves," Daniel Ortega proclaimed triumphantly at the July 19 celebration of the revolution's ninth anniversary.[1] Surviving eight years of Reagan was a great accomplishment for the Sandinistas; surviving the next American president promised to be much easier, especially if that president was Michael Dukakis. Despite choosing Senator Lloyd Bentsen, a longtime supporter of the contras, as his running-mate, Dukakis had made his opposition to the contra policy abundantly clear. In his acceptance speech at the Democratic convention he declared that the "greatest threat to our national security in this hemisphere is not the Sandinistas," but drugs. President Ortega suggested in July that if Dukakis were elected, there would be "hope for a new dialogue with the United States."[2]

That dialogue was now the paramount goal of Sandinista foreign policy. The Sandinistas were desperate for help to resuscitate their failing economy, which in 1988 had become too grave to ignore. It was no longer a question of hoping for higher coffee prices or a good cotton crop or a few million dollars more in aid from the Scandinavian countries. Neither private nor state-owned businesses were exporting enough to begin to meet the nation's needs. Nicaraguan goods could not compete in foreign markets because of high labor and production costs, bad management, and a lack of capital investment in equipment and technology. Crop yields were steadily declining because of a lack of hard currency to buy fertilizer and other needed supplies, a problem made worse by the American embargo.

To pay for a bloated state budget and a plethora of state subsidies, the government in 1987 had printed more currency and contributed to a hyperinflation which by the summer of 1988 was at least 10,000 percent. To respond to the crisis, the government had imposed new austerity measures in February 1988: a drastic devaluation of the currency, to make exports more competitive; cuts in the national budget, which by the end of the year would theoretically require thousands of lay-offs from state sector jobs; and a reduction of subsidies, resulting in increases in the prices of basic goods. The result of these austerity measures was a dramatic loss of purchasing power for the average Nicaraguan and a sharp decline in the standard of living from already low levels. Worse still, from the Sandinistas' point of view, those Nicaraguans hurt the most by these austerity measures were the core of the revolution's constituency: the urban workers and state-sector employees. All the pain caused by the austerity measures in February, moreover, had not improved the situation. Further "adjustments" were required in June and then again in the fall. The currency had to be further devalued more than half a dozen times over the course of the year.

Whether any amount of foreign assistance could have helped the Nicaraguan economy under Sandinista rule is debatable. But Nicaraguan government officials believed large amounts of foreign aid were essential to their survival—to prop up the failing currency, to help meet the foreign debt, to obtain additional loans, to encourage investment and attract business—and it was quite obvious that the money could come only from the United States and the West. The Soviet Union had reached the limits of its generosity, in terms of economic assistance. While in 1979 the Sandinistas had sought to reject the "notion of reconstruction based on massive infusions of foreign capital," therefore, it was precisely such infusions they hoped for in 1989 when a new American president took office.

Even as they cracked down in the last months of 1988, therefore, the

Sandinistas were aware that a time of bargaining with the Nicaraguan bourgeoisie lay ahead. First, they knew that any agreement with the United States would involve providing more political "space" to the opposition. Second, any resuscitation of the economy required the active participation and cooperation of the bourgeoisie, the independent businessmen, managers, and technocrats that the revolution had so badly alienated. Socialism as an economic strategy was all but discredited in Nicaragua. Even Soviet officials were advising the Sandinistas to move away from a command economy toward freer markets, and the Sandinistas, independently of Soviet advice, had begun to enact their own form of *perestroika*. As Carlos Chamorro, the editor of *Barricada*, wrote in September, "the new economic policy has invalidated a series of concepts that for years represented . . . a road map towards . . . the Revolution's economic agenda. . . . 'Social control,' 'secure channels,' 'price controls,' 'government subsidy,' 'preferential prices for the peasantry,' etc., are banners of a bygone era that has been left behind by reality." Chamorro noted approvingly that "efficiency is finally becoming a guiding parameter in decisionmaking." The Sandinistas' "survival economy" was in many respects a program to aid private producers, especially of the most profitable exports like meat and coffee, at the expense of consumers and workers. While Chamorro and other Sandinista leaders worried that the sectors of society most hurt by the changes—that is, "those who neither own nor run businesses"—would turn against the revolution, they agreed that the "change was unassailable and necessary." More and more the Sandinista government was taking advice from bourgeois technocrats, and the "predominant emphasis these days," Chamorro noted, was the "unquestionable importance that is being attached to the need to restore 'management skills.'"[3] Tomás Borge lamented that "these eight years of war have caused the FSLN's political decline," but even Borge agreed that political and economic compromises with the opposition were unavoidable.[4]

The crackdown at Nandaime and the repression that followed may have been, paradoxically, the first step in the Sandinistas' new strategy of compromise with the bourgeoisie. It was precisely because the Sandinistas recognized their increasing economic reliance on the private sector that they determined to limit its political "space" in the summer and fall of 1988, lest the bourgeoisie's power grow overwhelming in the coming difficult phase of the struggle.

The risks were similar to those the Sandinistas faced in the early days of the revolution, when their alliance with the bourgeoisie, so necessary for gaining the acquiescence of the West in the revolutionary triumph, had nevertheless posed a threat to the consolidation and further advancement of the revolution. Then the Sandinistas had feared that in the process of reconstructing the nation's devastated economy, the bourgeoisie would use the financial power of its imperialist allies to strengthen its own political power at the Sandinistas' expense. Then the Sandinistas had sought economic independence from the West to avoid the "shackling" of their economy to "the extortionist policies of imperialism." They had abandoned the moderation of "tercerismo" in favor of a more rapid consolidation of revolutionary power. The pretense of nonalignment had given way to a conspicuous effort to win full membership in the Soviet bloc.

Nine years later, however, the Sandinistas were reversing themselves. Instead of seeking economic independence from the West they were in desperate need of economic reintegration. Instead of relying solely on the strength and resources of an ascendant Soviet bloc, the Sandinistas were hedging their bets as that great empire appeared to fall behind in its long competition with the United States. Instead of brazenly defying American power, the Sandinistas, with as much dignity as possible, were bending to the new correlation of forces. They were not moving away from the strategy of "tercerismo," as the crackdown after Nandaime made it appear, but back towards it.

Whether the Sandinistas' new strategy could work depended on the willingness of the United States to ease the political, military, and economic pressures on Nicaragua in return for greater political "space" for the bourgeois opposition. In the summer of 1988, the prospects for such a deal appeared bright. The polls in July showed Michael Dukakis ten points ahead of Vice President Bush. The Sandinistas were under no illusion that even a Dukakis administration would embrace them,[5] but a Democratic president was more likely than a Republican to agree to "normalize" relations with a Sandinista government. As the Sandinistas cracked down on their opponents, therefore, they looked forward hopefully to a victory by Michael Dukakis, which would allow them to lift the repression a bit without fear of renewed American pressure.

Those hopes melted away in September and October, however, along with the Massachusetts governor's lead in the polls. By the beginning of October a Bush victory seemed likely, and the Sandinistas quickly began adjusting their strategy to this unfortunate change of circumstances.

It was not all bad news. The Sandinistas knew that the election of Reagan's Vice President would not necessarily mean a continuation of Reagan's policy toward Nicaragua. They recognized, as most American observers did, that Bush did "not have the same commitment that President Reagan had to the Nicaraguan counterrevolution."[6] His campaign revealed that he was wary and weary of the battles with Congress, and his chief adviser, James Baker, was known to have insisted that White House officials avoid controversial battles over contra aid during the election season.[7] Bush's few declarations of support for the contras were assumed, in Washington and in Managua, to be directed at a suspicious Republican right wing. "Even if Mr. Bush wins," Ortega speculated, "he will not make the same mistakes Reagan made." The next administration, "whether Republican or Democrat," would have learned "from the failures, mistakes, and discrediting of the Reagan administration's policy."[8]

Nevertheless, despite Bush's personal lack of enthusiasm for the contras, the Sandinistas also knew it would be very difficult for the Republican president simply to "extricate himself" from his party's long-standing policy of support for the rebels.[9] "What's important is to understand that President Bush can't abandon the contras," Daniel Ortega declared.[10] Bush's strategy would be to continue supporting the rebels "to try to win as many important concessions as possible from the revolution."[11]

Even before Bush's victory on November 8, therefore, the Sandinistas set out on a two-pronged strategy to meet the more difficult challenge posed by a Bush administration. On the one hand, they tried to persuade Bush advisers of their desire for a peaceful settlement of the U.S.-Nicaraguan conflict. In public the Sandinistas spoke warmly of the President-elect, contrasting his presumed "pragmatism" with the zealotry of his predecessor. Daniel Ortega publicly hinted at a possible deal on issues "which supposedly worry Washington the most," like the "alleged shipment of weapons by Nicaragua to revolutionary movements in various countries."[12] At international gatherings Ortega took every opportunity to seek out Bush, and Sandinista officials practically pleaded with Bush advisers for the beginning of even an informal dialogue. The Sandinistas' overtures were systematically rebuffed: President-elect Bush was not about to begin "normalizing" relations with the Sandinistas before his inauguration. The Sandinistas nevertheless hoped their entreaties would eventually bear fruit. Given Bush's difficulty with the Republican right wing, Humberto Ortega recalls, the Sandinistas knew they would have to "provide concessions for a long time without expecting anything in return."[13]

While trying to woo the Bush team, therefore, the Sandinistas also tried to speed up the diplomatic process during the last months of 1988 in an effort to present the new administration with a *fait accompli* by January. Starting in October, they pressed for an early summit of the five Central American presidents to reach final agreement on a plan to disarm the contras, dismantle their bases, and establish an international force on the border with Honduras to verify the removal of rebel forces.[14]

The waning influence of the United States in Central America, made more visible by the humiliating failure of Shultz's initiative in July, had opened a broad avenue for the Sandinistas' diplomacy. The "Tegucigalpa bloc" of Honduras, Guatemala, El Salvador, and Costa Rica was splintered. Guatemala's President Cerezo joined the Sandinistas in urging the Honduran government to accept a border verification agreement. President Duarte, who had been so energetic in the diplomatic activities of 1987, was suffering from inoperable cancer and took little part in the diplomatic maneuverings throughout the fall and winter of 1988. The Honduran government was facing new presidential elections and was looking for relief from its support of the contras.

The Hondurans, in fact, were facing their worst fear: the contras abandoned, angry, and armed on Honduran territory, and the United States washing its hands of the controversial project. Since the cease-fire in March, some 10–12,000 contras and their families had fled Nicaragua.[15] The Honduran military refused to sign a new U.S.-Honduran military protocol until the United States promised to solve the refugee problem. On October 4 the Honduran foreign minister made an impassioned plea at the United Nations for an international peacekeeping force to expel the contras. Reagan officials understood the Honduran's proposal as a "cry of anguish," and so did the Sandinistas.[16]

The Sandinistas wanted an early summit to take advantage of the diplomatic climate before the United States recovered its influence. If the five Central American governments reached agreement on dismantling the contras, it would be "impossible" for the next president to "keep the sovereign resolutions of the five chief executives off his agenda."[17] President Cerezo supported an early summit, and neither the Salvadorans nor the Hondurans seemed inclined to stand in the way.[18]

To the Sandinistas' chagrin, it was President Arias who stepped in to disrupt their plans in the waning weeks of the Reagan administration. When the five foreign ministers tentatively scheduled a summit for the end of October, Arias forced its postponement to the end of November. Then he forced the further postponement until January. On January 6

Arias demanded yet another delay until after President Bush's inauguration at the end of that month. Arias held off the summit despite the fact that rapid progress was being made by the five foreign ministers toward an agreement on border verification. By the beginning of December the agreement was completed and ready for signature. Arias alone stood in the way of the dismantling of the contras during the critical months between Bush's election and his inauguration.

Arias made no secret of his intentions, which were to ensure that the Sandinistas made good on their promises to enact democratic reforms and that American power was brought to bear to force their compliance. Arias declared that approval of a border verification agreement without corresponding domestic reforms by the Sandinistas would make "a mockery of the peace process." He insisted that the five presidents had to agree on "firm and irreversible mechanisms that guarantee the observance of [democratic] principles and values." To do less, his spokesman warned, would "tell the world, and particularly people in Washington, that the peace plan isn't working." This in turn "could lead the new administration to adopt a more radical position."[19] Once again, Arias used the threat of American aid to the contras to demand more concessions from the Sandinistas. While the Sandinistas, and Cerezo, cried out for the Central Americans to show independence from the northern power, Arias insisted that "the only way we can move forward is with Washington's support." He said he opposed any agreement that excluded the United States, and once the foreign ministers had reached accord on border verification, he insisted that further discussions must await elaboration of "the general outline" of the Bush administration's policies.[20]

President Arias's actions during this period provided the most compelling evidence of his true goals. If he had sought only the dismantling of the contras and not been concerned about democratic reform in Nicaragua, as many of his conservative critics in the United States and in Costa Rica believed, he could have accomplished this goal merely by letting events take their natural course between October of 1988 and January of 1989. If, on the other hand, he believed American support for the contras was a hindrance to a democratic outcome in Nicaragua, as his liberal supporters believed and as he himself often stated, he would not have delayed the summit long enough for the Bush administration to take office. By doing so, he insured that the United States and the contras would continue to play a role in shaping whatever agreement was eventually struck with the Sandinistas.

The Sandinistas condemned Arias for his hostile actions. "No one has designated Costa Rica as the referee in this matter," Ortega complained, warning that postponement of the summit would kill the peace process.[21] Arias was "bury[ing] Esquipulas" and had "subordinated Central American interests and decisions to a strategy that could very well be designed at the White House."[22]

By the end of 1988, however, the Sandinistas were diplomatically isolated. They had been wounded by unrelated events, both natural and man-made. On October 22 Hurricane Joan had struck Nicaragua's Caribbean coast, exacting millions of dollars in damage. The effects of the hurricane played havoc with the Sandinistas' efforts to control government spending, and the inflation rate leapt higher. The Sandinistas seized on the disaster as an excuse to redouble their pleas for economic assistance from Europe, but their clumsy requests—often made as self-righteous demands—only drew attention to their isolation. The West Europeans provided little new aid and, influenced by the United States and President Arias, withheld further aid pending the enactment of democratic reforms.[23]

Elections in Latin America brought further problems. In Mexico the inauguration of President Carlos Salinas had led to a change of policy by the Sandinistas' closest non-communist ally. Salinas was intent on repairing Mexico's weak economy, and an improved relationship with the United States was the chief goal of his foreign and economic policies.[24] The Sandinistas' longtime protector in the Mexican Foreign Ministry, Bernardo Sepulveda, was replaced by a new minister who wasted no time in staking out an unhelpful, neutral course in the Central American conflict.[25] In Venezuela, Carlos Andres Pérez was elected president on December 4 and on February 1 would begin his second term after six years out of office. While American conservatives chiefly remembered Pérez's assistance to the Sandinistas in their struggle against Somoza, both the Sandinistas and President Arias remembered Pérez's later disenchantment with the young revolutionaries and his support for the rebellious Edén Pastora. The Sandinistas, in fact, were almost as wary of Pérez as they were of Bush.[26]

When 1989 began, therefore, the Sandinistas were in a corner. Diplomatically isolated, economically prostrate, politically besieged, Sandinista leaders knew they would have to take dramatic action. They decided to make the most momentous and dangerous decision of the revolution. On February 1 Daniel Ortega traveled to Caracas for the inauguration of President Pérez armed with new proposals for "repatriating" the contras. In meetings with Pérez, Arias, and Spain's Felipe Gonzalez, Ortega was sternly warned that the Sandinistas would suffer economic collapse, diplomatic isolation, and perhaps a renewal of the contra war if they did not move quickly and decisively toward free elections.[27] But Ortega did not need to be lectured. He had come to Caracas prepared to compromise. He told Pérez and Arias that the Sandinistas now understood it was "important to hold elections in Nicaragua," and they planned to do so. Pérez and Arias demanded explicit guarantees that the Nicaraguan opposition would be granted fair terms for competing in the elections and a specific timetable for the campaign and the vote.[28] Arias also demanded that the Sandinistas move up the date of presidential elections nine months, from November to February 1990.[29] Ortega agreed. He demanded in return only that the contra army be dismantled well in advance of the elections.

With the Sandinistas' commitment to elections, Arias finally allowed the meeting of Central American presidents to go forward in the middle of February. On the first day of the summit held at the Tesoro Beach resort in El Salvador, Ortega announced that elections for president, National Assembly members, and municipal officers would be held in Nicaragua no later than February 25, 1990. Ortega also agreed to reform the electoral and media laws "in such a way as to guarantee political organization and action in the broadest sense for political parties," and to do so by April 25, 1989. Parties would begin organizing after April, and a six-month period of campaigning would begin on August 25. In sharp contrast to the 1984 elections, the Sandinistas agreed to invite international observers to "all election districts . . . for the purpose of certifying the integrity of the process" throughout the ten-month electoral period.

In return for these concessions, the Sandinistas won agreement by the five presidents to move ahead with the dismantling of the contras. They agreed to formulate a plan within 90 days for the "voluntary demobilization, repatriation or relocation" of the rebels and their families. Of greatest importance to the Sandinistas, the five presidents called on all "extra-regional" governments "which either openly or secretly supply aid to irregular forces" to halt such aid "immediately" and to provide only assistance which "contributes to the goals of this document."

The Sandinistas were delighted with the outcome of the summit. Although they had tried to play down the significance of the contras, and recently had begun calling them "an unburied, stinking corpse," it was clear to journalists attending the summit that the demobilization agreement had become "a near obsession for Sandinista leaders."[30] *Times* reporter Lindsey Gruson shared the Sandinistas' expectation that the new agreement was "likely to increase pressure on Congress not to vote any more money to supply food, medicine and nonmilitary equipment to the rebels." The Sandinistas' American lawyer, Paul Reichler, declared triumphantly after the summit that the rebels were finally "not only dead but buried."[31]

Part Six

DOWNFALL OF THE SANDINISTAS

57

"We Need Compromise; We've Had Dissension"

The fate of the contras still rested with the American Congress and the new American president, George Bush. Coming less than a month after Bush's inauguration, the Tesoro Beach agreement took the new team of administration officials by surprise. Secretary of State James Baker had spent his first weeks in office establishing the new administration's relationships with European allies. He was traveling in Europe when the agreement was announced. At the time of the summit, there was no assistant secretary for Latin America. Elliott Abrams had been asked to leave immediately along with most other Reagan appointees, and his replacement, Bernard Aronson, had not yet taken over. The Tesoro Beach summit, as the Sandinistas had hoped, presented the Bush administration with what appeared to be an unwelcome *fait accompli*.

To fervent supporters of the contras, the latest Central American agreement was another "sellout" of the contras. In their view, the Sandinistas had offered vague promises of future actions in exchange for the demise of the rebels within a matter of months. The new Vice President, Dan Quayle, immediately called the agreement a "ruse" to keep Nicaragua under a "Marxist-Leninist dictatorship."[1] Republican conservatives openly criticized Secretary Baker for being "out of the picture" during the Central American negotiations. They urged President Bush to declare his "objections and reservations" about the Tesoro Beach agreement and to seek authority for giving the contras new arms if the Sandinistas failed to abide by it. Liberals like Congressman Bonior, on the other hand, objected to renewal of contra aid in any form. They argued that the contras could survive on the aid they had long enough to be disarmed.[2]

From the point of view of senior Bush officials, the Tesoro Beach agreement was most unwelcome because it threatened to drag them back into the mire of the contra aid controversy. This was the last thing President Bush and Secretary Baker wanted. Their goal upon taking office had been to remove Nicaragua from the agenda of Washington politics as quickly as possible.

The Sandinistas had been right to see in Bush a reluctant supporter of President Reagan's controversial Nicaragua policy. As a presidential candidate, Bush had steered away from strong pronouncements beyond what was necessary to appease right-wing Republicans. As President, Bush clearly had none of the ideological fervor of his two predecessors, whose policies toward Nicaragua had flowed, sometimes inadvertently, from broad but clearly articulated general principles. Bush abhorred ideological pronouncements and avoided declaring the principles by which his policies would be guided. He enunciated, instead, a tone and a manner of doing business that was non-partisan and non-confrontational. In response to the ideological warfare that had riven the American government for two decades, Bush in his inaugural address called for an end to rancor and partisan struggle. "We need compromise," Bush declared, "we've had dissension. We need harmony; we've had a chorus of discordant voices."

At his inauguration, in fact, Bush openly cast off the Reagan mantle and made clear that his style of presidency would bear no resemblance to that of his predecessor. He implicitly endorsed the Democrats' criticism of the Reagan administration's political tactics, "in which not each other's ideas are challenged, but each other's motives." He sought to dramatize the difference by literally reaching out to the Reagan administration's arch enemy. "To my friends—and yes, I do mean friends—in the loyal opposition—and yes, I do mean loyal: I put out my hand. I am putting out my hand to you, Mr. Speaker. . . . For this is the thing: This is the age of the offered hand. . . . [W]hen our fathers were young, Mr. Speaker, our differences ended at the water's edge." In his inaugural address, Bush talked not about what American foreign policy ought to be, but about the bipartisan agreement that was required to conduct it effectively. His choice of secretary of state underlined this new emphasis. James Baker was a renowned "pragmatist," a master politician with an unsurpassed reputation for deal-making across partisan and ideological divides.

Nicaragua had been the most divisive of all the ideological controversies of the Carter and Reagan years, the most extreme manifestation of the "wounds" from Vietnam that Bush sought to heal. And, of course, Bush had special reason to want to be rid of this divisive issue. Even as Bush was preparing his inaugural address, the trial of Oliver North was about to begin, and the shadow of the Iran-contra scandal hung over the new administration. The press was filled with speculations about several of Bush's advisers and about the new President himself. As they had in the 1988 campaign, Bush and Baker wanted to change the subject as quickly as possible.

Senior Bush officials had known, of course, that they would have to confront the Nicaragua issue early, and they were not unprepared for the new political crisis. Even during the transition period Baker and his top foreign policy advisers, Robert Zoellick and Dennis Ross, had begun devising a strategy that would allow Bush to escape from the controversial policy without great political cost. The Tesoro Beach agreement only hastened the need for deft political maneuvers.

The problem Bush officials faced was how to steer a safe course between the irreconcilable positions polarizing the Congress. On the one hand, as Baker's closest adviser, Robert Zoellick, later recalled, the "idea of arming the contras was a dead letter. There was no political support for it." On the other hand, Baker also knew that conservative Republicans refused to let the contras be abandoned while the Sandinistas ruled Nicaragua. But even the savvy Baker was surprised to learn just how hard it would be to strike a compromise in the Congress. "The divisions on the hill," Zoellick recalls, "were bloody."[3]

Fortunately for the Bush administration, the Sandinistas had already provided the best possible solution to the American political puzzle. By finally agreeing to hold fair elections, the Sandinistas gave the Bush administration a chance, in Zoellick's words, to "reframe the debate, to seize the high ground." Baker and his advisers could focus all attention on the elections as a fulfillment of the Arias plan and the accords of the Central American presidents. Rather than continue the Reagan administration's emphasis on military pressure, the Bush administration could emphasize diplomacy and democracy. Fair elections in Nicaragua, in Zoellick's view, could be a "rallying point" for both sides in the ideological conflict. By focusing on the goal of free elections, Baker and his advisers hoped a majority in Congress would agree to continue providing the contras with "humanitarian" aid to keep them intact while the Sandinistas fulfilled their promises. Zoellick and others believed the contras could "play their role" of keeping pressure on the Sandinistas merely "by their very existence" as a "viable armed force."[4]

According to the Tesoro Beach agreement, the United States should not have provided any aid to the contras except to help them disarm and resettle. But Baker was undeterred when he went to Congress to seek a year-long extension of the "humanitarian" aid program that was due to expire in March. In addition to his own skills as a political deal-maker, Baker had a number of advantages as he opened negotiations with the Democrats. For one thing, the Bush administration, like any administration in its first months in office, would likely be given a chance to try its own hand at solving the Nicaraguan puzzle. Democrats, of course, wanted assurances that the new administration would not simply continue the policy it inherited. Baker quickly obliged by declaring that the Reagan administration's policy had "failed." The Bush administration insisted it was seeking support for something entirely new and different.

Another advantage on Baker's side was the changed political circumstances of the Democratic Party's leading politician, Jim Wright. The Speaker of the House was a different man from the one who had battled Ronald Reagan so effectively for so many years. At the beginning of 1989 Wright was deeply embroiled in a scandal that would shortly end his career. Although the charges filed against him in the House Ethics Committee concerned financial malfeasance, investment deals with favored constituents, an unusual book contract, and jobs for his wife Betsy, Wright believed, with good reason, that his vigorous opposition to the Reagan administration's policies in Nicaragua had been the chief cause of the Republican assault. Since his venture into personal diplomacy with Daniel Ortega in November 1987, Wright believed, there had been "a determination on the part of certain people in the other party to see to it that I was removed."[5] President Bush, therefore, knew well when he offered his hand on inauguration day that Wright would grasp it gratefully. The Speaker shared the Bush administration's desire to settle the Nicaragua matter quickly and quietly. Wright's eagerness for cooperation opened a broad path for Secretary Baker.

Perhaps Baker's greatest asset as he sought renewed "humanitarian" aid for the contras was that everyone in Washington believed that the

Bush administration's principal goal was to put the Nicaraguan mess behind it, not to force the Sandinistas from power. Senator Majority Leader Robert Byrd called the new request for aid "a face-saving way out for a new administration to cut off a loser inherited from the past administration . . . a way for some to ease the feelings of guilt in letting the contras now twist slowly in the Central American wind."[6] Unlike the Reagan administration, the *Washington Post*'s John Goshko wrote, the Bush administration had apparently "resigned itself to the hope that the Managua government can be induced to take steps, such as permitting greater internal political liberalization and not interfering in the affairs of its neighbors, that will allow an uneasy truce with the United States."[7]

These public perceptions of the Bush administration's strategy were largely accurate. Bush officials would have been delighted to see the Sandinistas lose the elections in February 1990, but that was not what most counted on. Nor was that how Bush officials intended to measure the success or failure of their policy. As Robert Zoellick later recalled, senior Bush officials believed that "the most probable outcome" of the elections would be a victory by the Sandinistas. According to Ambassador Crescencio Arcos, another close adviser to Baker on Central American affairs, "No one, not in the State Department, not in the CIA, not in the White House, believed the Sandinistas would let themselves lose the elections."[8] As far as the Bush administration was concerned, the elections in Nicaragua would indeed lead to "an uneasy truce" with the Sandinistas.

Without much hope for a Sandinista defeat, Baker and his advisers had a more plausible, and familiar, goal in mind. They hoped that the elections would produce "an opening" in Nicaraguan society and that a "viable opposition" would emerge to contend with the Sandinistas for control of the country. Their strategy was to implant, in Zoellick's words, a "virus of democracy" in the Nicaraguan political system which, over time, would weaken the hold of the Sandinistas. "We didn't have to win the elections to have a success," Zoellick recalled. "We could contain and preoccupy the Sandinistas through the electoral process."[9]

Such a strategy may have aimed at eventually undermining the Sandinistas, but in the near term it conformed well to the Sandinistas' own plans. The Ortegas had already determined to take the risk of holding an election. They had already decided to allow a political opening, knowing this was the price for "normalization" with the United States. If in the long run Bush officials hoped the Sandinistas would fall victim to the democratic "virus," the Sandinistas were prepared to take their chances. Meanwhile, the Bush administration's strategy promised an end to the long confrontation between the United States and Nicaragua.

The Bush administration's plans, for this reason, won support from most Democrats in Congress, as well. If the price for burying the contra policy was one more vote for contra aid, most Democrats were prepared to pay it. Baker's and Bernard Aronson's three weeks of negotiations with Congress, therefore, although arduous, passed with the minimum of public dissension. Liberal House Democrats, who still mistrusted the Bush administration's motives, wanted a chance to cut off aid to the contras after six months if the new administration's policy proved to be "really designed to continue the old policy under different rhetoric." Fortunately for Baker, Speaker Wright did not want to hold even one floor debate on Nicaragua, and the Liberals quickly found themselves bargaining without the support of their leaders.[10] Baker clinched the deal by reaching what he called a "gentleman's agreement" with the liberals: Congress could veto the release of remaining aid after November 30 if any one of the chairman of four congressional committees or the four leaders in both houses simply wrote a letter to the President requesting that the aid not be released.[11] The congressional leaders plainly had little intention of exercising this right.

The "Bipartisan Accord" announced on March 24 extended "humanitarian" aid to the contras "at current levels" (i.e., $4.5 million per month) through February 28, 1990, "noting that the government of Nicaragua has agreed to hold new elections under *international supervision* just prior to that date."[12] As usual, both sides in the debate interpreted the new agreement to suit their needs. Republican congressman Mickey Edwards said the purpose of the new aid was to "keep the contras alive," ready to take up arms again if the Sandinistas reneged on their commitment to hold fair elections; Congressman Obey declared that the new legislation "ends the contra war." On April 13 the House and Senate voted overwhelmingly to approve legislation providing the contras $66 million in "humanitarian" aid and the means of delivering it through February 28, 1990.[13]

The bargain reached in Washington in March ran roughshod over the agreement reached by the five Central American presidents in February. The Sandinistas strongly objected to the fact that the Bipartisan Accord denied them their sole victory at Tesoro Beach: the promise of disbanding the contras months before the elections. Daniel Ortega lamented that the bipartisan agreement reached in Washington only "reaffirm[ed] the policy that the strong may do whatever they wish, regardless of the will of the others."[14] President Arias also objected at first, but when he visited Washington on April 3, arriving on a U.S. Air Force plane provided by President Bush, Arias decided simply to declare victory. The Bush administration, he said, wanted "to give diplomacy a chance, which is precisely what I asked the Reagan Administration to do two years ago. What the Americans are now saying to me is: 'Our policy didn't work. Your approach was right.'"[15]

The only other obstacle in Central America was the Honduran government, which wanted the contras removed from its territory. But Secretary Baker had already solved this problem earlier in March.[16] State Department officials explained to the Hondurans that they had little choice but to go along with the Bush administration's plan for aiding the contras, since the alternative was no American assistance to the contras and an angry rebel army looking for ways to feed itself in Honduran territory.[17] The Hondurans bent immediately to this logic. In the middle of March Foreign Minister López Contreras agreed that it was of "great importance to Honduras that these armed groups do not become orphans of humanitarian aid."[18]

With the Bipartisan Accord approved in both Washington and Central America, the only serious threat to the Bush administration's new strategy was the possibility that the Sandinistas might not hold fair elections. If they reneged on their commitments and it became clear that the opposition did not have a reasonable chance in the elections, the administration would once again be left open to attack by conservative Republicans. Once again, it would face demands for a renewal of military aid to the contras. For the next ten months, the Bush administration had to do all it could to make sure that the opposition ran a credible campaign and that the Sandinistas gave the opposition a fair chance.

From the beginning, this seemed to be a formidable assignment. In April the Sandinista government promulgated new electoral and media laws as required by the Tesoro Beach agreement, but not in such a way as to satisfy the opposition or U.S. officials.[19] The new laws gave the Sandinistas control of the important Supreme Electoral Council (SEC), which would oversee the elections, interpret the laws, and select the local electoral boards. Throughout Nicaraguan history, government control of this central electoral apparatus had usually determined the outcome of elections. Opposition leaders loudly complained that they were denied "equitable participation" in overseeing the electoral process, as called for in the Tesoro Breach agreement, but the Sandinistas refused to bend.[20]

On other matters, the Sandinistas were more forthcoming, although not enough to dispel the impression that they were trying to manipulate the system as much as possible to their own advantage. The Nicaraguan government met its commitment to allow the opposition access to foreign funds and equipment—no small concession for a sovereign government—but then required that 50 percent of all foreign funds be provided directly to the Electoral Council for the purposes of "perfect[ing] the electoral system." In this way, the Sandinistas hoped either to limit the amounts provided by the United States Congress or to make sure that whatever was given to the opposition provided funds for the government as well. The Sandinistas also used a classic tactic of the Somozas, penalizing opposition parties for their boycott of previous elections. They decreed that at least 50 percent of government campaign funds would be distributed to parties according to the percentage of votes they had received in the 1984 elections. All but one of the major opposition parties had boycotted those elections. The Sandinistas also rejected the opposition's demand for absentee voting by the hundreds of thousands of Nicaraguans living in exile.[21]

The new media laws severely limited the opposition's access to government TV and radio stations.[22] The Sandinistas dismissed the opposition's demand for a license to run its own private television station. While the new law did away with prior censorship and restricted the government's ability to close down newspapers and radio stations, it also allowed the Ministry of the Interior to close down media outlets for up to four days and to impose penalties for the broadcasting of information "contrary to the interests" of the country.[23]

Opposition leaders charged that the Sandinistas were creating the framework for a "rigged" election. According to one of Baker's top aides, Bush officials also had serious doubts about the Sandinistas' intentions.[24] They feared that the Sandinistas simply lacked sufficient incentive to make the necessary concessions. For Bush officials, this meant that some means had to be found to "make up for the leverage we lost in Central America when military aid to the *contras* was ended."[25]

58

New Thinking

Baker and his advisers turned for help to an unusual source, the Soviet Union. They believed they had reason to hope that the Sandinistas' longtime strategic ally might be willing to help. Dennis Ross and other analysts of Soviet foreign policy believed that important changes were occurring under the leadership of Mikhail Gorbachev and his foreign minister, Edouard Shevardnadze. In their view, accompanying Gorbachev's drive for *perestroika* and *glasnost* at home had been some remarkable "new thinking" about Soviet policy toward the United States and the rest of the non-communist world. In the increasingly open Soviet press, intriguing suggestions had been made by Soviet writers throughout 1988. Two Soviet authors had argued that "it would be expedient to gradually abandon our global rivalry with the USA and refrain from the costly support of unpopular regimes, political movements, parties, etc."[1] Another writer blamed Brezhnev's aggressive policies in the Third World for the breakdown of détente in the late 1970s and argued that the Soviet Union would do well to promote "a favorable international situation for profound transformations in the Soviet Union's economy and socio-political system."[2]

In October 1988 a young Foreign Ministry official, Andrei Kozyrev, took the argument to its furthest extreme. In one of the fullest elaborations of "new thinking" yet seen in print, he wrote that the Soviet Union

641

no longer had any reason to be in "a state of class confrontation with the United States or any other country," and, as far as the Third World was concerned, "the myth that the class interests of socialist and developing countries coincide in resisting imperialism does not hold up to criticism at all, first of all because the majority of developing countries already adhere or tend toward the Western model of development, and second, because they suffer not so much from capitalism as from lack of it."[3] The articles seemed more than just idle discussion; perhaps they were hints of a new official policy. Gorbachev in his speech to the UN General Assembly in December 1988 declared the need for "de-ideologizing relations among states." The Soviet people, he explained, were not abandoning "our convictions, our philosophy or traditions, nor do we urge anyone to abandon theirs. But neither do we want to be hemmed in by our values." By the beginning of 1989 "new thinking" appeared to be winning out in the struggle with the "old thinking" of the Brezhnev era.

One tenet of the "new thinking" was that ideological solidarity was to play a smaller role in the determination of Soviet foreign policy and that economic considerations were to play a much larger role—presumably not welcome news for a poor, 'socialist-oriented' country like Nicaragua. Senior Bush officials were convinced that the economic crisis in the Soviet Union practically required a lessening of aid to Nicaragua. Deputy Secretary of State Lawrence Eagleburger believed that Gorbachev and his colleagues "realized they are overextended" and were "beginning to try to pull back." Nicaragua, Eagleburger believed, was one place where the United States "could persuade the Soviets to begin to draw back."[4]

By the beginning of 1989, the intriguing rhetoric had not been matched by any notable change of Soviet behavior in Central America, however. Under the military protocols between the Soviet Union, Cuba, and Nicaragua, signed in 1987, Soviet military aid had continued to flow to Nicaragua, and the levels of aid in 1988 were only slightly lower than in the record-breaking year of 1987. At $515 million and 19,000 tons, Soviet deliveries far outstripped the most extreme years under the "old thinking," and this heavy flow came during a period when the United States was providing no arms to the contras. In the last meeting between Elliott Abrams and his Soviet counterpart, chief of the Latin American Directorate in the Soviet Foreign Ministry, Yuri Pavlov, the Soviet official had rejected Abrams's suggestion that the Soviet Union reduce military aid to Nicaragua and responded instead with the usual Soviet offer to end aid to Nicaragua when the United States ended all aid to Central America.

Pavlov showed signs, nevertheless, that he personally was a devotee of the "new thinking," and this intrigued State Department officials. Pavlov expressed a measure of disdain for the Sandinistas, and as he bade Abrams farewell he handed him a copy of Andrei Kozyrev's ground-breaking article.[5] Despite the continuing high levels of Soviet military aid to Nicaragua, therefore, American officials saw Pavlov's actions as a signal that the Soviet Union might finally be prepared to be more cooperative with the United States in Central America.

During the transition between the Reagan and Bush administrations, officials in the Moscow embassy and in Washington wrote proposals for taking advantage of the confluence of circumstances: a new administration in Washington, no prospect of renewed military aid to the contras, and a possibly more pliant Soviet leadership eager to continue with President Bush the warming of relations begun under Reagan. Bush officials believed a special "window of opportunity" existed during the first months of the new presidency.[6]

Baker wanted to make Central America the first test of Gorbachev's new foreign policy. The State Department's strategy was to seek the cooperation of the Soviet Union both to reduce its aid to Nicaragua and to put "pressure on its clients"—Cuba and Nicaragua—to abide by the agreement of the Central American presidents.[7] This meant giving the Soviets "tangible signs that they will pay a real price in bilateral relations if they obstruct our Central American diplomacy."[8] Expectations of Soviet cooperation ran high. As a sign of the importance Bush officials placed on the Soviet relationship, Bernard Aronson, chosen in the spring to replace Elliott Abrams as assistant secretary of state for inter-American affairs, made his first overseas trip not to Latin America but to Moscow.

In a letter to Gorbachev at the end of March, President Bush declared that "continuing high levels of Soviet and Cuban assistance to Nicaragua" would inevitably affect the nature of U.S.-Soviet relations. He suggested a more hopeful course lay in "an initiative by the Soviet Union and Cuba to shut off the assistance pipeline feeding armed conflict in the region." Such a move would "pay large dividends in American goodwill. It would suggest that the Soviet Union was prepared to promote a political settlement in the region through deeds and not simply slogans."[9] The idea was to subject the Soviet government to what Secretary Baker described as "Chinese water torture" on the subject. As he explained the strategy to President Bush: "We'll just keep telling them over and over—drop, drop, drop—that they've got to be part of the solution in Central America, or else they'll find lots of other problems harder to deal with."[10]

The first test of this new policy came in April, when Gorbachev visited Fidel Castro in Havana. The Bush administration and the leaders of Congress pointedly declared in their Bipartisan Accord that this meeting represented "an important opportunity for both the Soviet Union and Cuba to end all aid that supports subversion and destabilization in Central America." Bush officials had high hopes that Gorbachev would use the meeting to send a signal that he, too, desired cooperation in Central America.

The Bush administration's expectations of Gorbachev, however, proved overly optimistic. Although American Soviet experts had been right to detect in Gorbachev and Shevardnadze a desire to be cooperative with the United States, if possible, they greatly overestimated the changes Gorbachev was willing to make in Soviet policy toward Cuba and Central America. While Yuri Pavlov and other officials in middle levels of the Soviet Foreign Ministry favored reducing Soviet aid to Cuba and to Central American revolutionaries, Gorbachev took a different view. As Pavlov later recalled, "Gorbachev had his own ideas . . . that reflected the Soviet establishment's firm resolve to keep Cuba as a reliable political friend and a strategic asset in the game of superpower politics." Gorbachev and his colleagues in the Politburo shared "an unwavering loyalty to the Soviet Union's ideological allies in Cuba and Castro."[11]

Far from wanting to chastise or rein in Castro, as demanded by the Bush administration, Gorbachev traveled to Havana in April 1989 to smooth over differences that had broken out between the two close allies. The most significant breach had arisen over *perestroika* and *glasnost*, the Gorbachev-sponsored reforms which Castro had publicly repudiated, fervently believing they would lead to the undoing of communism throughout the Soviet empire.[12] Unfortunately for Gorbachev, a majority of his colleagues in the Soviet hierarchy shared Castro's concerns.[13] In Havana, therefore, Gorbachev hoped only to explain his views and to try to persuade Castro of the wisdom of reform. But he planned to make it clear to Castro, and to the United States, that the Soviet Union would not impose its brand of reform on Cuba. As Pavlov recalled, "the U.S. administration had to be informed that Gorbachev was not going to follow Washington's insistent advice—to use Cuba's dependence on Soviet economic aid as leverage to pressure Havana. . . . Nor was Gorbachev thinking of reducing, at Washington's prodding, Soviet-Cuban military cooperation."[14]

Gorbachev was also unwilling to cooperate on the matter of greatest interest to the Bush administration: Soviet and Cuban military aid to Nicaragua and the Salvadoran guerrillas. Gorbachev and most senior Soviet officials viewed Central American issues as but a subset of the Soviet-Cuban relationship, and for many years Soviet policy in Central America had effectively been made in Havana, not in Moscow. Although it might seem strange that the small client state thus dictated policy to its superpower patron, it was nevertheless the case that the Cubans were "unwilling to grant Moscow equal status in [Central American] affairs, as they felt entitled to play the role of senior partner." Gorbachev and other senior Soviet officials were content with this arrangement, although Foreign Ministry officials under Shevardnadze yearned for the "de-Cubanization" of Soviet policy in Central America.[15]

In Havana at the beginning of April, therefore, Gorbachev disappointed Bush officials. Rather than put pressure on Castro to reduce arms shipments to the Sandinistas and the FMLN, Gorbachev adopted Castro's policy. He offered to cut off arms to Nicaragua if the United States did the same in El Salvador and the rest of Central America. As Pavlov recalled, "clearly the proposition was a nonstarter and had a purely propagandistic value."[16] In addition, Gorbachev called Baker's Bipartisan Accord to renew aid to the contras "regrettable." He declared the Soviet Union's opposition to the "export of revolution," but he also declared his support for "the autonomy of individual socialist countries," a phrase the Sandinistas found especially gratifying.[17] Asked by journalists in Havana about the Bush administration's request that he tame Castro's revolutionary activities, Gorbachev responded tartly: "You start from the point of view that [Cuba] is a colony. I feel that this is not an appropriate question."[18]

The Bush administration responded angrily to Gorbachev's statements. If the Soviets were serious about not supporting the export of revolution, the White House spokesman declared, they should "pressure their client states and revolutionary groups they support to do the same."[19] Over the next few weeks, however, American and Salvadoran officials detected a significant *increase* in the amount of Soviet and Cuban arms flowing to the FMLN. On May 2 President Bush vehemently denounced this continuing Soviet support for "terrorism" in Central America.[20] "The Soviet Union must understand that we hold it accountable for the consequences of this intervention—and for progress towards peace in the region and democracy in Nicaragua."[21]

Private conversations with Soviet officials were friendlier but no more productive. When Assistant Secretary Aronson complained to Pavlov about continuing Cuban support for the FMLN, Pavlov promised only that "we will talk to our Cuban friends," but he noted that while Soviet officials often tried to explain "the changes in the world every time we meet with the Cubans . . . Castro is not someone with whom one uses the word 'must' if one is serious about changing his behavior. Fidel doesn't take orders from anyone." And, Pavlov pointed out, Castro had "no interest in seeing an improvement in Soviet-U.S. relations," much less at the expense of Castro's personal project, the Sandinista revolution.[22] When Aronson asked more directly about the Soviet Union's own arms supply policy, Pavlov suggested that he and the Soviet Foreign Ministry were far from able to control that policy.[23]

By the beginning of May, the Bush administration's "Chinese water torture" had had no visible effect on Soviet policy. Meanwhile, Bush and Baker were ready to resume high-level talks with the Soviets on arms control and other important issues. Baker's first trip to Moscow was scheduled for May 10, and this visit would inaugurate the new policy of "re-engagement." Baker had decided that the Bush administration was appearing too "passive in the face of the great strategic changes."[24] The administration's earlier promise to link progress in U.S.-Soviet relations to Soviet policy in Central America was about to become a problem—for the Bush administration, not for Gorbachev. "Time is not on our side," Baker's advisers wrote on the eve of his trip to Moscow. "We must convince the Soviets not that we are in trouble and desperately need them to throw us an anchor [sic], but that it is *they* who risk being seen as a spoiler."[25]

On May 6, the day before Baker left for Moscow, Gorbachev finally answered Bush's March 27 letter. Bush officials found the response disturbingly enigmatic. Gorbachev "note[d] the positive trends in Central America, including the intention of your Administration and the U.S. Congress to 'give diplomacy a chance.'" He declared that "in order to promote a peaceful settlement of the conflict, and bearing in mind that the attacks by the contras' troops against Nicaragua have stopped, the U.S.S.R. has not been sending weapons to [Nicaragua] after 1988."[26]

Gorbachev's claim was incomprehensible to Bush officials. American intelligence reports showed that weapons were flowing to Nicaragua in the first four months of 1989 at about the same rate as the previous year. White House spokesman Marlin Fitzwater accused Gorbachev of playing a "p.r. game." There was no "evidence of a cutoff. The military aid is still coming in." Sandinista officials insisted that the Soviet Union had not informed them of any shift in policy.[27]

In fact, as Yuri Pavlov later revealed, Gorbachev's declaration on May 6 was not truthful. At the end of 1988 the Soviet Foreign Ministry had recommended a temporary suspension in the delivery of "heavy weapons to Nicaragua" and a show of "restraint in the deliveries of light weapons." Foreign Ministry officials like Pavlov thought this was an appropriate response to the suspension of U.S. military aid to the contras in February 1988. What officials at Pavlov's level did not know at the time, however, was that Gorbachev and Shevardnadze had approved a different policy and that the Soviet Union had continued throughout the first six months of 1989 "in violation of its declared policy" to transport weapons to Cuba that "were destined for further shipment to Nicaragua . . . in accordance with the existing Soviet-Cuban arrangement."[28]

Soviet policy raised the central question for the Bush administration. Was President Bush really prepared to hold U.S.-Soviet relations hostage to Soviet behavior in Central America? At the time Gorbachev's letter arrived in Washington, the answer was already becoming clear. The Bush administration was under pressure to resume talks with the Soviet government. America's West European allies were growing anxious and impatient, as Gorbachev offered one new arms control proposal after another.[29] In April President Bush rather sharply declared that the United States would be "ready to react when we feel like reacting,"[30] but the President and his secretary of state were intent on speeding things up. Baker was especially sensitive to charges that he had not taken control of foreign policy, except to negotiate the accord on Nicaragua, and had allowed the United States to drift for almost five months. He wanted to announce new U.S.-Soviet initiatives.[31] In Moscow on May 10, he told Gorbachev and Shevardnadze that the President and he were "ready and anxious" to resume negotiations on all matters. Baker and Shevardnadze began discussions about a Bush-Gorbachev summit and agreed to make a firm decision by the time of their next meeting in the United States in September.[32] On May 12 President Bush in his first major address on foreign policy declared his hope of taking American policy "beyond containment" to "welcome the Soviet Union back into the world order." Less than two weeks later the President promised "to seize every, and I mean every, opportunity to build a better, more stable relationship with the Soviet Union."[33]

As the Bush administration's zeal for resuming talks with Gorbachev grew, its inclination to chastise the Soviet Union publicly about Cuba and Nicaragua diminished. Even in private, the United States softened its stance. In May Baker asked the Soviet government to "lend its support through deeds as well as words to convince Nicaragua and Cuba—*in whatever manner [you] choose*—to halt all aid for subversion in Central America and to comply fully with Esquipulas."[34] Baker asked Gorbachev's permission to announce that the Soviet Union had indeed agreed to cut off arms to Nicaragua. When Gorbachev demurred, suggesting the United States open negotiations with Castro, Baker let the matter drop.[35]

Baker came to Moscow with incentives as well as demands. "We would not expect you to take these steps unless there were benefits," he told Shevardnadze. The benefits were an American promise to improve relations with Nicaragua as the Sandinistas took steps toward free and fair elections. The Bush administration would respect the results of the February 1990 elections if the Sandinistas won, and then afterwards it would "normalize" relations with the Nicaraguan government, resume economic assistance, lift the trade embargo, and end all aid to the contras. The Soviets could take credit, Baker argued, for "ensuring the long-term survival of the Sandinistas."[36] The American government referred to Baker's offer as the Five Points.[37]

Soviet officials, of course, welcomed American promises to normalize relations with Nicaragua. Yuri Pavlov asked that the United States give the Sandinistas clear signs of approval and tangible rewards when they took the right steps. "The more evidence Managua sees that the U.S. is willing to coexist with them after the elections, assuming they win," Pavlov told Assistant Secretary Aronson, "the easier it will be to create a free and fair election." Gorbachev had made a similar proposal to Bush concerning Cuba. Castro, he said, also favored "normalizing" relations.[38] Pavlov did his best to steer the Bush administration away from the idea of pressuring the Sandinistas and toward what he considered a more promising and, for the Soviets, less compromising approach. Pavlov used the Bush administration's promises to convince a skeptical Cuban government that the Soviets knew what they were doing. He told the Cubans, "the Americans have made certain promises. It is our belief that it serves the purposes of U.S. policy, as formulated by the Bush Administration, to stop the war in Nicaragua and settle the Nicaraguan crisis through political means." As Aronson recalls, "the Soviets wanted desperately for us to normalize relations with the Sandinistas, so we told them they had to make the elections fair."[39]

In what way the Soviets were to make the elections in Nicaragua fair, however, was unclear. While American officials hoped the Soviets would at least hold the Sandinistas to high standards of compliance with their promise to hold a fair election campaign and a fair vote, this was something the Soviets readily admitted they were incapable of doing. As Pavlov had once reminded American officials, the Soviet Union, which had never held a fair election of its own, was in no position to tell the Sandinistas how to hold one. As a practical matter, the Soviet ambassador in Managua could hardly advise, much less pressure, Sandinista leaders on such questions as electoral and media laws, the registration of opposition political parties, the fair distribution of campaign funds, the means for monitoring voter registration, and counting the votes. On these minute questions, each of which was important to the American goal of ensuring fair participation by the opposition, the Soviet Union could be of no help whatsoever, except perhaps to suggest that the Sandinistas should try to satisfy the international observers like Presidents Arias and Pérez. The Sandinistas, however, did not need this advice from the Soviets. They lived in the Western Hemisphere, felt the pressures from Arias, Pérez, and Bush directly, and had already made the critical and dangerous determination to try to meet their standards. After all, they needed their "seal of approval" from the West, not from the Soviet Union.

Bush officials were inclined to go along with the Soviet's softer approach. "We knew they had to be careful with the Sandinistas," Robert Zoellick later recalled. "I personally was loathe to second-guess them." What that meant, however, was that the Bush administration's strategy of using the Soviet Union to pressure the Sandinistas to hold fair elections amounted to very little. The Soviet Union served chiefly as a messenger, delivering the Bush administration's assurances that it would leave a freely elected Sandinista government in peace. As Zoellick put it, "we weren't asking the Soviets to do that much."[40]

59

"The Elections Will Show the World What We All Want the Nicaraguan Sandinist Revolution to Show"

During the months preceding the elections, therefore the most significant pressure came not from the Soviets but from the contras—even in their weakened condition. By May the Sandinistas were angry and frustrated that, despite the Tesoro Beach accords, no steps had been taken even to begin dismantling the rebel army. The 30 days during which the five Central American governments were to have proposed a plan to demobilize the contras had expired. The election of the conservative Alfredo Cristiani as president of El Salvador in March threatened to delay implementation of a demobilization plan indefinitely. Ortega warned that Cristiani, the leader of the right-wing alliance, intended to "sabotage" the Tesoro Beach accords.[1] On April 29 Ortega wrote an angry letter to President Arias complaining about the delays and also about Arias's continued interference in Nicaraguan domestic affairs.[2] The Sandinistas claimed to see the "meddlesome hand of Washington" behind the delays and insisted that the ratification of the demobilization agreement should occur "as soon as possible" rather than await a summit which "we do not even know if it will be held."[3]

The Sandinistas took out their frustrations on their political opponents in Nicaragua. In response to demands by the opposition and their foreign supporters for a reopening of the dialogue on electoral reforms, Ortega declared that the Sandinistas were "not willing to continue participating in senseless discussions with the opposition parties. . . . There will be no new concessions! . . . The reforms to the laws have already been made—and that is that!"[4] On June 21 the government confiscated the coffee plantations of three leading opposition businessmen, including the brother of COSEP leader Enrique Bolaños.[5] Daniel Ortega advised other producers to learn the proper lesson, "because if they do not, they run the same risk."[6] In early July Sandinista police banned an opposition rally in Ocotal and broke up another rally in León.[7] Chief of state security, Lenin Cerna, warned that "if demonstrators hold a rally with the expressed intention of attacking the police, the authorities and the revolutionary people, we will not be able to predict what will happen in such a situation. We cannot guarantee that people will not be killed or injured."[8] The Sandinistas were not "afraid of class struggles," Daniel Ortega declared. "We have the instruments of power to finish off whole sectors of our society quickly. We've made concessions to them, but we know we are living with scorpions in our shirt. If the scorpion gets too excited, we will crush him."[9]

The Sandinistas' crackdown was designed, in part, to speed up progress toward demobilization of the contras. They knew Bush, Arias, and Pérez wanted a successful election process with full participation by the opposition. And indeed, when opposition leaders responded to the crackdown in June by warning they might not participate in the elections, Pérez and Arias jumped into the breach.[10] They demanded concessions of Ortega, but they also assured him that compromise would be rewarded. Pérez told Ortega that he "would like to see a broad agreement reached with the opposition parties so that the elections will show the world what we all want the Nicaraguan Sandinist Revolution to show, that is, a process in which democracy is really the main factor." After a nine-hour meeting with Arias in San José on July 15, Ortega promised to hold another meeting with the opposition to "refine" the electoral rules.[11] With the summit of Central American presidents finally scheduled for August 5 in Honduras, Ortega at the end of July called for a public meeting with the opposition parties on August 3 to settle their differences.

At the meeting, the Sandinistas made a number of compromises, although they again rejected the opposition's chief demand for a change in the membership of the Supreme Electoral Council. The government offered to provide amnesty for political prisoners, but not until the contras had been fully demobilized and relocated out of Honduras. It agreed to suspend recruitment of youths for the army from September through February, but offered no change in the conscription law. Nor would the government grant a new license for a television station; it promised to provide a half-hour every evening on government-run television during the campaign to be shared among all the opposition parties. The two sides reached agreement on a number of measures concerning the monitoring and counting of votes, the sharing of voter registration lists, and the participation of the opposition on local electoral boards.

In exchange for these concessions, the Sandinistas demanded and received the opposition's agreement on two important points: The opposition formally and irrevocably agreed to register and participate in the elections, thus ending any further threat of blackmail. And the opposition called on the Central American presidents to approve the plan for the demobilization of the contras at the upcoming summit.

There was much private grousing among opposition groups after the meeting that their representatives had wilted under pressure and given away too much. Even before the meeting, an editorial in *La Prensa* called it "another show" designed for "others."[12] The opposition negotiators, however, had little choice but to agree to participate in the elections. Violeta Chamorro, a likely candidate for the presidency, had declared on July 24 that "the 1990 elections will never be the 1984 elections. Abstention and withdrawal should be considered equivalent to cowardice and treason."[13] As for the contras, the opposition leaders fully expected the Central American presidents to agree on a demobilization plan on August 5, no matter what happened at the meeting in Managua on August 3. The opposition feared this would be its last chance to win any concessions from the Sandinistas before the contras were eliminated.

With the August 3 agreement in his pocket, President Ortega traveled to Tela, Honduras, for his reward. President Arias did not even wait to learn the results of the August 3 meeting before declaring that the demobilization of the contras would be the "main issue" at the Tela summit. And he insisted that the demobilization had to begin prior to the February elections.[14] President Azcona's desire to rid Honduras of the contra army was clear to all observers. On July 27 Azcona had declared that "we are the party most interested in having this demobilization take place. . . . We want the contras to return to Nicaragua as soon as possible."[15] Only President Cristiani opposed a demobilization agreement, but not out of concern for the contras. Like Duarte, he insisted that any demobilization of the contras had to be tied to a simultaneous demobilization of the FMLN guerrillas. On this point, however, the Salvadorans were isolated. President Arias was eager to strike the deal with the Sandinistas, and on

August 3 he insisted that the two issues had to be considered separately at the summit.

Despite an ostentatious last-minute effort by the Bush administration to delay demobilization at least until the February elections, the five presidents agreed to complete demobilization of the contras no later than December 8.[16] The date was chosen with the U.S. Congress in mind. Since Baker's "gentleman's agreement" gave Congress the right to block further aid to the contras after November 30, the Sandinistas hoped Bush would have no choice but to allow the demobilization to go forward. In addition, President Azcona had demanded assurances that the disarming and resettlement of the contras would be undertaken by an international force of the United Nations and the OAS, not by the Honduran army. At Tela the presidents agreed to seek creation of such a force within 30 days.

––––––––––

Bush officials were surprised and dismayed. They had expected an agreement on demobilization but not such an early deadline. Secretary Baker called Arias to complain that American conservatives would revolt against the agreement. Congressman Mickey Edwards worried that the Democrats "now have all kinds of excuses not to give the permission needed for aid to go forward."[17] In Honduras the contras were declaring they would "return to the mountains" of Nicaragua rather than lay down their weapons.[18] The confrontation over contra aid, dormant since April, was about to erupt once again.

In response to this difficult predicament, the Bush administration chose simply to ignore the latest agreement as it had ignored the last. On August 8 presidential spokesman Marlin Fitzwater ambiguously explained that the administration's policy "is and has been that we would not like to see demobilization before the elections. However, that being the case, we still support the process; we support demobilization."[19] The Bush administration seized on the word "voluntary" in the Tela Accords and argued, as it had in March, that the Central American plan really did not require the contras to be demobilized against their will. Demobilization was "a voluntary process which depends on Nicaraguan willingness to create safe, democratic conditions."[20]

As in March and April, Democrats in Congress responded to the tone of the administration's statements more than to the content. Senator Dodd declared that Congress and the administration were "singing from the same hymnbook."[21] Once again the assumption that Bush and Baker were more concerned about outraged conservative Republicans than about the fate of the contras elicited sympathy and a degree of cooperation from Democrats. Dodd described what he considered the Bush administration's greatest fear: "Ronald Reagan is making a speech in Topeka and he says, 'Jim Baker and George Bush have sold out the contras.' They just can't handle that."[22]

Leading Democrats themselves were not prepared to force the contras to demobilize. Whatever the terms of the latest Central American accord, the underlying consensus in the American political system remained firmly entrenched. Even liberal Democrats shied away from demanding the contras be forced back to Nicaragua before fair elections had been held. Senator Claiborne Pell, the chairman of the Senate Foreign Relations Committee, said that although he did want aid to the contras "ratcheted down as much as possible," he did not want to "force the contras back to Nicaragua against their will."[23] Both parties and both branches of government in Washington still looked to the February elections as the answer to the problem. The matter of aid to the contras was set aside until November, much to the Sandinistas' displeasure.

The focus of international attention returned to Managua, where the Sandinistas' political opponents took the first steps toward mounting a campaign for the February elections. Some opposition leaders regretted the deal they had struck with the Sandinistas on August 3 and criticized the negotiators who had signed the "pact." Opposition leaders did not trust the Sandinistas to abide by their promises, but beyond these suspicions, most of these opposition leaders quietly feared they were destined to lose the elections no matter what the rules of the campaign.

No one knew better than Nicaraguan opposition leaders how small and ineffective their party organizations were, how riven by factional rivalry and personal ambition, how limited their reach outside Managua and a couple of Pacific Coast cities. Even in the days of Somoza these same parties had feared a true test of their strength—which was why they had preferred a plebiscite on Somoza's rule rather than a straightforward electoral contest that would measure their own popularity. In light of such fears, many opposition leaders believed their participation in the 1990 elections could serve only to give the Sandinistas the international legitimacy they craved and which the world seemed ready to accord them. César later recalled that many in the opposition believed the elections "would be like

1984, that we would never win, we won't be given the freedom to campaign. We'll just legitimize the Sandinistas." There was general fear that the recent agreement with the government might prove to be nothing more than the first and decisive step toward guaranteeing Sandinista rule in perpetuity. Antonio Lacayo, the opposition's campaign director, recalls that most of the opposition believed in August that there was no chance of beating the Sandinistas.[24]

Unity was the primary goal of most of the opposition, and of its foreign supporters, but past years and recent months had shown that unity was not the opposition's most notable attribute. The Sandinistas sometimes liked to argue that proof of their government's pluralism was the existence of 21 political parties. At other times they pointed out that most of these parties could hold national conventions in a closet. The existence of so many parties was more a sign of the futility of organized political opposition under Sandinista rule than of the vitality of the democratic system. No more than three or four parties could claim any nationwide following or political apparatus. The two main Nicaraguan parties, the Liberals and Conservatives, had splintered into factions. As in the days of Somoza, both parties had a faction that served officially in the legislature as a recognized opposition, and several other factions that refused to do so. A third national party, the Social Christians, were the cousins of the Christian Democrats who had ruled in El Salvador under Duarte and in Guatemala under Cerezo. The Nicaraguan Social Christian Party was also splintered into at least three factions, one of which participated in the Sandinista-dominated National Assembly. Of Nicaragua's 21 political parties, in fact, over half consisted of splinter groups from the three main tendencies.

These factions were organized chiefly around individuals, and the most common reason for the creation of new party factions had been less a matter of ideological divergence than the refusal of one party leader to accept subservience to another. Such divisions diluted whatever strength the Liberals, Conservatives, and the Social Christians might have had. The Communist Party and the Nicaraguan Socialist Party each commanded a small following. The remaining parties bordered on the microscopic, although their tiny size did not save them from breaking down into factions, as well. Thus there were two factions laying claim to the banner of the Central American Unification Party, a movement which would have been fortunate to claim 5,000 followers throughout the entire country.

The splintered opposition was the Sandinistas' best weapon in any election. Some opinion polls showed that the Sandinistas might claim a devoted following among the population of no more than 35 percent, but no other single party could claim more than 5 percent. Were every opposition party in Nicaragua to run its own presidential candidate in the 1990 elections, the Sandinistas could coast to victory. Even if the three main tendencies each raised a unified banner among its factions, the three presidential candidates would divide the opposition vote among themselves and give the Sandinista candidate a decisive plurality. Any hope of defeating the Sandinistas in a fair contest lay in ignoring established party mechanisms and uniting all the opposition factions under a single slate of candidates, in effect, turning the elections into a referendum on Sandinista rule. Yet the task of uniting all the many factions at times seemed almost impossible.

Competing personal and factional ambitions were only one source of cleavage among the opposition groups. Mutual suspicions and jealousies existed between those opposition leaders who had remained in Nicaragua throughout the 1980s, opposing the Sandinistas from within, and those who had left the country to form exile movements in Costa Rica or in Miami or to join the contras. The politicians who had stayed to run their parties during the years of Sandinista repression claimed moral superiority over those who had departed for the safety of San José and the United States. The return of self-exiled politicians like Alfredo César and Alfonso Robelo to take part in the 1989 campaign was hardly to be welcomed by those who could be displaced as leaders of their parties inside Nicaragua. Within weeks of his return to Managua in July, for instance, César engineered a coup within the tiny Social Democratic Party, making himself the party's leader in place of Guillermo Potoy. In early April the opposition parties in Managua quickly agreed that any nominee for the presidency had to come "from inside Nicaragua," a statement designed mostly to exclude César, whose ambitions for the presidency or leadership of an opposition bloc in a new National Assembly were well-known.[25]

Another division existed between those parties which portrayed themselves as progressive representatives of the poor and working classes and those which represented the more conservative Nicaraguan business class. One of the strongest opposition groups in Nicaragua was not a party at all, but the alliance of businessmen under COSEP. COSEP's leader, Enrique Bolaños, had openly opposed the Sandinistas from inside Nicaragua for a decade, had spent months in jail as a result and believed he had as much right to the presidential nomination as any political party leader—indeed more, since COSEP had long been the financial backbone of the opposition movement. Communist Party leader Eli Altamirano was not alone in insisting, however, that Bolaños was not a "suitable" candidate precisely because he represented the "private enterprise sector." Aside from the reasons of their own ambition for the nomination, many party leaders feared the opposition could not win a class-based campaign that pitted the Sandinista Party of "workers and peasants" against the Nicaraguan business elite.[26] Many conservatives, on the other hand, opposed the more progressive parties and their leaders for having been too timid in opposition to the Sandinistas' socialist policies. Conservative party leaders and businessmen had not forgotten the roles played by Violeta Chamorro, Alfonso Robelo, Alfredo César, and Liberal Independent Party leader, Virgilio Godoy, in the early years of the Sandinista revolution. While COSEP's leaders and some Conservative Party politicians had been sitting in Sandinista jails, these members had been serving in the government, signing decrees confiscating COSEP's properties and businesses and limiting freedom of the press, undermining non-Sandinista labor unions, and generally adding a veneer of legitimacy to Sandinista rule. Such mutual antagonisms were unlikely to vanish overnight.

Sandinista leaders expected that the many "contradictions" among the opposition parties made it impossible "even to imagine" that the opposition parties could "unite for the elections." The Sandinistas were not deluded about the extent of their own support in the country, but as Carlos Nuñez explained, "the FSLN is the only party in this country that has enough support to win the elections by itself. The other parties cannot wage a civic struggle against the FSLN if they go it alone."[27] The Nicaraguan government, moreover, had many means of exacerbating the "contradictions" without in any way compromising a fair electoral process. Indeed, this was one reason the Sandinistas were so willing to accede to intrusive foreign demands concerning the campaign and the vote. The main thrust of the Sandinistas' electoral strategy was not to repress the opposition but merely to help it along toward its inevitable self-destruction.

Despite its severe weaknesses, however, and despite efforts by the Sandinistas to keep it divided, the opposition in Nicaragua did begin in the late spring of 1989 to forge a remarkable degree of unity. The core of the opposition coalition was the handful of parties, unions, and business groups of the Coordinadora, which had remained united for more than seven years. By April this core of conservative organizations had also attracted an additional half-dozen parties from across the ideological spectrum, including several, like the Communist and Socialist parties, which had never before allied with the Coordinadora.[28] The Sandinistas were surprised to see the development of this strange alliance—known as the "Group of 14"—and they predicted its rapid unraveling.[29] But the opposition coalition surprised everyone, including the opposition leaders themselves, by remaining unified throughout the summer months. At the end of June the 14 parties formally united into the Nicaraguan Opposition Union (UNO) and pledged to support a single government platform and single slate of candidates for president and vice president in the 1990 elections. At the August 3 meeting with opposition leaders even Daniel Ortega was forced to deal with UNO as the main opposition group, virtually ignoring the other parties.[30]

The cohesion of the opposition coalition against all odds owed much to the intervention of foreign governments. From the beginning of the campaign Presidents Arias and Pérez, the Bush administration, and even President Cerezo of Guatemala pressed the opposition parties to unify,[31] and behind these exhortations lay the promise of millions of American dollars. By the fall of 1988 Congress had appropriated over $3 million dollars for the fiscal year ending September 30, 1989, to support opposition media, unions, and party organizations; on June 1, 1989, the Senate approved an additional appropriation of $3 million; and in September the Bush administration planned to ask Congress for considerably more for the five months between the end of September and the February 25 elections. The Bush administration wanted to provide this support to a united opposition, not to individual factions, and this provided a strong incentive for the parties to preserve their new alliance.

The greatest test of UNO's cohesion, however, came in August when the opposition alliance had to agree on candidates for president and vice president. As the deadline for making nominations approached, the opposition parties, business, and labor organizations did break down into distinct, mutually antagonistic blocs, although not those publicly promoted by the Sandinista media. By the middle of August three leading candidates for the presidential nomination had emerged, each representing a different set of interests within the opposition coalition.

The most prominent candidate was Violeta Chamorro, owner of *La Prensa* and widow of the martyred Pedro Joaquín Chamorro. Of the three blocs, Chamorro's was the most openly clannish, and in this respect perhaps the most traditionally Nicaraguan. Chamorro's closest advisers were her son-in-law, Antonio Lacayo, and Lacayo's brother-in-law, Alfredo César. Not closely associated with any political party, nor with any distinct political doctrine, Violeta Chamorro represented more than anything else the traditional ruling aristocracy of Nicaragua. Another contender, Virgilio Godoy, was a life-long politician and leader of the Liberal Independent Party, which was created in 1944 in opposition to Anastasio Somoza's Nationalist Liberal Party. He was a presidential candidate in the 1984 elections. Within UNO, Godoy generally commanded the support of the more "progressive" parties. Godoy had served as labor minister in the early years of the Sandinista revolution—thus earning the enmity of the conservative non-Sandinista labor unions represented in the UNO coalition.[32] Insofar as ideological questions mattered in the selection of candidates, Godoy stood for a compromise between Sandinista socialism and the stringent free-market prescriptions of COSEP. That businessmen's alliance had its own candidate in Enrique Bolaños, one-time president of COSEP and consistent hard-line opponent of the Sandinistas and their economic and political policies. Within UNO Bolaños was strongly supported by the more conservative factions. He stood for implacable opposition to the government and for sweeping reversal of all its policies in the event of an opposition victory.

The real contest for the nomination at the end of August came down to a battle between Chamorro and Bolaños, with Godoy as a possible compromise candidate. Both Chamorro and Bolaños had their strengths and weaknesses. Bolaños was the better speaker, had a much better grasp of economic and political issues, and had long ago proved a much tougher fighter than Chamorro. But Bolaños's strengths were also potential weaknesses. His uncompromising nature, and his tendency to denounce not just the Sandinistas but also those who were insufficiently stalwart in their opposition to them, threatened to divide the shaky UNO coalition, many of whose members had been the targets of Bolaños's invective.

Chamorro's weaknesses were obvious. Her emotional and physical resilience in a long, arduous campaign was open to doubt. In past moments of crisis, she had shown a recurring tendency to back down from confrontations, often citing reasons of poor health.[33] Even her closest supporters acknowledged her questionable fitness for the presidency. As César had declared when he returned to Managua in June, "The man or woman chosen to govern the country will not necessarily be the best one."[34] On the other hand, Chamorro was unlikely to offend anyone. Her attraction was precisely her nonpolitical quality; she was "above politics." Supporters compared her to Corazón Aquino, another martyr's widow, who had once said, "What do I know about running a country?" For these reasons, Chamorro was the candidate best suited to the kind of campaign most Nicaraguan opposition leaders and their foreign supporters agreed ought to be run. Because of her lack of party affiliation and clear political doctrine, Chamorro's candidacy came closest to fulfilling the opposition's general desire to make the elections a plebiscite on the Sandinistas rather than a test of the opposition's own popularity in the country. César argued that "because . . . these are not normal elections . . . we have to choose the person who best represents the desires the Nicaraguan people will express. . . . we must choose someone the Nicaraguan people can identify as a symbol of the change they want in the 1990 elections."[35] A Chamorro campaign might keep the electorate's attention focused solely on the failings of the incumbent government without raising the issue of what the opposition might do should it take power.

The choice between Chamorro and Bolaños involved issues far more complicated than simply who would make the better candidate, however. Surrounding the entire nominating process was the more fundamental question of what the opposition could realistically expect to achieve in the elections. One thing opposition leaders did not expect to achieve was victory. When UNO leaders wrote their government platform in the summer of 1989, Antonio Lacayo recalls, "they didn't think it was possible to win." The platform was more a statement of principles than a plan opposition leaders ever expected to implement. Instead, according to Lacayo, "UNO was planning to take 30 percent of the votes in the National Assembly" and to carry on their opposition to Sandinista policies from there.[36]

If the best the opposition could hope for was a minority share of power in the National Assembly, an important question was what kind of role it planned to play after the defeat. On this point there were even starker differences between Bolaños on the one hand, and Chamorro and Godoy on the other.

Throughout 1989 Managua had been rife with talk about a new bargain between the Sandinistas and their longtime opponents in the aristocracy and bourgeoisie—a return, as some saw it, to "tercerismo." The Ortega brothers had spoken to many opposition political and business leaders about what Humberto Ortega called a new "social pact" in Nicaragua. The idea, as he later described it, was to forge a "social pact with the economic sectors, to try to create better conditions for the political parties, to remedy the excesses of the Sandinistas."[37] Daniel Ortega spoke of yielding "shares of power" to the opposition after the elections. On July 19 he declared the elections could not transfer power in Nicaragua, but he also declared that "the people want power to be shared by the Executive Branch, the Legislative Branch, and the Judicial Branch. The power shared by the Legislative Branch and the Executive Branch is what is at stake at the forthcoming elections."[38] These were subtle but clear hints that the Sandinistas were expecting the elections to yield the opposition greater representation in the National Assembly and that the Sandinistas were willing to work constructively with that opposition, if the opposition was willing, in turn, to accept the fact of the "people's power."

Many opposition leaders saw in the Sandinistas' statements the possibility of gaining a measure of influence after an electoral defeat. The Sandinistas, it seemed, finally understood that they could not effectively run the economy by themselves. As one opposition leader put it, "The country can no longer survive with all political power concentrated in one party. Apparently even the Sandinistas now accept this. Once the election is over, what will probably emerge is a government of national unity."[39] The former contra leader and presidential candidate Arturo Cruz expected the final outcome of elections to be "some kind of coalition government . . . some kind of understanding between the Sandinistas and the opposition." The old Conservative Party stalwart, Emilio Alvarez, told reporters that "even if the opposition wins, we are going to have to negotiate with the Sandinistas. . . . The Sandinistas control the army, and that is a reality we are going to have to deal with."[40]

The opposition blocs that appeared most willing to entertain suggestions of a new "social pact" were Violeta Chamorro's and Virgilio Godoy's. Alfredo César, who backed Chamorro, spoke often about the proper role of the opposition in a "civilized country." In a civilized country, he argued, "the group that loses the elections is not erased from the country's political life, but becomes a responsible opposition." The government, therefore, had to share "the responsibility of leading the country with the opposition." And the opposition should be "responsible for the country's fate through its participation in the Legislative Assembly or Congress and through the work that its members do in the posts they occupy." The Sandinistas, César argued, could not insist any longer that "they are the chosen ones and that the Nicaraguan opposition has nothing to say about our country's future." They had to allow the opposition to participate in shaping Nicaragua's future.[41]

César's specific reference to the "posts" that an opposition might occupy in a Sandinista government after the election fed rampant rumors that a bargain had already been struck between the government and the Chamorro group to provide the latter with cabinet posts in a government of "national reconstruction" after the elections. The Sandinistas, in Arturo Cruz, Jr.'s, opinion, wanted a "credible loser" who after the election would "sit[] down with Daniel Ortega to negotiate the composition of [the] Cabinet." Cruz told an American interviewer, "You will be surprised at how many [in the opposition] will be willing to collaborate in this government of national reconstruction."[42]

Virgilio Godoy was portrayed by his own supporters as the man most capable of working out an arrangement with the Sandinistas. "Godoy knows the Sandinistas from inside," one opposition leader declared. "He is one of the few politicians in Nicaragua who has the qualities of a statesman. If there is any kind of negotiation after the election, he would be an ideal negotiator." Godoy himself baldly stated that the Sandinistas had "offered the opposition 3 of the 35 cabinet ministries." He denied that UNO leaders had accepted such a deal, but like César and Antonio Lacayo he spoke of "the national reconciliation concept . . . in the sense of institutional conditions that would produce a new peaceful spirit of coexistence."[43]

The Chamorro group and Godoy, while doing what they could to run a successful campaign, were also preparing for what would come after their likely defeat. The opposition's political platform for the coming campaign dwelt heavily on the need for national reconciliation, stability, and peace, the inclusion of all groups and political tendencies in a common effort to restore the economic well-being of the country. As Lacayo recalls, UNO had not written its platform "with the purpose of implementing the program, but with the setting forth of ideals" which it hoped the Sandinistas would honor after Daniel Ortega was re-elected. "It was a program of national compromise with all sectors of society."[44]

Antonio Lacayo had more reason than most to hope for improved cooperation between the Sandinistas and the bourgeois opposition, at least on economic matters. His own company, seized from him at gunpoint by the Sandinistas in 1982, had been partially returned to him in the summer of 1988—even in the midst of the political crackdown after

Nandaime. The Sandinistas were now Lacayo's business partners, inasmuch as the government owned significant shares of the company which they allowed him to run. In February 1989 Lacayo was reportedly "back in favor" with the government, and Lacayo himself boasted of his good fortune. "The private sector has a brilliant future here," he told American reporters in February. "The people who kicked me out at gunpoint are now my partners. That makes me believe that ideology can give way to reality."[45]

Not everyone in the opposition believed in the new "social pact." Enrique Bolaños stood for uncompromising opposition to the Sandinistas. While Chamorro, César, Lacayo, and Godoy spoke of a national reconstruction government involving cooperation among all sectors of society, Enrique Bolaños wondered aloud why the opposition should do anything to ease the dire straits in which the Sandinista government now found itself. To Bolaños, the Sandinistas' appeal for cooperation was an act of pure cynicism. It was as if the Sandinistas were saying, "'now we are drowning, and we can't continue annihilating you, but I need a life preserver so that I can regain my strength and then go on annihilating you.'" Bolaños suggested instead that a vote should be held "to ask the Nicaraguan people whether [the Sandinistas] deserve to be thrown a life preserver or a yoke?"[46]

Bolaños was the favorite of the more conservative parties that had long dominated the Coordinadora—the six parties that were now the core of the UNO coalition.[47] According to the rules of the nominating process, however, a candidate needed to win ten votes for nomination. And among the eight parties that had been added to the Coordinadora to form UNO, Bolaños was far less popular. The Communist, Socialist, and other self-proclaimed "progressive" parties opposed the businessmen's candidate. The result was a stalemate. Bolaños's chances of picking up four more votes for the necessary ten were slim. But with six secure votes out of 14, he had enough support to block the candidacy of anyone else. During meetings of UNO at the end of August, five successive ballots failed to produce ten votes for any candidate. On August 31 UNO's efforts to nominate a presidential and vice-presidential candidate broke down in acrimony.

At that point, powerful foreign interests intervened to secure Violeta Chamorro's victory over Bolaños. President Arias, according to Alfredo César, "intervened openly to get Violeta nominated," and Arias himself recalls that he "did everything to get Violeta as the candidate."[48]

Venezuela's President Pérez, a close friend of the Chamorros, had un-abashedly told reporters: "You know that I admire and love Violeta very much."[49] It was widely known in Managua, moreover, that Chamorro was also the preferred candidate of the Bush administration.

The intervention of Presidents Arias, Pérez, and Bush in favor of Vio-leta Chamorro's candidacy may have had more than one motive. Arias claimed he wanted the candidate with the best chance of defeating the Sandinistas in February.[50] But most observers did not expect an opposi-tion victory in February 1990. Given the likelihood of a Sandinista vic-tory, an opposition led by Chamorro, César, and Lacayo offered the best hope of ending the civil strife in Nicaragua. These opposition leaders had cooperated closely with the Sandinistas in the past and had pronounced their willingness to do so again in the future. The Sandinistas had made clear by their actions which group they wanted to do business with: Their confiscation in June of properties belonging to the Bolaños family and to prominent Bolaños supporters was in sharp contrast to the treatment op-position leaders like Lacayo were receiving. For the Bush administration, which preferred to see the opposition win the elections, but failing that wanted to put the Nicaraguan controversy behind it, Chamorro's candi-dacy offered the perfect solution. Chamorro was the candidate most likely to cooperate in a national reconciliation after a Sandinista victory. En-rique Bolaños was the least likely.

When the balloting resumed at the beginning of September, after the heavy intervention of foreign powers, the nominating procedures had been changed. Rather than voting on individual candidates, the parties voted for combined tickets of president and vice president, and the only two tickets up for decision were Chamorro-Godoy and Chamorro-Bo-laños. The weight of foreign influence showed in the final vote. President Arias recalls he had a "hard time telling Godoy to be Number 2 and telling Bolaños to get out."[51] When the voting ended on September 2, the ticket of Chamorro-Godoy had won.

Bolaños was bitter in defeat. His supporters cried foul, claiming the nominating procedures had been "fixed," and that some parties had been given "gifts" in exchange for their votes.[52] The Sandinista radio stations spread allegations that Alfredo César had been in charge of distributing dollars on behalf of the American government. They charged that "the arrival in Nicaragua of counterrevolutionary politician Alfredo César was aimed at securing the imposition of [Chamorro]."[53] A prominent Bolaños supporter called the Chamorro ticket "an empty shell" and, referring to Chamorro's well-known frailty, doubted that it would "be able to withstand the pounding of the rain." There was some question as to whether Bolaños and his followers would even support the new ticket. But on September 7 all the UNO factions, including Bolaños's supporters, signed a document pledging their full support for the Chamorro-Godoy ticket.[54]

60

"A Policy That Is Anachronistic"

The selection of UNO's candidates ended the first phase of the electoral process. The opposition coalition had survived the challenges to its unity, both from within and without, and the selection of Chamorro had given the opposition a jolt of enthusiasm and even optimism, despite the grumblings of Bolaños. Everyone recognized that Chamorro, whatever her failings, was a more unifying force than Bolaños ever could have been. Yet more difficult challenges lay ahead, in the registration and formal campaign phases of the electoral process. UNO had proven itself capable of resolving disputes among a small group of party faction leaders, albeit not without significant foreign intervention. The question now was whether it had the ability and the resources to gather the support of the Nicaraguan population.

In September the Bush administration tried to provide the resources. After several false starts, the administration on September 21 asked Congress to provide $9 million in direct and indirect aid to the Nicaraguan opposition.[1] Secretary Baker insisted on the importance of doing "everything possible to level the playing field" in an election that "pits an underfinanced democratic coalition against an authoritarian state." Bush officials said the new aid was particularly urgent to help the opposition register its supporters in October. The bill met opposition in Congress, however. Conservatives were reluctant to lend legitimacy to the seemingly inevitable Sandinista victory and opposed giving millions of dollars to the Sandinista-controlled Supreme Electoral Council.[2] Liberals denounced the aid as an improper intervention in Nicaraguan politics. Senator Dodd argued that Daniel Ortega, unlike Marcos or Noriega, had "a real popular base in his country."[3] Senator Harkin declared that Violeta Chamorro would become known as "the best candidate the United States can buy."[4] Bush officials insisted that much of the aid would be used for ""non-partisan technical support of the election process" and for other "non-partisan" purposes,[5] but liberal opponents rightly insisted that any money that went to the opposition aided Mrs. Chamorro's campaign.[6]

The main question before Congress concerned the appropriateness of U.S. intervention on the opposition's side in the February elections. Majorities in both houses favored such intervention. Congressman McCurdy spoke for most members when he declared that the United States had "a chance now to do something openly for a free democratic process in supporting democrats as opposed to supporting a Marxist government." He implored the House Democratic leadership not to be "beholding to the left on this" and not to let "Sandinista supporters" in Congress block the aid bill.[7] The House passed the administration's request 263–156, with 99 Democrats voting in favor and 145 against. The Senate passed the bill after the White House twisted the arms of reluctant conservatives.[8] Republicans who favored the bill argued it was essential to seize "the moral high ground," so that if and when the Sandinistas stole the elections, the United States would be in a position to criticize them.[9]

Although the administration and Congress brought down criticism upon themselves and upon the opposition for this violation of Nicaraguan sovereignty, it is questionable whether the U.S. government actually succeeded in intervening in any important way.[10] The Senate did not pass the bill until October 17, and the delays prevented any of the aid from reaching the opposition in time to make a difference during voter registration in October. American journalists reported from Managua in the middle of October that the opposition's political organization was operating "on a shoestring" and appeared "practically broke." While the Sandinistas had campaign offices "in almost every city and town" in Nicaragua, with banners and flags hanging from lampposts and public buildings, UNO had opened offices in only about half of Nicaragua's 16 departments and even in Managua was "practically invisible." The Sandinistas had party members posted at nearly every one of the 4,394 registration centers, while UNO had observers at only half. Observers agreed that "UNO's organizational travails could not be worse."[11]

Opposition leaders complained that "with all this talk about money from the United States, everyone thinks we must be rolling in cash. The truth is we have nothing." The National Endowment for Democracy eventually provided the opposition over $1 million from the previous year's congressional appropriation,[12] and the opposition received some unknown sums of money through private fund-raising.[13] But the vast majority of the money approved by Congress in October did not reach the opposition in time to make much difference in the campaign. After Bush signed the legislation at the end of October, it took administration officials a month to develop accounting procedures and standards and then to send the money to the appropriate agencies for distribution. The opposition filed legal papers with the Nicaraguan government on November 2, and the government approved them on November 11, but then on January 9 it informed the opposition that the papers were incorrect. UNO purchased $800,000 worth of automobiles and other supplies, but these were impounded by the Nicaraguan Customs office. Most of the money and supplies remained blocked until late January, when the Nicaraguan government finally released them after strong protests by foreign election monitors. By then there were only about three weeks left in the campaign.[14]

The Sandinistas were annoyed at the brazen intervention of both the U.S. President and Congress in support of the Chamorro campaign, and they took full advantage of the long debates in Congress to accuse their opponents of serving as paid tools of the United States government, just like the contras. But the Sandinistas did not fear that American aid would make a great difference in the February elections. Their polls showed Ortega maintaining a comfortable margin over Chamorro, and throughout the fall and winter of 1989 they exuded confidence in the certainty of their victory. The Sandinistas' only concern was that the Bush administration would not accept their victory and would try to declare the elections tainted.

To guard against this the Sandinistas went to extraordinary lengths to win international and American approbation of the electoral process. They organized their own voter registration drive, which was so successful that it made the opposition's failure to do so beside the point. Some observers had expected the Sandinistas to prefer a low turnout, on the assumption that the 35 percent of hard-core Sandinista supporters would be more effectively mobilized than the disorganized UNO supporters. But the Sandinistas, confident of victory, wanted to ensure that the world saw a massive turnout of Nicaraguans in what they promised would be the freest elections in Nicaraguan history. By the end of October an astonishing 1.7 million out of an estimated 1.9 million eligible voters had registered. Not all the credit for the high turnout belonged to the Sandinista campaign. The Nicaraguan people showed that they were as eager to cast their vote as the Salvadoran people had been in 1984.

More proof of the Sandinistas' confidence was their prodigious effort to ensure that the 1990 elections would be the most closely and extensively monitored in Latin American history. In July the United Nations accepted Nicaragua's invitation to monitor the campaign and the voting, the first time in its history that the international body had agreed to monitor elections in a sovereign state. Later that summer, former President Jimmy Carter also accepted the Sandinistas' invitation to monitor the elections. Just a few months earlier, Carter had led a delegation of election monitors in Panama. His declaration of fraud in the May 7 Panamanian elections had played a decisive role in severely tarnishing that attempt by General Noriega to remain in power, and Carter came to Nicaragua with international recognition as a credible election witness. By the end of September, international observers were descending on Nicaragua in ever-increasing numbers.

In contrast to similar efforts in the Philippines, El Salvador, and Panama, observers in Nicaragua intended to monitor closely political conditions throughout the campaign. On October 1, the first day of voter registration in Nicaragua, dozens of UN and OAS teams spread out across the country to oversee the registration process. United Nations technicians established a satellite communications network to maintain contact with hundreds of observers throughout Nicaragua during the five months leading up to the February vote. By November, the number of UN observers doubled, and in February it increased again to 160 full-time observers. Although unable to monitor the majority of polling stations on the day of the vote, UN officials believed that by selecting at least 10 percent of the stations, and by certifying the vote totals from these samples, they would be able to provide a "clear statistical picture" that would reveal "any irregularities" elsewhere in the country. The OAS planned to supply a similar number of observers, thus spreading the net wider.[15]

The Sandinistas intended to let these international missions have a fairly free rein in Nicaragua throughout the campaign so that there could be no doubt of the election's legitimacy. In September and October, both Carter and UN representatives publicly declared that, despite some irregularities and disagreements between UNO and the Supreme Electoral Council, the electoral process was proceeding in a fair and free manner. The Sandinistas, though not complying with every demand of the opposition, tried to satisfy the observers they had invited. Elliot Richardson, the head of the UN delegation, stated at the end of October that no "undue benefits have accrued" to the Sandinistas and that with the registration of 21 political parties "the most important phase of the campaign" had come to a "satisfactory conclusion."[16]

Daniel Ortega hoped the presence of the UN and Carter missions would deprive "the U.S. extreme right-wing groups" of "arguments and weapons against Nicaragua" and that "the confirmation of free elections in Nicaragua would eliminate pretexts that justify policies of isolation, especially policies of economic isolation." President Carter, fresh from his denunciation of Noriega in Panama, would "certify the rightwing's defeat" in Nicaragua.[17] And after February there would be a new "understanding between the United States and Nicaragua.... The effect that the Nicaraguan elections will have in the United States and in the international community will open political, economic, and financial doors that will facilitate our country's reconstruction."[18]

The foreign observers agreed that while their primary mission was to ensure that the elections were fair, their secondary mission was at least as important: to ensure that the United States accepted the results of those elections. In pursuit of this goal, the United Nations had made an unusual decision to select an American, Elliot Richardson, to lead the UN observer delegation in Nicaragua. United Nations officials hoped that the participation of this life-long Republican would "eliminate any doubt about the impartiality of the verification process, particularly for conservative Americans, whose opinion is considered important to broad acceptance of the election results." Jimmy Carter also believed he had a special role in ensuring that the Bush administration and Republican congressmen accepted the likely results of the February vote. He hoped that his certification of the elections would lead to an "immediate improvement in the relationship between the United States and Nicaragua," by which he clearly meant an improvement in the relationship between the United States and the Sandinistas.[19]

As the day of the vote grew nearer, and as the Sandinistas' grew ever more confident of victory, the Nicaraguan government invited more and more observers to witness the elections. Most of these were groups sympathetic to the Sandinista revolution, similar to the groups that had witnessed the 1984 elections. The American group, Witness for Peace, exhorted its followers to "do everything we can to convince the Bush administration and Congress of the fairness of the electoral process and the legitimacy of the outcome." The statement concluded: "May the revolution continue."[20]

As the Sandinistas moved ahead in the election process, they were increasingly angry to find no parallel progress in the demobilization of the contras. By late September the Tela agreement was proving as ineffective as the Tesoro Beach agreement earlier in the year, and the biggest obstacle remained the Bush administration's refusal to cut off "humanitarian" aid to the contras and replace it with assistance for demobilization and relocation. Until that happened, and until the contras saw they had no choice but to be "voluntarily" disarmed and relocated, neither the Central American governments nor the United Nations and OAS were prepared to take steps to force the contras out of Honduras against their will.

The United Nations revealed its helplessness in September and October. Missions traveled to Central America for consultations and planning, but no forces arrived to take charge of the Honduran-Nicaraguan border. Much to the Sandinistas' dismay, moreover, UN and OAS officials fully accepted the U.S. insistence on the "voluntary" nature of any contra demobilization, if only because these international bodies had no desire to enforce an involuntary demobilization.[21] Since any deployment of UN forces had to be approved by the UN Security Council, where the United States had a veto, the American delegation in New York was able to delay the deployment merely by raising legitimate questions about its size, cost and precise role. To the Sandinistas, it appeared the United States was stalling.[22]

Not until October 13 did UN officials visit the contra camps in Honduras, and the trip proved a disaster. The head of the UN delegation warned the contras they could "only stay as long as the Honduran government lets you. . . . You are Nicaraguan and not the objects of a [U.S.] policy that is anachronistic and has been abandoned by the country that helped you."[23] The threat was as hollow as it was annoying to American ears. Contra leaders responded defiantly that they would demobilize only "when there is democracy in Nicaragua"—which was to say, never.[24] In Washington outraged Republicans demanded that the Bush administration denounce the UN for its rhetorical excesses. Bush officials met with UN Secretary General Pérez de Cuellar and "read him the riot act," and he quickly apologized for any misunderstanding.[25] The Sandinistas were appalled. Humberto Ortega, in a fit of pique, offered the services of the Sandinista army to remove the contras from Honduran soil if no other force was willing to do so.[26]

Most observers continued to regard the contras as a moribund "anachronism," but the Sandinistas persisted in their fear of the contras' continuing survival. While the *New York Times* referred to "the pin pricks of contras who no longer pose a credible military threat," the Sandinistas still considered the contras the spearhead of American policy, as well as the armed wing of UNO. Their constant denunciations of the links between the opposition political parties and the armed guerrillas were not mere election propaganda.[27] The Bush administration provided money to UNO and to the contras as if they were two sides of the same coin. Throughout the campaign UNO leaders went out of their way to associate themselves with the contras and even resisted pressure from Jimmy Carter to sever the connection. The Sandinistas, with their usual attention to the simple question of who held the guns, recognized with cool objectivity that so long as the contras remained a force-in-being, they would be arrayed on the side of those who now challenged the Sandinistas at the ballot box, and they would be a tool available to the United States whenever it chose to use it.[28]

The Sandinistas were acutely conscious of the dangers the contras would pose under a variety of different electoral outcomes. The "social pact" Humberto Ortega had in mind had no place for an armed opposition. If the Sandinistas won the election, but the opposition gained a substantial base of power in the assembly, the UNO coalition would continue to use the contras as a lever to enhance its political power. If the Sandinistas won the election, but the Bush administration found grounds to declare the vote fraudulent, aid to the contras might be resumed. And should the impossible occur and the Sandinistas lose the election, the continued existence of the contras would be extremely perilous.

It was with such considerations in mind that Humberto Ortega began in the fall of 1989 to make clear his intention to retain control of the Sandinista army—no matter who won the elections in February 1990. Sandinista officials pointed out that "not even in Poland, despite the change of government, has the army been dismantled, and we are not going to do so either."[29] In November Tomás Borge related that when Humberto Ortega was asked if he would be worried if Chamorro won the election, "Humberto answered that the one who should be worried is she."[30] Ortega publicly declared that if the opposition did win the elections, it would have to respect the Sandinista Front and the army because "without the Sandinistas, no one can govern Nicaragua."[31]

Given their fears of a future struggle against the contras, the Sandinistas were understandably displeased to find that the one concrete result of the Tela agreement had actually been the reinfiltration of as many as 3,000 armed rebel fighters back into Nicaragua between August and October.[32] The contras, to be sure, were returning not to fight but to hide. Faced with the possibility of a forced demobilization at the hands of the United Nations, many contras fulfilled their vow to "return to the mountains" rather than give up their arms. The reinfiltration troubled the Sandinistas for several reasons, however. First, the more contras there were in the mountains of Nicaragua, the fewer there were to be demobilized in Honduras. Second, the contras would be difficult to root out of their lairs among the supportive rural population, forcing the Sandinistas either to accept an almost permanent guerrilla force in the mountains or to pay the high political price necessary to deprive the contras of their peasant supporters.

The Sandinistas were especially unhappy to see the contras back in their strongholds during the electoral campaign. In remote regions of Nicaragua where the city-based UNO parties could never hope to reach, the contras represented the sole organized opposition force. Journalists traveling in the hills of Matagalpa and other northern provinces learned from local government officials and church workers that the contra fighters had been "campaigning actively for UNO, encouraging people to register to vote and generally singing the praises of opposition presidential candidate Violeta Chamorro."[33] The Sandinistas themselves tried to frighten peasants away from the voter registration tables in these areas, using the alleged threat of contra attacks as an excuse. At the end of October peasants living near San Marcos "accused Government troops of staging mock combat near voter registration stations . . . to frighten away voters likely to cast their ballots against the Government." One man said the Sandinistas had intimidated hundreds of voters by bringing troops into town and firing weapons to defend against a purported contra attack. The local townspeople, however, who described themselves as supporters of the contras, didn't believe the government reports. "We knew that the commandos weren't going to attack. If they're going to do anything here, we certainly would know about it long before the Government." Throughout the campaign the Sandinistas charged that the rebels were trying to intimidate the peasants into voting for UNO.[34]

As early as August 16, Daniel Ortega had warned that a large reinfiltration of contras would force the Sandinistas to end their unilateral cease-fire and renew the war. August and September passed without an official resumption of the fighting, but the number of clashes between contra and Sandinista units increased. Most of these clashes were undoubtedly instigated by the Sandinistas, since the contras' strategic situation was too perilous to support a renewal of the war.[35] Sandinista army units played cat-and-mouse with the rebels, sending small units into rebel-controlled areas to flush out the contras in the hope of then bringing larger forces in for the kill. While there were no major engagements, and the contras undertook no offensive operations, there were constant skirmishes and occasional ambushes of Sandinista convoys.

By October, with no progress toward demobilization of the contra army in sight, the Sandinistas were looking for the right opportunity to capture the world's attention. On October 21 the Sandinista Defense Ministry reported the ambush in Matagalpa of two Sandinista army trucks filled with reservists, allegedly on their way to register for the vote. All the soldiers were armed, but according to the Sandinista report the contras surprised the convoy, killing 15 reservists and wounding another 9.[36] The contras denied the attack,[37] claiming two Sandinista units had mistakenly clashed. In the wake of the October 21 ambush Sandinista leaders ostentatiously held an "emergency" meeting of senior commanders to discuss measures for increasing "military defense against increasing criminal attacks" by the contras.[38] Daniel Ortega emerged from that meeting to declare that the Bush administration would now have to make clear whether it was "in favor of the electoral process or of the war." The Bush administration's decision would "determine whether or not the Nicaraguan electoral process proceeds successfully."[39]

Ortega's angry protests met with silence in Washington and Latin America, however, and the Sandinistas were compelled to take more dramatic steps. A few days after the ambush Ortega traveled to San José for the centennial celebration of Costa Rican democracy—a gala affair to which President Arias had invited many world leaders and where he hoped to display himself and Costa Rica in the best light. At Arias's celebration the democratic transformation of the hemisphere was manifest. Carlos Andrés Pérez, Spain's Felipe Gonzalez, Argentina's newly-elected President Carlos Menem, and President Bush were all in attendance, and so too was Violeta Chamorro, whom Bush took the occasion to embrace publicly. Communist governments were out of favor. Fidel Castro was conspicuously not invited. Daniel Ortega arrived in military uniform, with the Sandinista red bandanna around his neck, and seemed out of place. Arias in his opening address to the conference declared that "we have often seen how those who led struggles against dictators themselves use the name of freedom to establish dictatorships of a different ideological view."[40] When the friendly conference ended, and after Ortega had seized opportunities to meet and have his picture taken with Bush, the Nicaraguan leader announced that as of October 31 the Sandinistas intended to end the unilateral cease-fire and strike hard at contra forces in Nicaragua.

Although Sandinista officials had been hinting at such a step for weeks, the announcement set off an explosion of indignant denunciations. Latin leaders upbraided the Sandinistas for their crass, undiplomatic behavior. Arias declared the decision "lamentable. The ball is in the political court, not in the military court." The UN Secretary General called for moderation and expressed hope that the Sandinistas would continue the cease-fire. In Washington, liberal Democrats railed at Ortega. Congressman Obey complained that the Nicaraguan president was "a fool and always has been."[41] President Bush called Ortega "an animal at a garden party." On October 31 the Senate voted 95–0 to condemn the Sandinistas' "totally unjustified" action. Bush officials could scarcely conceal their delight; according to the White House spokesman, they were "incredulous that [Ortega] made such a blunder."[42]

Many observers immediately assumed the Sandinistas were looking for an excuse to cancel or postpone the elections. Bush called Ortega's threats a "shameful blow to democracy"[43] Nicaraguan opposition leaders said the Sandinistas' feared defeat at the polls and preferred to fight the contras. Few observers seemed to understand that the Sandinistas were, on the contrary, more concerned about the rebels than about the elections and that their decision to abrogate the cease-fire was a calculated if somewhat desperate attempt to force the United States to abide by the terms of the Tela agreement and to end direct support for the rebels. Daniel Ortega quickly admitted that he had "touched a wasp's nest" with his dramatic announcement at San José, but he and other officials insisted it had been the only way to grab the attention of the Bush administration and the American Congress. "It was a shock tactic. What we are looking for is a commitment to dismantle the contras by December 5. If we had not done this, it would never have happened."[44]

The logic of the Sandinistas' strategy was sound, even if the execution was flawed. In their extreme state of weakness, having made every concession demanded by the United States, the Sandinistas had few bargaining chips left to force compliance with their own demand that the contras be eliminated prior to the elections. The threat to disrupt the elections and resume the war was all that remained. Clearly, good behavior was getting them nowhere. The more the Sandinistas endeavored to satisfy American and international opinion concerning the elections, the more the United States and the world tried to evade the delicate issue of the contras in the hopes that the elections would solve the problem. The Sandinistas hoped President Bush or the Congress would end "humanitarian" aid to the contras rather than jeopardize the elections. The key to the Sandinistas' strategy was the "gentleman's agreement" that allowed Congress to block further aid to the contras on November 30. "When the U.S. Congress approved the law providing funds for the contras," Ortega explained, "they provided themselves a way out."[45] The solution to the crisis the Sandinistas had created was to cut off the aid. Ortega declared that "whether or not the electoral process moves along in Nicaragua will no longer depend on us."[46]

Although their actions at the end of October seemed a rash "blunder" to most observers, the crisis they provoked was carefully orchestrated to avoid an irreparable breach with the Bush administration. They quickly invited Presidents Arias and Pérez to settle the dispute and claimed to see signs that the Bush administration was willing "to negotiate the cease-fire and the contra's demobilization." Daniel Ortega correctly speculated that Bush did not want "to reactivate the contras militarily."[47] The offensive the Sandinista army launched after November 1 was ill-prepared and clearly not designed to annihilate contra forces in Nicaragua; it bore no resemblance to "Operation Danto" of March 1988.[48]

The Sandinistas had guessed that the elections meant more to the Bush administration than defending the contras, and they were right. After Ortega's announcement at San José, Secretary Baker quickly declared that "what we are trying to avoid is the Sandinistas seizing on something like this as an excuse to deny the Nicaraguan people free and fair elections."[49] Even when the Sandinistas launched their offensive,

Marlin Fitzwater said the Bush administration would not seek arms for the contras to defend themselves: "We don't want to go that route. We want to get free elections."[50] Contra leaders were bitter, complaining that the "whole debate" in Washington was "about whether the contras should be killed with their stomachs full or their stomachs empty."[51] The Sandinistas' assessment of the Bush administration was vindicated. As one official observed, "Daniel gave them the choice of war or elections, and faced with that choice, they took elections very clearly."[52]

The Bush administration preferred to let the Sandinistas suffer the political consequences of their actions rather than start a row with Democrats in Congress. Even pro-contra Democrats were eager not to give the Sandinistas "an excuse to cancel the elections or remove international observers." Where the Sandinistas miscalculated, however, was in expecting Democrats in Congress to demand a change of policy from the Bush administration. According to Ortega, it was liberal Democratic advisers who had counseled him to abrogate the cease-fire and force the Congress to act. Arias suggested he "get rid of" such advisers.[53] The international outcry over Ortega's announcement was so great that even liberal Democrats in Congress were shaken and had no stomach for demanding an end to "humanitarian" aid to the contras. Senate Majority Leader Mitchell called Ortega's announcement a "very unwise move." The Bipartisan Accord signed in March "contemplated continued assistance through the elections. And we intend to honor that."[54]

Far from acting too recklessly, the Sandinistas may have erred in not acting recklessly enough. Their strategy had depended on creating genuine fears in Washington and Latin America that the elections would be canceled and the war resumed, but they had too quickly deflated the crisis. Their American lawyer, Paul Reichler, had assured reporters almost immediately that the elections would be held on schedule and that the Sandinistas were "not even remotely considering canceling or postponing the elections or interrupting the electoral process." The offensive against the contras was too small to threaten their annihilation, so the Bush administration and Congress could return to complacency without fear that either the elections or the contras were seriously in danger.[55]

61

Old Thinking

A frustrated Humberto Ortega looked for other ways to force the Bush administration's hand. He decided to remind Bush officials, and Salvadoran President Cristiani, that the Sandinistas could cause as much discomfort in El Salvador as the continuing existence of the contras was causing in Nicaragua. "Because of the re-entry of the contras into Nicaragua," Humberto Ortega recalls, "we reactivated our support for the FMLN."[1] In September and October deliveries of arms from Nicaragua to El Salvador became bolder and more visible.

For the Bush administration, the continuing supply of weapons from Nicaragua and Cuba to the FMLN guerrillas posed a problem. Bush officials were keen to reduce the level of conflict in El Salvador and the controversy it engendered in the U.S. Congress. There was nothing Bush officials could do to the Sandinistas, however, since resuming military aid to the contras was out of the question. Once again, therefore, Bush officials turned to the Soviet Union to help solve the problem in Central America.

By the summer of 1989, however, the Bush administration's public demand for a "linkage" between Central America and all other issues in U.S.-Soviet relations was becoming an embarrassment to the President. Assistant Secretary of State Aronson's conversations with his Soviet counterpart, Yuri Pavlov, had been very friendly, but American intelligence officials reported that during the first eight months of 1989 Nicaragua had received an estimated 12,000 tons of Soviet military equipment at an estimated value of $350 million. At that rate, Nicaragua would receive $525 million worth of military goods in 1989, $10 million *more* than in 1988. Aronson had urged the Soviet government to show more understanding of the Bush administration's position. "You cannot escape it," he told Pavlov. "No one will ever believe that you cannot control your allies when your assistance sustains their very existence." Nevertheless, in the middle of September a Soviet shipment of four Mi-24 attack helicopters arrived at a Nicaraguan port after stopping in Cuba.[2]

The embarrassment for the Bush administration lay not only in the fact that the weapons still flowed to Cuba, to Nicaragua, and to El Salvador. The other problem was that, despite this, the President and his secretary of state wanted to renew in earnest the U.S.-Soviet rapprochement begun under Reagan. Pressures from Congress and from European allies had been mounting all year. On September 18 Senator Majority Leader George Mitchell called for "a more energetic and engaged policy" toward Gorbachev. Baker, very sensitive to such criticisms, had already decided to increase the pace of talks with the Soviet government and was recommending compromises on a number of American positions to move the negotiations forward.[3] A meeting between Baker and Soviet Foreign Minister Shevardnadze was scheduled for the end of September in Wyoming, and Baker hoped to agree there on a firm date for the next summit. As far as Central America was concerned, whatever "window of opportunity" might have existed at the beginning of the year was closing fast. The credibility of the administration's "linkage" was waning. Bush risked angering the conservative Republicans whom the policy had, in part, been meant to appease.

Just days before Baker's meeting with Shevardnadze in Wyoming, the State Department spokeswoman, Margaret Tutwiler, unleashed a vitriolic assault on Soviet policy in Central America. Declaring that the level of arms transshipped though Cuba to Nicaragua had "increased dramatically" in 1989, Tutwiler said it was "inexplicable to us why the East bloc feels that it must provide Nicaragua with even more weapons while a cease-fire is in effect than it provided the Nicaraguans when they were actively engaged with contra forces." Tutwiler also charged that Nicaragua and Cuba were continuing to supply weapons to the guerrillas in El Salvador, in violation of the Esquipulas agreements as well as Soviet pledges. At a press conference in Montana, President Bush himself chastised the Soviet government for a policy that was not "very kind and gentle."[4]

The sharp rhetoric, however, proved only a prelude to the more quiet severing of the "linkage." Baker reportedly pressed Shevardnadze hard at Wyoming, but the Soviet foreign minister's less-than-satisfactory responses did not prevent the two sides from reaching important agreements in most other areas of negotiation. The two ministers signed seven bilateral accords in Wyoming, made progress toward agreement on nuclear arms reductions, and announced plans for a summit between Bush and Gorbachev for the spring or summer of 1990. Privately, they also agreed on what was to be an historic "mini-summit" off the coast of Malta in December.

On the subject of Central America, Shevardnadze reiterated Gorbachev's assurance that no new weapons were being sent to Nicaragua in 1989, but Baker won no further concessions regarding Soviet indirect aid through Cuba to Nicaragua and from Nicaragua to El Salvador. Baker told reporters afterwards that the Soviets were "committed to using their influence to do what they can to stop the flow of weapons to the insurgency in El Salvador," but he also noted "an increase in Soviet-bloc weapons and military equipment" reaching Nicaragua.[5] In more plaintive tones than earlier in the year, Baker said, "We would simply like to see the Soviet Union do as much as it possibly could with Cuba to stop that flow." By the end of October, however, 16,000 tons of military equipment worth an estimated $480 million had been delivered to Nicaraguan ports.[6] At that rate the total for 1989 would reach 19,200 tons worth $576 million dollars, compared to 19,000 tons worth $515 million in 1988.

Bush officials chose to look on the bright side. After the ministerial meeting at Wyoming, Foreign Minister Shevardnadze made an unscheduled one-day trip to Managua. Bush officials waited expectantly for what they hoped would be a stern Soviet message to the Sandinistas, and in Managua American journalists detected trepidations among Sandinista leaders. Shevardnadze's meeting, however, produced nothing new. In separate communiqués, the Nicaraguan government committed itself to stop receiving "armaments from the Soviet Union to Nicaragua" until after the February elections. This statement, of course, left room for continuing indirect shipments through Cuba. The Soviet communiqué merely repeated that the Soviet Union had halted arms shipments to Nicaragua.[7]

Meanwhile, the State Department sent subtle signals of approval to the Sandinistas, indicating America's willingness to accept a Sandinista victory if elections were fair. When Daniel Ortega reached agreement with opposition leaders on August 3, for instance, Baker declared the

United States "very pleased," and in September he authorized a visit to Managua by one of his closest aides, Assistant Secretary of State Janet Mullins. This first formal meeting between a senior American official and senior Sandinista officials in years was taken as an important signal by the Sandinistas. Paul Reichler expressed hope that it would lead "to more direct contacts between the Administration and the Government of Nicaragua, and ultimately to the normalization of relations."[8] On September 22 Jimmy Carter was able to inform President Ortega that the Bush administration was prepared to begin a "step-by-step increase in embassy personnel" and that such a suggestion by the Sandinistas would be "well-received." Assistant Secretary Aronson, Carter wrote, "is prepared to work this out."[9] On October 8 Baker stated that the Bush administration would "accept the results of a free and fair elections without regard to [our] preferences with respect to who should have won the election." Baker and Aronson, convinced that the Soviets were keeping pressure on the Sandinistas to hold free and fair elections, fulfilled their part of the bargain.[10] As one journalist privy to the thinking of Baker and Aronson later put it, "a pattern began to form. The Soviets posed a number of tests for the U.S., and Washington passed most of them."[11]

It was perhaps unfortunate for the Bush administration that the Soviet government would not pass the one test posed by the Americans. Soviet arms continued flowing to Nicaragua, and the Sandinistas were providing some of those arms to the FMLN. Yuri Pavlov tried to soothe Aronson by pointing out that the kind of light weapons that were being delivered to the FMLN "could not tip the balance in Central America." He even cited the flow of weapons as a sign of Soviet restraint and goodwill. After all, there had been "no introduction of SAM [surface-to-air] systems in El Salvador."[12] Soviet officials reported that Shevardnadze had obtained "firm assurances" from the Sandinistas that they were not supplying weapons to the FMLN, but when Aronson said the United States could prove otherwise, Pavlov insisted that the Soviet government could not accuse the Sandinistas of shipping arms based on U.S. intelligence reports alone. "To go to the Sandinistas and say the U.S. had developed evidence of their violations would not do for us."[13] The Bush administration hoped for a "smoking gun" that would prove, without the aid of American intelligence, what everyone knew was occurring.

That "smoking gun" appeared on October 18, when a truck carrying weapons from Nicaragua to the Salvadoran guerrillas was captured by the Honduran army. The driver of the truck admitted to having delivered arms to the Salvadoran guerrillas throughout 1989. Aronson summoned Soviet Ambassador Dubinin to the State Department, presented the new evidence of gun-running from Nicaragua, and demanded a response. The Soviet government, however, refused to accept the evidence. On October 30 Foreign Minister Shevardnadze wrote to Baker dismissing the American claims as providing "no grounds for accusing the Sandinista *leadership* of violating its commitment to end assistance to rebel movements."[14]

Shevardnadze's response, in effect, challenged Baker either to cause an open breach between the two governments or to back down. Baker chose the latter course. He complained to Ambassador Dubinin that Shevardnadze's response was "the same old stuff," a relic of "old thinking," but he diplomatically suggested that perhaps the fault lay with the Sandinistas, not with the Soviets. He told Dubinin, "The Sandinistas are tooling you around badly. . . . It is hard for me to believe Minister Shevardnadze wrote this letter. I hope that someone else did."[15] Planning for the December summit, meanwhile, went forward without delay.

The captured truck was only the beginning of the problem, however. By the end of October it was clear that the Sandinistas' arms shipments to the guerrillas were fuel for a new "final offensive" against the Salvadoran army and the Cristiani government. On October 30 FMLN guerrillas launched a spectacular mortar attack against the Defense Ministry in San Salvador, and by the middle of November the conflict in El Salvador was once again blazing out of control. Both the Salvadoran army and the guerrillas carried out assassination attempts against one another, and the shadowy "death squads" began killing suspected guerrilla sympathizers. As the Bush administration's hopes for a negotiated settlement faded, its anger at the Soviets grew. On November 18 Baker declared that Soviet policy in Central American remained "the biggest obstacle to a full, across-the-board improvement in relations." With the Bush-Gorbachev "mini-summit" at Malta less than three weeks off, Pavlov flew to Washington for consultations with Aronson.[16]

A week after Baker's speech, another "smoking gun" fell from the sky. A small plane carrying weapons from Nicaragua to the FMLN guerrillas crashed at a landing strip in El Salvador, and the pilot and cargo were seized by the Salvadoran army. This shipment included 24 Soviet-made SA-7 surface-to-air missiles, the first time such weapons had ever been delivered to the Salvadoran guerrillas. President Cristiani suspended diplomatic relations with Nicaragua citing the "genocidal . . . and treasonous behavior of Daniel Ortega."[17] The Bush administration could scarcely believe the Sandinistas' audacity; and Bush officials could only wonder at the Soviet policy that had permitted this shipment to occur on the eve of the summit.

At least the Sandinistas' purposes were easy to discern. The delivery of the missiles to the FMLN was a deliberate and carefully considered message to the Bush administration that the Sandinistas were prepared to cause as much difficulty as possible in El Salvador so long as the United States continued to support the contras. Sandinista leaders made little effort to hide their involvement. Officials told reporters that the missiles were sent "to deal a powerful but precise blow to the American-backed Salvadoran military . . . placing America's extensive involvement in El Salvador at risk from weapons whose supply is controlled from Managua." The virtue of the SAM missiles from the Sandinistas' point of view was their *undeniability*. Unlike the unfortunate truck shipment, the delivery of SAM missiles did not require a capture or a crash to be discovered: From the moment the first SAM was fired at the first Salvadoran army helicopter, the United States would know with certainty that the Sandinistas had delivered them and that the decision to do so had been made personally by Humberto Ortega. Roger Miranda, Humberto Ortega's chief staff aide, had told American officials and journalists in late 1987 that the Sandinistas had the "arrows," that they had trained the guerrillas in their use, and that they had come very close to delivering them in 1987, but had held back.[18] After the plane crash, Sandinista officials made sure that American journalists understood that the delivery was not the act of some subordinate, but had been "designed and personally overseen by major Sandinista leaders, including Humberto Ortega." On November 27 Ortega himself ridiculed the "big fuss" that was being made because "some arrows have turned up in El Salvador." He reminded reporters that the first "arrows" in Central America had been used by the U.S.-backed contras against Sandinista helicopters.[19]

If the Sandinistas' reasons for delivering the weapons were clear, however, the policy of the Soviet government baffled American observers. The delivery of the SAM missiles directly contradicted Pavlov's earlier claim that the absence of such weapons in the FMLN's hands was a sign of Soviet restraint. Either the Soviet government had no control over the delivery of the missiles, in which case Pavlov had misled Aronson in suggesting that it did, or Soviet officials approved the delivery of the missiles, in which case by Pavlov's own logic the Soviet government had deliberately chosen not to show restraint—less than two weeks before the Malta "mini-summit" between Bush and Gorbachev. The much-heralded "new thinking" of Soviet foreign policy was little in evidence in the one part of the world where it seemed to make the most sense. It was the *Washington Post*, not just conservative Republicans, which insisted that "Mikhail Gorbachev cannot be allowed to continue posing as a good-willed, hand-wringing outsider."[20]

The puzzle of Soviet policy toward Nicaragua became even more complicated when American intelligence officials reported at the end of November that the Soviet freighter *Ivan Ilyich* had left Leningrad bound for Nicaragua with a cargo of four Mi-17 helicopters. If delivered, it would be the second Soviet shipment of helicopters to Nicaragua in less than three months and the most direct violation yet of Gorbachev's pledge, recently reaffirmed by Shevardnadze in Managua, not to make such deliveries. The Bush administration kept news of this shipment to itself.[21]

The news of the SAM missile delivery infuriated Bush officials, but with the eagerly awaited "mini-summit" between Bush and Gorbachev just days off, Secretary Baker did nothing that might upset the burgeoning partnership. White House officials declared that Bush would urge Gorbachev to "stop feeding Fidel Castro."[22] On November 28 the Soviet ambassador officially denied any "attempts to link us directly or indirectly with this incident. [There] is no reason for creating a crisis situation." Baker responded with a letter to Shevardnadze, in which he declared that "this latest incident calls into question your government's undertakings toward mine. . . . If the commitments we make cannot be kept, we have little basis on which to proceed. . . . The time has come for [you] to stand up and . . . use your influence to put a final and definitive end to Nicaraguan and Cuban military and logistical assistance to the FMLN." The letter practically accused the Soviet government of lying, and in a public statement the next day Baker actually used the word. But tough as Baker's statement was, he again provided the Soviet government the excuse it needed to close the matter without a rupture. "Either the Nicaraguans are lying to the Soviet Union, or the Soviet Union is lying to us. We prefer to believe it's the former."[23] The more likely answer was that everyone was lying to everyone else. Castro and the Sandinistas occasionally misled the Soviets.[24] But, as Pavlov later acknowledged, the Soviets had been giving the Americans inaccurate information about arms deliveries throughout the year.[25]

On stormy seas off the coast of Malta on December 2, President Bush insisted that Central America was "like a gigantic thorn" in their shoes as the two leaders tried "to walk smoothly along" toward better relations.[26] Gorbachev responded by reading a sentence from prepared notes: "We have assurances—firm assurances from Nicaragua—that no deliveries using certain aircraft were actually carried out." Pavlov, commenting later on this exchange, offered insight into the entire Soviet approach to American pressures concerning Nicaragua. Note the "very precise wording" of Gorbachev's statement, Pavlov explained. "[Gorbachev] said, 'We have assurances' from the Nicaraguans, which in fact we did. But he didn't say we believed them."[27]

The problem of Central America did not prevent the two leaders from declaring success at the summit. At an unprecedented joint news conference, Bush said "We stand at the threshold of a brand new era of U.S.-Soviet relations." When questioners raised the issue of Nicaragua, Gorbachev repeated that he had "assurances" from the Sandinistas. Bush said he was "accepting" the Soviet leader's claim, but he didn't "believe that the Sandinistas have told the truth to our Soviet friends." Motioning to Shevardnadze, Bush said he did not want to challenge the Soviet foreign minister's word. "I am saying that [the Sandinistas] have misled Mr. Shevardnadze when they gave a specific representation that no arms were going from Nicaragua into El Salvador." The next day, Secretary Baker argued not only that the Soviets had been misled, but that they were apparently powerless to affect Cuban and Nicaraguan policies in any case. "The Soviet Union has told us they are leaning on Nicaragua and Cuba not to send weapons to the FMLN, but that has not worked," Baker said, "so we are encouraging them to lean even harder. We have no reason to disbelieve them. . . . We believe them when they say they are leaning on these people, and yet the weapons do continue to find their way in."[28]

After Malta, Bush and Baker were attacked by conservatives for not demanding more from the Soviet leader. Days after the summit, Baker called Shevardnadze to make "it absolutely clear" that there would be a political price to be paid if the Soviet Union were not more cooperative, and he made clear who was to pay it. The Bush administration, Baker explained, had exposed itself to conservative criticism by offering economic cooperation at the summit without any concessions from the Soviets on Central America.[29] The Soviet foreign minister promised "to have a *very* serious conversation with the Nicaraguans and Cubans." According to diplomats in Managua, Ambassador Nikolaenko did meet with Ortega and reportedly delivered a stern rebuke—for allowing the missile shipment to occur on the eve of the summit.[30] According to Sandinista accounts, the Soviet ambassador warned that the Nicaraguan government would be held to blame "if Soviet-American relations seriously deteriorated" as a result of such embarrassing incidents.[31]

The FMLN's latest "final offensive" had ended unsuccessfully in El Salvador, so there would be no further need for arms deliveries before the February 25 elections. The Sandinistas were calling for dialogue in El Salvador as they turned their attention to the electoral challenge at home. The next summit of Central American presidents was set for December 11. Moreover, the U.S. Congress on November 30 approved the continuing supply of "humanitarian" aid to the contras through the end of February. The Sandinistas' gambit had failed, and they had little reason to continue pressing the point with the Bush administration.

The year's worth of exchanges between the American and Soviet governments ended with a fitting coda. After the Malta summit and Secretary Baker's telephone call to Shevardnadze, the Soviet freighter *Ivan Ilyich* bearing helicopters for Nicaragua was abruptly ordered to turn back to Leningrad.[32] According to Pavlov, the Soviet government "believed quite seriously that the course of U.S.-Soviet relations was in jeopardy. We had to act."[33] Pavlov did not explain, however, why the Soviet government was still worried about the course of relations *after* the successful conclusion of the Malta summit, while during the week *before* the summit Soviet officials had blandly brushed off Baker's complaints about the SAM missile shipment to El Salvador. In any case, the *Ivan Ilyich* turned around again a few weeks later and at the end of January delivered its cargo to Nicaragua. On February 1 Secretary Baker told members of Congress that he had been assured by Soviet officials that the four helicopters would be "committed to civilian use." As for Soviet pressures on Cuba, the State Department on February 20 confirmed reports that Cuba had received six new MiG-29s from the Soviet Union.[34]

Despite the Bush administration's later claims to the contrary, any Soviet pressures on the Sandinistas must in the end have had little effect. Since Soviet officials made clear, even to the Bush administration, that they had no intention of using economic and military aid as a means of pressuring their allies, the Sandinistas never had to fear that their arms supply or their economic assistance would be cut off. In the long term, Soviet aid might well decrease on all fronts, but this grim future was an inevitable fact of life for the Sandinistas, no matter what course they took. Far from making them susceptible to Soviet pressures, it made the Soviet Union less and less relevant to the Sandinistas' survival. The Sandinistas considered the Soviet Union a spent force, and their entire strategy in 1989 and 1990 consisted of changing horses in mid-stream, of creating an opportunity to jump from the declining Soviet bloc and to seek legitimate status in the Western community. The Sandinistas were not blind to the events swirling around them. The Eastern European empire was crumbling with each passing month. Communist governments were falling, with or without Soviet acquiescence. If the Soviet Union would not or could not protect its allies in Poland, Czechoslovakia, East Germany, or Hungary, with the might of the Red Army present on their very soil or just across the border, how was it going to protect the Sandinistas or the Cubans in a hemisphere dominated by American power?

In facing this global hurricane, to be sure, Fidel Castro and the Sandinistas chose two entirely different courses. Castro battened down the hatches and turned into the wind. He was convinced Gorbachev was making a tragic mistake, and he did not intend to be brought down in consequence. The Sandinistas, however, led by the Ortega brothers, tried to sail along with the new prevailing winds. If the United States was going to be the winner in the global struggle, the Sandinistas were determined to make their peace with the United States. In the end, the most important role the Soviet Union played was simply to be collapsing. As Tomás Borge put it at the end of January: "At the beginning of our struggle, the world was different. Today, our colored dreams of that time are in contrast with the present black-and-white dreams."[35]

The Sandinistas continued to be far more concerned about the contras than about the policy of the Soviet Union. The rebel army, protected from annihilation by the shield of world opinion, was completing a decade-long political evolution toward a genuine campesino army unlike anything seen in Nicaragua since the days of Sandino. At the end of 1989 a group of young military leaders under "Franklyn" formed a new "civil-military" commission to take over direction of the contra army. Composed exclusively of commanders, with only Aristides Sanchez as a civilian "adviser," the new leadership had cast off Enrique Bermúdez and Adolfo Calero, while the other members of the old contra directorate— Alfredo César, Alfonso Robelo, Azucena Ferrey, and Pedro Joaquín Chamorro—had long since returned to Managua politics.[36]

For the first time in its history the contra movement was openly led by fighters who had made their way up through the ranks. The 29-year-old

Franklyn, a former coffee farmer, had become the latest to fill the Sandino-like role of rebel chieftain in the northern and central country-side of Nicaragua. He and other young commanders had finally managed to complete the generational coup that had been quashed in the summer of 1988. This time, the U.S. government had not stood in the way, but assisted in the transformation of the movement by shutting off all funds to the contra Directorate headquarters in Miami at the end of 1989.[37] What remained were the fighters themselves, led by a mixture of former campesinos, former Sandinistas, and former Guardsmen, now speaking with their own voice. As one of the veteran American officials put it, "What we're seeing now is what we wished had happened five years ago."[38] The contras had finally been "purified" of most of their CIA and National Guard taint. This was both a weakness and a strength. The new complexion of the contra leadership made it much harder for the Sandinistas to denounce them as "Somocists" with any credibility. On the other hand, however, this campesino army had little in common with any of the political factions wrestling for power in Managua.

———

At the December 11 Central American summit meeting at San Isidro de Coronado, Costa Rica, Daniel Ortega made one final attempt to force at least the start of the contras' demobilization before the elections. The meeting occurred at a time of high tension in the region. The furious rebel offensive was just winding down in El Salvador. The Sandinistas had not restored the cease-fire in Nicaragua, and talks with the contras had broken down. On December 10, the eve of the summit, the most violent episode in the Nicaraguan election campaign occurred. A group of Sandinista supporters wielding machetes attacked an UNO rally in Masatepe, killing one opposition supporter and hacking off the arms of several others.[39] The opposition demonstrators responded by going on a rampage, unhindered by the Sandinista police, and attacking the homes of local Sandinista leaders. As the summit opened at San Isidro de Coronado, Costa Rica, President Arias lamented that his peace process had "regressed like never before."[40]

Despite the tensions, the five Central American presidents managed to find common ground for agreement in what had almost become a ritual of symbolic trades. Once again, Ortega appeased the Salvadoran president by publicly repudiating the Salvadoran guerrillas. This time he went further than ever before, not only demanding that the guerrillas give up their armed struggle and accept a cease-fire, but also paying unprecedented homage to the right-wing President Cristiani. In a statement practically dictated by the Salvadorans, Ortega joined the other presidents in expressing "decisive support of Salvadoran President Alfredo Cristiani and his Government . . . the product of democratic, pluralistic and participatory processes." The statement was the widest breach yet between the Sandinistas and their Salvadoran "cousins," and the most damaging to the latter. President Cristiani was clearly thrilled to return home with such a victory, and Humberto Ortega and other Sandinista leaders spent many weeks apologizing and attempting to explain away their public betrayal of the FMLN.[41] In return the Sandinistas got most of what they wanted: a joint call by the five presidents on the United States to cease supplying aid to the contras immediately and to provide it instead to the international monitoring and verification organizations. The Sandinistas had also wanted to set a new deadline for demobilization of the contras, perhaps in January. But the other presidents were not about to force a confrontation with the contras now that the elections were so near, and least of all was the Honduran government prepared to do so. The Sandinistas, therefore, had to settle for the demand that the United States cut off aid to the contras. This was another hollow victory, since the Bush administration had no intention of cutting off the contras now that Congress had approved aid through the elections.[42]

The summit at San Isidro, in fact, did little more than set aside all other issues pending the completion of elections in Nicaragua. There was a tacit understanding among all the governments involved that these other issues, such as the fate of the contras, U.S.-Nicaraguan relations, and even the war in El Salvador, would be determined by the outcome of the elections in Nicaragua. If the Sandinistas won, the guerrilla struggle in El Salvador would continue and the guerrillas could reassess their strategy. If the Sandinistas lost, the Salvadoran guerrillas themselves recognized that their own prospects would be dire. As one guerrilla commander told reporters before the Nicaraguan elections, "It would be a disaster if the Sandinistas were to lose. It would cause the regional balance of power to shift. We would be isolated." Already some FMLN leaders were saying they had learned from the Sandinistas' mistakes and that if they ever gained power, they would allow a greater role for the private sector and immediately seek good relations with the United States.[43]

If there were any doubts that the Sandinistas saw the February elections as their only salvation, such doubts should have been dispelled soon after the San Isidro summit. On December 20, the United States invaded Panama to remove Manuel Noriega from power and bring him to trial in the United States on drug smuggling charges. Had the Sandinistas sought an excuse to avoid the elections—as many assumed was the case after they abrogated the cease-fire in November—they could not have hoped for a better excuse than the American invasion of a neighboring Latin state. The Sandinistas vehemently denounced the intervention, expressed their solidarity with the people of Panama, and took the opportunity to put their own army on alert in case of an American assault on Nicaragua. Humberto Ortega even had a statement released warning opposition leaders that they would be the first executed if the Americans invaded—reminiscent of his warning, years before, that opposition leaders would be the first "hanging from the lampposts." When American soldiers entered the Nicaraguan ambassador's residence in Panama in search of weapons or the fleeing Noriega, Ortega ordered Sandinista army tanks to surround the American embassy in Managua, and the Foreign Ministry expelled 20 American diplomats in protest. Not once, however, did the Sandinistas suggest the invasion of Panama would have any effect on the February elections. On the contrary, within a week of the invasion Daniel Ortega embarked on his formal campaign, a campaign he and his colleagues confidently expected to win.

62

"Everything Will Be Better!"

The Sandinistas prepared themselves for the challenge of the 1990 electoral contest more thoroughly and conscientiously than for any other event in their history. In the early 1980s they had underestimated the threat posed by the contras and had been slow to repair their deficiencies in meeting it. In the mid-1980s they had overlooked the signs that their economic measures were failing badly, and were costing them heavily in rural Nicaragua; it took several more years of deepening crisis to prompt the Sandinistas to shift their policy. In the months leading up to the February 1990 vote, however, the Sandinistas neither underestimated the dangers nor failed to act swiftly and skillfully to meet them. The vanguard Sandinista Front, which to many observers seemed suited only for guerrilla war, adopted the style of Western political parties as if born to it. For men who had long spoken with contempt of the "bourgeois" democratic process, the Ortega brothers and their advisers proved in many ways more adept in that system than in their own.

The Sandinistas devised an elaborate campaign, drawing fully on the latest Western advice and technology. They put their vast party organization to work, making it a more effective election machine than anything seen in Nicaraguan history. They hired foreign consultants. They devised campaign themes to make the most of their strengths and to soften their sharp edges. In the parlance of political advertising, the Sandinistas

691

repackaged their image. Daniel Ortega transformed himself from a rather dour commander to a smiling celebrity, and the collective, opaque leadership of the nine gave way, for the purposes of the campaign, to the celebration of Daniel's candidacy.

The financial and technical aspects of the Ortega campaign awed both foreign journalists and Nicaraguan opposition leaders. As one American journalist reported at the end of January, "billboards featuring Ortega hover over nearly every major intersection in the city . . . pro-Sandinista slogans are scrawled on hundreds of buildings . . . Sandinista activists campaign door to door, handing out Hula-Hoops, candy, backpacks and T-shirts." Signs of the new "kinder, gentler Daniel Ortega" were everywhere. "The image of Ortega photographed cheek-to-cheek with his 2-year-old daughter, Camila, is now ubiquitous. At rallies, Ortega now appears in civilian dress rather than familiar olive green fatigues, poses for Polaroid snapshots with beauty contestants and has taken to dancing on stage, Bruce Springsteen-style, with female fans."[1]

After years of conflict with the hierarchy of the Catholic church, the Sandinistas and Ortega found religion again and sought at least the pictorial blessings of the Church and Cardinal Obando. In December Ortega was photographed carrying flowers to an altar, embracing a priest, and taking communion. On New Year's Day he delivered his address seated next to a nativity scene. On January 30, he agreed to several old demands of Cardinal Obando, including the release of all remaining political prisoners. Ortega made the announcement standing side by side with the cardinal.[2]

Abandoning the long, theoretical lectures of the past, Sandinista rallies and speeches appealed to Nicaraguan workers and campesinos in language and symbols they supposedly could understand. In a country fanatically devoted to baseball, Ortega urged voters not to "foul the ball to the right or the left" by voting for the opposition parties, but to hit a home run right down the middle by voting for the Sandinistas. He described the opposition coalition as an indigestible "tamale cooked by Bush . . . poorly-made and poorly-wrapped," or as a bag filled with "a dog, a hen, a cat, and a Yankee" who would tear each other to pieces. At rallies the Sandinistas gave away baseball equipment and stereos. When Ortega went to visit neighborhoods he was preceded by Sandinista "advance" teams who entertained the local residents with music and dancing girls. For large Sandinista rallies, public buses and government trucks carried thousands of campesinos and public employees, on paid leave, from their jobs or

homes. When the opposition held its rallies, the state television ran popular movies like *Batman* or the championship fight between Mike Tyson
and "Buster" Douglas, and the municipal buses ran more sporadically
than usual.

The Sandinistas made use of some of the most advanced campaign
technologies yet seen in Latin America. They conducted private polls
constantly and shaped their campaign carefully in response to them. The
Times's correspondent reported that the Sandinista campaign "sent out a
half-dozen mailings targeting distinct groups of voters, including house-
wives, professionals, people over 50 and artisans. Telegrams are being delivered to all registered voters on their birthdays. A computerized telephone system is dialing numbers all over the country with a recorded
message from Ortega reminding voters to check Box No. 5." The government-run television was "peppered with sights and sounds of the Sandinista campaign: a smiling Ortega kissing babies, white doves, children in
Sandinista T-shirts swaying to reggae rhythms and party followers chanting the party's campaign slogan."[3]

Fidel Castro and Cuban officials had warned the Sandinistas from the
beginning that the U.S.-backed opposition would have all the money and
the latest campaign technology. One Cuban official had told Miguel D'Escoto, "You can't beat the gringos at their own game. . . . The opposition
will have the best U.S. campaign advisers behind it. They will clobber
you."[4] The Sandinistas had taken these warnings to heart. They, too,
hired American advisers and acquired the necessary technology, and they
were proud of their American-style campaign. "It's a populist, media-
image campaign that has worked on all levels," one party spokesman told
reporters. "It was put together by research, the way it's done in the U.S. or
France." Castro had warned Daniel Ortega that elections were "a risky
business. . . . If you get into the game, you should be prepared to lose."
But Ortega had responded, "We will win, Comandante. If we do things
right, we will win."[5]

In all tangible respects, the Sandinistas had done things right. They
spent lavishly on the elections. To foreign observers the Sandinista campaign appeared "to enjoy nearly unlimited resources."[6] By February the
Sandinistas were publicly claiming to have spent $7 million on their cam-
paign. That figure did not include such costs to the government as the
use of public buses and military trucks for transportation of supporters to
and from rallies, the use of state-owned media for promoting Ortega's
candidacy and attacking the opposition, and the use of public employees

and government buildings for campaign work. The Sandinistas had no reason to spare expense on the campaign. Compared to the cost of fighting the contras or the suffering caused by continued international financial isolation, the price of the election was insignificant and well worth it.

The Sandinistas' campaign was not all glitter. Ortega and his advisers did not try to evade the obvious "issues" of the 1990 election, including even the most prominent and damaging one: the Sandinistas' dismal handling of the economy. The economic conditions in Nicaragua had improved in some respects since the end of 1988, but in ways that tended to make the government less rather than more popular with the Nicaraguan people. The hyperinflation of 1988 had been brought more or less under control in 1989: from an annual rate of over 30,000 percent inflation had dropped to about 1500 percent. This first and necessary step back towards a sounder economy had required large layoffs of government employees, to cut government spending, and was accompanied by a sharp recession, resulting in the loss of still more jobs outside the public sector. Industrial production in Nicaragua fell by 20 percent or more in 1989. Consumers and workers were angry; salaries were frozen while the price of goods continued to rise. To bring inflation under control, the Sandinistas had been forced to harm their strongest supporters, the urban workers and public-sector employees of Managua and other large Pacific Coast cities. To increase production and exports, the government had had to help their bitterest enemies—the small urban entrepreneurs, market vendors, and independent growers.

More than many incumbent parties in other countries would have, the Sandinistas accepted a measure of responsibility for the failed economy, admitted past mistakes, and promised to do better in the future. The acknowledgment of error became almost a campaign theme for Ortega, although at large rallies his frank admissions elicited confused responses from the Sandinista Party faithful. Accustomed to shouting in unison: "Sandinista Directorate, give us your orders!" they did not quite know what to answer when Ortega asked "Is the government's work perfect? Tell me the truth: Yes or no?" (Some shouted "No!" others shouted "Yes!") "Are there mistakes or are there no mistakes?" ("There are!"— "There are not!") "There are mistakes," Ortega insisted. "Of course there are mistakes. . . . There are failures, and there are mistakes. . . . We will not deceive ourselves. . . . We know that everything is not all right. We have problems; there are mistakes; there are failures . . . aside from the war, aside from the aggression."[7] The Sandinistas' campaign slogan,

"Everything will be better!" was among other things an acknowledgment of past mistakes. Everything would be better, the Sandinistas argued implicitly, because the Sandinistas themselves had changed.

Many foreign observers considered that campaign slogan, which was painted on almost every wall in every city in the country, to be a vague and vacuous theme. The Sandinistas, however, could not exactly ignore the dismal condition the country was in. And their promise was not really vacuous. The Sandinistas offered sound explanations about why everything would be better. The elections by themselves would solve most of Nicaragua's problems. Once the Sandinistas gained the legitimacy of an electoral victory, the war against the contras would end, and this, along with the end of Nicaragua's diplomatic and economic isolation, would open the way to national recovery.[8] Everything would be better, above all, because the Sandinistas would have made their peace with the Americans. The Sandinistas promised to seek "excellent relations" with the United States, or "at least an appropriate relationship of mutual benefit in the diplomatic and commercial areas." They argued that the Bush administration was prepared to normalize relations with Nicaragua. As Humberto Ortega explained, a central goal of the campaign was to convince the Nicaraguan people "to appreciate how we Sandinistas are able to establish a solid, respectful relationship with the United States that is beneficial to the people of Nicaragua."[9] The editors of *La Prensa* sneered that after ten years of "unnecessary distancing of relations" between the two countries, the Sandinistas were now making improved relations their "great electoral offer."[10]

Rapprochement with the United States meant peace in Nicaragua, and peace provided the answer to one of the most damaging popular complaints against the government: the draft. The Sandinistas refused to match Chamorro's very popular pledge to eliminate the military draft altogether after the elections, but Humberto Ortega and senior military officials assured Nicaraguans that, with the end of the war, military service would no longer mean death and maiming for Nicaraguan youths. On the contrary, one official explained, "Our youths and their families should realize that military service is good for them. . . . [It] will mean that they will have better opportunities to study"; it would give them the skills and discipline to prepare for their future "professional life."[11]

The Sandinistas promised not only a change in their relations with the United States, but also a change in their relations with the non-revolutionary and even counterrevolutionary elements of Nicaraguan society.

Everything would be better because of the new "social pact" the Sandinistas were inaugurating even before the February vote. The Ortega campaign openly appealed to sectors of Nicaraguan society they had in the past attacked as enemies of the revolution. "The ticket represents . . . all social sectors," Ortega declared, "and all economic sectors of Nicaragua. So, you must tell your friends, relatives, and neighbors about this even if some of them are involved with UNO. Some are confused, and they must know that it does not matter if you are not an FSLN militant; it does not matter if you think like a Conservative, or a Liberal."[12] Sandinista officials appealed to the middle class, the vendors, and the small independent producers not just with slogans but with economic incentives. The Sandinistas even courted "Somocistas," knowing well that many of the campesinos and small landholders of northern Nicaragua were old Somoza supporters. Ortega expressed his sympathy for those "people who were Somozists out of need, not because in their hearts they felt anything for Somoza. . . . We have many people working for us who once served for Somoza, but they are the poor people."[13] Indeed, one reason that Ortega made such a point of the Sandinistas' past errors was precisely to convince those who had suffered under Sandinista policies that the government really did understand its mistakes and would correct them. Throughout the campaign the Sandinistas made a point of promising, once again, that there would be no more confiscations of land after the elections. In Boaco, a stronghold of independent growers and contra supporters, Ortega gave a "guarantee" that the Sandinistas had "completed the period of land confiscations which had been necessary during these past 10 years of revolution."[14]

The Sandinistas devoted most of their campaign to these "positive" themes, but they did not neglect to attack the opposition. Ortega charged that Violeta Chamorro and UNO were puppets and mercenaries of the Bush administration. A vote for UNO was a vote for the United States and its policies of aggression against Nicaragua. When asked if he would debate Mrs. Chamorro, Ortega declared he would debate Bush, since "he is the true opposition we face." The Sandinistas insisted, and many foreign observers shared this view, that one of Chamorro's greatest weaknesses was her close association with the United States government.[15] After the invasion of Panama, this liability was thought to be particularly severe.

The Sandinistas also did their best to link the opposition closely with the contras. Sandinista media often referred to the opposition as the "GN-UNO;" the 'GN' stood for Guardia Nacional. When the Sandinistas complained about contra attacks in the countryside, they referred to them as "armed campaigning" on behalf of UNO. After every attack, and especially after the well-publicized ambush on October 21, the Sandinistas repeatedly called on UNO candidates to denounce and repudiate the contras.

UNO, in short, was the party of the Somozists, of the National Guard, of obedience to American imperialism. In all respects it represented a return to the past. The peasants would not vote for the return of their old masters; the urban workers would not vote for the return of the old bankers and factory owners; the masses who gained their voice in the revolution would not vote for the return of the elite oligarchy to rule their lives.

Each facet of the Sandinistas' attack on the opposition resonated especially well with many American observers, who tended to share the assumptions behind these campaign themes. Thus it was widely agreed that Violeta Chamorro suffered from her close association with the United States, and even more from UNO's ties with the contras. Many polls taken during the campaign supported these claims, and it was assumed that one of Chamorro's most difficult tasks would be to shed these various stigmas.

Yet Chamorro and UNO did not try to shed them. On the contrary, their actions tended generally to reinforce them. Chamorro went out of her way to appear to be President Bush's preferred candidate and the one whom Bush would reward with financial aid and a lifting of the trade embargo. As one of her first acts in the campaign, she flew to Washington to be photographed with Bush and to obtain assurances from him that the United States would help Nicaragua if she won. She and other UNO leaders refused to respond to Sandinista criticisms on this point, not even to assert the kind of independent nationalism that most American observers would have expected. Chamorro's only effort to avoid the label of "America's puppet" was to flaunt, as well, the support of Carlos Andrés Pérez and President Arias. After meeting with Bush she toured Europe to show that her access to all Western capitals, and to Western capital, was better than Ortega's. Chamorro and her advisers believed their close association with the United States was more beneficial than harmful, and for the same reason that the Sandinistas believed it important to promise better relations with the United States. As the editors of *La Prensa* put it, "the popularity [in Nicaragua] of the idea of normalizing friendly relations with the Bush administration" was apparent to both campaigns.[16]

Even the embarrassing debates in Congress over the Bush administration's $9 million aid proposal may have aided the Chamorro campaign. As one journalist reported from Managua, "Well-publicized foreign donations to the opposition parties here have been interpreted by many Nicaraguans as proof that the opposition, not the Sandinistas, has better access to the foreign money necessary to relieve Nicaragua's crisis."[17] The Sandinistas themselves soon came to recognize that their own campaign promise of better relations with the Americans unfortunately made a better case for Chamorro's election than for Ortega's. In the end the Sandinistas wound up having to make contradictory arguments: They promised, on the one hand, that everything would be better with a Sandinista victory because Nicaragua would benefit financially from improved relations with the United States; but, on the other hand, they rejected the opposition's identical argument on the grounds that the United States could not help Nicaragua. Three days after Chamorro traveled to Washington and won President Bush's support for a lifting of the trade embargo, Ortega cited President Bush's warning to Latin leaders that the large American budget deficit precluded increases in foreign assistance. "If the United States cannot help its friends resolve their problems," Ortega argued, "then the UNO should not come here with the story that it is going to solve Nicaragua's economic problems with the Yankees' assistance."[18]

The Chamorro campaign's refusal to repudiate the contras was even more surprising to American and foreign observers. Jimmy Carter, attempting to "lessen tensions" on both sides in the campaign after the December 10 violence at Masatepe, directly asked UNO leaders to "condemn the contras and ask them to come out" of Nicaragua. "The contra presence is deadly," Carter stated, and "the contra-UNO relationship is a very sensitive point." Right up until the end of the campaign, most American journalists assumed that the contras were "vastly unpopular" and that Chamorro hurt herself by not denouncing them.[19]

Again, however, both UNO and the Sandinistas understood why a repudiation of the rebel army would have hurt more than helped the opposition. The Chamorro campaign advisers knew as well as the Sandinistas that many thousands of campesinos and landholders in northern and central Nicaragua supported the contras. Indeed, in some areas of Nicaragua the rebels, many of whose leaders were from local families, had more popular support than UNO, whose leaders were as distant in race and class as in geography from the local campesinos. At an opposition campaign rally in Matagalpa, journalists reported that a "roar of approval greeted the introduction of three former contra chieftains." The crowd itself was swelled by contra fighters "in from the bush to hear the speech."[20] The contras and their supporters were a large and important "core constituency" of Chamorro's, no less than the Sandinista militants, union members, and government employees were a large and important "core constituency" of the Sandinista Party. It was no more in the interest of UNO to repudiate the contras, even after acts of violence, than it was for the Sandinistas to repudiate their followers who attacked opposition demonstrators with machetes.

The opposition took the same course as the Sandinistas, not alienating its supporters but trying to reach out to adherents of the other camp by softening the edges of the campaign. Tomás Borge and other Sandinista leaders tried to frighten the beneficiaries of the revolution by warning that UNO would take all those benefits away if it won and would persecute those who had given allegiance to the Sandinistas. In response, UNO tried in its own campaign to allay the fears of the Sandinistas' "core constituency" that a Chamorro government would turn back the clock and erase all aspects of the revolution. UNO leaders pledged not to take away the jobs of public-sector employees, not to take confiscated land away from the peasants, and not even to strip the army of its officer corps below the very senior levels. Whether these promises seemed any more credible to UNO's intended audience than Sandinista promises of a new "social pact" did to theirs may be doubted, but both government and opposition made an effort at least to blunt the hostility of the other camp in the hope of attracting the largest portion of wavering voters.

Both Ortega's and Chamorro's advisers believed the best way to make this appeal to the majority of voters in Nicaragua was to promise a national reconciliation following the election, a social compact in which no one would be excluded, ignored, or persecuted. On this all-important campaign issue, Chamorro had a distinct advantage. Not having been in power for very long, she had not had much opportunity to incur the resentment of anyone.[21] The Sandinistas, on the other hand, had a record to overcome of hostility, threats, and occasional persecution against the bourgeois class. Their ten-year fight with the contras had become a fight to the death, and the contra fighters had repeatedly sworn never to lay down their arms while the Sandinistas remained in power. And who would have a better chance of persuading the United States to cease its aid to the contras: a President Ortega or a President Chamorro? If peace and national reconciliation were the goals, Chamorro seemed to have a better chance of attaining them than the Sandinistas. Beyond these rational calculations, the images and symbols of the campaign also favored UNO. Ortega's civilian dress and baby-kissing during the last three months of the campaign could not erase the image of Ortega in military dress, reviling in angry rhetoric the counterrevolutionary elements of Nicaraguan society. Violeta Chamorro, on the other hand, was the embodiment of national reconciliation: a member, with Ortega, of the original junta of the government of national reconstruction; the widow of a martyr whom both the Sandinistas and their bourgeois opposition claimed as their own. Obviously no one had a better claim to the unifying symbol of Pedro Joaquín than Chamorro herself, and the Sandinistas' showed their concern about this by pettily referring to her always by her maiden name, Barrios.

In the end, the Sandinistas themselves implicitly acknowledged their disadvantage on this important issue by advancing an argument that was more of a threat than a promise of harmony. A Chamorro government would not be able to achieve national reconciliation, the Sandinistas insisted, because the Sandinistas themselves would not allow it. As Tomás Borge put it, the opposition could not

> govern because there have been deep transformations in Nicaragua that it would try to reverse, causing serious social consequences. For example, with the existing Revolutionary Armed Forces ... how can the officers obey hare-brained orders imparted by those who are appointed ministers of defense and the interior? Since these structures are revolutionary, UNO will attempt to destroy them, causing chaos in Nicaragua. This would be a country without a government. Therefore, an UNO victory will neither be convenient for the United States nor for the very few supporters of that electoral alliance.[22]

Although on the issues UNO appeared to hold its own with the Sandinistas, and even to have an advantage, this was subsumed by the many and more obvious disadvantages. Especially to foreign observers, the subtle question of whether Chamorro was hurt or helped by her close ties to the United States was difficult to answer; the "issues" of the campaign, in general, seemed to outsiders ill-defined and poorly articulated. Much clearer and more easily measured was the striking inferiority of UNO's campaign in terms of resources, organization, and unity.

The Cubans' warnings proved to be an exaggeration of the Nicaraguan opposition's resources and abilities, and of their American backers' capacity to provide them. As sophisticated and richly endowed as the Ortega campaign was, the Chamorro campaign was both unsophisticated and under-financed, despite the $9 million U.S. aid package. Large portions of the money voted by the U.S. Congress in October did not reach the opposition until near the end of January, due in part to bureaucratic delays in Washington and to legal tangles in Managua. Estimates of the resources ultimately available to the Chamorro campaign varied, but it is unlikely the opposition received much more than $4 million in equipment and cash. Much of this went to supply the opposition with the kinds of things the Sandinistas already had for free—vehicles, office furniture and equipment, and salaries for campaign workers.

The financial support for *La Prensa* and independent radio stations through the National Endowment for Democracy may have largely compensated for the Sandinista Party's control of Nicaraguan state-owned media. But a few hundred thousand dollars paid to the independent unions could not match the campaign work done by the much larger Sandinista unions. In short, the American assistance went some way toward "leveling the playing field" between the resources of the FSLN-dominated government and that of the opposition. The Sandinistas, however, had taken their campaign to a new and unanticipated level, and the Chamorro campaign had no means of competing on that level.

Subsequent charges by some of the Sandinistas' American sympathizers that the Bush administration "bought" the election for Violeta Chamorro were absurd. The opposition probably spent a little more than half of what the Sandinistas' spent, and that did not include the "free" campaign resources available to the Sandinistas by virtue of their control of the government. If large sums of money were reaching UNO campaign officials, they were not being used for the campaign.[23] Throughout the campaign American and other foreign journalists were stunned by the contrast between the two campaigns. As late as February, one American observer described the opposition's efforts as "almost invisible once you get a short distance from Managua," while another reported on the very same day that "in Managua, which has nearly a fourth of the nation's voters, UNO's campaign is virtually invisible."[24]

If the opposition failed to mount a strong campaign in the crucial months of November, December, and January, however, the problem was not only lack of funds. Some of the problem lay with the candidate herself, some with bad organization in the campaign, and some with fissures in the UNO coalition that had opposition leaders expending much energy in internecine battles.

In the five months between her nomination and the vote, Chamorro spent an average of one week per month outside of Nicaragua. Some of the time spent abroad was important in gathering and demonstrating American, Western European, and Latin support for her candidacy. An equal amount, however, was the result of Chamorro's frail physical condition. In September she took a week-long trip to Costa Rica, Miami, and Caracas. At the end of October she left Nicaragua to spend a week in Houston for medical treatment, and then two weeks more traveling to Washington and Europe to obtain foreign support for her candidacy. The campaign officially opened in December, but on January 2 Chamorro fell and broke her knee. She immediately traveled to Houston again for surgery, spent two weeks in the United States and a third privately convalescing in Managua. Almost all of January was lost, and when Chamorro finally returned to the campaign at the end of that month there were only three-and-a-half weeks left.

Chamorro's long absences, besides squandering precious campaign time, also provided the occasions for debilitating fights within the opposition coalition. Although the Sandinistas continued to harp on supposed splits between the left-wing and right-wing parties of UNO, the real division that emerged in the months after Chamorro's nomination was between the presidential candidate's small circle of friends and relatives and the rest of the UNO political party leaders. These disagreements were about power and prestige, not ideology.

The political leaders who had come together to form UNO in the summer of 1989 believed they were the leaders of the opposition. When they chose Violeta Chamorro as their presidential candidate, they believed they were choosing a figurehead or, less kindly, a puppet.[25] As the presidential campaign came to dominate the opposition's activities, however, and the backroom bargaining and compromises of the pre-campaign period ceased to have relevance to the struggle, the center of power shifted from the UNO party leaders to the presidential candidate and her small circle of close, and closely related, advisers. Chamorro became a national and international celebrity. She had the open support of powerful foreign leaders like George Bush and Carlos Andrés Pérez, and it was for her candidacy that money was raised. As one of Chamorro's advisers told reporters, "the presidential candidate transcends the coalition. She is the one who at the end of the day must make the decisions." As Violeta herself explained, "I am the boss."[26]

In Nicaraguan political circles it soon became clear that the route to power, whether the opposition won or lost the elections, was through the Chamorro clique, not through UNO. But that route was largely closed to those who were not relatives or devoted friends of Violeta. The UNO party leaders who saw their power fading rapidly after September 2 were especially troubled to watch the meteoric rise of Alfredo César—former Sandinista, former contra, and now fastened to Chamorro's rising star along with his brother-in-law and her son-in-law, Antonio Lacayo. On September 9, Chamorro named Lacayo as her campaign manager. César was named to the UNO Political Council. At the end of September, César also succeeded in having himself designated as UNO's candidate for president of the National Assembly, the equivalent of the American Speaker of the House, should the opposition win a majority in the legislature.[27] Whether the opposition won or lost the presidential elections, therefore, César would be the leader of the opposition in the Assembly.

While UNO political party leaders watched César's rise with concern and annoyance, members of the Chamorro circle viewed with similar irritation the behavior of vice presidential candidate Godoy. The experienced party politician and 1984 presidential candidate could barely hide both his disdain for Chamorro and his sense that, by rights, the presidential nomination ought to have been his. His public praise for her was often faint. She was, he said, a woman of "impressive unpretentiousness." A good public speaker himself, Godoy was compelled to acknowledge that Violeta Chamorro's speeches were "not very sophisticated," though she spoke "a language that anyone can understand." Asked about her weakness as a candidate, as he was constantly, Godoy would sometimes say that she would be good at drawing the women's vote.[28] It soon became clear to all observers that the relationship between the presidential and vice presidential candidates was not a close one.

The split between the Chamorro circle and Godoy and UNO had only one notable effect on the campaign itself. Godoy and UNO party leaders began to take a harder and harder line against the Sandinistas, against any post-election cooperation, and even against some aspects of national reconciliation. The gap between the Chamorro circle and Godoy and

UNO grew most noticeable in the last days before the vote, when Godoy provocatively warned of an uprising by UNO supporters against a Sandinista fraud. At a time when Jimmy Carter and the UN were seeking assurances of peaceful acceptance of the results by all sides, Godoy's comments stood out as especially disruptive. The Sandinistas noted the divergence and went out of their way to praise Chamorro's conciliatory spirit and to condemn the "hotheads" within UNO.

————

The debilities of the UNO campaign, physical and political, did not obscure all its successes. Chamorro, when she was able, played her part in the campaign perfectly. She appeared at rallies on crutches, seated on the back of a pick-up truck, dressed completely in white, moving her arms in the air to embrace the crowds. Her speeches were short, unmemorable, and as Godoy noted, "not very sophisticated." But she was an effective symbol. She was known to be a deeply religious, even somewhat mystical woman, and an unquestionably religious aura surrounded the crippled mother dressed in white. As the weeks passed, the crowds at the UNO rallies grew bigger and more enthusiastic. From the 5,000 that greeted Chamorro at the first rally in Juigalpa in early September, the numbers that came just to see Chamorro steadily increased, climaxing in the enormous rally of more than 200,000 in Managua on the last day of the campaign. Some observers detected a mounting wave of support for her campaign throughout the final weeks.

What these observers detected, however, did not appear in most of the independent polls. Throughout the campaign what became known as the "war of the polls" favored the Sandinistas. In the fall of 1989, both government and opposition media printed the results of polls that favored their respective candidates. By December it was the polls conducted by more respected, neutral organizations that began to attract attention, and the majority of these showed Ortega with a commanding lead. Both sides considered the polls extremely important, and for similar reasons. If the Sandinistas' victory appeared inevitable, so the thinking went, potential supporters of the opposition might not trouble to cast their vote, either out of a sense of futility, or out of a vague fear of retribution by the victorious Sandinistas. In their respective campaigns, the Sandinistas labored to make their victory appear a foregone conclusion, while UNO candidates tried to convince supporters that their vote would make a difference and, more important, that it would not be held against them. The opposition had no political slogan to match the Sandinistas' "everything will be better"; the most effective slogan of the Chamorro campaign was, "your vote is secret."

The Chamorro campaign was shattered, therefore, and the Sandinistas were elated, when three successive polls in January and February showed Ortega with a huge lead. On January 24 the firm of Greenberg-Lake released its poll showing Ortega ahead of Chamorro by margin of 51 percent to 24 percent, with 16 percent undecided. The Sandinistas were particularly delighted that this extraordinary poll had been conducted by an American firm, for in a country where the population almost instinctively regarded the will of the United States as decisive, the poll lent an aura of inevitability to the Sandinistas' victory. The opposition was obviously badly shaken by the poll, because the day after its release the UNO campaign openly charged for the first time that the Sandinistas intended to commit fraud during the February 25 vote. The charge included a summation of all the complaints UNO had been making about the campaign for weeks, but coming the day after the disastrous poll results it was widely seen as an effort by UNO to prepare the ground for a cry of foul after its inevitable loss on February 25.

The opposition had some grounds for complaint about the way the campaign had proceeded. American journalists confirmed allegations by UNO officials that the Sandinistas tried to intimidate opposition supporters, with the result that many UNO candidates and poll-watchers around the country resigned in the course of the campaign.[29] When the Sandinistas and international observers responded that the contras may also have been engaging in acts of intimidation against Sandinista supporters, thus balancing both the blame and the damage done,[30] UNO leaders complained that they had no control over the contras while the Sandinistas certainly had control over State Security officials.

Despite the validity of these complaints, however, even opposition leaders had to admit that the Sandinistas had behaved much better than they ever expected. *La Prensa* and the opposition radio stations had been allowed complete freedom of expression. Chamorro and Godoy had held their rallies with a minimum of interference from the government, and the *turbas divinas*, with the exception of the brutal incident at Masatepe in December, had been more or less controlled throughout the campaign—proof after ten years that the Sandinistas could control "the masses" when they so chose. Near the end of the campaign Alfredo César acknowledged to reporters that "we expected it to be really a lot more troublesome than we've had." The chairman of the Supreme Electoral Council, Mariano Fiallos, challenged foreign journalists to "Go around and see if you see any sign of widespread fear. You see demonstrations, people putting flags everywhere, painting the walls. You don't see signs of electoral fear in Nicaragua."[31] The international observers led by Jimmy Carter and Elliot Richardson had little patience with the opposition's complaints and saw in them only the opposition's fear of inevitable defeat. Carter called UNO's complaints "highly exaggerated," and he bluntly accused the opposition of "laying down a marker so if they lose they can say, 'Well, there were some irregularities.'"[32]

Nevertheless, Carter and his colleagues took up UNO's complaints in the interest of insuring the validity of the February 25 vote.[33] At the end of January, Carter won commitments from the Sandinistas finally to make the American aid available to the opposition, to prevent any "campaigns of intimidation" against UNO officials and supporters, and to limit the use of government property and state-owned media for the Ortega campaign. Carter noted that he had "a great deal of leverage over" the Sandinistas precisely because they were "looking for a victory on the 25th" and wanted the election "to be certified as being honest." Carter left little doubt what outcome he expected on the 25th. In comments to reporters on February 7, Carter said the problem that most concerned him was the demobilization and repatriation of the contras after a Sandinista victory. He did not find it necessary to discuss the equally vexing problem of what might happen to the Sandinista army after an UNO victory.[34]

Many opposition leaders were not entirely convinced of Carter's impartiality, although they appreciated his efforts on their behalf. They blamed Carter for the Sandinista victory in 1979, and one UNO official suggested that Carter must "share the guilt" for what had happened in Nicaragua. In asking Carter to present UNO's complaints to Ortega, that official also commented wryly that Ortega "listens to you. He is a good friend of yours." In response, Carter smiled and said, "I am a friend of all Nicaraguans."[35]

The Sandinistas responded to the January 25 poll by taking further steps to insure that their victory would be accepted by the international community and by the Bush administration. Not only did Ortega immediately accede to almost all of Carter's requests, but the Sandinistas also moved quickly to allow a new flood of election observers to watch the voting on February 25. Days after the Greenberg-Lake poll was released the Sandinistas began authorizing new delegations, even those that were known to be hostile to them.[36] At the end of January the Sandinistas agreed to authorize an increase in the number of OAS observers from 110 to 400.

The Greenberg-Lake poll had its effect in the United States, as well, where Bush officials began, under questioning by Congress, to set forth the conditions necessary for a normalization with the Sandinistas after the elections. Thus Secretary Baker explained to the Senate Foreign Relations Committee on February 1 that a Sandinista victory by itself would not guarantee improved relations between Nicaragua and the United States. If the administration determined that the election was "free and fair," Baker stated, "and we determine that they have indeed stopped their support of subversion in neighboring countries . . . then we would be prepared to normalize our relations with that government."[37]

Baker's statements aimed primarily at warning the Sandinistas that normalization would not be automatic if they won. Observers in Washington and Managua, however, took the statements as the Bush administration's acceptance of an inevitable Sandinista victory. Days later Tomás Borge declared that "even the Americans . . . believe in our victory," and throughout the month of February, the Bush administration's alleged acceptance of the pending Sandinista victory became a staple of Daniel Ortega's campaign rhetoric.[38] At a rally on February 16, Ortega interpreted the Bush administration's statements as grudging acceptance of the inevitable: "The President saying: Even though I do not like the elections in Nicaragua, and even though I will not like the electoral results, I am willing to recognize those electoral results." Ortega asked his fellow Nicaraguans to give "praise for Bush because Bush is helping us bury [UNO]!"[39]

The inevitability of a Sandinista electoral triumph appeared even more irrefutable when a second American poll was released on February 20, just five days before the vote. The prestigious *Washington Post*/ABC News survey showed Ortega leading Chamorro by 16 points, 48–32. Senior Bush officials like National Security Adviser Brent Scowcroft were convinced that "the Sandinistas are going to win. The only question is how brazen they will be."[40] Two days later Secretary Baker testified again before Congress and reiterated the Bush administration's conditions for better relations with the Sandinistas. "[I]f you're going to assume there is a Sandinista victory," Baker explained, ". . . it's very important before we talk about normalizing relations that we see a sustained period of good behavior in terms of subverting their neighbors. The government of the

United States must be satisfied that there will continue to be open political space in Nicaragua."[41] The next day a distinguished group of former American officials, led by McGeorge Bundy and Sol Linowitz, called for "full normalization" of relations with Nicaragua if the elections were fair, including the establishment of full diplomatic relations, support for the resettlement of the contras, a lifting of the trade embargo, and help in obtaining international financial aid for Nicaragua.[42] On the day of the vote, a State Department official confided to a reporter that there was a "constituency" in the State Department "that wants normalization with the Sandinistas if there is nothing grotesque [in] the elections, they make the right noises and discontinue support for the FMLN."[43]

By Election Eve, few in Nicaragua or in the United States doubted the outcome. The international observers were openly predicting a Sandinista victory. Former governor of Arizona, Bruce Babbitt, a member of Carter's observer team, saw not "much evidence to the contrary." The Sandinistas, Babbitt found, had "played this election like a pinball machine, shaking and jiggling it to improve the score, but never quite enough to light up the 'tilt' sign."[44] Many leading Nicaraguans were no less persuaded of the coming Sandinista victory. Arturo Cruz, returning to Nicaragua on February 23 to cast his vote, expressed confidence that the Sandinistas were genuinely offering a "political opening and that the hard and radical rhetoric at the start of the revolution is becoming more pragmatic." The election itself, he said, was not as important as what followed: a "process of national reconciliation, in which, if President Ortega is reelected, the opposition will play the role of censor from Congress."[45] Cardinal Obando also believed that the Sandinistas had changed and had become "more pragmatic." If the elections were honest, the cardinal declared, "the winner must be respected." Obando predicted that the Bush administration would "start conversations with" the Sandinistas if Ortega won.[46] Even members of the Chamorro campaign showed hints of resignation amidst the usual confident bombast of the political contest. "We won't lose either way the election goes," campaign spokesman and former contra spokesman Ernesto Palazio told reporters. "The revolution is over, finished. The Sandinistas have had to choose between ideology and power, and they can't go back."[47] Virgilio Godoy, although effusively optimistic throughout the campaign and regularly guaranteeing a two-to-one victory by the opposition, later admitted that he and his colleagues never expected victory: "There were so many obstacles. We had to overcome the Sandinistas, the fear that they have long instilled in the Nicaraguans, and even our own divisions. We had the whole Sandinista apparatus against us—its radio stations, its newspapers, and its television networks. We were also confronted by a large part of the international community and the hostility of many diplomats in Managua."[48]

As the Sandinistas grew more confident of victory, they began to prepare the ground for the domestic and foreign policies they intended to carry out after the elections. In the three weeks before the vote, Sandinista officials spoke constantly of national reconciliation. The vague campaign theme of preceding weeks became a virtual invitation to the opposition to cooperate in what officials from Arce to Borge to Nuñez called a "concerted effort" to rebuild the country's economy. Sandinista officials spoke of negotiating "fundamental agreements" with the opposition after the elections and did not rule out the distribution of ministries to opposition officials.[49] The day before the vote, Ortega said his first domestic priority after the election would be "to call on all Nicaraguans to take part in national reconciliation, to put in motion the socioeconomic forces to develop the country, and to appeal to the international community to support the Nicaraguan process."[50]

The Sandinistas also took the first steps toward the post-election negotiations with the Bush administration. On February 24 Ortega declared that his first foreign policy priority after the elections would be to open negotiations with the Bush administration on "the matter of sending Nicaraguan weapons to the Salvadoran guerrillas." He named Spain's Felipe Gonzalez as "mediator between the United States and Nicaragua."[51]

The United States appeared to reciprocate. On February 25, the day of the vote, President Bush told reporters at Camp David that "whoever wins" the elections would find "a better climate" for improved relations with the United States. In words that the Sandinistas could reasonably assume were meant only for them, Bush declared "I would love to see Nicaragua living peacefully, not trying to subvert its neighbors and giving its people a shot at democracy. Once all that was sorted out, I can guarantee there will be better relations with Nicaragua."[52] Daniel Ortega, after casting his vote that day, declared that the Bush administration was "getting ready to reach an understanding with Nicaragua that will permit the normalization of relations."[53]

This was a fair assumption. Throughout the first year of his presidency, when revolutionary changes were sweeping through the communist world, President Bush had shown a readiness, and even a fondness, for doing business with communist leaders bent on reform. He opposed radical change, even when led by democrats. In Poland, Bush admired General Jaruzelski and mistrusted Lech Walesa. In Hungary he appreciated the efforts of the reform-minded communist government and considered their more radical opponents too immature to rule. In the Soviet Union, he placed his trust in Gorbachev and had no use for Boris Yeltsin.[54] The gradual reform of communism, by the communist dictators themselves, was something the Bush administration had welcomed and encouraged. Developments in Nicaragua seemed to fit the global pattern of 1989—it was not until 1990 and 1991 that "reform communism" proved ephemeral and was overthrown everywhere by anti-communist forces. The Sandinistas had every reason to believe that their behavior was conforming to the Bush administration's wishes and that their elections would bring them the rewards they sought.

63

February 25, 1990

On the day of the vote, Managua thronged with spectators and foreign journalists. For this one moment Nicaragua had become the
center of the world's attention. Everyone knew that the Nicaragua's Election Day likely marked the end of one era of American intervention in
Nicaragua and the beginning of another era of American withdrawal. If at
the end of the day the Sandinistas remained in power, they would have
won a remarkable triumph against the world's superpower. Most of the
thousands of foreigners in Managua on February 25 had come to witness
that triumph.

The most important foreign witness was Jimmy Carter. He would be
the one to certify before the world that the victory had been clean, and
therefore he had the greatest power to keep the Sandinistas honest. As
Carter himself put it the day before the vote, "It would indeed be a hollow
victory if [the Sandinistas] got the most votes and then I went before the
world media and said in my opinion this vote was . . . false."[1] The actual
task of monitoring the election was carried out by the UN and OAS observer missions. From the time the polls opened at 7:00 a.m. to when they
closed in the evening, some 700 official election observers traveled
throughout the country by jeep, helicopter, on horseback, and on foot. By
the day's end, more than half of the 4,394 polling stations had been visited by observers from the UN, OAS, and Carter teams. More than 1,000

unofficial observers and invited delegations were also present, as well as 1,000 foreign journalists. Reports of irregularities were scarce, and when investigated many turned out to be minor or non-existent. In some places lines of voters moved slowly, but turnout was high. Some campesinos in rural areas walked miles to vote, beginning their trips at 3:00 a.m. Before any results became known, international observers were satisfied that the election was largely free of fraud.

The Sandinistas and their international supporters spent most of the day preparing for the evening's victory celebration. American celebrities and politicians were on hand to mark the occasion. Ex-Congressman Jim Wright came as representative of a Texas Hispanic organization. Nicaraguan-born Bianca Jagger attracted much attention and was seen singing revolutionary anthems. As late as 10:00 p.m., Sandinista organizers were still preparing for the mammoth festival, complete with "huge loudspeakers, balloons, ska and salsa music, and all the other trimmings that had for months drawn immense crowds to their rallies."[2] When the polls closed in the evening, Daniel Ortega was working on his acceptance speech.

The Supreme Electoral Council had been scheduled to announce returns at 10:00 p.m., and the journalists waited expectantly for information about whatever small percentage of the vote had been counted. No word came, however, and another hour passed without an appearance by the electoral council's chairman. On Sandinista-controlled radio stations, the political commentary that had droned on throughout the day was suddenly replaced by continuous music. Preparations for the celebrations continued, but rumors began spreading. The Sandinista Directorate was understood to be meeting in secret. At the opposition headquarters, Chamorro's supporters who had spent the day out among the people sensed the possibility of an upset. The silence from the Sandinistas confirmed their suspicions. In both government and opposition circles, there were whispers that something astonishing was occurring.

————

In fact, senior Sandinista officials knew by 10:00 p.m. that their year-long strategy had turned into a disaster. At 9:00 p.m. the UN observers' "quick count" of less than 10 percent of the vote showed Violeta Chamorro winning a broad and decisive victory throughout the country. The Sandinistas' own figures showed a closer margin, but they knew their defeat was almost certain. The Sandinista Directorate had called an emergency meeting to discuss their predicament. They had ordered the Supreme Electoral Council to withhold any news about the early returns and told the council chairman to delay his scheduled 10:00 p.m. appearance before the international press. They had ordered the radio stations to cease commentary and to play only music. In the view of American observers on Jimmy Carter's delegation, the Sandinista Directorate was considering "whether to go the route of Chile (reluctant capitulation) or of Panama (cancel the election)." As the hours passed, word of a possible crisis spread.[3] Since 9:30 p.m. Jimmy Carter had been "frantically" trying to reach Ortega by telephone, but Ortega would not speak to him.[4]

If the Sandinistas considered tampering with the vote count, or canceling the election, they were caught in a trap of their own devising. All their elaborate efforts to ensure the international legitimacy of their electoral victory now left them no escape from their defeat. Especially critical was the UN's independent "quick count" of the voting. Had the Sandinistas been in full charge of counting and announcing the vote, as in 1984, they could have found ways to delay announcement and change the results. Jimmy Carter and the United Nations observers, with the results of the "quick count" in their hands by 9:00 p.m., made any such stalling or tampering impossible. Some members of the press had been given samples from the "quick count" already. If the Sandinistas themselves did not acknowledge their defeat quickly, it would be announced and certified for them by the election observers and witnessed by the world.[5]

Although Carter would later insist that the Sandinistas never contemplated ignoring the results of the voting, his own actions at the time told a different story.[6] Just before midnight, Daniel Ortega finally returned Carter's phone call. Carter and his delegation went to meet Ortega at the Sandinistas' headquarters, uncertain about how the Sandinistas intended to respond to their calamity. "The question on the minds of Carter and the other observers was whether Ortega would accept the results." According to Carter's aide, Robert Pastor, the Sandinistas' own count showed them behind, but not by as much as the UN's "quick count," and the Sandinistas wanted to wait for a more complete tally before conceding. Ortega emphatically demanded that Violeta Chamorro not declare victory or even release preliminary results, a demand which Carter readily transmitted to the opposition leaders. Ortega insisted he needed time to prepare Sandinista militants for the bad news, but his request for delay may also have been designed to delay the announcement of results long enough to tamper with the more than 50 percent of the votes that re-

mained uncounted. Carter sensed the danger. He insisted that the Sandinistas accept their defeat publicly, and sooner rather than later. He
"made clear that the count was decisive and would not deviate."[7] Election Night had been "tense," he acknowledged, and when 2:00 a.m. had
passed and the Sandinistas had still not permitted release of the preliminary results, he worked hard to get them to change their minds. "The key
factor," he told reporters, "was the United Nations quick count." Thanks
to that small but powerful statistical sample, the Sandinistas' loss was
recorded before they had any chance to undo it.[8]

At 2:00 a.m. the Supreme Electoral Council chairman, Mariano Fiallos, finally appeared before the international press and began reading
aloud the results of the first 6 percent of the vote from samples across the
country. As the stunned listeners heard the early returns, they realized
that Ortega and the Sandinistas had lost the election. Sandinista supporters stood in stunned silence or wept. Soon the question that circulated
throughout Managua was whether or not the Sandinistas would actually
accept their defeat. As morning approached, and as the returns made
clear the size of the Sandinistas' defeat, Ortega made no statement conceding the election. Violeta Chamorro, under instructions from Jimmy
Carter, did not want to claim victory before Ortega's concession speech.
Her advisers worried, however, that if she did not claim her victory soon,
it might be taken away from her.

The Sandinistas had only a brief time to decide how to respond to the
disastrous electoral outcome. They could annul the elections, as Noriega
had done; or they could simply refuse to recognize Chamorro's election
and continue governing by decree and by force. But the cost of either
course promised to be oppressively heavy. The same reasons the Sandinistas had held elections in the first place—to escape international isolation, economic catastrophe, and the grinding war against the contras—
must have played a part in their ultimate decision to respect the
catastrophic reults of those elections. What future lay before the Sandinistas if they went the way of Noriega and tried to rule without any domestic or international legitimacy? They would become international pariahs,
shunned in Europe and most of Latin America. The chances were good
that the Soviet Union might cut them off entirely, but even if the Soviets
maintained current aid levels, the Sandinistas had already determined
that these were insufficient to keep the economy from hitting bottom. In
the United States, meanwhile, the Bush administration would have little
choice but to assume a posture of unremitting hostility to the Sandinistas.

The United States had just invaded Panama to remove Noriega. If the Sandinistas ignored their own elections, the Bush administration would at the very least have to seek renewed aid for the contras, whose ranks were likely to be bolstered by a fresh crop of elite politicians, including, perhaps, the unseated President Chamorro. If they tried to undo the results of February 25, the prospects for the Sandinistas' future were clear: war, poverty, and isolation.

It was not in the nature of Humberto Ortega or his brother Daniel to take such a bloody and perhaps suicidal course. The Sandinistas were not the Khmer Rouge, willing to wipe out their country in order to rule it. Rather, they sought to make the best of the situation, to salvage what they could from the disaster. And for Humberto Ortega, there was something well worth salvaging: the Sandinista army. No sooner were the election results known than Ortega began negotiations with Chamorro's advisers to preserve the army and his position as its leader. But Chamorro's victory itself, he had decided, could not be undone.

At 6:00 A.M. on February 26, therefore, Daniel Ortega emerged to concede defeat to Chamorro. The victory of UNO's candidate, and the electoral defeat of the Sandinistas, was official.

Shocked as most observers were by the election results, the full magnitude of the Sandinistas' loss did not become clear until results were released to the world over the coming days. The Sandinistas had not only lost the election. They had been buried under a landslide. The more than 90 percent of registered voters who cast their ballots had given Chamorro 55 percent to Ortega's 41 percent. Even more surprising than the margin of victory was the breadth of support for Chamorro and the opposition. The Sandinistas won only one of nine administrative regions across Nicaragua.[9] Chamorro beat them handily in rural and urban areas alike. In rural provinces she won by margins of two-to-one or more, but she also did surprisingly well in urban areas long considered to be Sandinista strongholds.[10] In Masaya, the so-called "cradle of the revolution," UNO won by 10 percent.[11] Chamorro even won in areas with high concentrations of Sandinista soldiers, assumed by both sides to be fervent supporters of the revolution.[12]

The Sandinistas were more stunned than anyone as they read through the returns and discovered which groups had apparently turned against the revolution. An intense period of self-criticism began, in which different Sandinista officials explained how the revolution had alienated the peasantry, the army, the youths, as well as the bourgeoisie, the middle

class, and the elite. They considered the "faults" of the revolution's domestic policies to have been "certain sectarian positions and outright im-
positions" on the Nicaraguan people.[13] Daniel Ortega admitted a great
deal of "rigidity in our methods, and a lack of communication between
government officials and the population regarding our economic policies."[14] Sandinista theorists focused particularly on the "arrogance" of the
revolution, which had taken popular support for granted without working
to earn it, which had insisted that only the revolution's leaders knew the
proper way to run the country, and which had grown distant from the
very people the revolution was meant to serve. "The breach was of such
magnitude that the illusion of belief was created, a phenomenon among
the rank and file and Sandinist leadership, that election victory was certain. . . . This 'certainty' that the people had internalized the campaign issues of the FSLN and would vote for them inherently expresses and did
express a certain arrogance in our language, a form which the people rejected."[15] The theorists, trained to make rational analyses of social behavior, did not shield their eyes from the crushing rejection of the revolution
by the campesinos of northern and central Nicaragua. In the regions of
Boaco and Chontales, where the Jorge Salazar forces had roamed and
fought for more than six years, Chamorro and the opposition defeated the
Sandinistas 68 percent to 28 percent. In Matagalpa and Jinotega, where
"Suicida" and "Tigrillo" had reigned as warlords, the margins were 58 percent to 37 percent.[16] Daniel Ortega himself blamed the revolution for
"not knowing how to work with the peasant populations in the border
areas."[17]

Nicaragua's youth, it was soon widely understood, had voted against
Daniel Ortega because he had not, like Chamorro, promised an end to
the draft even though he had promised an end to the war. Sandinista observers also realized that the campaign's implicit and sometimes explicit
theme—that everything would be better because the Sandinistas were
going to repair relations with the Bush administration—had backfired.
The Nicaraguan people understood perfectly well that if the answer was
better relations with the United States, then a Chamorro government was
far more likely to achieve that goal.

The Sandinistas accepted the reasons for their defeat more soberly
than their defenders in the United States. Liberal critics of the Reagan
and Bush administrations, who had portrayed the election as a referendum on American intervention, had to restate the election's meaning almost overnight. The common argument of American leftists after the

election was that American policy under Reagan and Bush had bludgeoned the Nicaraguan people into submission. Although they supported the Sandinistas with their "hearts," Nicaraguans voted them from power in order to bring an end to the war and the American economic embargo.

There was little doubt that the Nicaraguans who voted against the Sandinistas hoped thereby to end the war and put an end to economic hardship. The idea that they supported the Sandinistas in their "hearts," however, was a fantasy that the Sandinistas themselves no longer believed. There is no escaping the reality that the majority of the Nicaraguan people wanted the Sandinistas out. The stunningly inaccurate pre-election polls had revealed that what foreigners had long heard from Nicaraguans about their government was probably always suspect. Many critics of Reagan's policies had tended to believe that the only opponents of the Sandinistas were on the payroll of the CIA and indeed that without American meddling there might have been little or no popular opposition to the Sandinista revolutionaries who did, after all, "embod[y] the best of everything that three and a half million people . . . might dream of."[18] The election decisively proved the fallacy of this judgment.

The great disparity between the election results and the pre-election polls had revealed that "many Nicaraguans clearly feared to express their true sentiments to strangers," and this had been true not only during the campaign, but probably throughout the years of the Sandinista revolution. And as one journalist in Managua put it, "The implication that many interviewees lied to pollsters shattered another myth: That the Sandinistas were not associated with widespread repression."[19] It turned out that the most important role of the foreign observers may have been to guarantee the secrecy of the vote in Nicaragua. As one woman in Masaya explained her own surprise at the decisions of her neighbors to vote for the opposition: "I thought I was going to be in the minority. I thought it was going to be just like 1984, when the vote was not secret and there were not all these observers around."[20] As had always been the case in Nicaraguan history, there was an enormous difference between an election that was internationally supervised and one that was not.

The main debate in the United States was not over whether the Nicaraguan people had voted with their "hearts" or their "stomachs." The consensus among conservatives, moderates, and even most liberals was that the election of Chamorro and the defeat of the Sandinistas was a great triumph. What they disagreed about was who and what policy deserved the credit for this triumph. The Nicaraguan elections were viewed in the context of the great clash that had consumed Washington for more than a decade. Conservatives claimed that the result was a vindication of Reagan's policies of supporting the contras; liberals charged that it was only the abandonment of those policies that had worked. Conservatives praised Reagan; liberals praised Arias; and the Bush administration, with some justification, praised itself. On February 27, Assistant Secretary Aronson called reporters to his office to explain in detail how the Bush administration had "turned lemons into lemonade" in Nicaragua.[21]

CONCLUSIONS

64

Power, Diplomacy, Democracy

After so many years of bitter controversy, the most difficult thing for all sides to accept was that the elections in Nicaragua were the result of a confluence of forces, circumstances, and contradictory policies. American support for the contras had been essential. The Sandinistas had never intended to hold elections at all when they first came to power: Their dream and their passion was for socialism. In the absence of external pressures, they would not have put their power at risk in a "bourgeois election." As the years passed, the pressures on them grew, and they were forced to set aside their dreams for a while. Their youthful revolutionary spirit was not tempered by age and maturity, however, but by painful adversity. It was not the responsibilities of ruling that made moderates of the Sandinistas, as Viron Vaky and other Carter officials had predicted, but the very real danger that, unless they moderated their revolution, they might cease ruling altogether. For a revolutionary leader in the tradition of Lenin, as for most dictators of any stripe, falling from power is the only real and irremediable error.

What could threaten the Sandinistas' hold on power? Economic calamity, no matter how severe, and diplomatic isolation, no matter how stark, were not enough to threaten a regime in Managua—as Somoza and the Sandinistas had both known in 1979. No Nicaraguan government had ever been driven from office, or been forced to hold an election that

721

could be lost, except by rebel guns or by foreign intervention. Guns alone could force the Sandinistas from power, and guns alone, therefore, provided sufficient pressure to force them to make changes to preserve power. That was why the Sandinistas, from the days when they were a growing rebel army to the day when they became an opposition party, never relinquished control over the weapons of war. That was why they clung tenaciously to their alliances with Cuba and the Soviet Union, despite the price they paid in the American Congress. That was why they refused to accept limitations on weapons in a Contadora treaty, despite the opportunity it presented to undermine American support for the contras. The Sandinistas, contrary to the assumptions of many American observers, were prepared even to employ the risky tactic of a fair election rather than make concessions on the strategic question of military power. This fact alone should be sufficient proof that the contra army was the only threat capable of forcing moderation on the Sandinistas.

What of the assertion, long a staple of Reagan's critics, that the contras were too weak to defeat the Sandinistas and were, therefore, too weak even to affect their policies? Such arguments consistently ignored the main point, which the Sandinistas themselves never lost sight of. As long as the contras were armed and in the field, the possibility of overthrow existed. If the contras could not overthrow the Sandinistas, the Sandinistas could also not defeat the contras, so long as the United States and Honduras provided them aid and sanctuary. The Sandinistas apparently understood better than many American military officials and analysts the dictum of Clausewitz: "So long as I have not overthrown my opponent I am bound to fear he may overthrow me. Thus I am not in control; he dictates to me as much as I dictate to him."[1] It is impossible to know if the contras could ever have defeated the Sandinistas, just as it is impossible to know whether the Sandinistas could ever have defeated the National Guard. In both cases the government capitulated, or self-destructed, before the truth could be known. In both cases, however, it was clear that the armed rebels played decisive roles.

If the contras were essential to the outcome on February 25, however, they were not sufficient by themselves to bring about that outcome. President Reagan's policies, if continued unchanged, would probably not have led to fair elections in February 1990. The Sandinistas were faced throughout their years in power with a set of calculations of probabilities. Great as the contra threat might have become if Reagan had been allowed to pursue his policies unhampered by Congress, it would probably never have been enough to convince the Sandinistas to accept surrender. Hard as the fight may have been, the Sandinista army of 70,000 men would have continued to fight so long as they had guns to fight with. Nor, probably, would the Sandinistas have held the kind of election they held in February 1990 without some strong indication that they would be let alone if they won. The Sandinistas believed, with good reason, that Reagan would have accepted nothing less than their ultimate defeat and removal from power— no matter how many elections they won. The weighing of risks and benefits which the Sandinistas made in 1989, therefore, would have produced a different answer if Reagan were still in power or if Bush had appeared to be in complete agreement with Reagan's old policies. Reagan's policies, unmodified by the Arias plan or by Congress, would probably have meant many years of inconclusive struggle in Nicaragua.

President Reagan lacked complete control over American policy toward Nicaragua, however, so the Sandinistas faced a far more complicated calculation of risks and benefits. The ongoing battle in Washington between Reagan and the Congress, between Republicans and Democrats, and between liberals and conservatives created, quite unintentionally, an American policy that offered the Sandinistas routes of escape even as it chased them into corners. Because liberals in Congress lacked the votes to end contra aid definitively, moderates had stepped in to approve it conditionally. Some of the conditions affected the Reagan administration and the contras, but others more significantly affected the Sandinistas. To justify both their measured support of the covert war and their measured opposition to it, the moderates in Congress set up tests for the Sandinistas to meet. If they signed a Contadora agreement, if they negotiated with the contras, if they allowed more political privileges to their political opponents, if they held elections—then they could defeat the contras in the United States Congress. In Washington, these compromises bridged unbridgeable gaps and allowed political leaders to avoid the most difficult choices between intervention and non-intervention, between anti-communism and anti-anti-communism.

Nor was it surprising to find that in the United States, in the 1980s as in the 1920s, the ultimate compromise and most popular locus for consensus had to do with democracy. That a democracy should be left behind in Nicaragua was the one point of agreement between those who favored achieving it by force and those who favored achieving it by peaceful means. President Arias stepped in and brilliantly seized upon this formula as the central element of his peace proposal. The Arias plan succeeded where Contadora had failed in undoing Reagan's policy precisely and only because it made democratization the sole issue for American policy. Brilliant though Arias's plan was, it was nothing more than a codification and implementation of the American political consensus.

The modification of Reagan's policies imposed by Arias and the Congress thus gave the Sandinistas an alternative to the grim choice between perpetual war and disastrous surrender. The Arias plan opened a door of escape, one that promised salvation even though it also meant an abandonment of purer revolutionary visions. And ironically, although the contras were probably not strong enough to fulfill the more ambitious goal set for them by the Reagan administration, they were strong enough to make it more attractive for the Sandinistas to risk walking through the door rather than continue stubbornly to resist all reform of the revolution. It was ironic that Arias and liberal members of Congress, who had always claimed that the contras were useless and even counterproductive, consistently used the threat of renewed contra aid to convince the Sandinistas to do what was necessary to satisfy the American consensus. Gradually, as their situation worsened, the Sandinistas came to see the benefits of such a course.

Here the other elements of pressure also played a critical role. Not just the contra war, but the devastated economy, the diplomatic isolation, and the rapidly decreasing strength of the Soviet Union all combined to convince the Sandinistas that the risk of holding the election demanded by Arias and the United States was better than the risk of not holding an election. The Soviet Union did not put any serious pressure on the Sandinistas to hold elections, as Bush officials claimed, but it did not have to. By their obvious collapse as a superpower, the Soviets did all the persuading the Sandinistas needed.

The Bush administration played a critical part in the events that led to the Sandinistas' defeat, although not the one for which it later took credit. Neither cooperation with the Soviet Union, nor endorsement of the Arias plan, nor assiduous diplomacy in Europe convinced the Sandinistas to go through with the elections. By making clear that it wanted no further part in Nicaragua's affairs, that it sought the first politically safe opportunity to rid itself of the contras and, above all, that it was perfectly prepared to allow the Sandinistas to survive unharmed after a fair election, the Bush administration provided the final inducement to the Sandinistas. This had not been a ploy or a trick. Bush officials did not hope, as Reagan officials would have, that the Sandinistas would fail to meet the test on February 25. Such a ploy would not have worked. The evident sincerity of Bush's desire to be rid of the Nicaraguan mess convinced the Sandinistas that the risk of the elections was worth taking. Here the Soviets did play an important part: They were the bearers of the message from Bush and Baker that fair elections would lead to normalization of relations with the United States.

In retrospect it is possible to count and measure all the forces and decisions that contributed to the Sandinistas' defeat at the polls on February 25. One is tempted to see in this complex array of pressures and counterpressures a coherent strategy on the part of someone, whether Arias, or Baker, or perhaps Alfredo César. Some few individuals, notably Arias and Bernard Aronson, claim to have known all along that the Sandinistas would lose the election.

The final outcome, however, was the result of a terrible and almost inexplicable miscalculation by the Sandinistas. One thing is certain: If the Sandinistas had believed they would lose a fair election on February 25, they would not have held a fair election. They were "prepared to continue the policy of democratization," one Soviet Foreign Ministry official frankly recalls, "only as long as it did not interfere with the task of retaining power in their hands."[2] All the Sandinistas' actions since the early 1980s, all their hard-line policies and all their moderate reforms, had aimed at one goal: the preservation of power. In this, the Sandinistas were no more nor less worthy of condemnation or praise than any of Nicaragua's rulers since Zelaya. The determination to preserve power is normal for Nicaraguan rulers, as it has been for rulers of most nations throughout history. In human affairs the voluntary abdication of power is the rare exception. Only because they were sure of victory did the Sandinistas embark on their path to defeat. Only because everyone else also believed they would win was their decision to hold elections seen not as a capitulation to American pressure but rather as the ultimate sign that American pressure had failed.

Those who claim to have predicted the outcome on February 25, therefore, are suggesting not only that they knew the Sandinistas would lose a fair election, but that they also knew the Sandinistas themselves would remain foolishly confident of their victory until the last minute. Any "plan" to undermine the Sandinistas in this way would have had to include this remarkable piece of self-delusion by the government. Perhaps

Arias did watch in amazement as the Sandinistas boasted of their inevitable victory. That their disastrous miscalculation was part of his original plan, however, is hard to believe.

In the end the Sandinistas were their own executioners, the victims of their own blindness. Fidel Castro had warned them against holding the elections. "The people," he pointed out sagely, "can make mistakes." It was the Sandinistas who made the greatest mistake, however, by ignoring their own nation's history. Every Nicaraguan government that had ever submitted itself to a fair vote had been thrown out of office by the Nicaraguan people.

Of course, the Sandinistas' larger mistake came much earlier, at the very beginning of the revolution. History must record that their brazen challenge to American hegemony was folly. If the Sandinistas had been sensible, they would have taken a moderate course from the beginning, especially in foreign policy. But nations and their leaders don't always do what is in their best long-term interest. In retrospect the Sandinistas acknowledge that it was foolish to place their bet on the Cubans and the Soviets and to assume that the United States was in a state of permanent decline and retreat. But who in the world did not share that assumption in the late 1970s and early 1980s?

The very inconsistency of American policy under three very different American administrations may have added considerably to the Sandinistas' difficulties. What one American scholar has written of U.S.-Soviet relations in the seventies and eighties seems to apply well to U.S.-Nicaraguan relations, that a "disorderly mix of policies did more to destabilize" Nicaragua "than any single line of policy, consistently applied, would have been able to do."[3] In the case of Nicaragua the "disorderly mix of policies" derived both from the unique circumstances of the late Cold War and from the more timeless elements of the relationship between this great power and its small neighbor.

65

The Ambivalent Power

The elections of February 1990 marked the end of a period of American intervention in Nicaragua which had begun in the late 1970s. The 13-year involvement, like the long American intervention earlier in the century, was liquidated by a President eager to cast off a divisive burden whose original purpose no longer held any significance. With successful democratic elections in Nicaragua, the Bush administration prepared to depart from further involvement in Nicaraguan affairs with the same alacrity with which President Hoover sought the withdrawal of American marines after the 1932 elections.

In Nicaragua, however, the election of Violeta Chamorro on February 25 was not the end but rather the beginning of one of those complicated and unsettled periods that have occurred so frequently in Nicaragua's history, especially in the wake of an American intervention and withdrawal. The 1932 election had allowed the United States to withdraw from the "Nicaraguan mess," but that withdrawal set off a struggle for power which ended when the head of the army, Anastasio Somoza, overthrew the elected president and seized control of the nation. In 1990, another phase of Nicaragua's political struggle began, and it continues today.

After the election, the "social pact" planned by Humberto Ortega was enacted even though the Sandinistas had lost the election. An agreement between Violeta Chamorro's top advisers, Antonio Lacayo and Alfredo

César, and Humberto Ortega created a new governing coalition. It was in many ways a fulfillment of the original *Tercerista* vision, although now the Sandinistas were not exactly "hegemonic." The more conservative politicians within the UNO coalition were, of course, excluded from the new power arrangements. Vice President Godoy was stripped of his few powers, and the UNO coalition which dominated the new Assembly went into opposition against the Chamorro-Sandinista alliance.

The other excluded group was the rebel army. The contras' new leadership was disdained by Chamorro's government as "a bunch of Indians." A week after the February 1990 elections, the contras were told by American officials to lay down their arms and return to Nicaragua. The rebels were reluctant. Not only did they fear reprisals from the still-intact Sandinista army, but they also did not trust the new Chamorro government. As one contra told the Americans, the "white oligarchs" in power in Managua had never shown the smallest interest in the cause of a "bunch of Indians." Nevertheless, the contras ultimately complied and laid down their weapons.[1]

The most important consequence of the deal struck between Lacayo, César, and Humberto Ortega was that Ortega retained command of the national army, just as he had once threatened to do during the campaign. The consequences of that fateful decision, which the Bush administration reluctantly accepted, have yet to be seen.[2] Whether Nicaraguans will continue to try to settle the question of power at the ballot box, or whether force and intrigue will persist as the deciding factors in Nicaraguan political culture, must be left for the future to determine.

———

Most American observers believe that in the post-communist, post–Cold War era whatever happens in Nicaragua will be a matter of indifference to the United States. They are mistaken. If the history of the past century has taught anything, it is that the United States remains caught in a continuous cycle of intervention and withdrawal in this hemisphere, and especially in Nicaragua. The reasons for this are complex and fall outside the usual paradigms by which analysts explain and interpret American foreign policy. Efforts to attribute American interventions in Nicaragua to economic imperialism, to idealism, to strategic interests, or indeed to any one set of interests alone cannot account for involvements as diverse in style and purpose as Taft's, Wilson's, Coolidge's, Carter's, and Reagan's. The latest American intervention conducted under Reagan began as a product of the Cold War and American anxieties about Soviet encroachment in the Western Hemisphere. But the equally decisive intervention that came before, under Carter, was about something else entirely: It was a response to American feelings of guilt about and responsibility for the birth and continuance of the Somoza dynasty.

What could be more different than these motives for intervention, and yet how similar were the results. In both cases the leadership of the country changed hands as a direct consequence of American disapproval and of its superior power. José Santos Zelaya, Emiliano Chamorro, José Maria Moncada, and Anastasio Somoza García would have had no difficulty in recognizing the America that conducted these policies toward Nicaragua from 1977 to 1990. They were the policies of a great power exercising its will, however harshly or mildly, to enforce certain principles of behavior in both the external and internal affairs of a small, troublesome neighbor. Nothing could be more natural than such behavior by a great power, and Nicaraguans from the Somozas to the Sandinistas have seen American hegemony as the natural, if not necessarily desirable, state of affairs.

Yet this impulse to hegemony is only half the story of American policy toward Nicaragua. For every exercise of the great power's prerogative, there has been an equally strong recoiling from the use of power. While the United States cannot escape behaving as the hegemonic great power, it is also a great power with a democratic conscience, a strong anti-imperialist streak, and an unwillingness to adopt the role of policeman anywhere for more than a brief time. American policy toward Nicaragua has been shaped by the tension between the impulse to exercise moral, economic, strategic, and philosophical hegemony and the equally powerful impulse to reject both the responsibilities and the moral costs of such a role.

Often these two conflicting tendencies have been blended into one inherently contradictory policy: from Henry Stimson's intervention as a means of withdrawal in the 1920s, to Jimmy Carter's "non-interventionist" undermining of Somoza in the 1970s, to the bifurcated policy of aggression and conciliation pursued jointly by Ronald Reagan and the Democrat-controlled Congress in the 1980s. The most common characteristic of American policy throughout this century has been neither intervention nor non-intervention, but rather a virtually simultaneous intervention and withdrawal. Americans have been unprepared to make a full and continuous commitment to Nicaragua's political development, yet they have been equally incapable of remaining aloof.

The frequent American attempt to implant democratic institutions in Nicaragua and elsewhere in the hemisphere has been partly a product of this American ambivalence about power and its use. American administrations have intervened in this hemisphere for any number of reasons, but the only outcome of intervention deemed legitimate by the conscience of the American people has been one that leaves elected government behind. The violation of another nation's sovereignty, though it may have been deemed necessary for the protection of American interests, has only been justified in American eyes by the restoration or establishment of the only kind of sovereignty recognized by the American creed: the sovereignty of the people.

The implantation of democracy has usually aimed at another goal, as well. Every administration forced to intervene in Nicaragua has hoped that the installation of democracy would by itself do away with any need for further intervention, since a functioning democracy, by its very nature, is most likely to conform to the "American order" in the hemisphere. Democratic governments are least likely to challenge American strategic, economic, political, or philosophical hegemony because they are most likely to benefit from it.

For the United States to steer a country like Nicaragua along a steady course toward democracy, however, would seem to require something other than spasmodic interventions followed by hasty withdrawals. Perhaps it might be best for both countries if Nicaraguans were left to themselves to develop more effective and equitable means of sharing and transferring power. Or perhaps, absent a sudden transformation of Nicaraguan political culture, it might be better for both countries if the United States pursued a consistent policy, one that accepted the inescapable facts of American hegemony and one that assumed responsibility for the development of democratic institutions and the peaceful transfer of power in Nicaragua. The more the United States assumed such a role, the less it would have to use its power. A steady, low level of involvement, making subtle use of American influence, would probably obviate the need for the kinds of forceful interventions that have caused so much controversy over the years. After all, the exercise of only a little American influence would probably have prevented the first Somoza from upsetting the nascent electoral system established in the late 1920s. Not much more would have been necessary to manage the transition from the Somoza dictatorship to a more moderate, democratic government in 1979.

In the 1990s, a steady involvement by the United States could help fore-stall developments that may eventually threaten Nicaragua's peace again.

A realistic appraisal of the American people, however, leaves little room to hope for such a consistent application of American influence. The discipline forced upon American policymakers by the Cold War in the 1980s was probably an aberration. The ambivalence in the American soul has made such steady intervention almost impossible to sustain. Americans have preferred to view themselves as a people who stay out of the affairs of others, except when emergencies arise. They have been re-luctant to acknowledge their own insistence on maintaining hegemony and their enjoyment of its fruits. Their foreign policy in the future, there-fore, is likely to be one neither of consistent intervention, nor of consis-tent non-intervention. If the past is any guide, the only consistency in American policy in this hemisphere will be the endless cycle of interven-tion and withdrawal.

NOTES

Introduction

1. William Appleman Williams, *The Tragedy of American Diplomacy* (New York, 1959).

Chapter 1

1. Walter LaFeber, *Inevitable Revolutions: The United States in Central America* (New York, 1984), 40.

2. For a good account of these events, see Dana G. Munro, *Intervention and Dollar Diplomacy in the Caribbean, 1900–1921* (Princeton, 1964), 146–159.

3. Hubert Herring, *A History of Latin America* (New York, 1961), 464.

4. As one American official explained, "since the marines were regarded as a symbol of the American government's determination to prevent a revolution, the Liberals did not dare revolt. The Conservatives gave them no opportunity to win elections." Dana G. Munro, *The United States and the Caribbean Republics, 1921–1933* (Princeton, 1974), 161.

5. Senator William Borah, a leading Republican isolationist in the 1920s and 1930s, later called the treaty "as pronounced and unconscionable an act of imperialism as ever disgraced the records of any nation." *Congressional Record* [hereafter CR], 69th Cong., 2nd Session, 1927, Vol. 68, pt. 2:1557, quoted in Sergio Ramírez and Robert Edgar Conrad, eds., *Sandino: The Testimony of a Nicaraguan Patriot: 1921–1934* (Princeton, 1990), 16.

6. Munro, *The United States and the Caribbean Republics*, p. 216.

7. Ibid., p. 162.

8. Secretary Kellogg was not willing to "exert the strong pressure on the Conservatives that would have been necessary to persuade them to relinquish control of the government." Secretary Kellogg was also unwilling to guarantee American support for a new provisional government during the two years before the next presidential elections. Ibid., p. 205.

9. Kellogg to Dennis, Dec. 8, 1926, *Foreign Relations of the United States* [hereafter FRUS], 1926, Vol. II, pp. 810–11. (Washington, 1952) Munro, *The United States and the Caribbean Republics*, p. 210.

10. Munro, *The United States and the Caribbean Republics*, p. 212.

11. Quoted in Neill Macaulay, *The Sandino Affair* (Durham, NC, 1967), 31–32.

12. CR, 69th Congress, 2nd Session, 1927, Vol. 68, pt. 2:2290). Ramírez and Conrad, p. 15.

13. State Department officials shuddered at the President's mention of the alternative canal, a threat they deemed nonexistent. They found the President's warnings about the danger to American economic interests surprising . . . because our economic interests in Nicaragua were insignificant. Notwithstanding the criticisms of Senator Wheeler, American banks had several years earlier given up their controlling interests in the Nicaraguan bank and railway. See Munro, *The United States and the Caribbean Republics*, pp. 215–16.

14. Claude M. Fuess, *Calvin Coolidge, the Man from Vermont* (Boston, 1940), 415.

15. Henry L. Stimson, intro. and commentary by Paul H. Boeker, *American Policy in Nicaragua: The Lasting Legacy* (Princeton, 1992), 19–20.

16. Ibid., pp. 6 and 4–5.

17. See Gen. José Maria Moncada, *Estados Unidos en Nicaragua* (Managua, Tipografía Atenas, 1942), 7–9; Macaulay, p. 38.

18. Henry L. Stimson, *American Policy in Nicaragua* (New York, 1927), 76–79.

19. By his deal with Stimson, Moncada was effectively vaulting over the traditional Liberal and Conservative oligarchs, the Sacasas and Chamorros. See Arturo Cruz, Jr., "One Hundred Years of Turpitude," *New Republic*, Vol. 197, Number 20, November 16, 1987, 34.

20. Stimson and Boeker, *American Policy in Nicaragua: The Lasting Legacy*, p. 24.

21. Ibid., pp. 25–26.

Chapter 2

1. Sandino later complained bitterly to Moncada that "you always frowned on me when you were commander in chief. . . . It appears that you were jealous of me." Letter to General José Maria Moncada, May 24, 1927, in Sergio Ramírez and Robert Edgar, eds., *Sandino: The Testimony of a Nicaraguan Patriot: 1921–1934* (Princeton, 1990), 70. Conrad, The description of Sandino's personality comes from J. B. Pate, "Information Furnished by Humberto Torres . . . Who Served as an Officer in Sandino's Army," November 6, 1928, U.S. Marine Corps Historical Archives, Nicaragua: Box 10, folder 3. Quoted in Neill Macaulay, *The Sandino Affair* (Durham, NC, 1967), 57. It should be noted that Torres later defected from Sandino's army and undoubtedly bore a grudge against his former commander. However, Torres's depiction of both Sandino's flaws and virtues formed part of the common view. Even some of Sandino's closest allies found the young, dynamic leader thoroughly frustrating at times.

2. The Nicaraguan historian, Arturo Cruz, Jr., writes: "All of the leaders in those days mixed convenience, doctrine, and imagery more or less indiscriminately." Arturo Cruz, Jr., "One Hundred Years of Turpitude," *New Republic*, Vol. 197, Number 20, November 16, 1987, 33.

3. Donald Clarke Hodges, *Sandino's Communism: Spiritual Politics for the Twenty-first Century* (Austin, Tex. 1992), 24.

4. Sergio Ramírez, "Sandino: Clase e ideologia, in Augusto Sandino, *El pensamiento vivo* (Managua, 1984), 2:433–34, quoted in Ramírez and Conrad, p. 18.

5. Hodges, p. 19; see Macaulay p. 160.

6. See Anthony Lake, *Somoza Falling: A Case Study of Washington at Work* (Amherst, Mass., 1990) 56.

7. Sandino letter of July 17, 1927, in Ramírez and Conrad, p. 86.

8. Sandino letter of September 2, 1927, in Ramírez and Conrad, pp. 95–97.

9. Sandino later claimed the letter was a ploy to prove to his nervous followers that the Yankees were "bandits." He reviles "two miserable and cowardly intellectuals of Managua,"

who harped on this and another similar letter to embarrass Sandino: "With eyes fired up like two wild animals, tongues extended and dripping, they have sat over these two notes, unable to understand or appreciate the sacred breath that quickens the minds of men willing to sacrifice their lives in fateful times." (Ramírez and Conrad, p. 67)

10. See Message to Gabriela Mistral, April 10, 1929, Ramírez and Conrad, pp. 59–67.

11. As Neill Macaulay writes, "The election was hard-fought and fair. Despite Sandino's terrorism and propaganda, 133,000 of his countrymen cast their ballots on November 4, 1928—fifty thousand more than in the last American-supervised election in 1924." Macaulay, p. 129.

12. Macaulay, p. 212.

13. Dana G. Munro, *The United States and the Caribbean Republics, 1921–1933* (Princeton, 1974), 253.

14. See, for instance, Walter LaFeber, *Inevitable Revolutions: The United States in Central America* (New York, 1984), 66–67 and Lake, p. 65.

15. U.S. marine quoted in Lester D. Langley, *The Banana Wars: An Inner History of American Empire, 1900–1934* (Lexington, KY, 1983), 23.

16. See Macaulay, pp. 144, 177–78, 220–21.

17. Ibid. p. 180.

18. Quoted in Macaulay, p. 199.

19. Munro, p. 247; Macaulay, pp. 112–13.

20. CR, 70th Congress, 1st Session, 1928, 69, pt. 5:5037–38, quoted in Ramírez and Conrad, p. 16.

21. Richard Millett, *Guardians of the Dynasty* (Maryknoll, NY, 1977), 145–47.

22. See Macaulay, p. 247, and Millett, p. 150.

23. Macaulay, p. 248.

Chapter 3

1. For an account of these events, see Richard Millett, *Guardians of the Dynasty* (Maryknoll, NY, 1977), p. 158.

2. Press release issued by the Department of State, January 2, 1933, *FRUS*, 1933, Vol. V, pp. 848–49.

3. Ambassador Arthur Bliss Lane to Secretary of State Cordell Hull, August 29, 1935, *FRUS*, 1935, Vol. IV, pp. 868–70.

4. Hull to Lane, February 26, 1934, *FRUS*, 1934, Vol. V, pp. 538–39.

5. He reported to Hull that "there has been at times some question in my mind as to how the Hands Off and 'Good Neighbor' policies should or may be reconciled." Lane to Hull, May 4, 1934, *FRUS*, 1934, Vol. V, pp. 552–54.

6. Hull to Lane, September 26, 1935, *FRUS*, 1935, Vol. IV, pp. 872–73.

7. Lane to Hull, September 28, 1935, *FRUS*, 1935, Vol. IV, pp. 874–75.

8. Memorandum by the Assistant Chief of the Division of Latin American Affairs (Willard Beaulac), October 1, 1935, *FRUS*, 1935, Vol. IV, pp. 877–79.

9. Sumner Welles reaffirmed his government's commitment to non-interference. "[I]f the situation should become so critical as to threaten life and property," Welles told the Salvadoran minister, "and if requested by all contending factions, this Government would consider the possibility of rendering some assistance." However, the United States "would not act alone, but only in company with a group of nations, and that even under these circumstances this Government would not take the initiative." Assistant Secretary of State (Sumner Welles) to the Minister in Nicaragua (Boaz Long), May 19, 1936, *FRUS*, 1936, Vol. V, pp. 821–22.

10. Hull to Long, June 11, 1936, *FRUS*, 1936, Vol. V, p. 841.

11. Note from Sacasa, Chamorro, and Diaz to Hull, November 30, 1936, *FRUS*, 1936, Vol. V, pp. 844–47.

12. Quoted in Walter LaFeber, *Inevitable Revolutions: The United States in Central America* (New York, 1984), 69.

Chapter 4

1. "Nicaraguan Bishops Accuse Government of Resorting to Widespread Torture," Alan Riding, *New York Times* [hereafter NYT], March 2, 1977, p. 1.

2. The stated goal of the human rights legislation passed in 1976 was to "promote and advance human rights and avoid identification of the United States" with governments that deny such rights to their people. See the Foreign Assistance Act of 1961 (As Amended), Sec. 116 and Sec. 502B.

3. Speech by Jimmy Carter to the B'nai B'rith Convention, Washington, D.C., September 8, 1976.

4. Address by President Carter at Commencement Exercises at Notre Dame University, May 22, 1977.

5. Riding later told Robert Pastor that he had suspected Carter's human rights policy was meant "just to needle the Russians" and so he had sought a good test case in Latin America. See Robert A. Pastor, *Condemned to Repetition: The United States and Nicaragua* (Princeton, 1987), p. 53.

6. See floor statement of Congressman David Obey (D-NY), CR, June 23, 1977, p. 20585.

7. Floor statement of Congressman Charles Wilson (D-TX), CR, June 23, 1977, p. 20579.

8. When the chairman of the House Appropriations Subcommittee, Clarence Long, asked Under Secretary of State Lucy Benson, "What would be the reaction of the State Department if this committee were to suspend all aid to Nicaragua, in view of some of the gross violations of human rights that have taken place there? What would be lost to the United States and would there be a violation of our security interests?" she replied, "I cannot think of a single thing." See testimony of Under Secretary Lucy Benson before the House Appropriations Subcommittee on Foreign Operations, March 24, 1977.

9. See letter from Assistant Secretary of State Terence Todman quoted in the floor statement of Congressman John Murphy (D-NY), CR, June 23, 1977, p. 20582.

10. Human rights activists blamed their defeat on the work of lobbyists hired by Somoza and on their own disorganization, but the most important reason for their defeat was that the White House and the Democratic Party leadership had supported Wilson and the effort to restore military aid to Somoza in the foreign aid bill.

11. "Somoza and His Foes Both Looking to U.S. for Aid," Alan Riding, NYT, July 26, 1978, p. A3.

12. The end of Fiscal Year 1977 required that the administration either sign the previous year's military assistance agreement or see those funds returned to the Treasury.

13. Ironically, because the law did not make the same requirement for immediate action on the economic assistance approved by Congress that it did for the military aid, the administration could delay its decision on the release of all economic aid to Nicaragua without losing the funds. In a further irony, Congressman Koch had used the fact that Nicaragua was going to be receiving U.S. economic assistance to point out how comparatively small the cut in military aid was. See the floor statement of Congressman Ed Koch (D-NY), CR, June 23, 1977, p. 20590.

14. The figure was cited in U.S. House Appropriations Committee, Foreign Assistance and Relations Programs Appropriations Bill, 1978, Report no. 95-417, June 15, 1977, p. 65. Cited in Pastor, p. 49.

15. As Robert Pastor writes, "there was no specific policy toward Nicaragua early in the Carter presidency; there were only human rights policies that applied to Nicaragua." Pastor, p. 53.

Chapter 5

1. See Robert A. Pastor, *Condemned to Repetition: The United States and Nicaragua* (Princeton, 1987), p 55. Pastor bases his account on interviews with close Somoza advisers, Luis Pallais and Max Kelly.

2. "An Interview with Somoza's Foe, Now Dead," by Charles W. Flynn and Robert E. Wilson, NYT, January 13, 1978, p. A23.

3. Interview with Tomás Borge by Soledad Cruz, *Juventud Rebelde*, [Havana] February 10, 1980, Joint Publications Research Service 75341, pp. 173–177.

4. "The FSLN Program of 1969," in Robert S. Leiken and Barry Rubin, eds. *The Central American Crisis Reader* (New York, 1987), p. 149.

5. Tomás Borge, Carlos Fonseca, Daniel Ortega, Humberto Ortega, and Jaime Wheelock, *Sandinistas Speak* (New York, 1986), p. 56.

6. FSLN, Political-Military Platform, quoted in David Nolan, *The Ideology of the Sandinistas and the Nicaraguan Revolution* (Coral Gables, Fl., 1984), p. 78.

7. See Dennis Gilbert, *Sandinistas: The Party and the Revolution* (New York, 1988), pp. 28–30.

8. Borge et al., *Sandinistas Speak*, p. 56.

9. See "Nicaraguan Rebels Launch Major Drive," Alan Riding, NYT, October 20, 1977, p. A3; "Nicaraguan Rebels Deny Marxist Aim," Alan Riding, NYT, October 26, 1977, p. A9; "In Nicaragua This May Be the Twilight of the Somozas," Alan Riding, NYT, October 30, 1977, Week in Review, p. 3.

10. Panama City ACAN 1955 GMT 28 Oct 77, "FSLN Movement's Splits," FBIS, VI. 2 Nov 77, P19.

11. Panama City ACAN 0105 GMT 7 Nov 77, "Publisher Says Somoza 'Must Be Excluded' from Dialogue," FBIS, VI. 7 Nov 77, P4.

12. A report from Havana warned that "in the face of the development of the revolutionary movement, North American imperialism is carrying out a number of maneuvers aimed at finding a semi-democratic deadlock for the Nicaraguan situation." Havana International Service 0000 GMT 4 Nov 77, "Havana Report on U.S. Role in Nicaragua," FBIS, VI. 4 Nov 77, P5.

13. Pastor, p. 55. The statement is a paraphrase of what Somoza told a former Costa Rican President, Daniel Oduber, who later recounted the conversation to Pastor.

14. Paris AFP 0118 GMT 7 Jan 78, "Somoza Rejects Demands," FBIS, VI. 9 Jan 78, P5.

15. Paris AFP 1955 GMT 8 Jan 78, "Sandinist Communiqué Rejects Proposed Dialog," FBIS, VI. 10 Jan 78, P5.

16. See Shirley Christian, *Nicaragua: Revolution in the Family* (New York, 1985), pp. 52–53.

Chapter 6

1. Chamorro's widow alternately blamed Somoza and the Sandinistas for the murder, usually depending on her own political leanings at the time. Obviously both Somoza and the

Sandinistas had powerful motives for wanting Chamorro dead. Given subsequent events, however, the murder helped the Sandinistas enormously and ruined Somoza. If Somoza ordered the assassination, he was a monumental fool. Of course, a third option is that neither ordered the assassination, and that it was carried out by people with economic, not political motives. At the time of the murder, *La Prensa* had been running an exposé of a Nicaraguan company. There are allegations that the company's owners ordered the murder.

2. Shirley Christian, *Nicaragua: Revolution in the Family* (New York, 1985), p. 55.

3. Panama City ACAN 0130 GMT 22 Jan 78, "10,000 March to Cemetery," FBIS, VI. 23 Jan 78, P4.

4. Panama City Televisora Naciónal 2315 GMT 14 Jan 78, "Opposition Union President Interviewed," FBIS, VI. 16 Jan 78, P11.

5. Buenos Aires LATIN, "FSLN Blames Chamorro Death on Somoza Dynasty," FBIS, VI. 17 Jan 78, P5.

6. Panama City Televisora Naciónal 2315 GMT 24 Jan 78, FBIS, VI. 25 Jan 78, P6. The January 24 communiqué was signed by the Nicaraguan Development Institute, the Nicaraguan Chamber of Commerce, the Nicaraguan Construction Chamber, the Chamber of Industries of Nicaragua, the Customs, Storage, and Shippers Chamber of Nicaragua, the Cotton Growers' Cooperative of Managua and the Nicaraguan Organization of Publicity Agencies.

7. Author's interview with Xavier Zavala, January 17, 1989.

8. Panama City ACAN 2315 GMT 26 Jan 78, "Private Sector Urges Somoza Resignation," FBIS, VI. 27 Jan 78, P9.

9. "Respectable Rebels Threaten Somoza Dynasty," Alan Riding, NYT, January 29, 1978, Week in Review, p. 4.

10. "We have to go constitutionally," Xavier Zavala recalls arguing, "because it is the only channel for change." He meant it was the only safe channel. Author's interview with Xavier Zavala, January 17, 1989.

11. Buenos Aires LATIN 2006 GMT 8 Feb 78, "Somoza Tells Brazilian Magazine He Will Not Resign," FBIS, VI. 9 Feb 78, P6.

12. Panama City ACAN 1705 GMT 6 Feb 78 "No Voting Results Yet, Situation Apparently Normalizing," FBIS, VI. 7 Feb 78, P10.

13. "Newspaper of Slain Nicaraguan Editor Leads Strike," Alan Riding, NYT, February 1, 1978, p. 3.

14. Paris AFP 2301 GMT 6 Feb 78, "FSLN Vows to Continue Military Operations," FBIS, VI. 8 Feb 78.

15. Panama City ACAN 1847 GMT 28 Jan 78, "Somoza Speech in Corinto," FBIS, VI. 31 Jan 78, P5.

16. "Somoza Acts Secure As Strike Continues," Alan Riding, NYT, January 31, 1978, p. 5.

17. "U.S. Neutrality Heartens Nicaraguan Rebels," Alan Riding, NYT, February 5, 1978, p. 3.

18. "The goal of the strike," recalls Zavala, "was to get Somoza with international pressure." Author's interview with Xavier Zavala, January 17, 1989.

19. Letter from Pérez to Carter, cited in Robert A. Pastor, *Condemned to Repetition: The United States and Nicaragua* (Princeton, 1987), p. 60.

20. Havana International Service 2310 GMT 21 Jan 78, "Havana Comments on Nicaraguan Political Crisis," FBIS, VI. 23 Jan 78, Q2.

21. Havana Domestic Television Service 0100 GMT 12 Jan 78, "Commentary Discusses Chamorro Death, Situation in Nicaragua," FBIS, VI. 18 Jan 78, Q1.

22. Anastasio Somoza, *Nicaragua Betrayed* (Belmont, Mass., 1980), pp. 102–4.

23. Human Rights Report on Nicaragua prepared by the Department of State and submitted to the Senate Foreign Relations Committee, February, 1978.

24. As a result of the political attacks on the human rights policy throughout 1977, from both Democrats and Republicans, the Carter administration was now emphasizing, in *all* its statements on human rights, "constructive and cooperative" efforts to persuade other regimes to improve their treatment of citizens rather than "confrontation."

25. Testimony of Deputy Assistant Secretary of State, Sally Shelton, before the International Relations Subcommittee on International Organizations, February 16, 1978.

26. Testimony of Terence Todman before House International Relations Subcommittee on International Development, March 9, 1978.

27. "Nicaraguan Dissidents Say U.S. Does Not Appreciate Gravity of Crisis," Alan Riding, NYT, March 5, 1978, p. 14. See testimony of Mr. Swihart before the House International Relations Subcommittee on Inter-American Affairs, March 15, 1978.

28. Testimony of Terence Todman, March 9, 1978.

Chapter 7

1. "New Approach to Foreign Policy," address by Jimmy Carter to the American Chamber of Commerce in Tokyo, Japan, May 28, 1975.

2. Ibid.

3. "Venezuela to Urge Investigation by O.A.S. of the Somoza Regime," Graham Hovey, NYT, February 8, 1978, p. A3.

4. Testimony of Congressman Charles Wilson (D-TX), before the International Relations Subcommittee on International Organizations, February 16, 1978, U.S. 95th Congress, House Committee on International Relations, 92, Part 4, p. 97.

5. Testimony of Congressman Charles Wilson (D-TX), before the International Relations Subcommittee on International Development, March 9, 1978, U.S. 95th Congress, House Committee on International Relations, 49, Part 2, p. 2.

6. Testimony of Congressman Charles Wilson, Feb. 16, 1978, p. 82.

7. Even the *Washington Post* was criticizing the administration for unfair treatment of Somoza: "[C]ountries regarded as important for strategic, economic or political reasons, such as Iran, South Korea, the Philippines and various black African states, are to be mildly criticized but not officially penalized for shortfalls in human rights. But a little unimportant country like Nicaragua is to be both criticized and penalized; Nicaragua we note, has made major strides *forward* in rights in the last year, chiefly to appease the United States. For its pains it is not only faced, as a logical consequence of the loosening up, with growing internal unrest but is also now subjected to fresh humiliation at the hands of the United States. There is a double standard, or a triple or quadruple standard, and that is unacceptable." See "Human-Rights Report Cards," *Washington Post* [hereafter WP] editorial, February 8, 1979, p. A18.

8. Testimony of Congressman Charles Wilson, March 9, 1978, p. 2.

9. Robert A. Pastor, *Condemned to Repetition: The United States and Nicaragua* (Princeton, 1987), p. 66.

10. "Somoza Comments on Chamorro Case, Other Topics," FBIS, VI. 13 Mar 78, P3.

11. "PCN Denounces Ambassador's Statements," FBIS, VI. 14 Mar 78, P5.

12. Author's interview with Augusto Montealegre, September 7, 1989.

13. "Anti-Somoza Strike Halts Most Business in Managua," Alan Riding, NYT, July 20, 1978, p. A3.

14. By early 1978 it had become routine to send such letters to any dictator who made even token gestures toward reform. See Pastor, p. 67: "Generals Pinochet of Chile and Videla of Argentina—leaders responsible for much worse repression than Somoza—had received such letters."

15. Anastasio Somoza, *Nicaragua Betrayed* (Belmont, Mass., 1980), pp. 143 and 140.

16. "Somoza and His Foes Both Looking to U.S. for Aid," Alan Riding, NYT, July 26, 1978, p. A3.

Chapter 8

1. "Nicaragua Question," WP editorial, August 3, 1978, p. A22.

2. "'Commander Zero': Payoff Political," Associated Press, in WP, August 25, 1978, p. A15.

3. Untitled story, Alan Riding, NYT, August 28, 1978, p. 31.

4. The communiqué stated that: "The anti-somocista struggle process has counted on the participation of the wealthy people of the Conservative Party, who at all times, have sold themselves to Somoza; on the newly rich people of the Social Christian Party who have been begging Somoza for legalization of their party, and on the old rich people of the Constitutionalist Liberal Party who endorse the dialogue with Somoza. The other rich people like the business people, industrialists and the great financial capital, until a few months ago, did not have a major participation in the anti-somocista struggle. It wasn't until after the offensive of October 1977 that these forces—with the exception of the financial capital—were all in favor of a dialogue with the tyrant." (Communiqué quoted in Anastasio Somoza, *Nicaragua Betrayed* [Belmont, Mass., 1980], pp 159–61.)

5. Panama City ACAN 1839 GMT 26 Aug 78, "Somoza's Cousin Says Government Strengthened by Attack," FBIS, VI., 28 Aug 78, P7.

6. Managua Domestic Service 2018 GMT 24 Aug 78, "Somoza Addresses Nation," FBIS, VI., 25 Aug 78, P7.

7. Ibid.

8. Robelo reported this invitation to his colleagues at the MDN at the end of August, according to Xavier Zavala. Author's interview with Xavier Zavala, January 17, 1989.

9. "Somoza Vows to Finish Term; Planes Bomb 3rd Largest City," Karen DeYoung, WP, August 30, 1978 p. A1.

10. Tomás Borge et al., *Sandinistas Speak*, (New York, 1986), p. 69.

11. "With Moderates Split, Marxists Lead Fight Against Somoza Regime," by Karen DeYoung, WP, August 31, 1978, p. A17.

12. "He Was Crying, 'Don't Kill Me, Don't Kill Me!" Karen DeYoung, WP, September 20, 1978, p. A1.

13. Ibid.

14. "Venezuelan Asks OAS Intervention," WP, September 20, 1978, p. A1.

15. David Binder, NYT, September 13, 1978, p. 13.

16. Declassified testimony of Assistant Secretary Viron Vaky before a closed "Executive session" of the Senate Foreign Relations Committee, September 13, 1978.

17. Author's interview with Viron Vaky, February 16, 1989. Also see Anthony Lake, *Somoza Falling* (Boston, 1989), p. 115.

18. Robert A. Pastor, *Condemned to Repetition: The United States and Nicaragua* (Princeton, 1987), p. 79; and see Lake, p. 115.

19. Lake, pp. 115 and 116, and Pastor, p. 82.

20. White House transcript of "Interview with Zbigniew Brzezinski for Latin American Editors," September 22, 1978. Quoted in Pastor, pp. 88–90.

21. Lake, p. 117; Pastor, p. 86.

22. See CR, September 26, 1978, pp. 31777–78, remarks by Congressman Larry McDonald (D-GA).

23. Once again, however, Congressman Wilson succeeded in restoring the aid, this time in the House-Senate Conference meeting on the foreign aid bill.

24. Floor statement of Senator Frank Church (D-ID), quoted in the *Washington Post*, September 23, 1978, p. A9.

25. "Crisis in Nicaragua," WP, editorial, August 29, 1978, p. A14.

26. In his account of the Carter administration's policy toward Nicaragua, Robert Pastor has argued that domestic political pressure, from both right and left, "neither constrained nor changed," but rather "reinforced" the administration's preferred approach. "The conservatives had less influence on the Administration than the liberal bloc, but neither shaped the White House approach." See Pastor, p. 99.

It is difficult to support this contention, however. It would seem that, on the contrary, the administration's policy, or lack of policy, was very much the product of political pressures from all sides.

27. Pastor, pp. 83 and 84.

28. "Street Fighting Spreads Through Nicaragua," Karen DeYoung, WP, September 12, 1978, p. A10.

29. Pastor paraphrases Christopher as objecting that "the option had so many unattractive qualities that we didn't want to do it if we didn't have to." Pastor, p. 84.

30. For description of these events, see Pastor, pp. 88–89.

31. Pérez's conversations with William Jorden and Vaky, quoted in Pastor, pp. 86–87.

32. Quoted in Pastor, p. 89.

33. The transcript of the conversation between Somoza and Jorden is excerpted in Somoza's memoirs. Somoza did tape all his conversations with American officials, as Pastor suspected.

34. The first choice was William D. Rogers. Somoza complained that Rogers had "stated biased opinions about the Somoza family." See Pastor, pp. 91–92.

Chapter 9

1. State 252512 Cable from Vaky to Bowdler, October 4, 1978. Vaky wanted to authorize Bowdler to press Somoza to resign "substantially" before 1981, but was overruled by Christopher.

2. Ibid.

3. Ibid.

4. Author's interview with Viron Vaky, February 16, 1989.

5. Quoted in Pilar Arias, *Nicaragua: Revolución Relatos de Combatientes del Frente Sandinista* (Mexico, 1981), pp. 169–70.

6. This was suggested by the mediators. Managua 5142, October 18, 1978. Bowdler to Vaky.

7. Buenos Aires LATIN 0554 GMT 20 Oct 78, "Somoza Accuses Foreign Governments of Arming Opponents," FBIS, VI. 23 Oct 78, P1.

8. Author's interview with Viron Vaky, February 16, 1989.

9. Declassified Secret Memorandum from Robert Pastor to Zbigniew Brzezinski, October 31, 1978.

10. Ibid.

11. Robert A. Pastor, *Condemned to Repetition: The United States and Nicaragua* (Princeton, 1987), p. 104.

12. Anastasio Somoza, *Nicaragua Betrayed* (Belmont, Mass. 1980), p. 195.

13. Managua 5621, November 6, 1978; Managua 5421, October 28, 1978.

14. Panama City ACAN 2346 8 Nov 78, "Opposition Leader Predicts Somoza's Departure or Bloodbath," FBIS, VI. 9 Nov 78, P6.

15. "Three Mediators Leave Managua for Home," Alan Riding, NYT, November 13, 1978, p. A11.

16. "Somoza Seeks Votes on Foes' Strength; Opposition Refuses," Alan Riding, NYT, November 12, 1978, p. A1.

17. Report to the Secretary of State on the work of the International Commission of Friendly Cooperation and Conciliation, Annex 11, 1979.

18. Somoza, p. 207.

19. *Public Papers of the Presidents, Jimmy Carter, 1979* (Washington, 1980), Vol. 2, p. 1993.

20. Managua 5776, November 11, 1978. Bowdler to Vaky.

21. "On the Brink in Nicaragua," WP editorial, November 11, p. A16.

22. Managua 5778, November 11, 1978, Bowdler to Vaky.

23. Pastor, p. 105.

24. Anthony Lake, *Somoza Falling* (Boston, 1989), pp. 155–56.

25. Panama City ACAN 0115 GMT 17 Nov 78, "FAO Says Delaying Tactics Used In Mediation," FBIS, VI. 20 Nov 78, P9; Managua 5954, November 20, 1978. Bowdler to Christopher and Vaky.

26. Panama City ACAN 1840 GMT 23 Nov 78, "Archbishop Asks for Continuation of Peace Negotiations," FBIS, VI. 24 Nov 78, P12.

27. Panama City ACAN 0430 GMT 22 Nov 78, "FAO Suspends Talks with Mediation Commission," FBIS, VI. 22 Nov 78, P8.

28. Paris AFP 1847 GMT 27 Nov 78, "International Mediators Threaten to Leave in 72 Hours," Paris AFP 2256 GMT 27 Nov 78, "Government Rejects Mediators' Deadline," FBIS, VI. 28 Nov 78, P5.

29. Managua 6424, December 7, 1978.

30. Managua 6427, December 8, 1978.

31. Managua 6628, December 16, 1978.

32. "Rebels Hobnob with Bankers," by Marlise Simons, WP, December 20, 1978, p. A16.

33. For a transcript of this meeting see Somoza, pp. 325–33.

In June 1979, General McAuliffe and a State Department official had to answer searching questions from a conservative congressman who had received reports about this meeting with Somoza—no doubt from Somoza himself, who had taped it.

Rep. Carroll Hubbard (D-KY): Did you suggest to President Somoza that he resign?

General McAuliffe: No, sir.

Mr. Hubbard: You never made that suggestion to President Somoza?

Gen. McAuliffe: No, sir. We discussed—

Mr. Hubbard: Did you discuss his resignation?

Gen. McAuliffe: Discuss what?

Mr. Hubbard: His resignation.

Gen. McAuliffe: Not in that tone. . . . [O]ur discussion was to advise General Somoza of our support; that is to say, our military support, U.S. military support, Department of Defense support, for the process of negotiations leading toward a plebiscite which was then alive and under active consideration. . . . It was perhaps not clear, or not made clear to General Somoza that we on the military side supported that process. That was the purpose of my visit.

See the transcript of hearings by the House Committee on Merchant Marine and Fisheries, Subcommittee on Panama Canal, June 7, 1979.

34. Pastor, pp. 112 and 113.

35. See "Congressman Denounces U.S. Nicaraguan Efforts," Karen DeYoung, WP December 7, 1978, p. A26.

36. See Pastor, p. 114, for an account of this meeting. Pastor was not present, but he has interviewed both Murphy and Carter and provides a persuasive case that Carter made no concessions to Murphy *in the meeting*.

37. Pastor, pp. 115 and 116.

38. Ibid., p. 118.

39. Ibid., p. 119.

40. Lake, p. 179.

41. Pastor, p. 122.

42. "Somoza Jogs as U.S. Tries to Set Pace," Karen DeYoung, WP, January 14, 1979, p. A1.

43. "Somoza Says U.S. Is Pressing His Overthrow," Karen DeYoung, WP, February 22, 1979.

44. Vaky letter to Lee Hamilton, September 8, 1979, reprinted as Appendix 4 to a hearing held by the House Foreign Affairs Subcommittee on Inter-American Affairs, June 26, 1979.

45. Testimony of Viron Vaky before the House Foreign Affairs Subcommittee on Inter-American Affairs, June 26, 1979, p. 44.

46. Vaky letter to Hamilton, September 8, 1979.

Chapter 10

1. Henri Weber writes that "within the context of a fruitful strategic debate, a kind of functional division of labor developed among the three groups." Henri Weber, *Nicaragua: The Sandinista Revolution* (Paris, 1981), p. 57.

2. See discussion by Henry Ruiz in GACETA SANDISTA 1 Jan 79 pp 8,9, "Sandinist Commander Reviews Faction Strategies," FBIS, VI. 1 February 79, P6–P7.

3. A CIA report of May 2, 1979 stated that Castro had concluded by the fall of 1978 that "the prospects for revolutionary upheaval in Central America over the next decade or so had markedly improved largely because of the weakened position of Nicaragua's Somoza and the ripple effect his removal would have on other countries in Central America." Castro had, as a result, increased the training of guerrillas on Cuban territory, urged all Central American guerrilla groups to unify, and in the case of Nicaragua he had begun an extensive arms supply. See CIA report of May 2, 1979. Reprinted in CR May 19, 1980, pp. 11653–55.

4. CIA report of May 2, 1979. Reprinted in CR, May 19, 1980, pp. 11653–55.

5. Daniel and Humberto Ortega, and Victor Tirado of the *Terceristas*; Tomás Borge, Bayardo Arce, and Henry Ruiz, of the GPP; and Jaime Wheelock, Carlos Nuñez, and Luis Carrión, of the Proletarian Tendency.

6. See David Nolan, *The Ideology of the Sandinistas and the Nicaraguan Revolution* (Coral Gables, Fl., 1984), p. 98.

7. Havana International Service 0000 GMT 3 Feb 79 PA, "FSLN Commander Hugo Torres Vows to 'Continue Fighting,'" FBIS, VI. 5 February 79, P10.

8. Pastor, 65; Author's interview with Humberto Ortega, May 26, 1990.

9. See Frederick Kempe, *Divorcing the Dictator: America's Bungled Affair with Noriega* (New York, 1980), p. 97.

10. CIA report of May 2, 1979. Reprinted in CR, May 19, 1980, pp. 11653–55.

11. The irony of Costa Rican outrage was not lost on the American Ambassador, Marvin Weissman, who cabled to Washington on October 12, 1978: "Incredible as it appears, otherwise responsible Costa Ricans cannot see any inherent contradiction in the continuing presence and activities of Sandinistas, detained or otherwise, currently giving numerous press interviews, and the Civil Guard "sweeping" the border area, albeit with limited effectiveness. Nor can they accept relating FSLN activity, past or present, to [Nicaraguan National Guard] activity, past or present. They see themselves only as put upon by Somoza." (San José 04339, October 12, 1978).

12. The entire operation a few years later became the subject of a Costa Rican National Assembly investigation, which brought no charges of personal enrichment against former President Carazo.

13. Pastor, p. 76.

14. Declassified Secret Memorandum from Viron Vaky to the Acting Secretary (Christopher), September 9, 1978.

15. Declassified Secret Memorandum from Robert Pastor to Zbigniew Brzezinski, June 5, 1979.

16. Pastor, p. 128.

17. According to Humberto Ortega, "We undertook operations that did not fit within a specific political-military plan but they did serve the purpose of continuing to motivate the masses, to keep the mass movement going in the cities, which, in turn, allowed us to gain in strength." See Tomás Borge et al. *Sandinistas Speak*, (New York, 1986), p. 70.

18. Paris AFP 0024 GMT 12 Apr 79 PA, "Situation Deteriorating," FBIS, VI. 12 Apr 79, P6.

19. San José Radio Reloj 1314 GMT 16 April 79, "Witness Recounts Execution of 40 Hospitalized Youths," FBIS, VI. 17 Apr 79, P2.

20. UPI, April 17, 1979.

21. "Nicaraguan Rebels Begin Major Drive," Alan Riding, NYT, June 2, 1979, p. 1.

22. Pastor, p. 132.

23. Testimony of Gen. Dennis P. McAuliffe at a June 7, 1979, hearing of House Merchant Marine and Fisheries Subcommittee on the Panama Canal.

24. Managua 2535, June 8, 1979; Declassified Secret Memorandum from Robert Pastor to Zbigniew Brzezinski, June 8, 1979.

25. "Nicaraguan Towns Fall to Rebels," Alan Riding, NYT, June 8, 1979, p. 8.

26. Pastor, p. 135.

27. Somoza wrote in his memoirs, "Somewhere in Israel there is a large consignment of arms and ammunitions which could have saved Nicaragua." Anastasio Somoza, *Nicaragua Betrayed* (Belmont, Mass., 1980), p. 239.

28. Emphasis added. Pastor, p. 128.

29. CIA report of May 2, 1979. Reprinted in CR, May 19, 1980, pp. 11653–55.

30. See Kempe, p. 96.

31. "Nicaragua on Edge as Rebels Prepare," Alan Riding, NYT, March 21, 1979, p. 2.

32. According to Pastor, "Whenever information [about Costa Rican involvement in arms deliveries] was received ... the U.S. Ambassador was instructed to meet with Carazo and [Minister of Public Security] Echeverría to express U.S. concern." Pastor, p. 128.

33. See Kempe, p. 96.

34. Ibid.

35. Anthony Lake, *Somoza Falling* (Boston, 1989), pp. 217–18.

36. See testimony of Col. James C. Thomas, USAF (ret.) before the House Committee on Merchant Marine and Fisheries, Subcommittee on Panama Canal, June 7, 1979.

This should be contrasted with Pastor's assertion that American "intelligence was weak because State and CIA gave the region low priority." Pastor, p. 128.

37. Emphasis added. Pastor, pp. 132–34.

38. Declassified Confidential Memorandum from Robert Pastor to Zbigniew Brzezinski, June 5, 1979.

39. Ibid.

40. Pastor, pp. 132–34.

41. McAuliffe said there were "reports which relate to Cuban arms; and there are some reports that relate to Panamanian involvement. . . . It depends upon whether you are talking about the Government of Panama or Panamanian nationals who have been found to have done some of this." See testimony of General Dennis P. McAuliffe, House Merchant Marine and Fisheries Committee, Subcommittee on Panama Canal, June 6, 1979.

When President Carter met with 100 members of Congress on June 11 to lobby for the Panama Canal legislation, he was more candid: "I have enquired to the Panamanian leaders as to whether or not they were interfering in the internal affairs of Nicaragua. They replied that they are not. I cannot deny, however, that Panama and Venezuela . . . might very well have given aid to the dissident groups opposing Somoza. . . . But I can't comment on whether or not Panama has given aid to the opposition forces in Nicaragua. My guess is that they have. It is a common procedure, apparently, by many other governments that disavow any desire to become involved in the internal affairs of Nicaragua." (Quoted in Pastor, p. 136)

42. "The Canal and the Guns," Rowland Evans and Robert Novak, WP, June 8, 1979, p. A19.

43. See Shirley Christian, *Nicaragua: Revolution in the Family* (New York, 1985), p. 113: *Sandinistas Speak*, p. 77.

44. Lopez Portillo, for his part, called Castro "a liberator who has become not only a guide and ruler but also a living institution." "Castro, Citing Blockade, Lays Poor Relations to U.S.," Alan Riding, NYT, May 19, 1979, p. 2.

45. Nicaraguan Foreign Minister, Julio C. Quintana, told reporters he believed the "primary actor" in influencing Mexico was Castro, and the "supporting actor" was Carazo.

46. "Mexico Presses U.S. to End Somoza Aid," Alan Riding, NYT, May 22, 1979, p. A13.

Chapter 11

1. Paris AFP 2100 GMT 23 Apr 79, "FPN Seeks Unity to Overthrow Somoza," FBIS VI. 25 April 79, P4.

2. Managua 2463, June 1, 1979.

3. Eli Altamirano, the leader of the Nicaraguan Communist Party, was also arrested. Unlike Robelo and Córdova Rivas, however, Altamirano was sentenced to six months in jail.

4. Shirley Christian, *Nicaragua: Revolution in the Family* (New York, 1985), p. 111.

5. Paris AFP 1639 GMT 3 Jun 79, "Church Condemns Terrorism But Calls It Legitimate," FBIS, VI. 4 June 79, P9.

6. Managua 2473, June 1, 1979.

7. "The honest businessmen [will] show their patriotism by participating in the general strike. . . . Any Somoza followers owning stores or businesses and refusing to participate in this total blackout will be accountable to our units, squads and Sandinist [words indistinct] [who] have precise instructions to enforce this ordinance." Radio Sandino 1835 GMT 1 Jun 79, "Businessmen Asked to Participate in General Strike," FBIS, VI. 4 June 79, P9.

8. The American embassy reported that "the strike has been very effective, reaching the proportions of the height of last year's national work stoppage." Managua 2488, June 4, 1979.

9. *Public Papers of the Presidents, Jimmy Carter, 1979* (Washington, 1980), Vol. pp. 948–49.

10. Author's interview with Viron Vaky, May 24, 1989. A decision by the administration in May to allow the IMF to go forward with the loan, delayed since the end of 1978, was not meant to support Somoza, as many liberal critics of the administration argued, but to preserve the "non-political" nature of the international lending agency. On the other hand, approval of the loan did help Somoza, whether or not that was the intention.

11. "More Pressure to Oust Somoza Weighed," by John Goshko, *Washington Post*, June 13, 1979, p. A20.

12. Author's interview with Viron Vaky, May 24, 1989.

13. According to Pastor, Brzezinski argued in a meeting of senior officials that "events in Nicaragua would impact on U.S.-Soviet relations and on the President's domestic political standing, particularly in the South and West." Robert A. Pastor, *Condemned to Repetition: The United States and Nicaragua* (Princeton, 1987), p. 142.

14. Zbigniew Brzezinski, *Power and Principle* (New York, 1983), p. 321. For Brzezinski's views on the Soviet threat in the Third World, see also pp. 188, 318, 342–44, and 517.

15. San José Radio Reloj 2197 GMT 11 Jun 79 PA, "Meeting with Somoza," FBIS, VI. 12 Jun 79, P5.

16. San José 2441, June 11, 1979.

17. Pastor, p. 139.

18. The Carter administration had tried to discuss the matter with Robelo prior to his acceptance, presumably to dissuade him, but when Bowdler suggested to Robelo on June 15 that they meet in San José or Mexico City, Robelo had declined. Vaky letter to Congressman Lee Hamilton, September 8, 1979, reprinted as Appendix 4 to a hearing held by the House Foreign Affairs Subcommittee on Inter-American Affairs, June 26, 1979.

19. *Washington Post* reporter Karen DeYoung wrote that "the list is notable for its exclusion of the more doctrinaire Marxist Sandinista leaders and the inclusion of Robelo, a U.S.-favored left-centrist who has denounced the guerrillas in the past." "Andean Nations Provide Sandinistas a Diplomatic Opening," Karen DeYoung, WP, June 18, 1979, p. A20.

20. Author's interview with Viron Vaky, May 24, 1989.

21. Pastor, p. 135.

22. See Pastor, p. 158.

23. Assistant Secretary Derian argued that supporting a non-Sandinista alternative would "appear as our having opted for the status quo out of fear of social and political change, even when that change incorporates clear non-Marxist democratic elements." The Carter administration would be "forced into an East-West prism in order to defend our policies, lumping all elements as Cuban-Castroist, when they are not and when the democratic countries of the hemisphere do not view them as such." Secret Memorandum [declassified] from Assistant Secretary of State Patricia M. Derian to Acting Secretary Warren Christopher, June 18, 1979.

24. Vaky cabled his ambassadors in the region asking them only to seek support for a resolution in the OAS that would call for a cease-fire, a halt in the flow of arms to Nicaragua, "and if possible, a high level [foreign Ministers] mission to Somoza designed to urge and help shape a peaceful transition." State cable 153522 6-15-79.

25. At an interagency meeting on June 19, according to Pastor, "Brzezinski said . . . events in Nicaragua would impact on U.S.-Soviet relations and on the President's domestic political standing in the South and the West." As a *New York Times* editorial on June 20 put it, "President Carter can do without the title of midwife to a Central American radical regime." "Saving Nicaragua From Somoza," NYT editorial, June 20, 1979, p. 22.

26. See Richard C. Thornton, *The Carter Years: Toward a New Global Order* (New York, 1991), p. 381; Brzezinski, p. 342; and Jimmy Carter, *Keeping Faith: Memoirs of a President* (New York, 1982), p. 247.

27. Pastor, p. 141.

28. As Vaky recalls, while the State Department originally proposed going to the OAS for this uncontroversial purpose, the "NSC jumped on for different reasons." Author's interview with Viron Vaky, May 24, 1989.

29. Pastor, p. 144.

30. *American Foreign Policy, Basic Documents* [hereafter AFPD], 1977–1980. (Washington, 1983), Document 698.

31. Pastor, p. 133.

32. Ibid., p. 147.

33. "Vance Proposes Replacement of Somoza Rule in Nicaragua; Asks for an O.A.S. Peace Force," Graham Hovey, NYT, June 22, 1979, p. A1.

34. Pastor, pp. 147–48. Pastor was not present at the meeting, but later interviewed Brzezinski, who gave him this account of what was said.

35. Pastor, p. 151.

36. San José Radio Reloj 2146 GMT 18 Jun 79 PA, "Reconstruction Government Members Hold News Conference," FBIS, VI. 19 Jun 79, P5; Radio Sandino (Clandestine) to Nicaragua 0300 GMT 18 Jun 79 PA, "Junta Members Issue Messages Upon Accepting Positions," FBIS, VI. 19 Jun 79, P14.

37. San José Radio Reloj 0100 GMT 21 Jun 79 PA, "Communiqué Issued," FBIS, VI. 21 Jun 79, P4.

38. Managua 2699, June 19, 1979. Eventually the Council was expanded to 33 members, from whom the Sandinistas could still count on a slim majority.

39. Managua 2861, June 28, 1979.

40. See Pastor, p. 158.

41. Pastor, p. 157.

42. Pastor, pp. 156–57.

43. Managua 2919, June 30, 1979.

44. State 186183, July 19, 1979.

45. Pastor, pp. 151 and 156.

46. See Pastor for cable, p. 169.

47. Pastor reports that at a meeting on June 23 officials agreed that the Guard would need support, but "there was no discussion about either the magnitude or the kind of support that would be needed." Pastor, p. 148–49. "If we had armed the Guard," Vaky recalls, "it would really have plunged Nicaragua into civil war, and it would have been seen by the Latins as an effort to block the Sandinistas." Author's interview with Viron Vaky, May 24, 1989.

48. Pastor, p. 153.

49. Managua 3017, July 6, 1979.

50. State 175767, July 7, 1979.

51. Anatasio Somoza, *Nicaragua Betrayed* (Belmont, Mass., 1980), pp. 337–38.

52. Pastor, p. 170.

Chapter 12

1. Robert A. Pastor, *Condemned to Repetition: The United States and Nicaragua* (Princeton, 1987), p. 161.

2. Panama City ACAN 1806 GT 11 Jul 79 PA, "Nicaraguan Junta Meets with Former President Figueres," FBIS, VI. 12 Jul 79, P6.

3. Vaky letter to Congressman Lee Hamilton, September 8, 1979, reprinted as Appendix Y to House Foreign Affairs Subcommittee on Inter-American Affairs hearing, June 26, 1979, p. 77. The decision to let Panama and Costa Rica take the lead was due also to the fact that Bowdler was ill for several days at the beginning of July. He did not return to the mediation effort until July 7.

4. Pastor, p. 152.

5. Anastasio Somoza, *Nicaragua Betrayed* (Belmont, Mass., 1980), p. 337.

6. The *Washington Post* attacked the congressman: "For a legislator to take up a part as a free-lance negotiator . . . lending his presence and prestige and advice to the foreign party involved in a delicate adversary proceeding with his own government is very odd." "Mr. Murphy in Managua," WP editorial, July 6, 1979, p. A18.

7. Somoza, p. 347.

8. Somoza responded to Pezzullo's implicit threat with a warning of his own: "Don't force me to resign and walk through the bush. Because if you don't give me an alternative to go where I think my other country is, the U.S., my alternative is to resign and go to the bush. And then you have a Sandino again, all over again, and this poor goddamn country will never have peace." Somoza, p. 341.

9. Somoza, pp. 346–47.

10. "U.S. Asks Rebel Junta to Add Moderates," Alan Riding, NYT, July 2, 1979, p. A3.

11. "I am like a tied donkey fighting with a tiger," Somoza told reporter Karen DeYoung. "Even if I win militarily, I have no future." Somoza talked about getting another job: "I've got my education. I might find some place. What can a retired general, a retired president do?" "Somoza Agrees to Quit, Leaves Timing to U.S.," DeYoung, WP, July 7, 1979, p. A1.

12. Paris AFP 2003 GMT 10 Jul 79 PA, "U.S. Said to Use Somoza Resignation as Blackmail Tool," FBIS, VI. 11 Jul 79, P7.

13. "U.S. in Role of Key Nicaraguan Arbiter," Alan Riding, NYT July 10, 1979, p. A3.

14. "U.S. Presses Effort to Broaden Makeup of Nicaraguan Junta," Alan Riding, NYT, July 6, 1979, p. A1.

15. "Somoza's Departure Reported Delayed," Alan Riding, NYT, July 8, 1979, pp. 1, 7.

16. Pastor, p. 170.

17. Paris AFP 1606 GMT 18 Jul 79, "Reconstruction Government Junta Installed in León," FBIS, VI. 19 Jul 78, P7.

18. D'Escoto declared, "The only way to characterize this is blackmail. They're trying to bargain with the blood of our people. This can only result in the prolongation of the war and anarchy." "Latins Pressing Nicaraguan Left for Concessions," Alan Riding, NYT, July 9, 1979, p. A1.

19. See Shirley Christian, *Nicaragua: Revolution in the Family* (New York, 1985), p. 126.

20. Ibid., pp. 126–27.

21. "U.S. Contacts Rebel Junta, Plans Food Aid to Nicaragua," Karen DeYoung, WP, July 11, p. A10.

22. Karen DeYoung reported that "Borges [sic], a self-declared Marxist-Leninist, is considered a pragmatist. . . . As interior minister, political analysts said, Borges will also serve as director of police functions and thus will be in a better position to keep mavericks from his faction in line." "Nicaraguan Rebel Junta Names 12 to Provisional Cabinet," by Karen DeYoung, WP, July 15, 1979, p. A13.

Alan Riding also wrote that "Mr. Borge should be in a position to control the most radical elements among the rebels." "Nicaraguan Junta Selects Its Cabinet," Alan Riding, NYT, July 15, 1979, p. 1.

23. Once again, it was Violeta Chamorro, not the Sandinistas, who suggested that the Nicaraguan people were not ready for elections and that it might be at least three years before elections could be held. Chamorro argued that the Nicaragua people had to be "educated, taught to read and told what a voter's card and electoral register are." She justified her controversial position, as she almost always did, by saying "if he were alive my husband would do what we are doing." Paris L'HUMANITE 4 Jul 79, p. 7, "National Reconstruction Government Members Interviewed," FBIS, VI. 10 Jul 79, P8.

24. "The 72-Hour Document", [hereafter 72-Hour Document] translated and reprinted by, the Department of State, 1986.

25. Panama City Circuit RPC Television 1800 GMT 13 Jul 79 PA, "Former Venezuelan President Pérez on Nicaraguan Crisis," FBIS, VI. 16 Jul 79, N1-N2.

26. Viron Vaky, testimony before House Foreign Affairs Committee, Subcommittee on Inter-American Affairs, June 26, 1979.

27. Ibid.

28. Author's interview with Viron Vaky, September 1, 1989.

29. "Nicaraguan Endgame," WP editorial, July 5, 1979, p. A10.

30. "A Devastated Nicaragua Faces Years of Rebuilding," Alan Riding, NYT, July 4, 1979, p. A3.

31. Pastor, p. 173.

32. Columnist William Safire noted the apparent similarity between the Carter administration's strategy and Fidel Castro's. Citing the leaked intelligence report of May 2, Safire argued: "Our secret intelligence reports that when Fidel Castro met with the Nicaraguan communist leaders in March, he 'urged them to play down the Marxist nature of their program at this point and to offer to join with non-Marxists in forging a broad coalition.' Incredibly, that Castro strategy is also the Carter Administration's plan. By urging the overthrow of Somoza and his replacement with a coalition, Mr. Carter thinks he can prevent a Communist takeover—while Mr. Castro knows that any such coalition would be a quick transition to absolute Communist rule. We are still pretending there is some 'moderate' solution, when the hard choice is between an undemocratic right and an antidemocratic, dangerous left." ("Stranger Than Fiction," editorial by William Safire, NYT, July 5, 1979, p. A17)

33. "U.S. Presses Effort to Broad Makeup of Nicaraguan Junta," Alan Riding, NYT, July 6, 1979, p. A1.

34. Somoza managed to reach only Warren Christopher, however, who told him to meet with Ambassador Pezzullo. The next day, when Wright called to complain that Vance had not kept his word, Brzezinski was enlisted to explain to a fellow conservative Democrat what the administration was up to. As Pastor relates the conversation: "When informed [by Brzezinski] that the United States had asked Somoza to resign, Wright protested that asking a head of state to step down was extreme. Brzezinski explained that the circumstances were extreme, and the longer Somoza stayed in power the more ominous the outcome." (Pastor, p, 179)

35. See Christian, p. 135.

36. "Nicaraguan Junta Assumes Role in Jubilant Managua," Karen DeYoung, WP, July 21, 1979, p. A1.

37. San José Radio Monumental 2129 GMT 18 Jul 79, "First Official Pronouncement," FBIS, VI. 19 Jul 79, P10.

Chapter 13

1. "We did not think that [the Guard] was going to disintegrate so easily as it did," Moises Hassan explained on July 22. "Ephemeral President Urcuyo did us a big favor in allowing it to continue fighting until it suffered a decisive defeat." Paris AFP 0055 GMT 22 July 79, "Hassan Assesses State-Army Relations," FBIS, VI., 23 Jul 79, P11.

2. State 186183, July 19, 1979.

3. While some American journalists reported that Daniel Ortega was the only "official" Sandinista of the five, two days after the triumph junta-member Hassan stated matter-of-factly what all Nicaraguans knew—that "three of the five members of the junta are in complete agreement with the leadership of the Sandinista National Liberation Front." Hassan told reporters that "Alfonso Robelo and Violeta Chamorro feel less close to the guerrillas who won power than the others."

See, for instance, "Uneasy Alliance of Rebels, Businessmen to Rule Nicaragua," Karen De-Young, WP, July 22, 1979, p. A14; Paris AFP 0055 GMT 22 Jul 79, "Hassan Assesses State-Army Relations," FBIS, VI. 23 Jul 79, P11.

4. Emphasis added. Managua Domestic Service 0015 GMT 29 Jul 79, "Sandinist Staff Discusses National Security, Defense," FBIS, VI. 30 Jul 79, P2.

5. Milan L'UNITA 3 Aug 79, p. 11, "L'UNITA Interviews Sergio Ramírez, Daniel Ortega, Jaime Wheelock," FBIS, VI. 13 Aug 79, P9.

6. The Sandinistas had drawn "imperialism and the reactionary bourgeoisie into a colossal ambush" in which the crisis of the dictatorship became, "of necessity, the crisis of the economic order." The Sandinista Front had raised "the highly unifying anti-Somoza banner while at the same time routing the military underpinnings of the bourgeois system of domination, with the help of the bourgeoisie itself." 72-Hour Document.

7. Rio de Janeiro O GLOBO 19 Aug 79, p. 31, "Interior Minister Borge Interviewed by Brazilian Paper," FBIS, VI. 23 Aug 79, P4.

8. They were confident that "the power of the arms of the Sandinista People's Army" would assure "the irreversible character of the conquests and goals achieved so far." 72-Hour Document.

9. 72-Hour Document.

10. Ibid.

11. Shirley Christian, *Nicaraguan: Revolution in the Family* (New York, 1985), p. 142.

12. The Civil Defense Committees, copies of the Committees for the Defense of the Revolution established by Castro in Cuba, had served as support organizations for the guerrillas during the war, informing them of National Guard movements and identifying Somoza functionaries in each town.

13. Paris AFP 1753 GMT 28 Jul 79, "Reconstruction Work Underway Despite Problems," FBIS, VI. 30 Jul 79, P12.

14. Managua Cadena Panamericana de Radiofusión 1917 GMT 20 Jul 79, "Reconstruction Government Members Address Managua Welcoming Rally—Daniel Ortega Address," FBIS, VI. 23 Jul 79, P7.

15. Panama City Domestic Service 1848 19 Aug, "Members of Estelí Local Junta Elected 19 August," FBIS, VI. 22 Aug 79, P7.

16. Valerie Miller, *Between Struggle and Hope: The Nicaraguan Literacy Crusade* (Boulder, Colo., 1985), p. 25.

17. Managua Cadena Panamericana de Radiofusión 1917 GMT 20 Jul 79, "Reconstruction Government Members Address Managua Welcoming Rally—Alfonso Robelo Address," FBIS, VI. 23 Jul 79, P6.

18. Frankfurt Frankfurter Rundschau 20 Jul 79, p. 2, "Interview with Alfonso Robelo," FBIS, VI. 23 Jul 79, P9.

19. The pastoral letter itself was not broadcast over the Catholic church's radio station until August 6 because the station was under the government's orders to broadcast the flood of official communiqués and decrees.

20. Paris AFP 2225 GMT 6 Aug 79, "Church Urges Reinstatement of Civil Liberties," FBIS, VI. 7 Aug 79, P4.

21. Panama City ACAN 2058 GMT 13 Sep 79, "Sandinist Front Directorate Disowns New 'Sandinist' Party," FBIS, VI. 14 Sep 79, P4.

22. Paris AFP 0035 GMT 21 Sep, "Social Democratic Party Challenges Junta Decree," FBIS, VI. 24 Sep 79, P10.

23. Managua Radio Sandino 2200 GMT 23 Sep 79 PA, "New Party Secretary Describes Fear of Sandinism," FBIS, VI. 10 Oct 79, P8–P9.

24. Panama City ACAN 2058 GMT 13 Sep 79, "Sandinist Front Directorate Disowns New 'Sandinist' Party," FBIS, VI. 14 Sep 79, P4.

25. Managua Radio Sandino 1800 GMT Sep 27, "Sandinists Announce 'Death To Somozism' Program," FBIS, VI. 28 Sep 79, P4.

26. The number of these "unfounded" arrests was so great that Borge later acknowledged "abuses by certain members of the army . . . in which neighbors are arrested because of personal quarrels, with the neighbors physically abused and in some cases tortured." "This has been done," Borge said, "without the knowledge of the government and the Sandinist National Liberation Front." Managua Radio Sandino 1800 GMT 14 Nov 79 PA, "Borge Discusses False Charges, Immigration, Penal System," FBIS, VI. 15 Nov 79, P8.

27. Managua Radio Sandino 1800 GMT 28 Sep 79, "Ortega Promises 'Strong Hand' Against Reactionaries," FBIS, VI. 2 Oct 79, P8.

28. On September 24, an exasperated Tomás Borge complained that "those idiots want us to decree socialism and other crazy things. Socialism cannot be decreed." Panama City ACAN 0107 GMT 25 Sep 79, "Borge Refuses to Label Revolution 'Communist,'" FBIS, VI. 26 Sep 79, P12; Managua Radio Sandino 1800 GMT Sep 24 79, "Borge Criticizes Fake Social Democrats, Ultraleft," FBIS, VI. 26 Sep 79, P12.

29. Panama City ACAN 1941 GMT 9 Oct 79 PA, "Newsmen Arrested, Warning Issued," FBIS, VI. 11 Oct 79, P5.

30. Managua LA PRENSA 21 Oct 79, pp. 1, 9 PA, "PCD Issues Communiqué on Government Measures," FBIS, VI. 1 Nov 79, P6.

31. The destroyed Nicaraguan economy obviously provided "fertile ground" for "anti-Sandinista agitation. . . . The reactionary sectors of the bourgeoisie can find a magnificent opportunity to confuse the masses and even to organize them in blocs of resistance" against the revolution, particularly in areas where land had been taken over by the government. 72-Hour Document.

32. Managua BARRICADA 22 Oct 79, p. 3 PA, "Editorial Reponse" [First part of editorial: "Regarding the PCD Communiqué"] FBIS, VI. 1 Nov 79, P7–P9; and Managua BARRICADA 23 Oct 79, p. 3 PA, "Editorial Reponse" [Second and last part of editorial: "Regarding the PCD Communiqué"] FBIS, VI. 1 Nov 79, P9–P10.

33. Managua Radio Sandino 1200 GMT 23 Oct 79 PA, "Restrictions on State Council Membership Noted," FBIS, VI. 26 Oct 79, P14.

34. Paris AFP 1853 GMT 28 Oct 79 PA, "Robelo Announces Collective Socialization Process," FBIS, VI. 29 Oct 79, P15.

35. Managua BARRICADA 22 Oct 79, p. 3 PA, "Editorial Reponse" [First part of editorial: "Regarding the PCD Communiqué"] FBIS, VI. 1 Nov 79, P7–P9; and Managua BARRI-

CADA 23 Oct 79, p. 3 PA, "Editorial Reponse" [Second and last part of editorial: "Regarding the PCD Communiqué"] FBIS, VI. 1. Nov 79, P9–P10.

36. Managua Domestic Service 2223 GMT Oct 3 79 PA, "Agrarian Reform Minister Wheelock Speaks at Rally," FBIS, VI. 5 Oct 79, P2.

37. One of these was Carlos Coronel. Author's interview with Carlos Coronel, May 27, 1990.

38. Author's Interview with Humberto Ortega, April 11, 1991.

39. Panama City ACAN 1526 GMT 2 Aug 79, "Sandinistas Honor Fighters with New Ranks," FBIS, VI. 7 Sep 79, P7.

40. Author's Interview with Humberto Ortega, April 11, 1991.

Chapter 14

1. *Robert A. Pastor, Condemned to Repetition: The United States and Nicaragua* (Princeton, 1987), pp. 192–93.

2. Declassified Confidential Memorandum from Cyrus Vance to the President, January 7, 1980.

3. Testimony of Viron Vaky before House Foreign Affairs Committee, Subcommittee on Inter-American Affairs, September 11, 1979, pp. 3–4.

4. Pastor, p. 194.

5. Statement by Thomas J. O'Donnell quoted in Hans Binnendijk, ed., *Authoritarian Regimes in Transition*, pp. 147–48.

6. Pastor, p. 194.

7. Deputy Secretary of State Warren Christopher, testimony before the House Appropriations Subcommittee on Foreign Operations, September 11, 1979.

8. See NYT, July 26, 1979, p. 8, for press conference transcript.

9. Christopher testimony, September 11, 1979; Pastor, p. 194.

10. "U.S. Walking Softly," John Goshko, WP, July 25, 1979, p. A1.

11. Managua 3288, July 21, 1979.

12. Vaky testimony, September 11, 1979, p. 7.

13. Testimony of Lawrence Pezzullo; statement by Congressman Dante Fascell (D-FL), Ibid., p. 29.

14. Vaky testimony, September 11, 1979, p. 3.

15. Ibid. p. 25.

16. Ibid. p. 29.

17. "U.S. Debates Aid to Latin Rightists to Bar Takeovers," John M. Goshko, WP, August 2, 1979, p. A1.

18. Speech by Secretary of State Cyrus R. Vance before the Foreign Policy Association, New York, September 27, 1979. AFPD, 1977–1980. Doc. 692.

19. Address by President Carter to the nation, October 1, 1979, AFPD, 1977–1980. Doc. 712.

20. Author's interview with Humberto Ortega, April 11, 1991.

21. 72-Hour Document.

22. Ibid.

23. The American representative in Havana, Wayne Smith, cabled to the State Department that although Castro's public statements "may have been disingenuous in nature and soporific in intent," they were also a "pragmatic recognition of reality." "Castro cannot," Smith argued, "urge Nicaragua to close doors to assistance he himself cannot possibly offer even though

he recognizes provisions of such assistance will give us an advantage which will be difficult to counter." Havana 6623, 27 July 1979.

24. Ibid.; Milan L'UNITA 28 Jul 79, p. 14, "Interior Minister: Revolution 'Cannot Be Exported,'" FBIS, VI. 7 Aug 79, P5.

25. Robelo said the move toward a socialist system would be responsible, respectful of freedom, "a gradual move without hasty measures which can affect production." The effort counted on the "cooperation of the progressive bourgeoisie," Robelo said. "We cannot do without their knowledge."

26. Panama City ACAN 1931 GMT 10 Nov 79 PA, "State, Church Discuss Participation in Revolution," FBIS VI. 15 Nov 79, P10, P13.

27. These "abuses" had been carried out without the knowledge of the Sandinista Front, he said, adding that there were "always black sheep in any revolutionary process." Managua Radio Sandino 1800 GMT 14 Nov 79 PA, "Borge Discusses False Charges, Immigration, Penal System," FBI, VI. 15 Nov 79, P8.

28. Managua Domestic Service 0330 GMT 15 Nov 79 PA, "Borge Warns Against Enemies, Vows Respect of Human Rights," FBIS, VI. 16 Nov 79, P8.

29. Luis Carrión Cruz interviewed by Francis Pisani, cited in Henri Weber, *Nicaragua: The Sandinista Revolution* (Paris, 1981), p. 69.

30. Author's interview with Humberto Ortega, April 11, 1991.

31. Sandinista Directorate-member, Henry Ruiz, became Minister of Planning, replacing a prominent member of the financial community, Roberto Mayorga. The Ministries of Industry, Commerce, and Agriculture were then subsumed under the Ministry of Planning, thus removing other moderates from their positions. Jaime Wheelock became Minister of Agriculture, replacing another private-sector politician and landowner, Manuel José Torres.

32. As Henri Weber describes the Sandinistas' actions, "As the regime began to consolidate itself, and as the relationship of forces shifted in its favour, so the initial compromise with the bourgeoisie regularly came up for redefinition. . . . Clearly, the November compromises had not been intended as a permanent brake on social reforms." Weber, pp. 79 and 80.

33. The same was true with land seizures. "In the agricultural sector, the [government] (with Jaime Wheelock's Agrarian Reform Institute taking the lead) appears to be continuing land seizures despite the derogation of Decree 3. . . . It appears that Wheelock is actively seeking to expand his economic and political power by encouraging peasant land takeovers." Managua 1051, March 3, 1980; Managua 1093, March 4, 1980.

34. Paris AFP 0416 GMT 15 Feb 80 PA, "Robelo Invites Masses to Join His Party," FBIS, VI. 21 Feb 80, P13.

35. Managua 3382, July 28, 1979.

36. Managua Cadena Panamerica de Radiofusión 1905 GMT JU1 20 79, "Government Minister Borge Speech," FBIS, VI. 23 Jul 79, P8.

37. "U.S. Planning Loans and Other Aid for Nicaragua," Marlise Simons, NYT, August 17, 1979, p. A8.

38. Testimony of John Bushnell, February 26, 1980 before the Appropriations Subcommittee on Foreign Operations.

39. Vaky testimony before House Committee on Foreign Affairs, Hearing and Markup and on "Special Central American Economic Assistance," 96th Cong. 1st Session, November 27 and December 11, 1979, pp. 5–6; Bushnell testimony, February 26, 1980.

40. Vaky testimony, September 11, 1979, p. 4.

41. Bushnell testimony, February 26, 1980; Vaky testimony, September 11, 1979, p. 28.

42. Vaky testimony, September 11, 1979, p. 3.

Chapter 15

1. Statement of Congressman Robert J. Lagomarsino (R-CA) before House Committee on Foreign Affairs, Hearing and Markup on "Special Central American Economic Assistance," 96th Cong. 1st Session. November 27 and December 11, 1979, p. 18.

2. CR, February 26, 1980, p. 3852.

3. Panama City ACAN 1740 MT 28 Feb 80 PA, "*Barricada* Criticizes U.S. Handling of Loan," FBIS, VI. 29 Feb 80, P7. See also Bayardo Arce's statements describing the conditions as "absurd" and "childish." Paris AFP 0244 GMT 29 Feb 80 PA, "Bayardo Arce Comments on U.S. Conditions for Granting Loan," FBIS. VI. 29 Feb 80, P8.

4. As one scholar has put it, the law "presupposed worker participation in detecting disinvestment and economic sabotage." Dennis Gilbert, *Sandinistas: The Party and Revolution* (New York, 1988), p 112.

5. "Sandinista Policies Draw Criticism in Nicaragua," Terri Shaw, WP, April 3, 1980, p. A30.

6. Managua 1531, March 31, 1980.

7. "Sandinista Policies Draw Criticism in Nicaragua," by Terri Shaw, Washington Post, April 3, 1980, p. A30.

8. Managua 1753, April 12, 1980.

9. Managua 1876, April 22, 1980.

10. Minutes earlier the House had rejected a House-Senate conference agreement on aid for the international development banks, and the Democratic leaders feared they did not have enough votes on the Nicaragua conference report, either. Majority Leader James Wright told reporters that "the leadership doesn't like to get rolled twice in a row." *Congressional Quarterly Weekly Report* [hereafter CQ], April 19, 1980.

11. The description of the timing and content of the junta's meetings is largely Robelo's, from an interview he gave on April 28 to Radio Corporación in Managua. Managua Radio Corporación 1815 GMT 28 April 80, "Robelo Interviewed on Differences with Junta," FBIS, 30 Apr 80, P6-P13. See also Christian's account of these events, pp. 172–73.

12. Madrid YA 3 May 80 p. 10, "Ramirez: Armed Strength Guarantees Revolutionary Process," FBIS, VI. 9 May 80, P15-P16.

13. Robelo's account of the Sandinista comandantes voting on Ortega's behalf matches the information received by the American Embassy, although the Embassy may itself have gotten Robelo's version. See Managua 1898, April 22, 1980. There is no question, however, that Robelo and Chamorro voted against the Sandinista plan, and yet it was "approved" by the junta.

14. Told by an interviewer days later that she did not look "like a sick person," Chamorro responded, "God has given me the gift of being unusually strong." Madrid YA 29 Apr 80 p. 11, "Chamorro: Pluralism Still Feasible Option," FBIS, VI. 12 May 80, P15. Chamorro had, however, broken her ankle the day she resigned.

15. On April 20, the Sandinistas told the paper's news editor, and a strong supporter, Danilo Aguirre, to organize a work stoppage and occupy the plant—much like the workers' occupations of other bourgeois businesses. The Sandinistas demanded that a sympathetic editor, Violeta's son Xavier, be placed in charge of the newspaper. They threatened to confiscate not only *La Prensa*, but also the personal properties of its owners, if their demands were not met. Jaime Chamorro Cardenal, *La Prensa: The Republic of Paper* (New York, 1988), p. 28. Chamorro writes that he later learned that the Sandinista effort to put *La Prensa* in the hands of Xavier Chamorro and Danilo Aguirre was an organized plan by the Sandinistas called "Operation Trojan Horse." See Shirley Christian, *Nicaragua: Revolution in the Family* (New York, 1985), p. 177.

16. Christian, p. 174.

17. Ibid.

18. Managua 1940, April 24, 1980.

19. Panama City ACAN 0051 GMT 25 Apr 80, "COSEP Meets with FSLN to Analyze Country's 'Crisis,'" FBIS, VI. 29 Apr 80, P12.

20. Managua 1898, April 22, 1980.

21. See Shirley Christian for account of this and subsequent events concerning Pezzullo's role during the crisis, pp. 180–86.

22. Christian, p. 172.

23. From *La Prensa*, May 26, 1980. Cited and paraphrased in Henri Weber, *Nicaragua: The Sandinista Revolution* (Paris, 1981), p. 81.

24. Christian, p. 181.

25. Christian, p. 182. Interview with Ernesto Palacio, February 15, 1991.

26. Christian, p. 183.

27. Xavier Chamorro and Danilo Aguirre were given a new newspaper to run, *El Nuevo Diario*.

28. Letter inserted into the record by Senator Jesse Helms, May 19, 1980, pp. 11662–63.

29. Managua 2237, May 13, 1980.

30. Managua 2108, May 6, 1980; O'Neill's statement was, in fact, surprisingly harsh: "If there's any hope of saving Nicaragua, I'm all for it. But it's got to be proven to me that it's worth trying to save." CQ, May 17, 1980.

31. When the two names were announced, COSEP issued a statement praising the two men, but making clear that COSEP had nothing to do with their selection, that they did not represent specific "sectors" of Nicaraguan society, and their appointments, alone, were not enough to solve Nicaragua's critical problems. Managua 2325, May 19, 1980.

32. Christian, p. 186.

33. As Weber writes, "The MDN's blackmailing threats of a split had come sorely to grief." Weber, p. 81.

34. CR, May 19, 1980, pp. 11651–59.

35. Ibid. p. 11646.

36. Statement by the President on signing P.L. 96-257, May 31, 1980, AFPD, 1977–1980, Doc. 706.

37. The Carter administration had requested an additional $25 million for Nicaragua, including about $5 million in military assistance. The House quickly stripped away the military aid, however, by a vote of 267–105.

38. Quoted in *Congressional Quarterly Almanac, 1980* (Washington, 1981), p. 319.

39. CR, June 5, 1980, pp. 13486, 13488, 13494.

40. Stephen Neal of North Carolina, Bill Alexander of Arkansas, and Kent Hance of Texas.

41. Managua Radio Sandino 0300 GMT 7 Jun 80, "Report on Activities of U.S. Congressional Delegation," FBIS, VI. 9 Jun 80, P8.

42. Managua Radio Sandino 1200 GMT 10 Jun 80, "Loan Delay Explained," FBIS, VI. 11 Jun 80, P10–P11.

43. Managua EL NUEVO DIARIO 7 Jun 80, pp. 1, 10, "Junta Member Cruz Speaks on Trip to Washington," FBIS, VI. 13 Jun 80, P7.

44. Managua LA PRENSA 5 Jun 80, pp. 1, 12, "Ramírez Says Government Will Not Backtrack on Confiscation," FBIS, VI. 12 Jun 80, P6.

45. Panama City ACAN 1815 GMT 8 Jun 80, "Humberto Ortega Addresses Rally Against Reaction," FBIS, VI. 10 Jun 80, P13; Managua Radio Sandino 1200 GMT 9 Jun 80, "Revolutionary Leaders Speak at Nandaime Rally," FBIS, VI. 11 Jun 80, P11–P12.

46. Panama City ACAN 1627 GMT 10 Jun 80, "Robelo Says MDN Will Join State Council," FBIS, VI. 11 Jun 80, P12; Managua LA PRENSA 30 May 80, p. 5, "MDN Official Reports Threats in Jinotega, Matagalpa," FBIS, VI. 11 Jun 80, P13; Managua Radio Sandino 1800 GMT 11 Jun 80, "Workers Resent Being Called 'Mobs' by *La Prensa*," FBIS, VI. 12 Jun 80, P10.

47. Alexander's report, datelined "Managua, June 1980," was reprinted in CR July 2, 1980, p. 18341.

48. The July 2 vote was the toughest yet for the administration because the aid, controversial by itself, was imbedded in an even larger controversy over a large emergency foreign aid supplemental. The Senate version contained a foreign aid provision including the $75 million for Nicaragua, as well as additional funds for international financial institutions. The House conferees, led by Appropriations Committee Chairman Jamie Whitten from Mississippi, refused to accept the Senate's foreign aid provision because, they charged, it had evaded normal appropriations procedures, and Whitten's committee. The Senate had, in effect, inserted the Fiscal Year (FY) 1980 foreign aid appropriations bill, which had been stalled, into the omnibus supplemental. Whitten had consistently voted against aid for Nicaragua, in any case, but this maneuver drew his ire. Congressman Charles Long, the chairman of the Appropriations subcommittee responsible for foreign aid, ultimately offered an amendment on the House floor agreeing to accept some of the Senate's package, including the aid to Nicaragua. Congressman Bauman fought the amendment, as did Whitten. The final passage of aid to Nicaragua came on a vote of 198–196.

49. "Should the divisions between radicals, moderates, and rightists in government, church, business and unions burst into open conflict," Alexander warned, "the stakes for the United States become enormous indeed." If the private sector were to "go under," Alexander argued, Nicaragua would turn sharply to the left. Then, "it is a fair surmise that El Salvador would follow Nicaragua into the revolutionary camp," then maybe Guatemala, then Costa Rica "would be faced with moving to the left," then conditions in Panama might lead to a "Castro-type regime under Torrijos," then Honduras would have "little choice" but to turn in a revolutionary direction. Lest anyone find this analysis an apocalyptic "replay of the domino theory," Alexander insisted it was "a fair assessment of the situation that exists today in Central America." "Reason dictates, therefore, that the Congress move swiftly to extend the requested $75 million reconstruction loan as a signal to the communists that we do not intend to leave Nicaragua to their tender mercies."

Alexander's report, datelined "Managua, June 1980," was reprinted in CR, July 2, 1980, p. 18341.

50. Ibid.

51. Paris AFP 2220 GMT 30 Jun 80, "Police Conduct Raids in Preparation for 19 Jul," FBIS, VI. 2 Jul 80, P21.

52. In an increasingly predictable pattern, these arrests were followed by widespread popular complaints of false accusations and disappearances, people "crying or openly expressing their anger," and then by apologies from the Sandinista police for "errors" committed in the course of the operation. Paris AFP 2220 GMT 30 Jun 80, "Police Conduct Raids in Preparation for 19 Jul," FBIS, VI. 2 Jul 80, P21; Managua EL NUEVO DIARIO 6 Jul 80, P. 4, "Police Chief Admits Errors in '19 July Operation,'" FBIS, VI. 14 Jul 80, P17.

53. Managua Domestic Service 1800 GMT 21 Jul 80, "Junta Members Comment on Domestic, International Issues," FBIS, 24 Jul 80, P12 and P16.

54. Panama City ACAN 1622 GMT 3 Aug 80, "Junta to Hold Elections When 'Appropriate,'" FBIS, VI. 5 Aug 80, P11.

55. Managua Domestic Service 2302 MT 23 Aug 80, "Ortega: Junta Will Stay in Office until 1985," FBIS, VI. 25 Aug 80, P13.

56. Managua Domestic Service 2133 GMT 23 Aug 80, "Costa Rican President's Speech," FBIS, 25 Aug 80, P17.

57. Managua Domestic Service 2154 GMT 23 Aug 80, "Ortega Saavedra Speech," FBIS, VI 25 Aug 80, P18; see Christian, p. 198.

58. Managua 4135, August 29, 1980.

"With the 23 Aug election pronouncement and this followup campaign of gag laws the FSLN has seized the political initiative. The three decrees can be used to disarm critics of FSLN governmental and economic performance, areas the leadership is highly sensitive about. Apparently, the measures reflect FSLN fear of *La Prensa*'s proven potential of dominant strength in even an economic crunch. The political parties face an immediate future without the central democratic institution, elections, around which they traditionally organize, but political activity is not totally banned and they remain capable of pressuring the FSLN."

59. *Barricada*, September 16, 1980. Cited in Gilbert, p. 42.

60. Managua Domestic Service 2312 GMT 15 Sep 80, "Victor Tirado Lopez," FBIS, VI. 17 Sep 80, P11, P10, P10, and P11.

61. Managua LA PRENSA 12 Oct 80, pp. 1, 12, "Robelo Sees Totalitarian Tendency in Government," FBIS, VI. 21 Oct 80, P11.

62. Managua Domestic Service 0230 GMT 11 Nov 80, "Leaders Discuss MDN Rally, Border Incidents," FBIS, VI. 12 Nov 80, P7-P11. According to Robelo, Borge said "I want to make clear that we have the arms and are never going to put them down. We will use them to maintain this revolution." To which Robelo responded, "I guess that means I either have to stay as a vegetable or leave." Borge told him, "Continue doing what you are doing. Maybe some day we can see things differently." As told to Shirley Christian, p. 208.

63. Christian, p. 208. Weber, p. 83.

64. Madrid EFE 0830 GMT 10 Nov 80, "Junta Members, Robelo Interviewed on Peruvian TV," FBIS, VI. 12 Nov 80, P11.

65. Quoted in Weber, pp. 66–67, fn 6.

66. Quoted in Gilbert, p. 113.

67. Madrid FE 0154 GMT 12 Nov 80, "COSEP Criticizes Government; Ramírez Responds," FBIS, VI. 13 Nov 80, P10.

68. Ibid.

69. Managua Domestic Service 1817 GMT 13 Nov 80, "Junta Members Address Student Rally in Capital," FBIS, VI. 14 Nov 80, P5.

Chapter 16

1. See Department of State, *Nicaraguan Biographies: A Resource Book* (Washington, 1988), p. 35.

2. Antonio Chavarría, aka "Dumas" and Diogenes Hernández, aka "Fernando." See *Nicaraguan Biographies*, pp. 46, 50.

3. Sam Dillon, *Commandos: The CIA and Nicaragua's Contra Rebels* (New York, 1991), p. 49.

4. Ibid. p. 50.

5. Managua LA PRENSA 2 Sep 80. pp. 1, 9, "Cattleman Speaks Out on Behalf of Private Enterprise," FBIS, VI. 11 Sep 80, P17.

6. Managua Radio Sandino 1715 GMT 11 Sep 80, "Assassination Plot Denounced," FBIS, VI. 12 Sep 80, P3.

7. Managua Radio Sandino 1715 GMT 11 Sep 80, "Officials Hold News Conference on Larios Case," FBIS, VI. 15 Sep 80, P16.

8. See Bob Woodward, *Veil: The Secret Wars of the CIA, 1981–1987* (New York, 1987), p. 113.

9. This discussion is based heavily on Shirley Christian's excellent account of the early formation of the armed counterrevolution. Shirley Christian, *Nicaragua: Revolution in the Family* (New York, 1985), pp. 197–215.

10. Edgar Chamorro with Jefferson Morley "Confessions of a 'Contra,'" *New Republic*, August 5, 1985.

11. See Christian pp. 203–8.

12. Christian, p. 204. See also "Nicaragua Shaken by Violent Death of Businessman," Christopher Dickey, WP, November 23, 1980, p. A1.

13. Christian, pp. 204 and 205.

14. Pastor, p. 221.

15. Ibid., p. 222.

16. See "Inside the Sandinista Regime: A Special Investigator's Perspective," Department of State Publication 9466, October 1986; and Christian, p. 211.

17. Christian, p. 212.

18. "Confessions of a 'Contra'," by Edgar Chamorro with Jefferson Morley, *The New Republic*, August 5, 1985.

19. "Nicaragua Shaken By Violent Death of Businessman," Christopher Dickey, WP, November 23, 1980, p. A1.

20. Christian, p. 212.

21. Paris AFP 1634 GMT 22 Nov 80, "Junta's Cruz Rebuts Dissenters of Revolution," FBIS, VI. 24 Nov 80, P15.

22. The *New York Times* ran a story on November 19, 1980, on page 11. The story was written from Washington by Juan de Onis, however, not from Nicaragua (see "Security Forces in Nicaragua Kill Key Business Leader," Juan de Onis, NYT, November 19, 1980, p. A11.) even though Alan Riding had filed a story from Managua on November 15 on another subject.

23. "An Urgent Question for Nicaragua," NYT editorial, November 21, 1980, p. A30.

24. "Security Forces in Nicaragua Kill Key Business Leader," Juan de Onis, NYT, November 19, 1980, p. A11.

25. Remarks by President Carter before the Tenth Regular Session of the General Assembly of the Organization of American States, Washington, D.C., November 19, 1980. AFPD, 1977–1980, Doc. 696, p. 1314.

Chapter 17

1. Cited in Robert A. Pastor, *Condemned to Repetition: The United States and Nicaragua* (Princeton, 1987), p. 217.

2. Managua Radio Sandino 1200 GMT 23 Jun 80, "Arce Accuses AFP, *La Prensa* of Misrepresentation," FBIS, VI. 24 Jun 80, P16.

3. Managua Radio Sandino 1800 GMT 25 Jun 80, "*La Prensa* Accused of Being 'Counterrevolutionary,'" FBIS, VI. 27 Jun 80, P13; Managua Radio Sandino 1200 GMT 28 Jun 80, "Ortega Criticizes *La Prensa* for 'Sowing Distrust,'" FBIS, VI. 2 Jul 80, P17.

4. Letters and documents belonging to the Salvadoran guerrillas, captured by the Salvadoran army in November 1980 and January 1981, shed light on both the increasing involvement by the Sandinistas in the Salvadoran conflict and on the Sandinistas' attitudes toward their role in the support of revolution in Central America. The documents were prepared by State Department officials and were released to the press in February 1981 as part of a "White Paper"—"Communist Interference in El Salvador: Documents Demonstrating Communist

Support of the Salvadoran Insurgency"—that later became a source of controversy during the Reagan administration. Critics charged that the White Paper was filled with errors and did not provide evidence to support its interpretations and conclusions. However, the guerrilla documents themselves were acknowledged as authentic by the Salvadoran guerrillas and have never been a matter of dispute. The report was released as Department of State Special Report No. 80, February 23, 1981, and appears as Document 670 in AFPD, 1981. The captured documents appear in a documentary annex in AFPD, 1981—Supplement.

5. Document D of "Communist Interference in El Salvador."

6. Memorandum from Robert Pastor to Zbigniew Brzezinski, September 3, 1980.

7. CQ, August 30, 1980, p. 2608 cites a "State Department official" as the source of the information on the administration's decision to postpone.

8. Memorandum from Robert Pastor to Zbigniew Brzezinski, September 3, 1980.

9. In 1982, staff members of the Permament Select Committee on Intelligence, Subcommittee on Oversight and Evaluation, investigated what the CIA was reporting to the President at this time, in an effort to discover whether the agency had done an acceptable job collecting intelligence on the issue. According to a later report by the House Intelligence Committee, "the intelligence community reached, and communicated quite clearly, a view that did not support the Administration's position." See Report of the Permanent Select Committee on Intelligence, subcommittee on Oversight and Evaluation, 97th Cong., 2nd Session, September 22, 1982. The citation appears on page 6.

10. Emphasis added. Memorandum from Robert Pastor to Zbigniew Brzezinski, September 3, 1980.

11. Memorandum from Zbigniew Brzezinski to President Carter, September 9, 1980.

12. See Pastor, p. 217.

13. Cited in CQ, October 4, 1980, p. 2955. Assistant Secretary of State, Brian Atwood, sent out once again to respond to the onslaught, called Young's and Bauman's accusations of illegality by the President "outrageous charges."

14. Memorandum from Anthony C. E. Quainton to Deputy Secretary Warren Christopher, October 7, 1980.

15. Ibid.

16. Managua 4660, September 27, 1980.

17. Document J of "Communist Interference in El Salvador."

18. Associated Press, October 9. Printed in WP, October 10, 1980, p. A5.

19. Managua BARRICADA 15 Jun 80, p. 3, "Arce Views Importance of Anniversary Fete, Other Issues," FBIS, VI. 24 Jun 80, P9. The Sandinistas did continue to let the Salvadoran guerrillas operate a clandestine radio station in Nicaragua. See Department of State, "*Revolution Beyond Our Borders*": Sandinista Intervention in Central America (Washington, 1985); Pastor, P. 220.

20. Fidel Castro, *Obras escogidos, 1954–1962*, vol. 1 (Madrid, 1976), p. 131. Cited in Jorge I. Dominguez, *To Make a World Safe for Revolution: Cuba's Foreign Policy* (Cambridge, Mass., 1989), p. 116.

21. Author's interview with Humberto Ortega, April 11, 1991.

22. As Jorge Domínguez has written, support for revolutions abroad had also been "consistent with Cuban leaders' beliefs that the march of history is headed toward revolution, that such support enhances their own and Cuba's international influence, that it gives Cuba leverage with its Communist allies, and that it is a prime weapon in the struggle against the U.S. government." Castro did not support revolutions blindly or without regard to Cuba's own interests, but he did support them consistently as "part of a strategy to defend Cuba's own interests and to advance its radical ideology." Domínguez, p. 146.

23. Arturo Cruz Sequieva, "The Origins of Sandinista Foreign Policy," in Robert S. Leiken, ed., *Central America: Anatomy of Conflict* (New York, 1984), p. 104.

24. FSLN Unification Documents, p. 105. Cited in Dennis Gilbert, *Sandinistas: The Party and the Revolution* (New York, 1988), p. 162.

25. Document K of "Communist Interference in El Salvador." The Salvadoran guerrillas used code words for certain countries: "Lago" was Nicaragua; "Esmeralda" was Cuba.

26. Cynthia Arnson argues that "Reagan's election apparently helped to resolve a long-standing debate within the Sandinista directorate over aid to revolutionaries. . . . [T]he Sandinista leaders believed that the new administration would seek to undermine their revolution regardless of the conduct of the government. There was no reward for restraint." Cynthia J. Arnson, *Crossroads: Congress, the Reagan Administration, and Central America* (New York, 1989), p. 49. Christopher Dickey writes that the Sandinistas "opened the floodgates . . . as the election results came in." See Christopher Dickey, *With the Contras: A Reporter in the Wilds of Nicaragua* (New York, 1985), p. 75. This view is shared by others who claim that even before Reagan took office, his anti-communist rhetoric had provoked the Sandinistas into extreme actions. See, for instance, Gilbert, pp. 163–64.

27. George Gallup, Jr., explaining his organization's failure to predict Reagan's victory, later argued that Reagan's lead had materialized only after the Gallup organization stopped polling. Surely the Sandinistas had no way of knowing who would win the election when they resumed shipment of the weapons. See Everett C. Ladd and G. Donald Ferree, "Were the Pollsters Really Wrong?" *Public Opinion* (December/January 1981), p. 17.

28. Document K of "Communist Interference in El Salvador." The Salvadoran guerrillas used code words for certain countries: "Lago" was Nicaragua; "Esmeralda" was Cuba.

29. Pastor, pp. 225 and 225–26.

30. State 9158 to Managua, January 14, 1981.

31. Pastor, p. 226.

32. State Department Press statement, cited in Arnson, p. 50; Pastor, p. 227.

33. Pastor, p. 228.

34. Author's interview with Humberto Ortega, April 11, 1991.

Chapter 18

1. Jeane J. Kirkpatrick, "U.S. Security and Latin America," *Commentary*, January 1981, pp. 35–39.

2. Daniel Yankelovich and Larry Kaagan, "Assertive America," *Foreign Affairs*, Vol. 59, No. 3, 1981, pp. 696–713.

3. See CQ, January 31, 1981, p. 220.

4. Other prominent liberal senators defeated in the 1980 elections were Birch Bayh of Indiana, Frank Church of Idaho, Gaylord Nelson of Wisconsin, John Culver of Iowa, and Warren Magnuson of Washington.

5. "House Democrats Seeking to Limit Involvement by U.S. in El Salvador," Hedrick Smith, NYT, March 1, 1981, p. A1.

6. In a vote of the Democratic Party Caucus, liberals deposed the moderate Democratic chairman of the Foreign Affairs Subcommittee on Latin America, Gus Yatron, in favor of one of their own, the younger and more liberal Michael Barnes.

7. Alexander M. Haig, Jr., *Caveat: Realism, Reagan, and Foreign Policy* (New York, 1984), pp. 95, 123.

8. Author's interview with Craig Johnstone, January 31, 1991.

9. "Congressional Leaders See Threat to El Salvador and Back Military Aid Pledge," CQ, February 21, 1981, p. 359.

10. State Department Daily Press Briefing, January 23, 1981. The State Department was obviously caught unprepared in the throes of the rough transition between administrations. The Assistant Secretary of State for Latin America, William Bowdler, had been summarily dismissed by the incoming Reagan officials.

11. Secretary Haig told a foreign official that the United States had "absolutely firm evidence of massive Cuban intervention in El Salvador via Nicaragua" and that President Reagan considered "this intervention totally unacceptable and [was] prepared to take whatever steps are necessary to terminate it." State 30214, February 5, 1981.

12. *Washington Post* reporter, Christopher Dickey, has written: "The Nicaraguans had acted with incredible indiscretion." By January 14, five days before Reagan's inauguration, "U.S. intelligence had picked up an avalanche of incriminating evidence." Christopher Dickey, *With the Contras: A Reporter in the Wilds of Nicaragua* (New York, 1985), p. 105.

13. See Bob Woodward, *Veil: The Secret Wars of the CIA, 1981–1987* (New York, 1987), p. 116.

14. Haig, pp. 112 and 125.

15. Author's interview with Robert McFarlane, January 23, 1991.

16. Author's interview with McFarlane, January 23, 1991.

17. Haig, pp. 124 and 129.

18. "Applying Pressure in Central America," Don Oberdorfer, WP, November 23, 1983, p. A1.

19. As then-Assistant Secretary of State Thomas O. Enders later recalled, "this was a period when the White House wanted to stay as far away as possible from Central America. Author's interview with Thomas Enders, August 28, 1990.

20. Haig, pp. 127–28.

21. "Applying Pressure in Central America," Don Oberdorfer, WP, November 23, 1983, p. A1.

22. His declaration at the White House that "I am in charge," though not intended as a play for power, widened the already large gap of mistrust between the Secretary of State and the President's political advisers, and it did nothing to strengthen Haig's arguments for aggressive actions in Central America.

23. Haig, in McFarlane's opinion, was in a "funk" about Central America, and the issue receded to the back of a pressing set of international and domestic problems. He traveled to the Middle East in late spring, and when he returned the summer was dominated by the proposed sale of AWACS aircraft to Saudi Arabia, by the difficult decision of what to do with the MX missile, by battles with Congress over the defense budget, and then by the assassination of Egyptian President Anwar Sadat. Author's interview with Robert McFarlane, January 23, 1991.

24. Arturo Cruz later recalled that Pezzullo's remarks "hammered persistently on my mind. Ambassador Pezzullo, I venture to say, had developed sincere feelings of sympathy for my country. . . . [H]e pleaded, amicably and candidly, that the government in Managua refrain from aiding insurrection in the neighboring nations. The ambassador stressed that this was important for Nicaragua's own well-being." "Nicaragua's Imperiled Revolution", *Foreign Affairs*, Summer 1983, p. 1041.

25. CR, 97th Cong. 1st Session, April 2, 1981, p. 6206.

26. Department of State, "*Revolution Beyond Our Borders*": Sandinista Intervention in Central America (Washington, 1985), pp. 21–22.

27. "Nicaragua Seeking Accord in El Salvador," Alan Riding, NYT, February 12, 1981, p. 11.

28. According to one Salvadoran guerrilla leader, the units under his command received "99.9 per cent of our arms" from Nicaragua throughout 1981 and 1982. Comandante "Montenegro" told the *New York Times* that "urban commandos and 200 guerrillas under his command in Guazapa received monthly arms shipments from Nicaragua that were trucked across Honduras, hidden in false panels and floors. . . . Each truck, he said, carried roughly 25 to 30 rifles and about 7,000 cartridges of ammunition." "A Former Salvadoran Rebel Chief Tells of Arms from Nicaragua," NYT, 12 July, 1984, p. A10.

29. Author's interview with Thomas Enders, August 28, 1990; see Roy Gutman, *Banana Diplomacy: The Making of American Policy in Nicaraguan, 1981–87* (New York, 1988), p. 37. See also "*Revolution Beyond Our Borders,*" p. 22, which argues that shipments resumed before the April 1 decision.

30. Roger Miranda and William Ratliff, *The Civil War in Nicaragua: Inside the Sandinistas* (New Brunswick, NJ, 1993), p. 141; Haig, p. 47.

Chapter 19

1. Managua 432, January 28, 1981.

2. Madrid EL PAIS 3 Feb 81, p. 4, "Ramírez on El Salvador Policy, Domestic Tasks," FBIS, VI. 9 Feb 81, P22.

3. "Fearful Nicaraguans Building 200,000-strong Militia," NYT, Alan Riding February 20, 1981, p. 2.

4. Managua Radio Sandino 0200 GMT 30 Jan 81, "Cuadra on Somozist Border Threats, Honduran Stance," FBIS, VI. 3 Feb 81, P17; Managua 432, January 28, 1981.

5. Managua Radio Corporación 1600 GMT 26 Feb 81, "COSEP-INDE President Presents 1980 Economic Report," FBIS, VI. 3 Mar 81, P15.

6. Managua Radio Sandino 1700 GMT 24 Jan 81, "U.S. Aid Cutoff Sparks Comments on Problems," FBIS, VI. 26 Jan 81, P19.

7. Managua Radio Sandino 1200 GMT 2 Jan 81, "Borge Notes Priority Tasks for Coming Year," FBIS, VI. 5 Jan 81, P11.

8. Managua 0905, February 25, 1981. On March 3, after extensive foreign mediation convinced the Sandinistas that the costs were outweighing the benefits, the government acquitted José Estaban González in an "act of revolutionary generosity."

9. Once the leader of a Sandinista-sponsored organization of Atlantic Coast Indians, Fagoth had turned against the government along with most of the Indian and Creole population on the Atlantic Coast. The embassy reported that Fagoth was "highly popular among the Indian tribes of the coast and he was playing a key role in coordinating their resistance to Sandinista intrusions into traditional patterns of life." Managua 0876, February 24, 1981.

10. "Criticisms of the Sandinistas," according to the embassy report, "fell into the following categories: racial resentment against Spanish/Indian outsiders who are increasing the central government's intervention into every day life; antipathy toward the "godless" Sandinistas by people who have strong attachment to their religious faith and institutions; strong attachment to principles of free enterprise and resentment against government intrusions into economic life; complaints about inflation and unemployment; and resentment against the Cubans." (Managua 0876, February 24, 1981)

11. Managua 1055, March 5, 1981.

12. Hassan's removal, it was widely rumored, was a device intended to dilute the appearance of a purge of moderates on the junta.

13. Panama CITY ACAN 1625 GMT 26 Jan 81, "Cruz Expresses Support for Activities of Parties," FBIS, VI. 27 Jan 81, P26.

14. "[W]hen there were problems at the Human Rights Commission," as a Radio Sandino commentator later put it, "or when *La Prensa* was closed down or when there was any problem with Robelo or when there were problems at the Nicaraguan Democratic Movement headquarters, they always resorted to him [Arturo Cruz]. They viewed him as a kind of lifesaving device." Managua Radio Sandino 1927 GMT 13 Aug 81, "Junta's Córdova Rivas Interviewed on Role," FBIS, VI. 20 Aug 81, P13-P14. Cordova Rivas, the last remaining non-Sandinista on the junta, assured Radio Sandino's listeners that he would play no such role. Whatever Córdova Rivas might have represented before the victory of the revolution, as a member of the junta he had completely abandoned his former moderate allies and was renowned for being more Sandinista than the Sandinistas. He frequently began public statements with "Lenin used to say . . ." (for instance, see Managua Domestic Service 1557 GMT 1 May 81, "Junta's Córdova Rivas," FBIS, VI. 4 May 81, P15) and in vying for the leadership of his Conservative Party he once suggested that conservatives could "rob from Marxism-Leninism." (See Managua 0905, February 25, 1981.) A cartoon in *La Prensa* showed Córdova slipping into a supermarket of ideologies at night to steal the book on communism.

15. Managua BARRICADA 7 Mar 81, pp. 1, 5, "Cruz on Unity, Desire for Good Relations with U.S.," FBIS, VI. 19 Mar 81, P20. Cruz did, however, harshly criticize the business groups and "dissident" political parties he was presumed to represent. Asked if his resignation would harm the moderates, Cruz expressed irritation: "What happens here is that there are a few people who want to foil the revolutionary process." He hoped that with the new government reorganization, "the dissident groups can be treated with a lot of political force."

16. Panama City Radio Continente 1258 GMT 16 Mar 81, "Robelo: Sandinists 'Totalitarian Dictatorship,'" FBIS, VI. 18 Mar 81, P18.

17. Paris AFP 1737 GMT 15 Mar 81, "Situation 'Tense,'" FBIS, VI. 16 Mar 81, P21.

18. Managua 1217, March 15, 1981.

19. Robelo charged that Borge had tricked him into going ahead with the rally, which the government had banned in November, only to substitute "people's power" for government edict as a means of attacking the opposition. Panama City Radio Continente 1258 GMT 16 Mar 81, "Robelo: Sandinists 'Totalitarian Dictatorship,'" FBIS, VI. 18 Mar 81, P18.

20. Ibid.

21. The events of March had barely been covered by the American press—the *New York Times* recorded Robelo's "night of terror" on March 15 with a two-inch column in a corner of the obituary page.

22. The question came in response to Haig's description at the beginning of March of the Soviet Union's "four phase" strategy, and therefore the spokesman was trying to undo the perception that the Reagan administration considered Nicaragua irredeemably communist.

23. Managua 1571, April 3, 1981.

24. COSEP protested that once again the government had "amended the basic statute of the republic unilaterally and without consultation, thus arbitrarily changing for its own benefit and for the second time the composition of the State Council." Managua Radio Corporación 2300 GMT 5 May 81, "Sectors Continue to React to State Reorganization," FBIS, VI. 6 May 81, P19.

25. Managua Radio Sandino 0300 GMT 22 May 81, "Government Suspends Radio Corporacion Newscasts," FBIS, VI. 22 May 81, P15.

26. Managua Radio Corporación 2300 GMT 8 Jul 81, "Curia Protests Suspension of Mass TV Transmission," FBIS, VI. 9 Jul 81, P12.

27. Managua Domestic Service 1614 GMT 19 Jul 81, "Daniel Ortega Speech," FBIS, VI. 20 Jul 81, P6.

28. Managua 2086, May 8, 1981.

29. See Shirley Christian, *Nicaragua: Revolution in the Family* (New York, 1985), pp. 222–23.

30. Managua 3002, July 10, 1981.

31. Managua 3274, July 29, 1981.

32. See Roy Gutman, *Banana Diplomacy: the Making of American Policy in Nicaragua, 1981–87* (New York, 1988), pp. 19–38.

33. CR, July 30, 1981, pp. 18614–5.

34. Matters were complicated, to say the least, by the fact that the Right also had allies in the military.

35. The price, however, was that Enders and other officials had on occasion to look the other way when the military committed atrocities against suspected leftists and peasants.

36. AFPD, 1981, Docs. 657 and 694.

37. Statement by ABC news reporter John McWhethy in an interview with Secretary of Defense Caspar Weinberger, August 2, 1981. AFPD, 1981, Doc. 698.

38. Roger Miranda and William Ratliff, *The Civil War in Nicaragua: Inside the Sandinistas* (New Brunswick, NJ, 1993), pp. 141–42.

39. A censored copy of the March 9 finding reads: "Provide all forms of training, equipment and related assistance to cooperating governments throughout Central America in order to counter foreign-sponsored subversion and terrorism. [(deleted portion)] Encourage and influence foreign governments around the world to support all of the above objectives." The censored finding appears in "Report of the Congressional Committees Investigating the Iran-Contra Affair," [hereafter I-C Report] Appendix A: Volume 2, Source Documents, p. 1156.

40. This required another finding in December.

41. Although the Sandinistas were unpopular in Nicaragua, he argued, the "average Nicaraguan likes most of the changes he has seen and, while critical of many Sandinista faults, would gladly defend the revolution's positive achievements." Pezzullo opposed American assistance to the armed groups in Miami and Honduras because "any alternative to the Sandinistas that looks like Somocismo would be immediately repudiated by all Nicaraguans." Managua 2086, May 8, 1981.

42. Author's interview with Thomas Enders, August 28, 1990.

43. See Christopher Dickey, *With the Contras: A Reporter in the Wilds of Nicaragua* (New York, 1985), p. 107 and footnote on page 291. Dickey quotes one anonymous adviser to Casey who said that the CIA director was "deeply concerned about the Agency, deeply concerned that he not get it in trouble." Gutman cites Pezzullo's impression after a meeting with Casey in early 1981 that Casey agreed with him, although Gutman suggests that Casey may have been concealing his true opinions from Ambassador Pezzullo. Gutman, p. 63.

44. See Gutman, p. 66, quoting an aide to Helms who was present at the meeting.

Chapter 20

1. Christopher Dickey, *With the Contras: A Reporter in the Wilds of Nicaragua* (New York, 1985), p. 110.

2. The Sandinistas submitted a transcript of this conversation to the International Court of Justice in its suit against the United States in 1984–85. See International Court of Justice, year 1986, 27 June 1986, "Case Concerning Military and Paramilitary Activities in and against Nicaragua (Nicaragua v. United States of America)." It is quoted extensively in the dissent by Judge Schwebel of the United States, beginning on page 488, paragraph 156. See also Roy Gutman, *Banana Diplomacy: The Making of American Policy in Nicaragua, 1981–87* (New York, 1988), pp. 68–70.

3. Enders made clear that even the buildup of Soviet arms in Nicaragua was of secondary importance. He said only that "we should be glad if attention could be paid to the question of the arms race in Central America." The United States might "suggest a few ways of resolving this problem," if the Sandinistas wished, but Enders declared that "it is for each individual country to settle the question of the number of soldiers and the quantity of arms it should have."

4. The transcript provided by the Nicaraguan government to the International Court of Justice ended in the middle of the next sentence, in which Ortega said, "In March you transmitted reports to us which were very valuable in halting the flow. . . ." Why the Sandinistas did not provide a complete transcript, and why the transcript ended where it did can only be matters for speculation.

5. Roy Gutman makes much of Enders's "accusatory and threatening" tone in the meetings and quotes Daniel Ortega recalling that "I would say the principal problem that we had in the meeting with Enders was his arrogance. Because he was as arrogant as he was tall." Gutman, p. 73.

6. See Bob Woodward, *Veil: The Secret Wars of the CIA, 1981–1987* (New York, 1987), p. 165.

7. Author's interview with Robert McFarlane, August 28, 1990.

8. Woodward, p. 165. There is no evidence that Haig was talking at this point about "plans" to support a contra force, since there was no such plan in August of which Haig was aware. More likely, he was still talking about his plans for a more comprehensive approach to Cuba and Central America.

9. "U.S., in Secret Dialogue, Sought Rapprochement with Nicaragua," Don Oberdorfer, WP, December 10, 1981, pp. A1, A12.

10. Gutman (p. 73) suggests that the August 31 message introduced a precondition, and therefore "upped the ante," but that precondition had already been clearly stated almost three weeks earlier. This ultimatum represented no change from Enders's statements in Managua, when he had asked the Sandinistas to take immediate steps to cut back the flow of arms or "I could not suggest to my government that we pursue the line we have discussed."

11. The eight-paragraph draft statement explicitly addressed Nicaraguan concerns about exile training camps in the United States and listed the American neutrality laws that could be applied to limit these activities. The draft statement concluded that "the United States will vigorously enforce its laws in this regard." WP, December 10, 1981.

12. The statement, which was expressly based on the Rio Treaty of "reciprocal assistance," committed the United States not to use force or the threat of force against Nicaragua and not to permit acts of aggression against Nicaragua to be launched from American soil. The same principles would apply to Nicaragua's relations with its neighbors. Ibid.

13. Ibid. Gutman quotes one NSC official, Major Robert Schweitzer, saying the timing of the exercise was "a deliberate attempt to stick it in their eye," but these particular exercises had been a regular occurrence for years, and they were tiny compared to the maneuvers in the Caribbean ordered by the Carter administration in 1980. See Gutman, p. 73.

14. Enders also prepared a draft proposal for arms reductions in the region, which would have required the Sandinistas to return some weapons, particularly the T-55 tanks, to the Soviet Union and promise not to import any more. The proposal was never sent, however. It was shown to Ambassador Cruz, who objected that it was insulting. Enders withdrew the proposal, and Cruz never told his superiors in Managua about it. Gutman cites the "insulting" proposal as one element in the eventual breakdown in the negotiations, but it is hard to see how that could be true since, according to Cruz, the Sandinistas never saw the proposal. See Gutman, pp. 74–76.

15. Author's interview with Thomas Enders, August 28, 1990.

16. Cruz believed that "despite its peremptory nature, the U.S. position vis-à-vis Nicaragua was defined by Mr. Enders with frankness, but also with respect for Nicaragua's right to choose its own destiny." Arturo J. Cruz, "Nicaragua's Imperiled Revolution," *Foreign Affairs*, Summer 1983, pp. 1041–42.

17. As he told Enders after the meeting with Ortega, "The deal is if they will commit themselves to no export of revolution and to limiting the size of their armed force and their weaponry, we would on the other hand be willing to guarantee that we would not invade" and would prevent Nicaraguan exiles from training in the United States. The guarantee, Pezzullo suggested, would be an American pledge to close down the training camps in Florida and a mutual non-aggression pact that would include an American promise not to organize an anti-Nicaraguan alliance in Central America. Gutman, p. 68.

18. Edén Pastora Gómez, "Nicaragua 1983–1985: Two Years Struggle Against Soviet Intervention", *Journal of Contemporary Studies*, Spring/Summer 1985, pp. 10–11.

19. Years later, even Bayardo Arce had to admit that Enders was the "most serious person who spoke with us." Gutman, p. 72.

20. See, for instance, the assertion by Congressman Michael Barnes in 1986 that Reagan's policies "pushed the Sandinistas . . . into the willing embrace of the Soviets." CR, March 19, 1986, p. H1380.

21. The statement is a paraphrase of a similar portrayal of the world by Andrei Zhdanov at the founding congress of the Cominform in 1947. See Arturo Cruz Sequeira, "The Origins of Sandinista Foreign Policy," in Robert S. Leiken, *Central America: Anatomy of Conflict* (Elmsford, NY, 1984), p. 109.

22. Boris Ponomarev, "The Inevitability of the Liberation Movement," *Kommunist* (Moscow), No. 1 (January 1980), pp. 11–27, quoted in Jiri and Virginia Valenta, "Sandinistas in Power," *Problems of Communism*, September-October 1985, pp. 16–17; see also Francis Fukuyama, *Gorbachev and the New Soviet Agenda in the Third World*, RAND, June 1989, pp. 12–13.

23. Author's interview with Humberto Ortega, April 11, 1991.

24. Author's interview with Humberto Ortega, May 26, 1990.

25. Managua Radio Sandino 1643 GMT 28 Apr 81, "[Sergio] Ramírez Speech," FBIS, VI. 30 Apr 81, P16.

26. See Shirley Christian, *Nicaragua: Revolution in the Family* (New York, 1985), pp. 222–23. She has the date of this speech as June 23, 1981. Most other commentators have it as August 25, 1981. See Cruz, in Leiken, p. 103fn.

27. Interview with Tomás Borge in *Bohemia*, April 20–26, 1981.

28. Managua Domestic Service 1752 GMT 19 Jul 81, "Interior Minister Tomás Borge's 19 July Speech," FBIS, VI. 21 Jul 81, P9. Borge added that his statements did "not mean that we export our revolution."

29. As Daniel Ortega later put it, under Somoza "the right to strike was a necessary instrument," but "from 19 July onward, there has been no justification for strikes in this country, because relations have changed totally." Managua Sistema Sandinista Television Network 0030 GMT 17 Nov 81, "Ortega, Ramírez Appear on 'Face the People,'" FBIS, VI20 Nov 81, P5.

30. Panama City ACAN 0117 GMT 2 Oct 81, "Radio Corporación Suspended for 48 Hours," FBIS, VI. 2 Oct 81, P8.

31. *Miami Herald*, October 13, 1981.

32. Sergio Ramírez, asked in April 1981 if the American people would support President Reagan's policies in Central America, noted that there had already been a "great popular movement . . . against U.S. intervention in El Salvador. . . . Groups of religious men and women, intellectuals, students and workers are demonstrating in the United States." Ramírez understood

the American fear of "another Vietnam" and expressed confidence that just as "the Vietnamese people communicated with the U.S. people during their glorious war, so too are the Nicaraguan people communicating with the U.S. people." Managua Sistema Sandinista Television Network 0030 GMT 7 Apr 81, "Junta Members on U.S. Policy, Relations with USSR," FBIS, VI. 8 Apr 81, P13.

33. In conference with the House in December, the bill's language was changed to read "to the maximum extent feasible." See Cynthia J. Arnson, *Crossroads: Congress, the Reagan Administration, and Central America* (New York, 1989), p. 75; CR, October 20, 1981, p. 24489.

34. Ibid., pp. 24489–90.

35. Interview with Bruce Cameron, January 26, 1991; the account of the luncheon is also in Arnson, p. 75.

36. "Sandinistas Send Envoy to Soothe Capitol Hill," Terri Shaw, WP, October 29, 1981, p. A20; "Toward a Police State," WP editorial, November 9, 1981, p. A14.

37. As Enders later put it, "We were starting to see some indications of regressive tendencies that got strengthened at about that time." See Gutman, p. 79. Of Enders's claim that Sandinista domestic behavior helped push the administration to give up on the diplomatic effort, Gutman writes that "the argument was somewhat contrived. Enders himself had told Ortega that Nicaragua's internal political system was not a subject for negotiation; in addition, none of the events cited [i.e., the Ortega "lamppost" speech, the closings of *La Prensa*, and the arrests of the COSEP leaders] caused a great political stir in the press or in Washington." Yet there *was* a "stir," and administration officials, including Enders, were just as aware of these events as were the *Washington Post* editorialists, Flora Lewis, or Senator Kennedy.

38. Author's interview with Thomas Enders, August 28, 1990; "Revolution Beyond Our Borders"; "U.S., in Secret Dialogue, Sought Rapprochement With Nicaragua," Don Oberdorfer, WP, December 10, 1981, pp. A1, A12.

39. Author's interview with Thomas Enders.

Chapter 21

1. "Contras and CIA: A Plan Gone Awry," Robert C. Toth and Doyle McManus, *Los Angeles Times*, March 3, 1985, p. A1.

2. Christopher Dickey, *With the Contras: A Reporter in the Wilds of Nicaragua* (New York, 1985), p. 291fn.

3. The Argentines' motives were clear. The Argentine guerrilla group, the Montoneros, had made a base for themselves in Nicaragua, and the Argentine military considered that its war against the Montoneros now extended to the Sandinistas.

4. Roy Gutman, *Banana Diplomacy: The Making of American Policy in Nicaragua, 1981–87* (New York, 1988), p. 57.

5. Ibid., p. 80.

6. "Contras and CIA: A Plan Gone Awry," by Robert C. Toth and Doyle McManus, *Los Angeles Times*, March 3, 1985, p. A1.

7. "Haig Won't Rule Out Anti-Nicaragua Action," John Goshko, WP, November 13, 1981, p. A16.

8. This package of aid formed the core of President Reagan's proposal in early 1982 for a "Caribbean Basin Initiative."

9. "Reagan Backs Action Plan for Central America," Don Oberdorfer and Patrick E. Tyler, WP, February 14, 1982, p. A1.

10. The President also approved plans for the use of American military forces, including "a petroleum quarantine and/or retaliatory air reaction against Cuban forces and installations."

Such actions, however, would come only in response to "unacceptable military actions by Cuba." According to one newspaper account of the discussions, the contingency plans were seen by policymakers "as a way of letting A1 [Haig] down easy." "Applying Pressure in Central America," Don Oberdorfer, WP, November 23, 1983, p. A1.

11. "The Argentines are already training over 1,000 men." One aspect of the plan was to "work with foreign governments as appropriate" to conduct political and paramilitary operations "against [the] Cuban presence and Cuban-Sandinista support infrastructure in Nicaragua and elsewhere in Central America." "U.S.-backed Nicaraguan Rebel Army Swells to 7000 men," Don Oberdorfer and Patrick E. Tyler, WP, May 8, 1983, p. A1.

12. Ibid.

13. Author's interview with Thomas Enders, August 28, 1990; Bob Woodward, Veil: The Secret Wars of the CIA, 1981–1987 (New York 1987), p. 173.

14. "U.S. Approves Covert Man in Nicaragua," Patrick E. Tyler and Bob Woodword, WP, March 10, 1983, p. A1. "Nicaragua: Hill Concern on U.S. Objectives Persists," Patrick E. Tyler, WP, January 1, 1983, p. A1.

15. See WP, May 8, 1983. When Casey briefed the two intelligence committees, he apparently said that "no Americans and no mercenaries were to be involved."

16. Author's interview with Thomas Enders.

17. Alexander M. Haig, Jr., Caveat: Realism, Reagan, and Foreign Policy (New York, 1984), pp. 132–33.

18. Ibid., p. 136.

19. "U.S. Nearing Decision on Nicaragua," Michael Getler and Don Oberdorfer, WP, November 22, 1981, P. A1.

20. "What about Nicaragua?" WP editorial, November 25, 1981, p. A20.

21. Much confusion remains about this 500-man force, which was presumably separate from the more than 1,000-man contra force being organized by the Argentines. According to news reports about the finding, the finding had also called for the creation of a 500-man force of Latin Americans to undertake special actions in Nicaragua and elsewhere in Central America against Cuban and Sandinista targets, for the purpose of sabotaging the arms flow to El Salvador. With regard to this special force, the CIA would "work primarily through non-Americans to achieve the foregoing, but in some circumstances [the] CIA might (possibly using U.S. personnel) take unilateral paramilitary action against special Cuban targets." The CIA requested $19 million for the program, but emphasized that "the program should not be confined to that funding level or to the 500-man force described. . . . More funds and manpower will be needed." It is not clear what this 500-man force was supposed to be, but it does not appear to have ever been created. See WP, May 8, 1983.

22. Ibid.

23. Quoted in Gutman, p. 86.

24. WP, May 8, 1983.

25. The finding was later declassified, but was heavily deleted. See Cynthia J. Arnson, Crossroads: Congress, the Reagan Administration, and Central America (New York, 1989), p. 77fn.

26. CR, June 24, 1986, Extension of Remarks, p. 15294; see statement of Congressman Goodling, CR, June 12, 1985, p. H4159.

27. See WP, May 8, 1983.

According to Chairman Boland's report, "From the Committee's first briefing, in December 1981, on the program to support the anti-Sandinista insurgency, serious concerns were expressed by members of the Committee. These concerns went to the number and tactics of the insurgents to be supported, whether these insurgents would be under U.S. control and the possibility of military clashes between Nicaragua and Honduras." Amendment to the Intelligence

Authorization Act for Fiscal Year 1983—U.S. House of Representatives, 98th Congress, 1st Session, Dept. 98–122, Pt. 1. Report submitted by Mr. Boland to accompany H.R. 2760, the bill to amend the Intelligence Authorization Act for 1983.

28. Boland report, pp. 7–8.

29. AFPD, 1981. Doc. 662.

Chapter 22

1. See Cynthia J. Arnson, *Crossroads: Congress, the Reagan Administration, and Central America* (New York, 1989), p. 86: "as in 1981, there was little support for ending aid to the Salvadoran government, an action which was seen as paving the way for guerrilla victory."

2. Congressman Wright worked closely with the administration in trying to persuade Salvadoran political and military leaders to appoint a moderate as interim president despite the right wing's electoral victory.

3. Memorandum quoted in NYT, November 5, 1981, p. A10.

4. In January 1981 Secretary Haig had decried "our propensity to apply to these emerging states Western standards which resolutely ignore vast differences in their social cultures, political development, economic vitality, and internal and external security." AFPD, 1981. Doc. 1.

5. Address by President Reagan to the British Parliament, London, June 8, 1982. AFPD, 1982. Doc. 4.

6. Kirkpatrick argued that Nicaragua probably stood "in first place as a human rights violator in that very troubled region." Testimony by Ambassador Jeane J. Kirkpatrick before the Subcommittee on Western Hemisphere Affairs of the Committee on Foreign Relations, March 1, 1982, p. 76.

7. Address by President Reagan before the Permanent Council of the Organization of American States, February 24, 1982. AFPD, 1982. Doc. 672.

8. Senator Paul Tsongas, a liberal Democrat from Massachusetts and a harsh critic of the administration's policies in Central America, said "[I]t seems to me that those of us who support better relations with Nicaragua have an obligation to send a message. If this kind of oppression and violation of human rights continues, there will be a price to be paid among those in this country like myself who are more pro-human rights than perhaps the Government of Nicaragua would suspect." Tsongas insisted only that other nations in Latin America with equally bad records—he cited El Salvador, Chile, Argentina, and Guatemala—receive the same scrutiny from the Reagan administration. Statement by Senator Tsongas at a hearing of the Subcommittee on Western Hemisphere Affairs of the Committee on Foreign Relations, March 1, 1982, p. 70.

9. "Indian Rights, Rediscovered," NYT editorial, March 5, 1982, p. A26.

10. Author's interview with Craig Johnstone, January 31, 1991.

11. Ibid.

12. "The urgency in dealing with this Finding," one official wrote in mid-July to National Security Adviser William Clark, "derives from the fact that the opposition group under Eden Pastora has been developing quickly and that additional actions not covered by previous authority [i.e., the December 1 finding] are now being proposed." See Memorandum from Donald Gregg to William P. Clark, July 12, 1982. I-C Report, Appendix A: Volume 2—Source Documents, pp. 1019–22.

13. The CIA director had a tendency to mumble unintelligibly, although some congressmen believed he did so intentionally when he did not wish to be understood.

14. CR, 97th Cong., 2nd Session, March 11, 1982, p. 3951; CR, March 15, 1982, p. 4167.

15. "Nonintervention," WP editorial, March 11, 1982.

16. As Cynthia Arnson writes, a conviction "shared even by administration policy critics [was] that the Nicaraguan government had aided the Salvadoran guerrillas, despite occasional pauses and official denials, and that defeat of the Salvadoran insurgents was consistent with U.S. interests." Arnson, p. 72.

17. Enders reported on February 1 that "We have watched as the FMLN headquarters unit was developed on Nicaraguan soil, clandestine logistics routes perfected, geurrilla training camps set up. The number of Cuban military advisors in Nicaragua doubled during 1980 to between 1,800 and 2,000. Munitions and weapons resupply to the insurgents in El Salvador is again approaching levels reached before the 'final offensive.'" AFPD, 1982. Doc. 668.

18. In successive editorials on January 9, February 19, and March 11, the *New York Times* argued that while the guerrillas "may" be getting guns from Nicaragua, "there is no proof of large-scale smuggling across the borders"; that the Sandinistas "deny any major arms traffic to El Salvador"; and finally that the administration had not produced its promised "'overwhelming and irrefutable' evidence that Nicaragua is supplying significant quantities of Cuban and Soviet arms to guerrillas in El Salvador." Citing the flaws in a 1981 "White Paper," the *Times* suggested that skepticism of the administration's claims was warranted. See "A Need for Nuance in Nicaragua," NYT editorial, January 9, 1982, p. 24; "A Domino Has Two Sides," NYT editorial, February 19, 1982, p. A30; "The Nicaraguan Picture," NYT editorial, March 11, 1982, p. A30.

19. CR, March 11, 1982, p. 3951.

20. The chairman of the Senate Intelligence Committee, Republican Senator Barry Goldwater, released a similar statement shortly afterward.

21. A report by the House Intelligence Subcommittee, charged with "oversight and evaluation" of the intelligence agencies' work, later described the briefing given to the committee by intelligence officials on March 4 as "based on a skillful and professional examination of data obtained from various sources. The analysis was impressive and of definite value to policymakers." Repeating the increasingly familiar complaint that "an excessive zeal" by administration officials led to "several instances of overstatement and overinterpretation," the subcommittee report nevertheless concluded that "these inaccuracies were of little intrinsic importance" and were "not likely to misinform anyone seriously." See staff study by the Subcommittee on Oversight and Evaluation of the House Permanent Select Committee on Intelligence, entitled, "U.S. Intelligence Performance on Central America: Achievements and Selected Instances of Concern," pp. 8–9.

22. As one guerrilla leader told Alan Riding, "The junta [of the Salvadoran government] says the elections are possible because the war is controllable, but we will defeat the elections ... by making the war felt at all levels everywhere." "Salvadoran Rebels' Aim Is to 'Defeat' Election," Alan Riding, NYT, March 2, 1982, p. A7.

23. Managua Domestic Service, February 21, 1982.

24. Department of State, "*Revolution Beyond Our Borders*": *Sandinista Intervention in Central America* (Washington, 1985), pp. 10–11.

25. "A Former Salvadoran Rebel Chief Tells of Arms from Nicaragua," NYT, July 12, 1984.

26. Senator Tsongas's statement is quoted later in CR, May 6, 1982, p. 9069.

27. The editorial went on to say that Nicaraguan air power was "not quite as feeble as Sandinist leaders maintain," that the size of the Sandinista armed forces as revealed by American intelligence could not "be reconciled with Sandinists' assertions that their new army is no bigger than Somoza's old one," and that the aerial photographs showing destroyed Indian villages suggested that they had been demolished "in not quite as gentle a fashion as Sandinists claim." The *Times* argued, however, that "[n]one of this comes as a shattering surprise, and taken as a

whole it is cause for concern but not alarm; for all the aerial photographs, this is hardly a reprise of the 1962 missile crisis." "The Nicaraguan Picture," NYT editorial, March 11, 1982, p. A30.

28. Arnson, p. 71.

29. According to the *Washington Post* columnist Philip Geyelin, Barnes "was vigorously pressured by Speaker Tip O'Neill not to push a stronger amendment publicly [stronger than the amendment Boland was to write in the committee]. . . . Instead everything was to be done quietly, behind closed doors." WP, April 17, 1983.

30. See Amendment to the Intelligence Authorization Act for Fiscal Year 1983—U.S. House of Representatives, 98th Congress, 1st Session, Rept. 98–122, Pt.1. Report submitted by Mr. Boland to accompany H.R. 2760, the bill to amend the Intelligence Authorization Act for 1983, p. 8.

31. See Memorandum from Gregg to Clark, July 12, 1982, p. 1021. Some officials argued that a new finding was unnecessary because the earlier finding already covered such actions as supporting Pastora's "democratic revolution." See handwritten note by Vice Admiral John Poindexter on the Gregg-Clark memorandum.

Chapter 23

1. See Glenn Garvin, *Everybody Had His Own Gringo: The CIA and the Contras* (Washington, 1992), pp. 41–42.

2. The story of "Suicida" is the basis for Christopher Dickey's *With the Contras: A Reporter in the Wilds of Nicaragua* (New York, 1985). The following discussion of Suicida is from that book, and also from the articles Dickey published in the *Washington Post* after his trip into Nicaragua with the contras.

3. For instance, a former National Guard second lieutenant, Luis Alfonso Moreno, known as "Mike Lima," graduated from the military academy and entered active duty in the infantry one month before Somoza's fall. See *Nicaraguan Biographies: A Resource Book*, Special Report No. 174, United States Department of State, Bureau of Public Affairs, January 1988 Revised Edition, p. 54.

4. See Sam Dillon, *Commandos: The CIA and Nicaragua's Contra Rebels* (New York, 1991) pp. 53–56.

5. Typical of these fighters was Julio César Sánchez, known as "Kaliman." Under Pastora, Sanchez commanded 100 men in the fight against Somoza on the Southern Front from 1978 to 1979. After the revolutionary victory he became a lieutenant in the Sandinista army, but in September 1980 he deserted the army and left for Costa Rica, where he joined up with Chamorro. Another such fighter was Arturo Salazar, "Omar," who had joined the FSLN in 1977, fought in the "Battle for Managua" in June 1979, and after the war was assigned to the security detail of Tomás Borge and then of Edén Pastora when the latter became vice minister of the interior. He left with Pastora in June 1981 and in 1982 took up arms again on the Southern Front. Like most of the Southern Front commanders, "Omar" and "Kaliman" did not join the FDN in the summer of 1981. They stayed with their colleagues in Costa Rica, while the CIA, attracted by the more urbane, social democratic image of the old Southern Front fighters, tried to lure them to the FDN's ranks. Other Southern Front commanders who turned against the Sandinistas in 1980 and 1981 were Aquiles Miranda, aka "Pedro Rafa," and a Panamanian, José Antonio Brath-Waite, aka "Jhonny," who fought with the Panamanian "Victoriano Lorenzo" internationalist brigade led by Hugo Spadafora. *Nicaraguan Biographies*, pp. 46, 52.

6. Antonio Chavarría, aka "Dumas" and Diogenes Hernández, aka "Fernando." See *Nicaraguan Biographies*, pp. 46, 50.

7. See "Latin Border Area Becomes Volatile," Alan Riding, NYT, February 21, 1982, p. 21.

8. "Nicaraguan Troops Uproot Indians after Rebel Forays," John Dinges, NYT, January 5, 1982, p. A1.

9. Garvin, p. 44.

10. See Dickey, p. 131.

11. "Nicaragua to Impose Tax," NYT, p. A10.

12. "Journey to Moscow Expected to be Crucial to Nicaragua's Future," Christopher Dickey, NYT, May 5, 1982, p. A18.

13. "Nicaragua Accuses ex-Junta members of Plot," NYT, June 19, 1982, p. 5.

14. "Disenchanted Hero of Sandinistas Emerges As Leader of their Foes," Alan Riding, NYT, July 27, 1982, p. 1.

15. "Rebels Seek Peasants' Support," Christopher Dickey, NYT, April 15, 1983, p. A1.

16. "With Nicaraguan Rebels: Rosaries and Rifles," Peter R. McCormick, NYT, May 13, 1983, p. A1.

17. Luis Carrión Cruz interviewed in *Barricada*, June 20, 1990.

18. "Humiliation of Priest Fires Nicaragua," Raymond Bonner, NYT, August 21, 1982, p. 2.

19. "Paper Closes Down Again in Nicaragua," NYT, August 14, 1982, p. 3; "Two Die in Catholic Protests in Nicaragua," Raymond Bonner, NYT, August 18, 1982, p. A3.

20. "Sects Under Attack in Nicaragua," NYT, August 12, 1982, p. A3.

21. The grave was discovered in 1990 by Marta Patricia Baltodano, a Nicaraguan human rights lawyer who had worked for the Nicaraguan independent human rights commission and later for a group that monitored the human rights behavior of the contras. See Nina Shea, "Uncovering the Awful Truth of Nicaragua's Killing Fields," WSJ, August 24, 1990, p. A11.

22. "3 Years After Somoza's Downfall, Difficulties Engulf the Sandinists," Alan Riding, NYT, July 7, 1982, p. A1.

23. "Venezuelan Urges Pluralism in Nicaragua," Christopher Dickey, WP, July 20, 1982, p. A18.

24. "Significantly," Alan Riding reported in February, "the three countries that contributed most to the Sandinist victory in 1979—Venezuela, Panama, and Costa Rica—seem particularly disillusioned with recent developments in Nicaragua." "Nicaragua Pressed to Reduce Soviet-Bloc Ties," Alan Riding, NYT, February 16, 1982, p. 2.

25. "[T]he most prominent Sandinists have said they are Marxist-Leninists," the party's statement proclaimed, "and they should therefore belong to another International not ours." Ibid.

Chapter 24

1. Alan Riding, *Distant Neighbors: A Portrait of the Mexicans* (New York, 1984), p. 493.

2. As Riding notes: "Cuba has never sponsored guerrilla movements in Mexico, and . . . there is an explicit—though unwritten—understanding that neither government will meddle in the other's internal affairs." Ibid., pp. 497–98 and 498.

3. Managua Domestic Service 1724 GMT 21 Feb 82, "Lopez Portillo Speech," FBIS, VI. 22 Feb 82, P6–P8.

4. "If the bands of Somozist guardsmen who are operating along the border between Honduras and Nicaragua are disarmed . . . thus eliminating a real threat to this country's safety, one could believe that the Nicaraguan Government will simultaneously give up both the purchase of weapons and airplanes and the use of its scarce resources to maintain military troops on a scale that worries bordering and nearby countries."

5. Managua Domestic Service 1724 GMT 21 Feb 82, "Lopez Portillo Speech," FBIS, VI. 22 Feb 82, P6–P8.

6. CR, 97th Cong., 2nd Session, February 23, 1982, p. 2010.

7. Haig insisted that the proposal lacked "one fundamental ingredient," a commitment by the parties to a "termination of illegal activities which are the cause of the tensions." AFPD, 1982. Doc. 673.

8. AFPD, 1982. Doc 614.

9. AFPD, 1982. Doc. 679.

10. CR, March 10, 1982, p. 3759.

11. AFPD, 1982. Doc. 680.

12. NYT, March 15, 1982, p. A1; "Nicaragua Leader Blasts U.S. at U.N., Offers Negotiations," Michael J. Berlin, WP, March 26, 1982, p. A1.

13. Managua Domestic Service 1640 GMT 25 Mar 82, "Ortega Gives Speech at UN Security Council," FBIS, VI. 26 Mar 82, P12.

14. Author's interview with Arturo Cruz, Jr., April 30, 1993.

15. "Soviets Pledge Economic Aid for Nicaragua," Dusko Doder, WP, May 10, 1982, p. A20; "Soviet Signs Nicaragua Aid Pact," NYT, May 11, 1982, p. A8.

16. Roger Miranda and William Ratliff, *The Civil War in Nicaragua: Inside the Sandinistas* (New Brunswick, NJ, 1993), p. 142.

17. Author's Interview with Arturo Cruz, Jr., April 30, 1993.

18. Ibid.

19. As Jaime Wheelock analyzed the American political situation, "the people of the United States do not wish to attack Nicaragua. . . . [A] large number of U.S. congressmen are against an interventionist and aggressive policy. . . . U.S. public opinion, the main newspapers and the three main television networks are opposed to intervention. . . . [T]hose organized through the churches . . . do not approve of the U.S. Government's policy." Managua Domestic Service 0600 GMT 20 Mar 82, "Wheelock Comments on Relations with U.S.," FBIS, VI. 24 Mar 82, P12–P13.

20. "Nicaragua Asks Security Council to Rebuke U.S.," Alan Riding, NYT, March 20, 1982, p. A1.

21. CR, March 10, 1982, p. 3759.

22. In polls taken by the *Washington Post* and ABC news in March, 21 percent of those asked supported military aid to El Salvador, while 72 percent opposed it. The poll showed that only 65 percent of those asked knew that the United States was supporting the government of El Salvador and not the rebels. "Majority in Poll Opposes Reagan on El Salvador," Barry Sussman, WP, March 24, 1982, p. A1.

23. As Ramírez recounted the conversation, Barnes, who was "a friend of ours and a straightforward and honest man" told Ramírez "in a worried tone, that we were perhaps going too far by decreeing a state of emergency here and that he could assure us that a U.S. invasion would not occur, that the United States is opposed to it, that the conditions for it do not exist." Madrid YA 11 Apr 82, pp. 14–15, "Sergio Ramírez Sees Invasion as 'Certain'", FBIS, VI. 20 Apr 82, P13.

24. Columnists Evans and Novak reported "a steady stream of warnings from White House politicians to keep off the firing line and thereby avoid the trigger-happy label of 1980 campaign vintage." "Suspicions on a Leak," Rowland Evans and Robert Novak, WP, March 19, 1982, p. A23.

25. AFPD, 1982. Doc. 670.

26. Arturo Cruz, Jr., who in 1982 worked in the Sandinista Party's International Department, recalls that he drafted papers on negotiations with the United States "based on three

principles: that the negotiation process was a tool to buy time for the revolution; that the nego-tiators we chose had to be weak, so they could not make any decisions; that our negotiating strategy had to be based on the dynamic of American fears and anxieties so that we could take advantage of American dissension over Central America." Arturo Cruz, Jr., *Memoirs of a Counterrevolutionary* (New York, 1989), p. 141.

27. AFPD, 1982. Doc. 619, p. 1304.

28. "Mexican Officials Obtain U.S. Plan for Region," Alan Riding, NYT, August 16, 1982, p. A8.

29. The Sandinistas would have to make their airports, military installations, ports, borders, and "sensitive zones" accessible to visits by representatives of the OAS or other regional organizations.

30. Enders and Johnstone had no objection to calling for some democratic reform in Nicaragua, but they "wanted it reasonably soft." Johnstone recalls that he and Enders had no objection to an overthrow of the Sandinistas, but he maintained that "it wasn't clear we had the resources.... The contras were not started for the purpose of achieving democracy in Nicaragua.... It was overreaching. To those of us who didn't think the contras could win, it was foolish to set forth on a foreign policy that had no possible end." Author's interview with Craig Johnstone, January 31, 1991.

31. Roy Gutman's assertion in *Banana Diplomacy* (New York, 1988) that the inclusion of this eighth point was "the first impact of the new hard-line policy on diplomacy" and that it was a "remarkable demand" which was "incompatible" with the other demands because it "implied a change of government" greatly overstates the significance of the addition of this point and its effect on the 1982 negotiations, such as they were. (See Gutman, pp. 95–98.) For one thing, Reagan officials continued to make clear that the only *sine qua non* for an agreement was the Sandinistas' commitment to end aid to the Salvadoran guerrillas. The point concerning democracy was not intended as another *sine qua non*.

More importantly, however, Enders and Johnstone believed the Sandinistas did not intend to reach an agreement with or without the eighth point. (Author's interview with Johnstone.) Gutman, however, does not even explore the question of whether the Sandinistas would have agreed to the Reagan administration's plan without the eighth point. He argues that "logically, American policy could aim either at replacing the Sandinistas or at negotiating a security accord with them, but not both." He neglects to note that another possibility existed, that in 1982 neither kind of settlement was possible. His assertion that Enders's acquiescence to the "hard-liners" on this new point "signified that Enders had temporarily thrown in the towel on negotiations," but the reason had far more to do with the Sandinistas' response to his more limited offers than to zealous "hard-liners" in the Reagan administration.

32. "Managua, in Turnabout, Seeks U.S. Talks," Don Oberdorfer, WP, April 25, 1982, p. A33; "Nicaraguans Respond to U.S. Proposal," Christopher Dickey, WP, May 9, 1982, p. A21.

33. "U.S. Stalling on Negotiations with Nicaragua," John M. Goshko, WP, April 17, 1982, p. A1.

34. "Sandinist Leader Sees War on Way," Raymond Bonner, NYT, August 29, 1982, p. A11.

Chapter 25

1. "Mexican Officials Obtain U.S. Plan for Region," Alan Riding, NYT, August 16, 1982, p. A8.

2. Glenn Garvin, *Everybody Had His Own Gringo: The CIA and the Contras* (Washington, 1992), p. 63.

3. "Mike Lima" had scarcely served in the Guard. He graduated from the academy one month before the Somoza government fell.

4. Sam Dillon, *Commandos: The CIA and Nicaragua's Contra Rebels* (New York, 1991), p. 73; Garvin, p. 64.

5. "Nicaragua-Honduras Clashes Said to Increase Along Border," Richard Halloran, NYT, July 27, 1982, p. 3; AFPD, 1982. Doc. 694.

6. AFPD, 1982. Doc. 696.

7. AFPD, 1982. Doc. 699.

8. "Honduran Chief 'Too Busy' to Attend Peace Talks," Alan Riding, NYT, October 10, 1982, p. 6.

9. Garvin, pp. 67–68.

10. See ibid., pp. 68–69; Dillon, p. 75.

11. Dillon, p. 76.

12. "A Secret War for Nicaragua," *Newsweek*, November 8, 1982, pp. 42–53.

13. "U.S. Backing Raids Against Nicaragua," Philip Taubman, NYT, November 2, 1982, p. A6.

14. CR, 97th Cong., 2nd Session, December 8, 1982, pp. 29458–59.

15. Of the 13 members who rose in support of the Harkin amendment on December 8, the most senior was Congressman Dellums, elected in 1970; six were elected in the Watergate class of 1974. Only one congressman, Mickey Leland from Texas, came from the South.

16. CR, December 8, 1982, p. 29466.

17. Ibid.

18. "[I]t goes without saying that there is no one for whom I have a higher respect than the gentleman from Massachusetts," Harkin responded, "but there are things that bother me. As I said in our private conversations, 'Yes, I have faith in you; yes, I have faith in our Intelligence Committees to exercise their proper function.'" CR, December 8, 1982, p. 29467.

19. CR, p. 29457, December 8, 1982.

20. The House Democratic leadership scuttled it, probably to relieve their party members from having to go on the record in support of or in opposition to Harkin's careful phrasing.

21. "State Dept. Aides Said to Question Acts in Nicaragua," Leslie H. Gelb, NYT, April 7, 1983, p. A1.

22. CR, December 8, 1982, p. 29467.

23. See Edgar Chamorro with Jefferson Morley, "Confessions of a 'Contra,'" *New Republic*, August 5, 1985, p. 20. When Edgar Chamorro later broke with the FDN, he said he had changed his mind about the Guardsmen in the movement.

24. Captain Roberto Sánchez, the Sandinista army spokesman, noted in the fall of 1982 that Bermúdez had never been identified with what the Sandinistas call "war crimes" committed under Somoza. "Exiles Opposing Managua Seek Wider Support," Edward Cody, WP, December 8, 1982, p. A1.

25. Ibid.

Chapter 26

1. This was the estimate provided to journalists by a Sandinista military commander in the northeastern zone, Captain Rodrigo González, at the end of January. "Guarded by AK-47's, Sandinistas Take to the Fields," Alan Riding, NYT, January 26, 1983, p. 2. In another report, Sandinista officers said that in December and January two groups of about 300 fighters each moved into the area around Jalapa. "Sandinistas Brace for a Lengthy Battle," Edward Cody, WP, April 3, 1983, p. A1.

2. "U.S. Ties to Anti-Sandinistas Are Reported to be Extensive," Philip Taubman and Raymond Bonner, NYT, April 3, 1983, p. 1.

3. NYT, January 26, 1983.

4. Other estimates put the number of troops led by Suicida at 1,200 in early 1983. See Glenn Garvin, *Everybody Had His Own Gringo: The CIA and the Contras* (Washington, 1992), p. 86.

5. Ibid., pp. 72–75.

6. "Well-armed Units Show Strong-holds," Christopher Dickey, WP, April 3, 1983, p. A1.

7. "Rebels Seek Peasant Support," Christopher Dickey, WP, April 5, 1983, p. A1.

8. The Sandinistas did not help their cause with these religious campesinos when they insulted the Pope during his visit to Managua at the beginning of March. Borge's Interior Ministry had orchestrated the event by placing thousands of Sandinista and "people's church" supporters in the front rows, while preventing thousands of anti-Sandinista Catholics from attending. Throughout the homily, the Pope was repeatedly interrupted by a chorus of shouts of Sandinista slogans, also planned in advance. The Sandinistas had even connected the microphones of Sandinista supporters to the main loudspeakers. At times, the Pope was completely drowned out by shouts of "People's power!" and "We want peace!" He responded by angrily calling out "Silence!" several times. When the Pope concluded his sermon, the *Washington Post* reported, "the entire Sandinista National Directorate was on its feet, with Interior Minister Tomás Borge and Defense Minister Humberto Ortega clapping and shouting in time with the crowd, "Power to the people." "Protest of Papal Visit Part of Anti-Church Plan, Nicaraguan Says," Joanne Omang and Don Oberdorfer, WP, June 19, 1983, p. A14; "Pope Heckled During Mass in Nicaragua," Christopher Dickey, WP, March 5, 1983, p. A1.

9. "With Nicaragua's Rebels: Rosaries and Rifles," Peter R. McCormick, NYT, May 13, 1983, p. A1.

10. "Baptism of Fire for Armed Sandinista Village," NYT, March 31, 1983, p. A13.

11. After one battle witnessed by a *New York Times* reporter in May, a contra commander noted proudly that the fighting had taken place where Sandino had once ambushed a column of American marines. NYT May 13, 1983.

12. "New Rebel Raids Heighten Fears in Nicaragua," Edward Cody, WP, March 28, 1983, p. A1.

13. NYT, January 26, 1983.

14. "Nicaragua Tour Suggests Fighting is Modest," Edward Cody, WP, March 25, 1983, p. A30.

15. "Nicaraguan Sees a Salvador Link in Rebel Attacks," Alan Riding, NYT, March 25, 1983, p. A5.

16. "Nicaraguan Official Reports Invasion by 1,400 Rebels," Augustin Fuentes, WP, March 22, 1983, p. A1.

17. "Sandinistas, Rebels Facing a Stalemate," Karen DeYoung, WP, July 2, 1983, p. A1.

18. "Sandinists on the Border Tell of an Ebb in Clashes," Stephen Kinzer, NYT, April 17, 1983, p. 3.

19. WP, April 3, 1983.

20. Garvin, p. 64.

21. This according to Sandinista officials. "Nicaragua Reports a New Drive by Guerrillas," Marlise Simons, NYT, May 4, 1983, p. A7.

22. "Honduras-Based Unit Holds Town," Brian Barger, WP, June 15, 1983, p. A1; "Sandinistas Say Honduras Plays Major Role in Fighting," Stephen Kinzer, NYT, June 13, 1983, p. 10.

23. WP, July 2, 1983.

24. See Garvin, p. 95; Sam Dillon, *Commandos: The CIA and Nicaragua's Contra Rebels* (New York, 1991), pp. 82–84.

25. The *Washington Post'* Karen DeYoung was caught in just such an ambush at the end of May. "As one soldier lying next to me with his face in the dirt behind a tire explained, the contras have two types of ambush. One is to take a single point in the road, which vehicles can sometimes run through with minimum damage. The other is a much more sophisticated operation designed to hit a convoy such as ours, where a substantial force is positioned to definitely stop the first vehicle. When those behind it put on their brakes to try to turn around, other forces positioned along their flanks and behind the last vehicle open fire. We clearly were victims of the second type. . . . We lay there . . . under fire . . . for about an hour and a quarter until other government troops fanning through the hills pushed back the contra forces. Back in Jalapa, we realized we could not leave because the town was virtually surrounded." WP, May 24, 1983, p. A1.

One contra commander told the *New York Times*'s Peter R. McCormick that the Sandinistas "relied too heavily on trucks for movement. But he also said the Sandinistas were very well equipped, especially in artillery." NYT, May 13, 1983.

26. "Cuban Commander in Nicaragua Post," Leslie H. Gelb, NYT, June 19, 1983, p. A1.

27. "Soviets Speed Up Nicaragua Arms, U.S. Officials Say," Michael Getler, WP, July 2, 1983, p. A1.

28. "Nicaragua Rebels Inflict Heavy Damage at Border," Stephen Kinzer, NYT, June 19, 1983, p. A10.

29. "Nicaraguans Hope for Aid in Defense," Marlise Simons, NYT, July 17, 1983, p. A9.

30. "Nicaragua Hastens Land Redistribution as Pressures Mount," Marlise Simons, NYT, July 19, 1983, p. A1.

31. See Managua LA PRENSA 16 Jan 83, pp. 1, 12, "Opposition Leaders to Meet with Area Presidents," FBIS, VI. 26 Jan 83, P10; and also (Clandestine) Voice of Sandino 0000 GMT 3 Feb 83, "Opposition Delegation Visits Venezuelan Leader," FBIS, VI. 8 Feb 83, P17.

32. See statement by Adan Fletes, Managua Radio Sandino Network 1200 GMT 3 May 83, "Political Leaders on New State Council Session," FBIS, VI. 5 May 83, P12.

33. Managua Domestic Service 0306 GMT 5 May 83, "Carlos Nuñez Tellez Addresses State Council," FBIS, VI. 11 May 83, P9–P10.

34. Managua Domestic Service 0306 GMT 5 May 83, "Carlos Nuñez Tellez Addresses State Council," FBIS, VI. 11 May 83, P9–P10.

35. Foreign Minister D'Escoto feared the creation of "a Central American bloc against Nicaragua." Paris AFP 2134 GMT 27 May 83, "D'Escoto Expresses 'Concern' over Contadora," FBIS, VI. 31 May 83, P25.

36. "Nicaragua Says Reagan Has Declared 'War' On It," Michael J. Berlin, WP, May 10, 1983, p. A14.

37. The final resolution asked only that the Secretary General keep the Security Council "informed" about progress in the negotiations. See copy of resolution, NYT, May 20, 1983, p. A3.

38. Or as D'Escoto put it, the resolution "anchors our case here." "U.S. and Nicaragua Clash at the U.N.," Bernard D. Nossiter, NYT, May 20, 1983, p. A3.

39. D'Escoto acknowledged that the final resolution was "very minimal" compared with the "situation we denounced." The American delegation led by Ambassador Jeane Kirkpatrick lobbied hard with moderate members of the Security Council, and D'Escoto afterwards complained that "there was this great American pressure" on some Council members. The fact that France, whose government had been openly critical of American policy in Nicaragua, stood

with the United States and Great Britain on the final draft was particularly troubling to the Sandinistas. Ibid.

40. Arturo Cruz, Alfredo César, Leonel Poveda, and other former Sandinista officials declared at the end of June that it was "necessary to institutionalize democracy so that people can express themselves without having to resort to violent methods." San José LA NACION 2 Jul 83 p. 16-A. "Former Sandinist Officials Issue Statement," FBIS, VI. 18 Jul 83, P16–P18.

41. Contadora Declaration of Cancun, July 17, 1983.

42. July 17 statement by Ortega reprinted in CR, July 27, 1983, pp. S10959–60; "9 Latin Ministers Fail to Achieve Accord On Region," Richard J. Meislin, NYT, July 31, 1983, p. 1.

43. See Gutman, p. 166.

44. AFPD, 1983. Doc. 636.

45. Havana International Service 1800 GMT 11 Sep 83, "Havana Cites D'Escoto on Contadora Meeting, Results," FBIS, VI. 13 Sep 83, P17.

46. "Foes of Sandinistas Rally in Managua," Stephen Kinzer, NYT, September 4, 1983, p. 3.

47. Ibid.

Chapter 27

1. The liberal columnist Mary McGrory argued that "if the president admits that we are subsidizing the raids, he could admit to breaking the law." Mary McGrory, "The Administration Knows about Nicaragua—but Isn't Telling," WP, March 31, 1983, p. A3.

2. CQ, April 9, 1983, p. 703; without explicitly declaring that the law had been broken, Leahy told reporters that "if one is to believe the detailed accounts seen in the press in recent days, the Administration is actively supporting, and perhaps even guiding, a large-scale anti-Sandinista guerrilla movement now involved in open combat inside Nicaragua. From reported statements of some anti-Sandinista leaders, the undisguised aim of their military campaign is to overthrow the present Government of Nicaragua." "Reports of Anti-Sandinist Aid Worry Senators," Martin Tolchin, NYT, April 6, 1983, p. A9.

3. NYT, April 6, 1983. The *Times* put an additional twist on the legal question by suggesting that it was the contras' use of American arms in an offensive inside Nicaragua that violated the law. "Members of the Senate Intelligence Committee . . . said that a majority of Senators on the panel think that the CIA has insufficient control over the paramilitary forces that it supports in the region. As a result, the senators said, units based in Honduras and Costa Rica that have received United States assistance, including money, advice and military equipment, have put some of that equipment to use during their current offensive in Nicaragua." "Moynihan Questions CIA's Latin Role," Philip Taubman, NYT, April 1, 1983, p. A3.

4. Ibid.; "Washington's Role Troubles Congress," Don Oberdorfer, WP, April 3, 1983, p. A1.

5. Barnes's amendment stated that no U.S. agency "may provide any assistance of any kind or otherwise make any expenditures of funds . . . for the purpose or which would have the effect of supporting, directly or indirectly, military or paramilitary operations in or against Nicaragua by any nation, group organization, movement or individual." Such legislation, Barnes correctly argued, would amount to an "airtight" ban against any support for the contras. CQ, April 9, 1983, p. 703.

6. "Nicaragua: Hill Concern on U.S. Objectives Persists," Patrick E. Tyler, NYT, January 1, 1983, p. A1; NYT, April 1, 1983; WP, April 3, 1983.

7. "The Coming Showdown on Central America," Philip Taubman and Martin Tolchin, NYT, April 10, 1983, IV, p. 1.

8. Shultz later complained that "a covert operation was being converted to overt by talk on Capitol Hill and in the daily press and television news coverage. But because the program was nominally secret, I and others in the administration could not openly defend it." George P. Shultz, *Turmoil and Triumph: My Years as Secretary of State* (New York, 1993), p. 289.

9. He said that many of his colleagues were worried about news reports that the Reagan administration was supporting guerrillas in Nicaragua, and he wanted to talk to the chairmen of the intelligence committees "to hear from them on a confidential basis what's going on." NYT, April 6, 1983.

10. A legal opinion presented by the Intelligence Oversight Board to the President on April 6, 1983, stated that "the words 'for the purpose of . . .' are critical to understanding the Boland Amendment. . . . [It is] beyond reasonable doubt that Congress was referring to the 'purpose' of the CIA and DoD, not the purpose of the individuals and groups receiving assistance from the CIA." The opinion also showed the peculiarity of this law which purported to govern an administration's thoughts, but not its actions or the consequences of its actions. "[I]t is not legally relevant whether the Government of Nicaragua is in fact eventually overthrown . . ." the oversight board explained. "Assistance provided to pressure Nicaragua to cease its intervention in El Salvador—even if it resulted in the fall of the present regime—would not be unlawful; while assistance given to overthrow that regime, even if totally ineffective or actually counterproductive, would violate the law." See Opinion of the Intelligence Oversight Board, Apr. 6, 1983, pp. 12–15. I-C Report, Appendix A, Volume 1.

11. The President did not seem to realize that it was only his own intentions that mattered, not the contras' capacities. See Reagan statements in NYT, April 15, 1983, p. A12.

12. Congressman Bill Young warned that the debate in Congress was "going to be one-sided, and the side that's doing all the talking will prevail." CQ, April 9, 1983, pp. 703–4.

13. Citing "a good deal of confusion and misinterpretation in the press," the committee's chairman, Senator Goldwater, reminded reporters that "a key element of this law relates to the purpose of the U.S. government and not the expressed purpose of the recipients of any such support." "House Panel Votes Ban on U.S. Aid in Nicaragua War," Margot Hornblower and Patrick E. Tyler, WP, April 13, 1983, p. A1; "House Unit Votes Against Move Aid for El Salvador," Martin Tolchin, NYT, April 13, 1983, p. A1; Shultz, p. 301. Enders, testifying before the SFRC that same day, also drew members' attention to the phrase in the Boland amendment that said "for the purpose of."

14. "The Administration Knows about Nicaragua—but Isn't Telling," Mary McGrory, WP, March 31, 1983, p. A3.

15. "Congressman Faults Support by U.S. for Anti-Sandinistas," Philip Taubman, NYT, April 8, 1983, p. 10.

16. "U.S. Still Favors Latin Peace Talks," Stuart Taylor, Jr., NYT, April 11, 1983, p. 3.

17. "The Ferment Over Central America," Philip Taubman, NYT, April 25, 1983, p. A14.

18. "Boland is Center Stage, Like it or Not," Steven V. Roberts, NYT, May 1, 1983, VI, p. 2.

19. "Key House Member Fears U.S. Break Law on Nicaragua," Martin Tolchin, NYT, April 14, 1983, p. A1

20. NYT, May 1, 1983.

21. The figure of $80 million was simply the amount the Reagan administration requested for the covert program for the contras. It did not, therefore, derive from any calculation of what amount of money might actually be needed to perform the intended purpose of "overt" interdiction, a point which Republicans took great pleasure in making.

22. Shultz, p. 292.

23. Ibid., p. 285.

24. Ibid., p. 305.

25. Ibid., p. 292.

26. Shultz himself considered Foreign Minister Sepulveda a "mercurial, irascible, ... clever political operator who was no particular fan of the United States." Shultz, p. 301. Later in his memoirs, Shultz acknowledges that Sepulveda was "biased in favor of the Ortega regime and would never be helpful to us." Shultz, p. 951.

27. Although Shultz believed his principles "tracked well with" the San José declaration of October 1982, they were far less demanding and specific. On the subject of democracy, for instance, which was at the heart of the San José declaration, Shultz's and Sepulveda's principles called vaguely for "the prospect of a free expression of the political will of the population as the basis for government office." See Shultz, pp. 301–2.

28. Shultz was off to the Middle East to negotiate a settlement in Lebanon. Shultz, pp. 301–2.

29. Shultz, p. 297.

30. Ibid., p. 292.

31. Ibid., pp. 285–86.

32. Ibid., p. 305.

33. Ibid., p. 299.

34. Ibid., pp. 306–8.

35. NYT, May 5, 1983, D22.

36. Shultz, p. 314; Shultz comments in his memoirs that he "could not imagine getting hold without replacing Enders." He also exhibits no particular fondness for Enders, an "independent operator" who had tried to exclude everyone from policymaking, including, according to Shultz, the secretary of state. Shultz, p. 305.

37. Memorandum from Secretary Shultz to President Reagan, May 25, 1983. I-C testimony of Secretary of State, George P. Shultz, exhibit GPS-1, p. 454. Roy Gutman, in describing Shultz's position on negotiations, quotes this memorandum but inexplicably omits this sentence. Gutman thus claims that Shultz's policy, which Reagan then approved in a subsequent response, was to support the contras to achieve the more limited goal of getting the Nicaraguans to "mind their own business," when it is obvious that Shultz's statement is more complicated than Gutman would like to concede. See Gutman, *Banana Diplomacy* (New York, 1988), p. 133.

38. Ambassador Kirkpatrick told reporters on July 26 that the exercises were planned in response to a "very significant escalation" of Soviet arms and Cuban personnel in Nicaragua. "We simply feel this effort at escalation and military buildup is dangerous and unacceptable to the peace of the region." According to Kirkpatrick, American intelligence officials reported that Nicaragua received 11 shiploads of heavy weapons from the Soviet bloc during the first six months of 1983, compared with 14 shiploads during all of 1982. "'Finding' Backs Covert Action," Fred Hiatt, WP, July 27, 1983, p. A1.

39. WP, July 2, 1983.

40. "U.S. Reports Sharp Rise in Arms Aid to Nicaragua," Richard Halloran, NYT, August 2, 1983, p. A8.

41. Shultz, pp. 310–11.

Chapter 28

1. CQ, April 30, 1983, p. 819.

2. Wright and other party leaders feared "the Democrats had played into Reagan's hands by setting themselves up as the fall guys for a potential 'Who lost El Salvador?' campaign." "New Potential for Dividing Democrats," David Broder, WP, May 8, 1983, p. A1.

3. "Reagan Fights Ban on Covert U.S. Aid to Sandinistas' Foes," Hedrick Smith, NYT, April 30, 1983, p. 1.

4. "House Panel Bars Aid for the C.I.A. Against Nicaragua," Martin Tolchin, NYT, May 4, 1983, p. A1.

5. CQ, May 7, 1983, pp. 874–75.

6. Cynthia J. Arnson, *Crossroads: Congress, the Reagan Administration, and Central America* (New York, 1989), p. 124.

7. CQ, June 4, 1983, pp. 1109–1111; CQ, June 11, 1983, p. 1175.

8. "Casey Asks Panel: Who Said 'the C.I.A. Lies'?" NYT, May 27, 1983, p. A27.

9. See O'Neill, pp. 369–71. O'Neill explained "where my passion about Central America comes from. In fact, I have a special course—the Maryknoll priests and nuns, who are there as missionaries and health care workers. These people don't care about politics; their only concern is the welfare of the poor. And I haven't met one of them who isn't completely opposed to our policy down there." O'Neill kept in close touch with an aunt who had entered the Maryknoll order in 1920.

10. "CIA and Diplomats are Grilled on a 'Secret War,'" Patrick E. Tyler, WP, May 13, 1983, p. A24.

11. O'Neill referred to the "debacle of 1981." O'Neill, p. 346.

12. "House Panel Puts Off Vote on Nicaraguan Covert Aid," Margot Hornblower, WP, May 19, 1983, p. A24; NYT, May 27, 1983.

13. CR July 27, 1983, 98th Cong., 1st Session, p., 21200.

14. Author's interview with McFarlane, January 23, 1991.

15. Congressman Fascell shared Wright's bitterness. "It is not that we did not give them a chance, because they were all up here and they were all telling us what good guys they were. We put money up for them. We did all kinds of things. They ran all the moderates out. They went back on everything. They refused to have elections, and finally the U.S. Government cut off the money." CR, July 27, 1983, p. 21183.

16. "Reagan-Hill Compromise on Nicaragua is Seen as Unlikely," Joanne Omang and Don Oberdorfer, WP, July 15, 1983, p. A1.

17. "Imagine if the House Hadn't Voted Against the Secret War," Mary McGrory, WP, August 2, 1983, p. A3.

18. John M. Barry, in what is virtually an authorized biography, writes of Wright's passion to become Speaker: "The Speaker was second only to the President in power, and in some ways more powerful. All his life he had wanted such a chance. From boyhood he had wanted to be President, had tried twice for the Senate en route to that prize and had been disappointed, and only a few years earlier finally, on his fiftieth birthday, had acknowledged to himself for the first time that he would never attain that goal. Now it was as if he could be born all over again, as if everything he had once dreamed of and finally given up on was again possible." See John M. Barry *The Ambition and the Power: Jim Wright and the Will of the House* (New York, 1989), p. 15.

19. On issues of importance to younger members elected in the wake of Watergate and Vietnam, Wright's record was far from perfect. During the war, Wright sponsored a resolution supporting President Nixon's policies. In the generational debates over reform of House rules, in which the younger Democrats fought to change the formal seniority system, weaken the older committee chairmen, and strengthen the position of junior members, Wright stood firmly on the wrong side. Wright once made an emotional speech in support of one of the party's old guard, a Texas colleague. See Barry, pp. 14–15.

20. According to Barry, O'Neill decided Wright would represent a good regional and ideological counterbalance to his own northern, liberal roots.

21. In 1976, his voting record had agreed with the liberal lobby group, Americans for Democratic Action, only 30 percent of the time; in 1982, it rose to 55 percent; and in 1983, it was 72 percent. CQ, April 7, 1984, p. 777.

22. A reporter for the *Congressional Quarterly* called "Wright's about-face on the MX missile a significant example of how he has conformed his voting record to the wishes of younger, liberal Democrats." CQ, April 7, 1984, p. 777.

23. Ibid.

24. "The Unmaking of a Hawk," Bill Peterson, WP, July 28, 1983, p. A25.

25. CQ, June 11, 1983, p. 1174.

26. CQ, June 25, 1983, p. 1293. Not all the Florida Democrats took this route. Freshman congressman Larry Smith said he refused to be "painted as a communist sympathizer . . . and I will not accept the mantle of blame if our policy does not work and I disagree with the way that policy has been formulated or implemented." CQ, June 11, 1983, p. 1175.

27. "A Tightrope Act on Aid to Nicaragua," Philip Taubman, NYT, June 20, 1983, p. A12.

28. "House Vote Backs Halt in Covert Aid to Sandinista Foes," Steven V. Roberts, NYT, July 29, 1983, p. A1.

29. WP, July 15, 1983.

30. It was scorned by liberals, however, who accurately charged that the panel selected, though bipartisan, generally favored the views of the administration.

31. "U.S. Said to Plan Military Exercises in Latin America," Philip Taubman, NYT, July 19, 1983, p. A1.

32. "Reagan Latin Remarks Ignite Debate," David S. Broder, WP, July 27, 1983, p. A1; "Latin Move by U.S. Hit by O'Neill," Don Oberdorfer, WP, July 26, 1983, p. A1; "Panama, Venezuela Call U.S. Maneuvers Ill-timed," Fred Hiatt, WP, July 22, 1983, p. A14.

33. "Vote on Aid Cutoff: A House Divided and Confused," Steven V. Roberts, NYT, July 30, 1983, p. 3

34. Shultz, p. 311.

35. The Reagan administration did not like Mica's call for the OAS to verify the Sandinistas' compliance, believing the OAS was unreliable. Reagan officials supported the amendment offered by Republican Congressman Bill Young, which would have ended aid to the contras only after the Sandinistas agreed with their Central American neighbors to end aid to the Salvadoran guerrillas, subject to "effective multilateral verification." CR, July 27, 1983, p. 21197.

36. CR, July 28, 1983, p. 21413–15; Congressman Henry Hyde suggested that "the unwisdom of [the Boland-Zablocki amendment] has obviously been seen by the chief sponsor of that legislation because we have moved now to a position of tolerating aid to the paramilitary forces inside Nicaragua, but first we have to stop for 30 days." p. 21417. From the other side, Congressman Ted Weiss, the very liberal Democrat from New York City, criticized the Solarz-Boland amendment for bestowing congressional approval on illegal covert operations. CR, July 28, 1983, p. 21425.

37. CR, July 28, 1983, p. 21428.

38. Ibid., p. 21458.

39. See CQ, July 30, 1983, pp. 1536–37, for quotes by Mica and Snowe.

40. NYT, July 30, 1983.

41. CR, July 27, 1983, p. 21189.

42. "Behind the House Vote on 'The Secret War,' a Low-profile Insider," Don Oberdorfer, WP, August 6, 1983, p. A13.

43. CR, July 27, 1983, p. 21172.

44. See O'Neill, pp. 369–71.

45. "Senate Panel Compromises on Nicaragua," Patrick E. Tyler, WP, May 7, 1983, p. A1.

46. "More Aid to Nicaraguan Rebels Backed," NYT, September 21, 1983, placed in *Congressional Record* by Moynihan, CR, November 3, 1983, p. 30621.

47. CR, November 3, 1983, p. 30621.

48. CR, November 3, 1983, p. 30620.

49. Intelligence finding signed by President Reagan on September 19, 1983. I-C Report. Appendix A. Volume 1, p. 472.

50. NYT, September 21, 1983.

51. This could be little surprise, since the administration's script had now been virtually dictated by the committee. CR, November 3, 1983, p. 30621.

52. NYT, September 21, 1983.

53. Two Democrats voted against the administration's plan and the release of funds: Senator Patrick Leahy of Vermont and Senator Joseph Biden of Delaware.

54. "U.S. Covert Actions Said Not Unusual," Joanne Omang, WP, September 23, 1983, p. A1.

55. Senator Leahy made the, by now obligatory, comment that he held "no brief for the Sandinista regime, but whatever one thinks about it, it is the internationally recognized government of a sovereign nation. It should not be the function of the United States to overthrow regimes because it does not like their ideological character." CQ, November 5, 1983, p. 2294.

56. CR, November 3, 1983, p. 30620.

57. Citing the legal opinion of Eugene V. Rostow, then professor of law at Yale University, Senator Moynihan expressed the view that "the doctrine of self-defense embraces lawful defense of others. . . . In short, a covert assistance policy based upon reciprocating the Sandinista's export of revolution is arguably a justifiable, proportional response to the Government of Nicaragua's breaches of law." CR, November 3, 1983, pp. 30620–21.

58. Ibid.

59. CQ, November 26, 1983, pp. 2486–87.

60. CQ, November 19, 1983, p. 2411.

61. See Bob Woodward, *Veil: The Secret Wars of the CIA, 1981–1987* (New York, 1987), p. 263: "'Casey wants something that makes news,' Clarridge said [to Motley]. . . . Casey wanted the contras to 'do the urban bit.'. . . not just . . . for domestic political consumption in the United States. It was to establish credibility within Nicaragua for the contras. This sounded reasonable to Motley." Woodward, p. 281.

62. Author's interview with McFarlane, January 23, 1991.

63. Ibid.

64. Ibid.

65. Estimates in Glenn Garvin, *Everybody Had His Own Gringo: The CIA and the Contras* (Washington, 1992), 77.

66. "Nicaraguans Fight Rebels in East," NYT, September 20, 1983, p. A3.

67. Paris AFP 0223 GMT 19 Aug 83, "AFP: Humberto Ortega Reports New Contra Offensive," FBIS, VI, 19 Aug 83, P12–P13.

68. NYT, August 26, 1983, p. A1.

69. Shultz, pp. 312–13.

70. Ibid., pp. 319–20.

71. "Rebel Aircraft Attack Managua, Bombing Airport and Residences," NYT, September 9, 1983, p. A1.

72. Ibid.

73. "Costa Rica Cools to Nicaragua Rebels," Marlise Simons, NYT, September 20, 1988, p. A3.

74. "Nicaraguan Rebel to Seek Money in U.S.," Marlise Simons, NYT, September 19, 1983, p. A3.

75. "Nicaragua Evacuates Port Raided by Rebels," NYT, October 13, 1983, p. A13.

76. "Sandinistas Under Siege," Richard J. Meislin, NYT, October 17, 1983, p. A1.

77. "U.S. Officials Say C.I.A. Helped Nicaraguan Rebels Plan Attacks," Philip Taubman, *NYT*, October 16, 1983, p. 1.

78. Author's interview with Craig Johnstone, January 31, 1991.

79. Specifically, Johnstone wanted to do something to convince the Sandinistas to move the FMLN's command and control center out of Nicaragua. "We wanted to make this a discrete issue in the relationship," Johnstone recalls, and they were looking for a discrete tactic of their own that they could "swap" for this Sandinista concession. Author's interview with Johnstone. Secretary Shultz must have approved the plan, although in his memoirs he claimed not to remember.

80. Ibid.

Chapter 29

1. "Before Grenada, talk in the Directorate of an American invasion in the immediate future was more propagandistic than a reflection of real concern. That changed with Grenada, when the FSLN saw that the United States was still willing to invade a Latin American country [sic] and that U.S. strategy would be to strike massively in an effort to achieve victory in a matter of days." Roger Miranda and William Ratliff, *The Civil War in Nicaragua: Inside the Sandinistas* (New Brunswick, NJ, 1993), p. 224.

2. San José Radio Reloj 0100 GMT 15 Jan 84, "Defense Ministry Reports Clashes in North, FBIS, VI. 18 Jan 84, P16.

3. Managua Domestic Service 1930 GMT 17 Jan 84, "Defense Report; Humberto Ortega News Conference," FBIS, VI. 18 Jan 84, P10.

4. San Pedro Sula TIEMPO 21 Feb 84, p. 16, "FDN Spokesman Discusses Fighting, Elections," FBIS, VI. 23 Feb 84, P15; MDS 0300 GMT 23 Feb 84, "[Julio Ramos] Views Rebel Strategy," FBIS, VI. 24 Feb 84, P20.

5. Managua Radio Sandino Network 1200 GMT 28 May 84, "Military Activity, Contra Casualties Reported," FBIS, VI. 29 May 84, P20.

6. Accounts of the battle of San Juan del Norte appeared in both Costa Rican and Sandinista-controlled newspapers. Paris AFP 1552 GMT 14 Apr 84, "EPS Counteroffensive Anticipated," FBIS, VI. 16 Apr 84, P21; Panama City ACAN 2121 GMT 16 Apr 84, "Reportage on Situation at San Juan Del Norte," FBIS, VI. 17 Apr 84, P19; Panama City ACAN 1739 GMT 18 Apr 84, "ARDE Admits Retreat," FBIS, VI. 19 Apr 84, P13; Panama City ACAN 1752 GMT 20 Apr 84, "Army Girds for Attack," FBIS, VI. 23 Apr 84, P13.

7. Rome IPS 7 Apr 84, "Government Warns of Impending Attack in North," FBIS, VI. 11 Apr 84, P21.

8. Managua Radio Sandino 0127 GMT 13 Apr 84, "Judges Meet in 'First National Congress,'" FBIS, VI. 17 Apr 84, P13.

9. Managua Domestic Service 0045 GMT 15 Apr 84, "Daniel Ortega Discusses Rebels, U.S., Costa Rica," FBIS, VI. 16 Apr 84, P7. Ortega repeated that the attack was "the strongest ever by the U.S. Government, pushing in from the north, from Honduras, in the Departments of Nueva Segovia, Jinotega, and Northern Zelaya, and also from the south, in Rio San Juan Department."

10. Tegucigalpa Cadena Audio Video 1145 GMT 8 Mar 84, "Troops, Tanks Deployed to Honduran Border," FBIS, VI. 8 Mar 84, P15.

11. Roy Gutman, *Banana Diplomacy* (New York, 1988), p. 213.

12. Author's interview with Humberto Ortega, April 11, 1991.

13. San José Radio Impacto 0000 GMT 15 May 84, "FDN President Comments on Contra Groups' Unity," FBIS, VI. 16 May 84, P22; Tegucigalpa LA TRIBUNA 18 May 84, p. 52, "Calero on New Fronts," FBIS, VI. 21 May 84, P20.

14. Managua Domestic Service 2330 GMT 5 Jun 84, "H. Ortega Scores U.S., Outlines Defense Policy," FBIS, VI. 7 Jun 84, P15–P19.

15. Panama City ACAN 1957 GMT 24 May 84, "Purpose of New FDN Front in South Discussed," FBIS, VI. 31 May 84, P26.

16. Author's interview with Humberto Ortega, April 11, 1991.

17. Managua Domestic Service 0300 GMT 15 Jun 84, "Daniel Ortega on U.S. Attitude, USSR Visit," FBIS, VI. 15 Jun 84, P13.

18. For a thorough discussion of this gradual transformation, see Francis Fukuyama, "Moscow's Post-Brezhnev Reassessment of the Third World," RAND, February 1986. Fukuyama cites the death of Mikhail Suslov in 1981, for instance, as an "important change that was a necessary condition for Gorbachev's de-ideologized foreign policy. . . . Long the ideological standard-bearer and 'conscience' of the party, Suslov protected a number of key specialists in the bureaucracy and seems to have played an important role in encouraging Soviet support for radical states and movements in the Third World" (pp. 22–23). Other key figures who had warmly greeted the Sandinistas upon their rise to power in 1979 and 1980, like Boris Ponamarev, whom Fukuyama calls a "hard-line ideologue," were on their way out (p. 25).

19. See Fukuyama, p. 19: "Andropov was implicitly making the . . . argument that the USSR must attend to its own developmental needs ahead of those of its allies in the Third World."

20. "By the late summer of 1984," Seweryn Bialer argues, "well before the election campaign was over, the Soviets knew that they would have to deal with Reagan." Seweryn Bialer, *The Soviet Paradox: External Expansion, Internal Decline* (New York, 1986), p. 327.

21. Author's interview with Humberto Ortega, April 11, 1991.

22. Ibid.

23. Managua Domestic Service 2317 GMT 4 Dec 83, "State Council Final Session Held in Managua," FBIS, VI. 5 Dec 83, P10.

24. The speech was intended to be a private explanation by the Sandinista party leader of why the Sandinistas had decided not to run for the presidency on the same ticket as the socialists. Apparently without Arce's knowledge, the speech was tape-recorded and printed in a Spanish language publication, *La Vanguardia*, on July 31, 1984. The *Economist* reported in August that Daniel Ortega confirmed the authenticity of the speech as reprinted. See Department of State publication 9422, "Comandante Bayardo Arce's Secret Speech before the Nicaraguan Socialist Party."

25. See Arce speech, p. 4.

26. Author's interview with Humberto Ortega, April 11, 1991.

27. The Coordinadora included the two non-Sandinista unions, the Conservative, Social Christian, Social Democratic parties, a splinter of the Popular Social Christian party, and COSEP, still the most influential coalition of those private businessmen who remained in Nicaragua.

28. Managua La Prensa 26 Dec 83, pp. 1, 10. "Private Enterprise Council Issues Election Study," FBIS, VI. 5 Jan 84, P19–P23. The document was signed by two unions, four political parties, and the six business organizations represented by COSEP.

29. "Nicaraguan Elections Likely in '85 Despite New Snag, Diplomats Say," Hedrick Smith, NYT, February 6, 1984, p. A1.

30. "Sandinista Democracy? Unlikely." Arturo José Cruz, NYT, January 27, 1984, p. A27.

31. NYT, February 6, 1984.

Chapter 30

1. Two members of the panel quietly dissented from this recommendation. The report conspicuously "differed" with the Reagan administration in emphasizing the importance of improving the human rights record of El Salvador—but just a few weeks after the report, Vice President Bush warned the Salvadoran military that abuses would not be tolerated by the United States.

2. The exception was Henry Cisneros, the mayor of San Antonio. The hawkish Democrat was the president of Boston University, John Silber.

3. Duarte won a close race against the right-wing candidate Roberto D'Aubuisson—thanks in no small part to some financial intervention by the CIA.

4. CQ, March 31, 1984, p. 705.

5. Memorandum for Robert C. McFarlane from Secretary of State George P. Shultz, December 20, 1983. I-C Report, Appendix A, Volume 1, pp. 87–88.

6. At the beginning of 1984, Motley noted several signs that the Sandinistas might be yielding under American pressure—their acceptance of the Contadora Group's 21 objectives, their stated intention to begin reducing the number of Cuban advisers, to reduce their support for the Salvadoran guerrillas, to begin a dialogue with their political opponents in Nicaragua, and to hold elections. AFPD, 1984. Doc. 496.

7. George P. Shultz, *Turmoil and Triumph: My Years as Secretary of State* (New York, 1993), p. 403; Author's interview with M. Charles Hill, April 26, 1991.

8. Shultz, pp. 403, 414.

9. Ibid., pp. 402–3.

10. Quoted in Roy Gutman, *Banana Diplomacy* (New York, 1988), 210.

11. Shultz, p. 423.

12. Memorandum from McFarlane to President Reagan, February 21, 1984. I-C Document N16894.

13. Memorandum from President Reagan to Shultz, Weinberger, Casey, and Vessey, February 21, 1984. I-C Document N16897.

14. Actually, the committee approved $7 million in new direct funding for the program and gave the CIA authority to draw up to $14 million more from the contingency fund, but only after the agency explained its intended use to the two intelligence committees.

15. At the beginning of April, *New York Times* columnist Anthony Lewis chastised Moynihan in a column entitled, "Say It Ain't So, Pat." Noting Moynihan's "crucial role" in "rallying Senate votes" for the covert program, Lewis asked why the Democratic senator was "lending his talents to such a dubious cause [when] . . . opposition to the covert aid program [was] one program on which all leading Democrats are agreed this election year."

16. CQ, April 7, 1984, pp. 768–69.

17. See Bob Woodward, *Veil: The Secret Wars of the CIA, 1981–1987* (New York, 1987), p. 320, and Joseph E. Persico, *Casey: from the OSS to the CIA* (New York, 1990), p. 374 for two similar accounts of this sequence of events on the Senate floor. Woodward's account has an intelligence committee staff member, not Senator Cohen, stop Goldwater from continuing to violate security regulations on the Senate floor.

18. Transcripts of William Casey's briefings of the committee show that on March 8 and March 15, the CIA director told the committee that "mines have been placed in the Pacific harbor of Corinto and the Atlantic harbor of El Bluff, as well as the oil terminal at Puerto Sandino." The problem was that Casey never said precisely who had been laying the mines. Committee members had repeatedly asked for, and been given, assurances that there would be no direct American involvement. Casey's terse description did not arouse the members to seek more details.

19. "Moynihan to Quit Senate Panel Post in Dispute on C.I.A.," Bernard Gwertzman, NYT, April 16, 1983, p. A1.

20. Woodward, pp. 325–26.

21. AFPD 1984, Doc 526.

22. The idea for the trip had been only two weeks under discussion. Shultz had raised it with President Reagan during a visit by Mexico's President de la Madrid on May 15; he raised it again on May 23. Reagan "didn't say very much." Shultz had also discussed the idea with Casey, Weinberger, and McFarlane, who were all "unenthusiastic," he recalls, but made no effort to block the trip. Shultz found a much more enthusiastic response from James Baker, who appears to have used his influence to persuade the President. At the end of May, Baker told Shultz the President was "warming up to the idea," and by May 31, Shultz had Reagan's formal approval to meet with Ortega in Managua. See Shultz, pp. 402–8.

23. The minutes of the June 25 meeting were taken by Constantine Menges. They were later declassified and made available to the public during the trial of Oliver North.

24. Kirkpatrick even made the unique suggestion that if money could not be found right away, then the administration should "consider using the anti-Sandinistas elsewhere for the time being, for example, in El Salvador to help defend against the coming guerrilla offensive."

25. Minutes of NSC meeting, June 25, 1984.

26. Ibid.

27. Menges actually reports in his memoirs that Shultz "lost" in this meeting. Constantine C. Menges, *Inside the National Security Council: The True Story of the Making and Unmaking of Reagan's Foreign Policy* (New York, 1988), p. 127. Clifford Krauss also states that at the June 25 meeting, Shultz was "outgunned," and although "Shultz pleaded with Reagan and his fellow foreign policy advisers," Reagan sided with Weinberger and Kirkpatrick and "negotiations with Managua were scotched before they got off the ground." See Clifford Krauss, *Inside Central America: Its People, Politics, and History* (New York, 1991), The minutes of the June 25 meeting do not support Krauss's or Menges's interpretation.

28. Menges, p. 103.

29. Menges believed "that the unintended result of the [State Department's] secret plotting would have been just what the president predicted: a communist Central America and, in turn, the very real possibility of a communist Mexico and Panama." Menges, p. 95.

30. Quoted in Lou Cannon, *President Reagan: The Role of a Lifetime* (New York, 1991), p. 381.

31. Arturo Cruz, Jr., *Memoirs of a Counterrevolutionary* (New York, 1989), p. 141.

32. Craig Johnstone assumed, nevertheless, that the Sandinistas recognized that the Reagan administration would have to make real concessions if Nicaragua showed a willingness to negotiate, and he even sent such a message to the Sandinistas through the Nicaraguan embassy in Washington. According to Gutman, the Sandinistas claim they never received this message. Roy Gutman, *Banana Diplomacy* (New York, 1988), 221–222.

33. Shultz, p. 416–17. Tinoco did indeed lack authority to negotiate, but according to Tinoco this only meant that he "was not in a position to say immediately that [the State Department's proposal] was a disaster." Gutman, p. 221.

34. It should be noted that the Sandinistas continued to supply the Salvadoran guerrillas with weapons at least until 1993—when caches of such weapons were discovered in Managua. This practice continued, therefore, three years *after* the Sandinistas both held and lost fair elections!

35. Author's interview with Ambassador Harry Shlaudeman, April 9, 1991.

36. Ibid.

37. Shultz, pp. 416–7 and 418.

38. Peter W. Rodman, *More Precious Than Peace: The Cold War and the Struggle for the Third World* (New York, 1994), pp. 64–65.

39. See Roger Miranda and William Ratliff, *The Civil War in Nicaragua: Inside the Sandinistas* (New Brunswick, NJ, 1993), p. 159.

40. "Differences Reported at Parley in Panama," NYT Aug 29, 1984 p. A10.

41. Gutman, p. 227.

42. As Gutman put it, the substance of the September 7 draft agreement was "questionable. Security elements that would affect the United States . . . would be subject to removal on a fixed timetable, but those aspects affecting Nicaragua were largely left to subsequent negotiations. Verification procedures had no teeth"; Shultz, p. 422.

43. "As long as we are a country being attacked, like we are now in such a beastly manner, it is totally inconceivable, unacceptable that we should be asked to disarm." "Nicaragua Spurns Disarmament Plea," NYT, September 9, 1983, p. 14.

Chapter 31

1. "Nicaragua's Debt to the OAS," WP editorial, July 17, 1984, p. A18.

2. Letter from Wright et al., to Daniel Ortega, March 20, 1984. The letter, which began "Dear Comandante," caused a stir among conservatives in Congress like Congressman Newt Gingrich of Georgia, who attacked Wright for more than a year for the letter's ingratiating tone and offers of assistance.

3. Stephen Kinzer, *Blood of Brothers: Life and War in Nicaragua* (New York, 1991), p. 242.

4. Gutman and others have argued that the nine points "amounted to the framework for a constitution," suggesting that such matters should have been the subject of the electoral campaign and not the precondition. In the opposition's opinion, however, democratic elections could not take place in a wholly undemocratic environment. This had been precisely the complaint of the FAO when Somoza proposed elections to solve the nation's and his own political crisis. See Ray Gutman, *Banana Diplomacy* (New York, 1988), p. 238fn.

5. Arturo J. Cruz, *Nicaragua's Continuing Struggle* (New York, 1988), pp. 2–3, 4–5.

6. Ibid., p. 9.

7. Ibid., p. 30fn.

8. Ibid., pp. 7–8.

9. Kinzer charges Cruz with weakness for holding this position. "If he had been serious about running, and if he had been able to summon the necessary fortitude, he could have seized the gavel, proclaimed that as nominee he was now empowered to make decisions, and insisted that the campaign proceed. But in the first of a series of actions that made many of his admirers wonder if they had misplaced their confidence in him, he quietly accepted the split decision of Democratic Coordinator leaders, and refused to register his candidacy." Kinzer, p. 242.

10. See AFPD, 1984. Doc. 513.

11. Author's interview with Johnstone, January 31, 1991.

12. "White House Quits Rebel Aid Battle," Philip Taubman, NYT, July 25, 1984, p. A1.

13. See CQ, August 4, 1984, p. 1885.

14. See Arce speech to Nicaraguan Socialist Party, above, p. 303.

15. Cruz, p. 10.

16. Robert S. Leiken published his account of these events in an article entitled, "Nicaragua's Untold Stories," in the October 8, 1984 issue of the *New Republic*.

17. Ibid.

18. See Gutman, p. 243.

19. See Leiken. "Nicaragua's Untold Stories." See also Gutman, p. 243. "One of the most striking facts about the Chinandega rally was that no one in Washington seemed to know about it. No U.S. reporter was present."

20. Cruz, pp. 11–12.

21. Leiken, "Nicaragua's Untold Stories."

22. Roger Miranda and William Ratliff, *The Civil War in Nicaragua: Inside the Sandinistas* (New Brunswick, NJ, 1993), pp. 233–34.

23. Cruz, p. 13.

24. See Gutman, p. 243.

25. Cruz, p. 14.

26. See Robert S. Leiken, "The Sandinistas' Tangled Elections," in Mark Falcoff and Robert Royal, eds. *The Continuing Crisis: U.S. Policy in Central American and the Caribbean* (Washington, 1987), pp. 386–87. Leiken's article was originally printed in the *New York Review of Books*, December 5, 1985.

27. Cruz attributes the new set of demands to his conversations with the Colombians. Gutman attributes the new demands directly to Johnstone. See Gutman, p. 244.

28. Cruz, p. 15.

29. See Leiken, in Falcoff and Royal, p. 387.

30. Cruz, p. 15.

31. See Leiken, in Falcoff and Royal, p. 387.

32. "Sandinistas' Foe Back in Managua; Claims Backing of Latin Presidents," John Lantigua, WP, Sept 14, 1984, p. A31.

33. "Managua Mediation Said to Fail," John Lantigua, WP, September 19, 1984, p. A21.

34. Cruz, p. 16.

35. "Nicaraguan Police Aid Opposition Leader," WP, September 20, 1984, p. A39.

36. See Leiken, in Falcoff and Royal, p. 387.

37. "Moment of Truth in Nicaragua," Stephen S. Rosenfeld, WP, September 21, 1984, p. A21.

38. "Nicaragua Vows to Sign Contadora Peace Plan," John Lantigua, WP, September 22, 1984, p. A17.

39. "U.S. Voices Skepticism on Nicaraguan Move," NYT, September 23, 1984, p. 21.

40. El Salvador's President Duarte at first publicly declared his willingness to sign the September 7 draft. "Let us do something," he suggested at a press conference on September 22. "Let us sign the document." Shlaudeman had to visit Duarte and explain the Reagan administration's strategy for addressing the new crisis. See Gutman, p. 230.

41. Shultz, p. 422.

42. "Treaty Impasse Viewed as Omen of New U.S.-Nicaragua Tensions," Philip Taubman, NYT, October 2, 1984, p. A1.

43. See Gutman, p. 230.

44. Shultz, p. 422.

45. Tinoco recalls that "in a period of about one month, the administration was in a very difficult situation." Quoted in Gutman, p. 229.

46. Tinoco recalls "our impression was that it probably would be difficult for the United States to accept that." See Gutman, p. 229.

47. Author's interview with Ambassador Harry Shlaudeman, April 10, 1991.

48. "U.S. Plays Contadora Catch-Up," Joanne Omang, WP, October 15, 1984. See Menges, p. 185.

49. Menges writes: "It seemed to me that State planned to use the opportunity to persuade the four friendly Central American countries and Nicaragua to *sign its new draft treaty!* . . . By

this point I no longer had *any* doubt: State was trying to bring about a false peace agreement just before the U.S. presidential election!" Menges warned McFarlane about this "sixth attempted end run around the president's policy," but McFarlane was supporting Shultz's efforts and treated Menges as an eccentric annoyance. See Menges, p. 153. Emphasis in original.

50. Shultz, p. 422.

51. Ibid., p. 423.

52. See the Brasilia communiqué of Contadora foreign ministers, November 19, 1984. AFPD, 1984. Doc. 548.

53. "Treaty Impasse Viewed as Omen of New U.S.-Nicaragua Tensions," Philip Taubman, NYT, October 2, 1984, p. A1.

54. "Nicaraguan Acquiescence on Peace Plan Puts U.S. on Defensive," Joanne Omang, WP, September 27, 1984, p. A7.

55. Cruz, p. 22.

56. See Leiken, in Falcoff and Royal, p. 388.

57. Gutman, p. 252.

58. Ibid., p. 249

59. "I was working out of the same room as the CIA guy," Johnstone later told Gutman, "and unless some other part of the Agency was trying to undermine him, we were giving the same advice: take part if you can get fair terms." See Gutman, pp. 249–50.

60. Cruz's son Arturo, Jr., was called by the CIA station chief in Costa Rica and sternly told to advise his father to reject the deal. Interview with Arturo Cruz, Jr., April 2, 1991.

61. According to Robert Leiken, Ortega "told several newspaper editors that the Sandinistas had tapped the opposition's phones and were aware that the CDN right wing was reluctant to accept the Rio conditions. By the same means, the Sandinistas also learned that officials in the CIA were urging the rightists in the CDN to torpedo the Rio agreements." Leiken, in Falcoff and Royal, p. 389.

Cruz writes "we were hampered by the fact that telephone conversations between our delegation in Rio and [Coordinadora] headquarters in Managua were tapped by the Sandinista state security, so that the Sandinistas knew all our comments and reactions. This gave the government an enormous advantage because they could plan their strategy accordingly." Cruz, pp. 25–26.

62. "Talks on Vote Date Broke Down over Letter, Nicaraguan Says," Don Oberdorfer and Joanne Omang, WP, October 2, 1984, p. A12.

Ortega attributed his information to a long, private conversation between Cruz and Arce. But Cruz denies holding any private conversations with Arce. It is more likely that Ortega was relaying information obtained from Sandinista phone taps of the conversations between Cruz and the Coordinadora leaders in Managua.

63. Cruz, p. 25; this is the account of Augustín Jarquín, as told to reporters from the *Washington Post*. See ibid. Gutman presents the same account of events, see pp. 250–51: "[Cruz] went through Arce's paper point by point, wrote in changes of wording, then agreed to it. He conditioned his signature upon a 'vote of confidence' by the Coordinadora in Managua. If they did not back him, he would withdraw as their candidate."

64. Cruz, p. 28.

65. See ibid., p. 27 and Gutman, p. 251.

66. Gutman, p. 252; Cruz, p. 28.

67. Sergio Ramírez later declared that "extending the campaign was never a position for us." Gutman, p. 252.

68. Ibid., p. 232.

69. Quoted in ibid., p. 252. In some interviews, Cruz has himself complained about the pressure he felt from the CIA. In his only written account of the elections, however, Cruz states that "with regard to my own part in the elections, it has been alleged that the Americans had persuaded me not to participate. On the contrary, the only suggestions I received from personalities in Washington were intended to convince me of the usefulness of participating despite the flagrant absence of guarantees that the elections would be fair." See Cruz, p. 3. Note that Cruz refers only to "personalities in Washington," thus avoiding mention of CIA officials operating in Central America.

70. Kinzer, p. 244.

71. Cruz, p. 29.

72. See Gutman, p. 255.

73. Cruz, p. 29.

74. See Kinzer, p. 248.

75. Ibid., p. 247.

76. Gutman, p. 255.

77. Author's interview with Humberto Ortega, April 11, 1991.

78. Gutman quotes Johnstone: "It was unbelievable. A moderate [Ortega] undercutting a hard-liner [Arce]," p. 251fn. It appears that the Borge faction may actually have been prepared to postpone the elections, on the assumption that Cruz would do well and embarrass and weaken the Ortegas.

79. Author's interview with Augusto Montealegre and Rafael Solís, April 10, 1991.

Chapter 32

1. I-C Report, p. 444.

2. The President might have complained, on a somewhat higher plane, that the Boland restrictions were an unacceptable and possibly unconstitutional restraint on presidential prerogatives, but having agreed to the creeping encroachment on his conduct of the secret war against Nicaragua at successive stages over the previous two years, the President's case, as a political matter at least, was not strong.

3. "Countdown in Nicaragua," WP editorial, October 2, 1984, p. A18.

4. "Saving Nicaragua from Civil War," Robert S. Leiken, WP, November 1, 1984.

5. CR, October 11, 1984, S14205.

6. This interview with the *Times*, it should be noted, took place just after a meeting of senior officials and the President on June 25, at which Shultz expressed his opposition to efforts to solicit money from third countries for the contras. Apparently he believed that the contras could and should find money without American assistance.

7. George P. Shultz, *Turmoil and Triumph: My Years as Secretary of State* (New York, 1993), p. 428.

8. "If we can continue to fund the *contras* (or, if necessary, alternative benefactors are found), negotiations can proceed at a measured pace with the U.S. in the background." I-C exhibit GPS-1B, p. 467.

9. McFarlane I-C testimony, May 11, 1987, p. 15.

10. I-C exhibit 30, p. 458.

11. Recalling a meeting of senior foreign policy advisers to the President held on June 25, Secretary Shultz said he had expressed the view that "there would be ways of doing it [seeking third-country assistance for the contras] that would be unlawful, and I perhaps had—I am not sure about this—but in my mind, the proposal that I had seen was for us to be essentially a conduit."

12. McFarlane I-C testimony, p. 17.

13. Author's interview with McFarlane, February 19, 1991. McFarlane says he believed Shultz "never had any hangups" about the general idea of soliciting third-country support, "at least he never presented it to me."

14. Author's interview with McFarlane.

15. McFarlane I-C testimony, p. 18.

16. Shultz, p. 428.

17. Ibid., p. 420.

18. Letter reprinted in Robert S. Leiken and Barry Rubin, eds., *The Central American Crisis Reader*, (New York, 1987), p. 301.

Chapter 33

1. The main thrust of Mondale's attack responded to Hart's suggestion that the United States had no interests worth fighting for in the Persian Gulf.

2. As part of illustrating his disapproval of past and current American support for dictators, Hart told two reporters that the late Nicaraguan dictator, Anastasio Somoza, used to feed political prisoners to caged panthers to amuse his dinner guests. The two reporters, Morton Kondracke and Michael Kramer, investigated the matter to assure themselves that it was not true.

3. NYT, September 18, 1984, p. A1.

4. George P. Shultz, *Turmoil and Triumph: My Years as Secretary of State* (New York, 1993), p. 428; Roy Gutman, *Banana Diplomacy* (New York, 1988), p. 280. In a memorandum to McFarlane on December 4, North writes of "internal differences" and an "internal debate on the merits of whether or not we would pursue a further attempt to obtain funds for the Resistance movement." See North-McFarlane memorandum, December 4, 1984, I-C exhibit OLN-256.

5. McFarlane I-C testimony, May 11, 1987, pp. 5, 20.

6. Memorandum from Stanley Sporkin, General Counsel, to Deputy Director of Central Intelligence [hereafter DDCI], December 27, 1984, I-C exhibit CG-65.

7. CQ, January 19, 1985, p. 119.

8. "U.S. Considers Alternatives for Aid to Nicaragua Rebels," Bernard Gwertzman, NYT, January 26, 1985, p. 3.

9. A memorandum for McFarlane at the end of January stated that "Absent the existence of a new state or the transfer of U.S. recognition from Managua to a new capital held by the resistance, we would need to persuade Congress to alter a number of basic principles ingrained in this body of law [i.e. foreign assistance legislation] in order to accommodate a program for the Nicaraguan opposition. Moreover, the committees of competent jurisdiction for such an overt program (Foreign Affairs/Defense) are likely to be more hostile to helping the resistance in this manner than the intelligence committees have been in the past." Memorandum to Robert C. McFarlane, January 31, 1985. I-C Document N18824–18831. See also Memorandum from Stanley Sporkin, General Counsel to DDCI, December 27, 1984.

10. Memorandum from North to McFarlane, January 15, 1985. I-C Document N45086–93, Poindexter Deposition Exhibit 24.

11. This suggestion appears to have been less connected to the contras' needs than to an effort to shape perceptions in Congress. The low amounts of aid previously requested by the administration tended "to create a mind set in Congress that the threat to our security is not as great as we have articulated." Ibid.

12. A memorandum to McFarlane on January 31 expressed the "concern that the request for more than the already appropriated $14M may deny us the use of the expedited procedures

as provided for" in the 1984 legislation. In other words, changing the dollar amount could give House leaders the excuse to consider the legislation under normal procedures, which could delay any vote for months. Memorandum to McFarlane, January 31, 1985. I-C Document N18824–18831.

13. Memorandum from Stanley Sporkin, General Counsel to DDCI, December 27, 1984.

14. See Memorandum from North to McFarlane, January 15, 1985. North argued that the problem could be "overcome by a careful record of consultation with the concerned committees of Congress (Intelligence and Appropriations)." He also recommended that the President sign a new finding authorizing such solicitations, on the grounds that a new finding would be "tactically useful in building support with members of Congress."

The CIA's general counsel had agreed that "with congressional approval a third nation option does provide certain possibilities," although he argued it was not "a real option other than it provides Congress with a way to save face and buy back into the Nicaraguan program." Memorandum from Stanley Sporkin, General Counsel to DDCI, December 27, 1984.

Given both North's and McFarlane's knowledge of the solicitation of Saudi Arabia by the latter in the spring of 1984, which they apparently shared with few others in the administration, this recommendation seems to have been an effort by North to gain explicit congressional approval, *ex post facto*, for what was already occurring. The memorandum to McFarlane stated that consultations with Congress were important "to assure that we would not be subject to charges of circumventing or violating the statutory prohibition." Memorandum from North to McFarlane, January 15, 1985.

15. "Reagan Reports New Latin Threat," Gerald M. Boyd, NYT, January 25, 1985, p. A1; Note from Donald R. Fortier to McFarlane, January 22, 1985, I-C exhibit OLN-257.

16. McFarlane testified in 1987 that it "struck me that the sentiment of the Congress on that score was pretty clear just in what Don Fortier and I had heard in talking to members . . . and I did know that the Congress preferred we not do that [i.e., raise money from third countries]. . . . And if you know because you have been told by Dante Fascell, '[expletive deleted] it, don't raise the money,' you better not raise the money." See Note from Fortier to McFarlane, January 22, 1985, I-C exhibit OLN-257, and McFarlane I-C testimony, May 11, 1987.

17. McFarlane I-C testimony, May 11, 1987.

18. "Hondurans Wary of U.S. Policy," Joanne Omang and Edward Cody, WP, February 24, 1985, p. A1; "Honduras Reported Reluctant to Aid Niaraguan Rebels Alone," James LeMoyne, NYT, January 28, 1985, p. A3.

19. "Bush, Visiting Honduras, Attacks Sandinistas," James LeMoyne, NYT, March 17, 1985, p. 19.

20. CQ, January 26, 1985 p. 150.

21. "Reagan Reports New Latin Threat," Gerald M. Boyd, NYT, January 25, 1985, p. A1; memorandum to MacFarlane, January 31, 1985. I-C Document N18824-18831.

22. "Nicaragua Steps Up Harassment of Opposition," Robert J. McCartney, WP, December 3, 1984, p. A1.

23. "Nicaraguan Opposition Leader Faults Reagan's Hard Line," Joanne Omang, WP, November 15, 1984, p. A27; CQ, November 17, 1984, p. 2966.

24. CQ, January 19, 1985, p. 119.

25. Robert Leiken, who had developed close ties to Cruz during the 1984 electoral campaign, told an aide to McFarlane in January that Congress could be persuaded to pass some form of aid to the contras. Walter Raymond wrote McFarlane on January 19 that Leiken, whom he described as a "rock-ribbed liberal," believed "we have a fairly good chance of winning the Contras fight on the Hill if we play our cards right." See Memorandum from Walter Raymond, Jr. to McFarlane, January 19, 1985, I-C Document N32617.

26. "Administration to Press Congress for New Aid to Nicaraguan Rebels," Philip Taubman, NYT, January 5, 1985, p. 1.

27. "U.S. Seeks Nicaraguan Solution," Joanne Omang, WP, Jan 28, 1985, p. A1.

28. See Constantine C. Menges, *Inside the National Security Council: The True Story of the Making and Unmaking of Reagan's Foreign Policy* (New York, 1988), p. 200.

29. According to Gutman, "on one occasion early in 1985, [Motley] had convinced Shultz to approach Weinberger, Casey, and Vessey and ask each to appoint a representative to thrash out a deal in their name. Motley, Ikle, Moreau, and the CIA representative spent two and a half hours in a conference room and emerged with agreement on the guidelines for a Contadora treaty. A few hours later, Weinberger vetoed the deal. Apparently, Ikle had changed his mind. 'Schultz threw up his hands,' said a source close to Motley." See Gutman, p. 278.

30. "Shultz Says Nicaraguan People Have Fallen 'Behind Iron Curtain,'" Bernard Gwertzman, NYT, February 20, 1985, p. A8; CQ, February 23, 1985, p. 342.

31. Speech by Secretary of State George P. Shultz before the Commonwealth Club of California, San Francisco, February 22, 1985. AFPD, 1985, Doc. 539.

32. See "A Bone in His Throat," by Tom Wicker, NYT, February 22, 1985, p. 27.

Gutman, however, does not see a shift in Shultz's behavior. He calls Shultz's February 22 speech "a considered statement" in which Shultz "went out of his way to leave open the possibility for a negotiated solution." To support this claim Gutman specifically cites the sentence in which Shultz declares it "immaterial" whether change in Nicaragua comes through negotiations or through "the collapse of the Sandinista regime." According to Gutman, Shultz with this speech "struck back" at the "hardliners" in the administration who had been responsible for Reagan's recent strong statements. See Gutman, p. 273.

33. Quoted in Cynthia J. Arnson, *Crossroads: Congress, the Reagan Administration, and Central America* (New York, 1989), p. 172.

34. In his second inaugural address, given just 19 days earlier, the President had limited himself to declaring only that "America must remain freedom's staunchest friend." He made no mention of "freedom fighters."

35. Remarks by President Reagan at a dinner for the Nicaraguan Refugee Fund, Washington, D.C., April 15, 1985. Reprinted in 1985 CQ Almanac, p. 12-D.

36. Speech by Secretary of State George P. Shultz before the Commonwealth Club of California, San Francisco, February 22, 1985. AFPD, 1985, Doc. 539.

37. On March 20, in fact, the House Foreign Affairs Subcommittee on Asia, led by its chairman, New York Democrat Stephen Solarz, approved $5 million in military assistance to the non-communist rebels in Cambodia.

38. AFPD, 1985. Doc. 540.

Chapter 34

1. "Nicaragua Rebels Accused of Abuses," Larry Rohter, NYT, March 7, 1985, p. A1. See also "Contra Atrocities, or a Covert Propaganda War?" Jim Denton, WSJ, April 23, 1985, p. 30. Another New York lawyer, Paul Reichler, had put Brody on the case. Reichler's firm, Reichler and Applebaum, was on retainer for the Sandinistas when Reichler, as he told one reporter, originated the plan to send a team of "professional attorneys to Nicaragua to conduct an objective, independent investigation of Contra atrocities."

2. According to the testimony of Mateo Guerrero, director of the Nicaraguan National Commission for the Promotion and Protection of Human Rights (CPPDH), who defected to the United States in 1985. The CPPDH, which was under the control of the Foreign Ministry,

handled the Brody trip and paid Brody's expenses. See "Nicaraguan Defects," George Gedda, WP, August 21, 1985, p. A13.

3. "Rights Report on Nicaragua Cites Recent Rebel Atrocities," Joel Brinkley, NYT, March 6, 1985, p. A10.

4. The Arms Control and Foreign Policy Caucus charged in a report on April 18, 1985, "Who Are the Contras?" that 46 out of 48 top positions in the FDN were held by former Guardsmen. The report accurately counted the number of guardsmen in senior positions, especially those based in Honduras, but failed to take account of the rising importance of non-Guardsmen leaders in the field, especially in the growing Jorge Salazar Regional Command. Still, there was no denying that, as James LeMoyne wrote, "National Guard officers formed the nucleus of the [FDN]" since "besides Mr. Bermúdez, the heads of logistics, intelligence, operations, special warfare and training and several key combat units are all former National Guardsmen." See "Nicaragua Guerrillas Ponder Chances Without U.S. Help," James LeMoyne, NYT, March 18, 1985, p. A1.

5. "Nicaragua Guerrillas Ponder Chances Without U.S. Help," James LeMoyne, NYT, March 18, 1985, p. A1.

6. AFPD, 1985. Doc. 540.

7. NYT, March 18, 1985.

8. See North-McFarlane memorandum, November 7, 1984, I-C exhibit RCM-31.

9. See Calero I-C testimony, May 20, 1987, p. 12.

10. Calero testimony, May 20, 1987. pp. 12–13. I-C exhibit APC-3; Secord testimony, May 5, 1987, p. 52.

11. Ibid.

12. Secord testimony, May 5, 1987, p. 52.

13. The BLIs were made up of draftees who underwent several months of rigorous training in counterinsurgency warfare. The regular army remained in defensive positions around Managua and other large urban areas of the Pacific Coast, ostensibly to guard against American invasion.

14. For accounts of the BLIs composition, modus operandi, and increasing use at the beginning of 1985 see: "In Remote Nicaraguan Zone, Rebels Strike Boldly," Stephen Kinzer, NYT, January 23, 1985, p. A2; Managua Radio Sandino [hereafter MRS] 1200 GMT 2 Feb 85, "Defense Ministry Reports on EPS 15–31 Jan Actions," FBIS, VI. 6 Feb 85, P8; "On the Trail of the Contras," John Lantigua, WP, February 26, 1985, p. A12.

15. For Sandinista actions, including laying of mines, see statements by Sandinista Army Intelligence chief, Julian Ramos, in "Honduras Border Scene of Clashes," Bill Keller, NYT, May 19, 1985, p. 1. See also statements by Humberto Ortega in Managua BARRICADA [hereafter MB] 10 Oct 85 pp. 1–14, "H. Ortega Interviewed on U.S. Policy, Contras," FBIS, VI. 28 Oct 85, P19–P34.

16. "Nicaraguan Rebels Said to Get Missiles," James LeMoyne, NYT, May 4, 1985, p. A4.

17. See "Civilians Quit Border Zone," John Lantigua, WP, April 8, 1985, p. A23. See also "Honduras Border Scene of Clashes," Bill Keller, NYT, May 19, 1985, p. 1.

18. Acording to a "visiting military analyst", quoted in "Sandinistas Pin Hopes on Congress," Larry Rohter, NYT, March 3, 1985, Sec IV, p. 1.

19. MRS 1300 GMT 3 Feb 85, "Arce on Increasing Armed Force, Combat Readiness," FBIS, VI. 5 Feb 85, P13.

20. On January 23, Hugo Torres, the Sandinista army political chief, described the objective for the year: "to break up the mercenary forces and eliminate them" by enrolling thousands of new recruits and forming new combat detachments "until we have a formidable force that

will overwhelmingly hit the mercenary army." Managua Barricada 23 Jan 85, p. 5, "Commander Torres Discusses 1985 Defense Tasks," FBIS, VI. 25 Jan 85, P12.

21. "In Remote Nicaraguan Zone, Rebels Strike Boldly," Stephen Kinzer, NYT, January 23, 1985, p. A2.

22. Another reason for the increase in numbers of fighters was that the CIA was no longer placing a ceiling on the number of recruits.

23. Stephen Kinzer reported that by the beginning of April as many as 50,000 young men had fled the draft. See "Nicaraguan Men Fleeing Draft Fill Honduran Refugee Camp," Stephen Kinzer, NYT, April 11, 1985, p. A1.

24. Of 1,000 residents in one Honduran refugee camp, Kinzer reported that 75 percent were draft evaders. Kinzer also reported that only a few had apparently left to join the contras. Ibid.

25. "Contras Press for Funds," Edward Cody, WP, February 18, 1985, A1.

26. An Interior Ministry official traveling with the Simon Bolívar Irregular Warfare Battalion in Jinotega complained of the local populace: "These people are uneducated. The contras come through and tell them that we are planning to take away their land, that we are against God, that we kill old people and turn them into soap, and the people sometimes believe them." See "On the Trail of the Contras," John Lantigua, WP, February 26, 1985, p. A12.

27. San José Radio Impacto 1830 GMT 20 Feb 85, "EPS Reportedly Shells 15 Jinotega Communities," FBIS, VI. 21 Feb 85, P25.

28. Managua International Service 0000 GMT 17 Mar 85, "Government Resettles More Than 20,000 People," FBIS, VI. 20 March 85, P11. They also depopulated some areas near the southern border with Costa Rica where Pastora's small forces had been operating.

29. "Nicaraguans Shift Peasants," Edward Cody, WP, March 17, 1985, A1.

30. "Civilians Quit Border Zone," John Lantigua, WP, April 8, 1985, p. A4; ibid.

31. "Contras Press for Funds," Edward Cody, WP, February 18, 1985, A1; "Nicaragua Guerrillas Ponder Chances Without U.S. Help," James LeMoyne, NYT, March 18, 1985, p. A1; "Nicaraguan Rebels Appear Ready to Fight on Even If Aid Is Cut Off," James LeMoyne, NYT, April 23, 1985, A1.

32. Secord testimony, May 5, 1987, p. 52.

33. This was later cited as a possible violation of the Boland amendment, although there may have been some agreement between the CIA and the intelligence committees that "defensive intelligence" designed to prevent a "holocaust-type situation" could be provided. See letter from Casey to Senator Durenberger, March 18, 1985, I-C exhibit OLN-333A.

34. North letter to Calero, February 1985, I-C exhibit OLN-258.

35. Including the candidate eventually elected, José Azcona Hoyo.

36. Memorandum from Motley to Shultz, February 7, 1985. Declassified document number 808 contained in collection compiled by the National Security Archives [hereafter NSA], *Nicaragua: The Making of U.S. Policy, 1978–1990* (Washington, 1991).

37. Less noted was the fact that Gorman supported continued assistance to the contras, contending that "the answer [in Nicaragua] lies in some kind of combination of pressures and diplomacy." The contra war, he said, had "drawn off the energies of the Sandinistas and has diverted one heck of a lot of money." "Whatever you were investing in those 16,000 fighters," Gorman told Congress, "you got more than your money's worth." He predicted the contra forces could increase by another 8,000 if given financial support. Without renewal of funds, however, "the campaign will begin to peter out, wear down." "The nature of the beast is that you join what you think is a winning cause." See "U.S. General Says Nicaragua Rebels Cannot Win Soon," Bill Keller, NYT, February 28, 1985, A1.

38. Ibid.

39. Ibid.

40. MB (Special Supplement) 10 Oct 85, pp. 1–14, "H. Ortega Interviewed on U.S. Policy, Contras," FBIS, VI. 28 Oct 85, P19–P34.

41. AFPD, 1985. Doc. 538.

42. As early as November 7, 1984, North and Alan Fiers, the CIA officer who replaced Dewey Clarridge as chief of the Central America Task Force, discussed the possibility of a "liberation government" in which Arturo Cruz and Adolfo Calero would "share authority." North-McFarlane memorandum, November 7, 1984, I-C exhibit OLN-255.

43. McFarlane I-C testimony, May 11, 1987, p. 20.

44. Arturo J. Cruz, Jr., "General Points for a New Strategy," private notes, 1984, p. 27. Quoted in R. Pardo-Maurer, *The Contras, 1980–1989: A Special Kind of Politics* (New York, 1990), pp. 14–15.

45. "Nicaraguan Rebel Keeps Command as Shifts Buffet His Forces," Edward Cody, WP, February 28, 1985, p. A23.

46. Paid advertisement in San José LA PRENSA LIBRE 27 Feb 85, p. 3, "FDN Forces Proclaim Loyalty to Calero, Bermúdez," FBIS, VI. 8 Mar 85, P15.

47. North-McFarlane memorandum, April 1, 1985, I-C exhibit OLN-260.

48. "The Tercerista plan offered a social democracy," Cruz said, "but later came deception." Guatemala City Radio-Television Guatemala 0400 GMT 18 Mar 85, "Arturo Cruz Discusses Dialogue, Unity," FBIS, VI. 21 Mar 85, P12–P16.

49. Calero always referred to the "infamous Third Way, which did so much damage to the country." See San José Radio Impacto 1830 GMT 16 Feb 85, "FDN's Calero on Struggle Against Government," FBIS, VI. 19 Feb 85, P15.

50. McFarlane I-C testimony, May 11, 1987, pp. 5, 20; Letter from North to Calero, dated February 1985, I-C exhibit OLN-258.

51. Document reprinted in Robert S. Leiken and Barry Rubin, eds., *The Central American Crisis Reader* (New York, 1987), p. 305.

52. Guatemala City Radio-Television Guatemala 0400 GMT 18 Mar 85, "Arturo Cruz Discusses Dialogue, Unity," FBIS, VI. 21 Mar 85, P12–P16.

53. Cruz, however, insisted the agreement "has nothing to do with the aid from Congress." "Rebel Leaders Demand Talks with Sandinistas," Edward Cody, WP, March 3, 1985, p. A25.

54. "Anti-Sandinistas Call for a 'Dialogue,' | " James LeMoyne, NYT, March 3, 1985, p. A14. Even so, only the persuasion of North and McFarlane convinced Calero to agree to a proposal that was the work of others with quite different goals than his. On Calero's attitude toward the unity agreement, see North memorandum to McFarlane, April 1, 1985, I-C exhibit OLN-260, cited in Gutman, p. 275. North told McFarlane (North-McFarlane memorandum, April 1, 1985, I-C exhibit OLN-260) that Calero "personally wrote several of the democratization conditions." This may be true, but there were no demands in the final document that had not been made before by the Democratic Coordinadora. See especially the Coordinadora's nine-point document in December 1983, p. 304, above.

Gutman describes the goals of the document as "disingenuous," but this was only true for Calero and the Americans. Cruz, Coronel, and others who signed the document were sincere in their ultimate goals, though crafty in their means of achieving them.

55. MRS 1200 GMT 4 Mar 84, "Obando Y Bravo Said to Endorse Contra Document," FBIS, VI. 5 Mar 85, P13.; The Nicaraguan Episcopal Conference formally endorsed the proposal on March 22. Managua LA PRENSA 23–24 Mar 85, p. 1, "Episcopal Conference Offers to Mediate Peace Talks," FBIS, VI. 26 Mar 85, P5.

56. Managua Domestic Service [hereafter MDS] 2135 GMT 7 Mar 85, "Communiqué Alleges Cruz Involvement in CIA Plot," FBIS, VI. 8 Mar 85, P6.

57. MRS 1300 GMT 10 Mar 85, "State Security Summons Opposition Leaders," FBIS, VI. 11 Mar 85, P9. The ten leaders were: Jaime Chamorro Cardenál, editor of *La Prensa*; Eduardo Rivas Gasteazoro of the Coordinadora; Enrique Bolanos and Rene Bonilla of COSEP; Luis Rivas Leiva of the Social Democratic Party; Ramiro Gurdian of UPANIC, the organization once headed by Jorge Salazar; Mario Rappacioli and Miriam Arguello of the Conservative Party; Carlos Huembes of the Confederation of Nicaraguan Workers; and Rodolfo Mejia Ubilla of the Liberal Constitutionalist Party.

58. MDS 0001 GMT 11 Mar 85, "Ortega Speaks on CIA Maneuvers to Unite Contras," FBIS, VI. 11 Mar 85, P8.

59. North-McFarlane memorandum cited in Gutman, p. 275.

60. CR, April 23, 1985, p. H2375.

61. McCurdy interviewed by Arnson, p. 176; Arnson, p. 176.

62. Emphasis in original. "A Fair Offer to the Sandinistas," WP editorial, March 17, 1985, p. E6.

Chapter 35

1. CQ, April 6, 1986, p. 631. By the middle of March, some Reagan officials believed they might be short as many as 50 votes. NYT, March 13, 1985, p. A7.

2. See North-McFarlane memo, April 1, 1985, I-C exhibit OLN-260.

3. "Two Factors Led To Reagan's Plan," Gerald M. Boyd, NYT, April 5, 1985, p. A8. Dole told Reagan at the meeting that he intended to bring the budget proposal to the Senate floor during the week of April 22, which left a brief "window" for consideration of the contra aid proposal.

4. The "Nicaraguan Freedom Fund, Inc." would be established as a tax-exempt corporation to receive the contributions for humanitarian aid, while the "current donors" [i.e., Saudi Arabia] would "agree to provide additional $25–30M to the resistance for the purchase of arms and munitions." North-McFarlane memorandum, March 16, 1985, I-C exhibit RCM-36. North also recommended that McFarlane discuss this "fallback option" with Secretary Shultz, but McFarlane, unbeknownst to North, had still not told Shultz about the Saudi gifts.

5. "Another Vietnam," WSJ editorial, April 16, 1985, p. 30. Menges believed that "the president could *guarantee success* by speaking on national television." But if not, at least "the American people and history [could] judge whether the Democratic majority in the House had acted wisely." Constantine C. Menges, *Inside the National Security Council* (New York, 1988), pp. 203, 207.

6. One official told reporters that the President "can't win on the [contras], and he can't afford to lose on the budget. It's really a question of piorities." The *Washington Post's* Lou Cannon reported that Michael Deaver, budget director David Stockman, and political adviser Ed Rollins all opposed a speech on Nicaragua. Chief of Staff Don Regan agreed with Senator Dole that the President should give a speech on the budget instead. "Buchanan Urges Speech on Nicaragua," by Lou Cannon, WP, April 18, 1985, p. A1.

7. Contra aid, McFarlane told reporters on April 17, "has to be sustained in this country in successive votes to come." See CQ, April 20, p. 708.

8. "[E]ven if there had been a need for money," McFarlane testified at the Iran-Contra hearings in 1987, "I felt strongly that this had to be a matter which the administration could sustain through the Congress and the American people and that we couldn't continue to rely on foreign sources for it." McFarlane I-C testimony, May 11, 1987.

9. Memorandum from McFarlane to Max L. Friedersdorf, March 8, 1985, I-C exhibit OLN-105. According to McFarlane's contemporaneous notes of the meeting, he told Hyde "why these are just not tenable alternatives—for the freedom fighters or for us."

10. North opposed this extension of the contras' original deadline, fearing that "urging the resistance leaders (particularly Calero) to accept a major delay . . . will result in a breakdown of the unity we have achieved." See North-McFarlane memo, April 1, 1985, I-C exhibit OLN-260.

11. McFarlane wrote to Reagan on April 2: "It is likely that the Sandinistas will reject this offer out of hand—at least initially." McFarlane-Reagan memorandum, April 2, 1985, NSA Doc. 1010.

12. "O'Neill Calls Plan Ruse; Republicans Optimistic," Steven V. Roberts, NYT, April 5, 1985, p. A9.

13. CQ, April 6, 1986, p. 631.

14. "Nicaragua Scorns Proposal for Rebel Talks," Joel Brinkley, NYT, April 6, 1985, p. 1.

15. President's Remarks to the Nicaraguan Refugee Fund, Washington, DC, April 15, 1985.

16. In a March 20 memorandum to McFarlane, North made a detailed list of all activities planned by Citizens for America during the period April 8–17. The memorandum also listed some 80–90 other "public diplomacy" actions that were to have taken place between February and the date of the vote. See North-McFarlane memorandum, March 20, 1985, I-C exhibit OLN-217; see CQ, April 20, 1985, p. 716.

17. This event involved a private fund-raiser named Spitz Channell in Nicaraguan issues for the first time. Later in the year, and especially in 1986, Channell became a close collaborator with North in raising funds, both for public relations and for aid to the contras; CQ, April 20, 1985, p. 716.

18. Cynthia J. Arnson, *Crossroads: Congress, the Reagan Administration, and Central America* (New York, 1989), p. 178; See also Robert Parry and Peter Kornbluh, "Iran-Contra's Untold Story," *Foreign Policy*, Number 72, Fall 1988, pp. 3–30.

19. The efforts of the Coalition for a New Foreign and Military Policy have been described in detail by one of the coordinators of the effort, Cindy Buhl, in remarks delivered to a conference of the Latin American Studies Association on April 8, 1991. A copy of the unpublished remarks was provided to the author by Ms. Buhl.

20. Buhl, p. 1; this was the view of Bishop James Malone of Youngstown, Ohio; see "Religious Groups Orchestrate Opposition to 'Contra' Aid," Gerry Fitzgerald, WP, April 23, 1985, p. A18.

21. See Buhl, p. 4 and ibid.; CQ, April 20, 1985, p. 716.

22. Movie and television stars, singers and song-writers like Julie Andrews, Ed Asner, Jackson Browne, Mike Farrell of the TV show "M*A*S*H*", Robert Foxworth of the nighttime soap opera "Falcon Crest," and Darryl Hannah, star of the previous year's hit movie "Splash," either traveled to Nicaragua, personally lobbied members of Congress in Washington, or signed letters against contra aid, their activities coordinated by the Coalition for a New Foreign and Military Policy. See CR, April 23, 1985, pp. S4544–48; "Nicaragua Hosted 21 from Capitol Hill as Contra Vote Neared," John Lantigua, WP, April 23, 1985, p. A18; CQ, April 20, 1985, p. 716; and Buhl, p. 5.

23. Buhl, p. 3.

24. At the beginning of March, 135 House Democrats went on retreat to discuss the party's problems. At about the same time, a group of moderate and conservative Democratic politicians, mostly from the South and West, formed the Democratic Leadership Council with the aim, according to co-founder Senator Sam Nunn of Georgia, of undoing the public perception that "the party has moved away from mainstream America." See CQ, March 9, 1985, pp. 456–57.

25. The Republican Whip, Trent Lott, warned explicitly that "the slogan would be 'Who Lost El Salvador?' if the Democrats defeated Reagan and the Nicaraguan government exports its leftist revolution to its neighbors." See CQ, April 20, 1985, pp. 707, 708, 709.

26. See Arnson, pp. 181–82. "Despite the apparent thirst for a showdown with the president . . . several liberal and moderate Democrats were concerned that contra opponents be able to vote for a policy alternative and not just against the administration. The search for 'what to do about the Sandinistas'—as much a quest for political cover as for a positive policy—began before and in anticipation of the president's formal request for $14 million."

27. "Nicaragua Hosted 21 from Capitol Hill as Contra Vote Neared," by John Lantigua, *Washington Post*, April 25, 1985, p. A33. CR, April 23, 1985, H2378.

28. Younger liberal Democrats had already proved their power in January when they unseated the long-time chairman of the House Armed Services Committee, Melvin Price, who had the full backing of O'Neill and Wright, and replaced him with the younger Les Aspin, whom O'Neill personally disliked. See John M. Barry, *The Ambition and the Power: Jim Wright and The Will of the House* (New York, 1989), p. 33.

29. Especially after Wright's support for the Reagan administration's policy in El Salvador in 1984, his lukewarm opposition to the MX missile that same year and then his endorsement of Reagan's Strategic Defense Initiative in 1985.

30. See Barry, p. 32. Wright clashed more and more with Congressman Stenholm, who represented a part of Texas that included Wright's hometown.

31. CQ, April 20, 1985, pp. 707, 708, 709; CQ, April 20, 1985, pp. 707–9.

32. Congressman Jim Jones of Oklahoma, for instance, wanted to give the contras humanitarian aid for 90 days, assess the Sandinistas' behavior, and then have Congress vote again to decide whether or not to provide military aid. CR, April 23, 1985, p. H2421.

33. Senator Nunn was receiving the Henry M. Jackson Award from the Coalition for a Democratic Majority along with Congressman Les Aspin. His speech was reprinted in CR, April 23, 1985. pp. S4594–95.

34. Reagan had already put a request for military aid for the contras in his Fiscal Year 1986 budget. See CQ, April 20, 1985, pp. 707–09.

35. See Arnson, interview with Kirk O'Donnell, p. 181.

36. CR, April 23, 1985, p. H2339.

37. Ibid., pp. H2447 and H2451.

38. Ibid., p. H2340; Ibid.

39. Ibid. H2378.

40. It is worth noting, in connection with assertions by Menges and others that Reagan could have won a vote for military aid if he had tried harder, that only 167 Republicans voted for "humanitarian" aid, three less than the 170 Republicans Menges counted as "solid" for *military* aid. Menges, p. 230.

41. Congresswoman Collins of Illinois insisted "We must unequivocally cut off all aid to the Contras," and Congressman Conyers of Michigan expressed the liberals' concern that any bill containing contra aid would produce a compromise with the Senate that went much further than the Barnes-Hamilton amendment. CR, April 24, 1985, pp. H2466, H2460.

42. For some reason, this story which was written by Stephen Kinzer and dated April 23, did not appear in the *New York Times* until April 25, a day after the House completed its voting. See "Sandinista Leader Says He Plans to Visit Moscow Soon to Seek Aid," Stephen Kinzer, NYT, April 25, 1985, p. A8.

43. "Senator Objects to Trip," by Shirley Christian, NYT April 25, 1985, p. A8.

44. Bayardo Arce later defended the trip to Moscow on the grounds that "without the agreement on oil supplies that was reached there, Nicaragua would have come to a standstill." Stockholm DAGENS NYHETER 20 Jun 85, p. 13, "Arce Discusses Ortega's Visit to Moscow," FBIS, VI. 3 Jul 85, P11–P12.

45. There is some reason to question this version of events, however. Ortega and other Sandinistas acknowledged that the dates for the trip were set long before the vote in the Congress was scheduled, which means the trip was also set before the Sandinistas' oil crisis reached acute proportions with the Mexican cancellation on April 16. Vice President Sergio Ramírez later told reporters that the trip had been planned long in advance and was undertaken because "this was the proper time to carry out the visit." (See "Nicaraguan Leader Predicts U.S. Will Broaden Embargo," Stephen Kinzer, NYT, May 15, 1985, p. A6.) Possibly, Ortega's trip to Moscow was a normal state visit, but after the congressional outcry, the Sandinistas found it necessary to call it an emergency visit.

46. Since the beginning of the year, the Sandinistas had been unable to make their payments to Mexico, virtually their sole supplier. They feared Mexico would cut them off, and on April 16 Mexican President de la Madrid notified Henry Ruiz officially that Mexican deliveries of oil would indeed be suspended. Roy Gutman, *Banana Diplomacy* (New York, 1988), p. 289.

47. According to Bayardo Arce, they had "discussed the effects this trip to Moscow could have [on the U.S. Congress] before President Ortega went," and Arce suggested the Sandinistas "did not understand the extent to which the visit could be exploited. . . . It is possible that we made a mistake." Stockholm DAGENS NYHETER 20 Jun 85, p. 13, "Arce Discusses Ortega's Visit to Moscow," FBIS, VI. 3 Jul 85, P11–P12.

48. As it happened, after completing his 14-day tour of the Soviet bloc countries, Ortega extended his trip to include Western European countries, as well, in an effort to repair the political damage in the United States. But it was too late. See "Ortega Visits Spain, Wins Continued Aid," by Karen DeYoung, WP, May 12, 1985, p. A22.

49. Ruiz had a good relationship with the Soviets, and Soviet leaders surely would have understood the need for a less prominent delegation so soon after the vote in Congress. There were two trips in the first three months of 1980, for instance, during which trade and economic agreements were signed between the two countries with little publicity. The implausible explanation given by a Sandinista official to Roy Gutman was that Ortega "had to conclude an agreement very formally and at the highest levels to avoid the risk of a U.S. naval blockade that would block the supply of oil." Gutman, p. 289.

50. See Vernon V. Aspaturian, "Nicaragua between East and West: The Soviet Perspective," in Jiri Valenta and Esperanza Duran, eds., *Conflict in Nicaragua: A Multidimensional Perspective* (Boston, 1987).

51. Author's interview with Humberto Ortega, May 26, 1990.

52. See Francis Fukuyama, "Moscow's Post-Brezhnev Reassessment of the Third World" RAND, February 1986, p. 9.

53. Ponomarev retired in 1986 and was replaced by longtime Soviet ambassador to the United States, Anatoly Dobrynin.

54. *New York Times* correspondent Larry Rohter reported that each day, "to sorrowful strains of Chopin and Tchaikovsky, nightly news broadcasts praised 'Comrade Chernenko' as a 'great sateseman and untiring fighter for the cause of world peace and solidarity.'" See "Sandinista Government Viewed as Leftist Hybrid," Larry Rohter, NYT, March 23, 1985, p. A3.

55. CR, June 6, 1985, S7591.

56. "Contra Aid Vote Presages Renewed U.S. Role," Margaret Shapiro, WP, June 14, 1985, quoted in Arnson, p. 185; "Nicaragua Rebels Gain Some Backing," Bernard Gwertzman, NYT, May 3, 1985, p. A1.

57. McCurdy had been "livid" at what he considered the betrayal of his moderate group by liberal Democrats. He felt he had "taken these guys out on a limb electorally. . . . When [the liberal Democrats] backed off, we said, the hell with them." Arnson interview with McCurdy, Arnson, p. 184.

58. See CR, June 12, 1985, p. 15400; "Speaker Says House May Aid 'Contras,'" Margaret Shapiro and Joanne Omang, WP, May 7, 1985, quoted in Arnson, p. 185; Arnson interview with Kirk O'Donnell, Arnson, p. 185.

59. "Anti-Managua Aid Is Seen As Likely," Steven V. Roberts, NYT, May 5, 1985, p. 4; "O'Neill Is Firm on Aid to Rebels and Says Embargo Is Premature," Bernard Gwertzman, NYT, May 4, 1985, p. A4.

60. As O'Donnell explained, the Ortega trip made it all the more difficult to reconcile the divergent positions of the liberals and moderates in the party and to avoid forcing the moderates to cast "votes that could defeat them in an election." Arnson interview with Kirk O'Donnell, Arnson, p. 185.

61. McCurdy and other southern Democrats deny that it was Ortega's trip that created the demand for contra aid. "Ortega's trip was just a smokescreen," Congressman Cooper of Tennessee later insisted. "The deciding factor was the way the liberals sabotaged the very policy they had voted for." See Arnson interview with Cooper, Arnson, p. 185. At the beginning of June, McCurdy told an audience of conservative Democrats: "It is often said that the Ortega visit to Moscow was the reason that many people in the House changed their minds about aid. That is just not the truth. Our meeting occurred before that trip actually took place, nor would that trip have made a difference." See transcript, "Towards a New Policy for Nicaragua," a conversation with Senator Sam Nunn and Representative Dave McCurdy, Coalition for a Democratic Majority, [hereafter CDM] June 3, 1985, p. 3. Quoted in Arnson, p. 185.

62. Senator Durenberger also strongly supported an embargo, and had even proposed a "naval blockade" of Nicaragua to block Soviet arms shipments. "If we oppose the regime in Managua, why do we buy Nicaraguan beef and bananas?" Durenberger had asked at the end of March. A few days after Nunn's speech, Senator Lloyd Bentsen, a moderate Democrat from Texas and like Nunn a member of the intelligence committee, joined Republican moderates Kassebaum and Cohen in submitting legislation calling for "a total trade boycott and embargo against Nicaragua." If aid to the contras was controversial, Bentsen argued that his proposal was "one way we can be more nearly unanimous in expressing our disapproval" of the Sandinistas' behavior. CR, April 22, 1985, p. S4483.

63. "Dole Ponders Nicaragua Trade Embargo," Robert Pear, NYT, April 28, 1985, p. 3; "President Orders Halt to Trade with Nicaragua," Joanne Omang, WP, May 2, 1985, p. A1.

64. "Reagan Expected to Place Sanctions Against Nicaragua," Joanne Omang, WP, May 1, 1985, p. A1.

65. "Summit Partners Criticize Sanctions Against Nicaragua," Lou Cannon, WP, May 4, 1985, p. A16.

66. Co-sponsors of the legislation were Congressmen Richardson (D-NM), Robinson (D-AK), MacKay (D-FL), Bustamante (D-TX) Darden (D-GA), Daniel (D-VA), Mollohan (D-WV), Watkins (D-OK), Glickman (D-KS), and Jones (D-OK).

67. The only provision in McCurdy's bill not already explicitly agreed to by the President was that if the Nicaraguan government agreed to a cease-fire and a dialogue with the contras and suspended the State of Emergency, the President would respond by suspending military maneuvers in Honduras and off the coast of Nicaragua.

68. Other co-sponsors were Senators DeConcini, Durenberger, Lugar, and Nickles.

69. Aronson was a former speechwriter for Vice President Walter Mondale and a Democratic consultant close to Nunn.

70. Bernard Aronson, "Another Choice in Nicaragua," in *New Republic*, May 27, 1985, pp. 21–23, reprinted in CR, May 23, 1985, p. E2424–25.

71. Senator Nunn, CR, June 6, 1985, p. S7629.

72. Congressman Jones (D-OK) CR, June 12, 1985, p. H4137–8.

73. Ibid.

74. "Twin Threats to Democracy in Nicaragua," Robert S. Leiken, NYT, October 27, 1985, Sec. IV, p. 23.

75. Aronson was closer to Senator Nunn than to McCurdy, and his positions, though consistent with McCurdy's, often reflected Nunn's more aggressively conservative approach. Bernard Aronson, "Another Choice in Nicaragua."

76. Congressman Jim Jones, (D-OK), CR, June 12, 1985, p. H4137–8.

77. CR, June 12, 1985, p. H4152.

78. Bernard Aronson, "Another Choice in Nicaragua."

79. CR, June 12, 1985, p. H4137.

80. Bernard Aronson, "Another Choice in Nicaragua."

81. See McCurdy statement, CQ, May 11, 1985, p. 876. Senator Nunn said his amendment "moves American promotion of military action to the back burner." CR, June 6, 1985, p. S7629.

82. See CR, June 12, 1985, pp. H4137–38.

83. CR, June 12, 1985, p. 15383.

84. CR, June 12, 1985, p. 15409.

85. Spratt interviewed by Arnson, p. 186. It is only fitting, given the nature of this debate, that Spratt nevertheless voted not only for the McCurdy amendment, but also for the Boland amendment, which would have prevented aid from going to the contras "as a fighting force."

86. Emphasis added. Letter from President Reagan to Congressman Dave McCurdy, June 11, 1985. Reprinted in CR, June 11, 1985, p. 15203.

87. According to Gutman, in dictating the terms of the new policy to President Reagan "McCurdy stopped short of demanding a return to Manzanillo because his advisers and members of his coalition were divided on the merits of requiring negotiations of an administration that was dead set against them." Gutman, p. 290.

88. According to Gutman, "McCurdy thought he had a sufficient commitment by Reagan [to negotiations] to back the aid package." (Gutman, p. 290.) But in light of Gutman's claim, on the very same page, that McCurdy and his advisers knew the administration was "dead set against" negotiations, this is unlikely. Nor does McCurdy claim, in his floor speech on June 12, that he had any commitment at all from the President concerning bilateral negotiations, although he approvingly read large excerpts from the President's June 11 letter. CR, June 12, 1985, p. H4137.

89. CR, June 12, 1985, pp. 15399–400.

90. This estimate counts 137 Republicans and 26 Democrats (23 from the South) who had voted in July 1983 to continue military aid to the contras, then voted against the Boland amendment after the mining scandal in 1984, then for the Michel and McDade amendments in April and June of 1985. In addition, there were ten new conservative Republicans as a result of the 1984 elections (eight in the south) for a total of 173.

Then one must consider seven additional southern Democrats and one Republican—Democrats Thomas, Hatcher and Rowland of Georgia, Gibbons of Florida, English of Oklahoma, Ortiz of Texas, and Sisisky of Virginia, and Republican Coughlin of Pennsylvania. Their votes on the eight key votes in 1985 were as follows: On April 23–24, 'Yes' on the President's proposal (a vote on which only hard-line conservatives voted yes), 'Yes' on Barnes-Hamilton, 'Yes' on Michel, and 'Yes' on passage of the legislation as amended; on June 12, 'No' on Boland, 'No' on Gephardt, 'Yes' on McDade, and 'No' on Hamilton. In 1984, moreover, Congressmen Thomas, Rowland, English, and Sisisky voted against Boland after the mining, a hard-line conservative position. One is inclined to believe that these members certainly, and the other two probably, would have approved military aid to the contras if that was the proposal placed before them, which would have raised the total number of votes for military aid in June of 1985 to 182. The reader, however, may judge for him- or herself.

91. By virtue of their votes over the previous three years against every Boland amendment and in favor of all proposals to aid the contras.

92. CR, June 12, 1985, p. 15414; Arnson, p. 187, quoting from Nunn's CDM speech, op cit.; Richardson interviewed by Arnson, p. 187.

93. Every southern state with the exception of Tennessee (58–42) voted for Reagan by a margin of 60–40 or more.

94. Congressman Sam Hall did not vote in June, having been named as a federal judge by the Reagan administration at the end of May. Hall would certainly have voted for the humanitarian aid; the other eight southern states had voted far more consistently: 30–12 in favor of contra aid in 1983; 28–8 in favor of contra aid in 1985.

95. Quoted in Arnson, p. 188. In the last days before the vote, the House Democratic leadership tried in vain to calm these fears by releasing a poll of southern voters which, they claimed, proved it was safe to vote against President Reagan on contra aid. But southern Democrats could have taken little comfort from learning that their constituents opposed by a margin of only 51–37 percent the use of *American* troops to *overthrow* the Sandinistas to "prevent Communism from spreading in Central America." Poll cited in "Democrats Denounce Policy Toward Nicaraguans," NYT, June 6, 1985, p. 8. A national poll taken at the beginning of June showed that respondents favored "humanitarian" aid to the contras by a margin of 62–30, while opposing military aid by 66–24. See "Of Two Minds," Steven V. Roberts, NYT, June 9, 1985, Sec. IV, p. 1.

96. Arnson, p. 187.

97. Ironically, in neither Cambodia nor Angola was the Reagan administration prepared to begin providing covert support to guerrillas.

98. *Congressional Quarterly Almanac 1985*, p. 51.

99. CR, June 12, 1985, p. 15396.

100. Ibid., p. 15397.

Chapter 36

1. New shipments of arms bought through Richard Secord arrived in April (the so-called "slow boat from China" bearing the contras' first anti-aircraft missiles), and at the end of May. Jane Mayer and Doyle MacManus, *Landslide: The Unmaking of the President*, (Boston, 1988), p. 143

2. "Nicaragua Rebels Getting Advice from White House on Operation," Joel Brinkley and Shirley Christian, NYT, August 8, 1985, p. A1.

3. Ibid.

4. "White House Defends Legality of NSC Contact with Contras," Joanne Omang, WP, August 9, 1985, p. A1.

5. Ibid.

6. WP, August 13, 1985, quoted in Mayer and MacManus, p. 149.

7. McFarlane I-C testimony, Exhibit 40A.

8. Ibid., Exhibit 40B; ibid., Exhibit 40C.

9. Ibid., Exhibit 41.

10. "McFarlane Backs Aide on Contra Role," Jonathan Fuerbringer, NYT, September 6, 1985, p. A3.

11. Mayer and MacManus, p. 148.

12. "Frustration, Resignation and the C.I.A.," Charles Mohr, NYT, October 1, 1985, p. A24.

13. CQ, November 16, 1985, p. 2388.

14. See Mayer and MacManus, p. 148. When Barnes returned to his office, he told his aides: "I've just met a man who's afraid he's going to jail."

15. McFarlane I-C testimony, Exhibit 41C.

16. Arnson writes that Congress "lacked the will . . . to compel the release of information" due to what she calls a "defensive mentality." See Cynthia J. Arnson, *Crossroads: Congress, the Reagan Administration, and Central America* (New York, 1989), pp. 190–91.

17. Emphasis added. "Frustration, Resignation and the C.I.A.," Charles Mohr, NYT, October 1, 1985, p. A24.

18. See letter from Congressman Hamilton to William Casey, December 4, 1985, and letter from Senator Durenberger to Hamilton, December 5, 1985. McFarlane I-C testimony, exhibits 77 and 77A.

19. "Change in Bill May Help Contras," Robert Parry (AP), WP, September 15, 1985, p. A9.

20. "Perhaps," because somehow the solicitation of third countries had to be for "humanitarian" assistance, whatever that might mean. "Humanitarian" assistance now included trucks, helicopters, and communications gear.

Chapter 37

1. "Sandinistas Press Attacks on Rebels," Stephen Kinzer, NYT, June 4, 1985, p. A1; "Civilians Quit Border Zone," John Lantigua, WP, April 18, 1985, p. A23.

2. NYT, June 4, 1985.

3. Mexico City NOTIMEX, 1845 GMT 1 May 85, "Defense Ministry Reports Contras Casualties," FBIS, VI. 2 May 85, P20.

4. The number of Sandinistas who crossed the border varies depending on the source. LeMoyne's sources told him "elements of five battalions," ("Amid Signs of Battle, Questions About Its Scale in Honduras," James LeMoyne, NYT, March 29, 1986, p. 4) but a report from the American ambassador in Honduras to Washington estimates that "two Sandinista companies" crossed the border. (Tegucigalpa 6693, May 18, 1985.) Another U.S. official told the *New York Times* that 200 Sandinistas had been seen. ("Honduras Border Scene of Clashes," Bill Keller, NYT, May 19, 1985, p. 1.)

5. NYT, March 29, 1986. p. 4; "Anti-Sandinistas Are Curbed," (Reuters) NYT, May 17, 1985, p. A11.

6. According to Julio Ramos, chief of Sandinista military intelligence. NYT, May 19, 1985.

7. Ibid.

8. Tegucigalpa 6693, May 18, 1985.

9. NYT, May 19, 1985.

10. Tegucigalpa 6693, May 18, 1985. James LeMoyne also reported, in the *Times* at the beginning of May, that the Hondurans' "chief concern was that the rebels would remain inside Honduras, prompting Sandinista attacks that embarrass the Government and occasionally cause civilian casualties." See "Nicaraguan Rebels Said to Get Missiles," James LeMoyne, NYT, May 4, 1985, p. A4.

11. Tegucigalpa 6693, May 18, 1985.

12. "Anti-Sandinistas Are Curbed," (Reuters) NYT, May 17, 1985, p. A11.

13. NYT, May 19, 1985.

14. Ibid.

15. Tegucigalpa 6693, May 18, 1985.

16. Paris AFP 1234 GMT 30 May 85, "Offensive Launched Against Pastora's Forces," FBIS, VI. 31 May 85, P10; Managua Radio Noticias 1200 GMT 31 May 85, "Five EPS Members Captured in Costa Rica," FBIS, VI. 3 Jun 85, P13; MRS 1200 GMT 5 Jun 85, "Defense Ministry Reports Bombing of La Penca," FBIS, VI. 6 Jun 85, P14.

17. NYT, June 4, 1985.

18. MB (Special Supplement) 10 Oct 85, pp. 1–14, "H. Ortega Interviewed on U.S. Policy, Contras," FBIS, VI. 28 Oct 85, P19–P34.

19. "White House Tells Nicaragua to Stop 'Aggressive' Moves." Bernard Weinraub, NYT, June 5, 1985, p. A1.

20. Hamburg DPA 1544 GMT 24 Jun 85, "Army Deploys Soviet-Made Tanks Around Managua," FBIS, VI. 25 Jun 85, P12; Paris AFP 0214 GMT 26 Jun 85, "Armored Vehicles, Tanks Moved to Leon, Chinandega," FBIS, VI. 26 Jun 85, P3.

21. See Madrid EFE 1950 GMT 20 May 85, "Sandinist Army Captures Contra Command Post," FBIS, VI. 28 May 85, P10; and "Nicaraguan Rebels Appear Ready to Fight On Even If Aid Is Cut Off," James LeMoyne, NYT, April 23, 1985, A1.

22. See "Nicaragua Rebels Open a New Front," Stephen Kinzer, NYT, Sept 2, 1985, p. 1.

23. MDS 0300 GMT 7 Jun 85, "Contras Hit Near Honduran, Costa Rican Borders," FBIS, VI. 7 Jun 85, P11.

24. See MB 6 Jun 85 p4, "Defeat of 'Jorge Salazar' Command Reported," FBIS, VI. 12 Jun 85, P9.

25. Ibid.

26. MB 27 June 85, p. 5, "BLI Troops Continue San José de Bocay Operations," FBIS, VI. 3 Jul 85, P14–P15.

27. "Nicaragua Rebels Reportedly Kill 29 soldiers in Stepped-Up Attacks," (AP) NYT, July 31, 1985, p. A2.

28. MRS 1750 GMT 18 Jul 85, "Mercenaries Repelled by EPS in Nueva Segovia," FBIS, VI. 19 Jul 85.

29. MB 24 Jul 85 p. 12, "Militia Neutralizes Contra 'Resurgence' Plan," FBIS, VI. 26 Jul 85, P21.

30. MDS 0130 GMT 5 Aug 85, "Sandinist Army Breaks up Contra Plan in Estelí," FBIS, VI. 5 Aug 85, P10.

31. Managua Sistema Sandinista Television Network 0200 GMT 30 Jul 85, "Clashes Near Estelí Kill 4 Contras, 29 EPS Members," FBIS, VI. 31 Jul 85, P21.

32. "Nicaraguan Rebels Blow Up Bridge," WP, August 1, 1985, p. A23.SJRI 1353 GMT 1 Aug 85, "FDN Destroys Viejo River Bridge, Isolates Towns," FBIS, VI. 6 Aug 85, P11.

33. MRS 1205 GMT 2 Aug 85, "Defense Ministry Update on La Trinidad Situation," FBIS, VI. 5 Aug 85, P9.

34. "Rebels Briefly Hold Town in Northern Nicaragua," John Lantigua, WP, August 2, 1985, p. A1.

35. Ibid. "FDN Destorys Viejo River Bridge, Isolates Towns."

36. MDS 0130 GMT 5 Aug 85, "Sandinist Army Breaks Up Contra Plan In Estelí," FBIS, VI. 5 Aug 85, P10.

37. NYT, Sept 2, 1985.

38. "Contra Attack Said to Kill 51 Nicaraguan Soldiers," John Lantigua, WP, August 8, 1985, p. A1.

39. See NYT, Sept 2, 1985; and MDS 0235 GMT 3 Aug 85, "Communiqué Issued on Military Successes," FBIS, VI. 6 Aug 85, P9.

40. FBIS, VI. 8 Aug 85, P22.

41. NYT, Sept 2, 1985.

42. Stephen Kinzer, *Blood of Brothers: Life and War in Nicaragua* (New York, 1991), p. 293.

43. NYT, Sept 2, 1985.

44. MB 19 Aug 85, p. 7, "Army Commander Discusses Military Situation," FBIS, VI. 21 Aug 85, P10.

45. MRS 1200 GMT 9 Aug 85, "Borge Calls Contra Action in North 'Propaganda,'|" FBIS, VI. 12 Aug 85, P19.

46. NYT, Sept 2, 1985.

47. Kinzer, p. 294.

48. See MRS 1200 GMT 9 Aug 85, "Borge Calls Contra Action in North 'Propaganda,'" FBIS, VI. 12 Aug 85, P19; and MRS 1240 GMT 8 Aug 85, "Commander Torres Says 2,500 Contras Killed in 1985," FBIS, VI. 12 Aug 85, P19.

49. Buenos Aires REUTER 2301 GMT 16 Aug 85, "Army Preparing for Big Guerrilla Offensive," FBIS, VI. 19 Aug 85, P13.

50. Bogota EL SIGLO (NICARAGUA HOY Supplement) 11 Sep 85 p. 4, "FDN Issues Report on August Operations," FBIS, VI. 25 Sep 85, P15. The Sandinista Defense Ministry confirmed fighting in Chontales, Jinotega, and Matagalpa departments, see MEND 22 Aug 85 pp. 1, 10, "Defense Ministry Report on 15–21 August Clashes," FBIS, VI. 23 Aug 85, P13.

51. Panama City ACAN 0257 GMT 24 Aug 85, "Army Begins 'Second Phase' of Counterinsurgency," FBIS, VI. 26 Aug 85, P15.

52. MDS 0615 GMT 14 Sep 85, "President Ortega Issues Communiqué," FBIS, VI. 16 Sep 85, P25.

53. "Honduras Says It Hit a Copter from Nicaragua," James LeMoyne, NYT, September 14, 1985, p. 3; "Honduras Sends Troops to Border Area," James LeMoyne, NYT, September 15, 1985, p. 3.

54. MDS 0628 GMT 14 Sep 85, "Suazo's Comments Noted," FBIS, VI. 16 Sep 85, P26.

55. MRS 1200 GMT 20 Sep 85, "200 Peasant Families Resettled in Region 1," FBIS, VI. 25 Sep 85, P13.

56. Paris AFP 0104 GMT 15 Oct 85, "Cuadra on Possible Honduran Border Offensive," FBIS, VI. 16 Oct 85, P10.

57. Ibid.

58. MB (Special Supplement) 10 Oct 85, pp. 1–14, "H. Ortega Interviewed on U.S. Policy, Contras," FBIS, VI. 28 Oct 85, P19–P34.

59. MRS 1200 GMT 15 Aug 85, "Humberto Ortega Discusses Mobilization, Dialogue," FBIS, VI. 16 Aug 85, P11; MB (Special Supplement) 10 Oct 85, pp. 1–14, "H. Ortega Interviewed On U.S. Policy, Contras," FBIS, VI. 28 Oct 85, P19–P34.

60. MRS 1200 GMT 15 Aug 85, "Humberto Ortega Discusses Mobilization, Dialogue," FBIS, VI. 16 Aug 85, P11; "Nicaragua Resumes Draft for Rest of '85," John Lantigua, WP, September 3, 1985, p. A21.

61. MB (Special Supplement) 10 Oct 85, pp. 1–14, "H. Ortega Interviewed On U.S. Policy, Contras," FBIS, VI. 28 Oct 85, P19–P34.

62. Ibid.

63. NYT, April 23, 1985.

64. Asked by the *Washington Post*'s Joanne Omang if the Sandinista plan was simply to ignore the contras, Ortega responded, "Our strategy is not to ignore them, but rather to coexist with them." MB (Special Supplement) 10 Oct 85, pp. 1–14, "H. Ortega Interviewed On U.S. Policy, Contras," FBIS, VI. 28 Oct 85, P19–P34.

65. Paris L'HUMANITE 11 Apr 85 p. 8, "Interior Minister on Nation's 'Abnormal' Status," FBIS, VI. 23 Apr 85, P21.

66. MB (Special Supplement) 10 Oct 85, pp. 1–14, "H. Ortega Interviewed On U.S. Policy, Contras," FBIS, VI. 28 Oct 85, P19–P34.

67. Report by William Thiesenhusen, delivered at hearings sponsored by Congressman Robert Kastenmeier at the University of Wisconsin in Madison. Reprinted in CR, July 15, 1985, pp. S9466–67.

68. "Nicaragua Set to Sign Debt Payment Accord," NYT, June 17, 1985, IV, p. 4.

69. MDS 1952 GMT 8 Feb 85, "FSLN Message on U.S. Threat, Budget Measures," FBIS, VI. 11 Feb 85, P10.

70. MRS Newtwork 1200 GMT 7 Feb 85, "Nuñez Remarks," FBIS, VI. 8 Feb 85, P10.

71. Managua Radio Noticias 1200 GMT 7 Feb 85, "Deputies Stage Walk-out," FBIS, VI. 8 Feb 85, P11.

72. MDS 1952 GMT 8 Feb 85, "FSLN Message On U.S. Threat, Budget Measures," FBIS, VI. 11 Feb 85, P10.

73. "Sandinistas Are Showing Surprising Staying Power," Stephen Kinzer, NYT, June 9, 1985, p. E3.

74. "Ortega Calls U.S. Move 'Positive,'" Karen DeYoung, WP, May 13, 1985, p. A14.

75. NYT, June 9, 1985.

76. MB (Special Supplement) 10 Oct 85, pp. 1–14, "H. Ortega Interviewed On U.S. Policy, Contras," FBIS, VI. 28 Oct 85, P19–P34.

77. Interview with Borge in June, reprinted in Managua LA PRENSA 11 Nov 85, pp. 2,5, "Interior Minister Borge Interviewed on Revolution," FBIS, VI. 27 Nov 85, P18.

78. "Sandinista Portrait: Poet, Militant, Bible Devotee," Stephen Kinzer, NYT, September 3, 1985, p. A2.

79. San José Radio Impacto 1830 GMT 3 May 85, "PSC Chairman Jarquín Reports 1 May Repression," FBIS, VI. 9 May 85, P19.

80. "Nicaraguans Welcome Cardinal," Robert J. McCartney, WP, June 15, 1985, p. A14.

81. Panama City ACAN 1843 GMT 22 Jun 85, "Obando Y Bravo Sunday Transmission Banned," FBIS, VI. 24 Jun 85, P20.

82. "Sandinista Retain the Upper Hand," Stephen Kinzer, NYT, September 9, 1985, p. A6.

83. MB 3 Dep 85 p. 5, "Humberto Ortega Discusses Defense Issues," FBIS, VI. 5 Sep 85, P18.

84. NYT, September 2, 1985.

85. Managua BARRICADA 20 Mar 85, p. 16, "La Prensa Editor Advocates U.S. Aid to Contras," FBIS, VI. 22 Mar 85, P11.

86. Ibid.

87. See Kinzer, p. 296.

88. "Nicaraguan Crackdown Seen Aimed at Church," Edward Cody, WP, October 17, 1985, p. A1.

89. See Kinzer, p. 297.

90. "Nicaragua Arrests 134 for Aiding Guerrillas," WP, October 20, 1985, p. A25.

91. Kinzer, p. 296.

92. Quoted by Don Kowet, "Ortega Says His 'Victory' Justifies Denial of Rights," *Washington Times*, October 23, 1985. Kowet article reprinted in CR, October 23, 1985, p. E4778.

93. "Ortega Has No Use for Friends," Mary McGrory, WP, October 29, 1985, p. A3.

94. While "not closing the door" on bilateral talks, Shultz insisted they were not "appropriate under the circumstances." "Shultz Rejects Resumption of Talks with Sandinistas," Richard J. Meislin, NYT, July 27, 1985, p. A3.

95. MDS 0234 GMT 14 Sp 85, "D'Escoto Views Results of Contadora Meeting," FBIS, VI. 16 Sep 85, P29.

96. MRS 1930 GMT 4 Nov 85, "Foreign Ministry Document on Contadora," FBIS, VI. 8 Nov 85, P14.

97. Panama City ACAN 0122 GMT 27 Nov 85, "Tirado Lopez Decries 'Isolation' of Regime," FBIS, VI. 29 Nov 85, P15.

98. MRS 1200 GMT 30 Nov 85, "Ambassador Outlines Position," FBIS, VI. 2 Dec 85, P11.

99. "Instead of continuing with this process of trying to accommodate the Contadora document to U.S. interests," the Sandinista ambassador to the OAS declared, the Contadora ministers "must face the United States in an open and firm way. Contadora should tell the United States: Gentlemen, if you want to contribute to this peace process, stop all the attitudes or actions of aggression against Nicaragua and let us create the appropriate climate." Ibid.

Chapter 38

1. "Cubans Fighting Contras, Hill Told," Joanne Omang, WP, December 6, 1985, p. A1.

2. "Sandinistas Seen Turning Away from Liberal Allies," Edward Cody, WP, February 16, 1986, p. A25.

3. "Congress Resisting New Aid for Nicaragua's Insurgents," Shirley Christian, NYT, Dec 24, 1985, p. A4.

4. "Aid to Anti-Sandinistas Weighed," Shirley Christian, NYT, January 16, 1986, p. A4.

5. See account of January 10, 1986 NSC meeting in the Report of the Congressional Committees Investigating the Iran-Contra Affair, p. 64. The memorandum upon which the committees base their account was not made public. Unfortunately, the committee report is elsewhere filled with errors and skewed interpretations, and the reader must be cautious of its summaries of meetings when orginal documents are unavailable.

6. See statement of Frank C. Conahan of the General Accounting Office at hearings of the House Foreign Affairs Subcommittee on Western Hemisphere Affairs, March 5, 1986, p. 12.

It would be more accurate to say that the State Department could not satisfy the GAO. The State Department said the proof of deliveries was in the CIA reports, but the GAO did not have access to those reports, which could be seen only by members of the intelligence committees.

7. See Barnes statement at March 5, 1986 hearings, p. 23.

8. Administration officials suspected that the Honduran President Suazo was also holding up the shipments to force the United States to acquiesce in his continuation in office, even though he lost to José Azcona Hoyo in November elections.

9. Statement of Frank C. Conahan of the General Accounting Office, p. 13.

10. Testimony of Robert Duemling, at March 5, 1986 hearings, p. 35.

11. WP, December 6, 1985.

12. CIA officials thought the contras were a bit spoiled—"if they didn't have good boots they'd leave"—and were too dependent on outside support. Author's interview with the CIA's Central American Task Force chief, Alan Fiers, March 8, 1991.

13. "Contra Raids Reported Trailing Off," Stephen Kinzer, NYT, February 21, 1986.

14. "Contra Forces Now Viewed As a Much-Reduced Threat," James LeMoyne, NYT, March 6, 1986, p. A1.

15. See Jane Mayer and Doyle MacManus, *Landslide: The Unmaking of the President, 1984–1988* (Boston, 1988), p. 199.

16. When NHAO officials found what had happened they forced the contras to pay for the flight. See Report of Iran-Contra Investigating Committees, p. 65.

17. Ibid., p. 67.

18. Despite North's frequent references to the CIA as the "gang that couldn't shoot straight."

19. See, for instance, the editorial by Congressman Stephen J. Solarz, "It's Time for the Democrats to Be Tough-Minded," NYT, June 20, 1985, p. A27.

20. See Roy Gutman, *Banana Diplomacy* (New York, 1988), 318. "[A]fter McFarlane's departure," Gutman writes, "Shultz had few allies in the administration. He turned his focus to U.S.-Soviet affairs." The *Times'* Shirley Christian also suggested that Shultz dissented from the course the administration was taking, but was "counted among the silent." "Reagan Aides See No Possibility of U.S. Accord with Sandinistas," Shirley Christian, NYT, August 18, 1985, p. 1.

21. Testimony by Secretary Shultz at hearings of Senate Foreign Relations Committee, February 27, 1986, p. 11; "Shultz Assails Nicaragua in Asking Aid for Rebels," David K. Shipler, NYT, February 28, 1986, p. A6.

22. Peter W. Rodman, *More Precious than Peace: The Cold War and the Struggle for the Third World* (New York, 1994), p. 412.

23. Author's interview with Bruce Cameron April 19, 1991.

24. Evidence of this came in the summer of 1986, when Congress designated the State Department, i.e., Abrams, as overall policy coordinator of the $100 million contra program.

25. On November 26, 1985, Congressman Richardson published an angry editorial in the *New York Times*. He had been bombarded by criticisms from church groups in his district after his vote for contra aid in June: "My switch disappointed my constituents, my colleagues, even my wife and sister. . . . I have since been plagued by second thoughts." The situation in Central America had grown worse, he complained, not better. "What I had hoped to do with my vote was signal the Sandinistas that they must take the peace process seriously. I wanted them to know that progressive Democrats like myself were eager for them to mend their undemocratic ways." Since his hopes had not been realized, Richardson favored an end to all aid for the contras and an effort by the Reagan administration to seek peace with Nicaragua. President Reagan, he argued, had not "stuck to his part of the bargain" and had to be "convinced that arming the contras, directly or indirectly, is not the answer, and that actively promoting a peace process is more critical." "Bridging the Gap with Nicaragua," Bill Richardson, NYT, November 26, 1985.

26. Letter to the President from Congressman Jim Slattery (D-KS) et al., February 3, 1986, reprinted in CR, February 5, 1986, pp. 1770–71. In March, the presidents of the five Central American countries were supposed to meet for a new round of negotiations. Actually, the meeting did not occur until May.

27. "Against Arms for the 'Contras,'" Dave McCurdy, NYT, February 5, 1986, p. A27.

28. Richardson, "Bridging the Gap with Nicaragua." As the contras withdrew in droves from Nicaragua, Richardson wrote, "Mr. Ortega surely must recognize that Nicaragua is growing more and more isolated and that the contras are growing stronger."

29. Formed in the summer of 1985 to add mom"mentum to the stalled negotiations. The Support Group included Peru, Uruguay, Argentina, and Brazil.

30. "The Caraballeda Message Toward Central America's Peace, Security, and Democracy," printed in Report of the Committee on Foreign Affairs, U.S. House of Representatives on H. Con. Res. 283, entitled "Supporting the Contadora Process," February 26, 1986, pp. 54–57.

31. The Sandinistas only had to begin a "progressive reduction" in foreign military advisers, renew negotiations in Contadora, make a commitment to "avoid aggression" along with the other Central American countries, and "freez[e] the purchase of weapons." This latter requirement did not address the weapons already "purchased" and in the pipeline, not to mention those not "purchased" at all, like most of the weapons provided by the Soviet bloc.

Theoretically, the proposal also called on the Sandinistas to stop aiding the guerrillas in El Salvador, but since the Sandinistas officially denied doing so, and since the cessation of such support was to take place before signature of the treaty that was supposed to verify such a cessation, the only consequence of the injunction to cease aiding guerrillas in the region was to block the American aid to the contras about to be voted upon openly by the U.S. Congress.

32. MDS 1800 GMT 6 Feb 86, "D'Escoto Sends Note to Contadora, Support Groups," FBIS, VI. 7 Feb 86, P8.

33. "Against Arms for the 'Contras,'" Dave McCurdy, NYT, February 5, 1986 p. A27.

34. Testimony by Secretary Shultz at hearings of Senate Foreign Relations Committee, February 27, 1986.

35. In the Republican ranks alone, they claimed, some 40 northern and midwestern moderates were "solid" against the aid proposal. If even 20 of these actually voted against the President, the Democrats had only to keep defections from their own ranks below 55. "U.S. Plan for Contra Military Aid Condemned by House Democrats," NYT, February 21, 1986, p. A4.

36. "Inside the White House Contra Aid Command Post," David Hoffman, WP, March 18, 1986.

37. "The Contras Need Our Help," Patrick J. Buchanan, WP, March 5, 1986, p. A19.

38. "Reagan Steps Up His Drive to Give $100 Million to Nicaragua Rebels," Bernard Weinraub, NYT, March 6, 1986, p. A1.

39. "Mudslinging over Contras," R.W. Apple, NYT, March 12, 1986, p. A5.

40. See "Reagan's Resolve: Contra Aid a Must," Bernard Weinraub, NYT, March 7, 1986, p. A6; and "2 House Units Bar Contra Aid Plan And One Backs It," Steven V. Roberts, NYT, March 7, 1986, p. A1.

41. Statement by Senator Nancy Kassebaum, CQ, March 8, 86, p. 536.

42. CQ, March 22, 1986, p. 650.

43. "Intense Lobbying Efforts Focus on Swing Votes," Edward Walsh, WP, March 18, 1986, p. A1.

44. "White House Raises Stakes as Contra Vote Looms—Key House Members Still Unpersuaded," Milton Coleman and Edward Walsh, WP, March 9, 1986.

45. "Reagan Sees a 'Moral Obligation' by U.S. to Aid Nicaraguan Rebels," Gerald M. Boyd, NYT, March 11, 1986, p. A1.

46. NYT, March 7, 1986.

47. Ibid.

48. "Reagan Aides Open Compromise Talks on Aiding Contras," Bernard Weinraub, NYT, March 9, 1986. p. 1.

49. CQ, March 15, 1986, p. 600.

50. "2 in Congress Offer Compromise Plans on Aid to Nicaraguan Rebels," Steven V. Roberts, NYT, March 13, 1986, p. A4.

51. Quoted by Congressman Michel, CR, March 19, 1986, p. H1325. Habib told Senator Lugar that the Sandinistas would not involve themselves in useful negotiations unless Congress approved military aid. Richard Lugar, *Letters to the Next President* (New York, 1988), p. 195.

52. Reagan made this statement only indirectly, allegedly quoting the comments of Clare Booth Luce before her death.

53. Speech by President Reagan on March 16, 1986. Reprinted in CQ, March 22, 1986, pp. 671–73.

54. Democratic response to President Reagan's March 16 address, delivered by Senator Sasser, reprinted in CQ, March 22, 1986, p. 672.

55. An ABC poll on the day of the speech showed 30 percent in favor and 54 percent opposed to the aid; on March 25 it was 42 percent and 53 percent.

56. "Intense Lobbying Efforts Focus on Swing Votes," Edward Walsh, WP, March 18, 1986, p. A1; CQ, March 22, 1986, p. 651.

57. Congressman Breaux, a Democrat from Louisiana who supported contra aid but was no hard-core conservative, told reporters that the selection of Habib was a "very important and very positive move" which had "picked up some votes" for the President. "Party Leaders Say Reagan Will Have to Accept Deal on Nicaragua," Steven V. Roberts, NYT, March 12, 1986, p. A4.

58. CQ, March 22, 1986, p. 649. According to Arnson, O'Neill "saw that he needed the votes of the Democratic moderates to beat the president's proposal." Cynthia J. Arnson *Crossroads: Congress, the Reagan Administration, and Central America* (New York, 1989), p. 193.

59. CQ, March 22, 1986, p. 651.

60. As Cynthia Arnson puts it, O'Neill and the House leadership had been reduced to devising "narrow tactical maneuvers" to hold the moderates without "push[ing] the liberal wing into open rebellion." Arnson, p. 190.

61. "Reagan Reported to Lack 10 Votes on Aid to Rebels," Steven V. Roberts, NYT, March 19, 1986, p. A1.

62. CQ, March 22, 1986, p. 650.

63. "Reagan Defeated in House on Aiding Nicaragua Rebels," Steven V. Roberts, NYT, March 21, 1986, p. A1.

64. CQ, March 22, 1986, p. 650. Rowland once told Republican supporters in his district who questioned his lack of ideological consistency, "Unless you can vote three times, I need Democrats and independents to win." See CQ, January 5, 1985, p. 15.

65. CQ, March 22, 1986, p. 650.

Chapter 39

1. MDS 1736 GMT 5 Apr 86, "Humberto Ortega Discusses Military Struggle," FBIS, VI. 8 Apr 86, P15.

2. "U.S. Army Copters Carry Hondurans to Border Region," James LeMoyne, NYT, March 27, 1986, p. A1.

3. The contra forces had just been re-supplied and were preparing to enter Nicaragua when the attack came. Ibid.

4. Ibid.

5. See testimony of Elliott Abrams at a hearing of the Western Hemisphere Subcommittee of the House Foreign Affairs Committee, April 8, 1986, p. 34.

6. NYT, March 27, 1986.

7. "Honduran Troops Sent to Nicaraguan Border," AP, NYT, March 20, 1986, p. A8.

8. See State Department briefing paper, "Chronology Of Nicaraguan Incursion into Honduras, March 1986," submitted at a hearing of the Western Hemisphere Subcommittee of the House Foreign Affairs Committee, April 8, 1986, p. 9.

9. On March 21 Abrams and Galvin, the head of U.S. forces in Panama, had traveled to Tegucigalpa where Honduran officials, according to Abrams, asked "whether the commitment that the President had made to former President Suazo [after the previous year's incursion] . . . was still binding." American and Honduran military officials discussed "likely Honduran emergency requirements in the event of a Sandinista attack," including the possibility of emergency aid under the 506(a) provision. Honduran military officials, recalling their difficulties the previous year in transporting forces rapidly to the front, discussed the need for American assistance in providing airlift in the event of a crisis. National Securiy Adviser Poindexter informed Reagan that "in Honduras, we are prepared to provide expedited and, if necessary, enhanced secu-

rity assistance to deal with their border problem." See ibid; testimony of Elliott Abrams at a hearing of the Western Hemisphere Subcommittee of the House Foreign Affairs Committee, April 8, 1986, p. 14; and Memorandum from John M. Poindexter to President Reagan, March 20, 1986, I-C exhibit OLN-274.

10. "Honduran Peasants Confirm Report of Battle," James LeMoyne, NYT, March 28, 1986, p. A1; Managua International Service 0200 GMT 23 Mar 86, "Honduran Army Units Reportedly on Alert," FBIS, VI. 24 Mar 86, P16.

11. See testimony of Elliott Abrams at a hearing of the Western Hemisphere Subcommittee of the House Foreign Affairs Committee, April 8, 1986, p. 34.

12. Transcript of White House Press Briefing, March 25, 1986, p. 3.

13. The *New York Times'* headline on March 25 was "Hondurans Meeting Amid U.S. Reports of Nicaraguan Raid."

14. On March 24 President Azcona's spokesman told reporters "at this time we know nothing about these reports," and the Honduran foreign minister, Carlos Lopez Contreras, repeated that "we know nothing official at this time." "Hondurans Meeting Amid U.S. Reports of Nicaraguan Raid," by Stephen Kinzer, NYT, March 25, 1986, p. A1.

15. On March 25 President Azcona announced on Honduran radio and television that an incursion into Honduran territory had indeed occurred, involving approximately 1,500 Sandinista troops, and that he had therefore asked the United States for assistance and would do so again when "necessary to defend the nation." (See transcript of hearing of the Western Hemisphere Subcommittee of the House Foreign Affairs Committee, April 8, 1986, p. 34.)

The next day, his foreign minister, Carlos Lopez Contreras, told CBS evening news that the Nicaraguan incursion did "not represent a major threat to the security of Honduras." "The U.S. Denies Putting Pressure on Hondurans," Bernard Gwertzman, NYT, April 4, 1986, p. A1.

16. See "Honduras Tells of U.S. Pressure," James LeMoyne, NYT, April 3, 1986, p. A1.

17. Ibid.

18. At the insistence of Abrams, however, the American ambassador in Honduras told Azcona "you don't have a choice now." See Roy Gutman, *Banana Diplomacy* (New York, 1988), pp. 324–25.

19. The American ambassador in Honduras, John Ferch, was ill and in bed on March 24 and 25. Deputy Assistant Secretary William Walker shouted over the telephone to the embassy's chargé d'affaires: "You have got to tell them to declare there was an incursion." See Gutman, p. 324.

20. See transcript of hearing of the Western Hemisphere Subcommittee of the House Foreign Affairs Committee, April 8, 1986, p. 27.

21. See State Department briefing paper, "Chronology of Nicaraguan Incursion into Honduras, March 1986," submitted at a hearing of the Western Hemisphere Subcommittee of the House Foreign Affairs Committee, April 8, 1986.

22. "U.S. Army Copters Carry Hondurans to Border Region," James LeMoyne, NYT, March 27, 1986, p. A1. See also Frank McNeil, *War and Peace in Central America: Reality and Illusion* (New York, 1988), p. 224. In his memoirs, McNeil is highly critical of most aspects of the Reagan administration's policy in Nicaragua, including its actions in response to the incursion. In recounting the errors he believes the Reagan administration made, however, he becomes confused. On the one hand, he writes critically that "twice, in the spring of 1986 and the spring of 1988, the administration rushed to bail out the Sandinistas by hype and overreaction, making our Honduran ally look bad in the process." On the other hand, his next sentence states that "on an earlier occasion, the administration did something sensible, and used U.S. helicopters to ferry Honduran troops to remote border areas, a signal to the Sandinistas to clear out, which they did." McNeil may be referring to the use of American helicopters to ferry Hon-

duran troops in December 1986. In both March and December of 1986, however, American actions had the same effect on the Sandinistas, causing them to call off their attacks and retreat back across the border. See McNeil, p. 224. Accounts of this episode have been filled with errors or unfounded assertions. Roy Gutman writes that "the Honduran army refused even to call a state of alert" after the incursion (p. 324), but the Honduran armed forces were placed on alert on March 19 when they first detected Sandinista military activities near the border. When the immediate danger of an attack on March 21 in the Choluteca region appeared to pass, the air force alone remained on alert. Gutman makes no mention of the Nicaraguan-Honduran border tensions in the days leading up to the incursion.

Gutman writes that the fighting in Honduras lasted "two to three hours" (p. 324), a statement contradicted by numerous accounts of the fighting, from Honduran and American officials, from journalists like LeMoyne who interviewed local peasants, and even from experts called to testify before Congress against the administration. Professor Richard Millet, a consistent critic of this and other Reagan administration polices in Latin America, testified at the April 8 hearings that the fighting lasted "several days." (See transcript of April 8 hearings, p. 56.)

The Majority Report of the Committees Investigating Iran-Contra, in addition to erroneously declaring that the Sandinista troops had "pursued Contra fighters into Honduras," which the Sandinistas themselves contradicted, also states that the Sandinista troops "began to retreat across the border by March 24 . . . and were back in Nicaragua before President Reagan signed the authorization for emergency military assistance [on March 25]," (p. 382.) a statement which, like Gutman's, is contradicted by most accounts of the fighting.

Gutman, in a continuing effort to attribute almost all actions by the Reagan administration which he deems controversial to the hidden power of Oliver North, writes that Elliott Abrams's mission to Honduras on March 21 "was apparently thought up by North." (p. 324.) He deduces this from the fact that North drafted the memorandum from Poindexter to Reagan explaining the purpose of the mission. He does not mention, however, that the decision to send Abrams and Galvin was taken at a meeting of the National Security Planning Group (NSPG), although Poindexter's memo states this. The NSPG was a group of the highest-level officials from all the agencies concerned with national security and usually included the secretaries of state and defense, the director of the CIA, the Vice President, and the assistant to the President for National Security Affairs, in this case Poindexter. The fact that North drafted Poindexter's memo to the President is meaningless. North was probably Poindexter's notetaker at the NSPG meeting. The decision to send Abrams and Galvin to Central America was most likely that of the President's senior foreign policy advisers.

23. "Nicaragua Reports Successes," NYT, March 28, 1986, p. A1.

24. "Nicaragua Leader Warns of Risks in Use of U.S. Forces in Honduras," Stephen Kinzer, NYT, March 29, 1986, p. 1.

25. Tegucigalpa Cadena Audio Video 1227 GMT 3 Apr 86, "Ortega Discusses Contras, Recent Border Incident," FBIS, VI. 4 Apr 86, P5.

26. At a stormy committee hearing on April 8, long after the Sandinistas had acknowledged their actions and intentions in the incursion, Congressman Peter Kostmayer railed at Elliott Abrams for his "audacity and the audacity of this administration. I just spent a week in my congressional district where an increasingly large number of people are coming to regard the administration as simply being entirely untruthful on this matter." See statement of Congressman Kostmayer (D-PA) at a hearing of the Western Hemisphere Subcommittee of the House Foreign Affairs Committee, April 8, 1986, p. 28.

27. This allegation was repeated years later in the Majority Report of the Iran-Contra Committees, see p. 382. Among other facts ignored was that four days in advance of the attack the Nicaraguan government had closed border and customs posts and instructed truck drivers

to move at least eight kilometers back from the Honduran border. Honduran authorities, in response, had evacuated residents of El Espino and forbidden journalists from entering the area. See Panama City ACAN 2221 GMT 22 Mar 86, "Commercial Trucks Backed Up at Nicaraguan Border," FBIS, VI. 24 Mar 86, P11.

28. CQ Almanac 1986, p. 402.

29. "No responsible country," he declared, could "negotiate matters related to the purchase of the necessary means for its defense, or the restriction of these, under circumstances of aggression." MRS 1200 GMT 8 Apr 86, "D'Escoto Says U.S. Blocking Peace Efforts," FBIS, VI. 9 Apr 86, P16.

30. MDS 1232 GMT 12 Apr 86, "President Oretga Issues Message on Contadora," FBIS, VI 14 Apr 86, P14.

31. Tunnerman predicted on April 15 that the President would indeed "obtain some kind of aid during these debates." MDS 1426 GMT 15 Apr 86, "Ambassador to U.S. on Contra Aid Debates," FBIS, VI. 17 Apr 86, P12.

32. Emphasis added. Ibid.

33. The three Democrats were Congressmen Barnes, Richardson, and Slattery, all opponents of military aid to the contras. Quoted in Cynthia J. Arnson, *Crossroads: Congress, the Reagan Administration, and Central America* (New York, 1989), p. 196.

34. According to the *Congressional Quarterly*, O'Neill was angry after an administration official had leaked a cable from the American ambassador in Argentina criticizing O'Neill's behavior. This explanation is plausible but unnecessary. O'Neill had promised to attach McCurdy's bill to the supplemental and was fulfilling that promise. It wasn't O'Neill's fault that Reagan wanted to veto the supplemental, and it wasn't his job to make it easy for McCurdy to pass contra aid, which O'Neill vehemently opposed. As a small concession to McCurdy, the Speaker left open the possibility of detaching the contra aid bill from the supplemental if the latter were defeated, but then the McCurdy measure would once more lack a vehicle.

35. "Democrats' Fear of Voting," Mary McGrory, WP, April 13, 1986.

36. CQ, April 19, 1986, pp. 835–6.

37. CQ, April 19, 1986, p. 837.

Chapter 40

1. Managua International Service 0015 GMT 22 Apr 86, "Further Ortega Contadora, U.S. 'Aggression' Remarks," FBIS, VI. 22 Apr 86, P13.

2. The letter added that the administration "would not feel politically bound to respect an agreement that Nicaragua was violating." Letter to Congressmen Barnes, Richardson, and Slattery from Philip Habib, April 11, 1986, AFPD, 1986. Doc. 458.

3. Constantine C. Menges, *Inside the National Security Council* (New York, 1988), p. 296.

4. "The Contadora Treaty? Communists Don't Comply," Jeane Kirkpatrick, WP, May 26, 1986, p. A21.

5. Statement read by Larry Speakes, May 22, 1986, AFPD, 1986. Doc 459. See also "Honduran Doubts Nearness of Central American Treaty," Linda Greenhouse, NYT, May 23, 1986, p. A6.

6. "Habib Called Wrong, Imprecise, in Letter on U.S. Latin Policy," Joanne Omang, WP, May 24, 1986. Actually, Abrams's suggested change was impossible in the context of the Habib letter. The Contadora draft could not be interpreted to mean that support for insurgents would cease upon "implementation" of the treaty. The political turmoil created by the Habib letter could only have been avoided if the State Department officials had not tried to interpret the Contadora treaty at all but merely stated American policy.

7. CQ, May 31, 1986, p. 1224.

8. Menges, p. 296.

9. "Pentagon Fears Major War If Latins Sign Peace Accord," Leslie H. Gelb, NYT, May 20, 1986, p. A1.

10. "They Were Expendable," William Safire, NYT, May 26, 1986, p. A19.

11. Managua International Service 0440 GMT 25 Apr 86, "Ortega Speaks on Regional Issues, U.S. Role," FBIS, VI. 25 Apr 86, P2.

12. Mexico City EXCELSIOR 27 Apr 86, pp. 1, 10–11, "Excelsior Interviews President Ortega," FBIS, VI. 20 May 86, P12.

13. Constantine Menges predicted that "Mexico would use this gathering of heads of state to propagandize for its phony treaty." Menges, p. 294.

14. Managua Radio Noticias 1200 GMT 6 May 86, "Security Cited on Ortega's Absence from Inaugural," FBIS, VI. 7 May 86, P3.

15. "Nicaragua Balks at Latin Peace Accord," Stephen Kinzer, NYT, May 15, 1986, p. A8.

16. "Dates have been set on previous occasions and expectations were created, and then this gives the image that the negotiations are not progressing." Paris AFP 2016 GMT 10 May 86, "Ortega Qualifies Agreement with Contadora Act," FBIS, VI. 13 May 86, P13.

17. Paris AFP 2016 GMT 10 May 86, "Ortega Qualifies Agreement with Contadora Act," FBIS, VI. 13 May 86, P13; Panama City ACAN 1944 GMT 12 May 86, "Ortega Receives Soviet, Other Delegations," FBIS, VI. 14 May 86, P8.

18. Paris AFP 2207 GMT 14 May 86, FBIS, VI. 15 May 86, P5.

19. MB (Special Supplement) 10 Oct 85, pp. 1–14, "H. Ortega Interviewed on U.S. Policy, Contras," FBIS, VI. 28 Oct 85, P19–P34.

20. CR, April 16, 1986, p. H1874.

21. See the account of the meeting between Reagan and President Miguel de la Madrid on January 2, 1986, "Reagan Sees Mexican Today; Nicaragua May Be on Agenda," William Stockton, NYT, January 3, 1986, p. A4. Although the Mexican government's position, stated many times by Foreign Minister Sepulveda, was that the United States should talk directly to the Sandinistas and end aid to the contras, de la Madrid appears to have avoided such requests in his meeting with Reagan.

22. MB (Special Supplement) 10 Oct 85, pp. 1–14, "H. Ortega Interviewed On U.S. Policy, Contras," FBIS, VI. 28 Oct 85, P19–P34.

23. MDS 1225 GMT 19 May 86, "Ortega Comments on Panama Negotiations," FBIS, VI. 21 May 86, P7.

24. As Daniel Ortega put it, "Let us see what armaments can be described as offensive weapons and then let us negotiate regarding the offensive weapons. But we cannot negotiate the defensive weapons." Offensive weapons, as the Sandinistas defined it, were advanced fighter aircraft like those in the Honduran arsenal. The Sandinistas' extensive supply of tanks and attack helicopters, however, were defensive. MDS 1225 GMT 19 May 86, "Ortega Comments on Panama Negotiations," FBIS, VI. 21 May 86, P7; Panama City ACAN 2128 GMT 17 May 86, "Officials Discuss Posture on Contadora," FBIS, VI. 19 May 86, P5.

25. Menges repeats this prediction, retrospectively, in a book written several years later. For some reason he includes this "prediction" without commenting on the fact that events did not unfold as he claims to have feared. Menges, p. 294.

26. Managua International Service 2317 GMT 26 May 86, "Ortega Discusses Esquipulas Summit Meeting," FBIS, VI. 27 May 86, P10.

27. MDS 1200 GMT 3 Jun 86, "Ortega Blames U.S. for Contadora 'Sabotage,'" FBIS, VI. 5 Jun 86, P16.

28. Panama City ACAN 1458 GMT 5 Jun 86, "D'Escoto: U.S. 'Wants to Impose' Democracy," FBIS, VI. 6 Jun 86, P7.

29. "Set Own Pace, U.S. Tells Latin Chiefs," Gerald M. Boyd, NYT, May 28, 1986, p. A3.

Chapter 41

1. CR, June 25, 1986, p. H4262.

2. CR, June 25, 1986, p. H4238.

3. For Arias's rebellion, see below, pp. 500–506. See statement by Congresswoman Snowe. CR, June 25, 1986, H4270.

4. CR, June 25, 1986, p. H4248.

5. Notes of meetings provided to author by Bruce Cameron.

6. Cerezo said, "If they don't accept pluralism, we are going to have problems still. . . . We should establish Central American control of elections." And Duarte said, "We (the four elected presidents) all believe Central America will not have peace unless all five countries are democracies."

7. Unpublished memoirs of Bruce Cameron, provided to the author by Mr. Cameron. Chapter 7, p. 19.

8. Ibid. p. 20.

9. CR, June 25, 1986, p. H4262.

10. The four were Bustamante, Snowe, Ray, and Rowland. Congressman Frenzel was apparently persuaded by Ray and Snowe to support the $100 million.

11. See Cameron, Chapter 7, p. 21. "After what he saw and heard on his trip, he believed he could and should make a deal with the Administration and the Republican leadership exclusively."

12. See statement of Congressman Carper, for instance, CR, June 25, 1986, p. H4242.

13. Edgar Chamorro had criticized Calero after he was pushed aside in the FDN leadership, but except for confirmed critics of the contras, Chamorro's criticisms of Calero had little impact in the United States.

14. "Nicaragua Guerrillas Ponder Chances without U.S. Help," James Lemoyne, NYT, March 18, 1985, p. A1.

15. "Contras Debate How to Widen Group's Appeal," James LeMoyne, NYT, May 23, 1986, p. A1; "Rift Develops within Nicaraguan Rebel Group," Dennis Vollman, *Christian Science Monitor*, October 15, 1985, p. 1. When Cruz's supporters launched their campaign for contra reform through the press, Bruce Cameron recalls, "Our reporters of choice were James LeMoyne of the *New York Times* and Dennis Vollman of the *Christian Science Monitor*." Cameron, Chapter 3, p. 23.

16. As Arturo Cruz, Jr., wrote at the beginning of 1986, the creation of UNO so far had only conferred "legitimacy on the operation, not even of the FDN as such, but on the operation of Calero as the new *caudillo.* . . . What has prevailed by force of arms is Calero's *caudillismo.*" Cruz, unpublished notes.

17. NYT, May 23, 1986.

18. For instance, Owen noted that NHAO was putting money in dollars into the FDN's Miami accounts, leaving the FDN to convert it into Honduran lempiras. Suppliers were paid according to the official exchange rate of 2 to 1, but the black market rate was 2.75 to 1, leaving about a 37 percent profit. "Adolfo admitted to [NHAO Director Robert] Duemling . . . he is splitting this 50–50 with Aquiles Marín, and A[dolfo] C[alero]'s share is going to the war effort. Would you by chance know who Aquiles Marín is?" See Owen letter to North, March 17, 1986, NSA Doc (2493).

19. Ibid.

20. Unpublished Penn Kemble and Bruce Cameron paper, strongly influenced by Arturo Cruz, Jr., entitled "From a Proxy Force to a National Liberation Movement."

21. "Dispute Hampers Nicaragua Rebels," James LeMoyne, NYT, Nov 4, 1985, p. A1.

22. All funds received by the contras, both public and private, were to be placed in a common UNO account, rather than in bank accounts controlled by Calero; a new secretary general of UNO was to be appointed, replacing the Calero ally then in that job, and the powers of the secretary general were to be expanded; Calero's FDN representative in Washington was to be replaced by a Cruz loyalist, an UNO official, and transferred out of the country; and Cruz was to be named "Coordinator" of UNO.

23. Cameron, chapter 5, pp. 6–8.

24. Ibid., p. 11.

25. Ibid., pp. 6–8.

26. Ibid.

27. At one point Bermúdez told his troops not to worry about any agreements he might make with the new political organization because they meant nothing. Unfortunately for Bermúdez, his comments were taped by a journalist and quickly became public. See Cameron, chapter 4, p. 3.

28. Cameron, chapter 6, p. 3.

29. Once negotiations had begun, if Abrams decided after 30 days that the FDN was not negotiating in good faith, then the FDN would face another cutoff. See "Contras' Backers Lose a Close Vote on House Debate," Jonathan Fuerbringer, NYT, April 16, 1986, p. A1; and Cameron, chapter 6, pp. 5–6.

30. Cameron memorandum of conversation, July 1, 1986.

31. "In those staff meetings," Bruce Cameron later recalled, "Cruz's two assistants felt powerless to insist upon their positions. They saw their man as someone who would quit, leaving them with no position. Thus the FDN representatives easily outmaneuvered them." Cameron, chapter 6, pp. 6–7.

32. Ibid.

33. Another view is that Robelo may have aspired to a stronger position within the Directorate. R. Pardo-Maurer, an UNO official from 1986–88, later wrote: "Robelo . . . could at times derive an advantage by steering an intermediate position and thus on more than one occasion undercut Cruz. His actions were as compatible with a view that the pace of reform should be cautiously managed as with the hope that the two heavyweights would knock each other out, leaving the ring to himself." R. Pardo-Maurer, *The Contras, 1980–1989* (New York, 1990), p. 56.

34. Reagan officials told him to settle the differences with Cruz, "or we'll have to work it out for you." "Contras' Centrists Said to Gain Power," Julia Preston, WP, May 29, 1986.

35. Cameron, chapter 6, pp. 6–7.

36. Panama City ACAN 0141 GMT 30 May 86, "Details of Contra Reorganization Outlined," FBIS, VI. 30 May 86, P10.

37. "Basic Accords of the United Nicaraguan Opposition," May 29, 1986.

38. "Contras See a Long-Term Need for Aid," James LeMoyne, NYT, May 30, 1986, p. A3.

39. See Memorandum from Bruce Cameron to Spitz Channel, July 2, 1986, Iran-Contra Channel deposition exhibit, p. 585. Congressman Ray was "an absolute tiger on contra reform. He personally went to Miami to evaluate the outcome of the contra meetings."

40. CQ, May 24, 1986, p. 1167; speech by Senator Richard G. Lugar at the National Press Club, June 17, 1986. Reprinted in CR, June 19, 1986, p. S7981.

41. "Rivalry Threatening to Split Contras," James LeMoyne, NYT, May 16, 1986, p. A3.

Chapter 42

1. Their consolation was that they could vote against military aid on the second vote 90 days later.

2. The GAO, examining subpoenaed bank records of the NHAO suppliers and distributors, still could not account for substantial amounts of money which the NHAO director insisted had gone for supplies to the contras. Checks written to the Honduran Armed Forces chief and other local officials in the amounts of several hundred thousand dollars also raised eyebrows and spurred charges of illegal behavior. NHAO officials insisted that almost all goods paid for arrived in the hands of contras, monitored by the CIA, and the GAO report stated only that NHAO could not prove where the money had gone. Nevertheless, many congressmen, those who supported contra aid as well as those who opposed it, were angered by the discrepancies.

3. CR, June 25, 1986, p. H4271.

4. Ibid., p. H4268–9.

5. Ibid., p. H4238. In the Skelton-Edwards amendment, Reagan supporters had agreed not to release larger weapons until after the presidential determination in February. According to McCurdy's bill, the President would be free to introduce the so-called "heavy weapons" if Congress approved the aid in October.

6. After the vote, McCurdy told reporters that "the second vote in October was probably what killed it. People don't want to vote on this in October, before the election. They want to get it behind them." See "Reagan Allies in Vote Were Compromise, Fatigue," Edward Walsh, WP, June 27, 1986.

7. "[W]e have had plenty of votes and plenty of debate already," Congressman Frenzel of Minnesota complained. "We ought to move on to other business." CR, June 25, 1986, p. H4245.

8. CR, June 25, 1986, p. H4270.

9. See remarks of Congressman Carper (D-DE), who voted against the Skelton-Edwards amendment and against the Hamilton amendment. CR, June 25, 1986, pp. H4241–2.

10. McCurdy told Bruce Cameron he believed "the bill as passed was okay and he was satisfied." Cameron, chapter 7, p. 29. The ever-skeptical Cameron, who supported McCurdy's bill and opposed Skelton-Edwards, goes on to write: "I agreed, but neither of us believed our own words. We had too much experience with the Administration."

11. See, in particular, the interesting study of congressional votes on contra aid by William M. Leogrande and Philip Brenner, "The House Divided: Ideological Polarization over Aid to the Nicaraguan 'Contras,'" *Legislative Studies Quarterly*, Vol. 18, No. 1 (February 1993), pp. 105–36.

12. "Senate Approves Reagan's Request to Help Contras," Steven V. Roberts, NYT, March 28, 1986, p. A1.

13. "Nicaragua at Top of List for Return of Congress Tomorrow," Steven V. Roberts, NYT, April 7, 1986, p. A11.

14. "Reagan Rallied for Aid Till the Hill Surrendered," Joanne Omang, WP, January 2, 1987, p. A1.

15. A March 6 poll showed 47–34 approved of Reagan's handling of the "situation in Central America," compared with 40–47 in May 1985; the same poll showed 37–47 approval of Reagan's handling of Nicaragua. ABC News Poll, quoted in CR, June 25, 1986, p. H4274–5.

16. "Robb Recommends 'Tough Diplomacy,'" Phil Gailey, NYT, May 7, 1986, p. A26.

17. "Bradley and His Interest in Foreign Affairs," Jonathan Fuerbringer, NYT, April 20, 1986, p. A56.

18. CQ, June 28, 1986, p. 1443.

19. CR, June 25, 1986, p. H4248.

Chapter 43

1. For information on the purchase of airplanes, see Richard Gadd deposition, pp. 219, 231. [Depositions, testimonies, and exhibits in the following notes refer to the Report of the Congressional Committees Investigating the Iran-Contra Affair. Some documents are contained in the collection produced by the National Security Archives (NSA), *The Making of U.S. Policy: Nicaragua, 1978–1990* (Washington, 1991).]

2. North arranged for an alternative means of delivery twice in April, asking a Southern Air Transport pilot to fly military supplies to southern Front forces after completing a delivery in the north for NHAO. See Gadd deposition, pp. 33–35; also Exhibit OLN-88.

3. Secord testimony, 5/5/87, 64.

4. Dutton deposition, p. 471.

5. Message from North to Fortier, April 21, 1986. Exhibit OLN-5.

6. See Cruz's list of demands in early 1986, as recorded in Cameron, chapter 3, pp. 21–22.

7. See cable from the CIA's Central American Task Force (hereafter C/CATF). March 15, 1986. Exhibit 21. See also Memorandum from Owen to North, March 28, 1986, NSA Doc. (002558).

8. "Contras Expecting Showdown on Feud," James LeMoyne, NYT, May 11, 1986, p. 3.

9. "Rivalry Threatening to Split Contras," James LeMoyne, NYT, May 16, 1986, p. A3.

10. See North message to Secord, April 8, 1986. Exhibit OLN-88.

11. Secord later testified that "the FDN were husbanding their limited resources very tightly and didn't seem to want to donate any of their ammunition, weapons, communications, food, and so forth, uniforms to the southern front. So we were forced to buy some limited quantities of arms which we flew to El Salvador from Portugal and stored in a warehouse there for air drop purposes." Secord testimony, p. 63. Owen reported to North on March 28 that Aristides Sanchez, Calero's lieutenant, "did not want to supply the South" and had blocked the release of supplies for that purpose. Owen concluded that "the FDN cannot be relied on to provide material in a timely manner [to the southern front.]" See Memorandum from Owen to North, March 28, 1986, NSA Doc (002558).

12. Calero testimony, 5/20/87, 40–42.

13. North message dated April 21, 1986. Exhibit OLN-5.

14. In March Rob Owen reported to North that Secord's operation was "now openly discussed on the street" in Central America, and allegations about corruption and incompetence in the new resupply effort were widespread. Letter from Owen to North, March 17, 1986. Exhibit RWO-13.

15. Calero testimony, 5/20/87, 40–42.

16. See testimony of Alan Fiers, 8/5/87, 49–50.

17. PROF note (inter-office communication) from Poindexter to Don Fortier, May 2, 1986. Exhibit JMP-5. It is not clear that Reagan was referring in his comments to North's diversion scheme. Indeed, Poindexter's message raises doubts about whether President Reagan had seen and approved North's "diversion" memo (see below), which was drafted at the beginning of April.

18. Notes from NSPG meeting on May 16, 1986, paraphrased by Mr. Belnick, Abrams testimony, 6/2/87, 103–10.

19. Fiers testimony, 8/5/87, 49–50. Fiers later testified: "That was the option I was pushing. I pushed that very hard. I said, let's go to the committees, let's go to Congress, let's tell them our problem."

20. Shultz testimony, 7/23/87, 43–46; Fiers recalls Casey telling him after the meeting, "I'm not going to break my pick on that one, I'm sorry." See Fiers testimony, 8/5/87, 49–50.

21. Burghardt memorandum for McDaniel, "Minutes of the May 16, 1986 National Security Planning Group Meeting," [Iran-Contra Committee Documents N 10288 through 10299, at N 10298].

22. Presumably, if there had been a response by someone, this would have come out in the Iran-contra hearings, where this meeting was covered in some detail.

23. Minutes of NSPG Meeting of May 16, 1986, quoted by Arthur Liman in Poindexter Senate Deposition, pp. 311–13. Shultz later commented on his change of heart from two years earlier, when he had opposed seeking aid from other countries: "The whole atmosphere had changed. Congressional attitudes had changed. And so I thought under those circumstances, it was perfectly proper to do it, in fact, perhaps even desirable if we could do it in the right way." Shultz testimony, 7/23/87, 43–46.

24. It has never been established that President Reagan ever actually saw the "diversion memo." It has, therefore, been impossible to establish Reagan's awareness of the Iran-contra connection.

25. PROF message from North to Poindexter, May 16, 1986. Exhibit JMP-51.

26. PROF message from Poindexter to North, June 1986. Exhibit JMP-52.

27. See Hakim deposition, pp. 437, 508.

28. Ibid., pp. 407–8.

29. Hakim testimony, 6/3/87, 222; Hakim deposition, pp. 407–408.

30. Secord claimed that the $2 million was to insure future planes that would be used in ongoing arms sales to Iran. Hakim characterized the money as a "reserve." The counsel for the Senate investigating committee, Arthur Liman, tried to suggest that it was really just profit.

31. Message from North to McFarlane, April 21, 1986. Exhibit OLN-4.

32. Message from Secord to North, April 21, 1986. Exhibit RVS-3.

33. See composite of ledgers from CSF, the company Hakim used to manage the accounts. Exhibit OLN-17.

34. Hakim deposition, p. 499.

35. As Secord testified, "There were a lot of big, big maintenance problems with the aircraft that were not anticipated, which, of course, caused the expenditure of a lot more money for spare parts than had been anticipated." Secord testimony, 5/5/87, p. 64.

36. Secord testimony, 5/7/87, pp. 176–77.

37. As Secord later testified, "So, we sweated and spent a lot of money for nothing over a long period of time." Secord testimony, 5/5/87, 62.

38. See Tambs testimony, 5/28/87, pp. 172, 236, 264.

39. According to flight logs. See I-C Report, Table 3.1, pp. 79–81.

40. See Dutton deposition, p. 493. See also the report prepared in the summer of 1986 by Robert C. Dutton. Exhibit RCD-14.

41. North message to Poindexter, July 15, 1986. Exhibit OLN-198. "All seriously believe that immediately after the Senate vote the DRF [Democratic Resistance Forces, i.e., contras] will be subjected to a major Sandinista effort to break them before the U.S. aid can become effective."

42. And Secord never did buy the $2 million worth of food for the contras.

43. Fiers testimony, 8/5/87, 38–40. North claims it was William Casey's idea that Secord's operation should be purchased by the CIA. (See North testimony, 7/14/87, 140.) If so, and

there is no evidence to support North's claim, the CIA director did not manage to overcome the objections of his subordinates.

44. Dutton testimony, 5/27/87, pp. 52–58.
45. Gadd deposition, pp. 232–34.
46. Shultz testimony, 7/23/87. pp. 46–48.
47. PROF message from North to Poindexter, May 16, 1986. Exhibit JMP-51.
48. Exhibit JMP-14.
49. See I-C Report, p. 141fn.
50. Poindexter testified that "Chairman Hamilton indicated that he was not going to push that, his committee did not have to issue a report at that time, and he did not intend to." Hamilton did not contradict Poindexter's account. Poindexter testimony, 7/17/87, pp. 30–32.
51. Notes taken at meeting by Steven K. Berry, Associate Counsel to the committee, in a memo to the files, September 3, 1986. Exhibit OLN-127.
52. Message from Bob Pearson to Poindexter, August 6, 1986. Exhibit JMP-15.
53. Theodore Draper, *A Very Thin Line: The Iran-Contra Affairs* (New York, 1991), p. 346.
54. Rodriguez tesimony, 5/27/87, pp. 265–70.
55. See account of a meeting between Rodriguez, Bermúdez, Bustillo, Secord, and North in late April. Richard Gadd, House deposition, 5/1/87, pp. 36–39.
56. Dutton testimony, 5/27/87, pp. 49–51.
57. See Gregg, Senate deposition, pp. 19–21; Watson, Senate Deposition, pp. 60–64; Rodriguez testimony, 5/28/87, pp. 39–40.
58. Fiers testimony, 8/5/87, pp. 40–42.
59. Bustillo by this time was insisting that if and when Secord's people left, they would have to leave the aircraft and other supplies behind, since in his view they belonged to the contras. See Dutton deposition, p. 497.
60. Message from Robert Earl to Secord, August 13, 1986. Exhibit RVS-3, #25.
61. Message from Secord to Earl, August 13, 1986. Exhibit RVS-3, #25.
62. Message from Secord to North, August 13, 1986. Exhibit OLN-100.
63. Secord, testimony, 5/5/87, p. 76.
64. Hakim deposition, pp. 203, 205.
65. Tambs testimony, 5/28/87, pp. 172–76.
66. Exhibit RVS-3, #30.
67. North message to Poindexter, September 25, 1986. Exhibit OLN-203.
68. Managua BARRICADA 29 Aug 86 p 5, "Contras Making 'Spy Flights' into Country," FBIS, VI. 3 Sep 86, P13.
69. See message from Dutton to North, September 9, 1986. Exhibit RCD-6.
70. Ibid., September 11, 1986. Exhibit RCD-7.
71. Dutton deposition, pp. 498–99.
72. Dutton testimony, 5/27/87, pp. 119–24.
73. See Dutton deposition, pp. 501–2.
74. Bustillo complained to Dutton about his decision to send two planes at a time on mission, and he asked whether Secord's people were "merely trying to impress someone." Message from Dutton to North, September 11, 1986. Exhibit RCD-8.
75. See Secord testimony. Exhibit RVS-3, #29; Dutton message to North, September 13, 1986. Exhibit RCD-9.
76. Dutton deposition, p. 505; see Dutton message to North, September 17, 1986, quoted in I-C Report, p. 75.
77. Dutton deposition, p. 504.
78. Poindexter message to North, September 13, 1986. Exhibit JMP-60.

79. See Abrams testimony, 6/2/87, p. 44.

80. Hakim testimony, 6/5/87, pp. 181–84.

81. See the statement of Congressman Foley: "the only funds that were distributed from the accounts of Mr. Hakim and General Secord that resulted from the diversion of funds were applied to the so-called southern front, most of them for the purpose of aircraft and the payment of salaries and that about $600,000 or so was the amount of the supplies that were provided to the southern front." (Foley statement in examination of Poindexter, 7/20/87, 21–25.) See also the statement of Senator Heflin: North testimony, 7/13/87, 187–90.

82. North testimony, excerpted in CQ, July 11, 1987, p. 1525.

Chapter 44

1. "Who Was Betrayed?" George J. Church, *Time*, December 8, 1986. Quoted in Lou Cannon, *President Reagan: The Role of a Lifetime* (New York, 1991), p. 705.

2. "46% Approve Reagan's Work, Down 21 Points," Richard J. Meislin, NYT, December 2, 1986, p. A1.

3. Testimony he intended to give to Congress was found to be inaccurate, prompting a threat of resignation by the State Department's legal adviser.

4. As for the alleged diversion, Hollings advised the President to say he considered it Iran's money, not covered by the Boland amendment, and to claim that getting Iran to give money for the contras had seemed "a pretty good deal" at the time, although now he saw it was a mistake. Hollings Press Conference, December 3, 1986, transcript reprinted in CR, January 6, 1987, S123.

5. Interview on ABC News: "This Week with David Brinkley," Decenber 7, 1986, reprinted in CR, January 6, 1987, pp. S126–S129.

6. "Republican Leader in Senate Asserts Iran-Nicaragua Affair Hurts G.O.P.," Steven V. Roberts, NYT, December 2, 1986, p. A14. Some observers suspected Dole of political motives in repeatedly calling for more inquiries, since Vice President Bush, his main opponent for the 1988 nomination, presumably had to worry about what might come out of such investigations.

7. Although a majority also believed Reagan still had more integrity than most public officials. According to his wife, Reagan "never had his integrity questioned before. And that really, really bothered him." See Cannon, p. 718.

8. "New Poll Shows 47% Hold View Reagan Is Lying," Gerald M. Boyd, NYT, December 10, 1986, p. A1.

9. CQ, March 7, 1987, p. 408.

10. One might compare Reagan's last two years with President Eisenhower's, which included the U-2 crisis, an aborted summit with Khrushchev, and the election of John F. Kennedy.

11. Senator George Mitchell of Maine, CQ, March 7, 1987, p. 410.

12. In December Nancy Reagan, Stuart Spencer, and Michael Deaver enlisted the help of Robert Strauss, the former Democratic national chairman and renowned Washington power broker, to advise the President and, in particular, urge him to fire Don Regan. Perhaps, as Lou Cannon writes, "Strauss did not come to the White House as a Democrat," but the invitation was a signal that the salvaging of the President was to be a bipartisan affair. See Cannon, pp. 722–25.

13. And who soon made known his desire to make the CIA directorship a "non-partisan" appointment like the FBI post.

14. A few days after his appointement, Baker held a meeting with leading conservatives "to quiet them down and to calm them down." Baker reportedly told the conservatives he had

no agenda of his own and that the "President is the President." See "Reagan Moves on from Iran Affair," NYT, March 6, 1987, p. A1.

15. See William S. Cohen and George J. Mitchell, *Men of Zeal: A Candid Story of the Iran-Contra Hearings* (New York, 1988), p. 16. See also "Everyone Wants a Seat on the Iran Arms Panel," Steven V. Roberts, NYT, December 5, 1987, p. A32.

16. The final report was filed in the Senate in November 1987, a year after Meese's revelations.

17. Senator Hollings declared "we're really interested in the institution of the presidency, we're interested in President Reagan. He restored the presidency in this country. The people trust him. I trust him." Transcript of interview on "NBC Today," December 3, 1986, reprinted in CR, January 6, 1987, p. S122.

18. See Cohen and Mitchell, p. 45.

19. Ibid., p. 17.

20. John M. Barry, *The Ambition and the Power* (New York, 1989), 4.

21. The words are John M. Barry's. See Barry, pp. 4–5. Barry's *The Ambition and the Power* is virtually an authorized biography of Jim Wright, inasmuch as Wright cooperated throughout, allowing Barry to sit in on private meetings throughout his years as Speaker and share his private thoughts as events unfolded. Barry nevertheless writes with some critical distance from his subject and claims Wright did not exercise any control over the book's content.

22. Dissatisfaction with Aspin went beyond his vote for contra aid in June 1986, and Aspin later apologized for paying too little attention to his colleagues, but it was widely understood that his support for contra aid had played an important role in the Caucus's decision. No one contradicted Congressman Cheney when he declared in March that Aspin "had his chairmanship temporarily stripped from him because he had the tenacity and the temerity to join with the Republicans last year and support us and vote with us on the Contra package." CR, March 11, 1987, p. H1225.

23. Barry, pp. 124–25.

24. See Barry, pp. 80–81. Bonior "had run the Democrats' efforts to kill funding of the Nicaraguan contras. He had lost on the issue, but had run the operation so well—orchestrating the media and lobbying by outside groups—that Coelho planned to model all his whip task forces on Bonior's approach."

25. Barry, p. 126.

26. One of the more liberal Southerners, Senator Terry Sanford of North Carolina, had promised in his 1986 campaign to support the President's policy in Nicaragua.

27. CQ, February 7, 1987, p. 237.

28. Senator Lowell Weicker, a liberal Republican and contra aid opponent from Connecticut, chastised the Democrats for their trepidation. "Even in [Reagan's] present slightly weakened political state," Weicker complained in early March, "too many of my friends on both sides of the aisle are unwilling to stand up to the President of the United States. . . . [W]e still want to tread softly on Contra aid. Many do not know whether even now it is politically smart to actively oppose it and to vote against it." CR, March 10, 1987, p. S2897.

29. The columnist Jack Anderson reported that according to sources present at a January 5 staff meeting Carlucci said, "I don't see how the contras can win. We need a serious review of our policy now." Anderson went on to write that Carlucci's statement indicated to those present "that he is ready to dump the contras at the first opportunity." "Carlucci Signals New Policy on Contras," Jack Anderson and Dale Van Atta, WP, January 14, 1987, p. C11. After Anderson's column Carlucci, under attack from conservatives outside the administration, had to reaffirm that he "strongly support[ed] the democratic forces in Central America [and] support

the president, because he's right." "Carlucci Endorses Aid to Contras," Joanne Omang, WP, January 24, 1987, p. A17.

30. Author's interview with George P. Shultz, December 6–7, 1991.

31. Charges to which he later pleaded guilty in a plea bargain with the special prosecutor.

32. "Delay Contra Aid Bid, Michel Urges Reagan," Joanne Omang, WP, February 24, 1987, p. A13.

33. Reagan later wrote in his memoirs that "McFarlane, Poindexter, Casey, and . . . North knew how deeply I felt about the need for the Contras' survival as a democratic resistance force in Nicaragua." Ronald Reagan, *An American Life* (New York, 1990), p. 486.

34. "The Kemp-Michel Row," Rowland Evans and Robert Novak, WP, April 1, 1987, p. A23.

35. Ibid.

Chapter 45

1. "Contras Say Cash Came from Associate of North," James LeMoyne, NYT, January 10, 1987, p. 5.

2. Bruce Cameron, unpublished memoirs in author's possession, p. 78.

3. "Contra Crisis Worsened by Feuding Leadership," Joanne Omang, WP, February 5, 1987, p. A10.

4. "Contra Political Chief Will Quit Triumvirate," NYT, February 8, 1987, p. 13.

5. "Key Contra Demands Reduction of Rightist's Role," Elaine Sciolino, NYT, February 14, 1987, p. A5.

6. "4 Latin Leaders Ask Nicaragua for Joint Talks," James LeMoyne, NYT, February 16, 1987, p. 1.

7. WP, February 5, 1987; "Ousted Contra Leader Vows to Seek New Post," Julia Preston, WP, February 27, 1987, p. A34.

8. "Leading Contra Quits Alliance Amid Disputes," Joseph B. Treaster, NYT, February 17, 1987, p. A1.

9. "The Contra Shake-Up," James LeMoyne, NYT, February 18, 1987, p. A1.

10. Helms insisted that Calero was "the only person within UNO who truly represents the freedom fighters. The others are subservient to the State Department." "Senate Committee Votes to Halt Aid to Contras," Helen Dewar, WP, February 19, 1987, p. A16.

11. "Contra Leader Withdraws Threat to Resign," James LeMoyne, NYT, February 20, 1987, p. A11.; "Contra Chief Asks Deadline on Change," James LeMoyne, NYT, February 19, 1987, p. A6.

12. "U.S. Plays Down Split in Contras," Elaine Sciolino, NYT, February 18, 1987, p. A6. Cruz's son was convinced his father had long since determined to resign no matter what happened. In one meeting of Cruz's advisers, Arturo Cruz, Jr., erupted in anger: "He wants out. Don't you see that? Let him go!" Cameron, p. 80.

13. "Top Contra Quits, Saying Changes Were Blocked," James LeMoyne, NYT, March 10, 1987, p. A1.

14. "Cruz Resigns Contra Post, Takes Swipe at Rival Leader," Joanne Omang, WP, March 10, 1987, p. A6.

15. Ibid.; "Democrats in House Move to Postpone Aid to Contras for 6 Months," Linda Greenhouse, NYT, March 10, 1987, p. A7.

16. As one Cruz adviser noted ruefully, Cesar understood that if he was to be the "bright shining liberal light of the contras," then Cruz "had to be disposed of." Cameron, p. 80.

17. "Cruz, Contra Chief Who Quit, Says Aim Is to Force Changes," James LeMoyne, NYT, March 11, 1987, p. A1.

18. From unpublished diary and memoirs of Arturo Cruz, Jr., a copy of which was provided to the author.

19. "Cruz, Contra Chief Who Quit, Says Aim Is to Force Changes," James LeMoyne, NYT, March 11, 1987, p. A1.

20. Included among the funds that had to be traced were the $27 million in "humanitarian" aid, much of which the GAO had already reported could not be fully accounted for; the $60 million in combined military and "humanitarian aid," which the CIA had assiduosly documented but would not complete its accounting of until after any vote on the remaining $40 million would be held; and finally all the money that had been spent for or by the contras resulting from private fund-raising efforts and the "diversion" from the Iran arms sales. The latter monies could not possibly be accounted for until the congressional investigating committees finished their work in the fall, if ever. It is doubtful that all the expenditures on behalf of the contras will ever be fully accounted for.

21. John M. Barry, *The Ambition and the Power* (New York, 1989), p. 128.

22. The law passed in the summer of 1986 made provision for a straight up-or-down vote on disapproval under "expedited procedures," i.e., without amendments or delay.

23. At a meeting of the House Democratic Caucus, one Democrat called the plan "duplicitous" and another said it was a "cheap shot." Barry, p. 128. The chairman of the House Rules committee, Florida Congressman Claude Pepper—a strong supporter of aiding the contras—opposed overriding the existing law, and Pepper voted against it in his committee. CR, March 11, 1987, p. H1224.

24. By accepting Bonior's plan, Barry explains, Wright "reveal[ed] the kind of House he intended to lead.... Rejecting Bonior's maneuver would mean [Wright] would allow the House to work its will. Manipulating procedure meant he would drive his agenda, and that of the Caucus, through the House." See Barry, p. 128.

25. Statement by Congressman Gingrich, CR, March 10, 1987, p. H1145; days before the vote Bonior reported that the moratorium was "turning up people we never saw before." Barry, p. 129.

26. Democratic Congressman Glenn English of Oklahoma, for instance, a consistent supporter of contra aid since 1983, voted for it because he "felt that taxpayers' money should be accounted for." Congressman Robert F. Smith of Oregon, a Republican who had always supported the administration's policy, told reporters that while "supporting freedom fighters in Nicaragua is a policy I still endorse, I can't in conscience support the extension of the $40 million until I get an accounting of the money from the Iran-contra affair." And Republican Congressman Raymond McGrath of New York, another steady supporter, told reporters that back in his district, "They're all asking where the money is and, frankly, I want to know too. I want to know where that money went before I give more to the same people." All three of these members, however, voted for contra aid the next time it was proposed by the administration.

"In 1st Test, House Freshmen Toe Party Line," Edward Walsh, WP, March 13, 1987, p. A13.

27. Congressman Bustamante, the Democrat from Texas, declared his position was "very much in doubt, not only on the accountability issue but the question of what [the contras] are doing down there." Perhaps, he suggested, "six months from now, after we have found out where the money went and who received it, I may again support some form of military assistance. But I certainly cannot do so now."

Republican Congresswoman Olympia Snowe of Maine told Abrams she had "serious questions" about the administration's goals and the contras' chances of success. On the next contra aid measure, Congresswoman Snowe voted for aid; Congressman Bustamante voted against it.

See WP, March 13, 1987. CR, March 10, 1987, p. H1121; "Delay Contra Aid Bid, Michel Urges Reagan," Joanne Omang, WP, February 24, 1987, p. A13.

28. Majority Leader Byrd tried to bring up the more appealing "moratorium" proposal but could not muster the necessary votes to stave off threatened filibusters by conservative Republicans. Byrd fell well short of attracting the 60 votes necessary to invoke cloture. See "Senate Refuses to Block Contra Aid," Helen Dewar, WP, March 19, 1987, p. A1; and "Filibuster Threatened," Anne Swardson and Helen Dewar, WP, March 20, 1987, p. A4.

29. Three of the four Democrats who replaced Republicans in the South voted against Weicker's resolution, so opponents of aid gained only one vote there. The Democrats had picked up five new seats outside the South, but contra aid opponents gained only two new supporters, since three of the Republicans replaced had voted against aid anyway. Supporters of aid, meanwhile, gained two new votes of their own, one in Missouri and another in Nebraska (where a Republican replaced Senator Zorinsky, who died on March 6.) And Senator Bradley of New Jersey continued his northeastern apostasy by voting against Weicker's resolution. The result was that, while the total number of contra aid supporters in the Senate slipped from 53 to 52, the number of Democratic supporters actually rose from 11 to 14.

The Senate vote in March 1987 was no aberration, moreover, as the subsequent 51–48 vote in favor of the administration's request in February 1988 would show.

30. CQ, March 21, 1987, p. 511; three Republican moderates in the Senate wrote the President warning that they might no longer support contra aid unless the administration recognized that "disproportionate emphasis on the military aspect of U.S. policy is counterproductive." Letter from Senators Kassebaum, Cohen, and Rudman, March 24, 1987.

31. WP, March 19, 1987.

Chapter 46

1. To win his own party's nomination, Arias had had to fend off the ambitions of two former presidents, one of whom, José Figueres, was the founder and hero of the party. The party thus split into factions, and even after Arias secured the nomination, he ran with only tepid support from the party's most powerful figures. Author's interview with Oscar Arias, February 25, 1992.

2. "Everyone told me, we wish you could win, but the U.S. says you have no chance." Author's interview with Oscar Arias, February 25, 1992.

3. Stephen Kinzer, *Blood of Brothers: Life and War in Nicaragua* (New York, 1991), p. 343.

4. "Costa Ricans Vote Today in a Tight Presidential Race," James LeMoyne, NYT, February 2, 1986, p. 3.

5. The great majority of Costa Ricans were "anti-Nicaraguan," and since the killing of two Costa Rican border guards by Sandinista troops in May 1985, hostility to the Sandinistas had reached new heights.

6. LeMoyne wrote before the election that both candidates favored contra aid. See "Costa Ricans Vote Today in a Tight Presidential Race," James LeMoyne, NYT, February 2, 1986, p. 3. In an interview a few years later, Arias denied that he supported contra aid in his campaign, but claimed, rather implausibly, that the question was never asked. Author's interview with Oscar Arias, February 25, 1992.

7. Kinzer writes, "In the last weeks of his campaign, [Arias] made a special effort to portray himself as the peace candidate, pledging to keep his country out of the conflicts shaking Central America." Kinzer, p. 343.

8. Author's interview with Oscar Arias, February 25, 1992.

9. San José LA REPUBLICA 4 Feb 86, p. 3, "President-elect Outlines Foreign Policy," FBIS, VI. 13 Feb 86, P2.

10. San José Cadena de Emisoras Columbia 0503 GMT 3 Feb 86, "Arias News Conference." FBIS, VI. 3 Feb 86, P4.

11. MRS 0000 GMT 4 Feb 86, "Costa Rica Election Result 'Complication' for U.S.," FBIS, VI. 5 Feb 86, P20.

12. San José Radio Reloj 0100 GMT 16 Feb 86, "Arias Sanchez Favors Resumption of Nicaraguan Ties," FBIS, VI. 18 Feb 86, P1.

In its apology, the Sandinista government said it "deplores that the actions it was forced to take to defend its territory and the national sovereignty of Nicaragua from the actions of mercenary forces coming from other countries resulted in the death of two Costa Rican civil guards, and that this action to defend the country, which is constantly being subjected to a permanent aggression, has provoked the unpremeditated overflight of Costa Rican airspace by Nicaraguan aircraft." MDS 0305 GMT 14 Feb 86, "Reestablishment of Ties with Costa Rica Reported," FBIS, VI. 14 Feb. 86, P9.

13. Panama City ACAN 1915 GMT 22 Feb 86, "Arias' Contra Remarks Draw Various Reactions," FBIS, VI. 24 Feb 86, P1.

14. Asked to comment, Monge said "I will not comment for the time being because I don't want it believed that there is a conflict with the president who will succeed me on 8 May." Panama City ACAN 1915 GMT 22 Feb 86, "Arias' Contra Remarks Draw Various Reactions," FBIS, VI. 24 Feb 86, P1.

15. Panama City ACAN 1915 GMT 22 Feb 86, "Arias' Contra Remarks Draw Various Reactions," FBIS, VI. 24 Feb 86, P1; San José LA PRENSA LIBRE 22 Feb 86, p 10, "Editorial Criticizes Arias," FBIS, VI. 3 Mar 86, P2.

16. Author's interview with Oscar Arias, February 25, 1992.

17. Panama City ACAN 2125 GMT 9 Mar 86, "Arias' Regional Tour Excludes Nicaragua," FBIS, VI. 12 Mar 86, P1.

18. Hamburg DPA 0037 GMT 15 Mar 86, "Costa Rica's Arias Urges Coooperation for Peace," FBIS, VI. 17 Mar 86, P1.

19. See San José Radio Reloj 0100 GMT 19 Mar 86, "Arias on Contra Aid, Elections in Nicaragua," FBIS, VI. 20 Mar 86, P1; and "U.S. Legislator in Managua Backs Use of Advisers," Stephen Kinzer, NYT, March 24, 1986, p. A2.

20. Madrid EL PAIS 20 Mar 86, "President-elect Arias Reviews Regional Conflict," FBIS, VI. 4 Apr 86, P2.

21. Ibid; San José Radio Reloj 0100 GMT 19 Mar 86, "U.S. Ambassador to Decide Date of Arias Trip," FBIS, VI. 20 Mar 86, P1.

22. Abrams cited Arias's "second Cuba" statement in a press briefing at the State Department. See Press Briefing by the Assistant Secretary of State for Inter-American Affairs (Abrams), March 3, 1986, AFPD, 1986. Doc. 452.

23. San José LA PRENSA LIBRE 22 Apr 86, p. 10, "Arias' U.S. Policy May Ease Peace Process," FBIS, VI. 30 Apr 86, P1.

24. Azcona praised Arias at a meeting with President Reagan right after the Esquipulas summit. See White House Press Briefing, May 27, 1986, AFPD, 1986. Doc. 444.

25. Mexico City NOTIMEX 1458 GMT 10 May 86, "Arias Discusses Contadora, Domestic Concerns," FBIS, VI. 12 May 86, P1.

26. Mexico City NOTIMEX 1525 GMT 2 Jun 86, "Comments on Contadora," FBIS, VI. 3 Jun 86, P3.

27. San José Radio Reloj 0100 GMT 3 Jun 86, "Arias Discusses Contadora with Gen. Galvin," FBIS, VI. 4 Jun 86, P1.

28. Havana International Service 2300 GMT 2 Jun 86, "Arias Becoming Reagan 'Spokesman' In Region," FBIS, VI. 4 Jun 86, Q3.

29. MDS 1200 GMT 3 Jun 86, "Ortega Blames U.S. for Contadora 'Sabotage,'" FBIS, VI. 5 Jun 86, P16.

30. Managua International Service 1338 GMT 23 Jun 86, "Ortega States Position on Contadora Proposal," FBIS, VI. 24 Jun 86, P5.

31. See Managua Domestic Service 0304 GMT 26 Jun 86, "Report On Vote," FBIS, VI. 26 Jun 86, P4; and also Managua Domestic Service 0451 GMT 26 Jun 86, "Ortega Statement," FBIS, VI. 26 Jun 86, P4.

32. Managua Radio Sandino 1310 GMT 13 Jul 86, "Ortega Discusses Defense in Chinandega," FBIS, VI. 14 Jul 86, P15.

33. Managua Radio Sandino 1940 GMT 30 Jul 86, "Foreign Ministry Communiqué on New ICJ Suits," FBIS, VI. 31 Jul 86, P9.

34. Paris AFP 0132 GMT 22 Jul 86, "Government Communiqué Replies to Ortega 'Attacks,'" FBIS, VI. 22 Jul 86, P1.

35. San José Domestic Service 0102 GMT 20 Aug 86, "Arias Sanchez' 100 Days Speech to Nation," FBIS, VI. 22 Aug 86, P1.

36. Paris AFP 1907 GMT 27 Aug 86, "Arias Discusses Contadora, Contra Presence," FBIS, VI. 28 Aug 86, P1.

37. San José LA REPUBLICA 15 Aug 86 p 4, "Arias: Sandinists Responsible for C.A. Situation," FBIS, VI. 25 Aug 86, P1.

38. Managua Domestic Service 1728 GMT 18 Aug 86, "Discusses Dominican Visit," FBIS, VI. 19 Aug 86, P16.

39. Managua Domestic Service 1746 GMt 27 Nov 86, "Ortega Berates U.S. Policy toward Nation," FBIS, VI. 28 Nov 86, P4.

40. Author's interview with George P. Shultz, December 6–7, 1991.

41. Statement by President Reagan, December 4, 1986, AFPD, 1986. Doc. 433.

42. Recall Gutman's condemnation of the Reagan administration's insistence on democratization as a policy goal.

43. For a variety of reasons, however, it would be more than a year before that money was delivered.

44. See report by the Center for International Policy, reprinted in CR, June 24, 1987, S8621–S8625. Interview with Costa Rican official, Melvin Saenz, May 14, 1987.

45. San José LA PRENSA LIBRE 4 Feb 87, p. 2., "Arias, Rivera react to Nicaraguan Communique," FBIS, VI. 11 Feb 87, P1.

46. Bogota *El Tiempo*, February 4, 1987, in FBIS, VI. February 9, 1987, P6; San Salvador Canal Doce Television, February 13, 1987, in FBIS, VI. February 17, 1987, P12; see report by the Center for International Policy, reprinted in CR, June 24, 1987, S8621–S8625.

47. Tegucigalpa Voz de Honduras Network 1130 GMT 24 Mar 87, "Foreign Minister Lopez Discusses Arias Proposal," FBIS, VI. 26 Mar 87.

48. "Carlucci Endorses Aid to Contras," Joanne Omang, WP, January 24, 1987, p. A17; see report by the Center for International Policy, reprinted in CR, June 24, 1987, S8621–S8625.

49. Quoted in *Excelsior*, January 20, 1987 and *La Vanguardia*, February 1, 1987, in FBIS, VI. February 17, 1987, P10; see report by the Center for International Policy, reprinted in CR, June 24, 1987, pp. S8621–S8625.

Mexico City XEW Television Network 0530 GMT 6 Feb 87, "Arias Interviewed on Regional Diplomacy," FBIS, VI. 10 Feb 87, P1.

50. Interview with Melvin Saenz, adviser to Foreign Minister Madrigal on May 14, 1987. Quoted in report by the Center for International Policy, reprinted in CR, June 24, 1987, pp. S8621–S8625.

51. Author's interview with George P. Shultz.

52. Ibid.

53. Habib went on to explain that "You have to define the cease-fire. Is it going to be a cease-fire in place? What place? What about supplies? Can you be resupplied? What can you be resupplied with? Can you move? Can you not move? What about monitoring it? Who is going to monitor it? How are they going to monitor it? What are the terms of the right to settle disputes, for example? How do you settle disputes?" Habib testimony before House Foreign Affairs Subcommittee on Western Hemisphere Affairs, July 9, 1987, p. 6.

54. See Habib testimony before House Foreign Affairs Subcommittee on Western Hemisphere Affairs, July 9, 1987, pp. 6–7, 19.

55. "Dodd, Shultz Trade Barbs on Policy," Don Oberdorfer, WP, February 25, 1987, p. A10; CQ, February 21, 1987, p. 315.

56. See report by the Center for International Policy, reprinted in CR, June 24, 1987, S8621–S8625.

57. Author's interview with Secretary George P. Shultz, December 6–7, 1991.

58. Author's interview with Oscar Arias, February 25, 1992.

59. Mexico City XEW Television Network 0530 GMT 6 Feb 87, "Arias Interviewed on Regional Diplomacy," FBIS, VI. 10 Feb 87, P1.

60. "This is why I am trying to stop that war," he explained to reporters. Mexico City XEW Television Network 0530 GMT 6 Feb 87, "Arias Interviewed on Regional Diplomacy," FBIS, VI. 10 Feb 87, P1.

61. Paris AFP 2219 GMT 13 Mar 87, "Arias to Send Delegation to Nicaragua on Proposal," FBIS, VI. 16 Mar 87, P2.

62. Oslo ARBEIDERBLADET 7 May 87 p 18, "Arias Assesses Prospects for Peace Plan," FBIS, VI. 14 May 87, P2.

63. At the first Esquipulas summit in May 1986, for instance, and when he endorsed the Duarte proposal in March 1986.

64. San José Radio Reloj, FBIS, VI. February 16, 1987, P2; see report by the Center for International Policy, reprinted in CR, June 24, 1987, S8621–S8625.

65. Managua Domestic Service 0057 GMT 30 Mar 87, "News Conference Held," FBIS, VI. 30 Mar 87, P10.

66. Sofia OTECHESTVEN FRONT 13 Apr 87, pp 5, 7, "Interview with Interior Minister Borge," FBIS, VI. 22 Apr 87, P6.

67. Managua International Service 2314 GMT 18 Feb 87, "Government Communiqué on San José Meeting," FBIS, VI. 19 Feb 87, P10. "Managua Warms to New Peace Plan," Stephen Kinzer, NYT, February 22, 1987, p. 16.

68. Buenos Aires DYN, April 14, 1987, in FBIS, April 17, 1987, p. A1; see report by the Center for International Policy, reprinted in CR, June 24, 1987, pp. S8621–S8625. See also Panama City 0122 GMT 21 Mar 87, "Abadia Says Contadora Supports Arias Plan," FBIS, VI. 26 Mar 87, N1.

69. Havana International Service 2300 GMT 16 Mar 87, "Arias Tries to Get Support for 'Alternative' Plan," FBIS, VI. 1 Apr 87, Q3.

70. "Reagan, in Speech on Ellis Island, Makes a New Plea for Contra Aid," Gerald M. Boyd, NYT, May 4, 1987, p. A1.

71. NYT, June 18, 1987, p. A13; NYT, June 19, 1987, p. A7.

72. Tegucigalpa Voz de Honduras Network 1130 GMT 24 Mar 87, "Foreign Minister Lopez Discusses Arias Proposal," FBIS, VI. 26 Mar 87.

73. Panama City ACAN 0146 GMT 23 Apr 87, "Foreign Minister Discusses Arias Peace Plan," FBIS, VI. 24 Apr 87, P2; ibid.

74. "U.S. Officials Split over Costa Rican Peace Plan," Elaine Sciolino, NYT, March 19, 1987, p. A11.

75. Panama City ACAN 0022 GMT 3 Apr 87, "Salvadoran President Pledges Support to CDN Mission," FBIS, VI. 7 Apr 87, P9.

76. He claimed that, as a Costa Rican, he had a hard time discussing such things as the implementation of cease-fires, since Costa Rica didn't have those kinds of problems. San José Radio Reloj 0100 GMT 25 Mar 87, "Comments on Habib Meeting," FBIS, VI. 30 Mar 87, P1.

77. According to Costa Rican officials, Arias had already decided to stick to his original text and would consider changes only when they were offered at the summit meeting. See report by the Center for International Policy, reprinted in CR, June 24, 1987, S8621–S8625.

78. Panama City ACAN 2356 GMT 23 Apr 87, "Madrigal Travels to Counter Proposal Opposition," FBIS, VI. 24 Apr 87, P1.

79. San José LA REPUBLICA 21 May 87, p. 8, "Minister Rivera on Plan," FBIS, VI. 1 Jun 87, E1.

80. See NYT, March 19, 1987; George P. Shultz, *Turmoil and Triumph: My Years as Secretary of State* (New York, 1993), pp. 956–57.

81. Author's interview with George P. Shultz, December 6–7, 1991.

82. Oslo ARBEIDERBLADET 7 May 87 p 18, "Arias Assesses Prospects for Peace Plan," FBIS, VI. 14 May 87, P2.

83. San José Radio Reloj 0100 GMT 28 Apr 87, "President Arias Receives U.S. Envoy Habib," FBIS, VI. 30 Apr 87, P2.

84. Rome AVANTI! 6 Jun 87, p. 20, "Italian Paper Interviews Arias on Peace Plan," LAT 16 Jun 87, E1.

85. San José LA NACION 8 May 87, pp 4a, 5a, "President Arias Comments on Economy, Peace," FBIS, VI. 18 May 87, P1.

86. San José Radio Reloj 2120 GMT 1 May 87, "President Addresses Nation on May Day," FBIS, VI. 6 May 87, P2.

87. See Habib testimony before House Foreign Affairs Subcommittee on Western Hemisphere Affairs, July 9, 1987, p. 9.

88. Panama City ACAN 0117 GMT 20 Jun 87, "Foreign Minister on Decision," LAT 22 Jun 87, E4.

89. Panama City ACAN 0051 GMT 13 Jun 87, "Foreign Ministers View Suspension of Summit," LAT 15 Jun 87, E2; Panama City ACAN 0151 GMT 13 Jun 87, "Arias Accepts Postponement of Esquipulas Meeting," LAT 15 Jun 87, E1.

90. The Sandinistas charged that Duarte's demand for a postponement was part of an American maneuver, since Duarte had made the demand just one day after a visit from Habib. Habib vigorously disputed this allegation as "disinformation." See Habib testimony before House Foreign Affairs Subcommittee on Western Hemisphere Affairs, July 9, 1987, p. 7.

91. Quoted in report by the Center for International Policy, reprinted in CR, June 24, 1987, pp. S8621–25.

92. Panama City ACAN 0117 GMT 20 Jun 87, "Foreign Minister on Decision," LAT 22 Jun 87, E4; NYT, June 24, 1987, p. A11.

Chapter 47

1. See "Still in the Game," Mary McGrory, WP, July 23, 1987, p. A2. Those who could be said to have "lost" were those Democrats and moderate Republicans who took a critical stance toward the Reagan administration and its private associates. For the House Republicans and conservative Senate Republicans, who saw their role as defending the Reagan administration and who expressed general approval of the actions of North and the other witnesses, the hearings were arguably a success.

2. Senator Paul Trible of Virginia was normally considered a conservative senator, but during the hearings he followed the lead of Rudman and Cohen, seeking to distinguish himself as a disinterested critic of the Reagan administration's activities. He changed his approach after North's testimony.

3. CQ, May 9, 1987, p. 885.

4. CQ, May 2, 1987, p. 822.

5. CQ, May 30, 1987, p. 1130.

6. The 17 included all 11 Senate and House Republicans, three of the six Democratic senators (Nunn, Boren, and Heflin,) and three of the nine House Democrats (Fascell, Jenkins, and Aspin.) Of these only Aspin's continued support for contra aid was in doubt.

7. "Republicans on Iran-Contra Panel at Odds over Best Tactics to Use," Fox Butterfield, NYT, May 26, 1987, p. A1.

8. William S. Cohen and George J. Mitchell, *Men of Zeal: A Candid Inside Story of the Iran-Contra Hearings* (New York, 1988), p. 57.

9. Ibid., p. 63.

10. Ibid., pp. 50, 65.

11. With $8 million still sitting in his Swiss bank accounts even as he testified, Secord had seemed an easy target for Senate committee lawyer Arthur Liman, who intended to show that Secord had been "lining his pockets at the expense of both the Contras and the American people." After just two days of testimony, however, Secord had, in Cohen's and Mitchell's words, "seized control of the hearings, portraying himself as a righteous patriot who had been betrayed by his government." "Thousands of letters, telegrams, and phone calls" flooded the offices of committee members, complaining about Liman's appearance, his "abrasiveness," and his religion. Senators who questioned Secord with varying degrees of aggressiveness also came in for attack. "The Senate offices of Boren, Trible, and Rudman were flooded with angry letters, telegrams, and phone calls, berating them for joining forces with 'that New York Lawyer.'" See Cohen and Mitchell, pp. 70, 72, 75–76.

12. Ibid., p. 77.

13. Ibid., p. 165.

14. Ibid., p. 157.

15. "In New Poll, Most Say North Is Telling Truth," NYT, July 11, 1987, p. A1.

16. CQ, August 8, 1987, p. 1774; CQ, July 18, 1987, p. 1564.

17. Cohen and Mitchell, p. 157. Statement by Senator Mitchell excerpted in Cohen and Mitchell, pp. 169–72. The weekend before he was due to question North, Mitchell recalls, "I was disheartened, not confident of my ability even to discern the proper message, let alone frame and deliver it." Ibid., pp. 166, 168–69.

18. Ibid., pp. 164, 168.

19. An ABC/*Washington Post* poll on July 15 showed respondents divided 43–46, compared to 29–67 in early June. See "Polls Find an Increase in Support for Contras," NYT, July 17, 1987, p. A7; and "What Neighbors Know," WSJ editorial, July 17, 1987, p. 18. Richard Wirthlin, the President's pollster, reported in the third week of July that support for contra aid had risen from 40–60 against to 48–46 in favor since North's testimony. See "President May Seek

More Contra Aid," Gerald M. Boyd, NYT, July 20, 1987, p. A6. Only the *New York Times*/CBS News poll showed little increase in approval for contra aid, 35–51. See "New Poll Finds Majority Still Think Reagan Lied," NYT, July 18, 1987, p. 1. But another *New York Times*/CBS poll a week later showed an increase to 40–49. See "Support for Contra Aid Continues to Increase," NYT, July 24, 1987, p. A9.

20. CQ, July 18, 1987, p. 1568.

21. Ibid., p. 1569.

22. John M. Barry, *The Ambition and the Power* (New York, 1989), p. 303.

23. The White House, Buchanan wrote, needed to adopt "more of the mindset of Ollie North . . . get off the defensive and go on the attack; the President must not only make the case for the contras, but against the Congress." See "You've Won, Mr. President; Now Pardon Ollie and John," Patrick J. Buchanan, WP, July 19, 1987.

24. CQ, July 18, 1987, p. 1569; "President May Seek More Contra Aid," Gerald M. Boyd, NYT, July 20, 1987, p. A6.

25. Boren said there was "too much on the record" for Abrams to rebuild "a relationship of trust" with Congress. Congressman Fascell, another contra aid supporter, agreed, and Senator Rudman surmised Abrams would be the administration's "fall guy." "Congress Might Not Aid Contras If Abrams Continues in His Post," David E. Rosenbaum, NYT, June 4, 1987, p. A1.

26. "Abrams Is Backed by Shultz," Gerald M. Boyd, NYT, June 10, 1987, p. A14. "Shultz Rebuffs Call for Abrams' Ouster," Joe Pichirallo, WP, June 26, 1987, p. A16.

The White House made no comment and referred reporters to Shultz's statements. See "Democrats Seek Abrams's Ouster," Jonathan Feurbringer, NYT, June 13, 1987, p. A3.

27. Congressman Hyde believed the White House had been "stupid" in its handling of the new Speaker. "They should be stroking him at every opportunity. He's someone they could work with." Jack Kemp agreed: "I wouldn't say this publicly—I wouldn't want to get him in trouble with his liberals—but I think Wright leans toward the contras." See Barry, p. 311.

The columnists Evans and Novak wrote at the end of June that "close friends insist" that Wright "secretly . . . may favor aid because of genuine concern about communist gains in Central America and the inevitable Soviet influence that comes with it—major concerns in his own state of Texas." "The Hill's Ship-Watchers," Rowland Evans and Robert Novak, WP, June 29, 1987, p. A13.

28. Barry, pp. 312–13, 312.

29. Barry characterizes Wright's thinking as follows: "Politically, Democrats needed a policy to be *for*. If the worst case happened, if Democrats ended contra aid and the extreme left of the Sandinista junta took command and started a wave of executions, Republicans could smear Democrats for a generation." See Barry, p. 313.

30. As Wright's biographer puts it, "everything in [Wright's] personality drove him forward." See Barry, p. 316.

31. See Barry, pp. 315, 322.

32. "The Latin Peace Plan According to Wright," Wayne King, NYT, August 11, 1987, p. A14.

33. President Arias, meanwhile, reaped the political harvest for his refusal to join the conspiracy. He sneered at his erstwhile critics in the conservative Costa Rican press, "I can imagine the coarseness of today's editorials if the Costa Rican president had participated in the Irangate hearings instead of opposing aid for the contras." San José LA NACION 8 May 87, pp 4a, 5a, "President Arias Comments on Economy, Peace," FBIS, VI. 18 May 87, P1.

34. "Reagan's Troubles Worry Central Americans," William Branigin, WP, June 22, 1987, p. A1. James LeMoyne recorded these fears as early as December 1986, when he wrote of Honduran concerns that "with a Democratic majority in Congress and the Iran-contra controversy

on his hands, President Reagan is less able than ever to guarantee continued support for the rebels or to help Honduras should the rebel war fall apart." See "Honduras Eager to Have Rebels Out," James LeMoyne, NYT, December 10, 1986.

A senior Honduran diplomat later told Roy Gutman that "the scandal debilitated the standing of the U.S. government before the eyes of the Central American governments. . . . Many got worried about what the contra program means for future relations with a Democratic Congress and for a possible Democratic administration." Roy Gutman, *Banana Diplomacy* (New York, 1988), p. 348.

35. WP, June 22, 1987.

36. Author's interview with Oscar Arias, February 25, 1992. Philip Habib also noted that Duarte was "determined to protect his own interests, and El Salvador has very specific interests." See Habib testimony before House Foreign Affairs Subcommittee on Western Hemisphere Affairs, July 5, 1987.

37. The threat posed by the Guatemalan guerrillas to Cerezo's government was much smaller.

38. Duarte asked repeatedly whether the plan would really force the FMLN to abide by its terms. For instance, in an interview on June 12 Duarte had questioned the plan's call for negotiations with opposition groups: "If I call on the rebels to participate in a dialogue in a capital city garrison within the 60-day deadline specified in the [plan] . . . and the rebel fronts claim that they do not like the place selected, or do not show up, that kind of maneuver or 'trick' will spoil the effort." See Hamburg DPA 2208 GMT 12 Jun 87, "Duarte Discusses Esquipulas, Ochoa Statement," LAT 15 Jun 87, F1.

39. Author's interview with Oscar Arias, February 25, 1992.

40. See below, p. 532.

41. Author's interview with Alan Fiers, March 8, 1991.

42. This time the Honduran army responded by bombing Sandinista positions in northern Nicaragua and calling for American assistance in ferrying troops to the border region. The Reagan administration quickly fulfilled the Hondurans' request, with far less controversy than in March, and the Sandinistas withdrew.

43. NYT, December 10, 1986; CIA officials "thought the reinfiltration would be tough, but it was like a hot knife through butter." Author's interview with Alan Fiers, March 8, 1991.

44. "Divisions Detract from Contra Advances," William Branigin, WP, January 29, 1987, p. A21; Panama City ACAN 2156 GMT 28 Feb 87, "Ortega Says 6,000 Contras Infiltrated, Repelled," FBIS, VI. 2 Mar 87, P11.

45. WP, January 29, 1987.

46. This view was shared by retired American General Paul Gorman. Gorman told Congress at the end of January that the Sandinistas did not "regard the contras as a serious threat." He dismissed the administration's goal of forcing the Sandinistas to accept sweeping reforms as unrealistic: "I think they've got the situation under control. [W]hy should they be considering changing their ways of doing business?" "Contras Need a Success Soon, Crowe Says," George C. Wilson, WP, February 13, 1987, p. A31.

47. In the first week of June, the Nicaraguan Defense Ministry reported that contra forces of as many as 500 had attacked five different towns. MRS 1930 GMT 4 Jun 87, "EPS Begins Offensive Against Contras in Region 6," LAT 9 Jun 87, I3.

48. "Loss of Soviet-Made Copters Hurts Sandinista Operations," Julia Preston, WP, June 26, 1987, p. A1.

49. "Pentagon Says Contras Get 'Tactical Initiative,'" NYT, August 14, p. A8.

50. Sandinista army officials reported 372 "battles" in the month of June between EPS troops and contras throughout north, south, and central Nicaragua in the departments of

Jinotega, Matagalpa, Zelaya, and Rio San Juan. MRS 1200 GMT 7 Jul 87, "EPS Communiqué Monthly Military Report," LAT 14 Jul 87, I9; Author's interview with Alan Fiers, March 8, 1991.

51. The Sandinistas formally acknowledged these three areas of contra control when they announced a unilateral truce in these three zones in September. See "Ortega Declares a Unilateral Truce in Some Areas," NYT, October 1, 1987, p. A7, and p. 552 below.

52. Managua BARRICADA 20 Apr 87, pp. 1, 4, "Peasant Evacuation 'Strategic Blow' to Contras," FBIS, VI. 22 Apr 87, P5.

53. Ortega acknowledged that "certain sectors . . . reject our [revolution's] victory because they are manipulated by landowners . . . who reject revolutionary changes." MDS 1553 GMT 15 Jul 87, "Defense Minister Delivers 8th Anniversary Speech," LAT 17 Jul 87, I3.

54. Roger Miranda and William Ratliff, *The Civil War in Nicaragua: Inside the Sandinistas* (New Brunswick, NJ, 1993), p. 243.

55. The official figures of the Sandinista government may have understated their economic problems and the amount of the budget devoted to defense. For the purposes of this narrative, however, the official figures suffice to show the magnitude of the problem.

56. MDS 1555 GMT 19 Jul 87, "Ortega Delivers 19 Jul 8th Anniversary Speech," LAT 20 Jul 87, I1.

57. Only Sweden and Norway increased aid to Nicaragua in 1987. "For Nicaragua, Soviet Frugality Starts to Pinch," Stephen Kinzer, NYT, August 20, 1987, p. A1. See ibid.

58. Mexico and Venezuela, meanwhile, remained wary of selling oil to Nicaragua when previous shipments still had not been paid for. A trip by Sandinista leaders to friendly oil-producing states like Iraq, Iran, Libya, and Algeria in June and July proved futile. See Mexico City EXCELSIOR 24 Jun 87, pp 1-A, 18-A, 32-A, 35-A, "Ortega Interviewed on Central American Dialogue," LAT 8 Jul 87, I1; "For Nicaragua, Soviet Frugality Starts to Pinch," Stephen Kinzer, NYT, August 20, 1987, p. A1.

59. See "A Nicaraguan Reports Serious Shortage of Oil," NYT, August 19, 1987, p. A9; NYT, August 20, 1987.

60. MDS 1553 GMT 15 Jul 87, "Defense Minister Delivers 8th Anniversary Speech." LAT 17 Jul 87, I3.

61. "At the moment when the two superpowers are negotiating," Daniel Ortega argued, "and when it is obvious that they may very soon reach an agreement on withdrawing and scrapping medium-range and short-range missiles in Europe, which would open the possibility for a summit between Reagan and Gorbachev," there remained the "real danger" of an American invasion. Belgrade POLITIKA 28 Jun 87, p. 9, "Daniel Ortega Grants Interview to POLITIKA," LAT 17 Jul 87, I2.

62. In Ortega's words, "Reagan is probably thinking of a strategy that will permit the United States to arrive at overall agreements with the USSR on the subject of missiles, and, at the same time, may be thinking of a strategy to destroy the Nicaraguan revolution by any means." Mexico City EXCELSIOR 24 Jun 87, pp 1-A, 18-A, 32-A, 35-A, "Ortega Interviewed on Central American Dialogue," LAT 8 Jul 87, I1.

63. Miranda and Ratliff, p. 159.

64. His two top lieutenants were still Joaquín Cuadra and Oswaldo Lacayo.

65. "Humberto Ortega held a protocol meeting with a newly appointed U.S. military attaché in Managua," Miranda recalls, "a very rare occurrence, and tried to send a message to Washington that he was ready to talk." Ortega also talked to an aide to the Panamanian dictator, Manuel Noriega, and asked for a meeting with General Galvin, the commander of American forces in Latin America. During a Sandinista military parade in November 1986, in which the full arsenal of Soviet-supplied weapons was proudly displayed, Humberto Ortega rode in

the procession's only American vehicle: a Jeep Renegade. He told Miranda, "I want to show the Americans that despite all this Soviet hardware, I can ride in a Jeep." According to Moises Hassan, "Daniel Ortega got to the point where he would set ambushes for American officials. He would lurk in dark corners until an American official showed up, and then jump out and try to engage him in conversation." Miranda and Ratliff, pp. 159–60. Ratliff interview with Moises Hassan, May 2, 1991.

There is no evidence, however, that the Ortegas were prepared to offer anything new in any dialogue. At the beginning of August, Daniel Ortega repeated the Sandinistas' long-standing refusal to discuss anything other than bilateral "security" issues with the United States—an offer Secretary Shultz predictably rejected.

Humberto Ortega's former adviser, Carlos Coronel, believed that Ortega was merely keeping all his options open, equipping himself to survive any turn of events. Author's interview with Carlos Coronel, May 26, 1990.

66. Panama City ACAN 1842 GMT 21 Jun 87, "Arias to Attend Summit Despite Ortega Decision," LAT 22 Jun 87, E3.

67. President Azcona told reporters after his meeting with Arias that the Honduran government believed the plan "should be more far-reaching, should be developed more in some areas, and that, perhaps, the sequence of events mentioned there should be changed." But he denied that Honduras was trying to undermine the plan. Tegucigalpa Cadena Audio Video 1130 GMT 27 Jul 87, "President Azcona Comments on Summit, Arias Plan," LAT 28 Jul 87, H1.

For Arias's statements on Duarte, see Paris AFP 0013 GMT 29 Jul 87, "Arias Says Presidential Summit Obstacles 'Lifted,'" LAT 30 Jul 87, E1.

68. Author's interview with Oscar Arias, February 25, 1992.

69. Tegucigalpa Cadena Audio Video 1130 GMT 27 Jul 87, "Costa Rica's Arias Discusses Visit, Peace Plan," LAT 29 Jul 87, H1.

70. Tegucigalpa Radio America 1720 GMT 1 Aug 87, "Hold News Conference," LAT 3 Aug 87, BB4.

71. Hamburg DPA 2131 GMT 4 Aug 87, "Foreign Ministers Meeting Opens in Guatemala," LAT 5 Aug 87, BB1.

72. Nicaraguan Foreign Minister D'Escoto said he hoped the summit could achieve some agreement, "no matter how minimal in scope." Hamburg DPA 2131 GMT 4 Aug 87, "Foreign Ministers Meeting Opens in Guatemala," LAT 5 Aug 87, BB1.

Vice Foreign Minister Tinoco recalls that the Sandinistas "didn't expect an agreement" at the summit, but rather some kind of "communiqué." Gutman interview with Tinoco. See Gutman, p. 348.

73. "Accord Raises Honduran Misgivings on U.S. Ties," Lindsey Gruson, NYT, October 1, 1987, p. A6. He told reporters he expected no agreement at the summit. See Panama City ACAN 1842 GMT 5 Aug 87, "Azcona Withholds Comment on Reagan Peace Plan," LAT 6 Aug 87, H1.

74. San José Radio Reloj 0100 GMT 4 Aug 87, "Arias Optimistic about Summit, Stresses Agenda," LAT 7 Aug 87, E1.

Chapter 48

1. John M. Barry, *The Ambition and the Power* (New York, 1989), p. 320.

2. Roy Gutman, *Banana Diplomacy* (New York, 1988), p. 346.

3. Author's interview with George P. Shultz, December 6–7, 1991.

4. Barry, pp. 320, 327.

5. Barry, p. 334.

6. Congressman Hyde agreed that if the Democrats' "enthusiasm for no aid goes, say, from ten to seven, that will be very useful." See Barry, pp. 330, 335.

7. Barry, p. 336. There was certainly ambiguity. On August 5, Elliott Abrams declared that the plan called for the "fighting parties, the resistance and the Sandinistas, to sit down [and] negotiate a cease-fire." The next day, however, the President's spokesman, Marlin Fitzwater, said that while the contras would have a veto over any cease-fire, they did not necessarily have to be part of the negotiating process. This was, however, as Habib insisted, a logical contradiction. If the contras had a veto over the cease-fire, then one way or another they would have a say in setting its terms. For Fitzwater and Abrams statements, see "U.S. and Managua Openly Disagree on a Peace Plan," Steven V. Roberts, NYT, August 7, 1987, p. A1.

8. Gutman, p. 346; Barry, p. 336. Later, in a list of 21 points administration officials drew up to explain their "interpretation" of the agreement, they interpreted the plan to call for presidential elections in advance of 1990. Wright rejected the 21-point "interpretation," however, and it never became a part of the administration's official policy.

9. "House Speaker Warmly Embraces the Latin Plan," Stephen Engelberg, NYT, August 8, 1987, p. 4.

10. Barry, p. 336.

11. See Barry, pp. 331–32.

12. This point later became embroiled in controversy. Wright's original draft of the plan called for "bilateral" talks with all the countries, including Nicaragua. Shultz later changed that—ironically at the request of Senator Dodd—to "multilateral" talks with all five Central American governments simultaneously. NYT, August 7, 1987.

13. "Latin Peace Plan Is Put Forward by Administration," Linda Greenhouse, NYT, August 5, 1987, p. A1; Barry, pp. 340–41.

14. At a meeting of the Nicaragua task force on August 4, Barry recounts, liberals "tore into" Wright over the peace plan. Barry, p. 339.

15. Baker conversation with Kemp recounted in Barry, p. 344.

16. "Reagan Unveils Initiative for Peace in Nicaragua," David Hoffman and Helen Dewar, WP, August 6, 1987, p. A1.

17. Abrams quoted in Gutman, pp. 346–47; Abrams told the Republicans, "If you're for democracy, this plan will bring it—but only as a contract, not as a negotiating position." Quoted in Barry, p. 343.

18. Barry, p. 343.

19. "U.S.-Nicaragua Talks Rejected," John M. Goshko, WP, August 7, 1987, p. A18. See also NYT, August 7, 1987.

20. Ortega said he hoped the U.S. Congress was not so "naive as to not understand that if it supports this as an ultimatum to Nicaragua, it would be a declaration of war on Nicaragua." MDS 1657 GMT 6 Aug 87, "Ortega News Conference," LAT 7 Aug 87, BB3.

21. Author's interview with Oscar Arias, February 25, 1992. Wright had obviously been misled by Arias's ambassador, Guido Fernandez, who perhaps had not wished to discourage the powerful Speaker from his peacemaking efforts.

22. See Barry, p. 348; and "The Latin Peace Plan According to Wright," Wayne King, NYT, August 11, 1987, p. A14. As Gutman writes, "Wright transformed the Wright-Reagan plan into a blank check for Arias to use as he saw fit." Gutman, p. 347.

Wright also called on the Reagan administration to accept Daniel Ortega's request for an immediate "unconditional dialogue" with the United States, even though the Wright-Reagan proposal specifically called for talks with the Sandinistas only *after* they had agreed to the plan and negotiated a cease-fire, and even though Ortega made clear that an "unconditional dialogue" meant no discussion of internal democratic reforms in Nicaragua—which lay at the heart of the Wright-Reagan plan. Wright nevertheless complained to Shultz and Baker that "when you give a guy X days to respond and he says the next day let's talk, and you say no, then that's a problem." "Ortega Calls for Talks; Shultz Spurns Proposal," William Branigin, WP, August 7, 1987, p. A1. "Sandinistas and Rebels Differ Sharply on Proposal," James LeMoyne, NYT, August 7, 1987. "U.S.-Nicaragua Talks Rejected," John M. Goshko, WP, August 7, 1987, p. A18. See also NYT, August 7, 1987.

23. According to Congressman Kemp, for instance, "When the Central American democracies saw the U.S. back away from our commitment to the contras, they lost confidence in our determination to see a free and independent future for the region." "Kemp Rips Peace Plan, Urges Contra Aid Push," Mark Lawrence, WP, August 14, 1987.

In his memoirs, Constantine Menges quotes himself telling Congressman Kemp on August 4: "The four friendly Central American leaders will *perceive* this as a decision by Reagan—their anchor of stability in all these years—to give up on the Nicaraguan freedom fighters" (emphasis in original). Menges calls the Wright-Reagan plan the "eighth end run" by Shultz and the State Department. See Constantine C. Menges *Inside the National Security Council* (New York, 1988), pp. 325–26.

24. In the words of the Salvadoran foreign minister, Reagan "did not want to remain behind in formulating a peace plan." FBIS-LAT-87-181 18 September 1987, p. 13.

25. The Wright-Reagan plan made only one reference to guerrilla groups other than the contras, and even so it was buried among a number of issues to be left for future negotiations—"after the cease-fire is in place, negotiations among the Governments of the United States, Costa Rica, El Salvador, Honduras and Nicaragua shall begin on reductions in standing armies in the region, withdrawal of foreign military personnel, restoration of regional military balance, security guarantees against outside support for insurgent forces, and verification and enforcement provisions."

Foreign Minister Acevedo cited as the main difference between the two plans that "one is a multilateral plan in which all the Central American countries promise to make the same decisions, and the other is a bilateral plan—a plan that only involves Nicaragua and the United States." FBIS-LAT-87-181 18 September 1987, p. 13.

As Evans and Novak later wrote, "The Guatemala plan is consciously tilted toward regimes now in power, including communist Nicaragua's. That explains support from El Salvador's President José Napoleon Duarte, who gets the same protection against communist insurgents besieging his regime that the Sandinistas have against U.S.-backed contra. 'Let's face it,' an administration realist told us, 'the presidents who wrote this plan acted in their own interests as incumbents not as anticommunists.'" "So Long, Contras," Rowland Evans and Robert Novak, WP, August 14, 1987, p. A27.

26. According to Salvadoran Communications Minister Julio Adolfo Rey Prendes, as quoted in "The Latin Peace Plan According to Wright," Wayne King, NYT, August 11, 1987, p. A14.

27. Emphasis added. "Duarte Pledges to Fight Pessimism toward Pact," Julia Preston, WP, August 23, 1987, p. A21.

28. Salvadoran guerrilla leaders complained angrily that Arias had "made a suit for one person," the contras, but were "trying to make someone else wear it." "Risky Initiative," Stephen Kinzer, NYT, August 23, 1987, Section IV, p. 1.

29. Daniel Ortega later told his brother Humberto: "Reagan's announcement of his proposal just before we met had a lot to do with our reaching an agreement. When he put out a proposal without even consulting the presidents of the area, he stung everyone's pride. Before we began our discussions, I proposed that we reject Reagan's plan out of hand, and it was ac-

cepted unanimously." Roger Miranda and William Ratliff, *The Civil War in Nicaragua: Inside the Sandinistas* (New Brunswick, NJ, 1993), p. 265.

Wright believed Ortega alone had sabotaged his peace proposal and was "livid." See Barry, p. 356.

30. "Ortega Shows a Stronger Hand in Nicaragua," Stephen Kinzer, NYT, October 4, 1987, p. 19. Accounts differ over whether the directorate explicitly gave Ortega power to sign an agreement. Miranda recalls that "Prior to his departure, the Directorate had given him permission to act independently, but no one expected he would be signing a treaty." Miranda and Ratliff, p. 35.

31. Author's interview with Oscar Arias, February 25, 1992.

32. The account is from an anonymous Central American "official" who was present at Esquipulas and is quoted in "Costa Rican Chief Warns Nicaragua on Press Freedom," Stephen Kinzer, NYT, August 12, 1987, p. A1.

33. Ortega demanded proof from Duarte, who in turn supplied Salvadoran intelligence reports, as well as a letter from Castro thanking the Sandinistas for their aid to the FMLN. Ortega responded by reminding Duarte of his government's now-scandalous role in Secord's resupply operation. NYT, August 12, 1987.

34. See Miranda and Ratliff, p. 147; Ortega also told Duarte that for some time "the FMLN has asked us to send anti-aircraft missiles to them, but that we have not done so even though the United States is sending them to the Contras, as a way of showing our willingness to negotiate this point." Humberto Ortega was surprised by his brother's admissions: "You told him that?" To which Daniel responded, "Yes, it seemed to me stupid at these high levels to continue denying it to Duarte. It's all very well to deny it publicly, but at this level of discussion, we would lose respect." According to Ortega, this confession "did something to change Napoleon Duarte's attitude." Miranda and Ratliff, pp. 147–48.

35. "Duarte Pledges to Fight Pessimism toward Pact," Julia Preston, WP, August 23, 1987, p. A21.

36. See Gutman, p. 349.

37. "Duarte Offers to Meet Rebels on Sept. 15 for Talks," James LeMoyne, NYT, August 14, 1987, p. A8.

38. "The Latin Peace Plan According to Wright," Wayne King, NYT, August 11, 1987, p. A14.

39. The Esquipulas accords urged that "a cessation of hostilities be arranged" and that governments "undertake to carry out all actions necessary to achieve an effective cease-fire *within a constitutional framework*." The last phrase, long a staple of the Contadora agreement and insisted upon by the Sandinistas, ruled out talks with the outlawed contras.

40. Habib had told Central American officials that "the continuation of nonlethal aid for a reasonable period of time would be reasonable even after a suspension of military assistance . . . given the fact that the presumption would be that a cease-fire would be in place and there would be the necessity of supporting with food, clothing, medicine, the forces involved." See Habib testimony before HFAC Subcommittee on Western Hemisphere Affairs, July 9, 1987.

41. Indeed, the accords did specify one step that had to be taken before the 90-day deadline: the establishment of "national reconciliation committees." Within 20 days of signature, the governments were to form commissions made up of representatives from the government, church, and unarmed opposition that would "determine whether the process of national reconciliation is actually underway, and whether there is absolute respect for all the civil and political rights" guaranteed under the agreement. The timing of the formation of the national reconciliation committees, of course, added to the ambiguity. As Cardinal Obando later asked, what

were the committees supposed to do before the end of 90 days if democratic reforms were not to begin taking effect until the 90-day period ended?

Chapter 49

1. George P. Shultz, *Turmoil and Triumph: My Years as Secretary of State* (New York, 1993), p. 960. Habib declared "We're home free" when he read the text of the agreement. See Roy Gutman, *Banana Diplomacy* (New York, 1988), 349.

2. Shultz, pp. 961, 960.

3. See Gutman, p. 350.

4. "Bush Taking Some Positions at Odds with White House," Gerald M. Boyd, NYT, August 13, 1987, p. A10.

5. "Dole Wants Pledge for Contras," NYT, August 13, 1987, p. A10; "Wright Says Third Party Could Speak for Contras," Michael R. Gordon, NYT, August 10, 1987, p. A7.

6. "Weinberger Opposes Aspects of Latin Peace Plan," Elaine Sciolino, NYT, August 12, 1987, p. A8.

7. Shultz, p. 961; when presidential spokesman Marlin Fitzwater announced plans for the President to meet the contra leaders at the White House in the last week of August, he told reporters: "Make no mistake about it. We want to demonstrate to conservative leaders and to the [contra] directorate and to the nation that the President will not desert the contras"; and, he might have added, in that order. "Reagan to Meet Contra Heads," NYT, August 21, 1987, p. A6.

8. See Gutman, p. 351; Shultz, p. 961. Shultz recalls that conservatives "simply did not trust me or Habib or anyone else to negotiate effectively with Communists."

9. "Lawmakers Fault Shultz on Contra Aid," John M. Goshko, WP, February 3, 1988, p. A12.

10. "Reagan Favors Contra Aid until After Cease-Fire," Steven V. Roberts, NYT, August 16, 1987, p. 5.

11. "Habib Quits Post as Special Envoy; Rift Is Reported," Michael R. Gordon, NYT, August 15, 1987, p. 1.

12. The signatory governments committed themselves to "carry out all actions necessary to achieve an effective cease-fire within a constitutional framework." It could be argued, as Habib had, that an "effective" cease-fire could not be arranged without the agreement of both warring parties, but in the case of Nicaragua the limiting phrase, "within a constitutional framework," intentionally ruled out talks with the extra-constitutional contras.

13. As Secretary Shultz put it, the contras would have to declare themselves "satisfied that a cease-fire is going to be accompanied by such things as amnesty, release of political prisoners, the freedom of religion, freedom of the press and a process definitely under way that is going to lead to the kind of electoral system that we are advocating." Shultz made this statement on August 7 and possibly did not know that what he was saying bore no relation to what was contained in the text of the agreement signed that morning. "House Speaker Warmly Embraces the Latin Plan," Stephen Engelberg, NYT, August 8, 1987, p. 4.

14. "New Contra Plan Called a Threat to Latin Accord," Neil A. Lewis, NYT, September 11, 1987, p. A1.

15. NYT, August 8, 1987.

16. Wright placed $3.5 million for the contras in the 40-day continuing resolution, but at that point the amount of money was less important to the administration than the continued authorization for the CIA to keep supplying and advising the contras. And although the money was ostensibly for "humanitarian aid," it was to be delivered by the CIA along with weapons that had already been bought with the $100 million and which were enough to last almost to

the end of the year. Between September 30 and the end of November, contra attacks grew in size and number.

17. CQ, August 15, 1987, pp. 1892–93.

18. Daniel Ortega, Sesion Extraordinaria No. 47, Protocolo 1740, "Estrategia 1988," p. 2. This document cited in an early draft of Roger Miranda and William Ratliff, *The Civil War in Nicaragua: Inside the Sandinistas* (New Brunswick, NJ, 1993). One may speculate that Castro told Ortega the Sandinistas could do what they needed to do in Nicaragua, but that their support for the FMLN had to continue.

19. The missiles were not delivered until 1989. For those observers who liked to categorize Sandinista comandantes as either "moderates" or "hard-liners," it is interesting to note that the supposedly "moderate" Humberto Ortega acted without the knowledge of the "hard-line" Bayado Arce, who had nominal responsibility for relations with the Salvadoran "cousins," as the Sandinistas called them. See Miranda and Ratliff, pp. 40–41.

20. Miranda and Ratliff, p. 35. Ortega, secret Protocolo 1740, p. 2.

21. Ortega, secret Protocolo 1740, pp. 7–8.

22. Ortega, secret Protocolo 1740, p. 2.

23. The two were Lino Hernandez, head of the independent Human Rights Commission, and Alberto Saborio, a lawyer and secretary general of the Nicaraguan Conservative Party. See Paris AFP 1859 GMT 16 Aug 87, "Interior Ministry Arrests Opposition Figures," LAT 17 Aug 87, 12. "Managua Breaks Up 2 Protests for Peace Pact," NYT, August 17, 1987, p. A4.

24. MDS 1800 GMT 19 Aug 87, "D'Escoto on Lifting State Of Emergency," LAT 20 Aug 87, I1. There seems to have been some debate and confusion within the Directorate over this decision. On August 17, Vice Minister Tinoco apparently told the Guatemalan foreign minister that the emergency decrees had already been lifted. The Guatemalan government promptly made the news public, and it had to be denied in Managua. Panama City ACAN 2145 GMT 18 Aug 87, "ACAN Cites Tinoco on Lifting State of Emergency," LAT 19 Aug 87, I1; Panama City ACAN 0023 GMT 19 Aug 87, "Officials Deny Action," LAT 19 Aug 87, I1.

25. Statement by Congressman Peter Kostmayer. "With Dole in Lead, It's Senators vs. Ortega in Lively Debate," Stephen Kinzer, NYT, September 2, 1987, p. A8.

26. John M. Barry, *The Ambition and the Power* (New York, 1989), p. 373.

27. The opposition complained about Ortega's other choices for the commission, however, whom they considered "collaborationists."

28. On August 30 Omar Cabezas told a rally of party militants in Nagarote: "There is going to be more space for the right wing. We have to be on the ideological offensive." "Anti-Sandinistas Asking TV Licenses," Stephen Kinzer, NYT, September 3, 1987, p. A7. On September 2, Bayardo Arce told Sandinista Defense Committee organizers that "the signing of the peace accord is not just a new element in domestic and regional politics, but a matter of transcendent historical importance. It is a situation absolutely different from the one we have lived with until today. Naturally we have to prepare ourselves for this eventuality." There would be "full freedom for internal political forces to express their views and to seek support for their positions." "Nicaraguans Say Changes Are to Come," Stephen Kinzer, NYT, September 6, 1987, p. A15.

29. "Sandinistas' Foes Stage a Rally," NYT, September 7, 1987, p. 5.

30. According to Chamorro's account, "I told Daniel that if we were talking about censorship, there was nothing to talk about." See "Managua's Bid to Censor Is Reported," Stephen Kinzer, NYT, September 22, 1987, p. A3.

31. "Anti-Sandinista Paper Reopens, Defiant and Exultant," Stephen Kinzer, NYT, October 2, 1987, p. A3.

32. "Managua Braces for Return of Dissent," Stephen Kinzer, NYT, September 29, 1987, p. A3.

33. "Nicaragua: Peace Path Has Pitfalls," Stephen Kinzer, NYT, September 25, 1987, p. A3.

34. "Sandinista Foes Are Dubious," Stephen Kinzer, NYT, September 29, 1987, p. A6.

35. "They realize that the eyes of the world are fixed on *La Prensa*," Jamie Chamorro told reporters, "so they had to let us reopen. But freedom for *La Prensa* does not mean freedom of the press." "Press Curbs Remain, Nicaraguan Editor Says," Stephen Kinzer, NYT, October 22, 1987, p. A10; NYT, September 25, 1987.

36. "Wright Says Award for Arias Dooms Aid for Contras," Neil A. Lewis, NYT, October 14, 1987, p. A14.

37. CQ, October 10, 1987, p. 2445.

38. After talking with Arias privately, even Congressman Newt Gingrich claimed to have been "won over." CQ, September 26, 1987, pp. 2297–98.

39. "White House Opposes Move," NYT, September 23, 1987.

40. In the north, from a 240-square-mile area of Nueva Segovia east of Quilali, and from the area north of San José de Bocay in Jinotega; in the center of the country from a 240-square-mile area of central Zelaya province 165 miles northeast of Managua, and in the south, from the region around Nueva Guinea near the conjunction of the three provinces of Chontales, Rio San Juan, and southern Zelaya.

41. NYT, September 23, 1987.

42. NYT, October 14, 1987.

43. See Ibid. Committee officials later told Arias they had intended primarily to arm the Costa Rican President in his battle against President Reagan. Arias recalls with amusement that "Reagan was responsible for my prize." Author's interview with Oscar Arias, February 25, 1992.

44. Author's Interview with Oscar Arias, February 25, 1992.

45. "Latin Officials Adopt Guidelines for Carrying Out Peace Accord," by James LeMoyne, NYT, October 29, 1987, p. A16.

46. On October 28 the White House announced it would be "flexible" on the timing and size of its request, so long as the Congress assured "continuous funding" for the contras through the duration of the negotiations. "Reagan Delay Expected on Contra Aid Request," Elaine Sciolino, NYT, October 29, 1987, p. A16.

47. "Arias Is Insisting Sandinistas Talk with Rebel Chiefs," by Stephen Kinzer, NYT, October 15, 1987, p. A1.

48. Oslo AFTENPOSTEN 19 Oct 87, "Ortega Reiterates Contra Talks Rejection," FL-212 3 Nov 87, p. 12.

49. "Sandinistas Pressed on 2 Key Points," by Stephen Kinzer, NYT, October 26, 1987, p. A3,.

50. "Sandinistas Urged by Arias to Yield on Contra Talks," James LeMoyne, NYT, October 29, 1987, p. A1.

51. MDS 2238 GMT 29 Oct 87, "FSLN Communiqué on Esquipulas Compliance," FL-210 30 Oct 87, p. 14.

52. Statement by State Department spokesman Charles Redman. CQ, November 7, 1987, p. 2720.

53. CQ, November 7, 1987, p. 2720.

54. The Sandinistas, however, had obviously already made their decision at the meeting on October 28–29, before Ortega left for Moscow.

Chapter 50

1. "For Contras in One Area, Growing Civilian Support," Lindsey Gruson, NYT, November 5, 1987, p. A1.

2. "Contras Back to 'Fortress' in Northern Nicaragua," by William Branigin, WP, October 4, 1987, p. A29.

3. "For Contras in One Area, Growing Civilian Support," by Lindsey Gruson, NYT, November 5, 1987, p. A1.

4. "Released American Says Contras 'Own' Vast Zone," by Julia Preston, WP, November 3, 1987, p. A25.

5. "Contras Are Reported to Establish a Foothold in Central Nicaragua," Stephen Kinzer, NYT, September 13, 1987, p. 1.

6. The Rama Road runs east from the Atlantic port of Bluefields to the Pacific Coast and was used to ship Soviet-supplied weapons overland from the port.

7. "Contras Attacking in Bid to Force Talks," by Stephen Kinzer, NYT, October 17, 1987, p. 3; "Contra Attacks Leave a Message in 5 Towns," by Stephen Kinzer, NYT, October 24, 1987, p. 1.

8. "Contras and Nicaraguan Cardinal Meet," James LeMoyne, NYT, October 26, 1987, p. A3.

9. "Can the Contras Go On?" by James LeMoyne, NYT, October 6, 1987, Section 6, p. 32.

10. CQ, November 7, 1987, p. 2721.

11. MRS 1630 GMT 2 Sep 87, "H. Ortega News Conference," FL-173 8 Sep 87, p. 8.

12. John M. Barry, *The Ambition and the Power* (New York, 1989), pp. 495–96; see also "Offer to Wright on Nicaragua Talks Reported," by Michael R. Gordon, NYT, November 8, 1987, p. A3.

13. Barry, 498.

14. For his team Wright selected Ambassador Paul Warnke, who had negotiated the SALT II Treaty for the Carter administration; Ed King, who was a close adviser to Senator Dodd and an outspoken opponent of aid to the contras; Richard Pena, Wright's personal emissary to the talks at Esquipulas; and Wilson Morris, Wright's press spokesman.

15. For instance, he strengthened the Sandinistas' promise to lift the State of Emergency when the contras complied with the plan. Barry, pp. 500–501.

16. "Wright Has Talks with Both Parties in Nicaragua War," Neil A. Lewis, NYT, November 13, 1987, p. A1.

17. "Ortega Proposes Talk with Reagan and the Contras," Stephen Kinzer, NYT, November 11, 1987, p. A1.

18. Barry, p. 501.

19. Ibid., pp. 500–501.

20. Ibid., p. 505.

21. Wright also said, "The cardinal is the single most qualified person and commands respect. He must have more moral authority than just a messenger. Where? I have no opinion. It should be wherever the cardinal wishes. As for my help, we are at the cardinal's disposal. He is free to choose anyone." Ibid.

22. Cheney said Wright's action had "radicalized House Republicans." See Barry, p. 510; Michel declared that Wright was "absolutely wrong," and Democratic Congressman Dan Rostenkowski, a rival of Wright's in the party hierarchy, told television interviewers that he had "never seen it done before." "Rep. Michel Joins Critics of Wright," WP, November 16, 1987, p. A17.

23. "What Is Jim Wright Doing?" WP editorial, November 16, 1987, p. A12.

24. Wright statements quoted in Barry, pp. 509, 512–13.

25. "House G.O.P. Leaders Delay Vote on Contra Aid," Neil A. Lewis, NYT, December 3, 1987, p. A6.

26. The American press was also slow to understand what was going on. The *Times's* Stephen Kinzer depicted Ortega's acceptance of the four advisers as another concession by the Sandinistas. "Ortega vs. Contra Aid: Sandinistas Near Victory," by Stephen Kinzer, NYT, November 18, 1987, p. A10.

27. "Nicaraguan Cleric Seeks to Define Mediator Role," Julia Preston, WP, November 22, 1987, p. A22.

28. "Nicaragua Frees 985 Prisoners," Julia Preston, WP, November 23, 1987, p. A1.

29. "Nicaraguan Foes Urged by Cardinal to Renew Talks," by Stephen Kinzer, NYT, December 7, 1987, p. A8.

30. In a Sunday homily, the cardinal called on the government to show "flexibility" and to "use language that is conducive to a climate of peace and tranquility." "Nicaraguan Foes Urged by Cardinal to Renew Talks," by Stephen Kinzer, NYT, December 7, 1987, p. A8.

31. "Arias Seeks Halt of All Contra Aid," Karen DeYoung, WP, December 10, 1987, p. A41.

32. "Ortega Warns the Opposition," NYT, December 14, 1987, p. A12; "Sandinistas Warn Opposition Not to Push Too Far," by James LeMoyne, NYT, December 17, 1987, p. A10.

33. Because according to the Nicaraguan constitution any proposed changes had to be considered in two consecutive legislative sessions, the opposition complained that the Sandinistas' postponement of the issue ensured that no changes could be adopted for at least another year. See "NYT, December 17, 1987"; "Nicaraguan Parties Quit Dialogue," William Branigin, WP, December 16, 1987, p. A46.

34. Barry, p. 481.

35. Barry, p. 495. The pressures on Wright at the beginning of November went beyond the issue of Nicaragua. Wright was by then under scrutiny in the press for his dealings with certain savings and loan institutions. He was having difficulties fighting both the White House and members of his own party over the budget and taxes. Some of his efforts to seize control of the House had created bitterness in both parties. See Barry, pp. 430–95.

36. CQ, November 7, 1987, pp. 2720–21.

37. "Reagan Aides Seek Way for Congress to Help Contras," Neil A. Lewis, NYT, November 29, 1987, p. 1.

38. "Senate Approves Bill on Spending with Contra Aid," Jonathan Feurbringer," NYT, December 13, 1987, p. 1.

39. Barry, p. 552.

40. WP, December 13, 1987, p. A1. Ortega probably confirmed the report in order to hide his own embarrassment and to preempt the sensational story in Washington. In fact, Ortega had begun trying to preempt the story as early as the first week of November and had been ignored.

41. "U.S. to Challenge Soviet over Help for Nicaraguans," Neil A. Lewis, NYT, December 15, 1987, p. A1.

42. Part of the compromise called for a week's suspension of arms deliveries on January 12, so the Central American presidents could meet without American military aid flowing to the contras. The delay was only symbolic, however, since it would have no effect on the contras' supply of weaponry.

43. CQ Almanac, 1987, p. 113.

Chapter 51

1. See Francis Fukuyama, "Moscow's Post-Brezhnev Reassessment of the Third World" RAND, February 1986.

Fukuyama noted three new themes in Soviet writings and statements beginning in the early 1980s: the pressure of economic constraints on Soviet Third World policy driven by the need to concentrate on domestic economic development; awareness of the damaging effect of past Soviet Third World activities on U.S.-Soviet relations, particularly since Reagan; and a critique of the Marxist-Leninist vanguard party as a solution to the problem of securing long-term influence in Third World.

Fukuyama noted, as well, however, that Nicaragua seemed to be an exception to the general Soviet trend. See Fukuyama (1986), p. vii.

2. As Henry Ruiz told reporters in August, "If there is a complaint that I consider legitimate, it is from countries like the Soviet Union and East Germany, which have been generous to our people. In a subtle and delicate way, they have told us that we could do much more with the resources we have." Another Sandinista official expressed embarrassment about Sandinista mismanagement and recounted a perhaps typical horror story. "We had a Soviet group that produced a paper showing that they had sent us a certain amount of tons of steel over the last year, and they wanted to see the projects where the steel had been used. We had no idea where to take them, and there was no way to find out. They couldn't believe it." Both quotations are from "For Nicaragua, Soviet Frugality Starts to Pinch," Stephen Kinzer, NYT, August 20, 1987, p. A1.

3. "A Gorbachev Signal on Nicaragua?" Tad Szulc, NYT, September 6, 1987, IV, p. 15. For a similar view, see Nicola Miller, *Soviet Relations with Latin America, 1959–1987* (Cambridge, England, 1989), p. 216. The Moscow Communist Party boss Boris Yeltsin, Szulc suggested, had delivered this message to the Sandinistas during a visit to Managua in March.

4. Szulc, "A Gorbachev Signal on Nicaragua?"

5. See "Moscow to Increase Supply of Oil Donated to Nicaragua," NYT, September 8, 1987. The impression that the Soviet Union was withholding oil from Nicaragua would not die, however, as the *New York Times* ignored even its own reports and declared on October 1 that Moscow had "refused Managua's requests to step up the deliveries of oil and other vital supplies." See "Shevardnadze, in Brazil, Backs Latin Peace Plan," Marlise Simons, NYT, October 1, 1987.

6. See above, p. 555.

7. When Shevardnadze was asked in 1991 about the 1987 military aid agreement, he said he could not remember it. Yurii Pavlov, the Soviet official in charge of Latin American affairs in the Foreign Ministry, did remember the agreement, however. Pavlov said the agreement did not have the approval of the Foreign Ministry but seemed to have been hatched by the Soviet military as part of what Pavlov says was its competition with Gorbachev's central government. Both officials were interviewed by William Ratliff. Interviews contained in early draft of Roger Miranda and William Ratliff, *The Civil War in Nicaragua:Inside the Sandinistas* (New Brunswick, NT, 1993).

8. Miranda and Ratliff, p. 36.

9. See Alvin Z. Rubinstein, *Moscow's Third World Strategy* (Princeton, 1988), 254.

10. As Rubinstein has written, the Soviets saw "useful political gains in U.S. estrangement from important Latin American countries and West European social-democratic elites; in intensification of anti-Americanism among Third World critics; and in the absorption of American domestic political groups with an issue that diverts attention from Soviet activities in Afghanistan, Eastern Europe and the Middle East." See Rubinstein, pp. 217–18.

11. Thus on November 1, as the Sandinistas were privately preparing to begin indirect talks with the contras and had already ratified this decision in their meetings of October 28, a commentator in the Soviet army journal *Krasnaya Zvezda* was in perfect step, declaring that the American demand for "direct talks" with the contras was unacceptable. FBIS-SOV, November 12, 1987, p. 33. Cited in Mark N. Katz, *Gorbachev's Military Policy in the Third World* (New York, 1989), p. 50. As Katz has noted, "Under Gorbachev, Soviet commentary on Nicaragua has for the most part echoed the views of the Sandinista leadership." Katz, p. 50.

12. For an insight into Soviet thinking, see the account of Oleg Gordievsky, who reports that the KGB took "delight" from the "long-drawn-out black comedy of the Iran-Contra scandal" and from the "wave of anti-Americanism in Latin America and beyond" in response to U.S. policies. The KGB official who advocated Soviet support for the Sandinistas in the early years "basked . . . in reflected glory from Central America" and was promoted as a result of the perceived success of the policy. See Christopher Andrew and Oleg Gordievsky, *KGB: The Inside Story* (New York, 1990), pp. 562–63.

For a similar view, see Rubinstein, pp. 217–18, 254.

13. Part of the reason for the week's delay was a desire by State Department officials not to have the Miranda testimony obscured by the summit; a more important part, however, was the White House officials' desire to avoid having the summit overshadowed by Miranda's testimony.

14. "Shift on Contras Seen in Congress," Joel Brinkley, NYT, December 16, 1987, p. A17.

15. "Buildup Would Imperil Region, U.S. Aide Says," NYT, December 14, 1987, p. A12.

16. See Don Oberdorfer, *The Turn: From the Cold War to the New Era: The United States and the Soviet Union, 1983–1990* (New York, 1991), pp. 268–69.

17. "In Nicaragua, Economy Is Hobbling Sandinistas," James LeMoyne, NYT, December 20, 1987, p. 20.

18. Julia Preston illustrated the results of the inflation as follows: In 1981, 700,000 Nicaragua córdobas worth $25,000 could buy a "pleasant working-class home" in Managua; in the late spring of 1987, 700,000 córdobas were worth $87.50, enough to feed a family for a month; in January 1988, 700,000 córdobas were worth $16.00, enough to buy "one tiny pair of tin earrings." See "Inflation Runs Away in Managua," Julia Preston, WP, January 22, 1988, p. A1.

19. On December 30, the cardinal proclaimed: "Unfortunately, I have to say the amnesty in its broad sense has not been achieved nor has the state of emergency been lifted, and steps yet remain to be taken toward democratization." "Contras Seek Direct Meeting with Cardinal," Julia Preston, WP, December 31, 1987, p. A12; see also "Obando Warns 2 Sides on Nicaraguan Talks," NYT, December 20, 1987, p. 20.

20. "Nicaraguan Conflict Appears to Be in a Stalemate," Bernard E. Trainor, NYT, December 22, 1987, p. A18.

21. The contras did not destroy the mine works in Siuna, however, after local residents gathered in the church implored the fighters not to remove their chief source of employment.

22. "Raids by Contras on Three Towns Called Hard Blow," James LeMoyne, NYT, December 23, 1987, p. A1.

23. "The Contras Are Interested," WP editorial, January 2, 1988, p. A18.

Chapter 52

1. "Nicaragua Offers Talks with Contras," William Branigin, WP, January 17, 1988, p. A1.

2. "Salvadoran Rebels Still Based in Nicaragua, Monitors Told," Julia Preston, WP, January 7, 1988, p. A29.

3. In October 1987, Speaker Wright had warned President Azcona that Democrats had controlled the House for over 30 years, and while "the members of the Appropriations Committee" were "amenable to helping" the Honduran government, Democratic leaders "would look with very great disfavor on anything that slowed the peace process." John M. Barry, *The Ambition and the Power* (New York, 1989), p. 494.

In January 1988, Colin Powell and Abrams visited the four presidents to tell them, and particularly Duarte and Azcona, that if they believed the Sandinistas had not complied they had better say so. The future of contra aid, the future of American policy in Central America and thus, Powell and Abrams suggested, the future of American assistance to their countries depended on a clear condemnation of the Sandinistas at San José.

Congressmen Coelho and Foley then warned the four governments that it was the Congress that would decide how much money each of them received, not the administration. Barry, p. 586.

4. The most "eloquent and forceful arguments," according to Bonior, were made by Congressman Lee Hamilton who, though a consistent opponent of contra aid, could speak for and had the respect of moderates in the party. "Concessions to Affect Hill Contra-Aid Vote," John M. Goshko, WP, January 18, 1988, p. A1; "Arias Acknowledges Peace Plan Is Stalled," William Branigin, WP, January 15, 1988, p. A23.

5. WP, January 15, 1988.

6. Ibid.

7. Goshko, "Concessions to Affect Hill Contra-Aid Vote"; CQ, January 23, 1988, pp. 145; WP, January 17, 1988; "Next Hill Vote May Seal Fate of Contra Aid," John M. Goshko, WP, January 20, 1988, p. A1.

8. CR, February 3, 1988, pp. H119–20.

9. Ibid., p. H181.

10. See statements by Congressman Richardson, CR, February 3, 1988, pp. H119–20, and Congressman Scheuer, CR, February 3, 1988, p. H96.

11. Two of the most outspoken moderate Democrats in these weeks, for instance, were Congressmen Slattery of Kansas and Carper of Delaware, whose voting records over the years placed them squarely in the liberal bloc of consistent opposition to aid for the contras.

12. As one Democratic supporter of contra aid asked her moderate colleagues, "How many of you believe that voting on this issue a month from now is going to be any less difficult than it is today? . . . This is a very controversial issue and there is no comfort zone in which we can make a stand." CR, February 3, 1988, p. H92.

13. Daniels's equally conservative replacement was not named until June.

14. Biaggi was facing indictment, and eventual conviction, on racketeering charges in connection with the Wedtech scandal. It cannot be assumed that Biaggi would have voted for the administration's request. His voting record was erratic. Unlike the more moderate McCurdy Democrats, Biaggi supported the Michel amendment in April 1985 and the military aid bill in June 1986. Unlike conservative southern Democrats, he voted against military aid in March 1986.

15. Dyson himself told reporters about his conversation with Reagan and about his demand. See "Md., Va., Lawmakers Are Feeling the Heat," Eric Pianin, WP, February 3, 1988, p. A13; and CQ, February 6, 1988, p. 238.

16. "Contra Aid Concession Offered," Lou Cannon and Tom Kenworthy, WP, February 3, 1988, p. A1.

17. MRS 1644 GMT 14 Feb 88, "President on Economic Issues, U.S. Policy," FBIS-LAT-88-030, 10 February 1988, p. 13.

18. "Managua Frees 7 Opponents Jailed after Meeting Contras," Julia Preston, WP, January 19, 1988.

19. "Managua of Two Minds on Lifting of Emergency," Julia Preston, WP, February 1, 1988, p. A17.

20. Ibid.

21. Managua Radio Corporacion 1200 GMT 8 Feb 88, "10,000 Workers in Antigovernment March," FBIS-LAT-88-029, 12 February 1988, p. 6.

22. See reports by Julia Preston: "Roundup of Draftees Sparks Disturbances," WP, February 10, 1988, p. A1; "Sandinista Revolution Divides People of Masaya," WP, February 11, 1988, p. A37. See also Paris AFP 1818 GMT 10 Feb 88, "Demonstrators Renew Protests," FBIS-LAT-88-028, 11 February 1988, p. 18; Managua Radio Catolica 1300 GMT 11 Feb 88, "City 'Practically under Siege,'" FBIS-LAT-88-028, 11 February 1988, p. 19.

23. Only nine members present in the House in both 1986 and 1988 actually changed their stance regarding military aid—six switched from support of military aid to opposition; and three from opposition to support. The administration thus lost only three votes among members present in both the 100th and 101st Congresses. The administration lost the six votes because anti-contra Democrats won in 11 districts previously held by pro-contra Republicans, while pro-contra Republicans replaced anti-contra Democrats in only five districts. Of the 13 freshman Democrats who replaced Republicans in 1986, 11 voted with the party against the administration's request in 1988; and of the eight freshman Republicans who replaced Democrats, six voted with the President. Two pro-contra Republicans were replaced in 1986 by Democrats who voted for the administration's request in 1988 (Congresswoman Patterson of South Carolina and Congressman Pickett of Virginia.) Two anti-contra Democrats were replaced by Republicans who voted against the administration in 1988 (Congresswoman Morella of Maryland and Congressman Houghton of New York.) One pro-contra Democrat was replaced by a pro-contra Republican (Congressman Inhofe of Oklahoma.) The net difference between the 100th and 101st Congresses, therefore, was a loss of six votes for military aid to the contras.

24. Congressman Pickle, CR, February 3, 1988, p. H209; Congressman Carper, CR, February 3, 1988, p. H141; Congressman Richardson, CR, February 3, 1988, pp. H119–20;

25. CQ, January 30, 1988, p. 201.

26. Ibid.; "Democrats Set Alternative Contra Plan," Lou Cannon and Tom Kenworthy, WP, January 28, 1988, p. A1.

27. "Ortega Says War Is on Despite Vote," Julia Preston, WP, February 5, 1988, p. A1.

28. Wright told reporters the contras' decision "may slow us down." CQ, February 13, 1988, p. 292.

29. "Democrats Offer Reagan Role in Contra Aid Plan," John M. Goshko and Lou Cannon, WP, February 10, 1988, p. A30.

30. "Democrats Near Contra Aid Package," Don Phillips and Joe Pichirallo, WP, February 18, 1988.

31. (The FBIS translation has Ortega referring to Operation "Ganso," but the name may have been misheard. At all other times, the Sandinistas referred to the operation as "Danto".) MRS 1613 GMT 15 Dec 88, "H. Ortega, Tinoco Hold News Conference 15 Dec," FBIS-LAT-88-242, 16 December 1988, p. 16.

32. According to Bosco Vivas, a member of Obando's mediating team, "The government never indicated it would give a positive response. The government said it had decided not to take up the cardinal's proposal." According to Cardinal Obando, a telephone call from Ortega in Managua was made "asking that the proposal not be discussed at that time." Accounts of the confusing sequence of events can be found in Panama City ACAN 1953 GMT 21 Feb 88, "Obando States Cease-Fire Agreement 'Not Easy,'" FBIS-LAT-88-035, 23 February 1988, p. 21; Managua Radio Catolica 1353 GMT 23 Feb 88, "Obando y Bravo Comments," FBIS-LAT-88-036, 24 February 1988, p. 10; "New Proposal in Nicaraguan Truce Talks," Julia Preston, WP,

February 19, 1988, p. A16; "Nicaraguan Peace Talks Suspended," Julia Preston, WP, February 20, 1988, p. A1; and "Mistrust among Nicaraguans Impedes Talks," Julia Preston, WP, February 21, 1988, p. A26.

33. If the contras and Sandinistas agreed to a cease-fire, aid to the contras would continue at a rate of $4 million per month through the end of the year. As a symbolic concession to liberals, the aid was to be delivered by the Defense Department instead of the CIA before a cease-fire; after a cease-fire, the aid program would be administered by the U.S. Agency for International Development.

34. "House Democrats' Plan Loses Narrowly," Tom Kenworthy, WP, March 4, 1988, p. A1.

35. The moderate Democrats had at least voted for some contra aid, while the Republicans, as Congressman Mica put it, had "walked away" from the contras. Ibid.

36. "White House Plans Contra Aid Package," Lou Cannon, WP, March 8, 1988, p. A4; "Defeat of Contra-Aid Bill in House Suggests Issue Has Reached Stalemate," Tom Kenworthy, WP, March 5, 1988, p. A17.

37. "Contra Leaders Criticize U.S. Officials' Handling of Aid Politics," Julia Preston, WP, March 16, 1988, p. A7.

Chapter 53

1. MDS 0139 GMT 20 Sep 88, "Ortega Comments on Talks with Contras," FBIS-LAT-88-183, 21 September, 1988, p. 13.

2. WP, March 17, 1988, p. A1.

3. "Ortega Says Congress Hurt the Contras," Stephen Kinzer, NYT, March 12, 1988, p. A3.

4. "White House Pressures Congress on Contra Aid," Tom Kenworthy, WP, March 15, 1988.

5. "Nicaragua Again Adopts Stance of the Underdog," Julia Preston, WP, March 20, 1988, p. A29.

6. "Contra Aid Offensive Fizzles amid Contradictions," Lou Cannon and Tom Kenworthy, WP, March 16, 1988, p. A7; with special report filed by Julia Preston from Miami.

7. See account of meeting in John M. Barry, *The Ambition and the Power* (New York, 1989), 598. Another account comes from Congressman Robert Dornan, CR, March 30, 1988, p. H1360.

8. Reagan actually agreed "in principle" to send the 82nd airborne before Azcona's official request arrived in Washington. "Troop Decision Made Early," Lou Cannon and Don Oberdorfer, WP, March 18, 1988, p. A1; "Reagan Orders U.S. Troops to Honduras," Lou Cannon and Don Oberdorfer, WP, March 17, 1988, p. A1.

9. The Sandinistas told the reporters they were at the junction of the Coco and Bocay rivers, in an effort to prove that the Sandnistas had not crossed into the Honduras across the Coco. But actually the journalists may have been taken to the junction of the Bocay and Amaka rivers, nearly identical in appearance but a few miles further south, where there was no fighting.

10. "Aides Say Attack Halted Short of Contra Supplies," George C. Wilson, WP, March 23, 1988.

11. MRS 1613 GMT 15 Dec 88, "H. Ortega, Tinoco Hold News Conference 15 Dec," FBIS-LAT-88-242, 16 December 1988, p. 16.

12. Statement by Congressman Barney Frank (D-MA), CR March 23, 1988, p. H1137.

13. "Deployment Alarms Democrats," Tom Kenworthy, WP, March 17, 1988, p. A1.

14. CR, March 17, 1988, p. S2389.

15. "Senate Votes to Send Assistance to Contras," Tom Kenworthy, WP, April 1, 1988, p. A4.

16. "Wright's High-Risk Strategy on Central America Pays Off," Tom Kenworthy, WP, April 4, 1988, p. A1.

17. CQ, March 19, 1988, p. 696.

18. WP, April 4, 1988. Wright referred MacKay's bill to committee, effectively ruling out any rapid action. Byrd declared there was no "legislative vehicle" to which to attach Boren's proposal. "Reagan Again Vows Support for Contras," Lou Cannon and Tom Kenworthy, WP, March 23, 1988, p. A23.

19. Calero quoted in R. Pardo-Maurer, *The Contras, 1980–1989; A Special Kind of Politics* (New York, 1990), p. 105.

20. MDS 0139 GMT 20 Sep 88, "Ortega Comments on Talks with Contras," FBIS-LAT-88-183, 21 September, 1988, p. 13.

21. Author's interview with Alfredo César, August 24, 1992.

22. Ibid.

23. "Aid Cutoff Cited as Key to Accord," Julia Preston, WP, March 25, 1988; author's interview with César.

24. Author's interview with César; "'There Was a Special Nationalism,'" Julia Preston, WP, March 26, 1988, p. A17.

25. Author's interview with César.

26. WP, March 26, 1988; Author's interview with Cesar.

27. WP, March 25, 1988.

28. CQ, April 2, 1988, p. 839.

29. Ibid., p. 835

30. "AID Ready to Move Contra Aid 'Into the Region,'|" Julia Preston, WP, April 6, 1988.

Chapter 54

1. "Contra Leaders Face Resistance to Accord," Julia Preston, WP, March 27, 1988, p. A27.

2. "Contras Challenge Sandinistas at Talks," Julia Preston, WP, March 29, 1988, p. A1.

3. "Contras Reject Bid to Disarm, Question Case-Fire Process," Julia Preston, WP, April 18, 988, p. A1.

4. "Encamped Contras Await Food, News of Fate," Wilson Ring, WP, May 8, 1988, p. A22.

5. See Sam Dillon, *Commandos: The CIA and Nicaragua's Contra Rebels* (New York, 1991), pp. 218–25, for an account of these events.

6. This last point was confirmed by the observers, Baena Soares of the OAS and Cardinal Obando y Bravo. See "Sandinistas, Contras Adjourn Talks," Julia Preston, WP, May 1, 1988, p. A26.

7. "Contras Beset by Divisions, Supply Shortages in Field," William Branigin, WP, May 7, 1988, p. A1; WP, May 8, 1988.

8. "1,500 Contra Dissenters Said to Hole Up in Camp," Wilson Ring, WP, May 10, 1988, p. A15.

9. For a good account of these events, see Dillon, pp. 224–25.

10. "Ortega Denounces 'Pseudo-Leaders' of Labor," Stephen Kinzer, NYT, May 2, 1988, p. A13; "Ortega Threatens to Attack If Contras Refuse to Bend," *Washington Times*, May 2, 1988.

11. CQ, May 7, 1988, p. 1238.

12. See CR, May 18, 1988, p. E1598; and see statement of Congressman Cheney, CR, May 26, 1988, p. H3669.

13. CR, May 26, 1988, p. H3665.

14. Interview with César printed in *La Prensa*, May 23, 1988, p. 1.

15. "Sandinista Police Batter, Arrest Dozens of Strikers," Sam Dillon, *Miami Herald*, April 30, 1988; "New Plan Paralyzes Nicaraguan Economy," Julia Preston, WP, March 5, 1988, p. A16.

16. "Sandinistas Hold Leaders of Opposition after March," Glenn Garvin, *Washington Times*, May 5, 1988.

17. Statement by Luis Sanchez Sancho, a leader of the Socialist Party, quoted in "Nicaragua Taking a Tougher Stand on the Opposition," Stephen Kinzer, NYT, May 16, 1988, p. A1.

18. CQ, May 21, 1988, p. 1385.

19. Wright in his March 30 letter had promised to grant such a request if the President found the Sandinistas were "acting in violation of the terms of the cease-fire agreement." See Wright letter of March 30, 1988, CQ, April 2, 1988, p. 841.

20. "Superdiplomat Jim Wright," WP, May 8, 1988, p. B6.

21. "Sandinista: Not Blocking Contra Aid," John M. Goshko and Don Phillips, WP, May 13, 1988, p. A19.

22. Paris AFP 2210 GMT 26 May 88, "RN Presents Proposal to Government at Talks," FBIS-LAT-88-103, 27 May 1988, p. 9.

23. See p. 365 above.

24. See p. 304 above.

25. CQ, June 18, 1988, p. 1666.

26. "Contras Say U.S. Backs Settlement as Talks Resume," Julia Preston, WP, June 8, 1988, p. 23.

27. "Managua Offers Plan for Political Reforms," Julia Preston, WP, May 29, 1988, p. A29.

28. As the Sandinistas themselves pointed out, agreement in the national dialogue was not the same as the enactment of political and military decisions. As Vice Foreign Minister Tinoco explained on May 25, "we are talking about discussing these points to attain political agreements. This does not mean we will draft laws at the national dialogue, because . . . laws are drafted and approved by the National Assembly. . . . [W]e want to attain basic agreements that will lead to the drafting of laws that *could* be approved by the National Assembly in accordance with our Constitution." MDS 0000 GMT 26 May 88, "Tinoco on Proposal, Talks," FBIS-LAT-88-102, 26 May 1988, p. 11; emphasis added.

29. WP, May 29, 1988; "Sandinistas, Contras Report Chill in Talks," Julia Preston, WP, June 9, 1988, p. A32.

30. For Reichler's account of these discussions, see "Peace Terms Prove Too Costly at Managua Negotiations," Julia Preston, WP, June 11, 1988, p. A18; for Humberto Ortega's account, see "Ortega Says Nicaragua to Continue Cease-Fire," Julia Preston, WP, June 12, 1988, p. A1; Cesar's account is from interview with the author, August 24, 1992.

31. John M. Barry, *The Ambition and the Power* (New York, 1989), p. 628.

32. "Contras Say U.S. Backs Settlement as Talks Resume," Julia Preston, WP, June 8, 1988, p. 23.

33. See "Ortega Says Nicaragua to Continue Cease-Fire," Julia Preston, WP, June 12, 1988, p. A1.

34. Author's interview with César, August 24, 1992.

35. Managua BARRICADA 11 Jun 88, p. 3, "Tinoco Comments on Talks with Contras," FBIS-LAT-88-116, 16 June 1988, p. 14; WP, June 9, 1988.

36. See Stephen Kinzer *Blood of Brothers: Life and War in Nicaragua* (New York, 1991), p. 379. The *Post's* Julia Preston concurred that "the Sandinistas did not feel pressed to offer in their final proposal more than vague assurances to guarantee the contras' safe and fair participation in electoral politics," while the contras' "internal discord and disarry" prevented them from making a counterproposal that was more than a "farewell gesture." See "Peace Terms Prove Too Costly at Managua Negotiations," Julia Preston, WP, June 11, 1988, p. A18.

Chapter 55

1. "Who's Derailing Peace for Nicaragua?" letter from David E. Bonior to *Washington Post* editorial page, June 19, 1988, p. C6; CQ, June 11, 1988, p. 1628.

2. "Contra Leaders Ask Administration to Seek New Aid from Congress," John M. Goshko, WP, June 17, 1988, p. A20; CQ, June 18, 1988, p. 1664.

3. Statement by Congressman Edwards quoted in "Reagan Blames Sandinistas for Collapse of Peace Talks," Bill McAllister, WP, June 11, 1988, p. A20.

4. CQ, June 18, 1988, p. 1664.

5. WP, June 17, 1988; CQ, June 18, 1988, p. 1664.

6. Wright's press spokesman, Wilson Morris, expressed doubt that a vote could be held before September. See CQ, June 18, 1988, p. 1665.

7. "Contras Express Hope for Non-Lethal U.S. Aid," John M. Goshko, WP, June 16, 1988, p. A12.

8. This would not have been the only issue where the interests of Bush's re-election were affecting Reagan's policies at about this time. For the role of Bush and his advisers in the administration's dealings with the Panamanian dictator, General Manuel Noriega, see Frederick Kempe, *Divorcing the Dictator* (New York, 1990), pp. 313–14; WP, June 17, 1988.

9. "U.S. Seeking Way to Keep Contras Viable," David B. Ottoway, WP, July 3, 1988, p. A31.

10. Paris AFP 1535 GMT 3 Jul 88, "Arias on Diplomatic Offensive for Nicaragua," FBIS-LAT-88-128, 5 July 1988, p. 15.

11. Allegations of a massive CIA campaign to "destabilize" the Sandinista government—a program the Sandinistas referred to as the "Melton Plan"—were fanciful. Opposition leaders had been receiving funds from the CIA to support political activities since 1979. The biggest shift in U.S. policy in 1988 was the arrival of Ambassador Melton and his more activist approach, especially compared to his more inert predecessor, Ambassador Harry Bergold.

12. This meeting did occur on July 14. It is not clear that the opposition leaders called for mediation, but they did mention the plan for a national front. See San José Radio Reloj 1200 GMT 15 Jul 88, "Arias Meets Nicaraguan Opposition Leaders," FBIS-LAT-88-138, 19 July 1988, p. 9.

13. Stephen Kinzer, *Blood of Brothers: Life and War in Nicaragua* (New York, 1991), p. 381.

14. Ibid., p. 383; see also Managua LA PRENSA 11 Jul 88, p. 2, "LA PRENSA Comments," FBIS-LAT-88-134, 13 July 1988, p. 23.

15. MDS 1921 GMT 10 Jul 88, "Further on Riot," FBIS-LAT-88-132, 11 July 1988, p. 20.

16. "U.S. Expels Nicaraguan Ambassador, Seven Staffers," WP, July 13, 1988, p. A1.

17. "Arias Critical of Actions by Nicaragua," Jake Dyer, WP, July 14, 1988, p. 24; "Ortega: Contra Aid Means Military Showdown," Julia Preston, WP, August 5, 1988, p. A1.

18. Specifically, Gutman argued that the contras had "provok[ed] a crisis" by "breaking off the talks" in Managua on June 9. See "How the Contras Created Shultz' Credibility Gap," Roy Gutman, WP, August 7, 1988, p. B1.

19. WP, August 5, 1988; "Sandinistas Move against Opponents," William Branigin, WP, August 1, 1988, p. A1.

20. Emphasis added. "Senate Condemns Actions of Nicaraguan Leaders," Helen Dewar, WP, July 14, 1988, p. A24.

21. Senator Dole presented a proposal for new military aid, but even his plan would not provide the aid until after a second vote in September, and even Dole's proposal was too extreme for Senate Democrats.

22. "Expelled U.S. Envoy Advocates Contra Aid to Pressure Nicaragua," John M. Goshko, WP, July 14, 1988, p. A24.

23. The bill was sponsored by Democrats in an effort to show unity in the party in light of the divided Democratic presidential ticket—Governor Michael Dukakis was a staunch opponent of aid to the contras, his running mate Lloyd Bentsen an equally staunch supporter. The Democrats and Senator Dole sought White House support for the bill, but conservative Republicans and White House political advisers saw no reason to help the Democrats solve their political problems with an inadequate bill. The bill passed 49–47 without a single Republican vote.

See "Senate Democrats Draft $18 Million Contra Aid," Chris Adams, WP, August 1, 1988, p. A1; "Dole Taunts Democrats over Contra Differences," Helen Dewar, WP, August 3, 1988, p. A10; "Senate Seeks to Avoid Election-Year Showdown over Contra Aid," Helen Dewar, WP, August 7, 1988, p. A24.

Chapter 56

1. MDS 1533 GMT 19 Jul 88, "Ortega Extends Cease-Fire on 9th Anniversary," FBIS-LAT-88-139, 20 July 1988, p. 23.

2. Panama City ACAN 1601 GMT 24 Jul 88, "Praises Dukakis Speech," FBIS-LAT-88-142, 25 Jul 1988, p. 20.

3. Managua BARRICADA 20 Sep 88, p. 3, "Sandinist Power Threatened," FBIS-LAT-88-212, 2 November 1988, p. 24.

4. Managua LA PRENSA 29 Aug 88, pp. 1, 8, "Borge Cited on FSLN's 'Political Decline,'" FBIS-LAT-88-171, 2 September 1988, p. 10.

5. "[W]hether [the next] administration is Democrat or Republican," Ortega predicted, "it will try to impose its criteria on Nicaragua; it will try to make decisions regarding Nicaraguan domestic affairs." Even the Democrats had "their own strategy concerning the revolution" which was "not aimed at strengthening the revolution but at trying to weaken it." MDS 1808 GMT 8 Nov 88, "Ortega, Ramirez Comment on U.S. Elections," FBIS-LAT-88-217, 9 November 1988, p. 13; MDS 0447 GMT 9 Nov 88, "Ortega on Bush Victory," FBIS-LAT-88-127, 9 November 1988, p. 16.

6. MDS 0447 GMT 9 Nov 88, "Ortega on Bush Victory," FBIS-LAT-88-127, 9 November 1988, p. 16.

7. The contra issue, Baker said publicly, was "easily demagogued by the other side." CQ, November 5, 1988, p. 3191.

8. See MDS 2216 GMT 18 Aug 88, "Ortega on Talks, U.S. Elections, Radio Catolica," FBIS-LAT-88-161, 19 August 1988, p. 14; and MDS 1800 GMT 22 Aug 88, "Ortega on U.S. Action, Next Administration," FBIS-LAT-88-163, 23 August 1988, p. 9.

9. Mexico City EL DIA 30 Nov 88, pp. 1, 16, "Ortega Discusses Regional, Domestic Situation," FBIS-LAT-88-235, 7 December 1988, p. 18; MDS 1804 GMT 31 Dec 88, "Ortega Delivers 1988 Year-End Speech," FBIS-LAT-89-001, 3 January 1989, p. 23.

10. "Ortega Offers Proposal to Repatriate Contras," Julia Preston, WP, February 2, 1989, p. A27.

11. MDS 1804 GMT 31 Dec 88, "Ortega Delivers 1988 Year-End Speech," FBIS-LAT-89-001, 3 January 1989, p. 23; Managua BARRICADA 31 Dec 88, pp. 1,6,7, "Ortega Discusses Foreign, Domestic Issues," FBIS-LAT-89-004, 6 January 1988, p. 10.

12. Paris AFP 2355 GMT 22 Dec 88, "Ortega to Present Peace Proposal to Bush," FBIS-LAT-88-247, 23 December 1988, p. 14; Managua BARRICADA 31 Dec 88, pp. 1,6,7 "Ortega Discusses Foreign, Domestic Issues." FBIS-LAT-89-004, 6 January 1988, p. 10.

13. Author's interview with Humberto Ortega, May 24, 1990.

14. The Sandinistas had reason to believe, based on the record of the past, that groups like Amnesty International and Americas Watch were likely to be more critical of the human rights policies of the governments of El Salvador and Guatemala than of the Sandinistas.

15. See the statements of the Honduran justice minister reported in Panama City ACAN 1359 GMT 8 Sep 88, "Further on Contras," FBIS-LAT-88-175, 9 September 1988, p. 12.

16. Lopez also wanted the border between Honduras and El Salvador patrolled and FMLN forces cleared from Salvadoran refugee camps. "What Happens to Contras in Honduras When Reagan Is Gone?" John M. Goshko, WP, October 18, 1988, p. A4. To the Sandinistas, the Hondurans seemed "determined to escape from a curse" and were "acting out of desperation." In November, according to Ortega, Azcona approached him directly for help in dealing with the contras. "Azcona was very concerned, and asked me: What do I do about the contras, who are such a problem? I told President Azcona that we will take them in. Let us present a repatriation plan to the United Nations, the UNHCR, the Red Cross, and other international organizations so the refugees will not be afraid and will rest assured that nothing will happen to them." "Ortega Delivers 1988 Year-End Speech."

17. Managua BARRICADA 2 Dec 88, p. 3, "Editorial Analyzes Verification Problems," FBIS-LAT-88-240, 14 December 1988, p. 16.

18. Cerezo called on the Central Americans to adopt a "position that must be supported and respected by any U.S. administration." MRS 1937 GMT 23 Sep 88, "Ortega, Cerezo Meet, Comment on C.A. Summit," FBIS-LAT-88-186, 26 September 1988, p. 18.

19. "Arias Asks Delay in Central America Meeting," Stephen Kinzer, NYT, January 8, 1989, p. 8.

20. San José LA REPUBLICA 19 Oct 88, p. 2, "Madrigal Blames Nicaragua for Summit Delay," FBIS-LAT-88-207, 26 October 1988, p. 12; Panama City ACAN 1229 GMT 30 Sep 88, "Castro's Role," FBIS-LAT-88-191, 3 October 1988, p. 8; "Arias Asks Delay in Central America Meeting," Stephen Kinzer, NYT, January 8, 1989, p. 8; MDS 0210 GMT 7 Jan 89, "Ortega Speaks at Ceremony Honoring Jakes," FBIS-LAT-89-005, 9 January 1988, p. 20.

21. Arias had apparently not even consulted with the Hondurans or Salvadorans. The Nicaragua and Guatemalan governments immediately rejected Arias's proposal, and for a brief moment, President Duarte seemed to take no position, thus allowing Ortega to demand respect for the "majority" opinion among the five governments. The Honduran and Salvadoran governments, however, soon came around to support postponement of the summit. Managua BARRICADA 8 Jan 89, pp. 1,5," Foreign Minister's Reaction," FBIS-LAT-89-007, 11 January 1989, p. 33.

22. "Ortega Speaks at Ceremony Honoring Jakes"; Paris AFP 0048 GMT 11 Jan 89, "Ortega's Statement on Summit Postponement," FBIS-LAT-89-007, 11 January 1989, p. 32.

23. Arias openly criticized "the great indifference shown by the European democracies" who had been hesitant to "raise their voices in censuring governments that have not complied with the agreement." In October Arias had traveled to Spain to receive a prize for his peacemaking; before he left he declared that "Spain's voice must be heard again in Central America."

Panama City ACAN 1229 GMT 30 Sep 88, "Castro's Role," FBIS-LAT-88-191, 3 October 1988, p. 8.

24. The newly elected President Salinas was about to launch a thorough reform and privatization of the Mexican economy. He sought a closer economic partnership with the United States and was not about to do anything that might sour the relationship with the new American President. Even before Salinas's inauguration, the Mexican government had "absented itself from Central America" due to its serious economic problems. As H. Rodrigo Jauberth has written, Mexico had "exhausted its role and its presence in the region." See H. Rodrigo Jauberth, "The Mexico-Central America-United States Triangle and the Negotiations Process," in Jauberth, Gilberto Castañeda, Jesús Hernández, and Pedro Vuskovic, *The Difficult Triangle: Mexico, Central America, and the United States*, (Boulder, CO, 1992) p. 80.

25. In January, with the Sandinistas desperate for support in their demand for an early summit, the new Mexican foreign minister would say only that the date for the summit was less important than the results achieved. MRS 1200 GMT 27 Jan 89, "Mexico's Solana Cited on Peace Process," FBIS-LAT-89-018, 30 January 1989, p. 25.

26. After talking to Perez by telephone in January, Ortega suggested that "we should not entertain great hopes" about the meetings Arias and Pérez planned to hold around the inauguration ceremonies in Caracas. Managua Sistema Sandinista Television Network 0200 GMT 10 Jan 89, "Ortega Talks with Pérez, Duarte on Summit," FBIS-LAT-89-008, 12 January 1989, p. 14; Paris AFP 0048 GMT 11 Jan 89, "Ortega's Statement on Summit Postponement," FBIS-LAT-89-007, 11 January 1989, p. 32.

27. It apparently helped that the new American Vice President, Dan Quayle, was in Caracas denouncing the Sandinistas in the strongest terms. Alfredo César was present in Caracas and spoke with his friend Carlos Andrés Pérez and with Arias about their meeting with Ortega. According to César, Pérez, Arias, and Gonzalez told Ortega, in effect, "Look at this guy [Quayle]. Bush will be tough. This is your opportunity. If you don't deal with us, you'll be in trouble with the Americans." Author's interview with César, August 24, 1992.

28. See the account of this meeting in Andres Oppenheimer, *Castro's Final Hour: The Secret Story Behind the Coming Downfall of Communist Cuba* (New York, 1992), p. 205.

29. Arias's own term as president expired in March 1990, and he apparently wanted to make sure he was still around to see the Sandinistas carry out their promises.

30. "A Latin Peace Plan Not So Broad: Ball in Nicaragua's Court," Mark A. Uhlig, NYT, February 16, 1989, p. A12.

31. "Latin Presidents Announce Accord on Contra Bases," Lindsey Gruson, NYT, February 15, 1989, p. A1.

Chapter 57

1. "Quayle Criticizes 5-Nation Pact on Contras' Guerrillas," John M. Goshko, WP, February 25, 1989, p. A17.

2. CQ, February 18, 1989, p. 345.

3. Author's interview with former Under Secretary of State Robert Zoellick, January 20, 1995.

4. Ibid.

5. CQ Almanac, 1989, p. 40. This was not quite true. Gingrich had determined to pursue Wright earlier in 1987, but Wright's actions in November did help incite broader Republican support for Gingrich's efforts, especially from party leaders like Congressman Cheney.

6. CQ, April 15, 1989, p. 833.

7. "Nicaraguan Plan Shifts U.S. Emphasis to Diplomacy—and Compromise," John M. Goshko, WP, March 25, 1989, p. A11.

8. Author's interview with Under Secretary of State Robert Zoellick, January 20, 1995; author's interview with Ambassador Crescencio Arcos, April 5, 1995.

9. Author's interview with Zoellick.

10. CQ, March 18, 1989, p. 596; CQ, March 11, 1989, p. 538.

11. Given the 1983 Supreme Court ruling against a one-house veto, this "one-member veto" sent the new White House counsel, Boyden Gray, into a fit of public outrage. But Baker argued that the compromise was a "gentleman's agreement," not a law, and therefore not unconstitutional. The four committees were the Senate Foreign Relations Committee and Senate Appropriations Subcommittee on Foreign Operations, and the House Foreign Affairs Committee and House Appropriations Committee on Foreign Operations.

12. Emphasis added. International supervision was the strongest possible term for international monitoring of the elections. The Tesoro Beach agreement referred to observers "participating" and "certifying" the "integrity" of the elections. In 1978, Somoza had rejected international "supervision" of the plebiscite as excessively intrusive of Nicaragua's sovereignty, and President Carter had agreed.

13. The votes were 309–110 in the House; 89–9 in the Senate.

14. "Ortega Attacks Aid for Contras," Mark A. Uhlig, NYT, March 28, 1989, p. A6.

15. Madrid EFE 2042 GMT 5 Apr 89, "Arias Discusses Meeting with President Bush," FBIS-LAT-89-065 6 April 1989, p. 24.

16. "Bush to Seek $40 Million in Humanitarian Aid for Contras," Don Oberdorfer, WP, March 14, 1989, p. A23.

17. Baker's aides told reporters that the Honduran government had been assured that the United States would not leave Honduras "holding the hands of 11,000 armed contras." "U.S. Envoy Urges Hondurans to Let the Contras Stay," Robert Pear, NYT, March 14, 1989, p. A1.

18. "Baker to Contras: No Raids," Don Oberdorfer, WP, March 15, 1989, p. A28.

19. Managua LA PRENSA 14 Mar 89, pp. 1, 12, "Opposition Claims on El Salvador Accords Cited," FBIS-LAT-89-051, 17 March 1989, p. 26; Managua Radio Noticias 1200 GMT 15 Mar 89, "PSC President on Need for National Dialogue," FBIS-LAT-89-050, 16 March 1989, p. 27; MDS 2101 GMT 17 Mar 89, "Ortega Speaks on Country's National Dialogue," FBIS-LAT-89-052, 20 March 1989, p. 43.

20. President Ortega would choose the five members of the SEC from slates proposed by the National Assembly. Two members would be chosen from opposition parties, two to represent the government, and the fifth would be "neutral." The opposition, therefore, expected Ortega to choose among the more conciliatory opposition candidates and to select a 'neutral' who was not really neutral, thus giving the government control of the electoral council.

21. While the Sandinistas' new law allowed exiles to vote, however, it required that they return to the country to do so.

22. During the last 80 days before the elections, all the opposition parties were to share 30 minutes each day on the two government-owned television stations. Since any number of tiny parties might be participating in the elections alongside the main opposition coalition, and since some of these tiny parties would invariably be backed secretly by the Sandinistas, this rule gave the Sandinistas the means of limiting the access of their more dangerous foes.

23. "New Nicaraguan Law Eases Curbs on Press," NYT, April 25, 1989, p. A8.

24. "U.S. Calls New Nicaragua Laws Inadequate," NYT, April 26, 1989, p. A9; author's interview with Robert Zoellick, January 20, 1995. "We always doubted [the elections] would be free and fair."

25. State Department document quoted in Michael Kramer, "Anger, Bluff—And Cooperation," *Time*, June 4, 1990, p. 39.

Chapter 58

1. Aleksey Izyumov and Andrey Kortunov, "The Soviet Union in the Changing World," *International Affairs*, August 1988. Cited in Francis Fukuyama "Gorbachev and the New Soviet Agenda in the Third World," *RAND Corporation Report*, June 1989, pp. 14–15.

2. Cited by Mark N. Katz in Kurt M. Campbell and Neil S. MacFarlane, ed. *Gorbachev's Third World Dilemmas* (New York, 1989), p. 41.

3. The article, "Confidence and the Balance of Interests," was written by Andrei Kozyrev, who would later become Russian foreign minister under Boris Yeltsin. His article is cited in Fukuyama (1989), p. 20.

4. Testimony of Deputy Secretary of State-designate Lawrence Eagleburger to Senate Foreign Relations Committee, March 15, 1989.

5. Author's interview with Elliott Abrams, March 19, 1990.

6. The discussion that follows is based on interviews with Bernard Aronson, Eric Edelman, and Alex Wolf in 1990.

7. State Department document quoted in Michael Kramer, "Anger, Bluff—And Cooperation," *Time*, June 4, 1990. p. 39.

8. Quoted in Michael R. Beschloss and Strobe Talbott, *At the Highest Levels: The Inside Story of the End of the Cold War* (Boston, 1993) p. 57.

9. The Bush letter is excerpted in Kramer, p. 39.

10. Beschloss and Talbott, p. 57.

11. Yuri Pavlov, *Soviet-Cuban Alliance, 1959–1991* (Coral Gables, FL., 1994), pp. 130–31.

12. As Pavlov recalls, Castro had come "to an early conclusion that perestroika was acting like the AIDS virus, destroying the immunological defense of the socialist political system." Pavlov, p. 111.

13. Pavlov, p. 177. "The conservative majority of the Politburo and Secretaries of the CPSU Central Committee, Oleg Baklanov, Vladimir Kryuchkov, Yegor Ligachev, Ivan Polozkov, Nikolai Ryzhkov, Oleg Shenin, and others, shared Castro's ill feelings about the radical course *perestroika* was taking."

14. Pavlov, p. 127.

15. Ibid., pp. 101, 142.

16. Ibid., p. 135.

17. "Gorbachev's 'Gift' to Bush in Nicaragua," Robert S. Leiken, NYT, May 18, 1989, p. A31.

18. "Gorbachev Eclipsed," Bill Keller, NYT, April 6, 1989, p. A1.

19. "U.S. Dismisses Call by Gorbachev to End Latin America Arms Aid," Bernard Weinraub, NYT, April 6, 1989, p. A14.

20. "President Accuses Nicaragua," David Hoffman, WP, May 3, 1989, p. A1.

21. White House transcript of President Bush's speech to the Council of the Americas, May 2, 1989.

22. See Kramer, pp. 40–41,44.

23. Pavlov sometimes responded to Aronson's questions by saying "let me tell you what I am informed the Ministry of Defense says" about the flow of arms. Author's interview with Eric Edelman, March 10, 1990.

24. Quoted in Beschloss and Talbott, p. 55.

25. Kramer, p. 39.

26. Ibid.

27. A Sandinista Foreign Ministry official told reporters that the Nicaraguan government did not have copies of the "supposed" letter from Gorbachev to Bush and wanted to wait for more information "so that we can react with more care on such an important topic." "U.S. Questions Moscow Pledge on Sandinistas," Bernard Weinraub, NYT, May 17, 1989, p. A1.

28. Pavlov, p. 211. Shevardnadze, according to Pavlov, "was aware of the real situation."

29. "Soviets Indicate Intent to Relax Their Posture in Central America," Don Oberdorfer, WP, May 14, 1989, p. A28; See also Don Oberdorfer, *The Turn: From Cold War to the New Era: The United States and the Soviet Union, 1983–1990* (New York, 1991), p. 348; as early as February, the British government began urging Baker to "get back in the game." See Beschloss and Talbott, p. 31.

30. Oberdorfer, p. 334.

31. Baker was worried "about the politics of it all. Look who's getting the big cheers [i.e. Gorbachev and Shevardnadze]. Look who's getting the big yawns [i.e. Bush and Baker]." Beschloss and Talbott, p. 38.

32. WP, May 14, 1989.

33. Oberdorfer, p. 349.

34. Emphasis added. Kramer, p. 40.

35. Beschloss and Talbott, pp. 65–66.

36. Ibid., p. 62.

37. Kramer, p. 40; WP, May 14, 1989; The Sandinistas, when they received a written text of the American proposal from the Soviet government, called it the "non-paper"—a diplomatic term connoting an informal agreement between two governments not meant for public consumption. Author's interview with Humberto Ortega, May 24, 1990.

38. Kramer, p. 41; Beschloss and Talbott, p. 59. As the authors suggest, "Gorbachev was essentially asking Bush to solve the Castro problem himself." The same could be said about the Sandinista problem.

39. Pavlov quoted in Oppenheimer, 210; author's interview with Bernard Aronson.

40. Author's interview with Robert Zoellick, January 20, 1995.

Chapter 59

1. Panama City ACAN 1505 GMT 9 Apr 89, "Ortega on Cristiani Plan 'to Sabotage' Pact," FBIS-LA-89-067, 10 April 1989, p. 24.

2. Managua LA PRENSA 5 May 89, p. 10, "Costa Rican President Arias Replies to Ortega," FBIS-LAT-89-093, 16 May 1989, p. 37.

3. Managua BARRICADA 10 May 89, p. 3, "Contra Demobilization Plan Reported, Assessed," FBIS-LAT-89-091, 12 May 1989, p. 24; Madrid EFE 2105 GMT 23 May 89, "Ortega Urges Prompt Demobilization of Contras," FBIS-LAT-89-099, 24 May 1989, p. 18.

4. MRS 1235 GMT 19 May 89, "Ortega: No More 'Senseless' Opposition Talks," FBIS-LAT-89-097, 22 May 1989, p. 18; MRS 2015 GMT 19 May 89, "More on Ortega Speech," FBIS-LAT-89-097, 22 May 1989, p. 18.

5. Agrarian Reform Minister Jaime Wheelock explained that the government's decision was purely political. The owners had assumed a "confrontational position" and "attitudes that promote anarchy among themselves and other producers." MRS 1202 GMT 22 Jun 89, "Decree Explains Government Action," FBIS-LAT-89-120, 23 June 1989, p. 23.

6. Panama City ACAN 1904 GMT 22 Jun 89, "Ortega: Coffee Growers 'Chickens,'" FBIS-LAT-89-120, 23 June 1989, p. 25.

7. Panama City ACAN 2314 GMT 8 Jul 89, "UNO March Canceled Because of 'Repression,'" FBIS-LAT-89-130, 10 July 1989, p. 27.

8. MRS 1938 GMT 22 Jun 89, "Official Denounces COSEP "Plan,'" FBIS-LAT-89-120, 23 June 1989, p. 23.

9. Panama City ACAN 1904 GMT 22 Jun 89, "Ortega: Coffee Growers 'Chickens,'" FBIS-LAT-89-120, 23 June 1989, p. 25; "Nicaragua's Rulers Live by Revolution," Julia Preston, WP, July 2, 1989, p. A1.

10. Panama City ACAN 1629 GMT 7 Jul 89, "UNO Not to Send List for Regional Councils," FBIS-LAT-89-130, 10 July 1989, p. 27.

11. Managua Sistema Sandinista Television Network 0200 GMT 11 Jul 89, "Venezuelan President on Nicaraguan Elections," FBIS-LAT-89-133, 13 July 1989, p. 38; "Ortega Offers Election Talks," Mary Speck, WP, July 16, 1989, p. A20.

12. Panama City ACAN 2349 GMT 29 Jul 89, "Ortega to Demand Contra Demobilization," FBIS-LAT-89-145, 31 July 1989, p. 29.

13. Managua LA PRENSA 25 Jul 89, pp. 1, 12, "Violeta Chamorro Willing to Run for President," FBIS-LAT-89-144, 28 July 1989, p. 28.

14. Panama City ACAN 2308 GMT 3 Aug 89, "[Arias] Supports Early Demobilization," FBIS-LAT-89-150, 7 Aug 1989, p. 24.

15. San Pedro Sula TIEMPO 27 Jul 89, p. 3, "Security Council Approves Contra Demobilization," FBIS-LAT-89-144, 28 July 1989, p. 26.

16. On August 2 Aronson traveled to Guatemala to meet with Honduran, Salvadoran, Guatemalan, and Costa Rican officials. President Bush and Secretary Baker made several phone calls to President Azcona and Arias. Their efforts, reminiscent of many similar efforts by the Reagan administration, sparked accusations from House and Senate Democrats that the Bush administration was trying to undermine a diplomatic settlement at the Tela summit. Charges abounded that the administration officials had threatened Honduras with a reduction of aid. (Conservative Republicans charged in response that aides to Senator Dodd were making the same kinds of threats from the other direction.)

17. "Democrats Warn U.S. Must Support Contras' Eviction," Robert Pear, NYT, August 9, 1989, p. A1.

18. Panama City ACAN 0115 GMT 28 Jul 89, "Contras Reject Proposed Demobilization Plan," FBIS-LAT-89-144, 28 July 1989, p. 27.

19. "U.S. Endorses Contra Plan as Prod to Democracy in Nicaragua," John M. Goshko and Ann Devroy, WP, August 9, 1989, p. A16.

20. NYT, August 9, 1989.

21. WP, August 9, 1989.

22. "Bush, Resisting the Answers," Mary McGrory, WP, August 8, 1989, p. A2.

23. NYT, August 9, 1989.

24. Author's interview with Alfredo César, August 24, 1992; author's interview with Antonio Lacayo, August 24, 1992.

25. Managua Sistema Sandinista Television, "Alfredo César Elected PSD Secretary General," FBIS-LAT-89-068, 11 April 1989, p. 21; Panama City ACAN 1312 GMT 10 Apr 89, "RN, Opposition Parties Resume Meetings," FBIS-LAT-89-068, 11 April 1989, p. 22.

26. Panama City ACAN 1907 GMT 10 Apr 89, "Communist, Contra Leaders Embrace," FBIS-LAT-89-068, 11 April 1989, p. 23.

27. Managua EL NUEVO DIARIO 1 May 89, pp. 5, 6, "Nuñez Interviewed on Election Campaign," FBIS-LAT-89-088, 9 May 1989, p. 31; MRS 1930 GMT 16 Aug 89, "Sandinistas to Report Election-Related Moves," FBIS-LAT-89-160, 21 August 1989, p. 18.

28. To the ranks of the stalwart conservative opposition groups, therefore, were added the Liberal Independent Party of Virgilio Godoy, the Nicaraguan Communist Party, the Nicaraguan Socialist Party, and the Popular Social Christian Party of Mauricio Díaz. All four of these parties had run candidates in the 1984 elections and had since held seats as a "loyal opposition" in the National Assembly.

29. Carlos Nunez expected that the "Group of 14" would dissolve into two blocs—the eight parties of the Coordinadora, and what he referred to as the "Group of Six." The "Group of Six" would then form the nucleus of a "centrist" bloc of opposition, neither conservative and "Somocista" nor pro-government. Managua EL NUEVO DIARIO 1 May 89, pp. 5,6, "Nuñez Interviewed on Election Campaign," FBIS-LAT-89-088, 9 May 1989, p. 31.

30. Managua Radio Corporacion 2300 GMT 26 Jun 89, "National Opposition Unity Anounces Formation," FBIS-LAT-89-123, 28 June 1989, p. 29; see "Opposition That Needs All the Help It Can Get," Daniel Wattenberg, *Insight*, October 2, 1989.

31. Cerezo publicly advised opposition leaders that "if you maintain unity, it will be very difficult to defeat you." Managua LA PRENSA 12 Apr 89 pp. 1, 12, "Cerezo Desires Implementation of True Democracy," FBIS-LAT-89-071, 14 April 1989, p. 20.

32. Ramiro Gurdian attacked Godoy's "Marxist background," which he said had hurt the "working class." Panama City ACAN 1930 GMT 4 Sep 89, "UNO Nomination Process 'Fixed,'|" FBIS-LAT-89-172, 7 September 1989, p. 19.

33. When she left the Sandinista junta in 1980, for instance, she had attributed her decision to health problems rather than to any political differences with the Sandinistas. See p. 137 above.

34. Managua Radio Católica 1800 GMT 13 Jun 89, "Opposition Leaders Roundtable on Elections," FBIS-LAT-89-115, 16 June 1989, p. 28.

35. Ibid.

36. Author's interview with Lacayo, August 24, 1992.

37. Author's interview with Humberto Ortega, May 24, 1990.

38. Mexico City Red Nacionál 13 Imevisión Televisión 1300 GMT 19 Jul 89, "Ortega on 1990 Elections, Revolution's Future," FBIS-LAT-89-138, 20 July 1989, p. 42.

39. Statement by Luis Humberto Guzman, quoted in "Anti-Sandinistas Predict Coalition," Stephen Kinzer, NYT, September 10, 1989, p. 6.

40. NYT, September 10, 1989.

41. Managua Radio Católica 1800 GMT 13 Jun 89, "Opposition Leaders Roundtable on Elections," FBIS-LAT-89-115, 16 June 1989, p. 28.

42. Cruz speculated in September that "Daniel will 'reelect' himself, and then . . . he will offer concessions to the internal opposition on the basis of the economic Cabinet." While the Sandinistas would maintain control of the "security apparatus, the army [and] the ideological apparatus," they would offer the opposition posts at the "Central Bank, the Ministry of Finance and [in] foreign trade." Cruz quoted in Wattenberg, "Opposition That Needs All the Help It Can Get."

43. Statement by Roger Guevara Mena, quoted in "Anti-Sandinistas Predict Coalition," Stephen Kinzer, NYT, September 10, 1989, p. 6; Managua LA PRENSA 14 Sep 89, pp. 1, 12, "Chamorro, Godoy News Conference Reported," FBIS-LAT-89-180, 19 September 1989, p. 26.

44. Author's interview with Antonio Lacayo, August 24, 1992.

45. "Sandinistas Rehabilitate Businessman," Mary Speck, WP, February 22, 1989, p. A24.

46. Managua LA PRENSA 3 Feb 89, pp. 1, 12; 4 Feb 89 pp. 1, 12, "Enrique Bolaños Predicts 30,000 Layoffs," FBIS-LAT-89-054, 22 March 1989, p. 23.

47. Managua Radio Corporacion 1200 GMT 29 Aug 89, "Six Parties to Back Bolaños as Candidate," FBIS-LAT-89-167, 30 August 1989, p. 21; Panama City ACAN 1930 GMT 4 Sep 89, "UNO Nomination Process 'Fixed,'" FBIS-LAT-89-172, 7 September 1989, p. 19.

48. Author's interview with César, August 24, 1992; Author's interview with Arias, February 24, 1992.

49. Managua Sistema Sandinista de Television Network 0200 GMT 11 Jul 89, "Venezuelan President on Nicaraguan Elections," FBIS-LAT-89-133, 13 July 1989, p. 38.

50. President Arias later declared that he chose Chamorro because "I needed a candidate who could win." Author's interview with Arias.

51. MRS 1200 GMT 1 Sep 89, "UNO Postpones Presidential Candidate Election," FBIS-LAT-89-170, 5 September 1989, p. 23; author's interview with Arias.

52. Panama City ACAN 1930 GMT 4 Sep 89, "UNO Nomination Process 'Fixed,'" FBIS-LAT-89-172, 7 September 1989, p. 19; MRS 1200 GMT 4 Sep 89, "UNO Parties Receive U.S. Funds," FBIS-LAT-89-171, 6 September 1989, p. 19.

53. The Sandinistas often referred to Chamorro as "Mrs. Barrios," her maiden name, to avoid the association with her martyred husband. MRS 1200 GMT 4 Sep 89, "U.S.-Imposed. Candidates Denounced," FBIS-LAT-89-171, 6 September 1989, p. 19.

54. MRS 1200 GMT 7 Sep 89, "UNO Dissident Parties Switch Support to Godoy," FBIS-LAT-89-174, 11 September 1989, p. 25.

Chapter 60

1. At first, the administration had considered providing money to the opposition through the CIA, but the House intelligence committee forced it to give assurances that this would not happen. Then, at the beginning of September, the administration proposed providing the opposition $3 million through the National Endowment for Democracy, but some Democrats objected that the nature of the proposed aid violated the Endowment's charter because it was to be provided to an individual candidate. Finally, the administration changed the language and split the aid proposal in two, providing some through the Endowment and the rest through the Agency for International Development. This was the $9 million proposal the administration presented on September 21. See CQ, July 15, 1989, p. 1798; "U.S. Delegation Meets Nicaraguan Chief," Robert Pear, NYT, September 13, 1989, p. A3; "U.S. Drops Plan to Finance Nicaragua Opposition Leader," Thomas L. Friedman, NYT, September 16, 1989, p. A3; "U.S. Revises Plan to Aid Opposition in Nicaragua Vote," Robert Pear, NYT, September 22, 1989, p. A1.

2. NYT, September 22, 1989, p. A1.

3. NYT, September 16, 1989.

4. "Congress Adopts Nicaraguan Aid Bill," Helen Dewar, WP, October 18, 1989, p. A4.

5. I.e., "infrastructure development and training" for opposition parties, for voter registration and "get-out-the-vote drives," for "democratic education programs of labor, civic and business organizations and independent media," for election monitoring and for the financing of international observer missions. NYT, September 22 1989; NYT, September 16, 1989.

6. For instance, any aid to the "independent media" meant aid to *La Prensa*, which was the organ of the Chamorro candidacy, or to opposition radio stations which were as openly pro-UNO as the government-owned stations were openly pro-Sandinista.

Moreover, the arrangements finally worked out by the National Endowment for Democracy involved providing money to an organization established in Nicaragua on October 17, the Institute for Electoral Promotion and Training (IPCE). Although the money provided was to be "non-partisan" in character, the five board members of the IPCE were Alfredo César, Luis Sanchez, Guillermo Potoy, Silviano Mamatomors, and Adan Fletes, all leaders of the UNO coalition. See William I. Robinson, *A Faustian Bargain: U.S. Intervention in the Nicaraguan Elections and American Foreign Policy in the Post-Cold War Era*, (Boulder, Co., 1992), p. 63.

As Congressman Obey put it, "I know that when money goes in to help my party, it helps me." CQ, October 7, 1989, p. 2655.

7. CQ, September 16, 1989, p. 2406.

8. An amendment by Senator Harkin, prohibiting any aid from being provided to the Sandinista government, picked up a few Republican votes but still lost 59–40.

9. CQ, October 21, 1989, p. 2812.

10. In the most detailed attack on U.S. policy toward the Nicaraguan elections, William I. Robinson concentrates almost exclusively on how the administration, the National Endowment for Democracy, and the Congress planned to intervene in the elections, and he does a thorough accounting of the amounts of money appropriated for this purpose. He does not adequately address the question of when the aid was received by the opposition and whether it came in time to make a difference in the campaign. Moreover, while asserting that the U.S. aid "deeply influenced the electoral process," he admits that "to what extent it determined the outcome itself is open to question." Acknowledging that his book "does not attempt to provide an overall analysis of the Nicaraguan elections," Robinson asserts that "whether the outcome would have been different had the United States not intervened in the Nicaraguan elections is less important than that the results were determined, not on election day, but in the ten years of conflict with the United States that preceded the election." See Robinson, p. 2.

11. "Nicaraguan Opposition Operating on a Shoestring," Lee Hockstader, WP, October 13, 1989, p. A1.

12. Ibid.; on September 15, the NED board of directors approved $1.5 million in grants for Nicaragua. Once again the NED's president declared that the money would be used "to strengthen democratic institutions, processes and values in Nicaragua," but not to finance specific campaigns. "U.S. Seeking $3 Million More for Sandinistas' Foes," Robert Pear, NYT, September 10, 1989, p. 8; "U.S. to Pare Aid in Nicaragua Vote," Robert Pear, NYT, September 29, 1989.

13. An organization known as the Carmen Group appears to have handled most of the fund-raising efforts for UNO. According to Robinson, who carefully documented the Carmen Group's *planned* expenditures, "exactly how much of the Carmen budget categories were actually fulfilled . . . is not known." Robinson, p. 127.

14. See CQ Almanac, 1989, p. 584.

15. "In Nicaragua, the Election Observers Are Coming!" Mark Uhlig, NYT, October 2, 1989, p. A10.

16. "U.N. Group Reports Campaign Is Going Smoothly in Nicaragua," WP, October 24, 1989, p. A32.

17. MDS 0254 GMT 17 Sep 89, "Ortega on Carter Visit, Campaign," FBIS-LAT-89-179, 18 September 1989, p. 20; Panama City ACAN 1551 GMT 16 Sep 89, "BARRICADA Welcomes Carter Arrival," FBIS-LAT-89-179, 18 September 1989, p. 19.

18. MRS 1450 GMT 26 Sep 89, "President Ortega Holds News Conference 26 Sep," FBIS-LAT-89-187, 28 September 1989, p. 9.

19. NYT, October 2, 1989; "In Managua, Carter Says He Is Satisfied with Nicaragua's Election Plans," Lee Hockstader, WP Sepetmber 17, 1989, p. A40.

20. "Sandinistas Stage Last Rally in Capital," Lee Hockstader, WP, February 22, 1990, p. A26.

21. After a meeting with officials of the International Verification Commission (CIAV) on September 15, Deputy Foreign Minister Tinoco objected to the officials' "use the term 'voluntary demobilization.' Their interpretation is not correct." But CIAV officials told Tinoco they lacked coercive powers to force the contras to demobilize. MRS 1226 GMT 16 Sep 89, "Tinoco Talks to CIAV about Contra Return," FBIS-LAT-89-179, 18 September 1989, p. 23.

22. MRS 1514 GMT 8 Nov 89, "[Ortega] Discusses Current Situation," FBIS-LAT-89-216, 9 November 1989, p. 15.

23. "Nicaraguan Rebels Urged to Disband," Lee Hockstader, WP, October 14, 1989, p. A1.

24. Enrique Bermúdez expressed the views of thousands of contra fighters when he declared that "expecting the Sandinistas to democratize is like expecting the devil to be converted into a Catholic." Panama City ACAN 0201 GMT 16 Aug 89, "Bermúdez Addresses Contras," FBIS-LAST-89-179, 18 September 1989, p. 18.

25. "U.N. Chief Repudiates Contra Remark," John M. Goshko, WP, October 17, 1989, p. A24.

26. Panama City ACAN 0045 GMT 17 Oct 89, "Humberto Ortega Offers Help to 'Oust' Contras," FBIS-LAT-89-199, 17 Oct 1989, p. 40.

27. "Foolish, and Thuggish, in Nicaragua," NYT editorial, October 30, 1989, p. A26; on October 27, Ortega declared, "We are facing a terrorist offensive from a counterrevolution endorsed by the UNO and financed by the United States." "Ortega Declares He Will Abandon Nicaraguan Truce," Lindsey Gruson, NYT, October 28, 1989, p. 1.

28. As Vice Foreign Minister Tinoco explained Sandinista thinking, "For the United States, at this moment the contras guarantee the purity and honesty of the electoral process"; should Chamorro win the elections, the Bush administration would "maintain the contras to guarantee the term of Violeta Chamorro." Panama City ACAN 1900 GMT 25 Nov 89, "Tinoco Says Army Not to Disband after Elections," FBIS-LAT-89-226, 27 November 1989, p. 37.

29. Ibid.

30. "Sandinista Army Faces New Issues," William Branigin, WP, December 7, 1989, p. A46.

31. Madrid EFE 0342 GMT 18 Sep 89, "Humberto Ortega Statements in Mexico Reported," FBIS-LAT-89-179, 18 September 1989, p. 24.

32. "Contra Infiltration Confirmed," John M. Goshko, WP, November 3, 1989, p. A1.

33. "In Rural Nicaragua, War Dominates Politics," Lee Hockstader, WP, November 12, 1989, p. A31.

34. "Nicaraguans Begin Sweep against Contra Stronghold," Mark A. Uhlig, NYT, October 28, 1989, p. 5; Sandinista officials told American journalists that contra fighters were telling peasants they had a machine that could read a voter's identification card and discern how he voted. See "In Rural Nicaragua, War Dominates Politics," Lee Hockstader, WP, November 12, 1989, p. A31.

35. The *Washington Post*'s Lee Hockstader, traveling with contra forces in September, reported the forces "in dire straits," on the defensive, hiding in the mountains and avoiding Sandinista army probes. "Our strategy is to avoid being trapped and ambushed," one commander told Hockstader. "Once trapped in these mountains, we could be easily eliminated." "Contras Maintaining Presence in Nicaragua," Lee Hockstader, WP, September 22, 1989, p. A29.

36. "Contra Ambush Kills 18 Nicaraguan Troops," NYT, October 23, 1989; Panama City ACAN 2257 GMT 23 Oct 89, "More on Ortega Discussion of 'Contra' Attacks," FBIS-LAT-89-204, 24 October 1989, p. 9.

37. Tegucigalpa EL HERALDO 25 Oct 89, p. 41, "RN Denies Sandinist Charges on Fighting," FBIS-LAT-89-208, 30 October 1989, p. 38.

38. Managua BARRICADA 23 Oct 89, p. 5, "Communiqué on Ortega Meeting with Military," FBIS-LAT-89-205, 25 October 1989, p. 9.

39. Ibid.; Panama City ACAN 2257 GMT 23 Oct 89, "More on Ortega Discussion of 'Contra' Attacks," FBIS-LAT-89-204, 24 October 1989, p. 9; MRS 1200 GMT 24 Oct 89, "Ortega Comments on Involvement," FBIS-LAT-89-206, 26 October 1989, p. 14.

40. "Ortega Declares He Will Abandon Nicaraguan Truce," Lindsey Gruson, NYT, October 28, 1989, p. 1.

41. NYT, October 28, 1989; Paris AFP 2359 GMT 28 Oct 89, "De Cuellar 'Deeply Concerned,'|" FBIS-LAT-89-208, 30 October 1989, p. 35; "Anger with Ortega Unites Policy Makers in U.S.," Robert Pear, NYT, November 2, 1989, p. A12.

42. "Ortega Now Says End to Rebel Aid Can Save Truce," Lindsey Gruson, NYT, October 29, 1989, p. 1.

43. "Bush Assails Ortega for Cease-Fire Stand," Ann Devroy and Lee Hockstader, WP, October 29, 1989, p. A1.

44. "Ortega Seems to Retreat Further from War Threat," Mark A. Uhlig, NYT, October 31, 1989, p. A11; NYT, October 29, 1989.

45. MRS 1514 GMT 8 Nov 89, "[Ortega] Discusses Current Situation," FBIS-LAT-89-216, 9 November 1989, p. 15.

46. MDS 1203 GMT 1 Nov 89, "President Ortega Suspends Unilateral Cease-Fire," FBIS-LAT-89-211, 2 November 1989, p. 18.

47. Hamburg PDA 2010 GMT 28 Oct 89, "President Returns, Comments," FBIS-LAT-89-208, 30 October 1989, p. 33; "Why I Ended the Cease-Fire," Daniel Ortega Saavedra, NYT, November 2, 1989, p. A31.

48. The most *Barricada* could report on November 2 was that an army company, backed by militias, had attacked a group of 30 rebels in Nueva Segovia. As of November 6 in the area around Rio Blanco, where the October 21 ambush took place, the Sandinista army claimed still to be mobilizing for an offensive, but had not yet launched an attack. See "Nicaragua Mounts Offensive," Lee Hockstader, WP, November 3, 1989, p. A1; "Blast That Ended Truce Resounds in Nicaragua," Lee Hockstader, WP, November 7, 1989, p. A17.

49. "Ortega Announces End to Cease-Fire," Lee Hockstader and Ann Devroy, WP, October 28, 1989, p. A1.

50. "Anger with Ortega Unites Policy Makers in U.S.," Robert Pear, NYT, November 2, 1989, p. A12.

51. San Pedro Sula TIEMPO 31 Oct 89, p. 36, "Contras Declare 4,000 Troops in Nicaragua on Alert," FBIS-LAT-89-210, 1 November 1989, p. 20; "Pact in Nicaragua: U.S. Resists Too," Robert Pear, NYT, November 3, 1989, p. A8.

52. "Nicaragua Shaping a Risky New Strategy to Gain Leverage against U.S.," Mark A. Uhlig, NYT, December 7, 1989, p. A3.

53. NYT, October 29, 1989. See "The Peace Plan Wears Thin in Nicaragua," Lindsey Gruson, NYT, November 5, 1989, IV, p. 1.

54. "Continue Contra Aid Until Elections, Senate Chiefs Agree," NYT, October 30, 1989, p. A8.

55. NYT, November 2, 1989; Proof of the mildness of the offensive was that the contras on November 3 asked to delay the start of negotiations until November 13. "Contras Agree to Talks, but Ask for Delay," Wilson Ring, WP, November 4, 1989, p. A19.

Chapter 61

1. Author's interview with Humberto Ortega, May 24, 1990.

2. Daniel Ortega immediately acknowledged receipt of the helicopters and insisted on Nicaragua's right to receive military aid from any country it wanted. The Soviet ambassador in

Nicaragua, when asked about the shipment's origin, would say only "I do not have that information. I do not know where they got it, and I cannot speculate." Panama City ACAN 2217 GMT 19 Sept 89, "Ortega Confirms Receipt of Soviet Matériel," FBIS-LAT-89-181, 20 September 1989.

3. Don Oberdorfer, *The Turn: From the Cold War to the New Era: The United States and the Soviet Union, 1983–1990* (New York, 1991), p. 371.

4. "U.S. Says East Bloc Increases Arms Shipments to Nicaragua," David B. Ottaway, WP, September 19, 1989, p. A24.

5. "Shevardnadze Will Visit Cuba, Nicaragua, Raising U.S. Hopes," Don Oberdorfer, WP, September 28, 1989, p. A44.

In fact, on October 5, the *Washington Post* reported that the CIA estimated there had been a 20 percent decline in Soviet arms shipments up to that point in 1989 from the 1988 rate. The dip in supplies, however, proved temporary. There were additional shipments at the end of the year.

6. CQA, 1989, p. 473; figures were Pentagon estimates, cited in "Sandinista Army Faces New Issues," William Branigin, WP, December 7, 1989, p. A48.

7. "Soviets Reducing Arms for Managua," Mark A. Uhlig, NYT, October 16, 1989, p. A13.

8. "U.S. Delegation Meets Nicaraguan Chief," Robert Pear, NYT, September 13, 1989, p. A32.

9. Letter from Jimmy Carter to Daniel Ortega, September 22, 1989, reprinted in William I. Robinson, *A Faustian Bargain: U.S. Intervention in the Nicaraguan Elections and American Foreign Policy in the Cold-War Era* (Boulder, CO., 1992), 267.

10. CQ, October 21, 1989, p. 2809; Author's interview with Aronson November 10, 1990.

11. Michael Kramer, "Anger, Bluff—And Cooperation," *Time*, June 4, 1990, p. 41. Kramer's account of U.S.-Soviet cooperation on the Nicaragua issue in 1989 is virtually an authorized version of events as seen through the eyes of Baker and Aronson. Kramer's article was based on extensive interviews with American and Soviet officials and on examination of classified documents. Both the documents and the officials were made available to Kramer at the express direction of Secretary Baker. In Kramer's words, "Their motive is no mystery: it reflects pride in what they have accomplished and offers insurance against the day when old animosities re-emerge and citizens in both countries question the value of superpower cooperation."

12. Kramer, p. 44.

13. Ibid., p. 40.

14. Ibid., p. 44. Emphasis added.

15. Ibid.

16. Ibid.

17. "El Salvador Cuts Ties to Nicaragua," Douglas Farah, WP, November 27, 1989, p. A1.

18. According to Miranda, Humberto Ortega had promised the "arrows" to FMLN leaders, but had been overruled by the rest of the Directorate because he had acted without consulting them. Roger Miranda and William Ratliff, *The Civil War in Nicaragua: Inside the Sandinistas* (New Brunswick, NJ, 1993) pp. 40–41.

19. "Nicaragua Shaping a Risky New Strategy to Gain Leverage against U.S.," Mark A. Uhlig, NYT, December 7, 1989, p. A3; MRS 2230 GMT 27 Nov 89, "Humberto Ortega on Central American Peace Efforts," FBIS-LAT-89-227, 27 November 1989, p. 17.

20. "Managua's Intervention," WP editorial, November 28, 1989, p. A24.

21. Kramer, p. 38.

22. "How a Plane Crash Upended Peace Plans for Central America," Larry Rohter, NYT, December 3, 1989, Section E, p. 2.

23. Kramer, p. 44.

24. See Yuri Pavlov, *Soviet-Cuban Alliance, 1959–1991* (Coral Gables, FL., 1994), p. 150.

25. See p. 647 above.

26. Oberdorfer, p. 379.

27. Kramer, p. 44.

28. "Bush and Gorbachev Hail New Cooperation," David Hoffman, WP, December 4, 1989, p. A1.

29. "Baker, in a Call to Shevardnadze, Asks Action on Central America," Thomas L. Friedman, NYT, December 11, 1989, p. A10.

30. Emphasis in original. Kramer, p. 44; NYT, December 7, 1989.

31. Kramer, p. 45.

32. Ibid., p. 38.

33. Kramer, pp. 44–45.

34. Baker told the Senate Foreign Relations Committee that "while we know in the past helicopters such as this have been converted after they arrive in Nicaragua and used for military purposes, we have been told by the Soviets that this is not going to be the case in this instance." Statement of Secretary of State Baker to Senate Foreign Relations Committee, February 1, 1990; "Cuba Received New Soviet MiGs, State Dept. Says," WP, February 21, 1990, p. A17.

35. Vienna DER STANDARD 5 Feb 90, p. 3, "Borge Discusses Political Situation, Elections," FBIS-LAT-90-025, 6 February 1990, p. 19.

36. American journalists nevertheless typically referred to the new contra leadership as consisting of "right-wing elements" because they were opposed to demobilization before the elections. See "Hard-Line Contra Group Complicates Peace Talks," Ethan Schwartz, WP, November 11, 1989, p. A29.

37. Adolfo Calero, now denied even access to the contras' camps in Honduras, denounced the "coup d'état" which he said had been "promoted by the U.S. State Department." The charge was fair: two former deputies to Elliott Abrams, Cris Arcos and Dan Fisk, now serving under Aronson, had finally completed the mission of "contra reform" begun in 1986, although the final product was not what most adherents of reform had originally expected.

38. "Contras Turning to Younger Leaders," Mark A. Uhlig, NYT, November 5, 1989, p. 16.

39. The events were witnessed by an American delegation. Robert Beckel, Walter Mondale's 1984 campaign manager and an opponent of contra aid, told reporters that "What we saw was an outrage. There was no doubt among any of us at the scene that the violence was instigated by the Sandinistas." See "Honduran Leader Walks out on Talks," Mark A. Uhlig, NYT, December 12, 1989, p. A3.

40. "Central American Leaders Seek to Revive Peace Plan," William Branigin, WP, December 11, 1989, p. A23.

41. Humberto Ortega insisted it was "not right" to say that "we sell out our friends. . . . It happens that as a government our stances are undoubtedly different from the stances of a guerrilla movement." MRS 1200 GMT 18 Dec 89, "Humberto Ortega Feels Total Peace 'Very Close,'" FBIS-LAT-89-242, 19 December 1989, p. 12.

42. Although David Bonior declared that the administration "can no longer live with the fiction that it is supporting the peace process while bypassing the Central American presidents," the State Department spokesman declared only that "we will want to study further the language in the final communiqué and learn more precisely from the participants the meaning and intent of the agreement they reached." Marlin Fitzwater told reporters that the Bush administration "remained to be convinced" about the sincerity of the Sandinistas to abide by their

commitments. "5 Latin Leaders Urge Disbanding of Contras and Salvadoran Rebels," Mark A. Uhlig, NYT, December 13, 1989, p. A14.

43. The Salvadoran guerrilla leaders, interviewed by Douglas Farah in Colombia, insisted on anonymity. See "Salvadoran Rebels Isolated," Douglas Farah, WP, February 27, 1990, p. A17.

Chapter 62

1. "Nicaraguan Opposition: Outsmarted and Outspent," Lee Hockstader, WP, January 25, 1990, p. A29.

2. "Prisoners to Be Freed, Ortega Says," Lee Hockstader, WP, January 31, 1990, p. A14.

3. "Crowds Cheer Nicaraguan Opposition," Lee Hockstader, WP, February 19, 1990, p. A1.

4. For conversations between Cuban and Nicaraguan officials, see Andres Oppenheimer, *Castro's Final Hour: The Secret Story Behind the Coming Downfall of Communist Cuba* (New York, 1992), pp. 206–8.

5. Ibid.; WP, February 19, 1990.

6. WP, February 19, 1990; The *Times*'s Stephen Kinzer also reported the Sandinistas "lacked for nothing . . . with seemingly unlimited funds." See Stephen Kinzer, *Blood of Brothers: Life and War in Nicaragua* (New York, 1991), p. 390.

7. It was no less an amusing scene for a campaign when the Sandinista crowds finally understood the appropriate response. Ortega: "Have we made mistakes?" The crowd, in unison: "Yes!" See for an example MDS 2100 GMT 26 Nov 89, "[Ortega] Comments on Regional Situation," FBIS-LAT-89-226, 27 November 1989, p. 30.

8. As one Sandinista official explained, in public debate with a Chamorro adviser: "Here are the reasons why we are justified in thinking that all will be better. First, to legitimize the electoral process . . . will lead to the end of the war. The end of the war will bring two basic conditions for the Nicaraguan economy. For the first time we will be able to earmark huge financial, economic and material resources that have been assigned to the war effort for reconstruction and peace. Moreover, the United States may continue refusing its bilateral aid, but will not be able to block aid from multilateral organizations and other friendly nations indefinitely, who have limited this aid owing to the geopolitical circumstances imposed by the United States." Managua Sistema Sandinista Television Network 0000 GMT 18 Jan 89, "FSLN, UNO Candidates Debate Economics," FBIS-LAT-90-015 23 January 1990, p. 35.

9. Managua BARRICADA 20, 21 Dec 89, "Humberto Ortega on Prospects for Peace," FBIS-LAT-90-016, 24 January 1990, p. 34.

10. Managua LA PRENSA 5 Feb 90, p. 2, "Ortega's Sincerity Questioned," FBIS-LAT-90-028, 9 February 1990, p. 18.

11. MRS 2030 GMT 24 Jan 90, "EPS Official on Elections, Military Service," FBIS-LAT-90-017, 25 January 1990, p. 11.

12. MRS 0008 GMT 5 Dec 89, "Ortega to Propose New Contra Withdrawal Date," FBIS-LAT-89-232, 5 December 1989, p. 13.

13. MDS 1700 GMT 19 Nov 89, "Ortega Speaks on El Salvador, Upcoming Elections," FBIS-LAT-89-223, 21 November 1989, p. 26.

14. MDS 1942 GMT 16 Feb 90, "Ortega Holds Campaign Rally in Boaco," FBIS-LAT-90-034, 20 February 1990, p. 22. In February, Agrarian Reform Minister Jaime Wheelock declared that "private businessmen can rest assured that farming property will be respected because their property-ownership titles, deeds, and rights are sacred to the revolution. As of 1990, there will

be no confiscations or expropriations." Managua BARRICADA 14 Feb 90, p. 9, "Commander Wheelock Proclaims End of Confiscations," FBIS-LAT-90-033, 16 February 1990, p. 37.

15.　See, for instance, "Sandinistas Seem Changed by Election Campaign," Lee Hockstader and William Branigin, WP, February 25, 1990, p. A1. "In Nicaragua, where resentment of armed interventions in this century is deep, Chamorro's perceived link with Washington has hurt, polls have shown."

16.　Managua LA PRENSA 5 Feb 90, p. 2, "Ortega's Sincerity Questioned," FBIS-LAT-90-028, 9 February 1990, p. 18.

17.　"A Sandinista Promise Gone Sour Alienates Nicaragua's Working Class," Mark A. Uhlig, NYT, November 7, 1989, p. A10.

18.　Managua BARRICADA 12 Nov 89, p. 5, "Ortega Speaks at Chichigalpa Rally 11 NOv," FBIS-LAT-89-219, 15 November 1989, p. 50.

19.　Managua BARRICADA 16 Dec 89, p. 5, "Carter Meets Political Party Representatives," FBIS-LAT-89-242, 19 December 1989, p. 16; see, for instance, "In Nicaragua, a Widow's Calling," Myra MacPherson, WP, February 20, 1990, p. C1.

20.　"In Nicaragua, Too Little Too Late," Rowland Evans and Robert Novak, WP, February 21, 1990, p. A21.

21.　Ortega found it necessary to remind voters that Chamorro had taken part in the same objectionable activities for which the Sandinistas were now apologizing. Chamorro had also "signed confiscation decrees—she did sign them or maybe she did not know what she was signing. She is denying all that now. She also signed confiscation decrees." MDS 2349 GMT 8 Nov 89, "President Ortega Gives FSLN Anniversary Speech," FBIS-LAT-89-216, 9 November 1989, p. 19.

22.　Managua BARRICADA 7 Feb 90, pp. 3, 4, "Borge Touts FSLN as Party to Overcome Crisis," FBIS-LAT-90-029, 12 February 1990, p. 19.

23.　It is possible, of course, that large sums of money found their way no further than into the pockets of UNO campaign officials. If so, however, this was overlooked by a large team of auditors from both Congress and the Bush administration. Perhaps much of the private money raised on UNO's behalf was misused, but there does not appear to have been very much private money raised in any case.

24.　"U.S. Accused of Overstating Managua Election Offenses," John M. Goshko and A1 Kamen, WP, January 25, 1990, p. A29; "Nicaraguan Opposition: Outsmarted and Outspent," Lee Hockstader, WP, January 25, 1990, p. A29.

25.　The pledge Chamorro signed when she accepted her nomination of September 2 spelled out very precisely the relationship between the candidate and the opposition coalition: Both Chamorro and Godoy were to be subordinate to the UNO Political Council, a five-member coordinating body elected to represent the 14 parties. The two candidates pledged to "strictly obey" the decisions of this "permanent consultative council" both during the campaign and after the elections. If Chamorro won the elections, the government formed would not be Chamorro's government, but an "UNO coalition government . . . formed with representatives of all parties." San José Radio Impacto 2144 GMT 2 Sep 89, "Parties Agree on Document," FBIS-LAT-89-170, 5 September 1989, p. 24.

26.　"Candidate Chamorro Names Ex-Contra as Chief Adviser," Mary Speck, WP, November 23, 1989, p. A64; Managua Radio Corporación 2300 GMT 21 Nov 89, "Chamorro Appoints Alfredo César 'Main Adviser,'" FBIS-LAT-89-225, 24 November 1989, p. 30.

27.　Paris AFP 0528 GMT 29 Sep 89, "Designates César Candidate," FBIS-LAT-89-189, 2 October 1989, p. 31.

28.　Paris AFP 1628 GMT 12 Sep 89, "UNO Vice Presidential Candidate Interviewed," FBIS-LAT-89-180, 19 September 1989, p. 26.

29. See the reports by William Branigin and Lee Hockstader, "Nicaraguan Campaign Seen as Relatively Free and Open," Lee Hockstader, WP, February 17, 1990, p. A21; "Nicaraguan Neighbors Feud as Election Nears," William Branigin, WP, February 24, 1990, p. A21.

30. Carter's statement on December 16 was "The contra presence is deathly, tension is high, and all the political parties must do everything within their power to lessen the harassment." Managua BARRICADA 16 Dec 89, p. 5, "Carter Meets Political Party Representatives," FBIS-LAT-89-242, 19 December 1989, p. 16.

31. WP, February 17, 1990.

32. Richardson declared that despite charges of intimidation, "It's fair to say that there is a wide discrepancy between the prevalence of these charges and the production of any evidence of such actual intimidation." "U.S. Observer Team Disbands before Nicaraguan Elections," Helen Dewar and Don Podesta, WP, February 8, 1990, p. A1.

33. Carter even told the Sandinistas that "60 percent of [UNO's] representatives were intimidated." Managua BARRICADA 2 Feb 90, pp. 1, 6, "Further on Arce Meeting with Baena Soares," FBIS-LAT-90-024, 2 February 1990, p. 35.

34. Paris AFP 0140 GMT 29 Jan 90, "Carter Meets with Ortega," FBIS-LAT-90-019, 29 January 1990, p. 35; "U.S. Observer Team Disbands before Nicaraguan Elections," Helen Dewar and Don Podesta, WP, February 8, 1990, p. A1.

35. Managua BARRICADA 16 Dec 89, p. 5, "Carter Meets Political Party Representatives," FBIS-LAT-89-242, 19 December 1989, p. 16.

36. On January 30, for instance, the international organization of conservative parties, the International Democratic Union, received permission to send a 25-person delegation to Managua on February 23. Managua LA PRENSA 30 Jan 90, p. 3, "IDU Delegation to Observe Electoral Process," FBIS-LAT-90-023, 2 February 1990, p. 32.

37. Statement of Secretary of State Baker to Senate Foreign Relations Committee, February 1, 1990.

38. Santiago FORTIN MOPOCHO 7 Feb 90, p. 16, "Borge Discusses Mistakes, Elections, Soviet Aid," FBIS-LAT-90-033, 16 February 1990, p. 36.

39. MDS 1942 GMT 16 Feb 90, "Ortega Holds Campaign Rally in Boaco," FBIS-LAT-90-034, 20 February 1990, p. 22.

40. "The Trouble with Change," *U.S. News & World Report*, p. 35.

41. "Baker Sets Conditions on Nicaraguan Relations," John M. Goshko, WP, February 23, 1990, p. A19.

42. "Renewed U.S.-Nicaragua Ties Eyed," John M. Goshko, WP, February 24, 1990, p. A23.

43. "U.S. Officials View Fair Vote as Chance to Close Old Issue," James M. Dorsey, WP, February 26, 1990, p. 7A.

44. "Poll Position," Bruce Babbitt, *New Republic*, March 19, 1990, p. 17.

45. Managua EL NUEVO DIARIO 24 Feb 90, p. 16, "[Cruz] Comments on Elections," FBIS-LAT-90-038, 26 February 1990, p. 32.

46. Panama City ACAN 1912 GMT 22 Feb 90, "Obando y Bravo Notes Changes in Sandinists," FBIS-LAT-90-037, 23 February 1990, p. 27.

47. "Crowds Cheer Nicaraguan Opposition," Lee Hockstader, WP, February 19, 1990, p. A1.

48. Paris LE FIGARO 27 Feb 90, p. 4, "Godoy Discusses Election Results 25–26 Feb," FBIS-LAT-90-042, 2 March 1990, p. 32.

49. Borge said the problem of getting opposition ministers into the government was not the Sandinistas, but the "primitivism" of most opposition leaders, who are "confirmed anti-Sandinistas." See Vienna DER STANDARD 5 Feb 90, p. 3, "Borge Discusses Political Situation,

Elections," FBIS-LAT-90-025, 6 February 1990, p. 19; Panama City ACAN 1343 GMT 13 Feb 90, "FSLN Offer to Negotiate with UNO Viewed," FBIS-LAT-90-031, 14 February 1990, p. 14.

50. Panama City ACAN 0000 GMT 25 Feb 90, "Ortega Views 'Future Negotiations' with U.S.," FBIS-LAT-90-038, 26 February 1990, p. 10.

51. Ibid.; Panama City ACAN 0120 MT 25 Feb 90, "Ortega on Spanish Role as 'Mediator' with U.S.," FBIS-LAT-90-036, 26 February 1990, p. 10.

52. When Bush spoke of "Nicaragua," he meant the Sandinista government. Elsewhere in his statement, for instance, Bush said that "We've had difficulty because Nicaragua has said that they're not giving arms to the FMLN. Now they say, 'Well, if we're elected we won't give arms to the FMLN.'" "Bush Says Climate Will Warm If Fair Vote Is Seen," Neil A. Lewis, NYT, February 26, 1990, p. A6; "Opposition Claims Win in Nicaragua," William Branigin and Lee Hockstader, WP, February 26, 1990, p. A1.

53. MDS 2103 GMT 25 Feb 90, "Ortega Comments Further on Elections, Contras," FBIS-LAT-90-038, 26 February 1990, p. 13.

54. See Michael R. Beschloss and Strobe Talbott, *At the Highest Levels: The Inside Story of the End of the Cold War* (Boston, 1993), pp. 86–89, for Bush's views on Jaruzelski and Walesa; pp. 90–92, for his views on Hungary; and p. 103, for his views on Yeltsin.

Chapter 63

1. "Nicaraguan Future Tied to Elections, Carter Says," *Baltimore Sun*, February 25, 1990, p. 4B.

2. "Letter from Managua," Alma Guillermoprieto, *New Yorker*, March 26, 1990, pp. 83–93.

3. "Poll Position," Bruce Babbitt, *New Republic*, March 19, 1990, p. 17.

4. "Jimmy Carter's Second Chance," *U.S. News & World Report*, March 12, 1990, p. 35.

5. "Poll Position," Bruce Babbitt, *New Republic*, March 19, 1990, p. 17.

6. Carter told reporters on February 27 that "there was never any question about whether they would accept the results of the election." "Sandinista Leaders, Facing Defeat, Didn't Argue, Carter Says," Mark A. Uhlig, NYT, February 28, 1990.

7. "Carter Played Pivotal Role in Hours after Polls Closed," Lee Hockstader, WP, February 27, 1990, p. A19.

8. *U.S. News & World Report*, March 12, 1990, p. 35.

9. The Sandinistas won only in a "special zone" of 15,000 voters in Rio San Juan.

10. "Election Shattered Many Sandinista Myths," William Branigin, WP, March 2, 1990, p. A26.

11. "Letter From Managua," Alma Guillermoprieto, *New Yorker*, March 26, 1990, pp. 83–93.

12. The opposition won in one neighborhood of Managua where the career military made up more than 80 percent of the electorate. According to one international observer, "There were a number of polling stations where over 15 percent of the vote was military personnel, but the vote still went to the UNO." "Hard-Line Sandinista Hints He'll Accept Defeat," Mark A. Uhlig, NYT, March 2, 1990, p. A1.

13. Panama City ACAN 1948 GMT 20 Mar 90, "FSLN's Wheelock Confirms Weapons Distribution," FBIS-LAT-90-055, 21 March 1990, p. 21.

14. Santiago ANALISIS 19–25 Mar 90, pp. 50–52, "President Ortega Discusses Electoral Defeat," FBIS-LAT-90-026, 30 March 1990, p. 23.

15. Managua BARRICADA 3 Jul 90, p. 3, "FSLN 'Arrogance,' Control Blamed for Defeat," FBIS-LAT-90-168, 29 August 1990, p. 28.

16. WP, March 2, 1990.

17. Santiago ANALISIS 19–25 Mar 90, p. 50–52, "President Ortega Discusses Electoral Defeat," FBIS-LAT-90-026, 30 March 1990, p. 23.

18. Letter from Managua," Alma Guillermoprieto, *New Yorker*, March 26, 1990, pp. 83–93.

19. WP, March 2, 1990.

20. "Ortega Spurned in an Old Stronghold," Larry Rohter, NYT, March 5, 1990, p. A3.

21. Several newspapers and magazines carried stories based on Aronson's briefing. The most notable of these was published in *Time* by Michael Kramer. See Michael Kramer, "Anger, Bluff—And Cooperation," *Time*, June 4, 1990, pp. 38–45.

Chapter 64

1. *On War*, Book I, Chap. 1, p. 77.

2. Yuri Pavlov, *Soviet-Cuban Alliance, 1959–1991* (Coral Gables, FL., 1994), 144.

3. Stephen Sestanovich, "Did the West Undo the East?" *National Interest*, Spring 1993, No. 31, pp. 26–34.

Chapter 65

1. Author's interview with Ambassador Crescencio Arcos.

2. At the beginning of 1995, Humberto Ortega finally resigned and turned the army over to his second-in-command, General Joaquín Cuadra Lacayo.

SELECTED BIBLIOGRAPHY

Andrew, Christopher and Oleg Gordievsky. *KGB: The Inside Story*. New York, 1990.

Arias, Pilar. *Nicaragua: Revolución Relatos de Combatientes del Frente Sandinista*. Mexico, 1981.

Arnson, Cynthia J. *Crossroads: Congress, the Reagan Administration, and Central America*. New York, 1989.

Ashby, Timothy. *The Bear in the Back Yard: Moscow's Caribbean Strategy* Lexington, MA, 1987.

Barry, John M. *The Ambition and the Power: Jim Wright and the Will of the House*. New York, 1989.

Belli, Humberto. *Breaking Faith: The Sandinista Revolution and Its Impact on Freedom and Christian Faith in Nicaragua*. Westchester, IL, 1985.

Bemis, Samuel Flagg. *The Latin American Diplomacy of the United States*. New York, 1943.

Beschloss, Michael R. and Strobe Talbott. *At the Highest Levels: The Inside Story of the End of the Cold War*. Boston, 1993.

Bialer, Seweryn. *The Soviet Paradox: External Expansion, Internal Decline*. New York, 1986.

Binnendijk, Hans, Peggy Nalle, Diane B. Bendahmane. *Authoritarian Regimes in Transition*. Washington, 1987.

Booth, John A. *The End and the Beginning: The Nicaraguan Revolution*. Boulder, CO, 1985.

Borge, Tomás, Carlos Fonseca, Daniel Ortega, Humberto Ortega, Jaime Wheelock. *Sandinistas Speak*. New York, 1986.

Bradlee, Ben. *Guts and Glory: The Rise and Fall of Oliver North*. New York, 1988.

Brzezinski, Zbigniew. *Power and Principle*. New York, 1983.

Bugajski, Janusz. *Sandinista Communism and Rural Nicaragua*. New York, 1990.

Cannon, Lou. *President Reagan: The Role of a Lifetime*. New York, 1991.

Carter, Jimmy. *Keeping Faith: Memoirs of a President*. New York, 1982.

Chamorro Cardenál, Jaime. *La Prensa: The Republic of Paper*. New York, 1988.

Christian, Shirley. *Nicaragua: Revolution in the Family*. New York, 1985.

Close, David. *Nicaragua: Politics, Economics, and Society*. London, 1988.

Cohen, William S., and George J. Mitchell. *Men of Zeal: A Candid Inside Story of the Iran-Contra Hearings*. New York, 1988.

Cruz, Arturo J. *Nicaragua's Continuing Struggle*. New York, 1988.

Cruz S., Arturo J. *Memoirs of a Counterrevolutionary*. New York, 1989.

Deaver, Michael K. with Mickey Herskowitz. *Behind the Scenes*. New York, 1987.

Drew, Elizabeth. *Campaign Journal: The Political Events of 1983-1984*. New York, 1985.

873

United States. Dept. of State. *"Revolution Beyond Our Borders": Sandinista Intervention in Central America.* Washington 1985.

——. *"The 72-Hour Document": The Sandinista Blueprint for Constructing Communism in Nicaragua: A Translation.* Washington,1986.

——. *Nicaraguan Biographies: A Resource Book.* Washington, 1988.

——. *Report to the Secretary of State on the Work of the International Commission of Friendly Cooperation and Conciliation for Achieving a Peaceful Solution to the Grave Crisis of the Republic of Nicaragua,1979.* Washington, 1979.

Dickey, Christopher. *With the Contras: A Reporter in the Wilds of Nicaragua* New York, 1985.

Dillon, Sam. *Commandos: The CIA and Nicaragua's Contra Rebels.* New York, 1991.

Dominguez, Jorge I. *To Make a World Safe for Revolution: Cuba's Foreign Policy* Cambridge, Mass, 1989.

Draper, Theodore. *A Very Thin Line: The Iran-Contra Affairs.* New York, 1991.

Duncan, Raymond W. and Carolyn McGiffert Ekedahl. *Moscow and the Third World under Gorbachev.* Boulder, CO, 1990.

Eich, Dieter and Carlos Rincón. *The Contras: Interviews with Anti-Sandinistas.* Hamburg, 1984.

Falcoff, Mark and Robert Royal. *The Continuing Crisis: U.S. Policy in Central America and the Caribbean.* Washington, 1987.

Fuess, Claude M. *Calvin Coolidge, the Man From Vermont.* Boston, 1940.

Garvin, Glenn. *Everybody Had His Own Gringo: The CIA and the Contras.* Washington, 1992.

Gilbert, Dennis. *Sandinistas: The Party and the Revolution.* New York, 1988.

Gutman, Roy. *Banana Diplomacy: The Making of American Policy in Nicaragua, 1981-87.* New York, 1988.

Haig, Alexander M., Jr. *Caveat: Realism, Reagan, and Foreign Policy.* New York, 1984.

Herring, Hubert. *A History of Latin America.* New York, 1961.

Heyck, Denis Lynn Daly. *Life Stories of the Nicaraguan Revolution.* New York, 1990.

Hodges, Donald Clarke. *Sandino's Communism: Spiritual Politics for the Twenty-first Century.* Austin, Texas, 1992.

Horelick, Arnold L., ed. *U.S.-Soviet Relations: The Next Phase.* Ithaca, NY, 1986.

Jauberth, H. Rodrigo, Gilberto Castañeda, Jesús Hernández, and Pedro Vuskovic. *The Difficult Triangle: Mexico, Central America, and the United States.* Boulder, Colo., 1992.

Jordan, Hamilton. *Crisis: The Last Year of the Carter Presidency.* New York, 1982.

Katz, Mark N. *Gorbachev's Military Policy in the Third World.* Washington, 1989.

Kempe, Frederick. *Divorcing the Dictator: America's Bungled Affair With Noriega.* New York, 1990.

Kinzer, Stephen. *Blood of Brothers: Life and War in Nicaragua.* New York, 1991.

Korbonski, Andrzej and Francis Fukuyama, eds. *The Soviet Union and the Third World: The Last Three Decades.* Ithaca, NY, 1987.

Kornbluh, Peter. *The Price of Intervention: Reagan's War Against the Sandinistas.* Washington, 1987.

—— and Malcolm Byrne. *The Iran-Contra Scandal: The Declassified History.* New York, 1993.

Krauss, Clifford. *Inside Central America: Its People, Politics, and History.* New York, 1991.

LaFeber, Walter. *Inevitable Revolutions: The United States and Central America.* New York, 1984.

Lake, Anthony. *Somoza Falling: A Case Study of Washington at Work.* Boston, 1989.

Langley, Lester D. *The Banana Wars: An Inner History of American Empire, 1900-1934.* Lexington, KY, 1983.

Ledeen, Michael A. *Perilous Statecraft: An Insider's Account of the Iran-Contra Affair.* New York, 1988.

Leiken, Robert S. *Soviet Strategy in Latin America.* New York, 1982.

——. *Central America: Anatomy of Conflict.* Elmsford, NY, 1984.

—— and Barry Rubin, eds. *The Central American Crisis Reader.* New York, 1987.

Macaulay, Neill. *The Sandino Affair*. Chicago, 1967.

Mayer, Jane and Doyle McManus. *Landslide: The Unmaking of the President, 1984-1988*. Boston, 1988.

McFarlane, Robert C. with Zofia Smardz. *Special Trust*. New York, 1994.

McNeil, Frank. *War and Peace in Central America: Reality and Illusion*. New York, 1988.

Menges, Constantine C. *Inside the National Security Council: The True Story of the Making and Unmaking of Reagan's Foreign Policy*. New York, 1988.

Miller, Nicola. *Soviet Relations With Latin America, 1959-1987*. Cambridge, England, 1989.

Miller, Valerie. *Between Struggle and Hope: The Nicaraguan Literacy Crusade*. Boulder, Colo., 1985.

Millett, Richard. *Guardians of the Dynasty*. Maryknoll, NY, 1977.

Miranda, Roger and William Ratliff. *The Civil War in Nicaragua: Inside the Sandinistas*. New Brunswick, NJ, 1993.

Moynihan, Daniel Patrick. *Came the Revolution: Argument in the Reagan Era*. New York, 1988.

Munro, Dana G. *Intervention and Dollar Diplomacy in the Caribbean, 1900-1921*. Princeton, 1964.

———. *The United States and the Caribbean Republics, 1921-1933* Princeton, NJ, 1974.

Muravchik, Joshua. *The Uncertain Crusade: Jimmy Carter and the Dilemmas of Human Rights Policy*. Lanham, MD, 1986.

———. *News Coverage of the Sandinista Revolution*. Washington, 1988.

Nolan, David, *The Ideology of the Sandinistas and the Nicaraguan Revolution*. Coral Gables, FL, 1984.

North, Oliver L.with William Novak. *Under Fire: An American Story*. New York, 1991.

O'Neill, Tip with William Novak. *Man of the House: The Life and Political Memoirs of Speaker Tip O'Neill*. New York, 1987.

Oberdorfer, Don. *The Turn: From Cold War to the New Era: The United States and the Soviet Union, 1983-1990*. New York, 1991.

Oppenheimer, Andres. *Castro's Final Hour: The Secret Story Behind the Coming Downfall of Communist Cuba*. New York, 1992.

Pardo-Maurer, R. *The Contras, 1980-1989: A Special Kind of Politics*. New York, 1990.

Pastor, Robert A. *Condemned to Repetition: The United States and Nicaragua*. Princeton, NJ, 1987.

Pavlov, Yuri. *Soviet-Cuban Alliance: 1959-1991*. Coral Gables, FL, 1994.

Persico, Joseph E. *Casey: from the OSS to the CIA*. New York, 1990.

Pezzullo, Lawrence and Ralph Pezzullo. *At the Fall of Somoza*. Pittsburgh, 1993.

Ramírez, Sergio and Robert Edgar Conrad, eds. *Sandino: The Testimony of a Nicaraguan Patriot: 1921-1934*. Princeton, 1990.

Rangel, Carlos. *The Latin Americans: Their Love-Hate Relationship with the United States*. New Brunswick, NJ, 1987.

Reagan, Ronald. *An American Life*. New York, 1990.

Regan, Donald T. *For the Record: From Wall Street to Washington*. New York, 1988.

Riding, Alan. *Distant Neighbors: A Portrait of the Mexicans*. New York, 1984.

Robinson, William I. *A Faustian Bargain: U.S. Intervention in the Nicaraguan Elections and American Foreign Policy in the Cold-War Era*. Boulder, CO, 1992.

Rodman, Peter W. *More Precious Than Peace: The Cold War and the Struggle for the Third World*. New York, 1994.

Rosset, Peter and John Vandermeer, eds. *Nicaragua: Unfinished Revolution: The New Nicaragua Reader*. New York, 1986.

Rubinstein, Alvin Z. *Moscow's Third World Strategy*. Princeton, 1988.

Schieffer, Bob and Gary Paul Gates. *The Acting President; Ronald Reagan and the Supporting Players Who Helped Him Create the Illusion that Held America Spellbound*. New York, 1989.

Schoultz, Lars. *Human Rights and United States Policy Toward Latin America*. Princeton, 1981.

———. *National Security and United States Policy Toward Latin America*. Princeton, 1987.

Shulman, Marshall D., ed. *East-West Tensions in the Third World*. New York, 1986.

Shultz, George P., *Turmoil and Triumph: My Years as Secretary of State*. New York, 1993.

Smith, Wayne S. *The Russians Aren't Coming: New Soviet Policy in Latin America*. Boulder, CO, 1992.

Somoza, Anastasio. *Nicaragua Betrayed*. Belmont, MA., 1980.

Speakes, Larry with Robert Pack. *Speaking Out*. New York, 1988.

Stimson, Henry L. introduction and commentary by Paul H. Boeker, *American Policy in Nicaragua: The Lasting Legacy*. Princeton, 1992.

Thornton, Richard C. *The Carter Years: Toward a New Global Order*. New York, 1991.

Congress. Senate Select Committee On Secret Military Assistance to Iran and the Nicaraguan Opposition; and House of Representatives Select Committee to Investigate Covert Arms Transactions with Iran. *Joint Hearings on the Iran-Contra Investigation, May 5 through August 6, 1987*. 11 Volumes. Washington, 1988.

———. *Report of the Congressional Committees Investigating the Iran-Contra Affair with Supplemental, Minority, and Additional Views*, November 1987. 100th Congress, 1st session. Washington, 1987.

———. *Report of the Congressional Committees Investigating the Iran-Contra Affair. Appendix A: Source Documents*. 2 Volumes. Washington, 1988.

———. *Report of the Congressional Committees Investigating the Iran-Contra Affair. Appendix B: Depositions*. 27 Volumes. Washington, 1988.

———. *Report of the Congressional Committees Investigating the Iran-Contra Affair. Appendix C: Chronology of Events*. Washington, 1988.

———. *Report of the Congressional Committees Investigating the Iran-Contra Affair. Appendix D: Testimonial Chronology*. 3 Volumes. Washington, 1988.

United States. President's Special Review Board, John G. Tower, chairman. *Report of the President's Special Review Board*. Washington, 1987.

Valenta, Jiri and Esperanza Duran. *Conflict in Nicaragua: A Multidimensional Perspective*. Boston, 1987.

Valenta, Jiri and Frank Cibulka, eds. *Gorbachev's New Thinking and Third World Conflicts*. New Brunswick, NJ, 1990.

Vance, Cyrus. *Hard Choices: Critical Years in America's Foreign Policy* . New York, 1983.

Vilas, Carlos M. *The Sandinista Revolution: National Liberation and Social Transformation in Central America*. New York, 1986.

Walker, Thomas W. *Nicaragua in Revolution*. New York, 1982.

———. *Nicaragua: The Land of Sandino*. Boulder, CO, 1991.

———, ed. *Revolution and Counterrevolution in Nicaragua*. Boulder, CO, 1991.

Walsh, Lawrence E. *Iran-Contra : The Final Report*. New York, 1994.

Weber, Henri. *Nicaragua: The Sandinista Revolution*. Paris, 1981.

Weinberger, Caspar. *Fighting for Peace: Seven Critical Years in the Pentagon*. New York, 1990.

Williams, William Appleman. *The Tragedy of American Diplomacy*. New York, 1959.

Woodward, Bob. *Veil: The Secret Wars of the CIA, 1981-1987*. New York, 1987.

Wroe, Ann. *Lives, Lies and the Iran-Contra Affair*. London, 1991.

INDEX